RUSSIA AND EURASIA

Navruz Nekbakhtshoev

T0284915

THE WORLD TODAY SERIES®

2024–2025

54TH EDITION

Navruz Nekbakhtshoev

Navruz Nekbakhtshoev has taught political science courses at St. Olaf College, and University of Nebraska Omaha. He earned his PhD in political science with a minor in Central Eurasian studies at Indiana University. His fieldwork for his dissertation was conducted in Tajikistan. Navruz has published some of his research on Eurasian politics in journals such as *Central Asian Affairs, Central Asian Survey, Development, Europe-Asia Studies, Journal of Peasant Studies, Nationalities Papers*. The courses that he teaches at University of Nebraska Omaha include, Comparative Democratization, and Politics in Authoritarian Regimes.

First appearing as a book entitled
The Soviet Union and Eastern Europe 1970,
revised annually, published in 1970
and succeeding years by

Rowman & Littlefield
An imprint of The Rowman & Littlefield Publishing Group, Inc.
4501 Forbes Blvd., Suite 200, Lanham, MD 20706
www.rowman.com

The World Today Series has thousands of subscribers across the US and Canada. A sample list of users who annually rely on this most up-to-date material includes:

Public library systems
Universities and colleges
High schools
Federal and state agencies
All branches of the armed forces & war colleges
National Geographic Society
National Democratic Institute
Agricultural Education Foundation
ExxonMobil Corporation
Chevron Corporation
CNN

Red Square, Moscow

Peter the Great, St. Petersburg

Contents

Introduction: Russia and Eurasia, 2024 vi

The Russian Federation 1
  The Land and the People 3
  History 9
  The Communist Era 35
  Stalin's Revolution of the 1930s 44
  The Post-Stalin Era 53
  The Brezhnev Era 56
  Government Transition 60
  The Gorbachev Era 62
  Foreign Policy under Gorbachev 71
  The 1989 Revolutions 73
  An Independent Russia Is Reborn 79
  Boris Yeltsin Remakes the Russian State 80
  The Putin Presidency 88
  Russian Foreign Policy since Independence in 1991 100
  Government of the Russian Federation 106
  Excerpts from the Russian Constitution 109
  Culture 112
  The Changing Economy 120

Eurasia 142
  The Collapse of the Soviet Union 142
  Commonwealth of Independent States 145
  Economy under the CIS 147
  Some Regional Problems of the CIS 151

Western Republics 154
  Belarus 155
  Ukraine 170
  Moldova 200

Transcaucasian Republics 218
  Armenia 219
  Azerbaijan 236
  Georgia 252

Central Asian Republics 270
  Kazakhstan 270
  Kyrgyzstan 287
  Tajikistan 302
  Turkmenistan 316
  Uzbekistan 328

Websites and Bibliography 343

Bayterek Tower, Nur-Sultan, Kazakhstan

Introduction: Russia and Eurasia, 2024

Russia's invasion of Ukraine, now in its third year, has evolved into a war of attrition. Ukraine's much-anticipated March 2023 counteroffensive made limited territorial gains due to dense Russian minefields, heavy artillery and air assaults. Russian missile, rocket and drone attacks resulted in heavy human casualties, destroyed homes and businesses, and caused severe damage to Ukraine's energy infrastructure. According to the UN, as of February 2024, an estimated 10,582 civilians, of which 587 were children, died in Ukraine. The war caused 3.7 million people to become internally displaced, and nearly 6.5 million to flee to neighboring countries. With damaged homes and power grids, nearly 14.6 million people who stayed in the county confront disruptions in access to water, electricity, heating, healthcare, education, social services and life-threatening freezing temperatures in winter. Both parties to the war continue to suffer heavy losses in troops and military equipment. According to a leaked US Department of Defense document, Russia has endured approximately 189,000 to 223,000 casualties, including up to 43,000 soldiers killed in action. Ukraine suffered 124,500 to 131,000 casualties, with as many as 17,500 killed in action. With neither side able to break the stalemate since the onset of Ukrainian counteroffensive, both sides changed their strategies from ground assaults to greater reliance on long-range missile and drone attacks. While Russia increased its strikes against power plants and urban targets, Ukraine, bolstered by Western military aid, uses drones and longer-range missile systems to attack Russian military supply lines and oil refineries.

Despite ongoing provision of military equipment, financial aid, and training, signs of "Ukraine fatigue" are emerging in some Western countries, leading to debates about the sustainability of long-term support. Sanctions on Russia remain in place and have been periodically expanded. While observers continue to debate their effectiveness, Russia's economy has shown resilience by pivoting towards Asian markets, particularly China and India, for trade and energy exports. Additionally, Western imposed export controls on crucial technology did not prevent Russia from leveraging third party countries to secure technologies such as semiconductors for use in military equipment. Meanwhile, conflict resolution remains elusive. The positions of both leaders have hardened, with president Volodymyr Zelensky of Ukraine insisting on full territorial restoration, including Crimea, while President Vladimir Putin of Russia, reelected in March 2024, refuses to relinquish occupied territories. This impasse has complicated peace negotiations, despite various attempts at diplomatic solutions.

The war in Ukraine has left the small post-Soviet states of Moldova, the Republic of Georgia and Armenia more vulnerable and insecure than ever before. With public opinion in these states growing more pro-European, Russia has intensified pressure on the governments of these states, using energy politics, disinformation campaigns, and leveraging separatist regions to maintain influence in what it considers its sphere of influence. Despite these pressure points, Moldova has made substantial progress toward European integration. The country managed to strengthen its ties with Romania and Ukraine to reduce its energy dependence on Russia. Meanwhile, the government in the Republic Georgia passed a controversial law, dubbed "foreign agents law," which requires NGOs and media outlets receiving funds from Western countries to register as "organizations acting in the interest of a foreign power," submit themselves to stringent audits, or face punitive fines. The passage of this law has become a significant obstacle in its EU integration process. Georgia also continues to navigate a complex relationship with Russia, balancing economic ties against the ongoing occupation of Abkhazia and South Ossetia. After losing Nagorno-Karabakh to Azerbaijan, the government in Armenia signaled its desire to distance itself from Russia. The shift was prompted by what the Armenian government perceives as Russia's failure to defend its interests during the conflict. Armenia froze its membership by ceasing to provide funds to the Russian led Collective Security Treaty Organization (CSTO) and ordered the removal of Russian troops from the country. However, the country's geographic distance from the EU, and its historical reliance on Russia for security and energy, makes it the least likely candidate to join the EU in the near to medium future. The government of Azerbaijan prioritizes security and military cooperation with Türkiye, which provided military support to help it win back the breakaway region of Nagorno Karabakh in a short but brutal war. The government supports Ukraine's sovereignty while avoiding direct confrontation with Russia, and Azerbaijani society has largely united in support of Ukraine. With Russia's invasion of Ukraine, Turkey emerged as the country's preferred ally and destination for youth migration, while attitudes toward Russia have become more complex and support for Western nations remains limited. However, unlike Armenia, Georgia, Azerbaijan is an authoritarian country.

Like their counterparts in the Caucasus, political elites in Kazakhstan, Uzbekistan, Turkmenistan, Tajikistan, and Kyrgyzstan have all been working to balance relations between major powers while pursuing economic development and maintaining domestic stability. Since Russia's invasion of Ukraine, Kazakhstan has strengthened ties with states in the Caucasus, Türkiye, and Europe, through investing in the Trans-Caspian International Transport Route (TITR) or Middle Corridor. Once completed, the project would serve as a trade and transport link connecting Southeast Asia, China, Central Asia, the South Caucasus, Turkey, and Europe. Beyond infrastructure development, Kazakhstan has also deepened political and security cooperation with Azerbaijan and Turkey, signaling a strategic shift in its regional partnerships and trade routes. The government of Kazakhstan supports the territorial integrity of Ukraine and public opinion views Russia in a negative light. Uzbekistan is actively diversifying its international partnerships, engaging with Western nations while facing pressure not to support Russia's aggression. Nonetheless, the country Uzbekistan remains significantly dependent on Russia for trade, labor remittances, and natural gas supplies. Unlike Kazakhstan, public sentiment toward Russia is mixed, with the older generation having a more positive view than the younger generation. During his official visit in May 2024, Putin called Uzbekistan a strategic and reliable partner and pledged to invest in the construction of a small nuclear power plant in the country, the first of its kind in Central Asia. Turkmenistan has remained largely isolationist but has increased natural gas exports to China and has been building a pipeline to supply gas to Southeast Asia. Tajikistan and Kyrgyzstan remain more closely tied to Russia economically and militarily, though Kyrgyzstan has seen political turmoil and shifts between pro-Russian and more independent leaders.

Domestically, the region has seen a mix of gradual reforms and continued authoritarianism. According to Freedom House's Nations in Transit 2024 report, the outlook for rule of law in many post-Soviet states remains grim, with Central Asia facing particularly severe challenges. All five Central Asian countries were classified as "consolidated authoritarian regimes," the lowest category in terms of individual rights and competitive political systems, joining Russia, Azerbaijan, and Belarus in this designation. Kazakhstan, Kyrgyzstan, and Uzbekistan all experienced declines in their rule-of-law scores in 2023, based on evaluations of various factors, including press freedom, judicial independence, and electoral processes. This trend underscores the persistent obstacles to democratic development and the entrenchment of authoritarian governance in the region. Economic challenges including high youth unemployment persist across the region. Key issues going forward include managing relations with Afghanistan, water resource disputes, and balancing ties with Russia, China, and the West amidst geopolitical competition. Regional cooperation through bodies like the Shanghai Cooperation Organization has increased but historical tensions remain.

The bulk of the text and overall structure of this book still belongs to its longtime author: M. Wesley Shoemaker. Thanks to April Snider and the team at Rowman & Littlefield for their work on this publication and their guidance. I look forward to contributing to this volume now and in the future.

Navruz Nekbakhtshoev
Omaha, NE
July 2024

Russia

Crimean Peninsula annexed by Russia, March 18, 2014

Russia

Area: 6,592,771 sq. mi. (17,075,200 sq. km.).

Population: 140,820,810 (2024 estimate).

Capital City: Moscow (metropolitan population: 12.7 million).

Other Major Cities: St. Petersburg (5.6 million), Nizhny Novgorod—formerly Gorky (1.3 million), Ekaterinburg—formerly Sverdlovsk (1.5 million), Samara—formerly Kuibyshev (1.3 million), Omsk (1.2 million), Kazan (1.3 million), Perm (1.1 million).

Climate: Russia lies within the temperate, sub-arctic, and arctic zones. Most of European Russia is within the temperate zone, while most of Siberia lies in the arctic zone.

Neighboring Countries: (counter-clockwise from the northwest) Norway, Finland, Estonia, Latvia, Belarus, Ukraine, Georgia, Azerbaijan, Kazakhstan, Mongolia, China, North Korea, Japan. Kaliningrad (separated from the rest of the nation) is lodged between Lithuania (north and east) and Poland (south).

Official Language: Russian.

Ethnic Composition: Russians (77.7%), Tatars (3.7%), Ukrainians (1.4%), Chuvash (1%), Bashkirs (1.1%), Chechens (1%), Other or unspecified (14.2%) (2010 estimate).

Principal Religions: Russian Orthodox 15–20%, Muslim 10–15%, other Christian 2% (2010 estimate).

Chief Commercial Products: Russia is a major industrial power. More than 80% of all export earnings derive from energy exports (in particular, petroleum and natural gas), with commercial and precious metals (including manganese, nickel, chromium, copper and lead, gold, silver, and platinum), plus diamonds and furs, making up much of the remainder. Almost alone among processed goods, the export of military equipment is also a major foreign currency earner. Imports include tropical produce, manufactured goods, including consumer goods and machinery, and some food items such as meats, fruits, and nuts. Russia is currently the world's second-largest exporter of petroleum, while it is a major provider of natural gas to Central and Western Europe.

Currency: ruble.

Per Capita Annual Income (Purchasing Power Parity): $39,753 (2023).

Former Political Status: Core of the Russian Empire for centuries to November 7, 1917; Russian Soviet Federative Socialist Republic, member of the Union of Soviet Socialist Republics, from 1922 to 1991.

Federal Structure: Under the 1993 constitution, Russia is defined as a Federative Republic consisting of republics, provinces, autonomous provinces, districts, autonomous districts and territories. Republics enjoy greater rights of self-government than other subdivisions and some of the republics have negotiated separate agreements with the national government. Much of this autonomy was curtailed after Vladimir Putin became president in 2000.

National Day: June 12 (Russia Day).

Head of State: Vladimir Putin, President (May 7, 2012).

Head of Government: Mikhail Mishustin (January 16, 2020).

National Flag: Three equal horizontal stripes of white, pale blue, and red (the same as used by the Russian Imperial Empire).

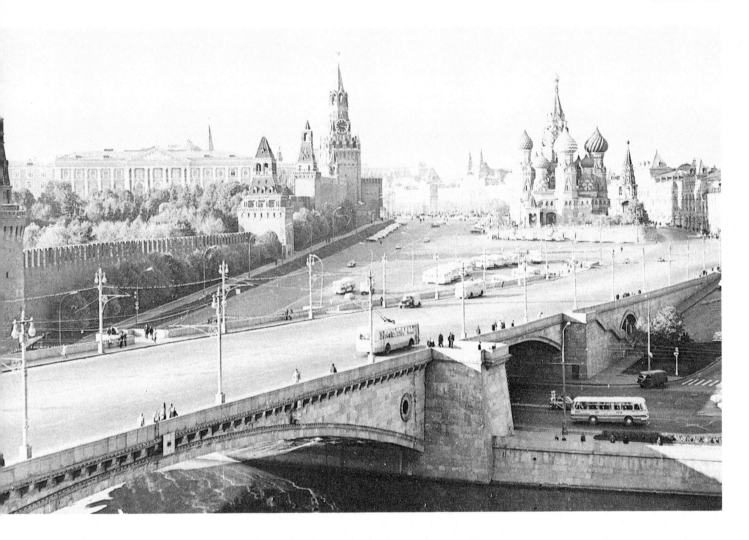

The Land and the People

The Russian Federation, which became a separate, independent nation in December 1991 after the collapse of the Union of Soviet Socialist Republics, consists of the Russian-speaking core of that former union. Still the largest country in the world, it stretches 5,500 miles (9,200 km.) from the Kaliningrad enclave in the west to the Kamchatka Peninsula in the east, encompassing the lands of historic Russia west of the Ural Mountains and all of Siberia. Expressed in another way, the Russian Federation reaches 172 degrees around the globe (from longitude 19°39'E to 169°W).

Until 2010, 10 time zones separated the Kaliningrad Region in the west from the Chukotka Peninsula in the east. In that year, the Russian government reduced the number of time zones from 11 to 9; the far eastern regions of Kamchatka and Chukotsk went from being nine hours ahead of Moscow to eight. Like most of the rest of Europe, Russia had traditionally moved clocks ahead one hour on the last Sunday of March and turned them back one hour on the last Sunday of October. However, Russia switched permanently to summer time in February 2011, and in 2014, it moved most areas back an additional hour accordingly, Russia is three hours ahead of Greenwich Mean Time all year round.

The heart of this enormous land is a seemingly endless plain that stretches from the Polish border in the west to beyond the Yenisei River in the east and into Central Asia in the south. This Eurasian plain, actually three interconnected plains partially separated by the low-lying Ural Mountains, is known as the Russian Plain west of the Ural Mountains. East of the Urals, it becomes the Western Siberian Lowlands. That part of the plain that extends across Kazakhstan and into Central Asia is known as the Turan Lowland.

The Russian Plain is part of the even larger East European Plain. It begins at the Baltic Sea in the north and extends to the Black Sea and the Caucasus Mountains in the south. Not totally flat, it is broken up by a series of higher elevations, the most significant of which is the Valdai Hills (also known as the Central Russian Upland), located in the northwest.

The somewhat higher elevations of the Valdai Hills give rise to several large rivers which, flowing outward to the sea, connect most parts of the Russian Plain. Although the Valdai Hills cover an area of only about 100 square miles, they are the birthplace of four rivers, including the two largest rivers of the Russian Plain, the Dnieper and the Volga. The other two rivers are the Western Dvina (known in Latvia as the Daugava) and the Lovat.

Today, the Valdai Hills form part of the border between the Russian Federation and the Republic of Belarus (formerly Byelorussia). However, this area, including the Pripet Swamps to the southwest, is usually accepted as the birthplace of all the Eastern Slavs, which include Russians. The Dnieper River flows west, then south, crossing the border into Belarus. It then continues southward, passing through the Republic of Ukraine before entering the Black Sea.

Russia

The Volga flows eastward, then southward, finally emptying into the Caspian Sea. The Western Dvina flows northward into Latvia, where it undergoes a name change and becomes the Daugava. It flows through Latvia into the Gulf of Riga, an arm of the Baltic Sea. The Lovat flows north into Lake Ilmen. When its waters leave the lake, they become the Volkhov, on which the historic city of Novgorod is located. The Volkhov, in turn, flows into Lake Ladoga. As the waters flow from the lake, they become the Neva River. The Neva, on which St. Petersburg is located, flows into the Gulf of Finland, another arm of the Baltic Sea.

The origins of the Russian state are associated with a north-south water trade route that arose in the 9th century using the western part of this river system. The major river involved was the Dnieper, along whose middle reaches the city of Kyiv is located. Ukrainians today prefer the spelling "Kyiv" for their capital city, which was also the capital of Kyivan Rus, the first Russian state. The other river system was the Lovat-Volkhov-Neva, and here the other important Russian city was Novgorod, located on the Volkhov at the

northern edge of Lake Ilmen. These two cities guarded the trade route, and their unification under a single ruler marked the beginning of the first Russian state.

There is one other river of the Russian Plain that needs to be mentioned, though its significance is more recent. The Don River lies between the Dnieper and Volga Rivers in the south. It flows into the Sea of Azov, an arm of the Black Sea. Because it is connected to the Volga by the Volga–Don canal, it provides a link between the Caspian and Black Seas.

The Western Siberian Lowlands, though nearly as large as the Russian Plain, have little of its importance, largely because of the climate. All of Russia lies quite far to the north, but most of European Russia benefits from weather patterns that give it a milder climate than its northern location would indicate. The warm waters of the Gulf Stream, pushing up through the English Channel and into the Baltic Sea, greatly modify the climate of northern Russia. Other weather patterns associated with the Mediterranean Sea have a similar effect on the southern part of Russia.

The influence of these weather patterns is not found east of the Ural Mountains.

Moreover, they are replaced by countervailing weather patterns whose effect is to make the climate even more severe than would be expected at similar latitudes. In addition, much of Siberia lies further north than the European part of the Russian Federation.

Nearly half of Siberia is situated north of the 60° parallel, the same parallel as St. Petersburg, and perhaps one-fifth of it lies north of the Arctic Circle. Another influence is that the land tends to slope downward from south to north, meaning that Arctic fronts can sweep unhindered southward across the landscape. This means also that Siberia's rivers flow from south to north—and their mouths in the north freeze earlier in the fall and thaw later in the spring than their more southerly upstream sections. The northern two-thirds of the Western Siberian Lowlands is, accordingly, a land of mixed evergreen forest and swamp.

This is the western third of a broad band of forest stretching from the Ural Mountains to the Pacific Ocean known as the Taiga. Agriculture is possible only in the south, in a fairly wide band just east of the Ural Mountains, but sharply

To keep the map simplified, names of the former, now independent, Soviet republics are not shown.

4

Russia

The first helicopter tour by an American journalist of the main harbor of Vladivostok (eastern coast of Siberia facing the Sea of Japan) produced this aerial view. In the foreground is a naval shipyard now serving the Russian Pacific fleet, with the aircraft carrier *Minsk* (center) undergoing maintenance. Courtesy of Bryan Hodgson © 1990 National Geographic Society

narrowing as one travels eastward, ending west of Irkutsk. It is easy to locate this fertile band on a map for here are found all of the major cities of western Siberia, connected by the Trans-Siberian Railway, which passes through the region.

The Western Siberian Lowlands are dominated by two great river systems, the Ob-Irtysh and the Yenisei. The Ob-Irtysh drains the western and central part of the plain; the Yenisei drains the eastern part plus the western edges of the Central Siberian Plateau. Because they both flow northward, their economic usefulness is very limited.

To the east of the Western Siberian Lowlands, the land rises and becomes known as the Central Siberian Plateau. Here the land is still mostly flat or slightly rolling, but the climate is much harsher, partly because of the higher elevation. In the north, the area is all treeless tundra, while the rest of the land is covered by evergreen forests, a continuation of the Taiga. The entire plateau is classified as an area of permafrost—the land is permanently frozen to a depth of 50–60 feet and in the short Siberian summers only the top 3–4 feet thaw. Subsistence agriculture is carried on in openings in the forests in the

south, but this is generally not an area suitable for agriculture.

The Lena River, mightiest of Siberia's rivers, divides the Central Siberian Plateau from the Eastern Siberian Mountains. The southern, upstream portion of the Lena River Valley has been developed somewhat more because of extensive mineral deposits that have been found in the area. Yakutsk, capital of the Republic of Yakutsk-Sakha, which is located on the banks of the Lena River, boasts a population of close to 350,000 inhabitants.

The Eastern Siberian Mountains are a series of ranges that run for 1,500 miles from west to east, up to the Bering Strait and the Pacific Ocean. Like the Central Siberian Plateau, it is an area of permafrost, with tundra in the north and taiga in the south. The tallest of these mountains is only about 10,000 feet in height, but the area is largely uninhabited except for wandering tribes of reindeer herders because of the extreme climate. Temperatures average above freezing for only about two months out of the year, partly because of the northern location, but also because of the effect of cold Arctic Ocean currents just offshore.

South of the Eastern Siberian Mountains, the Amur River forms the boundary between the Russian Federation and the People's Republic of China for a distance of about 700 miles before it turns northeastward and eventually empties into the Sea of Okhotsk. The Amur is the only major Siberian river to flow from west to east and the Amur River valley is the only area of extensive cultivation in the eastern part of Siberia. The amounts produced are insufficient to supply the population, however, so this, like the rest of Siberia, is a net food-importing area.

The last major feature of the Siberian landscape is a series of very high mountain chains that stretch all along the southern border. Starting from the west, they are the Altai, Sayan, and Yablonoi, plus the Stanovoi Mountains. The Stanovoi Mountains, which begin north of the Amur River, are separated from the Eastern Siberian Highlands by the Aldan Plateau. Together, the four high, rugged, mountain chains hem in the land and isolate Russian Siberia from its southern neighbors.

Natural Regions

The Russian Federation includes within its limits climatic belts varying from the

5

Russia

NATURAL VEGETATION

- Subtropical Forest
- Broadleaf Forest
- Fertile Steppe
- Dry Steppe
- Taiga
- Tundra
- Desert

temperate to the arctic, stretching from west to east in wide bands across the country. Two of these, the Tundra and the Taiga, are found primarily in Siberia. The Tundra stretches across the northern part of the land that borders on the Arctic Ocean from the Ural Mountains in the west to the tip of the Chukotka Peninsula in the east. It is almost entirely uninhabited and nothing but moss and swamp shrubs will grow there. Migratory herds of reindeer graze briefly in the southernmost part of the Tundra during the brief summer.

Immediately south of the Tundra is the Taiga, a zone of evergreen forest that begins at about Archangel in the west and gradually widens toward the east until it takes in an area as far south as Lake Baikal. The belt then bends somewhat northward before continuing on to the Sea of Okhotsk.

To the south of the Taiga is a zone of mixed forest which stretches from west to east across the entire country. West of the Urals, this takes in about two-thirds of the Russian Plain, reaching as far south as

Kyiv, capital of the Republic of Ukraine. On its southern edge, it gradually thins out, becoming mixed wooded steppe and grassy meadow. The northern slope of the Caucasus Mountains also belongs in this climatic zone.

The last vegetation zone is the steppe, or prairie area. The steppe begins as a 150-mile band north of the Black Sea and stretches eastward into Central Asia. Originally natural grassland, today this area is mostly cultivated land. The chief city of the Russian steppe is Stavropol, the main city of the region where Mikhail Gorbachev grew up.

The People

In the Russian decennial census, last conducted in 2021, the official population was 145.8 million. This was down from the immediate pre-independence population of 148.6 million. Russia's population decline has been the result of decades of low birth rates and high death rates. Numerous causes have been identified

as contributing to Russia's high mortality rate in the first two decades of independence including alcoholism, the social disruption caused by economic and social transition leading to high rates suicides and homicides, and an increase in chronic diseases such as cancer and cardiovascular diseases. In the late 2000s and early 2010s, population decline slowed due predominantly to decreased mortality rates. Fertility rates remain quite low.

But that is not the entire story; another part of the story is that immigrants are not counted in the population statistics. According to Statista, a German market research company (since 2014 Rosstat), more than half a million migrants enter Russia each year, most of them citizens from members of the Commonwealth of Independent States (CIS). With some countries excepted, none of the citizens of the CIS require visas to enter Russia; their numbers are therefore largely unknown. As indicated by the International Organization for Migration, most of these workers are economic migrants who work in Russia only during the warm months and return to their home republics over the winter.

The Russian government supports the idea that at least some of these migrants should be legalized, since they take jobs that would otherwise remain unfilled. Native-born Russian citizens are often hostile toward foreign workers, however—particularly those from the Caucasus and Central Asia—so the government has limited itself to calling on citizens to be more accepting of migrants. One of the benefits of the customs union which Russia, Kazakhstan, and Belarus inaugurated in December 2010 is that citizens of republics belonging to the customs union have the right to seek employment in any republic belonging to the customs union. That is one reason why the governments of Kyrgyzstan and Armenia joined in 2015.

Even though 77% of the population are ethnic Russians, the population of the Russian Federation is quite diverse. The state is home to numerous non-Russian ethnic groups and this is reflected in its federal structure—which divides the country into 21 republics, 49 regions, 6 territories, 10 autonomous areas, 2 cities of federal importance—Moscow and St. Petersburg, plus the Jewish autonomous region. After the collapse of communism in 1991, a number of the republics declared their "sovereignty" vis-à-vis the Russian Federation and several modified their names. For example, the Tatar Autonomous Republic became the Republic of Tatarstan, while the Yakutsk Autonomous Republic, changed its name to the Republic of Sakha (Yakutia). Former President Yeltsin actually supported the idea of local autonomy but, under Putin, much of this autonomy has been curtailed.

Ethnic Diversity: The Symbolism of Chechnya

In the area of the northern Caucasus, one group, the Chechens. seceded from the Chechen-Ingush Autonomous Republic to establish their own Republic of Chechnya. Under the leadership of Dzhokhar Dudayev, a former Soviet Air Force general, Chechnya then declared its independence.

President Yeltsin attempted to reassert Russian authority over the Republic of Chechnya in November 1991, but discovered he had neither the force nor the political support to carry it out. He backed down when the Russian Supreme Soviet refused to endorse his policy. Over the next three years, a series of attempts were made to get Chechnya to drop its independence bid, but without success. Chechnya also refused to sign the general Federation treaty which Yeltsin negotiated with the various republics in 1992. And General Dudayev refused to accede to the new

constitution of the Russian Federation, approved in December 1993, even though, under its terms, Chechnya would have had extensive autonomy, including its own constitution.

It has been suggested that one reason why the Chechens continued to hold out for independence is that most of the

republic's 1.3 million inhabitants are Muslims who wanted to separate from Russia for religious reasons. It is true that General Dudayev did, at times, make references to the creation of an Islamic nation. Yet that is not the only reason, for other Muslim-majority areas accepted the new constitution. In any case, President

European Russia's Heartland
showing principal cities

Russia

Yeltsin's patience was exhausted by December 1994; he then authorized the use of military force against the Republic of Chechnya.

Although greatly outnumbered, the Chechnyan defenders resisted strenuously and even managed to create a temporary stalemate. It took the Russian army approximately three months to capture Grozny, the capital and, even so, additional units had to be brought in to accomplish this. By April 1995, most of Chechnya had been brought under Russian control and a new Chechen government, headed by Salambek Khadjiev, a longtime opponent of General Dudayev, had been installed.

General Dudayev and his embattled forces retreated into the mountains in the south. They had not been finally defeated, however, so guerrilla fighting continued, with occasional Chechnyan forays even into nearby parts of Russia.

Though Russian forces managed to kill General Dudayev in April 1996, anti-war sentiment continued to grow in Russia, eventually forcing President Yeltsin to seek a way out of the impasse. In May, on the eve of the presidential elections, he announced a truce in the war. After his re-election, Yeltsin named General Alexander Lebed as his new security adviser and gave him responsibility for Chechnya.

Using his new authority, Lebed negotiated a settlement with the new Chechnyan leadership, agreeing to a withdrawal of all Russian forces from the republic in return for a Chechnyan pledge not to press for formal independence for five years. Although Lebed later lost his job, the agreement held until 1999, partly because

no one on the Russian side wanted to restart the war. As for the Chechnyans, they selected Aslan Maskhadov, the man who negotiated the agreement with Lebed, as their new president in January 1997, and he subsequently did his best to adhere to the agreement.

Unfortunately, Maskhadov often found his relatively moderate policies challenged by insubordinate military commanders, in particular the guerrilla leader Shamil Basayev, who dreamed of ridding the entire north Caucasus area of Russian influence and bringing it together in a new Islamic state. In August 1999, then, Basayev joined his forces with those of a radical commander of Jordanian origin by the name of Ibn al-Khattab and launched an invasion into neighboring Dagestan as a first step in accomplishing this ultimate goal. Russian military forces in Dagestan managed to drive the invading forces back into Chechnya after about six weeks of fighting, but a series of bomb explosions in Moscow and Rostov that killed about 300 individuals, which were blamed on Chechnyan terrorists, convinced Moscow to carry the war to Chechnya itself. Moscow, under the leadership of Yeltsin's Prime Minister Vladimir Putin, began bombing what it termed "strongholds of Islamic militants" in late September, at the same time breaking all links to Maskhadov's government in Grozny. Moscow launched its ground campaign against Chechnya on September 30.

As the war proceeded, hundreds of thousands of Chechnyan refugees fled across the border into neighboring provinces as Russian forces leveled Grozny

and other urban areas. It took the Russian forces about four months to overrun most of Chechnya, though several thousand of the remaining Chechnyan forces withdrew into the Caucasus Mountains region of southern Chechnya and remained undefeated. Russian military campaigns carried out after that time, plus periodic offers of amnesty, led to a reduction in the numbers of Chechnyan forces still holding out in the south, but guerilla attacks continued to occur in various parts of the republic.

Still, President Yeltsin's decision to again authorize the use of force against Chechnya should be viewed as something of an aberration. Yeltsin was, in fact, a consistent advocate of local sovereignty for the republics and other autonomous political subdivisions and it is this position that is essentially enshrined in the December 1993 constitution. Yeltsin's decision to take action in Chechnya resulted from his concern that Russia's authority in some of the other autonomous republics might be threatened if Chechnya were not punished for its challenge to Russian authority. There is at least some basis for this fear. There are still separatist tendencies in several of the republics, in particular Tatarstan and Bashkortostan, both of which have large Muslim populations and occupy a strategic location along the Volga River. Any movement toward independence in these republics would have to be viewed extremely seriously, for they are situated astride all the major railroad lines and oil pipelines connecting Siberia to European Russia. Thus the war in Chechnya was essentially a war on behalf of Russia's territorial integrity.

Vladimir Putin's election as president in March 2000 changed that equation in some respects. First of all, Yeltsin's selection of Putin as his successor was partly based on the actions he took with regard to Chechnya while he was serving as prime minister. Secondly, Putin made it clear after he became president that he intended to reassert the power of the center and bring all of the straying regions back into line. His Chechnyan policy has reflected this position. Militarily, the war against the rebels continued; at the same time, Chechnya has been reconstituted as a republic within the Russian Federation and given a new constitution.

As the war wound down in Chechnya, however, those opposing Russian rule carried the war to other areas of the North Caucasus. The new anti-Russian leadership is mostly radical Islamist; their program is to create an Islamic Emirate for the entire region of the North Caucasus. Supporters of radical Islam are to be found throughout the area of the North Caucasus. On January 24, 2011, a suicide bomber from Ingushetia, which borders

Chechnya to the west, killed 36 people at Domodedovo Airport, which is Moscow's busiest airport. The Chechen warlord, Doku Umarov (who died in mysterious circumstances in 2013) claimed to have ordered the bombing.

Chechnya has remained quiet, so quiet that the Russian government declared the war in Chechnya to be over in early 2009. Since 2007, the republic has been ruled by the autocratic Ramzan Kadyrov (first as president from 2007 to 2011, then as head of the republic since 2011).

History

The origins of both the Russian state and nation are found in the area north of the Black Sea and in the steppe lands to the north and east of that strategic body of water. Although there is evidence of human settlement in the area dating back to the Neolithic period of the Stone Age, significant history begins with the Slavs. These people were and are identified by a common or similar language rather than by any other common features. The Russians are part of an Eastern Slav group, the other members of which speak Ukrainian and Byelorussian (Belarusian).

The Poles, Czechs, and Slovaks belong to a second major group, the West Slavs. There is also a South Slav branch represented by the Bulgarians, Macedonians, Serbs, Montenegrins, Croats, and Slovenes.

Little is known about the original home of the early Slavs and many theories have been developed and discarded by scholars. As early as the beginning of the Christian era, however, Slavic people were found throughout most of the Russian Plain west of the Dnieper River and in Eastern Europe as far west as the Vistula River in what is now central Poland. References to the Slavs are also found in the writings of the Greek and Roman historians of the early Christian era, but very little is known about them in this time period. Essentially, they were cut off from classical civilization by the fact that they occupied only the center of the Russian Plain, the more southern part bordering the Black Sea not being suitable for medieval agriculture. The Slavs were traditionally an agricultural people and they left the grassy steppe of southern Russia to others.

The early political organization of the Slavs was basically tribal, with groups of self-governing villages cooperating in such areas as defense. By the 7th century, towns had begun to develop and trade between the tribes became more important. Kyiv, later the capital, was founded at about this time and probably owed its existence to the trade that had started along the Dnieper River. Located high on

ROAD FROM THE VARANGIANS TO THE GREEKS

the bluffs that overlook the western shore of the river, Kyiv was ideally located to dominate all such trade.

Novgorod, located at the northern edge of Lake Ilmen, was established somewhat

later. Begun as a trading post for amber and other products of the Baltic Sea area, it soon developed as a manufacturing center for jewelry, metals, and wood products. Its chief significance, however, was

9

Russia

Christian Orthodox (Byzantine) cross and pagan symbols

N.C.B.

1. Goddess
2. God of the Underworld
3. Hammer of a God
4. Sky God
5. Male God

as the northern terminus of the trade route known as the "Road from the Varangians to the Greeks." It was the existence of the trade route that led to the creation of the first organized Russian state.

"Varangian" was the old Slavonic word for a Norseman or Viking. Ancestors of today's Scandinavians, the Vikings were great seamen and from about the 7th century onward, they had been pushing out of Scandinavia, carrying out raids and explorations in all directions. Eventually they established settlements in eastern England, northern France and along the southern coastline of the Baltic Sea. This brought them into contact with Novgorod. According to tradition, Rurik, leader of one of these Viking bands, established himself at Novgorod in 862.

The story of the coming of the Vikings is told in *The Primary Chronicle*, a 12th century compilation of history from unknown earlier sources. According to the *Chronicle*, Rurik and his band of Varangians were invited to set themselves up as the local rulers—"Our land is great and abundant, but there is no order in it; come rule and reign over us." It is more likely that the Novgorodian merchants hired Varangians as mercenaries and then Rurik decided to take complete control himself. Twenty years later, Oleg the Norwegian, Rurik's successor, "set himself up as prince in Kyiv." Since he retained control in Novgorod, he then controlled the two chief cities of the "Road from the Varangians to the Greeks."

Kyivan Russia

This was the beginning of "Kyivan Rus," the first organized Russian state. Oleg lived until 913 and he spent the rest of his life extending his control over neighboring Slavic tribes and building up the trade route upon which the prosperity of the new state was based. His most spectacular gesture, according to Russian sources, was an attack on Constantinople which he launched in 907. Byzantine sources make no reference to such an attack but they do record that in 907 the Byzantine Emperor signed a treaty with Oleg which granted access to Byzantine markets on very favorable terms. Oleg was succeeded by Igor in 913; the latter was either the son or grandson of Rurik and from that time onward the descendants of Rurik sat on the throne of Kyivan Rus. The Rurikovichi ("sons of Rurik") dynasty later made the transfer when the capital was moved to Vladimir and, later to Moscow, so that it remained

the ruling dynasty of Russia until 1598, when Fedor, son of Ivan Grozny ("the Terrible"), died without an heir.

The first ruling family of Russia was thus Varangian in origin, but it must be emphasized that they became rulers of a land that had already developed an extensive "Slavic" culture. The Varangians were fine warriors and good leaders, but the Viking culture did not replace the native Slav culture. In fact, the opposite happened—the Varangian rulers were soon enveloped by Slavic culture.

This can be seen in the names of subsequent rulers. Igor was killed in 945 while on an expedition to collect tribute from a neighboring Slavic tribe. He was succeeded by his wife, Olga, because his son was still only a child. But that son, who succeeded to the throne in 962, was named Sviatoslav—the third generation of Varangian rulers already had Slavic names and, one can reasonably assume, were speaking the local Slavic language.

The subject of early Slavic culture is complex. It was indeed fairly well developed by this time, but it was centered on a belief in pagan Slavic deities. The trade connection between Kyivan Rus and Constantinople meant that the Russians were exposed to Byzantine culture and religion.

Constantinople was the leading city of Europe, the capital of the Byzantine Empire and the home of the Patriarch of Constantinople, leader of Greek Orthodox Christianity. It was a center of wealth, power, and culture. Further, the Orthodox Church was actively committed to a policy of conversion of the Slavs. Its missions had been active among the Bulgarians for some time and two Orthodox monks, Cyril and Methodius, had translated the *Bible* into Old Slavonic. In the process, they created the Cyrillic alphabet, which kept letters from the Greek alphabet for those sounds common to both languages but created new letters for sounds unique to Slavonic. The first written Slavic language was thus created.

Oleg permitted an Orthodox mission to open in Kyiv, but the first breakthrough did not occur until 955 when Olga underwent Christian baptism by missionaries from Constantinople. Her son, Sviatoslav, never converted, however, so Christianity remained a minority belief. The largest conversion to Orthodox Christianity occurred during the reign of Sviatoslav's son, Vladimir (978–1015). It was somewhat ironic that Vladimir was responsible for the conversion to Christianity, since he assumed the throne as a champion of the old Slavic gods. Paganism was a dying force, however. Poland, Hungary, and Bulgaria had already become Christian and the kings of Denmark and Norway

Russia

were converted shortly after Vladimir's accession to the throne.

Thus, when the Byzantine Emperor found himself faced with revolts in various parts of the empire and called upon Vladimir for assistance, offering his own sister to Vladimir as a bride, the offer was irresistible—Vladimir sent help and looked forward to the added power his anticipated bride would bring. But he found that the marriage could only take place if he converted to Christianity. Without hesitation, with the intent of allying himself with the most powerful state of that age, he underwent baptism in 988. After the marriage arrangements had been completed, he ordered the mass baptism of the entire population of Kyiv and began the construction of St. Sophia Cathedral. This church took its name from the 6th-century Hagia Sophia (Holy Wisdom) cathedral in Constantinople and became the first of the great Orthodox cathedrals built during the time of Kyivan Rus. The Byzantine style of architecture was thus introduced into Russia, a style that would remain dominant until Peter the Great introduced the neo-classical style at the beginning of the 18th century.

Kyivan Rus also officially adopted the Cyrillic alphabet at this time, and Vladimir ordered that schools be set up for the education of the sons of the upper classes. Kyivan Rus had, in fact, completely opened itself to Byzantine influence and, gradually, much of its culture was transformed.

Vladimir and his successor, Yaroslav (1019–1054), were responsible for much of this transformation; for this reason, the combined reigns of these Grand Princes is known as the height of Kyivan Rus. Influenced by the Byzantine example, the relationship of the Grand Prince to the people changed and, because of this change, Kyivan Rus could be, for the first time, defined as a nation. Earlier princes had merely levied tribute on the various tribes, each spring traveling about the country collecting goods, which were then traded in Constantinople. Vladimir replaced the tribute system with taxation. Yaroslav was responsible for having the Bishop of Kyiv named a *Metropolitan*, meaning that he became the head of an autonomous Russian Church. The Patriarch of Constantinople still retained the authority to *name* the Metropolitan, but this made Kyiv the religious as well as political capital of the state. Yaroslav's other important achievement is that he was responsible for the first Russian law code, the *Russkaya Pravda*.

After the death of Yaroslav, there was a period of decline, partly because of the "Rota" system, a method of inheritance in which all brothers inherited before any of the sons. The Rota system contributed to the division of the kingdom into separate principalities by encouraging competition for the throne among brothers and cousins. Occasionally, uncles and nephews struggled with each other to determine which would occupy the dominant throne of Kyiv. New Asian invaders, the *Polovtsy*, also appeared on the scene at about this time, contributing further to the decline of Kyiv.

Then, in 1169, Kyiv was captured by Prince Andrew Bogolubsky of Vladimir, a contender for the throne who, having obtained the title of Grand Prince, moved the capital to his own city of Vladimir. Kyiv thus lost its position as capital of the Russian states at this time.

It was then almost completely destroyed in 1240 by a massive invasion of Mongols (Tatars) led by Batu, grandson of the renowned Genghis Khan, founder of the Mongol Empire. Batu Khan would later establish his own capital at Sarai, near the mouth of the Volga River, and this became the origin of the "Golden Horde."

What came to be called the "Mongol Yoke" had to be endured by the Russians for the next 2.5 centuries until it was finally overthrown in 1480 by Ivan III, Prince of Moscow. A century earlier, Dmitry "Donskoi," Prince of Moscow, had defeated a "Golden Horde" force in a battle along the Don River (hence the title "Donskoi") in 1380, but Dmitry, fearing a Mongol punitive attack, then went to Sarai and renewed his oath of fealty to the "Golden Horde."

The Effects of Mongol Occupation

Historians disagree about the exact significance of the period of Mongol (Tatar) occupation. Generally speaking, the three-fold division is between those who point to the catastrophic effects of Tatar rule, those who feel it was beneficial, and those who feel that the importance of the occupation has been exaggerated.

It is hard to deny, however, that the strong, centralized and autocratic state that arose at Moscow between the 13th and 15th centuries differed greatly from the loosely organized confederation that had been Kyivan Rus. In addition, it is possible to point to specific developments, such as the legal concept of landholding, military techniques and organization, and forms of tax collection, as things taken over by the Muscovites from the Mongols. Certain Russian words also represent borrowings, although the words appear, in each case to be Chinese in origin. These include *chai* (tea) and *chin* (rank).

Some historians have also stressed the disruption of contact between the Russian people and important centers of culture such as Byzantium and the developing European states to the west that resulted from the Mongol conquest. It is certainly true that Russia missed most

19th-century drawing of a Mongol general

of the European Renaissance and the Reformation, but it is possible to exaggerate the extent of isolation as a result of the Mongol conquest. Moscow always maintained contact with the Byzantine Empire though its connection with the Patriarch of Constantinople. And in the 15th century, Ivan III obtained his wife, Sophia Paleologue, niece of the last Byzantine Emperor, through negotiations with the Pope; he also imported Italian builders to construct the "Faceted Palace" for him in the middle of the Kremlin.

Regardless of what judgment is placed on the effect of Tatar rule, there is agreement on one result—the growth and rise to power of a new center of leadership in the Russian lands: the Grand Duchy of Moscow. The emergence of this area as a leader compensated for the destruction of Kyiv and the breaking away of other states which remained detached from Russia for centuries.

To understand the contribution of the Tatars to the growth of Moscow, it is necessary to know of the way they exercised their power over the conquered Russian lands. With few exceptions, the Tatars usually left the native princes on their thrones and converted them into collectors of tribute and taxes. They also permitted them to continue to act as the law enforcement officials of their territories. Working as a tax collector for the Tatars was one of the many factors that helped to transform

11

Russia

MOSCHOVIA NVOVA TAVOLA.

An Italian map (1560) of the Principality of Moscow

Ivan the Great

Ivan the Great's most important military effort resulted in the capture of the powerful city of Novgorod, referred to in its own official title as "Lord Novgorod the Great." The most significant trading place in western Russia, Novgorod also possessed a unique form of government. Although a prince was the head of state, he was required to keep his throne outside the city walls; the internal affairs of the city were managed by the *Veche*, a broadly representative town council which could be summoned into session when any citizen rang the town bell. This early experiment in rudimentary democracy came to an end when Novgorod was absorbed by autocratic Moscow.

Ivan further achieved prestige in 1472 when he married Sophia Paleologue, niece of the last Byzantine emperor, killed when the Turks conquered Constantinople in 1453. Ivan occasionally styled himself *Tsar*, a Slavic contraction of the word *Caesar*, and he also added the titles *Autokratar* (Greek for "independent ruler") and *Gosudar* ("sovereign").

Several decades later in the early 16th century, the monk Philotheus of Pskov also developed the theory of the "Third Rome," which identified Moscow as the true capital of Christendom, in a line of succession through Rome and the recently fallen Constantinople. In later centuries, this doctrine became a justification for imperial expansion, although it had only a religious significance when first expounded.

Ivan the Terrible

The "ingathering of lands" was continued by Ivan the Great's successors. His grandson, Ivan IV (1533–1584) came to be known as "the Terrible." Actually the English word "terrible" is not an entirely accurate translation of the Russian word *grozny*, which is better described "the dreaded one." But there is much to justify Ivan's nickname regardless of the translation—he was a ruler impressive enough to inspire dread or awe and he was undoubtedly cruel and unpredictable enough to be called "the terrible."

Well-educated by comparison with other princes of his time, this shrewd man with a deep interest in theology was given to uncontrolled outbreaks of violence and cruelty. His pattern alternated between exaggerated acts of pious behavior and periods of unrestrained viciousness.

Ivan was a child of three in 1533 when his father died and he became the titular ruler of Russia. When his mother, Elena Glinskaya, died mysteriously five years later, Ivan found himself at the mercy of two competing boyar families: the Belskys and the Shuiskys. In their struggle for power, the two families paid public

the insignificant village of Moscow, first mentioned in the year 1147, into the center of a future empire. It is also important to point out that, first as pagans and later as Muslims, the Tatars exempted the Orthodox Church from the payment of all taxes and, in this way, contributed to the growth of its authority and power.

The Rise of Moscow

Moscow profited from its location close to frequently traveled river routes. Called Moskva in Russian, the city is located near the headwaters of the Daugara and Lovat Rivers that flow west and north and on the Moskva River that flows to the Oka River, the most important western tributary of the mighty Volga. The rise of the small principality of Moscow was made possible by the Rota—the traditional inheritance system—which encouraged battles to determine the successor to the throne and thus weakened Moscow's rivals for leadership. Moscow made its own contributions through a clever policy of expansion through purchase, conquest, service agreements with lesser princes, and, finally, clever dealings with the Tatar leaders that appeared to be part of a pattern of obedient behavior. Moscow also had to provide occasional military help to the Tatars in their battles to suppress rebellious princes and populations.

Moscow benefited also from the loyalty of the large landowners, called boyars

in Russian, and from the support of the Church. The boyars, whose lands suffered from the constant feuds among the lesser princes, wanted a strong prince who could enforce his authority and thus bring greater law and order to Russia. The Orthodox Church had transferred the seat of the Metropolitan, as the head of the Russian Church was known, from Kyiv to Vladimir in 1300. However, the Metropolitan Theognostus formally established Moscow as the seat of the Metropolitan in 1328 during the reign of the Grand Prince Ivan Kalita (i.e., Ivan "Moneybags"), thereby making it the spiritual capital of "all Russia." The Grand Prince of Moscow thus added to his status as a national leader and gradually came to be looked upon as the protector of the Russian lands against the Mongols.

As the power of the "Golden Horde" began to wane, the leading position of Moscow became less and less contested. The amount of territorial gain was tremendous—from the time of Ivan Kalita to the second half of the 15th century, the area of Moscow control expanded from about 600 to 15,000 square miles. In still further expansion, the ruler Ivan III ("The Great") added another 40,000 square miles by a combination of purchases, inheritance and conquest.

Ivan IV—the boy and the man

homage to Ivan, but ignored him in private. They exploited the state and pillaged the treasury. Ivan put an end to the situation in 1543 when the 13-year-old boy turned to his guards and ordered them to take Prince Andrew Shuisky away and kill him. At 13, Ivan was not yet ready to take the rule himself, but no one dared to oppose his will from that day onward.

Ivan was crowned "Tsar of All the Russias" in 1547, the first ruler to assume the title at the time of his coronation. In this same year, he married Anastasia Romanova, daughter of a minor boyar family. Ivan proved to be an energetic ruler whose reign was characterized by both reforms and military conquests. The reforms were, first of all, intended to reduce the traditional powers of the boyars, but they also included a new code of laws, the *Sudebnik*, issued in 1550, and an attempt to reform the Church through the calling of a church council in 1551.

Ivan was also responsible for creation of Russia's first parliament, the Zemsky Sobor ("Assembly of the Land"), which convened in 1550 and again in 1566.

Ivan defeated and annexed the Khanate of Kazan in 1552, thus giving him control over the middle Volga. Four years later, he attacked and defeated the Khanate of Astrakhan, adding those domains to his realm. This gave him control of the entire course of the Volga River and access to the Caspian Sea. To celebrate his victory over the Tatars, Ivan ordered the construction of St. Basil's Cathedral in what is now Red Square in Moscow.

Sometime during these years, Ivan also created the nucleus of a standing army to supplement the feudal levies provided by the boyars (nobility) in time of war (and thereby to decrease his dependence on the nobility). Five thousand of these *streltsy* (musketeers) were stationed in Moscow with another 7,000 in various border towns.

Problems began in 1558 when he decided to launch an invasion of Livonia—modern Estonia and Latvia—in an attempt to gain access to the Baltic Sea. When Livonia disintegrated, Poland-Lithuania and Sweden moved in to pick up the pieces and Ivan found himself at war with both of these nations plus Denmark. The war dragged on until 1582 and left Russia badly depleted.

The war also was at least partly responsible for Ivan's creation of the Oprichnina, a separate administration which was intended to finally destroy the traditionally separate power of the boyars. During the Livonian war, some of the boyars engaged in open treason and joined the side of Poland-Lithuania. One of the most distinguished of the boyars was Prince Andrei Kurbsky, one of Ivan's army commanders. He defected to the enemy side in 1564 after having been defeated by Lithuanian forces. The event is remembered through a purported fascinating exchange of correspondence between the tsar and the prince; the tsar called the prince a traitor, while Kurbsky maintained that he "chose freedom."

Ivan became determined to deal with all "traitors" and he threatened to abdicate as tsar unless he was given a free hand to deal with his enemies, both real and imagined, as he wished. His terms were spelled out in two letters he had delivered to the Metropolitan of Moscow. What Ivan proposed was to set up half of the realm as a personal domain, free from normal governmental administration and supervision by the "Chosen Council." In effect, half of Russia was to become Ivan's private property, and he would be free to take the lands of all the boyars located within the Oprichnina—"area set apart."

To enforce his will, he set up an *oprichnik* army of 6,000 men. Black-robed and riding black horses, each *oprichnik* had a dog's head fixed to his saddle and carried a broom, all to symbolize the tsar's determination to hound traitors and to sweep corruption from the land.

As Ivan obviously intended, the *oprichniki* struck terror throughout the land and the operation was successful from his viewpoint. The ability of the boyars to oppose the tsar was destroyed completely. The purges lasted seven years and, its purpose accomplished, Ivan dissolved the Oprichnina in 1572, after executing some of the chief executioners.

The Time of Troubles

Two years before his death in 1584, Ivan quarreled with his eldest son and namesake and, in a fit of passion, struck and killed him. He was succeeded, therefore, by his second son, Fedor, who was intellectually disabled. Under Fedor, actual power was exercised by a regency council headed by Boris Godunov. Little was accomplished during these years, but there is one thing that should be mentioned. In 1589, Boris Godunov managed to have Moscow recognized as an independent patriarchate. The first patriarch was the Metropolitan Job. When Fedor died in 1598, childless, and the Rurikovichi dynasty came to an end, the Patriarch Job was one of those who supported Boris Godunov as the new tsar.

There were a number of candidates but three men eventually emerged as serious contenders—Boris Godunov, Fedor Romanov, and Basil Shuisky. Each had some connection to the previous ruling family. Boris Godunov was married to

Russia

From Act I of Musorgski's opera Boris Godunov

the sister of Fedor; Fedor Romanov was the son of Nikita Romanov, brother of Anastasia, Ivan IV's first wife; and Basil Shuisky was descended from the elder branch of the Rurikovichi line.

To give legitimacy to the choice, the Patriarch proposed calling a Zemsky Sobor and allowing this popular assembly to select the new tsar. It chose Boris Godunov, who took the throne as Boris I (1598–1605).

Boris's reign started out well but, when a combination of early frosts and droughts produced widespread crop failures, the superstitious Russian people began to believe that they had made a mistake in choosing Boris, and opposition mounted to his rule. He managed to hold on to power during his lifetime but things began to fall apart when he died suddenly in April 1605. Within a month, his son, who had succeeded him, was overthrown by the first would-be Dmitry, an impostor who claimed to be the youngest son of Ivan IV.

This marked the beginning of a period of great turmoil in Russian history known as the "Time of Troubles." Dmitry (1605–1606) survived for approximately a year

before he was murdered by Basil Shuisky, who then ascended the throne as Basil I (1606–1610).

Basil, who represented the interests of the old *boyar* class, was unable to consolidate his control and was overthrown in 1610. Russia was once again without a tsar. In addition, a Polish army occupied Moscow while a Swedish army occupied parts of northern Russia. A number of Russian nobles proposed to offer the throne to Wladyslaw, the 15-year-old son of Sigismund, the Polish king. Sigismund rejected the offer and claimed the throne for himself.

This posed a basic threat to the power of the Russian Orthodox Church. Sigismund was a Roman Catholic and probably would have tried to force a union of the Church with the Roman Church. The Patriarch of Moscow, Hermogen, called urgently for the Russian people to drive out the Poles. A national revival to save "Mother Russia" began, led by Kuzma Minin, a wealthy commoner from Nizhny Novgorod. Minin assembled an army representing all classes of Russian society from *boyar* to serf and the Polish army was

driven out of Moscow. A Zemsky Sobor was then summoned and proceeded to choose Michael Romanov as the new tsar.

The First Romanovs

Michael Romanov (1613–1645) was a boy of 16 when he was elevated to the throne of Russia. The Zemsky Sobor wanted Michael's father, Fedor Romanov, as tsar, but that proved impossible for two reasons. The first was that Boris Godunov, after his own election as tsar, had forced Fedor to become a monk. He did this in order to remove a potential rival to the throne since Fedor, as a monk, would be ineligible for the throne. The second reason was that Fedor, now the Metropolitan Filaret, was in prison in Poland.

He had gone to Poland in 1610 as a member of the Russian delegation sent to negotiate with the Polish king with regard to his son Wladyslaw's accession to the Russian throne. When Sigismund decided to claim the throne for himself, he threw the entire Russian delegation into prison. When Filaret was finally permitted to return to Moscow in 1619, he was named Patriarch of the Russian Church

THE TEENAGE TSARS

Michael

Alexis

Fedor

and made co-ruler with Michael. He effectively ruled Russia until his death in 1633. Thus, Michael remained in the shadow of his father most of his life.

Michael was succeeded by his son, Alexis (1645–1676), who also was 16 when his father died. Like his father, he was a gentle person, easily dominated by those about him. Dominated in his youth by his tutor Morozov, he later fell under the influence of the Patriarch Nikon and, still later, by his last favorite, Artamon Matveev. Most of the accomplishments of his reign are more the product of these men than of Alexis.

Fedor III was the third Romanov Tsar (1676–1682), son of Alexis, who came to the throne as a boy of 14. An invalid, Fedor left most of the decision-making of the state to his advisers; he died after six years on the throne.

The first Romanovs were thus not very impressive, either as individuals or as rulers. Cautious and conservative, always looking to the past rather than the present or future, manipulated by those around them, their greatest contribution was that they survived. Yet this was a significant period since a number of things occurred during the reigns of these three tsars that would have an important bearing on subsequent Russian history.

The first thing is that the Russian state had to recover from the effect of the Time of Troubles and the Livonian War. The situation in 1613 was less than positive. The economy was in shambles with large parts of the countryside going untilled and whole villages abandoned. Rebellious peasants and gangs of soldiers from the

various disbanded armies roamed the countryside, robbing civilians and looting property. Novgorod was under Swedish occupation and Russia was still at war with Poland. Prince Wladyslaw of Poland continued to press his claim to the Russian throne.

Sweden agreed to return Novgorod in 1617 but, in that same year, Prince Wladyslaw invaded Russia at the head of a Polish army and laid siege to Moscow. The invasion actually helped Michael to establish his authority since he became identified with defense of the Russian homeland against the foreign invader. Wladyslaw's forces were driven out and a truce was signed between the two sides in 1618.

To further bolster his authority, Michael kept the Zemsky Sobor in more or less continuous session in Moscow and all-important decrees were issued under the joint authority of the Tsar and that body. This might have led to the creation of a permanent representative institution in Russia, but as he became more firmly established, Michael made less use of the Zemsky Sobor. A policy emerged whereby sessions were called only to discuss unusually important issues, such as whether Russia should go to war against Poland in the 1630s. A new Zemsky Sobor was also called to confirm Alexis's succession to the throne in 1645.

Alexis called two further sessions—in 1649 to issue a new law code and in 1651–1653 to address the question of war with Poland. It did not meet thereafter. The Zemsky Sobor was thus used to create and reinforce the authority of the Tsar at a time when that authority was not firmly

established. When this purpose was fulfilled, it was no longer called into session and so it just disappeared.

Another major development had to do with the revolt of the Ukraine against Polish rule and its acquisition by Russia. The area of the Ukraine had originally become part of the Principality of Lithuania in the 14th century. Subsequently, a dynastic marriage brought Poland and Lithuania together under a single monarch; they merged into a single state in 1569.

Poland was Roman Catholic and the Ukrainians were Russian Orthodox. Efforts to catholicize the Ukrainians were intermittent for a while, but this changed in 1589, when the Metropolitan of Moscow was raised to the rank of Patriarch and given authority over all Russian Orthodox believers. Poland refused to recognize the authority of the Patriarch within any of its territories and attempted to force all its Orthodox subjects to join a new "Uniate" church that recognized the authority of Rome.

In addition, economic pressure was applied as the estates of upper class Orthodox were seized and redistributed to Polish nobles while attempts were made to turn the mass of Ukrainian peasants into serfs.

Bogdan Khmelnitsky, who had himself lost lands to a Polish nobleman, was elected *Hetman* (chief) of the Zaporozhian Cossacks, a group of adventurous independent soldiers and mercenaries whose holdings were below the rapids (Zaporozhian means "beyond the rapids") along the lower reaches of the Dnieper River. He became the leader for Ukrainian autonomy. Khmelnitsky was successful

Russia

Nikon, patriarch of Moscow

to starve out the Russians by withdrawing the entire population from the Amur River valley. The matter was resolved in 1689 by the Treaty of Nerchinsk, whereby Russia gave up all claims to the area of the Amur River valley, but was conceded the rest of Siberia north of the Amur. Thus, by the end of the 17th century, Russian territory in the east extended to the sea.

The last development associated with the first Romanovs had to do with a church reform carried out by the Patriarch Nikon. Russian church books contained many errors that had crept in over the centuries as a result of mistakes of copyists. Nikon was determined to correct them according to the Greek originals. The changes were not very significant—correcting the spelling of the name Jesus, making the sign of the cross with three fingers instead of two, three Hallelujahs instead of two at a certain time during the worship service—but the old ways had been entrenched by tradition. Nikon found himself opposed by a significant element among the clergy who resisted the changes. Avvakum, the chief spokesman for the "Old Believers," called Nikon "a mocker of God and a heretic." Nikon retaliated by banishing the supporters of the old order.

A church council eventually approved Nikon's changes and Avvakum was sentenced to be burned at the stake. That, however, only resulted in a division in the church as the Old Believers continued to oppose the reforms. Since Tsar Alexis supported the measures, he became the "Anti-Christ" as far as the Old Believers were concerned, a term they applied to subsequent tsars as well. The government outlawed them as heretics but there were too many of them for this to be effective.

Nikon also insisted that the Church was superior to the secular state; however, he failed in this bid to challenge the power of the tsar. The church council that endorsed his changes in religious ritual deposed him as patriarch. Overall, the effect of the schism and of Nikon's failed effort to contest the tsar was to weaken the power of the church and to make it more dependent on the government for support. That soon became an important consideration, for it is unlikely that Peter the Great could have carried out many of his reforms against the united opposition of the church.

Peter the Great

Peter the Great (1682–1725) is usually conceded to have been the greatest of Russia's rulers and to have had a greater impact on the Russian land and people than any of his predecessors or successors. Yet, his was a disputed succession to the throne and for seven years after he became co-tsar in 1682, there was a serious

initially, but a defeat at the hands of Polish forces convinced him that the Ukrainians could not hope to maintain their independence for long. Believing that a victory by Poland would mean the end of the Orthodox Church and the enslavement of the people, Khmelnitsky offered to bring the Ukraine under Russian rule.

Tsar Alexis and his advisers discussed the matter for two years before accepting the offer because they recognized that, if they did so, it would mean war with Poland. The Zemsky Sobor finally decided in 1653 to incorporate the Ukraine into Russia and declare war on Poland. The war lasted until 1667, ending with the Truce of Andrusovo, under the terms of which Russia obtained all of the Ukraine east of the Dnieper and was permitted to occupy the city of Kyiv for two years. Russia never gave back Kyiv, however, and the terms of the truce were made permanent by the treaty of peace of 1686.

Another important territorial addition that occurred in the 17th century was the extension of Russian control over Siberia. The penetration of Western Siberia first occurred in the 16th century during the reign of Ivan IV, when the famous merchant family of the Stroganovs became interested in Siberian furs. It was this family that hired Irmak, an *ataman* of the Volga Cossacks, to explore east of the Ural Mountains. He led an expedition to the Irtysh River, defeated the Siberian ruler and claimed Siberia west of the Ob and Irtysh rivers for Russia.

Territorial acquisition was resumed in the 17th century. The Stroganovs continued to be involved, but now they were joined by other enterprising types; these merchant traders and explorers advanced from the Ob to the Yenisei, then from the Yenisei to the Lena. As they advanced, they left fortified trading posts behind them. By the middle of the century, they had reached the Amur River and had come into contact with the Chinese. The Chinese attempted

Peter I (Peter the Great)

in the village of Preobrazhenskoe outside Moscow, and it was here that he spent the next seven years.

Moscow's "foreign quarter" was located in a suburb near Preobrazhenskoe, and Peter, bored with life in the village, soon made the acquaintanceship of a number of foreigners who had come to Russia to take service with the Russian government. These included a Swiss, Franz Lefort, a Scot, Patrick Gordon, and a Dutchman, Franz Timmerman.

Another of Peter's diversions was to organize the young nobles assigned to him as playmates into opposing "toy regiments" and to have mock battles. He also discovered that a note dispatched to the Royal armory would bring him any piece of military equipment he asked for. So, he combined his two diversions, using Lefort, Gordon, and Timmerman, who were all military men, as advisers. Gradually Peter learned military engineering, artillery, and even geometry as part of these war games, and the "toy regiments" became more and more proficient. Eventually the two regiments were given the names of Preobrazhensky and Semenovsky and became the nucleus of a new army that Peter later created.

When Peter was 14, he found an old English sailboat that was in storage. He had it brought out and launched on a nearby lake. Soon he found a Dutch shipmaster to instruct him, and he began building other boats, working alongside Dutch carpenters from the foreign quarter. Peter also liked to sit in the foreign quarter drinking with his friends, so it is not surprising that his first mistress was the daughter of the Dutch innkeeper Mons.

Peter's mother disapproved of Peter's choice of pastimes and decided that he

question whether he would be permitted to rule in his own right.

The problem was that his father, Alexis, had married twice and Peter was born of the second marriage. Alexis' first wife, Maria Miloslavska, had given him two sons, Fedor and Ivan, as well as several daughters, including the ambitious and strong-willed Sophia. When Fedor came to the throne in 1676, he chose his advisers from among the Miloslavsky family and shunted the relatives of his step-mother, Natalia Narishkina, aside. When Fedor died in 1682, the next in line for the throne was Ivan, Fedor's younger brother. Ivan, however, was intellectually disabled, subject to fits, and nearly blind.

The Narishkin clan proposed that the 10-year-old Peter become the next tsar. Sophia recognized that this would mean her total exclusion from power; she appealed to the *streltsy*, the hereditary tsarist guard created by Ivan the Terrible, to intervene on behalf of the weak Ivan, suggesting that his life was in danger. She promised pay increases to the *streltsy* to encourage their support. They invaded the Kremlin, killed a number of Peter's relatives and demanded a reordering of

the succession to the throne. As a result, Peter and Ivan were named "co-tsars" and Sophia became regent and the real ruler of Russia. Peter and his mother were permitted to take up residence in a palace

The Winter Palace of the tsars in St. Petersburg

Russia

needed a wife to settle him down. He was therefore married at the age of 16 to Eudoxia Lopukhina, a rather pious and uninteresting young woman. Peter was distracted long enough for her to become pregnant, but within a few weeks he returned to his military games and his boats. Some years later, Peter banished Eudoxia to a convent. His son, Alexis, was partly raised in that convent, and he grew up hating his father and all he stood for.

In 1689, when Peter was 17, Sophia decided that she should become ruler of Russia in her own right and began making plans to dethrone both Ivan and Peter. Peter, learning of the plot, fled to the Trinity Monastery and called his "toy regiments" to his side. Sophia's support began melting away and she was forced to surrender power. Peter banished her to a nunnery.

Never particularly interested in the more ordinary aspects of governing, he turned the day-to-day control of Russia to his wife's relatives and returned to his military training. He participated in his first

military campaign in 1695–1696 which resulted in the capture of a Turkish fortress at Azov, at the mouth of the Don River. It was to seek allies for a general war against Turkey that Peter next organized a "Grand Embassy" to travel to Western Europe.

Peter accompanied the embassy in the guise of an apprentice shipbuilder, Peter Mikhailov. He went to Brandenburg-Prussia, Holland, England, and Vienna, capital of the Holy Roman Empire. He spent six months in Holland working as an ordinary shipbuilder.

Although he learned a great deal, he found no potential ally for a war against Turkey. Charles XI of Sweden had recently died, however, and several countries—Poland, Brandenburg-Prussia, and Denmark—were eager to go to war to despoil Sweden of territories won during the 17th century in the Baltic Sea area. This offered Peter an even better chance to gain a seaport, so he agreed to go to war against Sweden as soon as he could bring the war against Turkey to an end.

Peter was in Vienna when he learned of another revolt by the *streltsy*. Although the revolt had been quashed by the time he got back to Moscow, Peter took terrible revenge upon the mutineers. The leaders were beheaded and hundreds of others were tortured or killed and their bodies left to lie out on display as an object lesson for others. Sixteen *streltsy* regiments were ultimately disbanded; Peter had managed to destroy the political power of the *streltsy*, but he had also left himself without an army.

Peter is remembered as the "Great Westernizer" and it is true that he introduced many things into Russia from the West, particularly dealing with culture and manners. Peter was not an uncritical admirer of the West, however, and his primary motivation for introducing western styles was to make Russians more acceptable to Europeans. Thus beards, which were out of style in the West, were forbidden at court and Peter personally took a pair of shears and cut the hair of his chief courtiers. Nobles who chose to keep a

ROMANOV DYNASTY

MICHAEL

m. Maria (1) —**ALEXIS**— m. Natalia (2)
b. 1629 (1645–1676) (Regent 1689–1694)

Sophia (Regent 1682–1689)

FEDOR III b. 1661 (1676–1682)

IVAN V (Co-Tsar 1682–1696) b. 1666

m. Eudoxia (1) — **PETER I** — m. **CATHERINE I** (2)
"THE GREAT" (1725–1727)
(1682–1725)

ANNE (1730–1740)

Alexis

Anna

ELIZABETH (1741–1762)

Anna Leopoldovna (Regent 1740–1741)

PETER II (1727–1730)

PETER III (1762) Deposed and Murdered

m. **CATHERINE II** "THE GREAT" (1762–1796)

IVAN VI (1740–1741) Deposed

beard were required to pay a tax of 100 rubles and to wear a badge indicating that they had paid it. Peasants were permitted to keep their beards, but had to pay a fine of 1 kopeck each time they entered Moscow. Western-style clothing became mandatory for members of the upper classes. Women, previously kept in isolation, were now invited to public entertainments and dinners, and court balls were organized where men and women danced in the western manner.

Peter kept changing Russian ways of doing things all the rest of his life, but most of the other changes which he introduced might more properly be characterized as modernizations. He simplified the Russian alphabet, eliminating what he considered useless letters, and ordered that the new characters be used in all lay books. Church books continued to use the old style, which came to be known as Old Slavonic.

He also set up the first newspaper in Russia in 1703, established all sorts of technical institutes, laid the foundations for the Universities of Moscow and St. Petersburg, created the Russian Academy of Sciences, sponsored expeditions to explore the Kamchatka Peninsula, the Kuril Islands, and the Bering Strait, carried out extensive administrative reforms, established an iron industry, a munitions industry, textile factories, and in general encouraged the development of trade. He also brought the Russian Orthodox Church more under state control by replacing the position of patriarch with a secular head appointed personally by the tsar and turning priests into police informants.

In addition, Peter also built a modern army and navy and he fought a 21-year war with Sweden for control of the southern shores of the Baltic Sea. The war was ultimately successful, and Russia became established as one of the "great powers" of Europe as a result, but it was extremely costly. Taxes had to be increased on the peasantry and other commoner classes, while a lifetime service obligation beginning at age 15 was instituted for the nobility. Peasants were also drafted into the military for the first time. Although military service became a lifetime obligation for them, it did have the advantage that they ceased to be serfs upon taking the military oath.

After Peter's death, the term of military service for both nobility and commoners was reduced to 25 years. His proudest achievement was the city he built at the mouth of the Neva River on reclaimed swampland newly liberated from the Swedes. St. Petersburg, whose foundations were laid in 1703, was to be his capital, his chief seaport on the Baltic and his "window to the west." It was here—and at Tsarskoe Selo ("the Tsar's village"), twelve miles away—that he began the magnificent palaces which were to signify Russia's new great power status.

An Era of Palace Revolutions

One of Peter's greater disappointments was his son, Alexis, who in the normal course of events would have succeeded him. Alexis opposed everything that Peter stood for, however, and he made no secret of the fact that he planned to undo all of Peter's reforms if he came to power. He embarrassed his father further in 1716 by fleeing abroad and requesting sanctuary from the Holy Roman Emperor. Two years later, he returned home at his father's urging, where Peter forced him to renounce his claim to the throne, then had him put on trial for treason. He was found guilty and sentenced to death, but it was later announced that he had died while under interrogation.

Peter issued a decree abolishing succession of the oldest son or child of the tsar, which stated that the tsar would name his successor. He never got around to designating his own, however, and his sudden death left the succession unsettled. It was resolved by Prince Alexander Menshikov, one of Peter's close associates, who called upon the Guards regiments to support Catherine, Peter's second wife, as his successor. The Guards regiments, descendants of Peter's original "toy regiments," thus set a tradition of intervention which would continue throughout the 18th century. It was not until 1796, under Emperor Paul, that Peter's succession decree was finally repealed and primogeniture was reinstituted as the method of succession.

The weird succession to the throne of Russia following the death of Peter the Great at the age of 53 is best understood with the help of a diagram. The rulers between Peter the Great and Catherine the Great were as follows:

CATHERINE I (1725–1727), a peasant woman, Peter's second wife

PETER II (1727–1730), son of the dead Prince Alexis

ANNE (1730–1740), Duchess of Courland, half-niece of Peter I

IVAN VI (1741), half great-great nephew of Peter I

ELIZABETH (1741–1762), younger daughter of Peter I by his second wife

PETER III (1762), son of Elizabeth's older sister Anna and the Duke of Holstein, grandson of Peter I

This peculiar succession reflects the sequence of intrigues, plots, and coups by a series of advisers, court favorites, and lovers. The amazing thing is that Russia's international position did not decline during this period because other powers failed to take advantage of the internal upheaval.

Of these rulers, only one, Elizabeth, made any important contribution to Russian development. She consciously took up Peter's reforms where they had been left hanging in 1725 and carried them forward. It was Elizabeth who completed the Winter Palace in St. Petersburg, who hired the famous Italian architect, Rastrelli, to rebuild the Peterhof at Tsarskoe Selo and who established Moscow University. She also emulated Peter's foreign policy by signing alliances with Paris and Vienna and by intervening in the Seven Years' War against Frederick the Great of Prussia. She partially neutralized that accomplishment, however, when she named Peter III as her successor to the throne.

When he succeeded her at the beginning of 1762, he immediately set out to undo nearly everything she had accomplished. Although a grandson of Peter the Great, Peter III was German by upbringing and Lutheran in religion. He was not at all happy about becoming Tsar of Russia, a position for which he was unfit, both physically and mentally.

His marriage to the daughter of a minor German princely family, Sophie of Anhalt-Zerbst, had been arranged by his aunt, the Empress Elizabeth. It had been Peter the Great who had begun the practice of "arranged marriages" for political purposes (a pattern followed by German and other western European dynastic alliances), and she continued the policy. But the 1745 marriage remained "in name only" for nine years because, according to one story, the young Grand Duke had a physical disability which made it impossible for him to consummate the relationship.

The story goes that Peter had an operation to cure his disability, but Catherine, as the young Grand Duchess, was known after her conversion to Russian Orthodoxy, had already been urged by Empress Elizabeth to take a lover in order to assure an heir to the throne. In her memoirs, Catherine identified the young lover, Sergei Saltykov, as the father of her son, Paul. Whether true or not, Peter III evidently believed it because, when he became Tsar in 1762, he decided to disinherit Paul and send Catherine to a convent. This led to his overthrow and to his death in a coup d'etat which installed Catherine as Empress of Russia.

Catherine the Great (1762–1796)

Catherine had no personal claim to the Russian throne, but she did win the support of the Guards regiments—partly because her latest lover, Gregory Orlov, was an officer of the Guards. For 34 years, the growing Russian Empire was governed by a woman of great talent and even greater determination to excel in everything and to control all things. She was hardworking and devoted to matters of state. She saw herself as both a figure of the Enlightenment and as Peter the Great's

Russia

Catherine the Great

successor. She had a lively correspondence with Voltaire and Frederick the Great of Prussia and at one point she invited Diderot, the French encyclopedist, to St. Petersburg and set aside an hour each evening for conversation with him.

When she first came to the throne, she had great hopes for further reforms and she did a great deal to encourage culture and learning. At one point, she spent two years drafting instructions for a Legislative Conference which she called to draw up a new code of law. The instructions, heavily based on the writings of Montesquieu and other Enlightenment thinkers, were considered so radical that they were banned in France. The instructions were apparently also too radical for members of the Legislative Conference; they were unable to draft a new code based on them.

When Catherine first came to the throne, she expressed her dislike for serfdom. But she ultimately found that she could do nothing about it, for serfdom formed the economic basis of the nobility, the class that brought her to power and staffed the army and civil administration.

In her role as an enlightened despot, therefore, Catherine didn't accomplish very much. Her greatest achievements were in the area of public health

and education. She introduced a variolation procedure to prevent smallpox and opened hospitals, orphanages, and schools, including the famous Smolny Institute, which was Russia's first school for girls. Although her attachment to the ideals of the Enlightenment were overall rather superficial, she proved to be a good publicist whose writings and correspondence created a good impression of Russia in the West.

Something more should perhaps be said about her lovers. It is a matter of record that she had, over a period of many years, at least 21 lovers. In this regard, Catherine was not greatly different from other 18th century monarchs. The Empress Elizabeth, at whose court she grew up, had a succession of lovers who were given the official title of "Gentleman of the Bedchamber." Louis XIV of France was famous for his succession of official mistresses, known as "Ladies of the Bedchamber."

Catherine had more lovers than most, but only four had any significance insofar as Russian history is concerned. Two of these, the presumed father of Paul and the officer who helped her come to power, have already been mentioned. A third was Stanislaw Poniatowski, a handsome Polish nobleman whom she later made King of

Poland. The fourth was Grigory Potemkin (Poh-*tyom*-kin), who was responsible for a number of Russia's military victories during her reign, including the conquest and annexation of the Crimea. Potemkin became her lover and chief adviser—and there may even have been a private marriage ceremony. But when the two functions conflicted, he chose to remain her chief adviser—and over the next several years personally selected the young Guardsmen who became Catherine's "Gentleman of the Bedchamber."

Catherine deserves to be called "the Great" primarily because of her successful wars and because of Russia's extensive territorial expansion during her reign. Perhaps the most important of her territorial expansions is associated with her participation with Prussia and Austria in the three partitions of Poland that resulted in an end of the Polish-Lithuanian state.

The liquidation of Poland brought into the Russian empire all the lands which had been claimed as "Russian" during earlier history. This was not the only success of Catherine—under her leadership the first major victory was scored against the Ottoman Turkish Empire to the south, hastening the decline of a once-powerful foe. Russia obtained access to a considerable portion of the Black Sea in 1774 and secured the right of passage through the Turkish Straits into the Mediterranean. It was also recognized as the official protector of Orthodox Christians living under Turkish rule. Further expansion led to the acquisition in 1792 of a little-known fortress called Ochakov and the right to control the Crimean Peninsula. These events caused the first alarm in England over the possibility of Russian expansion into areas of interest to the British.

During the struggle between Great Britain and the American colonies, Russia played an important role in the League of Armed Neutrality. This was a group of nations that insisted on the right of passage of neutral ships across the Atlantic Ocean and other bodies of water in spite of British objections. Catherine followed with interest the developments in Western Europe and broke off relations with France after revolutionaries executed King Louis XVI. She apparently intended that Russia would be part of an armed intervention in France. She also entertained a greater scheme for the creation of a Christian empire out of Greece and other Turkish possessions, but nothing came of this.

The French Revolution and Russia

For a century prior to the French Revolution, Russia had been governed by a series of rulers committed to the concept of a "revolution from above." In the process, the nobility and urban classes had been transformed, but the peasantry—90% of the people—remained the same. It was this obstacle that Catherine was unable to overcome and when the French Revolution popularized the ideas of "liberty, equality, and fraternity" and announced the end of serfdom and legal distinctions based on class, this made the ideas of the French Revolution subversive within the Russian part of Europe.

An even greater difficulty was that Russian rulers from Catherine onward, educated in the Enlightenment traditions, agreed with many of the ideals of the French Revolution, but could not see how to achieve them in Russia without completely disrupting the very fabric of Russian society. All agreed, for example, that serfdom was a clearly seen evil and ought to be abolished, but none before Alexander II could bring himself to do so. As a result, the distance between convictions and actions widened, and the actions of Russian rulers became more and more conservative as the 19th century progressed. Half-hearted and partial reforms were still proposed and sometimes implemented, but they were never sufficient to transform the basic organization of the Russian society; the ideals of the French Revolution continued to be regarded as suspect and unworthy in Russia.

Further change was afoot in Western Europe—the Industrial Revolution—transforming social and economic relationships. As England, France and Germany industrialized, Russia, with a social and economic system that was incompatible with capitalism, fell further behind. In spite of all of its efforts, therefore, Russia's system of government and its role as a great power were both in decline throughout most of the 19th century. Even as its rulers attempted to catch up, Russia remained "on hold."

Romanov Monarchs after Catherine

We continue to refer to monarchs after Catherine the Great as Romanovs even though she was a German, and if her memoirs are correct, they are all descendants of Catherine and Sergei Saltykov. Before the Romanov dynasty ended its historical role, a sprawling and multinational Russia was ruled by six tsars—Catherine's son, Paul; his two sons, Alexander I and Nicholas I; Nicholas I's son, grandson, and great-grandson—Alexander II, Alexander III, and Nicholas II.

Paul I (1796–1801)

Paul, who succeeded his mother in 1796, had been alienated from her because he believed that she had usurped his rightful throne. He therefore spent the first part of his reign attempting to undo his mother's accomplishments. Possessing a military

Emperor Alexander I

mentality and a foul temper, his was an unstable reign that ended after five years in a coup d'état made on behalf of his son, who gave his advance approval albeit on the condition that his father's life was to be spared. Paul was murdered during the coup, a fact that was said to prey on Alexander's conscience and may explain some of his otherwise unexplainable actions. As one historian has pointed out, this was the last "indoor" assassination—the Tsar was killed in his bedroom by an "inside" group of high-ranking conspirators and officers of the Guards regiments. In the next century, "assassinations were to take place in the open street." With this last palace revolution, Russia drifted into the 19th century—loaded down with traditions of the past; autocratic rule; a privileged upper class; and with serfdom weighing as heavily as ever on the shoulders of the Russian people.

Alexander I (1801–1825)

Alexander I has always remained a puzzle to both historians and psychologists. In the beginning, he was inclined toward liberal ideas and determined to continue efforts to westernize Russia. But he ended up a political conservative and a religious mystical, dying at Taganrog, a small town on the Sea of Azov in southern Russia, where he had taken his wife because of her ill health. Typically for Russia, a legend developed that he didn't really die, but chose the life of a saintly hermit to ask

forgiveness for his sins. The fact that he was aware of the plot to kill his father before it occurred may have been the sin that later drove him to religious mysticism.

At the beginning of his rule, Alexander asked Michael Speransky, the outstanding statesman of that age, to draw up a plan of basic reforms, including a constitution, a modern code of laws, and an educational system. He even gave half-hearted consideration to abolishing serfdom; the only result was the law of 1803 that permitted the voluntary emancipation of serfs by landlords. Few made use of this opportunity.

On Alexander's orders, Speransky drew up a constitution which would have created a national legislature and guaranteed various civil rights. Most of the nobility opposed the plan, however. Needing the nobility's support in the approaching war with France, Alexander was forced to dismiss Speransky.

Alexander did carry out an administrative reorganization, turning the Colleges he had inherited from Peter the Great into Ministries and organizing them into something analogous to a cabinet, called the Committee of Ministers. In addition, he created an appointed legislature called the Council of State, to draw up legislation for the tsar's approval. None of these changes or new institutions actually restricted the tsar's authority, but they did regularize procedures and increase the size of the circle of advisers.

The War of 1812

The most famous achievement of Russia in this period was the spectacular defeat of Napoleon I of France after he launched his invasion of Russia in 1812. Earlier, Russia had been a member of the so-called Third Coalition that fought against Napoleon in 1805. Russia and its allies, Prussia and Austria, were beaten at that time and had to submit to rather harsh conditions of the Treaty of Tilsit, which, for Russia, included Russian adherence to Napoleon's "continental system." For the next seven years, relative peace and cooperation followed between Russia and France.

During this time, Russia expanded into areas along its borders, mainly at the expense of Persia and Turkey. Georgia, threatened by Persia, was annexed in the south. Bessarabia, to the southwest, was taken from Turkey. At the same time, Russia also seized Finland from Sweden, converting it into a Grand Duchy with the Tsar as ruler. It was also during this period that forts were established in "Russian America"—first in Alaska and then north of what is now San Francisco.

Mutual suspicions between France and Russia emerged in 1811–1812. Russia hated Napoleon's continental system, which prohibited Russia's large volume of trade

Russia

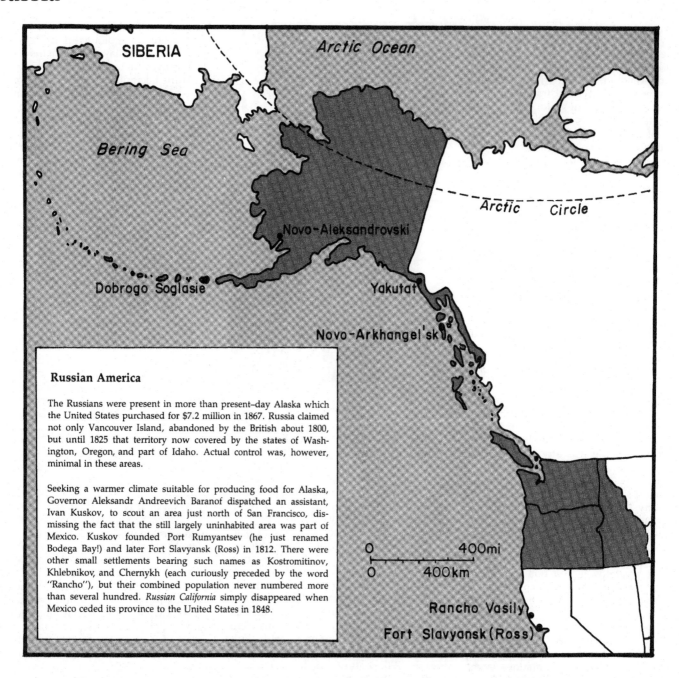

SIBERIA

Arctic Ocean

Bering Sea

Arctic Circle

Novo-Aleksandrovski

Dobrogo Soglasie

Yakutat

Novo-Arkhangel'sk

Russian America

The Russians were present in more than present–day Alaska which the United States purchased for $7.2 million in 1867. Russia claimed not only Vancouver Island, abandoned by the British about 1800, but until 1825 that territory now covered by the states of Washington, Oregon, and part of Idaho. Actual control was, however, minimal in these areas.

Seeking a warmer climate suitable for producing food for Alaska, Governor Aleksandr Andreevich Baranof dispatched an assistant, Ivan Kuskov, to scout an area just north of San Francisco, dismissing the fact that the still largely uninhabited area was part of Mexico. Kuskov founded Port Rumyantsev (he just renamed Bodega Bay!) and later Fort Slavyansk (Ross) in 1812. There were other small settlements bearing such names as Kostromitinov, Khlebnikov, and Chernykh (each curiously preceded by the word "Rancho"), but their combined population never numbered more than several hundred. *Russian California* simply disappeared when Mexico ceded its province to the United States in 1848.

0   400mi
0   400km

Rancho Vasily

Fort Slavyansk (Ross)

with Great Britain. Napoleon, worried that Russia would pull out of the continental system and ally itself with Great Britain, decided to invade Russia and did so on June 21, 1812, with an army of almost one-half million. The French constituted only about half of this force, with the remainder made up of levies from Austria and Prussia. A great number of Poles joined the effort, expecting Napoleon to liberate and restore to them all or most of the territory of the defunct Polish-Lithuanian commonwealth.

As in the past, the Russian peasant masses rallied to the support of "Mother Russia." Another significant factor in turning Napoleon's invasion into a major

defeat was the well-known Russian winter, which in 1812–1813 was unusually severe. This completely disrupted the extremely long supply lines of the French.

Hoping for a speedy surrender of the Tsar's forces, Napoleon remained in occupied Moscow until October and only began his departure west after the Russian winter had set in; before long, his *Grande Armée* was in tatters and without food. "Scorched earth" tactics and roaming bands of guerrillas were used against the invader by the Russian general, Mikhail Kutuzov. The departure of Napoleon's forces was not just a retreat—it was a rout. Russian troops pursued the small remnant of Napoleon's army all the way to Paris.

Russia played a major role at the Congress of Vienna which was convened to settle the affairs of Europe but Alexander I, who went to Vienna, did not get everything he wanted. Although Great Britain, Austria, and Prussia were allies with Russia so long as Napoleon remained a threat, they had their own goals which they pushed at Vienna. Britain and Austria in particular rejected Alexander I's proposal for reestablishment of a large Kingdom of Poland with Alexander I as king. The Kingdom of Poland actually established by the Congress of Vienna was much smaller than desired by Alexander I; substantial portions of the ancient Kingdom of Poland remained part of Austria and Prussia until after World War I.

Russia

Alexander I also proposed that the victors at the Congress of Vienna join together to form a "Holy Alliance" to guarantee the peace, guided by a spirit of Christian brotherhood. It was a rather unclear plan that had no important practical results in the field of international relations.

Of greater significance was the Quadruple Alliance, signed by Russia, Great Britain, Austria, and Prussia, which made provision for periodic conferences to review matters of common interest and to assure continued peace. The consensus about what it meant to maintain the peace settlement did not last very long, however. The British wished to limit international cooperation to international attempts to overthrow the status quo, while Russia, Prussia, and Austria argued for international cooperation to put down revolutionary movements within individual states. Great Britain broke with the other three nations on this issue in 1820, but Russia, Prussia, and Austria continued to cooperate.

Alexander I put domestic policies on hold during the War of 1812. After Napoleon's defeat, he turned his attention back to domestic affairs, but a large foreign debt and a budget deficit precluded major new programs such as had marked the earlier part of his reign. His antipathy toward serfdom continued, however, and in 1816 he abolished serfdom in Estonia. Another decree the next year ended serfdom in Courland, while a third decree abolished it in Livonia in 1819.

But Alexander I began to lose interest in secular change after he fell under the influence of a Russian monk known for his piety during the Napoleonic Wars. Another influence on him was Prince Klemens von Metternich, chief minister of the Austrian Empire, who persuaded Alexander that revolutionary forces threatened the political stability of Europe. Alexander began to collect more conservative advisers about him and, increasingly, to act on their advice. The most influential of these was General Alexis Arakcheev, who drew up and implemented plans for "military colonies" in the western part of Russia. Recruits assigned to the military colonies helped to support themselves by growing most of their food. Hated by both soldiers and officers, the military colonies were abolished by Nicholas I after Alexander's death.

Alexander also appointed religious conservatives to major posts such as the Ministry of Education with predictable results. A new regime of censorship was imposed and religious instruction was given a more prominent place in the curriculum.

The Decembrists

The end of Alexander's reign in 1825 is associated with the first Russian revolution—that of the Decembrists. Although this was exclusively a revolt by army officers and lasted only one day, it is labeled a revolution because the leaders had specific plans about changing the nature of the Russian state and society and did not merely wish to change rulers. The Decembrists were all nobles who had served in Western Europe and who wished to rid Russia of its backwardness. Their specific goals included the abolition of serfdom and the creation of a constitutional government. They were particularly aggrieved that Alexander I had granted a constitution to Poland and had permitted Finland to retain a constitution it had when it was annexed in 1809, but refused to grant one in Russia.

Organized into secret societies, they carried on discussions for a number of years, but were unable to agree on any specific action to take. They were galvanized into action by Alexander I's death, when no new Tsar was immediately sworn in as his successor. The confusion about the succession arose because Constantine, the nominal heir, had married a Polish countess and relinquished his claim to the throne—but this was not known. It was compounded by the fact that Constantine was in Warsaw, where he was regent, and all communications were by mail.

The matter was sorted out and Nicholas prepared to officially take over as tsar. On the appointed day, 3,000 "Decembrist" troops, assembled on the Senate Square, refused to take the oath to Nicholas, but then did nothing further. Nicholas surrounded the square with 10,000 loyal troops and demanded their surrender. When they refused, he ordered the artillery to fire on the insurgents, who then broke and ran. The revolt was over.

Nicholas I

The Decembrist revolt was therefore only a minor affair. Five of the top leaders were executed, while approximately 100 others were imprisoned and later exiled to Siberia. But what made it important was the myth that grew up about the Decembrists; Alexander Herzen, Russian revolutionary publicist, later took up the cause of the Decembrists and made them heroes to subsequent generations. Another importance of the Decembrist revolt was the breach it opened between the government and Russian liberals, who never forgave Nicholas for his harsh treatment of the Decembrists and remained alienated throughout his reign. Conversely, Nicholas was never able to overcome his suspicion that all liberals were potentially disloyal.

Nicholas I (1825–1855)

Nicholas was 29 years old when he became Tsar and ruled Russia for 30 years until his death in 1855. He was not particularly well educated and he had no practical experience in administration before he succeeded to the throne. His background was entirely in the military, where he held the rank of brigade general. He liked the military and during his lifetime he surrounded himself with soldiers, preferring them as advisers and chief administrators.

He distrusted public opinion and did not believe that solutions could arise from among the people. He therefore prohibited public discussion of current problems, and books, journals, and newspapers were censored. Since he also distrusted the bureaucracy but needed sources of information, he created "His Majesty's Third Section" as his eyes and ears; this organization was essentially a secret police organization.

However, he kept a report of the testimony of the Decembrists on his desk and conscientiously attempted to meet some of the criticism contained in their statements. One of his early successes was the new code of laws which was issued in 1833—the first new code since 1649. He was also deeply concerned about serfdom and appointed a series of secret committees to work on the problem—but he could not bring himself to the point of abolishing the system. He did, however, improve the lot of the State Peasants by commuting all labor service into taxes and by setting up local government for them. Just over 50% of all peasants were State Peasants—people who lived on state land rather than on the land of individual nobles.

Nicholas I's reign has also been referred to as "the reign of outer repression and inner liberation," since it was while he was upon the throne that Russian literature and culture first attained international stature and recognition. Great Russian writers of this period included the poet Alexander

23

St. Isaac's Orthodox Cathedral in St. Petersburg was commissioned by Tsar Nicholas I. It was designed by French architect Auguste de Montferrand and under construction from 1818–1858. The workers who applied the magnificent gold–mercury amalgam knew when they breathed the toxic fumes that they would die, often within two years

Russia

Pushkin, the novelist Mikhail Lermontov, author of *A Hero of Our Time*, and Nikolai Gogol, famous for novels, plays, and short stories. Nicholas I, who attended the premiere of Gogol's play *The Inspector General*, a biting satire on Russian officialdom, afterward commented "Everybody got what was coming to him and I got more than anyone."

Other Russian creative artists who began their work during the reign of Nicholas I included Ivan Turgenev, who wrote *A Sportsman's Sketches* during this time, and Mikhail Glinka, founder of Russian classical music and famous for his operas. The Bolshoi Theater, constructed in 1824, also provided a showcase for Russian ballet, comparable to that of France from where it came.

There were economic changes of some note as well, though the prohibitive tariff system adopted at the close of the Napoleonic Wars tended to isolate Russia from the momentous changes in Western Europe as a result of the spread of the Industrial Revolution. The continued existence of serfdom was another factor hindering change.

In spite of that, there was a dramatic growth in textile manufacturing in the province of Moscow and in and around the city of Lodz, in Russian Poland, during the reign of Nicholas I. Most of the early factories were relatively primitive, for powered machinery was beginning to be introduced only toward the end of his reign. This new industry was significant, however, because it was the first to make widespread use of free wage labor in Russia.

What made it even more interesting is that most of the workers were serfs who also compensated a master for labor services not performed in return for permission to take an outside job. The success of the new factories using wage labor foreshadowed the end of serfdom in Russia, for they established that free labor was more efficient than serf labor.

Nicholas I was also responsible for construction of the first railways in Russia, against the advice of his ministers. The first line, between St. Petersburg and Tsarskoe Selo, the royal palace complex located 12 miles away on the Baltic, was constructed as an experiment. The second line connected St. Petersburg with Moscow. Nicholas authorized a third line linking St. Petersburg and Warsaw, but the Crimean War intervened and the project was put on hold.

In foreign affairs, Nicholas fought a series of minor wars. Victory over the Ottoman Empire in 1828–1829 gave Russia the mouth of the Danube River and the eastern coast of the Black Sea. His troops were used again in 1830–1831 to put down a Polish insurrection. Nicholas then

punished the Poles by abolishing their constitution and declaring Poland an integral part of the Russian Empire. Troops were also dispatched to Hungary in 1849 to end a revolt there and force the Hungarians back within the Austrian Empire.

Two years before his death, Nicholas involved the Russians in his first major war, the Crimean War. The basis of the original quarrel with Turkey—Russia's claim to be the protector of all Orthodox Christians under Turkish rule—would not have justified a war involving three great powers, but Britain and France intervened because Britain believed that Russia was attempting to partition Turkey. The war began with naval attacks against coastal Russian towns on the Baltic Sea, the White Sea, and the Pacific Ocean, but the main attack came in 1854 when 60,000 allied troops began a siege of the Russian naval base at Sevastopol on the Crimean Peninsula.

Although faced with superior forces, the siege of the Russians lasted almost a year. One episode of the senseless loss of many lives is known to most pupils from Alfred Tennyson's "Charge of the Light Brigade." Tsar Nicholas died in the midst of the war, which was brought to an end by the Treaty of Paris in 1856. Russia had to surrender some territory, including Bessarabia, and give up the right to have naval forces or fortifications on the Black Sea.

Alexander II (1855–1881)

Alexander II, who succeeded to the throne upon the death of his father, Nicholas I, went down in history as the "Tsar Emancipator," the greatest westernizer since Peter the Great. Yet, he was not particularly well-liked during his reign, and he died the victim of a terrorist's bomb. The problem was that, though he saw the need for reforms, he wished to implement them in the form of another

Alexander II

"revolution from above," in the manner of previous tsars. Perhaps that was inevitable, but the result was that, first, his reforms were modified in their application by a conservative bureaucracy and, second, his unwillingness to involve the newly educated elites created by his reforms meant that he lost a chance to develop a popular constituency to support his measures.

Alexander II came to the throne much better prepared than his father, for Nicholas had appointed him to the State Council (the appointed legislative assembly created by Alexander I) and the Committee of Ministers (the Tsar's cabinet, also created by his predecessor). He held a series of military commands and had also sat on a committee on serfdom appointed by Nicholas. At the conclusion of one session, Alexander petitioned his father to abolish serfdom. Nicholas said he recognized that serfdom was a present, existing evil, but to touch it might perhaps create greater evils.

Russia's defeat in the Crimean War convinced Alexander that Russia could no longer afford to do nothing; its continued existence as a great power was now at stake. The industrialization that had spread across Europe in the first half of the 19th century had left Russia largely untouched. Serfdom, with its mass of peasant workers tied to the soil, was incompatible with industrialization. Russia stood still while Europe progressed.

Moreover, serfdom, which had been abolished everywhere else in Europe, had come to be viewed as a moral evil whose continued presence in Russia excluded it from the company of civilized Europe. This moral revulsion toward serfdom had been an important factor in the harsh terms applied to Russia in the Treaty of Paris. Alexander II thus had two important reasons to move for the abolition of serfdom.

Alexander appointed his first committee to consider ways to abolish serfdom in 1857. Four years later, in 1861, he gave his approval to the emancipation manifesto which immediately freed all serfs from personal bondage. Since Russia had an overwhelmingly agricultural economy, it was decided to free the serfs with a type of land tenure. Since the land legally was the property of the nobles, however, the law stipulated that the ex-serfs would get the amount of land they had worked for themselves before emancipation, but they would have to pay for it. Since the ex-serfs had no money, the government arranged to pay the nobles for the land and to have the ex-serfs pay off their debt to the government over a period of 49 years.

Direct and personal ownership of the land was not given to the peasants; the so-called peasant commune was to be collectively responsible for the payments of

25

Russia

Map labels: Murmansk, 1945, 1795, Minsk, 1793, Kiev, 1940, MOSCOW, Igarka, Yakutsk, Okhotsk, Petropavlovsk, 1783, Kazan, Samara, Ufa, 1864, 1810-29, Omsk, 1824, 1822, Caspian Sea, 1804-30, 1853, 1873, 1873, 1854, 1881, 1881, 1871, 1884, 1895, Irkutsk, Lake Baikal, 1858-60, Vladivostock

0   200   400 mi
0 200 400 km

Grand Duchy of Moscow and Russia in 1533
Year territory gained: 1533-98   1598-1689
1689-1725   1725-1801   1801-1945

THE GROWTH OF RUSSIA

its members and had the right to allot the land to peasant families. This was to be done according to the size of the family, and the allotments were open to revision every few years. Because of the financial responsibility, the commune hindered the attempts of the peasants to move away, causing overpopulation and land hunger in some areas.

Emancipation ended the control of the nobility over the serfs and necessitated the creation of local government and judicial institutions for the newly-freed peasants. Both of these reforms were carried out in 1864. The Zemstvo reform created elective councils at the district and provincial level and gave them responsibility for the local economy, health protection and education. Although voters were organized into three classes—nobles, townsmen, and peasants—and voted separately, the Zemstvo assemblies were genuinely democratic institutions in which all classes participated and they became an important voice for rural interests.

The judicial reform was even more radical, because it abolished traditional Russian judicial practices and created an entirely new system that introduced trial by jury, public trials, defense attorneys, and an independent judiciary, none of which had hitherto existed in Russia.

Cities were granted local government in 1870 along the lines of the Zemstvo reform. Elected city councils were created and an executive board was headed by a mayor. Although weighted voting systems meant that a relatively few large taxpayers could control the city council, the effect of the overall reform was positive.

An army reform, introduced in 1874, initiated the principle that every man, regardless of class, was liable for military service. The ordinary term of service was reduced to six years, schools for officers were modernized, and specific provisions were made to ensure that all enlisted men were taught how to read and write. Since illiteracy was quite high in Russia, the army thus became a significant adjunct to the nation's educational system.

Alexander also reorganized the secondary school system, granted autonomy to the universities and waived university fees for those too poor to pay. The Zemstvos had been given responsibility for primary education, but Alexander did approve a law calling for the establishment of a system of primary education throughout Russia. Many Zemstvos were slow to follow through on the Tsar's orders, but primary schools slowly came into existence; by 1914, Zemstvos were spending approximately one-third of their budget on primary education.

Alexander's economic reforms were—aside from serf emancipation—his most important measures, but they were more long-term and so took longer to show an effect. In addition, Alexander's commitment to industrialization was closely connected to his desire that Russia remain a great power. One of the major reasons for Russia's defeat in the Crimean War was the inability of the Russian government quickly to move men and supplies to the Crimean area. Because of the nature of the climate and the soil, getting about on land was nearly impossible for several months every year—roads turned into quagmires in the spring and fall. Russia's rivers were important transport links, but they were frozen during six winter months.

Alexander, whose mother and wife were both German and who visited Germany regularly, had been impressed by the extensive railway building in Germany in the 1840s and 1850s and the thrust this had given to German industrialization. The Tsar conceived of a similar program for Russia. But since there was little capital in Russia for investment and even fewer entrepreneurs—and the Russian government had no funds adequate for such railway construction—Alexander and his advisers set out to encourage the creation of private railway companies in Russia financed by foreign private capital investment.

Railway companies were permitted to bring in duty-free all equipment and material needed to construct a railroad; in addition, dividends and interest on stocks and bonds issued by the railway companies were guaranteed by the Russian government. Investors were, in effect, guaranteed against all losses.

The plan worked. By the time of Alexander II's death in 1881, approximately 7,500 kilometers of railroad had been constructed, metal-working and machine-building companies had sprung into existence, and the beginnings of a modern iron and steel industry had been laid. It was still only a beginning, but railroad construction continued in the 1880s and 1890s and, after a financial and political crisis that lasted for several years, again began between 1907 and 1914. By 1914, European Russia was covered by an extensive network of railways and the Trans-Siberian Railway had been built across the entire empire to Siberia and down to Vladivostok.

Alexander II was obsessed with Russia's defeat in the Crimean War and was determined to undo at least the more onerous clauses of the 1856 treaty. This became the main thrust of his foreign policy; his efforts to win over the French resulted in a friendship treaty between the two nations in 1857, but the Polish uprising six years later disrupted this relationship, since the French were sympathetic to the Poles. Alexander next turned to Prussia as a potential ally and this led to Russian support for German unification and a growing economic relationship between the two.

When the Franco-Prussian War broke out in 1870, the Russian government took advantage of the situation by denouncing the Black Sea clauses of the earlier treaty.

England protested, but agreed to drop the offending clauses when it became clear that the new German government supported Russia.

Russia and the Austro-Hungarian Empire tended to be rivals in the Balkan area and their relations had been strained since the Crimean War. However, Russia, Germany, and Austria signed an agreement in 1873—The Three Emperor's League—which brought them together in a quasi-alliance. It was Bismarck, the German Chancellor, who sponsored the agreement; he hoped to end the Russo-Austrian rivalry in the Balkans. Russia and Austria could, however, only agree to maintain the status quo, so when an uprising began in Bosnia in 1875 and quickly spread to Serbia and Bulgaria, relations between the two countries soured.

Russia and Austria signed the Reichstadt Agreement in 1876 whereby Austria agreed to remain neutral in case of war, while Russia agreed to a suitable territorial compensation for Austria and promised that it would not sponsor the creation of a single large Slavic nation. When war broke out between Russia and Turkey in 1877, Russian armies were victorious. In the ensuing treaty, Russia got back southern Bessarabia plus three small towns east of the Black Sea; Turkey agreed to recognize the independence of Serbia, Romania, and Montenegro. The remaining Slavic territories in the eastern Balkans would be organized into a single, autonomous state with an elected Christian Prince. No mention was made of any territorial compensation for Austria.

A bitter Austria threatened to go to war and England also objected to the terms of the treaty, sending its fleet into the eastern Mediterranean. War appeared imminent and Bismarck quickly agreed to host a conference of the powers in Berlin.

At the Congress of Berlin, the powers modified the terms of the treaty as follows: Bulgaria was reduced to one-third of its former size; another third was set up as the autonomous region of Eastern Rumelia; and the final third, Macedonia, was returned to Turkey. Austria received the right to administer Bosnia and Herzegovina and was allowed to station troops in the Sanjak of Novibazar. England got Cyprus. Even as modified, the Treaty of Berlin was a triumph for Russia for, with the return of Bessarabia, the last of the offending clauses of the 1856 treaty had been overturned. But instead, the Congress of Berlin was considered to be a humiliation for Russia and Alexander's foreign policy was judged to be a failure. The Three Emperors' League was dead; relations between Russia and Germany cooled; and Russia drew more and more into self-isolation for the next three years.

Although often at odds with the European powers, Russia was quite friendly with the United States of America. For example, the North was pleased to have squadrons of the Russian fleet pay visits to New York and San Francisco during the Civil War, though the Americans might have been less pleased had they known that the purpose of the naval visits was to avoid being trapped inside Russian bases in the event of a European war—they were not interested in helping the North. Even so, the North was determined to see the naval visits as evidence of the mutual friendship that existed between our two countries, and they also compared serf emancipation with America's abolition of slavery.

In this atmosphere, the United States government responded favorably when the Russian government suggested that it was willing to sell Alaska to America. After some negotiations, then, the United States purchased Alaska from Russia in 1867 for the sum of $7.2 million. Although this turned out to be one of America's greatest bargains, many Americans denounced it at the time as "Seward's Folly," a reference to the US Secretary of State who arranged the purchase.

In spite of Alexander II's preoccupation with relations with the West, the Russian nation continued to expand in Asia during his reign. In East Asia, China was involved in a struggle with the western powers encroaching on its coastal areas. Taking advantage of this, Russia coerced China into ceding it the regions around the Amur and Usuri Rivers. The city of Vladivostok,

Russia

meaning "Ruler of the East," was founded in 1860 as a symbol of Russian power on the Pacific shores.

Central Asia was another area of expansion for Russia in the 19th century. This was Russia's southern frontier and, as settlers pushed southward, they came increasingly into contact with central Asian peoples who resented their presence and showed this by carrying out periodic raids against Russian settlements. This would be followed in turn by punitive forays by the Russian army against central Asian settlements. As the raids continued, the army would begin building a new line of forts along the frontier and a new piece of territory would be added to the Russian empire.

By 1846, when a large part of Kazakhstan was incorporated into Russia, central Asia had been reduced to three independent Islamic khanates, Bokhara, Khiva, and Kokand. Great centers of trade and export in the middle ages which had made them legends of wealth and power, all three khanates had subsequently declined in importance. By the middle of the 19th century, their main cities had been reduced to regional trading centers and the khanates were pale shadows of their former selves. Moreover, the writ of their rulers extended mainly to the larger settlements and they made no significant attempt to control the undisciplined tribesmen of the countryside or to stop them from carrying out raids on Russian settlements across the border.

In the 1860s, the Russian armies began a final conquest of the area. Kokand, with its ancient cities of Tashkent and Samarkand, took three years to subdue. Its final conquest came in 1868. Bokhara fell the same year and Khiva was conquered in 1873.

Revolutionary Stirrings

While Russia was having general success in the area of international relations, the situation at home was deteriorating. Alexander II's promise of reforms brought a wave of enthusiasm among the people at the beginning, and even support from old revolutionaries such as Alexander Herzen in his exile in London. But disillusionment set in as implementation of the reforms began, for it became clear that, first, from the point of view of liberals, there were flaws in the legislation itself and, second, that a conservative bureaucracy would do its best to limit even further the benefits to come from the new legislation. Moreover, the very fact of reform from above brought a questioning of the status quo among educated Russians because it legitimated the question—"what further should be changed?" One writer who wrote on this theme was Nikolay Chernyshevsky, whose novel, *What Is To Be Done?*, became almost a sacred text for the questioning youth of the 1860s.

This questioning occurred mainly among the greatly increased numbers of young men streaming into the universities—as yet young women had to go abroad if they wanted a university education. Exposed for the first time to the latest scientific and philosophical theories from Western Europe—revolution, positivism, French Utopian Socialism—many of these young people began questioning everything about Russian culture and the Russian way of life. Although women were denied access to the universities, some of them soon became important leaders in this new movement.

We speak of this movement as *nihilism* and it was perhaps best summed up by the great Russian novelist Turgenev in his novel *Fathers and Sons*. Turgenev saw the development as a kind of generation gap, a clash between the ideas of the "fathers and sons."

The *nihilists* of the 1860s were in general not revolutionaries, but there were some exceptions. In 1866, one such "student" decided to shoot the tsar and he actually went to the garden of the palace, walked up to Alexander II, pulled out his revolver and shot at him. What saved Alexander II's life at that moment is that a worker in the gardens, seeing what was happening, grabbed his arm.

By the 1870s, the vague and somewhat negative revolutionary stirring of the previous decades merged into the so-called *Narodnik* (populist) movement. The *Narodniki* were heavily influenced by the writing of the French Utopian Socialists. Appalled by what they thought of as the evils of industrialism, they advocated a kind of agrarian socialism based on the traditional Russian peasant commune. The leadership expected to stir the Russian masses by going among the simple people, teaching them, but also learning from their supposedly pure and simple outlook which they allegedly had because they had not been "contaminated" by urban life. It became fashionable to "go to the people" to bring education and sanitary habits to the primitive, rural folk. Often the peasants repaid this by denouncing the uninvited tutors to the police.

Some of the populist leaders concluded that someone else would have to work for the peasants, because the masses were not mature and thinking enough to stage a general uprising against the Russian system. A decision was made to engage in acts of terrorism, the most spectacular of which was the attempt to kill the military governor of St. Petersburg. By the end of the 1870s, the revolutionary organization *Zemlya i Volya* (Land and Freedom) split into two major groups. One repudiated terrorism and violence and emigrated to

Alexander III

Russia

Switzerland. Taking the name "Liberation of Labor," it turned its attention more toward the emerging industrial working class and became the first Russian Marxist organization. The other, *Narodnaya Volya* (Will of the People), chose more terror in the somewhat questionable belief that removal of a few high personalities would change things in Russia. The Tsar was selected as the chief target for assassination. After several unsuccessful attempts, Alexander II was killed by terrorists in 1881. His murder occurred on the same day he signed a new decree granting a limited constitution and more political freedom to the people.

Alexander III (1881–1894)

The death of Alexander II brought to an end the age of reforms that originally began with Peter the Great. "Western" and "liberal" took on sinister meanings in the eyes of the government and upper classes. Alexander III, who was in narrow political terms a reactionary, believed it was impossible to come to terms with the liberals and that his father's assassination had partly resulted from his attempts to do so. He made it clear that liberals could expect nothing from him when, in his accession address, he declared his "complete faith in the strength and truth of autocracy" and that "for the good of the people" he would "maintain and defend the autocratic power from attack." He canceled his father's plans to introduce further liberal reform.

He was 36 when he came to the throne. A great bear of a man, he referred to himself as the "peasant Tsar," and he was very proud of the fact that he could straighten horseshoes with his bare hands. He was honest and hardworking, but intellectually somewhat dull. He recognized his limitations, however, and left many decisions to his ministers, supporting them and keeping them in office even when he didn't understand what they were trying to do.

His most important political advisers were Konstantine Pobedonostsev, Mikhail Katkov, and Dmitri Tolstoy. Curiously enough, all had been supporters of Alexander II's reforms. Pobedonostsev had helped to draft the judicial reforms, for example, and Tolstoy had been minister of education in the previous regime. Katkov had been a well-known westernizer and liberal.

By 1881, however, they had rejected their earlier admiration for foreign ideas and now sought Russia's salvation in its own past. Alexander III, strongly nationalistic with Pan-Slav leanings, accepted their advice about the need to Russify the minorities and to promote strongly the Russian Orthodox Church.

In Poland and in the Baltic provinces, Russian was made the language of instruction in the schools. Catholics, Protestants and Old Believers found themselves affected by government policies aimed at the conversion of these groups to Russian Orthodoxy.

Jews were treated more harshly. Earlier policies that had restricted their residence to the "Pale of Settlement" (sections of Poland that Russia had annexed in the 18th century), but which had been relaxed under Alexander II, were reintroduced. Limitations were placed on the entry of Jews to universities; they were excluded from most government service; and forbidden to acquire land in rural areas. In addition, in 1881, pogroms (violent attacks) against Jewish communities occurred and at times were supported by local officials. Repeated outbreaks caused a massive migration of Jews from the lands of Russian empire. Many came to America.

The nature of Alexander III's reign was thus quite different from that of his father. Yet, though he disagreed with his father politically, he was loath to undo the work which his predecessor had begun. The substance of reform survived, although the new Tsar did approve some amendments aimed at reducing popular participation. Provincial governors were, for example, given greater control over the Zemstvo assemblies and the franchise was changed to increase the representation of the nobility. The government also increased its administrative powers over the judiciary.

Alexander III shared his father's commitment to industrialization, so there was no essential change in economic policy. Government policy continued to encourage the construction of railroads, though more state-owned railroads were built in this period. Tariffs were also raised several times in order to encourage "infant industries." The policy worked in the sense that there was a good deal of foreign investment in Russia in the 1880s, but it also led to a tariff war with Germany from 1887 to 1893.

The policy of Alexander III toward the peasantry was probably his most important personal contribution toward the economic policy of his reign. Genuinely interested in the welfare of the peasantry, the Tsar set out to do what he could to improve their lot—at least insofar as that could be done within the framework of Russia at that time. The redemption debt was reduced in 1881 and again in 1884. Two taxes that weighed heavily on the lower class, the salt tax and the poll tax, were repealed. They were replaced by two taxes which applied mainly to the upper and middle classes: an inheritance tax and a tax on bonds.

The increase in population after emancipation had also reduced the average size of peasant allotments. To remedy this, the government set up a Peasant Land Bank to lend money. The bank also made loans to those who were willing to move to Siberia. In spite of these measures, the true state of Russia became evident in 1891 when crop failures led to famine in the countryside.

Although Russia remained at peace during the 13 years that Alexander III was on the throne, Russia's foreign relations were often abrasive, for, as one historian says of him, Alexander III attempted to obtain peacefully objectives that are usually obtained only as the result of a successful war. Russia's quarrels were primarily with Austria-Hungary and Germany and led to Alexander's decision to sign an alliance with France in 1892.

Alexander III's quarrels with Germany were of a two-fold nature, but they were exacerbated by his pan-Slav leanings. In the 1870s, Alexander III, then the heir to the throne, had supported pan-Slav aspirations in the Balkans and was deeply angered when Austria refused to accept the Treaty of San Stefano, negotiated at the close of Russia's victorious war against the Ottoman Empire in 1878. He favored a connection with Germany, however, and, in 1881, accepted his foreign minister's advice that a renewal of the Three Emperors' League was the only way this could be arranged.

Things went smoothly until 1885, when the Bulgarians, at that time protégés of the Russians, decided to carry through a union with East Rumelia without consulting with the Russian government. Alexander III "punished" the Bulgarians by withdrawing all Russian military advisers. When Austria took advantage of the situation to increase its own influence in Bulgaria, Alexander III felt betrayed and denounced the Three Emperors' League. His real quarrel, therefore, was with Austria. Alexander III still wanted a connection with Germany, however, and suggested a bilateral alliance with Germany in 1887, "not against Austria, but without Austria." This became the Reinsurance Treaty, which existed for three years, until 1890.

Alexander III also had a grievance with Germany having to do with economic relations between the two countries. In the 1880s, Germany was Russia's chief trading partner and the source of most foreign capital investment in the Russian economy. Russia had an adverse trade balance with Germany, which it attempted to solve by raising tariffs on the main goods coming in from Germany. This led a good number of German firms to open affiliates in Russian Poland as a way to retain the Russian market. However, this large German commercial presence in Russian Poland became another problem, because Russian nationalists felt it threatened Russian political control in this borderland area. In 1887, the Russian government issued a decree

Russia

Nicholas II and Alexandra

prohibiting foreigners from owning land in border areas such as Russian Poland, and Germany retaliated by an attack on Russian securities, known as the *Lombard Verbot*. Thus began an economic war that lasted until 1894 and brought the two nations as close to war as they were to come in the 19th century.

It was these poor economic-political relations with Germany which led Alexander III to sign an alliance with France in 1892. That alliance, still in force in 1914, would bring Russia and France into World War I as allies against Germany and Austria.

Nicholas II (1894–1917)

Alexander III has sometimes been referred to as the last Russian autocrat; whatever else can be said of him, it is generally agreed that he personified the policy of his reign. Nicholas II, by contrast, was a weak-willed individual who, all his life, was dominated by those about him. Moreover, he hated confrontations and got around them by seeming to agree with whomever he was talking. This made it extremely difficult for government ministers, for they never knew whether his approval of one of their suggestions was apparent or real. This also inclined him against strong-willed ministers, for that increased the possibility of disagreement. This trait became even more noticeable as he grew older, perhaps the result of the influence of his wife, Alexandra.

Alexandra called him weak-willed to his face and demanded that he stand up to his ministers. Other examples of her advice follow. Her influence came primarily toward the end of his reign, however, as she undoubtedly saw the future crumbling.

Nicholas II was 26 years old when he succeeded to the throne. Professing his admiration for his father, he retained his father's ministers and promised to continue his policies. Meeting with representatives of the Zemstvo of Tver, for example, Nicholas told them that:

"It has come to my knowledge that there have been heard in some Zemstvos the voices of those who have indulged in senseless dreams that the Zemstvos might participate in the direction of the internal affairs of the state. Let all know that I shall devote my energy to the service of the people, but that I shall maintain the principle of autocracy as firmly as did my father."

In spite of his promise, Nicholas did modify his father's policies in one area. He did not share his father's dislike for German culture and this showed up domestically in his reversal of his father's Russification policy as it applied to the Baltic Germans. It showed up internationally in the much better relations that developed with both Austria and Germany after 1894.

Russia was already in the midst of an economic boom when Nicholas came to the throne. The minister of finance was Sergei Witte (*Vi-teh*), a strong proponent of industrialization. Witte put the country on the gold standard, encouraged the inflow of foreign investment and pushed the construction of railroads. The boom lasted until 1899; by that time, the production of large-scale industry as a whole had doubled over the previous decade.

One ominous sign on the horizon was the lack of domestic entrepreneurs, however. Of 14 new steel mills built during the 1890s, only one was Russian. The other 13 were foreign-owned and had foreign management. Other branches of industry dominated by foreign capital included the electric and electro-technical industry, the gas industry, chemicals and dyes. Many metal-working and machine-building companies were also foreign-owned and run. Using the terminology of Karl Marx, whose economic theories were to have such a dynamic impact on Russia, it was *creating capitalism but very few capitalists.*

The Revolution of 1905

A worldwide financial crisis in 1899 halted the flow of new foreign capital into Russia, leading to a wave of bankruptcies and mounting unemployment. Just as business was starting to recover, the economy was set back by crop failures in the countryside in 1901–1902. A period of unrest followed, with strikes in the cities and peasant demonstrations in the villages. Illegal political parties began to appear and agitation for basic reforms increased.

Then came the Russo-Japanese War of 1904. It was badly fought, and the defeat of Russian forces at Port Arthur swelled the numbers of those who had come to believe that the government was unfit to rule.

In this tense atmosphere, the government made yet another blunder which set off the Revolution of 1905. Father Gapon, a Russian Orthodox priest who had started an organization for workers with the permission of the secret police, was asked by them to lead them in a march to the Winter Palace to present a petition for redress of grievances to the Tsar. The peaceful crowd of workers, accompanied by their wives and children, were fired upon by the police as they approached the Winter Palace.

Approximately a hundred people were killed and another hundred wounded. Although it had been one of the Russian Grand Dukes who had given the order to fire on the crowd—Nicholas II was not in residence at the Winter Palace at the time—Nicholas was blamed for what happened. Thus this event, which has gone down in history as "Bloody Sunday," had significance beyond the immediate deaths and injuries. On that day,

a myth died. The peasants had always thought of the Tsar as the "Little Father" who cared for his people. With the events of Bloody Sunday, that myth could no longer be sustained.

It triggered a wave of resentment and protests that continued throughout the spring and summer of 1905 and led, then, to a general strike that began in early fall. The strike established that Nicholas II's government had lost the confidence of all of Russian society, with the possible exception of the nobility and some of the military.

On the advice of Sergei Witte, Nicholas issued a manifesto promising constitutional government, civil liberties to all citizens and a national legislature (Duma). This was termed the "October Manifesto;" Nicholas also named Witte as his new chief minister.

Elections to the first Duma took place in March 1906. A plurality of the seats was won by members of the Constitutional Democratic (Cadet) Party, a liberal group supported by Russia's professional classes, because the more radical political parties boycotted the elections.

Learning that Witte had been sounding out Cadet representatives about joining his cabinet, Nicholas dismissed him as chief minister just before the legislature convened, replacing him with a colorless bureaucrat by the name of Ivan Goremykin. Perhaps Witte would not have been able to work with the Cadets either, but Goremykin never even tried.

As a result, there was a bitter clash between the representatives and the government, and Nicholas reacted by dissolving the first Duma. The second Duma was even more radical and it also was dissolved.

In calling for elections to a third Duma, Nicholas changed voting regulations to reduce the representation of those elements of the population that had been voting for more radical candidates. He also appointed Pyotr Stolypin as his new chief minister.

The change in voting made the new Duma less representative, but it also produced a body willing to work with the Tsar and his ministers. Stolypin turned out to be a strong individual who managed to save the Tsar from himself for the next several years.

Stolypin's name is particularly associated with a land reform whose goal was to break up the peasant communes and redistribute the land to the peasants as their private property. He hoped that, by giving the peasants something to lose, he would wean them away from their support of the radicals. But the reforms came too late and took too much time to implement; by 1914, only about 25% of the peasants had left the village commune, and fewer had managed

to exchange their scattered strips for a single, contiguous plot of land.

Stolypin was assassinated by revolutionaries in 1911. With his strong presence gone, Nicholas II again began to exercise a greater say in the government.

World War I

The good relations that Nicholas had cultivated with Germany and Austria came to an end in 1908 when a new quarrel erupted between Russia and Austria over events in the Balkans. Austria's annexation of Bosnia began the dispute, but it soon spread and involved Germany—because of its support of Austria. Russia then became a patron of Serbia, which had been anti-Austrian since the Karageorgovic dynasty seized the Serbian throne in 1903. The assassination by a Serbian nationalist of Archduke Franz Ferdinand, heir to the Austrian throne, in the summer of 1914 led Austria to declare war on Serbia.

The general system of alliances transformed this Balkan war into World War I and it was not long before the continent of Europe was aflame. Russian war plans were predicated on a war with Austria, and the Russian army had no plans drawn up at the beginning of the war for an attack

Russia

**Nicholas II:
A prisoner at Tsarskoe Selo, 1917**

on Germany. However, as the war began, the German military, working on the basis of the Von Schlieffen Plan, pushed rapidly through Belgium and into France, and soon threatened Paris. The French government then made a desperate plea to Nicholas II to launch an invasion into eastern Germany in order to take the pressure off France.

Nicholas II ordered three Russian armies to invade East Prussia in August 1914. The Russian armies, operating without a specific plan of invasion and both ill-prepared and poorly equipped, suffered a humiliating defeat. The action did

Grigori Yefimovich Rasputin

accomplish France's purpose, however, for the German Emperor responded to the invasion by pulling off forces from the right wing of the German armies invading France and ordered them to East Prussia. Shortly thereafter, the German forces were halted in the west and Paris was saved.

The Russian military was not that well prepared at the beginning of the war, but it did have fairly consistent success on the Austrian front in 1914 and 1915. It was, in fact, only when it came up against German forces that the Russian army proved to be not up to the task. However, a greater problem than the purely military one was the inability of the Russian government to work with the public organizations that were willing to assist in the war effort. Distrustful of the motives of these organizations, the government rejected their help and insisted on doing everything itself. The government thereby alienated a large part of the educated classes who were involved in these organizations, and such individuals tended thereafter to see every mistake and blunder of the government as a sign of its incompetence.

Tsar Nicholas made things worse for himself by assuming direct command of the armed forces in September 1915, leaving the Empress Alexandra in charge back in the capital. Although raised at the court of Queen Victoria, the German-born Alexandra had extremely conservative political ideas; more importantly, she was obsessed by the fact that her only son, Alexis, the heir to the throne, suffered from hemophilia, an incurable bleeding disease. Alexandra probably also suffered feelings of guilt, for hemophilia can only be inherited through the mother.

This led to another unhealthy influence in the palace, for Alexandra, seeking help for her son, put her complete faith in an itinerant Siberian self-styled monk called Rasputin—because she believed that Rasputin was sent by God, who could stop her son's bleeding when an attack started. Rasputin, often characterized as an illiterate, immoral, and filthy peasant, did apparently have some success in this regard, though no one knows how.

Many members of the educated classes of Russia objected to Alexandra's associating with such a man, but the real problem was that she soon began seeking Rasputin's advice on extremely important matters of state, and even dismissed officials who had anything negative to say about Rasputin. Such actions eventually convinced most educated Russians that the government was corrupt and incapable of governing competently. This also led several members of the Russian aristocracy, including two related to the royal family, to plan Rasputin's murder

in December 1916; they were successful in their plan, but by that time it was too late.

The effects of the war at first caused unrest mainly among the city dwellers who suffered from fuel shortages and high food prices caused by disrupted supplies. Soon the countryside also became restive. Major military defeats in 1915 and 1916 also contributed to a feeling that the government was incompetent. In addition, the demands of the military often overtaxed the hauling capabilities of the railroads, resulting in shortages of food in the cities.

By the beginning of 1917, the number of strikes and demonstrations was on the increase. Then food riots broke out in the capital city after bakeries began running short on flour, and bread became scarce in the stores. Troops summoned to restore law and order tended to side with the angry people. Nicholas was then advised by the Duma leaders that the only way to save the monarchy was for him to abdicate in favor of his son, Alexis.

Nicholas first considered doing so, but he then decided that it would be too great a burden on Alexis. He therefore changed the order of succession and named his brother, the Grand Duke Mikhail, as his successor. However, Mikhail refused the offer, and overnight the Russian monarchy came to an end. The royal family was put under arrest and sent to Ekaterinburg after the Bolsheviks came to power; they were executed by the Bolsheviks in July 1918 when it appeared that anti-Bolshevik forces might overrun Ekaterinburg. The order of execution may have been signed by Lenin himself.

An Experiment with Democracy

During the war years, the Duma had continued to meet periodically and to debate current issues. In September 1915, for example, the Duma had called for a government having the confidence of a majority in the legislature. Nicholas, ignoring this advice, instead, appointed himself commander-in-chief and went off to the front.

A second series of debates in October 1916 was even more negative in its evaluation of the government but they, too, represented points of view that the Tsar was not interested in hearing, so he ignored them as well.

By February 1917, however, the leaders of the Duma had come to the conclusion that they could no longer ignore their own responsibilities so, when Nicholas again issued a decree dissolving the Duma, they ignored the order and remained in Petrograd (changed from St. Petersburg in 1914). When the tsarist regime "evaporated," the Duma first organized a Temporary Committee with representation from all political groups except the extreme right and the extreme left. The Bolsheviks who had been elected to the Duma during the last elections in 1912 were, in any case, either in jail or in Siberian exile. The Temporary Committee then established a Provisional Government under the chairmanship of Prince Georgy Lvov, a liberal aristocrat.

It was intended that the Provisional Government would run the affairs of Russia until a Constituent Assembly charged with writing a constitution could be elected by the people. The Provisional Government lasted for a total of seven months and after July was headed by Alexander Kerensky, a moderate socialist, who held power until overthrown by the Bolsheviks on October 25 (or November 7 by the new calendar), 1917.

In order to understand how the Provisional Government came to be deposed, it is important to know that, on the very day that the Duma organized its Temporary Committee, the Provisional Executive Committee of the Soviet of Workers' Deputies also came into existence. This was actually a revival of the institution that briefly functioned as a socialist command post during the Revolution of 1905.

The Soviet was soon enlarged by adding representatives of the soldiers in revolt and it then became the Soviet of Workers' and Soldiers' Deputies. It was led by moderate socialists at this time, though Bolsheviks such as Joseph Stalin and Vyacheslav Molotov soon joined the deliberations. The moderate socialists, using Karl Marx as their guide, believed that Russia, a backward country in terms of industrial development, would have to go through a *bourgeois-democratic* stage before it could proceed to socialism. This *bourgeois-democratic* stage would bring Russia to the level of a mature, capitalist nation, at which time it would be ripe for a socialist revolution. The workers, or *proletariat*,

---

FROM LENIN'S "APRIL THESES"

(A few days after his return to Russia, Lenin published on April 7, 1917, a set of brief "theses" stating his view of the situation in the war-torn country. He outlined a program for the "second stage" of the revolution. Below are some excerpts.)

1. In our attitude toward the war, which unquestionably remains on Russia's part a predatory imperialist war under the new government of Lvov Company because of the capitalist nature of that government, not the slightest concession to "revolutionary defencism" is permissible.

The class-conscious proletariat can give its consent to a revolutionary war which would really justify "revolutionary defencism" only if (a) the power passes to the proletariat, (b) all foreign annexations be renounced in fact and not just in word, and (c) that a complete break be made in fact with all capitalist interests. . . .

5. There should not be a parliamentary republic—to return to a parliamentary republic from the Soviets of Workers' Deputies would be a step backwards—there must be a republic of Soviets of Workers', Agricultural Laborers' and Peasants' Deputies throughout the country, from top to bottom.

There also must be abolition of the police, the army and the bureaucracy. . . .

9. (c) [We must] change the Party's name. Instead of "Social Democracy," the world leaders of which have betrayed Socialism and deserted to the bourgeoisie . . . we must call ourselves a Communist Party.

10. There must be a new International. We must take the initiative in creating a new revolutionary International. . . .

---

would grow in numbers in the democratic capitalist period and would become aware of their power and historical role; another revolution would then usher in socialism.

Accordingly, the leftist parties, including the Bolsheviks prior to Lenin's return to Russia, gave their conditional support to the Provisional Government, although (except for Alexander Kerensky) refusing to serve in it. A peculiar pattern of power therefore emerged; although the Soviet enjoyed substantial support from the workers and soldiers, it reserved for itself the position of being a critic and "watchdog" of the revolution and refused to govern directly. Meanwhile the Provisional Government, the official governing body, had no mass following and was forced to rely on the Soviet for support. This was particularly true in matters involving the army. Although the Provisional Government was in nominal control of the

armed forces, the Soviet actually had representatives from all of the military units and its "Order Number 1," which granted full civil rights to enlisted personnel, also instructed them to form company committees to assume control of arms and keep them out of the reach of officers, in order to prevent a counter-revolution.

Lenin's Return

Events took a decisive new turn when Vladimir Lenin, the leader of the Bolshevik faction of the Social Democratic Party,, returned to Russia on April 3, 1917. A natural politician, Lenin believed strongly in the ideas of Marx, but he was, at the same time, flexible enough to deal with situations not covered by Marx. In line with ideas expressed in 1916 in *Imperialism, the Highest Stage of Capitalism*, Lenin believed that Russia was ready for the socialist revolution. He therefore proposed in his "April Theses" that the Provisional Government be pushed aside in favor of the new revolutionary government of the Soviets. He also called for an end to the war, arguing that the proletariat could "give its consent to a revolutionary war" only if "all power passes to the proletariat."

Lenin was aware that, at that moment, the Bolsheviks were a minority in the Soviet, but he fully expected to win over the masses to his ideas. In fact, many of his own Bolsheviks did not support his position when he first announced it, but they soon fell in line. His opposition to the war soon won him additional support because the Provisional Government continued to insist that Russia had an obligation to continue to fight Germany, an idea that was becoming increasingly unpopular. Another factor was the failure of moderate elements to deal with pressing internal problems such as distribution of land to

Demonstration against the Provisional Government, July 1917

Russia

Vladimir Lenin

peasants and creating an orderly supply of food. Propelled by Lenin's determined will and by simplified slogans such as "Peace, Bread, and Land," the Bolsheviks began their quest for power.

The opposition of the Bolsheviks toward continuing the war with Germany was especially helpful in winning additional support. The Provisional Government, besides failing to solve internal problems, made no real effort to get out of the unpopular war because it felt bound by an agreement with Russia's allies not to make a separate peace. Its decision to mount one more military offensive in July 1917 not only lost it additional support but it also contributed to the near collapse of army organization and morale. This played right into the hands of the Bolsheviks.

Lenin's slogan, "all power to the soviets," was picked up by radicals not under his control and it became the basis for an uprising known as the "July Days." Lenin considered it to be premature and tried to turn it into a peaceful demonstration. When it collapsed after three days, therefore, Lenin had to go into hiding across the border in Finland. In spite of this temporary setback, the influence of the Bolsheviks grew steadily, particularly among the soldiers and sailors.

After the "July Days," the Provisional Government tried to turn the anger of the people against Lenin and his followers by accusing them of being German agents. It further charged that Lenin had spent the war years away from Russia, mainly in neutral Switzerland; that he was an "internationalist" who had opposed the war from its very beginning in 1914; that he had returned to Russia with the assistance of the German army's High Command, who arranged for his travel through Germany in a sealed railway car; and that he had

been the recipient of sums of money from Germany since his arrival in Russia. Lenin never denied the first three charges and there is some evidence that the fourth accusation was true as well. But Lenin was never a German agent. The German army High Command helped Lenin to get back to Russia because he was a known opponent of the war and they hoped his presence in Russia would weaken the Russian resolve to continue the war. Any financial assistance they may have given Lenin was for the same reason. And Lenin was willing to take assistance from any source, provided it promoted his own particular goals.

Although Lenin was forced to remain in hiding because of these charges against him, the Bolsheviks continued to grow in popularity, primarily because of incompetence and failures on the part of the Provisional Government and the other political parties. One such case was the "Kornilov Affair."

General Lavr Kornilov had been appointed commander-in-chief of the armed forces shortly before with the support of Alexander Kerensky, who had been head of the Provisional Government since July 20, 1917. In late August, an unscrupulous financier by the name of Vasily Zavoyko convinced Kornilov, who was honest and patriotic but politically naïve, that Kerensky was willing to relinquish power to him as a way to combat the growing influence of the Bolsheviks. Meanwhile, Kerensky, learning that Kornilov had made plans to lead his troops to Petrograd, accused him of planning a coup and fired him.

When Kornilov refused to give up his post and issued a statement directed against the Provisional Government, Kerensky called upon the workers of the threatened capital, including groups that were known to be under Bolshevik influence, to come to his assistance. The "Kornilov Affair" ended with the arrest of the general. That seemed to strengthen Kerensky's position for a while but, in reality, the prestige of the Provisional Government had all but vanished.

Lenin's attitude at the time of the "Kornilov Affair" is reflected in his response to Kerensky's plea for support against Kornilov—"We will support him the way a noose supports a hanged man." Lenin apparently liked analogies about ropes and nooses; on another occasion, he characterized capitalists as being willing to "sell you the rope with which to hang them."

The Kornilov Affair rehabilitated the Bolsheviks and prepared the way for their

eventual seizure of power. In September, the Petrograd Soviet returned a Bolshevik majority; a week later, the Moscow Soviet did likewise. The new chairman of the Petrograd Soviet was Leon Trotsky. Although a longtime revolutionary and radical ideologist, he had only joined the Bolshevik faction in the summer of 1917. With Lenin still in hiding, however, it was Trotsky who took charge and actually carried out the coup d'état against the Provisional Government which was to go down in history as the "Great October Socialist Revolution."

However, even Trotsky later conceded that Lenin was the one indispensable individual in the Russian Revolution. It was Lenin who was convinced that the time was ripe to move against the Provisional Government and who persuaded the Central Committee of the Bolsheviks to begin preparations for the seizure of power.

Trotsky accepted that decision and set about to implement it. He persuaded the Executive Committee of the Petrograd Soviet that a Military Revolutionary Committee needed to be created for the defense of the revolution. This Military Revolutionary Committee then sent "political commissars" to each of the military units stationed in Petrograd. Their instructions were to persuade the soldiers and sailors to accept no orders from their officers unless they were countersigned by the political commissar of the Petrograd Soviet. In this manner, Trotsky managed to neutralize the entire Petrograd Garrison.

After many hesitations, the attempt to seize power was timed to coincide with the sessions of the All-Russian Congress of Soviets called for October 25, 1917 (November 7 by the new, Gregorian calendar). However, events came to a head a day earlier—the government had been tipped off about the impending *coup* and began to move some loyal troops into position. It also ordered the soldiers to occupy the premises where the Bolshevik newspaper *Pravda* (Truth) was printed.

By this time, the Bolsheviks were in control of the major military units of the Petrograd Garrison, and easily secured a number of important points. The seat of government in the Winter Palace was defended briefly by a small detachment of military cadets and a women's battalion but, when the guns of the cruiser Aurora were trained on the palace, resistance ceased. Most members of the Provisional Government were put under arrest. Kerensky escaped in disguise in a car flying the American flag. He died in New York in 1970.

The Bolsheviks march into Moscow

THE COMMUNIST ERA (November 1917–August 1991)

What Is Communism?

Communism, the official dogma of the Communist Party of the Soviet Union, was a modified version of a theory developed in the 19th century by Karl Marx and Friedrich Engels. Since the modifications are primarily those introduced by Vladimir I. Lenin, this dogma is also referred to as Marxism-Leninism. Let us begin with the theory of communism as developed by Marx and Engels.

First of all, Marxian communism includes, and to a great extent derives from, a theory of history called "historical materialism." According to this theory, the "mode of production in material life determines the general characteristics of the social, political, and spiritual processes of life." Marx illustrated the operation of this theory in the *Communist Manifesto* when he wrote that "the history of all hitherto existing society is the history of class struggles."

Marx, who was a heavy borrower of the ideas of others, took the basic mechanism for "historical materialism" from the dialectic of the philosopher Georg Wilhelm Friedrich Hegel. Hegel, concerned with historical change, developed a mechanism that focused on the evolution of ideas. His conclusion was that ideas evolved through a "dialectical" process based on the concepts of a thesis, antithesis, and synthesis. The original idea (thesis) is challenged by a second idea (antithesis). The challenge is resolved by a merging of what is true from both ideas to form a new idea (synthesis). The term "dialectic" refers to this process of conflict and reconciliation.

Marx borrowed Hegel's dialectical process but rejected his premise that ideas shape the nature of the real world. He concluded that Hegel had it backward; that it is the real world (materialism) that

determines what we think. Or as Marx phrased it in the *Communist Manifesto*,

Does it require deep intuition to comprehend that man's ideas, views, and conceptions, in one word, man's consciousness, changes with every change in the conditions of his material existence, in his social relations and in his social life? What else does the history of ideas prove, than that intellectual production changes its character in proportion as material production is changed? The ruling ideas of each age have ever been the ideas of its ruling class.

If the controlling mechanism is materialism, however, Hegel's original question, "what causes historical change?," still required an answer. Marx's answer was that historical change was the result of *changes in the mode of production*—and

35

Russia

that changes in the mode of production were themselves the result of "internal contradictions."

This explains why Marx saw all history as "class struggles." Each mode of production produces its own ruling class; as the internal contradictions bring about a change in the mode of production, a new class, representing the new mode of production, struggles to come to power.

Applying his ideas to the 19th century, Marx labeled the epoch as "capitalistic" and the ruling class as the "bourgeoisie." This class had been progressive within its own time for it had rid the world of feudalism and serfdom. Moreover, because of its identification with the economic idea of "free competition," it "historically, has played a most revolutionary part" and, in fact, "cannot exist without constantly revolutionizing the instruments of production." As a result,

the bourgeoisie, during its rule of scarce one hundred years, has created more massive and more colossal productive forces than have all preceding generations together. Subjection of nature's forces to man, machinery, application of chemistry to industry and agriculture, steam-navigation, railways, electric telegraphs, clearing of whole continents for cultivation, canalization of rivers, whole populations conjured out of the ground—what earlier century has even a presentiment that such productive forces slumbered in the lap of social labor?

And yet, said Marx, competition, the very mechanism that released those productive forces, produces internal contradictions within capitalism that doom it inevitably to eventual extinction. These internal contradictions, which Marx identified as "laws," are (1) the Law of Capitalist Accumulation; (2) the Law of the Concentration of Capital; and (3) the Law of Increasing Misery.

These "laws" are based on Marx's presupposition that *labor alone creates value and, accordingly, all profits are derived from unpaid labor time.* Their essence is that competition forces capitalists to invest more capital in labor-saving machinery, which results in a higher ratio of capital to labor and, Marx asserts, a consequent drop in profit; this leads to bankruptcies as less efficient capitalists are driven out of business. The effect of the operation of laws one and two is increased unemployment and a general lowering of employee wages as each capitalist attempts to increase his profits by increasing the amount of unpaid labor time.

As a result of the operation of these three "laws," capitalistic society eventually reaches the stage of monopoly capitalism, whereby nearly all wealth is in the hands

of a few capitalists and the overwhelming mass of the people have been driven down into the ranks of the proletariat. As Marx puts it,

And here it becomes evident, that the bourgeoisie is unfit any longer to be the ruling class in society, and to impose its conditions of existence upon society as an overriding law. It is unfit to rule because it is incompetent to assure an existence to its slave within his slavery, because it cannot help letting him sink into such a state, that it has to feed him, instead of being fed by him. Society can no longer live under this bourgeoisie, in other words, its existence is no longer compatible with society.

"At this point, the more or less veiled civil war . . . breaks out into open revolution, overthrowing the bourgeoisie and raising the proletariat to the position of the ruling class." Once in power, the proletariat will nationalize all the means of production and institute state planning to replace the now discarded mechanism of free competition. The state—"nothing more than a machine for the oppression of one class by another"—will wither away and mankind will have entered the highest and last stage of development, communism.

Marxism thus claims to be a scientific doctrine that, having mastered the general laws that govern human society, can apply them to understand the future. The logical test of Marxism is, therefore, whether the predictions that constitute Marx's "laws" subsequently came true.

In fact, none of Marx's predictions came true. The total number of capitalists continued to grow throughout the remainder of the 19th century as inventions such as the electric dynamo, the internal combustion engine, the light bulb, and the telephone brought whole new industries into being. As for Marx's proletariat, living standards improved as wages began an upward spiral that actually accelerated toward the end of the century. By 1900, it was generally conceded that Marx's Law of Increasing Misery was not operating, and among his followers efforts were being made to update and correct him.

Vladimir I. Lenin was not, properly speaking, one of these revisionists. He thought of himself as primarily a revolutionary, not a theoretician, but it was precisely for this reason that he wanted to know why the revolution had not yet occurred and what could be done to bring it about. He set forth his conclusions in *What Is To Be Done?*, a book he wrote in 1902. In essence, he argued that the revolution hadn't occurred because the proletariat wasn't capable of carrying out a socialist revolution; that, left to itself, it was only

"able to develop trade union consciousness." The revolution would be made by "a revolutionary youth, armed with Social-Democratic theory." What was needed, therefore, was an organization of full-time professional revolutionaries who, acting as "the vanguard of all the revolutionary forces," would bring about the revolution in the name of the proletariat.

Lenin thus presented an "organizational" solution to the question "what could be done to bring the revolution about?" This "organizational" solution had additional implications, however, for it effectively excluded the proletariat from control of the revolutionary party. Only individuals trained in Marxist ideology would have the necessary "socialist consciousness" to be able to provide proper guidance to the proletariat.

Lenin's position on the nature of the party became the chief issue at the Second Congress of the Russian Social Democratic Labor Party when it met in 1903. Lenin's supporters became known as Bolsheviks, while his opponents became known as Mensheviks. There was, in effect, a split in the party.

The Bolsheviks became a small band of professional revolutionaries, whose chief common characteristic was their personal loyalty to Lenin. Lenin's control was further reinforced in July 1917 when a Bolshevik party congress adopted the principle of *democratic centralism* as the basis of party organization. *Democratic centralism,* which remained the basis of Soviet Communist Party organization until Mikhail Gorbachev abandoned the concept in the late 1980s, meant in practice that subordinate party units were mere agents of the party leadership, bound to follow all instructions from above.

Lenin made a somewhat broader contribution to Marxist theory in 1916 when he wrote *Imperialism, the Highest Stage of Capitalism.* Most of the book is rather unoriginal, but it does contain an argument which tends to modify Marx's theory that the socialist revolution occurs in a country only after capitalism has been fully developed. According to Marx,

a social system never perishes before all the productive forces have developed for which it is wide enough; and new, higher productive relationships never come into being before the material conditions for their existence have been brought to maturity within the womb of the old society itself.

According to Lenin, however, imperialism created a new situation which called for a modification of Marx's statement insofar as colonial or semi-colonial people were concerned. Under imperialism, monopoly capitalists exploit backward, colonial peoples, first, as markets and, secondly, as a cheap source of raw materials. This exploitation permits the capitalists to pay their own workers higher wages than they would otherwise be able to pay, and accounts for the improvement in the lot of the workers, contrary to Marx's theory. At the same time, it has given a new form to the proletariat—which now included the "toiling masses of the backward countries."

Accordingly, every country that was subject to capitalistic exploitation was a suitable target for revolution, *regardless of the extent of its industrial development*. Russia was thus a proper target for revolution. The Russian Revolution of February 1917 further reinforced Lenin's conviction that Russia was ready for a socialist revolution. He returned to Russia in April 1917 and immediately began to implement his vision.

Creation of the New Soviet Regime

Although the coup d'état that brought the Bolsheviks to power was made in the name of the Second Congress of Soviets, it was actually carried out by the Military Revolutionary Committee of the Petrograd Soviet, and the Bolsheviks announced the overthrow of the Provisional Government before the Congress of Soviets convened on the evening of October 25/November 7. The Congress was dominated by the Bolsheviks and their allies, the Left Socialist Revolutionaries, however, so they accepted their new role and passed a resolution written by Lenin proclaiming the transfer of all power to the Soviets. Executive power was vested in a Council of People's Commissars (SOVNARKOM). The more moderate Socialist Revolutionaries and Mensheviks condemned the overthrow of

Karl Marx

the Provisional Government and walked out of the Congress of Soviets, leaving the Bolsheviks and their Left Socialist Revolutionaries in control of the revolutionary government.

Lenin became chairman, and he filled the other positions on the SOVNARKOM (equivalent to a cabinet) with Bolsheviks. Thus the Bolsheviks managed to clothe themselves in the legitimacy of the Soviet movement and to use it to gain political power in Russia. The Congress of Soviets, having installed the Bolsheviks in power, had completed its usefulness. A Central Executive Committee was therefore elected, composed of two-thirds Bolsheviks and one-third Left Socialist Revolutionaries, and given full authority to pass legislation in the name of the Congress, which now adjourned. Just in case that wasn't sufficient, the SOVNARKOM was authorized to issue decrees which would have the force of law.

Soviets had sprung up spontaneously over all Russia after the February Revolution, but they only existed at the local level and were not universal. In December 1917, a decree of the SOVNARKOM called for the creation of Soviets at the local, district, regional, and provincial level, these Soviets to replace the Zemstvos as organs of government. Soviet officials were in theory to be elected, but only workers and peasants had the right to vote.

Since the Soviets only recognized socialist political parties, all others had become illegal as of the creation of the new Soviet government. Mensheviks and Socialist Revolutionaries they soon found themselves subject to some repression as well. Menshevik newspapers were closed first, but this ban was soon extended to all opposition newspapers. By the spring of 1918, all opposition political parties had been outlawed and the Communist Party (the new name the Bolsheviks had adopted in March 1918) had become the sole legal party in Soviet Russia.

War Communism

The period of Soviet history down to March 1921 is usually referred to as the period of War Communism. Once it got itself organized, the new regime set out to communize the country—or at least those parts that recognized its authority, since at this time the various minority nationalities had broken away and were in the process of establishing separate governments.

First priority was given to the nationalization of the means of production. A decree on land, issued immediately after the takeover, abolished private property in land but permitted the peasants to continue to use the land, provided they did not make use of hired labor. Banks, railroads,

shipping, and foreign trade were nationalized almost immediately, and the Supreme Economic Council was set up to begin state planning. Another decree established worker control over production and distribution of industrial output. Lenin would probably have preferred to move more slowly with nationalization of the rest of the economy, but he found his pace forced by so-called "nationalizations from below" as individual workers expelled owners and seized control of factories on their own. By the spring of 1918, most industry had been nationalized. Meanwhile, the economy continued to deteriorate.

During the summer of 1918, the Soviet government implemented new policies aimed at further increasing Soviet control over the countryside. In June, the government created "Committees of Poor Peasants," and gave them the task of carrying "the class war to the village." The government also used these committees to help implement a policy of grain requisitioning, which essentially meant that the government took what grain it could find and seized it in order to be able to feed the cities. To be sure, the peasants received promises that they would receive manufactured goods from the cities in compensation, but there never was any surplus to distribute. The peasant response was to plant less the next year, setting the stage for a future famine.

In the cities, in the meanwhile, the government completed the nationalization of all major industries and placed them under the direction of the Supreme Economic Council. In November, the government extended its control over all internal trade. At about this same time period, partly in response to the beginning of the civil war and partly due to a continuing drop in production, new decrees were issued forbidding workers from leaving their jobs or striking. Even so, as the civil war progressed, more and more workers fled the cities and went back to their villages in search of food.

The Treaty of Brest-Litovsk

Of all the things Bolshevik propaganda had promised the people, peace had perhaps been the most significant. But the Bolsheviks also needed peace in order to have time to consolidate their government. They attempted a "decree on peace" on the very first day after seizing power, but that had no more than a propaganda effect. For real peace, they had to find a way to negotiate with those making war on Russia—the German Imperial General Staff. Preliminary negotiations resulted in the signing of a temporary truce in December. But when peace negotiations began in January, the German terms were so harsh that Trotsky, in charge of the

Russia

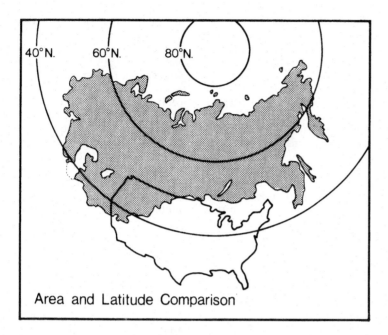

40°N. 60°N. 80°N.

Area and Latitude Comparison

negotiations as people's commissar for foreign affairs, rejected them out of hand. Lenin argued that there was no alternative to acceptance of the German terms, but it was not until the Germans began a new advance that he could get his associates to agree. The Treaty of Brest-Litovsk, signed on March 3, 1918, ended the state of war between Russia and the Central Powers, Germany, and Austria.

By the terms of the treaty, the Soviet government was obligated to give up any claim to Georgia (in the Caucasus area of southern Russia), the Ukraine (to the southwest, between Russia and Poland), and Finland (to the north). In addition, Poland plus Lithuania, Latvia, and Estonia, three small states located along the Baltic which were attempting to establish themselves as independent states, were recognized by the treaty as falling within Germany's sphere of influence. The Aaland Islands, in the Baltic Sea off the coast of Finland, were to be evacuated as well. Finally, the Turks, then allied with Germany, were given land in or near the cities of Kars, Ardahan, and Batum.

Profiting from Russia's weakness, the Romanians occupied the province of Bessarabia which had been a part of southwestern Russia. Altogether, the terms of the treaty meant a loss of 1.3 million square miles of Russian territory. This represented about 32% of the agricultural land, about one-third of the factories and approximately 75% of the coal and iron mines of Russia.

Harsh as the terms of the Treaty of Brest-Litovsk were, they gave the hard-pressed Bolsheviks an opportunity to consolidate their power in areas outside the two main cities of the country. Trotsky, who became

people's commissar for war after Brest-Litovsk, undertook the gigantic task of building an army to defend the revolution beginning in April 1918. But this was to be no revolutionary army. Known as the Workers and Peasants Red Army, it was based on conscription, authority, and discipline. Trotsky even recruited old tsarist officers to command the units he was creating, though they were now referred to as "military specialists" and their second in command was a political commissar whose job was to countersign all military orders to assure that they were not counter-revolutionary.

Intervention and Civil War

Russia's departure from the war with Germany was followed by a civil war within Russia, waged by elements opposed to the new regime. There had been, in fact, some fighting in the south during the early part of 1918, but most people date the real beginning of the civil war to the fighting which broke out between the Czechoslovak Legion and the Bolsheviks in May.

The Czechs were at that time in Cheliabinsk, in the Urals, making their way to Vladivostok by way of the Trans-Siberian Railway, from whence they intended to make their way to France in order to rejoin the war on the western front. The Soviet government had actually agreed to this arrangement in March, but a clash between Czech and Hungarian soldiers caused Trotsky to order the Czechoslovak soldiers to be disarmed. They refused to allow themselves to be disarmed, however, and began taking control of towns along the Trans-Siberian Railway as clashes between Czechs and

Bolsheviks spread. The French government intervened at this time to urge the Czechs to remain where they were, for the French were now planning an allied intervention. Allied forces were, in fact, already in the port cities of Murmansk, Archangel, and Vladivostok with the permission of the Soviet government. Their stated purpose for being there was to reclaim war supplies sent to the Russian government before it had left the war. Even as the Allies began to intervene, however, they were never in agreement about what they might accomplish by intervening. None of the Allies liked the Bolsheviks, to be sure, but probably only the French were totally committed to their overthrow. The result was a half-hearted intervention, in Winston Churchill's words, "a wretched half-measure." The Allies cooperated to some extent with anti-Bolshevik groups, but this assistance was never decisive.

The intervention was, in fact, a series of badly coordinated military efforts which, in European Russia, became tied in with the attempts of opposition groups to hold parts of the vast Russian territory and to form counter-governments in a series of uncoordinated attempts to overthrow the Bolshevik regime. Various groups were sponsored and supported by foreign powers. A period of short-lived resistance by former tsarist generals in the winter of 1918 was followed by a major effort of General Anton Denikin to deny the Soviet government access to the food and oil producing regions of the south. Elsewhere, an uprising against the Bolsheviks was staged by the right wing of the *Social Revolutionaries*, who were in favor of rejoining the war on the side of the Allies. After the Czech revolt, an anti-Bolshevik government was established in the Siberian city of Omsk by socialist elements. This was quickly taken over by Admiral Alexander Kolchak, who proclaimed himself "Supreme Ruler" of Russia. In still another area, General Pyotr Wrangel fought the Bolsheviks in the Caucasus, largely with French support. The British provided some support to both General Denikin and Admiral Kolchak.

The civil war dragged on until 1920, marked by heroism and cruelty on both sides. By that time, the allied intervention had come to an end and most of the anti-Bolshevik armies had been defeated. During the year also, Russia signed peace treaties with Estonia, Latvia, Lithuania, and Finland, recognizing their independence and establishing agreed boundaries.

Poland was another problem, however, for the Jozef Pilsudski government claimed Poland's "historic" boundaries and insisted that the Soviet government surrender all land west of the 1772 border—in other words, prior to the first partition of Poland. This included areas with significant

Byelorussian and Ukrainian populations and the Soviets therefore refused.

Pilsudski launched an invasion of the Ukraine in the spring of 1920, capturing Kyiv. His victory was short-lived, however. A Soviet counterattack drove the Polish army back out of the Ukraine and shortly thereafter a Soviet army was threatening Warsaw. But then the tide of battle turned once again, forcing the Soviet troops to retreat. The Soviets and Poles now agreed to a compromise territorial settlement, with the Poles getting much of what they wanted, and the Peace of Riga was signed in October 1920. The settlement left about 4.5 million Byelorussians and Ukrainians inside Poland a factor that continued to influence Soviet-Polish relations until 1939.

By 1922, the Communists extended Soviet control to Georgia, Armenia, Azerbaijan, and Siberia. The new Soviet state later added Central Asian territory that had previously been part of the Russian Empire.

New Economic Policy

With the end of the civil war and the war with Poland, a new situation existed. The economy had deteriorated over the preceding three years to such an extent as to make a mockery of Bolshevik claims to have improved the lot of the worker. Industrial output had fallen to 20% of its 1914 level and half of all industrial jobs had evaporated. Cities were being depopulated as people fled to the countryside to find food. The population of Petrograd had declined from a pre-war total of 2.3 million to 900,000. Agricultural output had also declined significantly, partly because of the ravages of the civil war, but also in response to the government's food requisition policy.

Neither the workers nor the peasants had supported the anti-Bolsheviks, but many were also unhappy with Bolshevik policies. They now felt free to put pressure on the government to change its policies. The result was peasant unrest, strikes by workers and, finally, a revolt of sailors at Kronstadt in early 1921. Lenin now recognized that some compromises were necessary and he announced a New Economic Policy (NEP) in March 1921.

The NEP, as it came to be called, reestablished a market economy in Russia. Food requisitions were to cease, to be replaced by a tax on agriculture to be paid with produce. After the individual peasant had paid the tax, he could dispose of the remainder of his crops as he saw fit. That meant that internal trade had to be reestablished within the private sector for, otherwise, the peasant would not have been able to dispose of his crops. An important feature of this era was the NEP-Man, the private trader who bought the peasant's

produce and furnished him with the products he wanted to buy. In the cities, private ownership of shops and factories employing fewer than 20 workers was also permitted. Money, which had largely lost its value, came back into use and a new currency was issued with gold backing.

The "commanding heights"—all large factories, mines, steel mills, transportation, banking, and foreign trade—remained in government hands, however. For that reason, 85% of all industrial workers continued to work in nationalized industry. But even government plants that were part of the "commanding heights" were formed into separate combines or trusts and ordered to operate on the basis of market principles. In addition, the government invited foreign capitalists to invest in Russia and it also recruited foreign technicians by offering contracts to come to Russia to teach their skills to Soviet workers. The Ford Motor Company opened a tractor factory in Russia at this time but, in general, the attempt to secure foreign capital investment was unsuccessful.

The NEP brought new life to Soviet Russia. By 1927, agricultural production had surpassed the levels of 1913 and consumer goods were again in ample supply. Only the large nationalized plants had not regained their pre-war levels—but even they had made great progress.

The NEP was never intended to exist for a long time, however, and Soviet state planning for industrialization continued throughout the period of the NEP. GOSPLAN, or the State Planning Commission, which subsequently became responsible for the Five-Year Plans, was actually set up on February 22, 1921, that is, immediately prior to the adoption of the NEP. Thus, one might say that Lenin ordered the beginning of planning to make it possible to eliminate the NEP at the very same time he was approving the new program.

Constitutional Arrangements

It was also during the period of the NEP that the Union of Soviet Socialist Republics (USSR) came into being—though most of the territories included in the new USSR had been under communist control since 1920. The first piece in the new constitutional structure was the Russian Soviet Federated Socialist Republic (RSFSR), created in July 1918 when the communists adopted the first Soviet constitution. As they extended their control to Byelorussia, the Ukraine, and the Caucasus, these areas were given similar constitutions and the designation of Soviet Socialist Republic. Although they had signed treaties with the RSFSR, they remained technically independent republics. That situation created all kinds of legal and bureaucratic

problems, so these four republics were brought together as the USSR in December 1922. The RSFSR institutions were then enlarged and somewhat modified to become "union" institutions. A new constitution for the USSR—essentially a copy of the 1918 RSFSR constitution—was drawn up and adopted in 1924. These constitutional arrangements were extended to Central Asia in 1924 with the admission of the Turkmen and Uzbek Republics to the USSR. By 1936, 5 more republics had been created, raising the number of union republics to 11. Then the Soviet Union added the 3 Baltic Republics plus Moldavia in 1940, spoils of its Non-Aggression Pact with Nazi Germany, bringing the number of republics to 15.

CONSTITUENT REPUBLICS OF THE USSR

1. Russian SFSR 1922
2. Ukrainian SSR 1922
3. Byelorussian SSR 1922
Transcaucasian SSR 1922
(Dissolved in 1936 into three constituent Republics, 4–6):
4. Armenian SSR 1936
5. Azerbaijan SSR 1936
6. Georgian SSR 1936
7. Uzbek SSR 1924
8. Turkmen SSR 1924
9. Tadzhik SSR 1929
10. Kazakh SSR 1936
11. Kirghiz SSR 1936
12. Moldavian SSR 1940
13. Lithuanian SSR 1940
14. Latvian SSR 1940
15. Estonian SSR 1940

The Struggle for the Succession

Lenin suffered a cerebral hemorrhage in May 1922 which left him incapacitated for several months. By September, he had recovered enough to be able to work again at his desk, but he then suffered a new apoplexy in December, followed by a third reoccurrence in March 1923 that left him speechless. He died on January 21, 1924. After his death, Lenin's body was embalmed and placed in a mausoleum in Red Square. Petrograd was renamed Leningrad in his honor at this same time.

Once Lenin's illness removed him from the active leadership of the party, a struggle broke out among Lenin's chief lieutenants to determine who would lead the party. In his "testament," Lenin himself identified six possible successors—Leon Trotsky, Lev Kamenev, Grigory Zinoviev, Nikolai Bukharin, Georgy Pyatakov, and Joseph Stalin. To the rank-and-file, Trotsky appeared to be the most logical choice, for he was the only one of Lenin's associates whose contributions to the revolution rivaled those of Lenin. In fact, according to

Russia

a document reported on by a Soviet historian, Lenin offered Trotsky the number two position in the government in 1922, but he turned it down. His reason, according to what he told the Central Committee in 1923, was that "we should not give our enemies the opportunity to say that our country was being ruled by a Jew."

As Lenin's deputy, Trotsky would have been in a good position to outmaneuver Stalin when Lenin's stroke set off a struggle for the succession. Instead, it was Stalin, Kamenev, and Zinoviev who formed a *troika* (a three-member team) with the express purpose of excluding Trotsky from the leadership.

Trotsky had his own levers of power—he was People's Commissar for War and a member of the Politburo—and he decided to carry the battle to the Party Congress. A great orator, he expected to win over the delegates to his side. Two things made that impossible. First, Lenin had gotten the Party Congress to outlaw factions in 1921. This meant that Trotsky could not do any pre-Congress organizing. Second, Stalin had been made General Secretary in 1922, and this gave him control over selection of the delegates to the Party Congress. Trotsky found the battle had been lost before it had begun.

Stalin later fell out with Kamenev and Zinoviev and this led them in turn to form a "United Opposition" with Trotsky against Stalin. But Stalin's control over the administrative levers of the party allowed him to defeat all three. Trotsky was expelled from the Politburo and then from the party; in 1928 he was exiled to Siberia, then a year later deported to Turkey. Stalin rapidly filled the Politburo with his supporters and was well on his way to establishing his "dictatorship over the party."

The struggles between Stalin and Trotsky involved apparent differences over policy and these were also aired during the period. Trotsky was an advocate of world revolution and he also wanted to end the NEP and embark on a rapid, large-scale industrialization of Russia. Stalin developed a theory of "socialism in one country" and defended the NEP. These turned out to be differences without a difference, however, for Stalin adopted Trotsky's policy on industrialization, but in more extreme form, immediately after eliminating Trotsky as a source of competition.

Foreign Policy during the NEP

When the communists first came to power in November 1917, their first consideration was to end the war with Germany. They considered it an "imperialistic" war that they had opposed from the beginning, but Lenin also recognized the need for peace in order to allow communism to be firmly established in Russia. Because

Leon Trotsky

of Russia's withdrawal from the war after the Bolsheviks came to power, France and England excluded Russia from the peacemaking at Versailles. Russia reciprocated by condemning the Treaty of Versailles and the League of Nations. Russia was thus hostile to the postwar settlement and the Allies responded by attempting to isolate the new government of Russia, and all that it stood for, diplomatically.

This didn't bother the Russian communists too much, for it essentially coincided with their own perception that the capitalistic countries would inevitably be hostile to the new Soviet government. In addition, Lenin was convinced that the world communist revolution predicted by Marx would break out at any moment and he was primarily concerned with what Russian communists could do to bring it about.

This led to the creation of the Communist International (COMINTERN) in March 1919 as a sort of coordinating body for the coming world revolution. Efforts such as these only reinforced the British and French in their opinion that Soviet Russia was a radical nation that had to be quarantined internationally.

With the adoption of the NEP in 1921, however, Russian policy began to change. The revolutionary tide in Europe had begun to ebb and Lenin opted for a policy which he called "peaceful coexistence." His emphasis was now on rebuilding the Russian economy and for that he wanted outside assistance. He therefore called for the establishment of trade and diplomatic relations with all countries willing to live in peace and offered to reopen the country to foreign capital investment.

The free market aspects of the NEP also helped to convince many people

that Russia was moving away from communism—and that, too, had a good effect abroad. Trade talks took place with England and Germany in 1921, but neither nation wanted to be the first to open diplomatic relations with Russia.

The breakthrough came in 1922 when the Allies called for an international conference to discuss reparations. The Soviets had to be invited because, according to the Treaty of Versailles, they were also entitled to reparations from Germany. The Genoa Conference failed to resolve the reparations issue (in fact, France refused to allow the subject to be raised), and this convinced the German delegates that they had nothing to lose by signing an agreement with Russia—particularly since the Soviets were willing to give up any claim to reparations from Germany. Over the weekend, the Russian and German delegates got together in the nearby town of Rapallo and signed an agreement reestablishing diplomatic relations between the two countries.

The Rapallo Agreement became the basis for a Russo-German relationship that was to continue throughout the 1920s and to serve the interests of both countries. What they had in common is that both were outcast nations who opposed the post–World War I settlement. Germany used the Russian connection to obtain concessions from England and France; for Russia, it served the purpose of ending its diplomatic exile. A major British trade delegation led by ex-Prime Minister Stanley Baldwin visited Russia in 1923, and this was followed by the resumption of diplomatic relations between the two countries in 1924. Italy, Austria, Greece, Norway, and Sweden followed almost immediately thereafter and before the year was out they had been joined by China,

Denmark, Mexico, and France. Of the major countries, only the United States continued to withhold diplomatic recognition. Although there were fairly extensive trade relations between the two countries, formal recognition did not come until 1933.

Building Socialism—the Five-Year Plans

Although Marx had written that "new, higher productive relationships never come into being before the material conditions for their existence have been brought to maturity within the womb of the old society itself," Lenin's revolution had brought the communists to power in an, at best, imperfectly industrialized country, one that obviously lacked the material conditions for communism. There could be no real guidance in Marx on how to remedy the lack, for Marx had never anticipated that this situation would arise. Lenin, guided by a reference in the *Communist Manifesto* to increasing "the total of productive forces as rapidly as possible" and, elsewhere, by references to *state planning* as the mechanism that would replace free competition as the driving force within a society under communism, did create the Supreme Economic Council in 1917 and the State Planning Commission (GOSPLAN) in 1921; he also linked the creation of large-scale industry with the electrification of the country. But he favored government efforts in this direction within the context of the NEP.

The policy of "socialist" industrialization was first proclaimed at the 14th Party Congress in late 1925, the first victory for Stalin's "socialism in one country." The measure did not come into effect immediately, however, for there were serious disagreements at the time as to how industrialization was to be carried out. Two years later, the Party Congress ordered GOSPLAN to prepare a Five-Year Plan for expansion of the national economy. This first Five-Year Plan went into operation in 1928.

The purpose of the plan was to carry out a large-scale, state-directed rapid industrialization. The priority was on heavy industry. Specifically, the government embarked on the construction of steel mills, opening of coal mines, building of dams for the production of hydroelectricity, and building of factories for the manufacture of a host of products, including tractors, agricultural machinery, automobiles, and chemicals. The goals for increased production were impressive: steel production was to go from 4.2 million tons to 10 million tons; coal from 35 million to 150 million tons; electric power from 5 million to 22 million kilowatt-hours. Some of these higher levels were to come from increased production at already existing plants, but it mostly involved new productive capacity.

Joseph Stalin, ruler of the Soviet Union

In all, the plan called for the creation of 1,500 new enterprises and a capital construction budget of 64.5 billion rubles. Such funds were not available to the state under the conditions of the NEP market economy. Stalin's solution was to phase out the NEP and to replace it with a "command model" which gave the state direct control over all economic activity. For the urban sector, this meant a return to the situation as it had existed under War Communism; for the villages, it meant an end to individual agriculture and the forcible creation of collective farms.

The Collectivization of Agriculture

Although collectivized agriculture eventually came to be an integral part of the economic system of nearly every communist country, Marx had, in fact, little to say about the organization of agriculture under communism. Some of the more pertinent references are found in the *Communist Manifesto*, where he referred to

the bringing into cultivation of wastelands, and the improvement of the soil generally in accordance with a common plan. . . . Establishment of industrial armies, especially for agriculture. . . . Combination of agriculture with manufacturing industries; gradual abolition of the distinction between town and country, by a more equitable distribution of the population over the country.

After the revolution, the communists took over the estates formerly owned by the Imperial family and organized them into state farms (*sovkhozy*). These units, owned and operated by the state, were run like "factories in the field," with the peasants receiving daily wages. The object was to turn the peasants into proletariat in line with Lenin's theory, expressed in *The Agrarian Program of Russian Social Democracy*, that hired agricultural workers belonged to the "working class." The communists also had in mind to create examples of good farming methods which the peasants could follow.

The *sovkhozy* represented—and until Gorbachev's agricultural reforms continued to represent—the communist ideal for organization of the countryside, but the

Russia

obligation to pay year-around wages means that they were expensive to run. The communists therefore developed a second type of farm organization which they called the *kolkhoz*. This was, in theory, a cooperative organization formed on a voluntary basis by a group of peasants. Land, livestock, and farm machinery were pooled and then became the property of the *kolkhoz*.

The unit was farmed collectively by the group of peasants, and all income after expenses and taxes was shared on the basis of the total number of workdays performed by each member of the collective. The farmers were permitted an individual "private plot" of not more than an acre for use as a garden. They also could keep a cow, pigs, and chickens. In the 1920s, the government offered special subsidies and favorable tax treatment to those who would join a *kolkhoz*, but they were not popular with the peasants and, by 1928, only about 1 peasant in 60 had joined.

The first Five-Year Plan called for 17.5% of the cultivated land to be organized into *kolkhozy*, which would have entailed persuading between four to five million peasants to join collective farms. There was strong resistance to the collectivization, however, and even the offer of seed, credit and the use of state-owned machinery brought a meager response, primarily among poorer peasants having little to lose.

The communists, recalling how the peasants had frustrated them during the period of War Communism, decided to force the issue. Peasants opposing collectivization were labeled kulaks (a traditional Russian term for a well-to-do peasant) and declared to be class enemies. Stalin set this new line in December 1929 when he called for the "liquidation of the kulaks as a class." Thousands of urban workers and student volunteers were sent into the countryside to agitate for the collective farms. When persuasion failed, special army and OGPU (secret police) units, assisted by local militias, began to use coercive measures to force the peasantry into the collectives. Committees of poor peasants were also set up to cooperate with the government and report on their wealthier neighbors. In effect, the communists deliberately promoted class warfare in the countryside.

At first, Stalin made it look as if the new measures of the government and party were only directed against the kulaks. In January 1930, a Politburo commission drew up quotas of 60,000 "malicious kulaks" to be sent to labor camps and 150,000 other kulak households to be exiled to the North, Siberia, the Urals, and Kazakhstan. The implementation of the quotas was assigned to the OGPU.

At the time, the Party theoreticians estimated that, of over 25 million peasant families, less than 1 million were wealthy enough to be labeled kulaks; accordingly, the OGPU plan called for 1 million kulak households to be stripped of their land and possessions and sent to labor camps or special settlements. Every village was assigned a quota by district authorities. Local Komsomol and Party activists then drew up lists of the "kulaks" in each village to be arrested and exiled.

By 1932, there were 1.4 million "kulaks" in the special settlements and an even larger number in labor camps attached to Gulag factories and construction sites. Overall, at least 10 million "kulaks" were expelled from their homes and villages between 1929 and 1932.

The progress of collectivization is shown by the following figures:

Year	Percent Collectivized
1928	1.7
Oct. 1929	4.1
Jan. 1930	21.0
Mar. 1930	58.0

A temporary halt was called in early 1930. Collectivization was slowed down and many *kolkhozy* were dissolved and the land was returned to individuals. This occurred after Stalin criticized those carrying out the forced collectivization in a famous article entitled "dizziness with success." But the program was soon resumed and those collectivized grew to 61.5% by the end of 1932. By the end of 1938, the 25 million peasant households were almost completely gathered into some 250,000 collective farms.

Because of extensive resistance to collectivization from the peasantry, the former voluntary nature of the *kolkhoz* ceased; the farm manager, formerly elected by the membership, was now selected by and subordinate to the higher Communist Party authorities.

In addition, Machine-Tractor-Stations (MTSs), which were directly controlled by the state, were set up in the countryside. The MTSs got all the new farm machinery that was being manufactured and, using their own crews, performed all of the mechanical labor on the collectives. They usually contained the local Communist Party cell as well, so they also exercised a control function in rural areas.

At the end of the harvest, each collective farm was required to deliver a set amount of its total production to the state at a controlled price. Next, a certain percentage of the total production was delivered to the MTS in payment of its services. Any remaining production was divided among the peasants according to the number of hours worked and the type of labor performed. In many years, the amount remaining to be divided was relatively small and the peasants had to rely on produce raised on the garden plots to feed themselves.

There were several important reasons for the collectivization of agriculture, but the most important reason was that it allowed the Communist Party to gain control of the countryside in a predominantly rural nation and to force the peasantry to serve the interests of the communist state. In one of his moments of candor, Stalin explained that, since Russia had no colonies to exploit, it could only find the funds for industrialization by taking them from its own people. And this is what was done.

[For a discussion of the man-made famine (Holodomor) in Ukraine and elsewhere in the Soviet Union in 1932–1933, see the historical section of the chapter on Ukraine entitled Collectivization and the Great Famine, beginning on page 170.]

During the period of the first Five-Year Plan, the living standard for the average Soviet citizen diminished by an estimated 35%, meaning that the living standard of the workers, the darlings of the Communist Party, suffered a drop during these years; but it was the peasantry whose privations during this period primarily paid for the first Five-Year Plan. As the government and the Communist Party saw it, however, by pouring 35% of the gross national product into new productive facilities, the government managed to more or less meet the goals of the plan. It should be noted, however, that Soviet production data for this period were notoriously unreliable. Managers were under tremendous pressure to "meet the plan" which caused many to resort to lying and deception in their record keeping.

Second and third Five-Year Plans followed and continued the process of industrialization. Nearly all of the investment continued to be in heavy industry, however, so the Soviet people saw very little change in their standard of living. But the heavy pace wore out the country, and criticism of Stalin's harsh policies increased even among his supporters. His reaction was to launch a purge—massacre—that eventually enveloped all parts of Russian society.

Terror and Purges

Stalin resorted to terror not only to deal with temporary emergencies; terror became a permanent and prominent feature of his style of governing. Lenin and other Bolshevik leaders had used terror on a smaller scale, and they had employed a special organization to combat "counter-revolution"—the Cheka. It came into existence soon after the Bolsheviks seized power. The name of the organization was changed several times; known by its Russian initials, it has been the GPU, OGPU, NKVD, MVD, MGB, and KGB. Whatever its name, however, its function was always the same—a secret police force looking everywhere for saboteurs, spies, and counter-revolutionaries. Abroad, it came to be used as an active espionage organization, more often than not in the guise of members of the Russian diplomatic corps.

Stalin changed the nature of the secret police, however, when, in the 1930s, he made them a major instrument of his ruthless purges. Stalin's first targets were the non-communist technicians and specialists, both Russian and foreign, who had been enlisted to help in the first Five-Year Plan. This had the effect of providing an excuse for failure to achieve some of the goals of the plan. Accused of espionage and sabotage, these technicians and specialists were convicted with the help of manufactured evidence and forced confessions.

Cauldron of intrigue: Hotel Lux in Moscow, where foreign Communists were housed during purges

The next group subjected to terror and liquidation were those peasants who were accused of sabotaging the collectivization drive. This action was officially known as the "liquidation of the kulaks as a class,"

but it actually affected millions who could by no stretch of the imagination be called "rich" peasants. Besides the million or so peasants who suffered death, there were others who filled forced-labor camps and were used in digging canals, mining gold, and other enterprises under unbelievably inhuman conditions.

What is known as the Great Purge lasted from 1934 to 1938 and differed from earlier periods of Stalinist terror. This time it was directed against the leading echelons of the Communist Party. The concept of a "purge" goes back to the era of Lenin, when it meant removal from the party only. It was Stalin who changed the meaning of the "purge," transforming it into an action that might include criminal prosecution, exile, or death. The Great Purge began in December 1934 with the assassination of Sergei M. Kirov, a member of the Politburo and Zinoviev's successor as first secretary of the Leningrad party organization. Although supporters of Zinoviev were blamed for organizing the murder, to this day it is not known whether there was a conspiracy or whether the shooter, Leonid Nikolaev, acted alone. Stalin may have ordered the murder himself. Kirov had questioned the breakneck tempo of change in the Soviet Union and was seen as a possible successor to Stalin.

Purge at the Top

In any case, Stalin used Kirov's death as an excuse to unleash a purge of suspect party members and, particularly, party leaders. Most significantly, the Society of Old Bolsheviks, whose members had worked closely with Lenin, was dissolved in mid-1935. A "verification" of party membership cards was ordered, and some 10% were expelled; by 1936, at least one-quarter of the membership had been dropped from the party.

Next came, in 1936, the first of three public trials, when 16 Old Bolsheviks, including Zinoviev and Kamenev, were charged with treason, convicted and executed. Mikhail P. Tomsky, leader of the communist trade unions, committed suicide.

In early 1937, at the second trial, 17 prominent communists, diplomats, economists, and writers, including Karl Radek, who had closely collaborated with Lenin, were tried as alleged German and Japanese spies. At the trials, an attempt was made to "expose" Trotsky and to condemn his activities abroad as being directed against the USSR. Thirteen of the accused were shot, while the other four were sentenced to long prison terms; none of them was ever heard from again.

Then, in June 1937, there was a brief press announcement which told of the secret trial and execution of Army Marshal

Mikhail Tukhachevsky and seven other leading generals of the Red Army. This was followed by a mass purge of officers which eventually included two of the five Soviet marshals, 13 out of 15 army generals, 62 out of 85 corps commanders, 110 out of 195 divisional commanders and 220 out of 406 brigade commanders. It has been estimated that 65% of all military officers holding the rank of colonel or above were liquidated.

The last of the public trials came in 1938 when several former Politburo members, including Nikolai Bukharin, Alexei Rykov, and N. M. Krestinsky, plus distinguished provincial party leaders were found guilty of treason and shot. The public "show trials" were the most spectacular aspect of the Great Purge because they included public "confessions," but they were only a minor aspect of the overall purge. Eventually, large numbers of trade-unionists, managers, intellectuals, and party and COMINTERN functionaries were arrested and liquidated. Finally, at one point, orders went out to the secret police to arrest an arbitrary percentage of the entire population. These individuals were given summary trials before being shipped off to prison camps in Siberia, where they provided the regime with a large quantity of unpaid labor. Finally, two different secret police heads, Genrikh Yagoda and Nikolai Yezhov, eventually became victims of the purges themselves. Yagoda was shot as a spy upon Yezhov's orders, while Yezhov was arrested in 1939 after Lavrenti Beria had replaced him as head of the secret police, and shot in 1940.

One observer has aptly called this period "a reign of terror without parallel in Soviet history" in which "no sphere of Soviet life, however lofty, was left untouched." The destructive fury of the Great Purge can only be explained on the assumption that Stalin was determined to eliminate once and for all any possible challenge to his personal power within the party leadership.

Russia

Death of a Commissar (1928)   Courtesy of K. S. Petrov–Vodkin

Stalin's Revolution of the 1930s

Marx had very little to say about the implications of his philosophical system insofar as the performing and creative arts were concerned, though it follows that, since the creative arts would be considered part of the superstructure of society, they must, according to Marx's general theory, reflect the social and economic environment in which they appear. Marx did indicate that the proletariat would take over that which was good in the previous bourgeois society, but he also stipulated that much would be discarded—and he made a specific attack on the bourgeois family. In most respects, however, Marx had conventional tastes in art and literature.

Lenin was also rather ordinary in his tastes, and his first people's commissar for education specifically proclaimed the right of individual creation. Lenin never permitted the printing of anything anti-revolutionary or anti-communist but, with that limitation, there was considerable artistic freedom in Russia during the NEP years. Among the excellent works produced in the 1920s were Alexander Blok's *The Twelve;* Mikhail Bulgakov's *The Master and Margarita;* Mikhail Sholokhov's *And Quiet Flows the Don;* poems by Boris Pasternak and Vladimir Mayakovsky; and, finally, the music of Dmitry Shostakovich.

In the schools, all sorts of experimental ideas were tried out—such as abolishing discipline—and courses in mathematics, chemistry, geography, and physics were phased out in favor of vocational education. Traditional family values also came under attack as divorce became a mere registration process and the emancipation of women from home life was stressed. Restrictions on religious life were relaxed after massive persecution of the Orthodox Church during the Civil War years.

All of this came to an end in 1929 when Stalin, launching his Five-Year Plan, decided that the creative arts had to be mobilized in support of the industrialization program of the Communist Party. Publishers were instructed on the types of books they were to publish. Specific "proletarian" goals were announced for art, music, and literature. Experiments in style were condemned and creative workers were informed that what they produced had to be intelligible to the masses. Themes suggested to the creative artists included industrial construction, the fight against external aggression and internal subversion and the glory of life on collective farms.

Schools were reorganized and traditional courses reinstated. Examinations were reintroduced, and teachers were again given control in the classroom. Family life was again emphasized and the parents were instructed that they were responsible for training and disciplining their children. Divorce became more difficult to obtain, and abortion was banned.

Socialist Realism

During this period also, the state developed a specific theory for the arts called *socialist realism*—defined as a portrayal of reality in its revolutionary development in order to remake and re-educate the workers in the spirit of socialism. What this meant in practice was that artists were to depict Soviet reality *as it would be, or should be*, rather than as it was. As one historian has expressed it, it was communism with a smiling face. No morbid or pessimistic themes were allowed; music was to be melodic and life was to be portrayed as good and getting better.

Militarized Communist Youth (1933)

Courtesy of A. N. Samokhvalov

The effect of these restrictions was predictable. Soviet paintings tended to be either poster art in the revolutionary style or Soviet versions of *Saturday Evening Post* covers. Favorite painting subjects included portraits of Lenin and Stalin, scenes from the Russian revolution and civil war, and landscapes that included factories or glamorized collective farms. Modern dance and jazz were outlawed and Soviet ballet returned to the classical style. Composers such as Shostakovich and Prokofiev began to base their compositions on folk music. Abstract and semi-abstract art were out, and this led to a purge of paintings in Russian museums. Artists whose works were now labeled decadent included Vincent Van Gogh, Paul Gauguin, Georges Seurat, Henri Matisse, Pablo Picasso, Marc Chagall, and Vasily Kandinsky. Their paintings were taken down from display and locked away in storerooms.

Soviet Foreign Policy in The 1930s

The Soviet Union had established friendly relations with Germany as a result of the Rapallo Pact in 1922 and those relations continued after Stalin came to power. Trade between the two countries actually increased after 1928 as the Soviet Union began its first Five-Year Plan. Political relations also remained good and the two nations signed an agreement in 1931 prolonging the Berlin Treaty on neutrality which the two nations had signed in 1926. The Soviet Union was willing to continue good relations even after Adolf Hitler came to power in 1933; it was Hitler's decision, not Stalin's, that changed the course of German-Soviet relations—and eventually led to a change in overall Soviet foreign policy.

The change in course by Hitler, plus his extreme anti-communist speeches, convinced the Soviet Union that it would have to seek new friends. Russia had always been an opponent of the League of Nations, but when Nazi Germany left the League, the Soviet Union decided to join. The Soviet Union became a leading advocate of "collective security" between 1934 and 1939.

Although it appeared that the Soviet Union was interested in active opposition to Nazism and Fascism, Stalin's actual policies at the time can best be described as isolationism with a substantial amount of appeasement. This reflected his caution and his obsessive fear of having to fight alone against a united capitalist world. The Soviet Union also chose a policy of appeasement toward Japan when it began to

assert its strength on the Asian mainland beginning in 1931. Although Stalin encouraged the Chinese nationalists and communists alike to resist the Japanese, he obviously considered events in East Asia to be less significant than what was happening in Europe and he was also unwilling to expose the USSR to direct Japanese attack. To lessen the threat of conflict, therefore, he arranged to sell the Russian share in the Chinese Eastern Railway to the Japanese-controlled puppet state of Manchukuo.

The main driving force behind Soviet foreign policy in the 1930s was the USSR's domestic industrialization program. Before 1934, therefore, foreign policy initiatives tended to be aimed at protecting the country from attack from abroad, and this took the form of negotiating non-aggression pacts with its neighbors. Thus, in 1932, it signed non-aggression pacts with Finland, Estonia, Latvia, Poland, and France. Its second main concern was to obtain access to modern technology and, complementary to that, to find markets for its grain, so as to be able to pay for foreign technology necessary for industrialization.

After 1934, the policy of the Soviet Commissar of Foreign Affairs, Maxim Litvinov, of cooperating with the Western democracies to oppose the growing menace of Nazi Germany led to mutual security pacts with France and Czechoslovakia, both signed in 1935. Soviet policy in the Spanish Civil War (1936–1939) took a slightly different direction. Here, the Soviet Union became actively involved as a supporter of the loyalist side against the insurgents led by General Francisco Franco. Although Great Britain and France opposed the Franco insurgency, they adopted a policy of strict neutrality. By comparison, the Soviet Union appeared to be supporting intervention in support of the loyalists, a position many

Kolhkoz Festival (1937)

Courtesy of S. V. Gerasimov

Russia

people in the West attributed to the fact that the Spanish communists constituted a major part of the loyalist forces. The fact that the COMINTERN helped organize "international brigades" to fight on the side of the Spanish Republic merely reinforced this interpretation, causing great disquiet in Great Britain and France.

In 1938, when Hitler demanded that areas of Czechoslovakia where German-speakers were in the majority be turned over to Germany, it appeared that the Soviet Union might be called upon to honor its mutual security pact and come to the aid of Czechoslovakia. However, France and Great Britain, after giving Czechoslovakia some initial support, eventually acquiesced in Hitler's demand and signed the Munich Agreement ceding the area of the Sudetenland to Germany.

It could not have pleased Stalin that the Soviet Union was not even invited to the Munich Conference, in spite of its mutual security pact with Czechoslovakia. But the British and French act of appeasement represented by the Munich Pact also went a long way toward convincing Stalin that a foreign policy based on cooperation with the West against Hitler was worthless. On the other side, there was an extremely negative reaction in the West to the gruesome purges Stalin was then conducting in the Soviet Union. Stalin probably realized that this Western revulsion would make any close cooperation between the Soviet Union and the Western democracies extremely difficult.

The appeasement policies of the Western Powers may have also led Stalin to suspect that they were hoping to encourage Hitler to attack the Soviet Union and thereby remove the threat from themselves. Some groups in the West did indeed nourish such hopes, although it never became the official policy of any of the Western governments.

Hitler's seizure of the rest of Czechoslovakia in March 1939 reinforced Stalin's perception that neither Great Britain nor France could be depended upon, since neither took any action, even though both had guaranteed Czechoslovakia's remaining territories. It is true that Prime Minister Neville Chamberlain condemned the German actions in Czechoslovakia in his Birmingham speech of March 17 and promised that his country would resist any further act of aggression by Germany, in particular against Poland—but Great Britain had made promises before and then ignored them. In March 1939, Stalin spelled out the position of the Soviet Union in a famous speech to the 18th Party Congress in which he declared that the Soviet Union was not willing to "pull the chestnuts out of the fire" for the benefit of others.

Stalinist die-hards demonstrating for their hero in late 1990s

Chamberlain's promise that Great Britain would resist any German aggression against Poland meant that Hitler had to expect war with Great Britain, and possibly France, if he pursued his objectives on Poland. On the other hand, the position of the Soviet Union now became all important. Hitler would need to come to an understanding with the Soviet Union before he could invade Poland, unless he was willing to chance the possibility of having to fight a war on two fronts.

As the crisis deepened, the Soviet Union became involved in two sets of negotiations in Moscow—official alliance discussions with the French and British on one hand and unofficial discussions under the guise of trade negotiations with Nazi Germany on the other. Stalin had to ask himself whether an alliance with Great Britain and France would deter Hitler—or whether it would only mean that the Soviet Union would be drawn into the war from the very beginning of an armed conflict.

The Nazi-Soviet Non-Aggression Pact

The German side had an offer that looked much more appealing—the division of Poland between Germany and Russia. From Stalin's point of view, this offered the opportunity to keep the Soviet Union out of the war and yet to receive the eastern third of Poland as a reward from Hitler for remaining neutral. In addition, Hitler was willing to recognize the Baltic area and Bessarabia as falling within the Soviet Union's "sphere of influence."

The agreement between the Soviet Union and Germany was announced on August 23, 1939. Though it came as a shock and surprise to the world, it was a logical, although risky, option for Stalin at the time. Soviet-Polish relations had never been particularly good, and the Soviet Union had no substantial reason to come to Poland's assistance. Moreover, what Stalin feared most of all was to be dragged into a war against Germany by Great Britain and France, and then be forced to bear the brunt of that war while those countries sat on the sidelines.

The Nazi-Soviet Non-Aggression Pact (aka Molotov–Ribbentrop Pact) gave Hitler a green light to invade Poland, which he did on September 1.

The fighting was mostly over by September 17, when Soviet troops entered from the east to claim the Soviet share of the spoils. The last member of the Polish government had already left the country to seek refuge abroad. The Soviet Union then claimed that its troops were entering a no-man's-land; Stalin even had the nerve to suggest to Hitler that he be permitted to state that Soviet troops were entering the former Polish territory in order to save the largely Ukrainian and Byelorussian population of the area *from the Germans!*

The Soviet side also suggested a change in the terms of the secret agreement. They wanted less Polish territory than what had been given them in the original deal, and asked instead to have Lithuania included in the Soviet "sphere" along with Latvia and Estonia. Hitler agreed and the swap was made. In October 1939, the Soviet

Union forced the three Baltic republics to sign offensive and defensive alliances which provided for the stationing of Soviet troops on their territory.

Finland also came under similar pressure, but the Finns resisted the Soviet demands. As a result, Stalin ordered the invasion of Finland in November 1939. Although the Finns managed to stop the first Soviet offensive—and in doing so to inflict embarrassing losses on the Soviet forces—the small country was forced to sue for peace after three months and to cede some Finnish territory to the Soviet Union.

The Soviet Union's use of military force against its small neighbor added to the bad reputation which the Soviet Union had in the West, already resentful of the Soviet deal with Hitler. Unrealistic ideas of coming to the assistance of Finland almost resulted in British and French declarations of war *against the Soviet Union*, at that time looked upon as an ally of Adolf Hitler. Fortunately for the future of Europe, the British decided against any such action when it became clear that they would be unable to provide any meaningful assistance to the Finns.

German troops conquered Denmark and Norway in April 1940, then began their sweep across France, Belgium, and the Netherlands in May. Their swift military success disturbed Stalin, who apparently expected a much longer involvement of German troops on the Western front. This is evident in the fact that he moved quickly to consolidate his hold on the territories he had obtained as a result of the Nazi-Soviet Non-Aggression Pact. In May 1940, the three Baltic republics were forced to join the Soviet Union. Next, Romania was asked to cede the province of Bessarabia, taken from Russia during World War I, and parts of Bukovina, about which there had been no clear arrangement with the Germans in 1939. The Soviet government also protested when Hitler sent German troops into Finland and signed an alliance with Romania which involved dispatching German troops to that country as well.

German Invasion of the Soviet Union: Operation Barbarossa

In late 1940 and early 1941, relations between the Soviet Union and Germany acquired an air of unreality. Stalin alternately

appeased and challenged Hitler, while the Führer, who had already ordered planning to begin for an invasion of the Soviet Union, tried to persuade Stalin to look to Iran and British India for future spoils. The Soviet Commissar of Foreign Affairs, Vyacheslav Molotov, who had replaced Litvinov, was presented with such a proposal during a visit to Berlin in late 1940, but the Soviets took the position that it was too early to discuss cutting up the British Empire.

By the autumn of 1940, Hitler was in a quandary. His plan for the invasion of England, Operation Sea Lion, had to be aborted when his air force was unable to gain control of the air over England. There was no immediate threat in the west, but also no chance to bring the British to the negotiating table. Was this the time to turn on the Soviet Union and, in another lightning onslaught, destroy his long-term foe in the east? On December 18, he answered that question by signing Operation Barbarossa "to crush Soviet Russia in a quick campaign even before the end of the war against England."

It mattered very little what the Soviet Union did at that point. However, one question arises with regard to what Stalin did prior to the German attack. He had received reports of an impending German invasion from many sources, but he ordered practically no preparations for the invasion, supposedly because he believed that they were bits of "disinformation" spread by the Western intelligence services to force a break between the Soviet Union and Nazi Germany. Stalin also probably figured that Hitler would not invade the Soviet Union, and thereby wage war on two fronts, without first presenting Stalin with an ultimatum.

Stalin made a major blunder in basing his foreign policy on his perception of Hitler's motives and not on what Germany was capable of doing.

Stalin's failure to improve the combat readiness of the Soviet armed forces during this period exposed millions of soldiers to slaughter and capture in the very first weeks of the war, launched by Hitler on June 22, 1941.

Ally of the West

Hitler's unprovoked attack changed the Soviet Union's international position literally overnight. British Prime Minister Winston Churchill, though a life-long enemy of communism, immediately welcomed the Soviet Union as an ally of Great Britain. The United States, not yet engaged in the war, also extended lend-lease to the Soviet Union in September 1941. There were, however, serious doubts in the West about Russia's ability to resist Hitler's offensive for very

Russia

long, and the speedy advance of German troops in July and August seemed to justify gloomy predictions. Although it was felt that the Soviet Union should be supported in its struggle against Germany because it was tying down masses of German troops, it did not appear that the Soviet Union was an important factor to reckon with at the time.

In this period, the Soviet government yielded to British pressure to reestablish relations with the Polish government-in-exile in London. However, even at this darkest time of military fortune, Stalin made it clear that the Soviet Union intended to retain all the territorial gains made as a result of the Non-Aggression Pact with Hitler.

The Nazi offensive consisted of three attacking forces whose destinations were Leningrad, Moscow, and the Ukraine. It achieved tremendous success in the beginning as Soviet units at the border disintegrated and Germany's mechanized armies swept eastward across the Russian plain, surrounding and conquering whole Soviet armies. Stubborn Soviet defenses halted the German armies for a time at Pskov and Smolensk, but reinforced German armies eventually overcame the Soviet defenders and continued their advance to the east. In the north, the Germans forces reached Leningrad in September and laid seige to the city. But the Germans were unable to close the ring entirely, so the city continued to be re-provisioned across Lake Ladoga, especially when it froze solid during the winter of 1941–1942. The ring of the blockade was broken in January 1943 and the siege was lifted by a German retreat a year later. About 800,000 people died in Leningrad during the blockade.

On the Soviet Central Front, the German forces got within 35 miles of Moscow before being ground to a halt by the Russian winter and a Soviet counter-offensive. In the south, Kyiv was captured on September 19. Between then and December, German armies overran the rest of the Ukraine, reaching as far east as the Donets River. However, Hitler, enraged that neither Leningrad nor Moscow had been captured, dismissed his chief generals in December and assumed personal command himself.

This was a gift for the Russians—Hitler, although occasionally capable of brilliant insights, was not a military strategist. In 1942, for example, he held his forces on the north and center on the defensive while he attempted to make a breakthrough in the south. His original goal was the oil fields of the Caucasus, an entirely logical one under the circumstances. But in June he ordered part of his southern armies to turn directly east and open a drive toward Stalingrad. Apparently, he intended to humiliate Stalin by destroying the city named after him. But Stalingrad (since renamed Volgograd) was a city of no particular strategic significance, while Hitler's diversion of part of his southern armies meant that the remaining forces were not strong enough to seize the Caucasus oil fields.

Stalingrad was reached in September 1942, after slow progress in the face of heavy Russian resistance. In late 1942, most of the city had been captured after bloody street-to-street fighting. Now, Stalin launched an artillery offensive that came up to the city from the East. The Soviet forces began an enveloping movement from both the south and north of the city and the German Sixth Army was soon encircled. The German forces could have broken out of the trap at this time, but Hitler ordered the 285,000 men trapped by the Soviets not to retreat. After attempts to relieve the army failed, the 90,000 survivors of the battle of Stalingrad surrendered on January 30, 1943. Later, Stalin would have them marched in triumph through the streets of Moscow.

After Stalingrad

The reversal of Soviet military fortunes represented by the victory at Stalingrad created an entirely new political situation. Although the Soviet Union remained heavily dependent on the lend-lease supplies that were flowing into Russia in very large amounts from the United States at the cost of many lives lost to German submarines, the Soviets developed the feeling that they had managed to live through the darkest moments of the war largely by their own efforts. It also did not help that the Allies now informed the Soviet Union that the "second front" in the West would have to be put off until 1944.

It was also at this time that another situation came to light which acted as a wedge between the Soviet Union and its Western Allies. In the spring of 1943, Germany announced the discovery of a mass grave in the Katyn Forest containing the bodies of thousands of Polish army officers who had fallen into the hands of the Soviet forces in September 1939. They had been shot in the back of the head, a standard method of execution practiced by the Soviet secret police. Alarmed by the discovery, the Polish government-in-exile in London asked for an investigation by the International Red Cross.

Stalin accused the Polish government-in-exile of aiding German propaganda and used this as an excuse to break off diplomatic relations. Soon a new organization was formed from among Polish refugees in the Soviet Union. This organization, the Union of Polish Patriots, became the nucleus of the Soviet-sponsored Lublin government, which was installed in power by the Soviet army after the liberation of Poland.

Wartime Conferences and the Occupation of Eastern Europe

The Soviet military occupation of Eastern Europe and the Soviet decision to set up communist governments in the area are usually considered to be important factors in the origins of the Cold War that developed between the Soviet Union and its Western Allies after World War II. The matter is somewhat more complex, however.

First of all, there were always differences between the Soviet Union and its allies over Soviet territories obtained as a result of the Nazi-Soviet Non-Aggression Pact of 1939. In particular, neither the United States nor Great Britain ever recognized the incorporation of Latvia, Estonia, Lithuania, and Bessarabia into the Soviet Union.

When the United States and Great Britain drew up the Atlantic Charter in 1941, setting forth their wartime goals, they stipulated there were to be no territorial changes without the freely registered approval of the people involved. They also promised to respect the right of all peoples to determine the form of government under which they would live. When, six weeks later, the Soviet Union gave its approval to the Atlantic Charter, American policymakers accepted that as a basis for cooperation. And in September 1941, although the United States was not yet at war, it extended a billion dollar "lend-lease" grant to the Soviet Union for the purchase of supplies in the United States. By the end of the war, the United States had shipped approximately $11 billion worth of equipment and supplies to the Soviet Union.

Presumably the Soviet Union signed the Atlantic Charter because it wanted the "lend-lease" agreement with the United States. Again, it would have been for the same reason that it agreed to the incorporation of the Atlantic Charter into the Declaration of the United Nations which the US, Great Britain, the USSR, and 23 other nations signed on January 1, 1942. That it never intended to apply the terms of the Atlantic Charter to territories annexed in 1939–1940 can be seen by the fact that it continued to pressure the US and Great Britain to recognize the incorporation of these territories into the USSR after signing the Atlantic Charter.

Another factor was Franklin D. Roosevelt's opposition to concepts such as "balance of power politics" and "spheres of influence." The United States was committed to allowing the peoples of Eastern Europe to set up their own freely elected governments and FDR attempted to bind

"The Big Three": Stalin, Roosevelt, and Churchill at Tehran

his allies to a similar position. What he forgot, however, was that Nazi Germany's defeat would bring about a power vacuum in Eastern Europe and, *one way or the other*, that power vacuum would be filled. But perhaps the most important factor influencing American foreign policy at this juncture was FDR's belief that Stalin didn't want anything for himself in Eastern Europe. As he commented to Ambassador William Christian Bullitt just prior to the Tehran Conference,

I have just a hunch that Stalin doesn't want anything but security for his country, and I think that if I give him everything I possibly can and ask nothing in return, noblesse oblige, he won't try to annex anything and will work for a world of democracy and peace.

Roosevelt's "hunch" seemed to be confirmed when he, Churchill, and Stalin met in Tehran in November 1943, for it was here that the "Big Three," in a general declaration which they drew up, promised an enduring peace in which "all the peoples

of the world may live free lives untouched by tyranny and according to their varying desires and their consciences."

In delineating spheres of military operations, however, Romania, Bulgaria, Hungary, Yugoslavia, Czechoslovakia, Poland, and Finland were designated areas of Soviet operations. If Roosevelt was right about Stalin, it wouldn't matter; but if he was not, he was putting his stamp of approval on whatever policy Stalin chose to carry out in Eastern Europe. Churchill, recognizing the potential danger in such an arrangement, pushed for an allied invasion up through the Balkans, but he was overruled.

Soviet troops began entering Eastern Europe in August 1944; by the time of the Yalta Conference in early 1945, Soviet armies occupied Romania, Bulgaria, Poland, and parts of Hungary and Czechoslovakia. The Yalta Conference was primarily concerned with the problem of Germany, and it was at this time that allied zones of occupation were established. The Soviet Zone would eventually become the German Democratic Republic.

Poland was also considered. Its eastern and western borders were established; the Communist Provisional Government was to be enlarged by the inclusion of democratic leaders from abroad, and the broadened Provisional Government was to hold "free and unfettered elections as soon as possible on the basis of universal suffrage and secret ballot." The rest of Eastern Europe was covered by a general declaration that other people of the region would be encouraged to

form interim governmental authorities broadly representative of all democratic elements in the population and pledged to the earliest possible establishment through elections of governments responsive to the will of the people.

It has often been charged that the United States essentially yielded to Soviet demands concerning territorial matters and the composition of the government of postwar Poland because it was eager for Soviet military assistance in the Far East. It is true that Stalin agreed at Yalta to enter

Russia

the war against Japan within 90 days of victory in Europe. It is also true that an American military study had estimated that, without Soviet assistance, the war against Japan would last until 1947 and might mean another million American lives. The study obviously did not take into consideration the development of the atomic bomb, and it is possible that Roosevelt didn't either. On the other hand, the essential fact is that the American armies were only approaching the Rhine River at the time when Soviet troops were in western Poland and approaching the German border at a point much closer to the main prize, Berlin. Political and strategic decisions made much earlier meant that the United States could only hope that the Soviet Union shared American perceptions about the future of Eastern Europe.

The Cold War

The Cold War essentially began when the Soviet Union, in occupation of Eastern Europe, began to implement its own understanding of the various wartime agreements. The problem arose over the differing Soviet and western Allied understandings of such terms as "democratic," "free elections," and "governments friendly to the Soviet Union." The United States, recognizing the Soviet Union's concern for its security, agreed that the Russians could demand governments "friendly to the Soviet Union" in Eastern Europe. The problem was that Stalin believed that any non-communist government would be *hostile* to the Soviet Union. The same thing applied to such terms as "democratic" and "free elections." According to communist dogma, both terms applied only to states in which communism prevailed.

Stalin was probably not certain that his Western Allies would permit him to communize Eastern Europe. He also recognized that it was necessary to mobilize as much popular support as possible for the new regimes he was installing. That is why "Popular Front" governments were installed nearly everywhere in Eastern Europe in the beginning and why they were normally headed by a non-communist. This transition phase lasted approximately three years. In the meantime, Soviet-Allied relations worsened as it became clear just what Stalin was doing.

It is difficult to pinpoint an exact date for the beginning of the Cold War, but revisionist historians who suggest that President Harry S. Truman's suspension of "lend-lease" assistance to the Soviet Union in May 1945 was motivated by anti-Soviet feelings place it too early. Actually, Truman was merely following the mandate of Congress which, in passing the original legislation, specified that it would continue only for the duration of the war.

Moreover, a quarrel over the political make-up of the new Polish government was resolved just prior to the Potsdam Conference (July 1945) when the US and Great Britain extended diplomatic recognition in return for Stalin's promise to add non-communist elements to it.

At Potsdam (a suburb of Berlin), the US and Great Britain threatened to withhold recognition from the communist-dominated governments of Romania and Bulgaria unless they were enlarged to include a broader political spectrum. But on the major topic, Germany, the Big Three were in general agreement on policies of disarmament and de-Nazification. The US and Great Britain also agreed that the Soviets were entitled to reparations from Germany, although they insisted that the Soviets extract them primarily from their own zone of occupation. That may have been hard on the East Germans, but did not affect the Soviets unduly.

In a 1946 speech delivered prior to new Supreme Soviet elections, Stalin began signaling an intent to reposition Soviet foreign policy away from the US and the West. It was a long speech, but its essence was that the alliance between the Soviet Union and the western democracies had been for limited purposes—to defeat fascism—and now that the purpose had been accomplished there was no longer any basis for co-operation. From now on, the emphasis would be on strengthening the "Soviet social order," which had established its superiority over any non-Soviet form of social organization.

If we place Stalin's comments into the context of the widespread destruction that occurred in the Soviet Union during World War II, they take on a more specific meaning. Large parts of the country had been occupied by foreign troops; and the effects of the actual fighting plus the Soviets' *scorched earth* policy during the retreat of 1941 and the willful destruction of the Germans as they retreated in 1943–1944, left very little intact in the western part of the Soviet Union. In addition, an estimated 26 to 27 million Soviet citizens had died during the war—9 million of them in action. The rebuilding of the Soviet Union was going to require tremendous sacrifices on the part of the Soviet people. Some who lacked a sufficient "proletarian consciousness" might be *seduced* by capitalist promises of a better life.

This provides the reason why, as Aleksandr Solzhenitsyn documented, hundreds of thousands of Soviet soldiers and prisoners of war were shipped off to labor camps in the Gulag Archipelago rather than being treated as heroes. They had become ideologically contaminated because they had seen and might bear witness to what Soviet propaganda endlessly

denied—*that even in devastated Germany the people were better off than those living in the land of the victorious proletariat.*

It also helps to explain Stalin's policy toward Eastern Europe. If these economies could be tied to the Soviet economy, exploitation would make the rebuilding much easier. To accomplish this, trade agreements and mutual friendship and alliance treaties were forged with the Eastern European countries as soon as new governments were formed, with the purpose of reorienting their trade toward the Soviet Union. By 1947, a third of the Soviet Union's imports were coming from Eastern Europe, and the figure continued to grow thereafter. Slowly, Eastern Europe was being cut off and isolated from Western Europe. When Winston Churchill made his famous speech stating that a curtain of iron had been erected between East and West by Stalin in 1946, he was partly referring to this phenomenon.

Though disturbed by developments in Eastern Europe, the United States continued to maintain an ambivalent attitude toward the Soviet Union. The two countries had, after all, been allies in World War II and the United States and the Soviet Union continued to be in basic agreement over policy toward Germany.

Something of a break in that pattern came in March 1947 when President Truman, in a speech to Congress, enunciated a policy toward Greece and Turkey that subsequently became known as the "Truman Doctrine." The Greek government was fighting a communist insurgency supported by Bulgaria and Yugoslavia, while Turkey was under pressure from the Soviet Union to cede certain frontier districts. In Truman's words, it was to be "the policy of the United States to support free people who are resisting attempted subjugation by armed minorities or by outside pressure." Neither communism nor the Soviet Union was mentioned, but the meaning was clear.

Three months later, Secretary of State George Marshall, speaking at the Harvard commencement, offered a broader response, insisting that

... our policy is directed not against any country or doctrine but against hunger, poverty, desperation and chaos ... governments, political parties or groups which seek to perpetuate human misery in order to profit ... politically will encounter the opposition of the United States ...

He thus spelled out a policy which later became known as the "Marshall Plan." The purpose of this was to assist Europe in the restoration of its destroyed economies, and it was to be open to all European nations. For a short while, it appeared that the Soviet Union was interested in the American offer, and Foreign Minister Vyacheslav Molotov even attended a preliminary meeting in Paris to discuss details. Czechoslovakia and Poland also expressed their interest. Then Molotov abruptly denounced the Marshall Plan as an attack on the sovereignty of Europe and announced that the Soviets would not participate after all. Czechoslovakia and Poland withdrew their applications as well. As American economic assistance began to pour into Western Europe, the gulf between East and West widened even further.

The Soviet Union recognized that a resurgent Western Europe might prove such an attraction that it would weaken the Soviet hold over Eastern Europe; it therefore decided to tighten its controls by organizing the Council for Mutual Economic Assistance (CMEA) in 1949. While Stalin was alive, the CMEA was used primarily as a tool to exploit the Eastern European economies. After 1953, however, it became more of a coordinating body to facilitate economic planning and effort.

A second reaction to the Marshall Plan was the creation of a successor organization to the COMINTERN, which had been dissolved in 1943. The Communist Information Bureau (COMINFORM) came into being in the fall of 1947 with its headquarters in Belgrade, Yugoslavia. This turned out to be a poor choice—a scant year later, Yugoslavia was expelled from the COMINFORM upon Stalin's orders because of Marshal Josip Broz Tito's objection to Moscow's meddling in Yugoslavia's domestic economic affairs.

Stalin would have driven Tito from power had he been able to. But Stalin had no Soviet troops stationed in Yugoslavia and the Yugoslavian Communist Party remained loyal to Tito. And, compounding his treason, Tito turned to the United States for support.

Concerned that there might be other Titos, Stalin ordered a purge of other communist parties of Eastern Europe. Individuals suspected of "national deviationism"—putting the interests of one's own country above the interests of the Soviet Union—were removed from office and sometimes put on trial and executed. As the number of executions grew, the American distaste for what was going on inevitably also grew, and so American-Soviet relations deteriorated even further.

The year 1948 also brought a direct Western-Soviet confrontation over Berlin, when Stalin cut off all land access routes between West Germany and Berlin. The Western response was an "airlift" that kept West Berlin supplied with food and fuel for nearly a year until Stalin lifted the blockade.

The Berlin Blockade was a double failure for Stalin, for it, plus the communist

coup d'état in Czechoslovakia, convinced the West that a more long-term response was needed. The North Atlantic Treaty Organization (NATO) came into being in April 1949 with General Dwight D. Eisenhower as Supreme Commander of the Allied Forces in Europe. Agreement was also reached on merging the three western zones of occupation of Germany, a decision that led to the founding of the Federal Republic of Germany in May 1949. Conceding defeat, the Soviet Union ended the Berlin Blockade in May 1949. Five months later, it organized a separate government for its own zone of occupation, which became the German Democratic Republic.

As the European situation turned into a stalemate, Soviet interest began to turn to the East Asia. Here, the victory of Mao Zedong's communists and the establishment of the People's Republic of China seemed to open new vistas for communist expansion. In mid-1949, *Pravda*, the Soviet Communist Party newspaper, carried a long article by Liu Shaoqi, one of the main leaders of the Chinese revolution, reporting on Asian communist parties. The article explicitly endorsed armed struggle as the primary tactic to be pursued by them. Since the article was followed by several similar articles, it soon became evident that the party line on armed struggle had changed. Thus, when the communist government of North Korea launched an invasion of the south in June 1950, the United States assumed that it was operating under Soviet direction. The United States, therefore, brought the matter before the Security Council of the United Nations, which declared the North Korean invasion to be an act of aggression and called upon all members of the United Nations to join in a united "police action" to defend South Korea. This action was possible because the Soviet delegate had been boycotting meetings of the Security Council since January 1950 in protest of the failure to seat communist China.

The Korean "police action" turned into a full-scale war that lasted until just after Stalin's death in March 1953. It soon became obvious that neither side would be permitted to resolve the issue by force, but too much prestige had been invested on both sides to allow for a compromise. News of the gray-haired old dictator's death was therefore greeted with relief, for it was hoped that a compromise might now be reached. The armistice came approximately four months later—on July 27, 1953.

Soviet Internal Political Developments during and after World War II

When Nazi Germany launched its invasion of the Soviet Union in June 1941, Stalin, recognizing that the vast bulk of the

Soviet citizenry had no particular reason to love communism, decided almost immediately to phrase his public messages in the language of Russian patriotism. Communist ideology almost disappeared from public utterances and World War II became the "Great Patriotic War." The Russian Orthodox Church offered its assistance and support, and Stalin in 1943 even went so far as to arrange for the election of a new Patriarch. The Russian Orthodox Church continued to benefit from its enhanced role after World War II as well although it remained very much under state control.

But if Stalin was willing to make nationalist gestures where large numbers of citizens were involved, he still retained his suspicious nature and he did not hesitate to make use of the secret police to uproot whole groups of the population when he became suspicious of their loyalty to the Soviet regime. Thus, the Crimean Tatars and the Volga Germans were forcibly removed from their homes in southern Russia and resettled in Siberia or Central Asia. As the war progressed, other ethnic groups who were suspected of being willing to collaborate with the Germans, or who deserted from the Red Army in too large numbers, were also affected.

After the war, the main task of the NKVD, as it was then called, was to screen and "reintegrate" Soviet citizens who had spent some time in Germany as prisoners of war or as forced labor. Many people also were deported from the areas acquired by the Soviet Union during and after the war. Millions of these people ended up in labor camps scattered across northern Russia and Siberia.

The Fourth Five-Year Plan, 1946–51

The stated economic goals of the fourth Five-Year Plan, initiated in 1946, were to restore war-ravaged areas of the country and to rebuild heavy industry and agriculture to their pre-war levels. These goals would have been challenging enough but, in February 1946, Stalin committed the nation to tripling industrial production in order to make the USSR "ready for every eventuality."

Although the Soviet Union announced in April 1951 that these goals had been met, Western scholars subsequently concluded that, while the assigned targets for raw industrial priority goods had been met, the production of low priority consumer goods fell far short of assigned goals. Agriculture, in particular, was an area in which production bore little relationship to stated goals. Most of the major grain-producing areas of the Soviet Union had, of course, been overrun by the Germans in World War II, and one effect of that was that the collective farms had been

Russia

dissolved and most farm machinery was destroyed. Yet the fourth Five-Year Plan allocated a pitiful 12.3 billion rubles to agriculture for 1946, while allocating 68.8 billion rubles to industry and a further 10 billion rubles to transport.

A famine beginning in late 1946 convinced the Party that something more would have to be done for agriculture, so a separate Three-Year Plan for agriculture was instituted in 1947. The goals—50% increase in the production of meat, milk, lard, eggs, and wool; a 20% increase in the number of cattle, hogs, sheep, and goats—were impressive but, ultimately, they were not achieved. And the reason is simple—heavy industry had first claim on resources and there weren't enough capital resources left over to finance stated agricultural needs.

When the Three-Year Plan for agriculture failed to increase agricultural production significantly, Nikita Khrushchev, who at that time was Party secretary in charge of agriculture, put forth a plan for amalgamating several small collective farms into single, larger collective farms. Khrushchev argued that amalgamation could cut costs and increase efficiency, making it possible to reallocate funds for the purpose of increasing production. The plan reduced the number of collective farms from 254,000 in April 1950 to 97,000 in October 1952. Khrushchev's original plan had also called for razing the old peasant village houses and moving all of the collective farm workers in new *agrogoroda* (literally, farm cities) consisting of high rise apartments. Although peasants were promised that the *agrogoroda* would come with theaters, parks, and other amenities, peasant opposition to the loss of their traditional village homes (and the garden plots attached to them) was strong enough that this aspect of the reform was never implemented. Still, this "reform" had an important effect on country life, even if there is no evidence that it increased efficiency in any way.

Cultural Purges and Anti-Zionism

One remaining aspect of this last period of the Stalin era should be mentioned here. That is the program of cultural and ideological "rehabilitation" that Stalin instituted beginning shortly after the end of World War II, remnants of which continued until his death in 1953. Some reference has already been made to the treatment of soldiers and prisoners of war who were shipped off to prison camps when they arrived back in the Soviet Union. That was because they had seen conditions in central Europe firsthand and could have told their fellow citizens how much worse it was in the Soviet Union.

But the loosening of restrictions during World War II meant that even citizens who had never left home had been exposed to "foreign influences" and become tainted. To counteract that, the Party launched a virulent anti-Western campaign in the summer of 1946. The man in charge of this Soviet "cultural revolution" was Andrei Zhdanov who, in explaining the campaign, said

> Does it suit us, the representatives of the advanced Soviet culture, to bow before bourgeois culture or play the role of its disciples? Our job is to scourge boldly and to attack bourgeois culture, which is in a state of miasma and corruption.

Among the Soviet creative artists whose works came under attack during this time were the poet Anna Akhmatova, the composers Sergei Prokofiev and Dmitry Shostakovich, the film director Sergei Eisenstein, the philosopher G. F. Aleksandrov, and the economist Eugene Varga.

Zhdanov died in 1948 and Soviet cultural policy then changed or, perhaps it might better be said, found another target. The targets were still intellectuals but, now, the target was Jewish intellectuals, who were accused of being unpatriotic, "rootless cosmopolitans." The real issue here appears to be that Israel emerged as an independent state in 1948 and some in the Communist Party worried that Jews, who often held important positions in society, might be more loyal to Israel than they were to the Soviet Union. Many Jewish intellectuals were arrested and, in 1952, several Jewish writers were executed without a trial.

Was Stalin personally involved in these events? The greatest evidence pointing in that direction is found connected with the so-called "doctors' plot" that developed during the last months of Stalin's life. The top echelons of the Communist Party had their own doctor-specialists whose job was to look out after their health. Many of these individuals happened also to be Jews. Stalin evidently came to believe that these Jewish doctors had drawn up a plan aimed at killing or undermining the health of leading Soviet officials. The investigation into the "doctors' plot" quickly came to an end after Stalin's death and Nikita Khrushchev stated in a "secret" speech in 1956 that the "doctors' plot" was fabricated from beginning to end.

The Post-Stalin Era

The Struggle for Succession

The announcement of Stalin's death came on March 5, 1953. It was a strange announcement, for it spoke of the need to prevent "any kind of disorder and panic." The disarray in the leadership which this indicates derived from the fact that Stalin had never permitted his lieutenants any independent authority and squelched any discussion of who his successor would be; now, for the first time, they were on their own. In his memoirs, Nikita Khrushchev reminisced about this period:

> Right up until his death Stalin used to tell us, "you'll see, when I'm gone the imperialistic powers will wring your necks like chickens." We never tried to reassure him that we would be able to manage. We knew it wouldn't do any good.

A Soviet history written in the 1980s characterizes the period of the 1950s as one of "restoration of Leninist norms and the collective principle in the work of the Party and state." There was actually a great deal of agreement in the Presidium about the need for modifications in the system. Some of these changes were inevitable. Stalin had concentrated all decision-making in his own hands—now, some decentralization was in order. The Central Committee, which had fallen into disuse, was revived and regular meetings scheduled. The various ministries were given a greater say in decision-making and there was a great deal of talk about streamlining and rationalizing the ministerial and planning bureaucracies.

In foreign affairs, the turn away from confrontation that led to an armistice in Korea also had an effect on Eastern Europe. In East Germany, the political leadership, concerned about the lack of domestic support, announced a "new course" aimed at reducing popular dissatisfaction. But before the "new course" could be put into action, worker demonstrations and strikes broke out in East Berlin and in other cities. When Soviet tanks were brought in to quell the demonstrations, the workers rebelled and had to be put down with force. June 17th, the date of the workers' rebellion in East Berlin, was subsequently established as a legal holiday in the Federal Republic of Germany. In July 1953, the Central Committee met in a plenary session to hear that Lavrenti Beria, head of the secret police and a top member of the party leadership since 1939, had been arrested. The charge was that he had been attempting a bid for total power based on his control of the secret police. To forestall such an attempt in the future, the secret police were brought firmly under party control by taking them out of the ministry of the interior and creating a separate committee for state security (KGB) directly accountable to the Presidium. The powers of the KGB were also somewhat restricted by the issuance of new regulations specifying when arrests could be made. Beria, who was executed in December, was to be the last leading communist to be physically eliminated after losing in a struggle for power. From 1953 until the collapse of communism in 1991, the maximum penalty was expulsion from the party.

The Beginning of the Khrushchev Era

In September, the first indication that Khrushchev might be a claimant for power came when it was announced that the title of the chief party post had been changed from *General* Secretary to *First* Secretary and that Khrushchev had been confirmed in this office. He now became a vigorous advocate of strengthening the party after years of Stalin's neglect.

The first sign of policy differences between Georgy Malenkov and Khrushchev also appeared in September—though in the carefully phrased way in which Party speeches were made this was easy to see only in retrospect. In August, Malenkov had addressed the Supreme Soviet, setting forth the future direction of the regime. Bidding to reverse Stalin's traditional emphasis on heavy industry, Malenkov's program called for additional investment in the areas of consumer goods and agriculture. His theme was that people had a "right to demand consumer goods of high quality."

Khrushchev, addressing a plenum of the Central Committee of the party after having been installed as First Secretary, argued that something had to be done for agriculture, but rejected a change in investment priorities to finance it.

The battle continued in 1954 and, in fact, became clearer. Khrushchev wanted to retain the priority of heavy industry and wanted to pour additional funds into modernizing defense—while greatly increasing agricultural production. He proposed to accomplish this through what later became known as the "virgin lands" program. What he proposed was that steppe lands in Kazakhstan that had traditionally been considered too dry for agriculture be plowed up and developed as state farms for the production of grain. Khrushchev's program was approved by a Central Committee plenum in March 1954; it was started in that year, but primarily was carried forward in 1955.

In the meantime, Khrushchev had continued his attacks against Malenkov and managed to get him removed as Chairman of the Council of Ministers in early 1955. His replacement was Marshal Nikolai Bulganin. Khrushchev had won a victory, but it was only partial. Bulganin belonged to the same faction on the Presidium as Malenkov.

Nikita Khrushchev

Russia

Although it is largely coincidental, the period of joint leadership by Bulganin and Khrushchev is associated with a number of breakthroughs in the foreign policy area. Calling for a resurrection of the old Leninist doctrine of "peaceful co-existence," the team of "B and K," as they became known to the West, engaged in a number of spectacular trips abroad, the most notable of which was a trip to Belgrade, Yugoslavia, to heal the breach with Marshal Tito. In a gesture to the West, the Soviet Union also agreed to end the joint military occupation of Austria, which regained its independence in 1955. This was the first withdrawal of Soviet troops without leaving a communist regime behind since World War II.

The good feeling engendered by the Soviet action in Austria was an important factor in producing the first meeting of major heads of government since the Potsdam Conference in 1945. This was the Geneva Summit of 1955. No specific agreements were reached but there was an exchange of views on German rearmament and reunification, European security, disarmament and the improvement of East-West contacts. The major Soviet proposal dealt with the opposing military alliances. It offered to disband the newly created (in May 1955) Warsaw Pact in return for the disbanding of NATO and the withdrawal of all "foreign troops" from the European continent. The proposal was so obviously one-sided that the West was unwilling to even consider it seriously. The summit was valuable from the Soviet point of view, however, for it signified that the West was willing to accept the Soviet Union as an equal in diplomatic discussions.

The 20th Party Congress, which met in February 1956, represented a new high for Khrushchev, for it confirmed that he had taken control of the party apparatus. It also represented a new foreign policy departure, for it was here that Khrushchev first articulated the view that war between capitalism and communism was no longer "fatalistically inevitable"—the view held by Stalin. Khrushchev justified his position on the basis of the emergence of socialism into a world system which made possible a worldwide peaceful transition to communism.

It appears, however, that the real basis for the change was Khrushchev's recognition that the existence of nuclear weapons had changed the basic nature of war and rendered it no longer "thinkable."

De-Stalinization

Khrushchev's most important speech at this Congress did not take place in the public session, however. In a separate "secret" session of the Congress, Khrushchev launched a major attack on the record of Stalin and what he called the "cult of personality." The speech set forth in great detail the many crimes of Stalin. Its content soon became known in the Soviet Union, however, and the actual text, first available in the West, has since been made public.

Khrushchev gave the speech to smash the "Stalin myth" and so gain the freedom to carry out wider changes in the system than conservatives favored. Khrushchev and his supporters apparently believed that it was possible to condemn Stalin's "errors" and at the same time maintain and even strengthen their own position. This was an effort to make communist rule more respectable by moving back toward older, "Leninist" norms. It signaled no basic change in the nature of communist rule, but it did suggest an end to harsh terror tactics.

The impact of Khrushchev's speech went far beyond what he had obviously intended. Stalin had defined the nature of communism for so long that the move to repudiate him unleashed forces which threatened the very foundations of Soviet power. Only weeks after the Congress, riots in Tbilisi, the capital of Soviet Georgia, resulted in the deaths of over a hundred persons.

The most serious and direct consequences of de-Stalinization occurred in Eastern Europe, however. In the Polish cities of Poznan and Warsaw, armed clashes occurred between the workers and police. In Hungary, university students demanded, and obtained, an end to compulsory Russian language instruction.

The situation continued to build in both countries. In October, a Polish Party plenum elected Wladyslaw Gomulka as First Secretary and called for internal reforms. In Hungary, the clash between university students and the Hungarian secret police led to large-scale fighting and, when it was ordered to intervene, to the disintegration of the Hungarian army.

The Soviet Ambassador to Hungary, Yuri Andropov, met with the new Hungarian government and arranged for the withdrawal of Soviet troops from Budapest on October 28. One week later, on November 4, they returned and put down the uprising. The Soviet intervention in Hungary brought revulsion abroad and a wave of resignations among prominent foreign communists. Jean-Paul Sartre of France and Howard Fast of the United States were among those who turned in their party cards at this time.

Khrushchev now began to downplay de-Stalinization, but he had lost the confidence of a number of the leading members of his own party. In June 1957, the Presidium voted seven to four to dismiss him as First Party Secretary. Khrushchev refused to accept the decision of the Presidium, however, and demanded that the full Central Committee be convened to vote on the matter. Khrushchev won in the larger forum and managed to obtain the removal of his opponents from the Presidium. Malenkov was sent to manage a remote installation in Central Asia while Molotov was named Soviet Ambassador to Mongolia. Nine months later, in March 1958, Khrushchev assumed the additional office of Chairman of the Council of Ministers (head of government).

One of those who benefited from Khrushchev's victory was Leonid Brezhnev, who became a full member of the Presidium in June 1957. Three years later, in May 1960, Brezhnev became Chairman of the Presidium of the Supreme Soviet (titular head of state). That same month, Alexei Kosygin and Nikolai Podgorny were promoted to full membership in the Presidium.

The 22nd Party Congress met in Moscow in October 1961. Its major theme was de-Stalinization. Following the Congress, Stalin's body was removed from alongside Lenin in the mausoleum on Red Square and buried outside the Kremlin wall. The city of Stalingrad had its name changed and became Volgograd, and other cities named after Stalin had their names changed as well. Yevgeny Yevtushenko, already well-known because of his poem about Babi Yar (where the Nazis carried out a massacre of Soviet Jews during World War II), now produced his poem entitled "The Heirs of Stalin" in which he spoke of those who

from rostrums, even heap abuse on Stalin
but, at night, hanker after the good old days

and warned that

As long as the heirs of Stalin walk this earth
Stalin, I fancy, still lurks in the mausoleum.

This was followed in November 1962 by the publication of *One Day in the Life of Ivan Denisovich*, Aleksandr Solzhenitsyn's bold novel about life in Stalin's concentration camps.

Writings with a specific political content were not published in the Soviet Union except with approval from high up, and it was said that Khrushchev authorized publication of Solzhenitsyn's book. But this was the surface reality. None of the "heirs of Stalin" denounced as criminals at the 22nd Party Congress suffered anything more than verbal abuse. However, Khrushchev decided to remove old Stalinists throughout the Communist Party by forcing retirement within all party committees. And in October 1964 they took their revenge by casting their votes for Khrushchev's ouster from power.

De-Stalinization was only one of several factors involved in Khrushchev's dismissal from power, however. Foreign policy was an issue and in particular, the Cuban Missile Crisis. It was an American who characterized Khrushchev's foreign policy as one of "overextension followed by capitulation" but this appears to have been the opinion of some of those on the Presidium itself. One of the few specific charges brought against Khrushchev in October 1964 was that he had caused a Soviet defeat at the time of the Cuban Missile Crisis. The theme of overextension was specifically taken up by Brezhnev the following month when he asserted that, in the future, Soviet foreign policy would take into consideration the "military power of the countries of the socialist camp."

The other chief issue was domestic. Khrushchev had staked a great deal on economic development and he had promised the Soviet people that the USSR would catch up with the United States economically by 1980. He had carried through a partial economic decentralization in 1957 when he created 105 new regional *sovnarkhozy* (economic councils). In November 1962, he announced a division of the party into separate industrial and agricultural sections, the object to turn the party into an economic administrative apparatus. This move threatened the power position of the regional first party secretaries and created a great deal of dissatisfaction throughout the party.

Khrushchev's agricultural failures also hurt his standing within the party leadership. After the initial success of his "virgin lands" program, agricultural production stagnated and the country began to suffer chronic food shortages. The 1962 division of the party was an attempt to deal with the problem administratively, but it was a failure. In August 1964, Khrushchev announced yet another reorganization of agriculture which he intended to submit to a November party plenum. But by this time the other members of the Presidium had had enough. On October 15, 1964, Moscow's TASS (the official news "wire") announced that Khrushchev had been relieved of his duties as First Party Secretary and Chairman of the Council of Ministers, and that Leonid Brezhnev had been elected First Party Secretary in his place. Alexei Kosygin became Chairman of the Council of Ministers. Anastas Mikoyan, who had succeeded Brezhnev as Chairman of the Presidium of the Supreme Soviet (titular head of state) in July 1964, retained that position until his retirement in December 1965; he was succeeded by Nikolai Podgorny, who continued to serve in that position until his death.

Soviet Foreign Policy under Khrushchev

Of key importance to the leadership of the Soviet Union was the problem of relations with the United States, the country which, after World War II, was the leader of the Western alliance. Stalin, knowing that he could not both keep control over Eastern Europe and continue good relations with the United States, chose confrontation. His successors, perhaps frightened at the turn that confrontation had taken and more aware of the threat that nuclear weapons represented, attempted to reach an accommodation with the West while retaining Stalin's empire. This led to some easing of tensions and to increased diplomatic contacts. A Geneva Summit Conference in 1955 after Stalin's death represented the culmination of this trend. No significant agreements were reached, but the "spirit of Geneva" continued to influence relations between the two powers for about five years.

The refusal of the United States to accept Soviet domination of Eastern Europe always remained a factor in US–Soviet relations, however, and when, as in 1956, the Soviet Union resorted to the use of force to retain its control, bilateral relations suffered. Not all of the Soviet Union's problems with regard to maintaining control were amenable to the use of force, however.

One such case was Berlin, established under separate four-power occupation in 1945. In the 1950s, West Berlin (representing a union of the three western zones of occupation) was a free enterprise, democratic island in the middle of a communized East Germany and it had become a place of refuge for East Germans fleeing communism. Determined to put an end to the constant drain of manpower, Khrushchev demanded in November 1958 that the occupation of West Berlin be terminated and that it be turned into a "free city" within the territory of the communist German Democratic Republic. Khrushchev's position, put in the form of an ultimatum, created the Berlin Crisis of 1958.

It is difficult to determine whether Khrushchev expected his viewpoint to prevail, but it did result in a four-power foreign ministers' conference in Geneva in May 1959 and an invitation to Khrushchev to visit the United States in September. Khrushchev stayed for 18 days, which included 3 days spent at Camp David in private conversation with President Eisenhower.

Though the talks produced only an agreement for additional summit level negotiations, the Soviets subsequently referred to them as having created the "spirit of Camp David." When Khrushchev returned to Moscow, he publicly characterized Eisenhower as a man who "sincerely wants to liquidate the Cold War and improve relations between our two great countries." That also led Khrushchev to suggest, in early 1960, that the Soviet armed forces would be reduced by about one-third.

This was the high-water mark in US-Soviet relations under Khrushchev. In May 1960, the Soviets shot down an American U-2 photo-reconnaissance plane that had penetrated deep into Soviet airspace. Khrushchev demanded an apology from Eisenhower and, when it was not forthcoming, he torpedoed a summit meeting scheduled to take place in Paris in mid-May. This also was one of the factors involved in Khrushchev's extraordinary performance at the United Nations General Assembly in September when he took off his shoe and banged it on his desk to show his disapproval of one of the speeches.

A meeting between Khrushchev and President Kennedy in May 1961 proved to be unproductive and, in fact, Khrushchev resurrected the Berlin Crisis by demanding a settlement by the end of the year. Further, he coupled this with a statement that the Soviet defense budget would be *increased* by one-third. Then, on August 13, 1961, the Soviet Union instituted a solution to the Berlin Crisis by beginning to

First Secretary Khrushchev and President Kennedy, Vienna, 1961

Russia

build a wall between West and East Berlin. Since the wall was being built on the territory of East Berlin, there was little that the United States and its allies could do other than to issue a diplomatic protest—but it obviously had a negative effect on US-Soviet relations. Barriers were later placed to totally divide East Germany from West Berlin. This was the first time in history that a fortified wall had been erected to keep people *in* instead of *out*.

The next test of wills came in October 1962—the Cuban Missile Crisis. In his memoirs, Khrushchev relates that:

It was during my visit to Bulgaria (May 14–20, 1962) that I had the idea of installing missiles with nuclear warheads in Cuba without letting the United States find out they were there until it was too late to do anything about them.

But the United States found out what the Soviet Union was up to as the missiles were being installed and demanded their removal. Khrushchev had to acquiesce, but he attempted to save face by claiming that he had preserved world peace and obtained (an oral) guarantee for Cuba's Fidel Castro against any future attempts to overthrow him by troops launched from the US. In fact, he did have some gains to show. In the final settlement, the United States confined its objective to the withdrawal of Soviet missiles, thereby conceding Castro's right to remain a Soviet ally and to retain a communist form of government if he wished. This was a tacit repeal of the Monroe Doctrine. In addition, the US afterward quietly began removing its intermediate range ballistic missiles from Turkey.

Moreover, in retrospect, the United States was as appalled as the Soviet Union at how close the two nations had come to all-out war and the result was further steps toward détente. This led to the installation of a Washington-Moscow "hot line" and the signing of a limited test ban treaty in 1963.

Domestically, however, Khrushchev drew different conclusions from the Cuban Missile Crisis and in March 1963 he pushed through a revision of the last two years of the seventh Five-Year Plan to allow for a large-scale deployment of Soviet ICBMs (intercontinental ballistic missiles). As he records in his memoirs,

the experience of the Caribbean crisis also convinced us that we were right to concentrate on the manufacture of nuclear missiles.

The Brezhnev Era

During the years that followed Khrushchev's ouster, the Soviet Union was governed by a relatively stable coalition of leaders that included Brezhnev, Kosygin, and Podgorny, but also included Mikhail Suslov, the party's chief ideologist, as well. Brezhnev gradually consolidated his position as first among equals, however, and, starting in the late 1960s, he became the dominant figure in foreign policy. Brezhnev's style of leadership can be characterized as undramatic, however; both his successes and his failures tended to be associated more with the system than with the man.

The immediate period following Khrushchev's departure was characterized by a reversal of many of his policies. Most importantly, the November 1962 division of the party into separate industrial and agricultural units was reversed and a unitary party structure was recreated. The regional economic councils created in 1957 were also gradually phased out and replaced by centralized ministries.

In 1965, at a Central Committee plenum, Brezhnev announced a change in agricultural policy which, he said, would place the emphasis on farm autonomy. The real thrust of the new program was *not* farm autonomy, however, but increased incentives—diffused in such a way that they probably had little economic effect.

Ever since their creation in the 1930s, collective farms had been required to deliver a set quota of grain to the government at artificially low prices. Brezhnev now lowered that quota by 11 million tons and increased the price that the government would pay for above-quota deliveries.

The price of various types of agricultural equipment was also lowered at this time. These changes increased retained earnings for the collective farm administrations, but they did not filter down in a meaningful way to the individual peasant.

Two other reforms did, however; peasants for the first time became eligible for old age pensions and were guaranteed a minimum monthly income. In addition, there was an attempt to encourage the production of more fruit, vegetables, and meat for sale in the free peasant markets of the big cities by easing restrictions and reducing taxes on small private plots.

Major changes in the industrial sector were also experimented with at this time. These experiments, collectively known as the Liberman Plan, were actually suggested in 1962 when a Kharkov (Ukraine) University professor by the name of Evsei Liberman wrote an article for *Pravda* setting forth general principles for economic reform. Under the Soviet economic system, manufacturing enterprises operated on the basis of detailed instructions drawn up by planning experts in centralized ministries. Liberman proposed that much of this planning be dismantled and that individual plant managers be given authority to run their enterprises themselves, subject only to overall production figures and fulfillment of delivery dates. Profitability, rather than the meeting of production norms, would be the new test of the efficiency of an enterprise, and supply and demand would replace the exchange of

Leonid Brezhnev

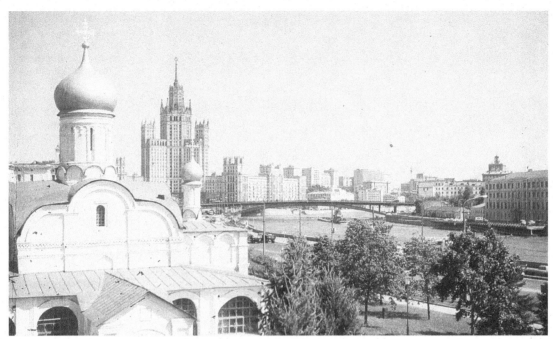

View of Moscow and the Moscow River

goods on the basis of pre-planned indexes. Wages and salaries would also be tied to the profitability of individual enterprises.

The Liberman article in *Pravda* had been personally approved and endorsed by Khrushchev, and in August 1964 the first test of the Liberman ideas began with an experimental tryout of the system in two textile plants. After Khrushchev's fall, Alexei Kosygin made the Liberman Plan his own and ordered that a reform program be drawn up for the entire economy. The new program was put into effect beginning in September 1965.

There was considerable opposition from among those who believed that it would tend to decrease the role of the party in the economy, however, and Brezhnev apparently aligned himself eventually with this group. As a result, the Central Committee plenum that instituted the reform also reinstituted central industrial and technical ministries, at least partially negating the reform from the very beginning. Libermanism was subsequently adopted by many Eastern European regimes, most notably Hungary, but in the Soviet Union it was phased out beginning in 1970.

Another program reversal that followed the ouster of Khrushchev was the gradual end of de-Stalinization, accompanied by a generally harder line on the cultural front. In September 1965, A. M. Rumiantsev, editor of *Pravda*, was dismissed after he came to the defense of Andrei Voznesensky, a Soviet writer who had been accused of *nihilism*. In that same month, Andrei Sinyavsky and Yuli Daniel were arrested and tried for publishing abroad works critical of the Soviet Union.

They were sentenced to seven and five years at hard labor.

One month later, in October 1965, a *Pravda* article by Professor Sergei Trapeznikov, chief of the Central Committee's department of science and education, characterized the Stalin era as "one of the most brilliant in the history of the Party and the Soviet State" and suggested it as a pattern for the theoretical and practical activity of the Party.

The decisions taken at the 23rd Party Congress (1966) confirmed the trend toward re-Stalinization. The Presidium again became known as the Politburo while the First Party Secretary resumed the title of General Secretary. Both names dated from the Stalinist era and had been dropped by Khrushchev.

The Dissident Movement

Re-Stalinization was accompanied by the rise of a dissident movement that grew in numbers and in significance in the late 1960s. In 1966, an underground journal, *Phoenix 61*, began to appear. Four writers associated with the journal were arrested at the beginning of 1967 and later sentenced. This, in turn, led to several public and private petitions of protest, signed by increased numbers of distinguished Soviet intellectuals. The situation was further worsened when Stalin's daughter, Svetlana Allilueva, defected in April 1967 and in a subsequent book, *Twenty Letters to a Friend*, expressed her solidarity with the Soviet intellectuals in their struggle for intellectual freedom. Also, about this time, two of Aleksandr Solzhenitsyn's novels, *In the First Circle* and *Cancer*

Ward, were published abroad—without Solzhenitsyn's permission, to be sure, but the mere fact of publication abroad was considered to be an act of dissidence.

As the dissident movement continued to grow, it gained a widening circle of recruits. In July 1968, Andrei Sakharov, a distinguished physicist and father of the Soviet Union's hydrogen bomb, allowed a manuscript of his entitled *Thoughts on Progress, Peaceful Coexistence and Intellectual Freedom*, to be published abroad. Sakharov had joined the ranks of active dissidents two years earlier when he wrote a letter to Brezhnev protesting the arrest of four persons whose crime was that they had protested against the trial of Sinyavsky and Daniel. Since Sakharov was a prominent member of the Soviet Academy of Sciences and a recipient of both the Stalin Prize and the Lenin Prize, nothing had happened then or subsequently when he signed a letter to the Party warning against a resurgence of Stalinism. In August 1968, however, Sakharov was removed from all secret work and transferred to another academic institute in Moscow; he and his wife were later sent to the official detention city of Gorky, where they remained until their release by Gorbachev in 1986.

The Soviet invasion of Czechoslovakia in 1968 brought both renewed protests and a harsher crackdown on dissidents. One of the seven individuals who staged a brief demonstration in Red Square against the invasion was Pavel Litvinov, grandson of Maxim Litvinov, Stalin's Foreign Minister in the 1930s. Litvinov was sentenced to five years internal exile in a Siberian village. After his return to Moscow in 1973,

Russia

Members of the famed Soviet National Ice Hockey Team of the 1980s

Litvinov and his wife applied for exit visas as Jews and emigrated shortly afterward.

One of the more interesting developments of the Brezhnev era was the adoption of a policy of allowing Jewish emigration. There were a little over two million Jews in the Soviet Union and the large majority of them considered themselves to be assimilated and at home. In 1970, for example, only 17.7% of all Jews listed either Hebrew or Yiddish as their mother tongue. There had always been some anti-Semitism in Russia, but the Soviet Union, to its credit, had seldom encouraged the attitude. In 1967, however, following Israel's defeat of the Soviet Union's Arab clients, Egypt and Syria, the Soviet Union unleashed a violent anti-Zionist campaign. For some of the Russian public, the distinction between anti-Zionism and anti-Semitism was too fine a difference to draw. As a result, an increasing number of Jews began applying for visas to emigrate to Israel; eventually over 100,000 Jews applied to emigrate. In 1968, the ministry of interior notified a few Jewish families that, if they still wanted to leave, they could. The flow of Jewish emigrants grew steadily thereafter, and by 1973 an average of 30,000 Jews were leaving every year.

The question of Jewish emigration became a foreign policy matter in 1974 when the US Congress, following the leadership of Senator Henry Jackson of Washington State, approved an amendment to the 1972 trade agreement on "most favored nation" status for the Soviet Union which made approval contingent on increased Jewish emigration from the Soviet Union. The Soviets, calling the Jackson Amendment interference in their domestic affairs, rejected the trade agreement in 1975.

Jewish emigration continued at a decreased level for a while after 1975, but then began growing again. By 1979, an average of 4,000 Jews were departing monthly. Then came a policy reversal. From a peak of 51,320 in 1979, the number of emigrants declined to 2,688 in 1982, the last year of Brezhnev's regime.

Non-Jewish dissidents did not, in general, have the right to apply for emigration but the Brezhnev regime rediscovered, in the period of the 1970s, that emigration or expulsion sometimes provided a suitable alternative to imprisonment for individuals too prominent to treat as ordinary criminals. Aleksandr Solzhenitsyn, expelled in February 1974, was the most famous of these, but the list of those given permission to go abroad temporarily who thereafter had their Soviet citizenship withdrawn was much longer. Thus, by the end of the Brezhnev regime in 1982, most individuals who had joined the ranks of the dissidents in the 1960s or early 1970s were either living abroad, in prison, a psychiatric hospital, or in internal exile.

A few new dissidents did appear in the late 1970s, particularly in association with attempts to demand implementation of the human rights provision of the Helsinki Accord, signed in 1975. They were small in number, however, and quickly rounded up. There was also some dissident activity in connection with the 1980 Summer Olympics and again at the time of the 1980–1981 Madrid follow-up conference to the Helsinki Conference on Security and Cooperation in Europe.

Yet the movement, although troublesome because of its international ramifications, was never more than an annoyance to the regime. The actual number of dissidents was always quite small. Thus, a Western study which attempted to identify all those who were in any way involved in the dissident movement was able to come up with names of only 3,400 persons for the period 1956 to 1975. The disturbing element from the point of view of the regime was that the dissidents originated in a social base that consisted essentially of the scientific-cultural intelligentsia. Their significance was that they said aloud what other people could only think.

A Regime in Crisis

A more serious problem in the long run was that the Soviet economy, which began a slowdown by 1970, continued in that pattern to the end of the Brezhnev era. Moreover, wage increases granted to the workers after 1965 exacerbated the situation for there was no accompanying increase in consumer goods.

The Five-Year Plan for 1971–1975 attempted to deal with this situation by calling for vast investment in agriculture and increased investments in consumer industry. For the first time in Soviet history, consumer goods were to be favored over heavy industry. But by the end of 1972, the planners had to admit that their priorities did not permit the planned investments in consumer goods and the plan was revised to renew the emphasis on heavy industry. The 10th Five-Year Plan (1976–1980) continued the revised priorities of the preceding plan. These targets were also not met.

The 11th Five-Year Plan (1981–1985) called for a slightly larger growth in consumer industry than heavy industry. Some of its goals, particularly those with regard to agriculture were unrealistic, however, and were never met. The essential problem—and it is one that the Soviets never solved—is that Soviet productivity slowed to a negligible rate in the 1960s and all the tinkering with the economy after that time did nothing to reverse that trend. Any effective economic reform would have had to decrease the role of the cadre of the Communist Party in the economy. Under Brezhnev, this was always unacceptable.

The Brezhnev era has one last characteristic worth mentioning. The Soviet Union had a huge bureaucracy which ran all things under the guidance of the Party. Khrushchev had feared that the bureaucracy was becoming ingrown and in 1961 he had sponsored a new Party statute which attempted to deal with the problem. Under the terms of the statute, there was to be a normal turnover of personnel on each of the Party committees, with a certain percentage of the membership to be replaced at each election. There was considerable opposition to this policy among Party bureaucrats and, at the 23rd Party Congress in

1966, the policy was reversed. Although a general clause was added stressing the intention of the Party to promote "energetic and competent young cadres," this was generally ignored in the period of the 1970s.

The result was an unparalleled continuity in office at all levels of government, and an aging Party and government elite. One can see how this operated with regard to membership on the Central Committee. In 1966, 76% of those elected at the 24th Party Congress were already full members. The percentage of full members reelected subsequently remained at this level. In fact at the 26th Party Congress in 1981, the figure was actually 75%; it would have been much higher, but the Central Committee was also growing during these years, having increased by 44 persons since the previous Congress.

Soviet Foreign Policy under Brezhnev

When Brezhnev replaced Khrushchev as Party chief in October 1964, a subtle change occurred in Soviet foreign policy. Without repudiating détente, Brezhnev began to speak about the necessity of maintaining Soviet defense potential at the highest possible levels. In July 1965, he spoke of a five-year defense plan to "increase the defensive might of the USSR." The subsequent 1966–1970 Soviet defense budget nearly doubled defense spending; it continued to grow in the period of the 1970s, though a CIA report issued in the middle 1980s indicated that the annual growth rate may have dropped somewhat for the period 1979–1982.

Brezhnev's push for increased defense expenditures was, from the Soviet point of view, entirely compatible with a policy of détente and, in some respects, a precondition for it. Cooperation between the two superpowers was made somewhat more difficult because of the United States' increasing involvement in Vietnam but, in spite of this, a treaty to ban nuclear weapons in outer space was negotiated in 1967. This was followed in 1968 by a treaty on the non-proliferation of nuclear weapons.

Negotiations to limit the size of both countries' strategic nuclear forces were to begin in 1968, but were canceled by President Lyndon B. Johnson after the Soviet-led invasion of Czechoslovakia. The Strategic Arms Limitation Talks (SALT) concept was revived by President Richard Nixon, however. This led to a visit by President Nixon to Moscow in May 1972 and the signing of the SALT-I accords. SALT-I primarily limited the deployment of antiballistic missiles (ABMs) but it also contained a five-year interim agreement freezing the number of land- and sea-based offensive missiles.

In late 1974, President Gerald Ford met with Brezhnev in Vladivostok and there the two leaders agreed on general guidelines for a SALT-II pact which would deal with strategic nuclear missiles. President Jimmy Carter reopened the SALT-II negotiations after he took office in 1977, but the Soviet Union was unwilling to accept the lower missile totals proposed by the American side. A new SALT-II agreement was finally initialed in 1979, but President Carter later withdrew the treaty from consideration by the United States Senate after a Soviet invasion of Afghanistan.

Military Intervention in Afghanistan

A group openly claiming to be Marxist-Leninist came to power in Afghanistan in a bloody coup in late 1978. The US government recognized the new regime, but became more and more disquieted by subsequent events. A large number of "advisers" were imported from the Soviet Union and the regime began an attempt to bring about a social revolution within the country. This produced strong resistance among the Afghan population, however, and it wasn't long before armed uprisings throughout the country threatened the very existence of the regime. In late 1979 therefore, the Soviet Union intervened with 80,000 Soviet troops to prop up the faltering Afghan communist regime.

But Afghanistan is mostly rugged mountain country with a population of about 20 million people; the Soviet troops were only sufficient to keep the communist regime from being overthrown, but not enough to put down the rebellion.

Soviet intervention in Afghanistan had an adverse effect on the Soviet Union's relations with most of the rest of the world, however. A number of countries, including the United States, boycotted the 1980 Moscow Olympics.

President Carter also announced a partial embargo on the sale of grain to the Soviet Union and began negotiating an agreement with Pakistan to provide military support to the mujahidin, the Afghan resistance. In addition, the Carter administration reversed its earlier position on the adequacy of American military power and began a new buildup of US forces. Further, it sponsored resolutions in the United Nations condemning the Soviet military presence in Afghanistan.

The Reagan administration continued and intensified most of these policies. Agreement with Pakistan was reached and significant aid began flowing to the mujahidin. Military budgets were greatly enlarged and the administration openly boasted about beginning a new arms race which they expected to win. The B-1 bomber aircraft, canceled by the Carter administration, was reinstated and a number of new weapons systems, including the multiple-warhead MX and the Trident submarine, were proposed.

This was the stick. At the same time, the Reagan administration stipulated its willingness to negotiate arms reductions and symbolized this by changing the name of the arms negotiations process from SALT—Strategic Arms Limitation Talks—to START—Strategic Arms Reduction Talks.

The START negotiations began in June 1982. The American position, set forth by President Reagan, called for a reduction of

Presidents Carter and Brezhnev exchange signed copies of the SALT II Treaty agreement, Vienna, June 1979

Russia

Mujahidin **resistance fighters look down on a village after a Soviet aerial attack. At left are terraced crop fields**

Courtesy of AP Images

missile launchers to 850 each (down from 2,000 for the US and 2,700 for the USSR) and a reduction of nuclear warheads by about a third. No more than half of the missile launchers could be land-based. Agreement on these points would lead to a second round of talks aimed at reducing other elements of the two nations' "balance of terror."

Brezhnev rejected Reagan's proposal in May 1982, apparently disturbed by its proposed limits on land-based ICBMs. His own proposal called for a two-thirds reduction in nuclear warheads, a ban on the development of new types of strategic weapons, and a freeze on strategic weapons at current levels, to begin concurrently with the negotiations. The United States rejected the freeze on the basis that it would codify existing Soviet advantages, but welcomed Brezhnev's willingness to negotiate. The United States and USSR were at least talking with each other in the area of strategic weapons.

One other area of American concern, that of theater nuclear weapons in Europe, remained totally stalemated. The problem dated from 1977, when the Soviet Union began installing SS-20 missiles in Eastern Europe. A mobile missile with three warheads, the SS-20 caused great concern among Western European leaders, and they began pushing for NATO to match these missiles.

In 1979, therefore, NATO voted for the emplacement of American Pershing II and Cruise missiles in Europe, if talks with the Soviet Union did not produce another solution. The Soviets refused to discuss the removal of their missiles, however, so President Reagan offered his Zero

Option—if the Soviet Union would pull its SS-20s out of Eastern Europe, then the US would refrain from installing Pershing IIs and Cruise missiles in Western Europe—in a public speech in September 1981. The Soviet Union had not yet responded as of November 1982, when Brezhnev died.

Government Transition

November 1982–March 1985

Prior to Brezhnev's death in November 1982, there was a widespread feeling that the last years of his regime had been ones of stagnation and even decline. Many felt that what was needed was a strong, vigorous, but tested leader who could get the country going again.

Konstantin Chernenko was Brezhnev's protégé and therefore represented continuity; Yuri Andropov, who had been head of the KGB for 15 years, was a man from outside Brezhnev's inner circle, and therefore represented change. The choice fell to Andropov. It turned out, however, that Andropov was a frail reed on which to lean: He was personally honest and hardworking, and he had attached to himself a number of younger individuals committed to change. But he was also suffering from a heart condition and diabetes, and was temporarily incapacitated only five months after becoming general secretary. Moreover, although a majority of the Politburo had chosen him over Chernenko, it soon became clear that there was no firm majority for reform. As a result, there were only three major policies associated with Andropov's name. The first of these was his campaign against corruption and slack

labor discipline. There was undoubtedly corruption and slack discipline, but if western observers were correct that these things were only symptoms and that the major problems were systemic—arising from or pertaining to the system *itself*—then Andropov's campaign was relatively meaningless.

Andropov was also interested in renewing the leadership of the Party by retiring older individuals and promoting younger men in their places. He succeeded to a certain extent at secondary levels, but the average age of the Politburo remained well past the usual age of retirement.

He also introduced two economic "reforms," a system of brigades for farm workers that permitted some wage differentiation based on actual production, and an experiment, limited to five ministries, in which work teams were set up in factories and encouraged to compete with each other. The factory reform was begun as of January 1, 1984. Both reforms constituted "tinkering with the system" and therefore made no significant contribution to higher productivity. They did represent Andropov's commitment to economic reform, however, and provided a beginning upon which Gorbachev could later build.

Foreign relations under Andropov deserve comment. He essentially represented a hard-line faction in this area, but he was extremely vigorous in his negotiating stance. Thus it was Andropov who issued the first formal reply to President Reagan's "Zero Option" speech of September 1981. In November 1982, shortly after becoming General Secretary, Andropov gave a speech in which he proposed to reduce

Pravda **announces Brezhnev's death**

the number of SS-20s in Eastern Europe to the same number of missiles held by Great Britain and France if, in return, NATO would cancel deployment of Pershing IIs and Cruise missiles in Western Europe. The offer was unacceptable because the British and French missiles, being part of their "national" arsenals, were not under NATO control. It did open the way for formal negotiations to begin, however.

The United States continued to push its Zero Option until March 1983. Then President Reagan gave another speech in which he introduced his "Interim Proposal." The proposal was that the United States and the USSR agree to an equal number of theater nuclear warheads on each side, with the expectation that talks on an eventual Zero Option would continue. The Soviets rejected this proposal.

Negotiations nevertheless continued and there was at least the possibility that an agreement would have been reached, except for the unfortunate circumstances of the Soviet shooting down of a commercial airliner, South Korean Flight 007, as it was leaving the large Soviet island of Sakhalin in the Far East in September 1983. The mutual recriminations that followed that event doomed the Theater Nuclear Weapons discussions.

In order to preserve their real or imaginary advantage, the Soviets embarked on a vigorous campaign to drive a wedge between the US and its Western European NATO allies through mountains of propaganda describing the horrors of nuclear war. This did, in fact, succeed in attracting the sympathies of a substantial number of well-meaning people in Western Europe and led to numerous anti-nuclear demonstrations. However, in November 1983, with no agreement in sight, the United States began delivering the first of the Pershing II and Cruise missiles to Western Europe. The Theater Nuclear Force discussions were then abruptly recessed by the Soviets in December 1983. They announced that they would not return to the negotiating table unless the United States agreed to withdraw all nuclear missiles emplaced in Western Europe.

Andropov fell ill at just about this point. He was last seen in public shortly before the downing of the airliner, and it is not known what role, if any, he had in foreign affairs during those last five months when he remained sequestered from the world.

This is the record which the members of the Politburo had to evaluate when they met to choose Andropov's successor in February 1984. The promise he represented had been largely unfulfilled, but even the pallid reforms instituted had been negatively received by a large part of the bureaucracy. In particular, Andropov's attempts to weed out incompetents and to promote younger persons to positions of higher responsibility threatened the security of the tenure of the "old guard" Party cadre, and they mobilized their forces accordingly. Chernenko, passed over once

Izvestia announces Andropov's death

precisely because he represented the politics of the waning years of the Brezhnev era, became their candidate.

The other two candidates were Mikhail Gorbachev and Grigori Romanov. Gorbachev and Romanov represented the younger generation of the Politburo and tended to be classified as economic specialists because both probably favored greater experimentation in the area of the economy. The Politburo chose Chernenko—although it appeared that Gorbachev moved into a clear number two position and was the heir apparent.

And how did Chernenko change things after becoming General Secretary? Serge Schmemann, Moscow correspondent for the *New York Times*, wrote, quoting from an interview he had with a knowledgeable figure in Moscow:

We have come to peace with Mr. Chernenko. He has contributed nothing new, the pace has slowed, the results are humble, but at least he has not turned back the clock.

Chernenko was a transitional figure, chosen to hold the fort a little longer before transferring power to a new generation. As such, his initiatives, or lack of them, reflected the will of a majority of the Politburo. When he first took over, there apparently were high-level disagreements on a number of policy issues, most importantly, on foreign policy. The result was several months of hibernation, exemplified by a Soviet boycott of the 1984 Summer Olympics in Los Angeles and a cancellation of a visit to China by Ivan V. Arkhipov, vice chairman of the USSR Council of Ministers.

General Secretary Konstantin Chernenko of the USSR

Russia

But Chernenko, who suffered from emphysema and a weak heart, disappeared from view for two months in mid-1984 and reportedly was brought back to Moscow in a wheelchair. It was shortly afterward that Foreign Minister Andrei Gromyko agreed to a meeting with President Reagan. The seriousness of Chernenko's illness had apparently broken the stalemate in the Kremlin and a new majority favoring negotiations with the US had emerged. At the beginning of November, it was announced that new high-level economic talks would be held in Moscow in January 1985. Two weeks later, Gromyko and Secretary of State George Shultz agreed to meet in Geneva in early January to discuss resumption of arms talks. It was also at about this time that Moscow announced that Arkhipov's delayed visit to China would take place in December.

The Moscow talks were inconclusive, but there was agreement to resume arms talks in Geneva beginning on March 12, 1985. Arkhipov's visit to China also resulted in some improvement in Soviet–Chinese relations.

These events occurred in Chernenko's absence, for he had disappeared from sight on December 27 and was never again seen in public. In February, it was officially confirmed that he was ill. A short television clip showed him voting in the Republic elections on February 24, but it appeared to have been "doctored," since its background matched another clip reported to be at another time and place. Fifteen days later, his death was announced. According to the official medical report, his death resulted from a combination of factors which included emphysema, a heart condition, and chronic hepatitis which had developed into cirrhosis. Evidently his death was quite expected, for the Central Committee had already met and decided on his successor.

The Gorbachev Era

A New General Secretary

The story of Gorbachev's formal installation as General Secretary is well-known—how Gromyko made the nominating speech at the meeting of the Central Committee and how he concluded his remarks with the observation that "Comrades, he has a nice smile, but he has iron teeth." No other candidates were presented to the Central Committee and acceptance was therefore assured.

In March 1987, however, a somewhat different report surfaced about a secret Politburo meeting which took place prior to the Central Committee meeting that installed Gorbachev as General Secretary. This report, which appeared in a Finnish newspaper, *Svomen Kuvalehti*, was based on an interview with Mikhail Shatrov, a Soviet playwright and Gorbachev adviser. According to Shatrov, nine persons were present at the Politburo meeting. With Gromyko as chairman and abstaining, the vote was tied four to four between Gorbachev and Viktor Grishin, Moscow party leader. Gromyko then intervened to cast the deciding vote.

Not every good story is true, of course, and according to Dmitri Volkogonov—who reviewed the files of that particular politburo meeting during preparation of his book *Autopsy for an Empire*—this is another example of a good story not supported by the written record, or at least not all of it. According to Volkogonov, Gromyko did nominate Gorbachev for the position of party General Secretary, Gromyko was later named Chairman of the Presidium of the Supreme Soviet (head of state), and Grishin and three other members of the Politburo did shortly afterward lose their seats on the Politburo. But Gromyko supported Gorbachev because he believed that only a young man could "pump new energy into the Party;" Gromyko was named Chairman of the Presidium of the Supreme Soviet because Gorbachev wanted to replace him as Minister of Foreign Affairs; and Grishin and three other members lost their Politburo seats as part of a remaking of the Politburo in Gorbachev's image.

Born on March 2, 1931, Gorbachev was at the time the youngest man on the Politburo. He was also the best educated, having graduated from Moscow University in 1955 with a degree in law. He later added a second degree when he earned the qualification of "agronomist-economist" from the Stavropol Agricultural Institute in 1967.

It was at Moscow University that Gorbachev first began to take an active interest in politics. He became the head of the Moscow University branch of Komsomol (Young Communists) and it was at this time that he joined the Communist Party. After graduation, Gorbachev joined the Stavropol Agricultural Institute. East of the Black Sea, this is an important agricultural district in southern Russia. It was also Gorbachev's home region, so he probably had political contacts there. He began work as a researcher, agronomist, and economist, but he soon moved over into full-time party work. By his 35th birthday, he was Stavropol party chief; four years later, he had become the party chief of the entire region.

Gorbachev was brought to Moscow in 1978 to become a member of the Central Committee Secretariat with responsibility for agriculture. A year later, he was made a candidate member of the Politburo; in 1980 he became a full member.

When Andropov became general secretary in 1982, he apparently began grooming Gorbachev as a possible successor. The first evidence of this came in May 1983 when Gorbachev made a visit to Canada. This was his first official trip outside the Communist Bloc and he acquitted himself very well. A trip to England in December 1984 was equally successful. Domestically, Gorbachev had been in charge of the CPSU Secretariat since at least October 1984. By March 1985, it was clear that Gorbachev was well-qualified to handle the General Secretary position.

In making his acceptance speech at the CPSU Central Committee meeting on March 11, 1985, Gorbachev broke no new ground but he did make a number of points which gave some indication of his thinking. First of all, he referred to "enhancing the independence of enterprises, raising their interest in the end product of their work." This implied a commitment to greater economic reform. Second, he made the assertion "we want a real and major reduction of the arms stockpiles." Although again somewhat vague, it appeared to be a commitment to pursue arms reductions talks with the United States with a definite goal in mind rather than simply exploring areas of disagreement.

Manipulation of the Politburo

The first order of business of the new leader was to consolidate his power base. He began the process a little over a month later, on April 23, at a special session of the Central Committee. Three men, all obviously Gorbachev allies, were promoted to full membership on the Politburo and one other individual was made a candidate member. The elevation of Viktor Chebrikov, the KGB chairman—already a candidate member—came as no surprise. But the promotions of Yegor Ligachev and Nikolai Ryzhkov were different, because both were elevated to full membership without having to go through the intermediate step of candidate member. Moreover, both worked in the Secretariat under Gorbachev and were closely tied to him personally. The other promotion, that of Minister of War Sokolov to non-voting candidate member, was probably an effort to appease the "old guard" and military at the same time. Sokolov, already 74, was viewed at the time as an interim appointee.

The April 1985 changes gave Gorbachev a firm majority and he used it to begin remaking the Politburo and the government. At the regular plenary session of the Central Committee on July 1, 1985, Grigori Romanov—another of Gorbachev's rivals for the position of general secretary—was retired from the Politburo "on health grounds." His Politburo seat went to Eduard Shevardnadze, first secretary for the

Russia

Georgian Republic. Gorbachev's promotion and Romanov's retirement had also created two vacancies in the Secretariat and these were filled by Boris Yeltsin and Lev Zaikov.

Some additional reasons for the changes became evident the next day when the Supreme Soviet met. One of its tasks was the selection of a new Chairman of the Presidium (often referred to in the West as the Soviet President), vacant since the death of Chernenko. It had been thought that Gorbachev would assume this position but, in a switch, he announced that, having been requested to devote all of his time to Party affairs, he was nominating Andrei Gromyko to the position. He then added that Eduard Shevardnadze would replace Gromyko as minister of foreign affairs. Gromyko thus got the honor of becoming head of state, while Gorbachev got a new minister of foreign affairs, untainted by any connection with previous Soviet foreign policies.

When he took over his new job, Shevardnadze was totally without experience in foreign affairs. He did have a reputation for being honest and hardworking, however, and had, it was said, waged an energetic and effective campaign against corruption and laziness in his native Georgia. Shevardnadze's appointment suggested that Gorbachev intended to have the principal voice in foreign affairs. That indeed proved to be the case, although Shevardnadze earned high marks during his tenure as foreign minister.

Gorbachev continued his rebuilding in the fall of 1985. In September, Nikolai Tikhonov stepped down as chairman of the Council of Ministers and was replaced by Nikolai Ryzhkov. A Gorbachev ally now occupied the office responsible for implementing economic reforms approved by the Politburo.

Additional changes occurred in October when Tikhonov retired from the Politburo and Nikolai Talyzin became a candidate member. Talyzin, a telecommunications specialist, became head of GOSPLAN at the same time. Now an individual closely associated with Gorbachev was also in charge of economic planning. The move was particularly significant, since Gorbachev had already rejected the draft Five-Year Plan drawn up by Nikolai Baibakov, the man whom Talyzin replaced at GOSPLAN. But Talyzin proved to be the wrong choice. At the mid-1987 meeting of the Central Committee, he was singled out for criticism by Gorbachev for failure to embark upon economic change with sufficient rapidity. Somewhat later, he was replaced at GOSPLAN and named permanent representative to the Council for Mutual Economic Assistance.

Economic leadership changes were particularly important to Gorbachev. As he made clear at the 27th Party Congress in February 1986, the Soviet leader intended an economic transformation of his country and was well aware of the human factor in any such transformation. This almost certainly is why he forced the resignation of the relatively young Grigori Romanov, an economic specialist, but also a conservative on programs of economic reform. Tikhonov, 81, and Baibakov, 75, on the other hand, were probably replaced primarily because of advanced age.

Having promoted four of his allies to the Politburo within six months of becoming general secretary and accepted the resignation of two others, it is clear that Gorbachev had carried out a rapid transformation of this ruling body. As it turned out, however, the transformation was not complete. In January 1986, Viktor Grishin resigned his Politburo seat and simultaneously turned over his position as Moscow City First Secretary to Boris Yeltsin. One month later, a number of other personnel changes were announced. Lev Zaikov became a full member of the Politburo while Boris Yeltsin and Nikolai Slyunkov

Gorbachev speaks at the Kremlin's Palace of Congresses

63

Russia

became candidate members. Two candidate members, Boris Ponomarev, 81, and Vasily Kuznetsov, 85, were edged into retirement.

There were also two interesting additions to the Secretariat at this time. The first of these was Anatoly Dobrynin, who had served as Soviet Ambassador to the United States since 1962. Gorbachev, probably hoping to make use of his extensive personal knowledge of the United States, appointed a new ambassador to replace him in Washington and added him to the Secretariat. The second addition was Alexandra Biryukova, who thus became the highest ranking woman in the Soviet Communist Party. Biryukova, whose background was that of a national trade union leader, had been a member of the Central Committee since the early 1970s, but this marked her transition to full-time party work.

Gorbachev's extensive changes since becoming General Secretary placed a new generation of leadership in power in the Soviet Union. At the 27th Party Congress in February 1986, this new leadership committed the Soviet Union to a Five Year and a Fifteen-Year Plan. The goal of the fifteen-year plan was to triple the rate of productivity growth by the year 2000 and at the same time double living standards. The goal for the five years 1986–1991 was less ambitious—basically an increased growth of approximately 1% over what had taken place during the previous five years. As the end of that plan came, however, it became clear that it had not been achieved.

Gorbachev's greatest problem was that, while the top leadership favored reform, the working level bureaucrats who had to implement any reform remained unconvinced, particularly when it involved the potential loss of their jobs. It was this opposition in both the party and administrative bureaucracy that explained why Gorbachev began waging a major public relations campaign following the 27th Party Congress designed to generate support for reform, going over the "heads" of the bureaucracy with a direct appeal to the people.

Glasnost, Perestroika, and Democracy

In the process, Gorbachev introduced three slogans, glasnost, perestroika, and demokratiya, which came to symbolize for the West what he wanted to accomplish in the Soviet Union. However, none of these words has the same meaning in Russian that they have in the West. For example, we have translated glasnost as "openness." The actual root of the word is "voice," thus a more appropriate translation might be "speaking out." That was what Gorbachev was stating when he used the term—that people who supported what he was trying to do should speak out to make their support known. His campaign resulted in a greater openness within Soviet society, but that was a by-product of what he sought to accomplish.

Gorbachev's second key word, perestroika, is usually translated as "restructuring." Again, the translation here is adequate, but also does not really reflect what was understood by the term within the Soviet Union. When Gorbachev first used the term, he meant it in the purely economic sense of reorganizing economic activity to make it more productive. At that point, the principles associated with it were "socialist" and "self-financing." But later people began applying it to all aspects of the society, speaking of the restructuring of science, the media, or even politics. Thus it became a synonym for general societal change.

Demokratiya or democracy, Gorbachev's third slogan, is perhaps the most difficult word to explain in the Soviet context. At least in the beginning, it did not mean democracy in the sense of political democracy, and it was not meant to challenge the monopoly of the Communist Party of the Soviet Union as the directing agent of Soviet society. Yet Gorbachev did mean greater popular participation in decision making at the local and possibly even up to the Republic level. Partly, this was once again an attempt to mobilize popular support behind his reform program, but it was also an attempt to give the people a feeling that they had a real stake in their country's future. Because more than one candidate was to be nominated for each position, it also gave the people somewhat more

The legendary summer palace—Tsarskoe Selo ("The Tsar's Village"), 15 miles south of St. Petersburg

Russia

control at the local level and moved toward something like genuine democracy.

Additional Politburo and Leadership Changes

This campaign was accompanied by changes in the Politburo related to Gorbachev's campaign for reform. The first such change came in December 1986, when Dinmukhamed Kunaev was dismissed as First Secretary for Kazakhstan. Accused of corruption, he lost his Politburo seat in January 1987. Kunaev may have been corrupt for it was the policy of the Brezhnev regime to co-opt non-Slavic leaders by not paying too much attention to what they did within their own jurisdictions so long as they remained loyal supporters of Moscow's policies nationally. On the other hand, he was dismissed primarily because he was an old-line conservative unable to adjust to Gorbachev's new technocratic vision.

But Gorbachev's decision to put his own man in charge backfired in this case. When word reached Alma-Ata, the Kazakh capital, that Kunaev had been dismissed and that he was being replaced by Gennady Kolbin, an ethnic Russian, violent rioting broke out and several persons were killed. Kolbin's appointment violated a long-standing tradition that the first secretary of a republic always represented the dominant ethnic group (i.e., in this case, the Kazakhs). Kolbin was later reassigned and a Kazakh was appointed first secretary in his place.

The next changes came at a plenary session of the Central Committee on June 26, 1987. Three men, Aleksandr N. Yakovlev, Nikolai Slyunkov, and Victor Nikonov, were added to the Politburo, while Dmitry Yazov, the new defense minister, became a candidate member. Yakovlev, who had studied in the United States in the late 1950s and served for a number of years as ambassador to Canada, quickly established himself as a strong voice for reform. Nikonov, a member of the Secretariat, had picked up the agriculture portfolio from Gorbachev when he became General Secretary. Slyunkov, who had been First Secretary of the Republic of Byelorussia, was considered to be a protégé of Ryzhkov's.

These additions to the Politburo must have strengthened Gorbachev politically, even though two stalwarts of the Brezhnev era, Heydar Aliyev and Vladimir Shcherbitsky, retained their positions.

Heydar Aliyev announced his resignation three months later, in October, ostensively because of ill health. Although there were some rumors earlier that Aliyev had suffered a heart attack, it is still not clear whether Aliyev left voluntarily or was pushed out. What was significant, however, is that Aliyev was the last Central Asian on the Politburo and his departure left Foreign Minister Shevardnadze as the sole non-Slav on the ruling body.

Aliyev's departure may have been voluntary, but the dismissal, in the same month, of Boris Yeltsin as first secretary for Moscow clearly was not. His dismissal, after a speech criticizing the pace of reform, came as something of a shock because he had been closely associated with Gorbachev up to that time. His "crime" was apparently that he favored a more confrontational approach with the bureaucracy than Gorbachev and wanted to force the pace of reform even against growing opposition. He was subsequently accused of holding the "political illusion" that reform "could be achieved through vigorous and honest guidance from above—that is, by using 'purified' but still high-handed methods."

It appears that Yeltsin fell victim to an emerging split in the top leadership ranks over the issue of how quickly economic reform should be implemented. Everyone in the top leadership accepted the necessity of economic reform in theory, but several wanted the reform to be as narrow and technical as possible. At this time, Ligachev, Chebrikov, and Yazov were the most outspoken exponents of this point of view. All three publicly criticized aspects of the reform. Gorbachev obviously felt that he needed their general support, however, and when Yeltsin took a confrontational stance and attacked Ligachev and others, Gorbachev abandoned him and he lost his leadership position in the party.

Even though Yeltsin was subsequently made first deputy chairman of the state construction committee, meaning that he was not totally disgraced, his dismissal had a chilling effect on the more outspoken reformers. In February 1988, Yeltsin lost his seat as an alternate member of the Politburo, though he retained his membership on the Central Committee.

However, the same Central Committee meeting that dropped Yeltsin also added two persons as alternate members of the Politburo. They were Yuri Maslyukov, 50, a defense expert, and Georgi Razumovsky, 52, an agricultural expert. Maslyukov subsequently replaced Nikolai Talyzin as head of GOSPLAN. Razumovsky, who was supposed to have close ties to Gorbachev, became a member of the Secretariat with responsibility for personnel.

And a New Definition of Democracy

The next event of significance in 1988 was the 19th All-Union CPSU Conference, which met in Moscow on June 28–July 1. Gorbachev, who presided over the conference, encouraged an atmosphere of open expression and, occasionally, debate among the delegates. The delegates eventually voted to accept six resolutions, the

Boris Yeltsin

most important of which called for "democratization of Soviet society and the reform of the political system."

The resolution provided only a bare outline of a new political system, but it did put the party on record as favoring a restructuring of the political system. Not everyone was happy with the resolutions, however. In August, two Politburo members, Yegor Ligachev and Viktor Chebrikov, gave speeches critical of the direction Gorbachev was taking the party.

Gorbachev responded by calling a meeting of the Central Committee which met at the end of September. The meeting led to a major reshuffle within the top leadership, several retirements, and some promotions. Among those retired were Andrei Gromyko, who also stepped down as chairman of the Presidium of the Supreme Soviet (informally, president), and Mikhail Solomentsev. Vladimir Dolgikh and Pyotr Demichev, who had been alternate members of the Politburo, were retired at the same time. The meeting also nominated Gorbachev as Gromyko's successor as Chairman of the Presidium of the Supreme Soviet, and this was subsequently confirmed by the Supreme Soviet.

Yegor Ligachev retained his seat on the Politburo, but he lost his position as chief ideologist and his informal position as Second Secretary, by virtue of which he had chaired meetings of the Secretariat. He gained the title of chairman of the agricultural commission. Chebrikov was removed as head of the KGB and made chairman of the legal affairs commission. Both moves were considered to be demotions.

Russia

The *das* have it: Gromyko is voted out as chairman of the Presidium of the Supreme Soviet. He sits dejected while Ryzhkov and Gorbachev vote "yes"

Vadim Medvedev, considered to be an ally of Gorbachev, was added to the Politburo and made chief ideologist. His official title was chairman of the ideological commission. In addition, Alexandra Biryukova, Aleksandr Vlasov, and Anatoly Lukyanov were made alternate members of the Politburo. Biryukova thus became the first woman on the Politburo since the Khrushchev era.

In yet another change, Anatoly Dobrynin was relieved of his duties as secretary of the Central Committee and sent into honorable retirement. Increasingly, Gorbachev's chief adviser on relations with the United States would be Aleksandr Yakovlev.

Although these personnel shifts helped Gorbachev to further consolidate his power, structural changes adopted at the same time may have had an even more important long-term significance. Essentially, the Central Committee voted to abolish the old Secretariat in the form in which it had previously existed—that is, as a body charged with implementing Politburo decisions. Instead, secretaries of the Central Committee were appointed as chairmen of six newly created commissions. In addition to those mentioned above, commissions were created for party building and cadre policy (Razumovsky), socioeconomic policy (Slyunkov), and international policy (Yakovlev).

The secretaries thus became responsible for longer-term policy planning, while shorter-term decisions became the prerogative of persons occupying state positions. The obvious purpose of the change was to remove the party from the day-to-day supervision of affairs and to have it concentrate on matters of broad policy. Similar instructions—that is, to stop interfering in the day-to-day affairs of the Soviets and the economy—were sent out to party secretaries at subordinate levels at this same time. The continuing evidence indicated that the new instructions had little effect on how party secretaries operated, however.

A Legislature?

The party had, in fact, long decided everything. If it were to be restricted to long-term planning, then a power vacuum would be created unless the governmental institutions were strengthened. This was the thrust of the reorganization plan which Gorbachev submitted to the Supreme Soviet in late November 1988. An elaboration of the outline approved by the party conference in June, it created a 2,250-member Congress of People's Deputies, to be elected on the basis of a competitive ballot. The new Congress, when it met, would elect a chairman of the USSR Supreme Soviet (informally, president), plus a two-chamber standing legislature, the USSR Supreme Soviet.

In effect, Gorbachev had redesigned the political system to allow for at least a partial transfer of power from the Communist Party to popularly elected legislative bodies. In addition, by creating strong executive ties to the new legislative bodies, he had partially freed himself from having to consult constantly with other members of the Politburo.

Elections to the Congress of People's Deputies took place on March 26, 1989, with the most interesting part being the campaign that preceded the actual election. Every candidate had to present an election platform, so the voters were able to choose between candidates based on issues. Most seats were contested. Of 1,500 seats, only 384 had a single candidate; the rest had two or more. Seven hundred and fifty other seats were filled by various officially recognized organizations, including 100 filled by the Communist Party. But, although only this small number was elected directly by the Communist Party, it is significant that 82% of all the candidates were members of the Communist Party and the party endorsed candidates in most of the districts.

Approximately 80% of those endorsed by the party won. The party was, therefore, in no way repudiated. However, a number of individuals who, a few years ago, were considered to be dissidents were among the winners. These included Andrei Sakharov and historian and writer Roy Medvedev. A third individual who won running against a candidate endorsed by the party was none other than Boris Yeltsin, who got almost 90% of the vote in a Moscow at-large seat. There were also some prominent losers. The highest ranking of those was Yuri Solovyev, first secretary for the Leningrad area, who failed to muster 50% of the vote, even though he was running unopposed. As a result, he eventually lost both his position as first secretary and his seat on the Politburo.

The new Congress was scheduled to convene at the end of May but, before that occurred, Gorbachev called a meeting of the Central Committee at the end of April and asked for the retirement of 110 people, or approximately one-third of the membership of that body. In turn, 24 persons were added to the Central Committee. In one sense, this was not a purge, however, as most of those who were retired from the Committee had already retired from the jobs that had earned them entry to the Central Committee in the first place. As one official associated with Gorbachev expressed it, since there was to be a genuine working legislative body for the first time, Gorbachev needed a Central Committee which was also made up of currently active individuals.

The Congress, when it did meet, proved to be lively but, ultimately, Gorbachev dominated the session. The Congress first grilled Gorbachev, then proceeded to elect him Chairman of the USSR Supreme Soviet (informally, President). The new USSR Supreme Soviet, the smaller, standing legislature, was then elected, and remained in session over the summer.

Although Gorbachev set the agenda and tended to dominate discussions, it established itself as a genuine independent voice and a valuable forum. Its televised sessions proved to be a national sensation. The second session showed itself to be even more independent and less subject to Gorbachev's control.

Gorbachev's greatest problem was to find groups who were not only loyal but were also committed to his programs. Again and again he made it clear that commitment to his goals came even before loyalty. This was shown once again in 1989, when he directed another major reshuffle. Three members of the Politburo, Viktor Nikonov, Viktor Chebrikov, and Vladimir Shcherbitsky, were "relieved of their duties" as Politburo members. They were joined in retirement by two alternate members, Yuriy Solovyev and Nikolay Talyzin.

Shcherbitsky was the last remaining member of the old Brezhnev Politburo (except for Gorbachev) and his dismissal had been long predicted. Chebrikov, Nikonov, Solovyev, and Talyzin, on the other hand, were early allies of Gorbachev who had shown a general lack of commitment to reform.

The additions were equally telling. Vladimir Kryuchkov, head of the KGB, and Yuriy Maslyukov, head of GOSPLAN, had both been early Gorbachev supporters. Their promotion to full membership appeared to give Gorbachev two strong allies on the Politburo. The two new alternate members, Yevgeny Primakov and Boris Pugo, were also viewed as Gorbachev loyalists though they later would turn on him. Primakov, chairman of the Council of the Union of the USSR Supreme Soviet, was also a member of the USSR Academy of Sciences with a doctorate in economics. Pugo, chairman of the Party Control Commission, and a former head of the Latvian Communist Party, was also a deputy of Latvia's Supreme Soviet.

Nationality Problems

The major agenda topic at the Central Committee Plenum at which these political changes were made was nationality policy. The Communist Party had always boasted that it had solved the nationality problems in the USSR but, in fact, the problems were merely suppressed.

Gorbachev's policies, which among other things encouraged people to get involved and to demand reform, and which also tolerated the creation of unofficial groups (but not alternative political parties) and promised economic autonomy to the individual republics, had led to the creation of national fronts in nearly every republic and other groups organized along ethnic or nationality lines whose function was to air grievances and demand redress. In the Caucasus region, this had eventually led to a state of virtual war between Armenia and Azerbaijan over the mixed area called Nagorno-Karabakh; in the Baltic republics, in Moldavia, and within Western Ukraine (where the Ukrainian Catholic Church is predominant), it had led to autonomy movements.

At the Central Committee Plenum, Gorbachev, arguing that "the need for profound changes is long overdue in ethnic relations," promised a new federation under which "the right of each ethnic group to enjoy all the fruits of sovereignty and to decide all issues of its development—economic, political, and cultural," would be guaranteed.

Gorbachev's position was endorsed by the Central Committee plenum, but the subsequent collapse of communist governments throughout Eastern Europe in the last three months of 1989—even though in one sense orchestrated by Gorbachev—changed the equation again and brought calls for even greater change.

A Distressed Economy

To make matters worse, the domestic economic situation had been deteriorating for some time; this added to the pressures as shortages of consumer goods continued to grow worse, producing greater public dissatisfaction. Reform-spirited communists, now organized into the Democratic Platform, threatened to split the party unless they got their way. Conservatives, on the other hand, reacted by urging a slowing down in the pace of reform.

In December 1989, Nikolai Ryzhkov, Chairman of the USSR Council of Ministers, brought in a new draft five-year plan that represented a clear retreat from economic change. It looked like the planners would remain in charge for another five years.

As had become his practice, it was at this moment that Gorbachev opted for more political reform. First of all, he accepted the idea of a multiparty system and formally proposed that the constitution be changed to delete the Communist Party's leading position. This was accomplished in January–March 1990.

Next, he proposed that, under the new circumstances, what the Soviet Union needed was an executive president, able to take action in an emergency without consultations with other bodies such as the Presidium of the Supreme Soviet.

This led, in March 1990, to creation of the office of President of the USSR, to which Gorbachev was subsequently indirectly elected through the new legislature. It also led to creation of a presidential council, which appears to have been an attempt to create a Soviet version of a national security council or, possibly, a "super cabinet." Its membership, originally 16, included the foreign, interior, and defense ministers, the head of the KGB, other government and party officials, and two prominent writers, Valentin Rasputin and Chingiz Aitmatov. In addition, the Chairman of the Council of Ministers sat as an ex officio member. It didn't work out and was later disbanded.

Russia

The first challenge which the new president had to handle came from Lithuania. Following multiparty elections which were won by Sajudis, the Lithuanian national front, the Lithuanian legislature installed Vytautas Landsbergis as president and passed a declaration of independence. Similar declarations were adopted by Latvia and Estonia, although in a somewhat different form. Gorbachev condemned all three as illegal and initiated a partial economic blockade of Lithuania. He then offered that, if the three republics suspended their declarations, talks leading to independence within two years could begin.

Gorbachev also said that he would not use force against would-be breakaway republics. The fact that he was scheduled to meet with President George H. W. Bush on May 30 obviously acted as a restraint on his actions. Although President Bush raised the subject, he apparently did not press it with vigor. The United States found itself in an awkward position at this time. The three republics had been incorporated into the Soviet Union as a result of the Nazi-Soviet Non-Aggression Pact signed in August 1939. In the Pact, Hitler had recognized these nations as being in the Soviet sphere of influence in return for a Soviet promise of neutrality when Hitler invaded Poland.

The United States had never recognized the incorporation of the three republics into the USSR and its legal position was that they were still sovereign nations. In fact, embassies of the three republics were still to be found in Washington, DC. At the same time, the United States favored closer relations with the Soviet Union.

However, the Soviet position articulated by Gorbachev was even more awkward. Although the Soviet government had repudiated the Nazi-Soviet Non-Aggression Pact and considered it invalid, it continued to maintain that the three republics were factually a part of the USSR and therefore had to apply for and receive permission to leave.

Rumblings of Change

Gorbachev also had other concerns. In the spring of 1990, elections in the Russian, Byelorussian, and Ukrainian republics produced a strong showing for the radical reformers, who won majorities in the largest cities, including Moscow and Leningrad. In Moscow, Gavrill Popov, a member of the Congress of People's Deputies and one of the leaders of the radical inter-regional group in the USSR Supreme Soviet, was elected mayor on the promise to move Moscow quickly toward a market economy.

Perhaps more important, Boris Yeltsin, was elected chairman of the RSFSR Supreme Soviet (popularly, Russian President) by that body on the third ballot in May. Gorbachev thus lost control of the all-important Russian Republic.

Essentially, all of this happened because the party had split into three factions, conservatives, Gorbachev supporters and democrats. The democrats wanted to move more quickly on reforms than Gorbachev did, and threatened to leave the party and form a new political party if Gorbachev didn't go along. Gorbachev, citing the need for party unity, urged them to stay. The conservatives, on the other hand, urged the democrats to leave.

This was the background to Gorbachev's other concern, the party congress which was scheduled to take place in late June/early July 1990. Gorbachev decided to use the party congress to remake the party, getting rid of the Politburo and replacing it with a larger, less powerful Presidium, the majority of whose members would be ex

Just weeks before his dream collapses, a giant portrait of Lenin, father of modern communism, rises in front of KGB headquarters in Moscow

Courtesy of Steve Raymer © National Geographic Society

Russia

officio—the party chairman and his deputies plus the 15 republic party secretaries. Gorbachev intended the new Presidium to concentrate on coordinating the activities of the party. Broad policy functions would then become the prerogative of the Soviet Government.

The draft made no mention of the office of General Secretary but it did specify that there would continue to be a secretariat. The leader of the party would be the "chairman," and he was to be elected by the party congress, as was the case under Lenin.

**Gavriil Popov,
former mayor of Moscow**

The draft was modified at the party congress but Gorbachev got most of what he wanted. The office of General Secretary was retained, but he was elected by the party congress. The Politburo was retained, but its membership and function were modified as Gorbachev desired.

The delegates also adopted a document called "Toward Humane, Democratic Socialism." Although the word socialism is in its title, the document actually moved the party a long way toward a rejection of what traditionally has been understood as Marxism-Leninism. Instead, the document spoke of the ideology of the party being based on "the legacy of Marx, Engels and Lenin, freed from dogmatic interpretation."

This document broke with traditional ideology in two basic ways. Socialism, it declared, should be based on individual, not collective, interests; and "private ownership must have a place in the system of forms of ownership" of equal validity with collective ownership. What this meant is that the Communist Party was

now claiming to represent the interests of Soviet citizens as individuals, not as members of a class or socioeconomic grouping. Thus Marx's entire class-based analysis was discarded. And granting private property equal status with collective property flaunted Marx's premise that ownership of the means of production provided the basis for exploitation of man by man. In ideological terms, this programmatic statement moved the Communist Party a long distance from Marxist-Leninist orthodoxy. It could still claim to be a socialist party, of course.

Two other issues preoccupied Gorbachev in 1990–1991, the economy and the negotiation of a new union treaty. The two issues were intricately linked to each other, since one of the demands of the republics was control over economic activity and natural resources. An economic plan that would devolve authority to the republics would go a long way toward meeting this demand.

That is why the Shatalin Plan, which proposed transforming the Soviet Union to a market economy in 500 days, had the support of 14 of the 15 republics. Proposed in August 1990 as an alternative to the government's plan to retain the old system of state orders for another 18 months, it even got Gorbachev's backing for a short while.

But Gorbachev backed down when Ryzhkov, chairman of the Council of Ministers, threatened to resign rather than take responsibility for implementing a plan he disagreed with. Gorbachev then told Ryzhkov to take the two approaches and combine them. The result, which was mainly the Ryzhkov plan, was approved by the Supreme Soviet in November. But Gorbachev's economic advisers were disappointed by the compromise and most left to work for Boris Yeltsin and the Russian government.

Gorbachev did get one good bit of news in October when he learned that he had been awarded the Nobel Peace Prize. Even that could not distract from worry about the economy, however. As Georgi Arbatov, the traditionalist director of the US and Canada Institute, commented at the time, "I am sure that he deserves the Peace Prize. I wouldn't think he has deserved the Nobel Prize for economics." Gorbachev's main problem with economic reform was that he was dismantling the old command system but was not replacing it with a functional market economy.

In late 1990, under prodding from the Supreme Soviet, Gorbachev changed the organizational structure once more. The presidential council and council of ministers were abolished and their place was taken by a strengthened council of the federation (created in March 1990) and a streamlined cabinet of ministers. There

continued to be a chairman who headed up the cabinet, but he was made directly subordinate to Gorbachev. These provisions were more or less implemented while some other provisions, such as Gorbachev's suggestion that the Congress of People's Deputies be replaced by a directly elected Supreme Soviet, were not.

Gorbachev lost his most valuable ally in December 1990 when Foreign Minister Eduard Shevardnadze resigned after charging that the Soviet Union was headed toward a dictatorship. He was replaced by Aleksandr Bessmertnykh, whose previous position had been Soviet ambassador to Washington. After his resignation, Shevardnadze became head of a new independent foreign policy research institute, the Soviet foreign policy association.

Gorbachev lost a second adviser in December when Nikolai Ryzhkov suffered a heart attack and resigned as chairman of the newly created cabinet of ministers. He was replaced by Valentin Pavlov, who had been Ryzhkov's finance minister. A conservative, Pavlov's first major action was to attempt to reduce the money overhang by a partial repudiation of the currency. All 50- and 100-ruble notes were withdrawn from circulation, with individuals given three days to redeem a limited amount related to monthly salary. Pavlov's overall economic program was a continuation of the Ryzhkov program. Gorbachev also dismayed many people when he appointed Gennady Yanayev, a Communist Party bureaucrat, as his vice president.

The Baltic Republics became the center of attention once again in January 1991, when ministry of the interior troops stormed the Lithuanian press center and a building occupied by the Lithuanian civilian militia on January 13, killing 14 people. Gorbachev's role in all this was ambivalent. He did not repudiate the attack, but claimed to have found out about it only after it happened. The following weekend, five more people were killed when ministry of interior troops seized the Latvian ministry of interior building.

The European Parliament then moved to block $1 billion in food aid to the Soviet Union, and a number of European nations began threatening other sanctions. In Washington, the Bush administration began discussing postponement of an upcoming summit meeting, which was in fact postponed, though publicly it was because of the Iraq conflict. Responding to this international pressure, Gorbachev backed down in early February and agreed to appoint a commission to consult with the Baltic Republics about their demands for independence.

Gorbachev's great concern was the national referendum on the question of the future of the USSR which was scheduled

Russia

The Supreme Soviet of the USSR discussing problems of stabilizing the national economy and transition to a market system, October 1990

for March 17, 1991. The question asked of the Soviet people was whether they considered it "necessary to preserve the Union of Soviet Socialist Republics as a renewed federation of equal sovereign republics, in which human rights and the freedoms of all nationalities will be fully guaranteed."

Six republics refused to participate in the referendum, and four other republics modified the question in some way. Gorbachev nevertheless claimed a victory on the basis of the 76% who voted "yes" among those who participated.

The next month, Gorbachev and the heads of the nine republics who had participated in the referendum announced their agreement on an outline for a new union treaty that would create a Union of Sovereign Soviet Republics. The draft called for a great deal of decentralization, particularly in the economic area, plus a remaking of the national government, including new elections for a national legislature and president. In early May, Gorbachev agreed to turn coal mines over to the Russian government as part of a deal to end a miners' strike.

Later in the month, Gorbachev also endorsed a new plan for economic reform drawn up by Grigory Yavlinsky, who had also contributed to the Shatalin Plan. This new plan called for significant international economic assistance to act as a "shock absorber of social costs and shocks" as the Soviet Union moved to a market economy.

Events tumbled on at a faster and faster rate. In May–June there was a resolution of differences over the CFE Treaty and a new immigration law was passed by the Supreme Soviet. It was announced that President Bush would travel to Moscow for a summit meeting sometime during the summer. And, in a new test of public opinion, Boris Yeltsin won 59% of the vote in a six-candidate race in his run for the newly created office of president of the Russian Federation. The official communist candidate came in a dismal third. Gorbachev, reversing his previous position, warmly embraced Yeltsin's victory.

Communist conservatives, evidently alarmed by this development, began to plot a "constitutional coup" against Gorbachev in late June. It took the form of a request by Premier Pavlov that the Supreme Soviet transfer from Gorbachev to him the power to rule by decree. The President, Pavlov explained, was "overworked." Pavlov's request was supported by Defense Minister Yazov, KGB Chairman Vladimir Kryuchkov, and Minister of Interior Boris Pugo.

The attempt failed. Forewarned of Pavlov's attempt to strip away some of his powers, Gorbachev counterattacked and defeated the move. In the process, however, Gorbachev did two things that he would later rue. He permitted all four of his disloyal subordinates to retain their positions of power, while he attacked their political arguments. He told these four representatives of the military-industrial complex that the Soviet Union was over-militarized and that "we have to remove this burden and turn the economy over to the people. Otherwise my mission will be useless and I will have to resign."

Gorbachev had a busy summer. In July, he traveled to London to meet with the "Group of Seven" (United States, Great Britain, Canada, Germany, France, Italy, and Japan). His purpose in requesting the meeting was to try to get a promise of economic assistance. He basically used the Yavlinsky Plan as the basis of his discussions. He got no promises of cash, though the Group did offer the Soviet Union some technical assistance and a "special associate status" with the International Monetary Fund (IMF) and World Bank.

President Bush came to Moscow at the end of July. The summit meeting included two days of discussions and a ceremonial signing of the completed START agreement. Gorbachev then left for a vacation in the Crimea with his family.

He planned to return to Moscow on August 19 since, the following day, he and the leaders of nine of the republics were to sign a new union treaty that conceded significant powers to the individual republics. Instead, Gorbachev was placed under house arrest on the evening of August 18. The next day, the world learned that a coup d'état had been launched by conservative communists in the top echelons of government—their goal to preserve the Soviet Union and the communist system. Among the top leaders were Pavlov, Yazov, Kryuchkov, and Pugo, the four participants in the attempted "constitutional coup" against Gorbachev in late June. They were joined this time by Vice President Gennady Yanayev. These five,

plus three other conservatives, took control as the "State Committee for the State of Emergency."

The coup lasted approximately 60 hours and eventually failed, thanks primarily to Boris Yeltsin and supporters of reform and democracy throughout the country. But the complicity of the Communist Party in the coup was so great that there were few objections when Boris Yeltsin, on the morning after the coup was defeated, banned Communist Party activities in the Russian Republic. Two days later, Gorbachev resigned as General Secretary and called upon the Central Committee to dissolve itself. He then issued a decree suspending the activities of the party and seizing all party property. After 74 years, the communist era had come to an end.

Foreign Policy under Gorbachev

Soviet foreign policy began changing in 1985, not only with regard to the United States, but with regard to the third world and Eastern Europe as well. Soviet support for a settlement in southern Africa led to an agreement to pull Cuban troops out of Angola. It was Soviet pressure on Vietnam that caused that country to pull its troops out of Cambodia. The Soviet Union also eventually halted the shipment of military equipment to Nicaragua and then tacitly supported the free elections that resulted in a non-communist government coming to power there in April 1990.

When Iraq invaded Kuwait, Gorbachev gave his support to the various UN Security Council resolutions demanding that Iraq

Soviet President Mikhail Gorbachev joins the Group of Seven leaders in London. Front row (L to R): President George H. W. Bush, President Mikhail Gorbachev, British Prime Minister John Major, French President Francois Mitterrand, German Chancellor Helmut Kohl. Back row (L to R): European Commission President Jacques Delors, Italian Prime Minister GiulioAndreotti, Canadian Prime Minister Brian Mulroney, Japanese Prime Minister Toshiki Kaifu, Dutch Prime Minister Ruud Lubbers Courtesy of Reuters/Bettmann

Russia

President-Elect George H. W. Bush, President Ronald Reagan, and General Secretary Mikhail Gorbachev check out their "where to stand" marks for a photo-taking session at Governor's Island, New York, December 7, 1988 Courtesy of AP Images

Soviet-East European relations were thus, for Stalin, an extension of domestic Soviet politics.

All of that began to change after Stalin's death. The new Soviet leadership, which had been subject to the same treatment during Stalin's lifetime, committed itself to a "new course" in intra-bloc relations. Modifying the previous relationship, they allowed Eastern European leaders greater independence and encouraged them to develop policies designed to win them greater popularity among their people. This was, they concluded, the best way to ensure the long-term success of communism in Eastern Europe.

There were limitations to this independence, of course. All were required to join the Warsaw Pact when it was established in 1955 and even Khrushchev, chief spokesman for this viewpoint, didn't hesitate to intervene militarily in Hungary in 1956, when the the reformist communist leader Imre Nagy called for free elections and removed Hungary from the Warsaw Pact. Khrushchev's decision to allow Gomulka to take power in Poland in 1956 was another part of this loosening of control.

Khrushchev sought to further integrate the Soviet and East European economies, but he permitted Romania to opt out when that country opposed the international division of labor proposed by the Soviet Union. Khrushchev also did nothing when, in April 1964, Romania claimed the right to develop its own policies. Romania would later go on to develop its own, independent foreign policy, though it always remained an orthodox communist society domestically.

Brezhnev intervened in Czechoslovakia in 1968 when that country's communist party moved to give up its monopoly of political power. He also put strong pressure on the Polish communist leadership to reverse its decision legalizing the independent trade union Solidarity in 1981. But he quietly permitted Hungary to implement a partly privatized economy in the 1960s.

Gorbachev's attitude toward Eastern Europe when he became General Secretary in 1985 appeared to be relatively orthodox, though from the beginning he tended to treat individual communist leaders as though he considered them partners in a common enterprise. His first plans for economic reform relied heavily on Eastern Europe as a source of new technology and he confidently expected them to join him in implementing similar reforms in their own countries. The Soviet Union already got many of the more sophisticated products that it imported, such as computers, computer software, and machine tools, from Eastern Europe, and he expected that they would want to upgrade their

pull out of Kuwait and then those authorizing the use of force against Iraq, even though Iraq had been a longtime ally of the Soviet Union. Gorbachev also presided over the demise of the Council for Mutual Economic Assistance and the Warsaw Pact, thus formally dissolving the ties that bound the various countries of Eastern Europe to the Soviet Union. And, of course, he presided over a series of military negotiations that helped to bring an end to the Cold War.

Changing Relations with Eastern Europe under Gorbachev

The pattern of foreign relations established by Stalin with Eastern Europe after World War II was one of almost total subordination on the part of the communist leaderships of those countries, exemplified

after 1948 by Stalin's campaign to remove from office those communist leaders who showed any independence whatsoever. During this period, Soviet ambassadors acted as virtual proconsuls, whose orders had the force of law.

Poland's Wladyslaw Gomulka, one of those who resisted and, as a result, was purged, described this phenomenon:

In this bloc of socialist states, it was Stalin who stood at the apex of this hierarchic ladder of cults. All those who stood on lower rungs of the ladder bowed their heads before him. . . . The first secretaries of the central committees of the parties of the various countries who sat on the second rung of the ladder of the cult of personality, in turn donned the robes of infallibility and wisdom.

technology and become a source of ever more sophisticated technology.

He was disappointed by the first response to his reform ideas. Only Hungary, already well along in its own reform program, was enthusiastic. For a while, he attempted to lead by example and by persuasion, speaking of his economic reform and pointing out its advantages on visits to Eastern Europe, but making no effort to coerce communist leaders into adopting the same approach. On the other hand, the Soviet Union did chide Eastern European leaders for the poor quality of their exports and it put behind the scenes pressure on them to upgrade the quality and technological level of their products, though with little success. Czechoslovakia and the German Democratic Republic, the Eastern European countries with the most developed economies, were both led by conservative leaders who believed that a program of economic reform would undermine their own legitimacy.

Gorbachev slowly came to realize that the Eastern European countries weren't going to provide the significant assistance in the area of technology that he had been counting on to help him with his own perestroika. Their unreformed economies simply weren't up to it. Finland, a noncommunist neighbor, proved to be much more valuable as a source of technology than any of the communist countries of Eastern Europe.

Meanwhile, the Soviet Union was providing Eastern Europe with energy supplies and raw materials below world prices, while receiving shoddy consumer goods and old technology in return. The question Gorbachev had to ask himself was whether the conservative and unreformed communist leaderships were more of a burden than an asset. Was Finland a better model? A number of articles appeared in the Soviet press at about this time discussing the merits of a "Finlandization" of Eastern Europe.

The 1989 Revolutions

Thus, we come to the events and decisions of 1989, when communism collapsed nearly everywhere in Eastern Europe. In country after country, ruling communist parties were first forced to compromise with their opponents and then, in most cases, to relinquish part or all of their power to them. Communism, a doctrine imposed from the outside by Soviet armies after the defeat of Nazi Germany, never was popular among the people of Eastern Europe. Yet the communist elites remained in power, partly because they controlled a monopoly of power and partly because they could always count on the support

and backing of the Soviet Union, spelled out after 1968 in the "Brezhnev Doctrine."

So, no one predicted the events of 1989, precisely because no one expected that the Soviet Union would permit such changes to occur in Eastern Europe. And that points out the most important difference about 1989—that the Soviet Union did not merely acquiesce in these changes; it was, in fact, an active agent in bringing them about. In hindsight, it was predictable. The Soviets had become economically exhausted and their only choice to continue control in Eastern Europe was military, which would have enraged world opinion.

Gorbachev had several times said things that sounded like a repudiation of the Brezhnev Doctrine after becoming General Secretary, but no one was certain whether he meant it. It was his intervention in Poland in the latter part of 1988 that gave the first indication that he meant what he had said.

Poland

After outlawing Solidarity in December 1981, General Wojciech Jaruzelski and the ruling Polish United Workers' Party introduced a program of economic reform to remake the Polish economy and to deal with the conditions that had brought Solidarity

October 1989: On a stone lion in front of parliament a Hungarian youth hoists the flag of his country—with the hammer and sickle surgically removed   Courtesy of AP Images

73

Russia

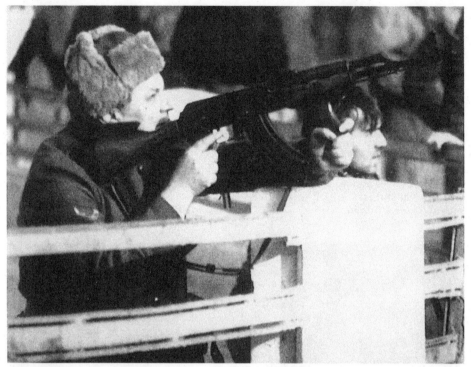

Bucharest, Romania, Christmas Eve 1989: A Romanian soldier points his rifle at enemy positions during street fighting
Courtesy of AP Images

into existence in the first place. That attempt at economic reform from above was unsuccessful and the government, under challenge from the official trade unions, collapsed in September 1988.

It was at this moment that the first indication of a reversal of Soviet policy occurred, in the form of a series of articles in the Soviet press portraying Lech Walesa and Solidarity in a favorable manner. This led to formal talks between the Polish government and Solidarity and the now famous April 1989 agreement re-legalizing Solidarity and setting new elections for June 4.

Those elections provided for only 35% of the seats in the Sejm (lower house of parliament) to be freely contested, but did include elections to a new Senate, all of whose seats were competitive. Solidarity took 99 out of 100 seats in the Senate, plus all of the open seats in the Sejm. In addition, most of the top *Communist* leaders, running unopposed for Sejm seats, were rejected because they failed to get 50% of the valid votes. These seats, reserved for communists, were filled in a second round of voting only because Solidarity instructed its supporters to endorse the new candidates.

The failure of the communists at the polls meant that they were in practice unable to form a government. Their allies, the United Peasants' Party and the Democratic Party, refused to support the communist candidate for Chairman of the Council of

Ministers and opened discussions with Solidarity. This led Lech Walesa to propose a Solidarity-led coalition government which would include communists. A second decisive Soviet intervention now occurred. After Mieczyslaw Rakowski, the new head of the Polish United Workers' Party, announced his opposition to such a coalition, he got a 40-minute telephone call from Gorbachev, the essence of which was that Gorbachev expected the Polish party to accept a Solidarity-led coalition government.

The psychological effect on the rest of Eastern Europe of the installation of a non-communist government in Poland was enormous; and even more important, it was known that Gorbachev not only gave his support to the change but actually intervened to help bring it about. This was seen as making change possible all over Eastern Europe. Surprisingly, Gorbachev continued to support change in Eastern Europe, even as those changes led to the collapse of communist governments throughout the region.

Hungary

After Poland, the next development occurred in Hungary, where a reform communist leadership had been installed in May 1988. Over the next year, opposition political parties were legalized and free elections were scheduled. New laws were also passed guaranteeing Hungarians the right to travel abroad and to emigrate. And in March 1989, Hungary signed a United

Nations protocol on refugees in which it obligated itself not to force refugees to go back home. In signing the protocol, the Hungarian government obviously had in mind Hungarian-speaking Romanians who were infiltrating across the border from Romania. By August 1989, however, tens of thousands of East German citizens had gathered in Hungary, drawn there by Hungary's decision to begin dismantling the barbed wire on its border with Austria. Refusing to return to East Germany, they wanted to go west.

The problem was a treaty that Hungary had signed with the German Democratic Republic in 1968 under which the Hungarian government promised to obtain clearance from the GDR before permitting GDR citizens to travel from it to a third country, a permission that was not forthcoming. The Hungarian government now decided to let the East Germans go, but there was some concern about the Soviet reaction. When informal sounding established *that the Soviet government would not object*, Hungary opened the border for the East Germans on September 10.

German Democratic Republic

The third break occurred in the German Democratic Republic, largely as a result of the decision of the Hungarian Government to allow East Germans to depart for the west. After the Hungarian action, other East Germans, unable to obtain visas to Hungary, began traveling in large numbers to Czechoslovakia, where no visa was required. Gathering in Prague, they began to inundate the grounds of the West German Embassy. Here they were given West German passports, but they still needed permission to depart Czechoslovakia for the west. The Czechoslovakian government, not wanting to be caught in the middle, requested clearance from the GDR government. The GDR eventually gave in and began arranging for trains to carry its citizens directly to West Germany.

The flight of hundreds of thousands of East Germans began to have repercussions at home, however. Protest demonstrations which were already occurring in a number of East German cities grew in size and number. The most organized of the demonstrations occurred in Leipzig. At first, the regime tried to handle the situation through the use of force. In addition to its usual riot police, it called out special "battle groups" of its party militia and fighting teams of the state security police, equipped with water cannons and armored cars. And on October 3, the East German government closed its borders with Czechoslovakia.

The matter came to a head on October 9 in Leipzig, when the local party leadership rejected orders from East Berlin to put down demonstrations scheduled for that day and instead called for a dialogue, promising to "use our full power and authority to ensure that this dialogue will occur, not only in the Leipzig area but with our national government."

At the Politburo meeting called to discuss the Leipzig decision, Egon Krenz, the number two man in the party, supported the Leipzig leaders over Erich Honecker's objections. This led to a Central Committee meeting eight days later and to Honecker's ouster as General Secretary on October 18.

Egon Krenz took over as General Secretary and promised reforms. He reopened the borders with Czechoslovakia and promised East Germans 30 days a year travel abroad. The flight through Czechoslovakia immediately resumed. Krenz next gambled that he could stabilize the situation by granting all citizens the right of unrestricted travel to the west, symbolized by the dramatic opening of the Berlin Wall on November 9, 1989. He accompanied this with promises of freer elections, economic liberalization, and power-sharing with other parties. Within a week, an estimated one-third of all East Germans had visited either West Berlin or West Germany.

After the initial euphoria, however, the pressure for change continued. On November 17, Hans Modrow, Dresden party chief, who had a reputation as a reformer, became the new head of government. Modrow proposed round-table discussions with the opposition and these began on December 7.

In the meanwhile, Egon Krenz and the other members of the Politburo submitted their resignations; a caretaker committee was appointed to run the party. At a special party congress that began five days later, Gregor Gysi, an attorney who had made his reputation as a defender of critics of the state and people caught fleeing the country, was appointed the new party leader. The delegates also voted to change the name of the party and to set the goal of the party as "democratic socialism."

At the congress, Hans Modrow spoke in favor of a confederation between the two Germanys. Helmut Kohl, the West German chancellor, had proposed a 10-point plan for unification in November, but this was the first time that any East German leader had endorsed the concept. Unification received another boost when Chancellor Kohl paid an official visit to East Germany on December 19. Kohl spoke in Dresden to cheering crowds and then he and Modrow joined the mayors of West and East Berlin in a ceremony opening a pedestrian crossing at the Brandenburg Gate.

Reunification was the big issue in the elections on March 18 and they were won by the conservative Alliance for Germany, led by the GDR Christian Democratic Union. On April 12, Lothar de Maiziere, leader of the Christian Democratic Union, became the first non-communist head of government, leading a "Grand Coalition" of the main non-communist parties, including the Social Democrats.

The new government immediately began preparing for German reunification. For a while, Gorbachev maintained that the Soviet Union would not agree to

November 11, 1989: With the Reichstag in the background, young Germans sit on the Berlin Wall in its final hours

Russia

German unification, unless Germany either suspended its membership in NATO or maintained its membership in the Warsaw Pact as well. After negotiations with the Federal Republic, however, he accepted continued German membership in NATO with the qualification that no foreign NATO troops would be stationed in the territory of the former East Germany. An economic, social and currency union went into effect on July 1 and final unification took place on October 3, 1990.

Czechoslovakia

Czechoslovakians had not reacted to the large numbers of East Germans fleeing west by way of their country, but subsequent events in East Germany did lead to the beginning of massive demonstrations in Prague. On November 17, 3,000 young people gathered near Wenceslas Square in Central Prague and began demanding free elections. The government reacted by ordering the police to put down the demonstration by force. It was a fatal mistake. The Czechoslovak people, aroused by the government's brutality, went into the streets in great numbers, singing, chanting, and demanding the ouster of Milos Jakes, the party General Secretary who had approved the police action. It was at this moment that Gorbachev intervened by sending a message that the Soviet government would not tolerate violence.

As the demonstrations continued and grew in size, a Central Committee meeting was called for November 24 and Milos Jakes and his entire Presidium resigned. The party had begun to crumble. Prime Minister Ladislav Adamec opened negotiations with the opposition, now organized as the Civic Forum. But Adamec, who wanted to retain a communist-dominated government, was forced to resign on December 6. His replacement, Marian Calfa, organized a new government in which the communists were in a minority.

The Czechoslovak parliament was subsequently purged and on December 28 Alexander Dubcek, leader of the 1968 Prague Spring, was elected chairman. The next day, Vaclav Havel, the Czech playwright whose opposition to the previous regime had landed him repeatedly in prison, was elected president. Czechoslovakia thus had its first non-communist president since 1948. Civic Forum won the multiparty elections that took place on June 6, 1990, while the communists were reduced to a tiny remnant.

Bulgaria

Change also came to Bulgaria, though at least in the beginning it was engineered to a greater extent from above. On November 9, Todor Zhivkov was forced out as communist party leader and replaced by Petar Mladenov. Zhivkov had been in power for 36 years. Mladenov, who had served as Bulgarian foreign minister for the previous 19 years, immediately instituted a policy of liberalization that soon led to legalization of opposition groups and the beginning of demonstrations in the streets. Broad-based talks began in January between the party and the opposition and a few days later the parliament voted to end the party's monopoly of power. At a hastily called party congress, the party voted to change its name and to become the Bulgarian Socialist Party. Mladenov also stepped down as party leader in April, after he had been elected to a new executive presidency.

Multi-party elections that took place in June were won by the ex-communists, but they had lost in the cities and the opposition, emboldened by this, continued their attacks on the government. In July, Mladenov was replaced by Zhelyu Zhelev, a leader of the opposition. After continued demonstrations, Dimitar Popov, a non-communist, was appointed prime minister. There was never any direct Gorbachev intervention in the political events occurring in Bulgaria in 1989–1990. However, Gorbachev's responses with regard to events in other parts of Eastern Europe were well known in Bulgaria; they undoubtedly were a factor influencing events in Bulgaria as well.

Romania

Romania experienced perhaps the greatest change of any country in Eastern Europe in 1989 when Nicolae Ceausescu, who had ruled the country since 1965, was overthrown in a violent uprising that ended in Ceausescu's death by firing-squad on December 25. Ceausescu, who was proud of his independence from Moscow, had rejected Gorbachev's policy of reform and made every effort to isolate his countrymen from events going on elsewhere in Eastern Europe. In November 1989, he had reaffirmed his policies at a party congress and had been reelected head of the party for a further five-year term. It was probably this reaffirmation of policies that was responsible for his downfall, for they had been responsible for a significant decline in the standard of living of Romanians over the previous nine years.

The revolt, which actually began as an ethnic dispute in the city of Timisoara, in the western part of Romania, spread to Bucharest, the capital, when Ceausescu called a mass meeting for December 21 to denounce the events in Timisoara. Instead, the people began shouting "freedom" and "democracy" and Ceausescu stalked off. That afternoon, the streets were full of people demonstrating against Ceausescu. That evening, Ceausescu ordered the secret police to begin firing on the people. A similar order to the army brought a refusal from General Vasile Milea, the Defense Minister. General Milea was executed the next morning, but the army now joined the revolution. Ceausescu and his wife fled the capital, but they were captured, brought back to Bucharest, and summarily tried and executed.

The Securitate, Ceausescu's secret police, fought on for a few days more but the army gradually managed to restore order. In the meantime, a group calling itself the National Salvation Front emerged as the new political leadership in the country. The Front, at first made up almost exclusively of former establishment figures who had fallen out with Ceausescu, was enlarged within a few days to take in various non-communist elements. It then began referring to itself as the Council of National Salvation. In the third week of January, the Council announced that multiparty elections would take place in May and that it intended to run its own candidates. This brought a condemnation from the leaders of the three largest opposition parties. After a series of negotiations, the Council agreed to make room for representatives of other parties. On February 1, the Council brought the representatives of 29 other political parties into the government coalition.

By this time, it had grown to approximately 180 members. It also underwent a name change and became the Provisional Council for National Unity. A new 10-member executive committee, headed by Acting President Ion Iliescu, also came into existence now. Meanwhile, the original National Salvation Front reorganized itself as a political party and announced that it, not the Council, would field candidates in the upcoming May 20 elections. As its candidate for president, it nominated Ion Iliescu. Most of the leadership of the Front had been members of the old Romanian Communist Party and the local branches of the National Salvation Front, set up at the time of the revolution, were largely made up of ex-officials. Thus, while the old communist party structure had collapsed, a large percentage of its membership transferred their loyalties to the National Salvation Front.

Eventually, some 80 political parties came into existence, though only 3 of them had any significant political support in the country. Two of these, both parties that were outlawed when the communists took over, were the Liberals and the Peasant Party. The third, the Hungarian Democratic Union, represented the interests of ethnic Hungarians. Although the opposition attacked the National Salvation Front because of its high component of ex-communists, there was, in fact, little to differentiate between them as far as programs were concerned. All were committed to the creation of a multiparty democracy and a market economy.

In the May elections, Ion Iliescu was elected president with approximately 83% of the vote while the National Salvation Front took 66% of the seats in the National Assembly. Election observers announced that there had been some irregularities in the voting but that, overall, the election was free.

An Overview

The events of 1989 and 1990 transformed east-central Europe and laid the basis for a new relationship with the Soviet Union. In the beginning, all of the new governments promised to remain in the Warsaw Pact and the Council for Mutual Economic Assistance (CMEA), but the basis for those organizations no longer existed. The CMEA was changing in any case, having agreed to carry on all trade in dollars as of January 1, 1991. This turned out to be so destabilizing that the CMEA effectively ceased to exist after the changeover and was formally dissolved on July 1, 1991. The military aspects of the Warsaw Pact were phased out in April after Hungary had announced that it intended to resign its membership; on July 1, 1991, the Warsaw Pact was also dissolved.

The Soviet Union pulled the last of its troops out of Hungary and Czechoslovakia in June 1991. It also signed an agreement with Germany to withdraw all Soviet troops by 1994 and gave a similar promise to Poland.

The various East European countries had begun to reorient their exports toward hard currency areas and away from the Soviet Union, a process that speeded up after the Soviet Union canceled standing orders with eastern European companies because of an inability to pay for the products in the now required hard currency. In a curious twist, the Economic Community actually helped to recreate some of those ties in 1991 as part of an agreement giving Hungary, Czechoslovakia, and Poland associate membership status in the EC (now the European Union). France, concerned about agricultural imports from east-central Europe, persuaded the EC to buy a part of the production from these countries for delivery to the Soviet Union.

US-Soviet Relations under Gorbachev

In 1985, the overriding factor in US-Soviet relations was the military rivalry between the two superpowers and how it was managed. Arms negotiations had occurred at intervals since the 1960s. There had been the occasional, successful negotiations, but the period 1979–1985 was basically one of stalemate. The two sides had continued to talk, but no agreements were reached. Meanwhile, the size of the

Foreign ministers meet in Bonn, West Germany, May 1990. Third from left is Foreign Minister Eduard Shevardnadze

arsenals continued to grow on both sides. Gorbachev's first policy speech after becoming General Secretary outlined a traditional Soviet position, but even that speech contained the phrase, "we want a real and major reduction of the arms stockpiles." The sticking point was President Reagan's Strategic Defense Initiative (SDI), launched in March 1983.

The SDI was a proposal to use emergent technology to develop a shield to stop incoming missiles, using a combination of laser beams, computers, satellites, and radar. SDI promised to reduce the threat of Soviet missiles to the United States. The failure of international negotiations gave it much of its political support, for it promised to achieve unilaterally what could otherwise be achieved only by successful negotiations.

The threat of having its missile force neutralized alarmed the Soviet leadership, and led to a Soviet proposal for talks on space weapons in mid-1984. The first discussions actually took place on March 12, 1985, one day after Gorbachev succeeded Chernenko as General Secretary. The beginning Soviet position was that the US cease *research* on development of a SDI system.

Officially, the Soviet opposition to American development of an SDI system was based on the premise that a successful one would give the United States a first strike capability *since it would not have to worry about retaliatory Soviet missiles*. The actual reasons for this opposition were far more complex, but were associated with Soviet weakness in the area of technological innovation and a Soviet recognition

that the western world was experiencing a technological revolution in the areas of computers and automation that was leaving the Soviet further and further behind.

This new computer technology had significant military applications and constituted, in fact, the heart of any successful SDI system. The Soviets thus feared SDI for the emerging technology it could produce. There was also the possibility of SDI "spin-offs" which could revolutionize conventional warfare, thus reducing Moscow's huge advantage in this area. It is no coincidence that Gorbachev's opposition to SDI internationally was coupled with a domestic program aimed at giving the Soviet Union mastery of advanced technology.

Although arms negotiations talks continued in Geneva, no progress was possible because of the deadlock over SDI. To break this, Reagan and Gorbachev decided to hold a summit conference in Geneva in November 1985. The talks were relatively cordial, and the two spoke privately for about five hours. There was no breakthrough on SDI, but Gorbachev did accept an invitation extended by Reagan to visit the United States in 1986.

Negotiations at Geneva continued in 1986. They were serious, and differences were narrowed, but a final agreement still remained beyond their grasp—because of SDI differences. When Gorbachev, as a consequence, postponed his visit to the United States, it was decided to hold a "pre-summit" in Reykjavik, Iceland. The two leaders met on October 11–12, 1986 for what turned out to be a wide-ranging discussion of the entire field of arms control.

Russia

No accord was reached, but the astonishing thing is how close they came, considering the topics discussed during that historic weekend. Concerning intermediate range ballistic missiles stationed in Europe, Gorbachev agreed to the US-proposed "zero option." On strategic offensive weapons, the two sides agreed to 50% cuts in five years and elimination of *all* such weapons in ten years.

Negotiations with regard to SDI proved to be most intractable, but even here progress was made in resolving differences. Thus, the Soviet position was that each side should agree to adhere to the ABM Treaty for 10 years; that during this time all SDI testing be confined to the laboratory, and that the two sides should negotiate about SDI stationing at the end of 10 years. Prior to the summit, the United States had been offering not to withdraw from the ABM Treaty for a term of 7.5 years. At Reykjavik, the US agreed to adhere to the ABM Treaty for 10 years if, during that same time period, strategic nuclear ballistic missiles were reduced to zero.

The two sticking points were the question of confining SDI testing to the laboratory and the question of whether the United States could begin deploying SDI at the end of 10 years without further negotiations with the Soviet Union. When agreement could not be reached on these two points, the negotiations fell through, because the Soviet position was that the arms-talks proposals were a single package, and agreement on any part of the package depended on acceptance by both sides of the *entire* package.

The first reaction to the Reykjavik summit was one of disappointment, but as both sides began looking back at what *had been accomplished*, the many areas of agreement became clear. In January 1987 the Soviet Union indicated its desire to continue discussions by naming a new chief Soviet negotiator at Vienna, Yuli Vorontsov, who held the rank of first deputy foreign minister.

Because of the lack of breakthrough, Gorbachev launched a new initiative on February 28. Reversing his position at Reykjavik, he called for urgent negotiation of a separate agreement on intermediate-range nuclear missiles. He accompanied this with the promise that once agreement on intermediate-range missiles was reached, the Soviet Union would withdraw its shorter-range missiles from East Germany and Czechoslovakia. In April, he further modified his proposal by indicating that the Soviet Union would eliminate all shorter-range missiles from Europe as part of an agreement on intermediate-range missiles. He was also quoted by TASS at this time as saying that he was ready to meet Reagan in order to "conclude" a treaty on intermediate-range missiles and to reach agreement on "key provisions" regarding strategic offensive arms, space defense, arms, and nuclear tests.

Negotiations between the two countries continued over the summer of 1987 but became stalled when the Soviet side insisted that West Germany's 72 Pershing 1A missiles (with US-controlled warheads) had to be included in the deal. This obstacle was removed in August when West German Chancellor Kohl agreed conditionally to dismantle the Pershing 1A missiles. It took a visit to Washington by Foreign Minister Shevardnadze in September and a visit of Secretary of State Shultz to Moscow in October, but the result was a draft agreement banning intermediate-range (and Soviet shorter-range) missiles, known as the INF agreement. It was this INF agreement that General Secretary Gorbachev signed when he made his first visit to the United States on December 8–11, 1987.

The successful conclusion of the INF treaty did not, as it turned out, provide enough momentum for agreement on strategic arms in time for President Reagan's visit to the USSR on May 29–June 2, 1988. As a result, the Moscow summit was largely ceremonial, though not less important for that reason.

Negotiations on strategic arms continued, but no agreement was reached, partly because of the change of American administrations and partly because of the complexity of the subject. There were other major developments in this area, however. The most important of these came in December 1988, when Gorbachev, during an address to the United Nations General Assembly, announced that the USSR would make unilateral cuts of 500,000 troops and 10,000 tanks, with 50,000 troops and 5,000 tanks to be pulled out of Eastern

Presidents Gorbachev and Bush at dinner aboard the Soviet Ship *Gorky*, off Malta, December 1989

Europe. He also promised that, in addition to the tanks, other equipment used in an attack, including river-bridging equipment would also be withdrawn.

The new Conventional Forces in Europe (CFE) talks—the enlarged version of the old MBFR talks—also began in Vienna in March 1989. The talks went very well from the beginning for it was the Soviet Union which proposed eliminating "imbalances and asymmetries" over a period of two years. Since they had an overwhelming advantage in ground equipment, their proposal meant that the Soviet Union would have to eliminate about 10 tanks for each tank eliminated by NATO.

The Soviet plan also suggested "equal collective ceilings which would be 10 to 15% lower than the lowest level possessed by either of the politico-military alliances." The ceiling proposed by NATO had been only slightly higher than this.

Finally, the Soviets also acknowledged the need for "the most stringent and rigorous verification, including inspections without right of refusal," thus meeting yet another of NATO's concerns.

A further significant breakthrough came in May 1989 when Gorbachev announced that the Warsaw Pact was prepared to withdraw from Eastern Europe 40,000 of 58,470 tanks, 42,000 out of 70,330 armored vehicles and 47,000 out of 71,500 artillery pieces, and finally that it was willing to "make similar reductions in manpower and other types of weaponry." This was precisely the area of NATO's greatest concern and, therefore, Gorbachev's offer was accepted with enthusiasm.

Two weeks later, President Bush, at a NATO summit in Brussels, proposed an equal ceiling of 275,000 troops which the two superpowers would be permitted to station in Europe outside their own territory and suggested that the CFE talks be expanded to include helicopters and land-based combat planes. He further called for demobilization of all troops to be withdrawn and for destruction of all equipment thus removed. Bush also suggested that it would "be possible to reach agreement in six months or even a year."

Since the Soviets had earlier suggested troop reductions and had wanted to include combat aircraft in the discussions all along, they welcomed President Bush's proposals. The CFE talks subsequently became stalled, however, partly because of the political changes that occurred in Eastern Europe in 1989. With non-communist leaderships in power throughout the region and with the German Democratic Republic moving toward unification with the Federal Republic of Germany, the old political basis of the Warsaw Pact no longer existed. In addition, the Soviet Union had agreed to withdraw its troops from Hungary and Czechoslovakia by the end of 1991 and those in Germany and Poland by 1994.

The CFE Treaty was initialed in November 1990 at a meeting of the CSCE. Shortly afterward, the Soviet armed forces leadership reclassified three divisions as naval forces and claimed that these divisions were not covered by the CFE, since naval forces had not been included in the discussions. The United States and other western nations objected and the treaty was put on hold. The disagreement was resolved in May 1991 when Gorbachev sent General Mikhail Moiseyev, the chief of the Soviet Staff, to Washington, DC, to work out a compromise. The compromise stipulated that the three divisions could be excluded from overall figures, provided commensurate reductions were made in forces not originally covered by the agreement.

Two months later, the US and the Soviet Union announced that they had reached agreement on a START Agreement and that it would be signed at the end of July when President Bush traveled to Moscow for a Summit Conference with President Gorbachev. The agreement, signed on July 31, 1991, required the two signatories to reduce the number of nuclear warheads to 6,000 each, though an involved method of counting raised this figure by about one-third. Nevertheless, it was the first treaty to achieve actual reductions in the number of nuclear weapons on each side. This was, it turned out, Gorbachev's swansong. Less than three weeks later, conservative communists tried to oust him in a coup. Although the coup was defeated, it discredited the Communist Party and led to the collapse of the Soviet Union a little over four months later.

An Independent Russia Is Reborn

Gorbachev still thought to save the union, even if under another name and with reduced powers, but it was not to be. By the end of August, 9 of the 15 republics were committed to independence. With the three Baltic Republics already receiving international recognition, Gorbachev called a special session of the Congress of People's Deputies for September 2. After three days of debate, the Congress accepted Gorbachev's proposal for the creation of a new interim government whose chief purpose would be to negotiate a new union treaty.

Gorbachev remained president of this new interim government, but final executive authority was lodged in a state council made up of Gorbachev and the leaders of the participating republics. A separate inter-republic economic committee, appointed by the state council, assumed the economic functions of the former Council of Ministers. Finally, a two-chamber legislature was established, the membership of the second chamber to be appointed by and represent the governments of the individual republics. In this chamber, voting would be by delegation, with each republic having one vote.

From the beginning, only 10 of the republics participated in the interim government. The first act of the state council was to recognize the independence of the Baltic Republics. Moldova refused to participate at all and Georgia sent only observers. In addition, over the next several days, all of the remaining republics other than the Russian Federation, Kazakhstan and Turkmenistan declared their independence. Later, even Kazakhstan and Turkmenistan would join the list.

Gorbachev knew that his new interim government existed on sufferance and that Boris Yeltsin's support was the first requisite. Gorbachev therefore dismissed all of his former advisers and accepted Yeltsin's advice on the make-up of his new government. He thus surrounded himself with liberals. He even appointed Ivan Silayev, prime minister of the Russian Federation, as chairman of the inter-republic economic committee, a post that effectively made him the caretaker prime minister of the union government.

Determined to save some form of union, he asked the reform economist Grigory Yavlinsky to draw up a plan for economic union and he and the state council began working on a plan for a new political union. Yavlinsky's draft for a new economic union was submitted to the state council in late September and won general approval. It was then submitted to the individual republics in October.

Most of the republics accepted the language of the economic union treaty, but the big exception was the Republic of Ukraine. Opposition was centered in the Ukrainian parliament, which drew up two pages of objections. The parliament demanded the right to set up an independent Ukrainian national bank, to issue a separate Ukrainian currency and, in general, to control its own fiscal policy. Later that same month, the Ukrainian parliament withdrew the mandate from its delegates to the USSR Council of the Republic and instructed them to participate as observers.

It came as no surprise, then, when the Republic of Ukraine decided to boycott the November 14 session of the state council, called to consider Gorbachev's draft for a new union treaty. In the event, only seven republics gave their preliminary approval to a new treaty creating a "Union

Russia

**President Reagan and General Secretary Gorbachev,
Reykjavik, Iceland, October 11, 1986**

of Sovereign States." Two weeks later, the state council met again, supposedly to initial the draft agreement. Instead, they voted to submit it to the individual republic legislatures for approval, a process that put the proposed treaty into severe jeopardy.

Up to this point, Boris Yeltsin had consistently maintained that he favored a continuation of the union. But he had also said that he could not envisage a union without the Ukraine. Yet Leonid Kravchuk, the Ukrainian leader, said on November 12 that he would "never sign" a treaty which contained "even the slightest hint of certain governing central bodies" and he had refused to participate in discussions in the state council on the new union treaty.

Yeltsin's own actions during this time indicate that he was also having second thoughts about the advisability of maintaining a strong center. At the end of October, he took over as his own prime minister and then announced that Russia would unilaterally begin a sweeping program of economic reform that included freeing prices, privatizing industry and land, and creating a strong Russian currency. He requested the Russian parliament to grant him the power to suspend Soviet laws that "hamper economic reforms." He also announced that, effective November 15, the Russian government would no longer finance union ministries which it did not utilize.

Yeltsin's program got the Russian parliament's endorsement on November 1. Two weeks later, he assumed control of Soviet diamonds and gold production and took charge of issuing oil export licenses. He followed this up with another decree taking over the remaining structures of the Soviet finance ministry, including its controls over foreign currency. This was accompanied by an announcement that Russia would no longer be responsible for any new debts incurred by the union government.

In effect, Yeltsin had begun a unilateral dismantling of the central government. This was carried a step further at the end of the month when Yeltsin stepped in and offered to finance the Soviet payroll after the central government had run out of funds. An integral part of the agreement was that Yeltsin henceforth controlled the union budget. He used his new power to order most central ministries to be closed.

Very little of the central government remained on December 1 when the Ukrainian people went to the polls to elect a new president and to vote on a referendum on independence. Leonid Kravchuk won the presidential race with 61.5% of the vote. Nearly 90% of all Ukrainians voted yes on independence.

"The independence of the Ukraine is a new political reality," commented Boris Yeltsin upon receiving the results of the Ukrainian vote. Yeltsin recognized that the draft union treaty drawn up by Gorbachev was dead, but he still felt that some kind of coordinating mechanism was necessary to handle the many problems of the now-separating republics. He therefore contacted President Kravchuk and Stanislav Shushkevich, president of Belarus, and suggested that the three presidents meet the following weekend to discuss the future. Shushkevich agreed to host the meeting and offered the use of a hunting lodge located not far from the Belarusian city of Brest. "We came to the conclusion," Shushkevich commented after the meeting, "that we had to sort out the concept of the kind of union we are capable of building."

The three leaders talked for two days, December 7–8. At the end of the second day, they returned to Minsk, where they signed an agreement creating a "Commonwealth of Independent States." Its most significant clause stated that "the USSR has ceased to exist as a subject of international law and as a geopolitical reality." This was, in effect, the Russian Federation's declaration of independence. Eight other republics—the sole holdout was Georgia—joined the CIS at a conference in Alma-Ata on December 21.

Gorbachev resigned as president of the USSR on December 25, turning the Kremlin and authority over the Soviet Union's nuclear arsenal to Boris Yeltsin. The Russian Federation succeeded to the Soviet Union's membership in the United Nations and its seat on the Security Council.

Boris Yeltsin Remakes the Russian State

Economic Reform

Boris Yeltsin launched his economic reform on January 2, 1992. One important aspect of this reform was the elimination of price controls, which resulted in an extremely high rate of inflation. Yeltsin also wanted to privatize quickly state-owned enterprises. Over the next several months, his government was mainly occupied with the implementation of that program, assuming the Soviet Union's international obligations, including its various diplomatic missions abroad, and carrying on negotiations with the other members of the CIS over economic relations and the future of the Soviet military forces. The republics had agreed to maintain strategic and nuclear forces under a single command, but three republics, Ukraine, Moldova, and Azerbaijan, opted from the beginning to establish their own national armies. Plans for a unified command under the CIS for the remaining forces were gradually discarded as the remaining republics moved toward creating their own national armies.

The original CIS agreement called for the republics to maintain a single economic space, but that proved impossible in practice. One problem was that the other republics wanted to buy more from Russia than it needed to buy from them. As a result, Russia had built up a positive balance of 1.2 trillion rubles with the other republics by the end of 1992. The Russian government abandoned its commitment to maintaining a single ruble zone for the CIS about the middle of 1992. In view of the growing trade imbalance coupled with Moscow's perception that the governments of the other republics were not doing enough to control spending, the Russian government began limiting the number of rubles they were willing to make available to the other republics and it began encouraging the other republics to develop their own currencies. Most eventually moved to do so, though in a number of cases "coupons" rather than a new currency were authorized.

A number of the other republics complained about the speed of Russia's economic reform, particularly the wide-ranging freeing of prices, but most grudgingly went along with it. At home, however, Yeltsin soon found that a majority of the members of the Supreme Soviet were also appalled at the speed of the reform. Even though they had, in December 1991, granted Yeltsin the right to rule by decree for the period of one year, by June 1992 they were strongly attacking his program and doing what they could to frustrate it or slow it down. Between June and December, they undermined his economic reform mainly through an enormous increase in credit, accomplished through taking control of the Russian State Bank. And in those same months, Speaker Ruslan Khasbulatov emerged as the chief spokesman for the anti-reform majority in the Supreme Soviet.

This raises an important question, for Khasbulatov had been elected chairman in 1991 with the support of reformers associated with Yeltsin; further, he had stood at Yeltsin's side in August 1991 in opposition to the attempted coup. Why did he

now abandon his former allies and throw in his lot with many of the same individuals he had opposed in August 1991? It appears clear that he did it, not primarily for ideological reasons, but because his own position was threatened. Khasbulatov was elected in 1990 to represent the autonomous republic of Chechnya. Since that time, Chechnya had declared its independence and was attempting to secede from Russia. An extremely ambitious individual, Khasbulatov's one chance for continued power on the national level was if secessionist movements were put down resolutely.

Thus he made common cause with a coalition of ex-communists and Russian nationalists dreaming about a restoration of the old Soviet Empire. Because he was an able man and a facile speaker, his joining the parliamentary opposition to President Yeltsin gave that grouping more success than it would have been able to achieve on its own.

That became clear in December 1992, when the Congress of People's Deputies met to decide what policy to take toward President Yeltsin and his reforms. At issue was whether to extend President Yeltsin's power to name his own government ministers and to issue decrees with the force of law. Under the leadership of Speaker Khasbulatov, the Congress failed by a narrow four votes to pass a constitutional amendment that would have stripped President Yeltsin of most of his powers. The Congress then voted a resolution condemning Acting Prime Minister Yegor Gaidar's reform program and calling his methods of work unsatisfactory. They subsequently rejected Yegor Gaidar as prime minister.

President Yeltsin stalked out of the Congress; he then threatened to organize a referendum on his policy of economic reform. Apparently frightened by the possibilities inherent in such a referendum, the Congress leaders proposed additional talks with Yeltsin. Valeri Zorkin, chairman of Russia's constitutional court, also offered his services as an honest broker during any talks. The result was a compromise whereby Yeltsin would retain his decree-issuing powers for another four months while a nationwide referendum on a new constitution would be scheduled for April. In return, President Yeltsin agreed to nominate as prime minister a person acceptable to the Congress. The Congress's choice fell on Viktor Chernomyrdin, a centrist who had been vice prime minister for oil and gas production since July. Chernomyrdin was undoubtedly a disappointment to the Congressional majority, however, for he continued the basic thrust of Gaidar's economic program.

Frustrated in its attempts to put an end to economic reform, the Supreme Soviet

continued its attacks on Yeltsin and his government. In addition, a majority of the Supreme Soviet began having second thoughts about a referendum which might lead to a new constitution and new elections which might see them removed from office. Things came to a head in February 1993 when Speaker Khasbulatov denounced the idea of a referendum. A few days later, Valeri Zorkin added his voice in opposition to a referendum. In addition, the leaders of Russia's regional governments, meeting with Yeltsin on February 9, told him that a referendum might lead to an explosion in the country. Faced with this widespread opposition, Yeltsin backed down and agreed to postpone the referendum indefinitely—provided a power-sharing arrangement could be reached with Khasbulatov and the Supreme Soviet. Yeltsin and Khasbulatov finally reached an agreement of sorts, subject to approval by the Congress of People's Deputies, which was reconvened on March 10.

But the full Congress was not in a mood to compromise. Rejecting Khasbulatov's efforts, the Congress voted to severely limit Yeltsin's right to rule by decree and canceled the referendum scheduled for April. Yeltsin temporized for seven days; he then went on national television on March 20 to announce that he would organize his own referendum to take place on April 25. The Russian people would be asked to cast a vote of confidence on his presidency and to approve a new constitution that would serve as a basis for new elections. In the meantime, Yeltsin added, he planned to ignore the Supreme Soviet and rule by decree.

Vice President Aleksandr Rutskoi and Valeri Zorkin, chairman of Russia's constitutional court, immediately denounced Yeltsin's plan as unconstitutional. On the other hand, at an emergency meeting of the Supreme Soviet the next day, the prime minister and the defense, security and interior ministers all threw their support behind Yeltsin. The Supreme Soviet then requested the constitutional court to rule on Yeltsin's plan. The court declared Yeltsin's decree to be unlawful on the basis of his television speech, since it had not yet received a copy of the decree itself. On that basis, Khasbulatov called for Yeltsin's impeachment and the Supreme Soviet voted to convene the Congress of People's Deputies on March 26.

A motion to impeach was supported by a majority of the Congress members voting, but fell 72 votes short of the two-thirds vote necessary to convict. Having failed to impeach Yeltsin, the Congress acceded to the idea of a referendum, but demanded that four questions be submitted to the people instead of Yeltsin's two: "Do you have confidence in the president? Do you approve

Russia

of the socioeconomic policy carried out by president and government in 1992? Do you think early presidential elections are necessary? And do you think early parliamentary elections are necessary?"

The Congress further stipulated that Yeltsin would have to win the votes of a majority of all registered voters on the first two questions in order to claim a popular mandate. Such a stipulation would have been almost impossible to obtain. In 1991, Yeltsin won 57% of all votes cast but that constituted only 42% of registered voters. The constitutional court subsequently ruled that Yeltsin could claim a victory on the first two questions if he won a majority of votes cast, but that the last two questions were constitutional and required the support of a majority of all registered voters to be binding.

In the event, Yeltsin won a 57.4% approval on the first question and 53.7% on the second. On the third question, 49.1% favored immediate presidential elections; however, 70.6% voted in favor of immediate parliamentary elections. Nevertheless, this constituted only 44.8% of the registered electorate, so it was not legally binding.

Yeltsin had won only a battle, not the war. Speaker Khasbulatov dismissed the voting results as meaningless and divisive and announced that neither he nor the Congress of People's Deputies were prepared to accept the results as decisive. Vice President Rutskoi, for his part, argued that:

there can be no talk of overall popular support. Those who said 'no' or remained silent are also Russian citizens, and we have to ask ourselves why they did so.

Rutskoi later added:

There is no popular support. That is why all these reform policies should be changed.

Yeltsin's reaction to his victory was predictably different. Saying that the referendum had created "a fundamentally new political situation" which required a new constitution, he summoned the political leaders from Russia's regions and republics to Moscow in April. Here he presented them with copies of a new draft constitution. Yeltsin proposed that each region and republic examine the draft and submit comments to him within a month. He asked them also to appoint two delegates to a constituent assembly which would convene to complete work on the document.

This procedure, not specified anywhere in the old Soviet constitution—which gave the power to amend to the Congress of People's Deputies—was Yeltsin's attempt to circumvent the opposition of the Congress of People's Deputies. The

585-member constituent assembly met for about a month. After closely examining and modifying the constitution, they approved it by a better than two-thirds majority and sent it on to President Yeltsin. He then submitted it to the 88 republics and regions for their approval.

As this was going on, the Supreme Soviet took up the government's draft budget and proceeded to gut it. Declaring that the budget was "anti-social," they increased spending to 40 trillion rubles ($40 billion), which according to the chairman of the Supreme Soviet's own budget committee would have meant a budget deficit of 25% of GDP. That would have destroyed the government's reform program entirely and unleashed hyperinflation. Not content with that, the Supreme Soviet tried to sabotage the privatization program of the government by voting to cancel a presidential decree requiring state-owned firms to swap at least 20% of their shares for privatization vouchers. Instead, it announced that from October these vouchers could be replaced by "privatization accounts" at the government-owned savings bank. Cutting short his holiday, President Yeltsin returned to Moscow and issued a new decree guaranteeing that privatization would continue. There was little he could legally do about the budget, however. He could veto it, but his veto could be overruled by a two-thirds vote in the Supreme Soviet.

President Yeltsin did, in fact, veto the budget twice over the next month and a half, but the Supreme Soviet was preparing to pass it for a third time on September 22. It was this which finally caused President Yeltsin, on the evening of September 21, to go on television to announce that the Russian parliament had been disbanded and that elections to a new parliament would take place on December 11–12. Within an hour, the rump Supreme Soviet, under Ruslan Khasbulatov's leadership, voted to strip Yeltsin of his powers, then installed Aleksandr Rutskoi, the vice president, as a rival president.

In the succeeding confrontation, Prime Minister Chernomyrdin and his cabinet, plus the police and the army, remained loyal to Yeltsin. The stand-off continued for nearly two weeks. The parliamentary forces, refusing to disband, barricaded themselves in the parliament building and began to collect arms. Yeltsin first surrounded the building with a cordon of police; he then ordered that electricity, heat, and water be cut off from the building.

Things turned violent on the night of October 3, when a mob broke through the police cordon and entered the parliament building. Urged on by Vice President Rutskoi, the mob attempted to seize Ostankino, the main television building. A number of television channels were

knocked off the air, but the mob never managed to gain control of the entire building.

President Yeltsin then called on the army to restore order and after some hesitation they agreed to do so. The first tanks arrived at the parliament building at 5:20 the next morning. They opened fire on the parliament building. According to official government data, 146 people were killed in this bombardment of the parliament, though the real number of victims may have been higher. Army troops then occupied the parliament and rounded up the last of the defenders. Khasbulatov and Rutskoi were arrested and imprisoned. That cleared the way for the December parliamentary elections. President Yeltsin set them for December 12 and enlarged the scope of the vote by specifying that the Russian people would also vote in a referendum on a new constitution and elect new regional and local councils.

December 1993 Elections

The results of the elections were a disappointment for the reformers, however. Although the people approved the new constitution, that was the last good news. It was the elections to the State Duma, the lower house of the Federal Assembly, that were the most disappointing. There were 450 seats to be filled, half by proportional representation and half by first-past-the-post voting. The largest vote getter for the proportional seats was the badly misnamed Liberal Democratic Party of Vladimir Zhirinovsky, the ultra-nationalist leader, which got 22% of the vote. The reform party of Yegor Gaidar, Russia's Choice, came in second with 20%.

Because Zhirinovsky's party did poorly in the first-past-the-post voting, however, Russia's Choice was the largest party in the State Duma with 76 seats. The New Regional Policy faction, formed after the election by individuals who had run without a party label, was second with 65 seats. The third-largest faction was Zhirinovsky's Liberal Democratic Party with 63 seats. Other parties included the Agrarian Party (53 seats), the Communist Party (45 seats), the Party of Russian Unity and Accord (30 seats), Yabloko (25 seats), Women of Russia (23 seats), and the Democratic Party of Russia (15 seats). The remaining 35 seats were held by independents not affiliated with any party.

That makes the result sound better than it actually was, however. Except for Yabloko, the party of reform economist Grigory Yavlinsky, nearly every one of the remaining parties was cool to reform; together they controlled a majority of the seats in the State Duma. Reflecting this fact, the man they selected as their speaker was Ivan Rybkin, a member of the Agrarian Party.

Russia

The situation in the Federation Council, the upper house of the Federal Assembly, was more positive for Yeltsin. Here a majority of the members supported reform. Vladimir Shumeiko, the Speaker, was a former deputy chairman of the Russian Council of Ministers.

One of the powers given to the State Duma in the new constitution is the right to grant amnesty. One of the first things the State Duma did after it met was to declare an amnesty to all those involved in the August 1991 and October 1993 attempted coups. This was widely seen as a rebuke to President Yeltsin, though it did have the advantage of cutting short what was turning into a long political trial.

Despite a stormy beginning, relations between the government and the legislature subsequently settled down into a form of cohabitation that occasionally became even cooperation. The best sign of this was the peace accord which President Yeltsin managed to get most of the factions in the State Duma to sign in the spring of 1994 giving the government two years of calm to focus on economic recovery.

War in Chechnya

That truce largely came to an end in December 1994 after President Yeltsin authorized the military to send troops into Chechnya to put down a separatist movement there. Curiously, however, it was his former supporters among the reformers who led the attack against the intervention. In January, the State Duma passed a resolution supporting a political solution in Chechnya and calling on the government to "take all necessary measures" to bring an end to the fighting. The resolution was in the form of a recommendation to the president, however, and lacked the force of law. Only 172 out of 450 members voted for a separate resolution which would have barred the army from fighting in domestic conflicts. Yet even those who objected to the use of force in Chechnya made it clear that they considered Chechnya to be an integral part of Russia.

Much the same was true of international opinion. Although the US government accused Russia of violating international agreements by failing to notify other countries about large-scale troop movements into Chechnya, it was also clear that it considered Chechnya to be strictly an internal affair.

The drop in Yeltsin's domestic and international popularity was not surprising. Most people were appalled by the news stories coming out of Chechnya and reacted accordingly. The decline would undoubtedly have been temporary had the Russian military been able to restore order in Chechnya and bring all fighting to an end. Unfortunately, this was not the

President Boris Yeltsin shares microphones with Chairman Ruslan Khasbulatov
Courtesy of NOVOSTI

case. In fact, General Dudayev managed to maintain a guerilla force in the mountainous areas of southern Chechnya and had twice showed—through terrorist raids on Russian hospitals in Budyonnovsk in June 1995 and in Kizlyar in January 1996—that he could make the Russian occupation of Chechnya costly.

December 1995 Elections

Yet the results of the legislative elections which took place in December 1995, though clearly not favorable to either President Yeltsin or his government, indicated that political opinion had changed very little since the previous elections in December 1993. The first thing about these elections was the extreme political fragmentation as each ambitious politician, it seemed, founded his own political party as a vehicle for his pretensions. Ultimately, 43 parties, blocs, and movements contested them. This proved to be self-defeating for a party needing a minimum showing of 5% of the national vote to enter the Duma on a party list. Since it was the liberal reformers who had splintered the most—often concentrating their venom on other reformers during the campaign—their final representation showed the greatest drop. The more disciplined Communist Party of Russia was the runaway winner with 22.3% of the vote—up 10 percentage points from 1993. Vladimir Zhirinovsky's ultra-nationalist Liberal Democratic Party came in second with 11%—though that was only half what the party had gotten in 1993. The only other parties to surmount

the 5% barrier were two reform parties, Our Home Is Russia, the party of Prime Minister Viktor Chernomyrdin, which came in third with 10%, and Yabloko, the liberal reformist party of Grigory Yavlinsky with 7%. Since only these four parties entered parliament on a party list, almost 50% of the votes were wasted because they had been cast for parties that failed to enter parliament on party lists.

Since only half of the seats were filled by party vote, the remainder being single-seat constituencies, there were several additional parties represented in the Duma. These included the Agrarians (21 seats), Power to the People (10 seats), Russia's Democratic Choice (10 seats), Congress of Russian Communists (5 seats) and Women of Russia (3 seats). A number of additional parties won one or two seats, and 76 individuals won as independents. Finally, the Communist Party of Russia won 58 single-constituency seats, Our Home Is Russia won 10 seats, Yabloko won 14 seats, and the Liberal Democrats won 1 single-constituency seat.

When parliament convened in January, it proved to be dominated by the Communists. Although they held only 149 out of the 450 seats themselves, they had a voting strength of 212 seats because of the support of a large number of individuals who ran and won as independents, meaning that they were just 14 seats short of a majority. After a stiff fight, they managed to elect one of their own, Gennadiy Seleznyov, a former editor of *Pravda*, as the new speaker of the Duma. They also obtained the chairmanships of more than a

Russia

third of the committees, including almost half of the major committees.

Although the position of the Communists was that economic reform has been a failure and should be ended, they were able, in fact, to find a lot of common ground with the government following the elections. One reason for this is that President Yeltsin also drew his own conclusions from the election results and essentially put economic reform on hold. Even more important, he got rid of the remaining reformers in his administration, replacing them with individuals more acceptable to the new majority in the Duma. Those departing included Anatoly Chubais, who as first deputy prime minister in charge of economic policy had been in charge of privatization, Sergei Shakrai, also a deputy prime minister, and Andrei Kozyrev, foreign minister.

But these dismissals were probably more symbolic than anything else, since all were ultimately implementers of Yeltsin policies rather than independent figures in their own right. More importantly, everyone understood that Yeltsin's term of office would expire in less than six months and that it would be the winner of the June 1996 elections who would determine the future course of government policy.

1996 Presidential Elections

The major candidates in the presidential race were Yeltsin, Gennady Zyuganov,

the Communist leader; Grigory Yavlinsky, founder of Yabloko; Vladimir Zhirinovsky, leader of the Liberal Democrats; and General Alexander Lebed, a Russian nationalist considered to be somewhat more moderate than Zhirinovsky.

From the beginning, Zyuganov was the favorite in the polls, first of all because the Communists had the best party organization and, secondly, because of the Communist Party's victory in the December 1995 Duma elections. Yeltsin, technically not a member of any party, had the additional disability of being the incumbent responsible for the dismal economic situation, the violent showdown with parliament in 1993, and the continuing Chechen conflict. Even he admitted that he could not be elected if the Chechen conflict were not settled by June. Another factor arguing for a Zyuganov win was that the Communists had no competitors on the left, while Zhirinovsky and Lebed were competing for the nationalist vote and Yeltsin and Yavlinsky were dividing the reform vote. Zyuganov was not expected to win a majority of the vote in the first round of voting, however; the important question, therefore, was who would come in second—and so get to run against Zyuganov in the second round.

From the beginning, Yeltsin's strategy was to win enough votes to come in second. Sensing that most Russian voters

wanted stability most of all, he told the electorate that the reforms had accomplished their purpose and now it was time for consolidation, not change. To make this point even clearer, he dismissed all of the reformers in the government and promised new, costly social programs that would benefit pensioners and others hurt by the collapse of the old command system. Reformers were extremely critical of him in the beginning, but he picked up the endorsement of a number of prominent reformers after they had pondered the various alternatives. He also picked up a surprise endorsement from the Women of Russia party and had the support of Our Home Is Russia, the party founded by Prime Minister Chernomyrdin.

Yeltsin's chances improved in March when the Communists pushed through a resolution in the Duma declaring the 1991 dissolution of the Soviet Union to be illegal. They almost certainly hurt their case also when they promised that a Communist victory would lead to extensive re-nationalizations and a rebuilding of state control over the economy.

The Russian public was well aware that any attempt to reestablish the Soviet Union was likely to result in many more Chechnyas. Except for Belarus, a Communist victory would have been viewed with dismay throughout the region and any attempt to recreate the Soviet Union would have been opposed. Even the various Central Asian republics, though they had rebuilt some of the military and economic connections with Russia that existed prior to 1991, made it clear that they wished to retain their political independence and would react negatively to any attempt to bring them under Moscow's control. All of the Caucasus republics felt the same way.

Yeltsin evidently read the Russian populace correctly. When the election finally took place, Yeltsin came in first with 35% of the vote to Zyuganov's 32%. The third-place winner was General Alexander Lebed, with 15% of the vote. Zhirinovsky and Yavlinsky trailed much further behind.

Courted by both sides, Lebed decided to throw his support to Yeltsin. Since the choice was now either Yeltsin or the Communists, the rest of the reformers came aboard as well. Yeltsin won in the second round with approximately 54% of the vote to Zyuganov's 41%. The remaining ballots were cast "against" both candidates.

Yeltsin was a very ill man during the electoral campaign. In fact, he suffered his fourth heart attack between the two rounds of election. The malady was kept from the public, which was only told that Yeltsin had a head cold. After he triumphed in the second round, his administration announced that he needed a

The Russian weekly, *Arguments and Facts*, predicts the outcome of the April 1993 referendum. Pictured are President Yeltsin and Ruslan Khasbulatov, chairman of the Russian Federation's Supreme Soviet

Russia

heart bypass operation. The only positive development during those months was that Yeltsin named General Lebed as his security adviser and Lebed used this authority to negotiate an end to the war in Chechnya. Yeltsin had a successful heart bypass operation on November 5, receiving five arterial grafts. Almost immediately after returning to work in January 1997, however, he developed pneumonia. Though this was apparently not directly connected to his heart bypass operation, it incapacitated him for a further six weeks.

Little got done in the government during the several months that he was ill. Prime Minister Chernomyrdin, supposedly in charge, ran the day-to-day affairs of government but he was no leader. Meanwhile the Duma, dominated by Communists and nationalists, attempted to take control of the country's agenda, and there were repeated calls for Yeltsin's resignation.

Economic Reform II: A "New Economic Order"

The calls ceased soon after Yeltsin's return in March, however, for he soon made it clear who was in charge. Moreover, Yeltsin had clearly decided that further reform was needed to deal with such continuing economic problems as the widespread failure of employees to be paid on time. He therefore brought Anatoly Chubais back into the government as first deputy prime minister, even though he was aware that Chubais had few friends in the Duma. Significant but symbolic as well, he appointed Boris Nemtsov as the other first deputy prime minister. Nemtsov, governor of Nizhny Novgorod province for the previous five years, had been among the first regional leaders to privatize small business enterprises and to promote land reform. As a result, Nizhny Novgorod, a closed city under the Soviets, had come to boast a fashionable pedestrian shopping mall, a glittery trade fair, a Coca-Cola bottling plant, a branch office of the accounting firm Price Waterhouse, and regular service by Lufthansa Airlines. Yeltsin was obviously hoping that Nemtsov could do something similar for the country. In any case, Yeltsin's selection of Nemtsov was undoubtedly a good political move, for the youthful Nemtsov was quite popular with the Russian people and provided a good "public face" for reform.

Over the summer, Chubais and Nemtsov pushed policies designed to lower the rate of inflation, (which had reached an annual rate of 2600% in 1992) pay off pension arrears, and carry out the sale of Svyazinvest, Russia's large telecommunications company. Their policies had some positive effect, but it became increasingly clear as time went by that some larger measures would be necessary to get the Russian economy growing again.

Russia's parliament building—The White House   Courtesy of NOVOSTI

Yeltsin sought to spell out just what was still needed in an address to the Federation Council, the Russian parliament's upper house, in September 1997. The message was an interesting one, for Yeltsin essentially pledged to put an end to the era of free-wheeling crony capitalism that had come in with the fall of communism in 1991. What was needed, Yeltsin said, was a "new economic order" in which government, not big business, made the rules. The speech, in other words, was an explicit attack on the new industrial barons and bankers who had bankrolled his reelection campaign. However, these same men were now attempting to extend their economic power even further and refusing to pay taxes to the state. This was, undoubtedly, their chief "crime," for the government had recently been able to collect only about 10% of GDP in taxes, which provided an insufficient amount of money to pay back wages and pensions and meet the government's pressing current needs. That same week, Boris Nemtsov reinforced Yeltsin's message when he warned the bosses of Avtovaz, a carmaker, that they had until October 1 to pay their back taxes or see the company forced into bankruptcy.

Two things now occurred that largely derailed reform, however. First, the economic crisis in Asia led to a worldwide decrease in investor confidence that resulted in some significant disinvestment in Russia in the fall of 1997. Second, Anatoly Chubais found himself caught up in a scandal when he and a team of colleagues agreed to accept a "publisher's advance" worth $450,000 for a book on privatization from a publishing firm linked to a bank that had made significant profits from participating in a number of privatizations overseen by Mr. Chubais. To his enemies, the "publisher's advance" looked like a bribe or a payoff. Chubais offered his resignation as first deputy prime minister and minister of finance on

November 15, but Yeltsin refused it, though he subsequently downgraded Chubais's position in the administration by stripping him of the minister of finance title.

Although President Yeltsin's administration had a few accomplishments over the next three months that he could point to—most salary and pension arrears were paid off by the end of the year and the 1998 budget was finally approved by the Duma in February 1998—this was essentially a period of drift. That came to an end toward the end of March when Yeltsin dismissed Prime Minister Chernomyrdin and his cabinet and appointed Sergei Kirienko, a 35-year-old junior minister, in his place. This also set up a confrontation with the opposition-controlled Duma, which had to confirm Kirienko before he could actually assume the job.

The only explanation that Yeltsin gave for his firing of Chernomyrdin—that he wanted the prime minister to "concentrate on political preparations for the forthcoming election," which would "decide the future of Russia"—didn't satisfy most people, so there were numerous speculations as to the "real" reasons. These ranged from speculations about Yeltsin's failing health to his anger at Chernomyrdin for moving too quickly to establish himself as a candidate for election to the presidency in 2000. None seemed adequate, particularly since they all had in common that they ignored the increasing drift of the previous three months. It appears more likely that Yeltsin, recognizing that this drift was discrediting reform in the minds of Russian voters, decided that some decisive action would have to be taken to get Russia back on track. His gamble was an extremely large one, but he did win the first part of his bet. The Duma, after rejecting Kirienko twice, finally confirmed him as prime minister by a vote of 251 to 25 on April 24. Kirienko needed 226 votes to win.

Russia

Anatoly Chubais   Courtesy of NOVOSTI

It is interesting to note which political parties voted for and against him. Gennady Zyuganov, the Communist Party leader, urged his followers to vote against Kirienko—and they did so during the first two rounds of voting. In the third round of voting, however, a significant number voted to confirm Kirienko. It helped that Duma Speaker Gennadiy Seleznyov, a member of the Communist Party, threw his support to Kirienko in the third round, arguing that "Russia will not forgive us if we sacrifice the State Duma over a nomination for the prime minister." Seleznyov was referring to the fact that, had Kirienko been defeated in the third round of voting, President Yeltsin would have been required by the constitution to dissolve the Duma and call for new elections.

Most members of Our Home Is Russia, the party led by Chernomyrdin, voted for Kirienko, even though a successful Kirienko might have threatened Chernomyrdin's own run for the presidency in 2000. Kirienko had the support of Vladimir Zhirinovsky and his Liberal Democrats, though Zhirinovsky also publicly negotiated for seats in the cabinet in return for his support. No public promises were made to him, though that is not to say that he expected to have no influence in the new government.

Curiously, perhaps the most consistent opponent was Grigory Yavlinsky, along with his Yabloko party. Yavlinsky, a self-billed reformer, had consistently opposed the government from 1993. However, the real reason for opposition to Kirienko was that Yavlinsky planned to run for the presidency in 2000 and a successful reform government would diminish his chances of winning. Yavlinsky and Yabloko refrained from taking part during the third

round of voting to make clear their united opposition to Kirienko.

Kirienko promised to put together a cabinet of technicians who would push through necessary reforms and get the Russian economy growing again, but the specific programs he laid out mainly dealt with additional subsidies for the energy sector. It must be assumed that Kirienko's program was really President Yeltsin's program and that he intended to change directions in order to win greater support for his government.

Political Crisis

If that is indeed the case, then, this time, President Yeltsin gambled and lost, for the Kirienko government was almost immediately overwhelmed by the economic crisis sweeping out of Asia. On August 17, the Kirienko government panicked and announced a series of economic measures that included a devaluation of the currency and a partial repudiation of Russia's massive debt. In response, President Yeltsin dismissed Kirienko as prime minister.

Viktor Chernomyrdin Courtesy of NOVOSTI

President Yeltsin then nominated Viktor Chernomyrdin as prime minister, but this time he did not get his way. A weakened Yeltsin had to agree to appoint a prime minister acceptable to the majority in the Duma. That turned out to be Yevgeny Primakov, an old bureaucrat who had been foreign minister in the two preceding cabinets.

Primakov served as prime minister from September 1998 to May 1999. During that time, the government printed new money to pay back wages of workers, thereby further depressing the value of the ruble. At the same time, the government negotiated with the IMF for several billion dollars' worth of loans. The IMF finally agreed, though primarily to prevent a total economic collapse in Russia. The Duma

approved a reasonably austere 1999 budget at the end of the year, but it continued to press the government to increase spending. Surprisingly, some privatization continued under the Primakov government, though primarily because the government was in desperate need of additional funds.

Primakov did calm the political atmosphere to some extent, since he was personally acceptable to the majority in the Duma. Yet the Duma continued to work on plans to begin impeachment proceedings against President Yeltsin, a step they finally took in May. It also did not help that Yeltsin was hospitalized several times in late 1998 and early 1999 because of a bleeding ulcer and appeared to be acting erratically in those periods when he did reemerge for a few days.

Things came to a head when the Duma leadership announced impeachment proceedings against President Yeltsin, to begin on May 13. The charges against the president included his being responsible for the dissolution of the Soviet Union and for taking unconstitutional actions against the Duma in October 1993. The Duma leadership had been threatening to impeach Yeltsin for months and Prime Minister Primakov had been attempting to negotiate an arrangement whereby the Duma leadership would drop impeachment proceedings in return for a guarantee from Yeltsin that he would allow Primakov's government to remain in power until new parliamentary elections in December. When it had become clear that Primakov had failed, Yeltsin dismissed Primakov as prime minister one day before the impeachment proceedings were to begin.

Gennady Zyuganov   Courtesy of NOVOSTI

President Yeltsin then nominated Sergei V. Stepashin as his candidate for the office of prime minister. Stepashin, whose background was in law enforcement, was an unlikely candidate for the office of prime minister, and most observers assumed that he would never be confirmed by the Duma. But Primakov's removal presented the Duma with a very unpleasant situation; should it vote to remove Yeltsin in impeachment proceedings before it confirmed a new prime minister, there would be no *constitutionally authorized* person available to assume power from Yeltsin upon his removal. Thus, it appeared that the confrontation between the president and the Duma had landed Russia in another crisis.

What happened next was something of an anti-climax, however, for the Duma leadership first opted to proceed with impeachment, then failed to win the required two-thirds majority on behalf of its motion to impeach. Having been frustrated in its attempt to remove Yeltsin, the Duma then voted to confirm Stepashin as prime minister by a lop-sided 298 to 55 on May 19.

Yet, only two months after he had been confirmed by the Duma, Yeltsin dismissed Stepashin as prime minister. Yeltsin never said why he decided to replace Stepashin, but it is suggestive—particularly considering what happened afterward—that Stepashin was fired only hours after he had flown back to Moscow from the Russian province of Dagestan, where Russian forces were fighting to repulse an armed invasion from neighboring Chechnya led by Shamil Basayev, one of Chechnya's more militant Muslim generals. The threat that Basayev represented was the possibility of a general Muslim rebellion against the Russian presence throughout the north Caucasus area.

What appears likely is that Stepashin's advice on Dagestan convinced Yeltsin that he wasn't up to the job of becoming president. This second point is supported by the fact that, when Yeltsin announced that he was nominating Vladimir V. Putin as Stepashin's successor, he praised him as

the person capable of consolidating society, the person who basing himself on the broadest political forces, is capable of ensuring a continuation of reforms in Russia.

Prime Minister Putin

Putin, a former KGB colonel who became associated with St. Petersburg Mayor Anatoly Sobchak, one of the early leaders of Russia's democratic movement, moved to Moscow in 1996 where he served as Yeltsin's deputy chief of staff, then head of the internal intelligence agency, before being named secretary to the Security Council in 1998.

Sergei Kirienko   Courtesy of NOVOSTI

Although little known before being named prime minister, Putin very quickly showed himself to be a force to be reckoned with. From the beginning, he took a hard line toward Chechnya, but he did not push for decisive military action until after a series of bomb attacks in Russian cities were blamed on militants from Chechnya, and even then he did not press for action until the Russian army indicated it was ready to move. Partly because of the bombings in Russian cities, the renewed campaign against Chechnya proved to be immensely popular, so Putin's popularity increased as the Russian military began to extend its control over the republic.

Although he had never stood for public office, Putin also showed himself to have a flair for politics as well. With new parliamentary elections set to take place on December 19, Russia's politicians prepared by building political alliances such as that represented by Fatherland-All Russia, which brought together Yuri Luzhkov, Mayor of Moscow; Aleksandr Yakovlev, governor of St. Petersburg region; Mintimir Shaimiev, boss of Tatarstan; and Yevgeny Primakov, prime minister in 1998–1999. A second, competing, political grouping, Unity, came into existence in September 1999 with the explicit purpose of increasing the political clout of regional leaders, and from the beginning its membership included many of the members of the Federation Council. Then, in November, Prime Minister Putin explicitly endorsed Unity, which then ran on a platform of supporting the government. A third new party, the Union of Rightist Forces, brought together most of Russia's reformers, including Kirienko, Nemtsov, and Gaidar. The Communist Party of Russia also set up an electoral alliance, For Victory, with the Patriots plus a faction of the Agrarians. Shortly before the

Yevgeny Primakov   Courtesy of NOVOSTI

elections, the Fatherland-All Russia bloc announced that it had agreed to "coordinate positions" in the new Duma with the Communist Party of Russia.

Six political parties surmounted the 5% barrier to win proportional representation seats in the December 19 elections. The Communist Party of Russia came in first with 123 seats (67 proportional seats plus 56 single mandate seats). Unity came in second with 72 seats (64 proportional seats plus 8 single mandate seats). Fatherland-All Russia came in third with 67 seats (37 proportional seats plus 30 single mandate seats). The Union of Rightist Forces came in fourth with 29 seats (24 proportional seats plus 5 single mandate seats). Zhirinovsky's Bloc won 18 seats (17 proportional seats plus one single mandate seat). Finally, Yabloko won 16 proportional seats. Eight other political parties entered the new Duma on the basis of winning one or more single mandate seats. Nine single mandate seats were won by Our Home Is Russia, led by Viktor Chernomyrdin, the former prime minister. The other 7 political parties won an additional 10 single mandate seats.

The largest significance of the December 1999 parliamentary elections was that they produced a Duma that was more centrist and reformist. As a result, although the Communist Party of Russia was still the largest party in the Duma, the defeat of its former allies meant that it had become an isolated minority no longer able to dominate the agenda of the Duma. This fact was obscured but not negated when Putin, in January 2000, brokered a deal for a division of the leadership positions in the Duma between Unity and the Communist Party of Russia that resulted in a communist, Gennadiy Seleznyov, being elected speaker. As it turned out, this agreement dealt only with process and not program. Putin subsequently negotiated agreements

Russia

with the smaller reform parties in which the government committed itself to support tax reform, passage of a land code, a labor law, and legislation limiting the right of legislators to immunity from criminal prosecution. Most of this program had already been achieved by the spring of 2001.

The Putin Presidency

Yeltsin's decision to resign as president as of December 31, 1999, made Vladimir Putin acting president and guaranteed that new presidential elections would have to take place within three months. They actually took place on March 26. Although eleven candidates competed in the election, Putin won in the first round of voting, garnering an impressive 52.5% of the vote—a 22% spread between himself and Gennady Zyuganov, the number two candidate, who polled just under 30%.

Putin was formally inaugurated as president in May and named Mikhail Kasyanov, his former deputy prime minister, as the new prime minister. Putin had not put forth any comprehensive program prior to his election, but he remedied that situation shortly after his inauguration—first of all, through the people he selected as members of the cabinet. Although Putin retained several ministers from his earlier cabinet, he placed liberals in charge of all the traditional top economic posts—finance, tax, and labor—and then created a fourth economic ministry—economic development.

In the following year, this group of ministers shepherded a new tax code through the Duma that created a 13% flat tax on all incomes. The flat tax was well received and greatly increased government revenues from income taxes. A new land code setting up procedures for the sale of non-agricultural land was passed by the Duma in March 2001.

In November 2001, the Duma passed a reform of the judicial code which, in addition to extending professional requirements for judges and establishing norms for disciplinary and criminal responsibility, mandated the nationwide establishment of jury trials by January 2003 for cases involving crimes such as murder and rape. Based on the experience of regions such as Inanovo, Moscow, and Saratov oblasts, where jury trials had been in use since 1993, the Duma passed follow-up legislation in July 2002 which made 3,500 changes in the criminal code aimed at making jury trials work better. Three of the most important reforms incorporated in the new legislation included the fundamental concept of presumption of innocence, the right to habeas corpus (i.e., anyone accused of a crime must be charged in

Vladimir V. Putin: president 2000–2008; prime minister 2008–2012; president 2012–

court within 48 hours), and a new role for the judge as a neutral arbitrator (not as a prosecutor's helper, his role under the old Soviet code). These reforms were gradually implemented over the remainder of 2002 and jury trials resumed formally in 61 Russian regions as of January 2003.

Through his appointments and subsequent actions, Putin established that he was, in some respects, an economic liberal. But it also became clear that, politically, he was a conservative. Although he always insisted that he was a democrat, the policies he pursued as president made clear that there was a strong streak of authoritarianism in his make-up. That became even more evident after his reelection in 2004.

The first of those policies, announced within days of assuming the presidency, was the division of Russia into seven federal administrative districts and the appointment of seven presidential representatives to head these new administrative districts. Putin intended that these seven men would eclipse regional governors and help to reassert the control of the center over the regions. Although this reform was not particularly effective in bringing the regions under centralized control, it did act as a complement to other policies that Putin implemented.

Putin's second announced policy was to remake the Federation Council (the upper house of parliament) by replacing regional governors with representatives elected from each region. Under the law passed in June 2000, each region would send two representatives, the first to be nominated by the governor with the consent of the regional legislature and the second to be elected from among candidates nominated by the legislature's speaker or by no less than one-third of the chamber's deputies. The reform, which was phased in over

the next 18 months, worked in some ways to strengthen the voice of the regions at the center, since the new Federation representatives remain permanently in Moscow, unlike the governors they replaced.

Putin's third policy program, which was actually launched soon after he became acting president, was more diffused, but its essence was to bring all of the regions into compliance with the Russian constitution and Russian Federation laws. The government used such terms as "harmonization of federal and regional legislation" and "conformity of all laws with each other," but the essence was that the center would no longer permit regions to have constitutions or pass laws that conflicted with the Russian constitution or Russian law. As a part of that, Putin had also, by April 2002, canceled 28 of the 42 power-sharing treaties that President Yeltsin had negotiated with regions such as St. Petersburg and Nizhny Novgorod and autonomous republics such as Komi, Bashkortostan, Sakha (Yakutia), and Tatarstan. In general, Putin's position was to negotiate new power-sharing treaties with autonomous republics while canceling those with regions. In addition, he forced several autonomous republics to redraw their constitutions to bring them into agreement with the federal constitution. These policies undoubtedly increased central control over the regions and autonomous republics and they led some commentators to express the worry that Putin's policies toward the regions might lead to so large an increase in the center's powers that Russia would cease being a federation in fact, even if not in name. That was still only a threat during Putin's first term in office, but that became an increasing reality after his reelection in 2004.

Chechnya

President Putin's policy toward Chechnya—in some ways his most controversial domestic policy—was related to his stated commitment to bring all of the regions into compliance with the Russian constitution and Russian Federation laws. Putin was President Yeltsin's deputy chief of staff in 1996 when General Lebed, as Yeltsin's security adviser, negotiated an end to the war in Chechnya—the terms of which specified the withdrawal of all Russian forces from Chechnya in return for a Chechnyan pledge not to press for formal independence for five years.

Aslan Maskhadov, elected president in 1997, found his policies, which were based on secular separatism, challenged by insubordinate military commanders who dreamed of ridding the entire north Caucasus area of Russian influence and uniting it in a new Islamic state. The chief spokesman for this point of view, Shamil Basayev, was originally a Chechen patriot who came under the influence of a radical commander of Jordanian origin by the name of Ibn al-Khattab in the middle 1990s. Khattab, who came to Chechnya in 1995, had fought along side Osama bin Laden as a teenager and the message he brought to Chechnya was of an international movement to free Muslims everywhere from foreign rule. In the case of Chechnya, this meant merging the two majority Islamic states of Chechnya and Dagestan into a single Islamic state. Under Khattab's tutelage, Basayev visited al-Qaeda training camps in Afghanistan on three separate occasions, then he and Khattab established their own training camp in Chechnya.

Islamic radicals had also been active in Dagestan since the early 1990s. One of them was a Jordanian cleric by the name of Khabib Abdurrakhman, who established a headquarters in the town of Karamakhi and here, heavily financed from outside, managed to build up an armed cadre of religious fundamentalists committed to jihad and turn the town into an armed enclave stockpiled with weapons. Khattab visited Karamakhi, even going so far as to take a local 17-year-old girl as his wife. Together, Abdurrakhman and Khattab plotted a takeover of Dagestan.

Basayev launched his invasion into Dagestan in August 1999, but the operation failed miserably within a few weeks as Russian troops drove the rebels under Basayev and Khattab back into Chechnya. Russian forces took control of Karamakhi in September and began purging the hamlet of radical Islamic forces. Most Dagestani, it turned out, rejected radical Islam, preferring to remain part of Russia.

But this marked the beginning of the second Chechnyan war. When Maskhadov did not immediately repudiate Basayev and Khattab, Moscow broke off all relations with his government; by October, 80,000 Russian troops had begun their ground campaign in Chechnya. Chechen forces soon had to abandon Grozny, the capital, and retreat southward into the Caucasus Mountains, though they remained undefeated. Khattab was killed by Russian forces in 2002.

The continuing conflict had significant diplomatic repercussions for Russia, first of all as it affected Russia's relations with Georgia and Azerbaijan and, secondly, with the countries of the European Union and, to a lesser extent, the United States. Russia was critical of Azerbaijan for permitting a representative of the Chechen rebel authority to maintain an office in Baku until October 2002. It was even more critical of Georgia, which it accused of allowing Chechen rebels to find sanctuary in the Pankisi Gorge, and it even threatened to carry "preventive strikes" against Chechen bases in Georgia. On the other hand, the European Union sponsored a resolution in the UN Human Rights Committee condemning Russia for human rights violations in Chechnya. The United States, which had frequently been critical of Russian military operations in Chechnya, announced in February 2003 that it was adding three Chechen rebel groups to its blacklist of terrorist organizations. That was undoubtedly viewed as good news by the Russian government, for this could be seen as an endorsement of the Russian position that the Russian army was fighting an "anti-terrorist" campaign in Chechnya. Even so, the overall US government position has always been that "the broader conflict in Chechnya cannot be resolved militarily" and human rights reports issued by the US State Department have criticized reports of mistreatment of citizens in Chechnya.

An incident in the latter part of 2002 also made it clear that the Chechen rebels had turned to terror tactics as an integral part of their war against Russia. It all began on October 23 in Moscow when a group of approximately 40 Chechen militants led by Movsar Barayev, a 25-year-old fledgling guerrilla leader, seized a packed Moscow theater, taking more than 800 persons hostage. Refusing to negotiate with the Russian authorities, Barayev demanded that all Russian military forces be withdrawn from Chechnya within one week. Armed with explosives strapped to their bodies and having placed additional explosives throughout the theater, the Chechen militants threatened to begin killing their hostages unless the Russian government complied with their ultimatum. The Russian authorities waited three days; they then used sleeping gas to resolve the hostage standoff. During the rescue action, all of the militants were killed while at least 129 hostages died as a result of a gas overdose.

The situation was made worse by the fact that Chechen President Maskhadov refused to condemn the hostage-taking while it was going on. It was further compounded when Shamil Basayev, whom Maskhadov had named to head his government's Military Committee in June 2002, claimed responsibility for the hostage taking. This was, of course, the same Shamil Basayev who started the second Chechen war when he launched his invasion of Dagestan in August 1999. President Putin responded by launching a massive retaliatory military operation in Chechnya, accompanying it with a promise to expand Russia's War on Terrorism, targeting "all places where terrorists and their ideological supporters and financial backers are based."

He also decided to put an end to any possibility of eventual Chechen independence by organizing a referendum in Chechnya on a new draft constitution establishing Chechnya as an autonomous republic within the Russian Federation. That referendum, which took place on March 23, 2003, received the overwhelming approval of the people voting in Chechnya and new elections, held in October 2003, resulted in the election of Akhmad Kadyrov as president.

These actions did not bring an end to the continuing conflict in Chechnya, nor did they prevent radical elements of the Chechnyan resistance from subsequently launching terror attacks in Moscow, in Chechnya, and in the neighboring republics of Dagestan, Ingushia, and North Ossetia.

Kadyrov himself was killed on May 9, 2004, when a bomb planted under the stands in Grozny stadium blew up as he was attending celebrations to mark the anniversary of the end of World War II. But Kadyrov's assassination did not change the Russian government's policy in Chechnya; in fact, his son, Ramzan Kadyrov, was appointed prime minister of Chechnya soon after his father's death. Ramzan Kadyrov was appointed acting president in February 2007; he later won election as president in his own right.

Aslan Maskhadov, the separatist leader, was killed by the Russian military in March 2005. Maskhadov's successor was Abdul-Khalim Sadulayev, a lesser-known Islamic fundamentalist, who was himself killed in June 2006.

The separatist cause in Chechnya was weakened by the loss of much of its top leadership, but the remaining leaders were determined to fight on—and to extend the war to other parts of the north Caucasus area. Meanwhile, an amnesty plan, announced after Shamil Basayev's death, was, according to the government, accepted by 647 former militants. Most of those who sought amnesty were low-level militants, however; no one knows how many militants continue to support the resistance.

Since President Putin's policies at the national level were aimed at strengthening the power of the central government in all of its dealings with the various political subdivisions, events in Chechnya were used as an argument to reinforce control at the center by stripping all of Russia's subdivisions of some of their autonomy, lest they turn into other Chechnyas. Thus, events in Chechnya have directly contributed to a growth in authoritarianism throughout Russia. President Putin stepped down as president at the end of his second term in May 2008, but he continued his policy toward Chechnya in his new role as prime minister. As the January 24, 2011, suicide bombing at Domodedovo

Russia

Airport, Moscow's busiest airport, indicates, however, the Russian government has been unable to bring an end to the North Caucasus insurgency. Putin's return to the presidency in May 2012 has not changed that equation.

Another problem, however, has emerged for Putin in Chechnya. Through his support of local strongman Kadyrov, Putin has created a potentially formidable regional rival. Kadyrov has established a brutal regime in the republic and has consolidated his control through heavily repressive acts. As detailed in Ekaterina Sokirianskaia's editorial in the *New York Times* on May 3, 2017: "Collective punishment is the hallmark of Mr. Kadyrov's repression. Relatives of those who displease the authorities are threatened, beaten, held hostage, expelled from the republic or have their homes burned down. Such methods were first applied to suspected rebels but have spread to regime critics, religious dissenters, even drunken drivers." In April 2017, Kadyrov's harsh rule gained worldwide attention as a result of an April 1 report in *Novaya Gazeta*, which documented evidence that gay men were being systematically arrested, tortured, and even executed by forces close to Kadyrov. As a result of these and subsequent reports, in May 2017 three French gay rights groups filed a complaint against Kadyrov in the International Criminal Court.

Media

Another policy area of the Russian government that has caused concern is the attitude toward the media, and in particular Russia's independent television network NTV. In 2000, when Putin was first elected president, Russia had three television networks—two state-run networks, ORT and RTR—and NTV, a privately owned network started in the mid-1990s by Vladimir Gusinsky. NTV, noted for its lively and critical news and current affairs programs, was a strong supporter of President Yeltsin and his policies until 1999, but it became a critic of the Russian government after Russian troops were sent back into Chechnya in that year. Not coincidentally, Vladimir Gusinsky came under increasing attack from the government shortly thereafter. Gusinsky, jailed briefly in the summer of 2000, fled to Spain upon his release, fighting extradition when the Russian government attempted to force his return. The Spanish government eventually refused to return Gusinsky but, at home, the Russian government moved against Gusinsky's media empire, arresting a number of the NTV's employees, including its finance chief, Anton Titov.

But the main attack was indirect. This attack was made possible by the fact that

Courtesy of *The Economist*

Gusinsky had received financial support from Gazprom, Russia's national gas company to start NTV—partly to show the Russian government's appreciation for Gusinsky's support of Yeltsin politically—and Gazprom got 46% of the NTV shares as a result. Gusinsky subsequently found himself in financial difficulties and borrowed an additional $300 million from Gazprom, pledging 19% of NTV's shares as collateral for the loan. When he was unable to repay the loan, Gazprom demanded the additional shares and sued the company in court when Gusinsky refused to turn them over. Gazprom won in court in April 2001; it then took control of the company and replaced its previous management.

All of this might have been viewed as a straight-forward business arrangement, were it not for the fact that Gazprom is partially owned—and effectively controlled—by the state. Did all of this happen because the government was determined to gain control of the sole independent television network in Russia? Would the government henceforth control this network as it already did the other two networks? Many of NTV's employees thought so and quit to work elsewhere after the new management took over. In addition, when Ted Turner offered to buy the 19% interest in NTV from Gazprom in return for a promise from the Russian government that NTV could continue to operate as an independent network, President Putin said that the government was not involved in the matter and so could make no such promises.

Although Gazprom's takeover of NTV certainly represented a loss for Gusinsky, it was less clear at the time that it was the result of a decision by President Putin to bring all of the media under government control. In fact, Michael Wines, writing

in the *New York Times* in April 2001, concluded that it did not. Wines wrote that, while Russians did not enjoy freedom as Westerners know it, a great media variety continued to exist in Russia.

There has been a continued loss of press freedom in Russia since 2001, however. The invasion of Ukraine resulted in intensified government crackdown on local independent news websites and social media platforms. Recently, the government passed a law that calls for up to 15 years of imprisonment for any content that includes "fake news" about the war. Roskomnadzor, the country's media regulator took the radio station Ekho Moskvy, and Dozhd TV off the air, after these news outlets continued to use the words "invasion" and "war" to describe Russia's attack on Ukraine, instead of Kremlin official phrasing "special military operation." Unwilling to tolerate censorship, *Novaya Gazeta*, the newspaper whose editor, Dmitry Muratov shared the most recent Nobel Peace Prize, suspended its operation. Russian authorites also banned Facebook and Instagram, and closed access to BBC, Voice of America and Radio Free Europe/Radio Liberty, and Deutsche Welle. In November 2004, Reporters without Borders issued a new press freedom index which ranked Russia 140th out of 167 countries. Commenting on the current situation, Mikhail Berger, editor in chief of *Yezhenedelnyi*, wrote in January 2005 that "it is amazing how the print media are willing to cater to the ruling elite's needs rather than to society's information needs." Dealing with the same topic, Igor Yakovenko, secretary-general of the Russian Union of Journalists, wrote about "the problem of the government monopoly of the media market [which] has not been resolved and has even grown worse." Vladimir Ryzhkov, an independent Duma Deputy, commented somewhat more cynically in April 2005 that "there are just two strategic resources for keeping power in this country—oil and television."

That evaluation is still valid. Freedom of the press as it is understood in the United States does not exist in Russia. On the other hand, the situation in Russia is not as bad as it is sometimes portrayed abroad. All national television broadcasts are under the control of the Russian government; much of the national press is controlled either by the government or by wealthy individuals allied with the government.

Independent newspapers and regional radio stations no longer exist, though the government moved to further restrict their freedom in 2013. It is also still possible to find most of the major western newspapers and newspapers for sale in Russia, at least in the major cities. An independent press can continue to publish only so long as it is careful to maintain a stance of genuine neutrality between the government and its political opponents; the danger comes when a radio station or a newspaper is perceived as being an instrument of the political opposition.

Putin Moves to Consolidate His Control: Battle with the Communists

In April 2002, there was a realignment of leadership positions in the Duma, which ousted the Communists from most of their committee chairmanships and threatened the position of the Duma speaker, Gennadiy Seleznyov, a member of the Communist faction. The genesis of this development goes back to October 2001, when two of the parties of the pro-government party coalition, Unity and Fatherland-All Russia voted to merge to create a new centralist political party, United Russia. This merger was completed in February 2002. Meanwhile, public opinion polls taken in October 2001 indicated that the Communist Party of the Russian Federation (KPRF) was losing support and would win fewer seats than Unity in any new legislative elections. This led Zyuganov, the Communist leader, to call an emergency congress of the KPRF to meet in January 2002 to deal with the situation. In spite of a warm letter from President Putin to the congress in which he referred to the KPRF as "a creative and constructive political association that united a considerable part of society," Zyuganov used the forum to launch a sharp criticism of President Putin's policies, while the congress adopted a resolution placing the KPRF in "irreconcilable opposition" to the government and its policies.

Since Putin's party, United Russia, together with the other parties of the pro-government coalition—the People's Deputy faction, the Union of Rightist Forces, and the Russian Regions group—controlled a majority of the seats in the Duma, it was only a question of what action they would take to counteract the Communist challenge. The move came in March 2002, when the government coalition threatened to replace Seleznyov as Duma speaker. That threat was subsequently withdrawn, but Seleznyov did lose the right to cast a deciding vote in the Duma Council, the organization which sets the agenda for the lower house. In addition, the coalition began to push for a reassignment of Duma committee chairmanships. That vote took place on April 3.

This realignment put a formal end to the working arrangement brokered between the pro-government United Russia and the Communist leadership in the Duma

Russian campaign poster for Vladimir Zhirinovsky's Liberal Democratic Party of Russia

as the Duma had organized itself after the December 1999 legislative elections. Under the new arrangement, seven of the nine committee chairmanships held by the Communists were transferred to pro-government political parties of the center and right. The pro-government coalition also voted to restrict Speaker Seleznyov's authority.

The 2003 Duma elections were scheduled to take place on December 7. With President Putin's popularity running at about 75%, it was a foregone conclusion that the pro-presidential United Russia would do well at the polls. But Putin was apparently determined to reduce the clout of the Communist Party and so his political operatives encouraged the creation of a new political alliance on the left led by Dmitry Rogozin, a nationalist who was chairman of the Foreign Affairs Committee of the Duma, and Sergey Glazyev, a member of the Communist faction in the Duma. This new party, which took the name Motherland, billed itself as a leftwing but patriotic party, thus presenting itself as an alternative to all those who had traditionally supported the Communists, but who were turned off by the position of total opposition adopted by the Communist Party. It also didn't hurt that the mostly government-controlled media gave the new party wide favorable coverage while largely ignoring the campaign of the Communist Party.

The December 7 vote brought a fundamental political shift with pro-government parties sweeping the field. United Russia, the pro-government bloc, took 37.1% of the vote, while the Communists came next with 12.7%. The other parties that surmounted the 5% hurdle to obtain proportional seats were Zhirinovsky's Liberal Democratic Party with 11.6% and Motherland with 9.1%. Support for the two so-called liberal or reform parties,

Yabloko and the Union of Right Forces, fell to under 5% so they lost their party representation in the Duma. In the final enumeration, United Russia took 300 of the 450 seats, which gave the government a two-thirds majority in the new Duma.

The results of the parliamentary elections were actually a prelude to presidential elections scheduled to take place on March 14, 2004. With his public approval ratings a consistent 70–75%, Vladimir Putin was always considered likely to win reelection, but the astonishing showing of the pro-government bloc in the December parliamentary elections convinced all of the potential major opposition candidates to drop out of the race.

Faced only with minor opposition, Putin never formally campaigned for reelection, though he did manage to create some excitement in February when he fired his prime minister, Mikhail Kasyanov, and named Mikhail Fradkov, a political unknown, as his replacement. Fradkov, a career bureaucrat, was a former head of the tax police and was serving as Russia's representative to the European Union when he was appointed prime minister. Putin said that he was changing prime ministers before the presidential vote because he wanted the Russian people to know precisely what they would be getting in his second term. However, the real message that Putin was sending had to do with the campaign that the government had launched the previous fall against the Russian oligarchs and, in particular, Mikhail Khodorkovsky, then head and chief shareholder of the energy company Yukos. When Kasyanov publicly objected to the government's decision to impound 44% of the shares of Yukos as a way to guarantee that it could collect on any future judgment against Yukos, most people were convinced that it was only a matter of time before Putin replaced him as prime

Russia

minister. Of course, Putin was also making it clear that it was he who would be totally in charge in the new administration.

The March 14 election came out as expected, with Putin garnering 71.2% of the vote. Communist Party candidate and Duma Deputy Nikolai Kharitonov came in second with 13.7% of the vote. The other two candidates, Sergey Glazyev and Irina Khakamada came in third and fourth with 4.1% and 3.9% of the vote.

A Shift toward Authoritarianism

President Putin promised at the time of his reelection to translate his landslide victory into a new season of reform, but the new policies introduced after that time all tended toward authoritarianism rather than reform. In September 2004, after the Beslan hostage crisis, Putin proposed to eliminate the direct election of governors and other regional executive-branch heads—including the heads of the so-called ethnic republics. In place of the election process, the president of the Russian Federation would submit the name of a candidate to the appropriate regional legislature, which would have to "give its consent" to the nominee before he was appointed to office. One can imagine how often a regional legislature would reject a candidate proposed to them by the president of the Federal Republic. However, should that occur, and the candidate be rejected a second time if resubmitted, the president would have the authority to appoint an acting regional head. If the

Original Königsberg University (now in Kaliningrad), where Immanuel Kant taught

candidate were rejected a third time, the president could dissolve the legislature and call for new elections. This particular "reform" was passed by the Duma in December 2004.

President Putin next submitted a bill to the Duma to change how deputies are elected. The new legislation abolished single-mandate districts and specified that all deputies would be elected from party lists according to a proportional-representation system. In addition, the new legislation banned the formation of electoral blocs to contest federal, regional, or local elections. The new legislation, which the Duma passed in April 2005, eliminated independent candidates and placed selection of all deputies in the hands of the political parties. Some democratic countries do have proportional-representation systems, but in the Russian system, where the largest political party is an instrument of the government with no party platform other than loyalty to the government and particularly the president, the possibilities for political manipulation of the electorate have proved to be enormous.

Another law, passed in December 2004, appeared to have as its purpose to limit the number of new political parties coming into existence. Under this legislation, a party had to have 50,000 members nationwide, while half of the regional branches had to have no fewer than 500 members each. A new party which failed to reach a sufficient membership will have to become a public association unless it achieved a minimum membership within the following year.

Another of Putin's second term "reforms" relates to nongovernmental organizations (NGOs) operating in Russia. The law, which went into effect on April 17, 2006, set new rules for the more than 400,000 NGOs operating in Russia. Essentially, the new law required foreign and domestic NGOs to re-register with a state body that would examine their work before deciding whether they would be permitted to continue operations. An important reason for the legislation was the fear that foreign money could promote the sort of popular revolt that led to the color revolutions in Georgia, Ukraine, and Kyrgyzstan. The legislation permitted the Federal Registration Service to prevent the funding of certain activities to safeguard the "constitutional" order. In addition, the legislation stated that NGOs could be closed if they threatened "Russia's sovereignty, independence, territorial integrity, national unity and originality, cultural heritage and national interests." Although a number of prominent NGOs initially had some difficulty in getting re-registered, most were successfully registered.

Two advisers to Putin during his first term in office who subsequently broke with

him are former Prime Minister Mikhail Kasyanov and Andrei Illarionov, who resigned as Putin's top economic adviser in December 2005. Kasyanov, who has often spoken critically about Putin's "restoration of Soviet order" since stepping down as prime minister, announced the formation of a new political movement, called the People's Democratic Union, in 2006. At the time, many people thought that Kasyanov was positioning himself for a political run for the presidency in 2008.

Illarionov, on the other hand, did not appear to have political ambitions and for that reason his criticisms of government policy had more resonance. Six days before he resigned, he told a press conference that Russia "is no longer a democratic country. It is no longer a free country." After his resignation, he criticized Putin for turning Russia into a corporate state. "Russia," he wrote in January 2006, "has become richer over the past six years but has seen its economic, political, and social freedoms diminish." But as Masha Lipman, editor of the Carnegie Moscow Center's *Pro et Contra Journal*, wrote in September 2005:

While public opinion polls show unrelenting discontent with government policies, Putin's own approval rating, which had dropped somewhat, popped back up to 70% in August.

It is true that criticism such as those of Illarionov had no effect on Putin's popularity, which according to polls continued to hovers between 70 and 80%. This was also reflected in regional elections that took place in March 2007. Putin's United Party won about 60% of the seats in 14 regional assemblies. The Communist Party came second with 12.5%. A Just Russia, the second pro-government party formed late in 2006 through the merger of the Party of Life, Motherland, and the Party of Pensioners, came in third with 12%. The other party to make a significant showing was Vladimir Zhirinovsky's Liberal Democrats, which took about 5%.

The December 2007 Duma elections took place under a pure proportional representation system. All candidates ran on a party list, while individual parties needed a minimum of 7% of the national vote in order to win seats in the Duma. Moreover, banding together with another party to form a coalition was no help; each was still required to meet the 7% minimum vote requirement.

Fifteen political parties were certified as eligible to participate in the election; four parties managed to surmount the 7% barrier. The election "campaign" was very interesting because United Russia, which billed itself as the party of government, refused to participate in any of the party debates. Instead, the party persuaded

President Putin to have his name placed at the top of the United Russia list and the party then turned the election into a referendum on Putin, placing huge billboards around Moscow proclaiming "Putin Is Our Choice" and "Moscow Votes for Putin." Helping their case, the press and television networks gave extensive favorable coverage of the United Russia candidates and either ignored or gave negative coverage to opposition parties.

The surprising thing, therefore, is that the makeup of the current Duma was quite similar to the old Duma elected four years earlier. United Russia did, it is true, win a larger percentage of the popular vote (64.3%), but it won only 15 more seats than it had won in 2003 (315 seats versus 300 seats).

The Communist Party won the second highest percentage of the vote (11.57%), which gave it 57 seats. The Liberal Democratic Party of Russia came third with 8.14% of the vote, but it also got 57 seats. A Just Russia came fourth with 7.74% of the vote, which gave it 38 seats. Although United Russia's 315 seats gave it the two-thirds majority needed to pass constitutional amendments on its own, the equally pro-government A Just Russia invariably voted the government line. Moreover, the Liberal Democratic Party is usually a fairly reliable supporter of government policies as well.

With the legislative elections out of the way, President Putin announced on December 10 that his choice as his successor was Dmitry A. Medvedev. The 42-year-old Medvedev then announced that he wanted Putin to serve as his prime minister and Putin agreed. Thus from the very beginning, Medvedev portrayed himself not only as Putin's man but also that his election would mean Putin would continue to have an important role in government

Medvedev held the rank of first deputy prime minister in the government at the time that he was chosen. He held the social portfolio in the cabinet. As it happened, President Putin had replaced his prime minister in September 2007, during the lead-up to the Duma elections. The new prime minister was Viktor Zubkov, a little-known bureaucrat who previously had been director of the Federal Financial Monitoring Service. Medvedev thus was much better known than his boss.

The presidential election was set for March 2, 2008. However, Medvedev never actually campaigned for the office; during the entire campaign, he gave only one "political" speech. On the other hand, the press and television channels daily reported on the important things he was doing in his current job. Again, huge posters appeared, this time with a photo of a smiling Medvedev standing next to President Putin, the colors of the Russian flag in the background, with the caption "2 Marta Vubory Prezidenta Rossii [2 March: Election of the President of Russia]." The message was clear; Medvedev was Putin's choice for the presidency.

On March 2, therefore, Medvedev received 70.28% of the vote, Gennady Zyuganov, his Communist rival, came in second with 17.72% of the vote. Vladimir Zhirinovsky, leader of the Liberal Democratic Party, came in third with 9.35% of the vote. Andrei Bogdanov, leader of the Democratic Party of Russia, came fourth with 1.3% of the vote.

Medvedev as President

Dmitry Medvedev was sworn in as president of the Russian Federation on May 7, 2008. Medvedev's first move as president was to name Vladimir Putin as his prime minister. On May 8, the Duma met and confirmed Putin as prime minister.

A public poll taken by the Levada Center, and released on May 6, found that 67% of the Russian people believed that President Medvedev would "act under the control" of Putin and his inner circle. When Russians were asked who should have power, 47% said Medvedev; when asked who they think will have real power in the country, only 22% said Medvedev.

Eleven months later, the BBC commissioned a poll that asked a similar set of questions. The results indicated that 15% of Russians believed that Medvedev was running the country; 27% thought Putin was; and 41% said that power was divided equally.

Those who thought that Putin was still making the major decisions pointed out that the office of the prime minister was reshaped in anticipation of Putin's taking the job. They pointed out that the Duma passed a law in April 2008 re-defining the powers of the future prime minister; it amended 150 laws and transferred 500 of the cabinet's former duties to lower government departments. The stated reason for the change was to free the prime minister of technical duties and to widen his authority as an independent political figure.

In addition, President Putin signed a decree on April 25 creating three new positions: personal press secretary for the prime minister; a head of the prime minister's protocol office; and a head of an office in charge of preparing the prime minister's public statements. The three positions were filled by presidential press secretary Dmitry Peskov, presidential aide Dmitry Kalimunin, and Anton Vaino, who served as Putin's head of protocol from 2003 to 2007.

Prime Minister Putin was also given responsibility for evaluating the country's governors, in effect determining whether they would remain in office. It was also reported that presidential envoys to the federal districts would "de facto be withdrawn from the system of the presidential administration and tied to the cabinet of ministers."

Putin was also named the new chairman of United Russia in 2008, which meant that he controlled the party that controlled the Duma. Under changes in United Russia's statute introduced on the eve of Putin's election, he was given virtually unlimited powers inside the party, including the power to name candidates for important positions. As Dmitry Babich, a Russian reporter, put it, "this means the new Russian prime minister will no longer be subject to the whims of the president."

They also point out that President Medvedev was on vacation at the time of the August war against Georgia. Prime Minister Putin made the decision to go to war and all subsequent decisions. President Medvedev, meanwhile, remained on vacation.

President Medvedev had a number of achievements during his four years as president, and he even publicly differed with Prime Minister Putin over a couple issues. He pushed through a number of constitutional political reforms, including extending the presidential term of office to six years, and he also issued a decree reestablishing the election of mayors.

As a lawyer, President Medvedev tended to seek legalistic solutions to problems vexing the country. Attacking the "legal nihilism" that pervaded contemporary Russia, he called for a law-based system and an independent judiciary. But not all of Medvedev's "solutions" led to greater democracy. For example, he submitted legislation to the Duma in February 2009 allowing "Kremlin-friendly regional legislatures to remove opposition mayors who were elected by popular vote," thus removing one of the remaining checks against the monopoly of executive power in the regions.

President Medvedev also made no objection when the government decided to file new charges against Mikhail Khodorkovsky for embezzlement of nearly 350 million tons of crude oil and laundering more than $20 billion of the proceeds, that is, as Masha Lipman, editor of the Carnegie Moscow Center's *Pro et Contra Journal*, put it "with stealing basically all the oil that Yukos produced during the same period covered by the first trial." Lipman concluded correctly that,

> *while Medvedev pledged to further the rule of law and judicial independence, after his first year in office there has no progress on either.*

At the end of his four years in office, that statement still remained basically

Russia

true but Medvedev did give a number of speeches and took several actions which seemed aimed as differentiating himself from Putin. For instance, in September 2009, Medvedev spoke to the Valdai Club, a group of international and domestic academics and journalists about his vision to change Russia. His goals included weaning Russia off its dependence on oil and gas revenues, a crackdown on corruption, more democracy, and a bigger focus on the individual in business and politics. He made little, if any, progress in any of these areas. Two months later, he gave another speech in which he argued

We have to admit that in previous years we failed to do enough to solve problems inherited from the past. We have failed so far to dismiss the economy's primitive structure, the humiliating dependence on raw materials, and to reorient production to people's real needs. High energy prices have lulled the country into a dangerous complacency, creating illusions that structural reforms could wait.

Finally, after a series of scandals involving endemic bribe-taking and documented cases of torture, Medvedev issued a decree calling for the staff of the 1.4 million strong Interior Ministry, which includes the police, Interior Ministry troops, investigators, and civilian officials, to be cut by 20% by January 1, 2012. In the decree, Medvedev said that disciplinary problems and law breaking by police officials had provoked widespread concerns in society and were undermining the authority of the state, making the reform essential. After issuing the decree, Medvedev gave an interview on television in which he explained that "A huge amount of complaints from our citizens have been piling up about the work of the Interior Ministry. We need rather tough and serious changes." As one commentator, writing about Medvedev's decree, pointed out, however, all previous attempts to reform Russia's notorious bureaucracy had failed.

An important change in policy came in March 2011 when President Medvedev decided that government officials should be removed from the board of directors of state companies. Among the government officials giving up their corporate jobs were Finance Minister Alexei Kudrin, who had chaired the supervisory committee of the bank VTB; Deputy Prime Minister Igor Sechin, who had been chairman of the board of directors of Rosneft, the state-owned oil giant; Transportation Minister Igor Levitin, who had been an adviser to Aeroflot; and First Deputy Prime Minister Viktor Zubkov, who had been chairman of the board of directors at Rosselkhozbank.

Although this move reverses the economic policy carried out by Putin when he

President Putin and Prime Minister Medvedev

was president, it is not clear that Putin opposed the change in direction represented by the new policy. Even though the new policy reduced the power of Sechin and his *siloviki* allies—themselves considered allies of Putin—Putin, in fact, made no public statement opposing the new policy.

Many people in Russia hoped that Medvedev would stand for reelection as president, but those hopes were dashed in September 2011 when a joint Medvedev-Putin statement made it clear that the two planned to switch jobs; Putin would become the candidate of the ruling United Russia party in the March 2012 presidential elections while Medvedev would become prime minister. Medvedev's "interlude" presidency between Putin's second and third terms shows that Putin adhered to the letter of the Russian constitution, which limits the president to two consecutive terms. However, as discussed below, Putin had not really given up power when he served as prime minister. Twice reelected for six consecutive terms since 2012, and having signed in April 2002 a law that would allow him to run for presidency two more terms, Putin is likely to remain in office untill 2036. If he stays in power until then, his tenure would surpass that of Joseph Stalin's 29-year rule. According to some observers, the reason Putin engaged in such constitutional power grab is because he wanted to avoid the possibility of becoming a lame-duck in 2024, which could have led to destabilizing power struggle among the elites.

Although public opinion polls made it clear that Putin remained extremely popular, popular demonstrations after the announcement showed that not everyone favored the switch. In fact, Finance Minister Kudrin showed his dissatisfaction with the switch by indicating publicly that he would refuse to serve as finance minister

under Medvedev. Kudrin had always been a loyal Putin follower, so he probably had hoped that he would be named prime minister in a new Putin administration. In any case, he was fired as finance minister, but Putin indicated he would have a role in a new Putin administration.

New parliamentary elections took place in December 2011. Because public opinion polls indicated that United Russia had lost a lot of its popularity, Prime Minister Putin formed the All-Russian Popular Front to bring in additional support for United Russia candidates. In the end, United Russia took 49.3% of the popular vote according to official results, which gave it 237 of the 450 seats in the Duma. There were, however, widespread charges of voter fraud which, in turn, led to several significant mass demonstrations in Moscow calling for new Duma elections. The public pressure, while noteworthy, did not result in new elections.

The Renewed Putin Presidency

Putin easily won reelection as president in the March 4 elections, but popular demonstrations continued to challenge those results. Nevertheless, Putin was sworn in as president on May 7, 2012, and that same day named Medvedev as his prime minister. Although the demonstrations were no real challenge to Putin's power or authority, they did mark the birth of opposition movements which could lead to genuine opposition political parties. There is also some indication the political elite was divided on how to respond to the continued protests. Part of the elite believed that increased pluralism was necessary in a rapidly changing society; others argued for a revival of the tough authoritarianism that characterized his second term as president. Putin accepted the argument of the hardline faction, for a whole series of laws cracking down on dissent were passed by the Duma over the summer.

The next event occurred in September when the Duma voted to strip Gennady Gudkov of his seat. Gudkov, a member of the A Just Russia party and a former KGB officer, had emerged over the summer as an advocate of the rule of law and freedom of speech. Putin evidently decided that he could not tolerate even one voice of dissent within the legislature and so Gudkov was expelled. The charge which led to his expulsion is that he was illegally running a business while serving in the State Duma. His expulsion caused a problem, however, for numerous Duma members were engaged in commercial activity. In fact, the Duma's commission on income subsequently looked into allegations that six United Russia members were engaged in commercial activity.

A more serious development occurred in October when the Duma overwhelmingly approved a new bill widening the definition of high treason. Treason had previously been defined as espionage or other assistance to a foreign state damaging Russia's external security; under the new law, the definition has been expanded to include moves against Russia's "constitutional order, sovereignty, and territorial and state integrity" plus the granting of "financial, technical, consulting or other help" to a foreign state or an international organization. That same month, the Russian government ordered the US Agency for International Development to close its Moscow office because it was using its international aid mission in Russia to meddle in Russian politics and influence elections.

Another law, passed by the Duma in July but which came into effect on November 21, 2012, requires all nongovernmental organizations (NGOs) that receive money from abroad and engage in political activity to register as "foreign agents." Use of the word "agent" suggested that the Russian government actually considered NGOs that received money from abroad to be extensions of foreign governments. A controversial aspect of this law is that it gives the government broad discretion in determining whether a particular activity by an NGO, even if it is non-political association by charter, qualifies as a political act. In April 2013, a court in Moscow fined Golos, the prominent Russian election-monitoring organization, for failing to register as a foreign agent. Prosecutors accused Golos of receiving money for the Andrei Sakharov Freedom prize it was awarded by the Norwegian Helsinki Committee in 2012. Golos insists that it turned down the money, which it says was lodged in a transit account prior to being sent back to the Helsinki Committee. Golos says it was targeted for uncovering widespread violations

in the 2011 parliamentary elections and the presidential vote.

Moscow's prosecutor-general also informed Memorial, a venerable and reputable human rights center, that it would have to register as a foreign agent, since it "receives financial support from abroad and is engaged in political activities." Transparency International's Moscow office also received notification from the Russian Ministry of Justice in April 2013 that they might also be required to register as a foreign agent if the organization received any financial resources from abroad. In May 2013, prosecutors formally warned the Levada Center—Russia's respected and independent pollster—that it was in breach of legislation requiring politically engaged NGOs that receive foreign funding to register as foreign agents. The warning came shortly after the Levada Center had released polls showing President Putin's popularity falling. The move threatens the Levada Center's continued existence; as Lev Gudkov, the center's director put it,

[The Center] is under threat of closure. In these circumstances, we cannot carry out independent research. We need sources of financing. We finance our own programs and projects by redistributing money we earn in other spheres. But now under this widened interpretation [of the NGO law], any of our partnerships—even if we work with an organization represented here in Russia but which potentially has a foreign source of financing—then we ourselves fall into the category of foreign agent.

President Putin has continued his assault against global NGOs that operate in Russia. In May 2015, he signed into law a bill that empowered Russia's prosecutor-general to designate as "undesirable" international NGOs that allegedly "threaten Russia's constitutional order, defense potential or security." According to the new law, those operating such NGOs can be subjected to heavy fines and imprisonment for up to six years. The law appears to give sweeping authority to the state to eliminate any NGOs that criticize official policies.

In recent years, the Russian government has also tried to control information that Russians can access through the Internet. According to the World Bank, as of 2020, 85% of Russians used the Internet. In November 2012, it introduced a blacklist of Internet sites to be blocked. During the Russian annexation of Crimea in March 2014 and the subsequent war in eastern Ukraine, websites that the Russian government found objectionable were blocked. In July 2014, the government introduced a law that required search engines, social

networks, and other forums to maintain computer records on Russian soil of everything published over the preceding six months. This legislation required Google to locate servers handling Russian traffic inside Russia. This legislation also stated that anyone whose Internet postings attracted more than 3,000 followers per day to register as a media organization. Such people were to be held legally liable for the accuracy of their postings and were obligated to disclose reader information to the Russian state. The new law applied to an estimated 30,000 Russian bloggers.

Between December 2011 and May 2012, as noted briefly above, in several mass demonstrations, tens of thousands of Russians protested fraudulent practices that reportedly occurred during the Duma elections of December 4, which were won by Putin's United Russia party. The demonstrators also criticized Putin's decision to run for a third term as president employing the slogan, "Russia without Putin." The rallies were organized largely through social media as occurred in the grassroots Arab Spring mass rallies that took place earlier in 2011 and toppled governments in Tunisia and Egypt and led to civil war in Libya. Following the Russian demonstrations against Putin, defenders of Kremlin policy have sought to use social media to their advantage. They have formed groups of paid, professional "Internet trolls" to spread pro-Kremlin propaganda and vilify the Kremlin's opponents using harsh rhetoric and distorted information. On June 2, 2015, Adrian Chen of the *New York Times* exposed a Russian "troll farm" operating in St. Petersburg.

One of the leaders of the street protests was Alexei Navalny, a prominent critic of Putin. In December 2014, he and his brother Oleg were convicted of embezzling funds from Russian companies. The convictions are widely viewed as fraudulent and politically motivated. Each brother was sentenced to 3.5 years in prison. Aleksei's sentence was suspended and Oleg was in a penal colony in the Oryol region. Oleg was further sentenced in absentia in February 2022 and his whereabouts are unknown.

Navalny emerged as the face of the Russian opposition to Putin. The March 26, 2017, anti-corruption protests that he organized across the country demonstrated his central role in the opposition. Unlike previous demonstrations, these protests were not limited to Moscow or St. Petersburg; there are reports of protests in 90 cities across Russia.

In December 2016, Navalny announced his intention to challenge Putin in the 2018 presidential elections. Less than two months later, he was found guilty in a retrial of the same crime he had been previously accused in 2014. This conviction for fraud

Russia

formally disqualified Navalny for running for office. Despite optimism that the politically motivated charge would be cleared, on December 25, 2017, Russia's central election committee determined that his case did not legitimate any special dispensation and therefore as a convicted felon, his name could not appear on the presidential ballot. Navalny's candidacy was not only attacked in the legal arena, he was also physically attacked. In two separate attacks in March and April 2017, unknown assailants sprayed a dye called zelyonka ("brilliant green") on his face. In the April attack, the chemical got into his right eye, causing him to lose 85% of his vision and seek medical attention in Barcelona. Navalny's supporters openly suspect that these attacks were carried out with the approval if not direct support of Kremlin.

In December 2013, President Putin issued a decree dissolving one of Russia's official news agencies, RIA Novosti, along with its international news broadcaster. The decree created a new agency in its place, Rossiya Segodnya (Russia Today). Putin then appointed Dmitry Kiselyov, a conservative news anchor, known mainly for his anti-gay views, to head up the new agency. (On June 30, 2013, Russia introduced a law that banned the promotion of same-sex relationships to minors.) In the words of the decree, the main mission of Rossiya Segodnya is to "highlight abroad the state policy and public life of the Russian Federation." The agency also broadcasts in English on American cable TV channels. At the same time, the Russian government is seeking to limit foreign ownership of broadcast media in Russia. In October 2014, the government ruled that by 2016, foreign ownership must not exceed 20%.

State run media carefully cultivates Putin's image as an idealized patriarchal figure. Images of Putin engaging in daring feats and physical prowess are offered alongside those of Putin showing his concern for his fellow citizens. Putin's softer side is especially promoted in the annual

**Alexei Navalny,
lawyer and political activist**

"Direct-Line" call-in show that he participates in, whereby Russian citizens ask him a range of personal and policy-oriented questions. Efforts to cultivate Putin's image can generate absurdities, for instance in April 2017 an image of Putin with painted eyes and lips which had become a popular meme was banned as "extremist material" by the Justice Ministry. According to an April 6, 2017, *New York Times* report, the image, which had become known as a "gay clown," was barred because it hinted at "an alleged nonstandard sexual orientation of the Russian president."

Following the invasion of Ukraine, the government shut down some news outlets, while other local broadcasters chose to closed down in the face of government censorship. in 2017, a new Russian media law established that any news organization that receives funding from abroad would be labeled a "foreign agent." As a result of this legislation, respected Western outlets such as the Voice of America and Radio Free Europe/Radio Liberty have been designated as foreign agents by the Justice Ministry, and therefore subject to additional government scrutiny. Domestic independent outlets are frequently the target of harassment and intimidation by government agents or those sympathetic to the government. For instance, in September 2017, journalist Yulia Latynina, a columnist for *Novaya Gazeta* who hosted a radio program on *Ekho Moskvy*, fled Russia after attackers set fire to her parked car. A few months before this incident, attackers had sprayed her home with a toxic chemical. In April 2018, an independent journalist named Maksim Borodin died after falling from the fifth-floor balcony of his apartment in Yekaterinburg. Borodin, who was an investigative journalist for the independent news site *Novy Den*, had just published the scoop of his career a few weeks prior to his death. His story on the deaths of Russian private military contractors fighting for Syrian president Bashar al-Assad had gained international attention. Although authorities quickly deemed Borodin's death non-suspicious, independent watchdog organizations, such as the Committee to Project Journalists have called upon the government to conduct a thorough investigation to ensure that his death was not linked to his reporting.

On February 27, 2015, Boris Nemtsov, a liberal former regional governor and deputy prime minister, who had become a fierce critic of Putin and especially of Russia's involvement in the war in eastern Ukraine, was shot dead near the Kremlin. The murder was condemned worldwide, and tens of thousands subsequently marched in a procession mourning Nemtsov. Five men from the North Caucasus were arrested in connection

with the murder, but they have denied involvement. The fact that President Putin dropped out of public view for eleven days without explanation shortly after the murder added to the mystery surrounding the matter.

In recent years, the space for independent civil society organizations has been drastically curtailed. A 2012 law established that NGOs which received foreign funding and engaged in political advocacy (a deliberately broad and vague term) were required to register themselves as "foreign agents." Although the Russian government has claimed that this law was passed in order to promote transparency, the label is clearly intended to imply that the organization is involved in counter-state activities and recalls terminology used during the Stalin era. Since 2014, the Ministry of Justice has been empowered to label NGOs as "foreign agents" without their consent. As of June 2016, more than 100 organizations have been labeled as such. Many NGOs that have been designated as "foreign agents" have complained of difficulties with gaining access to public institutions and staff recruitment as well as lengthy court battles. Since May 2015, prosecutors have been granted the power to designate foreign organizations "undesirable" and force them to disband. After winning the support of 54.2% of the party-list vote (in a very low turnout election in which fewer than 50% of voter's bothered to participate), United Russia secured 343 seats (out of 450) in the State Duma. With this victory, United Russia secured a super-majority that will enable it alter the constitution through a strict party vote. The election itself was marred by allegations of fraud. On September 21, 2016, the *Atlantic* magazine reported claims by Sergei Shpilkin, a Russian physicist and statistician, that data analysis reveal that as many as 12 million pro-United Russia ballots were falsely added to the final count.

Perhaps in part due to fraudulent election results, the legislative power of United Russia is out of step with its level of popular support, which is somewhat tepid. In the run-up to the most recent elections, public opinion polling found fewer than 50% support for the party. The low turnout in the election can also be interpreted as a signal of the limited popular appeal of United Russia.

In contrast to United Russia, Putin remains incredibly popular, with most opinion polls hovering around 85% approval. While some observers speculate that this level of support is somewhat soft, and may decline due to the challenging economic conditions, to date Putin's popularity has remained robust even as the Russian economy has experience contraction and slow growth over the past several years.

Since 2013, Russia has promoted the creation of a Eurasian Economic Union (EEU) under Russian leadership to counteract the attraction that eventual membership in the European Union holds for Eurasian nations (what Russia calls its "near abroad"). Russia fears that parts of the former Soviet Union might over time direct their trade more toward Europe and away from Russia. Under the auspices of its Eastern Partnership program, the EU was offering Belarus, Ukraine, Georgia, Moldova, Azerbaijan, and Armenia a free trade arrangement as part of an Association Agreement to be entered into by the individual states. Russia has applied various forms of pressure to prevent Eurasian states from joining the EU. For example, Russia issued threats to cut off the flow of natural gas to Ukraine and Moldova. Russia also threatened to ban the importation of wine and fresh fruit from Moldova and chocolate from Ukraine. But the main threats appear to have been political.

The EEU came into existence on January 1, 2015, with founding members Russia, Belarus, and Kazakhstan. Armenia joined the following day and Kyrgyzstan on May 8, 2015. Moldova has strong connections with EU member Romania and has thus resisted Russian pressure to join the EEU.

Consolidated Present, Uncertain Political Future

Following the 2016 legislative elections, Putin's United Russia party retained firm control of the Duma. More importantly, the 2016 elections were not marred by the same degree of urban protest that had accompanied the 2011 elections. The successfully managed legislative elections set up the 2018 presidential elections which were held on March 18. To no one's surprise, Vladimir Putin easily won reelection. He received 76.69% of the vote and won easily over the seven rival candidates. Of course, the most prominent opposition candidate, Alexei Navalny, was barred from running due to his criminal record. As a result, the choice on the ballot was between Putin and a collection of has-beens (such as Vladimir Zhironovsky) and never-were. Even more discouraging, the campaigns run by the rival candidates were notably lackluster and disengaged. Thus, many observers took to calling the event a plebiscite rather than a proper election. In essence, voters were given able to give thumbs up or down to one more term in office for Putin.

As a plebiscite, voters could opt to voice displeasure in one of two ways—they could vote for one of the rival candidates, thus reducing the percentage of the vote that Putin would win, or they could stay home completely, thus reducing turnout. From Putin's perspective, a low turnout election for his fourth term would have presented a tremendous challenge to his legitimacy. No doubt to his relief, 68% of the total electorate participated in the election.

New Constitutional Amendments and an Invigorated Opposition

Putin's landslide victory on March 18, 2018 raised questions about the future of the regime. As a result of the election, Putin would be president for the next six years, but then what? At At the time of the election, Putin was term-limited. In other words, it was assumed he would be entering the "lame duck" phase of his presidency and would have less control over various elite factions than he once did. The last time Putin had been in this position he helped to build-up the United Russia party as a mechanism to manage the temporary succession with Dmitry Medvedev.

In fall 2018, efforts to consolidate United Russia's dominance at the federal level ran into an obstacle in a handful of the 22 regions conducting regional elections. In two regions, Khabarovsk and Vladimir, LDPR gubernatorial candidates defeated United Russia incumbents. In a third region, Khakasia, a communist party candidate defeated a United Russia incumbent. The fact that these surprising election results occurred alongside widespread and well-publicized protests over pension reform legislation which substantially increased retirement age led some to speculate civil society during Putin's last term may not turn out to be as quiescent as he may hope.

On December 19, 2019, Putin seemed to indicate a strategy for managing the looming uncertainty associated with his impending term limit when he floated the idea of additional amendments to the Russian constitution at a press conference. Ultimately, a staggering 206 amendments would be brought forth. These amendments adjusted basic law in numerous ways including through strengthening the power of the presidency by granting the President the power to remove judges, cementing the definition of marriage as between a man and woman, establishing Russian as the state language, making explicit reference to God. However, the most important amendment was a change which reset Putin's term-limit clock, effectively allowing him to serve as President until 2036.

This package of amendments was passed through a "nationwide vote" held between June 25 to July 1, 2020. Voters were granted a simple yes-or-no choice in approving the entire slate. Although there was no campaigning permitted on behalf of the "no" vote, Russian media consumers were exposed to a great deal of content emphasizing the importance of a "yes" vote to the future of Russian children and the preservation of Russian culture and conservative values. One of the ads produced for social media was so explicitly homophobic that it was banned by YouTube. Unsurprisingly, the amendments passed with 78% of the vote in favor. Despite the ruling by the Constitutional Court that the process was legitimate, the European Parliament and Vince Commission have criticized the procedure used to enact the amendments. Most importantly, the amendment process appeared to violate the spirit of Russian law on the referendums. By law, before a referendum, the Russian public should be exposed to "for" and "against" campaigns, and their should a transparent process for counting votes cast. By referring to the vote as a "nationwide vote" rather than a referendum, the Russian government was able to skirt these requirements.

Despite the questionable legality of the amendment process, in April 2021 Putin signed the new amendments into law. Although he now has a means to legally remain President for 16 more years, this is not the only path for him to choose. If he stays in power until then, his tenure would surpass that of Joseph Stalin's 29-year rule. One reason Putin engaged in such constitutional power grab is because he wanted to avoid the possibility of becoming a lame-duck in 2024, which could have led to destabilizing power struggle among the elites. The amendments also protect Putin from prosecution if he was to step down and it paves a way for him to potentially retire to the State Council, a heretofore ceremonial body which formally advises the president but which was emboldened through some of the amendments. Fundamentally, these new amendments preserve Putin's strategic flexibility and cements his rule by undermining potential defections from his inner core.

Putin's pursuit of institutional flexibility comes at a time in which he is facing growing societal mobilization and invigorated opposition. Beginning in 2018, Alexei Navalny and his supporters began advocating for "Smart Voting." In essence, this is an effort to focus opposition votes strategically towards the most likely successful non-United Russian candidate in any given election regardless of political platform or ideology. This tactic has seemingly resulted in some successes at the local level. In 2019, United Russia lost 13 seats in the 45-person Moscow City Duma, although the party maintained its majority. In 2020, United Russia lost its majority in the Tomsk city council and in the Novosibirsk city council. In each of the 2020 elections, Navalny allies were able to win seats.

Before the Tomsk election was held, Navalny fell ill on a flight from the

Russia

THE SITUATION IN THE EASTERN REGIONS OF UKRAINE

8 June 2015 (00:00)

Siberian city to Moscow. He was hospitalized in Omsk after an emergency and put into a coma. Two days later he was transferred out of the country for treatment in Berlin, Germany. Lab work revealed that he had been poisoned by a new form of the nerve agent Novichok. Investigations into the incident by Bellingcat have implicated the FSB in the assassination attempt.

Navalny's dramatic return to Russia on January 17, 2021, resulted in his immediate detention at passport control. While he was detained, his newest film "Putin's Palace" spread through social media alleging corrupt links between the president an elaborate palatial estate being built on the Black Sea. Navalny's supporters took advantage of the public attention and announced a nationwide protest for January 23. Despite heavy police presence and widespread repression of protesters, even more turned out the following week during the second round of protests. On February 2, Navalny's sentencing to two and half years of prison further deepened opposition to the government and contentious acts. While the regime attempted to pass off the protests as the result of "pandemic fatigue," there was a growing sense of rift between Russian youth and the president.

Russia's Annexation of the Crimean Peninsula and the War in Ukraine

For President Putin, it was most important to convince Ukraine to join the EEU.

It could even be argued that the EEU had no real possibility of success as a counterweight to the EU unless Ukraine joined. Russia's relations with Ukraine improved in 2010, when the pro-Russian candidate Viktor Yanukovych was elected president of Ukraine. Several bilateral agreements were signed, the most important of which extended to 2042 Russia's lease on its naval base at Sevastopol on Ukraine's Crimean Peninsula. In return, Russia agreed to provide natural gas to Ukraine at a 30% discount from the European market price. The entire relationship with Ukraine, however, began to change in the autumn of 2013. In November 2013, shortly before Ukraine was to initial an Association Agreement with the EU, President Putin invited Ukrainian President Viktor Yanukovych to Moscow for talks. Putin apparently offered Yanukovych many financial incentives. (A few weeks later, Russia publicly offered to purchase $15 billion in Ukrainian bonds and to sharply reduce the price Ukraine would pay for Russian natural gas.) He probably also pointed out the damage Russia could inflict on the Ukrainian economy if Yanukovych continued with his negotiations with the European Union. In any case, in late November Yanukovych agreed to drop discussions with the EU right before he was scheduled to sign a partnership agreement in Vilnius, Lithuania. Yanukovych did not promise to join the Eurasian Customs Union. Nor did he rule out the prospect that Ukraine

might join the EU at some point in the future. He was trying to chart a course between the EU and Russia.

What Putin did not anticipate was that a significant part of the Ukrainian population would refuse to accept Yanukovych's decision to discontinue discussions with the European Union for an Association Agreement. The demonstrations they launched in the central "Euromaidan" (European Square) in the heart of Kyiv continued throughout the winter in spite of all attempts by the government to bring them to an end. And, in the end, they brought down Yanukovych's government and turned his own Party of Regions against him, causing him to flee Kyiv on February 21, 2014.

President Putin responded by characterizing the new government as a group of Fascists and sending Russian troops to occupy the Crimean Peninsula starting on March 1. On March 4, however, Putin denied that Russian troops were involved. (A year later, in a nationally-broadcast TV program, Putin flatly stated that he orchestrated Crimea's annexation.) On March 16, a hastily organized referendum on Crimea joining the Russian Federation was overwhelmingly approved by the population of Crimea. Two days later, in an ornate ceremony in the Grand Kremlin Palace, Putin announced that Crimea had joined Russia. The United States and the European Union have rejected both the Crimean referendum and its annexation by Russia.

Immediately following the annexation of Crimea, pro-Russian separatists in Ukraine's southeastern Donbass region formed demonstrations, and they took control of the cities of Luhansk and Donetsk. Fighting quickly ensued between the separatists and the Ukrainian army. In April, according to NATO, Putin moved 40,000 Russian troops up to Ukraine's eastern border. Putin threatened to intervene further in Ukraine. On April 17 on Russian national television, he explained his position by arguing that "large sections of the historical south of Russia" now "form the southeast of Ukraine. I would like to remind you," he added:

that what was called Novorossiya back in the tsarist days—Kharkov, Lugansk, Donetsk, Kherson, Nikolayev and Odessa—were not part of Ukraine back then. The center of that territory was Novorossiysk, so the region is called Novorossiya. Russia lost these territories for various reasons, but the people remained.

Putin's intentions at this time were unclear, and they remain so. By invoking the term "Novorossiya," which Catherine the Great had introduced to refer to lands that Russia had taken from the Ottoman Turks in the late 18th century, was he signaling that he desired to annex a large swath of southern Ukraine all the way westward to the Moldovan border?

Putin may pursue such a radical and de-stabilizing agenda; however, perhaps the most reasonable interpretation of his strategy is that he wants to transform Ukraine (minus the Crimea) into a decentralized federation along the lines of Bosnia and Herzegovina. In this scenario, Russia could exert its influence over the Donetsk and Luhansk regions, with their large ethnic Russian populations, and thereby prevent Ukraine from joining either the EU or NATO.

Putin's rhetoric and mobilization of troops near the Ukrainian border encouraged the separatists and further heightened tensions in eastern Ukraine. On May 11, 2014, the new, self-proclaimed Donetsk People's Republic and Luhansk People's Republic voted for independence in separate make-shift referendums that have not been recognized by any other country.

Fighting intensified in the Donbass region of eastern Ukraine between separatists and Ukrainian army troops in the late spring and summer of 2014. Between mid-June and mid-July, around a dozen Ukrainian helicopters and other military aircraft were shot down. Then, on July 17, Malaysia Airlines Flight 17 en route from Amsterdam to Kuala Lumpur crashed in the conflict zone killing all 298 people on board. The following day, President Obama stated that evidence indicated that the plane was shot down by a surface-to-air missile fired from territory controlled by separatists. Ukrainian intelligence produced an audio transcript of what it claimed was a phone conversation between a separatist commander at the crash site and a Russian intelligence officer, in which the commander confirmed that a separatist unit had shot down a civilian airliner. In addition, right around the time that the plane was destroyed a rebel leader boasted on Russian social media that insurgents had shot down a plane. Russian media, without citing credible evidence, asserted that the Ukrainian military downed the plane. The most likely explanation is that separatists, or possibly Russian military specialists supporting the separatists, mistook the civilian airliner for a Ukrainian military plane and destroyed it with a surface-to-air missile. The separatists were known to have the Buk anti-aircraft system, and the plane was headed toward Russia over territory controlled by the separatists. The final report on the air crash by the Dutch Safety Board released in October 2015 revealed that a Russian-made Buk missile brought down the plane.

Following the downing of the Malaysian jetliner, the EU, US, and a few other countries increased sanctions against Russia, which they first had introduced following Russia's annexation of Crimea. These sanctions were targeted to individuals and business and consisted of denial of visas and confiscation of assets. The sanctions were gradually ratcheted upward during the latter half of 2014 and on into 2015. Russia retaliated with targeted sanctions of its own and a total ban on food imports from countries that had sanctioned Russia.

In August 2014, Russian servicemen, tank columns, and self-propelled artillery guns entered Ukraine from Russia in support of the separatists. NATO claimed that over 1,000 Russian military personnel had crossed the border to join the fight. Russian government officials have consistently denied that active-duty Russian troops have been fighting in Ukraine. On April 16, 2015, President Putin stated: "I can tell you outright and unequivocally that there are no Russian troops in Ukraine." On occasion, Russian officials have said that Russian troops who have shown up in Ukraine went there on their own using vacation leave. In May 2015, the Atlantic Council think tank, which is based in Washington, DC, issued a detailed report on Russian involvement in Ukraine. It claimed that Russian training camps along the border with Ukraine were launching pads for intervening in Ukraine and that Russian commanders have ordered their troops to remove uniform insignia and conceal identifying markings of vehicles they drive over the border. The report further states that weapons and ammunition manufactured in Russia have appeared in Ukraine and that Russian forces in Ukraine have received covering fire from Russia.

The increase in fighting in the late summer of 2014 in the Donbass, especially around the cities of Donetsk and Luhansk, prompted the Organization for Security and Cooperation in Europe (OSCE) to sponsor talks in Minsk with the aim of achieving a cease-fire. On September 5, the "Minsk Protocol" was signed by representatives of the self-proclaimed Donetsk and Luhansk People's Republics, and of Russia and Ukraine. The Protocol called for an immediate and verifiable cease-fire and release of all prisoners, among other things. Two weeks later, the representative agreed to create a buffer zone 30 kilometers wide between the warring factions that would be free of heavy weaponry. However, the agreements collapsed by January 2015. The following month, Russian President Putin met in Minsk with Ukrainian President Petro Poroshenko and representatives of the Donetsk and Luhansk separatists, as well with French President Francois Hollande and German Chancellor Angela Merkel. They signed a new cease-fire, dubbed Minsk II, which reiterated much of the previous Minsk Protocol. Shortly after this new cease-fire was signed, the key small city of Debaltseve, located in the Donbass between Luhansk to the north and Donetsk to the south, fell to the pro-Russian separatists. In the southern part of the Donetsk region, fighting also took place near the city of Mariupol. If separatists were to take Mariupol, they might be able to secure a corridor of territory along the northern coast of the Black Sea connecting Russia with the Crimean Peninsula.

According to the United Nations Human Rights Office, by March 2015, more than 6,000 people had died in the fighting in eastern Ukraine, and OSCE monitors were detecting an increasing number of violations of the Minsk II accords. On May 5, 2015, Russian Foreign Minister Sergey Lavrov charged that the Ukrainian military was shelling the rebel-held city of Luhansk. At the end of the month, the Reuters news agency reported that Russia was massing troops and hundreds of pieces of heavy weaponry near its border with Ukraine. On June 4, Ukrainian President Poroshenko told his parliament that the Ukrainian military must prepare for a possible "full-scale invasion" from Russia. He added that there was a "colossal threat" that major fighting would resume.

Russian media have continued to refer to the Ukrainian government as "fascists" who are supported by Western powers. President Putin has often portrayed Russia as under a state of siege by the West. He has compared Ukraine's attempt to take control of the city of Donetsk from the separatists to the Siege of Leningrad during the Second World War, when Nazi Germany and Finland tried to starve and bombard Leningrad (now St. Petersburg) into submission. Close to one million Leningraders died during WWII. Putin grew up in postwar Leningrad, and his family suffered grievously during the siege. His older brother died of a starvation-related disease, and his parents almost perished as well. Russia's comparison of the Ukrainian government's attempt to wrest control of its eastern Donbass area from the pro-Russian separatists to Nazi aggression in WWII strikes a responsive chord in Russia. (The Soviet Union lost 26–27 million in the war or about 65 times the number of US war dead.) Putin's approval rating in Russia remains above 85%.

The Russian government is very keen to suppress news that contradicts its narrative that Russian troops are not involved in the war in Ukraine. In late May

Russia

2015, Putin signed a decree that made the death or wounding of a soldier in a special operation a secret during "peace time" as well as during a time of war. This legislation raises the possibility that anyone who disseminates information about Russian soldiers who were killed or wounded in Ukraine could be charged with a crime against the state. According to a report released in May by Russian opposition figures and journalists, at least 220 Russian troops have died in the fighting.

On February 24, 2022, Russia started Europe's first major war in decades by invading Ukraine from multiple fronts, targeting large cities, including Kiev, using artillery fire and air strikes. The official goal behind Russia's ground and air assault on Ukraine, which the Russian government calls a "special military operation," is the "demilitarization and denazification" of the Ukrainian government, but not occupation. Russian authorities have accused the Ukrainian government of oppressing the Russian-speaking population of the country—especially those residing in the Luhansk and Donbas provinces. Months prior to the miliary offensive, Russia amassed a total of 70,000 troops and military equipment along Ukraine's northern and eastern borders. Despite warnings by the US intelligence of an imminent attack, few people, including Ukrainian President Volodimir Zelenski, believed in such a scenario. As of April 28, more than 3,000 civilians were killed and more than 3,500 were injured. Additionally, the war created the fastest-growing refugee crisis seen since World War II. More than five million people fled Ukraine into neighboring countries, and a further 7.7 million people became internally displaced. Russian bombardment of major cities in the east and the south of the country has resulted in humanitarian issues. The destruction of roads and bridges has complicated efforts at evacuation of civilians trapped in certain areas with dwindling access to food, clean water, medicine, and electricity. The resistance of Ukrainian forces frustrated Putin's early belief in a swift victory over that country. After failing to take Kiev in the opening weeks of the war, Russian forces have concentrated their assault on the east and southeast part of the country. In the aftermath of the invasion, the United States and its allies imposed sweeping sanctions on Russia and Belarus for supporting Russia's war efforts. Negotiations between Russia and Ukraine have not gone far beyond establishing humanitarian corridors for civilians trapped in hardest-hit cities.

Russian Foreign Policy since Independence in 1991

After independence, the various ex-Soviet republics agreed to honor the various arms agreements signed by the now defunct Soviet Union. President Yeltsin, who took control of the Soviet Union's nuclear missiles after Gorbachev resigned, ordered that ICBMs be targeted away from American cities.

After President Bush proposed in his 1992 State of the Union speech that the US and the former republics of the Soviet Union eliminate all multiple-warhead missiles and reduce the number of permitted nuclear warheads to 4,500, President Yeltsin proposed that both sides end production of all new nuclear warheads and reduce the total number of long-range warheads to 2,500 on each side. Speaking at the United Nations a few days later, Yeltsin further proposed that the US and Russia jointly construct a global anti-missile shield. In that same speech, Yeltsin proclaimed that he considered "the United States and the West not as mere partners but as allies."

Yeltsin almost certainly recognized that the collapse of the Soviet Union would eventually mean an end to the unified Soviet armed forces, and might make Russia vulnerable to attack. Since that time, all of the newly independent republics have indeed opted for separate armed forces. In most cases, the new armed forces have been only lightly armed, which raises the question whether they would be able to defend their borders if attacked. As we saw in 2008 in the case of Georgia, the answer was a resounding no. In 1992, however, the Russian government was probably thinking about its long border with the People's Republic of China and so wanted the assurance of American and Western support should such a threat arise.

The United States government also announced in early 1992 that the Peace Corps would begin operating in the area of the former Soviet Union. Peace Corpsmen were to be sent to Russia, Ukraine, Armenia, and one Central Asian country. A separate program applied to the three Baltic republics. Some of those various programs have since been terminated, sometimes at the request of the country involved.

When Yeltsin came to the United States in June 1992, the highlight of the official visit was the signing of an agreement in principle setting a new limit of 3,000–3,500 nuclear warheads on each side. This agreement was then codified into the START II agreement, which the United States and Russia signed in Moscow in December 1992. START II remained in a state of limbo for the next three years, however, because of a problem with the government of Ukraine over START I. Although the United States and Russia had ratified START I and had begun implementing it, certain parts needed the cooperation of the government of Ukraine. But the Ukrainian legislature refused to implement the agreement, because, it was argued, there were no funds to commit to the cost of dismantling the nuclear missiles, estimated to cost at least $1.5 billion. The American Congress, which had already authorized $800 million to help defray the cost of dismantling nuclear missiles in the four ex-Soviet Republics that had them, eventually voted an additional sum of money and the Ukrainian government then signed off on the agreement. With START I finally on its way, START II was ratified by the US Congress in January 1996. The Russian Duma, on the other hand, did not get around to ratifying the agreement until the spring of 2000—after new parliamentary elections in December 1999 had changed the composition of the Duma. Pushing ratification through the Duma was one of Vladimir Putin's first victories, and he accomplished it while still acting president.

The US and Russia also worked out the broad outlines for an agreement for joint 1993 space flight during the Yeltsin visit in 1992. A Russian cosmonaut participated in a US shuttle flight in 1993 and a US astronaut began a lengthy stay aboard the Russian space station Mir in March 1995. In January 1996, the US government announced that cooperation was continuing on a planned international space station. To facilitate cooperation and reduce Russian costs, NASA had agreed to add three space shuttle missions, two to ferry supplies to the existing space station Mir and one to place in orbit a Russian science module. These were nine such joint missions through 1998. With the space station completed and having received its first occupants, Mir was allowed to plunge to earth in a controlled descent in early 2001. Cooperation in space has continued to develop since that time. It is, in fact, true the United States will be dependent on Russian delivery systems after the US shuttle is retired after its last flight in December 2011.

Another area of Russian–American cooperation for several years was that of ex-Yugoslavia. Russia originally supported sanctions against Serbia after war broke out in Bosnia; but it later adopted a rather ambivalent policy, sometimes refusing to support further actions against the Serbs. On the other hand, Russia played an important role in getting the Serbs to withdraw from the vicinity of Sarajevo in the spring of 1994 and it supported the effort that led to the agreement on Bosnia in December 1995. In addition, the Russian troops sent to Bosnia as a part of the implementation force took their operational orders from the American general who was the senior NATO military commander in Europe. The quirk was that the Russian troops came under his operational command as part of the American forces serving under him, not in his role as NATO commander.

It should be emphasized that Russia will always have an independent foreign policy that sometimes puts it into competition with the United States on specific foreign policy issues. For instance, Russia objected to American threats to launch retaliatory bomb attacks against Iraq after Saddam Hussein blocked United Nations inspections. It also supported the Kofi Annan mission to Iraq, which defused the situation, and promised to act as an advocate for Iraq in the future. Russia's "pro-Iraq" position is understandable if one recalls that it was owed several billion dollars by Iraq and wanted to be repaid.

A second illustrative case relates to Serbia's actions in its province of Kosovo in the 1990s. The United States threatened additional sanctions against Serbia after Serbian paramilitary units carried out attacks on Kosovan villages in an effort to put down an independence movement in the province. Russia condemned the killings of Kosovan villagers, but opposed additional sanctions. Here Russia's position is explained by the cultural connection arising from the fact that both countries are Slavic and Orthodox.

In 1998, NATO launched a new attempt to get Serbia to grant the Kosovans renewed autonomy. It achieved agreement on a cease-fire in Kosovo in November, but outbreaks of violence began to grow again in early 1999. NATO then sponsored new peace talks in France, which included a demand that Serbia restore autonomy to Kosovo. Serbia grudgingly agreed, but it was not willing to permit the stationing of NATO troops there to enforce the agreement. When NATO launched air strikes against ex-Yugoslavia in March 1999, Russia threw its support to the Serbs and temporarily withdrew its representatives from NATO. After the fighting was over, however, Russia joined in sending troops to Kosovo and subsequently reestablished its contacts with NATO.

Russia still tended to support Serbia, however. The Russian government consistently opposed granting Kosovo independence during United Nations discussions about the future of Kosovo and eventually stopped the United Nations from taking an official position on the issue. When Kosovo declared unilateral

independence, Russia threw its support to Serbia. President Putin subsequently used Kosovo's declaration of unilateral independence to justify his own decision to recognize the "independence" of South Ossetia and Abkhazia.

Russia's Relationship with Eurasia (except Ukraine)

An important part of Russia's foreign policy is concerned with Eurasia that area which Russia refers to as its "near abroad," a term they apply to the ex-Soviet republics other than the three Baltic nations. Russia had negotiated individual agreements with a number of republics after the collapse of the Soviet Union, but the Russian government's policy toward these republics began to change in 1993. Essentially, Russia began placing its emphasis on the Commonwealth of Independent States, demanding that relations between the various republics take place within that context. After that time, Georgia joined the CIS, Azerbaijan reactivated its membership, and a number of general agreements were negotiated dealing with a customs union, currencies, and military assistance. A number of the ex-Soviet republics, in particular Kazakhstan and Belarus, but most of the Central Asian republics as well, have tended to favor a close working relationship with Russia. These republics actively participate in the CIS's Inter-governmental Assembly and have also signed agreements establishing an economic union, a payments union, a customs union and CIS peacekeeping forces. Russia favored the CIS because it provided, in the Russian view, a framework for Russia's relations with the "near abroad."

From 2003–2005, Russia sought closer ties with, and more control over, Eurasia. Three major events sparked this change in policy and seem to have convinced President Putin that the West, especially the United States, posed a serious threat from which Russia would have to defend itself. That defense would come in the form of closer relations with the rest of the former Soviet Union. In 2003, Putin condemned the US-led invasion of Iraq, with which Russia had close economic relations, as a dangerous violation of Iraq's national sovereignty. (See section below on Russian reaction to the war in Iraq.) In addition, Putin contended that Ukraine's "Orange Revolution" of 2004–2005, which led eventually to the electoral defeat of the pro-Russian presidential candidate Viktor Yanukovych by the pro-Western Viktor Yushchenko, was secretly backed by the West. Thirdly, Putin saw a threat to Russian national security in the inclusion of Estonia, Latvia, and Lithuania into NATO in 2004. The three Baltic states had been part of the Soviet Union, and all three shared a border with Russia.

During the earlier period, Russia offered special economic concessions to the countries of the near abroad, in particular providing energy at or near the price inside Russia. But in December 2005, Gazprom, the government-controlled Russian natural gas company, informed the governments of Georgia, Ukraine, and Moldova that they would have to pay world market prices in 2006. Shortly afterward, the Russian government banned the importation of wines from Georgia and Moldova. (Russia's conflict with Moldova stems largely from Russia's support for the breakaway area of Moldova east of the Dniestr River.) Russia also instituted a visa requirement for Georgians entering Russia, though it specifically exempted residents from the breakaway regions of Abkhazia and South Ossetia from this requirement. Russia later ended its ban on Moldovan wines and fresh fruits and vegetables and it announced in May 2007 that it would begin issuing visas to Georgian citizens again. It did not reverse its position on natural gas prices, however, and it, in fact, enlarged the policy by extending it to Belarus.

Until March 2008, the Russian government had always paid at least lip service to the idea that it recognized the territorial integrity of the various ex-Soviet republics. In March 2008, however, President Putin announced that Russia was pulling out of the 1996 CIS agreement that prohibited the establishment of political or economic relations with the breakaway provinces of Abkhazia and South Ossetia. Putin then formalized this new foreign policy the next month by issuing a decree ordering the Russian government to establish formal political and economic ties with the two provinces.

This was mainly a legal change, since Russian military forces had been in control of the two provinces since 1992 and 85–90% of their inhabitants already carried Russian passports. However, it was these moves that led the Georgian government,

**Former Secretary of State
Condoleezza Rice in Moscow**

Russia

in August 2008, to attempt to regain control in South Ossetia.

The Russian government responded with a military invasion that led to a temporary occupation of all of northern Georgia. Russia then recognized the "independence" of the two breakaway provinces. After a truce, Russian forces were then withdrawn into the two enclaves and reinforced. Although technically still separate, they are, de facto, part of the Russian Federation.

The Russian government also supported the opposition revolutionary forces that overthrew President Kurmanbek Bakiev of Kyrgyzstan in 2010. In these two cases, Russia extended its influence in the area of the "near abroad," a fact that was not missed by other parts of the "near abroad." In Georgia, for example, nearly every opposition politician made at least one pilgrimage to Moscow, presumably to make the point that they weren't responsible for the 2008 war.

President Putin now claims the right to send Russian forces to assist Russian-speakers wherever they are to be found if they ask for assistance. As Putin expressed it, the collapse of the Soviet Union left the Russian nation as "one of the biggest, if not the biggest ethnic group in the world to be divided by borders"; that gave Russia the right to intervene in Crimea and, by extension, anywhere ethnic Russians or their culture are threatened. All of the post-Soviet republics of the "near abroad" have such Russian populations.

Putin and Russian Foreign Policy with the Rest of the World

When President Putin first came to power, he placed his major emphasis on domestic problems, so little changed in the international arena. Internal discussions between various factions did take place about the direction of Russian foreign policy, with the left and the nationalists pushing for reinvigoration of relations with old allies, while the more centrist and liberal parties urged greater engagement with the West. This changed almost completely after the terror attacks of September 11 against the United States and the subsequent American-led international campaign against terrorism.

President Putin quickly condemned the attacks and offered his government's fullest cooperation in Washington's war against terrorism. Putin set forth the position of the Russian government in a speech given on September 24. "Russia," he said:

is supplying and intends to continue to supply all the information we have about the infrastructure and the location of international terrorists and their training bases. Second, we are ready to offer Russian airspace for airplanes with humanitarian aid for the region where the antiterrorist action will be carried out. Third, we have agreed on this position with our allies, including Central Asian states.

There was a great groundswell of sympathy for the United States among ordinary Russians after the attacks of September 11, so Putin's strong support for America's war against terrorism was well received at home. But it was also true—as the Putin administration pointed out—that Russia and the states of Central Asia had been struggling with terrorism launched by radical Islamists for a number of years, and the United States-led campaign could assist that endeavor.

Nevertheless, the government did come in for a lot of criticism in October when it announced that it intended to dismantle its electronic espionage center in Lourdes, Cuba, and close its naval base at Cam Ranh Bay, Vietnam. Mainly, the government was taken to task for voluntarily giving up a major source of intelligence on the United States as part of a shift to a pro-American point of view, presumably in connection with Russian support for the international War on Terrorism. As the Russian government was careful to point out, however, the decisions to close Lourdes and Cam Ranh Bay had been taken prior to September 11 and reflected a determination that these bases were no longer worth the money they cost to maintain.

Putin's strong support for the war against terrorism greatly improved relations between Russia and the United States. It also brought him an invitation to visit United States in November 2001. The several-day visit cemented a relationship between the two presidents, though the wide-ranging discussions highlighted differences between the two nations even as they resolved some of them.

President George W. Bush announced that the United States would reduce its nuclear arsenal of strategic warheads from 7,000 to between 1,700 and 2,200 within 10 years. Putin, in turn, proposed a mutual reduction to 1,500 warheads. President Bush originally preferred unilateral reductions by the two nations, but eventually he gave in when President Putin expressed a strong wish for a mutual agreement. START III negotiations in Geneva subsequently produced an agreed text which was initiated by Presidents Putin and Bush during the latter's visit to Moscow in May 2002. The final agreed text was extremely short. Article I, the operative clause, reads:

Each Party shall reduce and limit strategic nuclear warheads, as stated by the President of the United States of America on November 13, 2001 and as stated by the President of the Russian Federation on December 13, 2001 respectively, so that by December 31, 2012 the aggregate number of such warheads does not exceed 1700–2200 for each Party. Each Party shall determine for itself the composition and structure of its strategic offensive arms, based on the established aggregate limit for the number of such warheads.

The Bush administration's desire to build an anti-missile shield led to negotiations between the two nations in the summer and fall of 2001. Since the 1972 ABM treaty banned any such defensive shield, the United States proposed revising the AMB treaty to permit work on such a missile shield. When negotiations made it clear that Russia opposed any change this major, however, the United States formally withdrew from the treaty. Though Russia had wanted to keep the treaty intact, the withdrawal was accepted calmly; as Prime Minister Kasyanov expressed it, "although we favor preservation of the treaty, US withdrawal from it would pose no threat to Russian national security."

Russia's strong support for the War on Terrorism raised the issue of its relationship to NATO in such a way that Russia could participate fully in formulating common policies on such subjects as terrorism and weapons proliferation. It was decided to replace the Joint Permanent Council, established in 1997 as a vehicle for Russian cooperation with NATO, with a new NATO-Russia Council where Russia would, in some respects, have rights equal to NATO's 19 member nations. The details were approved on May 28 at a Russia-NATO summit meeting near Rome. In theory, the new organization allowed for the full participation of Russia in the formulation of common policies outside the core mission of NATO.

Iraq policy is an area where there have been great differences of opinion between Russia and the United States. Russia has a long history of close relations with Iraq going back to the time when the Soviet Union was a major source of military equipment for Iraq. One legacy of that relationship is a multi-billion-dollar debt owed by Iraq to Russia. As part of that relationship, a Russian consortium negotiated multi-billion-dollar contracts with the Iraqi government in 2000–2001 to develop an oil field in southern Iraq. As late as September 2002, in fact, the Russian government announced a proposed long-term trade agreement between the two countries that was estimated to be worth $40 billion. The Russian government thus had a strong economic incentive to maintain good relations with the Iraq regime.

When the United States proposed a UN Security Council resolution to force

Iraq to disarm or face military action, the Russian government took the position that it would support requiring Iraq to allow UN weapons inspectors to resume their work, but would oppose any explicit endorsement of military action. UN Security Council Resolution 1441 was essentially drafted along those lines and it passed in November with Russia's full support.

Three months later, the United States began advocating for additional measures to be taken after it had become convinced that the Iraqis were not cooperating with the UN weapons inspectors. Russia reacted to the argument by joining the French and German governments in a statement supporting a continuation of the UN weapons inspection process.

A week later, President Putin explained the rationale for the Russian position. "The international community cannot interfere with the domestic affairs of any country in order to change its regime," he said, adding that "the only legitimate goal the United Nations can pursue in this situation is the disarmament of Iraq."

Russia condemned the invasion of Iraq in March 2003, and continued to oppose the war as major resistance continued. As the Iraqi regime collapsed, however, the Russian government softened its position.

When Condoleezza Rice, the US national security adviser, went to Moscow on April 7, it was clear that both sides were working to repair the frayed relationship. As President Putin said on April 11, "nobody liked the regime of Saddam Hussein, except Hussein himself."

Yet it should be pointed out that President Putin's statement was made during a joint press conference with French President Jacques Chirac and German Chancellor Gerhard Schroeder and that President Putin also endorsed the French-German position that the administration of Iraq should be under the aegis of the United Nations rather than of the US-led coalition.

The question of the United Nations role in postwar Iraq was resolved in May when the UN Security Council reworked, then passed, a draft resolution proposed by the United States and Britain. The resolution, which brought 13 years of Iraqi sanctions to an end, essentially recognized the US–British role as occupiers and rulers of Iraq until such time as Iraq had an elected government of its own. In a gesture to Russia and France, both of whom had big contracts under the previous oil-for-food program, the resolution specified that the sanctions regime would be phased out over a period of six months, during which old contracts would continue to be honored.

The question of who should be responsible for the administration of Iraq until such time as it had its own reconstituted

government was resolved by instructing the UN secretary-general to send a "special representative" to Iraq whose "independent responsibilities" would include, first, coordinating, promoting, and facilitating Iraq's reconstruction and, second, facilitating the "process leading to an internationally recognized, representative government." This gave a role for the United Nations in Iraq, a position already endorsed by the United States and Britain, while making it clear at the same time that the ultimate authority would rest with the occupying powers, the US and Britain. In the end, Russia supported this formulation, as did France and Germany.

President Bush had been long scheduled to pay an official visit to Russia in June to participate in the 300th anniversary celebrations of the founding of St. Petersburg. To smooth the path for the visit, President Putin dispatched Defense Minister Sergei Ivanov to Washington on May 21 with a message stressing Putin's view that Russian–American cooperation benefited the entire world by enhancing global stability and security and expressing his further wish that the Bush visit to St. Petersburg would move forth the bilateral dialogue between the two countries. Back home, Putin also persuaded the Duma to ratify the arms reduction treaty signed by Bush and Putin a year earlier which pledged the two sides to reduce their nuclear arsenals by two-thirds over the following 10 years.

In the end, the Bush visit went off smoothly, the one remaining issue of disagreement being Russia's sales of nuclear technology to Iran. While President Putin defended the sales to Iran, he also stated his own opposition to Iran's obtaining nuclear weapons. After that time, Russia offered to enrich nuclear fuel inside Russia for Iran—an offer Iran spurned. In the end, Russia supported a United Nations Security Council resolution threatening Iran with sanctions unless it agreed to give up nuclear fuel reprocessing. Russia also suspended sales of processed uranium fuel to Iran for a time, though it eventually provided fuel for the nuclear energy plant it was building for Iran.

Russia is one of six nations that signed an interim deal with Iran on April 2, 2015, to ensure that Iran does not develop nuclear weapons in exchange for an end to sanctions imposed on Iran. The deadline for a final deal is June 30. There is some speculation that Russia's support for the deal is half-hearted, because an end to sanctions would enable Iran to export more oil, which would likely drive down the price of oil further. Russia's economy largely depends on its own exports of oil.

Russia's position with regard to North Korea's nuclear program was similar.

Russia participated in six nation talks on the issue, but it was unwilling to support more stringent actions against North Korea.

But even as the United States found itself in disagreement with Russia on several issues in the last years of the Bush administration, the two nations continued to cooperate against the threat of terrorism, and this kept relations at a sort of even pitch. President Bush's official visit to Russia in May 2005 to mark the 60th anniversary of the end of World War II in Europe also helped to create positive atmospherics. President Bush went to Moscow again in August 2006 to attend a meeting of the G-8 Countries, hosted that year by Russia.

During the latter part of the Bush administration, three issues divided the United States and Russia. Two of these issues were long-standing: Iran and Kosovo. The third issue was the American plan to deploy missile defense systems in Eastern Europe. Related to that, Russia suspended its implementation of the 1998 revisions to the Conventional Forces Europe treaty in December 2007. Deputy Foreign Minister Alexander Grushko said that suspension of the Conventional Forces in Europe treaty did not mean that Russia would unilaterally build up its forces in Europe. He also proposed that the NATO–Russia Council be charged with responsibility for laying the foundation for a joint missile-defense system.

It should also be reported that Russia and the United States signed a long-awaited civilian nuclear pact on May 6, 2008, President Putin's last full day of his second term as president. The agreement established the legal basis for US and Russian companies to trade in nuclear materials. The agreement also opened the way for Russia to import, store, and reprocess thousands of tons of spent fuel which had been supplied by the United States for reactors around the world. The pact faced some opposition in the US Senate, however, so the Bush administration decided not to submit it to Congress at that time.

The Obama administration, which took office on January 20, 2009, was committed to establishing a new relationship with Russia. One of the first actions of Secretary of State Hillary Clinton, the was to visit Russia and there to publicly pledge to "reset" the relationship between the two countries. As part of that "reset," President Obama's administration announced that the United States had canceled plans for deploying elements of a missile defense system in Poland and the Czech Republic.

After that time, the two countries signed a new nuclear reduction treaty and renewed support for another treaty, signed during the Bush administration, which reestablished an earlier agreement for the reprocessing of enriched Russian nuclear

Russia

fuel in the United States. They also reached agreement on new sanctions to be applied to Iran because of Iran's ongoing violation of clauses of the Non-Proliferation Treaty, to which Iran is a signatory, although this is primarily because France, Great Britain, and Germany supported the American position.

In October 2012, Russia announced that it intended to allow the Nunn-Lugar weapons reduction and security agreement to lapse when it expired in May 2013, saying that it no longer needed to receive foreign aid and was concerned about leaks of nuclear security information. It subsequently ordered the United States Agency for International Development (USAID) to close down its offices in Moscow. Russia also terminated a bilateral agreement on cooperation in law enforcement and drug control in January 2013. Under the agreement, signed in 2002, the US government had provided financial assistance to help the Russian government combat drug and human trafficking, Internet-technology crimes, money laundering, corruption, and terrorism.

On the other side, the US government scrapped long-standing trade restrictions on Russia in December 2012, thus granting Russia permanent normal trade relations. However, the legislation included language banning Russians accused of human-rights violations from obtaining US visas and limiting their access to the US financial system. The legislation was triggered by Russian government actions toward Sergei Magnitsky, who died in prison in 2009 after accusing Russian government officials of fraud.

In February 2013, sharp differences emerged between Russia and the United States at the annual Munich Security Conference. As Vice President Joe Biden put it, the two countries "have serious differences on issues like Syria, missile defense, NATO enlargement, democracy, human rights." But," he added, "we continue to see opportunities for the United States and Russia to partner in ways that advance our mutual security interest and the interest of the international community."

The United States and Russia have continued to disagree over policy in a number of areas, notably with regard to Iran, North Korea, and Syria in recent years. Putin's government has publicly and militarily supported the embattled Bashar al-Assad regime in Syria. In September 2015, Russia initiated a series of air strikes aimed to disrupt rebel groups and assist the Syrian government in reclaiming lost territory. This intervention has further complicated US-Russian relations as the Russian targets have included both ISIS and US-backed insurgents. In March 2016,

Amnesty International released a report that accused Russian and Syrian joint operations as intentionally attacking civilian targets, including health facilities, in direct violation of international law. To date, Russia has denied these and other related accusations and claimed that they have only targeted terrorist groups.

The United States has also condemned the Russian military occupation of the Georgian provinces of Abkhazia and South Ossetia, and Russia's subsequent recognition of the "independence" of these two provinces; and it opposes the presence of Russian military forces in eastern Moldova.

The United States has also been disturbed by the trend toward authoritarianism in Russia, as well as the rather blatant disregard for the rule of law in Russia toward critics of the current government. But as Vice President Biden's statement would indicate, these differences of opinion did not have a major effect on Russian–American relations until the recent developments with regard to Ukraine. President Putin's blatant disregard for Ukraine's territorial integrity when it occupied and then annexed the Crimean Peninsula after the collapse of the Yanukovych government has resulted in American and European Union sanctions against Russia. The United States and the European Union also strongly reject Putin's assertion that Russia has the right to intervene on behalf of Russian speakers wherever they are to be found in defense of Russian language and culture. The greatst fear over possible Russian intervention in countries with Russian-speaking minorities (outside of Ukraine) exists in the small Baltic nations of Estonia, Latvia, and Lithuania. Each was part of the Soviet Union and shares a border with Russia. Over the past year, Russian air force and naval activity has increased markedly in the Baltic Sea, and an Estonian security service operative was abducted in September 2014 near the nation's border with Russia and has not been released. Russian hostile activity directed against any of the three Baltic states could spark an existential dilemma for NATO, as all three belong to the military alliance. An attack on any one NATO member is considered an attack on all 28 members.

It is no exaggeration to state that Russia's relations with the West are at their lowest point since the late Cold War over 30 years ago, just before Gorbachev rose to power. According to the opinion polling of the respected Levada Center, in late winter 2015, 81% of Russians held a negative view of the United States, and only 13% regarded the US positively. Opinions of the EU were similar: 71% negative and 20% positive.

That having been said, under the Trump administration, it was quite difficult to discern how US–Russian relations would evolve. There were allegations of Russian involvement in the Trump election campaign. At times, it appeared that President Trump sought to break with long-standing Russia policy and forge a relationship with Russia on the basis of his personal affinity with President Putin. For example, in June 2018, President Trump made a statement in support of Russia being permitted to rejoin the G-7, apparently without making any concessions. In March 2014, Russia was removed from the G-8 because of the annexation of Crimea, and aside from President Trump, no G-7 leader had floated the possibility of welcoming Russia back in without some sort of resolution to the dispute with Ukraine. Despite this rhetoric, however, the actual policy on Russia advanced by the Trump administration often resembled prior administrations. Throughout the spring of 2018, the US treasury department placed additional government officials and entities on the targeted sanction list, including Rosoboronexport—a state-controlled weapons trading company that has been involved in exporting weapons to Syria. Sanctions have also been leveled against individuals accused of working with the FSB to launch cyberattacks on the US. In March, former Russian intelligence Sergei Skripal and his daughter Yulia were victims of a nerve attack while living in the United Kingdom. It is widely believed the attack was orchestrated by Russian government actors. In response, the US joined with a number of other Western states in condemning the assault and expelled 60 Russian officials from the country. It also closed the Russian consulate in Seattle.

Russia's invasion of Ukraine caused a definitive rapture in its relations with the US. In response to Russia's aggression, the United States and its European allies, imposed a comprehensive economic sanction. As a result of these sanctions, major Russian banks have been removed from the international financial messaging system Swift, and Russia's central banks assets (worth $630 billion) were frozen. Sanctions also targeted high-ranking Russian officials including Vladimir Putin, and oligarchs close to him. In part because of the pandemic and accompanying slump in oil prices, Russian economy is in bad shape. The sanctions may have contributed to the rise in inflation from about 9% before the war to more than 17% in April 2022. As a result of the war in Ukraine, it is difficult to assess how the relationship between the United States and Russian might unfold. The United States wants to maintain a stable and predictable relationship with Russia and cooperate with it in areas central to US national interest, provided that Russia is willing to be a responsible global actor, meaning that it would not violate the territorial integrity or interfere in the democratic processes of other counties.

As Russian relations with the West have deteriorated some observers have noticed with consternation signs that Sino-Russian relations have improved. For instance, in May 2015, Russia and China engaged in joint military exercises in the Black and Mediterranean Seas. During the same month, Chinese president Xi Jinping attended the Victory Day Parade in Moscow before holding bilateral talks with President Putin. These talks were part of a negotiation over a gas deal worth $400 billion. Although the worsening relations with the West likely catalyzed some intensification of the engagement between Russia and China as Russia has looked for alternative sources of capital, Sino-Russian relations have been warming since the early 1990s when the two states finally settled long-standing border disputes that dated back to the Soviet era. With respect to the situation in Ukraine, China has tried to toe a careful line. It did not join Western countries in condemning Russia for the invasion, but neither did it help Russia evade Western sanctions. As such, one should not get overly carried away regarding a potential deep alliance between the two authoritarian regimes; to date, as Chatham House associate fellow Dr. Bobo Lo has said, the relationship has been more of an "axis of convenience" than anything else. In other words, relations between the two states have been guided more by pragmatism and availability than fundamental principles or ideals. For instance, the much discussed Shanghai Cooperation Organization (SCO), which in addition to Russia and China includes Kazakhstan, Kyrgyzstan, Tajikistan, and Turkmenistan, is less an anti-Western dictators club and more of a multinational forum to allow China to gain access to Central Asian energy resources and trade infrastructure.

Russia

A presidential bodyguard salutes Russian President Boris Yeltsin and Italian President Francesco Cossiga at the Quirinale Presidential Palace on December 19, 1991
Courtesy of Reuters/Bettmann

Government of the Russian Federation

Under the constitution approved in December 1993, Russia is a federation with a division of powers between the central government and the local governments. The federal government is delegated certain exclusive powers. Those powers which can be exercised concurrently by the federal government and the member units are specifically enumerated. The constitution then stipulates that the member units may exercise powers not mentioned in the constitution. The constitution thus achieved Yeltsin's intention to devolve considerable authority on the republics and regions.

Since 1993, federal relations in Russia have evolved in the direction of greater centralization. The collapse of the Soviet Union quickly ushered in a period of chaotic decentralization empowering local authorities. The early hopes that federalism would strengthen open society and improve accountability were in vain, as regional elites began to abuse political power, refuse to cooperate with each other and disengage from society. By the end of 1990s, decentralization reached such an extreme level as to leave Moscow with few levers of political influence on the regions. When Vladimir Putin became president,

he pushed through reforms to deprive regional elites of political financial autonomy and allow for greater federal intervention in regional affairs. The Beslan school terrorist attacks in 2004 gave Putin a pretext to introduce a new approach to state administration that he believed would be effective in the fight against terrorism. As a consequence, direct elections for regional governors were abolished in 2004. Thus, between 2004 and 2011, Moscow appointed the governors of all federal subjects or regions. However, in the wake of 2011 post-election (Bolotnaya) protests, the central government was forced to cede some power and allow for regions to elect their governors.

The President of the Russian Federation, directly elected by popular vote, is the head of state and the guarantor of the constitution. He is commander-in-chief of the armed forces. He conducts foreign policy and provides the general guidelines for domestic policy. He also has wide powers of appointment. In addition to the prime minister (technically, chairman of the government of the Russian Federation), he appoints and dismisses members of the cabinet, judges, the prosecutor-general of the Russian Federation, top commanders

of the armed forces, and diplomatic representatives. He has the power to call elections and dissolve the State Duma (as specified in the constitution), submit bills to the State Duma, and sign federal laws. He decides questions of Russian citizenship and may grant political asylum.

The prime minister proposes the members of his cabinet to the president and presides over meetings of his cabinet. Neither the prime minister nor members of his cabinet may be members of the State Duma. In case of a vote of no confidence in the prime minister, the president decides whether to dismiss the government or dissolve the State Duma and call for new elections.

The Court System

The constitution creates a court system modeled on western democracies. There is a Constitutional Court which reviews laws when requested to do so by the President of the Federation, the Supreme Court of the Russian Federation, the Supreme Arbitration Court of the Russian Federation and local legislative and executive bodies. The Constitutional Court will also accept original jurisdiction over cases of individuals who feel that their constitutional rights and freedoms have been violated.

The Electoral System

Until 2003, elections to the State Duma operated on a mixed system, with half of the 450 seats filled by proportional representation and half by first-past-the-post voting. President Putin then got the Duma to change the system to full proportional representation with individual political parties required to obtain a minimum of 5% of the total national vote in order to be awarded seats in the Duma. The 2003 elections, carried out under the new rules, resulted in the disappearance of the so-called liberal parties, Yabloko and the Union of Right Forces. On the other hand, United Russia took 300 of the 450 seats on the basis of winning 37.1% of the vote.

It came as a surprise, therefore, when President Putin submitted a request to the Duma in January 2013 for a major change in the rule for parliamentary elections. Essentially, Russia will go back to the system that was in force until 2003. Half of the Duma seats will be filled by direct elections of individual candidates with the other half to be filled on the basis of proportional representation. The December 2016 Duma elections followed the renewed rules.

Rather than a liberalization of the system, it has been suggested that President Putin was motivated to take this action by the falling popularity of United Russia. He may have hoped to overcome its unpopularity by endorsing individual candidates. As David Herszenhorn, writing in the *New York Times* put it,

> The proposal also comes just a year after allegations of widespread fraud in the parliamentary elections in December 2011 set off a wave of huge street protests in Moscow.

What Has Been Changed

One of the first things that Lenin did after coming to power in 1917 was to abolish the imperial Russian court system and create new people's courts staffed by communists and other revolutionaries. The Russian court system, created by Alexander II in the 1860s, was modeled on western judicial practices. It incorporated the concept of "equal justice under the law" and included an independent judiciary, trial by jury, public trials, and defense attorneys.

The Soviet court system was specifically created to defend the revolution. Judges and prosecutors were required to be members of the Communist Party and to be loyal implementers of the party line. Trials by jury were abolished. Guilt or innocence was determined by a judge, assisted by two ordinary citizens who were referred to as lay assessors. Their function was to support the prosecution. Defense attorneys existed, though their role differed from that of attorneys in western countries. With no presumption of innocence, a long legal tradition developed against an acquittal-oriented defense. The function of the defense attorney was therefore to negotiate for the most lenient sentence rather than to get the client off. This was reinforced by the fact that, under the law, defense attorneys had a lesser status than representatives of the state. Acquittals were almost unknown.

Midnight, with the Russian tri-color floating over the Kremlin after 74 years. St. Basil's Church is in the foreground
Courtesy of NOVOSTI

Russia

Attitudes toward the law underwent something of a change after Gorbachev came to power in 1985, particularly after he endorsed the concept of a "nation of laws." The first practical manifestation of this new thinking came in December 1989, when a law on judicial procedure went into effect giving individual republics the authority to increase the number of lay assessors on the bench. This was viewed by some as a move toward creation of a jury system. Defense attorneys were also permitted to establish a national Union of Advocates and the number of acquittals began growing slightly.

Gorbachev's main goal was to free the legal system from outside political interference. He wanted to create courts where fairness and objectivity were the rule and cases were decided exclusively on the basis of evidence presented in court. He made some progress, but most of the authoritarian system originally created in the 1920s and 1930s continued to exist even after his reforms.

The repudiation of communism and the emergence of an independent Russian government created a new situation, however. Moscow was full of talk about reforming the entire legal system in 1992–1993, but the quarrel between President Yeltsin and the Russian Supreme Soviet meant that little was resolved.

This began to change in December 1993 when a new Russian constitution was approved which made major modifications in the legal system. Under Article 120, judges are "independent and subject only to the Constitution of the Russian Federation and federal law." Article 121 makes them irremovable, while article 122 guarantees their inviolability. Article 123 reintroduced the concept of trial by jury. In addition, Chapter 2 of the constitution contains numerous individual legal rights, including "the right to have a case heard by a court with the participation of jurors in the cases provided for by federal law" (Art. 47); the right to receive qualified legal assistance (Art. 48); presumption of innocence (Art. 49); guarantees against double jeopardy (Art 50); and protection against self-incrimination (Art. 51).

Most of these changes and new rights required implementing legislation by the Duma before they could take effect, however. In the case of trials by jury, the Duma authorized implementation on an experimental basis in 9 of the 89 regional courts beginning in December 1993. In the first eight months of 1994, over 5,000 trials were held in regional courts; of that number, 99 were trials by jury. The experiment continued, however, and, in July 2002, the Duma adopted a new legal code governing the prosecution of criminal cases which, among other things, authorized

trials by jury throughout Russia beginning in January 2003. In addition, the new legal code guaranteed habeas corpus (i.e., anyone accused of a crime must be brought before a court within 48 hours) and the presumption of innocence. It also changed the role of the judge to that of a neutral arbitrator, and authorized defense lawyers to challenge the admissibility of evidence. Separately, the Constitutional Court ruled in July 2002 that a former procedure that allowed prosecutors or courts to overturn acquittals or to increase sentences on appeal was unconstitutional.

In related developments, a new Arbitration Procedure Code came into force on July 29, 2002, which broadened the sphere of competence of arbitration courts and established a procedure for transferring cases to them from courts of general jurisdiction. In addition, a new Civil Procedure Code went into effect in February 2003 which establishes new procedures for settling civil disputes such as those in the workplace and among family members. Together, these new codes complete the transformation from the judicial system set up under communism. As Justice Minister Yuli Chaika expressed it,

with the introduction of the new Criminal Procedures Code, the Civil Procedures Code, and the Arbitration Procedures Code, the role of the legal profession in defending the rights, freedoms, and interests of citizens has radically changed and immeasurably grown.

Yet a series of reports coming out of Russia in 2005 made it clear that Justice Minister Chaika was wildly optimistic about the effect of the new laws on the actual operation of the legal system. As an October 2005 report by Peter Finn, reporter for the *Washington Post*, put it, "the jury system remains the object of suspicion, even contempt, among prosecutors and some judges in Russia." Finn points out that, under Russian law, prosecutors can appeal verdicts and almost all not-guilty jury verdicts are appealed. He gave the example of a defendant who had been found not guilty by three separate juries and then quoted the leader prosecutor in the third trial as saying afterward: "He's guilty. We cannot leave an unlawful verdict in force."

The Supreme Court, which has the prerogative to propose legislation, called for a law restricting jury trials to murder cases. The Supreme Court's proposal was made in the fall of 2005. At about the same time, the Russian Department of Justice proposed legislation aimed at bringing defense attorneys under the control of the state. One part of its proposed legislation would give the state the right to demand "information which the lawyers obtain while providing legal assistance to their

clients"; a second part would bring the self-governing bar under state control by giving the state "direct control, as well as control via its territorial branches, over the activities of lawyers, law firms, and bar associations.

The hostility of many in the government to recent judicial reforms has gradually had an effect; in December 2008, President Medvedev signed new legislation eliminating jury trials for persons accused of what might be called political crimes, including terrorism, hostage taking, the organization of illegal armed formations, mass disturbances, treason, espionage, sedition, armed rebellion, and sabotage.

Criminality in the Russian Federation

Over the past several years, American newspapers have been full of stories about rising crime in Russia and the private security forces that have become necessary to cope with it. Many journalists seem to be at a loss to explain this new phenomenon, though they clearly tie it to the economic transformation that followed the collapse of communism. There is little doubt that we are learning a great deal more about crime in Russia then we did before 1992. On the other hand, it should be remembered that the Soviet Union never permitted any reporting on crime until the last years of the Gorbachev regime and the very existence of adequate reporting creates an image of a greater increase in crime than has been the case. Moscow is still, for most people, one of the safer cities of the world.

Another problem that was particularly important in the 1990s is that the police had been, under communism, responsible for suppressing the very sort of "economic crimes" which then constituted the emerging market system. Since many of the

**Hon. Yuri M. Luzhkov,
former mayor of Moscow**

EXCERPTS FROM THE RUSSIAN CONSTITUTION

Article 1

1. The Russian Federation—Russia shall be a democratic, federative, law-based state with a republican form of government.

Article 3

1. The multi-ethnic people of the Russian Federation shall be the bearers of its sovereignty and the sole source of authority in the Russian Federation.

Article 5

1. The Russian Federation shall be made up of republics, territories, regions, cities with federal status, the autonomous region and autonomous areas, all of which are equal members of the Russian Federation.

Article 8

1. A unified economic space, the free movement of commodities, services and finances, and support for competition and freedom of economic activity shall be guaranteed in the Russian Federation.

2. Private, state, municipal and other forms of property shall be equally recognized and protected in the Russian Federation.

Article 12

Local self-government shall be recognized and guaranteed in the Russian Federation. Local self-government shall be independent within the limits of its powers. The bodies of local self-government shall not be part of the system of the bodies of state authority.

Article 13

1. Ideological pluralism shall be recognized in the Russian Federation.

2. No ideology shall be established as a state or compulsory ideology.

Article 15

4. Universally acknowledged principles and standards of international law and international treaties of the Russian Federation shall be a part of its legal system. Should an international treaty of the Russian Federation establish rules other than those established by law, the rules of the international treaty shall be applied.

Article 27

1. Each person who is legitimately within the territory of the Russian Federation shall have the right to move freely and to choose where to live temporarily or permanently.

Article 35

1. The right of private ownership shall be protected by law.

Article 38

3. Able-bodied children who have reached the age of eighteen years shall take care of parents who are unable to work.

Article 40

1. Each person shall have the right to housing. No person may be arbitrarily deprived of housing.

Article 41

1. Each person shall have the right to health protection and medical assistance.

Article 43

3. Each person shall be entitled on a competitive basis and free of charge to receive a higher education in a state or municipal educational institution or at an enterprise.

Article 47

1. 2. A person accused of committing a crime shall have the right to have a case heard by a court with the participation of jurors in the cases provided for by federal law.

Article 49

1. Each person accused of committing a crime shall be presumed innocent until his/her culpability is proved in the manner specified by federal law and established by a court sentence which has become effective.

2. Defendants shall not be obliged to prove their innocence.

Article 59

3. In cases where the performance of military service runs counter to a citizen's persuasions of religion, and also in other cases specified by federal law, a citizen of the Russian Federation shall have the right to replace military service with alternative civilian service.

Article 81

1. The President of the Russian Federation shall be elected to office for a term of four years by the citizens of the Russian Federation on the basis of universal, direct and equal suffrage by secret ballot [terms were extended from four to six years in 2008].

3. The same individual shall not be elected to the office of President of the Russian Federation for more than two consecutive terms.

Article 83

The President of the Russian Federation shall:

a) appoint, with the consent of the State Duma, the Chairman of the Government of the Russian Federation;

b) be entitled to preside over sessions of the Government of the Russian Federation;

d) nominate for approval by the State Duma the Chairman of the Central Bank

of the Russian Federation and bring before the State Duma the issue of removing the Chairman of the Central Bank of the Russian Federation from office;

f) nominate judges to the Constitutional Court, Supreme Court and Court of Arbitration of the Russian Federation and the Prosecutor-General of the Russian Federation; and appoint judges to other federal courts;

g) organize and chair the Security Council of the Russian Federation, the status of which shall be defined by federal legislation;

k) appoint and dismiss the top commanders of the Armed Forces of the Russian Federation;

Article 86

1. The President of the Russian Federation shall:

a) be in charge of the foreign policy of the Russian Federation;

Article 87

1. The President of the Russian Federation shall be Commander-in-Chief of the Armed Forces of the Russian Federation.

Article 90

1. The President of the Russian Federation shall issue decrees and directives.

2. Decrees and directives of the President of the Russian Federation shall be binding for execution throughout the territory of the Russian Federation.

Article 95

1. The Federal Assembly shall consist of two houses—a Federal Council and a State Duma.

Article 103

1. The State Duma shall have the power:

a) to approve the nominee of the President of the Russian Federation to the office of the Chairman of the Government of the Russian Federation;

c) to appoint the Chairman of the Central Bank of the Russian Federation and to remove him from office;

f) to declare amnesty;

g) to lodge accusations against the President of the Russian Federation for the purpose of removing him from office by impeachment;

Article 105

1. The federal laws shall be adopted by the State Duma.

3. The federal laws adopted by the State Duma shall be submitted for consideration by the Federation Council within a period of five days.

5. In case of the disagreement of the State Duma with the decision of the Federation Council, a federal law shall be considered adopted if in the repeat

Russia

police officers who arrested such "criminals" remained on the police force after the collapse of communism, it should not be surprising if they were less than vigorous in enforcing the new legality.

It should also be pointed out that corruption became endemic in the last years of the Brezhnev era with many officials taking bribes to overlook black market activity. Payoffs became an important way to supplement salaries and the corruption reached high into the government and party.

The minister of the interior, Nikolai Shchelokov, and his deputy, Yuli Churbanov, who also happened to be the son-in-law of Brezhnev, were eventually accused of illegal transactions. Shchelokov committed suicide before being brought to trial, but Churbanov was found guilty and sentenced to several years in prison.

But the corruption was too pervasive for the arrests of these top people to put a stop to it. When, with the fall of communism, private economic activity became legal, many of these officials and ex-officials continued to demand protection money from the new capitalists in much the same way they had milked black marketers earlier. For example, *Izvestia* reported on May 6, 1994, that a group of senior ministry of interior officials had been charged with operating a protection ring for well-connected gangsters (i.e., ex-black marketers); among other things, the protection ring intervened to help killers, kidnappers, and thieves stay out of jail.

As a result of widespread police corruption or even, in some cases, antipathy to developing capitalism, most businessmen have felt that they could not depend on the police for protection. This spawned a whole new industry, private security companies, most of them started by retired Soviet soldiers, former members of *spetsnaz*, i.e., special interior ministry troops, or ex-policemen. The size of these security forces is sometimes enormous.

Moreover, foreign businessmen wanting to establish a presence in Moscow have often found that one of the first things they had to deal with was the matter of security. One such American businessman reported that he had been accosted by five men with pistols and a print-out of his firm's worth. They demanded 7% of future earnings. In this case, the businessman took the first flight back to New York. In the late 1990s, it was estimated that three-fourths of all private firms were paying 10% or more of their earnings in protection money.

There is some evidence that Putin attempted to improve the situation after he was elected president in 2000 but, if so, that improvement lasted for a relatively short time and eventually got even worse. In May 2002, a two-year study of corruption by the INDEM think tank concluded that Russians paid about $37 billion each year in bribes and unofficial fees, a sum equal to 12% of the Russian GDP. About 90% of the bribes were paid by businesses, with roughly 75% going to low-level local officials.

In February 2003, Mikhail Khodorkovsky, head of Yukos, one of Russia's larger oil companies, told President Putin that corruption costs Russia up to $30 billion annually and he gave an example of the sort of dislocations it causes. The prestigious Moscow Gubkin Oil Institute had only two applicants for each opening, even though the average starting salary for graduates was about $500 a month. At the same time, there were four or five applicants for each slot at the state tax academies, even though starting salaries for their graduates range from $150–$200. His point was that graduates of the state tax academies expected to more than make up the salary difference through bribes. This is obviously a heavy tax on the new market system.

Rising crime in the 1990s was, in part, a symptom of the disruptions and discontinuities arising out of Russia's transformation from a command system to a market

economy; another factor was that, under Yeltsin, there was no pro-reform majority willing to pass legislation establishing clear and easily enforceable property rights in the Duma.

That changed with the election of the new parliamentary elections in December 1999 but, even so, the Duma did not get around to passing a land code permitting the sale of non-agricultural land—thus making possible a resolution of who owns the land on which privatized enterprises and buildings are located—until March 2001. The Duma finally got around to passing legislation governing the sale of agricultural land in 2002, and it went into effect on January 27, 2003.

In June 2009, Sabine Leutheusser, a special European investigator commissioned by the Council of Europe, reported some progress in the Russian legal system, including pay raises for judges to reduce the temptation for corruption. But she also reported prosecutors with "almost unchecked" power to put people behind bars and subservient judges "subject to an increasing level of pressure aimed at ensuring convictions in almost cases."

A notorious example of corruption and politicization of the police and judicial system in the late 2000s was what happened to the investment fund Hermitage Capital. Hermitage was once Russia's largest foreign shareholder. It hired three Russian lawyers to handle what they thought was a routine tax case. Instead, they found evidence that top police and tax authority officials had quietly seized control of Hermitage firms and used them to arrange a $230 million tax refund.

It all began in June 2007 when police raided Hermitage's Moscow offices and those of its Moscow-based law firm, Firestone Duncan, looking for evidence, they said, of tax evasion by a Hermitage affiliate. Among items taken by the police were original corporate seals and founding documents.

In October 2007, the Hermitage lawyer learned of a $400 million judgment issued by a judge against three Hermitage affiliates, based on testimony of lawyers representing the firms who had essentially pleaded guilty in every case; however, none of the lawyers had ever worked for Hermitage. Hermitage then checked the government's corporate registry and found that it no longer owned the subsidiaries.

Sergei Magnitsky, a tax law expert at Firestone, Duncan, then investigated and found that the new owners used the original seals and founding documents taken by the police months earlier to affect a transfer of ownership. When Hermitage brought the situation to the attention of the Ministry of Interior, prosecutors responded by indicting Hermitage executives in absentia and disclosing the original tax inquiry had been initiated by the Federal Security Service.

Meanwhile, Hermitage learned that the new owners had filed for and received a $230 million tax refund on behalf of the former Hermitage affiliates; when Hermitage reported the fraud to the police

in July 2008, the police went after the Hermitage lawyers, summoning them to Kazan. Two of the Russian lawyers subsequently fled abroad, fearing arrest; the third, Magnitsky, remained in Russia.

Magnitsky was arrested in November 2008. He was charged with helping Hermitage evade taxes in 2001. This was patently false, since Magnitsky did not begin working for Hermitage until 2002. Magnitsky was repeatedly beaten in prison by eight guards while awaiting trial. He was denied medical care and died in jail of pancreatitis in November 2009.

Meanwhile, no charges were ever brought against the Ministry of Interior officials who got away with $230 million. And no one has ever looked into what role the Federal Security Service played in all this.

After a public outcry following Magnitsky's death, President Medvedev fired 20 senior prison officials. However, when Russia's prosecutor-general attempted to dismiss Anatoly Bagmet, who played a role in the investigation into Hermitage Capital's complaint about the fraudulent use of their companies, he was

overruled. It turns out that Mr. Bagmet's immediate boss, Aleksandr Bastrykin was a classmate of Prime Minister Putin in the law faculty of Leningrad University.

The next chapter in this saga occurred in April 2011 when the findings of a new investigation sponsored by William F. Browder, owner of Hermitage Capital Management, were published in a short documentary film released on YouTube. In 2015, Browder published a searing indictment of the Russian cover-up of Magnitsky's murder in a best-selling memoir, *Red Notice*. In 2012, the US government introduced the "Magnitsky Act," which imposed sanctions against 18 Russian officials accused of being responsible for Magnitsky's death. President Putin responded by halting American adoptions of Russian orphans.

In July 2013, in a bizarre and absurd ending to this case, the deceased Magnitsky was tried and convicted of tax evasion. This was the first posthumous conviction in Russian history and was a telling comment on the state of the Russian legal profession.

Russia

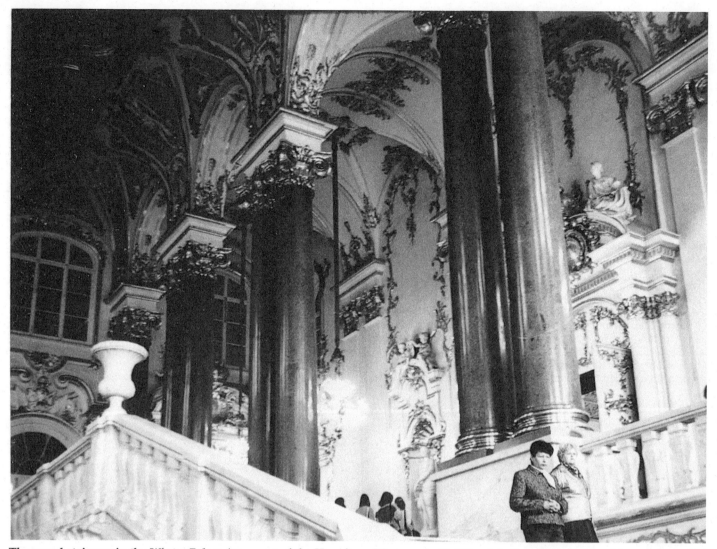

The grand staircase in the Winter Palace (now part of the Hermitage Museum in St. Petersburg). In 1732 Tsarina Anna commanded Italian architect Bartolomeo Rastrelli to build a four-storied Winter Palace of extravagant design and furnishings; it was built during the reign of Tsarina Elizabeth (1741–1762)

Courtesy of Miller B. Spangler

Culture

The failure of the August 1991 coup led to the repudiation of communism and the subsequent collapse of the Soviet Union, thereby giving birth to an independent Russian Federation committed to the goals of pluralism, democracy, privatization, and a market economy. These events marked the end of an era of official culture, but 70 years of indoctrination of the people with the philosophy of Marxism-Leninism cannot be overcome overnight. Proletarianism and socialism remain defining ideas for many people, and even terms like "socialist realism" have their supporters among conservatives. The old ideas live on, particularly among the old, among the peasants of the countryside, and among all segments of the population in the old industrial towns.

The greatest transformation has occurred in St. Petersburg and Moscow. Even in large cities, however, change is resisted. In St. Petersburg, for example, the Mariinsky Theater opened a new building in 2013 with state-of-the-art facilities and continues to host world-class ballets. Nonetheless, the Ballet, which since 1992 has been called the pre-revolutionary name of Mariinsky, is still known as the Kirov Ballet to some.

The fact that there is a continuing struggle over what to keep and what to change is not surprising. Throughout the Soviet era, at least two other cultures co-existed with, and sometimes challenged, the official version of Soviet culture. The first of these was pre-revolutionary Russian culture; the second was non-official culture. To these must be added religious culture, which survived in spite of official disparagement by the state, and today again flourishes. To

all of these, we should also add traditional Russian nationalism, whose proponents rushed in to fill the vacuum left by the repudiation of communism. With the demise of communism, all of these cultures have once again assumed their traditional roles in defining Russian culture; now it is Soviet culture that is tolerated and lingers on.

How much of Soviet culture will persist? Some "proletarian" authors and artists will undoubtedly continue to write or paint, although the Russian people have very little taste for political art after a steady diet of it for 70 years. But the fact is that there never was very much purely "Soviet" art and what there was of it was usually tied to specific political campaigns that quickly became outdated. Such art has a historical interest, of course, but it was by definition not made to transcend the age in which it was produced, and so it now lacks artistic interest.

great novels that people continued to read or the great artists that they admired were mostly pre-revolutionary. In effect, except for elements considered anti-revolutionary, the regime appropriated Russian culture to itself. Thus, poets like Alexander Pushkin and Mikhail Lermontov continued to be published throughout the Soviet period, along with short story writers like Nikolai Gogol, novelists like Ivan Turgenev, Fyodor Dostoyevsky, Leo Tolstoy, and Maxim Gorky, and playwrights such as Anton Chekhov.

Russian ballet, one of the "glories" of Soviet culture, continued to be dominated by classical French choreography. There were some experiments with modern dance after Stalin's death but, because they usually expressed revolutionary themes, they seldom rose to the level of art. Most Russian operas performed throughout the Soviet era were pre-revolutionary. All of this gave Russian culture the eerie aspect of being a museum of the past.

Things did get better after Stalin's death, but artists had been repressed so long by that time that very few of them were capable of great art. Still, some of these works are interesting for historical purposes. Ilya Ehrenburg's novel, *The Thaw*, is not a very good book, but everyone read it because of its message of hope.

To a certain extent, this period of liberalization was associated with the personal fortunes of Nikita Khrushchev. Although vocal in his own dislike for modern, especially abstract, painting, he encouraged writers who wrote works critical of the "distortions" of the Stalin era. He personally defended the book *Not by Bread Alone* by Vladimir Dudintsev. It was also he who authorized the publication of Aleksandr Solzhenitsyn's *One Day in the Life of Ivan Denisovich*.

Cultural controls were tightened again after Khrushchev's departure. This produced a great outpouring of unofficial Soviet culture. Some painters had always found their art to be unacceptable to the regime, so they had to find ways of supporting themselves by other means. The number of individuals able to afford paintings increased considerably after the death of Stalin, however; as a result, artists shut out of official exhibits were still able to find customers for their unofficial art.

The situation for writers was somewhat different. Unable to get works published, some resorted to circulating them in manuscript form. This was referred to in Russian as samizdat—literally, self-publication. Others, seeking a wider circulation, contrived to have a manuscript smuggled abroad, where it would be published, usually in translation. Having an unapproved manuscript published abroad was legally an anti-Soviet act, however, and a number

Russian artist in his St. Petersburg studio

Some of the work by revolutionary artists and novelists in the 1920s was an exception to this, but even that period had its darker aspects. Stifled in the new conformity, many artists fled abroad; others, like the poets Vladimir Mayakovsky and Sergei Yesenin, committed suicide.

The Association of Proletarian Writers was an annoyance in the late 1920s because of its intolerant attitude toward those who did not share its "proletarian" outlook, but that period appeared mild in retrospect after Stalin had instituted his authoritarian cultural controls and enforced his "socialist realism." Most of the great works of the 1920s were banned as "unproletarian" in the 1930s. These included the novels of

Mikhail Bulgakov, author of *The Master and Margarita* and *Heart of a Dog*, and the paintings of Andrei Malevich, who even in the 1920s had been forced to give up his earlier, abstract style.

Two exceptions were Dmitry Shostakovich, the composer, and Sergei Eisenstein, the film producer, who produced great works in the 1930s; however, both of them came under criticism in the periods of the 1940s and either had to revise their works or couldn't get them released at all.

But the fact is that most "Soviet" culture was actually pre-Soviet culture. There never were that many revolutionary artists; and most of these eventually found themselves stifled by the regime's tight controls. So the

Russia

of writers were imprisoned for this offense. Because of the Soviet Union's policy
of "socialist realism," nearly every great
work of Soviet literature written after 1930
had to be published abroad and almost
every Soviet Nobel Prize winner for literature was labeled a dissident.

In the early 1970s, the Brezhnev regime
added a refinement when it began expelling Soviet artists or stripping them of their
citizenship while abroad. The most famous
of those was Aleksandr Solzhenitsyn,
expelled from the Soviet Union in 1974.
Solzhenitsyn returned to Russia in 1994,
but he did not like the new openness. It was
only after Putin became president in 2000
that Solzhenitsyn found a system he could
like. As he said in a 2007 *Spiegel* interview,

> *Putin inherited a ransacked and bewildered
> country, with a poor and demoralized people.
> And he started to do what was possible—a
> slow and gradual restoration. These efforts
> were not noticed, nor appreciated, immedi-
> ately. In any case, one is hard-pressed to find
> examples in history when steps by one coun-
> try to restore its strength were met favorably
> by other governments.*

Solzhenitsyn died in August 2008,
shortly after Putin stepped down as president. Paying homage to the great writer,
Putin said of Solzhenitsyn that "his entire
long, thorny life journey will remain for us
a model of true devotion, selfless service
to the people, motherland and the ideals of
freedom, justice and humaneness."

A number of other artists who had been
given permission to travel chose to live and
work abroad. The pianist Vladimir Ashke-
nazy chose to live in England. The renowned
cellist-conductor Mstislav Rostropovich and
his talented wife settled in the United States.
Several top ballet performers defected
while touring abroad, while others, like the
Panovs, emigrated after long delays in waiting for permission to leave Russia.

The beginning of the Gorbachev era,
with its emphasis on glasnost, widened
the area of the permissible and brought the
publication of previously banned works.
Thus writings of Anna Akhmatova,
Boris Pasternak, Aleksandr Solzhenitsyn,
Mikhail Bulgakov, Vladimir Nabokov,
Osip Mandelstam, Vasily Grossman, and
Marina Tsvetaeva were all published. A
selection of Akhmatova's poems was put
out by the journal *Oktyabr*. Moscow's
Taganka Theater brought a play about
Pasternak and his novel, *Dr. Zhivago*, to the
Soviet stage, and the novel itself, for which
Pasternak received the 1958 Nobel Prize
for literature, was published beginning in
January 1988 by the journal *Novy Mir*.

Another example of greater freedom
for the arts under Gorbachev was the new
play by Mikhail Shatrov, *The Brest Peace*.

Performance of the Kuban Cossack Choir in Kranodar   Courtesy of NOVOSTI

Shatrov's play gives a detailed and fairly
sympathetic treatment of Leon Trotsky
and Nikolai Bukharin. Trotsky's name
had been anathema in the USSR after his
expulsion by Stalin in 1929; Bukharin was
executed in 1938 as part of the Stalinist
purges. What is perhaps most interesting about the play is that it was written in
1962, but the author had previously been
unable to get it performed or published.

Gorbachev eventually put his personal
stamp of approval on this new trend:

> *There should be no forgotten names or
> blanks. We must not forget names and it is
> all the more immoral to forget or pass over in
> silence large periods in the life of the people.*

As Gorbachev apparently intended,
part of this new "openness" turned into an

attack on Stalin. Thus a novel by Anatoly Rybakov published in 1986, *Children of the Arbat*, depicts Stalin as pathologically suspicious and politically obtuse. Like Shatrov's play, *The Brest Peace*, Rybakov's novel was written in the 1960s but he was not able to get it published earlier.

New plays with similar themes also began to appear by 1988. The best known was another play by Mikhail Shatrov, entitled *On, On, On*, which was published in the January 1988 issue of the literary monthly *Znamya*. A controversial play, it is full of suppressed details of Soviet history and is harshly anti-Stalinist. Interviewed about the play, Shatrov commented that

> *If you read my plays you will see that all of them are in essence about one thing: Stalin is not Lenin's heir. Stalin is a criminal of the kind the world has never had. He is not a Communist for me, because if he is a Communist, I have to leave the party immediately.*

Many Soviet intellectuals who shared Shatrov's point of view began pressing the party for a total repudiation of Stalin and a rehabilitation of his victims. Gorbachev was, in general, sympathetic but other members of the leadership, including Ligachev, Chebrikov, and Yazov, spoke out against what they termed the "one-sided" evaluation of Stalin. While willing to condemn such things as the 1930s purges, they argued that Stalin should be given credit for such things as industrialization and collectivization and the USSR's victory in World War II. In essence, their view of Stalin was that he was a good communist who had made mistakes.

The resulting division led to a battle in the Soviet media in which Shatrov, in particular, was accused of "inaccuracies," "juggling with the facts," and "departure from the truth." What more conservative reformers like Ligachev apparently feared is that excessive criticism of the past would weaken popular faith in the party. In the summer of 1990, after the final defeat of Ligachev at the 28th Party Congress, Gorbachev ended the controversy by issuing a decree rehabilitating Stalin's victims.

After 1990, artists were basically free to write or compose or paint what they wanted, free of party tutelage. Thus, with few exceptions, Gorbachev had brought an end to the long period of official supervision of the arts by the cultural affairs section of the Communist Party. These last few exceptions ended in August 1991 with the failure of the coup to unseat Gorbachev and reinstate a new orthodoxy. The complicity of the Communist Party in the coup led to its repudiation and Boris Yeltsin subsequently issued a decree in effect banning the party.

The collapse of the Soviet Union and the emergence of an independent Russian Federation with Boris Yeltsin as president marked the beginning of a new era in which Russian culture, free finally of all state controls, was free to develop as Russians wished it. This has already brought changes, not all of them laudable, to be sure. Culture now has to be much more "commercial," since it needs customers to survive. As some artists are beginning to recall with nostalgia, the old Soviet regime subsidized art as well as controlled it.

Perhaps that is why the government's attitude toward culture began to change soon after Vladimir Putin took over as president in 2000. Many changes occurred as a result in the change in political leadership, but the most important difference is that Putin reversed the "hands off" attitude that was so dominant a theme under Yeltsin and he began talking about the need to encourage patriotism. He also publicly endorsed creation of a youth organization modeled along the lines of the Komsomol, the communist youth organization of the Soviet Union. As another gesture in that direction, Putin authorized the use of the old Soviet flag by units of the military. Finally, he threw out the national anthem approved under Yeltsin—actually a piece of music written by Mikhail Glinka—and replaced it with the music from the Soviet anthem approved under Stalin. A contest held to provide new words for the music was won by Sergei Mikhailov, the 87-year-old poet who co-authored the original anthem during World War II. The text of the Russian (and old Soviet) anthem is as follows:

> *Russia our sacred state!*
> *Russia, our beloved country!*
> *A mighty will, a great glory*
> *[are] your inheritance for all time!*
>
> *[Refrain]*
> *May you be glorious, our free Fatherland.*
> *An eternal union of fraternal peoples.*
> *Popular wisdom given by our forebears.*
> *May you be glorious, country! We are proud of you!*
>
> *From the southern seas to the polar region*
> *Extend our forests and meadows.*
> *You are unique on earth! You are the only such!*
> *Native land protected by God.*
>
> *A broad space for dreams and for living,*
> *The years open up the future to us.*
> *Our loyalty gives strength to the Fatherland.*
> *Thus it was, thus it is and thus it will be forever!*

Faithful Muslims gather for Friday prayer at the central mosque in Kazan, capital of the Tatar autonomous region on the Volga River

Courtesy of Steve Raymer © 1991 National Geographic Society

Religion in the Russian Federation

Religion had a peculiar status in the now defunct Soviet Union. There was an

Russia

officially declared separation of church and state, and Soviet citizens had a constitutionally guaranteed freedom of worship. But communism, the ideology of the only legal political party, was militantly atheistic, so the constitution guaranteed the right of anti-religious propaganda as well. Official opposition to religion had its roots in the basic materialistic philosophy of Marxism, which held that spiritual matters were merely a reflection of material things and conditions. Karl Marx, in a famous phrase, stated that religion was being used by the ruling classes as an opiate, or drug, which dulled the ability of the masses to know their real problems and find the solution for them. Claiming to derive their views from scientific knowledge, communists saw themselves as secular and "this world" minded and opposed religion as "unscientific" and false. Since communists held that their value system represented "truth," they were extremely intolerant of all religious teachings, because of their competing claims to truth. In fact, communism had a comprehensive world outlook and set of beliefs which made it a sort of "religion" itself. It even promised paradise, though it was to be here on earth rather than in another world.

Communist theory held that communism represented a new "consciousness" on the part of mankind. To reach the stage of communism, therefore, it was necessary to "transform" the thinking of the people through a process of consciousness-raising or indoctrination. This process was to result in the emergence of a "new man," conditioned to living in a communist society.

Communists attached particular importance to the "educational" functions of the party. They were especially concerned with shaping the basic beliefs of the younger generation, since young people were still untainted with the corruptions of the previous system. Religious bodies, since they represented the values of the previous system, were forbidden to proselytize or to carry on any public functions other than the worship service itself. Churches, synagogues, and mosques were barred from all areas of education, including Sunday schools and catechism classes. Organized acts of charity were also forbidden and religious marriage ceremonies were banned. For a time, even the ringing of bells was forbidden.

Beyond that, the regime tended to differentiate in its treatment of individual religions depending on the total number of adherents and the role accorded it in pre-revolutionary Russia. The Orthodox Church, to which most Russians, Ukrainians, and Byelorussians belonged, had been one of the mainstays of the old system and a loyal tool of the tsarist governments. Moreover, the Orthodox Church

Patriarch Kirill, elected January 2009

adopted a strongly anti-Bolshevik position during the revolutionary upheaval of 1917 and the civil war that followed. Thus the Orthodox Church became a particular target. During the civil war, many members of the clergy, including the Patriarch, were arrested and quite a number were executed. All church buildings were nationalized and many were closed. In the 1920s, the party created an organization known as the League of Militant Atheists to carry on the battle against religion. Members of the league, lavishly supported by the regime, engaged in all sorts of anti-religious propaganda. One of the things they did was to turn Kazan Cathedral in St. Petersburg, a beautiful, neoclassical church built in the 18th century, into the Museum of Atheism.

Islam came under similar restrictions. Islam was considered to be even more dangerous than Christianity in some respects, since it recognized no distinction between the secular and the religious. In addition, the Muslim clergy were strong defenders of the traditional way of life, and so opposed most of what the communists were trying to do. Communists therefore did their best to stamp out Islam in Central Asia. Religious schools and mosques were closed and many of the Islamic clergy were imprisoned.

Nor did the regime cease its attacks on religion after it had consolidated its power. In the 1930s, Stalin ordered churches, synagogues, and mosques closed all over the country and he had a number of Moscow's historic churches torn down as a part of his rebuilding of the center of the city. Most of the remainder were turned into museums or converted to other secular uses.

As conditions became stabilized in the late 1930s, the Stalin regime adopted a somewhat less militant position toward religion. A dramatic turn occurred after the German invasion of the country in June 1941. The League of Militant Atheists was

dissolved and its printing facilities were actually turned over to the Russian Orthodox Church. Stalin had come to the conclusion that, in a crisis, the communist regime could make use of the support of the Church with its deep roots among the masses.

The regime tightened its control again after the end of the war, but this was mainly to guarantee that the church continued to serve the goals of the state. Internationally, members of the higher Orthodox clergy were frequently used as delegates to various international peace congresses. Domestically, the Patriarch and other members of the hierarchy were expected periodically to speak out in support of Soviet policy. The Islamic clergy, by this time tamed, was also used occasionally for diplomatic missions, mainly to the Middle East.

Even so, about 10,000 additional churches were closed between 1959 and 1964—about half the remaining total in the Soviet Union. In 1960, the Archbishop of Kazan was tried and sentenced to prison. That same year, the Metropolitan Nicholas of Krutitsy was deprived of his offices. And in Central Asia, historic mosques, sitting unused, fell further into disrepair. This policy of repression, associated mainly with the regime of Nikita Khrushchev, came to a partial end in 1964. The Brezhnev regime later permitted 500 of the closed churches to be reopened. Mosques were not reopened, but the most historic ones were given the classification of national treasures and the first efforts at restoration were begun.

The Brezhnev regime remained officially atheist, but it was a conservative regime that tended to accept religion as part of the status quo. Russian nationalism enjoyed something of a revival at this time as well, and that was often extended to include the Orthodox Church. As a result, it was the best-treated of all the organized religious groupings in the USSR under Brezhnev and saw even a modest growth in its nominal membership to more than 30 million. In the last years of the Brezhnev regime, church services were overflowing and, in a change from the past, many young people began attending services. Since most of this growth occurred in the period now known as "the era of stagnation," it was partly a symptom of the loss of faith in communism that was then only beginning to manifest itself.

Brezhnev died in November 1982, but the era of stagnation really lasted until March 1985, when Mikhail Gorbachev was appointed General Secretary. Although it was not immediately apparent, Gorbachev had an entirely different attitude toward religion than his predecessors as leader of the Communist Party of the Soviet Union. Although not a believer, his attitude may have been influenced by the fact that his mother was. But whatever the reason,

Religious procession in Moscow   Courtesy of NOVOSTI

Gorbachev set out rather systematically to end the party's traditional hostility toward religion. One of the points he made in justifying this change of position was that people needed moral values and that religion had an important contribution to make in this area. In 1988, official celebrations marking the millennium of Russia's conversion to Christianity symbolized this changed attitude on the part of regime.

In September 1990, the USSR Supreme Soviet passed new legislation prohibiting the government from interfering in religious activities. Another law required the state to reopen a place of worship on receipt of a petition signed by at least 20 believers. Some 4,000 new parishes opened between 1985 and 1991.

In another indication of this change, when Patriarch Pimen died in May 1990, one of those who spoke a eulogy at his funeral service was Anatoly Lukyanov, chairman of the USSR Supreme Soviet. And in 1991, Boris Yeltsin, the president of the Russian Federation, and Valentin Pavlov, the Soviet chairman of the Cabinet of Ministers, were among those attending Easter services at Epiphany Cathedral in Moscow. Easter services were also held at St. Basil's Cathedral on Red Square, even though it was still officially a museum.

Aleksy II, Pimen's successor as patriarch, died in December 2008. In a sign of the changes that have recently taken place in Russia, both Putin and President Medvedev kissed the patriarch during his lying-in-state. Alesky II's successor was Kirill, the church's long-standing external affairs director, who previously had held the title of metropolitan. The election took place in the rebuilt Cathedral of Christ the Savior, the original of which

had been demolished by Stalin in 1931. President Putin is Russia's first leader since the last tsar, Nicholas II, to identify as an Orthodox Christian. Relations between the Russian Orthodox Church (ROC) and Putin have been very strong. Kirill once called Putin's long tenure as president "a miracle of God." According to Reuters correspondents Gabriela Baczynska and Tom Heneghan, the ROC has built or restored 25,000 churches over the past 25 years, and claims about 200 million members worldwide. Next to Roman Catholicism, it is the largest denomination in Christendom.

Gorbachev's policy of religious toleration eventually came to be applied also to Muslim areas, though somewhat later because the Iranian revolution and the war in Afghanistan had created fears of an Islamic fundamentalism sweeping through Central Asia. The Soviet troop pullout from Afghanistan and the death of Iran's Khomeini reduced that threat, and paved the way for a changed policy toward Islam.

This brought the beginnings of a religious revival. Mosques were reopened all over Central Asia. In 1990, 14 new mosques were opened for services in Kokand, some while still under construction. For decades, a single mosque had served a Muslim population of 150,000 in that city. Elsewhere, mosques were being opened at the rate of almost one a day. In Uzbekistan, over 200 new mosques were opened in 1989–1990. Hundreds of students were enrolled in theological colleges and millions of copies of the Qur'an were distributed. And more than 1,500 Soviet Muslims made the pilgrimage to Mecca in 1990, the largest number in recent memory. As Muhammad Yusuf, the grand

mufti of Tashkent and Central Asia's senior Muslim leader said,

at first Muslims were rather passive and did not react quickly to what was happening elsewhere in the country. Now we are demanding the same privileges accorded to other religions.

Judaism represented a somewhat different situation because, under Soviet law, Jews were viewed as both a religious group and a nationality. Various factors made the situation complex, including a pre-revolutionary tradition of anti-Semitism which Lenin combated as being a tool of reaction. Stalin reversed this position in the late 1940s with his campaigns against "rootless cosmopolitan writers," and his later "doctors' plot." Anti-Zionism survived Stalin and continued to justify anti-Semitism under his successors.

In the past, religious practices of Soviet Jews were limited by the government, but the Gorbachev regime's changed attitude toward religion brought about a basic change of attitude toward Jews as well. In general, the restrictions on the practice of Judaism were abolished. Jews were authorized to set up religious schools and seminaries and to begin giving religious instruction to young people. One problem was the lack of trained rabbis. That was partially solved by bringing in rabbis from abroad. Hasidic organizations from the United States and Israel have also actively provided assistance of all sorts.

The failed coup of August 1991 created a new situation by bringing a repudiation of the Communist Party and a break up of the Soviet Union. The newly independent Russian Federation closed down the Communist Party and rejected its ideology. Religion is now considered to be a matter of conscience and as such beyond the purview of the state. In December 1991, President Yeltsin symbolized this new approach by issuing an appeal to heads of religious faiths and believers in which he condemned "the policy of spiritual genocide" of the previous regime and promised to

eliminate the consequences of the profoundly unjust policy of the many-year-long communist dictatorship with regard to believers [and] to hand over religious shrines, churches, and cloisters to those to whom they should rightly belong.

Catholics, Protestants, and other Christian communities have had greater problems since the government passed legislation aimed at restricting "sects," partly at the behest of the Orthodox Church. This has not stopped the growth of non-Orthodox Christianity, however. Christian Evangelicals, in particular, have

Russia

Russian school girls. School uniforms are no longer required attire
Courtesy of Miller B. Spangler

established many churches in Russia over the past 25 years.

The Muslims of the former Soviet Union, located mainly in the six republics of Central Asia, have their own independent governments to look after their interests. Muslims live in the Russian Federation, though they constitute a small percentage of the population. Guaranteed the same rights as other believers, most live in one of the autonomous republics or other autonomous regions, and they are to be found mainly in the Volga River Valley or in the area of the north Caucasus. However, a sufficient number live in Moscow to support six mosques, and a huge new mosque was completed in the hills overlooking the city in the fall of 2008. The growth in the number of mosques in Russia over the past decade or so has been phenomenal, in fact. In 1989, there were 98 mosques in all of Russia; at last count, there were more than 8,000 and the numbers continue to grow.

A problem for Islam is the struggle for dominance between the old-line moderate Islamic clerical leadership and a growing presence of Salafism that spread out from the area of the Northern Caucasus to other parts of Russia where there are significant Islamic populations. In the area of the North Caucasus, it took the form of a demand for creation of an Islamic Emirate that would operate under religious law and it produced a civil war that has gradually turned into a religious war. In the Russian Caucasus republic of Dagestan, Said-Afandi Artayev, a leading Sufi Muslim leader, was killed by a suicide bomber in August 2012.

In the Tatarstan republic, moderate leaders have attempted to counter the influence of Salafism by dismissing ultraconservative preachers and banning textbooks from Saudi Arabia. In July 2012, Ildus Faizov, the Chief Mufti of Tatarstan, was wounded by a car bomb; in a separate attack that occurred 20 minutes later,

Valiulla Yakupov, the Grand Mufti's deputy, was shot and killed. Yakupov was in charge of Muslim religious education for the republic's spiritual directorate.

The greatest current threat to Jewish culture in the Russian Federation is probably the large emigration that has occurred in recent years. For example, approximately 400,000 Jews left the Soviet Union in the last two years of its existence, 1990–1991. It then subsided for the next several years as Jews began to reconsider leaving. After the collapse of communism, a number of new Jewish high schools, newspapers, and theaters were opened, and an increasing number of individual Jews began speaking about the newly independent Russian Federation as a place that offered bright prospects for Jewish life. This trend was reversed after Russia's financial crisis began in August 1998. The Jewish population then stabilized at about 150,000 according to the 2010 census, though Jewish organizations say the number is larger.

The *New York Times* reported on the opening of a new Jewish Museum and Tolerance Center in Moscow in November 2012. The cost of the new state-of-the-art museum was underwritten by oligarchs, among them billionaire Viktor Vekselberg, though it was reported that President Putin had also contributed a month's salary toward the cost of the museum. At the opening ceremony, Berel Lazar, the chief rabbi, said that Jews "have never felt as comfortable in Russia as today."

Education

Russian education, like almost everything else in Russian society, is currently in a state of transition. The failure of the August 1991 coup brought about a repudiation of communism and the subsequent collapse of the Soviet Union itself. As a result, the regimentation in the area of education enforced by that old system also disappeared. The government of the

Russian Federation has not rushed in to assume the authority of the old center, so individual school districts find themselves very much on their own. The result is that individual schools are beginning to make changes and institute programs that, increasingly, set them off from other schools. Some school authorities fear that this is producing a fragmented, localized system, but others see this as another example of increasing pluralism in the society.

One of the changes already evident is an abandonment of the school uniforms worn by all school children under the old system. Most children continue to wear the uniforms, or parts of them, but they now also wear a variety of sweaters and jackets. Some schools have also begun offering classes in religious education. In other schools, educational reformers are asking how school systems can be changed to make them better able to serve the needs of a market economy.

An Historical Overview

Education in Russia saw many changes in the 74 years following the Russian Revolution of 1917. In the first years after the revolution, "progressive" methods were tried on all levels, with an almost total elimination of classroom discipline. Teachers were subjected to the rule of committees of pupils; there was much noisy activity and very little learning.

When the revolutionary fervor faded, education was reestablished along traditional lines, with uniform studies for all schools of the huge country and a strong emphasis on the sciences and mathematics. Elective courses were abolished in favor of a standard curriculum throughout the Soviet Union. Teaching was conducted in the native languages of the various Union Republics, but the content was centrally determined in Moscow.

A major problem of pre-revolutionary Russia was that more than 60% of the people could not read and write. This high illiteracy rate was vigorously attacked by the Soviet government and as a result, by 1928, more than half of the citizens were literate. The figure rose to 81% in 1939 and is now almost 100%.

For a while, the state-controlled school was looked upon as a counter-balance to the "reactionary" influences of traditional family ties; at the height of the purges in the 1930s, children were encouraged to report "subversive" activities of their own parents and other relatives. In the late 1930s, however, this approach was abandoned in favor of an emphasis on the Soviet family as the source of "correct" values. The events of August 1991 have reinforced this approach.

Because increasing numbers of Russian women were drawn into the workforce in the 1930s, a wide network of nurseries and kindergartens—usually run by individual factories—was created to take care of children of working mothers. These facilities were often crowded and not particularly well run, and it was not until the collapse of communism that privately-operated day care centers began to come into existence. That trend accelerated as the Russian privatization program was implemented in the 1990s. In addition, many factories now run their day care centers as commercial ventures, meaning that they are available, at a fee, to anyone who wants to use them, not just their own employees.

Regular schooling lasts for 8, 10, or 11 years, depending on where the student lives and his or her academic achievement—though this is changing. In June 2000, the ministry of education proposed a 12-year educational program for Russian students. One thing that held up implementation of the plan was an objection by the ministry of defense, which feared a shortfall in the number of conscripts if students stayed in secondary school for an additional year.

Children attend school six days a week, though the school day for primary students is relatively short, consisting of four 45-minute lessons. Additional after-school supervision is offered to children of working mothers. Such children are organized into "extended-day" groups and they remain at school until their parents come to take them home. After-school supervision was an area that felt the pinch of tight budgets in the 1990s, which led to a scaling

back of the amount of money going into education.

There are basically two types of secondary schools—general and technical—but a movement began in the late 1970s to merge the two. In 1978, for instance, the time reserved in the school curriculum for machine-shop practice was doubled. Senior pupils were also required to spend four hours a week at a factory or on a farm, receiving on-the-job training.

A new reform decree, issued in early 1984, carried this evolution further. Beginning in 1986, children started school at age six, one year earlier than previously, and they received greater vocational training as an integral part of their schooling. Each student was expected to master at least one basic mechanical skill before graduating, even though enrolled in an "academic course." Such compulsory vocation courses have largely disappeared under the new system, though vocational education may actually be more available for those who opt for it.

There were great fears even before August 1991 that Gorbachev's move to a market economy would have an adverse effect on the university system. Thus far, the collapse of the union government has had no such effect, mainly because the Russian government has taken over responsibility for institutions of higher education and continued to fund them.

The scarcity of funds during the 1990s, coupled with the policy of the Russian government that societal institutions

should, to the maximum extent possible, be self-supporting, brought about a number of changes after 1992. Universities instituted tuition fees to cover part of the cost of education, for example. Further, a number of new schools and universities have been created over the past several years. These have included some church schools and private schools. Some current state universities have also proposed turning themselves into private institutions. Thus, the growth of pluralism within the system is real, even if gradual.

The area of culture with the greatest freedom of expression under the old system was that of the natural sciences, mainly because the regime came to the conclusion that keeping scientists in a straitjacket in harmony with official dogma hampered Russia's ability to compete with nations with superior technology. Scientists were some of the most independent people in the Soviet Union and some of them spoke out courageously against the official pressures and Party-imposed limitations. One has only to think of Andrei Sakharov as an example.

The life sciences such as biology always had to put up with greater tutelage than the natural sciences, but even here the party eventually withdrew as an arbiter. The social sciences remained under official tutelage until 1985, but gained almost total freedom under Gorbachev. Sociology, not even recognized as a separate discipline until after Stalin's death, was also freed by Gorbachev.

Even history, always the most controlled of the social sciences, underwent the beginnings of a renaissance when Gorbachev called for new histories of the Communist Party and new schoolbooks that would restore names and historical periods that had been cloaked in official silence. "There should be no forgotten names or blanks either in history or literature," he said, adding that "history must be seen for what it is." In fact, Gorbachev's policy of glasnost had brought about so many changes in this area by 1988 that the history exams had to be canceled that year, since all of the history books were completely out of date.

Thus the older system of control had been greatly weakened even before the attempted coup of August 1991 brought the system down completely. Still, much that existed down to August 1991 had nothing to do with Communist ideology as such, but rather reflected traditional Russian cultural mores. For that reason, society continues to look and operate in much the same way it always did. The difference is that there is greater pluralism in the new system being created than there had been in the one being replaced.

A St. Petersburg school specializing in English. Russian students present Tom Sawyer, Becky Thatcher, and the fence painted white—with the dialogue all in English!

Courtesy of Miller B. Spangler

Russia

Democratic groups march through Moscow in September 1990 to demand immediate steps toward a market economy

The Changing Economy

The old command economy created by Stalin in the 1930s had already been seriously undermined—though not eradicated—by Gorbachev's policy of perestroika even before the failed coup in August 1991 brought about a repudiation of communism and a collapse of the Soviet Union. The end of the Union and the emergence of an independent Russian state transformed the situation completely. With the Union abolished, the old, centralized bureaucracy—which had dominated the economy for so long—came under the control of the Russian Federation, which gradually phased most of it out. The government of the Russian Federation retained some instruments of economic control, but it systematically set out to eradicate the old command system and replace it with a market economy based primarily on private enterprise.

This process of transformation was painful; but it was also even more difficult and challenging than anybody imagined as the process was launched at the end of the 1980s. Insofar as the economy was concerned, the last two years of Gorbachev's perestroika were a disaster.

The Russian Federation therefore inherited a system that was basically in collapse. Some of the symptoms were a hyperinflation in which the ruble, officially valued at about $1.75, actually traded at about one cent; a state trading system which was unable to provide the public with any goods because it could not obtain them at the low fixed prices it was authorized to pay—and much of what it did obtain was siphoned off for sale at a large mark-up on the black market; and a budget deficit that was over half the size of the overall budget. Overall industrial production was down approximately 10% over the preceding year as individual enterprises found it more and more difficult to obtain raw materials and component parts.

President Yeltsin launched his program to begin the transformation to a market economy and private enterprise on January 2, 1992 by abolishing state-set prices for most goods. Reflecting the hyper-inflation of the preceding months, prices jumped an average of 300–350% by the end of January. More goods began to appear in the shops, however—and even more frequently in kiosks along the streets—and prices started to drift downward, reflecting the increased supply and resistance among consumers to the higher prices. In particular, the lively street vending in the cities and towns made more consumer goods available.

The price increases permitted the government to begin phasing out subsidies to industry and agriculture, and allowed it to draw up a budget for the first three months of 1992 with a deficit reduced to 4.4% of the Gross Domestic Product. The government later lowered the Value Added Tax, which the Yeltsin government had instituted to replace the old turnover and sales taxes, from 28% to 15% as a way to lower costs to consumers. The value of the ruble stabilized, and then actually began to increase in value as demand for the ruble grew—in effect a vote of confidence in the government's program.

Freeing prices and moving toward a balanced budget were necessary first steps. President Yeltsin's government was also committed to achieving ruble convertibility as soon as possible and he had negotiated with the International Monetary Fund for a ruble stabilization fund, like the one created in 1990 to support the Polish currency. As an interim step, Yeltsin announced that the Russian Central Bank would set a single official value for the ruble based on the results of weekly currency auctions. He expressed his hope that the stabilization process could begin in the summer of 1992, after Russia was admitted to the IMF and World Bank.

Yeltsin also moved forward on other aspects of his economic reform. In February 1992, he announced plans to privatize 25% of state property by the end of the year. Under the plan, current employees were to receive shares equivalent to 25% ownership in state firms, while the remaining 75% would be sold at auction.

The government also decided that, in order to maintain a tightened fiscal policy, it would have to phase out most remaining subsidies. Even in this first stage of reform, however, approximately 90% of consumer goods and 80% of industrial goods were freed of direct administrative regulation. Controls were maintained over 12 basic food products, certain communal services, certain fuels, and some semi-finished products.

The government also announced that it would begin a liberalization of fuel prices after the winter heating season was over. Fuel prices were then to begin rising in steps until they reached world prices at the end of 1993. The government predicted that the economy would continue to decline until sometime in 1993, when a turnabout was expected.

In retrospect, the government's predictions on the amount of inflation that would be unleashed with the freeing of prices turned out to be unduly optimistic. By June 1992, the exchange rate for the ruble had declined to about 100+ to the dollar, there were money shortages throughout the country, and many individuals had not been paid for weeks. Other disruptions were occurring as well. Many of the state stores had closed down, while others had almost nothing to sell. Overall, more goods were available, but they were mainly sold from kiosks erected along the sidewalks, since most of these new, private entrepreneurs operated on a small-scale and, in any case, the state-owned buildings were still not available for private entrepreneurs to rent. Many of the items sold were imported also, since the state companies continued to deal only with other state companies. Some private shops did manage to find local suppliers, but it wasn't easy. The result was that ordinary individuals were ambivalent in their attitudes. There was still support for Yeltsin, but almost everybody had their complaints.

In this atmosphere, the Supreme Soviet, which five months earlier had granted President Yeltsin the power to rule by decree for one year, emerged as a center of opposition to Yeltsin's reforms. Under the leadership of Arkady Volsky, chairman of the Union of Entrepreneurs of Russia, and with the cooperation of Vice President Rutskoi and Ruslan Khasbulatov, chairman of the Supreme Soviet, the Supreme Soviet became the forum for blistering attacks on President Yeltsin's economic policies.

During the month of June, the Supreme Soviet voted down two separate attempts to pass a bankruptcy law, rejected a land reform law permitting greater private ownership, and refused to consider the draft constitution submitted by President Yeltsin. It also began putting extreme pressure on the government to loosen up on credit to state enterprises. About 25% of the members of the Supreme Soviet and the larger parent body, the Congress of People's Deputies,

were managers of state enterprises, but this was not viewed as a conflict of interest. In their rhetoric, in fact, the enterprise managers portrayed themselves as protectors of the workers' livelihoods.

By this time, industrial production had dropped by about 15% over the preceding year and President Yeltsin recognized that something would have to be done to prevent further declines. Accordingly, the government agreed to provide industry with an extra 320 billion rubles in credit. In addition, President Yeltsin issued a decree at the beginning of July canceling the accumulated debts of all state enterprises, a sum amounting to approximately 1.9 trillion rubles. The government also agreed to postpone scheduled increases in energy prices.

The conservative majority in the Supreme Soviet was not satisfied with these governmental actions. Moreover, Yeltsin continued to issue decrees that further implemented his program of economic reform. At the beginning of July, he issued a decree establishing a process for bankruptcy for enterprises defaulting on debts incurred after July 1. Another decree called for the privatization of all state-owned enterprises by July 1, 1995, exempting only state farms and certain defense and energy firms deemed vital to the country.

Coincidentally, the Supreme Soviet was presented with an opportunity to further undermine economic reform when Georgi Matyukhin, head of the Russian State Bank, resigned toward the end of June. Taking advantage of the fact that the old communist era constitution designated the parent Congress of People's Deputies as the highest authority within the system and made the chairman of the State Bank accountable to the Supreme Soviet, Speaker Khasbulatov and the Congress appointed Viktor Gerashchenko, former head of the USSR State Bank, as chairman of the Russian State Bank.

Gerashchenko immediately began issuing large amounts of credit to state enterprises. This policy, which Gerashchenko later said he had instituted at the behest of the Supreme Soviet leadership, had the full and vocal support of the members of the Supreme Soviet. The alternative, argued individual speakers, was massive layoffs of workers. Over the next five months, the chairman of the State Bank flooded the country with massive new credits, setting off an inflation that dropped the value of the ruble from about 100+ to the dollar to about 750 to the dollar.

Then in December the leaders of the Supreme Soviet convened the parent Congress of People's Deputies and used this forum to challenge Yeltsin directly. Here

President Yeltsin with alert bodyguards   Courtesy of NOVOSTI

Russia

they attempted to strip him of most of his powers; though they failed, they did manage to oust Yegor Gaidar as deputy prime minister and to force Yeltsin to accept a man of their choice, Viktor Chernomyrdin, as prime minister. In a surprise, Prime Minister Chernomyrdin turned out to be a disappointment to the parliamentary leadership, for he shortly became a convert to Yeltsin's overall economic reform.

Parliamentary opposition to Yeltsin and economic reform continued, however. In March 1993, the Congress of People's Delegates narrowly failed to impeach Yeltsin, then structured the referendum he had requested into a four-question query designed to undermine him. But in that they were to be disappointed, for the April 25 referendum actually provided a vote of confidence in Yeltsin and his economic program. Meanwhile, the parliamentary attacks continued.

Yeltsin's political struggle with the legislature undoubtedly consumed a great deal of his time but, surprisingly, his overall reform remained more or less on track. Much of the credit for this properly goes to Anatoly Chubais, the minister in charge of privatization, who announced in March 1993 that his ministry had managed to privatize 46,815 firms in 1992. The 1992 privatizations were largely limited to small firms, mostly retail shops. The first privatizations of large industrial firms occurred in December 1992 when the government transformed 18 large firms into joint-stock companies, then began exchanging shares of stock for some of the 144 million privatization vouchers which had been issued earlier to the general public.

This became the new pattern. In March 1993, another 249 large firms were privatized using this method, among them the automobile manufacturing company Zil. This industry, with 103,000 workers, was important not only because of it size, but because the privatization was supported by the management and employees. The voucher system of privatization continued over the next 15 months. When it finally ended in July 1994, more than 100,000 state companies had been transformed. These included 15,779 medium-sized and large enterprises, representing 62% of gross domestic production and employing 60% of the industrial workforce. In addition, the 85,000 shops represented 70% of the national total. Approximately 50,000–70,000 kiosks continued to operate in the major cities, but the more successful ones now began to buy or lease permanent shops. Perhaps the most interesting statistic of all is that approximately 40 million people had become shareholders in operating companies.

Privatization continued after July 1994, but enterprises were sold for cash, not vouchers. This led to significant infusions of foreign capital over the next couple years as investment firms began to pump money into the newly privatized Russian firms. Some 500–600 American firms had set up shop in Moscow by the end of 1997, sometimes alone and sometimes in joint ventures with Russian companies. The total amount of private American investment remained relatively small, however.

Although the privatization program was a success, general economic statistics for this period were more mixed. Overall production declined drastically in the first half of 1992, then leveled out in August 1992. Overall production began growing again after that, but sharp contractions in the military sector and a downturn in textile production, the latter caused mainly by a sharp increase in the cost of cotton imported from Central Asia, kept overall production figures below the December 1991 level. Subsequent government statistics seemed to indicate that the economy had taken a turn for the worse and that what was left of the state-run economy was collapsing.

That was probably misleading, however. First of all, as privatization was implemented, government statistics became less and less meaningful. As an article in the *New York Times* put it in August 1994, "Russian figures barely touch the growing private economy." A second point to take into consideration is that official retail trade turnover figures for this same period were actually stable. Finally, many of the remaining state-run firms, refusing to adjust or change, continued to turn out products that no one wanted to buy. Cutting out such production would actually be a help for the economy.

Still, statistics suggesting many firms in deep financial trouble were obviously a matter of concern for the government. President Yeltsin's response came in August 1994 when he signed a decree making available approximately $2 billion in state credits to firms, to use either for investment projects or to help them convert to other activities. Under the terms of the decree, enterprises were required to provide one-third of the money for conversion projects and half of the money for investment projects. Concurrently, the government announced that debts between companies totaled about $45 billion, and that a commission had been set up to deal with that problem.

The Russian Economy and Inflation

Inflation was the Russian economy's most persistent problem after prices were freed in January 1992. The problem was that, although the government was committed to a policy of relative fiscal austerity, political forces representing sectors of the economy hurt by the policy periodically managed to get the government to grant huge new credits to their ailing sectors. The argument used was always that such credits protected jobs that would be lost if the firms were forced out of business. Separate subsidies were also voted for agriculture each fall in response to threats by collective farmers that otherwise they would not harvest the crops.

The first flood of state credits began in June 1992, ordered by the Supreme Soviet and provided by the Russian State Bank. This brought a quick jump in inflation and a corresponding drop in the value of the ruble. By January 1993, inflation was running at 27% a month. A renewed restraint on credit then caused it to drop to 21% by March, and it then continued downward throughout the summer. The Russian government also got greater control over credit creation in April 1993 when the Russian State Bank agreed to work within

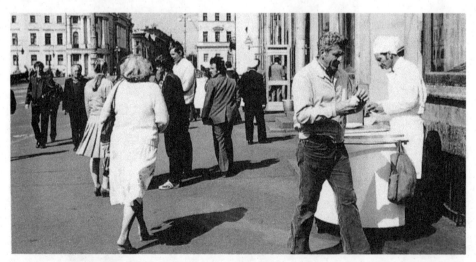

The ice cream vendor in St. Petersburg is a highly popular figure even in winter
Courtesy of Miller B. Spangler

For a century, the GUM Department Store flanking Red Square has been the Macy's of Moscow (in importance, if not quality)   Courtesy of Miller B. Spangler

restraints set by the government—though Gerashchenko, head of the State Bank, said that he agreed to the restraints because he believed that the government would find itself unable to live within them.

The government also received some psychological help when the industrial nations promised an additional $43 billion in the run-up to the April 25 referendum—even though a large part of that package included things such as loan facilities conditional on further reform, debt relief that would provide no new cash, and aid promised earlier and not yet delivered.

By September 1993, however, the battle between reformers and conservatives had been renewed in full vigor. After rejecting the government's budget, the Supreme Soviet attempted to force a budget on the government which would have destroyed the government's program of reform. This brought on the confrontation between the Supreme Soviet and President Yeltsin that ended with the legislature being disbanded with new elections set for December 1993.

Although inflation had dropped to 12% a month by December, reformers did badly in that month's elections to the new Federal Assembly. By January 1994, most reformers had withdrawn from or been forced out of the cabinet, with only

Anatoly Chubais remaining on as minister for privatization. Although Chernomyrdin continued as prime minister, the policy statement of the new government stressed a need for cushions against market forces and for investment in export industries, while downgrading the fight against inflation.

When the new budget was presented in March 1994, however, it appeared that the fight against inflation was not dead after all. In his budget message, Chernomyrdin warned that hyperinflation "means death" and announced that he had trimmed the budget from an estimated 17% of GDP to just over 10% of GDP. Why the reason for the change of emphasis? As it happened, the Russian government was in the middle of negotiations with the IMF for a $1.5 billion loan to help finance the continued transformation to a market economy. Following publication of the 1994 budget and inflation figures for March indicating that inflation was running at 7.8%, the IMF agreed to release the requested funds.

Inflation dropped further to 6.4% in May, then to about 4% in June, and it began to appear that Russia was close to establishing a stable economy. In fact, however, the government was once again under extreme pressure from conservatives to come to the aid of the ailing defense industries

and agriculture. Thus, beginning in July and continuing through September, the government made available an estimated 10 trillion rubles to these two sectors of the economy. Such a large influx of new money into the economy would normally have been accompanied by a downward drift in the value of the ruble. To counteract this trend, the Russian Central Bank spent some $2 billion between August and October to support and stabilize the ruble.

But the central bank's foreign reserves were not unlimited and it could not afford to dissipate all of its reserves. When it was forced to stop its support of the ruble in October 1994, the ruble all but collapsed, dropping in a single morning from 3,081 to the dollar to 3,926 to the dollar. Heavy intervention on the part of the Russian Central Bank brought the exchange rate down to 2,988 to the dollar, but Viktor Gerashchenko, president of the bank, coming under extreme criticism, submitted his resignation after President Yeltsin demanded his dismissal.

Following the events of October 1994, the government instituted a new stabilization policy. Furthermore, when it submitted its 1995 budget to the Federal Assembly, it indicated that it intended to utilize a new mechanism for financing the deficit. Instead of requesting credits from the central bank, the government pledged to finance the deficit through the issuance of government securities and/or external loans from the West. The government also reached an agreement with its 600 foreign bank creditors for the refinancing of $26 billion in loans. Finally, the Ministry for Privatization announced in October that foreign investment was coming into Russia at the rate of $400 million a month, four times what it had been at the beginning of 1994.

The Russian government asked for loans totaling $6.2 billion from the IMF, but discussions held in February 1995 failed to produce an agreement. The two decisive factors were undoubtedly a January inflation rate of 17.8%, a 12-month high, plus the military campaign that started in December in Chechnya and was still continuing at the time of the meeting. Everyone recognized that the cost of the campaign would inevitably increase the size of the budget deficit.

The IMF position was that the Russian government would have to make a greater effort to rein in inflation if it wanted any further credits. Perhaps in response, President Yeltsin signed several decrees which gave him unprecedented control over government spending. Meanwhile, inflation dropped in March to 9.9%, an encouraging sign.

Reacting to the government's new-found will to control its money supply, the IMF

Russia

agreed to make $6.4 billion available to the Russian government, with the restriction that the monies would be advanced on a monthly basis and would be subject to greater controls than previous loans. This worked. Inflation fell steadily throughout the year and had fallen to 3.2% per month by December 1995. Partly based on these results, economists predicted in early 1996 that the Russian economy would begin growing again for the first time since 1989.

These predictions, based on a continuation of the government's economic program, proved to be premature, for subsequent events changed the political, and therefore the economic, situation. First of all, the December 1995 Duma elections gave the Communist Party and their allies a plurality that was just 12 seats short of an absolute majority. Gennady Zyuganov, leader of the party, liked to point out when talking with non-Russians that his party was not the old Communist Party of the Soviet Union—that it was, in fact, founded during the last years of the Gorbachev era as a reform party. He would then add that the party accepted a market economy and private property.

But some of Zyuganov's other position statements, while vague, were less reassuring. Thus he described the situation in Russia in January 1996—"in our country, it's the mafia and corrupt bureaucrats who have power," then suggested re-nationalization of major companies—"We believe in a regulated market where every type of ownership—state, collective, partial, private—is allowed to have its place in the sun." To make the point clear, he added that privatized companies could stay in private hands "if they work well and are being run properly."

The relatively weak Duma could not, of course, unilaterally force a change of economic policy. But President Yeltsin, a candidate for reelection in the June 1996 presidential race, began desperately trying to reposition himself to increase his chances of winning. Meanwhile, Vladimir Kadannikov, Anatoly Chubais's successor as first deputy prime minister for economic policy, began pushing for additional subsidies for industry. As he put it, "directors of state enterprises have exhausted all inner resources that could help enterprises survive. Now the only thing left to do is deal with the financial and political environment."

Still, because most western economists continued to believe that Yeltsin's reelection would be preferable to a victory by Gennady Zyuganov, the IMF signed an agreement with Russia in February 1996 making available $10.2 billion in loans linked to a sweeping plan to proceed with privatization and trade liberalization, in the words of Michel Camdessus, the IMF's

managing director, to make the economic reforms "truly irreversible."

Yeltsin did win reelection in 1996, but this was followed by a period of almost six months when he was incapacitated, first by a heart bypass operation, then by a bout of pneumonia. Then, in March 1997, Yeltsin took charge again and appointed Anatoly Chubais and Boris Nemtsov as first deputy prime ministers. These two reformers managed to carry out a series of reforms in 1997, but Chubais then discredited himself by agreeing to take a large advance from a book company for a book on privatization. Chubais subsequently quit government and was appointed chief executive of Unified Energy Systems, Russia's giant electricity company.

Yeltsin also got a new prime minister, Sergei Kirienko, in April 1998. Unfortunately, this new, young reformer proved unequal to the job and was dismissed by President Yeltsin in August 1998. Essentially, Kirienko and his economic team were overwhelmed by the Asian economic crisis which began driving oil prices lower about the time that Kirienko became prime minister. The government attempted to address the problem with a 25-point anti-crisis program, but the Duma voted down several parts of the plan that would have raised government revenues. In spite of this, the government managed to obtain a promise of a further $17 billion in loans from the IMF in July, $12.6 billion of which was to be paid out to the Russian government during the last half of 1998. That appeared to provide the government with some room to maneuver, but it turned out not to be enough.

On August 17, Prime Minister Kirienko announced that the Russian government would discontinue support for the ruble, plus institute a whole series of measures which added up to a partial repudiation of outstanding Russian loans. These

measures included freezing the repayment of state securities up to December 31, 1999, placing "temporary" restrictions for Russian residents on large-scale foreign currency operations, and prohibiting non-residents from investing funds in short-time ruble assets. The effect of these measures was to destroy confidence in the ruble which, in turn, brought rising prices and sharp cuts in the availability of imported goods. It even appeared that the government might default on up to $200 billion in foreign debt.

President Yeltsin reacted by dismissing the Kirienko cabinet and attempting to reinstate Chernomyrdin as prime minister. But the fall of the Kirienko government, only four months after Yeltsin had forced Kirienko on the Duma, weakened Yeltsin's position and he had to agree to a new prime minister acceptable to the Duma. That turned out to be Yevgeny Primakov, the foreign minister in the previous two governments and an old Soviet bureaucrat. Primakov was confirmed as prime minister in September, though he had some difficulty assembling a cabinet acceptable to the Duma.

Those appointments made it clear that economic reform was dead in Russia for the foreseeable future. For example, the new minister of economics was Yuri Maslyukov, a member of the Communist Party. It is true that Maslyukov actually joined the Kirienko cabinet in July, but his portfolio at that time was trade, a far less sensitive position than that of minister of economics. In addition, Viktor Gerashchenko, who presided over the massive inflation in 1992, was reappointed Central Bank chairman.

Primakov remained prime minister for approximately nine months, but he never developed any clear economic policy that one could identify. However, the government did begin printing additional ruble

On Moscow's Arabat Street, models pose in some of the latest fashions

notes under Primakov—apparently in order to be able to pay back wages to workers—ignoring the contribution this was likely to make to future inflation. Granted, the continuing fall in oil prices throughout the fall placed the government under sharp pressure as its revenues continued to fall. As a result, the government drew up a budget that included billions in IMF and other loans, even as it failed to come to any agreement with the IMF.

In retrospect, it appears that Primakov was attempting to take Russia in the direction of "state capitalism," a sort of market economy heavily supervised by the state. For example, prices of essential foods and medicines were re-regulated, exporters were required to deliver 75% of all hard currencies to the state, and plans were announced to restructure the entire commercial banking system and bring it under greater government control. All of these actions could possibly be justified on a temporary basis as a reaction to growing unemployment, a general decline in incomes, and, in general, increased domestic distress. But if they were to become permanent policy, Russia would find its economy increasingly isolated internationally, and declining domestically.

His successor, Sergei Stepashin, stressed his commitment to reforming the economy but, as he only remained prime minister for approximately two months, apparently because of a disagreement with Yeltsin over the developing situation in Chechnya, his only accomplishment was to finalize an agreement with the IMF whereby that organization agreed to provide a $4.5 billion financial package, the first $640 million of which became available to Russia in August.

Stepashin's successor, Vladimir Putin, was confirmed as prime minister on August 16, 1999. His support for the war in Chechnya—a popular policy in Russia—won him wide popularity within the country. This may also explain why pro-government political parties made such an improved showing in the December 1999 parliamentary elections. And these two factors, together, probably explain why Yeltsin resigned as president on December 31, thereby elevating Putin to the position of acting president.

Program of the Putin Administration

Putin went on to win the presidency in March; he was inaugurated as president on May 7, 2000. Putin's economic views were largely unknown at this time. Of course, it was well known that he was not an economist but, rather, had made his career as a member of the KGB until 1994. He won the presidency largely on the basis of his dogged pursuit of the war in Chechnya and because he was perceived as a strong

George A. Cohon, vice chairman of Moscow-McDonald's and president/CEO of McDonald's Restaurants of Canada Ltd., with Russian crew members at McDonald's on Pushkin Square

leader who would restore Russia's national pride.

Four years later, as his first term was coming to an end, it was clear that Putin had given the country its most united, effective government since the collapse of communism. He was therefore reelected by a huge majority.

On the negative side, it had also become clear that, politically, Putin favored what he called "managed democracy," which included considerable government oversight, and sometimes ownership, over television and the press. On the other hand, Putin supported a fairly coherent program of economic reform throughout his first term of office, and he managed to get most of it enacted by the Duma.

Putin's policies were certainly important, but it helped that he became president just when the Russian economy had begun growing at a remarkable pace for the first time since the 1970s. Between 2000 and 2006, the Russian economy averaged a 7% growth rate and the economy grew almost fivefold, from $200 billion to $920 billion. Predictions were then being made that GDP would triple by 2010. At the same time, the growth in real incomes was even more impressive, averaging better than 8%.

On the other hand, it was also true that the fairly high levels of industrial production after 2000 were primarily—at least until 2008—the result of high energy prices rather than any major growth in manufacturing. It is also true that much of that growth occurred—again, at least until recently—in the Moscow metropolitan area, while most of the rest of the country lagged significantly behind. Monthly salaries also reflected this trend; as of February 2007, the average monthly salary in Moscow was $1,000, while it was $640 in St. Petersburg, and $325 nationally.

Still, it was becoming more and more expensive to do business in Moscow and,

as a result, capital began flowing to other areas, particularly regional capitals with a population of one million or more, such as Samara, Ekaterinburg, Novosibirsk, and Krasnoyarsk, where new malls, office buildings and apartment blocks were going up in large numbers. IKEA, the Swedish furniture maker, spent $100 million to open a huge new mall in Kazan and had plans to open a number of other malls in other provincial cities.

Russia had large trade surpluses between 2000 and 2008, most of which was attributable to higher world prices for petroleum and gas. Russia's trade surplus in 2005 was $120 billion. On April 1, 2006, the Russian Central Bank Chairman Ignatyev announced that Russia's gold and foreign currency reserves totaled $205.9 billion, giving Russia the fifth-largest reserves in the world. Just under two years later, in March 2008, the Russian newspaper *Rossiiskaya Gazeta* reported that government gold and foreign currency reserves had grown to $502 billion.

Because over half of all government revenues came from gas and oil exports, the budget surpluses were large enough to allow the government to set up a Stabilization Fund that reached $100 billion as of February 2007. The total would have been even larger, but the Russian government used $3.3 billion to pay off its debt to the IMF in 2006. Russia's debt to the Paris Club—$29.8 billion as of October 1, 2005—was also completely paid off in 2006.

On February 1, 2008, the Stabilization Fund was officially liquidated and its accumulated assets were divided between a Reserve Fund and a National Welfare Fund. The Reserve Fund, which is essentially a renamed Stabilization Fund, was assigned reserves of $125 billion; the National Welfare Fund received reserves of $32 billion. It was planned the Reserve Fund would continue to be the recipient

Russia

of windfall oil profits, with its assets kept segregated from the Russian economy. The National Welfare Fund, on the other hand, would act as a sovereign wealth fund; its assets would be invested in things like the Pension Fund and in corporate stocks and bonds. It was also suggested that some of the funds could also be used eventually to pay down the rapidly growing corporate debt of the many state-owned companies.

On the negative side, the large cash inflows resulting from the high price of oil contributed to an inflation rate which reached 11% in 2005 and remained at that same approximate rate or a little higher, in spite of government efforts to lower it. The ruble also gained considerably in value after 2005. These two developments, inflation and a more valuable ruble, threatened the competitiveness of the non-energy sectors of the economy.

One area of particular concern to the Russian government was that of capital flight, estimates of which ranged between $200 and $300 billion for the period 1991–2001. The trend began to reverse in 2002–2003, dropping to $9–10 billion for 2002 and less than $3 billion in 2003. But capital flight grew fourfold in 2004, mainly as a result of the arrest of Mikhail Khodorkovsky on charges of fraud and tax evasion and the government's largely successful campaign to dismantle Yukos, his oil company, through exorbitant tax liens that, for one year, were larger than the total revenues of the company. Khodorkovsky, who had supported opposition political parties, remained in jail for a decade. He was pardoned shortly before the start of the 2014 Winter Olympics, which Russia hosted in Sochi.

According to the Economic Development and Trade Ministry, Russian businesses and banks took a record $19 billion out of the country in the first three months of 2005. Capital flight clearly grew after the Russian government began using its tax laws to punish those deemed to be opponents of the government. Even so, much of this outflow was the result of the various Russian companies, and in particular those in the energy field, using their huge profits to buy productive facilities abroad. This trend actually grew in 2006, but with one important difference—the trend now had the support of the Russian government.

Putin's Industrial Policy

The reason for the change is related to the Russian government's new industrial policy, originally launched in the energy area, of bringing the "commanding heights" of the Russian economy back under government control (for more on Russia's energy policy, see the section titled Putin's Energy Policy beginning on page 134).

In February 2006, President Putin issued a decree setting up the United Aircraft Construction Corporation as a joint-stock company, three-quarters of whose shares would be owned by the Russian government. The purpose of the move was to merge all Russian civilian and military aircraft producers into a single, state-owned, holding company. A press release issued at the time described the move as a way

to preserve and develop the research and production potential of the Russian aviation construction industry, to ensure the state's security and defense capabilities, and to pool the intellectual, industrial, and financial resources for implementing prospective programs to create technical equipment used in aviation.

The government also began consolidating the Russian airline industry, using state-owned Aeroflot to take control of the largest privately-owned airline companies through a series of mergers. In July 2006, German Gref, minister of economic development, drafted a decree on the "consolidation of regional airlines." By that time, Aeroflot had already absorbed several of its major domestic competitors, including Pulkovo, Krasair, and Sibir (also known as S7) Airlines, obtaining control through a series of share swaps involving shares the Russian State held in the companies. Other airlines that have since been absorbed include two Siberian airlines, Omskavia and Sibaviatrans, Moscow's Domededovo Airlines, and Samafra, which serves the Volga region.

The program also has an international component. In the spring of 2006, the state-owned Vneshtorgbank purchased $1 billion in stock of the European Aeronautic Defense and Space Company (EADS), which owns Airbus. The payoff came in March 2007 when EADS agreed to outsource 5% of the design and manufacture of the A-350 frame to the newly created United Aircraft Company; in return, Aeroflot signed an agreement to purchase 22 A-350 aircraft from Airbus.

Another state-owned industrial sector which has extended its control over areas that had been privatized in the 1990s is the Russian arms industry. In September 2006, Rosboroneksport, the state arms trader, purchased a 66% share in VSMPO-Avisma, the world's largest titanium maker. Titanium has, of course, both civilian and military usages. In January 2007, however, President Putin issued a decree giving Rosboroneksport a monopoly of all arms exports. At the time, there were 22 joint-stock companies operating in the arms and military hardware field; all of their foreign sales have since been handled by Rosboroneksport. All of this is probably

preliminary to their being absorbed by Rosboroneksport.

Similarly, the Russian Federal Ministry for Industry has drawn up plans to unite 20 of the leading heavy-machinery manufacturers and the leading tank and artillery manufacturing companies in a single new holding company controlled by the state. The Russian State is already a majority stockholder in a number of these companies; the state intends to purchase majority stockholdings in the remainder of the companies.

A similar consolidation has also begun in the aluminum industry; in this case, however, RusAl, the company taking over its rivals, is owned by Russian billionaire Oleg Deripaska. RusAl took over its chief rival, Sual, in October 2006 with the blessing of President Putin. RusAl became the world's largest aluminum company at about this same time when Deripaska took over Swiss-owned Glencore—all of this with the blessing of the Russian government.

Part of Putin's industrial policy also appears to be to permit and even encourage private investment in non-strategic sectors of the economy. Here the best example is probably the United Energy System (UES), the state-owned Russian company that provides electricity for the entire country. In March 2007, UES announced that it was hoping to raise $15 billion from the sale of 15 major asset sales.

Essentially, Russia's non-nuclear power generation stations were organized into 21 new power generation companies, all of which became candidates for privatization. Nuclear power generation stations, on the other hand, remained under control of the Atomic Energy Agency (for more on nuclear power developments, see the section entitled Nuclear Power, beginning on page 137).

The first of the sales occurred in March 2007 when Norilsk Nickel, the Russian nickel mining giant, paid $3.1 billion for a 38% share in OGK-3, which operates power plants in several parts of Russia. Norilsk's interest in obtaining power generation plants is obvious, considering the role that energy plays in the manufacture of nickel. In a separate deal with UES, Gazprom recently acquired a majority interest in Mosenergo, which operates electric power plants in the Moscow area.

As for non-energy parts of the Russian economy, industrial areas that showed strong growth until 2008 include microbiology firms, polygraph companies, and crystal and ceramic manufacturers. The advertising market also boomed, with television advertising reaching $900 million. After an 8.5% drop in GDP in 2009, Russia began growing again in early 2010. The recovery was slower than expected, but did reach 4% in 2011, dropping to 3.6% in 2012. Growth slowed again in 2013 as energy prices remained stagnant and then slowed down further in the first quarter of 2014. In May 2014, the IMF cut its growth forecast for 2014 to 0.2%.

There have been some fairly important turnarounds as well. Russian banks, which have been notoriously weak, often operating primarily as conduits for channeling public funds to favored firms, showed significant improvement after a banking reform launched by President Putin in 2002. Even so, the *Economist* reported four years later that "all but 100 or so of Russia's banks are tiny, or dormant, or are 'pocket' institutions serving the needs of at most one or two controlling shareholders."

The largest Russian bank is Sberbank, the government-controlled savings bank. Vneshtorgbank and Gazprombank, the second and third-largest banks, are also state-controlled; together, these three banks account for approximately 40% of all bank-held assets. In 2012, the government reduced its stake in Sberbank to 50% plus one share; it raised $5 billion through selling 7.58% of the shares to the public. Between 10–15% of the shares were sold in Russia; the remainder were marketed in dollars on foreign exchanges in the form of global depository shares. VTB, which is 75.5% owned by the state, also announced in November 2012 that it planned to raise as much as $3 billion by selling off new shares in the first half of 2013. This dropped the government's stake in VTB to about 65%.

There are 42 foreign-owned banks operating in Russia and collectively they control about 7% of the banking market. Because the Russian government only allows foreign banks to operate branches through subsidiaries that must be registered in the country, nearly all foreign banks maintain a presence in a single city, usually Moscow.

The two largest are the US-based Citibank and the Austria-based Raiffeisen International Bank. Raiffeisen, which has been operating in Russia since 1996, greatly expanded its operation in Russia in 2006 by purchasing the privately-owned Russian Impexbank for $550 million. By buying Impexbank and turning it into a subsidiary, Raiffeisen obtained 190 new branches across the country and 350 consumer-finance outlets in supermarkets and shopping centers. Other foreign banks could take this same route, but Russian bank assets are no longer cheap; Raiffeisen paid almost three times book value for Impexbank.

Russian Minister for Economic Development and Trade Gref announced in November 2006, however, that subsidiaries of foreign banks will be barred from Russia, but "100% companies are permitted to operate on the Russian market with

a 50% stake in combined banking capital." It is not certain how this has affected the banking industry.

A February 2011 *Economist* report on Russian banks indicated that state-owned banks had begun raising capital by selling a portion of their shares on international exchanges. VTB Bank, Russia's second biggest bank, easily raised $3.3 billion by selling 10% of the bank's equity. There is a consolidation going on but there also appears to be a concerted effort to build up the investment banking arms of Sberbank. For example, Sberbank took over Troika Dialog, a brokerage, local asset manager, and investment bank, in February 2011. When the Bank of Moscow, at the time 64% owned by the city of Moscow, came on the market in 2011, Alfa-Bank, Russia's largest private bank, called for a public auction. Instead, the state-owned VTB Group took over the bank in May 2011. VTB also purchased Bank of Moscow shares held by Goldman Sachs. VTB also took over TransCreditBank at about this same time. According to data compiled by Bloomberg, the various deals gave state-owned banks 60% of the domestic market for underwriting corporate bonds, up from 34% in 2010.

At the same time and perhaps not co-incidentally, a number of international banks have begun closing their branch offices in Russia. At least six European and US banks cut back or closed operations in Russia 2010–2011. Morgan Stanley sold its local mortgage unit in 2010. Spain's Banco Santander closed its Russian retail banking operations in December 2010. Barclay's, a British bank which had purchased a Russian lender in 2008, announced in February 2011 that it intended to sell its Russian retail operations. And in April 2011, HSBC Holdings announced that it was closing its Russian retail banking operations, retaining only an office for corporate lending.

It is clear that, in some cases, the decision to close retail operations in Russia was the result of financial pressures that had nothing to do with Russia. This was almost certainly true with regard to the Barclay's decision, for example. But in other cases, the difficulty of doing business in Russia, in addition to the competitive pressures, were factors in these decisions.

It is clear that some international banks are still happy to be doing business in Russia. This is particularly true of those banks specializing in corporate and investment banking rather than in

Russia

retail lending. Citigroup, which has retail operations in about a dozen Russian cities, is one of those. ZAO Raiffeisenbank, which is owned by Austria's RZB Group, is another successful bank. After a pre-tax return of 52% in 2009, the 2010 return of 18% was perhaps disappointing but still rather good; Raiffeisenbank also expected its 2011 return to be an improvement over 2010. Other successful international banks include UniCredit of Italy and Rosbank, 75% owned by France's Société Générale. The secret is to find an unexploited niche. As the *Economist* pointed out in its February 2011 report on Russian banking, "the industry will be dominated by state-owned banks for a long time to come."

Another part of the story is that Sberbank has begun expanding beyond Russian borders. In the fall of 2011, for example, Sberbank agreed to pay $800 million for Volksbank of Austria's operations in Slovakia, the Czech Republic, Hungary, Slovenia, Croatia, Ukraine, Serbia, and Bosnia. The purchase made Sberbank the largest bank operating in Eastern Europe as measured by its total assets of $368 billion at the end of 2011. Through its former Volksbank branches, Sberbank now manages $6.9 billion in loans to customers in Eastern Europe.

Sberbank has also begun extending its influence in many parts of the former Soviet Union by buying up local banks in these countries. As a result, it has become the largest foreign bank in Kazakhstan and is one of the largest in Ukraine. Although Sberbank's expansion beyond the Russian borders is probably driven by commercial motives—there is little chance that it can further expand its already extensive retail network in Russia—the prospect of a Russian-controlled bank amassing power beyond Russia's borders gives some of Russia's neighbors pause.

Private Direct Capital Investment

Russia did not do well in attracting private direct capital investment when it opened up its economy after 1992, but that situation changed under Putin. In January 2006, former Deputy Prime Minister Zhukov announced that the inflow of private capital in 2005 exceeded Russian capital outflows for the first time since 1991. The net inflow was $300 million. Zhukov said that the private sector brought $77 billion into Russia in 2005; $39 billion—or just over half of that total—represented foreign loans by Russian companies. Five Russian companies were, in fact, responsible for $28 billion of this borrowing—Rosneft and Transneft, two oil companies, plus Sovkomflot, Russian Railways, and Alrosa. An additional $16.7 billion came

Russians line up in front of McDonald's in Moscow for a "Beeg Mak"

into the country in the form of direct foreign investment. In April 2008, it was reported that net foreign inflow reached $82 billion in 2007; $47 billion of this figure was in the form of foreign direct investment, while the remainder represented foreign borrowing by Russian firms.

The foreign companies investing in Russia included Coca-Cola, which purchased the Russian juice-maker Multon for $600 million; the Dutch brewer Heineken, which made $750 million in acquisitions during the year; Nestlé's, which invested $120 million in an instant-coffee factory that opened in Krasnodar in November 2005; Whirlpool Corporation, which built a plant to manufacture washing machines in Russia; American Express, which launched its first ruble credit cards in December 2005; Amway Corporation, which began selling cosmetics and detergents in Russia in March 2005; the Austrian Bank Raiffeisen, which purchased the Russian private bank Impexbank for $550 million; and the Deutsche Bank, which paid $420 million for UFG, a Moscow investment bank.

Boeing, which has invested $2.1 billion in Russia since 1991, announced in April 2005 that it planned to invest $2.5 to $3 billion in Russia's aviation sector over the following five years. That same month Toyota announced that it was planning to construct its first automobile plant in

Russia. The plant, which was built in St. Petersburg, represented an investment of $142 million; production began in 2007; currently Toyota assembles about 50,000 Camry cars a year there. The remaining $21.9 billion mainly represented share issues of Russian companies floated on foreign exchanges.

Of course, there are also the companies who have been operating in Russia for a number of years. These include the Ford Motor Company, which sold 115,985 vehicles in Russia in 2006, and General Motors (GM), which sold 111,458 vehicles in 2006. GM invested an estimated $300 million in a plant near St. Petersburg which was intended to produce up to 230,000 cars per year for the Russian market. However, the plant never came close to reaching this capacity and was idled in 2015, 7 years after it opened, when GM pulled out of the Russian market. In late 2018, GM decided to sell off the plant to Unison Auto Russia, a contract assembler which is a subsidiary of Belarusian company CJSC Unison.

One should also mention Avon, one of the early pioneer American companies investing in Russia; Avon is currently the largest-selling cosmetics company in Russia.

Another major investor in the Russian economy is the Swedish furniture-maker IKEA, which opened its first store in Russia in 2000 and since that time has poured $4 billion into the country. One unusual part of IKEA's operations strategy is that it builds malls that always include 30 or more stores whenever it opens a new IKEA. In 2009, it completed its 12th and largest mall, in the city of Samara. This latest mall, which has 1.2 million square feet of space and 200 shops, has caused IKEA to rethink its Russian strategy, however. One year later, IKEA had still not received permission to open the mall; local government officials continued to insist that the facility violated numerous safety regulations and other rules. IKEA concluded that corruption was the root of the problem; IKEA company officials point out that one new requirement is that the mall be able to withstand near-hurricane force winds, even though there is no history of such weather conditions there. In addition, IKEA's Russian manager was informed by a Samara official that a particular local construction company could "quickly help" fix the alleged deficiencies. IKEA has always refused to pay bribes and this has caused it difficulties in the past; in 2004 in Moscow, local officials also forced a delay because of alleged safety problems. In that case, IKEA officials appealed directly to President Putin, who made the problem go away.

The Strategic Sectors Law

On May 7, 2008, in one of his last acts as president, Vladimir Putin signed two pieces of legislation which, collectively, are referred to as the Strategic Sectors Law. The first, Federal Law No. 57-FZ, carries the title "On the Order of Foreign Investment in Companies of Strategic Significance to National Security and Defense." The second, Federal Law No. 58-FZ, carries the title "On Amendments to Certain Legislative Acts of the Russian Federation and the Termination of Certain Provisions of Russian Federation Legislative Acts due to the adoption of the Federal Law on the Order of Foreign Investment in Companies of Strategic Significance to Natural Security and Defense."

The Strategic Sector Law spells out 42 activities which are considered to be "strategic," that is, new foreign investment in any of these areas requires the approval of the Russian government if such investment would result in the foreign investor gaining control of the strategic company; in the case of a "subsoil strategic company," permission would be needed if the investment gave the foreign investor 10% or more of the company. The 42 activities covered by the Strategic Sectors Law include geological study and exploration/extraction in subsoil areas of "federal significance"; activities which affect the levels of precipitation in the atmosphere; activities related to military technologies,

ammunition or explosives, including explosives for industrial use, and the production of special metals and alloys used in military technologies; encryption, including the distribution or maintenance of encryption technology; electronic surveillance equipment; use of nuclear facilities, radioactive materials or waste, or the construction of nuclear facilities; air safety and aviation technology; media related activities, including television and radio networks; large-scale printing or publishing; fixed line telecommunication services industries registered as a "natural monopoly," with exceptions; and fishery activities. The regulations pertaining to development involving subsoil areas, which are particularly restrictive, pertain to deposits of uranium, diamonds, quartz of high purity, rare-earth minerals of the yttrium group, nickel, cobalt, tantalum, niobium, beryllium, lithium, metals of the platinum group, recoverable reserves of oil of 70 million tons or more; reserves of gas of 50 billion cubic meters or more; vein gold reserves of 50 tons or more; and copper reserves of 500 thousand tons or more.

Clearly, the dominant purpose of the Strategic Sectors Law is to give the Russian government the legal authority to control and restrict future investment in large segments of the Russian economy. However, some of the implications of the law may work to discourage foreign investment in Russia because of the indirect effects of the law. For example, Russian companies with some foreign ownership may not be permitted to participate in tenders and auctions for the right to use subsoil or subsoil plots deemed "federally significant." Further, under the terms of the legislation, the Russian government could deny a mining license to a foreign investor subsoil user whose geological study identified a mineral deposit of "federal significance." The legislation does not make it clear what would happen at that point. Finally, subsoil companies will no longer be able to enter into service agreements in order to carry out exploitation of the subsoil. The legislation does specify that investors have the right to compensation for geological expenses and the return of the license fee if a license is terminated.

Many international companies will probably conclude that they can live with the new limitations on investment spelled out by the Strategic Sectors Law; some have already concluded, in fact, that it is better to have the limitations spelled out in law than to have to deal with the same policies carried out on an ad hoc basis, as has been the case in the past three years or so. Thus the law will not stop foreign investment in the Russian economy, though it will obviously channel it into

the areas deemed desirable by the Russian government.

Since passage of the Strategic Sectors Law, Russia has been badly hit by a worldwide economic downturn, which has hit Russia even more than most. That was partly because of a severe drop in the market price for petroleum, down to under $40 a barrel at one point. But it was more than that; in the fall of 2008, Russian private companies owed $437 billion in foreign debt and a sharp drop in profits meant that many companies were unable to service their debts and international banks in many cases refused refinancing or new loans. Many of these firms would have gone under if it hadn't been for the intervention of the Russian government, in particular the $280 billion stimulus plan it adopted in 2009.

But as a side effect of this, the Russian government has begun rethinking how much foreign involvement should be permitted in the energy field. In September 2009, Prime Minister Putin met with executives from Shell, ExxonMobil, and other companies in Salekhard, a city in the Yamal-Nenets district that is rich in untapped deposits of natural gas. "We are ready for broad partnership and that is why we invited you here," Putin told the executives, according to the official transcript. "We want you to feel like members of our team, participants in the process."

In August 2011, ExxonMobil announced that it had reached a sweeping partnership with Russia's state-owned Rosneft for exploration of projects on Russia's Arctic Sea shelf in the Kara Sea, in the deep waters of the Black Sea, and in complex, tight rock formations in Western Siberia. According to Rosneft's estimates, the East Prinovozemelsky field holds oil reserves of 35.8 billion barrels, plus 10.3 trillion cubic meters of natural gas. ExxonMobil will be providing the technology and putting up $3.2 billion to finance exploration in the Kara Sea. Rosneft will get access to special technologies not currently available in Russia and, in addition, ExxonMobil will allow Rosneft to participate in ExxonMobil projects in deepwater exploration off the coast of Mexico and in tight oil fields in Texas.

Other Problems

There are also continuing weaknesses that have nothing to do with the current economic downturn. A major long-term problem is the scarcity of small businesses in Russia. Currently, small and medium-sized companies employ only 22% of the labor market; in countries with longer-term market economies, the figure is usually closer to 65%. At President Putin's urging, the Duma passed legislation aimed

Russia

at cutting red tape for small companies; indications thus far suggest that the new legislation has not solved the problem.

Another problem is that there are at least 300 Russian "monocities" that have grown up around a single plant that furnishes heat, income and social security. Many of these factories are outdated with equipment sometimes dating back to World War II. The high energy prices of the period 2000–2008 concealed the fact that Russia's industrial production was actually declining during this same period because it was so uncompetitive. Although Russian industrial salaries are low, that does not offset the fact that the industrial workforce is nearly seven times less productive than the American worker. Nearly all of these factories are money-losing propositions today, but the Russian government has forced the firms to keep the factories open, in some cases also shoring up the main companies with economic assistance. What these factories need to make them competitive is large investments for modern technology—several hundred billion dollars' worth—which neither the companies nor the Russian government have.

Health is another long-term problem. Russia reported 70,000 new cases of HIV infection in the first 10 months of 2001, which is 1.6 times as many as reported in 2000. A second problem is tuberculosis. The disease has spread rapidly throughout Russia over the past decade, particularly in prisons, and drug-resistant strains have been appearing in greater numbers. The Red Cross estimated in 2001 that 130,000 new cases developed each year in Russia, and 30,000 people were dying annually from the disease. USID and the International Federation of Red Cross and Red Crescent are currently supporting a three-year, $3.4 million program in Russia to address this problem.

Finally, 20.8 million Russians, or about 14.6% of the population, live below the official poverty line—meaning that they have monthly incomes of less than 2,451 rubles ($81.70). Although there has been a sharp decrease in those living below the poverty line over the past five years or so, Russia still has a long way to go yet to reach the standard of living found even in neighboring countries to the west such as Poland and Hungary. In July 2007, *Rossstat*, the federal state statistics service, reported that the average monthly income was $544, rising above the $500 mark for the first time. The report added that "wages are climbing by 20–27% annually and have jumped 750% in the past eight years."

In April 2008, the former Health and Social Development Minister Tatyana Golikova announced that the cash incomes of Russians had grown by 25% over the past two years in real terms; she added that six million Russians has seen their incomes grow to more than the minimum subsistence level in those same two years. The number of unemployed also shrank by nearly one million people as well.

The Impact of the Worldwide Economic Crisis on Russia

On June 11, 2008, the International Energy Agency announced that Russia's oil production had hit 9.5 million barrels per day in the first quarter, edging past Saudi Arabia's 9.2 million barrels to become the world's largest producer of crude. As the worldwide economic crisis set in over the summer, however, crude oil prices began to drift lower; peaking at $147 a barrel in July, they had dropped to $95 a barrel by the middle of September. And in the intervening three months, international investors had withdrawn an estimated $35 billion out of Russia. Some of those investors were retrenching; others were worried about the recent investment climate in Russia, in particular the problems that BP had been having with its Russian subsidiary, TNK-BP. Russia's invasion of Georgia on August 8, 2008, was another contributing factor. Even President Medvedev has admitted that the war was responsible for up to a quarter of the stock markets' losses.

By the middle of September, the Russian stock markets had lost 55% of their value since their record high in May, losing 25% of their value in three days in September. The Russian government only prevented a collapse by pledging $120 billion to prop up markets and banks. However, Russian reserves amounted to $600 billion at this time, the country was running a budget surplus, and the government had other reserve funds of at least $172 billion. Taxes on the energy sector were responsible for nearly half the federal budget, however, which prompted former Finance Minister Alexei Kudrin to suggest that the budget would remain balanced even if the price of oil fell to $70 a barrel. It eventually fell to under $40 a barrel.

By the end of October, the value of stocks on Russian stock exchanges had fallen by 85%; the capitalization of Gazprom, Russia's largest company, had dropped from $350 billion to less than $100 billion. It was, of course, the rich who were losing much of their wealth—since most ordinary Russians owned no shares whatsoever.

However, a major problem was that Russian companies and banks had borrowed an estimated $437 billion abroad. When the ruble began dropping in value, the cost of servicing these, mostly dollar-denominated, loans soared. In addition, many companies had pledged shares in their companies as collateral for loans; as the price of shares dropped, the companies had to either pay off the loans or turn over shares of stock. Some of the oligarchs were caught in this squeeze as well. Oleg Deripaska, whose range of businesses included aluminum, aerospace, financial services, mining, and timber, was forced to surrender 20 million shares of the Canadian auto maker Magna to the French bank BNP Paribas. Deripaska was also about to lose a 25% stake in Norilsk Nickel until the Russian government stepped in with a $4.5 billion loan.

The Russian government always requires something for any assistance that may be provided. The *New York Times* illustrated the point when it reported in its June 5, 2009, issue about a trip Putin had made to the town of Pikalevo, a one-factory company town, which existed because of local deposits of alumina. Putin came because the workers had not been paid for three months. It turned out that the owner of the factory (with two other businessmen) that processed alumina was the oligarch, Oleg Deripaska, who had shut down the plant in December 2008 because the plant had been losing $300 on each ton of ore it produced. Putin's solution, which he set forth in a televised meeting inside the factory, was to require Deripaska to reopen the alumina plant and to agree to pay the workers their lost wages. In the television presentation, Putin addressed Deripaska and the other two owners directly, saying:

I wanted the authors of what happened here to see it with their own eyes. Addressing these authors, I must say that you've made thousands of residents of Pikalevo hostages to your ambition, your non-professionalism and maybe your greed. Thousands of people. It's totally unacceptable.

The price of crude oil hovered between $70 and $80 a barrel in 2010, but the series of Arab revolutions that began in early 2011 in Tunisia and then spread to Egypt, Yemen, and Libya, drove the price of crude to about $125 a barrel. That higher price could not be sustained. By June 2012, crude oil was selling for $93 a barrel.

Stocks on the Russian stock market gained back about 30% of their pre-2007 value in 2010 and another 24% in 2011. Prices stagnated thereafter, but they dropped by 20% since the beginning of 2014, not primarily for economic reasons but because of President Putin's decision to send Russian troops into Crimea and then annex it to Russia.

In the summer of 2013, President Putin proposed a program of government investments in mega-projects that included two ambitious rail upgrades and a new major highway—in all a government investment of about $43.5 billion. Since the government was currently running a deficit at the time, the moneys were to be taken from the country's sovereign wealth funds. The spending plans were never carried out. Instead, the government adopted a new three-year budget in September 2013 that called for reduced spending to bring the budget closer into balance. Similarly, President Medvedev's earlier plans for government investment to diversify the economy have been cut from the budget. Perhaps because of worries about possible popular discontent, big pension increases to keep elderly voters happy remain in the budget.

The Impact of Western Sanctions and the Sharp Drop in the Price of Oil on Russia's Economy

The Russian economy has been significantly weakened over the past few years by the sharp drop in the world price of oil and by the imposition of sanctions by the EU, US, and a few other countries in response to Russia's annexation of Crimea and support of pro-Russian separatists in the war in eastern Ukraine. Experts have warned the Russian government since at least 2000 to diversify its economy and not depend so heavily on the export of oil and, to a lesser extent, natural gas, which combined accounts for approximately two-thirds of Russian export revenue. During his tenure as president, Medvedev supported the idea of economic diversification. For example, he proposed creating a huge information technology center—in his words "something along the lines of Silicon Valley—in a Moscow suburb. However, with the price of oil rebounding sharply to over $100 per barrel after the economic crisis of 2008–2009, Russia had little incentive to curtail its dependency on energy exports. Beginning in the latter half of 2014, the price of oil dropped sharply. If the price peaked at $115 per barrel on June 19, 2014, it bottomed out at $27.10 on January 20, 2016. The drop occurred because supply outstripped demand. In an overall weak global economy, the US significantly boosted oil production, and Saudi Arabia chose to keep its output high to grab market share.

Following Russia's annexation of Crimea in March 2014, the US, EU, and several other countries froze the foreign assets of selected Russian officials and refused to grant them entry visas. When Russia supported the separatists in the emerging war in eastern Ukraine, and especially after the shooting down of the Malaysian jetliner on July 17, the sanctions were repeatedly ratcheted upwards to include more individuals and Russian businesses. In addition, Russia's ability to borrow from Western banks was restricted as was the sale to Russia of arms and technology for the oil industry. Moreover,

Western companies have been curtailing their activity in Russia. For example, in March 2015, General Motors announced that it would indefinitely close its assembly plant in St. Petersburg.

Russia's gross domestic product (GDP), which grew at a relatively robust rate of 4.4% in 2011, dropped to only 0.7% in 2014 and contracted by 3.7% in 2015. In 2016, the economy contracted by another 1.2% in the first quarter. In December 2014, President Putin blamed the sanctions for 25–30% of Russia's economic problems. Russia's economic decline is reflected in the value of its currency, the ruble. During 2012 and 2013, the ruble exchanged at a steady rate of about 30 to the US dollar. During the last four months of 2014, its value dropped steadily reaching a low of 80:1 in mid-December. The ruble then rose somewhat in value before dropping back to 70:1 by the end of January 2015. Fluctuations in the value of the ruble track closely with the changing price of oil. As the price of oil dropped in the winter of 2016, the ruble once again traded at 80 to 1 US dollar.

In March 2014, Russia responded to the initial Western sanctions with sanctions of its own against a small group of Western officials. Then, in August, Russia banned imports of vegetables, fruit, dairy products, and most kinds of meat from those countries that had sanctioned it. The food ban was a surprising move, as it limited what Russian consumers could purchase and drove up prices. Overall inflation in Russia surpassed 15% in 2015. Russian invasion of Ukraine in February 2022 further exacerbated the economic situation of average Russians. As a result of Western sanctions, consumer prices rose from 11% in February to 19% in April of 2002. However, for the first time since Russia's invasion of Ukraine, inflation dropped below 4% in March 2023. As forecasted by the World Bank, inflation is likely to rise due to an increase in consumer demand, commodity prices, and ongoing supply bottlenecks caused by the pandemic. For its part, the Bank of Russia, expressed concern that weaker rouble, significant labor shortages and wide budget deficits would contribute to rising inflation. Although the official poverty rate in Russia, as reported by the World Bank, has been slowly declining from 12.6% in 2018 to 12.1% in 2020, the rate will be sensitive to the severity of the pandemic and Western sanctions. In December 2022, the EU imposed its toughest sanction on Russia yet, by banning it from importing its seaborne crude oil and blocking insurers from covering its cargoes of crude. The ban on insureres applies to tankers carrying Russian oil globally. Without insurance, tankers would not risk delivering Russian oil. Following

the ban on crude, as of December 2023, the EU embargoed imports of refined oil products from Russia. Additionally, the EU, the G7, and Australia imposed a price cap on Russian crude oil at $60 per barrel. Collectively, these measures would force Russia to export its oil over long distances to a small number of buyers, thereby driving down Russia's revenue per barrel.

The Russian government responded to sanctions by intensifying import substitution efforts, deepening economic ties with China, India, and other non-Western partners, and expanding the use of alternative payment systems to bypass SWIFT. Russia's import substitution policy to stave off the effect of comprehensive economic sanctions has had mixed success. Some domestic industries, such as food and agriculture, which received state subsidies, were able to produce alternatives to Western imports. For example, state investments in this sector reduced the import bill for meat by 70% compared with 2013. However, the bans on Western food imports have also resulted in reduced competition, driving up prices.

Under import substitution policy, Russia has struggled even more to build competitive heavy and high-tech sectors. For example, AvtoVAZ, Russia's largest carmaker, which is owned by Renault, had to suspend operations after it was unable to source parts. Cars and vehicle components remain Russia's biggest imports. According to the central bank of Russia, as of 2021, 65 percent of enterprises in the country were dependent on imports for their manufacturing. According to the study by the Gaidar Institute for Economic Policy, more than 60% of firms in Russia reported that they were unable to find domestic alternatives for goods that they used to import prior to Western sanctions. While in the medium and long-term the economic crisis and associated reduction of foreign goods from markets may spur domestic production and encourage long needed diversification, in the short term it has caused a great deal of domestic pain, especially amongst the states most vulnerable citizens. In all, these measures have only partially offset the negative effects of sanctions. The ruble has remained volatile, inflation persisted above target levels, and economic growth stagnated. While Russia has avoided economic collapse, the sanctions have contributed to a widening technological gap with the West and increased Moscow's economic dependence on Beijing.

What Is Being Changed: A Look Back at the Old Soviet Command Economy

The most distinctive feature of the now defunct Soviet economic organization was the reliance on a rigid central plan for the national economy. This is in contrast to a

Russia

market economy, which relies on the independent or semi-independent decisions of many producers. In theory, a rigidly planned economy was supposed to avoid the ups and downs—inflation and depression—of a free market economy. Marx and Engels charged that a market economy amounted to "anarchy of production."

In practice, centralized planning proved to be difficult. For many years, economic targets and goals were met by lavish investments of capital and labor. Progress was identified with the rate of growth of specific key industries—coal, steel, and heavy industry in general—and a high percentage growth rate for overall industrial production. Quantity was stressed over quality.

Such a growth strategy produced an economy that led the world in the production of a long list of industrial products, including coal, steel, cement, manganese and chrome ores, locomotives, metal-cutting lathes, and mineral fertilizer. Yet it also produced an economy that, from the point of view of the consumer, was an economy of scarcities. Some consumer goods were not manufactured at all while others were obtainable only after a long waiting period. Still, there were important improvements in the availability of consumer goods over the years. By the time Gorbachev became general secretary in 1985, for example, most Russian families had a color television set.

Although the Soviet standard of living improved between 1960 and 1985, it was still only about 37% of the level of the United States—and probably falling. Moreover, it was even below the level of the neighboring countries of Eastern Europe. From the point of view of the consumer, an even more important problem was that Soviet goods were of such poor quality that they could not be sold abroad.

Gorbachev was already aware of the weaknesses in the system when he came to power in 1985. During his first year as general secretary, he put together a team of younger and better-educated individuals and, at the 27th Party Congress in February 1986, he put the party on record as favoring economic reform. He then began to give substance to this commitment.

It soon became clear that many party members objected to any major modification of the economic system on ideological grounds, however. As Gorbachev pointed out at the 27th Party Congress:

Unfortunately, there is a widespread view that any change in the economic mechanism is to be regarded as virtually a retreat from the principles of socialism.

Gorbachev was faced with a major contradiction. Gorbachev's own chief source of authority was his leadership of the party.

Moreover, since the party controlled the levers of power, economic reform was possible only with the party's support. Yet how could he use the party to direct his program of economic reform if the party was itself the chief opponent of that reform? Gorbachev's two-fold answer was to remake the party in terms of personnel, organization and ideology while, at the same time, restructuring the system so that the party was no longer in direct control.

The process began in 1987 with the introduction of three slogans which came to symbolize his campaign for reform—openness (glasnost), restructuring (perestroika), and democracy (demokratiya). Unfortunately, his successes in political reform were not matched in the economic area.

In June 1987, Gorbachev outlined future economic plans to a Central Committee Plenum. Here he called for "cardinal reform" in the *financing and credit systems*. He also spoke of the need for "development of self-management," and "fundamental change in the style and methods of work." Factories should, he urged, be "self-financing" and more efficient so as to reduce their workforce.

That same Central Committee session approved a "Law on the Socialist Enterprise" which went into effect on January 1, 1988. Under the terms of the law, 60% of Soviet industrial and agricultural production began working under a new system of "economic accountability" in which individual enterprises became responsible for obtaining their own raw materials and fuel and were expected to compete with other enterprises for business.

While they now had the right to dispose of any profits earned by the enterprise, they also became responsible for replacing obsolete machinery and paying the wages of their employees. Subsidies to money-losing enterprises were supposed to be phased out and such enterprises were to be permitted to go bankrupt, if they could not begin turning a profit. Companies were also to be able to get rid of surplus workers, so unemployment became another possibility. All of this was supposed to be in effect by the end of the 1986–1990 Five-Year Plan.

The system was never fully implemented, however. In 1988, 90% of the output of factories was still produced for "state orders." Two years later, state orders still controlled nearly 90% of industrial production. The state was also supposed to gradually withdraw from direct control of most economic activity, with GOSPLAN relinquishing its control over individual enterprises and concentrating on long-term planning. Some of that happened. In 1987, for example, the number of centrally planned indicators was reduced from 46,000 to 22,000. It was supposed to be

further reduced to 3,500 indicators in 1988, though it cannot be verified that this second reduction took place. Ministries and departments were supposed to be reduced by approximately one-third and there was supposed to be a drop of approximately 100,000 in personnel. Again, reductions occurred but not in those magnitudes.

One problem was that the economic program had two major goals—a short-term goal of accelerating the growth rate of national income and a long-term one of promoting innovation and reconstruction—and they were in basic conflict with each other. The first goal required all out production, while the second goal could only be met by things like closing down assembly lines while obsolete machinery was being replaced by modern technology and enforcing higher quality standards by rejecting goods that failed to meet the new standards. That conflict, obvious by 1989, got considerably worse in 1990–1991, with the result that neither goal was met.

A second problem had to do with decentralization of decision-making authority within the system. Essentially, enterprises were given authority to set wages but no responsibility for paying them. As a result, they granted wage increases far in excess of increases in productivity, and the state had to make good the difference. It did this through the expedient of printing additional money. The increase in money in circulation first produced shortages as individuals used their higher wages to buy more goods. In a capitalist system, that would have led to inflation as prices increased to reflect additional demand. But all prices were controlled, and so could not increase. What happened instead was a loss of faith in the banking system and the currency itself.

The result was well summed up in February 1990 by Nikolai N. Slyunkov, a member of the Politburo, in remarks he made at the Central Committee Plenum:

The situation has deteriorated especially in the consumer market as regards both food and essential goods over the past two years.

A similar picture of the state of the Soviet economy is to be found in a poll published in the Moscow *Ogonek*, also in February 1990. Seventy-three% of all respondents said that they "constantly or quite often" experienced difficulty in locating food that they needed, while 60% reported that they spent over half of their income on food.

All of this economic distress put the government under extreme pressure. Everybody agreed that *something* had to be done but there was no consensus on what that something should be. The radical reformers wanted to push forward rapidly, while conservatives urged pulling back; Gorbachev fell somewhere in the middle. The draft Five-Year Plan submitted in December 1989 by Nikolai Ryzhkov, chairman of the Council of Ministers, represented a distinct pulling back, but there continued to be strong pressures to move more quickly.

Ryzhkov submitted a later version of his plan in May 1990. Saying that the state of the economy and the mood of the people did not permit any immediate changes, he proposed a continuation of the policy of state orders for another 18 months coupled with what he called price reform. They were, in fact, just price increases, since prices were not to be freed but simply raised. He characterized his program as "a transition to a regulated market economy." Radicals attacked his proposals and Gorbachev called them absurd, though he added that people were unprepared for market economics.

Economic reform was on the agenda at the 28th Party Congress in July 1990. After heated discussions, the party adopted a document called "Toward humane, democratic socialism," one of whose major points was that private property did not contradict communist ideology. Reflecting this change, Ryzhkov, in a speech given on July 20, spoke of moving toward a market economy. All references to the word "regulated" were dropped.

Then in August came the Shatalin Plan for a 500-day transition to a market economy. It had the support of Boris Yeltsin and the other radicals and was actually accepted by the Russian Supreme Soviet in early September. Gorbachev rather reluctantly endorsed the plan, but it came under attack by conservatives and Ryzhkov threatened to resign if the plan were adopted. Eventually, the USSR Supreme Soviet turned it down. Essentially the Soviet Union had no plan for economic reform.

Ryzhkov suffered a heart attack at the end of December and was replaced by Valentin Pavlov in January 1991. Pavlov, who had been finance minister under Ryzhkov, was a conservative. One of his more notorious "reforms" was to attempt to reduce the fiscal overhang by withdrawing 50- and 100-ruble notes from circulation. Since individuals were limited in the amount of bills they could redeem, Pavlov in effect reduced the overhang by expropriating a portion of the public's wealth. Its most important effect was to further reduce faith in the currency.

Real GNP fell by 10% in 1990, and shortages were even more pervasive than they were in 1989. Yet the stalemate continued. Conservatives were convinced that further moves in the direction of a market economy would disrupt the economy even more, while reform advocates argued that any action was better than no action. Gorbachev, no economist, didn't know what to believe. A joke he told reporters in November 1990 illustrated his position.

They say that Mitterrand has 100 lovers. One has AIDS, but he doesn't know which one. Bush has 100 bodyguards. One is a terrorist, but he doesn't know which one. Gorbachev has 100 economic advisers. One is smart, but he doesn't know which one.

By May 1991, Gorbachev had lost confidence in Pavlov's economic program and he began seeking outside advice. Grigory A. Yavlinsky, who had helped draw up the Shatalin Plan, now proposed a new plan whereby the western nations would provide substantial aid to the Soviet Union to help in its economic transition. Gorbachev endorsed this plan and used it as a basis for his meeting with the "Group of Seven" nations in July 1991. Though no specific overall sums were mentioned, Soviet economists talked about the need for $30 billion a year in grants and loans. The G-7 nations gave a cool reception to the general idea, though they promised assistance once transition to a market economy had begun. Before any further progress could happen, the August 1991 failed coup brought an end both to the Soviet Union and Gorbachev's leadership.

Agriculture

The failure of the August 1991 coup, although it gave Mikhail Gorbachev four more months as president, actually marked the beginning of the breakup of the Soviet Union and the emergence of Boris Yeltsin as head of an independent Russian Federation. What this meant insofar as agriculture was concerned is that the reforms that Yeltsin had been demanding for two years could finally be implemented.

This had a two-fold significance. First of all, the demise of the Soviet Union definitively ended the various central control mechanisms of the old regime. For the first time since the early 1930s, Russian peasants were on their own. Amazingly, they managed to plant even more winter wheat following the collapse of the ministry of agriculture than they had when it was telling them what to plant and when.

Yet while the peasants welcomed the end of bureaucratic control, they very quickly realized that being on their own meant an end to supports, credits, loans, and guidance. Moreover, although the reformers said that they wanted to break up the collective and state farms and create a private agriculture, the government offered almost no assistance to peasants who wanted to leave the collective and start on their own. It was in fact, another two years before President Yeltsin finally issued a historic decree granting Russians the right to buy and sell private land.

The reform of prices also turned out to be a negative factor insofar as agriculture was concerned. Two examples will illustrate this point. In 1991, one pound of wheat would buy two pounds of diesel fuel or fertilizer. By 1994, that same two pounds of fuel cost the equivalent of nine pounds of wheat, while a single pound of fertilizer sold for the equivalent of eight pounds of grain.

Although the government has been, on paper, largely successful in its campaign to break up the collective/state farm system—94% of the agrarian sector was officially classified as private by the end of 1994—the real situation is that, while collective/state farms are now "joint stock companies," they continue to operate in much the same way they always have. Moreover, the state continues to set the prices of many grains through Agroprom, its state buying agency, which still collects grain from the farms and delivers goods in return.

Farms are, to be sure, not obligated to sell to Agroprom, but the lack of alternative purchasing agents means that farms that do not want to sell to Agroprom have to find a way to market their goods on their own. At the Koltsovo joint agricultural enterprise, formerly the Suvorov Collective Farm, for example, all milk is still sold at fixed prices to the state. To the question, why not sell it elsewhere, the reply was:

Where will we get the fuel, the trucks? We did try once, but these thugs met us and suggested we go home.

According to the most recent figures, there are about 350,000 private farmers in Russia—out of 30 million people who depend on the land. Many of these private farms are, moreover, extremely small, and most lack adequate machinery to work their land. Most do not have access to credit, so they are unable to improve their holdings. They also control only about 4% of the agricultural land in the country.

One reason is that, although article 35 of the 1993 constitution promises that "the right of private property shall be protected by law," this remained only a theoretical right until January 2003, when a new law on agricultural land sales finally went into effect. Legislation permitting the sale of non-agricultural land was passed by the Duma in March 2001—but it explicitly exempted agricultural land sales. The new law remains controversial, however, and certain regions, including Krasnodar Krai, have indicated that the new law will not be implemented on their territories. In any case, most regions do not have land registers or land-quality surveys, so it will be

Russia

some time before significant amounts of land will become available for sale.

On the other hand, approximately 40 regions had passed their own local land laws setting up procedures for the purchase of land even before the new law came into effect. One such region is Saratov province, which passed a local land law in 1997. Since then, the authorities have conducted 335 auctions of land, selling 1,202 plots that comprise a total of 20,485 acres. To put those sales figures into context, the total amount of agricultural land in Saratov province is 25 million acres.

There are several reasons why this should be so. First of all, demand for land is small, since farmers can lease land for less than $4 an acre. Second, land mortgages do not exist, so it is not possible to borrow money to buy land. In addition, most farmers do not have the capital to buy the farm equipment which would be needed to work a larger piece of land. Finally, without a viable legal system, no one can be certain that they can keep what they buy.

One farmer in Saratov province, who owns 316 acres and leases an additional 9,815 acres, explained why he remains an exception as a private farmer:

Today, basically, land doesn't belong to anybody, and so nobody is interested in working on nobody's land and increasing the productivity of nobody's land. It's like if you rent an apartment and you renovate it at your own expense; you can still be thrown out in a month.

The transition to a genuinely privatized agriculture is likely to be long and arduous. In the first place, most ordinary peasants oppose change, fearing apparently that they will lose what they already have. Many are also older—the average age for collective farmers is over 50—and they don't want to start over. Thus real change may have to wait until the next generation of farmers takes over. In the meantime, the question appears to be whether the ex-collective farms can be turned into competitive enterprises. One sign of progress is that the central committee of the Agrarian Party, which had opposed privatization of land in the past, endorsed the concept of a new land code which would "guarantee the property rights of agricultural producers" in March 2000.

In 2001, the Russian government initiated a new program which, among other things, reduced taxes, set up a subsidized loan program, and made farm equipment available on least at very reasonable prices. The program also included some restrictions on agricultural imports. One effect of this program, plus rising prices on agricultural products, was the beginning

Moscow's Arbat Street in August 2008

of significant investment from Russian and foreign firms into Russian agriculture. Russian commodity traders, food processors, shipping outfits and the like began buying up or leasing farms with the intent of modernizing Russian agriculture and cashing in on the high grain and food prices. Foreign investment in Russian agriculture also nearly tripled between 2005 and 2007. In the case of foreign companies, the land must be leased, since the Russian Land Code forbids foreign nationals and companies, as well as Russian companies with more than half foreign ownership, to own farm land.

Three examples of this new type of agricultural holding companies would be RAV Agro-Pro, a Russian company with Israeli, US, and British funding, which has 370,000 acres under lease; Agro-Invest, an affiliate of Sweden's Black Farming, which has 900,000 acres under lease; and Alpcot Agro, a Swedish company, which has 120,000 acres under lease. *Business Week* reported in 2008 that large agricultural holding companies controlled some 10% of Russia's farm land. A number of larger Russian companies, particularly energy companies, have begun investing in agricultural enterprises as well. All of these companies are introducing modern technology and farming methods. One effect of this has been a doubling of farm productivity on these new farms.

Russia exported about three million tons of grain in 2001 and over six million tons in 2002. Unfortunately, Russia then had a partial grain failure in 2003; this led the government to ban all grain exports and begin making grain available from its reserves when the poor harvest began to translate into increased bread prices. But Russian farmers had a good year in 2004, producing 45 million tons of grain, the

largest harvest since 1991. After several good harvests, an extremely hot summer and an accompanying drought led to a sharp drop in production in 2010. As a result, the government banned the exportation of grain. Long-term, however, Russia is likely to once again become a major exporter of grain. This is certainly the continuing view of the Russian government. In September 2008, it announced that it was planning to form a state trading company to broker about half of the country's millions of tons of grain exports. This will, of course, expand the government's control over who buys Russian grains and how much they pay for them. Whether this would be a plus for Russian farmers is another question.

Russian agricultural production did, indeed, recover in 2011; the total grain harvest that year was 94.2 million tons. Russia exported 21.3 million metric tons of grain in the 2011–2012 market year, which ended on June 30. That included about 1.2 million tons of corn, as well as 600,000 tons of peas and legumes. Carryover stocks of wheat were about 11.5 million tons. Although Russia suffered partial drought conditions in several grain-growing districts, the 2012 grain harvest was still between 70 and 75 million tons; grain exports dropped by nearly half but still reached 12 million tons in 2012–2013.

Two new crops that have begun growing in importance are soy beans and rice. During the Soviet era, soy beans were cultivated in the Far East, but production dropped off during the 1990s. It began growing again after 2000 and 1.5 million acres were under cultivation by 2011. About half of all soy beans are still grown in the Amur Region, but southwestern Russia has now a significant producer as well. Soy beans are used mainly for cattle feed inside Russia, but Russia is also a major exporter of soy meal. Russian rice in produced the Krasnodar region. Production in 2012 was 1 million tons, down from 1.05 million tons in 2011. Total exports in the year to August 2012 were 151,400 tons. Russian rice is exported mainly to Turkey, Tajikistan, and Turkmenistan, with smaller sales to Egypt and Libya.

What Is Being Changed: Agriculture

When the Soviet Union introduced the collectivization of agriculture as part of its first Five-Year Plan, it was considered to be the first step in the creation of a modern, scientifically organized, mechanized agricultural system. Distinctions between city and the countryside were to be abolished and peasants were to become "proletarians in the fields." Until 1953, this remained largely a dream, although Khrushchev's plan for the creation of *agrogoroda*—loosely, "agricultural cities"—which he first put forward in 1950, showed that the dream had only been postponed, not abandoned. Khrushchev, as he consolidated his power after 1953, gave a great deal more emphasis to agriculture than had Stalin. Agriculture was placed much higher on the Soviet list of priorities and additional investments were directed into this area.

In addition, a program of consolidation of the collective farms, actually begun in 1950, continued under Khrushchev and, in the process, many were transformed into state farms (sovkhozy). The Machine Tractor Stations were also phased-out beginning in 1958 and their agricultural equipment was sold to the sovkhozy and kolkhozy. As the process of transformation and consolidation continued over the next two decades, the number of agricultural

units shrank until, by 1987, the number had dwindled to 22,900 sovkhozy and 26,300 kolkhozy, with slightly over half of the land being organized as sovkhozy.

Another innovation in agricultural organization, introduced in the early 1970s, was the "agro-industrial complex." Always considered experimental, their numbers nevertheless increased over the next decade until there were more than 9,000 of them in existence. Most tended to specialize in the production of a single crop—for example, grapes, which they also further processed into wine or raisins.

One Khrushchev policy innovation that was to have great consequences in later years was his decision, made in the late 1950s, to commit the country to a great increase in meat production. The large increases in the numbers of livestock and poultry that resulted from this policy led to a greatly increased demand for grain for use as animal feed. Between 1960 and 1980, the amount of feed grains used for livestock and poultry tripled, going from 40 million tons to 120 million tons.

Grain production also increased during this period, but it could not keep up with the constantly growing demand. In 1963, after a relatively poor harvest, the Soviet Union imported its first grain. It imported grain only intermittently during the remainder of the 1960s, but after 1972 it become a regular customer on the world grain market.

This concerned the Soviet leadership and under Brezhnev huge sums of money were poured into the agricultural sector. Capital investment in the 1970s was over 300 billion rubles, which was 2.3 times what had been invested in agriculture in the previous decade. Most of the

investment went into creation of a large artificial fertilizer industry.

None of this did any good. Grain harvests from 1979–1985 were uniformly dismal, averaging between 40 and 50 million tons below annual targets specified in the Five-Year Plan. As a result, the Soviet government stopped publishing overall grain production figures in 1980. No overall figures were published again until October 1986, when it was announced that the grain harvest for 1985 totaled 191.5 million tons. Although this figure was 47.4 million tons less than the target, it actually was an improvement over the trend for the period 1981–1985, when production averaged only 179.5 million tons.

Grain figures for 1987 and 1988 were higher, at 210 and 211.3 million tons, but dropped in 1989 to 195 million tons. The 1990 harvest, on the other hand, was magnificent, reaching 247 million tons, though a significant amount was lost before reaching the Soviet public. The 1991 grain harvest was a disappointing 180–185 million tons.

The important thing, however, is that the Soviet Union, year after year, imported an average of 40 million tons of grain because Soviet collective and state farms fell that much short in meeting the demands of the economy. Even in the bumper year of 1991, the government imported approximately 28 million tons of grain.

Western agricultural experts have believed for a long time that the basic problem was in the system itself—that a basic conflict existed "between a centrally planned and controlled agriculture and the evolution of a modern, highly productive agriculture." Before Gorbachev, Soviet planners always rejected this point of view and tended to blame it on Russian weather.

Western experts also point out three other problems which they feel contributed to the failure of Soviet agriculture. The first is that Soviet farm equipment was always breaking down. This is partly because Soviet tractors didn't last very long and partly because there was never a sufficient supply of spare parts for them. This is still an unsolved problem. A February 1992 report indicated that 200,000 tractors were standing idle because of a lack of spare parts.

The second problem is the lack of adequately trained and motivated labor in the countryside. Young, better educated individuals have been leaving the collective and state farms and seeking work in the cities for a long time. In the 1970s, 15 million workers left for the cities and that trend, though diminished, continued in the 1980s. The reason is that young people could see no opportunity for advancement on the collective or state farm. A large number of persons are still employed in agriculture, but many of these persons are

Prison photo of Mikhail Khodorkovsky, former head of Yukos Oil. After a second trial, he was sentenced to another seven years for "new crimes." He was pardoned shortly before the start of the 2014 Winter Olympics, which Russia hosted in the city of Sochi

Russia

women (12% of the workforce) and lesser educated, older men, precisely those elements which are least productive and least amenable to change.

The third problem is related: there is a terrible shortage of food-carrying railroad cars and storage facilities. Because of this a substantial part of annual production fails to reach city markets, and simply rots. When properly used, food-carrying cars, refrigerated and unrefrigerated, properly become a place of storage as they move over large distances.

Gorbachev had held the agriculture portfolio in the secretariat for a number of years before becoming general secretary. There were some reforms he had been urging for a number of years, and he began implementing them after 1985. In his keynote speech to the 27th Party Congress, Gorbachev spoke of the need to significantly extend "the independence of collective and state farms," and he proposed a two-fold plan for agriculture. State and collective farms would be assigned fixed annual quotas that would not be altered. All production in excess of the quotas could be used as the farms saw fit, including selling it "in fresh or processed form at the collective farm market or through cooperative trade."

Gorbachev described his proposal as "the creative use of the Leninist idea of a tax in kind"—a reference to Lenin's *New Economic Policy*. The idea had great potential, for it could have been manipulated to create a major free market for agricultural produce if the level of fixed deliveries were set low enough. In addition, 100% of the production of state farms had traditionally gone to the state. Including them in the proposal was a departure from past practice and a genuine decentralization as far as state farms were concerned. Including them was also important because slightly over 50% of all agricultural land belonged to state farms. The potential was never reached, however, largely because so many people were opposed to any general loosening of control, and they managed to sabotage the reform.

Another of Gorbachev's innovations was to suggest that the "brigade" or "team" system in agriculture might be extended by making them available at the level of families. Under this setup, a group of workers "contracted" to perform certain agricultural tasks as, for example, to cultivate a specified acreage or run a dairy. Remuneration, divided according to the individual contributions of the members of the brigade or team, was based on the productivity of the unit. Gorbachev's innovation was approved, but the problem was in the implementation. Some family contracts were certainly written, but anecdotal reports indicate that the idea was not widely implemented.

This is the background that produced a Central Committee Plenum on Agriculture that took place in March 1989. In his speech to the Plenum, Gorbachev argued that "the essence of economic change in the countryside should be in granting farmers broad opportunities for displaying independence, enterprise and initiative." To accomplish this, he proposed turning collective and state farms into "a supreme type of cooperative."

To accomplish this, he proposed that land, equipment and buildings be leased out to individual farmers for periods up to 50 years. The state and collective farms would continue to exist as some sort of co-ordinating agency, but would not directly control production.

Although conservatives such as Ligachev spoke up for lesser reforms, Gorbachev's plan was approved in principle. The Plenum also voted, once again on Gorbachev's initiative, to abolish Gosagroprom, the super-ministry for agriculture that Gorbachev had created in 1985.

In April 1990, the Supreme Soviet actually passed a new law allowing the leasing of land, equipment, buildings, and other property for 50 years. Private farms were now a possibility. A few braver peasants moved to take advantage of it. They often had difficulty with the management of their collective or state farm, but there were an estimated 100,000 private farmers in Russia by the beginning of 1992.

Natural Resources

The Russian Federation is well supplied with most of the raw materials necessary for industrial production, although the major source of minerals is Siberia. European Russia is less well supplied. The area of the Russian Plain has bauxite and lignite deposits, while anthracite and iron ore are found mainly along the western slopes of the Ural Mountains. The northern Caucasus has a petroleum field, an extension of the famous petroleum field centered on the city of Baku, in the Republic of Azerbaijan. Oil is also produced in the area between the Volga River and the Ural Mountains.

In Siberia, on the other hand, there are found some of the largest reserves of coal, petroleum, and natural gas in the entire world, plus gold, silver, diamonds, platinum, copper, lead, zinc, chromium, cobalt, tungsten, manganese, and uranium. Beginning in the west, there are the iron ore and anthracite coal deposits of the eastern Urals that are exploited by the cities of Magnitogorsk and Yekaterinburg (Sverdlovsk).

To the northeast is Russia's largest oil field, centered on the city of Raduzhny, in Tyumen Province. The Tyumen Field, located in the southern part of the West Siberian Plain, produced 6.1 million

barrels a day in 1992, more than any country other than the United States and Saudi Arabia. Small fields are found in the vicinity of Pechora, far to the north on the Barents Sea, and further to the east in an area known as the East Siberian Lowland. Both are extremely isolated areas and production costs are thus higher.

The rest of the Russian Federation produced another 2.13 million barrels a day in 1992, making Russian production 9.23 million barrels a day at that time. Daily production was approximately 1.3 million barrels a day higher in 1990. Production continued to decline after that time, dropping 11% in 1994 alone. A large part of the problem was the result of Russian government policy. Until March 1992, the government continued to sell petroleum for the equivalent of a dollar a barrel, not only domestically but to the former Soviet republics as well. Oil exported to Europe brought $18 a barrel, but oil companies got only 25% of the resulting revenues, the rest going to the government as a royalty.

At those prices, particularly with the virulent inflation raging in the country, the state companies producing the oil were not getting a sufficient return to replace worn out or broken equipment. Domestic petroleum prices were subsequently allowed to rise to 40% of world levels, but a new 50% royalty tax acted as a negative incentive.

Another disincentive was Russia's system of oil-export quotas, which required oil producers to sell 65% of their output at home, at prices 70% less than the world price. In an attempt to raise its own revenues, the government also instituted a $5 a barrel tax on oil exports. After strong pressure from the IMF and the World Bank, Russia ended quotas on oil exports as of January 1, 1995, though the new export tax of $3.75 a barrel instituted as an alternative depressed oil exports even further. Domestic oil prices then began to rise gradually toward world levels, and that produced some new investment in 1996–1997. That trend was reversed in 1998, however, and new investment only began to grow again after 2000.

Putin's Energy Policy

Somewhere during his first term, President Putin decided that privatization of the energy sector had not served the best interests of the Russian people. In particular, he was disturbed by the new wealth being amassed in the privatized energy sector even as the government remained starved for funds. It also bothered him that some of the new oil barons were using their wealth to finance opposition political movements. Putin concluded from all of this that the "commanding heights" of the energy sector had to be brought back under government control.

This led to the move against Mikhail Khodorkovsky and the eventual destruction of Yukos, the best run energy company in Russia. It also led to the government's decision to regain majority ownership of Gazprom, then primarily a producer of natural gas, and, in the words of its chairman—"to gradually transform it into a global energy company and a world market leader."

This was possible because a Gazprom-controlled subsidiary already controlled Russia's 150,000 kilometers of natural gas pipelines and Gazprom held a monopoly on gas exports—a sop given it in the 1990s when the government required it to provide gas domestically at low, controlled prices.

Most of Russia's reserves of natural gas are located in Siberia. Most of the natural gas is found in West Siberia, in the northern part of Tyumen Province. These are the Urengoi Fields. Some natural gas also comes from the area of the East Siberian Lowland. The production of natural gas has grown greatly in importance in recent years as new fields have been found and exploited.

Gazprom, now Russia's main producer of natural gas, is today the world's single biggest gas producer. About two-thirds of its gas goes to the domestic market at relatively low, government-controlled prices, however. Gazprom exports most of the rest to either Europe or Turkey. Gazprom could invest in developing untapped Arctic fields, but it has chosen not to do so—possibly because it lacks the necessary capital to do so. Instead, it has signed contracts to buy natural gas from Uzbekistan and Turkmenistan. This arrangement has been profitable for Gazprom up until recently because Gazprom has been able to obtain gas from these republics for about one-third of what it charged its customers in Central and Western Europe. Gazprom has recently increased the capacity of the Central Asian pipeline to accommodate these increased amounts, and it is currently constructing another gas pipeline with a capacity of 30 bcm per year to connect Central Asia and Russia.

In June 2006, Gazprom used its wholly owned subsidiary, Gazprombank, to purchase a 51% interest in Sibneftegaz, the owner of the large Beregovoye field in western Siberia. Sibneftegaz, a wholly owned subsidiary of the gas production company Itera, had not developed the field because Gazprom refused to give it access to its gas pipeline network, which meant that Itera had no way to get the gas to market. Two other independent gas producers, North Gas and Novatek, were similarly denied access to Gazprom's pipelines until they allowed Gazprom to buy into their companies. Gazprom currently owns 9.99% of Novatek.

Gazprom was willing to allow the Shell Oil Company to buy a 20% interest in Novatek as compensation for agreeing to sell Gazprom half of its interest in Sakhalin-2. As part of the deal on Gazprom's entry into Sakhalin-2, Gazprom signed a co-operation agreement with Shell allowing the latter to expand its resource base in Sakhalin outside the Sakhalin-2 project.

Gazprom became a major oil producer when it paid Roman Abramovich $13 billion for 72% of Sibneft in September 2005. Prior to the acquisition, Gazprom had produced 12 million tons of oil a year; after its acquisition of Sibneft, its annual production became 46 million tons a year. This put Gazprom in third place among publicly traded oil and gas companies, with a market capitalization of the St. Petersburg Stock Exchange of $224.6 billion. Because of the subsequent decline in the value of stocks on the St. Petersburg Stock Exchange, Gazprom's market capitalization was only $78 billion in May 2014.

Gazprom recently put the squeeze on TNK-BP, a 50–50 joint venture between British Petroleum and three Russian tycoons, over a Siberian gas field called Kovykta. TNK-BP's license required it to produce 9 billion cubic meters of gas a year; however, TNK-BP was forbidden to export gas and domestic demand was perhaps a third of the required output. TNK-BP proposed a joint management agreement on Kovykta with Gazprom, but Gazprom refused. In June 2007, under threat that the Russian government would revoke TNK-BP's license for the field, British Petroleum agreed to sell its stake to Gazprom for $900 million, somewhat more than the $500 million it spent developing the field.

With Gazprom's income dropping by 23% in 2009, however, Gazprom found itself unable to finance the purchase; in March 2010, with the Russian government once again threatening to strip TNK-BP of its license, the firm announced that it was in discussions with Rosneftgaz and hoped to sell its Kovykta gas field by the end of 2010. Rosneftgaz, which like Gazprom is a state-owned firm, owns a 10.97% stake in Gazprom, so the change in buyers is probably not significant.

In general, Gazprom has not spent significant sums to develop new fields, but has preferred to take over fields developed by other gas producers; most of its growth has been accomplished in this manner. As an exception, however, Gazprom is willing to develop new fields if foreign companies put up most of the basic capital in return for future deliveries of natural gas. One such development is in the area of Novy Urengoy, in western Siberia. Two German companies put up $1.5 billion to finance development of the field; Gazprom began shipping natural gas to Germany in 2010.

Gazprom thus represents the new model of Russian capitalism that has emerged since Putin became president in 2000; at the same time, it represents the contradiction which is inherent in that new model. Gazprom is a huge, largely state-owned and wholly state-directed company; at the same time, it is a publicly traded company whose stock is available for purchase by private investors. Since 2005, several more such companies have come into existence in Russia.

Another part of the picture is provided by the history of Rosneft, a state-owned oil company which went from being a middling oil firm in 2004 to Russia's second-largest oil producer in 2005. It then went on to become Russia's largest crude producer in May 2007 when it picked up Tomskneft, the last remaining Yukos subsidiary, at a bankruptcy sale. The sale included the Angarsk and Achinsk refineries plus the East Siberian Oil Company.

The secret behind Rosneft's growth is that 70% of its output comes from a subsidiary called Yuganskneftegaz, which until December 2004 was owned by Yukos. Rosneft therefore owes its growth to the destruction of the Yukos Oil Company. The Russian government forced the sale of Yuganskneftegaz in 2004 to pay for several billion dollars in tax liens against Yukos, the mother company. Yuganskneftegaz was purchased for $9.4 billion by a fictitious company set up by the Russian government; it was then immediately sold to Rosneft. After the sale, the Russian government magically reduced the tax claims against Yuganskneftegaz by $3.9 billion.

According to newspaper reports at the time, President Putin originally intended Yuganskneftegaz to go to Gazprom; worries about possible civil lawsuits against Gazprom by disgruntled Yukos stockholders led the government to create the fictitious company and arrange the resale to Rosneft. To pay off money borrowed to finance the purchase of Yuganskneftegaz, Rosneft made an initial public offering of $10.4 billion of its stock in London and in Russia in July 2006. With the company's oil reserves larger than those of ExxonMobil and its profits in 2005 almost five times higher than in 2004, many foreign investors were willing to forget how Rosneft got 70% of its assets.

The surprise, however, was that $1.1 billion of the shares were bought by Malaysia's state-run oil company, Petronas. The second government-run company to participate in the offering was the China National Petroleum Corporation, which took another $1.5 billion of the shares.

Although it is clearly the intent of the Russian government to obtain control over the "commanding heights" of the energy sector, it does continue to permit

Russia

PETROLEUM AND GAS DEPOSITS

Petroleum Deposits
Natural Gas Deposits
Petroleum Refinery

0   500   1000 Miles

individual private Russian oil companies to grow and prosper. The best example of this is Lukoil, the second-largest producer of crude oil in Russia.

One of Lukoil's attractions to the Russian state is that it has aggressively expanded abroad, opening the American market for Russian gasoline sales. Over the past several years, Lukoil purchased the Getty Petroleum Marketing Company plus ConocoPhillips stations in New Jersey and Pennsylvania (Mobil brand); Lukoil until recently operated over 2,000 service stations in 13 eastern states, all of them supplied with gasoline shipped from its Vysotsk terminal on the Baltic Sea near St. Petersburg. Pressed for funds because of the economic crisis, Lukoil arranged to sell 500 some stations in late 2008.

Although the general policy of the Russian government is to bring energy production under state control, until recently it had continued to encourage foreign investment in technically challenging projects, particularly those offshore or in the Arctic. The largest of the projects being developed by foreign capital is the offshore drilling east of Sakhalin Island in Eastern Siberia.

Although Russian state companies pumped oil from wells on Sakhalin Island beginning in the 1930s, it was only in the 1970s that large pools of oil and gas were discovered off Sakhalin Island itself. The government mapped the offshore recoverable reserves at the time, but it then lacked the money and the technical expertise to develop the field itself.

Oil production of 300,000 barrels a day began in October 2005; this grew to 550,000 barrels a day by 2008.

Shell also began building two 400-mile pipelines, one for oil and one for gas, that begin at two huge offshore drilling platforms in the Sea of Okhotsk off Sakhalin Island. The gas pipeline ends at Aniva, where a $2.5 billion liquefied gas plant has been constructed. The oil pipeline ends at a deepwater loading terminal on a bay 90 miles northeast of Japan.

The plan of the private companies was to export the oil to China, Japan, and South Korea, though ExxonMobil intended to ship some of its oil through an existing Russian-owned pipeline. Much of the natural gas was to be shipped to a terminal being built in northern Mexico.

From there, it was to be fed into a pipeline and shipped to California.

Now those plans are moot. In September 2006, Russia's Natural Resources Ministry wrote to the companies essentially demanding that the original agreements be rewritten. That same month, the Russian government withdrew its environmental approval for the Sakhalin-2 liquefied natural gas project. After some months of negotiations, Royal Dutch Shell and its two Japanese partners were forced to cede control of their Sakhalin-2 venture to Gazprom. Gazprom went on to complete the building of a liquefied natural gas plant in 2010, but it has placed on hold plans to expand the plant, possibly because of a reduction in overall world energy demand as a result of the global economic downturn.

Sakhalin-1 is still operating, but the Russian government awarded a bid to a small oil field near Sakhalin-1 to Rosneft rather than ExxonMobil in September 2006. It appears clear that non-Russian companies will be limited to a minority— and probably diminishing—role in the development of Russian energy in the future.

Oil and Natural Gas Pipelines

One of the Soviet Union's larger and more controversial industrial projects in the 1980s was a 3,400-mile pipeline constructed from the Urengoy fields of Siberia to Western Europe. The pipeline was largely constructed with Western technology and credits, with the Western European countries that have financed it—Great Britain, France, Germany, and Italy—receiving payment in future gas deliveries. The first gas began to flow to Western Europe in December 1983. In 2005, Russia and Germany signed a deal on the construction of two natural gas piplines, referred to as Nordsteam 1, that run under the Baltic Sea. Comissioned in 2015, Nordstream 1 is owned and operated by Nord Stream AG, whose majority shareholder is the Russian state company Gazprom. In 2015, Germany and Russia signed a deal for a second set of pipelines, referred to as Nordstream 2, to expand export capacity along the same route. Gazprom fully owns this $11 billion project. This deal took place after Russia had annexed Crimea and invaded Kharkiv, Luhanks, and Donets regions. Despite objections from the US and its other Western allies, the German government defended Nordstream 2 calling it a purely "commercial project" vital for its all-important industires, and stating that it did not make Germany or Europe vulnerable to Kremlin. For Russia, the successful completion of Nordstream 2 meant it would no longer be needed to pay $2 billion in transit fees to Ukraine to deliver gas to Europe through its territory. Nordstream 2 finished construction in 2021 and was due to go online in 2022, but the invasion of Ukraine in February 2022, led the German government to revoke its support for the project. While Nordstream 2 is put on hold, Germany, much to the consternation of Ukraine, contines to import gas through Nordsream 1.

In addition to gas, Russia has built East Siberia-Pacific Ocean (ESPO) oil pipeline system for exporting crude oil to the Asia Pacific markets to meet the growing energy needs of Japan, Korea, Taiwan, China, and India. Started in 2006 and completed in 2012, the 4,857-km ESPO oil pipeline sends oil from Taishet in eastern Siberia to the Pacific Ocean terminal at Kozmino, near Vladivostok. ESPO is planning to build a.spur that would l connect the pipeline to China. In the meantime, Russia has contracted to begin exporting oil to China through a pipeline which Kazakhstan recently built and connects Kazakhstan's western oilfields and western China.

Russia's oil pipelines are controlled by Transneft, a state-owned joint-stock company which has a network of about 50,000 kilometers of pipelines that carry more than 95% of the crude oil produced in Russia. As with the case of Gazprom, Transneft's shares are traded on the Moscow Stock Exchange; again, like Gazprom, 75% of its shares are owned by the Russian government, which actually owns 100% of the voting stock. Transneft is currently constructing the Baltic Pipeline System as a way of reducing Russian dependence on shipments through neighboring countries. It is also attempting to gain control of oil pipelines in other parts of the CIS and in Central and Western Europe for the same reason.

Until recently, a second state-owned company, Transnefteprodukt (TNP), controlled the pipelines which handled the export of refined oil products. In 2006, over 16 million tons of gas product was moved through TNP pipelines.

In April 2007, however, President Putin signed a decree transferring ownership of TNP to Transneft. As Putin's decree states, the purpose of the merger is "to create a unified system of transporting crude and products in order to protect the country's economic interests. Russia's long-term goal is to process more crude inside the country and thereby increase product exports, thereby diversifying away from dependence on exports of raw materials.

Coal and Lignite

The Russian Federation, and the Republics of Kazakhstan and Ukraine together contain almost 20% of the world's known reserves of coal and lignite. The three republics today account for nearly a quarter of all coal mined in the world. Russia's two largest coal fields, which are both located in Siberia, were developed by the Soviet government after 1917. Pechora, the first Siberian field developed, is in the far north at the beginning of the Ural Mountains, along the Barents Sea. More interesting—and more challenging—is a major new coal field located in the southern part of the Republic of Yakutsk-Sakha (formerly the Yakutsk Autonomous Republic), which the Soviet Union began developing in 1974 in a joint project with Japan.

The Republic of Yakutsk-Sakha in eastern Siberia has large deposits of gold, diamonds, gas and tin, in addition to coal. But it is also one of the coldest inhabited places on earth, with temperatures known to plunge to –60°C (–108°F). It is also extremely remote from the major populated areas of Russia.

This provides a problem for any form of development, but presents an especially difficult one in the case of a low value, bulk item like coal. As early as the 1930s, Soviet scientists had identified deposits of high-grade coking coal in the vicinity of the city of Neryungri, estimated to be as large as 300 million tons. It is an isolated area, however, and the Soviet government poured its limited development funds into more accessible areas. Then, in 1974, the Soviet government negotiated a joint project with a number of Japanese companies to develop the coal field. The Japanese companies provided the necessary technology and equipment, while the Soviet Union built a spur rail line to connect Neryungri with the Baikal-Amur Railway (BAM), a new railway constructed in the 1980s that runs parallel to but north of the Trans-Siberian Railway. The Japanese payment was in the form of deliveries of coal.

The project was eventually completed, though capital costs turned out to be four times the level of European Russia, and the project took several years more to complete than originally planned. As a result of the development, however, Yakutsk, the regional capital, has grown from a small settlement to 200,000 people. The potential for further development in this area is very great, though costs remain a significant factor.

Metal Ore Deposits

Russian deposits of iron ore are found, first of all, in the Ural Mountains and, secondly, in the mountains that form the southern border of Siberia, particularly in the area around Lake Baikal. There are vast deposits around Lake Baikal, but the iron mines of the Urals are extremely old and largely worked out, having been originally developed in the 18th century. But Russian iron ore deposits are lower in ore content than those of the Republic of Ukraine, particularly those of Krivoi Rog, where the pure iron content runs as high as 68%. Russia will continue to get much of its iron from the Ukraine for the next several years, but development of the iron deposits of the Lake Baikal area is a good possibility for the future.

With respect to other ferrous metals, the Russian Federation is remarkably endowed; it is the world's largest producer of manganese and chromium and has substantial reserves of nickel, titanium, and vanadium. On the other hand, there is a relative shortage of such important metals as cobalt, molybdenum, and tungsten, all of great importance in steel production.

Insofar as non-ferrous metals are concerned, copper mining resources, developed primarily since World War II, now produce about 12% of the world total. Tin is in relatively short supply; lead and zinc are available in relatively large quantities. Russia is the world's second-largest producer of gold, though production is down and the mines, at the moment still all state owned, have been having labor problems. The production of light metals such as aluminum is steadily growing; the known

Russia

deposits of aluminum ore are estimated to be adequate for at least 40 years.

The Role of Russia's Waterways

In discussing the natural resources of this country, mention must be made of the extensive system of waterways. Because of the difficulty in building roads in some areas, waterways played an important role in past centuries. The network of navigable inland waterways, totaling some 75,000 miles, is still of importance in reaching certain otherwise almost inaccessible areas, but the total volume of goods now carried by water is no more than 10% of the total. Practically no rivers remain open all year, and those that do suffer from seasonal shortages of rainfall which makes them too shallow.

The water resources of the Russian Federation have been used to construct hydroelectric power stations, including some of the largest in the world. An intricate system of canals, developed in the past, is still maintained and continues to play a significant economic role.

Paved roads continue to be scarce and the number of all-weather roads suitable for trucks is limited, so people and goods are still carried primarily by railroad. The Soviet Union was the first country to use jet airplanes for passenger traffic and certain remote areas can still be reached only by air; thus the network of air routes gets much use. Flights tend to be irregular and many times are simply canceled. Railroads have been designated a "Commonwealth" interest, and the newly independent republics are committed to maintaining the integrated network that had existed under the now defunct Soviet Union.

Nuclear Power

Until the nuclear accident at Chernobyl in April 1986, the Soviet Union had been committed to nuclear power as a major source of electric power. At that time, the USSR had a capacity of 17.5 million kilowatts generated from this source and it had 18 more nuclear power stations under construction. In addition, Russia had produced two prototype industrial fast breeder-reactors, plus two nuclear heat supply stations, each of which was designed to produce enough heat for a city with a population of about 400,000. The most important reason for this ambitious program was the severe lack of alternate energy sources in the area of European Russia. The nuclear accident at Chernobyl changed all that. Under growing public pressure, most of the nuclear power stations under construction were put on hold, and then later canceled entirely.

Chernobyl is a small town about 60 miles north of Kyiv, in the now independent Republic of Ukraine. The plant had four reactors, two with "containment" buildings and two without. An experiment was underway using one of the unprotected devices when a sudden burst of power surged through the reactor, causing a steam leak. This led to the formation of hydrogen gas, which then exploded, demolishing the roof of the plant and killing two workers. Unrestrained by containment, the released radioactive gases quickly spread into the atmosphere, leading to widespread contamination not only of Soviet territory, but of neighboring nations as well.

The world found out about the accident two days later when the Swedes, detecting increased radiation in the atmosphere, began making inquiries. After first denying that anything untoward had occurred, the Soviets finally admitted the fact of the accident. It is now known that the reactor which got out of control was an unusual type that made use of graphite in its core. The graphite caught fire when overheating occurred. There was at least a partial "meltdown" and the reactor continued to spew out radiation for about two and a half weeks before it began to be controlled.

About 300 radiation victims were brought to Moscow hospitals; 35 of these had suffered severe radiation exposure. Emergency bone marrow transplants were performed under the direction of an American surgeon. The death toll from radiation quickly reached 19 out of the 35; the *Times* of London later reported that the figure had grown to 31 and that 209 others "remained in hospitals or sanatoria suffering from various degrees of radiation sickness." Dr. Robert Peter Gale, the American surgeon who performed the emergency bone marrow transplants gave as his own estimates that there were "about 50,000 to 100,000 individuals who have received at least some dose [of radiation] that may be of long-term concern." Twenty years later, an April 2006 *National Geographic* report lowered this estimate considerably; as the article put it, it is now estimated that "the cancer fuse lit by Chernobyl will claim 4,000 lives."

Even so, that does not alter the fact that Soviet handling of the Chernobyl disaster was, at best, shabby—both with its delay in reporting what happened and its subsequent failures of communication. Primary blame was placed on local officials who "didn't have a true assessment of the accident."

The Soviet Union did carry out major modifications of the 14 other graphite-core nuclear reactors which it operated. It also announced that future reactors would have containment buildings and would be pressurized. That was not enough for an increasing number of Soviet citizens, however. Protests grew around the Soviet Union and, increasingly, republic governments began putting pressure on the central government to cancel nuclear reactor building programs in their republics. The Soviet government canceled the two reactors it had been planning to build at Chernobyl, and later stopped construction on a number of other plants in southern Russia, Armenia, and elsewhere, but it never abandoned its commitment to nuclear power.

The Russian people were not among the major protesters against nuclear power in the past, but there was an increasing movement in Russia in the 1990s urging that the government phase out nuclear energy. The government, concerned about the continuing energy shortages in the area of European Russia put the entire question on hold for the next several years.

The matter was reopened in November 2005 when President Putin appointed Sergei Kirienko as the new head of the Atomic Energy Agency. In his acceptance speech, Kirienko said that the government intended to build a new generation of nuclear power plants to replace the plants that would shortly have to be retired. Two months later, President Putin said that he wanted nuclear plants to provide one-quarter of Russia's energy needs to be provided by nuclear plants by 2030, up from the 16–17% derived from nuclear energy at that time. Kirienko, speaking two days later, said that Russia needed to build 40 new nuclear plants to meet the 25% figure. Russia currently has 35 nuclear reactors in operation.

In March 2006, Viktor Opekunov, who chairs the Duma's Atomic Energy Committee, said that the government intended "to consolidate the nuclear power industry and turn it into a 'vertically integrated holding' under state control." Two months later, TVEL was set up as a state holding company with control of all the enterprises that make up the country's nuclear power industry. The new head of TVEL is President Putin's own chief of staff, Sergei Sobyanin.

Another state-owned consortium, which may eventually become a part of TVEL, is Rosenergoatom. In June 2006, Rosenergoatom announced that it had begun constructing the world's first floating nuclear power station—carrying two nuclear reactors capable together of generating 70 megawatts—to provide electric power to populations in the area of the White Sea; the completion date is 2016. The consortium also indicated that the government planned to construct six additional floating nuclear power plants to provide power to other remote areas. These projects mirror other recent government actions to bring strategically important sectors of the economy under state control, as was done, for example, with oil and gas and the aircraft industry.

The government has also announced plans to bring all Russian uranium-producing enterprises together in a single holding company. The holding company also has plans for partnerships with partners from former Soviet republics. One such partnership already exists with the Republic of Kazakhstan. Inaugurated in December 2006, the joint venture will extract uranium for further processing in Russia. Two Russian companies, Teksnabexport and Atomredmetzoloto, have formed the joint venture with Kazakhstan's Kazakatomprom.

The Russian government has the problem of disposing of tons of radioactive plutonium and enriched uranium from warheads now being disabled because of the CFE and START agreements. Disposing of the warheads alone will eventually cost billions of dollars. The US Congress provided $400 million to help pay the cost of dismantling the missiles, but much more will be needed.

The Future

The foundation of Vladimir Putin's regime has long rested on ensuring a certain level of economic well-being coupled with restricted freedoms in exchange for political support. To his supporters in Russia, Putin has represented stability. The regime has always been attuned to public opinion, and has done everything to keep things the same, until it did not when it unleashed a full-scale war on Ukraine. While initially boosting Putin's popularity through nationalist fervor, the prolonged war has led to increasing economic hardships, international isolation, and military setbacks. These factors have gradually eroded public support, especially among younger and urban populations, who exited the country in droves to avoid getting swept up in government's mobilization campaign. The regime has responded by tightening control over media and dissent, while also intensifying propaganda efforts. However, cracks in the facade of unity are becoming apparent, with some elites quietly questioning the war's cost–benefit ratio. Despite these challenges, Putin's grip on power remains firm and is supported by a mix of repression, information control, and lingering patriotic sentiment among segments of the population.

Analysts agree that the war has changed the nature of the regime. Some argue that the war has accelerated Russia's decent from autocracy into a totalitarian state. Others dub the regime as "totalitarianism 2.0" in reference to how Putin's regime resembles the old Soviet order in politicizing the police force, subduing courts, and censoring the media. Still others speculate that Russia would emerge from the war as a country ruled by warlords and criminals. To the extent that analysts speculate about Russia's possible collapse after the war, they either paint an optimistic picture of a peaceful disintegration of the federation or violent separatist wars. Whatever happens with Russia, it is likely to ramify throughout the region. Hence, it is imperative that the neighboring states be prepared for any possible scenario to minimize the aftershocks.

Ukraine and the West, on the one hand, and Russia, on the other, are engaged in a fundamental test of wills. It would appear that Putin believes that time is on his side. He hopes that the world community over time will come to accept Russia's annexation of Crimea and the occupation of Luhanks, Donetsk, and Kherson oblasts, even though respect for established international boundaries is a cornerstone of the post–World War II international order. Putin seems absolutely determined that Russia retain control of Crimea and the aforementioned oblasts, but it is hard to imagine how the rest of the world can accept the annexation and occupation. Putin also appears to have calculated that Ukraine, Europe, and the rest of the world will eventually relent and negotiate a decentralization of Ukraine's governmental structure.

The invasion of Ukraine sustains Putin's popularity at home. His approval rating remains extremely high as Russians, especially those who receive their news from state-controlled television, largely accept Putin's explanation of the war. According to a poll conducted by the Levada Center in February 2023, 83% of respondents approved of Putin as president. At the same time, Putin's ever-increasing attempt to squelch opposition sentiment within Russia reveals his underlying insecurity over the future. The pro-Navalny protest of 2021 reveals that significant pockets of opposition to government policy exist, especially among the youth. Alexey Navalny's return to Russia and his subsequent arrest elevated his status in the eyes of many members of the public growing tired of Russia's recent economic and political stagnation. Ultimately, the failed assassination attempt of Navalny in August 2020 has to be seen as a self-inflicted wound for the regime since it transformed Navalny into a martyr for reform.

Eurasia

Five of the plotters: Interior Minister Boris Pugo and Vice President Gennady Yanayev (third and fourth from left)

The Collapse of the Soviet Union

It was early in the morning in Moscow on Monday, August 19, 1991, when Soviet television issued its news bulletin. Mikhail Gorbachev, alleged to be unable for health reasons to perform his duties, had been relieved as president. His powers had been transferred to his vice president, Gennady Yanayev, who was to exercise them in consultation with an eight-member "State Committee for the State of Emergency," composed of himself, the prime minister, the ministers of defense and interior, head of the KGB, two individuals representing the military-industrial complex, and the chairman of the Farmers' Union of the USSR.

A state of emergency was announced throughout in the country, demonstrations and protest meetings were banned and independent newspapers were closed. Subsequently it was revealed that Gorbachev had actually been in military custody since the preceding evening.

Although portrayed as an ordinary transfer of power resulting from the inability of the Soviet president to fulfill his duties, this was actually the beginning of an attempted coup d'etat, a fact that became clear as soon as one looked more closely at what was happening. First of all, if Gorbachev had really been ill, his vice president could have temporarily assumed his duties without further ado. It was not necessary either to declare a state of emergency or create a "State Committee for the State of Emergency" to supervise it.

Secondly, not only was every member of the "State Committee for the State of Emergency" a prominent conservative; this was the second attempt by four of them to assume Gorbachev's powers. Two months earlier, the prime minister, Valentin Pavlov, had asked the Supreme Soviet to give him the right to issue decrees that would not require Gorbachev's signature; his request had been supported by the ministers of defense and interior plus the head of the KGB. Gorbachev had to personally and energetically intervene to defeat this first maneuver of the conservatives. In retrospect, Gorbachev should have dismissed Pavlov and the other plotters at that time, but he evidently thought he could continue to control them and he desired to rule by consensus without breaking with the more conservative members of his government.

Now the plotters were trying again. They decided to make their move because Gorbachev, vacationing in the Crimea with his family, was due to return to Moscow that morning. A second consideration was that Gorbachev was scheduled to sign a new union treaty the next day that would transfer considerable powers to the republics. Communist traditionalists opposed the new union treaty and were determined to stop it.

That the pending union treaty was a major factor in the timing of the coup was made clear by the plotters when they issued their first statement announcing the removal of Gorbachev. Here they listed their aims as "overcoming the profound and comprehensive crisis, political, ethnic and civil strife, chaos and anarchy that threaten the . . . territorial integrity, freedom and independence of our fatherland" and referred specifically to the March 1991 "referendum on the preservation of the Union of Soviet Socialist Republics." Further, Yanayev's first action after assuming power was to cancel the treaty-signing ceremony. The question was, could the coup succeed?

In theory, it should have. The leaders controlled all of the traditional instruments of force within the country. Marshal Dmitry Yazov controlled the military as minister of defense; Vladimir Kryuchkov was head of the KGB and Boris K. Pugo controlled both security troops and the police as minister of the interior. They demonstrated this control by ordering tanks, troops, and armored vehicles into the major cities at the beginning of the attempted coup, ringing republic government buildings with troops and tanks, and seizing control of television and radio facilities.

Moreover, the coup leaders included, in addition to the prime minister, the first deputy chairman of the defense council (Oleg Baklanov), the president of the Association of State Enterprises and Industrial, Construction, Transport and Communications Facilities of the USSR (V. A. Staradubtsev) and the chairman of the Farmers' Union of the USSR (A. I. Tizyakov). Further, they had the support of the Communist Party and a significant percentage of officials throughout the country.

It must be noted that the coup would probably have succeeded two or three years earlier. What the leaders overlooked, however, was the significant democratization that had taken place over the preceding years. These moves had produced new leaders such as Boris Yeltsin, elected president of the Russian Federation in June 1991, and Anatoly Sobchak, mayor of Leningrad. An order was actually issued for the arrest of Yeltsin, but no attempt was made to take other democratic leaders into custody or even to dismiss them from their positions.

The attempt to arrest Yeltsin was bungled. Eluding his would-be captors, Yeltsin made it to the Russian Republic Parliament building by 10:00 a.m. and immediately began organizing opposition to the coup. His first step was to call a press conference to question the authority of the "State Committee for the State of Emergency." He followed this up with a decree ordering all Russian Republic citizens to obey the orders of the Russian Republic Government, rather than the orders of the unconstitutional "Committee."

In perhaps his grandest gesture, he then went outside where tanks ringed the parliament building, climbed up on top of one of them, and called for an "unlimited general strike" and mass civil disobedience. The soldiers, apparently devoid of orders about what to do in case of opposition, allowed Yeltsin to then climb down and go back into the Parliament building. Subsequently, thousands of Yeltsin supporters gathered around the structure and, forming a human shield, made it impossible for the coup leaders to move against Yeltsin and his democratic supporters without inflicting major casualties.

The coup leaders overlooked many things, but perhaps their greatest failure was in communications. They took the traditional action of seizing control of the radio and television stations (which abruptly acquired an air of unreality) and they closed down opposition newspapers, but they never gained control of telephone lines or stopped foreign reporters from filing their dispatches with their home organizations.

As a result, the democrats built up their own internal communications using computers and modems (a means for communication by telephone line from one computer to another). News of the coup and

growing opposition to it was broadcast to the Soviet Union by the BBC, Voice of America, and the rest of the international media. The Soviet people also learned thereby of the nearly universal condemnation of the attempted coup by world leaders. Western nations suspended aid programs and otherwise made it clear that its leaders would find themselves isolated internationally if they won.

What the leaders also forgot to take into account was the possibility that parts of the military and the KGB might be weaned away from loyalty to the attempted coup. In fact, however, as popular demonstrations grew, many individual commanders

adopted a passive stance or actively threw their support to Yeltsin and the forces of democracy. In Leningrad, 200,000 demonstrators gathered in the square outside the Winter Palace, while in Siberia coal miners announced a protest strike. Gradually, one after another of the Republic leaders came out against the coup.

When it became clear to the coup leaders that the Soviet people (1) would not accept their rule peacefully and (2) that they could win only through a ruthless use of force and a continuing regime of oppression that would leave the Soviet Union isolated internationally, one after another of the coup leaders lost his nerve

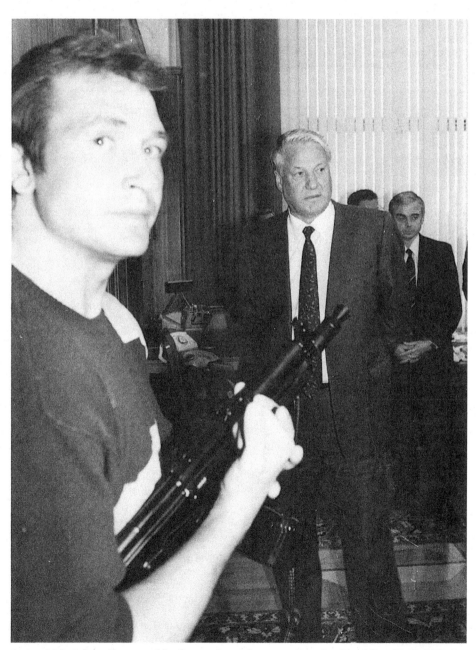

August 20: A heavily armed bodyguard watches over Russian President Boris Yeltsin inside the Russian parliament
Courtesy of Reuters/Bettmann

Eurasia

and the movement began to collapse. After approximately 60 hours, Gorbachev was freed, the troops were ordered out of Moscow, and an order went out for the arrest of the coup leaders.

Boris Pugo, minister of the interior, committed suicide as did, later, Marshal Sergei Akhromeyev, Gorbachev's chief military adviser, who was implicated in the attempted coup. Aleksandr Bessmertnykh, the foreign minister, was fired because of questionable loyalty despite his protests of innocence, which were even expressed by live satellite TV in the United States.

The Return of Gorbachev and Collapse of the Union

Gorbachev arrived back in Moscow Thursday morning to loud cheers but, though he claimed to be in complete control of the Soviet Union, it soon became clear that the three-day attempted coup had rung a death knell to the old system. Even as Gorbachev defended the Communist Party and promised to work for its renewal, Yeltsin issued a decree banning party activities in the Russian Republic and specifically prohibited party cells in military units, police units of the ministry of interior, and in the KGB.

Abruptly, on Friday, Gorbachev, speaking to the Russian Parliament, abandoned his earlier defense of the party and referred to the Central Committee as "traitors." On Saturday, he followed this up by resigning as general secretary and calling on the Central Committee to dissolve itself. He then issued a decree suspending the activities of the party and seizing all its property. This about-face created a serious problem of credibility.

The Soviet Union, which Gorbachev still hoped to save, was crumbling around him. Estonia had declared itself independent on August 19 and Latvia followed the next day. In the week following the defeat of the coup, four more republics followed with their declarations of independence: the Ukraine on August 25; Byelorussia (now Belarus) on August 25; Uzbekistan on August 26; and Moldavia (now Moldova) on August 27. Armenia set a referendum for a vote on independence for September 16.

Several of the other republics also promised to hold plebiscites to confirm their declarations. The most important of those was the Ukraine, which set its referendum for December 1. Thus, the situation was that, including Lithuania and Georgia, which had declared their independence even before the attempted coup, 9 of the 15 republics were committed to independence. If the republics really meant their declarations of independence, no viable union was possible. It was unclear whether their declarations of independence were real or only bargaining tools in preparation for negotiations on a new union treaty.

The Rise of Boris Yeltsin and Attempts toward Union

Crucially, Boris Yeltsin, president of the Russian Federation, still favored some form of union, and on August 28 he sent a delegation to the Ukraine to see what could be worked out. What he got was a provisional economic and military alliance which, the Russian and Ukrainian Governments announced, other "former subjects of the USSR" were welcome to join.

The next step came on September 2 when a special session of the Congress of People's Deputies met in Moscow, with the leaders of ten of the republics in attendance. Here Gorbachev proposed the creation of a new interim government to replace the discredited one over which he presided. After three days of debate, the Congress voted, in effect, to dissolve itself and transfer authority to a new executive council and legislature controlled by the participating republics.

Gorbachev remained president, but final executive authority was lodged in a State Council made up of Gorbachev and the leaders of the participating republics. A separate Inter-republic Economic Committee, appointed by the State Council, assumed the functions of the former Council of Ministers. Finally, a two-chamber legislature was established, the membership of the second chamber to be appointed by and represent the governments of the individual republics. In this chamber, voting would be by delegation, with each republic having one vote. This clearly interim government was to govern until a new union treaty could be signed by the individual republics bringing into being a proposed "Union of Sovereign States."

The first act of the State Council was to recognize the independence of Lithuania, Latvia and Estonia. It can be argued that recognition had become inevitable by this time, since most of the world, including the United States, had already recognized the independence of the Baltic Republics. Nevertheless, this was the first formal step in the breakup of the Soviet Empire. Even at this time, only 10 of the 12 remaining republics were supporting the interim government. Moldavia refused to participate at all and Georgia sent only observers. Neither appeared likely to sign a new union treaty. In addition, over the next several days, all of the remaining republics other than the Russian Federation, Kazakhstan, and Turkmenistan declared their independence. Later, even Kazakhstan and Turkmenistan would join the list.

The next three months were to prove decisive. Gorbachev, determined to save some form of union and, recognizing that Boris Yeltsin's support was absolutely vital, dismissed all of his former advisers and accepted Yeltsin's advice on the make-up of his new government, surrounding himself with liberals and even appointing Ivan Silayev, prime minister of the Russian Federation (i.e., the Russian state), as chairman of the Inter-republic Economic Committee, a post which effectively made him the caretaker prime minister of the union government. He then asked the reform economist Grigory Yavlinsky to draw up a plan for economic union which he presented in draft form to the State Council in September.

The leaders of ten of the republics attended the meeting and gave their general approval to the plan. The two missing leaders were the presidents of Moldova (formerly Moldavia) and Georgia. Zviad Gamsakhurdia, then president of Georgia, had made it clear that his government was pursuing a policy of complete independence and wanted nothing to do, even economically, with a union. The Moldovan government was undecided whether to participate in an economic union and so chose to abstain.

The other key republic was the Ukraine, led by Leonid Kravchuk, the former head of the Ukrainian Communist Party, who had repudiated the party and become a convert to democratization and a market economy. Kravchuk himself supported the idea of some form of continued union at first, but he came under increasing pressure from the Ukrainian parliament, which opposed supranational ties as a limitation on Ukrainian independence. In October 1991, the Ukrainian parliament drew up two pages of objections to the pending economic treaty, after which the Ukrainian Government announced that it would not sign the agreement without significant changes in the language. Among the changes that the parliament was demanding was the right for the Ukraine to set up its own national bank, issue its own currency and, in general, to control its fiscal policy.

The Ukrainian parliament then decided that the deputies selected to represent the Ukraine in the Union Supreme Soviet would participate only in the Council of the Republic and only as observers. It came as no surprise, therefore, when the Ukraine joined Georgia and Moldova in boycotting sessions of the State Council called to talk about a new union treaty.

Thus, only seven republics agreed, on November 14, to establish a new "Union of Sovereign States." The additional two republics not signing were Uzbekistan and Armenia. Two weeks later, when the State Council met again, supposedly to initial the draft agreement, seven republics were again present but, this time, Uzbekistan was represented while Azerbaijan was missing. And instead of initialing the treaty, they decided to submit it to their republic parliaments for approval, a process that put the proposed treaty into severe jeopardy.

By this time, Leonid Kravchuk had dropped his earlier general support for some continuation of the union. Having said on November 12 that the Ukraine would "never sign" a treaty which would contain "even the slightest hint of certain governing central bodies," because "the center has fully exhausted itself," he added two weeks later that he would "take no part in the . . . talks on signing a new Union Treaty" and "all allegations that I meant to join the treaty later are nothing but fiction."

All of that might have become more or less academic, had the December 1 referendum on Ukrainian independence gone differently. In fact, nearly 90% of all Ukrainians voted *yes* for independence. At the same time, Kravchuk proved himself to be in line with Ukrainian thinking and a popular politician by winning 61.5% of the vote in the concurrent race for the newly created office of Ukrainian president.

"The independence of the Ukraine is a new political reality," commented Boris Yeltsin upon receiving the results of the Ukrainian vote. And what Yeltsin meant when he used the phrase "new political reality" was that Gorbachev's draft for a political union was now dead. The Ukraine would not join and, as Yeltsin had already said, he could not conceive of a political union that did not include the Ukraine. As far as that goes, Gorbachev had said much the same thing, although he apparently still hoped that the Ukraine might still be persuaded to reverse its stand. Yeltsin had no such hopes.

Yet Kravchuk had said on a number of occasions that he favored some kind of coordinating mechanism to handle the many problems of the now-separating republics. The question was what sort of political structure the Ukraine was willing to accept to achieve that coordination. Yeltsin decided to find out. He contacted Kravchuk and Stanislav Shushkevich, president of Belarus, and suggested that the three presidents meet the following weekend to discuss the future of the union. Shushkevich agreed to host the meeting and offered the use of a hunting lodge located not far from the Belarusian city of Brest. "We came to the conclusion," Shushkevich commented after the meeting, "that we had to sort out the concept of the kind of union we are capable of building."

So, the three leaders talked for two days and, in the end, they produced the agreement, which they signed late in the day on December 8, 1991, in the Belarusian capital of Minsk, calling into being the "Commonwealth of Independent States."

Commonwealth of Independent States

The suddenness of the December 8 agreement probably shocked a lot of people, but two aspects of the agreement caused some disquiet in the beginning. The first was that the three signatories were the heads of the three Slavic republics of the old union, suggesting to some that they were creating a "Slavic Commonwealth," even though the agreement specified that membership was open to "all member states of the former USSR," plus "other states that share the goals and principles of the present agreement." The second cause for concern was that the agreement also specified that "the USSR has ceased to exist as a subject of international law and as a geopolitical reality."

The first issue was defused rather quickly when the leaders of the five Central Asian Republics met in Ashkabad, Turkmenistan, and there signed an agreement to become co-founders of the Commonwealth of Independent States. This led to a conference in Alma-Ata, Kazakhstan, on December 21, 1991, which was attended by the presidents of 11 of the republics, with President Gamsakhurdia of Georgia the sole hold out. Even Georgia sent an observer, however. The three Baltic Republics were not represented, having made it clear earlier that they would not join any new political union.

At Alma-Ata, the eleven presidents signed a protocol making all eleven republics co-founders of the Commonwealth of Independent States. An additional protocol and two accords were also signed dealing with subsidiary matters. They also signed a resolution supporting Russia's claim to the USSR's United Nations membership, including its permanent membership in the Security Council. They further agreed to meet again in Minsk on December 30.

The December 30 meeting was actually the first "session" of the executive bodies of the Commonwealth of Independent States and included separate meetings of the heads of state and heads of government. A total of 15 documents were negotiated and signed at these meetings, fleshing out the structures of the CIS and establishing certain forms of cooperation. Since the CIS was seen as a coordinating body, there was to be no "center" as such—no president or prime minister, no ministries and no legislature. Instead, using to some extent the structure of the European Community (EC), the leaders drew up documents creating a Council of the Heads of States and a Council of Heads of Government.

Another agreement created a "working group" as a sort of secretariat to "prepare organically and technically the holding" of the meetings of the two councils. Unlike the EC, however, they did not create the presidential commission and cadre of bureaucrats that plays such an important role in Brussels. In fact, possibly to underline that point, the CIS Heads of State agreed that the job of drawing up proposals on how this working group should be structured would be handled by a conference of CIS foreign ministers meeting in Minsk in early January.

Perhaps the most important topic discussed at the Minsk meeting was the future status of the armed forces. Immediately prior to the meeting, the defense ministers and chairmen of the committees for defense questions of the 11 member states had met in Moscow with Air Marshal Yevgeny Shaposhnikov, named Soviet defense minister following the August attempted coup and designated temporary commander of the union forces at the Alma-Ata meeting.

An earlier proposal to maintain a unified armed force became moot when it became clear that the Ukraine, Azerbaijan, and Moldova wanted to have their own armies. Thus, the agreement that actually came before the CIS heads of state was based on the concept of joint CIS armed forces. The signed agreement stipulated that each republic had the right to establish its own army; but it also provided for continuation of a unified army under CIS command which republics could participate in if they wished. National armies were to be limited to conventional forces, however; all 11 republic heads of state agreed that nuclear forces would remain under unified command. Nuclear weapons were at that time based in four different republics—the Russian Federation, Ukraine, Belarus, and Kazakhstan. All except for the Russian Federation had stated that they intended to go "non-nuclear"—that is, eventually to get rid of all nuclear weapons on their soil. In the meanwhile, it was agreed that the president of the Russian Federation would have primary authority over nuclear weapons with the other three republican presidents having a veto power on their use.

The Ukrainian government immediately set about creating its own armed forces, and also moved to extend its control over the Black Sea fleet as well. Azerbaijan also moved to take control of the Caspian Sea fleet.

Marshal Shaposhnikov, who also participated in the military discussions at the Minsk meeting, was named commander-in-chief of the CIS armed forces. A council of republic defense ministers was also created and charged with elaborating a common defense policy.

Eurasia

The presidents of Ukraine, Belarus, and Russia: (L to R) Leonid Kravchuk, Stanislav Shushkevich, and Boris Yeltsin in Minsk, Belarus, December 8, 1991

The CIS Heads of States also touched on the subject of foreign policy. In addition to a general commitment to coordinate policy, they signed an agreement which provided for the division of the former USSR's property held abroad, including embassy and consulate buildings.

Other agreements signed in Minsk included one that called for joint activities in the exploration and use of space, plus several that dealt with a number of regional issues which the various heads of state agreed to treat as matters requiring CIS cooperation. These included the problems of the Aral Sea, the consequences of the Spital earthquake [centering in Armenia], preservation of fish stocks in the Caspian Sea, and elimination of the consequences of the Chernobyl nuclear power station disaster.

Though he had very little faith in the viability of the Commonwealth of Independent States, President Gorbachev recognized it as a fait accompli. He therefore agreed to a wind up of the old union by December 31 and the transfer of the Kremlin and the state bank to Russian control. Yeltsin, meanwhile, issued a series of decrees taking control of all union ministries other than defense and atomic energy. Gorbachev himself resigned as president of the USSR on December 25. Separately the USSR Supreme Soviet held its own last session on December 26. The handful of deputies present, far less than a quorum since most of the republics had already withdrawn their deputies, recognized the Commonwealth of Independent States before voting itself out of existence.

Thus, the Union of Soviet Socialist Republics officially disappeared and the Commonwealth of Independent States came into being. The CIS did not, if fact, replace the USSR, since the individual independent republics see themselves as the collective heirs to the USSR. The CIS was not established as a sovereign entity, but rather as a coordinating body for the independent republics which make up its membership. For that reason, its significance, and even its viability, came under question at the time. In addition to Gorbachev, among those who publicly questioned whether the CIS had any chance for longtime survival were Eduard Shevardnadze, a former Soviet foreign minister and former president of Georgia, James Baker, and Henry Kissinger.

Their criticisms were to the point. The CIS had then, and still has, a weak structure. It is also true that the CIS has not been able to contribute much toward the solving the mammoth problems faced by the newly independent republics.

On the other hand, the CIS came into existence precisely because the apparatchiks of the old center acted as a major force holding back and frustrating necessary reforms. Creation of the CIS got rid of most of that particular countervailing force. There are still many people who question the long-term viability of the CIS but it must be pointed out that the CIS does provide a structure that has facilitated the negotiation of a number of multilateral agreements among individual members of the CIS in recent years.

Perhaps the greatest weakness of the CIS has been the political position of the

Republic of Ukraine which opted out of most of the multilateral agreements negotiated for the first decade or so after independence because it feared that Moscow could use the organization as an instrument for continued domination. That changed when Ukrainian President Leonid Kuchma was elected head of the CIS Heads of State Council at its Kyiv summit in January 2003. After that time, President Kuchma committed himself to revitalizing the CIS.

President Viktor Yushchenko, who replaced Kuchma at the beginning of 2005, had a fairly favorable attitude toward the CIS when he first came to power but events after that time changed his attitude. The first of those was Gazprom's decision to begin charging world prices for natural gas furnished to Ukraine, Georgia, and Moldova—but not Belarus. It had not escaped anyone's notice that the three states being charged much higher prices were precisely those states who had recently taken the most independent stances toward Russia. One can, of course, make the argument that Gazprom's decision to raise prices was economically justified, even if it is majority-owned and controlled by the Russian state. However, Russia's subsequent decision to ban the importation of wines from Georgia and Moldova appeared to be an even cruder attempt to put political pressure on these three governments. It is therefore no surprise that sentiment has increased in all three countries to withdraw from the CIS. If Russia took these actions for other reasons and never intended them as political acts, then it blundered badly. Moreover, the Russian decision to go to war with Georgia in 2008 over the two Georgian autonomous republics of South Ossetia and Abkhazia—and subsequently to effectively annex them while ostensively recognizing their "independence"—probably dealt a death-knell to the CIS.

Russia's new "answer" was the Eurasian Customs Union (ECU), formed with Kazakhstan and Belarus in July 2010 and formally launched at a Moscow summit in December 2010.

Possibly because the new customs union did not win as much support as Russia wished, Prime Minister Putin persuaded several of the CIS members to sign onto creation of a free-trade zone in October 2011. This separate agreement was initialed at the meeting of CIS prime ministers that took place in St. Petersburg. In addition to the three members of the Eurasian Customs Union, the republics that signed on to the new free-trade agreement included Armenia, Kyrgyzstan, Moldova, Tajikistan, and Ukraine. Representatives of Azerbaijan, Uzbekistan, and Turkmenistan were present at the meeting but they did not sign on to the free-trade agreement, suggesting that more time was needed to consider the implications of joining.

According to President Putin's grand plan, a third organization, the Eurasian Economic Union came into existence on January 1, 2015, bringing these various parts together in a organization modeled on the European Union. The essential purpose of the Eurasian Economic Union is to unite the various countries in the area of the former Soviet Union into an economic bloc under Russian leadership.

Membership in the Eurasian Economic Union includes Russia, Belarus, Kazakhstan, Armenia, and Kyrgyzstan. The former Kyrgyzstan President, Almazbek Atambayev, supported Kyrgyzstan's membership in the customs union and the Eurasian Economic Union, because of two benefits from membership—closer political relations with Russia plus the fact that membership would allow Kyrgyz citizens—many of whom work illegally in Russia each summer—the legal right to work in Russia.

Armenia had been negotiating an Associate Membership agreement with the European Union and by all accounts the agreement had already been initialed. Thus, it came as a surprise when President Serzh Sargsyan went to Moscow in September 2013 to meet with President Putin, announcing afterward that Armenia would cease negotiations with the European Union over Associate Membership and, instead, would join the Eurasian Economic Union. The deciding factor appears to have been President

Sargsyan's fear of renewed war with Azerbaijan and Armenia's dependence on its military alliance with Russia.

Like Armenia, Ukraine and Moldova were in discussions with the European Union about Associate Membership agreements that had developed out of the European Union's Eastern Partners program. President Putin was particularly determined to have both countries in the Eurasian Economic Union, however; to achieve this purpose, Russia began putting economic pressure on Ukraine and Moldova to drop the discussions with the European Union. Both countries were threatened with a cut-off of natural gas supplies if they continued their negotiations with the European Union. In Ukraine's case, Russia also embargoed Ukrainian chocolate and meat. In Moldova's case, it was wine and processed meat products that were embargoed. The Moldovan political leadership stood firm, however, and signed an Associate Membership agreement with the European Union in November 2013.

Ukraine's political situation was different. President Yanukovych had supported negotiations with the European Union, but he also favored good relations with Russia. Moreover, his political party, the Party of Regions, was pro-Russian in its orientation. Even so, it appeared that most Ukrainians were surprised when President Yanukovych flew off to Moscow in November 2013 to meet with President Putin; they were even more surprised when, after the meeting, he announced that Ukraine would pull out of the negotiations with the European Union. He added that Russia had agreed to provide Ukraine with a $15 billion loan to help the country with its economic difficulties. He did not commit Ukraine to joining the Eurasian Economic Union, but it was understood that his actions would produce that outcome.

President Yanukovych's actions set off demonstrations in Kyiv that lasted for three months and ended only when President Yanukovych fled the country. But that did not end the turmoil in Ukraine. First of all, President Putin refused to recognize the new political leadership that replaced Yanukovych; next, he sent elite Russian troops to occupy Crimea; finally, he followed these actions up by announcing the annexation of the autonomous republic to Russia. He also moved Russian troops up to the eastern border of Ukraine and began pointing out that large parts of Ukraine had once been known as "New Russia" and had been part of the Russian Empire under the tsars. Most of the world governments have condemned Russia's actions in Crimea and its subsequent support of pro-Russian elements in Eastern Ukraine. It is

Air Marshal Yevgeny Shaposhnikov arrives in Alma Ata, Kazakhstan, December 20, 1991
Courtesy of Reuters/Bettmann

still not clear whether Ukraine can survive as an independent country. But Putin's actions in Ukraine have almost certainly destroyed the last remaining usefulness of the Commonwealth of Independent States.

Economy Under the CIS

The economy of the old USSR was designed and built as a single economy, with all important decisions coming out of Moscow. In addition, the first principle of the planners was economies of scale which translated into "bigger is better." Since all enterprises were owned and run by the Soviet state, they deliberately set out to create monopoly situations in every part of the economy, since these were considered to be more efficient. Accordingly, all over the Soviet Union, single, large factories were built, designed to serve the needs of a large part of the country or even, sometimes, the entire Soviet economy.

Such factories, being part of the "union" economy, took their orders from their supervising ministry in Moscow; the republic government exercised no control whatsoever. This made for a highly integrated economic system, though it also made it highly vulnerable, since a single, badly run factory could disrupt a complete sector by failing to deliver acceptable products in good time. Two further factors were possible time delays and added transportation costs.

All of these factors were magnified tremendously in 1991 in the situation of a

Eurasia

collapsing Soviet Union. As the individual republics moved to establish their political independence, they also moved to take control of their own economies. But when they tried to do so, they found that, in many cases, a significant part of their industry was totally dependent on deliveries of raw materials and parts from other republics and could not operate without these continued deliveries. Moreover, the same was true with regard to factory output. Worst of all, in many cases, too, the customers were factories located in other republics.

Just how complicated this could get was explained in November 1991 by V. Razumov, deputy minister of the former USSR ministry of the chemical and petroleum refining industry, just after the ministry had been abolished on November 15. Razumov used the example of the plastic that goes into making refrigerators. "One of the many things that could make our life a little easier today," commented Razumov,

is refrigerators. But you can't make them in, say, Belarus, if you have no polystyrene, which is made in Kazakhstan. Kazakhstan cannot produce polystyrene unless ethyl benzene is supplied from Tataria. They cannot make ethyl benzene in Tataria if they have no benzene. And benzene is made from petroleum, which is extracted mainly in [the] Tyumen [region]. That is roughly the system that is currently just [barely] managing to supply plastic for refrigerators. It could easily be destroyed. The people of Tyumen will sell independently a little

more of their petroleum, the refinery workers a little more of the benzene produced from their supply of petroleum, and so on, with the quantities being reduced at each stage of the production of plastic. And it could easily turn out that the end result is that we get no refrigerators.

Razumov was dealing with a single example. Just how serious was this problem for the overall CIS economy? A Moscow Interfax "Soviet Business Report," issued on October 31, 1991, looked at the overall problem based on 1989 data, the latest obtainable. What the report established was that 20.3% of all domestic trade was inter-republic in 1989. What the report also pointed out, however, is that the smaller republics were most closely bound into the old command economic system, while larger republics like Russia and Ukraine were far less dependent on inter-republic trade.

Soviet Republics' Individual Share in Inter-Republic Trade (from 1989 data)

	Imports	Exports	Average
Russia	12.2%	13.0%	12.6%
Ukraine	26.2%	26.6%	26.4%
Kazakhstan	36.6%	20.6%	28.6%
Azerbaijan	23.6%	41.6%	32.6%
Uzbekistan	40.5%	28.8%	34.5%
Georgia	34.4%	40.3%	37.4%
Kyrgyzstan	42.8%	32.5%	37.7%
Turkmenistan	40.2%	35.5%	37.9%
Armenia	39.7%	37.2%	38.5%
Tajikistan	48.9%	32.8%	40.9%
Belarus	37.5%	46.3%	41.9%
Moldova	43.3%	43.3%	43.3%

There was clearly some deterioration in inter-republic trade in 1991, but the number of alternate producers in the USSR/ CIS was so limited that there was almost no likelihood that these figures had changed significantly by that time. What they make clear is that, except for the Russian Federation, there was a high level of mutual economic dependence among the republics which would lead to an almost total disruption if they were unable to work out some form of continued economic cooperation. A number of republics did negotiate bilateral trade agreements, but these did not work out very well, since suppliers and customers were seldom from a single republic or even from the *same* republic. An even more important problem was the matter of prices.

In the old Soviet Union, prices were largely symbolic, set by the state for reasons such as to subsidize development of individual industries or to discourage consumption, and having little or nothing to do with either the cost of manufacturing or the international market price of the articles. All of this was possible because it was then a closed system. In general, the prices of food, fuel, and raw materials were kept low, while the prices of most consumer goods were above world prices. The movement to world prices after 1992 tended to disrupt inter-republic trade; some of the poorer republics were unable to pay the greatly increased prices for food and fuel, while other republics did not want to pay world prices for merchandise that did not meet world standards.

An even more important factor was the failure of the plan that called for all of the republics to continue using the ruble as their common currency. The former union-wide banking system having collapsed, the individual republics were unable to come to an agreement at the CIS level on the transfer of funds between the republics. The result was a rapidly growing mountain of debt, much of it owed to Russia. In response, the Russian government first tried restricting credit to the other republics and, when this didn't solve the problem, effectively forced them off the ruble standard. The various republics later developed their own currencies, but the CIS was very slow in developing adequate mechanisms for the transferal of funds between republics. As a result, inter-republic trade dropped by as much as 70% in the period 1992–1994.

This was a transitional problem, of course, related to the fact that most economic activity in the CIS was still state-run. The real, long-term solutions were to be found in privatization and movement to a market economy. The various republican leaders were theoretically committed to move in this direction but, with the exception of Russia and, after 1993, Ukraine, the movement was extremely slow. Of the 12 members of the CIS, only Russia, Ukraine, and Kazakhstan had made a full transition to market economies by the latter part of the decade.

After significant progress in the first years, war and political instability slowed the process in Georgia and Armenia, though both have made further progress since about 2005. Belarus abandoned the process in 1994 when Alexander Lukashenko was elected president and this has largely remained Lukashenko's position ever since.

Moldova put the process on hold in 2000 after the Communist Party of Moldova returned to power. The party was, in theory, committed to eventually moving toward a

Russian sailor in St. Petersburg

market economy, but there was very little support for further privatization among the general population. The new Moldovan government, elected in August 2009, is committed to development of a full market economy, but there is still significant popular support for the old state-run system.

Kyrgyzstan made significant progress in the 1990s, and even became the first ex-Soviet republic to become a member of the World Trade Organization; however, progress has been slow since a near collapse of the economy in 1998. The least amount of progress is to be found in the three remaining states of Tajikistan, Turkmenistan, and Uzbekistan. Tajikistan was sidelined by a civil war for several years and it is one of the poorest of the Central Asian states. The government is committed to transforming the economy, but it has very little to work with. Turkmenistan and Uzbekistan both have authoritarian leaders who have tended to view significant societal change as a threat to their power. In the spring of 2002, Uzbekistan negotiated an agreement with the IMF which committed it to begin the process, however, and it has made some minimal progress since that time; Turkmenistan has also made some progress since President Gurbanguly Berdymukhammedov assumed power in 2007.

Developments Since 1992

The CIS heads of state and heads of government have continued to meet on a regular basis after 1992 and a significant number of agreements have been negotiated. In most cases, only a minority of the republics either signed on to the agreements or subsequently implemented them, however. In 1993–1994, the Russian government began pushing for greater military cooperation at the CIS level, particularly with regard to guarding the old borders of the USSR, and it was successful in encouraging cooperation in this limited area. By the beginning of 1995, all of the CIS members except Azerbaijan had negotiated agreements authorizing the use of Russian troops along the frontier. And even in Azerbaijan, where Soviet troops were withdrawn after the collapse of the Soviet Union, Russian troops later returned to police the truce line between Nagorno-Karabakh and Azerbaijan proper.

Russian forces are, in fact, still quite active in the ex-Soviet republics. Russian troops still guard parts of the Tajik international boundaries and they advise Turkmenistan's army and frontier forces. Armenia, which has good relations with Russia, has a military agreement whereby Russian troops guard the Armenian border with Turkey. Although Belarus and Kazakhstan maintain separate armies, they work in close tandem with the military forces of Russia. As one Russian colonel

commented, "the Belarusian army is virtually an adjunct of the Russian army." In the case of Kazakhstan, almost all officers are ethnic Russians and Russian is the language of command. It is probably wiser to think in terms of "influence" rather than "control," however. Such officers would undoubtedly support and even advise close cooperation with Russia, but there is no reason to believe they would disobey contrary orders deriving from the political leadership of their republics.

Ukraine held its participation in the CIS to a minimum during its first decade of independence and rejected any suggestion of "jointly" monitoring of CIS borders or CIS peacekeeping forces. Even so, the Ukrainian and Russian governments reached an agreement in early 1995 to divide the Black Sea fleet between the two countries, and the Ukrainian Government also agreed to share the Sevastopol naval base with Russia. Relations remained cool under President Yushchenko and the Orange Coalition but this changed in February with the election of President Yanukovych; since that time, The Ukrainian government has signed an agreement extending the Russian lease on the naval base at Sebastopol until 2042.

Russian–Georgian relations have been something of a special case. President Zviad Gamsakhurdia refused to join the CIS when it was originally established; he was overthrown in January 1992. The next three years were years of political instability; a Military Council ruled for several months. Eduard Shevardnadze, invited back to Georgia, was first made a member of the Military Council; he was named chairman of the State Council in March 1992, where he shared power with the prime minister. Finally, a new constitution, approved in the summer of 1995, reestablished the office of president; Shevardnadze won the subsequent presidential election in November 1995.

This was a period of great weakness for Georgia; with no real army, the government had no hope of regaining control over the revolting provinces of Abkhazia and South Ossetia. Shevardnadze therefore negotiated an agreement with the Russian government for a cease fire in Abkhazia; in return, the Russian government demanded that Georgia promise to join the CIS. Georgia later signed an agreement authorizing four Russian bases within its borders. The Georgian government hoped that cooperation with Russia would allow it regain control over Abkhazia and South Ossetia, though Russia actually continued to provide military support to the two secessionist provinces.

Mikheil Saakashvili forced the resignation of President Shevardnadze in November 2003 and won the subsequent

presidential election in January 2004. One year later, he negotiated an agreement with the Russian government which called for all Russian bases in the country to be closed by 2008. The Russian bases were closed on schedule but Georgian-Russian relations reached a new low by the beginning of 2008.

In March 2008, President Putin ordered Russian authorities to establish social, economic, and political ties with Abkhazia and South Ossetia, in effect rejecting Georgian claims that the two provinces were still part of Georgia. Russia formally recognized the "independence" of the two provinces in the summer of 2008 after a short war with Georgia. After that time, Georgia resigned its membership in the CIS and broke off diplomatic relations with Russia.

President Putin had long felt that what Russia needed was a zone in which Russia had preferential economic interests and privileges. By the beginning of his second term as president, he had come to the conclusion that the CIS structure did not provide such a framework. For several years, Putin tried to accomplish this through bilateral negotiations with other former Soviet republics. During his years as prime minister, he turned again to multilateral negotiations. The Customs Union comprising Russia, Kazakhstan, and Belarus came into existence on January 1, 2010. The Single Economic Space—again with the same three republics—came into existence on January 1, 2012.

But Russia had a rival in the European Union's Eastern Partnership program, with the original program including six republics—Belarus, Ukraine, Moldova, Georgia, Armenia, and Azerbaijan. Eventually this program offered these six republics the possibility of an Association Agreement with the European Union. Belarus soon pulled out and Azerbaijan put itself on the slow track, but Moldova, Ukraine, Armenia, and Georgia continued their negotiations until the summer of 2013. All came under strong pressure from Moscow to join the Eurasian Customs Union, but it appeared that all four were prepared to initial an agreement with the European Union instead.

But in September 2013, President Putin invited Armenian President Sargsyan to Moscow for talks. Following the discussions, President Sargsyan announced that Armenia would join the Eurasian Customs Union and there would be no further discussions with the European Union. Moldova came under similar pressure, with Russia issuing threats such as a cut-off of natural gas, unless Moldova dropped its talks with the European Union and joined the Eurasian Customs Union. Moldova resisted the Russian blandishments, however.

Eurasia

In November, Ukraine President Yanukovych received his invitation from Putin to come to Moscow. After the meeting, Yanukovych announced that Ukraine was dropping its application for an Association Agreement with the European Union. He did not say that Ukraine would be joining the Eurasian Customs Union, but he did announce that Ukraine would be receiving a $15 billion loan from Russia to deal with Ukraine's strained economic condition.

This set off the demonstrations in Kyiv that would last until February 2014 and, in the end, result in Yanukovych's fleeing the country. In turn, President Putin canceled the Russian loan and refused to recognize the new Ukrainian Government. He then sent his own military forces into Crimea and shortly thereafter announced the annexation of Crimea. As soon as Russia annexed Crimea, pro-Russian separatists in eastern Ukraine organized mass demonstrations and seized control of several cities. The separatists declared independent republics centered on two cities in the Donets River Basin (Donbass), Luhansk, and Donetsk. Russia has secretly supported the separatists with weaponry and military personnel. A new Ukrainian government under elected President Petro Poroshenko had attempted to reestablish control over the Donbass. Despite two attempted ceasefires in the area, the fighting continues. As of June 2015, about 6,400 have been killed in the conflict.

The new Ukrainian Government has indicated its intention to drop its membership in the Commonwealth of Independent States. Moldova is likely to follow suit. The CIS now appears to be dead.

Economic Cooperation

CIS Economic cooperation was a desirable goal and one that should have been easier to accomplish. When a CIS joint economic zone was mandated in 1994, however individual CIS members hesitated to implement it, so what cooperation has taken place over the years has been in the form of a series of bilateral and multilateral agreements. One of those was the Eurasian Economic Community (EEC), formed by Russia, Kazakhstan, and Belarus in January 1995. Kyrgyzstan and Tajikistan joined later. Separately, Russia and Kazakhstan signed an agreement calling for increased economic and military links.

Kazakhstan, Uzbekistan, and Kyrgyzstan also joined to form the Central Asia Customs Union, to which Tajikistan adhered in 1998. This was replaced by a new organization, the Central Asian Cooperation (CAC) in December 2001. CAC was meant to be a broader organization than the one it replaced, promoting political, economic, and military

cooperation among the four member states; the four presidents have met on several occasions since that time, but disagreements between individual members have prevented larger agreements.

In October 1999, all of the CIS members with the exception of Belarus discussed introduction of a CIS free trade zone at a CIS meeting at Yalta. They also signed preliminary documents that, among other things, reduced customs regulations. This proposal was a major topic of discussion at a CIS summit meeting that took place in Moscow in December 2001. President Putin told the other 11 presidents at that time that any kind of integration, political or military, must have a strong economic footing. He also promised that Russia would work on the regulations and legislation needed to establish a CIS free-trade zone.

The idea did not get very far as long as it was viewed as a concept being pushed by Russia. That changed somewhat after Ukrainian President Kuchma was elected head of the CIS Heads of State Council at its Kyiv summit in January 2003. In his acceptance speech, Kuchma argued that the best way to revitalize the Commonwealth of Independent States was to shift the emphasis from the political to the economic and he pledged that all of his efforts as president of the Heads of State Council would be focused on expediting the creation of a CIS free-trade zone.

This led to a meeting of the presidents of Ukraine, Belarus, Kazakhstan, and Russia in Moscow on February 22–23. Here, the four presidents designated their countries as "core" CIS members for the purpose of developing a CIS free-trade zone and committed their governments to cooperate in creating a single economic space within the CIS, which the other eight CIS members were invited to join. This initiative remained stillborn, however.

In July 2010, Russia, Kazakhstan and Belarus signed a new agreement calling for creation of a joint customs zone with a common external tariff; the agreement came into effect in December 2010 when the three presidents met in Moscow and signed a series of agreements creating a common economic space. When fully

implemented, citizens of the new customs union will be able to freely travel and work anywhere in the new customs union. This, plus the fact that there will be no internal tariffs, gives the idea a certain attraction for some of Russia's neighbors. Currently, the governments of Kyrgyzstan, Ukraine, and Moldova say that they are open to the idea of membership and are still weighing the advantages and disadvantages. Armenia has also shown an interest, though it does not share a border with any of the current member states. Russia's interest in the new customs union is primarily political; there appear to be few economic benefits in it for Russia.

Military Cooperation

One other form of regional cooperation is the organization known as GUAM, the name representing the four countries (Georgia, Ukraine, Azerbaijan, and Moldova) that were its founding members in 1996. Uzbekistan became the fifth member in 1999 and the organization then became known as GUUAM. Primarily a support group, and set up originally with the encouragement of the US government, GUUAM's main success was in coordinating member states' positions in arms-control negotiations over the issue of Russian troop levels. One other area where GUUAM played a role was in developing a coordinated position on east-west energy pipelines. Uzbekistan withdrew from the organization in 2012; it is hard to say today whether this organization any longer exists.

The terror attacks of September 11, 2001, and the subsequent United States–led War on Terrorism that began that fall also provided an organizational impetus to the member states of the CIS, as most of them soon became heavily involved through the granting of bases to the anti-terrorist coalition. But the Central Asian republics had already been dealing with the problem of terrorism prior to September 2001, and six of the states—Russia, Kazakhstan, Kyrgyzstan, Tajikistan, Armenia, and Belarus—had agreed in 1999 to create a CIS Collective Rapid Reaction Force under the auspices of the CIS Collective Security Treaty, signed in 1999. In September 2001, they signed a supplementary agreement calling for coordination of the work of their arms industries. In April 2002, the defense and foreign ministers of the six signatories met in Yerevan, Armenia, to discuss transforming the Collective Security Treaty into an international organization corresponding to the UN charter. On April 28, 2003, the six countries, meeting in Dushanbe, signed the final documents creating the Organization of the Treaty on Collective Security (ODKB). The ODKB was supposed to have been set up with its own budget, secretariat, military staff, and rapid-reaction

Aerial view of the Aral Sea

force. Its main military base was to be the Kant airfield in Kyrgyzstan. Addressing the Dushanbe meeting, President Putin said that, in addition to its main mission of combating terrorism, the ODKB would be used to deal with drug-trafficking, an increasing problem for the various Central Asian states. Some cooperation is continuing, but this has become just another organization dominated by Moscow.

In February 2002, at the CIS defense ministers meeting in St Petersburg, agreement was reached to restore an integrated CIS air-defense system. Colonel General Sergei Mikhailov, a Russian general, was placed in charge. Russia has been calling for greater coordination in the defense area and this may have been the result. As Russian Security Council Secretary Vladimir Rushailo said to the assembled security chiefs on April 11,

the success of our economic cooperation will also depend on how effective our cooperative action will be in the fight against international terrorism.

Terrorism was on the agenda again at the October 2002 meeting of the CIS heads of state in Chisinau. All CIS presidents attended the meeting except for President Saparmurat Niyazov of Turkmenistan. The 11 presidents approved the establishment of a joint anti-terrorism center in Central Asia.

The color revolutions of 2003–2004 brought some changes and, in general, a loosening of the CIS bond. President Putin apparently felt that the color revolutions threatened his own political leadership and he accordingly reduced official relations with Georgia and Ukraine to a minimum. Russia's invasion of Georgia, and its subsequent recognition of the "independence" of the two Georgian provinces of Abkhazia and South Ossetia, caused Georgia to break off diplomatic relations with Russia and to resign its membership in the CIS.

Russia's annexation of Crimea in February 2014 actually represents the culmination of a Russian policy that has, over the past several years, gradually changed from one of cooperation and partnership to one of domination. His apparent goal is now to recreate as much as possible of the old Soviet Union under Russian leadership. No one knows how much force he is willing to use to accomplish that goal.

Some Regional Problems of the CIS

Aral Sea. Kazakhstan, Kyrgyzstan, Turkmenistan, and Uzbekistan are members of the International Fund to Save the Aral Sea (IFAS), an organization which has been in existence since 1992. Following the CAC meeting in October 2002, the four presidents met to discuss the Aral Sea. Tajik radio, reporting on the meeting, said that the four countries had projects worth $300 million under way focusing on problems of water supply, irrigation, and land reclamation. As part of that, Kazakhstan indicated that it was currently implementing a $70 million project aimed as saving a section of the northern part of the Aral Sea.

In spite of more than a decade of discussions, the four republics do not have a plan to replenish the Aral Sea, nor have they been able to agree on how to manage their shared water resources in a coordinated and rational manner. The inability to agree on a program aimed at replenishing the Aral Sea is understandable, since any solution would have to include reductions in the amount of water each republic would be permitted to use.

In March 2008, the Uzbek government sponsored a conference on the Aral Sea, bringing together over 200 public figures, scientists, ecologists, and specialists from several countries and major international organizations. In his address to the conference, President Karimov stressed that the "environmental, social, economic, and demographic problems" linked to the Aral Sea concern not only issues of water security in the area, but "are of international and global importance in terms of their origins and the scale of consequences."

Bolat Nurgaliyev, secretary-general of the Shanghai Cooperation Organization, argued in his address that the problems of the Aral Sea region "can be resolved only by attracting serious financial aid from the international community."

Regional Water Problems. While the problems of the Aral Sea could certainly use some international assistance, the republics of Central Asia have other problems that they will have to solve themselves. For example, floods along the middle reaches of the Syr Dar'ya near the Uzbek-Kazakh border in February 2004 showed what can happen when countries carry out policies that ignore the need of their neighbors. Essentially the floods were man-made and resulted from a breakdown in the system of regional water management that had been established during Soviet times. At that time, a series of dams or reservoirs was constructed along the Syr Dar'ya and its tributaries for the joint purpose of producing hydroelectricity and storing water for irrigation.

With the disappearance of the Soviet Union, however, each republic took charge of dams or reservoirs on its territory and ran them to suit its own purposes. In the case of Kyrgyzstan, the primary purpose was to produce hydroelectricity, for which its greatest need was in the winter.

The Kazakh and Uzbek governments need water for irrigation during the spring and summer. In years past, in order to retain water in the upstream reservoirs when not needed for irrigation, they had agreed to provide electricity supplies to Kyrgyzstan during the winter and so reduce its need for hydroelectric power; in 2003–2004, however, those supplies were cut because the Kazakh and Uzbek governments had had a reduced need for water in the previous summer.

Faced with a shortage of energy, the government of Kyrgyzstan released water from its Toktogul Reservoir to generate hydroelectricity, and this led to flooding along the Syr Dar'ya downstream after the Chardara/Shardara Reservoir, jointly managed by the Uzbek and Kazakh government, reached its capacity.

A temporary solution was reached when Kazakhstan agreed to provide Kyrgyzstan with coal and fuel oil so it could make greater use of its thermal plants. It is clear, however, that a permanent solution will require the creation of some kind of transnational water consortium or an expansion of the responsibilities of the current IFAS. Such a consortium, which would have to include Tajikistan since it controls one of the important upstream reservoirs, might then provide the impetus for cooperation on the larger problem of the continuing destruction of the Aral Sea.

Some movement in this direction occurred in May 2008 when Kyrgyzstan hosted a meeting in Bishkek of officials from Kazakhstan, Tajikistan, and Uzbekistan to discuss plans to improve regional cooperation in the management and use of water and energy resources. The focus of the meeting was on the drastic decrease in the water level at the Kyrgyz Toktogul reservoir. As an interim measure, the officials, all deputy ministers of energy, adopted specific measures governing the use of the water and energy resources at the Toktogul reservoir. They are supposed to continue meeting.

Caucasian Regionalism. The continuing political instability of the area of the Caucasus can be explained largely by two factors, geography plus the astonishing ethnic diversity found throughout the area. Because of the extensive fighting that has taken place there over the past decade, Chechnya has come to symbolize this situation for the area of the north Caucasus, though in fact the neighboring Russian republics of Ingushia, North Ossetia, and Dagestan suffer from many of the same problems. To give just one example, a suicide bomber set off 66 to 132 pounds of explosives as he pulled next to the

Eurasia

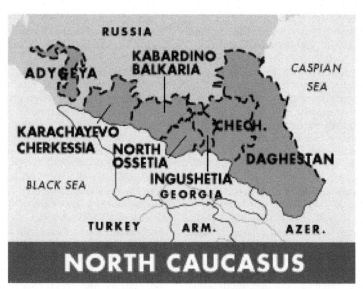

Map of the North Caucasus republics

limousine of Ingush President Murat Zyazikov on April 6, 2004. The attack failed because it was an armored limousine. That same day, there were two bomb explosions in Dagestan, one outside a police station in Khasavyurt and the other a car bomb that exploded on a residential street in Makhachkala. The attempted assassination of President Zyazikov may have been related to events in Chechnya, since Zyazikov is a supporter of President Putin while the political opposition in Ingushia has close ties with former Chechen President Maskhadov. Or both may have been carried out by Chechnyan radical Islamists committed to uniting the entire area of the north Caucasus under an Islamic Emirate.

An additional factor is that all of the peoples of the northern slopes have close ties of culture and blood with peoples living on the southern slopes of the Caucasus Mountains in Georgia. The best example of this phenomenon is South Ossetia, which fervently wants to unite with North Ossetia. Although most of these populations are Muslim, ethnic ties appear to be the decisive factor in their political orientations. Except for the Chechens, in fact, most of the populations of the north Caucasus appear to be satisfied to remain a part of the Russian Federation. Moreover, two of the Georgian separatist areas, South Ossetia and Abkhazia, have made numerous requests to be allowed to join the Russian Federation. To be sure, the separatist movements on both the northern and southern slopes of the Caucasus arose at the time of the collapse of the Soviet Union, though the reason for the movements along the southern slopes appears to be related to the rise of an extreme Georgian nationalism at this same time which threatened the traditional autonomy

of these ethnic non-Georgian areas. It also helped that the Russian military tended to encourage and support such movements, though an even more important factor was the political weakness of the Georgian government in the 1990s and the almost total failure of the economy.

As president, Mikheil Saakashvili has been successful in creating a strong central government and improving the economy but, his very success in strengthening the Georgian government was probably behind Russia's decision to go to war against Georgia and to establish formal legal ties with the Abkhazia and South Ossetia that is just short of formal annexation.

Caspian Sea. The countries bordering on the Caspian have not been able to agree on how to divide the seabed of the Caspian. The main question under international law is whether the Caspian is a sea or a saltwater lake. If it is determined that the Caspian is a saltwater lake, then, according to international law, its various resources can only be exploited on the basis of an agreement signed by all bordering states. On the other hand, if the Caspian is a sea, its resources would be divided into national sectors that each country would have the right to exploit as it pleases. Russia and Iran had until recently contended that the Caspian is a saltwater lake. Azerbaijan and Kazakhstan, on the other hand, took the position that it is a sea. Turkmenistan, the last of the states bordering on the Caspian Sea, has been divided on the issue. It first sided with Kazakhstan and Azerbaijan, then switched its position in 1996 and until recently was supporting the Russian-Iranian position. In 1998, Russia and Iran indicated that they might be willing to agree that the Caspian is a sea

if an appropriate division of the seabed could be worked out. However, Iran's recent claim to 20% of the seabed has been rejected by Azerbaijan.

Despite these disagreements Azerbaijan has signed agreements with a number of international oil companies for the development of what it considers its national sector. In September 2002, Azerbaijan signed an agreement with Russia delimiting the two countries' respective sectors of the Caspian Sea bed. Azerbaijan has also instituted talks with the Iranian Government concerning the Caspian Sea bed. Iran continues to insist on an equal division of the seabed, however.

Turkmenistan, which recently renewed diplomatic ties with Azerbaijan, has also opened discussions with Azerbaijan aimed at settling differences between the two countries about dividing the seabed. Since there are believed to be large oil and natural gas reserves in the area under dispute which cannot be exploited without an agreement, these particular discussions appear to have a greater chance of success than the Iranian talks.

Islam. Islam is the dominant religion of 6 of the 12 members of the CIS and together these 6 republics have a Muslim population of approximately 52 million. In addition, the Russian Federation is made up of several areas with large Muslim populations plus a few autonomous republics where the majority of the population is Muslim. In all, there are perhaps 20 million Muslims who are citizens of the Russian Federation.

The Soviet Union was extremely intolerant of overt religiosity and this applied particularly to the adherents of Islam. Although the government became much more tolerant of religion under Gorbachev, Islam was only beginning to recover somewhat when the Soviet Union collapsed.

All of the successor states were, and are, secular in their orientation. In a departure for Soviet Union, political elites in the newly independent states viewed Islam as part of their national heritage, and made sure that Islam was embraced in the nation-building efforts. However, they did not want Islam to supersede nationalism or be used to challenge their authority. The elites allowed the Saudis to provide money for the construction of new mosques and religious schools. Saudis have funded these projects with the goal to promoting a Wahhabi interpretation of Islam at the expense of local religious creeds. As an ultra-conservative religious reform movement which originated in Saudi Arabia, Wahabism calls for a return to "pure" Islam and the practices of the early generations of Islamic scholars. Proponents of Wahabism are notable for the unduly harsh enforcement of their beliefs, and their intolerance toward Muslims who practice their local traditions, such venerating Muslim saints and visiting their tombs or shrines. Since there were very few trained religious leaders in any of the new states of the CIS, the secular governments also permitted religious leaders to be sent in from abroad; many of these religious leaders were Saudis, though they were also recruited from other Muslim countries such as Jordan and Egypt.

Most of these teachers and religious leaders limited themselves to teaching the *Qur'an*, but some transmitted a political message that included a call for an Islamic government.

In Russia, these ultra-conservative religious movements were largely limited to the area of the North Caucasus, and particularly associated with Chechnya—though it should be emphasized that the manifestation of Wahabism in Chechnya is only a recent phenomenon and it was not responsible for the original Chechnyan War. Wahabism has also spread to neighboring Dagestan, which appears to have become the center of the Islamist uprising. Saudi inspired strain of Islam is still spreading in the area of the North Caucasus, but it may not be the dominant reason for rising discontent. Even in Chechnya, where a significant number of radical Arab fighters joined the rebel force, ordinary Chechens are more motivated by feelings of nationalism than Islam.

The situation is somewhat different in the Central Asian republics. After the breakup of the Soviet Union, Islam became a salient political force in the region. Religious-oriented social movements that arouse in the region advocated for a greater representation of Islam in politics. The three prominent Islamist organizations in the region included the Islamic Revival Party of Tajikistan (IRPT), the Islamic Movement of Uzbekistan (IMU), and the transnational Hizb-ut-Tahrir Islamic political party. In keeping with the Soviet tradition, however, incumbents did not allow Islamist organizations to participate in politics, causing these organization to remain in opposition. Founded in 1990, IRPT was the only Islamist organization in the entire post-Soviet space that was able to enter politics. Shortly after gaining independence, the authorities in Tajikistan banned IRPT. This move forced its members to join various opposition groups which fought against the government during the country's civil war. Following the peace accords in 1997, the government agreed to legalize IRPT. In 1999, IRPT was the second largest party in the parliament. However, under constant government repression the party was never able to meaningfully contest the ruling party in subsequent elections. In 2014, the government banned the party altogether. The IMU was founded in the 1990s by an Uzbek who took the name of Juma Namangani. He was killed in Afghanistan in 2001 but remnants of his organization continue to exist in Uzbekistan, Tajikistan, and Kyrgyzstan. A second, even more pervasive organization is the Hizb-ut-Tahrir, an organization that was founded in 1953 by Taqi al-Din al-Nabhani, a Palestinian who received an education in Islamic law in Egypt, and only recently introduced into Central Asia. In theory, an organization that eschews violence, its main platform is the creation of a new emirate that would bring all Central Asians together under a new Islamic regime. Outlawed in every Central Asian republic, its followers have been arrested in every country of Central Asia and even in Russia.

Although Islamist movements engaged in violence throughout central Asia, incumbent governments continue to overreact to their supposed threat. Central Asian regimes have always used the narrative of Islamic terrorism to justify their crackdown on political opposition. This tendency was especially pronounced in the wake of the September 11 terrorist attacks against the US. In exchange for their cooperation in the fight against terrorism in Afghanistan, the US government tended to ignore central Asian regimes' flagrant violation of human rights, and supported their persecution of Islamic groups.

Hizb-ut-Tahrir may have been a potential threat to the secular governments throughout the area, but only a minor one at best. As for terror attacks, until recently they had been traced to members of the IMU. It was believed that the IMU had largely ceased to exist after Namangani's death, but the terrorist attacks that took place in Uzbekistan between March 28 and April 2, 2004, raised the issue of whether the organization had been reconstituted. Uzbekistani officials were inclined to believe that the attacks, which involved at least two different female suicide bombers and resulted in the death of at least 44 persons, had to have been the work of the IMU. To date, these Islamic groups do not appear to have a large following in the region. Moreover, the region's populace, like their leaders, are hesitant to give Islam a greater role in politics.

WESTERN REPUBLICS

Showing principal cities (with Russian spellings)

The Republic of Belarus

Area: 80,150 sq. mi. (207,600 sq. km., about the size of Minnesota).

Population: 9,501,451 (2024 estimate).

Capital City: Minsk.

Climate: Temperate.

Neighboring States: Russia (east), Latvia, Lithuania (northeast), Poland (west), Ukraine (south).

Languages: Belarusian, Russian.

Ethnic Composition: Belarusian (83.7%), Russian (8.3%), Polish (3.1%), Ukrainian (1.7%), Other and Unspecified (3.3%) (2009 estimate).

Principal Religions: Russian Orthodox (48.3%), Catholic (7.1%), Other (3.5%), Non-believers (41.1%) (2011 estimate).

Chief Commercial Products: Grain, potatoes, cattle, agricultural machinery, motor vehicles, machine tools, oil, electricity, steel, coal, and metal production.

Currency: Belarusian ruble.

Per Capita Annual Income (Purchasing Power Parity): $27,718 (2023 estimate).

Recent Political Status: Part of the Russian Empire until 1917, became the Byelorussian SSR in 1919, part of the USSR (1922–1991).

Chief of State: Alexander Lukashenko, President (first elected July 10, 1994).

Head of Government: Roman Golovchenko, Prime Minister (Appointed June 4, 2020).

National Flag: A broad red horizontal band fills in the upper two-thirds of the field, with a second, green stripe filling in the bottom third; a white vertical stripe on the hoist side bears Belarusian national ornamentation in red.

National Day: July 3 (1944), the date Minsk was liberated from German troops.

The Land

The Republic of Belarus is the independent successor state to the Byelorussian Soviet Socialist Republic, established on January 1, 1919. It is located in the northwestern portion of the Russian Plain, just southwest of the Valdai Hills. The northern part of the republic is made up mostly of low, rolling hills. Dzyarzhynskaya Mountain, the loftiest point in the republic, is only 1,135 feet high. Most of the southern part of the republic is covered by a lowland area known as the Prypyats (Pripet) Swamp. Much of this area is a mixture of swamp and forest with a very low population density.

Four major rivers flow through Belarus. In the north, the Western Dvina River, which begins in the Valdai Hills, enters from the east and then flows in a mainly northwestern direction until it crosses into Latvia, there becoming the Daugava. The Dnieper River also enters Belarus from the east, then flows in a southern direction a short distance west of the eastern border. It actually forms the eastern border for a short stretch before entering Ukraine. The third of the rivers is the Prypyats, which enters from the south from Ukraine, then flows eastward just north of the southern border. It crosses into Ukraine shortly before emptying into the Dnieper.

The last of the rivers is the Nyoman [Nemunas], which begins in northwestern Belarus, a short distance west of the capital city of Minsk, and flows west and then north before crossing the border into Lithuania. A tributary of the Nyoman, the Neris (Villia), starts in northwestern Belarus just north of Minsk. It flows in a meandering northwestern direction before crossing the border into Lithuania. Originally covered in forests and fens, today Belarus is a mixture of forests and fields. Reclamation projects in the south have reclaimed about 6.25 million acres of swampland, thereby increasing the agricultural potential of this area, particularly for pasturage, although hemp is another major crop. The south also has over six thousand peat deposits.

The People

According to recent estimates, the country's population is 9.5 million. The current population growth rate is negative. Belarusians constitute more than 83% of this total. Russians, the largest minority group, are around 8.3% of the population. Other sizeable minorities include Poles, Ukrainians, Jews, and Lithuanians.

Belarusian belongs to the eastern Slavic family of languages. It is fairly modern in origin and arose primarily for historical reasons. Its ancestor is Slavonic, which had been spoken by all eastern Slavs as late as the 13th century. This area became part of the Grand Principality of Lithuania in the 14th century. After the Lithuanian Union with Poland in 1569, the upper classes became heavily Polonized and this, plus the several centuries of separation, eventually produced a language that was different from either Russian or Ukrainian. As a result of the industrialization of the 20th century, about three-quarters of the population now lives in urban areas.

History

The area of the Prypyats (Pripet) Swamp, in southern Belarus, is believed to be the original home of the eastern Slavic peoples. Spreading out from that point, they eventually occupied most of the Russian Plain. The first organized Slavic state, Kyivan Rus, came into existence as a trading state which controlled the "road from the Varangians (Vikings) to the Greeks." That "road" was the water system that permitted travel from the Baltic Sea in the north to the Black Sea and Constantinople in the south. The most important of those rivers was the Dnieper, which flows south through the eastern part of Belarus.

Kyivan Rus was destroyed by an invasion of the Mongols in 1238–41. The collapse of that first Slavic state left the northwest in a state of anarchy which ended in the first half of the 14th century when Gedaminas founded the Grand Principality of Lithuania. It had its capital at Vilnius but the state extended southward as far as the

Belarus

Black Sea, and included all of present-day Belarus. The majority of the people living in this state were Slavs and the language used at the court was old Slavonic, the language of Kyivan Rus.

This situation continued until 1569 when Lithuania became part of the Polish Kingdom as a result of the Union of Lublin. From that time onward, the upper classes became increasingly Polonized. When an independent Patriarchate was established at Moscow a few years later, the Polish King separated the Orthodox Church in Lithuania from Moscow and forced it to recognize the Pope as the head of the church, thereby creating the Uniate Rite of the Church. That situation continued for over 30 years before the Orthodox Church was allowed to begin operating again. After about 1625, therefore, you had a situation where the upper classes were Polonized and increasingly Roman Catholic and the peasants were Orthodox and enserfed.

The southern portion of the Orthodox lands broke away in 1654 and joined Russia; this became the Ukraine. But the northern Orthodox lands remained part of the Polish Kingdom until the three partitions of Poland in 1772, 1793, and 1795. These partitions gave the area of present day Belarus to Russia. From 1795 to 1918, therefore, these lands were part of the Russian Empire. Russia did not recognize Belarusian as a separate language, however, so Russian became the language of government while Belarusian was merely the local dialect of the peasantry.

The Russian Revolution brought about a collapse of the old Imperial Government and the various parts of the empire began to set up autonomous governments. On March 25, 1918, anti-communist leftists established the independent Belarusian Democratic Republic. Lenin and his Bolsheviks in Moscow refused to recognize the new republic and it was later overthrown by the Red Army. On January 1, 1919, the communist victors set up the Byelorussian Soviet Socialist Republic.

The then Byelorussians accepted their inclusion in the new Soviet regime and they remained loyal and subservient citizens throughout the Soviet era. In return, Moscow transformed the country industrially over the years. In addition, the republic was greatly enlarged in November 1939 when significant territories taken from Poland as a result of the Nazi–Soviet Non-Aggression Pact were added to the republic.

Gorbachev's program of glasnost and perestroika brought some changes in Byelorussia, but the majority of the communist leadership was conservative. A Byelorussian Popular Front was established but, harassed by the leadership of the republic, it found it difficult to build up support and it remained a minority movement. The Chernobyl nuclear accident in April 1986 created great fear throughout the republic, but the accident had actually occurred across the border in the Ukraine, so Belarusian officials were only blamed for not doing enough. They, in turn, blamed Moscow and otherwise helped keep a tight lid on news of the event.

When the attempted coup against Gorbachev began in August 1991, Nikolas Dementei, the first secretary of the Byelorussian Communist Party, made the mistake of supporting the coup leaders. When the attempt collapsed, therefore, Dementei was ousted from his position as chairman of the Supreme Soviet. On August 25, the Byelorussian Supreme Soviet declared the republic's independence, adopting the name *Belarus* (initially spelled Belorus). It then suspended the activities of the communist party.

Stanislav Shushkevich was elected chairman of the Belarus Supreme Soviet on September 20, 1991. He previously had held the position of first deputy chairman of the Supreme Soviet. He was a nuclear physicist by training, however, and "headed laboratories and departments of nuclear physics in various Minsk higher educational institutions." He was also a member of the USSR Supreme Soviet where he belonged to the liberal Interregional Deputies Group.

Shushkevich supported a continuation of some form of union as long as that appeared a viable option. After the December 1 referendum and elections in the Republic of Ukraine, however, Shushkevich joined with Presidents Yeltsin and Kravchuk in creation of the Commonwealth of Independent States on December 8.

Shushkevich had hosted the meeting at his hunting lodge and the agreement was signed in Minsk, the capital of Belarus.

Political Developments in Independent Belarus

Once Belarus had opted for independence, Shushkevich pushed for "the speediest introduction of market relations and private ownership." However, the Belarus Supreme Soviet, still filled with ex-communists, was really controlled by Vyacheslav Kebich, who held the position of prime minister. Kebich, much more conservative, advocated a "go slow" policy. Because Shushkevich attempted to govern by consensus, he was never able to bring about very much economic change. Over time, however, his relations with Kebich grew worse. In January 1994, Shushkevich informally supported an attempt to oust Kebich. Kebich won the vote of confidence 175 to 101. The legislature then voted 209 to 36 to dismiss Shushkevich as chairman of the Supreme Soviet. Although Shushkevich had been an advocate of the need for economic reforms, the most important reason for his ouster was his nationalism. Kebich, taking the position that the situation in Belarus had deteriorated after the collapse of the Soviet Union, wanted to rebuild economic ties to Russia. Shushkevich favored good political relations with Russia but opposed closer economic ties because he thought they would compromise Belarus's independence.

Following Shushkevich's ouster, the Supreme Soviet elected Myechyslaw Hryb as its new chairman in 1994. Under Hryb's leadership, the Supreme Soviet voted to adopt a presidential republic, and voted approval of a new constitution on March 4. This paved the way for new presidential

A typical Belarusian-style Orthodox Church; this one is in Mosar, Belarus

Marc Chagall's memory of his hometown Vitebsk (1922)

elections in June. These elections were won by Alexander Lukashenko, a former collective farm director without previous political experience. Lukashenko's winning platform called for rebuilding ties with Russia with the ultimate goal of merging the two economies.

Three months earlier, in fact, Prime Minister Kebich had negotiated an agreement with Viktor Chernomyrdin, the Russian prime minister, under which Belarus would begin reintegrating itself into the Russian economy. According to the terms of the agreement, Belarus was to lift all customs barriers with Russia; Belarusian "coupons" would be replaced by Russian rubles; and military bases in Belarus being used by Russian troops were to be leased to Russia free of charge. As the July elections would later confirm, the majority of the Belarusian population favored a policy of reintegration with Russia, particularly in light of its dismal experience running its own economy.

President Lukashenko continued to push the policy of reintegration with Russia after his election but, in fact, almost nothing changed because the Russian government decided that it would be too expensive for Russia to exchange Belarusian coupons for rubles, and backed out of the deal. The "coupons" were eventually replaced by Belarusian rubles.

Meanwhile, the Belarusian economy continued to decline with no sign of a reversal in sight. A $300 million standby loan from the International Monetary Fund was approved in July 1995, based on a government promise to begin a program of reform. When the government did nothing, however, the loan was eventually suspended. Since that time, Belarusian government has rejected any movement toward privatizing its massive state sector and, since 2005, has actually renationalized a number of private companies.

Belarusian citizens have often been given little incentive to invest in the political process. In the May 1995 elections,

for example, a majority of eligible voters turned out to vote in only 119 out of the 260 electoral districts, thus invalidating the results in the remaining districts. Since the new constitution specified that 179 delegates constituted a quorum, the new parliament was unable to meet. The crisis continued until new elections took place in November, with President Lukashenko meanwhile ruling by decree. The electorate did manage to vote in a new parliament the second time around; however, they gave a majority of the seats to communists and agrarians, both opponents of reform.

But Mr. Lukashenko's authoritarian manner made it impossible for him to work with even this "ideal" parliament; in essence, Lukashenko was even unwilling to consult with people who agreed with him. In August 1996, therefore, Lukashenko called for a "vote of confidence" in his policies in the form of a constitutional referendum to take place on November 7 (not coincidently the anniversary of the November Revolution). Under the terms of the referendum, Lukashenko was to be given a fresh five-year term of office, additional powers to rule by decree, authority to create an appointed upper house of parliament, and authority to appoint half of the members of the constitutional court.

Parliament, which opposed the referendum, tried to stop it but failed. When the vote finally took place, it did so under a general presumption that the outcome was rigged. Giving the charge added credence, Mr. Lukashenko's prime minister, Mikhail Chigir, resigned after the result was announced. Internationally, both the European Union and the United States refused to accept the validity of the referendum vote; in addition, Belarus's memberships in the Council of Europe and the OSCE Parliamentary Assembly were suspended at that time.

The IMF and the World Bank also ended all funding to Belarus in 1997. Most of the various members of the European Union suspended economic aid projects at the same time. Lukashenko's authoritarian style of governing was a factor, but an even more important reason is that these countries were convinced that foreign credits would just be wasted because Belarus had proved itself unwilling to introduce any real economic reforms. President Lukashenko's response to its international isolation was to announce that Belarus did not need foreign credits.

Meanwhile, union with Russia continued to be Lukashenko's answer to all of Belarus's problems. A union treaty negotiated by the Russian and Belarusian governments supposedly went into effect on June 11, 1997, but brought little change. President Lukashenko even told

an assembly at Almaty State University in September 1997 that "speculation on the full merger of Belarus and Russia was dreamed up by politicos who have nothing better to do," adding that Belarus would never give up its sovereignty.

There was some tangible progress toward union eventually, however. In October 1998, Russia and Belarus signed a military security agreement, described as a supplement to the union treaty, which led to some integration of the economic and political systems of the two countries during 1999. But Russian Foreign Minister Ivanov undercut the significance of this new union agreement by characterizing the documents as "a declaration, not a treaty of further unification." Blurring the situation further, Yugoslavia was formally invited to join the "union" after the beginning of NATO air strikes over Kosovo, though of course that did not happen.

In December 1999, a second union treaty was signed by Presidents Yeltsin and Lukashenko; in it, Belarus and Russia agreed in principle to form an economic and political union with its own separate executive and parliament, union citizenship, a single, common external tariff, and, by 2005 or so, a common currency and defense policy. Membership was also to be open to other republics that wanted to join.

This second union treaty has provided the theoretical framework for Russian—Belarusian relations since that time—though it is sometimes difficult to determine what has actually been implemented.

Although President Putin specifically endorsed the idea of a Russia-Belarus union after he became president, Russia has tended to be more hard-nosed toward Belarus under Putin. In April 2000, for example, the Russian government sharply repudiated an assertion by Lukashenko that the two countries intended to create a joint 300,000-strong military force in response to NATO's expansion. The Russian government has also expressed uneasiness about Lukashenko's human rights record—in particular, the fact that domestic political opponents suffer constant harassment and several simply "disappeared" during the first years of the Lukashenko regime.

Another concern that sometimes surfaces is the economic cost of union to Russia. One factor is that, because of the state of Belarus's still unreformed economy, most of Belarus's manufactured products are uncompetitive in Russia. In fact, a few years ago, Belarus even had to subsidize the cost of bread in areas near the Russian border because cheaper Russian breads had begun to monopolize the local market. At that time, Russia was providing a subsidy of up to a billion dollars a year through such mechanisms as providing gas and oil at the Russian domestic

Belarus

price. By 2002, the subsidy had grown to at least $2 billion a year.

This may explain why President Putin characterized Minsk's proposals for a common Belarusian-Russian state as "legalistic nonsense" in June 2002. Two months later, he told President Lukashenko that the two countries should establish equal market conditions and ensure the rights of both citizens and enterprises. He next proposed that unification of the two states proceed on the basis of the Russian constitution, with a single government and parliament. Pointing out that the Belarus's GDP is only 3% of the Russian GDP, Putin declared that "the future union state can only be a federation." Lukashenko rejected Putin's proposal, saying that it was tantamount to "dividing Belarus into seven parts, incorporating these parts into the Russian Federation, and granting these Belarusian parts equal rights with Russia's regions." Lukashenko then added that "to form union bodies on the basis of the Russian constitution—[that] is totally absurd."

The Russia–Belarus Union is not dead—the Parliamentary Assembly of the Russian–Belarus Union actually met for the first time in Moscow in January 2003, and it has met annually to approve a union budget since that time. In the early days of the Russian–Belarus Union, there had been discussions of the Russian ruble becoming the sole currency of the union, with a planned implementation date of January 1, 2005. Russia coupled the proposed currency union with a caveat—a single state bank—which Lukashenko ultimately rejected..

In August 2007, the Belarusian National Bank announced plans to peg the Belarusian ruble to the US dollar instead of the Russian ruble, as had previously been the case. The reason given was that the Russian ruble was increasing in value vis-à-vis the US dollar, and this was driving up the value of the Belarusian ruble and contributing to domestic inflation in Belarus. In 2016, the country introduced a new Belarusian ruble. This currency is allowed to float and is not pegged to any particular currency. The value of the BYN to the dollar fell to its lowest rate in in spring of 2022, in light of the Russian invasion of Ukraine. By fall that year, it recovered to its current rate of approximately 2.5 BYN to the dollar.

Yet the Russian government cannot just pull out of the union, since polls indicate that over 80% of all Russians favor closer relations with Belarus. Nor can Lukashenko agree to become part of Russia, since only 5% of Belarusians favor that approach.

Meanwhile, President Lukashenko continues his authoritarian method of rule at home. In 2000, he made a sham of

Hon. Stanislav Shushkevich

the parliamentary elections by pushing through a new electoral law which allowed him to disqualify dozens of candidates and rig the count.

Neither the United States nor the countries of the European Union recognized the results of the 2000 parliamentary elections. That did not stop Lukashenko from pursuing similar policies when he ran for reelection in September 2001. Months prior to the election, the government launched a series of attacks on the political opposition, portraying them as puppets of foreign interests. As part of this attack, the Belarusian government broadcast a television program in February 2001 which accused the US Central Intelligence Agency of providing support to the political opposition. All television broadcasts are controlled by the state, as are almost all newspapers.

Although the political opposition managed to unite behind a single candidate—Trade Union Federation leader Uladzimir Hancharyk—it probably never had a chance in spite of Lukashenko's growing unpopularity with the public. In fact, President Lukashenko announced prior to the vote that he would be satisfied if he received 75% of the vote and that turned out, not coincidently, to be the precise percentage he officially received. Again, neither the United States nor the various countries of the European Union recognized the validity of the voting.

The situation with regard to Russia was more nuanced. President Putin called up Lukashenko to offer congratulations on his election, but Aleksandr Veshnyakov, the chairman of Russian Central Election Commission, characterized the election as "far from being an example to Russia and other countries that have embarked on the path toward democracy."

As if to further emphasize that point, Lukashenko continued his attacks on Hancharyk and the Trade Union Federation after the election. Hancharyk was forced out as president of the Trade

Union Federation and, then, out of the country. He eventually settled in Moscow. Franz Vitko, his successor as Trade Union Federation leader, then came under pressure and he was, in turn, forced to resign in July 2002.

Two months later, the government completed its takeover of the Trade Union Federation; at an extraordinary congress of the union, delegates elected Leonid Kozik, the former deputy chief of the presidential administration, as the head of the renamed Trade Union Federation of Belarus (FPB).

After the vote, President Lukashenko addressed the congress of the FPB. "I came to the conclusion," he said, "that we need to [place our society] on three powerful pillars; the renewed trade unions, the powerful youth organization, and the [system of] soviets." The government had created the Belarusian National Youth Organization approximately one month prior to Lukashenko's speech. Lukashenko never spelled out what he meant by his reference to soviets. Even more interesting, Lukashenko made reference a little later in his speech to a fourth pillar—political parties. But society has not matured enough to handle having political parties, he added, characterizing current political parties as:

> something incomprehensible. If only I see—provided that I am still your president—or you let me know that such [comprehensible political parties] have crystallized themselves, we will make them the fourth pillar of our—as it is trendy to say nowadays—civic society.

With new legislative elections scheduled to take place in the fall of 2004, the government extended its control further

President Alexander Lukashenko

by sponsoring new legislation giving itself the authority to ban political parties, trade unions, or other organizations if found guilty of even a single violation of the law during rallies. To understand the significance of this legislation, it should be pointed out that the Belarusian High Court banned 54 nongovernmental organizations (NGOs) during the preceding year, almost all for technical violations of the law. The government also moved to restrict the influence of the few remaining independent newspapers at this time by making it difficult for them to distribute their newspapers.

In January 2004, Belarus's national postal service canceled a contract to distribute subscriptions of *Belorusskaya Delovaya Gazeta*, a prominent independent newspaper. Simultaneously, the Belarusian national press's retail-sales network refused to handle the newspaper at its newsstands. These moves came after the government had earlier suspended publication of the newspaper for three months.

Elections to the 110-seat Chamber of Representatives took place on October 17, 2004. In the lead-up to the elections, the government first denied registration to or disqualified nearly half of the opposition candidates, then harassed and intimated those it permitted to run. Since the ballot also included a referendum on lifting the two-term constitutional limit on the presidency, President Lukashenko had a personal interest in the outcome.

In the end, supporters of the president won all but 1 of the 110 seats, while it was declared that the presidential referendum had won with an 86% majority—even though an independent poll had indicated less than 50% support among the voters. The OSCE and the European Union rejected both the elections and the vote for the referendum. In March 2005, the European Parliament adopted a resolution on Belarus calling on EU member nations to recognize Belarus as a dictatorship and President Lukashenko as a dictator. US Secretary of State Condoleezza Rice echoed this position in April 2005 when she referred to Belarus as "the last dictatorship in Europe" during a visit to Lithuania.

This pattern continued for the next three years. New presidential elections were scheduled to take place on March 19, 2006. In December 2005, the legislature passed a new, tougher public-security law which made it a crime punishable by a jail term of up to two years for any public comment which would bring discredit to Belarus in the international arena. In the words of the new law, candidates guilty of this offense would be "removed from the election process." The government used its new powers to carry out a program of intimidation against the few remaining independent

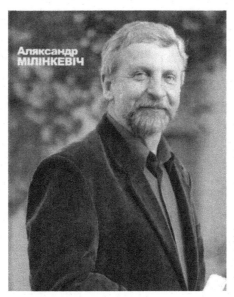

Dissident Alaksandar Milinkevich

newspapers, suspending one newspaper for three months, confiscating individual editions of other newspapers, and refusing to allow distribution through state-controlled kiosks in other cases.

The opposition probably never had a chance to win the election, but it did not help that they were unable to unite behind a single opposition candidate. In the end, the official tally gave Lukashenko 82.6% of the vote, with his chief presidential rival, Alaksandar Milinkevich, getting 6% of the vote. The other two presidential candidates together took 5.8% of the vote. The United States, the OSCE and the European Union refused to accept the results of the election. After that time, they coordinated on new sanctions against Belarus, including travel bans against those officials held responsible for the flawed voting process. There was, however, little more that these countries could do, since Belarus was already under sanctions for numerous acts of this nature in the past.

In May 2006, however Belarus got a rude shock when Energy Minister Alyaksandr Azyarets was invited to Moscow for talks with Gazprom on a natural gas price for 2007. According to a Gazprom spokesman, the gas price charged Belarus would depend on Belarus's steps to "satisfy the economic demands" of Gazprom. In essence, Gazprom wanted to buy Beltranshaz, Belarus's gas-pipeline system; if Belarus wouldn't sell, the price for natural gas would go from $47 per 1,000 cubic meters to $200 per 1,000 cubic meters. Negotiations continued for the rest of the year. Belarus eventually agreed to sell a controlling interest in the pipeline to Gazprom, but it wanted to continue to receive gas at the Russian domestic price. There was also disagreement on

the valuation of Beltranshaz, although the Dutch ABN AMRO Bank gave a valuation of $3.5 billion in December.

A new natural gas agreement was finally signed on December 31, 2006, but only after the Belarusian government threatened to pull gas for its own use out of the pipelines that carry natural gas to Poland, Lithuania, and Germany—much as the Ukrainian government had done in 2006. In the end, the Belarus government and Gazprom signed a five-year agreement on gas deliveries to Belarus. Under its terms, Belarus would pay $100 per 1,000 cubic meters of gas in 2007, with the price gradually rising to the European market level by 2011. Gazprom also agreed to pay $2.5 billion for a 50% stake in Beltranshaz, the gas pipeline company. In December 2007, Gazprom paid $625 million for a 12.5% interest in Beltranshaz; this payment was the first of four 12.5% installments to which were to be made between 2007 and 2010.

Even as the gas price argument was being resolved, the Russian government announced in December that it would begin charging a duty of $180 per ton on crude oil exported to Belarus. Here the problem was that Belarus had been importing Russian crude oil at the domestic Russian price for a number of years, refining it, and then selling it abroad at world prices.

The Belarusian government retaliated by placing a fee of $45 per metric ton on all crude oil shipped across Belarus en route to Western Europe. Russia then retaliated by cutting off all shipments of crude oil to Belarus in the first week of January. The impasse was broken a week later as the result of a telephone call to President Lukashenko by President Putin. Lukashenko agreed to drop the export duties Minsk had imposed on Russian oil shipments, and the two presidents agreed that their prime ministers would meet the following week to discuss several related issues.

Business Week estimated in January 2007 that Belarus would "pay approximately $1 billion more for energy in 2007 than last year." On the other hand, President Putin said on Russian television on January 15 that his country would continue to support Belarus, but at a "significantly reduced" level. Putin argued that the deal amounted to a $5.8 billion subsidy by Moscow and "is a payment by Russia for a calm and smooth . . . method of transition to a market relationship." Russia subsequently lowered its export duty on oil to Belarus from $180 to $53 per ton; in return, Belarus pledged to pay 70% of the export duty it receives for refined products.

At the end of January, a new agreement was announced that appeared to wipe out the new export duty entirely. According to the Belarusian petrochemical concern Belnaftakhim, it had an agreement with a

Belarus

Lukashenko propaganda: "Always There for You"　　　　　Courtesy of Maaike Göbel

number of Russian oil companies to purchase oil at some $240 a ton, including the oil export tax of $53 per ton. That was approximately what Belarus paid for oil in 2006.

In addition, the Belarusian government announced on February 5 that it had increased its tariffs for Russian oil in transit via Belarusian pipelines from $2.60 a ton to $3.50, a 34.6% increase. On the other hand, Belarus increased the crude oil export duty from $156.40 to $200.60 per ton on June 1, 2007. It also raised the export duty on a number of petroleum products by some 25% at this time. The purpose of these changes was to unify Russian and Belarusian duties on oil and oil products.

While these disagreements were going on, President Lukashenko began making noises about wanting to settle his disagreements with the west. By April, he was still resentful at Russia's decision to "switch to market economic relations":

How can you build good, human, brotherly relations, when they have bled you dry under the guise of the establishment of market relationships? How could I respond to this and what relations could I build with Russia?

At the same time, Lukashenko rejected European Union overtures aimed at improving relations because of the preconditions set by the EU for talks; as he put it, Belarus would not tolerate dictation and pressure exerted by the EU.

Although the Belarusian government continued to feel pressure from Gazprom to pay its oil and gas debts in a timely fashion, the Russian government has continued a general policy of support. In December 2007, Russia approved a $1.5 billion stabilization loan to Belarus. At about the same time, Gazprom indicated that it would

supply natural gas to Belarus in 2008 at a price of $119 per 1,000 cubic meters, a sharp discount from the European market price; the price was scheduled to rise to 80% of the European market price in 2009 but Belarus would not be required to pay the full European market price until 2011.

In the summer of 2008, things began to change in Belarus. The subsequent worldwide economic crisis reached Belarus in the fall and speeded up this trend.

New parliamentary elections were scheduled to take place on September 28. In July, President Lukashenko surprised many by appointing 42 opposition members to the district election commissions supervising the elections. There are 110 district commissions, so the 42 opposition commissioners constituted less than 3% of the total number of commissioners; nevertheless, it was a vast increase over 2004, when only one opposition representative was seated. President Lukashenko also approved an OSCE request to send more than 500 persons to monitor the parliamentary elections. Moreover, the president released political prisoners prior to the vote and permitted more than 70 members of the political opposition to participate in the ballot.

In the end, no single opposition candidate was seated in the 110-seat chamber, however. The most important reason for this outcome is probably that economic conditions in Belarus were still good in September. But there was also no real campaign. There were no debates on television, no election posters festooning the cities, and no political demonstrations. Finally, the OSCE noted in its preliminary findings that ballot counting occurred behind closed doors, making it impossible to monitor. Thus, no one knows whether there was an accurate count or not.

One important political change has occurred in Belarus, however. When the

European Union raised the possibility of abandoning its long-standing drive to isolate Belarus, the move was endorsed by the top leaders of Belarus's political opposition. For Aleksandar Milinkevich, who spoke at the European Parliament on October 8, the main factor was to secure Belarus's independence from Russia. And the Russian invasion of Georgia two months earlier was obviously on many minds, in the European Parliament and in Belarus. In fact, it may even have affected the thinking of President Lukashenko as well. Although Belarus's economic links to Russia are too all encompassing for any real reversal to occur, Russian–Belarusian relations deteriorated after President Lukashenko refused to join Russia in recognizing the "independence" of the Georgian provinces of South Ossetia and Abkhazia, even after Russia pledged $2 billion in credits to Belarus. When President Lukashenko continued to balk, the Russian government announced in May 2009 that it would withhold the last $500 million installment of the $2 billion loan. Russia also banned the importation of Belarusian dairy products in the summer of 2009.

In June 2009, the International Monetary Fund approved a $2.5 billion loan to Belarus though, as a condition of the loan, it required the government to devalue the Belarusian ruble by 20%; in the end, the Belarusian government devalued its ruble by more than 40%.

It was also about this time that President Lukashenko agreed to join the European Union's Eastern Partnership program, a program aimed at strengthening ties between the European Union and post-Soviet countries—an idea opposed by Russia. Shortly afterward, the Russian government announced that it was ending its special program with Belarus whereby Belarusian refineries paid only 35.6% of Russia's standard crude oil export tariff as of January 1, 2010.

At this moment, the Belarus–Russian alliance that was once intended to result in the creation of a single union state appeared to be dead. Instead, it has been replaced by a new entity which includes Kazakhstan. In January 2010, the governments of Russia, Kazakhstan, and Belarus signed a new agreement launching a customs union of the three nations. At that moment, it was a customs union in theory only, as the three republics had not yet agreed on unified trade regulations or customs codes. Nevertheless, the three republics signed a second agreement in December 2010 in which they committed themselves to the creation of a Common Economic Space. Belarus benefited from these discussions; after Belarus had signed on to the agreements, Russia removed all Belarusian oil duties.

Belarus held presidential elections on December 19, 2010. Lukashenko had only nominal opposition but he campaigned as though he might lose. One of his themes was that Belarus was a model economy. To emphasize the point, he ordered that salaries of workers in the state sector be increased by up to 50%. Lukashenko won with 79.7% of the vote and the raises went into effect. State-owned enterprises account for 70% of the economy, however, so demand for every sort of good increased rapidly, fueling inflation and leading to a sudden shortage goods; this, in turn, led to a shortage of foreign currency as traders attempted to meet demand by importing more goods from abroad.

By March, the government was running out of money, so Lukashenko turned to Moscow for a loan. Initially rebuffed by Moscow, the government temporized by beginning a series of devaluations of the ruble, which eventually led to a three-fold devaluation of the ruble by the end of the year. Eventually, the economy was more or less stabilized when Moscow agreed to a $3 billion loan—though technically the loan was made by the Russian-dominated Eurasian Economic Community Bail Out Fund. Belarus also received a $1 billion loan from the Russian State-owned Sberbank. As part of the deal, Belarus also agreed to sell its remaining half-ownership in Beltransgaz to Russian state-owned Gazprom.

President Putin made an official visit to Belarus in June 2012, his first official foreign visit since his election as president in March. He brought along news that Belarus would be getting another $440 million tranche of the $3 billion loan from the Eurasian Economic Community Bail Out Fund approved in 2011. During the visit, an agreement was signed for the construction of a new nuclear power plant in Belarus, with Russia providing the financing in the form of a $10 billion loan.

New parliamentary elections took place in September 2012. All 110 seats went to candidates from parties loyal to the president. Most opposition parties had pulled their candidates prior to the election and urged voters to stay away from the polls. The OSCE's election observation mission characterized the elections as "not competitive from the start." As Antonio Milososki, head of the election observation mission, put it:

A free election depends on people being free to speak, organize, and run for office. And we didn't see that in this campaign.

President Lukashenko won a fifth term in office in October 2015. Citing issues with vote counting and tabulation as well as legal ambiguity on the composition of electoral commissions, the OSCE's election observer report stated that the election "once again indicated that Belarus

The House of Government, Minsk

still has a considerable way to go in meeting its OSCE commitments for democratic elections." The report does positively note that all political prisoners were released by August 2015. It has been speculated that the prisoner releases represent an attempt to curry favor with the West in light of growing concern over Russian intentions.

President Lukashenko has followed very carefully Russia's annexation of Crimea from Ukraine in March 2014 and fighting between Ukrainian troops and pro-Russian separatists secretly backed by Russia. Lukashenko has been in power for more than 25 years, and Belarus remains closely linked to Russia. Russian energy subsidies keep the Belarusian economy solvent, and Belarus joined the Eurasian Economic Union together with Russia and Kazakhstan on January 1, 2015 (with Armenia joining the next day). At the same time, Russian aggression against Ukraine has given Lukashenko the opportunity to distance himself somewhat from Russia. Lukashenko condemned Russian annexation of Crimea, and Belarus did not join Russia's economic boycott on importing agricultural products from the European Union after the EU increased its sanctions against Russia following the downing of the Malaysian jetliner over rebel-held territory in eastern Ukraine in July 2014. Another way that Lukashenko has tried to separate himself from Putin has been by hosting two sessions of international peace talks on Ukraine. These efforts paid off. In February 2016, the European Union cited Belarus' efforts to improve human rights as justification for permanently ending five years of sanctions against the country. The decision formally lifted sanctions against three defense companies and 170 individuals, including President Lukashenko, who had experienced a travel ban and had their assets frozen. Despite the lifting of sanctions, critics of the regime maintain that Belarus' improved human rights record has largely been rhetorical. Independent journalists and opposition politicians are regularly

harassed by state officials. In Spring 2017, a wave of protests swept through the country intially catalyzed by a new tax levied on the unemployed. Although initially these protests were tolerated with remarkable restraint by the regime, by late March 2017, hundreds of protesters were being arrested. Additionally, prominent organizers and opposition politicians, such as 2010 presidential candidate Mikalay Statkevich, were also jailed.

In August 2018, Lukashenko announced a major government reshuffle. Most prominently, Prime Minister Andrei Kobyakov was replaced with Sergei Rumas, the former Belarusian Development Bank Chief executive. Lukashenko suggested that the move was spurred by frustration that the prior government was not adequately following his orders or improving social conditions across the country. Rumas' rise reflects a general trend in the Belorussian political system towards younger, more technocratic politicians. As noted by Ryhor Astapenia of Chatham House, following the 2019 parliamentary election, parliament is comprised of relatively younger and more professionalized politicians than in the past.

There is no change at the very pinnacle of the regime, however, and in August 2020 Lukashenko was elected president for the sixth time. Unlike in some previous cycles, Lukashenko was unable to enjoy a uncontested re-coronation as disputes over the integrity of the election prompted historically large demonstrations against his rule. Anti-Lukashenko protests had actually begun the previous May. When the dictator announced that he would seek another term, a popular blogger named Sergei Tikhanovsky organized a "slipper uprising" in which he encouraged citizens to rise up in order to flatten Lukashenko. Tikhanovsky compared to dictator to the antagonist in a children's poem called the "Mighty Cockroach." Tikhanovsky's provocative rhetoric proved attractive to many disgruntled Belarussians who

Belarus

President Lukashenko meets with President Putin in 2015

marched with slippers in hand ready to symbolically squash the cockroach but also gained the attention of the regime's security services. The blogger was arrested in late May and accused of being a foreign agent.

Tikhanovsky's arrest proved to be a catalyst for further contentious acts. Following more street demonstration in early June, the regime arrested Lukashenko's main opposition rival, Viktar Babaryka, supposedly for plotting a coup attempt. This arrest also proved to be insufficient to suppress the growing movement and in its wake, Tikhanovsky's wife, Sviatlana Tikhanovskaya announced her intent to run for president. The invigorated opposition quickly rallied behind her candidacy.

Soon after the polls closed, Lukashenko was declared the landslide winner. Tikhanovskaya disputed the results. At a press conference the next day, she declared herself the winner and stated that "[t]he authorities should think about how to peacefully hand over power to us." Unsurprisingly, the authorities never did and soon Tikhanovsky was exiled to Lithuania. Throughout August and into September, protests swept across the country with hundreds of thousands gathering in Minsk. Lukashenko was able to quell protests with a violent crackdown. Russia's pledge to deploy troops to demobilize protesters likely helped Lukashenko's embattled regime to survive this wave of contention.

Foreign Policy

General. The Government of Belarus adopted an official stance of international neutrality upon independence. To that end, it signed the Nuclear Non-Proliferation Treaty and, in February 1993, its legislature ratified the START I agreement. At that time, there were 81 nuclear-armed SS-25 missiles stationed in Belarus. Over the next two years, all but 18 mobile launchers were shipped to Russia to be dismantled. President Lukashenko then canceled the remaining redeployments in July 1995, saying that the decision to withdraw the missiles had been a "major political mistake." Belarus remained in technical violation of the START I agreement for the next two years before finally arranging for a transfer of the remaining missiles to Russia.

In general, Belarus has played a rather reticent role internationally, although it did negotiate agreements with the three Baltic Republics shortly after independence and made a point of establishing good relations with its western neighbors.

Belarus's foreign policy began to change after President Lukashenko was elected and began to reverse the reforms initiated by his predecessors. Things came to a head in September 1997, when the presidents of ten countries in the region sharply criticized Belarus for its retreat from democratic reforms. The meeting, hosted by the presidents of Poland and Lithuania and held in Vilnius, brought together the presidents of Belarus, Bulgaria, Estonia, Hungary, Latvia, Moldova, Romania, and Ukraine, plus Prime Minister Viktor Chernomyrdin of Russia. The meeting underlined President Lukashenko's isolation, for virtually everyone present was outspokenly critical of Belarus's policies under his leadership, both in its retreat from a market economy and its abandonment of democracy.

Russia. An active supporter of the Commonwealth of Independent States from the beginning, Belarus adopted a policy of favoring closer relations with Russia even before Lukashenko was elected president.

For example, Belarus signed an agreement subordinating its military policy to that of Russia in December 1993. In 1994, it signed a second agreement with Russia which was supposed to result in a common customs and currency zone, though it was never implemented. President Lukashenko then negotiated an agreement for full economic and political union in the spring of 1996, during the Russian presidential campaign, but this was never implemented either. Finally, Russia and Belarus exchanged ratifications for a Union Treaty in June 1997 which once again called for the unification of the two peoples.

But little changed, while relations between the two countries actually appeared to deteriorate when Belarus detained several TV journalists working for Russian Public Television (ORT) and charged them with entering the country illegally. Three of the journalists were released after Russia protested, but a fourth was detained for several months longer. In addition, two Belarusians working for ORT were arrested and put on trial. Relations turned even colder in October when Russia barred President Lukashenko from visiting two Russian regional cities. When Lukashenko protested, President Yeltsin replied that he would be happy to have Lukashenko visit—but only when the fourth Russian journalist was released.

Under President Putin, relations between the two countries were outwardly cordial, though, increasingly, Russian politicians complained that Russian support for Lukashenko was not only expensive but was actually detrimental to Russian interests in the long run. In addition, various individuals in the Russian government argued that Russia could maintain Belarus in its sphere of influence under another leader who would move Belarus toward economic reform and a market economy.

After his reelection in 2004, President Putin approved a Russian government decision to cut its subsidies of Belarus by moving toward charging Belarus the world market price for natural gas and crude oil as of the beginning of 2007. The move angered Lukashenko; it did not, in fact, represent a withdrawal of political support for Lukashenko. While nearly every other neighbor was appalled by the blatantly undemocratic nature of the 2006 presidential elections, President Putin congratulated Lukashenko and promised his support. Belarus's relations with Russia did not change significantly for the first two years after Dmitry Medvedev replaced Putin as president, but an agreement signed in December 2010 probably indicated a new warming of relations. After President Lukashenko signed off on membership on the Russian sponsored a free-trade zone arrangement called Common

162

Economic Space (whose membership also includes Kazakhstan), the Russian government agreed to drop duties on export of crude oil to Belarus. The Government of Belarus agreed, in turn, to send all duties on exported oil back to Russia. The agreement is expected to be worth between $2.5 and $4 billion year to Belarus, since Belarus will be paying the Russian domestic price for all domestically consumed oil and gas products; on the other hand, the agreement also ties Belarus even more firmly to Moscow. Since the Russian intervention in Ukraine, President Lukashenko has frequently publicly criticized Russian actions and attempted to redirect the countries foreign policy focus in a westward direction. Partially in response to changes in Belarus's visa regime to allow citizens of 80 countries visa-free travel, in Spring 2017 Russia initiated border checks on their shared border and began threatening to reduce oil imports into the country. By Fall 2017, however, it has appeared that Belarusian-Russian relations have somewhat stabilized as the two states conducted joint military exercises. Ultimately, despite Lukashenko's apparent desire to reduce Belarus's dependence on its powerful neighbor, his efforts are constrained by the fact that as of 2017 Russia accounts for more than 40% of Belarusian exports and around 60% of its imports. Indeed, Lukashenko implicitly acknowledged this dependence during a March 1, 2019 press conference. Although he stated that the long-speculated annexation of Belarus by Russia would never occur, he stressed that further integration of the two states is imperative.

The 2020 post-election protests, and Russia's invasion of Ukraine, had the effect of making Belarus more beholden to and reliant on Russia for political, economic, and military support. Following the unrest over the disputed presidential election, Russia provided Belarus with a $1.5-billion loan as a show of support. In return, Belarus hosted Russian troops and equipment, and participated in joint military exercises ahead of Russia's invasion of Ukraine. The incumbent regime's support for Russia's invasion of Ukraine contrast sharply with its criticisms and non-recognition of Crimea's annexation, which suggests that Minsk is likely to remain a difficult and unpredictable partner for Moscow to deal with. At present, the relationship appears to be rock solid even it comes at the cost of Belarus of living under fresh Western sanctions over its support for Russian aggression.

United States and European Union. Belarus's relations with the United States, good between 1991 and 1994, began to deteriorate after Lukashenko took over as president. They suffered a severe setback in September 1995 when border guards shot down a hot air balloon, killing its two American pilots, and they were made even worse after President Lukashenko absolved the military from any wrongdoing. Relations suffered a further setback in the spring of 1997 when Belarus accused an American diplomat of spying and expelled him. The United States subsequently withdrew its ambassador for consultations, though he later returned.

Another irritant occurred in June 1998 when President Lukashenko decided that the presidential compound at Drozdy was too small. Since the presidential compound was located in the middle of the diplomatic compound, Lukashenko's solution was to evict the ambassadors from the residences surrounding his compound. The ambassadors were first asked to move to other residences in the vicinity and, when they objected, they were told that the entire compound had become the "residence of the President of the Republic of Belarus," that they would require passes to enter the territory, and they would "have to comply with the special security rules of a presidential residence."

Following this, several ambassadors were denied reentry to the compound when returning from offices elsewhere in the city. Next, Lukashenko ordered that water and electricity be cut off from the residences. At this point, nine countries withdrew their ambassadors from Minsk "for consultations."

In addition, the European Union retaliated by placing severe travel restrictions on Belarusian state officials. A number of non-EU countries also adopted the travel ban—Bulgaria, Cyprus, the Czech Republic, Estonia, Hungary, Iceland, Norway, Romania, Slovakia, and Slovenia.

Among Belarus's western neighbors, only Poland and Lithuania continued to maintain diplomatic relations, and even these two countries publicly criticized Belarus's actions. Poland continued its contacts with Belarus because Bronislaw Geremek, the then Polish foreign minister, was also chairman of the OSCE, which had an important headquarters in Minsk. Lithuania declined to join the visa ban on Belarusian officials because it wanted to "soften the impact of [Belarus's] isolation on Lithuanian-Belarusian relations."

The controversy lasted until December 1998, when the Government of Belarus and the European Union reached a compromise of sorts. European Union ambassadors were to be given access to their old residences for a period of one month while they located and leased new apartments. In return, the government of Belarus agreed to compensate the countries for the expense and inconvenience that they had been put to. Essentially, the nations of the European Union largely yielded to Lukashenko's demands because of their belief that the political and economic situation in Belarus had worsened greatly in the second half of the year and it was advisable that their ambassadors return to Minsk in case of some sort of emergency.

A standoff between Belarus and the American government continued for several more months, but Ambassador Daniel Speckhard finally returned to his post in September 1999. According to the US State Department, Speckhard was ordered back to Minsk in response to Belarus's pledge to abide by the Vienna Convention and to pay compensation for losses suffered by the US embassy as a result of the ambassador's earlier eviction. "Having Ambassador Speckhard back in Minsk will enable us more effectively to promote

Wedding party at a public park in Minsk

Belarus

democracy and human rights, help those who support and work for the restoration of democratic rule, and promote other interests that we have in Belarus."

Relations between the United States and Belarus did not improve, however. When Michael Kozak, Speckhard's successor as US ambassador, arrived in Minsk on October 20, 2000, he was kept waiting for four months before being permitted to present his credentials to President Lukashenko on February 22. Lukashenko's refusal to meet Kozak for such a long time was widely viewed as a snub to the US government for its criticism of his regime and policies. Relations between the two countries deteriorated even further after the United States refused to recognize the validity of the September 2001 presidential elections.

Subsequently, Deputy Assistant Secretary of State Steven Pifer announced during a visit to Minsk that Belarus had made no progress in "key areas of democratization and that the human rights situation had actually deteriorated in previous months. "We see no progress toward democratic election reform. We see no evidence of steps to empower an independent Belarusian parliament or encourage functioning independent media." Pifer then added that the United States was willing to resume productive bilateral relations only if Belarus fulfilled the conditions it agreed to in joining such international organizations as the United Nations and the OSCE. What might be taken as Lukashenko's reply came the next month when the Belarusian government refused to allow Eberhard Heyken, the OSCE's new head, into Belarus.

The Belarusian government continued to pursue its intention to close the OSCE Advisory and Monitoring Group offices in Minsk through the expedient of refusing to renew visas for OSCE officials. That office officially closed as of December 31, 2002, but new discussions between the OSCE Parliamentary Council and the Belarusian government resulted in an agreement for a new OSCE office in Minsk to open as of the beginning of the year. The greatly reduced mandate of the new office calls for it to "assist the Belarusian government in further promoting institution building, in further consolidating the rule of law, and in developing relations with civil society in accordance with OSCE principles and commitments."

In November 2002, 14 of the 15 European Union states imposed a travel ban on President Lukashenko and seven other senior officials as a protest against human rights abuses in Belarus. In February 2003, the European Parliament passed a resolution condemning the Belarusian government's "indiscriminate attacks on the

media, journalists, members of the opposition, human rights activists, and any person who attempts freely to voice criticism of the president."

In March 2004, a joint US and EU mission that had come to Minsk in order to meet with government officials and representatives of the Belarusian political opposition issued a statement afterward in which it "noted with regret that Belarus has failed conspicuously to make progress toward meeting its OSCE commitments and thereby realizing an improvement in its relations with the European Union and the United States." The following month, the UN Human Rights Commission adopted a resolution condemning alleged human rights abuses by the government of Belarus. In November 2004, in response to "fraudulent legislative elections and presidential referendum" on October 17, the foreign ministers of the European Union voted to ban senior Belarusian officials from entering EU territory. This ban added 15 people to the list of 4 Belarusian officials banned in September 2004 in connection with the disappearance of political opponents.

Additional political sanctions were imposed by the United States, the European Union and the OSCE following the 2006 presidential elections; they have not had any effect on the actions of the Belarusian government, however.

On the other hand, Belarus was denied a seat on the United Nations Human Rights Council in May 2007 as a result of the combined opposition of the United States and the European Union. And in November 2007 a UN General Assembly committee adopted a resolution by a vote of 68 to 32 (with 76 abstentions) that criticized Belarus's human rights record. In addition, the European Union withdrew preferential trade tariffs for Belarus in June 2007 because of Belarus's failure to reform labor rights. European standard tariffs are three percentage points higher than preferential rates. That same day, the International Labor Organization issued a statement saying that Belarus had not made progress in giving workers the right to join trade unions.

Belarus picked a quarrel with the US government in January 2008 when it threatened to expel the US ambassador, apparently because the US Treasury Department had imposed economic sanctions against Belnaftakhim, Belarus's largest petrochemical company. In March 2008, Belarus recalled its ambassador in Washington and "urgently recommended" that the US government a similar action. After the US withdrew its ambassador "temporarily," Belarus withdrew all but seven of its diplomats from its embassy in Washington and demanded that the US do the same. On April 30, Belarus expelled 10

**Former Prime Minister
Andrei Kobyakov**

US diplomats, leaving the embassy to be staffed by 4 diplomats. Even before this action, the US had reduced the number of diplomats at the embassy from 32 to 14; because of the cut in staff, the Embassy also suspended the acceptance of visa applications from Belarusian citizens. The United States has not had an ambassador in Minsk since 2008.

The US government then took the position that "relations will be normalized when the authorities in Minsk release imprisoned opposition leaders." President Lukashenko subsequently released several minor political opponents, though Alexander Kozulin, a presidential candidate in 2006, who subsequently was sentenced to five years in jail for organizing demonstrations after the 2006 presidential vote, was not released until the summer of 2008. Finally, most other political prisoners were released in the spring of 2009.

One can say that Belarus began emerging from its 13-year exile under President Lukashenko in the spring of 2009. Belarus was among six states invited to join in the European Union's Eastern Partnership, whose first meeting took place in Prague in May 2009. That same month, President Lukashenko made a trip to Italy where he met with Pope Benedict XVI—and extended an invitation for the pope to visit Belarus. He also had dinner with Prime Minister Silvio Berlusconi while in Rome. But President Lukashenko's December 2010 decision to take Belarus into the Russian-sponsored Common Economic Space probably means that Belarus is moving back toward an eastern-oriented foreign policy for the near future. A European Union decision to renew sanctions against leading Belarusian officials after the rigged December 2010 presidential elections (where Lukashenko gave himself 80% of the vote) will have given him another push in that direction. And, in fact, President Lukashenko announced in January 2011 that Belarus had ordered the closure of the Minsk office of the Organization for Security and Cooperation in Europe

Belarus

(OSCE) after it criticized the results of the presidential elections. The OSCE was particularly critical of the Belarusian government's "detention of most presidential candidates and hundreds of activists, journalists, and civil society representatives" on election night. Referring to the ouster, a Belarusian foreign ministry spokesman said that, "the OSCE has fulfilled its mandate" in Belarus.

Since 2014, Russian actions have spurred a warming in Belarusian relations with the West, as the EU and US have no longer sought to isolate the authoritarian state. Following Belarus's decision to release its political prisoners in 2015, the EU permanently lifted most of its sanctions against the state in 2016. Sanctions placed on four members of Lukashenko's security services suspected of orchestrating political disappearances remain in place, however. In November 2015, the US eased some of its sanctions against Belarus, including those leveled against the oil company Belneftekhim, while leaving in place sanctions placed on a handful of elites accused of violating human rights, including Lukashenko. It is widely believed that the initial constraint that Belarusian authorities displayed in tolerating the Spring 2017 protest wave was directly due to the desire to maintain positive relations with the West. The unprecedented thaw in U.S.-Belarusian relations did not last long, however. The relationship sharply deteriorated when Lukashenko's security forces violently demobilized protesters, detaining 30,000 protesters following the disputed presidential elections in 2020. In response, the U.S Treasury slapped sanctions on 40 Belarussian officials, including those associated with the country's central elections commission, the interior ministry, and KGB for their role in suppressing protesters. According to these sanctions, the blacklisted officials cannot access their U.S.-based assets and are barred from visiting the U.S. or dealing with American citizens. More U.S sanctions followed when Belarus offered its territory for Russia to use as a launchpad to attack Ukraine. This time, the U.S sanctions were more sweeping as they targeted the country's banking, financial, defense, and security industries. Similarly, the EU restricted the provision of SWIFT services to major banks in Belarus and limited the amount of financial inflows from that country to the EU by prohibiting the acceptance of a deposits in excess of €10,000 from Belarusian residents and nationals.

Nature of the Regime

Belarus is an authoritarian regime. Formally, it has been a presidential republic since March 1994, when the Supreme Soviet adopted a new constitution which called for creation of a new executive official as head of state who would be called the president of the republic. Under the terms of the constitution, the president is the chief political figure within the new system. Charged with determining general policy, he is assisted by a prime minister who is responsible for day-to-day operations of the government.

President Lukashenko was elected under the terms of the 1994 constitution, but found that its terms constricted his actions. In November 1996, therefore, he sponsored a constitutional referendum which gave him an increased power to issue decrees, permitted him to create an upper house of parliament to be appointed directly or indirectly by him, gave him the right to appoint half of the members of the constitutional court, and extended his term of office to the year 2001. The government announced subsequently that the referendum had passed.

The constitutional referendum did not change the duties of the prime minister, who continues to be appointed by the president and must be confirmed by the legislature. He thus continues to preside over the cabinet, to oversee day-to-day operations of the government, and to be responsible for maintaining good relations with the legislature. The current prime minister is Sergei Rumas, who was appointed to that office on August 18, 2018.

The new National Assembly, which replaced the old Supreme Soviet, is a bicameral legislature, consisting of a lower house, the 110 seat Chamber of Representatives, and an upper house, the 64 seat Council of the Republic. The Council of the Republic is not elective but, instead, is made up of senators proposed either by regional councils (56 members) or appointed by the president himself (8 members).

Following the results of the most recent parliamentary elections, which took place on November 17, 2019, all 110 seats in the Chamber of Representatives were awarded to pro-government politicians. Thus, the fig leaf of pluralism which existed following the awarding of two seats to opposition candidates in the 2016 election has fallen away. Unsurprisingly, the 2019 election was criticized by the OSCE for failing to live up to international standards for democratic elections. As discussed earlier, in August 2020, Lukashenko won his sixth term in office. While this election was as unfair as previous ones, the galvanization of the opposition around the candidacy of Tikhanovskaya embattled the Lukashenko regime. Not only did Tikhanovskaya declare herself the rightful winner of the election, but her contestation of the results sustained a massive national protest movement.

Culture

Belarus has one prominent architectural monument from the period of Kyivan Rus, the Cathedral of St. Sophia in Polotsk, which dates from the 11th century. There are also two church-fortresses dating from the period of the Lithuanian Grand Principality, Maloye Mazheykava and Synkavichy. The 17th century saw the introduction of the Baroque style. The Jesuit church at Grodno exemplifies this new style and also the growing presence of Roman Catholicism, officially fostered by the Polish Government at this particular juncture in time.

Polotsk was long a center of learning and there are a number of names associated with it. Frantsyk Skaryna produced the first Belarusian translation of the Bible in the first quarter of the 16th century. The two editions of the Bible were actually printed in Prague and Vilnius. Symeon of Polotsk was a seventeenth-century poet who wrote in Belarusian.

Maksim Bahdanovich was an important poet of the late 19th century. Three poets of the early Soviet period are Ales Harun, Yanka Kupala, and Yakub Kolas. Kupala also produced a play, *Natives*, which was first produced in 1924. Kolas also produced a three-volume novel, *On the Crossroads*. Maksim Haretski was a novelist who wrote *The Quiet Current*. His diary was also published under the title of *On the Imperialist War*.

There was, in fact, a great outpouring of literature in the period of the 1920s. These included poets (Uladzimir Dubouka and Yazep Pushcha) and writers of fiction (Kuzma Chorny and Kandrat Krapiva). Stalin's introduction of socialist realism in 1930 brought a decline in the level of Belarusian writing, although some writers continued to be published. After World War II, a number of good composers appeared in Belarus. Dzmitry Lukas produced his first opera, *Kastus Kalinouski*, in 1947. Ryhor Pukst produced three operas between 1947 and 1955. Yauhen Hlebau produced an opera, *Your Spring*, in 1963 and a ballet, *Alpine Ballad*, in 1967. Yauhen Tsikotski and Yury Semyanyaka also wrote operas at this time. Belarus has both a conservatory of music and a philharmonic society. There is, in addition, the Belarusian State Theater of Opera and Ballet in Minsk, plus a state dramatic theater.

Belarus has a well-developed system of higher education. There are more than 40 institutes of higher education scattered throughout the republic, plus another 138 technical colleges. Until 2004, Minsk had been the home of the European Humanities University (EHU), founded after the fall of communism to promote Western-style teaching. It was closed in that year by orders of President Lukashenko. When this

165

Belarus

happened, the several European countries that had been providing financial support stepped in and helped the EHU move to Vilnius, Lithuania, where it has continued to survive. It currently has about 1,900 students, about half of them from Belarus. The Belarusian Academy of Sciences also has 32 scientific institutes in various parts of the republic. There is a comprehensive system of primary and secondary schools According to a 2010 report, Belarus turns out 4,000 information technology specialists every year, along with world-class specialists in mathematics and physics. With average engineer salaries running at only about $1,200 a month, IT outsourcing companies are beginning to show some interest in Belarus.

In August 2006, Deputy Education Minister Faryno reported that 4,006 schools would open for the new school year. Faryno's report revealed that only 20.5% of Belarusian schoolchildren would be instructed in Belarusian; in Minsk, only 4 out of 234 general-education schools instruct children in Belarusian. Two years earlier, official statistics indicated that 57% of all schools had the status of instructing in Belarusian.

Russian was made an official language in Belarus in 1995 and, from that time, the government began cutting its subsidies to publishing houses and authors producing texts in Belarusian. All of this reflects President Lukashenko's comment, made in 1994, that:

The people who speak the Belarusian language cannot do anything else apart from speaking the Belarusian language, because it is impossible to express anything great in Belarusian. Belarusian is a poor language. There are only two great languages in the world—Russian and English.

The republic also publishes approximately 200 daily newspapers, 130 of which are in Belarusian and the rest in other languages. However, Belarus's state postal system, which holds a monopoly over the distribution of subscription periodicals, denied distribution in the first six months of 2007 to major nationwide independent newspapers and many local independent newspapers. While addressing the National Assembly, President Lukashenko said that he was ready to "solve" problems encountered by private newspapers. But, in fact, he took no action, and it was almost certainly his policy that the postal service was reflecting in its decision.

About 80% of Belarusians have at least a nominal connection with the Russian Orthodox faith. Even under communism, when religion was officially discouraged, the Russian Orthodox Church occupied a special position. For the first few years after the collapse of communism, the state took a completely neutral position, but this began to change after Lukashenko was elected president in 1994. Religious repression began increasing under Lukashenko, but it was not until October 31, 2002—when Lukashenko signed a new law, "About the Freedom of Confessions and Religious Organizations"—that the state took formal responsibility for determining what religions are legal in the country. Essentially, the new law makes it illegal for worshippers of any faith to meet on a regular basis unless they are registered with the state. While it extends automatic legal recognition to 26 faiths, including Russian Orthodoxy, Roman Catholicism, Judaism, Islam, and Lutheranism, it requires unrecognized faiths to be registered with the state before they can begin to hold regular meetings. In addition, any unrecognized faith must have been active in Belarus since 1982 and have at least 10 separate congregations in order to qualify for registration.

Although Vladimir Lameko, vice chairman of the Belarus Parliament's committee for religious affairs, claims that "all religions are equal before the law," the new religion law singles out the Russian Orthodox Church as playing "a determining role" in national culture and government. According to its authors, a major purpose of the law was to protect the leading role of the Russian Orthodox Church against dangerous sects. Government actions even before the law went into effect bear that out.

In August 2002, for example, the government bulldozed a western Belarus chapel of the Russian Autocephalous Orthodox Church, a splinter organization separate from the main Russian Orthodox Church. One month later, several Minsk branches of the Full Gospel Pentecostal Church received word that their prayer services were illegal. The Pentecostal Church, with 450 registered churches and 200 unregistered ones, is the largest Protestant group in Belarus. Other faiths which have come under harassment by the state include the Hare Krishnas and the New Life Protestant Church. In addition, a small 150-member Hindu community has been denied registration on technical grounds. Meanwhile, the apartment being used as a community temple by the Hindus was broken into and ransacked. The group has also been repeatedly denied the right to hold public meetings. Several members have also been arrested.

The position of Jews in Belarus is somewhat peculiar, partly for historical reasons. Belarus, home of the 19th century Jewish Pale, was once home to some 800,000 Jews. But most of Belarus was occupied by the Nazis for most of World War II and, among their various atrocities, they destroyed the Minsk Jewish ghetto, killing up to 100,000 Jews in the process. Today, approximately 50,000 Jews live in Belarus.

Until around 2008, the government downplayed this history. That October, Belarus "marked" the destruction of the Minsk ghetto through three days of staged processions, memorial services, and an exhibition on the Holocaust, with art from children around the world. President Lukashenko himself launched the proceedings with a televised speech, stating that Belarus had a "great debt" to all those who fought against the Nazis.

Economy
Belarus has a fairly well-balanced economy, with an agricultural sector that is, in general, capable of feeding its population and a well-developed industrial base. Agriculture in the northern part of the republic concentrates on raising beef and

Reenactors demonstrate traditional rural life outside of Minsk

dairy cattle. The farms produce their own fodder and hay and otherwise, except for those areas set aside for growing flax, the land is in pasturage. In the center of the republic, the farms concentrate on pig breeding. The most important crop grown in this area is potatoes. In the south, there are once again many farms that specialize in the raising of cattle, either for milk or beef. Hemp is also grown in this area. Grain is grown throughout the republic. Some grain is imported into the republic, but mainly to be used as cattle feed.

The problem with agriculture is that about two-thirds of the peasants are still organized into collective farms, with most of the remainder in state farms. A few private farms were set up after that became possible, but the treatment they received from the state sector discouraged others from trying. The first post-independence Belarusian government favored a changeover to private agriculture, but that policy was repudiated by President Lukashenko after his election in July 1994.

Today, there are 2,381 state-run agricultural enterprises. In general, all production is sold to the state at low controlled prices that cover only part of the cost of production. To keep the farms operating, the state makes "loans" to cover part of the cost of planting and harvesting. In April 2004, Belarusian Television reported that more than 40% of all collective farms were losing money. Nor was Belarus's problem limited to grain production. The potato harvest was also down to one million tons, a drop of two-thirds from 1990. As Deputy Agricultural Minister Aleksandr Prakopau put it,

Our potato sector is facing what our sheep industry has already gone through and what our flax industry is going through right now. Our sheep breeding is dead. The flax industry is slowly dying.

According to Deputy Agriculture Minister Anatol Rubanik, the total debts of agricultural enterprises were the equivalent of $720 million in November 2001, up from $22.8 million at the beginning of 1999. Agricultural officials have been stressing for years that a radical change in the state's pricing policy was necessary if Belarus wanted to get agricultural production back to 1991 levels.

Agricultural leaders have advocated changes such as encouraging new technologies, upgrading farm equipment, and reforming farm collectives but President Lukashenko, who was a state farm manager before entering politics, does not favor such changes.

Lukashenko came up with his own program concerning collective farms in March 2004 when he issued a decree aimed at

attracting investment from Belarusian companies in state-owned collective farms. Such firms would receive deferments on lingering debts, tax arrears, and overdue utility bills owed by the collective farm taken over. Perhaps this new policy has had some affect; Statistics Minister Uladzimer Zinouski reported that the 2006 grain harvest was 6.5 million tons.

Belarus has very little heavy industry. In 1991, it was capable of producing about 1.1 million tons of steel a year, while it also manufactured machine tools, agricultural machinery, and motor vehicles. It also manufactured chemicals, paper, and bricks. There was a branch of industry that manufactured consumer goods such as watches, radios, televisions, and bicycles. Most of the rest of industry was associated either with textiles or processing of agricultural products. There was a flax-spinning industry and another that manufactured artificial silk. Shoes and boots were also made. Agricultural end products included sugar and preserves. Domestic energy supplies were limited mainly to peat, which was widely used in industry.

But Belarusian industry had two major weaknesses. It imported most of its raw materials from other republics and it was dependent on imports for most of its energy. As a result, industry came under severe economic pressure soon after independence and this so frightened the political leadership that economic reform never really got off the ground. Only about 5% of enterprises had been denationalized by July 1994 when President Lukashenko took office and halted the process completely.

In November 1997, President Lukashenko issued a decree giving the government the right to intervene in the affairs of private joint-stock companies, including forcing them to remain open even if they were unprofitable. Three months later, the government moved against what little private enterprise continued to exist by announcing that it was reestablishing state monopolies on oil, tobacco, and cars. The government denied that it was going back to "totalitarian planning" and characterized the new program as "indicative planning." The government also decided to turn to the printing presses to cover the shortfall in the budget.

If these moves were intended to shore up the failing economy, they did not work. By March 16, 1998, the zaichik was trading at 59,000 to the US dollar, down 25% from the previous week. By December 1998, the zaichik had virtually collapsed, with unofficial trading reaching nearly 400,000 to the US dollar. That the financial collapse of Russia played an important role in this collapse cannot be denied, since Russia had been the recipient of 70% of Belarusian exports before the crisis, and the drop in sales

to Russia forced Belarusian enterprises to reduce output or, in some cases, to cram storehouses full of unsold products.

But this is at best only a partial explanation. By the fall, there was also an acute shortage of foodstuffs and a number of regions began instituting rationing. In this case, one factor was that Belarus's grain harvest was down by about 1 million tons. Another factor was that Belarus exported $250 million in foodstuffs to Russia in 1998 as payment for natural gas imports.

But it also did not help that state-controlled food prices were set so low that collective farmers were forced to sell their produce to the state at about 50% of what it cost to produce. Under those circumstances, no one had any incentive to raise any more food than they could consume themselves.

Even before the crisis, in fact, relatively little local produce was available in the stores. Almost all food for sale in stores was imported. And when the zaichik collapsed, Belarus could no longer afford to pay for imported food.

President Lukashenko appeared not to understand what was happening to the Belarusian economy. Speaking to the nation in February 1999, he blamed "mismanagement" for the country's economic decline in 1998. He also outlined the country's economic priorities as closing the trade deficit (over $1 billion in 1998), halting spiraling inflation, maintaining economic growth, and reducing the number of unprofitable companies. All these are laudable goals, to be sure.

But as he had asked his ministers at a televised cabinet meeting shortly before, "Why are our people becoming poorer and poorer every month while we are so dynamically developing industry and agriculture?" None of his ministers was able to give him an answer.

Over the next two years, Lukashenko intensified the command aspects of the economy. In May 1999, for example, he signed a decree regulating prices and service charges; he next ordered the government to bring the Belarusian Union of Consumer Cooperation and the consumer trade sector directly under government control, thus effectively nationalizing trade in the countryside.

As the slide in the economy continued, Belarusian workers organized a number of rallies protesting the government's economic policies. None of this had any effect on government policy, however, and the situation in the countryside worsened through the rest of 1999. In January 2000, therefore, the government announced a plan to increase the productivity of the agricultural sector. It turned out, however, that the government's "plan" merely consisted in raising the prices at which the

Belarus

government purchased meat and milk. Responding to an annual inflation rate of more than 200%, the government also decided in January to trim three zeroes off the currency.

President Lukashenko made no major changes in policy until after his reelection in September 2001. He then appointed Henadz Navitski as his new prime minister and, in introducing him, announced that the new cabinet had been tasked with ensuring macroeconomic and financial stability, reformation of the state economic sector, and the development of entrepreneurship in the country. Lukashenko promised to liberalize economic relations and support private businesses, and he further promised that the government would reduce to the minimum direct interference in the activities of economic entities. Somewhat later, Lukashenko made it clear that it was the Chinese economic model that he had in mind as a model for Belarus.

Prime Minister Navitski was dismissed in December 2003; his successor, Syarhey Sidorski, had no greater success in his overseeing of the economy. But this is not surprising, since it is President Lukashenko who makes all important governmental decisions.

According to official Belarusian statistics, GDP grew at an 11% rate in 2004; industrial output rose by 15.6% while agricultural production rose by 12.9%. There was also a 40% rise in foreign trade, with exports to Russia accounting for 46.6% of exports. Belarus had a $4.7 billion deficit in trade with Russia, partly explained by the fact that it obtained almost all of its energy supplies from Russia. Belarus had an overall trade deficit of $2.6 billion in 2004. The government also announced that the average before-tax monthly wage rose from 299,859 Belarusian rubles ($139 at the then exchange rate) in December 2003 to 434,900 Belarusian rubles ($200 at the current exchange rate) in December 2004. Based on these figures, Belarus was making good economic progress and life was improving for ordinary citizens. Outside observers tend to be skeptical about official Belarusian statistics, however.

In March 2006, Siarhej Karol, a financial manager at American International Group, wrote that the Belarusian economic model:

seems to defy economic theory. An economy entirely consisting of the old, unreformed Soviet industrial base, manages to churn out high single digit growth in gross domestic product (GDP), provided guaranteed monthly income and full, if not always full-time, employment, even as it remains in a state of complete isolation from the modern world. That, indeed, is the puzzle of Belarus.

The decision of the Russian government to introduce market pricing in its relations with Belarus as of the beginning of 2007 further stressed the Belarusian economic model. Under the new policy, the 2008 price was $119 per 1,000 cubic meters of natural gas (versus $46.68 per 1,000 cubic meters in 2006), and the price was supposed to increase each year until 2011, when Belarus would be paying the European market price. The price increase may have cost Belarus an extra $1 billion in 2007, though this was partly offset by Gazprom's purchase of a 50% interest in Beltransgaz, Belarus's gas-distribution network, for $2.5 billion.

Russia was also upset that Belarus was importing and refining 17 million tons of oil from Russia, but exporting all but 4 million tons of the refined oil to Western Europe and selling it at world market prices. President Putin first threatened to place a duty on oil exported to Belarus of $180 per ton, though this was later reduced to $53. In fact, Belarus apparently ended up paying approximately the same price for oil in 2007 as it did in 2006. But Russia continued to press President Lukashenko to accept movement toward a market economy. As Kremlin policymakers saw it, Belarus was economically and politically dependent on Russia and President Lukashenko's policies were "bringing the country to a political and economic dead end. Russia had only to wait for 'the fruit to ripen and fall into its hands.'"

In the fall of 2008, the worldwide economic crisis reached Belarus. Exports declined sharply—dropping by one-third in January 2009; this was partly because the Belarusian economy was strongly tied to the Russian economy, also suffering a major economic decline at this time. Faced with this situation, President Lukashenko called on other countries for help. Russia agreed to provide a $2 billion loan, though it eventually canceled the last $500 million installment. Lukashenko even asked Washington for a loan of $5 billion, though to no avail. Lukashenko also made overtures to the IMF and the World Bank, both of which had ceased lending to Belarus in 1997. The IMF agreed to a $2.5 billion loan, though it required Belarus to devalue its currency by 20%; in fact, the ruble was eventually devalued by more than 40%.

Under pressure to raise cash, President Lukashenko also restarted a long-stalled privatization program, which has resulted in the sale of government stakes in two mobile-phone companies. It has also said that it would privatize some banks. Belarus has also enacted a number of regulatory reforms and tax relief measures since 2007 which, together, have eased the difficulty of doing business in Belarus. The moves have apparently increased foreign interest

in Belarus; the Belarusian government says that foreign investment in Belarus more than doubled in 2009. Total current foreign investment in Belarus is given as $4.8 billion. In March 2010, representatives from Microsoft, Cisco Systems, Honeywell, and Navistar visited Minsk for meetings with President Lukashenko and top business leaders. Microsoft opened a sales office in Minsk shortly after these meetings.

Lukashenko's decision, during the 2010 presidential campaign, to order a 50% increase in wages for all workers in the state sector led to such a huge growth in demand that Belarus found itself in crisis by March 2011. With the currency in collapse and shortages throughout the economy, President Lukashenko turned to Moscow for help. The Russian government made Lukashenko wait for several months before announcing a rescue plan in November 2011. Under the plan, Belarus got a $3 billion loan from the Russian-dominated Eurasian Economic Community Bail Out Fund and a $1 billion loan from Sberbank, owned by the Russian state. In addition, Belarus agreed to sell its remaining half ownership in Beltransgaz to Gazprom. Even after the bailout, however, the Belarusian government was forced to reintroduce price controls on foodstuffs. The government also announced that it would pass new laws to allow citizens to hold more than one job in order to be able to augment their incomes.

Although the economy had stabilized by the end of 2011, GDP growth was anemic in 2012; in spite of a five-year modernization program, Belarusian industry was finding it more and more difficult to compete with Russian industry. One sign of that is that increasing numbers of Belarusian workers were leaving to seek jobs in Russia. The situation was apparently particularly bad in the lumber of wood-processing industries. As a result, President Lukashenko issued a decree in December 2012 prohibiting workers in the wood-processing industry from quitting their jobs. According to the decree, workers who left their jobs would be sentenced to compulsory labor and returned to the production line. That was the stick; Lukashenko also promised to raise worker salaries from $140 a month to $400–500 during 2013.

Belarus is a major producer of potash, an ingredient of fertilizer. All production is under the control of the state-owned firm Belaruskali, one of the top three taxpayers in the country. Russia is also a producer of potash and in 2005 Belaruskali formed a marketing agreement with the Russian firm Uralkali to export all potash through a new company formed for that purpose, the Belarus Potash Company. At that time, the two companies controlled 40% of the global potash market.

Belarus

Uralkali was subsequently taken over by a Russian oligarch, Suleiman Kerimov, who greatly enlarged the company by buying up other potash producers. Kerimov then set his sights on taking over Belaruskali and in 2011 offered $10 billion for Belaruskali. President Lukashenko was willing to sell but wanted $30 billion for the firm.

To put pressure on Lukashenko, Uralkali began selling potash outside the 2005 agreement. In 2012, about 80% of Uralkali's potash exports were outside the 2005 agreement. One result was a steep drop in global potash prices.

Deeply angry, President Lukashenko first appealed to President Putin but got no satisfaction. He then rescinded the 2005 marketing agreement entirely in July 2013. One month later, Lukashenko ordered the arrest of Vladimir Baumgertner, general director of Uralkali. Baumgertner was arrested on the charge of "exceeding his authority" following a meeting with Belarusian Prime Minister Mikhail Myasnikovich, after negotiations on joint pricing of Russian and Belarusian potash exports collapsed. He was subsequently held "under house arrest" in Minsk.

In response, the Russian government suspended the import of Belarusian live hogs and pork products and announced a 20% cut in oil exports to Belarus. The Belarusian government then issued an order calling for the arrest of Suleiman Kerimov, who was in Russia. All of this cast a bad light on the Russian-sponsored customs union between Russia, Kazakhstan, and Belarus which is supposed to become the Eurasian customs union in 2015.

To resolve the dispute, President Putin ordered Russia's federal Investigative committee to open an investigation into Mr. Baumgertner on suspicion of abuse of power. Belarus had also complained about the $3 billion in annual oil products duties which had to be remitted to Russia,

arguing that they were a violation of the customs union that had existed between Belarus, Russia, and Kazakhstan since 2010. In October, Russia agreed to scrap the oil duty if Belarus would lift unspecified trading barriers. This seems to have resolved the dispute between the two countries. It is not clear if the potash dispute has been resolved, though it has been suggested that the Russian government would resolve it by buying out Suleiman Kerimov, thereby taking control of the potash industry.

As of 2022, Belorussian economic fortunes remain inextricable from Belorussian-Russian relations. After a series of bilateral talks failed to produce agreement over the price that Russia would sell oil to Belorussian refineries, Russia ceased nearly all oil shipments into its neighbor on January 1, 2020. At the heart of the dispute was the level of economic integration between the two states, with Russia arguing that it needed to see more of commitment to deepen the level of integration before it would continue to sell oil to Belarus at heavily subsidized prices. The standoff came to an end in April as the global price of oil spiraled to record lows.

The Future

President Lukashenko is often called "Europe's last dictator." He has been in power since 1994 and allows no serious political opposition. The contention over the August 2020 presidential election reveals eroding support for the Lukashenko regime. Against long odds, the opposition rallied around a single candidate and sustained massive national protest events for several months. While some of the energy of these protests have dissipated over the months that followed, the ability of the anti-Lukashenko sectors of society to continue to stage protests nearly a year after they began last May could be a sign of a galvanized civil society.

Belarus has enjoyed certain advantages from its close link to Russia since the collapse of the USSR in 1991 and Lukashenko's election in 1994. Most importantly, it has received very large energy subsidies from Russia in the past. However, Russia's economic troubles have spilled over to Belarus. When the Russian ruble dropped precipitously in 2014, so did the Belarusian currency which helped push the economy into recession. Grievances over the economic recession were a major cause of the large-scale protests witnessed in spring 2017. These protests and the government's initial permissive response demonstrate the tricky situation the government finds itself in. Because of a desire to gain favor in the West, the regime was unwilling to repress the protests as severely as it had in the past. Ultimately this led the government to concede to the protesters and delay implementation of Decree No 3. It is possible that this concession encouraged subsequent protests. Perhaps the new government comprised of young technocratic reformers will finally be able to carry out needed economic reforms. Ultimately, without economic liberalizing reforms at home and expanded trade ties with Europe, the long-term future of Belarus remains bleak. It is unclear, whether over the medium to long term, the comprehensive economic sanctions on Russia and Belarus would drive a wedge between these countries or bring them closer together. What seems certain, however, is that for the US to freeze sanctions against Belarus, the regime has to do more than disassociate itself from Russia in its war effort against Ukraine. The regime must respect human rights at home. At least that is how Ned Price, the US Department of State Spokesperson, sees it. At a press briefing held on May 20, 2022, he stated that the Biden administration will continue to use sanctions against Belarus as long as the regime engages in human rights abuses.

Ukraine

Area: 240,000 sq. mi. (621,840 sq. km.), twice the size of New Mexico.

Population of Ukraine: 35,661,826 (2024 est.).

Capital City: Kyiv (Pop. 3.017 million, 2023 est.).

Climate: Temperate.

Neighboring States: Russia (east), Belarus (north), Poland (northwest), Slovakia, Hungary (west), Romania, Moldova (west).

Languages: Ukrainian (only official language), Russian.

Ethnic Composition: Ukrainian (77.8%), Russian (17.3%), Crimean Tatar (0.5%), Jewish (0.2%), other (4.2%).

Principal Religions: Ukrainian Orthodox (Moscow Patriarchate, Kyiv Patriarchate, and Autocephalous) and Ukrainian Greek Catholic (Uniate).

Chief Commercial Products: Grain, potatoes, fruit, vegetables. Ukraine has some of the richest land in the former USSR. Highly developed fuel and power resources, iron and manganese ore, metal production, engineering, chemical production, gas, processed food, building materials. The nation has 60% of the former USSR's coal reserves.

Currency: hryvna.

Per Capita Annual Income (Purchasing Power Parity): $16,231 (2023 est.).

Recent Political Status: Part of the Russian Empire until 1917, Ukrainian Republic (1917–1922), Ukrainian Soviet Socialist Republic (1922–1991).

President: Volodymyr Zelensky (May 20, 2019).

Prime Minister: Denys Shmyhal (March 4, 2020).

National Flag: Two horizontal stripes, the top a light blue, the bottom yellow; the blue represents the sky, yellow the wheat fields.

National Day: August 24 (1991), Independence Day.

The Land

Ukraine is the independent successor to the Ukrainian Soviet Socialist Republic, a constituent republic of the Union of Soviet Socialist Republics. Ukraine declared its independence on August 24, 1991 and this was confirmed by a popular referendum that took place on December 1, 1991. The territory of Ukraine also includes the Crimean Autonomous Republic (created in 1991), which, however, has been occupied (and claimed) by Russia since February 2014.

Ukraine lies in the southwestern part of the Russian Plain. The chief feature of the landscape is the Dnieper River, which flows down through the center of the republic. There are two upland regions, a series of rolling hills in the southeast and the Volyn-Podol Plateau, which stretches from the Polish to the Moldovan border in the west. The only large mountainous area is along the western border, where the northern ridges of the Carpathian Mountains cross the republic. The southern tip of the Crimean Peninsula also has a small mountainous area, a western extension of the Caucasus Mountains. Mountains make up only about 5% of the total land surface of the republic.

Because so much of the republic consists of a level plain, the differentiation between the various parts is based on the amount of rainfall that each gets. The most rainfall occurs in the north and diminishes to the south. The northern part of Ukraine is actually a large swampland, called the Pripet Marsh, the major part of which lies across the border in Belarus. The Dnieper Lowland dominates the central part of the republic. It is flat in the west and gently rolling in the east. Its chief feature is the Dnieper River and its tributaries. This is the traditional grain basket of the republic, which extends as far south as the city of Dnipropetrovs'k, on the Dnieper River. Here the rainfall is adequate to support wheat and other grains without irrigation. In the area south of Dnipropetrovs'k, on the other hand, irrigation becomes necessary.

The area immediately north of the Crimean Peninsula is known as the Nogai Steppe. This area, plus the northern part of the Crimean Peninsula—referred to as the Crimean Lowland—were once grassy steppes, homelands of the Nogai and Crimean Tatars and pasturelands for their animals. Today a huge artificial lake on the Dnieper provides water for irrigation.

The southern shore of the Crimean Peninsula has a mild Mediterranean-type climate, with average January temperatures of 39°F. Summers are hot and dry. The northern shore of the Black Sea is much colder, with average January temperatures of 26°F. Spring comes early, however, usually at the end of January. Average January temperatures in Kyiv are 18°F. Temperatures are also lower in winter and higher in summer in the eastern part of the republic.

Soils vary somewhat throughout the republic, but rich *chernozems* (black earth soils), which cover the entire central part of the republic, make up about 65% of the total. To the north of the *chernozems* area are found mixed gray *podsol* and black earth soils, and eventually pure, gray *podsol* soils, which are less fertile and also acidic. South of the *chernozems* belt is an area of chestnut soils, not as rich as *chernozems* and tending to be saline as one nears the Black Sea. The vegetation also reflects this soil division. Forests are found only in the north, in the area of the gray *podsols*. Mixed forest and grassy steppe cover the *chernozems* area. Desert and semi desert plants grow in the chestnut soils of the south.

The People

In 2017, Ukraine was estimated to have a population of 44 million. This represents a decline of around 8 million people since independence. The decline in the population is the result of significant outmigration, as well as rising death rates (16.4/1,000 population) and falling birth rates (9.59/1,000 population). Experts believe that a major causative factor derives from the Chernobyl nuclear accident of 1986, which has contributed to male fertility problems, but other factors that have contributed to the decline in population would certainly include things like AIDS, tuberculosis, and even poverty. At the time, the World Bank estimated that the population would drop to 37 million by 2025, but by 2024 the population had already contracted beyond that estimate

Approximately 67.5% of the population speaks Ukrainian as their first language. Russian-speakers constitute the largest minority, making up 29.6% of the overall population; Russian-speakers are actually a majority in certain parts of eastern Ukraine and the Crimea. Reflecting this fact, Deputy Education Minister Viktor Ohnevyuk said in August 2005 that Russian is the language of instruction in 1,500 Ukrainian schools with a population of 1.2 million students, that is, approximately 20% of the school population. In addition, there are nearly a hundred smaller ethnic groups, including Belarusians, Moldovans, Crimean Tatars, Bulgarians, Hungarians, Romanians, Poles, and Jews.

Ukrainian belongs to the eastern Slavic family of languages, the other two of which are Russian and Belarusian. Ukrainian is derived from Old Slavonic, the language spoken by all eastern Slavs during the period of Kyivan Russian history. Ukrainian evolved after the split caused by the Mongol invasion in 1240. After 1240, the area that constitutes modern Ukraine was ruled directly by the Mongol Empire for a hundred years, before it was incorporated into the Grand Principality of Lithuania. The area east of the Dnieper River came under Russian control in 1654; the rest was added in the 18th century. It was this historic separation, and the connection with Lithuania and Poland between 1341 and the end of the 18th century, which resulted in the Ukrainian language.

The word Ukraine (no modifier) means "something that is on the edge or periphery" and describes Ukraine's position vis-à-vis Moscow. At various times in history, the land has also been referred to as Malorossiya, or "Little Russia."

History

Archaeological evidence indicates that the first settlement at the city of Kyiv, capital of modern-day Ukraine, was made in the 7th century (though there is a popular tradition that dates the founding to the 5th century). Kyiv, built on the western bluffs above the Dnieper River, commanded traffic on the river and soon became a regional trading center. At the end of the 9th century, then, it became the capital of the first organized Slavic state—historically known as Kyivan Rus—when Olaf the Norwegian conquered it and moved his headquarters there from Novgorod. Kyiv remained the capital of Kyivan Rus until 1169 when Yuri Dolgaruki, Prince of Vladimir, became Grand Prince and moved the capital to his own city of Riazan.

Although Kyiv lost its political preeminence at this time, it remained an important trading center until 1240, when it was sacked and virtually destroyed by the Mongols. At this time, all the craftsmen who had not been killed in the sack of the city were rounded up and sent to Sarai. All of southern Kyivan Rus was then incorporated into the new Mongol Empire and ruled from its regional capital of Sarai, located on the eastern bank of the Volga River, just north of the Caspian Sea. Though it remained the seat of the Metropolitan until 1300, Kyiv became a ghost city, occupied only by the churchmen associated with the St. Sophia Cathedral and the office of the Metropolitan.

The "Golden Horde," as the Russians called the Mongol government, appointed new Grand Princes to govern in the north, but the weight of the Mongol yoke brought a collapse of this line by the early 14th century. Slowly, then, Moscow rose in the northeast and built its leadership, all the time acting as agent for the "Golden Horde."

In the northwest, however, a new leadership rose, based on freeing as much of the area as possible from the Mongol yoke. The leader of this new state was the Lithuanian Prince Gediminas (Gedymin in Russian), founder of the Jagellon dynasty; however, the majority of the subjects of this new Grand Principality of Lithuania were eastern Slavs and this was exemplified by the fact that their language, Old Slavonic, became the official language of the court. As Gediminas extended his control southward, he freed Kyiv and the western territories as far south as the Black Sea from Mongol control.

Cossack House **by Serhiy Vasylkivsky (1854–1917)**

Ukraine

One effect of the Mongol control had been that most of the area of southwestern Kyivan Rus was virtually depopulated. Since this area remained subject to periodic attack from the Mongols, it remained a borderland for another 200 years where only the brave or the desperate dared to live. Increasingly, however, communities of Slavic speakers fleeing from oppression in either Lithuania or Muscovy area settled this area, adopting many of the habits of nomadic neighbors, particularly the use of the horse and methods of fighting. These became the Cossack communities of the southern steppe, one of the most important of which was the Zaporozhian Cossacks, with their settlements south of the cataracts on the Dnieper River.

These Cossacks had to fight constantly for their freedom, against nomads to the east and against encroachments from governments to the north. After the Grand Principality of Lithuania was merged with the Kingdom of Poland in the Union of Lublin in 1569, the combined Kingdom of Poland-Lithuania attempted to control this southern borderland area. The fighting prowess of the Cossacks was such, however, that the government was often willing to sign a treaty recognizing their status as Cossacks in return for military service to the Polish-Lithuanian state. At the same time, however, the government was giving out land to Polish noblemen and encouraging their settlement in this borderland area. These Polish noblemen brought the institution of serfdom with them—and there were constant efforts to enserf individual free peasants of the steppe.

At the end of the 16th century, religious differences emerged as a salient cleavage. The Cossacks were Orthodox, while the Polish nobility moving into the area were Roman Catholic. When the Patriarch of Constantinople recognized Moscow (Muscovy) as a separate Patriarchate at the end of the 16th century, he recognized the Russian Patriarch's jurisdiction over all Orthodox in the Slavic-speaking area, including those of the southwest under Polish-Lithuanian control. For political reasons, the Government of Poland-Lithuania refused to recognize this jurisdiction and outlawed the Orthodox Church within the area of its jurisdiction. Instead, it created the Uniate or Eastern Catholic Church, which used the traditional Orthodox service and the Old Slavonic language but recognized the spiritual leadership of the Pope.

Thus, the free peasants of Ukraine found themselves under a three-pronged attack in the first half of the 17th century—encroaching serfdom, Polonization resulting from the increasing numbers of Polish nobility establishing estates in the area, and attempts to destroy the independent Orthodox Church. The man who now rose to the leadership of the Ukrainian forces was Bodgan Khmelnitsky, a Ukrainian landowner elected Hetman (head) of the Zaporozhian Cossacks. Khmelnitsky defeated the Polish forces a number of times (which contemporary Ukrainian history calls the "War of Independence") and for a while apparently dreamed of creating an independent Ukraine. But it soon became apparent to him that the Ukrainian forces were not strong enough to sustain an independent Ukraine. Believing that a victory by Poland would mean the end of the Orthodox Church and the enserfment of the free peasants of Ukraine, he turned to Muscovy and offered to bring Ukraine under Russian control.

Tsar Alexis, then ruler of Muscovy, hesitated for some time before accepting the offer because he recognized that it would mean war with Poland. He finally accepted in 1653, however. This led to a war between Poland and Muscovy that began in 1654 and ended with the Truce of Andrusovo in 1667. Under the terms of the truce, Poland recognized Moscow's control over all lands east of the Dnieper River, plus temporary control of the city of Kyiv. Russia never gave Kyiv back, however, and the terms of the truce were confirmed by a peace treaty signed in 1686. Russia got the remaining parts of the Ukraine during the partitions of Poland in 1772 and 1793. Thus, the destinies of the Ukrainian people were tied to those of Russia primarily over the issue of religion (i.e., loyalty to the Orthodox Church). Cossacks also retained their freedom from serfdom, though there was some encroachment in this area in the 18th century.

Russian–Ukrainian relations were not always smooth. Part of the problem was that Ukraine had been guaranteed its own autonomous government with its own Hetman or ruler under the treaty of 1654, but Ukrainian leaders were not always happy with Moscow's policies as they affected Ukraine. Perhaps the most extreme example of this occurred in 1708, when Ivan Mazepa, Hetman of the Zaporozhian Cossacks since 1687, signed an alliance with Charles XII of Sweden (then at war with Russia) under which Ukraine was to become an independent nation under Mazepa's leadership. After Peter the Great's victory over Sweden at the battle of Poltova, he moved to curtail most of Ukraine's autonomy. There were three further Hetmans in the 18th century, all Russian nominees. The last Hetman was Kyrylo Razumovsky, younger brother of Empress Elizabeth's "Gentleman of the Bedchamber." Catherine the Great accepted his resignation in 1764.

Catherine the Great incorporated Ukraine directly into Russia by dissolving separate Cossack bodies and dividing the area into *guberniyi*. In 1793, when the remaining territories occupied by Ukrainians were taken from Poland in the second partition, the name *Ukraine* was

A country wedding day—complete with troubadours

dropped and all of the territory simply became part of Russia.

Ukrainian nationalism resurfaced in the 19th century with the founding of the secret Brotherhood of Saints Cyril and Methodius in Kyiv in 1846. The membership of the Brotherhood included two historians, Mykola Kostomariv and Panteleimon Kulish, plus the Ukrainian poet Taras Shevchenko. One year later, the organization was suppressed and its thirty members exiled to other parts of the empire.

Tsar Alexander II authorized the publication of a journal, *Osnova* (The Outset) in Ukrainian in 1861. In 1876, however, Alexander II prohibited the publication of journals or books in the Ukrainian language and closed all Ukrainian language schools. Thereafter, Ukrainian nationalists migrated abroad, either to Lvov (L'viv) in Austrian Galicia or to Switzerland. The Austrian Government permitted a Shevchenko Scientific Society to be founded there in 1872 and in 1890 a chair in southeastern European history was established at the University of Lvov (L'viv).

The first man appointed to fill the position was Mykhailo Hrushevsky, a Ukrainian historian. Hrushevsky eventually published a ten-volume *History of Ukraine-Rus*, whose major thesis was the continuation of Kyivan Rus-Ukrainian history and the separate development of the history of Muscovy-Russia. After the Revolution of 1905, when the Russian government lifted its ban against the publication of journals and books in Ukrainian, Hrushevsky moved back to Kyiv.

After the Russian Revolution of 1917, Ukrainian nationalists held a National Ukrainian Congress in Kyiv in April and elected a Rada (Council) headed by Hrushevsky. The Ukrainian Rada proclaimed an autonomous Ukrainian republic in June with Hrushevsky as president, Volodymir Vinnichenko as premier, and Symon Petlyura as minister of war.

After the Bolshevik revolution in November, the Ukrainian Rada called for convocation of a freely elected Ukrainian Constituent Assembly. Opposing this, the Bolsheviks announced formation of a Ukrainian Soviet Government on December 26. On January 22, 1918, the Ukrainian Rada proclaimed a "free and sovereign" Ukrainian Republic. The Central Powers signed a separate peace treaty with this government at Brest-Litovsk on February 9, but the Bolsheviks managed to seize Kyiv on February 8. After the Rada fled to Zhitomir, German and Austrian troops occupied most of Ukraine. The Rada and the Central Powers now came into conflict, whereupon the Central Powers overthrew the Ukrainian Rada on April 24 and appointed Pavlo Skoropadsky as Hetman of Ukraine.

After the collapse of Germany in November 1918, a five-man directorate took over in Ukraine, with Volodymir Vinnichenko as chairman and Symon Petlyura as commander in chief. A separate Republic of the Western Ukraine was proclaimed in L'viv. The Poles occupied L'viv about three weeks later, however, so this government fled to Ivano-Frankovsk. In January 1919, a union of the two Ukraines was proclaimed, but a Red Army occupied Kyiv the same day. On March 14, 1919, a Ukrainian Soviet Socialist Republic was formed under the leadership of Khristian Rakovsky. However, the whole of Galicia remained in Polish hands. The Bolsheviks were driven out of Kyiv by the anti-Bolshevik forces of General Denikin in September 1919. However, Denikin had a falling out with the Ukrainian nationalists because he was opposed to a separate Ukraine. After Denikin's defeat in December 1919, the Ukrainian Soviet Socialist Republic established its control over most of Ukraine.

Communist Control

In December 1919, Lenin, speaking of the equality of the Russian and Ukrainian peoples, proposed an alliance. The Ukrainian nationalists couldn't bring themselves to come to terms with the Bolsheviks, however. Instead, Petlyura allied himself with Jozef Pilsudski, the Polish leader, which led to a Polish invasion of the Ukraine in April 1920. The Poles occupied Kyiv on May 7. Pilsudski now began dreaming of a reconstructed Polish–Lithuanian–Ukrainian Commonwealth. But that vision was no more acceptable to Ukrainian nationalists than Lenin's offer had been, and the Polish forces were soon forced out of Ukraine. In December 1920, Lenin and Rakovsky, head of the Ukrainian Soviet Socialist Republic, signed an alliance uniting Soviet Russia and Ukraine. A peace treaty with Poland was signed on March 18, 1921. Under the terms of the treaty, Poland got to keep Eastern Galicia and Volhynia.

In December 1922, an All-Union Congress of Soviets representing the Russian, Ukrainian, Byelorussian, and Transcaucasian Soviet Socialist Republics agreed to form the Union of Soviet Socialist Republics. A constitution for the new union was adopted in July 1923.

In Ukraine, a Language Act of August 1, 1923, established the priority of Ukrainian over Russian. Hrushevsky was appointed president of the Ukrainian Academy of Science, founded in 1918. This period of Ukrainization came to an end in 1928 when Stalin forced the government to introduce Russian as the second official language. Two years later, "nationalist deviation" became a crime punishable by death when 45 intellectual leaders were put on

trial and charged with treason. Thirteen were sentenced to death and the rest were deported. Hrushevsky, though not one of the 45 accused, was also deported. As part of Stalin's grisly purges, additional trials were held in 1931 and 1933. Being a member of the Communist Party was no defense. Yury Kotsiubinsky, deputy premier, was shot in 1933; in 1937, Panas Lyubchenko, an ex-premier, was also shot; and in 1939, yet another premier, Vlas Chubar, was shot.

Collectivization and the Great Famine

The other program that was to wreak havoc on Ukraine was collectivization. Launched in 1929, the purpose of collectivization was to put an end to individual farming and organize all of the peasants into collectives controlled by the state. By mid-1932, 70% of all Ukrainian peasants were in kolkhozes (collective farms).

The origins of the Ukrainian famine of 1932–1933 can be seen in the rising grain quotas enforced during the period 1930–1933. In 1926, the best harvest year before collectivization, the Soviet Government obtained 3.3 million tons of grain from Ukraine. In the good harvest of 1930, the Soviet Government set a quota of 7.7 million tons for Ukraine. In 1931, the quota was again set at 7.7 million tons, but the harvest was poor and only 7 million tons were actually collected. But this marked the beginning of a famine in 1932, for only an average of 250 pounds per capita was left to feed the rural Ukrainian population until the next harvest. But even with widespread evidence of grain shortages throughout the republic, the quota was again set at 7.7 million tons for 1932—and this out of a harvest reduced by two-thirds by collectivization and poor weather.

When local officials complained that the poor harvest made it impossible to meet the state quota, Moscow's response was to issue a decree in August 1932 which spelled out the legal sanctions which were to be used to enforce the quota. The decree further specified that those guilty of offenses under the terms of the decree were to be considered enemies of the people and shot, unless there were extenuating circumstances.

Over a fourth of the officials staffing agricultural middle management were arrested because of their opposition to the quota; the actual collections were carried out by gangs of thugs sent into the villages to root out the hidden grain.

As the collection process stripped the villages of food, many of the peasants attempted to flee; lacking internal travel documents, they were stopped by guards at the border of the republic and prevented from entering Russia proper. In the end, most stayed in the villages and

Ukraine

Former President Leonid Kuchma

tried to find enough to survive on until the next harvest.

Although people had been dying all winter, death on a mass scale really began in March 1933. To keep the famine a secret, foreigners were forbidden to travel to Ukraine. The grain harvest collection in Ukraine was officially ended on March 15, 1933. Estimates of the total number of deaths vary greatly, but they certainly numbered in the millions. The famine served the interests of the Communist leadership in a peculiar way, however, for the many deaths broke the will of the Ukrainian peasantry; never again would they dare to challenge the will of the Soviet government.

The 1932–1933 famine is still a political issue in Ukraine. In November 2006, President Yushchenko submitted a bill to the Verkhovna Rada declaring the manmade famine to be an act of genocide against the Ukrainian people. Lawmakers from the Party of Regions and the Communist Party opposed the bill during the ensuing debate, arguing that it would only worsen relations with Russia. In the end, 233 deputies voted in favor of the bill. A memorial to the victims of the famine was dedicated in November 2008. In the shape of a towering candle, it sits on a hillside overlooking the Dnieper River. It is already a pilgrimage site.

Post–World War II Ukraine

The territory of Ukraine was considerably enlarged as a result of World War II. Those parts of Poland where Ukrainians lived, essentially eastern Galicia and Volhynia, were occupied by the Red Army beginning in September 1939 and incorporated into Ukraine later that year. Romania ceded Bessarabia and northern Bukovina to the Union of Soviet Socialist Republics in June 1940. Northern Bukovina and the Bessarabian districts of Hotin and Izmail went to Ukraine. On June 29, 1945, Czechoslovakia ceded Sub-Carpathian Ruthenia to the USSR, and this area was also incorporated into Ukraine.

The last addition to Ukraine came in February 1954 when Nikita Khrushchev marked the 300th anniversary of the Russo-Ukraine union by transferring the Crimea to Ukraine. In 1991, the Government of Ukraine granted the Crimea the status of an autonomous republic.

The Gorbachev program of reform instituted after 1985 found no immediate response in Ukraine, for Vladimir Shcherbitsky, first secretary of the Ukrainian Communist Party, was a Brezhnev stalwart who was quick to slap down any signs of dissent. He was removed in September 1989 and died soon afterward. His successor, Leonid Kravchuk, although also a product of the party apparatus, showed himself to be more "liberal" than his predecessor and more willing to make concessions on nationalism.

This made good political sense for Rukh, the national front movement, had come into existence by this time and it was challenging the Communists for the political leadership of the republic. By stealing a number of their positions, Kravchuk managed to turn back the Rukh challenge in the March 1990 elections. After the Communists had managed to hold on to 239 out of the 450 seats in the legislature, Kravchuk sponsored a declaration of republican sovereignty, which was adopted in July 1990.

In March 1991, Kravchuk agreed to hold a referendum on a new union treaty drawn up by Gorbachev, but insisted on rewording it to make it clear that Ukraine was unwilling to give up its claim to sovereignty. As the same time, Kravchuk worked to insulate Ukraine from Gorbachev's economic policies, suggesting in July, for example, that Ukraine intended to issue its own currency. The Ukrainian legislature also began taking more nationalistic stances, for example repealing a series of Soviet tax and foreign-trade laws.

When conservatives launched their coup d'état to overthrow Gorbachev in August 1991, Kravchuk compromised by refusing to recognize the authority of the leaders while, at the same time, not condemning them publicly. After the collapse of the coup, he resigned as first secretary of the Ukrainian Communist Party and banned the party from the republic. On August 24, he got the Ukrainian legislature to declare Ukraine independent, subject to a popular referendum scheduled to take place on December 1, 1991.

At this point, it appeared that Kravchuk favored some form of continued union, and Ukrainian delegates cooperated in creating the new interim government that the Supreme Soviet approved on September 5. Nationalist pressures continued to grow, however, and by October Kravchuk was

beginning to sound as though he wanted a completely independent Ukrainian state. In November, the Ukrainian legislature voted to "decertify" the Ukrainian deputies to the USSR Supreme Soviet; henceforth they were to participate as observers only. Meanwhile, Kravchuk had stated that Ukraine also intended to create its own national army.

The December 1 referendum and popular election for the office of President of Ukraine became the culmination of this increasing trend. Over 90% of all voters cast their ballots in favor of Ukrainian independence, at the same time giving 61% of their votes to Kravchuk to make him the first president of an independent Ukraine. Eight days later, Kravchuk met with the presidents of Russia and Belarus to declare the Union of Soviet Socialist Republics dead and create the Commonwealth of Independent States. Eight other republics joined the CIS on December 21, and Gorbachev resigned as president of the USSR on December 25.

The history of the CIS has been extremely uneven since its creation in December 1991 and Ukraine has contributed to that unevenness. Essentially, Ukraine, fearing a new domination by Russia, has mostly been only a half-hearted participant in CIS efforts to create independent structures that would permit continued cooperation between the ex-Soviet republics. For example, the Republic of Ukraine made it clear from the beginning that it intended to take control of all conventional forces stationed in Ukraine, including naval forces. There were no problems with the army, including nuclear forces, but a quarrel did arise with Russia over the Black Sea Fleet, headquartered in the Crimea. Ukraine first claimed the entire Black Sea Fleet, then only the conventional portion of it, while Russia took the position that dividing it would destroy it. The two countries worked out an arrangement for joint supervision of the Black Sea Fleet in 1992, but it wasn't until 1997 that they were able to reach an arrangement acceptable to both sides.

Another problem has been the status of the Autonomous Republic of Crimea. Crimea, which has a population of about 2.5 million, is about 67% Russian and 26% Crimean Tatar. Ukrainians actually make up only 26% of the population.

A majority of the Crimea population voted for Ukrainian independence in December 1991, but Russian nationalists in the Crimean legislature subsequently pushed for a vote of independence from Ukraine, with the real aim of joining Russia.

The Crimean legislature has actually been ambivalent on the issue, voting for independence and then modifying the vote to indicate that Crimea was a part of

Ukraine. The issue has also been fueled by Russian nationalists in Russia, who argue that Crimea ought to be returned to Russia, to which it belonged until 1954. In May 1992, the Russian Supreme Soviet actually passed a resolution declaring the 1954 transfer to be invalid. The Yeltsin Government repudiated the resolution, but the Supreme Soviet's vote was seen by Ukrainian nationalists as another example of Russia's traditional tendency to bully and dominate. The Friendship Treaty between Russia and Ukraine, signed in May 1997, presumably put an end to this problem because it includes an explicit Russian recognition of Ukraine's borders.

Ukraine's main problems after independence were economic, however, partly because until 1994, the leadership of the country remained in the hands of former communists opposed to significant economic change. President Kravchuk was, of course, first secretary of the Ukrainian Communist Party before 1991. His first prime minister, Vitold Fokin, was another old-line Communist bureaucrat who found himself beyond his depth in the new circumstances of a collapse of the old Communist system. Even as Ukraine's economic circumstances continued to grow worse over the next several months, the government did nothing to tackle the problems. By September 1992, inflation was outpacing even the Russian rate and, in spite of seemingly unlimited easy credit to industry, economic activity was down 18% over the preceding year. Faced with that situation, even the Supreme Soviet, dominated though it was by ex-Communists, was unwilling to continue to put up with Fokin's policies. On September 30, he and his cabinet were forced to resign.

President Kravchuk's first choice as his successor was another former Communist boss, Valentin Simonenko, but he was unacceptable to the Supreme Soviet. President Kravchuk then settled on Leonid Kuchma, a member of the Supreme Soviet who had

also been director of Yuzhmash, Ukraine's largest producer of nuclear missiles, since 1986. Although a longtime member of the nomenklatera, Kuchma had a reputation for being hard-driving and competent. Moreover, he took office with a mandate to step up the pace of economic reform if he so wished. In confirming him, the Supreme Soviet also gave him the power to rule by decree until May 1993.

Over the next year, Kuchma pushed through major economic reforms—issuing decrees on privatizing land, reforming income tax, and commercializing state-owned enterprises—aimed at addressing most of Ukraine's problems and moving the country toward a market economy. But Kuchma's policies brought loud objections from the legislature, which made several attempts to revoke his right to rule by decree. Over the next several months, therefore, Kuchma spent his time quarreling with parliament and getting very little accomplished. Parliament then refused to renew his right to rule by decree in May 1993. Kuchma remained on as prime minister until September, apparently hoping to work out some accommodation with parliament. He then resigned and was replaced by Youhym Zhiahilsky.

Zhiahilsky, an ex-Soviet enterprise director from the Donbass, never claimed to be a reformer and the policies he implemented as prime minister were in line with those favored by the hard-liners in parliament. Not surprisingly, prices increased 30-fold in 1993 and the government's budget was almost 90% of GDP. Having a large budget deficit to contend with, the government also instituted punitive taxes which suppressed economic activity. With company taxes levied on gross revenues instead of profits, it was not uncommon for companies to hand over more than 100% of their official profits as tax. This had the effect of driving most private economic activity underground. By the end of 1993, the

"underground" category was estimated to encompass 60% of the economy.

The Government of Ukraine withdrew from the ruble block in November 1992, at the prompting of Russia. From that time until the summer of 1996, its currency consisted of "coupons" that the government had begun issuing in the spring of 1992. The government had a new currency, the hryvna, already printed up but, because of a virulent inflation, did not dare to release it.

New parliamentary elections took place in March 1994. The result: 338 out of the 450 seats were filled, with the remainder to be filled in a second round of voting. Of the 338 seats filled, 163 were won by persons running without a party label. Most of these were prominent local people, usually former communists. Among parties, those associated with the old communist regime made the best showing. The Ukrainian Communist Party came in first with 86, followed by the Peasant Party, with 18 seats and the Ukrainian Socialist Party with 14 seats. Rukh, largest of the nationalist parties, won 20 seats while five other nationalist parties garnered 20 more seats among them. Six centrist parties won 17 seats. In general, persons representing the Communist Party of Ukraine, and their allies, did best in eastern Ukraine, while nationalists did best in western Ukraine. While most Ukrainians thus voted against change, Leonid Kuchma, leader of the centrist Interregional Reform Bloc won over 52% of the vote for president on July 10, 1994, defeating incumbent Leonid Kravchuk.

The Kuchma Era

Kuchma had run as a reformer and he signaled this by meeting with Michel Camdessus, managing director of the IMF on July 28, 10 days after taking office. This was, in effect, a follow-up of a meeting that Kuchma had had with Camdessus in Washington earlier that spring. During that meeting, Kuchma had invited Camdessus to come to Kyiv if Kuchma won the election and had concrete economic proposals ready. After the Kyiv meeting, Camdessus promised that the IMF would work with Kuchma to develop an economic program for the Ukraine aimed at keeping monthly inflation to single digits, reducing the budget deficit, and freeing prices.

This, in turn, would permit a start on implementation of the $4 billion aid package promised at the economic summit meeting in Naples earlier in the month. That promise had been conditioned on the Ukrainian Government's moving forward on programs such as land redistribution, privatization of state enterprises, elimination of price controls, and drastic cuts in the budget. Kuchma subsequently pushed

Kyiv, capital of Ukraine, on the Dneiper River

Ukraine

a far-reaching economic reform program through the legislature which promised large-scale privatization of state companies, cuts in the national budget and the removal of price controls on many goods.

Ukraine received its first IMF loan, for $371 million, in October 1994 and agreement was reached for a second loan for $1.5 billion in March 1995. With the payments deficit for 1995 expected to be $5.5 billion, however, the Ukrainian Government requested an additional $900 million from individual Western countries as well. The US government pledged $100 million, while additional funds eventually came from the members of the European Union. After some Western arm twisting, Russia also agreed to reschedule $2.5 billion in Ukrainian debts, and Turkmenistan took similar action on monies owed it for deliveries of natural gas.

Economic reform continued after that time, with the government gradually selling off state assets. With inflation slowly being brought under control, the Ukrainian Government was finally able to begin issuing its new currency, the hryvna, in the summer of 1996. However, the economy remained stagnant, the 1996 budget continued to run a large deficit, and the gross foreign debt at the end of 1996 stood at $8.5 billion.

The Ukrainian government did have promises of loans totaling approximately $4 billion from the West, including the IMF, if it carried through with a promised structural reform. President Kuchma worked hard to do so, though he was not always been able to get his proposals through the legislature. A particular example of this occurred in 1997 when the legislature delayed passage of the budget for over six months, threatening up to $3 billion in credits from the IMF.

Kuchma's policies had considerable support within the country but they were by no means universally liked. Another problem was that, until 1997, Kuchma was unable to get parliament to accept a prime minister who was in agreement with his economic policies. His first prime minister, Vitaliy Masol, an old Communist bureaucrat, often opposed specific elements of Kuchma's policy of economic reform. Kuchma retained him as prime minister because it would have been difficult to get any more liberal successor approved by the Communist-dominated parliament.

Masol stepped down in March 1995. He was replaced by Pavlo Lazarenko, a former state-farm boss from the Dnipropetrovs'k region of eastern Ukraine. Lazarenko served from July 1995 to July 1997, when he was replaced after a period of illness. His successor as prime minister was Valeriy Pustovoitenko, a former mayor

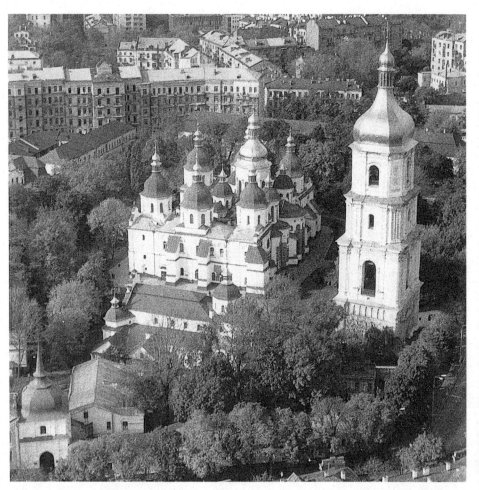

St. Sofia Cathedral, Kyiv, the city's oldest structure dating back to the times of the Kyivan Rus
Courtesy of NOVOSTI

of Dnipropetrovs'k. A leading member of President Kuchma's People's Democratic Party, Pustovoitenko was as committed to radical economic reform as President Kuchma. Confirmed as prime minister in August 1997, Pustovoitenko attempted to win support for his policies from members of parliament by involving them earlier in the process as new policies were being developed. This technique allowed him to get more new legislation approved by the legislature than his predecessors had managed to do.

One example is the election law which parliament approved in September 1997. With new parliamentary elections scheduled for March 1998, Kuchma wanted to get a new electoral law enacted establishing single member constituencies throughout country. Although the legislature rejected Kuchma's plan, the electoral law which it did approve provided for half of the seats in the 450-seat legislature to be filled by ballots cast in single-member constituencies, while the other half were to be elected by party lists.

The stakes in those elections were raised in November 1997 when the

parliament passed a resolution suspending privatization. Although the government adopted the position that privatization was already the law of the land so the parliamentary vote could not be binding, this was still a serious setback. The chief reason for the vote against privatization was that the parliament was controlled by individuals hostile to economic reform, but it is also true that the situation of the economy gave them an excuse. For example, GDP fell by 4% in 1997. This was an improvement over 1996, when the drop was 10%, but it still presented a negative picture. Moreover, the currency came under international pressure at this time and began dropping in value. The pressure on the currency was primarily a reaction to the economic collapse in Thailand, Korea, and Indonesia, but it was easy for opponents to blame it on economic reform.

The government countered with the argument that parliament's opposition was responsible for the continued fall of the currency. This argument, plus negotiations between the government and the legislature over the government's 1998 budget, persuaded the parliament to approve the budget and lift its ban on privatization in February 1998.

The results of the March 29, 1998, parliamentary elections were not encouraging, however; the Communist Party of Ukraine (CPU) and its left-wing allies increased their representation in the 450-seat parliament and now controlled a clear plurality of the seats. The CPU took 121 seats, while its left-wing allies, the Peasants/Socialists Bloc and the Progressive Socialist Party, took an additional 73 seats. Other parties in the parliament included the nationalist Rukh party (32 seats); the Greens (19 seats); the Popular Democratic Party, led by then Prime Minister Valeriy Pustovoitenko (17 seats); the Hromada party, led by former Prime Minister Pavlo Lazarenko (who in March 1999 went into exile in the United States) (16 seats); and the United Social Democrats, led by former President Leonid Kravchuk (14 seats). Independent candidates won 114 seats.

When the parliament met on May 12, however, it became clear that the Communists and their allies did not control an ideological majority in the legislature. Although only a simple majority of 226 votes was necessary for election, the Communists and their allies were only able to produce 176 votes for their candidate for the office of speaker. Meanwhile, several of the smaller political parties made a point of abstaining because they were pressing for the speaker and two deputy speakers to be elected on a single slate. That would have, of course, required some agreement in advance on the three candidates and given these parties some say in the selection. Since the left rejected this procedure, the legislature was unable to elect a speaker and so organize itself for nearly two months. The legislature finally elected Oleksandr Tkachenko, a member

of the *Peasants*/Socialists parliamentary group, as its speaker on the 19th round of voting on July 7.

Although a member of the left, Tkachenko met with President Kuchma soon after his election; after the meeting, he joined the president in calling for "constructive cooperation and concerted action." In addition, he expressed his own support for recent presidential economic decrees. There was, in fact, considerable cooperation between the president and parliament after that time, with the speaker one of those pushing for decisive action. The legislature even managed to pass the 1999 budget on December 31 after a compromise with the Communists provided more money for education and health care.

With the beginning of 1999, however, most political activity began to focus on the presidential elections which were due in the fall. Parliament passed a new law on presidential elections in January which stipulated that presidential candidates could be nominated by political parties or a group of at least 500 voters but that each candidate had to collect a million signatures from among Ukraine's 35 million eligible voters. The legislation also stipulated that a candidate needed to be positively supported by more than half of the voters who cast their ballots in order to win in the first round of voting. If nobody won in the first round, a runoff would follow. In this second round of voting, a simple majority of votes cast was required to win.

Thirteen individuals contested the October 31 vote. President Kuchma came in first with 36.36% of the vote, followed by Petro Symonenko, candidate of the Communist Party of Ukraine, with 22.32%. Symonenko won the endorsement of six of the losing candidates, including Oleksandr Moroz, the Socialist Party leader, who came

in third. He also received the endorsement of parliamentary speaker Oleksandr Tkachenko. However, Symonenko had openly acknowledged that he favored a return to Soviet-style government and intended to reverse those market reforms Kuchma had introduced. In the November 14 runoff, therefore, Kuchma won a convincing victory by obtaining 56.31% of the votes to Symonenko 37.76%.

President Kuchma took his victory as a popular mandate to speed up reform, something which would be very difficult if he continued to face a parliament controlled by the left. Kuchma therefore took his victory as a mandate for parliamentary reform. This became even more compelling when parliament rebuffed his attempt to reappoint Pustovoitenko as his prime minister. In the event, parliament did accept his second candidate, Viktor Yushchenko, confirming him by a vote of 296 to 12. Yushchenko, who was chairman of the National Bank of Ukraine at the time that he was appointed prime minister, was a pro-market reformer who argued for a reduction in government's role in the economy, massive privatization, and abolition of collective farms.

On January 15, 2000, Kuchma announced on national television that he had signed a decree to hold a nationwide referendum on April 16 involving six questions. The first was, in effect, a vote of confidence in parliament; the second would give the president the right to disband parliament if it failed to form a majority within a month or adopt a budget within three months; the third abolished legislators' immunity from criminal prosecution; the fourth and fifth reduced the size of the legislature from 450 seats to 300 seats and split it into two houses; and the sixth provided for the possibility to adopt the constitution via referendum.

A week later, the center and rightist parties organized themselves into a new parliamentary majority consisting of 242 deputies and voted to oust Oleksandr Tkachenko from the post of parliamentary speaker. However, Tkachenko, supported by the caucuses of the Communist Party, Socialist Party, Progressive Socialist Party, and Peasant Party, refused to recognize the new majority. The majority then met again on February 1 and elected Ivan Plyushch as the new parliamentary speaker. Still refusing to recognize the validity of the vote or to relinquish control, the left occupied the parliamentary building and held its own session of the leftist minority on February 3. Proclaiming all decisions of the parliamentary majority to be illegal, the leftists called on the international community for support.

Instead, a district court in Kyiv ruled on February 9 that former speaker Tkachenko

Mother Motherland statue in Kyiv memorializing the Soviet effort in World War II

Ukraine

and his supporters had taken illegal action by preventing the majority from entering the parliamentary building and by not allowing the newly elected parliamentary leadership to take its place in the parliamentary presidium. That brought an end to the confrontation, but the left, refusing to cooperate with the new parliamentary leadership, referred to the events of February 1 as a coup.

Speaker Plyushch has said that the majority was formed "to end any confrontation, assume responsibility, and follow the path the people voted for." President Kuchma referred to the election of the parliament's new leadership as a "momentous" event and promised that the government would seek cooperation with the legislature to show Ukrainians that the "six-year confrontation" in the country was over.

Meanwhile, the political left brought a challenge to President Kuchma's referendum before the constitutional court, but lost when the court ruled that the referendum could go forward. President Kuchma did later revise the terms of the referendum somewhat, dropping points one and six. Voting took place over a period of 10 days in April, with voters endorsing Kuchma's four referendum questions by margins of between 80 and 90%. In spite of this strong showing, none of the four proposed changes was ever implemented, since the amendments required a positive vote by two-thirds of the membership in parliament in order to go into effect.

In the spring of 2000, Prime Minister Yushchenko instituted a program that he described as "serious systemic reform." This included privatization of Ukraine's still largely state-owned industry plus a major campaign against corruption and inefficiency in the economy and in the government. During this period, the government managed to renegotiate its foreign debt, increase its foreign exchange reserves, and cut the annual rate of inflation to about 20% on an annual basis, still high but impressive if one recalls that the annual inflation rate five years earlier had been 377%. In addition, the economy grew by 6% in the first nine months of 2000 with industry growing at an even faster pace.

All of this progress was suddenly challenged by a political scandal that erupted on November 28 when Socialist Party leader Oleksandr Moroz accused President Kuchma and Interior Minister Yuriy Kravchenko of having organized the murder of a journalist by the name of Heorhiy Gongadze. Gongadze, editor of an independent Internet newspaper called *Ukrainskaya Pravda*, disappeared on September 16. Six weeks later, a headless corpse turned up who relatives identified as being the missing journalist. But the real bombshell came

A family folk dance group in Ukraine
Courtesy of NOVOSTI

from the fact that Moroz's "proof" was a number of tapes that, he said, had been made by a former member of the presidential security service by the name of Mykola Melnichenko. In one of the conversations on the tapes, two male voices, which Moroz identified as being President Kuchma and Interior Minister Kravchenko, discuss getting rid of Gongadze.

Moroz's revelations led to a splintering of the government's parliamentary majority and an effective end to progress on the government's reform program. The government originally denounced the tapes as fakes; after some individuals heard on the tapes verified their conversations, however, the government changed its position, arguing that the tapes were genuine but that they had been doctored. Kuchma himself has flatly denied any role in the disappearance of Gongadze.

The Ukrainian government subsequently invited FBI experts to come to Ukraine, presumably to give any assistance they could that would help solve Gongadze's murder. During the visit, which took place from April 8–15, 2002, the government arranged meetings with officials of the Prosecutor-General's Office, the Interior Ministry, and the Security Service, but refused to give the FBI experts access to the Gongadze file.

The explanation given by Ukrainian law enforcement officials was that they were unable to discuss any aspects of the case, share evidence, or conduct a joint site inspection, because "Ukrainian law prohibits sharing any information that is not in the public domain." These actions clearly

did not help to establish that the government was attempting to get at the truth of Gongadze's murder.

If the government appeared to be a little paranoid on the subject, it should be added that Gongadze's murder had become a major political issue, and those leading the attack were mainly from those parties which have opposed Kuchma and his policies all along. After the attacks began, Kuchma was forced to dismiss Interior Minister Kravchenko; next, Prime Minister Yushchenko was ousted in April 2001 after the opposition called for a vote of confidence in his government.

Yushchenko's defeat was a blow to Kuchma, since the president had called on parliament to support the prime minister prior to the vote. Essentially, the vote against Yushchenko was supported by the Communists and Socialists plus those pro-business parties that, prior to this time, had been allies of Kuchma. The fact that the pro-business parties voted against the prime minister was interpreted by many Ukrainians to mean that Kuchma wanted to get rid of Yushchenko and used this opportunity to do so. Although that is certainly a possibility, the argument is not convincing, since it was always a possibility that Yushchenko would join the political opposition if it became clear that the charge was true.

In fact, it appears that the pro-business political parties—which were really controlled by the oligarchs who emerged as a result of privatization—opposed Yushchenko because his efforts to stamp out corruption in the economic sphere had

178

begun to affect their business activities negatively. In the short run they benefited from Yushchenko's fall, since President Kuchma named Anatoliy Kinakh, leader of the Ukrainian Union of Industrialists and Entrepreneurs, as his new prime minister. Although, Kinakh promised to continue his predecessor's "market reforms and move to civil society," the government did little to move the program forward over the next year.

Instead, both the government and the opposition increasingly focused on the new parliamentary elections scheduled for March 2002. Kinakh's task here was to produce a parliamentary majority for the president. Although he ultimately failed in that endeavor, he did manage to hold the pro-Kuchma forces together and this, coupled with a lavish use of the prerogatives of the government during the campaign, allowed the pro-Kuchma forces to win a plurality of the seats in the new parliament.

There was also a fairly significant realignment of political forces during the year preceding the new parliamentary elections. It began when two prominent anti-Kuchma leaders, Yulia Tymoshenko, at that time leader of the National Salvation Forum, and Oleksandr Moroz, leader of the Socialist Party, proposed that Yushchenko join forces with them to create an anti-Kuchma electoral bloc. Instead, Yushchenko created his own Our Ukraine electoral bloc of reformers, liberals, and nationalists by bringing together Ukrainian nationalists associated with the two wings of Rukh, the Christian Republican Party, the Federation of Trade Unions, and a number of smaller liberal political parties. At the same time, Yushchenko was always careful to define his electoral bloc as an "alternative," not an opposition, to Kuchma, so as not to alienate those with whom he had worked as prime minister.

Fearful of the growing support for Yushchenko's electoral bloc and the threat this represented from the middle, President Kuchma sought to increase his own support on the left by appealing to the more Russified, urban, and industrialized populations of Eastern Ukraine. The chief competition for this vote was from the Communists—always among Kuchma's strongest opponents—whose principal platform advocated a return to the old Soviet way. The Communist program, which included a return to a socialist economy, nationalization of banks, introduction of a planned economy for state enterprises, official status for the Russian language, and a break of all relations with NATO, made Kuchma seem, by contrast, both more liberal and more western, so he was able to increase his support from among the more liberal elements in eastern Ukraine.

When the new parliamentary elections finally took place on March 31, 2002, Yushchenko's Our Ukraine bloc came in first in the popular vote with 23.52% (70 seats), followed by the Communist Party with 20.04% (59 seats). Kuchma's For a United Ukraine bloc came in third with 11.98% (36 seats). Three other political parties surpassed the 4% barrier to obtain proportional representation seats—the Yulia Tymoshenko bloc with 7.21% (21 seats), the Socialist Party with 6.93% (21 seats), and the Social Democratic Party-United, which ran a separate slate as an ally of President Kuchma, with 6.24% (18 seats).

In the races for the 225 single-mandate constituencies, however, Kuchma's better organized For a United Ukraine bloc came in first, winning an additional 66 seats. His ally, the Social Democratic Party-United, won five single constituency seats, giving it a total of 26 seats. Since President Kuchma could count on the support of at least 56 of the 93 "independents" who won individual seats, the pro-government bloc consisted of 182 seats at this point, making it the largest political force in the new parliament. The Our Ukraine bloc of former Prime Minister Yushchenko won 42 individual mandates and was, in addition, joined by five independents, putting it second with 117 seats. The Communist Party won five single mandate seats, which made it the third strongest party in the parliament with 66 seats (down from 112 seats in the previous parliament). The Yulia Tymoshenko bloc came in next with 22 seats.

With no single party or bloc in a position to organize the new parliament on its own, maneuvering began to create a coalition that would have enough votes to organize the parliament. The first move came in early May when President Kuchma appointed Viktor Medvedchuk, leader of the Social Democratic Party-United as head of the presidential administration. It was Medvedchuk who then managed to get Volodymir Lytvyn, the former head of the presidential administration, elected as parliamentary speaker later in May. But Lytvyn received only 226 votes, 1 vote more than the required minimum, and that 1 vote was cast by Mykhayko Potebenko, who had been elected to the parliament on the Communist Party ticket—an action for which he was subsequently expelled from the Communist Party. A number of other yes votes had come from political independents, however, since the nine groups forming the pro-presidential coalition claimed only 201 members.

Political maneuvering continued over the summer but things came to a head in September when the leaders of the Yulia Tymoshenko bloc, the Communist Party, and the Socialist Party called for massive

demonstrations to demand the resignation of President Kuchma.

Viktor Yushchenko, leader of Our Ukraine, was still attempting to form a majority centrist coalition at this time committed to creating a harmonious working relationship between the prime minister, the president, and the parliament and, on August 15, he had actually met with President Kuchma. As he hesitated, parts of the Our Ukraine bloc decided to participate in the planned demonstrations. Fearing the collapse of his political support, Yushchenko announced his support for the protest demonstrations and, at the last minute, joined the 20,000 demonstrators gathered in Kyiv's main square on September 16. However, Yushchenko's fence-straddling exasperated both sides and several members of his bloc later left to join the pro-presidential grouping.

It was on October 8 that Parliamentary Speaker Lytvyn announced the creation of a 231-member pro-presidential majority—consisting of Labor Ukraine-Party Entrepreneurs (42 deputies), Ukraine's Regions (37), the Social Democratic Party-United (37), Democratic Initiatives (20), Power of the People (18), European Choice (18), Popular Democratic Party (17), Ukraine's Agrarians (16), People's Choice (13), and United Ukraine (7), plus six deputies who left opposition caucuses. Three of those came from the Yulia Tymoshenko bloc, two came from the Communist Party, and one came from Our Ukraine.

Now that the pro-presidential forces were in control of parliament, President Kuchma decided that the time was ripe to change prime ministers. He therefore announced Kinakh's dismissal and in the accompanying official decree explained that he was taking this action in order to boost "cooperation" with parliament and "implement the proclaimed course of reforming the political system in the country." Kuchma's choice for the new prime minister was Donetsk Oblast Governor Viktor Yanukovych, who had close ties to the Ukraine Regions parliamentary caucus. Yanukovych was confirmed as prime minister on November 21, receiving 234 votes, 8 more than the minimum required.

During the confirmation process, Yanukovych had explained that he saw his most important task as "strengthening the positive dynamic and the tempo of economic growth. This progress must give the signal to the world that Ukraine is a country which is developing quickly and transforming into a democratic country."

Less than a month later, however, Yanukovych found himself involved in a major quarrel with the political opposition when the pro-presidential majority moved to dismiss National Bank of Ukraine Governor Volodymir Stelmakh and to

Ukraine

replace him with Serhiy Tihipko, leader of the Labor Ukraine-Party of Industrialists and Entrepreneurs parliamentary caucus.

The political opposition now threw their support behind Stelmakh and managed to defeat two attempts to replace him. Declaring that the political opposition would do everything in their power to prevent the dismissal of Stelmakh, Yushchenko declared that Stelmakh "is our last bastion, and we will not move away."

Responding to the opposition's attempts to obstruct the vote, the majority created an ad hoc commission for tabulating the vote made up solely of its own deputies. In addition, the majority held the roll call vote in the office of the permanent presidential representative to parliament rather than in the session hall itself. In a move to consolidate its control, the 229 majority deputies also voted to remove all opposition party members as chairs of parliamentary committees.

Declaring the two votes to be illegal, the four opposition parties began to block parliamentary proceedings and promised to continue to do so until the two votes were annulled. In the end, the government had the votes, however, and so got its way. It also helped that Yanukovych was willing to hold talks with the political opposition concerning President Kuchma's program of constitutional changes aimed at transforming Ukraine into a parliamentary-presidential republic.

Kuchma's proposed reforms would have transferred some presidential authority to parliament and enhanced the role of the prime minister; one important clause specified that all parliamentary seats would be allocated on a proportional basis. After a year of further debate, the legislature approved a separate bill mandating a fully proportional system of parliamentary elections in March 2004. However, the separate constitutional reform bill required a minimum of 300 votes to pass, and it received only 294.

In March, parliament passed legislation setting the presidential election for October 31, 2004. Although 24 candidates managed to qualify for the ballot, it was always understood that the race was between Prime Minister Viktor Yanukovych, leader of the pro-presidential coalition, and former Prime Minister Viktor Yushchenko, leader of the opposition coalition.

The campaign, which became rather vicious, perhaps reached its nadir on September 6 when Viktor Yushchenko disappeared, only to turn up a week later in Austria, being treated for a mysterious illness, which—three months later—was diagnosed as dioxin poisoning. Yushchenko would later make the accusation that he had been poisoned by the Ukrainian authorities, but, in fact, the Ukrainian Government

was never able to discover how he was poisoned or by whom. Nevertheless, the poison weakened him physically and caused his face to be covered by swellings; years later, photos of him show that he still bears the scars of the poisoning.

Because there were so many candidates on the ballot, the October 31 elections proved to be inconclusive, with Yushchenko and Yanukovych each winning slightly more than 39% of the votes. Since neither candidate had won anywhere close to 50% of the vote needed to avoid a runoff, a second round of voting was set for November 21.

In the period leading up to the runoff, several of the other presidential candidates threw their support to Yushchenko. Two important endorsements came from Oleksandr Moroz, leader of the Socialist Party of Ukraine, and former Prime Minister Kinakh, leader of the Party of Industrialists and Entrepreneurs.

Nevertheless, the Central Election Commission announced on November 22 that Viktor Yanukovych had won the runoff election, taking 49.42% of the vote to Yushchenko's 46.69%.

Yushchenko and the Orange Revolution

Yushchenko's supporters were particularly incensed because two separate exit polls had shown Yushchenko winning comfortably over his opponent. On November 22, a crowd estimated to be at least 100,000 gathered on Kyiv's Independence Square to protest, as they said, the government's falsification of the previous day's runoff vote. Pitching tents in the center of the city, the protesters

vowed to remain until Yushchenko was declared president. As the "Orange Revolution," as it came to be called, spread throughout the nation, city councils of various Ukrainian cities began adopting resolutions declaring Yushchenko to be the legal president. Later, the demonstrators also began a blockade of the parliament so that it was unable to meet.

Finally, roundtable talks to resolve the dispute took place in Kyiv on December 1; attending were the two contenders, President Kuchma, EU High Representative Javier Solana, OSCE Secretary-General Jan Kubis, Polish President Aleksander Kwasniewski, Lithuanian President Valdas Adamkus, and Russian State Duma Chairman Boris Gryzlov. The resulting document bound the two sides to eliminate the use of force in resolving the election crisis; unblock government offices that were being surrounded by pro-Yushchenko supporters; prepare proposals for concluding the presidential election in line with the ruling of the Supreme Court; prepare a new presidential election law, draw up a constitutional reform bill which would shift the balance of power from president to the parliament and prime minister; and work toward preventing an economic crisis in Ukraine.

On December 6, the Supreme Court invalidated a decision of the Central Election Commission certifying Yanukovych as the winner of the November 21 runoff; simultaneously, the court ruled that the second round of voting take place by December 26. Two days later, the parliament adopted a constitutional reform bill conforming to the December 1 roundtable guidelines plus amendments to the presidential

Ex-President Yushchenko, before and after his dioxin poisoning

180

Former Prime Minister Yulia Tymoshenko, now leader of the opposition. Sentenced to seven years in prison in 2012, she was released in February 2014

election law aimed at eliminating election abuse and fraud; passed by an overwhelming vote of 402–21, the legislation was signed into law by President Kuchma that evening.

That same day, the parliament dissolved the old Central Election Commission and then appointed a new Central Election Commission, which was sworn in immediately. The next day, President Kuchma sent Prime Minister Yanukovych on leave to campaign for the presidential runoff election, set for December 26.

That election was won convincingly by Viktor Yushchenko, who got 51.99% of the vote to Yanukovych's 44.19%. Reflecting the political geographic divide, Yushchenko won in 19 western and central oblasts and Kyiv, while Yanukovych won in nine eastern and southern oblasts and Sevastopol.

Yushchenko was sworn in as president on January 23, 2005; one day later, he appointed Yulia Tymoshenko as his prime minister. Tymoshenko, a recent political ally of Yushchenko, had served as energy minister when Yushchenko was prime minister. She was confirmed by parliament on February 4. The 373 votes to confirm constituted a strong vote of support for the new government's policies.

The new government passed a budget law in March 2005 which eliminated most tax and customs privileges, which had the effect of bringing more economic activity out of Ukraine's large shadow economy. But a 50% increase in crude oil prices during the first three months of 2005 caused gasoline prices to begin to rise in early April; and as the price of gasoline rose, confidence in the government fell.

Prime Minister Tymoshenko, who publicly charged that the fuel price increase was a "plot" by Russian oil traders—who controlled 75% of fuel supplies to Ukraine—to destabilize the government, attempted to deal with the fuel crisis using administrative and non-market levers. In mid-April, she ordered prices for gasoline to be stabilized at a level below 3 hryvnyas a liter. Simultaneously, the economics ministry informed Russian oil traders that the government would not guarantee their property rights for Ukraine's refineries unless they agreed to cut fuel prices.

The Russian traders did cut fuel prices—but Russian-owned oil refineries in Ukraine reacted by either significantly decreasing their daily output or halting it altogether because of "planned repairs." As a result, long lines began to appear at gasoline stations. President Yushchenko then accused Prime Minister Tymoshenko of incompetence in dealing with the fuel crisis and went on to suggest that she might consider resigning. Instead, the differences between president and prime minister were papered over after Tymoshenko agreed to try a more market—oriented solution. Parliament then abolished import

duties on fuel in May, which temporarily resolved the fuel crisis.

However, a larger policy difference soon arose between the president and prime minister concerning how to investigate alleged corruption in past privatizations of state industries. Tymoshenko, arguing the corruptness of the entire system of privatizations under Kuchma, wanted thousands of companies to be investigated and renationalized; Yushchenko, arguing for the need to build a market-oriented system that would encourage international investment, wanted a much narrower examination of past privatizations.

Ultimately the battle centered on two past privatizations, the Nikopol Ferroalloy Plant and the formerly bankrupt Severodonetsk Azot. A consortium controlled by Viktor Pinchuk, son-in-law to President Kuchma, acquired a controlling interest in the Nikopol Ferroalloy Plant in 2003; Worldwide Chemical, a subsidiary of New York-based IBE Trade, obtained 60% of the shares of Severodonetsk Azot in return for a promise to invest $180 million in the new company.

In August, the Kyiv appellate court nullified the Pinchuk consortium's 50% plus one share stake in the Nikopol Ferroalloy Plant and returned it to the state. A week later, the private industrial group Privat, which is allegedly supported by Prime Minister Tymoshenko, attempted a takeover of the company. President Yushchenko had no problem with the court's nullification of the Pinchuk consortium's stake in the Nikopol Ferroalloy Plant; however, he did intervene at this point, ordering the government to "resolve the conflict according to the law" and get the plant back into operation.

A lawsuit challenging the Severodonetsk Azot privatization was filed in a district court in Kyiv in March 2005. The court ruled against the privatization without permitting either the new investors or the state to testify. In August, the minister of industrial policy signed an order returning control of Severodonetsk Azot to the state. Armed with this order, dozens of men dressed in camouflage and body armor stormed and seized the headquarters of the company on September 2. According to a senior government official, "the order was based on a court case filed by a fictitious company, on behalf of a politician who stood to gain from the seizure."

On September 6, President Yushchenko ordered that Severodonetsk Azot be returned to its new investors until the matter was resolved in court. President Yushchenko's interventions in the two cases set off a whole series of charges and countercharges that led to several high-level resignations and, on September 8, to President Yushchenko's dismissal of Prime Minister

Ukraine

Tymoshenko and her cabinet. At the same time, the president accepted the resignation of Petro Poroshenko, his national security and defense council secretary.

Tymoshenko's successor as prime minister was Yuriy Yekhanurov (yeh-kay-NOOR-awf). Yekhanurov served as head of the state property fund between 1994 and 1997, in that position overseeing the initial stage of Ukraine's privatization. Elected to parliament in 2002 as a member of Yushchenko's Our Ukraine bloc, Yekhanurov was appointed governor of Dnipropetrovs'k Oblast in April 2005.

Yekhanurov was confirmed as prime minister on September 22, after President Yushchenko signed a memorandum of understanding with Party of Regions leader Viktor Yanukovych.

However, the government had been declining in popularity even before Tymoshenko's dismissal and this only accelerated afterward. A public opinion poll taken just before the first anniversary of the beginning of the Orange Revolution showed that more than half of all Ukrainians felt the new government had failed to keep the promises made a year earlier. The poll also indicated that only one in seven Ukrainians fully supported President Yushchenko.

Matters got even worse in December as gas prices continued to rise, especially after Gazprom announced that the price of natural gas sold to Ukraine would go from $50 per 1,000 cubic meters to $220–230 per 1,000 cubic meters. After Ukraine rejected Gazprom's demand for a price hike, Gazprom cut off gas supplies to Ukraine as of January 1, 2006.

Since Russian gas exports to Western Europe go by way of the Ukrainian pipeline, however, a half dozen Western European countries quickly complained of sharp drops in the gas they were receiving; Gazprom restored gas to the Ukrainian pipeline on January 2. The following day, Ukraine and Gazprom announced a face-saving compromise. Gazprom would set up a new trading company, RosUkr Energo, as a Swiss-based joint venture of Gazprom and Austria's Raiffeisen Zentralbank. RosUkrEnergo would purchase natural gas from Gazprom for $230 per 1,000 cubic meters and mix it with cheaper gas from Central Asia. The end result is that Ukraine would pay $95 per 1,000 cubic meters of natural gas.

From the beginning, the political opposition—led by Yulia Tymoshenko—condemned the gas deal and there were calls for the president's impeachment and the prime minister's resignation. On January 10, parliament actually voted to dismiss Prime Minister Yekhanurov, though President Yushchenko refused to recognize the vote as legal.

A Kyiv newspaper (June 9, 1995) reports on Presidents Kuchma and Yeltsin signing the treaty which permits the Russian Black Sea fleet to berth at Sevastopol on the Crimean Peninsula

This was the background to the March 29 parliamentary elections, the first in independent Ukraine to be contested under a fully proportional, party-list system. Under this system, voters no longer got to vote for individual representatives; instead, they chose between political parties. Voters determined the number of representatives awarded to each party; each party's leadership chose the candidates and determined their placement on the candidate list. Only parties that obtained at least 3% of the national vote received representation in parliament. In addition, members of the new parliament would serve for five years, one year more than previously. Lastly, the constitutional changes adopted in December 2004 reduced the powers of the presidency and increased the powers of the prime minister and parliament.

Four electoral blocs won seats in the new parliament. The Party of Regions, led by Viktor Yanukovych, came in first with 32.14% of the vote (186 seats). The Yulia Tymoshenko bloc (BYuT) came in second with 22.29% of the vote (129 seats). Our Ukraine came third with 13.95% of the vote (81 seats). The Socialist Party came fourth with 5.69% of the vote (33 seats, followed by the Communist Party with 3.66% of the vote (21 seats).

In mid-April the three parties of the Orange Coalition signed a protocol pledging to work toward creating a parliamentary majority. When the new parliament convened on May 25, however, the country remained in a state of political stalemate.

The chief stumbling block in the coalition talks was the question of who would become prime minister. Yulia Tymoshenko insisted that she was entitled to become prime minister again.

After three months of negotiation, an agreement by the three parties of the Orange Coalition was signed on June 22. Tymoshenko was to become prime minister, while Our Ukraine was given the right to name the parliamentary speaker and deputy prime minister. But Oleksandr Moroz, leader of the Socialist Party, felt that he was entitled to the office of parliamentary speaker so, when the Communists and the Party of Regions agreed to support him for that position, he abandoned the newly reconstituted Orange Coalition and signed a new "anti-crisis" agreement with the Communists and the Party of Regions. Those three parties then elected Moroz to the office of parliamentary speaker. The same coalition then went on to nominate Viktor Yanukovych, leader of the Party of Regions, as prime minister.

Political Coexistence: Yushchenko and Yanukovych

Ukraine's experiment in political coexistence had a rather acrimonious beginning with Yulia Tymoshenko calling for the two remaining parties of the Orange Coalition to give up their seats in order to force new elections. President Yushchenko's party, Our Ukraine, announced, however, that it accepted the legitimacy of the "anti-crisis" coalition and would go into the opposition.

Although President Yushchenko waited the constitutionally permitted 15 days before he announced that he would formally propose Yanukovych as prime minister, Yanukovych easily won confirmation as prime minister, receiving the positive votes of 271 of the 296 deputies that were present. What that vote masked, however, is that the Verkhovna Rada has 450 members and 154 deputies belonging to the Yulia Tymoshenko bloc and Our Ukraine boycotted the meeting. In the end, Yanukovych won with the support of the Party of Regions, the Socialists, and the Communists; only 30 Our Ukraine bloc deputies and six deputies from the Yulia Tymoshenko bloc voted for the new prime minister.

Thus, although President Yushchenko signed a declaration of national unity with the "anti-crisis" coalition and nominated five members of the Our Ukraine bloc for seats in the cabinet, the majority of the Our Ukraine bloc considered themselves to be in the opposition.

Discussions went on for another two months on whether the Our Ukraine bloc would formally join the government coalition; in September, however, one of the members of the Our Ukraine bloc, the Reforms and Order Party, announced that it was switching alliances and going into the opposition. This was the beginning of a split that eventually led most of the deputies belonging to the Our Ukraine bloc to reject an alliance with the governing coalition and formally join the opposition. Coalition talks ended on October 19 when the five Our Ukraine deputies in the Yanukovych cabinet tendered their resignations. One of the five, Interior Minister Yuriy Lutsenko, later withdrew his resignation and remained in the cabinet; he later resigned his membership in the Our Ukraine bloc.

The formal withdrawal of Our Ukraine exacerbated problems in relations that already existed between the president and prime minister. According to the constitution, two of the members of the cabinet, the defense and foreign ministers, are appointed by the president; in November, Prime Minister Yanukovych called on the president to dismiss them, saying:

How can I react to a minister who says he is in opposition to the government? What does this mean? This means he disagrees with the program the government is fulfilling. If you are a man, if you have principles, resign.

When the president took no action, the Verkhovna Rada voted to dismiss Foreign Minister Borys Tarasyuk on December 1. Shortly thereafter, the Verkhovna Rada voted to dismiss Interior Minister Lutsenko as well. The Verkhovna Rada then voted to install Vasyl Tsushko, head of the Socialist Party parliamentary caucus, as interior minister.

President Yushchenko refused to accept Tarasyuk's dismissal and appealed to the Constitutional Court, but Tarasyuk, a career diplomat, submitted his own resignation on January 30, saying that he refused to allow the foreign ministry to become hostage to unlawful actions of the government. The Verkhovna Rada then twice rejected President Yushchenko's next candidate for foreign minister, Volodymir Ohryzko, another career diplomatic official. After the second rejection, Our Ukraine and the Yulia Tymoshenko bloc walked out of the parliamentary session and announced that they would return only after the ruling coalition complied with demands their representatives had signed in President Yushchenko's presence the previous day.

Prime Minister Yanukovych then requested that the president propose a new candidate for the post of foreign minister. President Yushchenko nominated Arseniy Yatsenyuk, and he was confirmed as foreign minister on March 21. Members of Our Ukraine and the Yulia Tymoshenko bloc attended the session and cast their votes for Yatsenyuk, but they left the session hall immediately after the vote.

But by now the political opposition had begun to crumble. That same day, Anatoliy Kinakh, leader of the Party of Industrialists and Entrepreneurs, whose party was part of the United Ukraine bloc, joined the government as economy minister. The next day, it was announced that five deputies from the Yulia Tymoshenko bloc and six deputies from Kinakh's party had changed sides and joined the ruling coalition, which then renamed itself the national-unity coalition.

President Yushchenko believed that the government had acted unconstitutionally when it accepted individual opposition deputies into its ruling majority; according to the constitution, a government is put together by enlisting party factions, not individual members. On the other hand, the constitution gives the president only four circumstances when he may dissolve parliament and call for new elections and none of those circumstances appeared to apply to this situation.

President Yushchenko therefore met with Yanukovych in an attempt to get him to adhere to constitutional procedure; when he was rebuffed, he ordered the dissolution of parliament, accusing Prime Minister Yanukovych of usurping power. Mr. Yanukovych's supporters replied by calling an emergency session of parliament and passing a resolution declaring President Yushchenko's decree unconstitutional. Both sides then appealed to the Constitutional Court to resolve the matter, thus thrusting the Constitutional Court into the middle of the ongoing political battle.

One of the first acts of the Yanukovych government—carried out on August 4, 2006—had been to reconstitute the Constitutional Court, which had been inoperative since the preceding November when the terms of nine of the judges had come to an end. As prescribed by the constitution, the Verkhovna Rada had elected five judges, who then joined eight others already on the court. Five of the incumbents had been elected earlier by the Congress of Judges, while three other members had been named to the court by President Yushchenko in November 2005. Five judges were added later, bringing the court to its full complement of 18.

The newly reconstituted Constitutional Court soon came under attack from both sides; on April 10, five Constitutional Court judges asked the state to provide them with bodyguard services because of pressure being exerted on them.

More seriously, the Security Service announced on April 16 that it was investigating Syuzanna Stanik, the deputy head of the Constitutional Court, on a charge of possible corruption. She was charged after the Security Service had established that $12 million in property had been transferred to an unemployed close relative of Judge Stanik. Volodymir Lytvyn, former Verkhovna Rada speaker, probably summed up the public reaction when he said on April 20 that "I think we all acknowledge that the Constitutional Court does not exist in Ukraine. People are frankly saying [about the Constitutional Court]: You are all scoundrels."

US and Ukrainian officers in front of bomber earmarked for dismantling

Ukraine

On May 2, President Yushchenko dismissed Judge Stanik and a second judge, Valeriy Pshenichnyy. Yushchenko then appointed Vasyl Kostytskyy and Stepan Havrysh to replace the two dismissed justices. Judge Pshenichnyy refused to accept his dismissal, however, and he was reinstated on the court after a district judge in Donetsk suspended the president's decree dismissing him and Judge Stanik. Two weeks later, Ivan Dombrovskyy, the head of the Constitutional Court, resigned and his duties were entrusted to Judge Pshenichnyy. Constitutional Court Judge Dmytro Lylak then tendered his resignation on May 21. Three days later, the Verkhovna Rada dismissed Constitutional Court Judge Petro Stetsyuk. The next day, Judge Pshenichnyy announced that he had been able to assemble only 10 judges of the 18-judge panel; 12 judges are necessary for legally binding rulings. "The court has been paralyzed and demoralized," President Yushchenko announced on May 23;

I am forced to admit that the Constitutional Court is losing its constitutional legitimacy and, under the existing circumstances, cannot perform its function of ensuring the supremacy of the Basic Law in the country.

When it became clear that the Constitutional Court would be unable to resolve the constitutional situation, Yushchenko and Yanukovych attempted to resolve their differences in a series of meetings that also included Parliamentary Speaker Oleksandr Moroz. On May 27, the three announced that they had reached a deal on holding early parliamentary elections on September 30, 2007. President Yushchenko also agreed to suspend his decrees dissolving parliament so it could legally meet to adopt the necessary legislation.

The Orange Coalition Is Reborn

The September 30 parliamentary elections were essentially a rerun of the 2006 elections with the important difference that the Socialist Party failed to overcome the minimum of 3% of the national vote and so failed to enter parliament. As in the previous election, all seats were allocated on the basis of proportional representation.

The Party of Regions again came in first with 175 seats (34.37%), followed by the Yulia Tymoshenko bloc (BYuT) with 156 seats (30.71%). The slightly renamed Our Ukraine-People's Self-Defense Bloc (NUNS) got 72 seats (14.15%), followed by the Communist Party with 27 seats (5.39%), and the Lytvyn bloc with 20 seats (3.96%).

The two parties of the old Orange Coalition—the BYuT bloc and the NUNS bloc—together controlled 228 seats, which gave them just two more mandates than

Prime Minister Tymoshenko and her party faction hear the news of President Yushchenko's October 8 decree dissolving parliament. The dissolution decree was later withdrawn

the minimum number of votes needed to pass legislation. Worried about the dangers of such a small majority, President Yushchenko proposed that the five parties constituting the new parliament hold political talks with the aim of producing a government which could unite the country. However, Yulia Tymoshenko rejected any coalition with the Party of Regions, so the talks were stillborn. A larger coalition government having been ruled out, the two political factions of the old Orange Coalition decided to reconstitute their Coalition on the basis of their two-vote majority; an accord to this effect was signed on October 15.

The new parliament met for the first time on November 23. However, the BYuT bloc and the NUNS bloc were unable to create their planned parliamentary coalition because six NUNS bloc members refused to vote for the coalition agreement. President Yushchenko had to intervene to bring the NUNS bloc members into line; he then nominated Yulia Tymoshenko as prime minister on December 6. When the vote for confirmation came on December 11, however, Tymoshenko got only 225 votes, one shy of confirmation. Tymoshenko was finally confirmed as prime minister on December 18 by 226 votes, the exact number needed for her approval as prime minister.

Parliament remained deadlocked because of a disagreement among the parties over Ukraine's eventual membership in NATO, however. The government coalition favored a commitment to eventual NATO membership but the opposition, led by the Party of Regions, insisted that any decision about NATO membership be made on the basis of a popular referendum. Parliament essentially endorsed this position in March, with a number of BYuT

bloc members joining with the opposition to pass the legislation.

Parliament did manage to approve membership in the World Trade Organization. Ukraine was accepted as a member of the WTO in February 2008. The country will have a five-year transitional period to adjust to WTO regulations.

In April 2008, a new quarrel broke out between the president and the prime minister when Prime Minister Tymoshenko announced that her bloc wanted to amend the Ukrainian constitution in order to "balance the branches of powers" in the country. A week later, Prime Minister Tymoshenko, in Strasbourg for a session of the Parliamentary Assembly of the Council of Europe, told reporters that "we must untangle the functions of the executive and make Ukraine a traditional parliamentary republic."

At about the same time, the Yulia Tymoshenko bloc attacked the president for "blocking" the work of the coalition government. Prime Minister Tymoshenko joined the attack on April 21, accusing the president of blocking "by decree" around 20 government initiatives aimed at boosting transparency and fighting corruption. Tymoshenko was apparently referring to a presidential decree issued earlier in the month to cancel the sale of four regional electricity producers, claiming that the sale of key state-owned enterprises was unconstitutional. Tymoshenko subsequently tried on two occasions to remove the head of the State Property Fund, only to be blocked by a presidential decree. Tymoshenko also called for removal of the Prosecutor-General and the head of the Presidential Secretariat.

The struggle between the two leaders of the Orange Coalition took a new turn on May 13 when legislators loyal to Prime

Minister Tymoshenko physically blocked the speaker's chair when President Yushchenko came to parliament to give his state-of-the-nation address, forcing the president to cancel his address. Members of the Yulia Tymoshenko bloc were angry at Yushchenko for opposing the prime minister's program for dealing with an inflation then running at 30%. Tymoshenko, a populist, had greatly increased spending on social benefits; Yushchenko argued for a balanced budget and some reorientation of spending from social benefits to infrastructure. With the economy growing at a 5.6% rate, Tymoshenko opposed any cut in social benefits.

The Russian invasion of Georgia in August revealed new differences between the president and prime minister. Yushchenko was staunch in his support for Georgia and he even traveled to Georgia in a show of solidarity with President Mikheil Saakashvili. Tymoshenko, on the other hand, remained notably silent during the Russian-Georgian conflict.

But the difference that led to a temporary suspension in the coalition came on September 3, when Prime Minister Tymoshenko joined forces with the Party of Regions, the Lytvyn bloc, and the Communist Party to pass legislation expanding the powers of the cabinet of ministers at the expense of the office of the presidency. Calling the vote a "political and constitutional coup d'état," Yushchenko withdrew the support of the Our Ukraine-People's Self-Defense bloc from the coalition government. The formal collapse of the government came on September 16. That gave Tymoshenko 30 days to find one or more alternate coalition partners that would create a new majority or face new elections. In fact, President Yushchenko formally dissolved parliament on October 9 and called for new elections on December 7.

But it was not to be. Ukraine's economy, which had been growing so vigorously over the summer, suddenly went into sharp decline as the worldwide economic decline brought a sharp withdrawal of investment from Ukraine, and Ukraine's largest foreign currency earner, steel exports, plummeted as construction projects ground to a halt around the world. Cut off from foreign credit, Ukrainian banks came under pressure as depositors withdrew billions in anticipation of possible bank failures.

The Government of Ukraine then turned to the International Monetary Fund for assistance. The IMF offered to make $16.5 billion available to the Ukrainian Government, but only in return for assurances from the cabinet that the 2009 budget would be balanced. But Ukraine had no government to give such an assurance. Finally, on October 29, Yushchenko

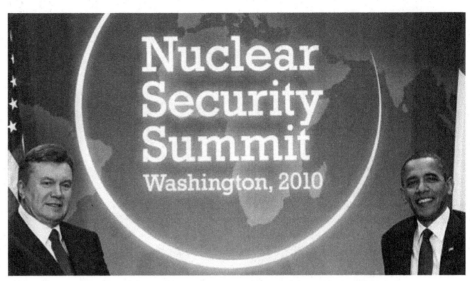

Then President Yanukovych visits Washington, April 2010

and Tymoshenko put aside their differences and cobbled together new legislation that met the IMF's requirements. The legislation cut welfare spending, placed a freeze on the minimum wage, and introduced measures intended to strengthen Ukraine's banks.

Two months later, Ukraine was hit by another crisis as Gazprom, Russia's natural gas monopoly, cut off all shipments of natural gas to the country, charging that Ukraine owed more than $600 million for past deliveries of natural gas. Gazprom also indicated that it intended to charge the market price for future deliveries of natural gas to Ukraine, which it said might be as much as $450 per 1,000 cubic meters. Gazprom continued to ship natural gas to Europe via Ukraine but, a week later, Prime Minister Putin ordered Gazprom to cut off all gas to the Ukrainian pipeline, thereby cutting off all shipments of gas to Europe via Ukraine.

The impasse lasted 18 days; it was resolved during direct negotiations between Prime Ministers Putin and Tymoshenko. Under the terms of the agreement, Ukraine would receive gas during 2009 at a price pegged to the price of oil, which, in essence, meant that Ukraine would be paying approximately $235 per 1,000 cubic meters of gas, up from $179.50 in 2008.

The two-week interruption in the supply of gas was a further blow to the Ukrainian economy, but the continuing contraction of the world economy probably had a greater effect. The steel, coal, and chemical industries, the mainstays of Ukraine's economy, were all badly hurt as export sales plummeted. Unemployment grew domestically as these industries shed workers, even as thousands of migrant workers were returning to Ukraine, having lost their jobs abroad. By March 2009, industrial production was

34% below what it had been in January 2008. As Anders Aslund, a senior fellow at the Peterson Institute for International Economic in Washington, wrote, "No other country has been as hard hit as Ukraine."

In early March, therefore, the Ukrainian legislature passed new legislation cutting the salaries of all the top governmental officials by half with the support of 374 of the 423 deputies. They also cut other prerogatives of government officials such as free public transportation, free use of state sanatoriums and free housing.

Even as the Ukrainian Government pushed through these changes in an attempt to respond to the worsening economic situation, the president and prime minister continued to have difficulty working with each other. In May, Prime Minister Tymoshenko again sought to replace the government coalition based on the BYuT and the NUNS bloc with a new government coalition allying the BYuT with Viktor Yanukovych's Party of Regions. As part of the coalition agreement, Tymoshenko proposed a series of constitutional changes aimed at further diminishing the power of the president while essentially turning Ukraine into a full parliamentary system. Among the proposed changes was that the president be elected by parliament rather than by popular vote. The attempt to form a new coalition failed partly because of the mistrust between the two political groupings but, also, because Viktor Yanukovych eventually decided that he preferred a popularly elected presidency.

Yushchenko, Tymoshenko, and Yanukovych were all candidates when new presidential elections took place on January 17, 2010. No candidate won enough votes to avoid a runoff election, but Viktor Yanukovych came in first with

Ukraine

35% of the vote; Yulia Tymoshenko came in second with 25% of the vote. Yushchenko got just over 5% of the vote. In the run-off election that took place on February 7, Yanukovych's margin of victory over Tymoshenko was about 3.5 percentage points; because 4.36% of he voters backed neither candidate, however, Yanukovych won only 48.95% of the popular vote.

The President Yanukovych Era

Yanukovych was inaugurated as president on February 25. At that time, Tymoshenko was still prime minister. Two weeks later, however, Tymoshenko's government collapsed when the Our Ukraine faction and the party led by Volodymir Lytvyn, speaker of the parliament, pulled out of the coalition. On March 11, a new coalition came into being consisting of the Party of Regions, the Lytvyn party, plus individual members of other parliamentary parties. To ease the process, the Party of Regions persuaded parliament to pass a law allowing individual lawmakers to break away from their parliamentary factions. And as part of the deal, Volodymir Lytvyn was reelected speaker of the parliament.

The new prime minister was Mykola Azarov, who for the past eight years had been Yanukovych's right-hand man in the Party of Regions. Born in the Russian city of Kaluga in 1947, Azarov graduated from Moscow State University with a degree in geology studies. He moved to Donetsk in 1984 to take up a position as deputy director of the Ukrainian State Geological Institute. He was first elected to the Ukrainian parliament in 1994. He actually helped form the Party of Regions, and was its first leader but, in 2002, stepped aside for Yanukovych, who became leader of the party and prime minister. An ethnic Russian, Azarov speaks almost no Ukrainian.

Elected democratically in elections recognized as fair by international observers, Yanukovych later appointed prosecutors to carry out investigations of opposition political leaders, including Yulia Tymoshenko, leader of the opposition—who subsequently was put on trial and given a seven-year prison sentence. As Clifford J. Levy wrote in a February 10, 2011, article in the *Washington Post*, "Ms Tymoshenko has been repeatedly interrogated by prosecutors who said they were examining official corruption during her tenure as prime minister." In fact, the "crime" she was charged with was negotiating the January 2009 natural gas agreement with Russian State-owned Gazprom that ended a 17-day standoff between Ukraine and Russia. Yulia Tymoshenko's trial and subsequent imprisonment may have removed a political opponent from the political stage, but Yanukovych

Ex-Prime Minister Mykola Azarov

has had to pay a political price as well. Domestically, Yanukovych's treatment of Tymoshenko united nearly all of the other political factions against him; internationally, the European Union said that Tymoshenko's seven-year sentence could have "profound implications" for relations. The European Union subsequently put a planned political association and free trade agreement with Ukraine on hold. In May 2012, a number of leaders of EU member countries let it be known that they would not be attending the Euro 2012 championship matches which were co-hosted by Ukraine and Poland.

The US State Department also condemned the Tymoshenko trial and conviction, and expressed its "serious concern about the government of Ukraine's commitment to democracy and the rule of law."

There were also reports of curtailed press freedom under the present regime. In August 2010, the International Press Institute wrote to President Yanukovych to "express its concern at the significant deterioration" in press freedom. In September 2010, William Burns, US Undersecretary of State for Political Affairs, told reporters in Kyiv that there are "grounds for concern" about freedom of press in Ukraine. And in August 2010, Chancellor Angela Merkel told President Yanukovych during his visit to Berlin that "in the area of press freedom and freedom of opinion, we had certain questions." A February 23, 2011, editorial in the *Washington Post*, titled "Slipping in Ukraine: How a democratic revolution can be reversed," accused Yanukovych of leading the retreat from democracy through his government's attacks on the free media and opposition political leaders. Its conclusion was that "the United States should be pressing harder to stop the democratic erosion."

New parliamentary elections were held on October 28, 2012. President Yanukovych's Party of Regions took 185 of the 450 seats. The All-Ukrainian Union "Fatherland" bloc—the core of which is the old Yulia Timoshenko Party—came in second with 101 seats. The Ukrainian Democratic Alliance for Reforms (UDAR) came in third with 40 seats. The Communist Party of Ukraine (CPU) was next with 32 seats. One further party, Svoboda (Freedom), won more than 5% of the proportional vote and ended up with 37 seats. In addition, 43 independents won individual constituency seats, while an additional 7 seats were won by small parties which had won no proportional seats. Five seats remained unfilled.

The Party of Regions managed to cobble together a legislative majority by adding the votes of the CPU plus those of a number of independents. International observers were highly critical of the 2012 parliamentary elections, however. US Secretary of State Hillary Clinton characterized the election as "a step backwards" and urged the Ukrainian Government to stop "the backward slide." Walburga Habsburg Douglas, head of the OSCE monitors, after criticizing the absence of Yulia Tymoshenko from the ballot, added:

Considering the abuse of power, and the excessive role of money in the election, democratic progress appears to have reversed in Ukraine.

The year 2013 marked the 1,025th anniversary of the adoption of Christianity by Prince Vladimir, ruler of Kyivan Rus, and the date was marked by celebrations to which President Putin was invited as an honored guest. Yet all was not well between the two nations. The issue was Ukraine's negotiations with the European Union for a Partnership Agreement which included a free trade agreement between Ukraine and the European Union.

Over the summer, the Russian government became alarmed because it had been putting great pressure on Ukraine to join the Russian-sponsored Eurasian Customs Union signed by Russia, Belarus, and Kazakhstan in 2010. When it became clear that President Yanukovych had actually initialed the proposed EU Agreement, the Russian government began to put economic pressure on the Ukrainian Government to change its mind. On July 29, Russia's chief health inspector, Gennady Onishchenko, announced a ban on imports of chocolates and other sweets from the Ukrainian confectioner Roshen. Three weeks later, Russian inspectors at the Ukrainian border began demanding that all trucks be completely unloaded and inspected item by item. They also began seizing and questioning the authenticity of documentation. All of this was part of a pattern of Russian pressure against Ukraine to persuade the Ukrainian Government to drop its application for an Association Agreement with the EU and join the Eurasian Customs Union instead.

There were complications, however. By all the evidence, most Ukrainian business leaders favored the EU Association Agreement and most of the Ukrainian people were leaning the same way. On the other hand, European leaders had made it clear that President Yanukovych would have to free Yulia Tymoshenko from prison before an Association Agreement could be signed. Moreover, the Ukrainian economy was teetering on the edge of bankruptcy and needed outside assistance, either from Russia or the IMF.

By November, President Yanukovych had not yet made up his mind and Tymoshenko was still in prison, though he had freed Yuriy Lutsenko, interior minister in Tymoshenko's government. On November 13, Prime Minister Mykola Azarov told his cabinet that "normalizing relations with Russia" was the nation's top priority. President Yanukovych then went to Moscow to meet with President Putin and here he announced that Ukraine would drop its application to sign an Association Agreement with the EU. Russia would, he said, lend Ukraine $15 billion and reduce the price of natural gas being furnished by Gazprom by 20%. There was also a report that President Putin had threatened to retaliate with severe trade sanctions if Ukraine signed an Association Agreement with the EU.

President Yanukovych did not say that Ukraine would be joining the Eurasian Customs Union, but most Ukrainians understood that that would be the likely result of his decision. His announcement therefore set off a series of demonstrations in Kyiv's central square that would continue until the following February and, in the end, result in Yanukovych's fleeing the country after he had been repudiated by his own Party of Regions and had much of his power taken away from him by a vote of the national legislature.

Yanukovych fled Kyiv on the evening of February 21, making his way to Donetsk in eastern Ukraine, accompanied by a small entourage. From Donetsk, he traveled to the Crimean Peninsula, where the Russian Fleet is located. Again finding no support, he disappeared, only to appear days later in western Russia.

The Ukrainian Crisis, 2013–2015: Revolution, Loss of Crimea, and War

Russian President Putin's desire to prevent Ukraine from joining the European Union (EU) and instead to draw it into his proposed, rival Eurasian Economic Union (EEU) helped spark the unrest that led to revolution in Kyiv. In the EEU, Putin wanted to create a Russian-dominated unified economic space in which goods, capital, services, and people could move freely throughout the member nations. Ukrainian President Yanukovych, who derived his support mainly from the large groups of ethnic Russians who resided in the country's eastern regions, tried to walk a fine line between Russia and the EU. Yanukovych expressed interest in joining a Russian-led customs union, which was weaker than the planned EEU, while simultaneously pursuing membership in the European Union (EU). In November 2013, he backed out of an Association Agreement, which would have set Ukraine on the path toward eventual EU membership. Shortly afterward, the Russian government offered to purchase $15 billion in Ukrainian bonds and cut significantly the price of natural gas that Ukraine bought from Russia. The Russian government likely also threatened Ukraine in the event that Yanukovych signed the agreement with the EU. Yanukovych contended that he was under extreme pressure: "We have big difficulties with Moscow. I have been alone for three-and-a-half years in very unequal conditions with Russia." On November 21, in reaction to the president's flip-flop, opposition politician Arseniy Yatsenyuk issued an appeal on Twitter to organize a protest rally in the heart of Kyiv. Thousands responded, and the protest movement grew in size during the ensuing winter.

In late January the opposition movement swelled to about 200,000 people in reaction to new government laws that severely limited freedom of speech and the right of assembly. Clashes between the protestors and Berkut riot police resulted in the first deaths. The precise chain of events that prompted Yanukovych to flee Kyiv the following month and wind up in Russia is not entirely clear. What is known is that during February 18–20, about 70 people, including at least 10 police, were killed and over 1,000 injured in armed clashes. The fact that police were among the victims indicates that they were not the only ones resorting to violence.

In an attempt to quell the unrest, Yanukovych met with Yatsenyuk, two other Ukrainian opposition politicians, the foreign ministers of Poland, Germany, and France, and a special envoy from Russia. On February 21, all except the Russian envoy signed a compromise settlement. The agreement called for: creation of a national unity government; early presidential elections (to be held no later than December 2014); constitutional reform that would curtail the powers of the president; an investigation conducted by the authorities, the political opposition, and the Council of Europe into the recent acts of violence; a promise that the authorities would not introduce a state of emergency; and a pledge that the authorities and opposition would refrain from the use of violence. The agreement offered a glimmer of hope for peaceful resolution to the crisis; however, within hours of signing the document, Yanukovych on February 22 fled to eastern Ukraine and then sought sanctuary in Russia. He claimed that his life was in danger in Kyiv but that he was still the legitimate president of Ukraine.

Why did Yanukovych flee Kyiv? On January 4, 2015, Andrew Higgins and Andrew Kramer of the *New York Times* published the results of a detailed investigation into this question. Based on extensive interviews with key players and examination of phone records and other documents, they concluded that the president fled after members of the Ukrainian parliament and the security forces deserted him. On February 20, 2014, Ukraine's Acting Interior Minister Vitaliy Zakharchenko allowed troops to fire on demonstrators, and over 50 people were killed. Then, according to Higgins and Kramer, the parliament late on February 20 ordered all security troops to return to their barracks. This decision showed that the president had lost the confidence of his former loyal supporters in the legislature. In addition, the commanders of the Berkut riot police suspected that the international investigation into the recent violence, which was mandated by the compromise settlement, would put the blame on the police. The police were also reportedly terrified by rumors that hundreds of guns had been seized in the western city of Lviv, which was a center of ardent Ukrainian nationalism and pro-European sentiment near the Polish border, and that those

Golden Gate of Kyiv, once part of the fortifications of medieval Kyiv

Ukraine

firearms were on their way to Kyiv to add to the weaponry that some protestors had already accumulated. Security forces in Kyiv then packed up and left Kyiv for eastern Ukraine leaving the presidential administration building and the president's palatial estate unguarded. When Yanukovych learned that his protection force had melted away, he too panicked, fled, and refused to return.

Another question that is crucial to understanding the Ukrainian Revolution of 2014 is: Who were the demonstrators and what were their motives? Without question, the large majority of protestors on the Independence Square (*Maidan*) in Kyiv were ordinary Ukrainians from all walks of life and of all ages who demonstrated peacefully and patiently over several months in favor of closer ties to Europe and a stronger democracy. A small minority, whose presence became more noticeable when the events turned violent starting in late January 2014, were militant and extreme nationalists. The "Right Sector" emerged at the beginning of the protest movement in November 2013 as an umbrella organization for several nationalist groups, and the symbols they carried and wore harkened back to Ukrainian struggles for nationhood in the 1930s and 1940s.

The leader of Right Sector, Dmytro Yarosh, views the controversial figure of Stepan Bandera as a national hero. Bandera was a Ukrainian nationalist from the area of Lvov in eastern Poland (present-day Lviv in western Ukraine), which had a large Ukrainian population. His life's goal was to create an independent Ukraine from the Ukrainian parts of eastern Poland and Soviet Ukraine. He was willing to collaborate with whoever would help him achieve that end. In 1939 when Germany invaded Poland, Bandera was

serving a life sentence for his role in the assassination of the Polish interior minister back in 1934. Bandera then worked with German intelligence in preparation for the German invasion of Soviet Ukraine in 1941. The Nazis, however, did not share Bandera's goal of creating an independent Ukraine. Eight days after Germany invaded the USSR, Bandera declared an independent Ukrainian state in Lviv and was promptly arrested by the Germans. He was incarcerated first in Berlin and then in the Sachsenhausen concentration camp. In 1944, Germany released Bandera to fight against the Red Army, which by then was rapidly retaking Soviet Ukraine and crushing any sentiment in favor of Ukrainian nationalism. Bandera's supporters fought against the Red Army and the Polish Communists, but Bandera himself remained in Germany. After Germany was finally defeated, some Ukrainian nationalists continued to wage partisan battles against the Soviet Union in western Ukraine into the early 1950s. The Soviet secret police (KGB) assassinated Bandera in Munich, Germany in 1959.

Some within the relatively small number of Right Sector demonstrators carried posters of Bandera in the Euromaidan Revolution, and it was Right Sector members and other ultra-nationalists who were particularly inclined to fight back against riot police in January and February 2014.

Russian news coverage of the Euromaidan demonstrations and the toppling of Yanukovych exaggerated and distorted the role played by extreme nationalist elements. Russian state-controlled media focused on Bandera and his links to Nazi Germany; blamed the demonstrators, not the riot police, for the violence; and dismissed the 2014 Ukrainian Revolution as a "neo-fascist coup."

Russian President Putin's policy toward Ukraine had clearly failed. Seven days after his ally Yanukovych fled Kyiv, Putin attempted to turn the defeat into a triumph by seizing control of the Crimean Peninsula, where 58% of the population was Russian, in a quick, efficient, and almost entirely bloodless military strike. Putin claimed that grassroots paramilitary troops had overthrown Ukrainian control of Crimea, but over a year later he publicly acknowledged that he had personally orchestrated the seizure of power. Exactly two weeks after Ukraine lost Crimea, on March 16, the people of Crimea were asked to vote in a referendum on whether they wanted to join Russia or to continue to be part of Ukraine but with enhanced autonomy. (There was no option of maintaining the status quo.) According to the official tally, more than 95% of voters favored union with Russia. Two days after the referendum, in an ornate ceremony in the Kremlin, Putin announced that Crimea had rejoined Russia.

Emboldened by the events in Crimea and as Russian troops massed along the border with eastern Ukraine, pro-Russian separatists took control of the eastern Ukrainian cities of Kharkiv, Luhansk, and Donetsk and surrounding territory. On May 11, 2014, the new, self-proclaimed Donetsk People's Republic and Luhansk People's Republic organized referenda for independence. Among those who showed up at the polling stations, the overwhelming majority voted in favor; however, the meaning of the vote was obscured in the Donetsk region, because there the people were asked to vote on "samostoiatel'nost'" which can be translated as either "independence" or "broad autonomy."

Three months after Yanukovych's flight from Ukraine, the people of Ukraine elected a new president. On May 25, Petro Poroshenko, a very wealthy businessman, who had served as Ukraine's Minister of Trade and Economic Development and before that as its Foreign Minister, won a resounding victory, taking 54.7% of the vote in a contest in which five candidates received at least 5% of the vote. He polled well in almost all parts of Ukraine, except in occupied Crimea, where no voting occurred, and in parts of the Donbass where pro-Russian rebels disrupted the vote. Former President Yanukovych made no attempt to return to Ukraine to run in the election. The Russian narrative that the Euromaidan Revolution had been the work of "neo-Nazis" was undermined by the fact that Dmytro Yarosh, the leader of ultra-nationalist Right Sector (some of whose supporters revere Stepan Bandera, who had opportunistically allied with Nazi Germany during part of WWII in the hope of creating an independent Ukraine),

Euromaidan protests, December 2013

Ukraine

received less than 1% of the vote. The left-wing populist and nationalist party, the Radical Party, was much more successful winning 7.4% of the vote and receiving 22 seats. With these seats it joined the coalition government until leaving in September 2015 in protest over a parliamentary vote to decentralize power.

On June 27, 2014, President Poroshenko signed the Association Agreement with the EU, which former President Yanukovych had refused to sign. The agreement opened much of the European market to Ukrainian exports. Poroshenko called the signing "the most important day" in Ukraine's history since the collapse of the Soviet Union. Poroshenko then scheduled early ("snap") parliamentary elections for October 26, 2014. With a healthy turnout except in occupied Crimea and the Donbass, the "Petro Poroshenko Bloc" won the most seats in the Supreme Council (Verkhovna Rada), the country's unicameral legislature, and promptly formed a ruling coalition government with four other pro-Western parties. The election confirmed that most Ukrainians desired firmer ties with Europe. The ultra-nationalist Right Sector won only one seat.

As Ukraine moved closer to Europe, fighting intensified in the Donbass region of eastern Ukraine between pro-Russian rebels and Ukrainian army troops in the late spring and summer of 2014. Poroshenko was determined to defeat the separatists in the Donbass. Between mid-June and mid-July, the separatists and/or their Russian partners shot down several Ukrainian helicopters and other military aircraft over Ukrainian territory. Then, on July 17, Malaysia Airlines Flight 17 en route from Amsterdam to Kuala Lumpur crashed in the conflict zone killing all 298 people on board. Ukrainian intelligence produced an audio transcript of what it claimed was a phone conversation between a separatist commander at the crash site and a Russian intelligence officer, in which the commander regretfully confirmed that a separatist unit had shot down a civilian airliner. Russian media, without citing credible evidence, charged that the Ukrainian military downed the plane. The most likely explanation is that separatists, or possibly Russian military specialists supporting the separatists, mistook the civilian airliner for a Ukrainian military plane and destroyed it with a surface-to-air missile. The rebels were known to have the Buk anti-aircraft system, and the plane was headed toward Russia over territory controlled by the rebels. The final report on the air crash by the Dutch Safety Board released in October 2015 revealed that a Russian-made Buk missile brought down the plane.

Ukraine has not been able to control its eastern border with Russia. In August 2014, Russian servicemen, tank columns, and self-propelled artillery guns entered Ukraine from Russia in support of the separatists. NATO claimed that over 1,000 Russian military personnel crossed the border to join the fight. Russian government officials have consistently denied that active-duty Russian troops have been fighting in Ukraine. On occasion, Russian officials have said that Russian troops who have shown up in Ukraine went there on their own using vacation leave. In May 2015, the Atlantic Council, a think tank based in Washington, DC, issued a detailed report on Russian involvement in Ukraine. It claimed that Russian training camps on the Russian side of the border with Ukraine were launching pads for intervening in Ukraine and that Russian commanders have ordered their troops to remove uniform insignia and conceal identifying markings of vehicles they drive over the border. The report further states that weapons and ammunition manufactured in Russia have appeared in Ukraine and that Russian forces in Ukraine have received covering fire from inside Russia.

The increase in fighting in the late summer of 2014 in the Donbass, especially around the cities of Donetsk and Luhansk, prompted the Organization for Security and Cooperation in Europe (OSCE) to sponsor talks in Minsk with the aim of achieving a cease-fire. On September 5, the "Minsk Protocol" was signed by representatives of the self-proclaimed Donetsk and Luhansk People's Republics, and of Russia and Ukraine. The Protocol called for an immediate and verifiable cease-fire and release of all prisoners, among other things. Two weeks later, the representative agreed to create a buffer zone 30 kilometers wide between the warring factions that would be free of heavy weaponry. However, the agreements collapsed by January 2015. The following month, Russian President Putin met in Minsk with Ukrainian President Poroshenko and representatives of the Donetsk and Luhansk separatists, as well with French President Francois Hollande and German Chancellor Angela Merkel. They signed a new cease-fire, dubbed Minsk II, which reiterated much of the previous Minsk Protocol. Shortly after this new cease-fire was signed, the key small city of Debaltseve, located in the Donbass between Luhansk to the north and Donetsk to the south, fell to the pro-Russian separatists. Fighting also took place near the city of Mariupol in the southern part of the Donetsk region on the coast of the Sea of Azov.

According to the United Nations Human Rights Office, by March 2015, more than 6,000 people had died in fighting in eastern Ukraine between the rebels and the Ukrainian army. The war has also produced waves of refugees. As of early June 2015, some 1.3 million Ukrainians have been displaced within the country. Nearly 900,000 others have fled abroad, mainly to Russia. Although the cease-fire has largely held since September 2015, there have been frequent violations by both forces and there are no meaningful signs that a resolution is forthcoming. Ukraine's loss of administrative control in its war-torn regions was underscored by its inability to hold scheduled local elections in October 2015 in Crimea, Donetsk, and Luhansk. Increasingly it is looking likely that Eastern Ukraine will become yet another "frozen conflict zone" in the post-Soviet sphere similar to Transnistria, South Ossetia, and Nagorno-Karabakh.

Politics in the Aftermath of Euromaidan
Petro Poroshenko's decisive victory in the first round of Presidential voting on

Apartment building in Luhansk Region destroyed in fighting

189

Ukraine

THE SITUATION IN THE EASTERN REGIONS OF UKRAINE

8 June 2015 (00:00)

May 25. 2014 masked how difficult it prove to be to govern Ukraine in the wake of the EuroMaidan Revolution. The foremost challenge was the ongoing war with Russia in the east. Despite inheriting a devastated military, early in his term Poroshenko assured Ukrainians that the war would soon end. Although heavy fighting has indeed ended, low level fighting continues nearly five years later. The gap between promise and realty overshadows Poroshenko's notable success in steering the rebuilding of the Ukrainian military.

Similarly, despite rhetorical promises to root out corruption, Poroshenko struggled to convince Ukrainians that significant enough steps were being taken to address its prevalence. Though some concrete steps were taken, such as the establishment of the National Anti-Corruption Bureau of Ukraine, whatever positive effects these efforts had were undermined by the widespread perception that regime insiders continued to exploit their positions for personal gain. When news broke in early 2019 that the first deputy chairman of the National Security and Defense Council's son was involved in a scheme to smuggle contraband military components from Russia to be sold to Ukrainian state companies, skepticism over Poroshenko's commitment to tackling corruption seemed justified. Poroshenko's decision to fire the smugglers father, close ally Oleh Hladkovskyy, did little to convince the public.

Frustration and dissolution with the slow progress under Poroshenko fueled the unlikely presidential campaign of Volodymyr Zelensky. Zelensky is a political novice who was previously best known as the star of the satirical television series "Servant of the People" (Sluha Narodu) in which his character, a teacher named Vasyl Holoborodko, unexpectedly wins the presidency after a video of him decrying corruption goes viral. Throughout the campaign, Zelensky exploited his television persona to present himself as an anti-establishment and anti-corruption reformer. He spent very little time articulating coherent policy platforms beyond his desire to clean up Ukrainian politics. Thus, his resounding win in the second round of the presidential elections on April 21, 2019, is better seen as a negative referendum on the direction of the country under Poroshenko than as a positive vote for the promises of Zelensky.

Constitutional Crisis and The Continuing Struggle with Corruption

Following the Euromaidan revolution, the government created several new legal institutions designed to address the state's corruption: the National Agency for the Prevention of Corruption (NACP), the National Anti-Corruption Bureau (NABU), and the Specialized Anti-Corruption Prosecutor's Office (SAPO). NACP is a regulatory body charged with establishing standards and maintaining compliance in order to prevent corruption. One of its chief tasks involves collecting and checking asset declarations of government officials. These official electronic declarations are free to download from the NACP website. NABU is an investigatory body charged with preparing cases against state officials for prosecution. SAPO is responsible for indicting and overseeing the investigations launched by NABU.

While the relatively slow roll-out of these bodies has frustrated some Ukrainians eager for immediate change, collectively the three institutions have achieved some measurable success. For instance, around a million officials submit their annual asset declarations every year, greatly increasing government transparency. NABU has also been involved in hundreds of investigations. However, rulings in 2020 by the Constitutional Court of Ukraine threatened to dismantle the government's institutional efforts to combat corruption. In a case associated with pro-Russian politician Viktor Medvedchuk and oligarch Ihor Kolomoisky the Court determined that NAPC lacked the constitutional authority to review declarations of public officials since it violated separation of powers. It also determined that the provision which established that the false declaration of income to NAPC as a criminal offense was too severe and struck this down. Finally, NABU was determined to be essentially unconstitutional.

The ruling was criticized by the Venice Commission (the Council of Europe's advisory body on Constitutional Law) for its lack of constraint as well as for its lack of disclosure of conflicts of interest regarding the fact that NABU were investigating some court members financial declarations to NACP. President Zelensky argued that the ruling threatened Ukrainian relations with the EU and on October 29, 2020, submitted a controversial bill which would have invalidated the ruling and sacked the entire bench. Although this bill was withdrawn, a bill restoring criminal penalties for false asset declarations to NAPC was passed in the Rada in December. In March 2021, in a constitutionally dubious move, Zelensky fired the Court's chairperson Oleksander Tupytskyi as well as judge Oleksandr Kasminin. These moves signaled Zelensky's plans to instigate long-discussed (and long-delayed) judicial reforms, which were put on hold yet again because of the unprovoked Russian military assault on Ukraine.

The War in Ukraine

On February 24, 2022, Russia invaded Ukraine. Russia's massive ground and air assault marked a major escalation in a Russo-Ukrainian war that started in 2014. As early as December 2021, the US officials found that Russia had amassed up to 170,000

Ukraine

UEFA EURO2012
POLAND-UKRAINE

Logo used for 2012 European
Soccer Championship jointly hosted
by Poland and Ukraine

troops east and north of the Ukrainian border in preparation for a multi-front offensive against that country at the start of 2022. Despite early warnings, Volodimir Zelensky denied that Russian attack was imminent and implored Ukrainians not to give in to panic. At the start of the new year, Zelensky finally acknowledged the possibility of invasion and stated that the reason he appealed for calm earlier was because he wanted to avoid "panic in the markets, panic in the financial sector," which, as he saw it, could have unsettled the country's economy. Diplomatic efforts by the US and the EU leaders did not help to avert the war. Ahead of the invasion, Moscow officially recognized the independence of Luhansk People's Republic and Donetsk People's Republic. In his address to the nation two days before the invasion, Vladimir Putin announced that Russia would launch a "special military operation" against Ukraine. He variously blamed NATO's eastward expansion closer to the Russian border and the oppression of the Russian-speaking population at the hands of the Ukrainian authorities for the onset of the war. As he put it, one of the main goals of the military operation is to "protect the people who have been subjected to abuse and genocide by the regime in Kyiv for eight years. And for this we will pursue the demilitarization and denazification of Ukraine and bring to justice those who committed numerous bloody crimes against civilians, including citizens of the Russian Federation." "Denazification" is a code for Putin's aim to overthrow the democratically elected government in Ukraine and install a puppet regime, and repress pro-Western activists and civil society groups. The idea that

the Ukrainian government is run by Nazis is absurd if only because Zelensky himself is Jewish and lost family members in Holocaust. Authorities in Russia deny that their country is at war with Ukraine. The country's media regulator ordered media outlets to use the phrase "special military operation" instead of "assault, invasion, or declaration of war" to describe Russia's assault; otherwise, it warned, they would risk being blocked and fined.

Russia has a much larger army and spends more on defense than Ukraine. Perhaps this gave Russian authorities confidence that their military would easily win in a conventional war and that Kiev could fall within 72 hours of Russian invasion. Russia used the territory of Belarus as a launch pad for a ground offensive on Kiev. However, the military operation was anything but a lightning coup. Almost four months into the invasion, Ukrainian forces were able to hold on to Kiev and through a series of counter offensives forced Russian troops to retreat farther into the east. After failing to capture Kiev, in April 7 Moscow began to redeploy its troops to the east and south of Ukraine, where it made early gains during the invasion. As of June 13, 2002, the countries are fighting a war of attrition and the momentum appears to be shifting in favor of Russia, which was able to gain control of major cities, including Kherson in the south, Mariupol in the south-east, and Donetsk and Luhansk in the east. As of the time of this writing, Russian forces appear to have gained a partial control over Severodonetsk, a city in Luhansk province. Meanwhile, Russian media was euphoric over the retreat of the Ukrainian forces from the city, and declared it a major victory. Considering that Russia's initial plan was to take over the country, including the entire Donbas region, which includes Luhansk and Donetsk provinces, the partial occupation of Severodonetsk is certainly a modest target to rejoice about. Nonetheless, control of this city would allow Russian forces to cross the Donetsk River farther north and encircle an estimated 10,000 Ukrainian defense force troops in Luhansk province. If Russia manages to take over the entire Donbas region, it would hold roughly a fourth of Ukraine, including its industrial heartland and most of its Black Sea coast.

Ukrainian resistance has been key in preventing Vladimir Putin to realize his plan for prosecuting a quick war and holding a victory parade in Kyiv thereafter. However, without Western support, it is unlikely that Ukrainian forces would prevail over Russian forces in the war of attrition, given that Russia redeployed a substantial proportion of its battle-tested forces to pursuing a limited objective of securing control over Donbas region. The US

alone contributed about $37 billion to the war. At the G-7 summit in Hiroshima from 19–22 May 2023, the US promised an additional $375 million in arms, including ammunition and armored vehicles. The US credibly committed to providing dozens of F-16 fighter jets and urged European partners to help Ukraine defend its airspace. Ukrainian defense officials called the aid a game changer as the country prepares for a much-anticipated military counter offensive to take back occupied lands this summer.

The prolonged fighting has taken a massive human toll. According to the UN Office of the High Commissioner for Human Rights (OHCHR), between February 24 and June 12, 2002, a total of 4,395 civillians were killed and 5,390 injured. OHCHR notes that the number of casualites is likely to be higher because the office does not receive timely information on the number of casualties in areas that experience intense fighting. Furthermore, OHCHR points out that, among other weapons, explosive weapons with wider impact area caused most of the casualties. According to Human Rights Watch (HRW), "Russian forces have repeatedly used cluster munitions in attacks that killed hundreds of civilians and damaged homes, hospitals, and schools since its invasion of Ukraine." Because these munitions kill indiscriminately, most armed forces in the world stopped using them. As the war drags on, Russia is likely to continue using tactics that would inevitably inflict pain on the civilian population. In addition to using cluster munitions, Russian forces laid seige to major cities and cut off supply lines and escape routes, all the while bombarding civilians with heavy artillery. All of this appears to be by design, as Russia wants to weaken the resolve of the Ukrainian self-defense units to fight. Russian unprovoked invasion has displaced nearly 12.8 million people, of whom 7.7 million people (about 17.5% of the entire population) have not left the country. The bulk of the displaced people found refuge in Poland, with the remaining resettled in other European countries. HRW documented several cases of war crimes perpetrated by Russian soldiers against civilians in the occupied areas of Chernihiv, Kharkiv, and Bucha. According to HRW "these include a case of repeated rape; two cases of summary execution, one of six men, the other of one man; and other cases of unlawful violence and threats against civilians between February 27 and March 14, 2022." Russian forces reportedly used chemical weapons in Mariupol, the site of the most devastating siege, against Ukrainian soldiers and civilians who took refuge in the Azovstal works, a vast Soviet-era plant, and held their position for 82

191

Ukraine

days, which was the Ukrainian authorities viewed as crucial in delaying Russian plan to seize the east and south of Ukraine.

Ukrainian resistance has been key in preventing Vladimir Putin to realize his plan for prosecuting a quick war and holding a victory parade in Kyiv thereafter. However, without Western support, it is unlikely that Ukrainian forces would prevail over Russian forces in the war of attrition, given that Russia redeployed a substantial proportion of its battle-tested forces to pursuing a limited objective of securing control over Donbas region. As of June 13, the US is set to deliver longer-range rocket systems that would allow Ukrainian troops to attack Russian guns and break Russian supply lines. For its part, UK committed to sending a further $130 billion in military support. In addition to other military hardware, Germany sent 2,500 anti-aircraft missiles. Some of the new weapons are unlikely to arrive soon enough for Ukraine to regain control of Severodonetsk, but they will be vital for retaking other towns in the east and south of the country.

Foreign Policy

When it declared its independence at the end of 1991, the Ukrainian government expressed the idea that it wanted to become part of Central Europe, and to that end expressed an interest in joining NATO and the European Union. Although it was one of the founding members of the Commonwealth of Independent States, it was extremely fearful of a continued Russian domination. As a result, its participation in the CIS was often nominal, and it several times refused to support CIS initiatives, even when it might have been in its economic interest to do so. Thus, Ukraine failed to sign agreements on payments and a customs union, it opted for "observer" status at the CIS's Intergovernmental Assembly, and it has refused to provide troops for CIS peacekeeping.

This fear of Russian domination has also affected Ukraine's ability to develop ties with the west. For example, the Ukrainian Government agreed to foreswear nuclear weapons but then balked at turning the weapons over to Russia. The legislature also refused to ratify the Non-Proliferation Treaty (NPT), apparently because of a fear that Ukraine might become subject to Russian nuclear blackmail at some time in the future. The stalemate was resolved in January 1994 when the Ukrainian Government signed a trilateral agreement with the United States and Russia, under which it stipulated that it would dismantle all missiles on its territory and deliver the warheads to the Russian government for destruction. Even so, Ukrainian legislators waited until November 1994 to ratify the

Former President Petro O. Poroshenko

Former Prime Minister Arseniy P. Yatsenyuk

NPT, and then coupled it with a stipulation that it would go into effect only after the United States, Russia, and Great Britain had provided assurances that they would respect Ukraine's borders and never use nuclear weapons against it. Ukraine was the last of the ex-Soviet republics to ratify the NPT.

These changes in foreign policy came about because of the election of Leonid Kuchma in July 1994. Kuchma personally lobbied the Ukrainian legislature for several weeks before the vote, insisting that the legislature's attempt to use the nuclear warheads as a bargaining chip was counterproductive and that Ukraine would get nothing from the west until it had fore-sworn nuclear weapons. As Kuchma told the legislature, "Ukraine today has no choice between being nuclear or non-nuclear. The process of world disarmament depends on our decision today." Ultimately his argument prevailed, with the final vote being a lopsided 301 to 8.

United States. After his election, the US government signaled its support by sending Vice President Al Gore to Kyiv following his visit to Poland to commemorate the 50th anniversary of the Warsaw uprising. Kuchma also received a warm welcome when he visited the United States in November 1994, plus a promise of $200 million in addition to the $700 million the United States had pledged earlier.

In addition, President Clinton extended the security assurances that the Ukrainian legislature had asked for in ratifying the NPT. Essentially, the United States Government decided that political stability in Ukraine was a critical element for peace in Europe and that economic aid was essential for the success of President Kuchma and his program of reform, a position that had strong support in Congress from both Republicans and Democrats. In May 1995, President Clinton paid an official visit to Ukraine after participating in ceremonies in Moscow commemorating the end of World War II in Europe.

During his visit to the United States in September 1996, Prime Minister Pavlo Lazarenko was quoted as saying that "integration with the West is the main thrust of our foreign policy." The Republic of Ukraine pursued that policy with regard to Western Europe and this brought membership in both the Council of Europe and the Central European Initiative, a regional trade forum, in 1996. Ukraine also joined NATO's Partnership for Peace. President Kuchma expressed support for Ukrainian eventual membership in both the EU and NATO.

US-Ukrainian relations deteriorated in 2002 over a charge that Ukraine had illegally sold highly sophisticated Kolchuga radar system to Iraq in 2000. Ukraine denied the allegations, but the United States blocked $55 million in previously approved aid to Kyiv in September. The basis for the charge was an audio recording made by Mykola Melnichenko in which a Ukrainian arms dealer tells President Kuchma that Iraq was seeking to buy four Kolchuga systems. In October, the United States sent investigators to Ukraine to probe the charges.

While this was going on, President Kuchma was discouraged from attending the November NATO conference in Prague and, when he insisted on coming, he was ostracized by the American delegation. Kuchma told a press conference in February 2003 that he regretted the state of poor relations with Washington. Asserting that Ukraine had proven its innocence to US and British experts probing allegations that Kyiv sold Kolchuga radar systems to Iraq, Kuchma added that "On my word, I do not know what else we need to do to change the mind of the United States."

That same month, the Ukrainian Government announced that it was sending a radiation and chemical battalion to Kuwait in support of United States objectives there. The Ukrainian government also contributed troops to the occupation after Iraq's defeat in the subsequent US–Iraqi war. These two actions largely restored Ukraine's relations to the United States.

Kuchma's successor, Viktor Yushchenko, was an even greater supporter of membership in the EU and NATO, even though polls indicated that a majority of Ukrainians were opposed to NATO membership. The United States strongly supported President Yushchenko, both because he was perceived as a democrat and because there was a pro-western orientation to his foreign policy. The United States also worked with Viktor Yanukovych, while he was prime minister, even though Yanukovych was perceived as being more pro-Russian than Yushchenko.

Relations have intensified since the Euromaidan Revolution. In 2014, President Barack Obama signed the Ukraine Freedom Support Act which outlined increased military and economic assistance to Ukraine while also providing for sanctions against parties responsible for the invasion. Although assistance from the US increased, despite the desire of many Ukrainians for lethal weapons, US military assitance primarily took the form of nonlethal aid and military training. It remains to be seen how the Trump administration will handle aid to Ukraine. Since assuming office, the Biden administration has committed $5.3 billion in security assistance to Ukraine, $4.6 billion of which was given in response to Russia's unprovoked invasion of that country. Among other types of military equipment, the US delivered more than 1,400 Stinger anti-aircraft systems, 6,500 javelin anti-armor systems, and 20,000 other anti-armor systems. On June 1, 2022, the administration committed another $700 million in security assistance to Ukraine.

CIS. Ukraine voted to join the CIS Interparliamentary Assembly in March 1999. Originally sponsored by the Communists, the resolution eventually won 230 votes and passage.

The Republic of Ukraine's relations with the Commonwealth of Independent States remained cool until 2003, when President Kuchma was elected to head the CIS Council. After that, Ukraine took the lead in pushing for the creation of a free-trade zone for the CIS. In another sign of increasing cooperation with its neighbors, the Republic of Ukraine signed a defense cooperation agreement with Azerbaijan in January 2003.

Ukraine's relations with the CIS cooled after Yushchenko became president, however; Yushchenko placed a strong emphasis on eventual membership in the EU and was unwilling to sign any agreements that might have gotten in the way of eventual EU membership. Under President Yanukovych, Ukraine's participation in the CIS became more active but Ukraine's basic policy did not change—or, at least,

not until November 2013 when President Yanukovych found himself maneuvered into a commitment into a possible future membership in the Russian-dominated Eurasian Economic Union. However, this brought demonstrations in Kyiv that, continuing until the following February, resulted in a collapse of Yanukovych's government and his fleeing to Russia. The strongly pro-EU stance taken by the leadership in the new government, coupled with Moscow's strong hostility, would suggest a very limited role for the CIS in Ukraine's future.

European Union. Ukraine has also cultivated good relations with Poland, Germany, and Greece. Among other things, this produced a five-year military cooperation agreement with Germany and a pledge that the Greek government would support Ukraine's eventual entry into the European Union. President Yanukovych has said that he wants good relations with the EU, but he has taken actions since he became president that would preclude actual EU membership. The European Union froze progress on an association agreement and free trade zone with the EU after the trial and imprisonment of opposition leader Yulia Tymoshenko. The unprovoked Russian invasion against Ukraine, brought the EU member states together in their support for Ukraine. Despite occasional disagreements over whether to support Ukraine, the block committed a total of "€4.1 billion to support Ukraine's overall economic, social and financial resilience in the form of macro-financial assistance, budget support, emergency assistance, crisis response and humanitarian aid." Additionally, the EU provided €1.5 billion in military assistance under the European Peace Facility and will raise a further €500 in security assistance. The EU support for Ukraine goes beyond security assistance, however. On May 30, the EU leaders agreed to impose a ban on the import of crude oil, coal, steel, and iron from Russia. As of the time of this writing, the leaders are contemplating imposing an embargo on Russian gas. Additionally, the EU banned Vladimir Putin and his associates from visiting the EU and froze their assets.

Russia. As it built up its relations with the West, Ukraine began to allow its relations with Russia to become warmer as well. Perhaps this reflected an increased sense of self-confidence in its own ability to deal on a level of equality with its much larger Slavic neighbor. In any case, a Ukrainian-Russian Friendship Treaty and an agreement on the disposition of the Black Sea Fleet were signed during President Yeltsin's May 1997 visit to Kyiv. The

Friendship Treaty included a mutual recognition of borders, thus affirming that the Crimea, with its large Russian population, was an integral part of Ukraine.

While Russia agreed to cancel part of the debt that Ukraine owed to Russia for past oil deliveries, Ukraine ceded most of the Black Sea Fleet to Russia and also gave Russia a long-term lease on the naval base at Sevastopol. Both agreed that neither could reach an accord with a third party that would threaten the other.

Although the Friendship Treaty and agreement were important in themselves, of greater long-term significance for Ukraine was the fact that Russia had recognized its borders. Of even greater importance was the fact that the Russian government was willing to treat with Ukraine as a sovereign equal.

Ukraine ratified the Friendship Treaty in early 1998; the Russian Federation Council finally got around to ratifying it in February 1999, but only after adding the proviso that it would not go into effect until Ukraine ratified three agreements on the Russian Sevastopol Black Sea Fleet. Kuchma hailed the Russian ratification and added, "I think it won't take long for the Ukrainian parliament to ratify the [agreements] accompanying the pact."

Ukraine's relations with the West tended to suffer during President Kuchma's last years in office, particularly after the release of the Melnichenko tapes. As a result, President Kuchma turned increasingly toward Russia in 2001, a situation that continued even after the events of September 11 brought a partial reversal of Ukraine's isolation after Ukraine signed on to the United States-led coalition against terrorism.

Thus while Kuchma spoke about enhancing Ukraine's relations with NATO and filling Ukraine's strategic partnership with the United States with specific content, he signed a series of agreements with Russia during this same time period; these included an agreement on a parallel operation of their power grids which would allow Russia to export electricity to the West, an agreement on Ukrainian debts for Russian gas, an agreement on the joint production of a new AN-148 passenger jet aircraft, and continuing talks concerning broad cooperation between Ukrainian and Russian military-industrial companies. Most of these agreements were economic in nature, of course, and beneficial to the Ukrainian economy. They also fitted in well with Kuchma's political strategy leading up to the 2002 parliamentary elections.

Russia's war with Georgia in 2008, and its subsequent recognition of the "independence" of South Ossetia and Abkhazia, inevitably affected domestic Ukrainian politics and its relations with

Ukraine

Russia as well. President Yushchenko took the side of the Georgians in the war and even visited Tbilisi to make clear his support. Viktor Yanukovych and his Party of Regions, on the other hand, argued that Ukraine should join Russia in recognizing the independence of South Ossetia and Abkhazia.

After his election as president in February 2010, Yanukovych started to reorient Ukrainian foreign policy. Although he expressed a wish to continue to strengthen relations with the European Union and the West in general, he also moved quickly to establish a new working relationship with Russia. Most importantly, he negotiated a treaty with Russia extending the Russian lease on the naval base at Sevastopol for a second 25 years after the current lease ran out in 2017. In return, the Russian government committed Gazprom to provide natural gas deliveries to Ukraine at a 30% reduction from the world market price. Yet even under President Yanukovych, Ukraine supported Ukraine's participation in the EU's Eastern Partnership program, and, in 2013, Ukraine was actively negotiating an Association Agreement, including a free trade agreement, with the EU.

That did not suit President Putin, who was determined to get Ukraine to sign on to the Russian-dominated Eurasian Customs Union. Russia put increasing pressure on Ukraine as the year progressed; finally, in November, President Putin invited Yanukovych to Moscow for talks. The result was Yanukovych's announcement, after talking with Putin, that Ukraine would end its talks with the EU about an Association Agreement with the EU. In return, Russia would lend Ukraine $15 billion and reduce the price that Gazprom was charging Ukraine for natural gas.

The announcement set off demonstrations in Kyiv that lasted until the following February and resulted in a collapse of Yanukovych's government and he himself seeking sanctuary in Russia. Relations between the two countries reached a new nadir when President Putin refused to recognize the new Ukrainian Government; next sent troops into Crimea; and, then, issued a decree annexing the Crimean Peninsula to Russia. Putin also ordered 40,000 troops to the Ukrainian border, while suggesting that large additional parts of Ukraine were once part of the Russian Empire (and might become so again). Elements of the Russian military were also sent into eastern Ukraine to work with pro-Russian elements there. This resulted in some pro-Russians seizing local governments, and even a local plebiscite to join Russia, but it got no further. All the polls indicate that most Ukrainians continue to support the idea of an independent Ukraine. The unprovoked invasion of Ukraine reinforced these sentiments. A telephone survey of 2,000 respondents conducted by the Kyiv International Institute of Sociology in May 2002, found that in all regions of Ukraine, the vast majority of residents reported having a bad attitude toward Russia. In the south, 90% of respondents reported having a negative view of Russia, and in the east that number was 85%. Additionally, the poll found that since the start of the war residents of the south and eastern regions of Ukraine tended to view Russia less favorably. For example, in early February, 45% of respondents in the south and 53% in the east had a good attitude toward Russia. By mid-May, however, that number declined to 10% and 15%, respectively. Another key finding is that 82% of respondents who continued to live in the occupied territories after February 24, 2022, reported having a negative attitude toward Russia, and only 6% had a positive attitude toward it. In the same poll, 82% of Ukrainians stated that they would not give up any of Ukraine's land to Russia, even if it meant the war would drag on, 10% reported that conceding territory was necessary to end the war, while 8% were undecided.

Nature of the Regime

The Republic of Ukraine has a presidential-parliamentary system with a popularly elected president who acts as spokesman for the nation and set general policy. How much power the president can exercise has always been a matter of contention in Ukraine. In 2004, a series of constitutional amendments stripped the president of much of his former authority. Then, in October 2010, President Yanukovych challenged the 2004 constitutional amendments in court. After the Constitutional Court nullified the 2004 amendments, Yanukovych persuaded parliament to reinstate the 1996 constitution, which returned Ukraine to a presidential form of government. In February 2014, however, as President Yanukovych's government was collapsing, parliament restored the 2004 constitution, stripping the president of most of his power.

The Ukrainian legislature, the Verkhovna Rada, has its own internal organization which is independent of either the president or the prime minister. Since 1996, half of the 450 members are elected in individual constituencies; the other half are elected under a proportional party-list system. Under this system, voters cast their ballots for a political party or electoral bloc rather than for individual representatives. The total number of votes for a party determines the number of representatives awarded to that party; each party's leadership draws up the party-list and so determines which candidates are placed on the candidate list and where they will be placed on the list. The higher up a name appears on the list, the greater is the likelihood that the individual will be elected. Only those parties or blocs obtaining at least 5% of the national vote are allocated seats in parliament.

Following the 2014 Ukrainian revolution and Yanaukovych's flight to Russia, Ukrainian voters went twice went to the polls. In May, businessman Petro Poroshenko was elected president and in October a new parliament was elected in snap elections. In these elections a newly formed "Petro Poroshenko Bloc" received the plurality of seats (132/450) followed by another new party, People's Front (82/450). The formerly powerful Party of Regions did not compete in the parliamentary elections, although many of its members joined the newly constructed "Opposition Bloc." After receiving only 8%% of the party line vote, the Opposition Bloc only won 29 total seats. These results clearly signalled Ukrainian voters had rejected the Yanukovych lineage. However, large portions of Ukraine were unable to participate: because of the war in eastern Ukraine and the Russian annexation of Crimea, 27 seats went unfilled (12 in Crimea and 15 in Donetsk and Luhansk).

In 2019, Ukrainian democracy achieved a major milestone with the peaceful transition of power from the defeated incumbent President Petro Poroshenko to newly elected Volodymyr Zelensky. 39 candidates competed in the first round of the election held on March 31. Given the large number of candidates, it is not surprising that no candidate came close to the 50% threshold needed to win the election outright. The two top vote getters in the first round, Zelensky and Poroshenko moved on to the second round held on April 21. The result of the second round was decisive: in a relatively high turnout election, Zelensky won more than 70% of the vote. Despite an intense campaign, Poroshenko acknowledged and honored the election results, peaceably allowing Zelensky to be inaugurated on May 20, 2019.

Culture

There is a rich cultural life in the Republic of Ukraine, but most of it belongs to a larger Slavic culture, except for a traditional Ukrainian folk culture. Ukrainian houses tend to be painted or whitewashed with traditional decorations worked into the wood trim and around the windows. The Ukrainian folk costume is often highly embroidered, with bright colors worked over white or black.

Ukraine

Wheat fields in western Ukraine

Historically, the Ukrainian Orthodox clergy has had greater contacts with the Greek Orthodox Church and so is closer to the Greek original. Despite these deep historical ties, in 1686 the Ukrainian church was pulled out of the orbit of Constantinople and into the orbit of the Russian Orthodox Church. With the consent of Constantinople, the Ukrainian church was put under the jurisdiction of the Moscow Patriarchate. In 2019, this more than 300-year arrangement formally came to an end when the spiritual leader of the Eastern Orthodox Church, Patriarch Bartholomew I, formally recognized the independence of the Ukrainian Orthodox Church from the Russian Orthodox Church. President Poroshenko attended the multi-hour ceremony in Istanbul underscoring the political significance of the recognition of the church's independence from Russia.

Ukraine began to develop a secular music in the 19th century. There are a number of 19th century operas with specific Ukrainian themes, such as Semen Hulak-Artemovsky's *A Cossack beyond the Danube*. Mykola Lysenko was an early 20th century composer who wrote the opera *Taras Bulba*. Two other composers of this period were Kyrylo Stetsenko and Mykola Leontovych. Lev Revutsky and Borys Lyatoshynsky were two composers of the early Soviet period. The cultural regimentation of the 1930s led to a cultural decline, but there was a revival of sorts after Stalin's death. More recent composers include Kostyantyn Dankevych, Yuliy Meytus, and the brothers Yuriy and Platon Maiboroda.

Ukrainian theater is primarily a 20th century phenomenon, primarily because censorship laws would not allow works in the Ukrainian language before 1905. Three pre-Soviet Ukrainian playwrights are Lesya Ukrainka, Volodymir Vinnichenko, and Oleksandr Oles. All wrote before 1905, but their works were not available in the Ukraine until after that time.

There was a flowering of Ukrainian theater in the period of the 1920s, the so-called period of Ukrainization. Mykola Kulish, who used expressionist techniques, was perhaps the most famous. As in opera, the introduction of socialist realism led to a decline in drama. A contemporary Ukrainian playwright of some fame is Oleksandr Korniychuk.

One interesting development since Ukraine became an independent republic is the matter of language. While it was a soviet republic, Ukrainian nationalism was discouraged and the Russian language was used as the language of instruction in all of the schools throughout the republic. Ukrainian was introduced as the language of instruction in over 1,300 schools in the first decade after independence. In 2017, President Poroshenko signed a new education law which sought to further cement the centrality of Ukrainian. By 2023, the Ukrainian language is to be the language of instruction at all levels, with some allowances for English or other official languages of the European Union. In the media, on the other hand, Russian continues to be the dominant language, with 57% of all publications printed in Russian.

Use of the Russian language remains a hotly contested political issue in Ukraine. In June 2012, the Ukrainian parliament passed legislation making Russian an official language in some regions alongside Ukrainian. The result: 234 deputies voted in favor with many of the remaining deputies vehemently opposed.

Economy

Ukraine has been the historical "bread basket" of Russia and, although industry today plays a larger role in the economy, agriculture continues to play an extremely important role. In recent years, Ukraine produced about 20% of all Soviet food. Grain, in the form of wheat and corn, is the most important crop, but others include potatoes, vegetables, fodder crops, fruits, and grapes. Sugar beets are the most important industrial crop. Cattle are raised for both milk and meat. Other important animals raised include pigs, sheep, and goats. Honey is another important product, as are silkworms.

In 1993, the government issued a decree breaking up the collective farms and turning the land over to private farmers; this created such a storm of protest in the legislature that the government retreated and ordered that the collective farms be reorganized as joint-stock cooperative farms.

The government also distributed 11 million garden plots among approximately two-thirds of the population. Although these garden-plots constituted only 14% of farmland, they accounted for 95% of the potato crop in 1996 and 82% of all vegetables. They also produced more than one-half of the country's meat and milk and two-thirds of its eggs.

The large, poorly managed cooperatives were in decline for several years, producing even less than the collective farms did under communism. Grain production in 1997 was approximately 37 million tons, lower than any year since 1985, and sugar beet production was the smallest in 30 years. Although farm privatization was the logical longer-term solution to these problems, the improved showing of the Communist Party and the Socialist/Peasants' Bloc in the March 29, 1998, parliamentary elections convinced the government that it would be unable to get such a program through the Verkhovna Rada.

However, Kuchma decided that his re-election victory in November 1999 had given him a window of opportunity to take action if he chose. In addition, his advisers informed him that Ukraine needed to import 1.5 million metric tons of grain between then and September 2000 if the country were to be guaranteed a continuous supply of bread. These two things, the opportunity and the threat, convinced Kuchma that it was time to act.

After several months of preparation, President Kuchma issued a decree in December 2000 that divided the land of the country's 11,000 cooperative farms into plots which were to be distributed among the country's 6.4 million farm workers. By October 2001, approximately 1.8 million Ukrainian farmers had received

Ukraine

certificates documenting the private ownership of their plots. To help complete the process, the World Bank agreed to loan the Ukrainian Government $120 million. This was later supplemented by a $14.5 million grant from the United States government. The money has been used to finance the issuance of another 5 million documents certifying property rights on land lots and to create a registration system for real estate rights.

The Ukrainian parliament also passed a Land Code in October 2001 specifically authorizing the buying and selling of farmland after 2004, though this legislation never went into effect. In October 2004, parliament passed new legislation extending an earlier moratorium on land sales until January 1, 2008. President Kuchma vetoed the legislation, but it was passed over his veto the following month. The moratorium was later extended to 2009. However, agro-industrial companies began to buy up or lease large areas of farmland after 2004, pouring money into them to modernize and mechanize them. This has produced increased farm productivity and normal grain surpluses.

Ukraine's grain harvest was 39.7 million tons in 2001, the best crop in 10 years. That allowed Ukraine to export about 7 million tons of grain, mainly to the Middle East and North Korea. Overall food exports in 2001 were valued at $1.8 billion, a 34% rise from 2000 and accounting for 12% of total exports. The 2002 harvest, at 36.7 million tons, was down slightly but still very good. This had a downside for farmers, however, since the increased production tended to drive down grain prices. Since meat and milk prices also declined in 2002, many cooperative farms were reported to have lost money. The news for 2003 was even worse; the total grain harvest dropped to 20 million tons after severe frosts destroyed more than 60% of the winter grain crop. When rising grain prices began to drive up the price of bread in the cities, the government intervened and began buying grain abroad. Fortunately, Ukraine had normal grain harvests over the next three years, producing 34.3 million tons in 2005 and 28.7 million tons in 2006. The 2007 grain harvest was reduced somewhat by drought, but there was no actual shortage of grain. However, rising world prices for grain caused the Government of Ukraine to limit the export of grain in the third quarter of 2007 in order to protect the domestic supply. Grain production has been increasing over the past several years, but a spell of extremely hot weather in 2010 led to a drought and a poor harvest, causing President Yanukovych to order an embargo on grain exports. The 2011 harvest was back to normal. A partial drought in

the Black Sea region in the summer of 2012 reduced the total wheat crop, but Ukraine still exported about 8.5 million metric tons of wheat.

The development of industry in the Ukraine goes back to the end of the 19th century when 14 steel mills were built on the steppe north of the Black Sea. Even today, the center of Ukraine's heavy industry is a belt that stretches from Krivoi Rog in the west to the border of the republic in the east. Here the republic produces cast iron, steel and rolled steel, and steel pipe. Other allied manufactures include diesel locomotives, freight cars, automobiles, giant airliners, seagoing vessels, electric generators, thermal and gas turbines, metallurgical equipment, and tractors.

Another major Ukrainian industry is coalmining, with huge reserves of anthracite and bituminous coal in the Donetsk Basin and brown coal in the Dnieper Basin. Originally developed in the 19th century and then greatly expanded under the Soviets, the industry is now a dead weight on the economy. With only seven of 176 mines able to operate without government subsidies, the mines cost the government about $500 million a year to keep going. Nor can the government just close down the mines, for this would lead to mass unemployment. It did close 90 mines using a $300 million loan from the World Bank in the period 1997–2002, but then put on the brakes. Although the World Bank expressed its willingness to provide another $100 million to finance the closure of an additional 40 to 50 mines, the government demurred after strong protests from local communities. An additional 30 mines were closed by 2011, but that still leave a lot of uncompetitive mines, all requiring government subsidies. The government would like to privatize the industry but, thus far, only two mines have been privatized.

The Republic of Ukraine produces a small amount of oil and gas, and it is very interested in expanding the industry as much as possible. Ukraine's state oil-and gas producing company, Ukmafta—which produces 93% of Ukraine's crude oil—produced almost 3 million tons in 2004, or about 62,800 barrels a day. Ukraine's current consumption is 290,000 barrels a day. According to the CIA World Factbook, Ukraine has proven reserves of 197.5 million barrels, so it could increase production further but probably not by very much.

Natural gas production reached 3.3 billion cubic meters in 2003 but, again, the Republic of Ukraine consumed 74.1 billion cubic meters of natural gas in 2001. Ukraine has been a large importer of natural gas from Russia but it now appears that Ukraine could reach natural gas

independence in the next decade or so. The new development is shale gas extraction, a technique developed in the United States but which is now being introduced in Ukraine. Ukraine has four major largely unexplored shale deposits. No one has any idea how much gas they may hold, but the potential appears to be great. Yuri A. Boiko, Ukraine's minister of energy and coal, met with American shale gas executives in Huston in early 2011. ExxonMobil, which owns the American shale producer XTO, signed a memorandum of understanding with the Ukrainian Government in early 2011. Chevron and Shell have also expressed an interest in helping Ukraine develop its shale gas deposits. In May 2012, it was announced that the Ukrainian Government had signed agreements with Chevron and Royal Dutch Shell which gives these two companies the rights to develop unconventional natural gas fields in Ukraine. Prime Minister Azarov announced at the time that Ukraine expected to increase natural gas production by as much as 25% by 2015.

Since that time, Italy's Eni SpA bought a stake in Ukraine-based LLC Westgasinvest, which holds about 1,500 square miles of land with potential shale-gas reserves.

Buttressing the case for developing Ukraine's shale gas deposits, Gazprom currently charges $346 per thousand cubic meters (tcm); in the United States, where shale gas development has greatly increased the amount of natural gas available, the benchmark price for natural gas is $153.30 per tcm. Also helping the situation, President Yanukovych has signed a shale gas exploration agreement with the United States; he has also reached an accord with the European Union on energy transport that opens Ukraine's pipeline system to western companies.

The Ukrainian food-processing industry includes the processing of granulated sugar, vegetable oils, and wine. Light industry includes textiles, the manufacture of ready-to-wear garments, and shoes.

The preponderant weight of heavy industry in the Ukraine's industry meant that a large percentage of its production was shipped to other republics—amounting to approximately 25% of the republic's gross domestic product. In return, it imported oil and natural gas, some raw materials, and a good percentage of its consumer goods. It was unable to maintain many of those markets after independence and lost, in fact, a fifth of its export market in the first year.

For the first 10 months after achieving independence, very little was done about the economy and the result was a disaster. By October 1992, inflation was running at 30% monthly, economic activity was down

18% over the preceding year, and the budget deficit was running at 44% of GDP. Prime Minister Vitold Fokin was forced out at the end of September and replaced by Leonid Kuchma.

Kuchma turned out to be a reformer. One of his first acts was to raise the central bank lending rate to 80% and to announce that the government would no longer provide inefficient state enterprises with soft credit. In November, he submitted an ambitious, market-oriented reform program to the Supreme Soviet, which called for a tight budget, a temporary wage freeze in state-owned enterprises, cuts in social welfare payments, a law forbidding the government to finance the budget deficit by printing money, and a commitment to begin large-scale privatization. Kuchma also wanted to break up inefficient enterprises and sell their pieces on the auction block.

However, Kuchma's program was opposed by the communist-dominated majority in the Supreme Soviet, and it began passing legislation negating what Kuchma was trying to do. It also imposed controls over wages and prices. Kuchma lost his power to rule by decree in May 1993 and resigned in September. After that, everything was put on hold.

New parliamentary elections in March 1994 reconfirmed communist control of the legislature, but Kuchma's victory in the July 1994 presidential elections brought in a whole new equation. Kuchma quickly announced concrete proposals for reform and arranged a quick meeting with Michel Camdessus, head of the IMF, to win the support of that organization. Kuchma subsequently pushed a far-reaching economic reform program through the legislature which promised large-scale privatization of state companies, cuts in the national budget, and the removal of price controls on many goods.

As a result, Ukraine got its first IMF loan in October 1994 and began receiving loans from individual western countries as well. As economic reform continued, some 11,000 state-owned enterprises were privatized through March 1995 and a further 8,000 large and medium-sized firms privatized in 1996 and 1997. Inflation was brought under control and this allowed the issuance of a new currency, the hryvna, in the summer of 1996.

Foreign investment also began to grow, though the amounts were still minimal. Ukraine received $335.5 million in foreign investment during the first half of 1997. The United States was the largest foreign investor (with $315 million), followed by Germany ($165.9 million), the Netherlands ($160.2 million), Great Britain ($130.9 million), Cyprus ($116.4 million), Russia ($114.2 million) and Liechtenstein

($103.1 million). Investments were mainly in the food industry, machine building, metal processing, finance and insurance, construction and construction materials, and the chemical and petrochemical industries.

Although the overall economy had not yet achieved positive growth by the end of 1997, the government was predicting a 0.5% growth rate in 1998. Some positive growth (0.1) was actually achieved during the first five months of 1998, but inter-national economic events overtook the Ukrainian economy soon after. The economic crisis in Russia in September then came on top of that and threatened Ukraine with the same events that were already occurring in Russia. But President Kuchma was determined that it not happen. As early as June, in fact, he had issued a package of economic decrees to steer the country past its economic crisis. He had little choice; at that time, he was faced with a paralyzed parliament unable to elect its own leadership. These decrees—which were designed to raise additional government revenue—lowered the value-added tax, simplified tax procedures for small businesses, and introduced a fixed rate tax on agricultural products.

Even so, the Ukrainian National Bank was forced to devalue the national currency, the hryvna, in July in order to stop the drain on foreign currency reserves. The hryvna continued to be gradually devalued in steps throughout the rest of the year, so there never was a collapse in the currency. It also helped that the IMF approved a new $2.2 billion loan to Ukraine in September, while the World Bank granted a $900 million loan that same month.

Because Russia was responsible for 44% of Ukraine's general trade turnover, however, there was no way that the Ukrainian economy could be unaffected by the Russian economic collapse. Thus, the Ukrainian economy shrank as Russian customers canceled orders for Ukrainian goods and Russian suppliers of key components shut down their production lines, leaving Ukrainian companies without the means to continue production. Metallurgical products, heavy machinery, and chemicals were particularly affected, for it was products of these industries that made up most of the trade with Russia. Other sectors were less affected. Ukraine thus suffered tremendous economic distress, but it escaped the general collapse that occurred in Russia.

The situation began to turn around in 2000. The economy began growing again for the first time since 1990, managing an impressive 6% growth during the year. The government also renegotiated its foreign debt and cut its annual rate of

inflation to 20%. The economy grew at an even faster 9% in 2001, while inflation dropped to 6.1%; industrial production was, in fact, up a whopping 14.2% over 2000. This spurt in growth was possible because there was still a great deal of unused capacity within the system. Wages have also remained low. According to the Ukrainian Government, the average worker earned the equivalent of $61.50 in October 2001. Lower-paid workers such as farmers, medical workers, and teachers earned even less than this minimum.

The economy slowed to a 4.1% growth rate in 2002, though industry continued to expand at a 7% rate and inflation had dropped to practically zero. Growth reached the torrid rate of 9.3% in 2003, in spite of the extremely poor grain harvest, fueled by a 15.8% growth in industrial production and a 28% growth in exports during the year. Helped by a bountiful grain harvest, Ukraine's GDP grew at a 12% rate in 2004.

The "Orange Revolution," which occurred toward the end of 2004, introduced an element of political instability that had a temporary negative effect on the economy, but the significant increase in energy prices in 2005 probably had a more significant effect. GDP growth decreased significantly as the year progressed, dropping to 3% by November.

The quarrel between President Yushchenko's and Prime Minister Tymoshenko, which became public in May 2005, was another negative factor; her dismissal in September 2005 further shook the political system. Gazprom's decision to begin charging Ukraine world market prices for natural gas, announced in December 2005, was a further blow.

The March 2006 parliamentary elections represented a partial repudiation of President Yushchenko and rehabilitated Yulia Tymoshenko. After hard negotiations, an agreement to reconstitute the Orange Coalition was reached on June 22 (with Yulia Tymoshenko set to become prime minister), but it fell apart one week later, when Oleksandr Moroz, leader of the Socialist Party, signed a new "anti-crisis" agreement with the Communists and the Party of Regions in return for their support for him for the office of parliamentary speaker. After Moroz was elected parliamentary speaker, Viktor Yanukovych, leader of the Party of Regions, became prime minister in August.

Prime Minister Yanukovych's government survived until the spring of 2007. But an attempt to reduce the prorogates of the presidency led President Yushchenko to dissolve parliament and call for new elections. These elections, which took place on September 30, 2007, were won

Ukraine

by a reconstituted Orange Coalition. Yulia Tymoshenko became prime minister again on December 18, 2007.

The economy continued to grow at a rapid pace until the fall of 2008 and then plummeted, as the worldwide economic crisis reached Ukraine. Ukraine's GDP dropped by about 15% in 2009, though the economy tended to stabilize toward the end of the year. The IMF agreed to extend a $16.5 billion loan to Ukraine in early 2009, and actually provided almost $11 billion in loans before it canceled the agreement in December 2009 because, it said, the Ukrainian Government had failed to get the budget under control. The agreement was later renewed after the government took action to reduce the huge Ukrainian budget deficit. In July 2011, President Yanukovych reached a new agreement with the IMF on a stabilization program, which required Ukraine to tighten the state budget and raise gas prices for consumers. In return, the IMF allowed Ukraine to draw against $15 billion in credits. The government instituted the required reforms, but Anders Aslund, writing about the "reforms," suggested that had not boosted "Ukraine's competitiveness or market freedom but instead benefited a few businessmen close to the president." Ukraine grew at a 4% rate in 2010 and 2011. Growth followed a similar pattern in the first half of 2012, but slowed in the second half of the year. Ukraine began 2013 in technical recession.

The Ukrainian economy has been devastated by the war. In 2015, the economy shrank 12% and inflation was over 40%. Nevertheless, there are glimmers of hope. In 2015, Ukraine negotiated $25 billion in loans, including $17.5 billion from the IMF. It hopes to attract another $15.3 billion from its creditors through debt restructuring. The head of an IMF mission to Ukraine in May 2015, asserted that economic austerity reforms were being implemented and that "economic stability is gradually taking hold." As a result of these stabilizing reforms, the World Bank estimated modest economic growth of 1% in 2016 and 2% in 2017. The inflation rate was also anticipated to slow down in the immediate future. Ukraine had a strong economy before the Russian invasion. In 2021, the country's economy expanded by 3.4%, its agricultural sector delivered a strong harvest, past macro-economic reforms resulted in high currency reserves and low debt-to-GDP ratio. At the outset of the war, the government slashed taxes to 2% to allow business to stay afloat, imposed capital controls to stabilize currency, removed value-added taxes and customs duties on imports to expedite the flow of humanitarian and military aid into the country. All of these measures allowed the country to weather the initial shocks of the war which forced over 4 million people to flee the country, and over 6 million people to become internally displaced. According to the World Bank estimates, Ukraine's economy is expected to shrink by 45% in 2022. The World Bank acknowledges that it is hard to calculate poverty rate during the war but projects that it would ". . . increase to 19.8 percent in 2022, up from 1.8 percent in 2021, with an additional 59 percent of people being vulnerable to falling into poverty." As the war drags on, the Ukrainian economy will incur higher costs in the form of higher consumer prices because of spiraling gas prices, and the inability to export commodities (including wheat) because of Russia's blockade of the country's Black Sea ports. Prior to the war, Ukraine's ports accounted for as much as 70% of the country's imports and exports. Through the port in Odessa, Ukraine used to export 5 million tons of grain. Together with Russia, Ukraine accounts for 30% of the world's wheat supplies. Since the start of the war, Ukrainian grain shipments from its Black Sea ports have stopped and more than 20 million tons of grain are said to be stuck in silos. As in other instances, Russia and Ukraine blame each other for the problem. Western countries and Ukraine blame Russia for blockading the Black Sea ports. Russia, for its part, claims that it does not control a section of the sea, which it labels as "safe corridor" that would reportedly allow access to the port in Odessa, and accuses Ukraine for laying sea mines that, Russia alleges, caused disruptions in grain shipment.

The economic carnage is going to mount with each passing day that Ukraine is unable to use its ports to export commodity. With the economy in bad shape, the Ukrainian government is unable to raise taxes to cover basic social services and pay soldiers's salaries. According the estimates by the Ukrainian authorities, the country would need an additional $5 billion each month to pay for those expenses. The damage to the country's infrastructure is estimated to have reached an equivalent of $94 billion. The reconstruction of the physical damage would require an upward of half a trillion dollars. Western countries and international financial institutions have approved funds for that purpose. The International Monetary Fund approved $1.4 billion in emergency loans, the World Bank offered $723 million in grants and loans and the European Commission proposed $9.5 billion in loans. The finance ministers of the G7 nations pledged $20 billion. The US is set to deliver $40 billion in military and humanitarian aid, of which $7.5 was earmarked for restoring the country's economy. It remains to be seen if these entities would be willing to sustain the same level of support in the event of a prolonged war.

The Future

There is a great deal of debate among Western analysts on the real causes of Russian unprovoked war in Ukraine. Some, such as John Mirsheimer, argue that NATO's expansion to the east is responsible for the war because it presumably provoked Putin to defend Russia's sphere of influence. Others, such as Stephen Kotkin, argue that Russia's invasion of Ukraine is not some kind of aberration. He notes that Russia in the 19th century behaved in much the same militaristic way. According to him, Russia has always viewed itself as a great civilization and has had the aspiration to surpass, or at least manage the power differential with the West, but it has never had sufficient capability to measure up to that aspiration. Through the invasion of Ukraine, Putin wants to make it clear to the West that Russia is a global power. Still others who followed Putin's February 21 speech believe that Putin started the war to expand Russia's borders to what they looked like before the Bolshevik revolution of 1917, meaning that he wants to restore the Russian empire. Concurrent with this, analysts contemplate about what the future holds for Ukraine.

In his speech to the nation on April 13, 2022, Volodymyr Zelensky stated that "The future of Ukraine directly depends on the strength of our resistance in all its forms." The manner in which the war played out largely supports this statement. Ukrainians have been able to mount a series of successful counter-offensives to prevent Russian armed forces from taking Kyiv, and force them to retreat to the east. The commitment by the US and the EU to support Ukraine with military and economic aid, and impose financial and economic sanctions on Russia helped Ukrainian forces in that effort.

However, as the war in Ukraine drags on, analysts predict that fatigue might set in, eroding Western support for Ukraine. Already, there was division in the US within the Republican Party over the amount of aid that should be sent to Ukraine. Reportedly, Vladimir Putin is skeptical about the Western staying power in this conflict. He wants to see the war to drag on until the day Western countries would, under pressure from their electors, who are bearing the brunt of war induced inflation, change their militant rhetoric and begin to force Ukraine to make major concessions to Russia. Perhaps, for this reason, speaking at the World Economic Forum in Davos, Switzerland, former U.S.

secretary of state Henry Kissinger suggested that the Ukrainian government should concede Crimea, and the regions of Luhansk and Donetsk as a condition for holding peace talks with Russia before the conflict widens. Likewise, French president Emmanuel Macron cautioned Ukraine against humiliating Russia by making maximalist demand that Russia withdraw to its February 2014, pre-Crimea annexation border with Ukraine. For its part, the Joe Biden made it clear that his administration would not impose any negotiating terms on Ukraine, but hinted that it would favor a negotiated settlement to the conflict.

The outcome of the war is likely to be determined by factors internal and external to Ukraine. Internally, much depends on whether Ukrainian troops can sustain the war, by continuing to combine conventional with irregular civilian resistance. Externally, military, economic and diplomatic support from the US and the EU would be crucial in ensuring that Ukrainian forces continue to hold ground. Already the US and the EU have committed substantial funds for military and economic aid. Whether Western countries continue supporting Ukraine at the same levels depends on how willing the domestic electorate is in putting up with the side effects of the war, including high gas and food prices. Additionally, it remains to be seen whether Western sanctions would cause sufficient economic pain as to force Putin to readjust his war plans.

Moldova

Area: 13,000 sq. mi. (33,843 sq. km., a little larger than Maryland).

Population: 3,250,532 3,599,528 (2024 est.).

Capital City: Chisinau (pronounced *Kee-shee-nau*, Pop. 487,707).

Climate: Moderate winters, warm summers.

Neighboring States: Romania (west). Ukraine surrounds the country on the other sides.

Official State Language: Romanian (Moldovan); Official Minority Languages: Russian, Ukrainian, Gagauz.

Ethnic Composition: Moldovan/Romanian (75.1%), Ukrainian (6.6%), Russian (4.1%), Gagauz (4.6%), Bulgarian (1.9%), others (0.8%) (2014 est.).

Principal Religion: Eastern Orthodox.

Chief Commercial Products: Grain, livestock, silk, honey, processed foods, wine and cognac. Over 70% of exports still go to other members of the Commonwealth of Independent States and Moldova is heavily dependent on energy supplies from these same republics.

Currency: leu/lei (singular/plural).

Per Capita Annual Income (Purchasing Power Parity): $15,670 (2023 est.).

Recent Political Status: Formed in 1940 by union of the Moldavian SSR, previously only an autonomous republic within the Ukrainian SSR, and most of Bessarabia, transferred to the USSR by Romania in 1940.

National Day: August 27 (Independence Day 1991).

Chief of State: Maia Sandu (December 24, 2020).

Head of Government: Dorin Recean (February 16, 2023).

National Flag: three vertical stripes, sky blue, yellow, and red. A right-facing golden Roman eagle, outlined in black with a red beak, is centered on the yellow. The eagle holds a yellow cross in its beak, in its right claw a green olive branch and in its left claw a yellow scepter. A heraldic device forming the body of the eagle pictures a bullhead, star, rose, and crescent, all in yellow outlined in black.

The Land

The Republic of Moldova is the independent successor state to the Moldavian Soviet Socialist Republic. The Moldavian SSR was created in August 1940 when Stalin merged Bessarabia, which he had forced the Romanian Government to cede to the Soviet Union in June 1940, with the autonomous republic of Moldavia, which was then part of the Ukrainian SSR. He gave it constituent republic status. In 1941, after Nazi Germany invaded the Soviet Union, Romania (then an ally of Nazi Germany) reclaimed Bessarabia. Soviet troops retook the territory in 1944 and the Moldavian SSR was reestablished. The republic was renamed Moldova in 1990. Moldova declared its independence on August 27, 1991.

The Prut River, a tributary of the Danube, forms the western border with Romania. The area immediately east of the Prut is somewhat elevated, with a flat highland in the north and rolling hills interspersed with deep flat valleys further south. The highest elevations are about 1,400 feet. The southern part of the republic is a low plain.

The chief feature of the eastern part of the republic is the Nistru (Dniestr) River, which originates in the Carpathian Mountains to the northwest and flows southward across western Ukraine, then forms the border between Moldova and Ukraine for some distance. At this point, the border shifts eastward, while the Nistru continues south and into Moldova. A major feature of the river is the 60-mile-long Lake Dubossary, created when a dam for producing hydroelectric power was built on the Nistru. The Nistru crosses back into Ukraine again shortly before it empties into the Black Sea. On its western side, the Nistru has a high bank, formed by the eastern slope of the Nistru uplands. Transnistria, the small strip of territory east of the Nistru, is a low plain.

Rainfall in the republic varies considerably but averages between 18 and 22 inches. Most of it falls in summer. Moldovan soils are mostly rich, black *chernozem* soils. About 40% of the land is covered by forest, most of it in the uplands.

Moldova

The People

Approximately 3.5 million people live in Moldova. Largely as a result of significant levels of emigration, the country has experienced high rates of negative population growth since achieving independence. It has been estimated that as much as half of the population live and work abroad, about half of them in European Union countries. Many of these émigrés have applied for and received Romanian passports because that gives them the right to work in EU countries.

Moldovan/Romanian speakers make up 75.2% of the population, followed by Russian speakers (16%), Ukrainian speakers (3.8%) and Gagauz speakers (3.1%). Gagauz is a Turkic language and is one of the three official languages of Gagauzia (along with Romanian and Russian), an autonomous region for members of the Gagauz ethnic group.

History

Moldova's modern history is really the history of Bessarabia, the name bestowed on the area between the Prut and Nistru (Dniestr) Rivers by the Russians at the beginning of the 19th century. But Moldova's history begins long before that. At the beginning of the 2nd century A.D., this area, and the area of present-day Romania, became the province of Dacia in the Roman Empire after being conquered by the Emperor Trajan. Although Rome soon lost control, 70% of the roots of the modern language—whether called Moldovan or Romanian—derive from the Latin language carried to the region by the Roman conquerors. Over the following centuries, the area was to know many masters. The eastern part came within the sphere of influence of Kyivan Rus in the 10th century. Later, independent Galician princes ruled. After 1240, it became part of the Mongol Empire for about 100 years. The Genoese built fortified commercial outposts on the Nistru (Dniestr) in the 14th century, though they never attempted to rule the area.

In the 15th century, an independent Principality of Moldavia came into existence which included the northern part of present-day Romania and all of Bessarabia. The Ottoman Empire soon extended its control over most of the area, however, along with the second Romanian Principality of Wallachia. In 1711, Peter the Great occupied part of Bessarabia during a short war with Turkey. He was forced to abandon the territory after his army fell into an ambush, however. Russia occupied the territory three more times in the 18th century, each time relinquishing it to the Turks. In 1812, Russian forces again occupied Moldavia and Wallachia after a new war broke out between the two countries;

Russia won and forced Turkey to cede the territory (which it called Bessarabia) in the Treaty of Bucharest.

After Russia's defeat in the Crimean War, it was forced to cede Bessarabia to Moldavia, at that time an autonomous principality under the Ottoman Empire, in 1856. After its victory in the Turkish War of 1877–1878, Russia took Bessarabia back and kept it until 1918. After the overthrow of the Tsar in 1917, a National Moldavian Committee was organized in Bessarabia in April. Its program included autonomy, use of the Romanian language, and land reform. After the Bolshevik coup d'etat in November, a government was established in Bessarabia, called the Sfatul Tarei. On December 2, 1917, the government proclaimed Bessarabia to be an autonomous constituent republic of the Federation of Russian Republics. The Bolsheviks occupied the capital, Chisinau (Kishinev) on January 5, 1918. Two weeks later, they were driven out and the Bessarabian Government then proclaimed itself an independent Moldavian Republic. Two months later, it voted for a conditional union with Romania. Unconditional union was voted on December 9, 1918. The Union of Bessarabia with Romania was recognized by the Treaty of Paris, signed by Great Britain, France, Italy, and Japan, on October 28, 1920.

The Union of Soviet Socialist Republics never recognized Romania's right to the province and refused to establish diplomatic relations with Romania until 1934. In the meantime, the frontier along the Nistru (Dniestr) was closed.

Under the terms of the Nazi–Soviet Non-Aggression Pact of August 23, 1939, Hitler recognized Bessarabia as being in the Soviet sphere of influence. The Soviet Union revived its claim to Bessarabia, but Romania rejected the claim until after the fall of France in June 1940. On June 27, the Soviet Union demanded the immediate cession of Bessarabia, plus the additional territory of northern Bukovina as "compensation for Romanian misrule in Bessarabia." Without an ally, Romania had to submit. Troops of the Red Army entered Bessarabia on June 28.

The central districts of Bessarabia were merged with part of the Moldavian Autonomous Republic, which then became the Moldavian Soviet Socialist Republic in August 1940. Ukraine was compensated for the loss of the Transnistria territory by receiving the Khotin district in the north and the Cetatea Alba and Izmail districts in the south.

Romania declared war against the Soviet Union in July 1941. Its war goal was to reclaim Bessarabia and to reincorporate it into Romania. This was accomplished by December 1942. Soviet forces reentered

Bessarabia in 1944 and its forces occupied all of Romania as well. Bessarabia was formally ceded back to the Soviet Union by the peace treaty signed between the two countries on February 10, 1947.

After Gorbachev launched his programs of glasnost and perestroika, a nationalist movement arose, which called itself the Popular Front of Moldavia. The ultimate goal of the front was union with Romania. In 1989, the legislature abolished use of the Cyrillic alphabet (see Russia), and restored the Latin alphabet which had been used prior to the republic's incorporation into the Soviet Union. On July 29, 1989, Mircea Snegur was elected president of the presidium of the Moldavian Supreme Soviet. Snegur was at that time first secretary of the Moldavian Communist Party, but he represented the democratic-nationalist faction of the party. In June 1990, the legislature adopted a declaration of republic sovereignty and changed the name of the republic to Moldova.

In March 1991, the Government of Moldova refused to participate in a referendum on continuation of the Soviet Union. It also refused to take part in subsequent discussions on a new union treaty. When conservatives launched their attempted coup against Gorbachev in August 1991, Moldova became a target also. The local military commander surrounded the capital of Chisinau (Kishinev) with troops and threatened to use them against the republic government. President Mircea Snegur refused to recognize the coup committee, however, and called on the people of Moldova to demonstrate in support of democracy and freedom; over 100,000 persons demonstrated in the capital. Following the collapse of the Russian coup, Moldova declared its independence on August 27. It also formally outlawed the Communist Party.

Independence

After it declared its independence as a separate state in August 1991, Moldova began to have problems with the area east of the Nistru (Dniestr) region, the latter motivated by a fear that the rest of Moldova intended to reunite with Romania.

Some violence occurred when the Moldovan government tried to reestablish its control east of the Nistru. The situation only calmed down after President Snegur threatened to resign if the Moldova Supreme Soviet insisted on using force to restore control. The government also repudiated the idea of immediate union with Romania.

This led to the opening of talks between the two sides. At first, the situation appeared to be hopeful, particularly after Igor Smirnov, the "Dniestr Moldavian" leader, said in October that he would

Moldova

The Republic of Transnistria

Dniestr-Moldova, the area east of the Nistru (Dniestr) River, proclaimed itself the "Republic of Transnistria" in August 1991, more or less simultaneously with Moldova's own declaration of independence.

The population of the area in 1991 was an estimated 600,000; according to the 2004 census, the population has since decreased and is now about 555,000. Moldovans/Romanians account for only 31.9% of the population; another 30.3% speak Russian while 28.9% speak Ukrainian. The Russian and Ukrainian speakers rejected Moldovan independence because they felt independence was merely the first step to merging with Romania. In fact, a separatist movement was organized in this area in 1989 in response to the republic government's declared intention to move toward independence.

A September 2 referendum that followed its declaration of independence showed that a majority of people of the area supported the policies of the breakaway republic. The region's capital is Tiraspol, which has 131,000 inhabitants. The region's other major cities are Bendery, with 76,500 inhabitants, and Rybnitsa, with 62,000 inhabitants.

Igor Smirnov was elected to the position of president of the new republic in December 1991, a position he retained until 2011. The new president was Yevgeny Shevchuk, a young man of 43 who was elected in December 2011. (In December 2016, Vadim Krasnoselsky became the third president of Transnistria.) In a statement issued after his election, Shevchuk said that

In foreign policy, we will focus our efforts on winning recognition for Transnistria and on friendship with our strategic partners in Russia.

There is also a 43-member elected legislature, called the Supreme Soviet. Since June 2012, the speaker of the Supreme Council has been Mikhail Burla.

In 1991, the Russian 14th Army was stationed here and at least some elements of the army actively supported the area's separation from Moldova. Most of the Russian forces and part of their equipment were later removed from the area, though there are still about 1,500 Russian troops stationed here.

In November 2003, the Russian government proposed that the problem of Transnistria's separatism be settled by creating a new federal government with Moldova and Transnistria as equal partners. The proposal, known as the Kozak memorandum, further proposed that Russian troops would remain in Transnistria for another 20 years.

Although the area is somewhat more industrialized than the rest of Moldova, it has always been clear to outside observers that the Transnistrian enclave is not viable as a separate entity without political and economic support from Russia. The Moldovan government has stood ready to grant the region autonomous status with the broadest rights, but it has always insisted on the eventual withdrawal of Russian troops. But a Russian troop withdrawal has always been opposed by the Transnistrian leadership, which might not survive without the Russian presence.

At this point, there is limited hope for a political settlement of this long-standing frozen conflict. In November 2017, the OSCE announced that progress had been made in talks that the organization had encouraged in Vienna between Moldova, representatives of the separatist region, as well as Russia, Ukraine, the US, and the EU. However, the limited scope of what was agreed to at this meeting—certification of university degrees, and an easing of telecommunications relations—only serves to underscore how far the principles remain from a true settlement.

be willing to join a federal Moldova, together with Moldova and Gagauzia. The Gagauz, a Turkic-speaking but Orthodox Christian people, had proclaimed a separate republic in southern Moldova in 1990. Like "Dniestr Moldavia," the Gagauz objected to the idea of merging with Romania.

Another favorable development occurred in October when President Snegur, breaking with the leadership of the Popular Front of Moldova, publicly pledged his support to the concept of an independent Moldova. "A union with another state is out of question," he was quoted as saying, adding "at present, Moldova promotes a policy pursuing the assertion of our independence internationally." Snegur also supported continued economic ties with the former Soviet republics.

The Moldovan presidential elections were scheduled to take place on December 8, 1991; the major issue in the campaign was the question of independence versus merging with Romania. There were originally two other candidates in addition to President Snegur—Grigore Eremei, the former first secretary of the Moldovan Communist Party and Gheorghe Malarciuc, a writer—but both candidates withdrew in the middle of November. The Popular Front of Moldova did not nominate a candidate since Mircea Druc, the head of the Front, did not meet the residence requirements; instead, the Front urged voters to boycott the election. The leadership of "Dniestr Moldavia" adopted the same position. "Dniestr Moldavia" and the "Republic of Gagauzia" held their own separate elections on December 1. Smirnov was confirmed as president of "Dniestr Moldavia" and Stepan Topal was elected president of Gagauzia. Neither area permitted voting in the December 8 Republican elections.

Because President Snegur was running unopposed in the December 8 elections, the fact that he got 98% of the vote came as no surprise. On the other hand, the results showed that 83% of all registered voters participated in the election, meaning that they rejected the Popular Front of Moldova's call for a boycott of the election. This gave President Snegur a great deal more leeway in dealing with the Front than he had had before.

Unable to resolve its differences with either "Dniestr Moldavia" or Gagauzia, the Moldovan government formally nullified the results of the December 1 elections in the two breakaway republics on December 11. Later, President Snegur offered to establish a free economic zone in "Dniestr Moldavia," if it would withdraw its declaration of independence. Neither carrot nor stick worked. The main issue remained the question of Moldova's merging with Romania. Even though President Snegur publicly supported an independent Moldova, the leaders of "Dniestr Moldavia" and Gagauzia remained convinced that union with Romania was still on the agenda.

Later in the month, President Snegur went to Alma-Ata and took Moldova into the Commonwealth of Independent States. Moldova did not agree to maintain a CIS military command, however, and began to create its own national army. The plan called for it to be a cadre army of about 12,000 persons, with a larger number of citizens serving in an army reserve.

In March 1992, a weekend of clashes that left 23 dead caused President Snegur to issue an ultimatum to "Dniestr Moldavia" to lay down their arms or face the use of force against them. Igor Smirnov, leader of "Dniestr Moldavia," then declared a state of emergency, closing the enclave to outside contact. According to reports, "Dniestr Moldavia" had by this time created its own 10,000-man militia to defend the enclave.

Meanwhile, the unstable political situation was contributing to a deteriorating economic situation. This led on June 1 to the resignations of the prime minister, Valeriu Muravschi, and his cabinet. President Snegur then nominated Andrei Sangheli, outgoing agriculture minister, as the new prime minister.

President Snegur was more concerned about establishing political control throughout all of Moldova than about the economy. Fighting with "Dniestr Moldavia" flared up again in June 1992 when President Snegur's troops tried to take control of the city of Tighina (Bendery). It appeared for a while that Moldova might find itself involved in a confrontation with Russia when elements of Russia's 14th Army, stationed in eastern Moldova, supported the "Dniestr Moldavia" forces. It turned out that it was only rogue elements of the 14th Army that were involved, however.

Moldova held its first parliamentary elections since independence on February 27, 1994; a week later, it held a referendum on whether Moldova should remain independent or seek unification with Romania. More than 90% of all voters supported the option of remaining an independent state within current borders. In the parliamentary elections, most of the parties that did well favored closer relations with Russia and reconciliation with the breakaway region of "Dniestr Moldavia." The Agrarian-Democratic Party got about 45% of the vote, while the pro-Russian Socialist Bloc got 25%. Andrei Sangheli, the prime minister, was the leader of the Agrarian-Democratic Party.

An aerial view of Chisinau

Courtesy of NOVOSTI

Subsequent Moldovan-Russian discussions resulted in an agreement, signed in October 1994, calling for a three-year phased withdrawal of the troops of the 14th Russian Army from the region of the self-declared "Transnistrian Republic." This agreement was never fully implemented, however. Although some elements of the 14th Russian Army were removed, significant Russian forces remained. The Russians claimed that the problem was logistical—how to get the 14th Russian Army's arms and equipment to Russia; this position was contradicted by Petru Lucinschi, the chairman of the Parliament, who claimed to have obtained the Government of Ukraine's agreement to allow everything to be shipped across its territory.

Periodic talks continued to take place between the Moldovan government and the leadership of the "Dniestr Moldavian Republic," but no agreement proved possible; the "Dniestr Moldavian" leadership did agree to allow the circulation of the leu, Moldova's official currency, along with Transdnistria's own largely worthless coupons, however. For its part, the Moldovan government offered the "Dniestr Moldavian Republic" autonomous republic status with its own parliament; even more important, the Moldovan government agreed that the area east of the Nistru had the right to opt out should Moldova ever decide to merge with Romania. The two sides also agreed to not use force against each other.

The issue apparently holding up final agreement was Moldova's insistence that defense should remain the exclusive prerogative of the Moldovan government. "They can have their own symbols and parliament—an autonomous republic," said Ion Gutsu, a deputy prime minister; "but Moldova must have a single domestic policy and army."

The Moldovan government reached an agreement with the Gagauz in August 1995. The Gagauz separatists, who had hitherto refused to recognize the authority of the government, demanding autonomous republic status for their own area, agreed to lay down their arms in return for a broad measure of autonomy.

New presidential elections were held on November 17, 1996. President Snegur stood for reelection but was opposed by several candidates. President Snegur and Petru Lucinschi, who at that time held the position of chairman of the Parliament, were the two highest vote-getters, but no candidate obtained a majority of the votes. In the runoff, Lucinschi won with approximately 53% of the vote.

Lucinschi, a Central Committee Secretary of the Communist Party of the Soviet Union in its final days, had by this time become a social democrat and as a centrist. It appears that Snegur lost because of a falling out earlier in the year with Andrei Sangheli, his prime minister. In April 1996, Snegur accused the Sangheli Government of incompetence and corruption and urged the parliament to dismiss it. Although there may have been other issues involved, the quarrel between Snegur and Sangheli began in March 1996 when Snegur accused the defense minister of corruption and attempted to have him dismissed; Sangheli, opposing the dismissal, carried the issue to the Constitutional Court and won. Sangheli then formed a tacit alliance with Lucinschi. A bitter presidential campaign followed, won in the end by Lucinschi.

Lucinschi appointed Ion Ciubuc as his new prime minister in January 1997. Because of the political make up of the legislature, the Ciubuc cabinet contained representatives of several parties and even two communists serving as individuals.

Moldova

Ex-President Vladimir Voronin, now leader of the Communist opposition in the legislature

The cabinet was essentially centrist—supportive of reform but aware that the reforms, although necessary, were hurting many individual Moldovans.

New parliamentary elections took place on March 22, 1998. The political situation in Moldova was still rather fluid, however, so the political parties that competed in these elections were rather different from those that competed in the 1994 elections. Fifteen political parties and electoral blocs—plus 70 independents—competed in the parliamentary elections. Only four of the contesting parties or blocs won representation in the parliament, however.

The largest winner was the Party of Moldovan Communists (PCM), which won approximately 30% of the vote and 40 seats. Although there were communists in the previous parliament and two of them even held portfolios in the previous cabinet, the PCM was a new party to the parliament, for it had still been banned at the time of the 1994 elections. The center-right but pro-reform Democratic Convention of Moldova (CDM), led by former President Snegur, came in second with approximately 20% of the vote and 26 seats. The pro-presidential For a Prosperous and Democratic Moldova (PMPD) bloc, led by Prime Minister Ciubuc, came in third with approximately 18% of the vote and 24 seats. The Party of Democratic Forces (PFD) won some 9% of the vote and 11 seats. The Agrarian-Democratic Party, the dominant party in the previous parliament (with 56 seats), fell below the minimum 4% barrier and so was eliminated from the new parliament.

Since no single party had a majority in the 101-seat parliament, negotiations began in early April for creation of a coalition government. The PCM opened negotiations by announcing its willingness to set up a coalition with the PMPD and the PFD; it rejected cooperation with the CDM.

Since such a coalition would have meant the end of reform, the PMPD did not respond to the overture of the PCM but, instead, opened discussions with the PFD and the CDM. These discussions were successful and resulted in an agreement on a coalition government which was announced on April 21. Under the terms of the agreement, each party was to receive government representation proportional to the number of votes each received in the March elections. The agreement also stipulated that the PMPD would have the chairmanship of the parliament, while the prime minister would be a member of the CDM. In addition, the three parties agreed to form a joint faction in the parliament, to be called the Alliance for Democracy and Reform, and elected former President Mircea Snegur as the joint faction leader. Dumitru Diacov was elected to the position of chairman of the parliament.

Although it appeared that Mircea Snegur, the leader of the CDM, would become prime minister, he opted, in the end, to remain in the parliament, so the incumbent, Ion Ciubuc, was reappointed as prime minister. In compensation, the CDM got one deputy prime minister slot plus the interior portfolio.

Moldova was badly affected by Russia's financial crisis which began in August 1998, however, and this led to increased inflation, a growing trade deficit, dropping foreign currency reserves and, finally, a sharp drop in the value of the currency unit, the leu. In the resulting crisis, the several parties were unable to agree on a single policy and this led to the resignation of Prime Minister Ciubuc and his cabinet on February 3, 1999. Mircea Snegur also resigned as leader of the governing Alliance for Democracy and Reform at the same time.

On February 5, President Lucinschi named Serafim Urecheanu, the mayor of Chisinau, as the new prime minister. Urecheanu attempted to set up a cabinet of "experts" not tied to the relative strength of the individual parties in the parliament, and he also called on the parliament to grant the government the right to rule by decree for at least two years. This attempt to curtail the power of parliament brought a negative reaction and Urecheanu was forced to give up his attempts to form a cabinet on February 17.

Two days later, President Lucinschi appointed Ion Sturza, a member of the pro-presidential PMPD, as the new prime minister-designate. Sturza, taking an opposite tack to that of the unsuccessful Urecheanu, promised that his government's structure would "reflect the expectations of the parliamentary majority." He also promised a "continuation of economic and democratic reforms." But Sturza got only 51 votes when parliament was asked to approve

his government on March 3, one vote short of the 52 votes necessary to win approval. Sturza lost because one of the parties of the government coalition, the Christian Democratic Popular Front (FPCD), refused to vote for the cabinet unless it was given two additional cabinet seats. President Lucinschi renominated Sturza as prime minister on March 9; this time, Sturza got 52 votes and was installed as prime minister, though that vote was also challenged, since the 52nd vote was an absentee ballot cast by a member of parliament detained in Transnistria.

In spite of his promise to reflect the "expectations of the parliamentary majority," Sturza's government was no more stable than its predecessor; however, the sharpest blow came in late October when four parliamentary deputies resigned from his political grouping, For a Prosperous and Democratic Moldova. Sturza submitted his resignation on November 9, shortly after losing a confidence vote in parliament. At issue was an agreement the government has signed with the IMF promising to privatize Moldova's wine and tobacco industries.

After Sturza's fall, the IMF froze all loans to Moldova and it appeared that the World Bank and the European Union would do the same. This led to six weeks of political maneuvering, during which parliament rejected two candidates as prime minister, before finally voting to confirm Dumitru Braghis on December 21, 1999. This represented a victory for the government, for Braghis had participated in drafting the program of the Sturza cabinet which had been rejected in November; moreover, the prime minister announced after his confirmation that he would not change the program drawn up by Sturza's outgoing cabinet. Braghis put together a cabinet of non-political technicians—in Braghis's words, "competent people, selected on the basis of professionalism"—with the expressed purpose of reducing the role of parliament in the government. In spite of that, 57 deputies voted for confirmation. Support came from the PCM (40 votes), the Christian Democratic People's Party (PPCD) (9 votes), plus eight independent deputies. Braghis, an engineer by training, headed the Moldovan Komsomol organization when the republic was still part of the Soviet Union.

Three and a half months later, Braghis managed to get his new budget through parliament—but only after he had threatened to resign if his program were not enacted. Parliament refused to pass the remainder of the government's program, however—in particular privatization of the wine and tobacco industries—even though the IMF had stipulated this as a prerequisite for additional funding.

Ex-Prime Minister Vasile Tarlev

In retrospect, that should have been expected, since the PCM, parliament's strongest block, opposed privatization.

By the summer of 2000, the economic situation in Moldova had become desperate. By IMF estimates, the economy had declined by 60% since independence in 1991. In Soviet days, a quarter of the country's earnings had come from high-tech plants serving space and submarine programs. Those had collapsed, leaving the country dependent on subsistence farming, some wine sales, and money sent home by emigrants. Average salaries, when paid, were $30 a month. Most rural people were destitute. Statistics showed that Moldova had become the poorest country in Europe, edging out Albania and Romania for that honor.

The essential problem was the stalemate in parliament. Responding to this situation, President Petru Lucinschi proposed creation of a "presidential" regime that would allow him to rule by decree. But parliament saw this proposal as a threat to its prerogatives; instead, it moved to reduce the power of the president, abolishing direct presidential elections and providing for the president to be elected by parliament.

President Lucinschi's term of office was scheduled to end in December; parliament held the first in a series of votes to elect his successor beginning on December 1. Vladimir Voronin, leader of the Party of Moldovan Communists, won 48 votes during this first round, and he continued to fall short in subsequent rounds of voting. Pavel Barbalat, candidate of the center-right, received 37 votes. When it had become clear that no candidate would win the necessary 61 votes, President Lucinschi dissolved parliament in mid-January and scheduled new parliamentary elections for February 25.

Those elections were won by the Party of Moldovan Communists with 50.7% of the popular vote and 71 seats of the 101 seats in parliament. Only two other parties cleared the 6% barrier for representation in parliament—the Braghis Alliance, headed by Prime Minister Braghis, which got 13.3% (and 19 deputies)—and the PPCD, which got 8.24% (and 11 deputies). Two prominent political parties—the Party of Revival and Accord, led by former President Mircea Snegur, and the For a Prosperous and Democratic Moldova, led by outgoing speaker Dumitru Diacov and former Prime Minister Ion Sturza—fell below the 6% barrier and so failed to win any representation in parliament.

Vladimir Voronin was elected as the country's new president on April 4, 2001 and took the oath of office three days later. Four days later, he named Vasile Tarlev as prime minister. Tarlev, an ethnic Bulgarian and a political independent, had served a stint as chairman of the Supreme Economic Council. He was also a businessman who served as chairman of the Moldovan Association of Producers. Essentially a technician, Tarlev's job has been to implement the large political decisions made by President Voronin.

At the time of his inauguration, Voronin indicated that Moldova's foreign policy would "undergo some modifications," but he saw "no serious obstacles" hindering the "continuation of reforms" domestically. He probably meant it when he promised to pursue a foreign policy "oriented toward the West, toward the East, and toward the international organizations"; however, his first foreign policy initiative was to propose to Russia that the two nations negotiate a new basic treaty to replace a treaty negotiated in 1990 but never ratified by the Russian Duma because it lacked provisions for safeguarding Russian interests of Transnistria. To deal with this problem, Voronin proposed that the new treaty specifically designate Russia as mediator in negotiations between the Moldovan government and the Dniestr Moldova authorities. At the time, it appeared that Voronin had gotten even more for Russia specifically condemned "separatism in all its forms" in the new treaty, signed by the two presidents on November 19, 2001. To reciprocate, President Voronin gave a promise, which was also written into the treaty, that "measures will be taken to satisfy the need for Russian language instruction" in Moldova.

This was, in fact, a major foreign policy coup. Russia subsequently shipped out about two-thirds of the ammunition and equipment held by the Russian 14th Army in Transnistria and afterward it consistently supported the principle of Moldova's territorial integrity in its communications with the Transnistrian authorities. This did not produce a settlement to the conflict, however.

President Voronin had two other foreign policy successes in the summer of 2001, though they appeared at the time to be less significant that his treaty with Russia. Moldova was admitted to the Stability Pact for Southeastern Europe in June and entered the World Trade Organization in July. Both of these initiatives had their origins under the previous government, of course, so they were not really the result of actions by the current government.

Voronin's domestic policy initiatives were less successful; in addition, his promise to Putin that he would satisfy the need for Russian language instruction in Moldova got him into trouble later. In September 2001, the government announced its intention to make the teaching of Russian language mandatory in all primary schools. The following month, the government announced that it was replacing a course in the "History of the Romanians" with a course in the "History of Moldovans."

In December, the Ministry of Education issued an order introducing mandatory Russian language classes in schools. Almost simultaneously, the leader of the Party of Moldovan Communists parliamentary group put forth an initiative at the Constitutional Court to introduce Russian as the country's second official language.

In response, the smaller of the two opposition political parties in the parliament, the PPCD, organized a series of anti-Russification demonstrations. As the protests continued, the government suspended the PPCD for one month; however, it was forced to rescind the suspension after international protests. After two months of protest, the government annulled its decision to introduce mandatory Russian language classes and introduced a "moratorium" on its earlier decision to replace the "History of the Romanians." President Voronin then sacked his minister of education after he told protesters that he had "made a mistake" in deciding to introduce mandatory Russian language classes. Two days later, the president accepted the resignation of his interior minister because, according to local analysts, he had refused to crack down on protesters.

Another issue which reflected badly on President Voronin was the government's handling of an application by the Bessarabian Metropolitan Church for registration in Moldova. The Bessarabian Metropolitan Church, which existed in Moldova between 1918 and 1940, is under the jurisdiction of the Bucharest Patriarchate. When it annexed the territory in 1940, Moscow created the Moldovan Metropolitan Church under the

Moldova

Moldovan family celebrating a special day

jurisdiction of the Moscow Patriarchate. After previous Moldovan governments had refused to register the Bessarabian Church, it had filed an appeal with the European Court of Human Rights (ECHR). In December 2001, the ECHR ruled in favor of the Bessarabian Church, stating that the Moldovan government had breached ECHR provisions on religious freedoms and the right of association when it refused to register the church. The Moldovan government appealed the ruling but a five-judge panel ruled against the appeal on March 25, 2002. The Bessarabian Church then applied for re-registration.

When the government stalled on the issue, the Council of Europe's Parliamentary Assembly issued a new order on April 24; two weeks later, the Council of Europe's Committee of Ministers approved a resolution calling upon the Moldovan government to report by July 31 on measures it had taken to register the Bessarabian Metropolitan Church. Most Moldovan officials still opposed registration of the Bessarabian Metropolitan Church, but the government, realizing that it had no choice, hastily drew up a draft law modifying procedures for registering religious organizations and submitted it to the parliament on July 11. On July 30, one day before the Council of Europe's deadline, the government announced that it had registered

the Bessarabian Metropolitan Church. Since that time, the Bessarabian Church has managed to open several dozen parishes in Moldova. By way of comparison, there are 1,200 Russian Orthodox parishes in Moldova.

The government's relations with the political opposition remained poor throughout its entire first term in office, both from those represented in the parliament and from within the general population. For instance, none of the opposition political parties was happy when the government proposed new legislation requiring political formations to reregister and prove that membership had not dropped below 5,000 members after the initial registration.

Press freedom also became an issue in the fall of 2002 after the Audiovisual Council withdrew the broadcasting licenses of several radio stations for violating broadcasting regulations. Three weeks later, the government ordered that the independent Voice of Bessarabia private radio station be closed down, despite (or possibly because of) the fact that the station was politically independent and had received support from the US Embassy in Chisinau.

A related issue was new legislation concerning the state-owned Teleradio Moldova. The original government plan would have transformed Teleradio Moldova into a public company, but the

government would have controlled the Board of Observers. After protests—and an appeal to the Council of Europe by opponents of the government plan—the government modified the legislation so that only 5 of the 15 members of the Board of Observers were to be appointed directly by the government.

In spite of all of the political bickering, however, the Party of Moldovan Communists managed to retain most of its popularity. A poll taken in December 2003 indicated that President Voronin was the country's most popular politician and that 64.4% supported the Party of Moldovan Communists.

However, an important part of President Voronin's program—his espousal of a pro-Russian foreign policy in return for Russia's support on "Dniestr Moldavia" issue—fell apart in November 2003 when the Russian side put forth a proposal for resolving the matter in the so-called Kozak memorandum. Essentially, the Russians proposed that Transnistria be given the status of a separate republic under a federal government with Russian troops remaining in Transnistria for another 20 years. Relations with Russia deteriorated after Voronin's rejection of the Kozak memorandum; this, in turn, apparently convinced Voronin that his foreign policy up to this time had been based on a false premise.

As a result, the next three years saw a reorientation in Voronin's foreign policy. The first step came in June 2004, when Voronin submitted a Declaration on Stability and Security Pact to the OSCE, requesting the various nations to recognize Moldova's territorial integrity. The declaration had been under discussion at the OSCE, but it had been opposed by the Russian government. Among other things, the document called for the removal of Russian troops from Dniestr Moldova. In October 2004, Moldova formally proposed that US and EU representatives be added as observers to the Dniestr Moldova negotiations.

Relations with Romania also improved during this period, partly because the government had begun to look toward eventual membership in the European Union and Romania was a little further along that same road. In connection with this, the government also approved a blueprint for a series of reforms designed to bring the country closer to EU standards. The European Commission approved the action plan in January 2004.

New parliamentary elections took place on March 6, 2005. Nine political parties, two voting blocs, and 12 independent candidates were registered to run in the elections. To win representation in parliament, independents had to win 3% of the overall vote, while parties had to garner 6%, blocs

Moldova

of two parties 9%, and blocs of three parties or more 12%.

The Party of Moldovan Communists (PCM) took 46.1% of the vote (56 seats), the Democratic Moldova Bloc (BMD) drew 28.1% (34 seats), and the Christian Democratic People's Party (PPCD) won 9.07% (11 seats).

One of the first responsibilities of the new parliament was to elect a president. It takes 61 votes to win the presidency. This became a problem for Voronin, when the leaders of the BMD and the PPCD announced that they planned to boycott the presidential vote. In fact, the BMD split over the issue when Dumitru Diacov and seven followers left the party to form a new group, called the Democratic Party (PD). When the vote for the presidency took place on April 4, Voronin won with 75 votes. He got not only the 8 votes of the PD but also the 11 votes of the PPCD. This never became a formal government coalition, but most of the parties that supported Voronin's reelection tended to cooperate with the government on most issues.

The Democratic Moldova Bloc later broke up; the main opposition then became known as Our Moldova Alliance, though there was a second opposition party which split off from the Our Moldova Alliance in October 2005 which was led by former Prime Minister Dumitru Braghis.

An IMAS-INC poll published in April 2007 shows some interesting things about the Moldovan population. While 53% expressed the view that the direction of economic policy was wrong, 49% expressed confidence in the government. President Voronin remained the country's most trusted politician and the Communist Party the most popular party. Publication

of the poll came as the government was discussing a reform of the Moldovan economy proposed by President Voronin that included tax advantages to companies that reinvested their profits, a tax amnesty, and the legalization of previously undeclared assets at a cost of 5% of their value. That probably indicated that a majority of the population was opposed to President Voronin's economic reforms but disliked every other Moldovan political figure even more.

A severe drought during the summer of 2007 had a negative effect on the Moldovan economy. Industrial production also fell during the period, though the drop was not necessarily connected with the drought. A more important factor was the loss of the wine market in Russia. President Putin promised President Voronin in 2007 that the ban on Moldovan wine would be lifted, but Moldova struggled to regain entry to the Russian market after the ban was lifted in May 2008. According to more recent statistics, over half of Moldova's exports go to various members of the European Union.

Local elections, which took place in June 2007, showed that the PCM remained the most popular party in the country. The elections also showed a drop-off in Communist support, however. Although the PCM polled 29% in mayoral elections, 14% ahead of its nearest rival, that was well down from the 41% the PCM polled in local elections in 2003. The one bright spot for the opposition was the mayoral race in the capital city of Chisinau. Here, the winner was Dorin Chirtoaca, the 29-year-old candidate of the Liberal Party.

In March 2008, Vasile Tarlev submitted his resignation as prime minister.

His successor was Zinaida Greceanii, the first woman to become prime minister of Moldova. Prime Minister Greceanii was born in the Tomsk Region of the Russian Federation. An economist with degrees from the Financial and Economic College in Chisinau and the State University of Moldova, her previous government positions included Deputy Minister of Finance (2000–2001); First Deputy Minister of Finance (2001–2002); Minister of Finance (2002–2005); and First Deputy Prime Minister (2005–2008).

New parliamentary elections took place on April 5, 2009; they were won by the PCM, which received just over 50% of the popular vote. That gave them 60 seats in the new legislature, while the opposition political parties took the remaining 41 seats. Among the casualties of the election was the PPCD, which failed to pass the minimum 6% barrier. The entire parliamentary membership of the PPCD had cast its votes for President Voronin in the previous election.

In fact, the report of the PCM victory set off violent demonstrations in Chisinau amid accusations that the Communists had stolen the election. Although the original demonstrations were organized by opposition political parties, they were quickly taken over by young people who said that they saw no future if Communists continued in control. During three days of riots, the demonstrators seized control of the president's office and set the parliamentary building on fire. The violent demonstrations appear to have been partly the result of a sharp generational and urban versus country split, with the elderly and rural citizenry supportive of the Communists and their promises of state assistance; the urban populations and young people favored greater integration with the West, in particular the European Union.

But Anne Applebaum, writing in the *Washington Post* on April 21, suggested another reason for why the demonstrations turned violent. She reported that

> *some of the most violent demonstrators were immediately identified, by Western observers and local politicians, as members of the Moldova security forces. One observer told me that it would have been difficult even to get on the roof of that parliament building without tools and preparation, let alone put up a flag.*

If true, that would indicate that the government deliberately set out to discredit the opposition by encouraging and arranging for violent acts. President Voronin's charge that Romania was trying to overthrow his government would fit in with this scenario.

Moldovan wine industry celebrated on a postage stamp

Moldova

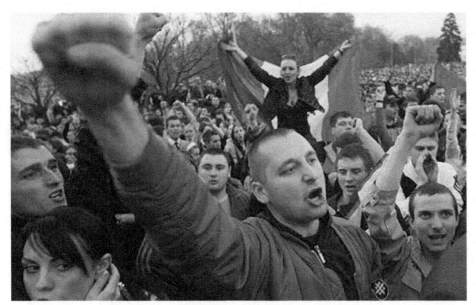

Moldova protest 2009

In any case, opposition political leaders called off the protests after the demonstrations turned violent. When President Voronin ordered the mass arrests of protestors, however, several hundred young people gathered outside government headquarters to demand the release of those arrested during the riots.

Protests went on for several days and were only defused after the Constitutional Court ordered a recount of the results of the parliamentary elections, as well as a verification of voter lists. The recount reaffirmed the Communist win.

The results presented a major problem for the PCM, however. Under the constitution, the parliament's first duty after it convened was to elect a new president. A three-fifths majority (61 votes) is needed to elect the president. Yet all three opposition political parties announced that they would boycott the election.

When the parliament convened on May 20, the PCM put forth Prime Minister Zinaida Greceanii as its candidate. The PCM also nominated a second candidate, but all 60 Communist deputies cast their ballots for Greceanii. Since opposition deputies had walked out prior to the vote, Greceanii failed to win election as president. The parliament did, however, elect Voronin as the new parliament speaker. The plan of the PCM was to have Marian Lupu, the former parliament speaker, named prime minister by Greceanii after she became president.

The parliament met again on June 3 to make its second and last attempt to elect Greceanii. According to the constitution, a second failure to elect a president would trigger new parliamentary elections. That attempt also failed, since the political opposition once again boycotted the voting.

Under the terms of the constitution, Vladimir Voronin, ex-president and newly elected parliamentary speaker, now became acting president, charged with organizing new parliament elections. After appointing Ziniada Greceanii as acting prime minister, he set July 29 as the date for new parliamentary elections.

At that moment, Voronin probably had every reason to expect that the PCM would win the July 29 parliamentary elections with enough votes that he would then be able to install Greceanii as president. However, that changed on June 12 when Marian Lupu, ex-speaker of parliament and Voronin's designated choice to become prime minister after Greceanii was installed as president, announced that he had left the PCM and had joined the Democratic Party as its new leader. Even so, there was a great deal of uncertainty about what this would mean. The Democratic Party was a left-wing party which had often cooperated with the PCM in the past; some commentators suggested that Lupu was a stalking horse for the communists and he would form an alliance with the PCM after the elections.

A poll taken shortly before the July 29 elections had some interesting findings, most of which seemed to favor the PCM. For example, over 80% of respondents described Moldova's relations with Russia as good and 77.9% said that they trusted Putin; 52% said that Russia should be Moldova's strategic partner. On the other hand, over 57% of respondents said that the best solution to Moldova's security was its neutrality, while 65% said that they supported membership in the European Union.

Since the elections took place under Moldova's system of proportional voting,

only those parties that got over 5% of the overall national vote qualified for seats; five parties passed this hurtle. The PCM came in first with 48 seats, down 12 seats from the April elections. The Liberal Democratic Party of Moldova (LDPM) came in second with 18 seats, followed by the Liberal Party (LP) with 15 seats. The Democratic Party (DP) came in fourth with 13 seats; astonishingly, in April (i.e., before Marian Lupu joined the party) that party had failed to win any seats in the parliament. Lastly, the Our Moldova Alliance (MNA) won seven seats.

The new parliament met for its first session on August 28. The PCM immediately called for a pause until September 4 for continued political consultations. However, the four opposition political parties, by this time formed into a coalition called the Alliance for European Integration, demurred. With 53 members, they had enough members to form a majority government and intended to do so. At this point, the 48 PCM members stood up and left the room. They would continue to boycott sessions of the parliament for the next several months.

The remaining members of parliament—all members of the Alliance for European Integration—then formed a commission for electing the speaker of parliament. All four factions supported Mihai Ghimpu, leader of the Liberal Party, for that post and he was elected with 53 votes. Under the terms of the constitution, Ghimpu could now become acting president until a new head of state was elected by parliament. The Alliance announced that Marian Lupu would be their nominee for the office of president.

Acting President Voronin at first refused to recognize the vote establishing the new government, going so far as to deny that the Alliance for European Integration existed; he then reversed himself and

Ex-Prime Minister Vlad Filat

Moldova

Marian Lupu, ex-Speaker of Parliament

Former President Nicolae Timofti, elected in March 2012

Former Prime Minister Iurie Leanca

submitted his resignation on September 14, though he made it clear that the PCM would not vote for Marian Lupu as president; as he put it, a new round of parliamentary elections in 2010 would be better for the country than "four years of governance by the new parliamentary majority."

Ghimpu was elected acting president on September 14, though the PCM immediately challenged the election. Three days later, after the courts confirmed the election, Ghimpu nominated Vlad Filat as prime minister.

Parliament held two votes to elect a new president in December but, with the PCM members boycotting parliament, the votes just confirmed the stalemate in parliament. In March 2010, Acting President Ghimpu, who also continued to be speaker of parliament, proposed an ad hoc commission of parliament to consider amending article 78 of the constitution pertaining to election of the president. Although the PCM was continuing its boycott of parliament, it agreed to appoint four members to the commission. The government coalition, Alliance for European Integration, stood for direct election of the president. The PCM wanted the election of the president to remain with the parliament; they proposed using a three-round voting procedure gradually lowering the voting minimum, so as to elect the president in the third round, if need be, by a simple majority. The Alliance for European Integration's plan for direct election of the president was submitted to a popular referendum in September 2010, whereupon the PCM called for a boycott of the vote. The referendum won a majority of votes cast but failed because fewer than 33% of the people went to the polls.

Presaging that vote, a political poll published in early May showed that the

PCM remained the most popular political party in Moldova, winning 28% support from among respondents. The Liberal Democratic Party (PLDM) came second with 25.5% support. The Democratic Party (PD) placed third with 13.4% support, followed by the Liberal Party (PL) with 7.6% support. The Our Moldova Alliance (NMA), drawing only 3.2% support, would not make it into the new parliament. So, the PCM remained the single strongest party but, without allies, it could not hope to form a new government.

The poll also indicated that, should Moldovans once again be given the right to elect their president, 21% would vote for Marian Lupu, 17% for Vladimir Voronin, and 14% would vote for Vlad Filat, the prime minister. Since the referendum failed, however, the Constitutional Court of Moldova ruled that parliament had to be dissolved and new parliamentary elections called.

Those parliamentary elections took place on November 28, 2010. As the May political poll had suggested, the PCM came first with 39.3% of the vote, giving it a total of 42 seats out of the 101 total. Three parties of the Alliance for European Integration—the PLDM the PD, and the PL—won the remaining 59 seats in the new parliament. The PLDM took 29.4% of the vote, giving it 32 seats. The PD came next with 12.7% of the vote, giving it 15 seats. And the PL got 10% of the vote, and the remaining 12 seats. Thus, support for the coalition had increased over past showings but it was still 2 votes short of the required three-fifths majority (61 votes) to elect a president.

The negotiations over creation of a new coalition government lasted over a month

and were described as painful. All knew that a reconstituted Alliance for European Integration would be unable to elect a president unless at least two communists broke ranks and voted for the coalition's candidate. Rumors were therefore rife that either the PLDM or the PD would join with the PCM to form a new government coalition. The PCM had actually proposed a coalition government to Martin Lupu, leader of the PD, but he rejected it because the communists had insisted that Moldova become part of a customs union with Russia. In the end, the reconstituted coalition came into being and the new government was formed on December 30, 2010. Vlad Filat, the prime minister in the old coalition, got the job again, while Marian Lupu was elected to the office of Speaker of Parliament. Since the office of president was vacant, he also became Acting President.

As discussions continued over how to elect a new president, the news broke that Prime Minister Filat had been meeting with ex-President Voronin aver a possible coalition government involving the PLDM and the PCM. The rationale was that, together, the two parties controlled 74 votes and could elect a new president. The proposal presumably involved Vlad Filat remaining on as prime minister, while a communist would be elected president. It is not clear whether Prime Minister Filat ever seriously considered the communist offer, but it did shake relations with his coalition partners for a while.

In February 2011, Moldova's highest court ruled that parliament could stay in power for its full four-year term even if it failed to elect a president. This would have left the country with an Acting President, but it did take some of the pressure off the government coalition and perhaps

Moldova

weakened the leverage of Voronin and the PCM.

Prime Minister Filat actually proposed a fairly far-reaching program for his new government, the only question being whether he would be given time to implement it. He proposed to reform the judiciary sector, law enforcement organs, and adopt a new constitution for the Government of Moldova. The main goal of the program, entitled, "European Integration, Democracy, Prosperity," was to continue the European course set by the Filat Government-1, most of whose members remained in the new team.

Politics remained in flux over the next several months, prompted partly by the economic situation of the country but also by the continuing inability to elect a president. The pro-European coalition did manage to get its candidate for mayor of Chisinau elected In June, but the coalition then almost broke up in October when Prime Minister Filat accused the Democratic Party of exercising too much power in the coalition, even going so far as joining with the Communist Party In demanding the dismissal of Prosecutor General Valeriu Zubco and Chairman of the National Commission for Financial Market Mihai Cibotaru—both Democratic Party members. There was even talk of a new government coalition being formed consisting of Filat's Liberal Democrats and the Communist Party.

Perhaps it was only idle talk. In any case, such talk ceased when three members of the Communist Party bloc in the parliament announced that they had left the bloc and might back a presidential candidate from the pro-European alliance for the presidency. The three deputies, Igor Dodon, Zinaida Greceanii, and Veronica Abramciuc, organized themselves as the Dodon group. In return for their votes, they wanted Igor Dodon elected as parliamentary speaker. This was unacceptable to the pro-European alliance.

After another futile attempt In December to elect a president and further talks, the Dodon group agreed to support a neutral candidate for the office. The choice fell on Nicolae Timofti, a 63-year-old career jurist, then chairman of the Supreme Council of Magistrates. Timofti was elected president on March 16, 2012, receiving 1 more than the 61 votes necessary to win election. Communist deputies boycotted Timofti's election.

In a statement after his election, Timofti pledged to maintain Moldova's pro-European Union outlook, arguing that it was the only way to bring prosperity to "the poorest country in Europe." In foreign policy, he promised that Moldova would maintain good relations with Romania and Ukraine; he also said that he wanted a "strategic relationship" with Russia.

Collapse of the Alliance for European Integration. On February 13, 2013, Prime Minister Vlad Filat announced that his political party, the Liberal Democrat Party, was leaving the three-party Alliance for European Integration. Vilat said at the time that the coalition had turned the country into an oligarchy with criminal clans.

One recrimination brought another. Marian Lupu, Speaker of Parliament and leader of the Democratic Party (one of the three parties of the coalition), retorted that Filat had failed to accomplish his responsibilities and brought the country to a political crisis. On March 5, the Communist Party proposed a vote of non-confidence in the Filat Government; the vote was carried by 54 votes, with 15 of the votes coming from members of the Democratic Party. Three days later, Filat submitted his resignation as prime minister.

All of these events were triggered by a December 2012 hunting accident in which a 34-year-old businessman, Sorin Paciu, was shot and killed. One of the individuals on the hunt was Prosecutor General Valeriu Zubco, who used his authority to cover up the shooting and accidental death. He was assisted in the cover-up by Appeals Court Judge Gheorghe Cretu. When Prime Minister Filat learned of the shooting and cover-up, however, he demanded that Zubco resign his office.

But by this time the issue had become political. Prosecutor General Zubco was a member of the Democratic Party and according to the coalition agreement that office was assigned to the Democratic Party to fill. But Filat attempted to use the hunting accident scandal as an opportunity to remove his greatest political enemy, Vladimir Plahotniuc, from his position as vice-chair of parliament by abolishing the position of vice-chair.

Meanwhile, the Democratic Party, seeing Filat's actions as an attack on the party, used their control of the prosecutor's office to dig up dirt on Filat's Liberal Democratic Party of Moldova (PLDM), which resulted in allegations being made against the PLDM ministers of culture and health. Filats reacted by pulling the PLDM out of the Alliance for European Integration; this, in turn, led to the vote of non-confidence that led to his resignation as prime minister.

Most of the rest of March was spent trying to reconstruct the Alliance for European Integration. When President Timofti offered Filat a reappointment as prime minister, it was the leadership of the Liberal Party which took the issue to the Constitutional Court, which ruled on April 15 that the reappointment of Filat as acting prime minister was an illegal act. President Timofti then named Foreign Minister Iurie Leanca as the country's caretaker prime minister on April 23.

Two days later, the Communist Party proposed the removal of Marian Lupu as speaker of parliament. This time, the Liberal Democrats joined with the Communists to vote Lupu out of office. It now appeared that the Alliance for European Integration was well and truly dead—killed not by political differences between and among the parties but by personal rivalries and differences by leading figures within the parties who then used their control of individual political parties to exact vengeance against personal enemies. Obviously a lot of hubris was also involved.

The Communist Party of Moldova began calling for new elections which they could hope to win since the parties of the Alliance for European Integration had so fully fallen out with each other.

Faced with the possibility of new elections, Vlad Filat and the Liberal Democrats established an informal coalition with the

1 Leu note, first printed in 1994

Communists and, together, they passed a series of measures in parliament designed to favor them in the new voting. They first voted to raise the electoral threshold from 4 to 6%, an action which threatened the continued existence of the Liberals, the smallest party in the current parliament. Next, they restored the right of Soviet-era passport holders to vote in the next elections, reversing a vote taken by the parliament two weeks earlier. This would presumably have benefited the Communists. Third, they gave the legislature the power to remove judges of the Constitutional Court if three-fifths of the legislative body supported the decision. The obvious purpose here was to remove those judges who had on April 15 ruled that Vlad Filat was ineligible to be reappointed prime minister. And in a final act of defiance, the Communist and Liberal Democratic deputies voted to reverse the appointment of Corneliu Gurin as the new Prosecutor General.

All of these actions brought swift condemnations from various European Union governments and Moldova came under strong international pressure to reverse the decisions. President Timofti's May 15 decision to formally name Iurie Leanca as prime minister designate—a mandate which gave him 15 days to form a new governing coalition and get it confirmed—was certainly part of Moldova's reaction to the international pressure. Fifteen days later, 58 deputies voted to confirm Leanca as prime minister after Communist deputies walked out of the session hall prior to the voting.

A strong spokesman for the European agenda, Leanca shepherded the final round of negotiations on Moldova's signing of an Association Agreement with the European Union. As Leanca commented in June 2013, "joining the EU is not an option, but a necessity." Reflecting this position, Moldova formally informed Russia in August that Moldova would not join the Putin-sponsored Eurasian Union. Three months later, Moldova initialed the Association Agreement with the EU on November 29.

Various spokesmen for the Russian government responded angrily to Moldova's opting for an association with the EU over membership in the Eurasian Union. Russian Foreign Minister Sergey Lavrov said in July that signing an Association Agreement with the EU would "affect the relations between Russia and the Republic of Moldova." A month later, during a visit to Chisinau, Russian Deputy Prime Minister Rogozin suggested that Russia might cut off the natural gas delivered to the country during winter. "We hope you will not freeze in winter," Rogozin warned. And in September, Russia banned the importation of Moldovan wines. The ban came into effect one day after a summit to

further Moldova's and other neighbors' ties with the EU.

President Timofti responded by calling Russia's move "unfriendly." And Prime Minister Leanca suggested that Russia's move conflicted with bilateral trade deals and World Trade Organization obligations. As it happened, the European Union liberalized Moldovan wine exports to the EU effective January 2014. And addressing the Russian threat to cut off natural gas exports, the Moldovan and Romanian Governments signed an agreement in August 2013 to begin construction of a joint pipeline to connect Moldova to the EU's network of natural gas. The first section of the pipeline was opened in 2014.

Moldova is one of the poorest countries in Europe. Its economy is largely based on agriculture. It has high unemployment, a large foreign debt, and significant corruption within the economy. Moreover, the country is heavily dependent on energy imports from Russia. It sits on a fault line between the European Union and the newly formed Eurasian Economic Union, which is dominated by Russia. As the Ukrainian crisis unfolded in 2013–2015, Moldova has moved resolutely to join the EU. It has received strong support for EU membership from Romania in particular. The historic ties between the two countries are very strong; the Moldovan language, in fact, is but a dialect of Romanian.

In late November 2013, Moldovan Prime Minister Lurie Leanca initialed the Association Agreement with the EU in Vilnius, the capital of Lithuania. This was the same agreement that President Yanukovych of Ukraine backed out of, which sparked demonstrations in Kyiv, which led to the Euromaidan Revolution. Then, on June 27, 2014, Moldova signed the agreement with the EU in Brussels, which included a free-trade pact. The

Controversial oligarch and former PDM chairman, Vladimir Plahotniuc

EU promptly lifted visa restrictions for Moldovans traveling to EU countries. Moldova's decision to seek eventual EU membership worsened its relations with Russia, which wanted Moldova to join its Eurasian Economic Union. Russia banned the import of Moldovan wine in 2013, and following the signing of the agreement in Brussels, Russia added import bans on apples, meat, and other food products from Moldova. Moldova responded by limiting Russian media broadcasts in Moldova, which are targeted mainly to the breakaway Transnistria region in eastern Moldova.

On November 30, Moldova elected a new parliament. A coalition of pro-European parties won a narrow victory; however, the pro-Kremlin socialists and communists finished first and third, respectively. The pro-European coalition saw a drop of 11% from the 2010 parliamentary elections largely due to the damage inflicted on the economy by the Russian sanctions, a major banking scandal, and the overall weak global economy.

Nevertheless, in May 2015, Moldovan President Timofti clearly stated that the country's four million citizens would prefer to join the European Union: "We can't deny the realities that exist in Moldova. We were part of a union where Russia predominated. We are a European country and our people have European aspirations. It has been understood that we can live much better in the European family than in any other political conjunction."

Since the November 30, 2014, parliamentary elections, the tensions between the pro-European and pro-Russian forces have been exacerbated by a prolonged period of political tumult. Following the elections, political wrangling between the Liberal Democratic Party of Moldova (PLDM) and the Democratic Party of Moldova (PDM) dragged on for months before a coalition government headed by Chiril Gaburici was formed in mid-February 2015. The coalition government proved unstable and collapsed less than four months later. The government formed in the wake, headed by Valeriu Strelet, was around for an even shorter period, lasting only three months. This was followed by another three months of wrangling between the political parties, until on January 20, 2016, a new government headed by Pavel Filip was sworn in.

The instability of the Moldovan governmental was exacerbated by social mobilization over political corruption. In 2014, around $1 billion (more than 10% of Moldova's GDP) was illegally transferred out of three of the country's largest banks and disappeared. The revelation of the banking theft spurred the organization of a new group calling themselves Dignity and Truth. Throughout 2015, the organization

Moldova

staged large street demonstrations on an almost weekly basis demanding investigation into the stolen money. Pressure from the street was influential in the collapse of the Strelet government and in the arrest of former Prime Minister Filat on corruption charges related to this scandal. However, there are clear limits to the power of the protesters, as demonstrated by the fact that Ilan Shor, a powerful businessman who is believed to be at the center of the scandal remains at large and is currently an elected mayor in the city of Orhei.

In 2015 and 2016, a series of rival demonstrations were held in Chisinau pushing for (and against) unification with Romania. While unification is highly improbable, for the demonstrators unity with Romania would represent the cementing of Moldova's status a European state. Furthermore, there is a sense that unification would help to stabilize the country's politics and solve some long-standing fiscal problems. The dream of unification took a significant symbolic hit when Igor Dodon won the second round of the presidential election held November 13, 2016. Dodon, a member of the pro-Russian Party of Socialists of the Republic of Moldova (PSRM), ran on improving relations with Russia. He also appears to have little sympathy for pro-unification efforts: in an interview in a Russian newspaper (*Komsomolskaya Pravda*) published on February 3, he accused the United States of promoting unification with Romania as a means to generate instability within the country.

In December 2017, the ruling PDM party reshuffled its government in an apparent attempt to boost domestic and European legitimacy. The leader of the party, Vlad Plahotniuc, claimed that the new government would be more technocratic, but it is best understood as an effort to clean up the party's image and dissociate the government from the massive bank corruption scandal. This action, as well as the passage of a new law in January 2018 banning Russian "media propaganda," were attempts to establish the PDM as the leading pro-Western party in the run-up to the February 2019 elections.

The February 2019 elections were the first in Moldova to utilize a mixed electoral system in which 50 seats were determined via a national party-list proportional vote, and 51 seats were determined via single-member districts. Results were inconclusive and marred by allegations of vote buying. The PSRM won a plurality of seats with 35, followed by the PDM's 30 seats, and the anti corruption alliance ACUM's 26 seats. Although in the past, the pro-West PDM and the pro-Russian PSRM worked together to pass the sweeping electoral reforms that established the

new mixed voting system over the objections of domestic civil society actors and the Council of Europe, forging a coalition in the wake of the fragmented election results was quite difficult.

In June, the pro-Russian PSRM formed an uneasy coalition with the pro-EU ACUM bloc (composed of PAS and DA), forcing the PDM into opposition. The government that formed, headed by ACUM co-leader Maia Sandu, only lasted for five months. Although the two blocs were able to put aside foreign policy disagreements, a dispute over the process to appoint the country's general prosecutor proved fatal, and on November 14, the Sandu government lost a no-confidence vote. The next day the PSRM formed a minority headed by Ion Chicu. The government gained approval in parliament based on the assurance from President Dodon that the new prime minister is not party operator; according to Dodon, Chicu is "a technocrat, a professional who has not been in any political party." Chicu reinforced this message with his claim to only seek to serve as caretaker until new elections can be called.

Not only did the post-election coalition wrangling reveal that foreign policy disputes can (at least occasionally) be transcended in Moldova, perhaps even more significantly it also resulted in Vladimir Plahotniuc's exit from political life. As the short-lived coalition was being forged, the powerful oligarch fled from the country, eventually making his way to the United States. In March 2020, the U.S. Embassy in Moldova announced that despite being formally banned in January from entering the U.S. due to "significant corruption," he had been able to get into the country. It also announced that the process for deporting Plahotniuc had begun. He has subsequently moved to Turkey. If, and when, he is repatriated he could face corruption charges in Moldova.

Dodon was defeated in the second round of the presidential election to Maia Sandu (the country's first female president) in November 2020. This election was largely contested on the familiar pro-west vs. pro-Russian lines, with Sandu demanding the Russian troops withdraw from Transdniestria. Due to the stark divisions between the factions, this election once again spurred a governance crisis as 20,000 protesters gathered in Chisinau demanding snap elections to enable the newly ascendant pro-Western faction an opportunity to regain control of parliament. The protests were successful: Prime Minister Chicu resigned on December 23, and early elections were scheduled for July 11, 2021, in which the Party of Action and Solidarity, founded by Maia Sandu in 2015, won a parliamentary majority. With PAS holding a solid majority in parliament,

Sandu finally has an opportunity to implement her political agenda of tackling corruption, reducing poverty and integrating Moldova with the EU. As part of the government's anti-corruption campaign, on May 24, 2002, Igor Dodon was detained on charges of treason and corruption. Dodon denied the charges as being politically motivated and his supporters took to the street to demand his release and accused the government of political persecution.

Foreign Policy

General. Moldova, when it achieved independence in 1991, adopted a policy of neutrality and it has adhered to that stance ever since. Although it became a member of the Commonwealth of Independent States, it has kept its membership at a nominal level and it has eschewed other regional organizations that have come into existence in recent years. Moldova has been active in world organizations such as the United Nations and it has had good working relations with the IMF and World Bank. President Voronin met with the president of both organizations in October 2002 while paying an official visit to Washington. In return, Voronin received World Bank President James Wolfensohn's promise of support for the reform process in Moldova. Most recently, Moldova has been working to improve relations with the European Union. In April 2005, the European Commission gave Moldova a grant of $11.77 million to improve public finance management, social services, and for projects in the agricultural sector.

Russia. Relations with Russia were correct but cool until the communists came to power as a result of the 2000 elections. One reason for this was Russia's support for the breakaway government in the area east of the Nistru (Dniestr) River. However, the communists postulated that it was necessary to improve relations with Russia in order to win its support and this paid off handsomely for a while. Russia committed itself to supporting Moldova's territorial integrity and it began pulling its military equipment, though not all of its troops, out of the area of Dniestr Moldova.

Things began to fall apart in November 2003 when Russia submitted its plan for unification of the two parts of Moldova. The plan, called the Kozak memorandum, called for the creation of a federal state with Moldova and Transnistria as equal partners, each with its own government. The memorandum would have also legalized the presence of Russian troops in Transnistria for another 20 years. President Voronin rejected the plan and Russo-Moldovan relations deteriorated after that time.

By February 2005, the situation had gotten so bad that the Moldovan government expelled 11 Russian citizens who had come to Moldova as observers for the parliamentary elections—according to the Moldovan government because the Russians were interfering in the election campaign and spreading disinformation. In response, the Russian Duma adopted a resolution calling for a boycott of Moldovan wine and tobacco and an increase in the price of energy exports to Moldova.

The Russian government did temporarily ban the importation of Moldovan wines and fruits and vegetables in May 2005. This ban was lifted, but it was then re-imposed on March 27, 2006. The ban on the import of Moldovan wines was lifted in November 2006; it was lifted on fruits and vegetables in March 2007, along with the ban on Moldovan meat. Moldova's total exports fell by 3.6% in 2006; however, Moldova's exports to CIS members (including Russia) accounted for only 40.3% of total exports, down from 50.5% in 2005.

Three agreements, reached in December 2006, show the then current state of Moldovan-Russian relations. In early December, Russia and Moldova signed an agreement on resumption of passenger rail traffic between their two republics via the Transnistrian region. Russia also agreed to accept rail traffic through the Moldovan-Ukrainian checkpoint; it was the March 2006 agreement with Ukraine on a common border checkpoint that brought the original Russian ban on rail traffic from Moldova. A few days later,

Gazprom agreed to provide natural gas to Moldova for $170 per 1,000 cubic meters in 2007, an increase of only $10 from what Moldova paid in 2006—though the agreement did state that the natural gas price would continue to increase until it reached the average European level in 2011. Eight days later, Moldova signed a bilateral agreement on Moscow's accession to the World Trade Organization. After the signing, President Voronin described Russia as Moldova's strategic partner; "Russia is our main economic partner, the main market for our goods and a supplier of energy carriers."

The victory of the Alliance for European Integration in the summer of 2009 brought some changes in Moldovan–Russian relations, but they were not as great as might have been expected. The new government was committed to integration with Western Europe, but they wished to continue good relations with Russia.

That was not always easy, since the Russian government sometimes used economic measures to put pressure on the Moldovan government to get it to see things its way. Russia had previously embargoed deliveries of Moldovan wine in March 2006, a ban that lasted for more than a year. Then, in June 2010, Russia's consumer rights watchdog Rospotrebnazor reported that it had detected pesticides in Moldovan wine after Acting President Ghimpu declared June 28 the Day of Soviet Occupation. In October 2010, Rospotrebnadzor rejected 655,000 liters of imported Moldovan wine.

In addition, Gazprom has billed the Government of Moldova for gas delivered to the pro-Russian government of Transnistria. Gazprom is currently charging Moldova $294 per 1,000 cubic meters, up by 12% from the fourth quarter of 2010. It should be added, however, that this price is in line with the December 2007 Russian-Moldovan agreement that Gazprom signed with President Voronin.

On the other side, Marian Lupu, the Acting President, announced in January 2011, that he favored the automatic extension of the Russian–Moldovan treaty signed in 2001; that treaty, which was to run for 10 years, expires in 2011 unless renewed. It is Acting President Lupu's position that Moldova's European integration does not contradict its cooperation with Russia.

In August 2012, the Moldovan government ratified a Free Trade Zone Agreement with CIS. One month later, Russian Prime Minister Medvedev issued a formal invitation to Moldova to join the Customs Union (also known as the Eurasian Union) created by Russia, Belarus, and Kazakhstan and due to come into existence in 2015. This was a major domestic political issue in Moldova since the Communist Party of Moldova was pressing strongly for Moldova to join the Eurasian Union, while the Alliance for European Integration favored signing the Association Agreement with the European Union. The Moldovan government formally informed the Russian government that it would not be joining the Eurasian Union on September 3, 2013; the government formally initialed the Association with the EU on November 29. Although the Moldovan government went out of its way to stress that it was committed to the best possible relationship with Russia, the feeling was not reciprocated. Having already cut off wine imports from Moldova in September and threatened to cut off natural gas exports, Russia began demanding that Moldova pay $4 billion for natural gas supplied to Transnistria and never paid for by the Transnistrian government. In March 2014, President Putin claimed that Moldova and Ukraine had instituted a "blockade" against Transnistria; he demanded that the "blockade" be lifted and raised the issue of sending in Russian troops to come to the aid of Russian citizens living in Transnistria. And in April 2014 Russia banned the importation of pork products from Moldova, citing quality concerns because the products of one Moldovan company were processed in an EU member state. Russia maintains a ban on all pork products from the EU, allegedly due to possible swine flu infection. Reflecting the various Russian actions, Moldovan exports to Russia decreased by 28.5% in the

Ex-President Voronin holds a joint press conference with Javier Solana, European Union foreign policy chief in Chisinau on April 24, 2009. Voronin's term as president ended later that year, but he remains the leader of the Moldovan Communist Party

Moldova

first two months of 2014 against the same period in 2013. Moldova is seeking to end its economic dependence on Russia, particularly its near-total reliance on Russian gas, which it used to receive at below market price. The country has found itself trapped in a cycle of debt before Russia's Gazprom, which raised gas prices following the invasion of Ukraine. Relations with Russia have deteriorated following the election of Maia Sandau, who has been actively trying to put the country on the path to joining the EU. In response to Russia's unprovoked aggression against Ukraine, in March 2022 Moldova formally applied for EU membership and synchronized its electricity grid with that of the EU. Moldova condemned the invasion of Ukraine and publicly supported the sovereignty and territorial integrity of that country. Perhaps, for these reasons, Russia increased gas prices for Moldova and threatened to block energy export to the country, which forced Moldova to seriously explore alternatives to Russian gas.

United States. The United States government gave its blessing to an independent Moldova from the beginning, but relations between the two countries have never been extensive. Yet the United States has supported IMF and World Bank loans to Moldova, a policy it continued under the Communist government. The United States also supports the reintegration of the area east of the Nistru (Dniestr) River in a new federal framework. After an official four-day visit to Washington in December 2002, President Voronin commented that Moldova "counts on US backing" in its efforts to shape a "unified, neutral, and demilitarized country." During his meeting with President George W. Bush, Voronin told him that Moldova would be sending five members of the Moldovan military engineering corps to participate in de-mining operations in Afghanistan. Relations warmed further in 2004, particularly after President Voronin proposed in October that the United States join the talks on Dniestr Moldova as an observer, along with representatives of the European Union.

Romania. Moldova's relations with Romania have been at the center of its politics since achieving independence in 1991. It was, in fact, the existence of political leaders arguing for union with Romania that led pro-Russian leaders in the area east of the Nistru (Dniestr) River to create their separate mini-state. Most Moldovan political figures long ago gave up any thought of merging with Romania, but the fact that the two countries share both a language and a religion (though not the same religious leadership) means that relations with

Romania are different than they are with any other country. In recent years, Romanian politicians have gone out of their way to respect Moldova's separate identity, and this has helped smooth relations somewhat, but there continue to be issues.

One of the more important is the decade-long struggle of the Bessarabian Metropolitan Church to receive permission to operate legally in Moldova. This church, which operated in Bessarabia between 1918 and 1940, was banned when Bessarabia was incorporated into the Soviet Union because it operates under the jurisdiction of the Bucharest Patriarchate. After the collapse of the Soviet Union, it applied to operate in Moldova, but previous governments refused to give it permission. As it continued to press its request for permission to operate in Moldova, the Moldovan government came to believe that the Romanian Government was behind the actions of the Bessarabian Church.

The communist government escalated the matter further when it accused Romania of interfering in Moldovan politics through its support of such things as the demonstrations against mandatory Russian language instruction and dropping the course on the "History of the Romanians" from the school curriculum. Relations reached their nadir in March 2002 when Moldova expelled the Romanian military attaché and Romania retaliated by expelling the Moldovan military attaché in Bucharest. The breach was partially healed when Romania appointed a new military attaché to its embassy in Chisinau in August.

In October 2002, President Voronin met with Romanian President Ion Iliescu in Beirut, and the two presidents discussed measures they could take to improve relations. Three months later, President Voronin gave an interview with Romania Radio in which he again took up the subject of how to improve Moldovan-Romanian relations. The main thing that Bucharest could do to improve relations, he said, was to renounce talk of the existence of "two Romanian states." A second condition for improving relations would be for the two countries to concentrate on economic rather than "all sorts of political or national problems."

Relations between the two countries improved enormously in the period 2005–2006 but turned negative again in 2007. The improvement was partly due to a new foreign policy orientation on the part of Moldova, which turned westward after relations with Russia deteriorated toward the end of 2003.

Several of the old differences appeared in 2007, however. In December 2007, Moldova expelled two senior Romanian diplomats for activities "incompatible

with their diplomatic status." Although the Moldovan government gave no other details, it was unofficially spread about that the diplomats funneled money to three newspapers that favored Moldova's becoming part of Romania. It may also have been a case of pique on President Voronin's part. When he visited the European Union's headquarters in Brussels in December 2007, he publicly accused Romania of "constant aggression." President Voronin took particular offense at Romania's refusal to recognize Moldovan and Romanian as separate languages.

Moldovan-Romanian relations had reached a low under the Voronin regime, but improved significantly under Acting President Ghimpu. President Timofti is more neutral in his attitude toward Romania but relations remain good. That probably suits most Moldovans since they have made it clear in poll after poll that they prefer an independent Moldova and oppose merging with Romania. In addition, the approximately 30% of Moldovan citizens whose ethnic background is other than Romanian are particularly opposed to becoming part of Romania. At the same time, Romania's standing offer of Romanian citizenship and a Romanian passport is proving to be attractive to many Moldovans, particularly since it allows them to freely travel and work inside the European Union. Moldovans traveling on Moldovan passports require visas to enter Romania and the European Union.

In November 2010, Romania and Moldova signed a border treaty, wherein, among other things, Romania recognized Moldova's borders. The treaty also dealt with technical things such as marking of the border, usage of water, railways and roads, fishing, hunting, and breaches of the border regime. Romania also strongly supports Moldova's future membership in the European Union.

Nature of the Regime

The Republic of Moldova has a presidential-parliamentary system, with the president recognized as spokesman for the nation and also responsible for setting general policy. Moldova has a unicameral parliament of 101 members. Formerly known as the Supreme Soviet, it is now known as the Supreme Council or parliament. Moldova's current constitution was approved in July 1994. The new constitution made some changes in the administrative divisions of the state, but otherwise mainly codified changes adopted after Moldova's declaration of independence in 1991. On one interesting point, however, the constitution created a Supreme Court but gave it no judicial review of legislative acts; instead, it created a separate

Moldova

Constitutional Court, which has sole authority for constitutional judicature.

The president was popularly elected until the fall of 2000, when, in reaction to President Petru Lucinschi's attempt to increase the powers of the office, the legislature amended the constitution to give itself the power to elect the president, thus creating in theory a parliamentary republic. However, the Party of Moldovan Communists (PCM) won the February 2001 parliamentary elections, so it was Vladimir Voronin, the PCM leader, who got to interpret and implement the constitutional reform. He chose the office of president (while retaining the position of head of the PCM), and he gave the office a much more powerful mandate than his constitutionally reserved ceremonial role.

When President Voronin's term of office was up in May 2009, the parliament failed to elect a new president in two separate votes. New parliamentary elections were then scheduled to take place on July 29 but, before they could occur, Marian Lupu, the PCM's designated candidate to become prime minister, resigned from the PCM and took over leadership of the reconstituted Democratic Party. The July 29 parliamentary elections were won by four opposition political parties including Lupu's Democratic Party. They won 53 parliamentary seats to the PCM's 48, and took power as the Alliance for European Integration. Their 53 seats were, however, not enough to elect a new president without PCM support. Since their candidate was Marian Lupu, the PCM withdrew from parliament rather than vote for an individual they referred to as a traitor and turncoat. Accordingly, the Speaker of Parliament held the additional position of acting president between September 2009 and March 2012. The stalemate was finally broken on March 16, 2012, when Nicolae Timofti was elected president.

In March 2016, the Constitutional Court ruled that parliament did not have authority to select the head of state, thus overturning the 16-year-old amendment that ended the popular election of president. Eight months later, in November 2016, Igor Dodon became the first popularly elected president in 20 years. The fact that Dodon is openly in favor of enhancing relations with Russia, puts him at odds with the current parliament and could result in continued tumult in Moldovan politics.

The president appoints a prime minister who must be confirmed by the legislature. The president also appoints members of the council of ministers on recommendation of the prime minister. The prime minister and members of the council of ministers must be approved by the legislature before they can take office, and the prime minister must retain the support of a majority in the legislature in order to remain in office. The prime minister handles day-to-day policy and presides over meetings of the council of ministers. The current prime minister is Pavel Filip, confirmed in office on January 20, 2016.

In a rather rushed process, the government overhauled its electoral system in summer 2017, moving from a proportional representation (PR) system to a mixed system that will include elements of first-past-the-post (FPTP). The ruling PDM party argued that the inclusion of FPTP elements would enhance representation by making representatives directly accountable to specific constituents. Furthermore, they argued that since other European states, most notably Germany, have mixed systems, the reform had genuine democratic intent. However, many domestic and international critics remained skeptical, suggesting that the reforms were initiated in order to extend the rule of the PDM despite the party's current widespread unpopularity. Critics alleged that the reforms were pushed through without generating widespread societal consensus and seemed designed to favor wealthy elites, such as PDM chairman and notorious tycoon Vladimir Plahotniuc, while weakening the prospects for smaller and new parties. In essence, these critics alleged that the reforms are likely to perpetuate, rather than reduce, the role of corruption in Moldovan electoral politics.

February 2019 witnessed the first election under the new mixed system. The election itself was competitive with 3 parties/coalitions receiving more than 25 seats in the 101 body parliament; however it was indecisive. After months of wrangling, an unlikely coalition government was forged between the pro-Russian PSRM and the pro-EU bloc ACUM. For a country whose domestic political fights often seem to revolve around foreign policy positions, this coalition may signal a new era of political possibilities. However, this particular coalition proved short-lived and led to the establishment of a minority technocratic caretaker government backed by the PSRM. Even this caretaker government proved short-lived; in the face of protester demands for new elections, Prime Minister Chicu resigned in December 2020, and Aureliu Ciocoi named acting Prime Minister. In snap elections that took place in July 2021, the Party of Action and Solidarity won a parliamentary majority. It remains to be seen whether these elections will finally allow for the formation of a somewhat durable ruling coalition.

Culture

The Republic of Moldova is primarily an agricultural society, with about 60% of the population still living in the countryside. On the other hand, Moldovan villages are large, averaging over 1,000 inhabitants, and fairly modern. All have electricity, for example, and most are supplied with natural gas as well. Because of the ethnic identity of most Moldovans, the culture of Moldova is similar to that found in Romania. Most people think of themselves as members of the Orthodox Church and that has become more important since all restraints on religion were lifted. The border with Romania is also now open, so that reinforces the connection.

Most Moldovans are literate, and there is a comprehensive system of primary and secondary schools throughout the republic. Around 70% of the children go to preschool before entering primary school.

The most prestigious institutes of higher education are the State University, the Nicolae Testimiteanu University of Medicine, and the Academy of Economic Studies, all located in Chisinau (Kishnev), plus the Aleco Russo Pedagogic University at Bain. There are several other institutions of higher education in other parts of the republic, including 10 private institutions of higher education founded since 1992. Two of the better-known ones are the Free University of Moldova and the Cooperative Commercial University. There are also 51 technical schools scattered throughout the republic.

The Moldovan Academy of Sciences was established in 1961. It has 17 research institutes under its jurisdiction.

Economy

The Moldovan economy is still predominantly agricultural, with approximately 40% of the people still employed on the land. Its mild climate and fertile soil, plus the extensive mechanization that has taken place since 1940, mean that agriculture is fairly productive, in spite of the fact that most land is still organized into successor organizations of the old collective or state farms.

President Lucinschi said in March 1998 that 700,000 land titles had been distributed, though the titles were for parcels of land varying in size from one to three hectares (2.5 to 7.5 acres). Saying that it was "high time to end the useless debates about land privatization," Lucinschi urged the country to accelerate reforms in the villages. His personal choice, he said, would be a model where peasants would work their land in "well-equipped peasant associations." The overwhelming victory of the Party of Moldovan Communists in the February 2001 parliamentary elections put the entire question of land tenure on hold for the foreseeable future, however.

Winter wheat and corn are the main grain crops grown. Wheat is consumed

Moldova

within the republic, while some of the corn is exported to other republics.

Other crops that have traditionally produced surpluses for export include sugar beets, tobacco, and sunflower seeds. Moldova also produces significant quantities of fruits, vegetables, berries, grapes, and walnuts, all of which have been exported to other republics in the past. Today, a majority of Moldova's exports go to countries in the European Union, though trade with Russia and Ukraine remain extremely important.

Moldova has a diversified industry, though the most significant branch is food processing. These include sugar refining, wine making (including champagne and brandy), oil pressing, canning, and the processing of essential oils. All of these branches have traditionally exported to other parts of the Soviet Union, though a March 2006 ban by the Russian government on the importation of Moldovan wine led the Moldovan government to seek new export markets among its neighbors to the west. Flour mills, dairies, meat processing, and candy making industries also exist, but these serve the domestic market.

Other light industry includes things such as the processing of pelts for fur coats, footwear, and textiles, particularly knitting and the processing of silk. There is relatively little heavy industry, though the republic does have some machine-building, including tractors, and it also manufactures building supplies, including bricks, tiles, cement, slate, and concrete blocks. In 2005, industry accounted for 23.9% of GDP and 14% of the labor force.

A draft privatization program submitted in January 1992 by the department for privatization to the Supreme Economic Council was rejected as being too narrow in scope. Cabinet members who participated in the discussion favored an alternate program drawn up by government experts. The disagreement appeared to be more political than economic. Parliament had set up the department for privatization as an agency separate from the cabinet, but several cabinet members wanted the cabinet to be in charge of privatization. Parliament, which wanted privatization to start immediately, opposed this. The disagreement caused privatization to be put on hold for the next year.

Another factor was the bad economic situation. By some estimates, real income dropped by two-thirds between 1990 and 1994. The first privatizations finally occurred in 1994, when the government finally began to implement a voucher program which privatized 940 companies; some new private companies also began to appear at this time. Currently, around 50% of the national economy is in private hands.

GDP growth, which had increased by 1.3% in 1997, turned negative again in 1998. The Russian financial crisis which began in August 1998 hit the Moldovan economy perhaps harder than any other former Soviet republic, probably because Moldova had continued to maintain most of its trade with Russia. Thus, even as the parliament was calling for a speed up in privatization of state enterprises and of the energy sector in September 1998, the government was reporting that the budget would no longer stand the effects of the Russian financial crisis and would have to be revised.

After three years of decline, the Moldovan economy began growing again in 2000, though by a pallid 1.9%; the trend continued in 2001, however, and has remained at or above the 6% level every year since. In 2010, the economy grew by 6.9%.

These growth figures are somewhat misleading, however. Moldova always has great difficulty finding markets for its exports, since they are mainly agricultural—wine, fruit, and vegetables.

A harsh blow came in March 2006, when the Russian government banned the importation of Moldovan wines, fruits and vegetables, and meat. The ban on fruits and vegetables was lifted after about nine months; the ban of Moldovan wine was also eventually lifted, but Moldova has not been able to regain only about one-half of its former share of the Russian market; moreover, a new Russian regulatory regime has meant additional expenses so Moldovan wines now cost more in Russia, thus decreasing their competitiveness.

The European Union's Common Agricultural Policy until recently tended to keep such products out; until recently, the European Union used a quota system to limit the total value of goods Moldova could export to the European Union. For example, 12% of Moldova's wine exports went to the European Union in 2008; that figure represented a 27% increase over 2007. However, 40% of the wine going to the European Union actually went to one country, Poland.

The European Union did grant individual trade preferences to Moldova in March 2008, which means that Moldova has received quotas for the duty-free export to the European Union of small amounts of products such as sugar, wine, and wheat. In 2011, the European Union granted additional quotas for wine, barley, corn (maize), and wheat.

Moldova suffered a 6% decrease in industrial production during the first half of 2006, though this situation reversed itself in the second half of the year. A bad drought in the summer of 2007 had a disastrous effect on agricultural production.

The situation might have been far worse but—according to a report of the

International Organization of Migration Moldovan—migrant workers sent home a record $1 billion in 2006. According to the report, one-third of Moldova's working-age population is employed abroad, and cash remittances account for 30% of the country's gross domestic product. The recent worldwide economic crisis meant that remittances from Moldovans working abroad fell somewhat in 2009, but then grew again to $1.3 billion in 2010. This report also indicated that almost half of all Moldovan workers are employed abroad. These remittances obviously remain extremely important for the Moldovan economy. The National Bank of Moldova reported in April 2013 that Moldovans working abroad transferred $1.5 billion to Moldavia through banks in 2012. They had transferred a further $202.7 million home in the first two months of 2013.

In the past, most Moldovan men tended to find work either in Ukraine or Russia, mainly in the construction industry or agriculture. This remains true, though the number of male Moldovans finding work inside the European Union has grown considerably in recent years. A December 2012 report by the Russian Federal Migration Service indicated that 529,467 Moldovan citizens were residing in Russia; most Moldovans live in and around Moscow. Moldovan women are found mainly in Western Europe, Turkey, or Israel, where they work as domestics, as agricultural workers, or in the sex industry.

About 80% of all Moldovans still live below the poverty line. The latest Moldovan government report on salaries, issued in March 2010, gave the average monthly salary as 2,699 lei ($211). The average salary of civil servants was somewhat less than that—2,375 lei ($186)—while the average salary in the banking and financial was higher—5,533 lei ($433). Workers in the agrarian and fisheries sector averaged only 1,294 lei ($101), however.

Moldova has received some outside assistance from international organizations such as the IMF. But the relationship has not been smooth because of the Moldovan government's inability to follow a consistent policy of reform.

To give one example, the IMF suspended a $190 million loan in the fall of 1997 because of the stalled reform process; it then agreed to unfreeze a $35 million tranche in January 1999, in view of the impact of the Russian crisis on Moldova's economy. It froze lending again in the summer of 2000 when the legislature deadlocked over privatization. After the Party of Moldovan Communists won an overwhelming majority in the February 2001 parliamentary elections, however, the IMF offered to open talks with Moldova; under an agreement reached in the summer of 2001, the

Moldova

IMF resumed its external financing for Moldova.

The World Bank also renewed its support to Moldova in 2001, providing $20 million for budget stabilization. Moldova was also admitted to the World Trade Organization in 2001.

In 2006, the Paris Club agreed to restructure the foreign loans Moldova received before December 31, 2000—worth about $150 million. In addition, the International Trade Committee of the European Parliament approved $58 million in economic aid to Moldova in January 2007. In 2008, the European Union also pledged $336 million for the period through 2010.

The situation changed fairly substantially after the new coalition government, Alliance for European Integration took power in September 2009. First of all, the European Union promised $2.6 billion—half in the form of nonreturnable grants. In October 2009, the IMF signed a new financing agreement and over the next several months dispersed $90 million to Moldova; then, on January 29, 2010, the IMF launched a new three-year program with Moldova which promised $574.4 million in credits, repayable in 10 years. The money is being used for restoring tax stability, combating poverty, and encouraging economic growth.

Prime Minister Filat visited Washington in January 2010 and while there signed an agreement with the Millennium Challenge Corporation for $262 million in aid. In March, Secretary of State Clinton first praised the European Union, IMF, and the World Bank for their support of Moldova, then added that the United States would be rendering "assistance to Moldova's leadership in its implementing democratic reforms and economic revival for the sake of improving the Moldovan people's living standard." Presumably that means more money in the future.

The banking scandal which dominated politics in Moldova in 2015 revealed the state's massive corruption problems and undermined the legitimacy of political and financial institutions. The street protests that followed the revelation of this scandal were further fueled by general frustrations over the state of the economy. In 2015, the Moldovan economy experienced a recession in part due to declining level remittances from migrants working in Russia and poor crop yields due to drought. The triple pressure from Covid-19 pandemic and the energy and the refugee crisis associated with the Russian invasion of Ukraine has dampened Moldova's economic growth and increased the cost of living. Whereas in February 2021, the month-on-month increase in consumer prices was 0.38%, in February 2022, that figure rose by 18.52% year-on-year and 2.7% month-on-month.

Moldova strongly depends on Russia for the import of its gas. Moldova uses Russian gas to generate electricity that powers the whole country. The electricity is generated in power plants located in Transdnistria. For many years, Moldova purchased Russian gas at far below market price. Moscow struck a deal with Moldova that as long as the latter allows the gas to flow to Transdnistria, the Russian state-backed gas supplier Gazprom would be lenient on the payments for the gas. As a result, Moldova has, reportedly, racked up $700 million in unpaid debt for past deliveries, which it disputes and is unable to repay, especially now that Russia raised gas prices. Although Moldova has maintained a neutral stance over the invasion of Ukraine, Russia's decision to raise the price may have had to do with Moldova's increasing Westward orientation, especially after the election of Maia Sandu. According to the World Bank, high gas prices would increase consumer prices and erode the competitiveness of Moldovan enterprises. Anticipating that Russia might scrap the current contract because of the unpaid debt, Sandu's government has been exploring the alternative option of importing gas from Romania. To support Moldova in that effort, the European Union provided the country 60 million euros to help it cope with rising fuel prices. Additionally, it made funds available to Romania to help that country increase its gas storage capacity to meet Moldova's energy needs.

Moldova economic challenges go beyond rising fuel costs, however. The influx of refugees from Ukraine and the fall in financial remittances from Russia have compounded the country's economic woes. Since the Russian invasion of Ukraine on January 24, an estimated 421,130 refugees have fled to Moldova, 101,331 of whom decided to stay in that country. In per capita terms, Moldova has been the largest recipient of refugees in Europe. Moldova has received financial and in-kind donations from the US and European Union to cope with the pressure. Nonetheless, the World Bank estimates that a protracted war in Ukraine could push 30 percent of the population below the poverty line. For comparison, prior to 2018, the Bank estimated that 12.8 percent of the population was below poverty line.

The Future

Moldova is an impoverished agricultural country riddled with corruption. In the wake of the theft of around $1 billion from three banks, many Moldovans recognized the need for deep and sweeping institutional reforms and took to the street in order to instigate these changes. To date, meaningful reforms addressing the state's endemic corruption remain distant as political infighting has paralyzed the governing process. Moldova has thus far defied Russia in remaining on track to join the European Union. The path to relative prosperity for Moldova leads through membership in the EU; strengthening the rule of law, especially with regard to business practices; and reforming the economy. Unfortunately, the Covid-19 pandemic, the refugee crisis and heavy reliance on Russia and Ukraine for the import of food and energy at a time when the war between these countries has disrupted the supply of these commodities have distracted the incumbent government from implementing these needed institutional reforms.

In May 2023, tens of thousands of Moldovans rallied in the capital Chisinau to support their government's drive toward Europe. That same month, the speaker of the Moldovan parliament, Igor Grosu, announced that Moldova would begin the process of withdrawing from the CIS's Interparliamentary Assembly. This body serves as a forum for economic and political cooperation and coordinates election monitoring in its member states. Moldovan officials claim that the CIS's Interparliamentary Assembly is an instrument through which Moscow tries to influence the legislative activity in the CIS area. Moldovan authorities have to overcome the hurdle of a divided public opinion over their quest to cut all ties with Russia. According to a poll conducted in April 2023, 40.6 percent of Moldovans would want to quit the CIS, while 41.2 percent would want to stay. Likewise, there is a split among political parties on the issue, while the ruling Party of Action and Solidarity (PAS) seeks to cut all ties with Russia, the three opposition parties, including Socialists, Communist Party, and the Shor Party, are supportive of Russia and want to stay in the CIS.

TRANSCAUCASIAN REPUBLICS

//Due to their shared histories as well as frequent geographical and cultural similarities, there is necessarily some repetition from one entry to the other.

Showing only capital cities and political boundaries

Armenia

Area: 11,503 sq. mi. (29,800 sq. km.), slightly smaller than Maryland.

Population: 2,976,765 (2024 est.).

Capital City: Yerevan (Pop. 1.095 million, 2023 est.).

Climate: Dry and highland continental.

Neighboring States: Georgia (north), Turkey (west), Nakhichevan Region of Azerbaijani (southwest), Azerbaijan (east), a slender border with Iran (southeast).

Language: Armenian.

Ethnic Composition: Armenian (98.1%), Yezidi (Kurd) (1.1%), other (.7%) (2011 est.).

Principal Religion: Armenian Apostolic.

Chief Commercial Products: Livestock, chemicals, textiles, wine, grain, footwear.

Currency: dram (introduced in Nov. 1993).

Per Capita Annual Income (Purchasing Power Parity): $20,781 (2023 est.).

Recent Political Status: The Armenian SSR was established in 1920; from 1922 to 1936 it was joined with Georgia and Azerbaijan into the Transcaucasian SSR, but reverted to status as a constituent republic of the former USSR. It declared independence on August 23, 1990.

National Day: September 21 (1991), Independence Day.

President: Vahagn Khachaturyan (since March 13, 2022).

Prime Minister: Nikol Pashinyan (since September 10, 2021).

National Flag: Three equal horizontal stripes, red, blue, and orange.

The Land

The Republic of Armenia (Hayastani Hanrapetut'yun), which emerged as an independent state as a result of the collapse of the Union of Soviet Socialist Republics in 1991, is located in a landlocked area south of the Caucasus Mountains. The ancient empire of which it is a remnant fell under the sway of various empires, the last of which was Ottoman Turkey. Russia obtained eastern Armenia from Ottoman Turkey in 1828, but western Armenia, an area of about 57,999 square miles (147,000 sq. km.) remained part of Ottoman Turkey. During World War I, policies carried out by Ottoman Turkey, including forced resettlement, resulted in an estimated 1 million Armenian deaths. That area, now largely devoid of Armenians, remains part of Turkey today. Mt. Ararat, traditionally associated with Armenia, is actually in this area, the highest peak in the mountain chain that forms the border between modern-day Turkey and Armenia.

Today, Armenia consists of 11,503 square miles (29,800 sq. km.). It borders on Turkey to the west, Iran to the south, Georgia to the north, and Azerbaijan to the east. Yerevan, the capital, is the largest city.

The second big city is Gyumri (formerly Leninakan), which was one of the cities badly damaged by the earthquake of 1988.

The area of Nagorno-Karabakh, a primarily Armenian-populated region located in western Azerbaijan, remains a preoccupation of Armenian leaders, largely as a result of events since 1988. As the Soviet Union began to fall apart during the last years of the Gorbachev presidency, the Armenian-dominated population of Nagorno-Karabakh began to press for separation from Azerbaijan and union with Armenia. Azerbaijan attempted to deal with the situation by abolishing Nagorno-Karabakh's autonomous status and placing it directly under the rule of Baku, and act that led the Nagorno-Karabakh leadership to launch a war against Azerbaijan in 1991. By 1994, Nagorno-Karabakh and Armenian forces controlled all of Nagorno-Karabakh plus a significant portion of western Azerbaijan. A cease-fire signed in May 1994 ended the fighting, but the two sides have since been able to make any significant progress toward a peaceful resolution of the problem. A second war over the region in 2020 plunged Armenia into political crisis. In this war, the aggressor state, Azerbaijan, was able to regain control of significant territory in Karabakh and the surrounding districts before a Russian-brokered ceasefire was signed. Public opinion of the current government plummeted as a result of the poor performance of the Armenia military and the unfavorable terms of the ceasefire,

leading to the official resignation of the prime minister, Nikol Pashinyan, on April 25, 2021. Notably, he was reappointed and sworn in approximately six months after his resignation.

All except about 10% of Armenia is extremely mountainous. Its "lowlands" are over 3,000 feet high, while the average height above sea level for the entire country is slightly over a mile high; its highest mountains are in the northwestern part of the country. Mt. Aragats, the highest peak, is 13,418 feet high. The northern part of Armenia consists of a series of ranges and elevated volcanic plateaus, into which deep river valleys have been cut.

In the east, the dominant feature is a high mountain lake surrounded by mountains. Lake Sevan, which is 525 square miles in size, lies at 6,200 feet, while the surrounding mountains soar to 11,800 feet. In the south is the Ararat Plain, only the northern half of which belongs to Armenia. The Ararat Plain is divided by the Aras River, which forms Armenia's southern border.

Armenia's rainfall varies considerably, with over 300 inches in the high mountains and an average of 80 inches on the Ararat Plain. Most of this precipitation falls in the form of heavy rains in the autumn and as snow in the winter.

Armenia's many rivers arise in the mountains in the north and west. Because of the sharp drop in elevation, they tend to be short and turbulent, with many waterfalls and rapids. Armenia accordingly has great hydroelectric power potential,

Armenia

estimated at nearly 22 billion kilowatt-hours a year. Four of these rivers—the Akhuryan, the Hrazdan (which flows out of Lake Sevan), the Arpa, and the Bargushat—provide water to irrigate the Armenian half of the Ararat Plain before emptying into the Aras River, itself a tributary of the Kura River, which flows into the Caspian Sea.

Since it lies at the northern edge of the subtropical zone, Armenia has long, dry, hot summers with long, mild, sunny autumns. Because of the elevation of most of the land, it also has a winter with average temperatures below freezing, though only the plateau and mountains in the north have really inclement weather.

In spite of its small size, Armenia has an unusually large variety of landscapes. Because of a combination of location and variation in altitudes, it possesses five different vegetation zones: semi desert, steppe, forest, alpine meadows, and high-altitude tundra. The semi desert landscape is found in the south at altitudes below 4,600 feet. This region, unless irrigated, produces only a scanty vegetation of mostly sagebrush and similar drought-resistant plants.

The land between 4,600 and 6,600 feet is mostly steppe, and here, if not watered, mainly drought-resistant grasses grow. The forest zone is found mostly in the southeast at altitudes between 6,200 and 6,600 feet, and in the northeast, at altitudes between 7,200 and 7,900 feet. Oak grows mainly in the southeast, while beech grows in the northeast.

The alpine zone lies above 6,600 feet, where thinning forests give way to mountain meadows. Such meadows are used as summer pastures for goats and sheep. Finally, above the alpine zone is the area of

Ex-President Robert Kocharian

tundra, where little grows other than cushion plants such as moss.

The Ararat Plain produces fruits such as figs, grapes, pomegranates, apricots, peaches, and melons. The plateau and the mountain valleys produce cereals and grains, tobacco, vegetables, and orchard crops such as cherries, apples, pears, almonds, and hazelnuts. Higher altitudes produce potatoes, grain, and fodder grasses.

The People

The estimated population of Armenia has fallen under 3 million. That figure does not include the out-migration of young, educated Armenians leaving to seek jobs elsewhere following the collapse of the Soviet Union, however; according to official estimates, there was an out-migration of at least 900,000–1,000,000 people after 1992. That trend appears to be reversing, however. In August 2007, Gagik Yeghanian, who heads the Armenian government's Department for Migration and Refugee Affairs, announced that, for the previous three years, more people had come to settle permanently in Armenia than had emigrated.

Armenians constitute 98.1% of the population, with Kurds, the largest minority, about 1.1%.

History

Armenians, who refer to themselves as the Hayk, are an Indo-European people who, it was traditionally considered, migrated into the area in the 7th century B.C., overrunning and conquering an earlier, high civilization. More recently, some Armenians have suggested that Armenians did not move into the area but were simply the successors of the same civilization that lived there. Whichever version is correct, they subsequently came under the influence of the Medes, Persians, and Greeks as they became part of these empires. The first Armenian Empire came into existence during the period of the rise of the Roman Empire. As the Roman Empire became ever more powerful, however, this empire disintegrated, and Armenia became a sort of buffer zone between Rome and the Parthian Empire.

The people of Armenia converted to Christianity about 301 A.D., the first country to establish Christianity as a state religion. Not surprisingly, the Armenian Orthodox Church is known for its ancient and rich liturgy. Under communism, the role of the Church was severely limited but today the Church is playing an important role, particularly in the cultural sphere.

An independent Armenian state first emerged around 190 B.C., but it was not until the middle of the 1st century B.C. that a united Armenian state was created

under Tigranes I the Great (ca. 94–ca. 55 B.C.). The first capital of this state was Artaxata, located on the Aras River not far from modern-day Yerevan. This kingdom lasted for almost 500 years, and it reached its pinnacle under Tigranes, who extended his kingdom eastward to include parts of modern-day Iran and westward to encompass Syria. His conquests brought him to the attention of the Roman General Pompey, who defeated him in battle in 66 B.C. Tigranes was forced to relinquish Syria and become an ally of Rome.

For the next 120 years, Armenia remained a buffer state between Rome and Parthia, each manipulating Armenia to achieve its ends. The area was annexed by the Emperor Trajan in 114, but abandoned by his successor, Hadrian. An army of Marcus Aurelius destroyed Artaxata in 163. Caracalla attempted to annex Armenia in 216, but his successor, Macrinus, abandoned the attempt and recognized Tiridates II as King of Armenia. The resurgent Persian Empire then began pressing Armenia from the east. In 238, it conquered Armenia and established it as a vassal state, holding it for 50-some years before another Roman Emperor, Diocletian, intervened and restored Tiridates III, son of Tiridates II, to the throne.

The reign of Tiridates III is extremely important for Armenian history, for this is when Armenia was converted to Christianity. Tiridates III was himself converted by St. Gregory the Illuminator and he made Christianity the official religion of the realm in 300 A.D. From this time onward, the Armenian patriarchate also became an important symbol of Armenian unity, holding the people together during periods of political instability.

Tiridates was later assassinated by his own court chamberlain in league with local nobles and Armenia split into two parts, with the smaller part gradually being absorbed into the Byzantine Empire. The larger part came under Persian domination in 428 when the Armenian nobility deposed their king and requested a Persian governor.

The religion of Persia at this time was Zoroastrianism and the Persian ruler made the mistake of attempting to impose it on the Armenians. An Armenian revolt in 451 caused the Persians to declare that they would not attempt to impose Zoroastrianism by force; a second revolt in 481–484 won Persian recognition of a native Armenian ruler and a Persian promise to honor Armenia's political and religious freedom in return for Armenia's agreement to provide military assistance to Persia when called upon.

The Armenians asserted their religious freedom even further in 554 when

Armenia

an Armenian Church Council got into a quarrel with the rest of the Christian Church over a minor point of dogma, the dyophysite formula enunciated by the Council of Chalcedon in 451. The Council of Chalcedon formulation was that Jesus Christ was both human and divine in one nature; the Armenian Church adopted the position at the second Council of Dvin that two natures, human and divine, existed in Jesus Christ in perfect unity. The Armenian Church, by rejecting the dyophysite formula of the Council of Chalcedon, isolated itself from the rest of Christianity and turned the Byzantine Empire into an enemy.

Armenia came under attack from the Arabs beginning in 640. Thirteen years later, Armenia came under Arab control as an autonomous region under its own native ruler. This situation continued for the next 300 years.

In the 10th century, however, a resurgent Byzantine Empire invaded from the west, effectively destroying Armenia politically. The final blow came in the 11th century when Armenia was invaded from the east by the Seljuk Turks. The Seljuk Turk conquest was complete by 1071, although a few minor Armenian kingdoms survived for a time in the more remote mountains. In the 12th century, part of northern Armenia was annexed to the Georgian Kingdom. However, Armenia was overrun again in 1236–42 by the Mongols.

Most of Armenia eventually became part of the Ottoman Empire and, after the fall of Constantinople in 1453, the Armenian bishop of Bursa was

Armenians fleeing Turkish lands in the early 20th century

transferred to Constantinople and appointed leader of the Armenian Church in the Ottoman Empire. The eastern area fell to the Ottoman Empire in 1516, but it soon became a battlefield as Persia and the Ottoman Empire fought for control. Persia gained control of the regions of Yerevan, Karabakh, and Nakhichevan as a result of the peace of 1620. In the mountainous region of Karabakh, however, five Armenian princes managed to assert their independence at the beginning of the 18th century. Forces of the Ottoman Empire occupied the area in the 1730s, but were driven out by the Persians.

Amid the swirling events that ultimately resulted in the end of the Ottoman Empire, Armenians claim that 1.5 million of their people were mercilessly slaughtered by the Turks in western Armenia in the late 19th and early 20th centuries, an estimated 1 million during World War I. Many Armenians fled the Ottoman Empire in the last 19th and early 20th centuries, and a substantial number of them migrated to the US.

Armenia under Russian-Soviet Rule

The Russians began to focus their attention on the area of the Caucasus at the beginning of the 19th century. A war between Russia and Persia beginning in 1809 gave Russia Georgia, northern Azerbaijan and Karabakh. In 1828, Yerevan and Nakhichevan were added. A large part of traditional Armenia still remained under Ottoman control, but the area that was to become modern Armenia had become part of the Russian Empire.

The Russian government tended to treat Armenians as co-religionists throughout most of the 19th century and being part of the Russian Empire meant that Armenians had greater access to western ideas than before. The 19th century therefore ushered in a cultural renaissance in Armenia.

This changed toward the end of the century, however, when the government of Nicholas II began to get worried about Armenian nationalism and introduced repressive measures to stamp it out. In 1897, hundreds of schools and libraries were closed and Armenian newspapers were banned. And since the Armenian Orthodox Church was closely associated in people's minds with Armenian nationalism, the government moved in 1903 to confiscate all property of the Armenian Church.

Armenian nationalists joined with Georgians and Azerbaijani to form the Trans-Caucasus Federal Republic in April 1918, but the new state collapsed in just over a month. An independent Armenia was then declared on May 26, 1918. The republic, which lasted until March 1922, had a bumpy independent existence as

it attempted to secure as much of the lands occupied by Armenians as it could. It fought short wars with Georgia and Azerbaijan—the latter over the area of Nagorno-Karabakh—and a war in 1920 with Turkey. The loss to Turkey in 1920 led to a change in government and the creation of the Soviet Republic of Armenia in December 1920.

The new government was established as a coalition of communists and nationalists, but the nationalists were soon eliminated and it became a purely communist government. In March 1922, this new government joined with Georgia and Azerbaijan to form the Transcaucasian Soviet Federated Socialist Republic. On December 30, 1922, it became a part of the Union of Soviet Socialist Republics.

The Transcaucasian Soviet Federated Socialist Republic was dissolved in 1936 when a new Soviet constitution was adopted and Armenia became the Armenian Soviet Socialist Republic. Armenia did relatively well as a part of the Soviet Union. Quite a bit of industry grew up around Armenia's chief cities, and individual Armenians held important positions in industry and the professions in major cities throughout the Soviet Union.

Yet Armenia was one of the first republics to "explode" after Gorbachev launched his program of glasnost. The most important reason for this was the Nagorno-Karabakh Autonomous Republic, the Armenian enclave in the neighboring republic of Azerbaijan. The situation in Nagorno-Karabakh is treated in greater detail under the Republic of Azerbaijan (See section on Nagorno-Karabakh immediately after the discussion of Azerbaijan's foreign policy). Suffice to say here that this became a galvanizing issue for the vast majority of Armenians when the Nagorno-Karabakh regional council petitioned in February 1988 to become part of Armenia.

Within weeks, the Armenian political leadership had endorsed the Nagorno-Karabakh position. The Azerbaijani leadership angrily rejected Armenia's claims on Nagorno-Karabakh and began to encourage popular demonstrations in support of its position. The demonstrations got out of control, however, and turned into an anti-Armenian move in the Azerbaijani city of Sumgait. Within weeks, an incipient state of war existed between Armenia and Azerbaijan.

Gorbachev dismissed the Communist Party leaders of both Azerbaijan and Armenia in May 1988, on the grounds that they had not acted quickly enough to control the situation. The new first secretary of the Armenian Communist Party leader was Suren Arutunyan, a Gorbachev loyalist who had spent the previous several years working in Moscow. He tried

221

Armenia

his best, but he was constantly caught between Moscow loyalists on the one side and nationalists organized as the Karabakh Committee on the other. In the process, the Armenian Communist Party lost much of its authority.

Armenia was hit by a natural disaster in December 1988, when a major earthquake killed over 25,000 persons and injured thousands more. Other thousands were left homeless. International aid poured in, but Armenians lost further faith in both the Armenian and union leadership when help was slow in coming.

The people applauded in January 1989 when Gorbachev announced that he had decided to suspend Azerbaijan's control over Nagorno-Karabakh and put the autonomous republic under Moscow's direct control. They suffered when the Azerbaijan Popular Front instituted its road and rail blockade against Armenia, but they refused to give in. They were, therefore, extremely angry when Gorbachev gave in to the Azerbaijan Popular Front's blackmail and requested the USSR Supreme Soviet to relinquish control back to Azerbaijan. Armenian delegates refused to participate in that vote.

Armenians now turned conclusively against the Communist Party. By the spring of 1990, there were an increasing number of armed clashes between Armenian nationalists and Soviet troops. In July, Gorbachev ordered all such vigilante groups to be disbanded, but then the Armenian Supreme Soviet defied Gorbachev, declaring that his order "contradicts the Armenian people's natural right to self-defense." In August 1990, the Armenian Supreme Soviet elected Levon Ter-Petrossian to the top post in the republic, chairman of the Supreme Soviet. Ter-Petrossian, a leader of the Karabakh Committee, was Armenia's first post-communist leader. On August 23, 1990, the Armenian Supreme Soviet followed this up by passing a declaration of Armenian independence.

Independence

Ter-Petrossian turned out to be a cautious leader in practice. He did not attempt to challenge Moscow but, again, his quarrel was not really with Moscow. The confrontation with Azerbaijan continued and Armenia continued to suffer from an Azerbaijani blockade of fuel and most other supplies, but it would not cede on the political question. In the spring of 1991, it boycotted discussions about a new union treaty. Armenia took advantage of the coup attempt against Gorbachev in August 1991 to reiterate its declaration of independence. This was followed by a popular referendum that received overwhelming approval. The Armenian

Supreme Soviet also created the office of president to be elected by popular vote. The election took place on October 16 and Ter-Petrossian won 83% of the votes. He formally assumed the office in December 1991.

Armenia accepted Russian–Kazakh mediation of the Nagorno-Karabakh dispute with Azerbaijan in September 1991 and agreed to yield its claims over Nagorno-Karabakh at this time. It subsequently recognized the independence of the Republic of Nagorno-Karabakh, however, so its confrontation with Azerbaijan continued.

Armenia agreed to join the Commonwealth of Independent States at the December 1991 founding meeting. Unlike Azerbaijan, it opted to not establish a separate republic army at that time, even though large numbers of Armenian "freedom fighters" were already involved in the fighting in Nagorno-Karabakh. Partly this was because it hoped to win CIS backing for its position on Nagorno-Karabakh; partly it was because the Azerbaijani blockade had been successful, and its economy was in terrible shape.

As a result of strains between individual CIS members and a continuing fear of being dominated by Moscow, however, most

CIS members began to create national armies in 1992. Armenia created a ministry of defense and an Armenian army and began to equip these forces with heavier equipment such as tanks, transferred mainly from Soviet forces.

The war between Azerbaijan and Armenia widened somewhat in the spring of 1992, when forces within Nagorno-Karabakh extended their control over areas formerly occupied by Azerbaijani forces. These same forces then overran Azerbaijani territory lying between Nagorno-Karabakh and Armenia, creating a corridor connecting the enclave with Armenia at the point where the two territories are the closest together. This had a military significance, since Armenia, which had been shifting supplies in by air up to this point, could begin bringing supplies in by truck.

Azerbaijan was going through a great deal of domestic political turmoil at this point, at least partly because of its military defeats. Azerbaijani forces in the enclave of Nakhichevan (cut off from Azerbaijan by a strip of Armenian territory), then began shelling Armenian villages across the border. This led to an Armenian attack on the enclave city of Sadarak, and so the war widened further. Fighting continued intermittently over the summer and into the fall, in spite of a series of truces negotiated with the assistance of international third parties; however, no further significant changes in the military situation occurred. But Azerbaijan maintained its blockade of Armenia, so the economic situation within Armenia deteriorated further.

The situation within Armenia became desperate in January 1993 when the sole gas pipeline leading into the country through Georgia was blown up. A new temporary pipeline was opened in February, however, and gas began flowing again from Georgia. But even with almost all Armenian factories closed because of a lack of energy, there was no sign that Armenians were ready to compromise or lessen their support for fellow Armenians in Nagorno-Karabakh. Demonstrations in Yerevan calling for President Ter-Petrossian's resignation and for new parliamentary elections did occur in February 1993, but many of the demonstrators were critical of the president precisely because he had not pursued the war against Azerbaijan firmly enough.

Russia brokered another cease-fire between Armenia and Azerbaijan in March 1994. Under the agreement, Russian troops were to be stationed around the borders of Nagorno-Karabakh and both sides were to withdraw troops, heavy guns and aircraft. The cease-fire lasted approximately six weeks before heavy fighting erupted in April. A new cease-fire eventually set in, however. With no solution to the problem of Nagorno-Karabakh in sight, however, Armenia remained cut off from its traditional energy supplies and its industries continued to operate only at an extremely low level.

Parliamentary elections, carried out in 1995, were won by President Ter-Petrossian's political party, but only after the government had moved to ban one of the opposition political parties. International observers later reported that the elections were unfair.

New presidential elections took place in September 1996, with President Ter-Petrossian a candidate for reelection. The president's chief opponent in the election was Vazgen Manukian, a former prime minister. The other candidates were Sergei

Badalian, leader of the Communist Party, and Ashot Manucharian, the president's former national security adviser. The two chief issues in the campaign were the continuing stalemate with Azerbaijan over Nagorno-Karabakh and the state of the economy. A cease-fire with Azerbaijan had largely held since 1994 and the economy, which had grown by 7% in 1995—albeit from an extremely low level—continued to expand at about the same rate in 1996.

President Ter-Petrossian won with just under 52% of the vote, but the results were tainted by widespread charges of voting irregularities during the election. In consequence, his opponents protested the result and thousands of demonstrators gathered near the presidential palace to demand that the president step down. After three days of demonstrations, the government called in the armed forces to break them up. Most of the opposition political leaders were jailed or went underground. All serious opposition was then banned.

Concerned about his growing unpopularity, President Ter-Petrossian dismissed his prime minister, Hrant Bagratian, in November 1996, supposedly because

Looking down the main boulevard in Yerevan

Courtesy of NOVOSTI

Armenia

Bagratian, who had been prime minister since February 1993, had become increasingly unpopular because of his close identification with painful economic reforms. He then appointed Armen V. Sarkissian as his new prime minister. It was certainly true that conditions for most Armenians remained severe, in large part because of the trade embargoes put into effect by both Azerbaijan and Turkey. Most outside observers were also convinced that Armenia could expect no significant longtime economic improvement unless it were able to reach a settlement of the conflict with Azerbaijan over Nagorno-Karabakh.

The Organization for Security and Cooperation in Europe (OSCE) put forth its terms for peace in November 1996. These terms, which became known as the Lisbon principles, essentially called for the restoration of Soviet era borders, broad autonomy for ethnic Armenians in the disputed region of Nagorno-Karabakh, and international guarantees of such a settlement.

The leaderships of both Armenia and Nagorno-Karabakh rejected the OSCE terms, but President Ter-Petrossian found himself coming under increasing international pressure to accede to the Lisbon principles in succeeding months. Recognizing that these demands from abroad threatened to weaken domestic support from among top military leaders as well as hard-liners within his own party, Ter-Petrossian, in March 1997, asked Robert Kocharian, then president of the unrecognized Republic of Nagorno-Karabakh, to become his prime minister.

The president and his prime minister worked closely together over the next several months, drawing up plans for economic reform. Then President Ter-Petrossian dropped a bombshell in September 1997 when he gave a press conference in which he admitted publicly for the first time that the status quo was untenable. He then went on effectively to endorse the OSCE Lisbon principles, suggesting that Nagorno-Karabakh could retain effective independence, but would technically have to remain part of Azerbaijan. The president had apparently become persuaded that all of his plans for economic reform would fail without peace.

But this was the beginning of the end for Ter-Petrossian. Not only did his opponents call him a traitor; he also came under severe attack from members of his own party and of the government, particularly from his military allies. One of his severest critics was his prime minister, Robert Kocharian, who essentially argued that Ter-Petrossian was wrong and that Armenia could rebuild its economy while continuing its support for an independent Nagorno-Karabakh.

President Ter-Petrossian's resignation came on February 3, 1998. Speaking on national television, he said that he was resigning in response to demands by "state bodies well known to you." Although he characterized his resignation as "the defeat of the honorable party of peace in Armenia," he argued that differences over Nagorno-Karabakh were just a pretext that hard-line forces were using to make him resign.

In line with the Armenian constitution, Robert Kocharian then became prime minister and acting president. He also became a candidate for election to a full term as president, in spite of the fact that, as a former president of Nagorno-Karabakh, he could hardly claim to have been a citizen of Armenia for 10 years as required by the constitution. Kocharian had the support of several political parties, organized as the Justice and Unity Bloc.

In the first round of voting, which took place on March 16, 1998, Kocharian won 38.82% of the vote, followed by Karen Demirchian, candidate of the Armenian Communist Party, with 30.62%. Vazgen Manukian, head of the National Democratic Union, came third with 12.22% and Sergei Baldalian came fourth with 11.02%. Since no candidate won a majority, a second round of voting took place on March 30. Here Robert Kocharian came in first with 59.7% of the vote.

Eleven days later, he chose Armen Darbinian, his 33-year-old finance and economy minister, as his new prime minister. Darbinian, who had also served as first deputy chairman of the Armenian Central Bank from 1994 until May 1997, when he became finance minister, was known internationally as an economic reformer. After becoming prime minister, he concentrated on domestic economic policy, with an emphasis on encouraging private enterprise. In June 1998, for example, he announced that the Armenian state airline company would be put up for international sale, arguing that "privatization is the only way to guarantee its efficient and competitive work."

This emphasis on privatization brought in $98 million in direct foreign investment during the first six months of 1998 and contributed to an annual growth rate of 6.7% during this period. Although this was impressive, the IMF resident representative cautioned that the growth took place from a "very low base."

The Armenian economy suffered something of a setback during the last half of the year, reflecting Russia's financial collapse in September. In particular, Russian investors sold off Armenian government bonds, thus causing a drop in value of the dram, Armenia's national currency. Armenia's tight fiscal and monetary policies saved the country from most of the effects of the Russian collapse, though economic growth was slowing as 1998 ended. In December 1998, the parliament passed a 1999 budget which had the approval of the IMF and the World Bank. Although it included a budget deficit of 5.3% of GDP, 95% of this deficit was covered by foreign loans.

Elections to the 131-member National Assembly, which took place on May 30, 1999, were won by the Miasnutyun (Unity) alliance, which took 41.67% of the vote. The Miasnutyun alliance was composed of the Republican Party of Armenia, headed by then Defense Minister Vazgen Sargsyan, and the People's Party of Armenia, led by Karen Demirchian, former first secretary of the Communist Party of Armenia. The Miasnutyun alliance won 29 of the 56 seats allocated under the proportional system plus 28 of the 75 seats allocated in single-mandate constituencies, giving it a total of 57 seats. By contrast, the former ruling Armenian Pan-National Movement squeaked into the National Assembly with a single seat. Because 32 deputies ran and won as independents, it was not difficult for the Miasnutyun alliance to put together a majority in the National Assembly. After the electoral results were in, Armen Darbinian submitted his resignation as prime minister. President Kocharian then named Vazgen Sargsyan as the new prime minister on June 10. Karen Demirchian was elected to the position of parliamentary speaker.

Prime Minister Sargsyan pledged to continue the liberal reforms begun by his predecessor, though he indicated that he would attempt to minimize the economic hardships they had caused for much of the population. He also promised to crack down on corruption and tighten the government's supervision of investment policy. International financial organizations liked Sargsyan's policies; in October 1999, the World Bank pledged a further $238 million to fund development projects in Armenia over the following three years while, at the same time, agreeing to disburse a third and final structural adjustment credit worth $23.5 million to help offset the country's budget deficit.

However, tragedy struck on October 27 when five gunmen burst into the parliament and began shooting. They killed Prime Minister Sargsyan, parliamentary speaker Karen Demirchian and his two deputies, a government minister, and two parliamentary deputies. Six other parliamentary deputies were seriously wounded.

The gunmen held about 40 persons hostage overnight before surrendering to the authorities the following morning. Three of the men were charged with terrorism aimed at undermining authority, but the reason for the attack never became clear. Although Nairi Hunanian, the leader of the assault, had earlier been associated with the Armenian Revolutionary Federation, a radical nationalist party, the party itself denied any connection with the attack. Hunanian, who had worked as a journalist, first said that the group was staging a coup, but later said that they only wanted to protest the country's economic collapse, for which they held Sargsian responsible.

Shocked by the events, the Armenian parliament met in emergency session on November 2 and elected People's Party member Armen Khachatrian as parliamentary speaker. Gagik Aslanian, also a member of the People's Party, and Tigran Torosian, of the Republican Party, were elected deputy speakers. Those two parties constituted the majority Miasnutyun parliament faction.

One day later, President Kocharian appointed Aram Sargsyan to succeed his murdered elder brother as prime minister. The 38-year-old Sargsyan had been elected a deputy to the parliament in May 1999 but had no other political experience. He turned out to be a disappointment as prime minister and lasted only six months. Within weeks of taking office, he became embroiled in a series of political assaults on the presidency; he was finally dismissed as prime minister on May 2, 2000.

His successor, appointed 10 days later, was Andranik Markarian, chairman of the Republican Party of Armenia, the larger of the two parties in the ruling Unity alliance. Markarian, a computer specialist, served a three-year term in prison in the 1970s for his membership in an underground nationalist party called the National Unity Party.

Markarian, in his first speech as prime minister, promised that "reform should be the main essence of economic change"; little changed under him, however. One reason is that the ruling Unity alliance largely disintegrated in September 2001 after the leader of the People's Party of Armenia (HZhK), the junior partner in the coalition, declared the Unity alliance to be defunct, called Markarian a stooge of President Kocharian, and called for new parliamentary elections. Following these events, over half of the membership of the HZhK defected to the opposition. Even the Republican Party of Armenia lost 11 of its members, reducing it to 46 deputies. Having lost its majority, the government only remained in power because the 20 member Kaynutyun (Stability) parliament group agreed to support the government without becoming part of the government coalition.

Intending to stand for reelection but without a party structure or organization of his own to back him, President Kocharian was dependent on the support of the oligarchs and power elites of the country. Two of the most important of his supporters were Prime Minister Andranik Markarian, leader of the Republican Party of Armenia, and Defense Minister Serzh Sargsyan. To widen his support, President Kocharian proposed a series of constitutional amendments—favored by most of the opposition political parties, particularly those on the left—whose effect would be to somewhat reduce the powers of the president. Although these amendments did not go as far as the left wanted—most argued for the replacement of the presidential system with a parliamentary system—it did increase Kocharian's popular support.

When the Armenian local elections took place on October 20, 2002, Prime Minister Andranik Markarian's Republican Party of Armenia won the post of mayor in 30 of Armenia's 37 towns and cities. Since Markarian was supporting President Kocharian for reelection, this indicated that he would be difficult to beat.

Realizing this, the political opposition began discussions aimed at uniting behind a single presidential candidate. In November, Stepan Demirchian, chairman of the HZhK, won the support of 15 other opposition political parties, but this opposition unity began to unravel in November when the National Accord Party, the Communist Party, and the Socialist Armenia bloc formed a separate alliance to field joint candidates in both the presidential and parliamentary elections. By the time the presidential voting took place on February 19, there were nine candidates vying for the presidency.

President Kocharian came in first but, because he won only 49.5% of the vote, he was forced into a runoff with Stepan Demirchian, who placed second with 28.2% of the vote. President Kocharian easily won the runoff on March 5 with 65.5% of the vote, but numerous irregularities were reported on by outside observers. Charging that the election was marred by legal, constitutional, and procedural violations, Demirchian requested the Constitutional Court to void the election. The Constitutional Court ruled against Demirchian, but it did order the Prosecutor General's Office to launch a criminal investigation into those irregularities.

With new parliamentary elections scheduled to take place on May 25, 2003, the political opposition made those irregularities the basis of its campaign as it attempted to discredit the pro-presidential parties. The opposition also gave a great deal of publicity to the fact that the Constitutional Court had recommended a "referendum of confidence" in the country's leadership.

Because the parties and blocs contesting the election were in basic agreement on all policy issues, the major issue became whether a candidate was a supporter or opponent of President Kocharian. Opponents were organized as the Artarutiun (Justice) bloc, which brought together the parties that had supported Stepan Demirchian in the presidential elections. The National Unity Party, headed by Artashes Geghamian, campaigned as part of the opposition, though its only major platform issue was its demand that the elections themselves be free, fair, and democratic. That put it in the opposition precisely because so many Armenians questioned whether Kocharian and his supporters were prepared to ensure that the ballot was truly free and fair.

In the end, the opposition won an impressive share of the votes, but failed to gain control of parliament. The three pro-presidential parties—the Republican Party of Armenia (HHK), the Armenian Revolutionary Federation, and the Orinats Yerkir—came in first, third, and fourth with 26.4%, 12.1% and 11.1% of the votes, giving them a majority of the seats in the parliament. The Artarutiun bloc pulled 14.3%, while the National Unity Party got 9.7%. The Communist Party of Armenia drew less than 5% and so failed to win any proportional seats. In addition to the proportional seats, the HHK won 12 single-mandate constituencies, and Orinats Yerkir six; the opposition Artarutiun bloc won three.

In a joint statement released after the election, the OSCE and the Council of Europe characterized the voting as "a marked improvement" over the February–March presidential election, but it still "failed to meet international standards in several key areas."

After several relatively quiet months, the opposition, led by Stepan Demirchian, began organizing demonstrations demanding a referendum on President Kocharian's rule. These political attacks escalated after the so-called "Rose Revolution" in neighboring Georgia led to the resignation of President Shevardnadze.

Hoping for a similar result, the Armenian opposition demanded that President Kocharian step down and permit new elections. As the demonstrations continued, the opposition bloc announced a boycott of parliament. The boycott was not total, however; the two dozen deputies from the Artarutiun bloc and the National Accord Party continued to attend debates on "crucial" issues such as constitutional reform and amending election legislation.

In 2005, the Armenian government submitted a set of draft constitutional amendments to the Parliamentary Assembly of the Council of Europe for its approval

Armenia

prior to bringing them up for discussion and vote in the legislature. The Council of Europe's Venice Commission endorsed the changes—as did both the European Union and the US government—but the political opposition was not mollified. When the constitutional amendments came up to a vote in the Armenian legislature, the opposition quit the chamber prior to the vote and thereafter urged a boycott of the November 27 referendum on the amendments.

In the end, the boycott was unsuccessful. According to the government, there was a 65.3% turnout for the referendum and a 93% positive vote for the amendments. The opposition claimed massive fraud, however, and began to organize mass rallies and demonstrations in an effort to overturn the result. The protests had no sustained mass participation, however, so Stepan Demirchian withdrew his support for the mass rallies in December 2005. Things then quieted down, though the opposition continued to boycott parliament.

With new parliamentary elections scheduled to take place in May 2007, signs of a political realignment began surfacing in 2006 in both the government coalition and in the opposition Artarutiun bloc. In May 2006, the Orinats Yerkir party pulled out of the government coalition after its leader, then parliament speaker Artur Baghdasarian, gave an interview to a German newspaper advocating future membership for Armenia in the EU and NATO. Baghdasarian was forced to resign as parliamentary speaker after being verbally abused by President Kocharian, presumably because Kocharian saw the parliament speaker's statement as a challenge to the president's pro-Russian foreign policy.

As it turned out, this did not affect the government majority because ten Orinats Yerkir party members left to form a new party pledged to continued cooperation with the government, while the six-member United Labor Party joined the government coalition at this time. And, in another development, Defense Minister Serzh Sargsyan formally joined the Republican Party of Armenia (HHK); he subsequently was appointed chairman of its governing council.

As for the political opposition, Stepan Demirchian, nominal leader of the nine-party opposition Artarutiun bloc, announced in April 2006 that his People's Party of Armenia was considering contesting the next elections on its own. His statement was probably triggered by rumors that at least three parties belonging to the opposition bloc had threatened to leave the bloc.

In fact, several opposition politicians formally joined pro-government

President Serzh Sargsyan (on the right) with ex-President Kocharian

political parties over the next several months. Another prominent opposition figure, Viktor Dallakyan, left the Artarutiun (Justice) bloc and joined the Prosperous Armenia party, the party of millionaire businessman Gagik Tsarukian, a close associate of President Kocharian. These defections reduced the size of the Artarutiun bloc to 12 seats.

The next change came in March 2007 when Prime Minister Andranik Markarian died suddenly of a heart attack. When Serzh Sargsyan, the former Defense Minister, was named his successor, people began almost immediately to speculate that Sargsyan would be the presidential candidate of the ruling HHK in 2008.

In the May 12 parliamentary elections, Prime Minister Sargsyan's HHK came in first with 33.8% of the proportional vote; the Prosperous Armenia party, headed by wealthy businessman Gagik Tsarukian, came in second with 15.1% of the vote. The Armenian Revolutionary Federation-Dashnaktsutiun (HHD) came in third with 13.1% of the vote. The other two parties to garner the minimum 5% of the vote needed to win proportional representation were the opposition Orinats Yerkir (Law-based State) party, which pulled 6.8% of the vote, and the Zharangutiun (Heritage) party of former US-born Foreign Minister Raffi Hovannisian, which got 6%. Factoring in wins in the 41 single-mandate seats, the final parliamentary distribution was: HHK

64 seats; Prosperous Armenia 25 seats; the HHD 16 seats; the Orinats Yerkin 10 seats; Zharangutiun 7 seats; and the Dashink (Alliance) party one seat.

Although the HHK could have formed a government on its own, Prime Minister Sargsyan wanted a government as broadly based as possible. The result was that the HHK and Prosperous Armenia formed a coalition government (which included a commitment to support a presidential bid by Prime Minister Sargsyan in 2008). The new HHK-Prosperous Armenia coalition then signed a cooperation agreement with the HHD under which the HHD got three cabinet seats (agriculture, education, and social security), but retained its freedom to field its own presidential candidate in 2008.

In the end, there were nine candidates on the ballot when the Armenian people went to the polls on February 19, 2008. Prime Minister Serzh Sargsyan took 52.76% of the vote, thus avoiding a second-round runoff. Coming second was former President Levon Ter-Petrossian with 21.51% of the vote. Former parliamentary speaker Artur Baghdasarian came in third with 16.7% of the vote, followed by Vahan Hovannisian, the candidate of the HHD, with 6.1%.

Although the Joint Election Observation Mission of the OSCE concluded that the ballot largely met international standards in 95% of the polling stations, the losing candidates, and in particular former President Ter-Petrossian, challenged the results and called for demonstrations to overturn the results. Large crowds continued demonstrating for 11 days before President Kocharian declared a state of emergency and instituted a curfew. Military police officers then moved in on the demonstrating crowds; in the subsequent confrontation, at least 8 persons were killed and more than 130 injured. Former President Ter-Petrossian then backed down and ordered his supporters to support the curfew.

President-elect Sargsyan subsequently signed a political cooperation agreement with Artur Baghdasarian, who had placed third in the February 19 presidential ballot. In return for his support, Baghdasarian was named secretary of the presidential council on national security.

Serzh Sargsyan was formally sworn in as president on April 9, 2008. He immediately named Tigran Sargsyan (no relation) as his new prime minister. A graduate of the Yerevan Economics Institute, Sargsyan studied at an institute in St. Petersburg before completing three years of graduate study in Washington, DC. After teaching economics at Yerevan State University, he was elected to the Armenian parliament, where he headed the committee for finance, loan, and budget issues. He then served as the head of the Armenian Bank Association from 1995 to March 1998, when he was made chairman of the Central Bank.

At this time, Prime Minister Sargsyan's government had the support of four of the five political parties represented in the Armenian parliament. They included the HHK, Orinats Yerkir (headed by former parliamentary speaker Artur Baghdasarian), Prosperous Armenia, and the HHD. The coalition agreement called for deepening democratic reform, speeding up economic development, strengthening the rule of law and freedom of speech, and launching a "comprehensive and effective fight against corruption."

For his part, Prime Minister Sargsyan promised that his government would focus on the need for "more ambitious programs" in future years; it was his clear intention to transform Armenia domestically. But subsequent international developments, both political and economic, meant that large parts of that program had to be put on hold.

The first of those "transforming" events occurred in August 2008, when Russia invaded Georgia to forestall an attempt by the Georgian government to regain control over the breakaway Georgian province of South Ossetia. The Russian invasion threatened Armenia economically because, with its borders with Azerbaijan

Ex-Prime Minister Tigran Sargsyan meets with Prime Minister Putin

and Turkey closed as a result of its conflict with Azerbaijan over Nagorno-Karabakh, Armenian exports went by railroad across Georgia and then out through Georgian ports. The Armenian government's first reaction was, therefore, to ask the Russian government not to take actions which would threaten Armenia's export lifeline. Russian troops did cut the main east-west Georgian road and briefly occupied Poti, Georgia's main port, but the railroad and port remained intact.

The Armenians had been happy with the close embrace of Russia and had cooperated as Russian investors took over most of the country's infrastructure. Armenians did, in fact, benefit from the flow of Russian funds into the country, with growth up to 2008 averaging 13% a year.

But the Russian invasion of Georgia sent a shiver of instability throughout the Caucasus, and caused some Armenian politicians to conclude that they had to do something to widen their options. As it happened, President Sargsyan had already extended an invitation to Abdullah Gul, the Turkish president, to travel to Yerevan for an upcoming soccer match between the Turkish and Armenian teams. Gul accepted and, after several months of subsequent negotiations, Armenia and Turkey announced on April 22, 2009, that they had agreed on a "comprehensive framework for the normalization of their bilateral relations."

However, this opening to Turkey brought a split in the government coalition. The HHD, which traditionally had taken a hardline position toward relations with Turkey, pulled out of the government coalition four days after the agreement with Turkey was announced. That still left the government with a large majority, but the HHD's departure did add to opposition forces in the parliament.

The Armenian government still wanted an agreement with Turkey, however and, in September, the two governments issued a joint statement affirming that they had agreed "to start political negotiations" aimed at establishing diplomatic relations. Approximately six weeks later, Armenia and Turkey signed two protocols which, when implemented, would have established diplomatic relations and opened the border between Turkey and Armenia.

Yet it turned out that the agreement was not as welcome a development as it first appeared. While Levon Ter-Petrossian, probably the most important of the opposition political leaders, backed the government, popular opinion appeared to be against the agreement if the numerous angry protests that occurred throughout Armenia were any indication; in addition, spokesmen for Armenian communities in the United States, France, and Lebanon strongly opposed plans to normalize relations with Turkey.

Nor was the agreement popular in Turkey. With most non-governmental politicians expressing opposition, many members of Prime Minister Recep Tayyip Erdogan's party began to distance themselves from the agreement. This led Erdogan to announce in March 2010 that Turkey's border with Armenia would remain closed until Armenia's quarrel with Azerbaijan over Nagorno-Karabakh was resolved. A few days later, Erdogan announced that the presence of an estimated 100,000 Armenian immigrants in Turkey "may no longer be tolerated." In response, President Sargsyan suspended parliamentary ratification of the protocols, though he was careful to say that Armenia had not "ended the process but had suspended it until the Turkish side" was ready to move forward. There has been no movement

Armenia

since that time, however, and it is unlikely that this will change any time soon.

Armenia's latest parliamentary elections took place on May 6, 2012. Eight political parties and one bloc fielded candidates but only four parties surmounted the 7% minimum necessary to win proportional seats. President Sargsyan's Republican Party came in first with 44.05% of the proportional vote, which gave them proportional 40 seats. Prosperous Armenia, the junior party in the government coalition, came in second with just under 31% of the vote, which gave them 36 seats. The Armenian National Congress, led by former President Ter-Petrossian, came in third with just over 7% of the vote, which gave them seven seats. The Armenian Revolutionary Federation (Dashnaktsutyun) pulled just over 7% of the vote and so got six seats. In addition, candidates of the Republican Party won 28 of the 41 single-mandate seats. The final results thus gave President Sargsyan's Republican Party (HHK) a total of 69 seats; Prosperous Armenia (BHK) came next with 37 seats. The Armenian National Congress won no single-mandate seats, so its total remained at seven. Of the remaining seats, five each went to the Heritage Party and the ARF (Dashnak); the Rule of Law Party holds a further six; and the last two were won by independents.

The coalition government which had been in existence prior to the elections was re-formed in May 2012 with Tigran Sargsyan remaining on as prime minister, but BHK withdrew its ministers shortly thereafter, apparently because it thought it deserved more ministerial seats than it was offered in the coalition talks. After that time, the BHK stood outside the government, but it also refused to cooperate with the opposition.

New presidential elections were held on February 18, 2013. President Serzh Sargsyan won reelection with 58.64% of the vote. His chief challenger was Raffi Hovannisian, leader of the Heritage Party and a former foreign minister. Although Hovannisian won 36.74% of the vote with the remaining votes split among five other candidates, Sargsyan had been heavily favored to win reelection because his two chief opponents, former President Levon Ter-Petrossian and Gagik Tsarukian, head of Prosperous Armenia, had declined to run. Even so, Hovannisian protested the election results and insisted that he had won the election. Thus for the fourth time in 17 years, a defeated Armenian had openly denounced the outcome of the ballot and declared himself to be the legitimately elected president.

On the other hand, the international community gave a generally favorable assessment of the vote with congratulations

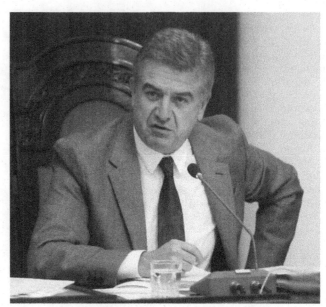

Former Prime Minister Karen Karapetyan

being offered to Sargsyan by both US Secretary of State John Kerry and European Union President Jose Manuel Barroso.

Prime Minister Tigran Sargsyan, who had held the office for six years, stepped down on April 2014, supposedly for personal reasons. However, his resignation came days after the Constitutional Court had declared a controversial pension reform to be unconstitutional. The reform legislation had been a major initiative of the Sargsyan cabinet.

Sargsyan was replaced by Ovik Abraamian in April 2014. Under his government, Armenia ushered in a Constitutional amendments, ratified via popular referendum, which transformed the government from a semi-parliamentary system to a parliamentary system. Abraamian was replaced by Karen Karapetyan in September 2016, the run-up to the first parliamentary election under the new constitution which were held on April 2, 2017. Abraamian, a member of the ruling Republican Party of Armenia, had been speaker of parliament before his appointment.

Armenia's Velvet Revolution

During debates prior to the 2015 referendum to transform the government to a parliamentary system, critics speculated that at the heart of the reform was a desire to provide an institutional means for then-president Serzh Sargsyan to remain in control once his presidential term limits expired. Not surprisingly, at that time the incumbent president denied any intent to serve as prime minister in the future. However, in confirmation of his critics fears, on April 16, 2018 Serzh Sargsyan was selected by the National Assembly to

serve as Prime Minister following his departure from the presidency. The opposition immediately accused Sargsyan and his Republican Party of "pulling a Putin," making reference to Russian President Putin's side-step of term limits by serving as prime minister between 2008–2012 before returning as president.

Although Putin's return to the presidency was marked by widespread protests in Russia, the transition was ultimately successful. Sargsyan's attempt to circumvent term limits, on the other hand, was not. Before the transfer of power even occurred, at least three different protest movements emerged attempting to mobilize society against the continued rule of Sargsyan. Ultimately the most successful of these movements was the #mystep protests organized and fronted by long term opposition politician and journalist, Nikol Pashinyan. Begun on March 31, the #mystep movement slowly marched the 120 kilometers from the city of Gyumri to the capital Yerevan. Along the way, Pashinyan and a growing number of supporters delivered anti-Sargsyan messages in the communities they passed through. The marchers reached Yerevan's central Republic Square on April 13, four days before Sargsyan would be sworn in as prime minister. Over the next several days, tens of thousands of protesters, comprising large numbers of young Armenians, gathered in the square to listen to Pashinyan's passionate speeches and to denounce the ruling elite's attempted power grab.

Perhaps out of a desire to avoid the criticism that followed from its repression of anti-regime protests in 2008, the government was initially permissive of the protesters. However, following a

Former President Serzh Sargsyan (L) shakes hands with Turkish Prime Minister Erdogan in Washington, DC, in April 2010

brief and acrimonious meeting between Serzh Sargsyan and Pashinyan, the protest leader was detained by police alongside 232 protesters. This pivotal action eroded the legitimacy of the government. The next day, April 23, the numbers joining in the protests increased with some Armenian military personnel leaving their barracks to support the movement. By 4:30 in the afternoon, Serzh Sargsyan announced his immediate resignation from the role of prime minister, stating that "Nikol Pashinyan was right. I was wrong." These events have been dubbed by participants as "Armenia's Velvet Revolution," recalling the non-violent protests that brought down Communist party rule in Czechoslovakia in 1989.

Sargsyan's resignation threw the government into a temporary crisis, with the ruling Republican Party and interim Prime Minister Karen Karapetyan initially refusing to concede further to the protest movement. After a nationwide strike paralyzed the country's infrastructure, on May 8, 2018, parliament selected Nikol Pashinyan as prime minister.

Pashinyan's capacity to enact his promised reforms and anti-corruption efforts was hindered by the fact that throughout the rest of 2018, parliament was dominated by Sargsyan's HHK. Following a dominating performance by the My Step Alliance in snap elections held for seats in the Yerevan City Council in September 2018, Pashinyan made the bold step to resign as prime minister in order to force early parliamentary elections. In elections held on December 9, the My Step alliance won in a land slide. With 70% of the vote, the alliance earned 88 seats in the 132-member parliament. The remaining seats were split between two parties, Prosperous Armenia and Bright Armenia.

Notably, Sargsyan's HHK party failed to cross the 5% electoral threshold. However, HHK elites could not credibly claim that the election results were unfair: the OSCE noted that that the election was genuinely competitive and that there was a "general absence of electoral malfeasance."

Following his legislative success, in May 2019 Pashinyan set his sights on remaking the judiciary. Following the release of ex-President Robert Kocharyan on bail while awaiting his trial on charges of overthrowing the constitutional order for ordering security forces to violently repress protesters in 2008, Pashinyan called on protesters to block access to the courts. He went on to argue that judicial reform was the next step of the Armenian revolution, and that sitting judges need to be publicly vetted in order ensure that they are clean of corruption or ties to the old elites. Pashinyan's revolutionary challenge also targeted elites in the disputed territory of Nagorno-Karabakh, who he accused of conspiring with former President Kocharyan (who had also been the leader of Nagorno-Karabakh) to undermine his regime.

In September 2019, the Constitutional Court ruled that the trial against Kocharyan was partly unconstitutional which only furthered Pashinyan anger against the body. Calling the Constitutional Courts decisions against his government a "threat to democracy," in February 2020 he called for a referendum to alter the make-up of the court. In essence, if passed, the referendum would dismiss the seven members of the court who were appointed before Pashinyan came to power. The referendum, scheduled for April 2020, has been delayed to summer 2021 due the declaration of a state of emergency to contain the novel coronavirus. With the obstruction to Pashinyan's court-packing

scheme, Kocharyan's trial was ruled unconstitutional by the sitting judges of the Constitutional Court in spring 2021. The former president soon thereafter announced his intention to return to politics and run in the June 2021 elections.

Pahinyan's political star plummeted to earth following the disastrous second Nagorno-Karabakh war in fall 2020. Armenian troops were unprepared for the war and were quickly overwhelmed by Azerbaijani forces resulting in the loss of significant territory. Pashinyan's signature on a ceasefire deal ceding the lost territory sparked days of protests and demands for the resignation of the prime minister. In February 2021, the sacking of a top general led Onik Gasparyan, the Chief of the General Staff of the Armenian Armed Forces, to circulate a letter signed by other army officers calling on Pashinyan to resign for destabilizing and weakening the country. Over the next months, Armenia fell into political crisis, as Pashinyan accused Gasparyan of attempting a coup and struggled with President Sarksyan to have the general dismissed from his post. Pashinyan announced his formal resignation as prime minister on April 25, 2021, and served as acting prime minister in the run-up to the June 2021 elections. The snap elections paved the way for Pashinyan's reelection as his party won the elections, receiving more than half of all votes. Since his return to premiership, Pashinyan has been preoccupied with Azerbaijan in negotiation over the status of Nagorno-Karabakh. As tensions between the two countries escalated, in March 2022 the Azerbaijani government sent the Armenian government a five-point plan to normalize relations. The plan calls on both sides to recognize each other's territorial integrity, abstain from threatening each other's security, demarcate state borders, and open transportation links between these countries. However, the plan did not mention anything about the status of Nagorno-Karabakh. In response, Armenia called for international mediation to discuss the plan. Two rounds of negotiations in Brussels, one in April and the other in May 2002, appear to have resulted in significant breakthroughs. After a long delay, the meeting between the commissions from each country took place in which they discussed border delimitation. After these meetings, the Armenian Foreign Minister Ararat Mirzoyan publicly stated the following:

"It is paramount for the Armenian side that the rights and freedoms of the Armenians of Artsakh are guaranteed, and the status of Nagorno-Karabakh is finally clarified. For us, the Nagorno-Karabakh

Armenia

conflict is not a territorial issue, but a matter of rights,"

The media in Azerbaijan construed his statement to mean that Armenia was ready to recognize Karabakh as part of Azerbaijan. The Armenian opposition capitalized on that to call street protests against the incumbent government. The latest in a series of protest took place on May 2, in which thousands rallied against government's reported willingness to compromise on Armenians' sovereignty over Nagorno-Karabakh. For its part, the government used security forces to demobilize protesters, detaining 244 demonstrators.

Foreign Policy

Azerbaijan. Armenia is technically at war with its eastern neighbor, Azerbaijan. Though there has been only sporadic fighting since a cease-fire signed in 1994, this continues to be a major factor in Armenia's domestic and foreign policies, since it colors its relationships with all of its neighbors. This situation got even more complicated in 1998 when Robert Kocharian, the former president of Nagorno-Karabakh, was elected president of Armenia. Kocharian's official position at that time was that Nagorno-Karabakh had to have the right to decide its own future status vis-à-vis the Azerbaijani government; at the same time, he also made it clear that he would not support any proposed settlement that would directly subordinate Nagorno-Karabakh to Azerbaijan. Kocharian's preferred solution was a "horizontal" arrangement between Nagorno-Karabakh and Azerbaijan based on "federative or confederative relations." It is not clear how such an arrangement would work out in practice but, in any case, Azerbaijan has always opposed granting Nagorno-Karabakh anything more than autonomy.

Serzh Sargsyan, who won election to the presidency in February 2008 (and re-election in February 2013), is also from Nagorno-Karabakh. Although he is considered to be more pragmatic than Kocharian, his position on Nagorno-Karabakh appears to be very similar to that of Kocharian.

President Kocharian met numerous times with Azerbaijani President Heydar Aliyev and then later with his son and successor, Ilham Aliyev but these discussions never produced any results. The OSCE Minsk Group became involved in 2002 but they never produced a breakthrough either.

Foreign matters were largely put on hold during Armenia's 2003 presidential and parliamentary elections. President Aliyev's subsequent death left relations between the two neighbors in limbo. When

Ultra-modern Zvartnots Airport in Yerevan

Ilham Aliyev, the son, won the presidency in November 2003, he retained most of his father's advisers, but spent the next year or so consolidating his control domestically. Meetings between the two presidents have continued to occur periodically, but the only result has been that both sides pledged themselves to a peaceful resolution to the Karabakh conflict. Serzh Sargsyan's elevation to the presidency in 2008 did not alter that situation.

In June 2012, renewed violence flared along the border of Armenia and Azerbaijan with five Azerbaijanis and three Armenians killed. This produced statements from both countries reiterating their positions. Armenia's Foreign Minister Nalbandian said that Armenia was willing to negotiate a settlement but blamed Azerbaijan "which has rejected and continues to reject . . . proposals to consolidate the cease-fire, to withdraw snipers from the line of contact, to create a mechanism on investigating cease-fire violations and incidents." A spokesman for the Azerbaijan foreign ministry replied by placing the blame on Armenia. "We have shown a very clear and concrete will . . . to start the peace process. Armenian occupying forces must leave so we can move forward in the peace process. That's the major and No. 1 obstacle."

Another irritant in Armenian-Azerbaijani relations occurred in September 2012 when Hungary repatriated Ramil Safarov to Azerbaijan. Eight years earlier, Safarov, in Hungary to participate in a NATO-sponsored English class, had crept into the dormitory room of a fellow student, an Armenian serviceman, and killed him with an ax. Convicted of that crime and given a life sentence, he was repatriated to Azerbaijan on the understanding that he would serve out 25 years of his life sentence. Instead, President Aliyev greeted him at the airport upon his arrival, granting him a pardon, a new apartment, eight years of back pay, a promotion to major, and the status of a national hero.

In late 2014 and early 2015, there was a spike in violence in the disputed region of Nagorno-Karabakh, and Armenia and Azerbaijan accused each other of violating the 1994 cease-fire that left pro-Armenian forces occupying the region. Reports of isolated killings in the region continued to surface. According to Radio Free Europe/ Radio Liberty, on January 26, 2015, Armenian President Sargsyan said that he remained open to negotiations and building "bridges of trust" with Azerbaijan but if tensions along the border continue to increase "hotheads [in Azerbaijan] can expect some surprises . . . we reserve the right to carry out preventative strikes."

In April 2016, four days of fighting over the territory resulted in more than 200 casualties. While the origins of the clashes remain murky, many observers have suggested that they were initiated by Azerbaijani forces in part as an attempt to seize some of the territory back as well as to test Armenian military resolve. By all accounts, the clashes have made a peaceful final resolution of the disputed territory even more unlikely, despite formal pronouncements to the contrary from both the Armenian and Azerbaijani presidents.

Turkey. Armenia has fairly good relations with Georgia and Iran, but its relations with Turkey have been cold until recently, partly because Turkey has tended to favor Azerbaijan in its war with Armenia. Although Turkey did recognize Armenia's independence in 1991, it never established diplomatic relations with Armenia and it has maintained an embargo on Armenian goods since 1993.

There have been some contacts, however. In October 1998, Suleyman Demirel, the Turkish president, invited President Kocharian to attend the 75th anniversary celebrations of the founding of the Republic of Turkey. Kocharian accepted the invitation, but there was no breakthrough. The atmosphere cooled once again in April 2006 when President Kocharian, in remarks made during ceremonies commemorating the 91st anniversary of the 1915 genocide of Armenians in Ottoman Turkey, publicly declared that "Ottoman Turkey and its legal successor bear full responsibility for this crime."

Another attempt at a rapprochement occurred in March 2007 when the Turkish government invited Hasmik Poghosyan, the Armenian Minister of Culture, to attend the inauguration of a recently restored 10th century Armenian church, located on an island in Lake Van. Poghosyan accepted the invitation, but he was criticized harshly inside Armenia by individuals who charged that Turkey was using its restoration of the church for propaganda purposes.

A breakthrough of sorts finally came in April 2009, when Turkey and Armenia announced an agreement in principle to normalize relations. On October 10, 2009, the two countries signed two protocols calling for establishment of diplomatic relations and opening the border between the two countries. However, after bitter recriminations and numerous demonstrations by opponents of the agreements back home in Turkey and Armenia, both countries put ratification of the protocols on hold. Turkey has said that it would be ready to ratify the protocols after Armenia's quarrel with Azerbaijan over Nagorno-Karabakh is settled; Armenia has said that it will be ready to ratify the protocols when Turkey is ready to move ahead on the issue.

The 100th anniversary in 2015 of the start of the mass killing of Armenians by Turks during the First World War did not prove to be a turning point in Armenia's relations with Turkey. The Turkish government continued to refuse to characterize the massive death toll as "genocide." It claims that there was no deliberate, systematic attempt during the war by the Ottoman Turkish government to eliminate the Armenian Christian minority. Turkey continues to acknowledge that large numbers of Armenians died as a result of the harsh conditions of war, just as hundreds of thousands of Muslim Turks also perished.

Russia. Armenia has always favored good relations with Russia and has seen active participation in the Commonwealth of Independent States as part of that policy. Russia and Armenia have signed a series of bilateral agreements in recent years whose purpose was to boost military cooperation. The most significant such document, signed in August 1997, was a treaty "on friendship, cooperation, and mutual assistance" under which Russia, for the first time, committed itself in an accord to defend an ally militarily in the event that the ally was attacked by a foreign country. The treaty also calls for coordination of military-technical policy, mutual development of defense industries, standardization of military hardware, and joint financing of military projects. This treaty was supplemented in 2001 by a bilateral agreement on the common use of Armenian and Russian forces for "ensuring common security." There are currently two Russian military bases in Armenia. Russia and Armenia have also discussed setting up a joint military unit whose primary focus would be terrorism. In August 2010, Russia and Armenia signed a new military agreement which extended Russia's basing rights in Armenia for another 24 years. The new agreement commits Russia to supplying Armenia with "modern and compatible weaponry and special military hardware." This is something less than a new security agreement, but it does suggest a further Russian tilt toward Armenia vis-à-vis Azerbaijan.

Russia and Armenia have negotiated a number of economic accords, including one that established a joint venture for the re-export of Russian gas to Turkey. Another, signed in March 2002, provided for the transfer of five state-run Armenian companies to Russia in payment of a $94 million debt that Armenia owed the Russian government. The Armenian parliament ratified this particular agreement in December 2002. In their joint statement after President Kocharian's three-day visit to Moscow in January 2003, Presidents Putin and Kocharian praised the level of bilateral political, economic, and military cooperation between their countries. Separately, President Kocharian characterized the relations as "close to ideal."

Russian investors have also greatly increased their holdings in Armenia in recent years. In 2006, the Russian state-owned Unified Energy Systems purchased the Armenian power distribution system for $73 million from British-registered Midland Resources Holding. In 2007, Russia's Mobile Telesystems paid $430 million for an 80% share of K-Telecom, Armenia's largest mobile-phone operator. In January 2008, Russian Railways acquired the rights to manage the Armenian national rail network for a 30-year period. Russian Railways has promised to invest a minimum of $570 million to upgrade the rail system. Armenia also received a $500 million loan from Russia in early 2009.

In 2011, Armenia decided to join a new Russian-sponsored free-trade zone, whose other signatories include Belarus,

ՍԱ ԵՐԵՎԱՆՆ Է

Ինչ գոյ գիշեր է. մեկն ինչ հիշել է.
Նա ինչ հուշել է անհուշելին.
Նա է իմ հուշար. անդրաակույսր
Նա է իմ լույսր` մութ գիշերին:

Նա. ով եկել էր. կյանքս բեկել էր.
Բախտս բեկել էր ինքն իր բախտին.
Բայց արդեն ուշ է. հուշր մշուշ է.
Սերր քնքուշ էր կեսգիշերին:

Ներս արի. ներս արի. ի՞նչ ես կանգնել.
Ի՞նչ ես հիմար ժպիտով թաքացել:

Սա Երևանն է. այսպիսի դու տեսանս ես.
Ուր քեզ սպասում են դեռ կեսգիշերին:
Ուր կամ սիրում են. կամ թունդ հայհոյում են.
Երբ հիշեցնում են անհիշելին:

Ներս արի. ներս արի. ի՞նչ ես կանգնել.
Ի՞նչ ես հիմար ժպիտով թաքացել:

Սա քո փողոցն է. կյանքիդ դպրոցը.
Ուր քեզ հիշում են. դեն չեն մոռացել:
Սա քո փողոցն է. կյանքիդ դպրոցը.
Ուր քեզ հիշում են. դեն չեն մոռացել:

Ինչ գոյ գիշեր է. մեկն ինչ հիշել է.
Նա ինչ հուշել է անհուշելին.
Բայց արդեն ուշ է. հուշր մշուշ է.
Սերր քնքուշ էր. կեսգիշերին:

1995

Sa Erevann e (This Is Yerevan), the lyrics of a song by Ruben Hakhverdyan, a famous contemporary Armenian singer and song-writer

Armenia

Kazakhstan, Kyrgyzstan, Tajikistan, and Moldova. This free-trade zone is supposed to be transformed into the Eurasian Economic Union (called EURASEC by Moscow) in 2015, an entity President Putin has sponsored as a countervailing organization to the European Union. Russia put quite a bit of pressure on Armenia to commit itself to EURASEC but, until 2013, Armenia appeared ready to opt for the EU's Eastern Partnership program instead. Talks with EU representatives had actually been concluded and Armenia was preparing to initial the agreement when President Sargsyan was invited to Moscow in September 2013. After Sargsyan's meeting with Putin, he announced that Armenia would join the current Customs Union and was ready to take part in the establishment of a Eurasian economic union. As President Sargsyan put it,

It is a rational decision stemming from the national interests of Armenia. This decision does not constitute a refusal to continue our dialogue with European structures. We intend to continue these reforms in the future.

In fact, of course, this put an end to Armenia's previous intention to sign the planned Association Agreement with the European Union.

In 2014, President Sargsyan moved Armenia closer to Russia and away from the prospect of eventual membership in the European Union. On October 10, in the Belarusian capital of Minsk he signed an agreement to join the Russian-dominated Eurasian Economic Union (EEU). This decision sparked unrest the same day in Yerevan, where thousands demonstrated against the agreement as well as against the nation's slow economic growth and ongoing corruption. Nevertheless, on January 2, 2015, Armenia joined the EEU. Armenia depends heavily on natural gas from Russia, and Russia continues to keep about 3,000 troops at a military base in Gyumri, Armenia, which is located about 72 miles north of Yerevan.

United States. Americans tend to be sympathetic to Armenia as is reflected in the aid program that the US government instituted in 1993. In 2006, the US government announced that $236 million had been allocated to Armenia under the Millennium Challenge program. Armenia continues to receive economic support from this program.

The events of September 11 and America's subsequent worldwide campaign against terrorism affected Armenia directly because the United States decided to partially waive Section 907 of the Freedom Support Act (that barred direct US government aid to Azerbaijan as long as that country maintained its embargo against Armenia and Nagorno-Karabakh) because of Azerbaijan's assistance in the war against terrorism. Following two days of talks during a visit to Washington in October 2001, Foreign Minister Vartan Oskanian expressed Armenia's disquiet at the partial lifting of Section 907, but said that Armenia understood the US government's need for flexibility in dealing with Azerbaijan for an effective fight against terrorism. Armenia's own commitment to the war against terrorism brought an invitation to Defense Minister Sargsyan to visit the United States in March 2002. During this visit, which Sargsyan described as marking "the beginning of American–Armenian military consultations," the United States offered training to Armenian military personnel and assistance in upgrading Armenian communications facilities.

In late 2019, U.S. Congress offered a symbolic gesture to Armenia and Armenians when it passed a resolution acknowledging the Armenian Genocide. For years, similar resolutions had failed to receive enough support in both houses, largely out of fear that any such vote would alienate Turkey, a NATO ally. However, anger over a Turkish incursion into Syria prompted Congress to change course. On April 24, 2021, U.S. President Joe Biden officially recognized the Armenian genocide on Armenian Remembrance day.

Iran. Armenia has excellent relations with Iran, and Iran is, in fact, Armenia's chief trading partner. The reason for cultivating good relations with Iran is not difficult to discover, however. At war with Azerbaijan and with Turkey enforcing an embargo against Armenian products, only Iran and Georgia remain. And Georgia has been nearly as badly off economically as Armenia. What has given Armenia the opportunity to develop such relations is that Iran has poor relations with Azerbaijan, partly because it fears Azerbaijani influences on Azeris within Iran, partly because Azerbaijan has welcomed American companies and their billions of dollars of investment.

Tajikistan. Armenia has also made major efforts to counteract its lack of relations with Azerbaijan and Turkey by building up its relations with other countries in the area. President Saparmurat Kocharian paid an official visit to Tajikistan in April 2002. Four bilateral documents were signed that included an Agreement on Friendship and Cooperation. The talks also covered bilateral military cooperation and regional security.

Turkmenistan. In March 2002, President Kocharian had conversations with President Saparmurat Niyazov of Turkmenistan which resulted in an agreement for Armenia to purchase two billion cubic meters of Turkmen gas annually. Because the gas has to be shipped by way of Iran, a new gas pipeline connecting Armenia and Iran had to be built; it was completed in March 2007.

International Organizations. Armenia was admitted to the United Nations at the same time as the other members of the Commonwealth of Independent States. It is also a member of the Council for Security and Cooperation in Europe, the IMF and World Bank, and a full member of the Council of Europe.

Armenia's long-term goal of joining the European Union received a boost in September 2002 when the Armenia-EU parliamentary commission expressed its support. The following month, the Armenia-EU coordinating council announced an agreement on creating "new mechanisms for broader EU engagement and political consultation." Already, the EU countries are collectively Armenia's largest trading partner.

Armenia's application for membership in the World Trade Organization was approved in December 2002. Armenia had applied for membership six years earlier, but its membership was held up while the government worked to draw up and pass a new customs code plus other legislation required by the WTO dealing with matters such as VAT and excise taxes.

NATO. Armenia was also granted observer status in the NATO Parliamentary Assembly in May 2002. In November, Armenia hosted a three-day NATO conference in Yerevan, a sort of preparatory conference to discuss military exercises scheduled to take place in Armenia in June 2003 under the Partnership for Peace program. The following month, a NATO delegation headed by former Supreme Allied Commander Europe General Joseph Ralston arrived in Yerevan for meetings with President Kocharian, Foreign Minister Oskanian, and Defense Minister Sargsyan. Ralston and Kocharian also discussed Armenia's participation in the Kosovo peacekeeping operation.

Armenia signed an individual Partnership Action Plan with NATO in 2005. President Kocharian made it clear at the time, however, that his government was "not going to join NATO." That was not really an issue, since NATO prohibits its members from hosting military bases from non-NATO members; Armenia hosts two Russian military bases.

The Nature of the Regime

The National Assembly instituted a modified proportional system prior to the 1999 legislative elections. At that time, 56 of the 131 seats were to be apportioned proportionally with the remainder elected in single mandate seats. In July 2002, the National Assembly raised the number of proportional seats to 75 and that system was used for the 2003 legislative elections. Since the new law kept the number of deputies at 131, the total number of single-mandate constituencies was reduced from 75 to 56.

In May 2005, parliament amended the electoral law again, to take effect at the 2007 parliamentary elections. Under this latest legislation, the proportion of parliamentary mandates distributed under the proportional system was raised to 90 and the number of single-mandate constituencies was reduced to 41.

The legislation also reduced from three to one the number of members which the president was empowered to name to the electoral commissions, and it transferred responsibility for maintaining accurate voter lists from the local authorities to the police. The changes, which were endorsed by the Council of Europe, were supposed to help minimize electoral fraud.

Serzh Sargsyan was formally sworn in as president on April 9, 2008. He immediately named Tigran Sargsyan (no relation) as his new prime minister. On February 18, 2013, he was reelected with 58.64% of the vote; he immediately re-appointed Tigran Sargsyan as prime minister.

In December 2015, a constitutional referendum changing regime from a semi-presidential system to a parliamentary republic passed with more than 63% of the vote. Under the amended constitution, beginning in 2018, the power of the prime minister will be expanded at the expense of the powers of the president. Although the amendments have drawn praise from some outside observers, the referendum was marred by accusations of fraud, vote buying, and low turnout. It was widely speculated that the referendum represented an attempt by the ruling Republican Party to help incumbent President Serzh Sargsyan circumvent formal term limits. Although he is only permitted to serve two terms as president, he could serve an unlimited number as prime minister. On April 2, 2017, the first parliament with the power to select the next president was elected. As could be expected, President Sargsyan's Republican Party of Armenia won the majority of seats in the reconfigured parliament; the party won 58 out of 105 seats (55%) after receiving 49.17% of the vote. Eight other parties and alliances competed in the election but only three others cleared the 5%

threshold. The Tsarukyan bloc won 31 seats after receiving 27.35% of the vote, the Way Out bloc won 9 seats, and the Armenian Revolutionary Federation won 7 seats. According to the OSCE's preliminary conclusions about the election they "were well administered and fundamental freedoms were respected." However, the OSCE's report also notes, that similar to the Constitutional Referendum, the parliamentary election was marred by "credible information of vote-buying, of pressure on public servants including in schools and hospitals, and of intimidation of voters to vote for certain parties." As discussed above, Serzh Sargsyan's planned transition from President to Prime Minister was derailed by massive street protests in April 2018. As a result of these protests, dubbed Armenia's Velvet Revolution, the regime is entering into a new phase: one headed by former opposition leader Nikol Pashinyan. In the wake of Pashinyan's selection as the new Prime Minister, the formerly dominant Republican Party has been weakened by defections, and as of June 2018 no longer held the majority in the National Assembly.

Culture

Traditional Armenian culture has deep historic roots with the first written literature dating back as far as the 5th century A.D. Two works that date from that period are Movses Khorenatsi's *History of Armenia* and Eznik Koghbatsi's *Refutation of the Sects*. The two themes represented by the works, history and religion, continued to be important in subsequent centuries, but they gradually began to be expressed in new forms.

Grigor Narekatsi, who lived in the 10th century, was Armenia's first great poet. A deeply religious man, his mystical poems and hymns heavily influenced the Armenian Orthodox Church and led to his canonization after his death.

A secular tradition began to emerge in the 16th–18th centuries with the appearance of popular bards (troubadours). Known as *ashugh*, they produced numerous love songs which are now known by the people. The 19th century saw the emergence of both the novel and the short story. Famous Armenian novelists include Hakob Paronian, Ervand Otian, and Hakob Maliq-Hakobian, whose pen name is "Raffi." Paronian also wrote plays, as did Gabriel Sundukian.

The communist era had a negative effect on Armenian culture; it rejected nearly every theme associated with traditional literature. Pre-revolutionary novelists and playwrights continued to be read and performed, but modern writers were required to conform to communism's "socialist realism," a requirement which turned them into party hacks.

There were some good Armenian writers during the 20th century, and these include Hovhannes Tumanian, Paruir Sevak, Avetik Isahakian, and Eghishe Charents. If none of these writers ever became known outside of Armenia, it is nevertheless true that the 20th century did produce Armenia's first great composer, Aram Katchaturian, probably because it was hard for Moscow authorities to apply "socialist realism" to classical music. Two lesser-known composers of this period were Komitas and Alexander Spendiarian. Two famous artists from this period were Martiros Saryan and Minas Avetisian. Armenia also has its famous actors, including V. Papazian and H. Nersisyan.

Famous Armenians living abroad who were considered to be part of Armenian culture included Charles Aznavour, a popular singer who lived in France; William Saroyan, a playwright who lived in the United States; and Atom Egoyan, a film director who lived in Canada.

Communism did leave behind an established society which will help Armenian culture to develop further in the future.

Former Foreign Minister Oskanian and Finance and Economy Minister Khachatrian in Washington, DC, March 2006

Armenia

There is both a state radio and television broadcasting system with studios in Yerevan. The city is also the site of a State Academic Theater of Opera and Ballet. Several drama theaters also exist, a national dance company, several orchestras, and a film studio.

Old folk arts such as dancing, singing, and artistic crafts were left undisturbed by communism. Thus, the new non-communist government has a firm basis on which to build. An Armenian Academy of Sciences runs a number of research institutes throughout the country.

Economy

Industry. Armenia today is overwhelmingly an urban and industrial society, with agriculture perhaps accounting less than a sixth of the national income. During the communist era, three fifths of the country's industries were located in and around the city of Yerevan; because so many of them were heavy, polluting industries, Yerevan became one of the most polluted cities of the former Soviet Union. These factories produced synthetic rubber, fertilizers, chemicals, nonferrous metals, machines, and equipment. Armenia was also the source for other polluting minerals, all of which produced badly polluted areas in the countryside. The government has begun dealing with this problem in recent years and change is now occurring. Some of the most polluting industries have been closed, but the greatest change has been in the development of new, non-polluting industries such as the new information technology sector.

It also has light industry—textiles, carpet-weaving, food processing, wine-making, fruit, meat-canning, and creameries. Medium industries include electrical equipment, precision instruments, and machine tools. Armenia is still also a large producer of cement, marble, pumice, volcanic basalt, and fireproof clay.

Industry, which makes up about 25% of the economy, suffered a sharp collapse between 1991 and 1993 and only began to recover in 1994. Although all of the post-communist economies suffered sharp drops as they began the transition to market economies, in Armenia's case this was exacerbated by its political quarrel with Azerbaijan over the Armenian-populated enclave of Nagorno-Karabakh. From the beginning of the fighting, Azerbaijan maintained an embargo against Armenia; as the war continued, it was joined by Turkey, which instituted a blockade against Armenian goods in 1993. As a result, Armenian industry had great difficulty obtaining energy supplies and raw materials.

Petroleum and gas, which formerly came from Azerbaijan and Turkmenistan, remained in short supply until Armenia negotiated a deal with Iran for the delivery of petroleum. A similar agreement was signed with Turkmenistan for the purchase of natural gas, though, at the time, there was no pipeline connecting Turkmenistan and Armenia. In December 2004, construction began on a gas pipeline connecting Armenia to Iran; the line was completed in March 2007. The Iranian pipeline provides (Iranian and Turkmenistani) natural gas to the thermal power plant in Hrazdan, recently modernized by a state-owned Iranian company.

Two high-voltage transmission lines connecting Armenia to Iran were also constructed in this same time period, with the second such line beginning operation in 2007. In this case, energy is actually exchanged between the two countries on a seasonal basis with Armenia exporting excess electricity in the spring and summer and importing it in the winter.

Armenia also reopened the Medzamor nuclear plant in 1995; it now relies on that source for much of its electricity, though it is under continuing pressure from the European Union to close the plant. Armenia also signed a trilateral agreement on energy with Georgia and Iran in late 2006, under which the three countries agreed to "synchronize" and link their power grids.

Agriculture. Agriculture contributes only about 15% of GDP, but it continues to provide employment for almost half the population, either in agriculture itself or in related industries. Armenia began replacing the republic's state and collective farms with private agriculture even before it achieved its independence in 1991. The government has also set up regional scientific centers to offer consulting services to farmers and engage in long-term agricultural planning, but growth has been hindered by a weak market infrastructure and a lack of machines.

Armenia's most valuable agricultural product is grapes, from which famous wines, brandies, and champagnes are made. Orchard crops are next in importance—peaches, apricots, apples, cherries, pears, pomegranates, walnuts, hazelnuts, and almonds are abundant. Tobacco is another important cash crop. Extensive mountain pastures support a significant dairy industry, plus many sheep for wool and meat. Pigs and poultry are also raised.

Foreign Capital Investment. Armenia launched a program of privatization based on vouchers in 1994, but the program was not very successful because it failed to inject new capital into enterprises or

change the way that they were managed. Accordingly, the government launched a new program in 1997 whose aim was to encourage greater foreign private capital investment in the country. That approach, which was further expanded in 1998, included the sale of a 90% interest in Armentel, the national telecommunications company, to a Greek consortium. It also resulted in a Canadian company investing $200 million in gold mining.

Total direct foreign investment reached $98 million in the first half of 1998, though it dropped off in the latter part of the year after the Russian market collapse. As an exception, General Motors announced in January 1999 that it planned to begin manufacturing minibuses, small tractors, and trucks in Armenia, and planned to sell its products throughout the region.

Growth was slower in 1999 and 2000, but picked up again in 2001 when GDP growth reached a torrid 9.1%. The Armenian government also launched another round of privatization in 2001 when it put 300 large and medium state-owned industries up for sale. Many of the firms were loss-making, however, so buyers were scarce. In the end, the government managed to sell about 225 of the firms, though this produced very little new money for the state. As an example, one of the firms put up for sale was the Armenian power grid which was crippled by losses of $50 million a year and a debt of some $100 million. The government accepted an offer to buy an 81.1% stake in the company for $40 million in August 2002. However, the buyer, a Canadian citizen whose company was registered in the Channel Islands, reneged on the deal. The Armenian government then negotiated a deal with the Daewoo Engineering group of South Korea, which assumed full management of the energy distribution network in December 2002. In September 2005, the Armenian government agreed to sell the network to Unified Energy Systems (UES), the Russian government-owned company. UES took final control of the network in September 2006. Although foreign investment has continued to grow since that time, it remains at a fairly low level, perhaps $300 million a year.

The economy grew at double digit rates between 2001 and 2008. Agriculture and capital construction were two areas of consistently faster growth, with industrial growth consistently much lower. Industry grew at a slower pace during these years.

Small and medium-sized firms now account for more than 40% of total GDP. One factor that inhibits industrial growth is that interest rates for small businesses have averaged 20% or more. The government began addressing this problem in December 2002 when it created a new state fund of

250 million drams ($430,000) which is being used to provide credit guarantees for small and medium-sized businesses.

While the economy was making progress in recent years, Armenia continued to run budget deficits of 2–3% of GDP which had to be covered by foreign loans. The 2008 budget envisaged revenues of 746 billion drams ($2.5 billion) and expenditures of 822 billion drams. The 76-billion-dram deficit was largely financed by domestic borrowing. Although defense spending for 2008 increased by 33% over 2007, expenditures earmarked for education, health care, social security, and other public services were increased as well.

Armenia originally proposed a balanced budget for 2009, but the worldwide economic downturn began affecting the Armenian economy by late 2008. From a 13% growth rate in 2008, the economy went into actual decline during the first quarter of 2009; by the end of the year, GDP had dropped by 14.4%.

Foreign Assistance. Armenia's economic policies have been supported by both the IMF and World Bank over the past several years. When Jerome Kremers, a senior IMF official, visited Yerevan in October 2005, he commended Armenia for its double-digit economic growth over the preceding five years. He then announced a three-year $33 million credit which was to be used to increase tax collection and customs revenues and reduce poverty. In March 2009, the IMF again came to Armenia's aid with a standby loan of $540 million. Roger Robinson, head of the World Bank's office in Armenia 2001–2006, stated as he was leaving that he had witnessed "a significant change in the quality of life" in Armenia over those five years and added that he believed economic growth could continue over the next 5 to 10 years, though he warned that it would require deeper "institutional reforms" dealing with governance, tax, and customs administration, as well as the overall business environment.

The European Union signed an agreement with Armenia in March 2004 providing Armenia with $25 million in the years 2004–2007. The EU has asked Armenia to decommission the Medzamor nuclear-power plant and has offered Armenia 100 million euros as an inducement to set a concrete date for doing so. Since Armenia receives 30% of its electricity from the plant, its position is that it can not do so until alternative energy sources are available. Since 2003, the Medzamor plant has been managed by RAO Unified Energy Systems, the Russian state electricity monopoly.

The United States Government announced in December 2005 that it had awarded Armenia a Millennium Challenge Grant worth $236 million which was to be made available over the succeeding five years. A total of $67 million was earmarked for rehabilitation of almost 600 miles of rural roads, while the remainder was to be used to finance irrigation projects and the introduction of higher-yield crops.

Recent Economic Developments. The worldwide economic crisis which began in late 2007 began to affect Armenia in the fall of 2008. The Armenian government attempted to maintain a stable exchange of the dram against the US dollar, but it was forced to allow the dram to float in March 2009. With a sharp drop in exports and a growing budget deficit, Armenia first applied for a $500 million loan from Russia, which it received; it next applied to the IMF, which agreed to extend a $540 million emergency standby loan in March 2009. Armenia's GDP dropped by an estimated 14.4% in 2009; this was largely because of the economy's heavy dependence on construction, which dropped 14% that year. Economic growth resumed in the first quarter of 2010, with industry showing a growth of industrial output of 9.7%. However, bad weather led to a 14.5% drop in agricultural output, with the result that total GDP growth was only 2.6% for the year.

Prime Minister Sargsyan, addressing his cabinet on December 30, 2010, acknowledged this development. "Economic growth is no longer ensured by construction and agriculture," he said; rather, "industry, modern technologies, and the information technology sector" would be "the main engines of economic development" in 2011–2012. Industrial output currently accounts for about a quarter of the country's GDP, while agricultural production only accounts for 12% of the country's economic output.

Since 2014, the Armenian economy has been negatively impacted by the Russian economic crisis. As reported by ARKA News Agency on October 4, 2010, Armenian Finance Minister, Vardan Aramyan acknowledged the sharp decline in remittances from migrant workers. Aramyan stated: "remittances to Armenia in 2014 and 2015 decreased by $700 million, and if we consider the current situation and the expected economic slowdown in Russia, we anticipate that the remittances will drop further by $140 million." In part due to the drop in remittances, as well as reduced level of exports in 2016 economic growth was a paltry .2%.

Armenia has made a concerted effort to attract foreign investment and to establish infrastructure to enable and encourage entrepreneurial activity. Due to these efforts, in the World Bank's 2017 Ease of Doing Business, the country was ranked 38th. This represented a higher rank than Belgium and Italy and trailed only a handful of non-Baltic post-Soviet states (Belarus, Kazakhstan, and Georgia). Despite these efforts, its isolated geographic location and endemic corruption have greatly limited its appeal for foreign investors. As a result, for the foreseeable future its economic fortunes will remain directly tied to the Russian economy.

The Future

Armenia's future remains clouded by the continuing quarrel with the Azerbaijan over Nagorno-Karabakh. The disastrous 2020 war with Azerbaijan has destabilized the regime. Following the Velvet Revolution in 2018, there was a tremendous degree of optimism surrounding the political situation in the state. Prime Minister Pashinyan had unified significant sectors of society and seemed poised to implement needed reforms to root out corruption. There was hope that his coalition could build sustainable democratic institutions. Most of that optimism has now dissipated in the wake of the Russian-brokered ceasefire as Pashinyan has faced mass defection from both public supporters as well as from elites. These defections spurred Pasinyan's resignation and the announcement of snap elections in June 2021. Pasinyan returned to office following his party's victory in those elections. His political survival in office is far from assured, however. His willingness to compromise on Armenians' sovereignty over Nagorno-Karabakh, has sparked periodic street protests and put his government at odds with de facto leaders of Nagorno Karabakh. It remains to be seen whether his negotiations with Azerbaijan will pave a path out of the current political crisis.

The Republic of Azerbaijan

Area: 33,428 sq. mi. (86,600 sq. km.), about the size of Maine.

Population: 10,650,239 (2024 est.)

Capital City: Baku (Pop. 2.4 mil) (2023 est.).

Climate: Generally dry, sub-tropical.

Neighboring States: Russia (north); Georgia (northwest); Armenia (west and east, where the Naxcivan (Nakhichevan) Region is separated from the rest of the country); Iran (south).

Language: Azerbaijani (Azeri).

Ethnic Background: Azerbaijani (91.6%); Lezghin (2%); Russian (1.3%); Armenian (1.3%); Talysh (1.3%); other (2.4%). Note: the predominately Armenian populated Nagorno-Karabagh region is not included in these numbers.

Principal Religion: Islam, principally Shi'a.

Chief Commercial Products: Agriculture—grain, cotton, rice, grapes. Industry—oil, natural gas, concrete, nonferrous metals, alumina, carpets, processed food (fish, caviar, and meat), wine, cheese.

Currency: manat.

Per Capita Annual Income: $21349 (2023 est.).

Recent Political Status: Democratic Republic of Azerbaijan (May 28, 1918–April 1920); Azerbaijan SSR, founded in 1920; part of Transcaucasian Federation (1922–1936); Constituent republic of the USSR (1936–1991).

President: Ilham Aliyev (since 2003, and elected to a fourth term April 11, 2018).

Prime Minister: Ali Asadov (since October 8, 2019).

National Flag: Three equal horizontal stripes, sky blue, red, and green, with a crescent moon and star superimposed in the center of the red.

National Day: May 28, 1918 (founding of the Democratic Republic of Azerbaijan).

The Land

The Republic of Azerbaijan (Azarbaycan Respublikasi), which was one of the 15 Soviet republics before the collapse of the Union of Soviet Socialist Republics in 1991, is located in an area south of the Caucasus Mountains along the western shores of the Caspian Sea. It covers an area of 33,428 square miles (86,600 sq. km.). Iran lies to the south, Armenia and Georgia to the west, and the Russian Federation to the north. It also includes the Naxcivan (Nakhichevan) Autonomous Republic, occupied mainly by Azeri but separated from the rest of Azerbaijan by the southeastern part of Armenia, and the Nagorno-Karabakh Region—which had the status of an autonomous republic until the Azerbaijani Supreme Soviet abolished it in November 1991—mainly occupied by Armenians.

More than 40% of Azerbaijan is lowlands, most of which are in the Kur River Valley, which runs in a northwest direction beginning at the Caspian Sea and ending in the mountains of Georgia. The Kur River actually originates in the Small Caucasus Mountains, which stretch along the border between Georgia and Turkey. It flows down through the high valley of central Georgia before crossing the border into Azerbaijan.

The Aras River, a southern branch of the Kur, originates in the Aras Mountains of Turkey. It forms the southern boundary between Armenia and Turkey, between the Naxcivan (Nakhichevan) Autonomous Republic and Turkey and Iran, and between Azerbaijan and the Iranian province of Azerbaijan. It then turns northeast and joins the Kur River.

The remaining lowland areas include the Lenkoran Lowland in the southeast, plus a strip of land beginning at the Apsheron Peninsula, which juts out into the Caspian Sea to the north of the mouth of the Kur River, and then running north along the western shores of the Caspian.

To the northeast of the Kur River Valley, the chain of the Great Caucasus Mountains runs southeast, ending just before the Apsheron Peninsula. Here the highest mountains are over 14,000 feet, though most of the territory is covered by foothills running perpendicular to the line of the higher mountain ridge and varying in height from 1,300 to 4,900 feet.

Southward across the Kur River Valley, the ground again flows upward, becoming foothills then rising to become the Small Caucasus Mountains, which mark the border between Azerbaijan and Armenia. The Karabakh upland, where the Nagorno-Karabakh Region is situated, is also in this area.

The annual rainfall of the Kur-Aras Lowland varies from 8 to 16 inches and so has the plant life of the steppe and the semi-desert. A well-developed system of dams and canals means that most of the lowland is irrigated, however, and today most of the area is devoted to the cultivation of cotton. The largest of these dams is the Mingechaur, built in 1953 along the Kur River in northwestern Azerbaijan. Mingechaur Dam, which is also a major hydroelectric station, forms a lake that covers an area of 234 square miles and has a storage capacity of 565 trillion cubic feet.

The Kur River Valley has a dry, subtropical climate with hot summers and mild winters. Southeast Azerbaijan, which receives the most rainfall of any part of the republic, has a humid, subtropical climate. Here the annual rainfall is about 50 inches, which falls mainly in the winter. The Naxcivan (Nakhichevan) Autonomous Republic, with altitudes between 2,300 and 3,300 feet, has a dry, continental climate, with cold winters and dry summers.

The Caspian Sea shoreline has a Mediterranean type climate, cool in winter and dry in summer. Forests are found on the upper slopes of the Great Caucasus and Small Caucasus Mountains. The main trees are beech, oak, and pine.

The People

According to the CIA World Factbook, the estimated population of Azerbaijan as of 2023 was 10.6 million. Azeris or Azerbaijani are a Turkic-speaking people. They migrated into the area in the 11th century as part of the Oguz Seljuk migrations. There are another 16.5 million Azeris living across the border in northern Iran, an important factor in Azerbaijani-Iranian relations.

Since its independence from the Soviet Union, the demographics of Azerbaijan have become steadily more ethnically homogeneous. For instance, in 1989, ethnic Azeribaijanis represented 82.6% of the population, and Russians 5.6%. As of July 2017, ethnic Azerbaijanis are estimated to be 91.6% of the population and Russians 1.3%.

History

After the Bolsheviks came to power in Moscow, national groups in Azerbaijan, Armenia, and Georgia got together and established the Transcaucasian Federal Republic on April 22, 1918. It collapsed after one month. In Azerbaijan, a National Council of the Tatars, dominated by the Mussavat (Nationalist) Party, announced the birth of the Democratic Republic of Azerbaidzhan on May 28, 1918. This government continued to exist until April 1920, when it was overthrown by the Red Army. The communists established the Azerbaijan Soviet Socialist Republic on April 28, 1920.

This was the beginning of Azerbaijani political history. Prior to that time, the Azeri were an undifferentiated Islamic people, first under Persian then under Russian rule, of the area of the Trans-Caucasus. Peter the Great was the first Russian ruler to take an interest in the area, when he occupied Baku in 1723. The coastal region actually became Russian in 1813 by the Treaty of Gulistan, under which Persia ceded the lands bordering the western shores of the Caspian Sea from the Lenkoran Lowland northward to Derbent. The interior was annexed by Russia in 1829.

Although Azerbaijan came under communist control in 1920, it remained theoretically independent until March 1922. It was then merged with Armenia and Georgia to form the Transcaucasian Soviet Federated Socialist Republic. The Transcaucasian SFSR became a formal part of the Union of Soviet Socialist Republics in December 1922. Fourteen years later, under the terms of Stalin's 1936 Constitution, the Transcaucasian SFSR was dissolved and the Azerbaijan Soviet Socialist Republic reemerged.

Azerbaijan was a pliant republic under the communists until Gorbachev's policy of glasnost began to challenge the old status quo. The situation had been building up over a number of years, however, in connection with jobs in the modern, industrial sector. Azeris were traditionally either nomads or farmers, so when the Baku oil industry was developed, most of the jobs went to Armenians or Russians. After the Russian Revolution, literacy campaigns gradually carried education to the countryside where most Azeris lived.

As more and more Azeris became educated, they began to be recruited for positions in industry and government. For a long time this was nominal, but the Brezhnev leadership, in particular, encouraged the development of native elites in the republics. This new Azerbaijani leadership founded numerous institutes of higher education and, increasingly, favored a policy of edging out non-Azeris and replacing them with Azeris. Thus there was a very distinct bias among the Azerbaijani political leadership to favor Azeri speakers. Armenians were a particular target of this policy.

Many Armenians from Armenia had taken jobs in the Baku area in the past. When they found themselves edged out of a job, however, they could always return to Armenia. This presented a different problem for the Armenians of the Nagorno-Karabakh Autonomous Republic, however, since this was a relatively poor area without significant industry. The Armenians of Nagorno-Karabakh also felt that the leadership at the republic level ignored needs of the autonomous republic. Thus they formally requested to be transferred to Armenian jurisdiction in February 1988.

When the Armenian Republic leadership supported Nagorno-Karabakh's request two weeks later, apparently spontaneous riots broke out in the Azerbaijani city of Sumgait which turned into a slaughter of Armenians. When this was followed by retaliatory moves against Azeris living in Armenia, the result was a dual stream of refugees, Armenians fleeing to Armenia and Azeris fleeing to Azerbaijan.

This first, open manifestation of Azerbaijani nationalism was exacerbated when Gorbachev dismissed the first secretaries of the Azerbaijani and Armenian Communist Parties in May 1988 for allowing the situation to get out of hand. The Azerbaijani educated classes, up to this time loyal supporters of the party, now began to think of the party as Moscow-dominated. Gorbachev aggravated the situation even further when he announced in January 1989 that he was suspending Azerbaijan's authority over Nagorno-Karabakh and putting the autonomous republic under direct Muscovite control.

That summer the Azerbaijan Popular Front was founded for the specific goal of safeguarding Azeri national interests. And the national interest was defined as meaning the territorial integrity of Azerbaijan. In a challenge to the Communist Party, the front launched a series of mass demonstrations and labor strikes in August.

In September 1989, the front organized a road and railroad blockade of Armenia. With 85% of Armenia's freight entering the country by way of Azerbaijan, this action brought Armenian industry almost to a halt. The success of the blockade also brought the front a political victory over the Azerbaijan Communist Party. On September 13, Abdul Vezirov, the first secretary, signed a protocol with the front in which he agreed to call a special session of the Supreme Soviet to pass a law on sovereignty. The law was passed 10 days later.

The fortress at Baku (ca. 1300)

Azerbaijan

Meanwhile the front threatened to maintain its blockade of Armenia until Moscow dissolved its special commission and allowed control over Nagorno-Karabakh to revert back to Azerbaijan. On November 28, the USSR Supreme Soviet voted to end Moscow's direct rule over Nagorno-Karabakh. The rail blockade was eased, but not lifted entirely.

In January 1990, a new series of killings of Armenians broke out in Baku, the Azerbaijani capital. The government declared a state of emergency to handle the matter. Gorbachev then sent in Soviet troops to restore order and to forestall a coup by the Azerbaijani Popular Front against the Azerbaijan Government. Soviet Defense Minister Dmitry Yazov later said that the Soviet troops were sent in "to destroy the organizational structure" of the Azerbaijan Popular Front. The Azerbaijan Communist Party leadership was changed as well. Ayaz Mutalibov, who had been prime minister up to this time, was installed as the new party leader and head of state.

Azeris were extremely angered by Gorbachev's actions. Elmira Kafarova, chairman of the Azerbaijani Supreme Soviet, referred to the events of January 1990 as "a gross violation of Azerbaijani sovereignty." More than a million people turned out for the funeral of the approximately 100 Azerbaijanis killed when Soviet troops entered Baku.

There were also rallies when Communist Party membership cards were burned, but Gorbachev kept the troops in Baku and eventually order was restored. Mutalibov survived as party first secretary, though he never dared to lift the state of emergency declared in January 1990.

Independent Azerbaijan

Mutalibov was abroad on a visit to Iran while an attempted coup against Gorbachev was going on. He never condemned the attempt, but, after it failed, he resigned as head of the party and issued a decree banning party cells in government and industry. The party later dissolved itself.

Mutalibov announced Azerbaijan's independence on August 30. He then had the Azerbaijan Supreme Soviet modify the constitution by creating a popularly elected, executive presidency. He was later elected president in an uncontested election.

Mutalibov remained under intense pressure from a growing political opposition, however. In September 1991, he created an eight-member Defense Council and appointed members of the Social Democratic Party, the National Independence Party, and the Popular Front to it. By this time, Tamerlan Karayev, leader of the Azerbaijan Popular Front, had been elected deputy head of the Supreme Soviet.

The front demanded that the Supreme Soviet be replaced by a temporary "National Council" which would prepare for new elections. When Karayev threatened to resign his post as deputy leader in October, Mutalibov agreed to the creation of a National Council and to a second demand that Azerbaijan establish its own army.

On October 18, 1991, the Supreme Soviet passed a law formally reestablishing Azerbaijan's independence. It declared the present government the legitimate successor to the Azerbaijan Democratic Government, overthrown by the communists in April 1920. The law further declared that "all acts and treaties concluded by the republic since April 1920" were considered invalid.

In early November, Mutalibov closed down the gas line to Armenia, cutting off the delivery of gas. Later in the month, when an Azerbaijani helicopter was downed over Nagorno-Karabakh, Mutalibov announced that he was calling an extraordinary session of the Supreme Soviet and would request them to dissolve the Nagorno-Karabakh government. At the same time, he cut all railway links with Armenia. The Azerbaijani Supreme Soviet endorsed Mutalibov's actions on November 26. By this time, Azerbaijan had its own defense minister and had created a military force of about 25,000. Mutalibov ordered his defense minister to restore order in Nagorno-Karabakh. Something approaching full-scale war existed in the area.

The Azerbaijan National Council met for the first time on November 29. Its first act was to pass a law putting all of Azerbaijan's borders under state control, to be guarded by Azerbaijani border guard troops. The purpose of the legislation was to give Azerbaijan control of its border with Armenia.

Meanwhile, the Armenian political leadership in Nagorno-Karabakh had declared the area to be an independent republic. A referendum, held on December 10, brought overwhelming popular approval.

The war between Azerbaijan and Nagorno-Karabakh continued for the next two months. All of Nagorno-Karabakh's connections with the outside were cut off and Azerbaijani troops carried out raids into the area from the east. There were reports that the city of Stepanakert had been virtually destroyed, but the Armenian leadership of Nagorno-Karabakh refused to give in. They were also being assisted by elements of the Armenian National Army, which had opened a corridor between Armenia and Nagorno-Karabakh.

When Mutalibov said that he was still seeking a political solution to the problem, the Azerbaijan Popular Front demanded his resignation on February 20, 1992, charging that the course of military actions in Nagorno-Karabakh was detrimental to Azerbaijan. As Azerbaijani nationalists continued to press the government to step up the fighting against the Armenians in Nagorno-Karabakh, Mutalibov resigned as president on March 6.

The Azerbaijan Popular Front never accepted Mutalibov's conversion to nationalism, and they never forgot that he was installed by Moscow after Soviet armed forces had been used against the front. Under their prodding, an Azerbaijani legislative

At prayer in the Mashtagin mosque

238

commission, appointed to investigate the events of January 1990, had concluded that Moscow had deliberately chosen Azerbaijan as a test case to see whether an independence movement could be crushed through the massive use of force. Forcing Mutalibov's resignation was therefore part of their revenge for the events of January 1990. They did not take any personal revenge against him, however. In addition to a grant of immunity against prosecution and a 10-man bodyguard, the legislature provided him with a pension of 10,000 rubles a month and a villa in the countryside.

Following his resignation, the legislature transferred presidential authority to the newly elected chairman of the legislature, Yagub Mammadov. One of the first acts of the new government was to launch new attacks against Nagorno-Karabakh. Their target was the city of Askeran, located not far from the capital city of Stepanakert. They were driven back by Armenian forces, however.

Ordinary Azerbaijanis reacted by calling for greater efforts to reclaim Nagorno-Karabakh. Mammadov, however, called for diplomatic efforts to get negotiations under way.

In March, Prime Minister Hasan Hasanov, said that

the chance of the conflict erupting into an all-out war and the chance of a political solution are 50–50. This depends on how much world public opinion realizes that the Armenian state terrorist army must immediately leave the occupied territory of Azerbaijan. If it continues its occupation of Nagorno-Karabakh, the chances of a military outcome will greatly increase.

In fact, Azerbaijani attempts to extend their control in Nagorno-Karabakh were unsuccessful. In May, forces of the Nagorno-Karabakh Defense Council managed to capture the Azerbaijani stronghold of Shusha and drive most Azerbaijani forces out of the enclave. Even as the Armenian and Azerbaijani Governments continued discussions aimed at bringing an end to the fighting, the Nagorno-Karabakh Defense Council forces captured a corridor across the Azeri territory separating Nagorno-Karabakh and Armenia, thereby creating a ground connection with Armenia.

Later in May, the war widened when fighting broke out along the border between Armenia and the Azerbaijani enclave of Naxcivan, separated from the rest of Azerbaijan by a strip of Armenian territory. According to Armenian reports, the fighting began after Armenian villages were shelled from across the border. Armenians retaliated by launching attacks on the Azeri villages of Sadarak and Lachin. Both Turkey and Iran protested

View of the port area of Baku
Courtesy of NOVOSTI

the Armenian "aggression" at this point, however, and a sort of quasi-truce settled in along the border.

The next development came on June 7, when the Azerbaijani population went to the polls to elect a new president. There were five candidates, but the easy winner was Abulfaz Elchibey, leader of the Azerbaijan Popular Front, who won 60% of the vote. Elchibey was 53 years old at the time of his election and a noted historian. He was also one of the founders of the Azerbaijan Popular Front.

Though the Popular Front came into existence as part of a popular response to Nagorno-Karabakh's demand that it be permitted to become part of Armenia, it claimed democratic credentials and was determined to break the old-line Communist leadership's hold on power. Strongly nationalist, it also opposed cooperation with the other former Soviet republics in the CIS. One of Elchibey's first acts as president was to announce that Azerbaijan would withdraw from the Commonwealth of Independent States and that Azerbaijan would deal with the other republics only on a bilateral basis. Elchibey was particularly incensed that several of the CIS members had negotiated a mutual security pact which included Armenia, though he had been cool to the CIS from its first inception.

Aside from that, however, Elchibey was relatively moderate in his actions after becoming president. This may be partly because he looked to Turkey as a model for his own government and the Turkish government was urging that course on him. He was committed to an economic reform based on free market principles, but did little in that direction, partly because of his continued preoccupation with Nagorno-Karabakh.

The struggle over Nagorno-Karabakh did not cause the bad economic effects in

Azerbaijan that it did in Armenia, but it did appear to preclude Azerbaijani leaders from thinking about anything else. Unfortunately for Elchibey, however, Armenian forces overran the northern part of the strip separating Nagorno-Karabakh from Armenia in April 1993, capturing the Azerbaijani regional town of Kelbajar and in the process bringing about 10% of Azerbaijan's territory under Armenian control. The defeat at Kelbajar also produced an estimated 100,000 new refugees for the Azerbaijani government to cope with.

This was a severe setback for President Elchibey, made worse by the fact that the Azerbaijani forces suffered a series of humiliating defeats when they attempted to regain control of the overrun territories in subsequent fighting.

President Elchibey then found himself challenged by his own forces when he tried to discipline one of the regional commanders, a 35-year-old army colonel by the name of Suret Guseinov. Instead, Guseinov rebelled and ordered his troops to march on Baku. As Guseinov's troops approached the capital, Elchibey fled to his home base in the Naxcivan enclave, leaving a political vacuum in Baku.

The Azerbaijani parliament now elected Heydar Aliyev to the position of chairman of parliament and acting head of state, and then called on Guseinov to negotiate an end to his uprising. After discussions, the matter was resolved when Aliyev agreed to nominate Guseinov as prime minister, and the parliament confirmed him in this position on July 1.

Although Aliyev and his allies had now taken effective control of the government, there remained the problem that Elchibey was still legally president. To remedy that situation, parliament voted to strip Elchibey of his authority; it then set a referendum for August 29 on the question whether he should remain president. More

Azerbaijan

than 90% of those going to the polls cast their ballots against Elchibey. This cleared the way for Heydar Aliyev to be elected president in new elections that took place on October 3, 1993.

President Aliyev continued to consolidate his power over the next year, but this threatened the position of Guseinov and led to a falling out between the two leaders. In October 1994, Aliyev fired Guseinov as prime minister and named Fuad Quliyev as his successor. Quliyev lasted for two years; he was then replaced by Artur Rasizade in November 1996.

New presidential elections took place in October 1998. Aliyev was heavily favored to win reelection from the beginning because the man considered the main oppositional leader, Rasul Guliyev, had lived in exile in the United States after he was ousted as speaker of the Azerbaijani parliament in September 1996. Although Guliyev announced his intention of running for president in January 1998, he eventually did not do so because he risked arrest if he returned to Azerbaijan. In the end, six candidates entered the race but, because all were second rank candidates, Aliyev swept the race with 76.1% of the vote. Etibar Mammadov, the runner-up, got 11.6% of the vote.

Although several candidates protested the poll results, Aliyev was sworn in as president on October 18, 1998. He then reappointed Artur Rasizade as prime minister, and the appointment was confirmed by the parliament on October 23. Since a large majority of the seats in the parliament were held by Yeni Azerbaycan, the political party founded by Aliyev in late 1992 as his personal power base, it was fairly clear that President Aliyev was thoroughly in political control of the country.

Yet, one should not forget that Aliyev twice had to put down armed rebellions and there were a number of attempts on his life. Azerbaijan was still a badly divided country where regional loyalties were strong and a significant percentage of the people lived below the poverty line. Although Azerbaijan could look forward to significant future revenues as foreign consortiums developed Azerbaijan's oil wealth, very little of that money had trickled down to the level of the ordinary citizen by this time.

There was also the continuing problem of Nagorno-Karabakh. Although there had been only occasional, and usually isolated, skirmishes after a cease-fire was signed in 1994, the Armenian and Nagorno-Karabakh Governments still controlled not only the entire territory of Nagorno-Karabakh, but, also, all Azerbaijani territory lying between Armenia and Nagorno-Karabakh—approximately 10% of the territory of Azerbaijan. The Organization

for Security and Cooperation in Europe (OSCE) continued to mediate the situation, but no plan had won the support of either side. President Levon Ter-Petrossian of Armenia was, in fact, forced out of office in February 1998 after he indicated his willingness to consider a 1997 OSCE plan.

President Aliyev was in a similar situation. He said that he would be willing to consider a corridor linking Armenia and Nagorno-Karabakh but he could not go further without losing domestic support. Meanwhile, the war created up to 750,000 refugees and internally displaced persons that the Azerbaijani government had to take care of.

President Aliyev underwent heart bypass surgery in the United States in April 1999, and he spent the next couple months recuperating. President Aliyev met twice with Armenian President Kocharian during the year to discuss a possible Nagorno-Karabakh settlement. Neither meeting produced any significant progress, though the atmospherics improved somewhat. Meanwhile the Nagorno-Karabakh ceasefire continued to hold, except for a three-hour exchange of fire in June 1999 in which two Azerbaijanis were killed and four injured near Mardakert.

When President Aliyev visited the United States in February 2000, his chief purpose was to persuade the United States to end the 1992 Congressional ban on United States government aid to Azerbaijan. The Clinton White House supported lifting the ban, but the US Senate refused to go along. It took the events of September 11, 2001, and Azerbaijan's offer to the United States of the use of its airspace during the antiterrorism campaign to get the Senate to reverse itself and partially waive the ban on aid. The waiver, signed into law on January 25, 2002, allowed Azerbaijan to receive some $50 million in aid in 2002. The chief benefit to Azerbaijan has probably been political, however.

Presidents Aliyev and Kocharian met twice in 2002, the second time on the sidelines of the NATO summit. Both characterized the talks as "useful" and Armenia even confirmed the existence of a new Karabakh peace proposal. A few days later, however, Armenia accused Azerbaijan of backtracking on Karabakh; two weeks later, the Armenian Foreign Minister condemned Azerbaijan at the OSCE Ministerial Council meeting in Porto, Portugal.

As the situation deteriorated, there was a military skirmish between Armenian and Azerbaijani forces in which one Azerbaijani soldier was wounded and another taken prisoner. The following week, President Kocharian reaffirmed his commitment to a peaceful solution to the Karabakh conflict, though he reiterated his position that it was impossible for the Armenian population

President Ilham Aliyev

of Karabakh to live within an Azerbaijani state. President Kocharian was reelected in March 2003, but nothing changed with regard to Karabakh.

In April 2003, President Aliyev collapsed during a speech at a military academy in Baku one month after returning from the United States, where he had been operated on for an inguinal hernia. On May 3, President Aliyev flew to Turkey for specialized medical care at the Gulhane Military Medical Academy in Ankara. In July, he traveled to the United States for further medical treatment.

At the beginning of August, he appointed his son, Ilham, as prime minister, while the Yeni Azerbaycan nominated both father and son to run in the October 15 presidential elections. President Aliyev pulled out of the presidential race on October 2. His death came shortly after the election.

President Ilham Aliyev

There were eight presidential hopefuls, including the leaders of three of Azerbaijan's most influential political parties. In the final tally, Ilham Aliyev polled 76.84% of the vote. Musavat Party Chairman Isa Qambar came second with 13.97%, followed by independent candidate Lala-Shovket Gadjieva with 3.63% and Azerbaijan National Independence Party Chairman Etibar Mammadov with 2.92%.

Word of Aliyev's victory brought several thousand Qambar supporters into the streets on October 16. They resisted when police and Interior Ministry forces attempted to disperse them. Fighting continued for three hours in and around the main square in Baku; at least two persons were trampled to death and several hundred persons were injured, including over 60 policemen. The result: 174 of the participants in the clashes were arrested, among

Azerbaijan

Nagorno-Karabakh, which declared itself an independent republic in December 1991, was for many years an Armenian enclave located in Azerbaijan with the status of an autonomous republic. The majority of the population of the enclave has always been Armenian, but not overwhelmingly so. However, today, as a result of refugee movements caused by the armed conflict that raged between 1992 and 1994, around 180,000 Armenians live here and make up approximately 90% of the population.

Nagorno-Karabakh's current problems began in February 1988 when the Nagorno-Karabakh regional council, feeling itself discriminated against by the Azerbaijani government, asked that the region become part of the Armenian SSR. The matter became an inter-republic dispute when Armenia endorsed Nagorno-Karabakh's request. While the two republics were still discussing the issue, nationalist demonstrations in Azerbaijan and Armenia turned to violence, producing hundreds of thousands of refugees on both sides. In January 1989, with the situation as bad as ever, Moscow suspended both the local provincial committee and Azerbaijan's control over Nagorno-Karabakh and instituted "a special form of administration" for the rebellious autonomous republic, thus putting it under Moscow's direct control.

This led to the birth of the Azerbaijan Popular Front, a political organization with a single plank that was at the same time a demand—that Moscow return Nagorno-Karabakh to Azerbaijani jurisdiction. The Front backed up its demand by organizing a blockade of railway traffic going into Armenia. Moscow, fearing further popular demonstrations, gave in to the demand and returned Nagorno-Karabakh to Azerbaijani control in November 1989.

In September 1991, Russia and Kazakhstan offered to mediate the dispute between Azerbaijan and Armenia. This produced a cease-fire agreement between the two republics and Armenia also agreed to give up its claim to the enclave in return for a promise by the Azerbaijani leadership that it would allow free elections in Nagorno-Karabakh and bestow additional autonomy on the enclave. The agreement also called for disarming illegal local militias and the right of Armenian and Azeri refugees to return to their homes.

But President Mutalibov of Azerbaijan never implemented the agreement, probably because of his fear of the nationalist opposition. Mutalibov, with little popular support of his own, deliberately appealed to nationalism in an attempt to outflank his nationalist opposition. When an Azerbaijani helicopter was downed in November 1991, Mutalibov suspended talks with Armenia, then called an emergency session of the Azerbaijani legislature and got it to abolish Nagorno-Karabakh's autonomous republic status.

In December 1991, Nagorno-Karabakh responded by holding a referendum on the question of independence, then declared itself an independent republic after the referendum received overwhelming approval. It also set up a new governmental structure at that time, essentially a presidential-parliamentary system of government with an 81-seat legislature (with 11 seats reserved for Azeris).

Nagorno-Karabakh remained under siege by Azerbaijani forces for the next two years. Turkey and Iran attempted to mediate the dispute and at least six truce agreements were actually signed, though none held. In 1992, after both Azerbaijan and Armenia had been admitted as members of the Conference on Security and Cooperation in Europe (now the Organization for Security and Cooperation in Europe), that group agreed to sponsor new negotiations. Although the talks initiated at that time failed to produce a breakthrough, the OSCE has continued to play the leading role in negotiations since that time, though without any success.

In 1993, the nature of the conflict changed when forces from Nagorno-Karabakh (with covert assistance by forces from Armenia) overran significant parts of Azerbaijan. As Armenian and Karabakh forces continued to advance during the summer and fall, a large part of western Azerbaijan was overrun and occupied. This brought a rebuke from the United Nations and a demand that Karabakh pull back from its occupied territories. Negotiations now reopened. Once again, a number of ceasefires were negotiated but it was not until 1994 that a cease-fire held. Technically, a state of war continues, though there have been only occasional outbreaks of violence along the cease-fire line since 1994. The cease fire agreement was violated most recently on April 2, 2016. A day of fighting led to at least 30 military deaths, and recriminations on both sides over which party was responsible for the renewed hostilities.

Meanwhile, the military forces of Armenia and Nagorno-Karabakh continue to occupy approximately 20% of Azerbaijani territory and the OSCE has continued its mediation efforts. In 1997, its Minsk Group, co-chaired by the United States, Russia, and France, produced a peace plan that called for a "phased" approach. Armenia would first withdraw from all occupied territory outside of Nagorno-Karabakh, where upon discussions would follow on the final status of Nagorno-Karabakh. The government of Azerbaijan accepted the proposal, not difficult to understand since the proposal essentially endorsed the Azerbaijani position. Surprisingly, President Ter-Petrossian of Armenia agreed to accept the proposal "as a basis for further talks." However, the leadership in Nagorno-Karabakh rejected the peace plan because it would have required Karabakh to withdraw all of its forces from Azerbaijani territory before any talks took place on Nagorno-Karabakh's final status.

The leadership of Nagorno-Karabakh has publicly stated that it is willing to trade territory for an assurance that Azerbaijan will not again invade the enclave. But Azerbaijan refuses to negotiate directly with Nagorno-Karabakh because it is unwilling to concede a separate status. President Aliyev did indicate, in July 1997, that Azerbaijan would agree to continued use of the Lachin transit corridor linking Nagorno-Karabakh and Armenia, but he made it clear that he would never accept an independent Nagorno-Karabakh.

A new twist came in March 1998 when Robert Kocharian, a former president of Nagorno-Karabakh who had been made prime minister of Armenia by President Ter-Petrossian, was elected president of Armenia. Kocharian argued that Armenia could never abandon its fellow Armenians in Nagorno-Karabakh. He also called for direct talks between the Azerbaijani and Nagorno-Karabakh leaderships (something Azerbaijan has always rejected). Although he did not call for recognition of Nagorno-Karabakh's independence, he did argue that any solution would have to exclude the possibility of any direct subordination of Nagorno-Karabakh to Azerbaijan.

In September 2020, the long-standing frozen conflict quickly thawed. With the backing of Turkey, Azerbaijan launched an offensive to reclaim territory surrounding Karabakh as well as territory in the southern, less mountainous, part of the region. Due to oil revenue and Turkish support, Azerbaijan's military had been significantly strengthened over the past decade. Its military superiority enabled the state to gain control of Shusha, the second largest city in Nagorno-Karabakh.

The war came to an end in November 2020 with a Russia-brokered cease fire which cemented Azerbaijani territorial gains. In total, the war resulted in more than 5,000 fatalities and tens of thousands of displaced persons. The fallout from this war was deep and ongoing for Armenia, Azerbaijan and Russia. From the Armenian perspective, the war was a disaster and it plunged the state into a political crisis which it has yet to resolve. From the Azerbaijani perspective, the war was a tremendous success and President Ilham Aliyev has exploited the "rally around the flag" effect of the war to bolster his legitimacy. For many observers, Russia has won the peace. Russia was able to establish itself as the peacekeeper in the region, ensuring that it would have a persistent military presence; under the terms of the ceasefire, for at least five years, around 2,000 Russian troops will maintain the peace between Azerbaijan and Armenia. In response to increasing tensions following the war, in March 2002, the government of Azerbaijan proposed a five-point plan for resolving the conflict, which the Armenian government, but not the whole population, looks increasingly likely to accept. Most importantly, the plan calls for both sides to recognize each other's territorial integrity. Omitted from the plan was any discussion about the status of Nagorno-Karabakh. In effect, it means Azerbaijan already considers Nagorno-Karabakh as its own and demands that Armenia acknowledge Azerbaijan's sovereignty over that territory. Azerbaijan denied Armenia's request to have the Minsk Group involved in the negotiation claiming that it outlived its mission because the territories in question are now under Azerbaijani government control and that there was no need to have talks about the status of Nagorno-Karabakh for which the Minsk Group was designed. The two sides ultimately agreed to have the European Council be the mediator. Two rounds of meeting in Brussels resulted in a significant progress, including a meeting between commissions from each country in which they agreed to cooperate on delimiting and demarcating their mutual border.

Azerbaijan

them 4 deputy chairmen of the opposition Musavat Party and Umid Party Chairman Iqbal Agazade.

President-elect Aliyev placed special blame for the rioting on Musavat Party Chairman Isa Qambar who, according to Aliyev, urged his supporters to resort to violence. Qambar's reply was that "people would not have protested if the elections had not been falsified."

The evaluation of the OSCE election observation mission was that the

voting had been "generally well administered in most polling stations but the overall election process still fell short of international standards in several respects. International observers noted a number of irregularities in the counting and tabulation."

That mild reproof was undoubtedly welcomed by the Azerbaijan Government, even though the OSCE issued a later statement deploring the arrests and detentions that followed the rioting.

As the government and the opposition faced off against each other in subsequent weeks, the government launched a crackdown that eventually led to the arrest of up to 1,000 persons, including opposition party leaders and members, democracy activists, journalists, and election officials.

One year later, seven of the leading opposition politicians were found guilty of inciting clashes between police and protesters following the 2003 presidential election. Rauf Arifoglu and Arif Haliji, both deputy chairmen of the opposition party Musavat, were sentenced to five years in prison. Panakh Huseynov, chairman of the People's Party of Azerbaijan and Serdar Djalaloglu, secretary-general of the People's Party of Azerbaijan each got four years. Musavat Party Deputy Chairman Ibrahim Ibrahimli and Umid Party

Chairman Iqbal Agazade were sentenced to three years. Lastly, Etimad Asadov, head of an organization representing veterans of the Nagorno-Karabakh war, got two years. Six months later, in March 2005, all were pardoned by President Aliyev in response to a representation made by a visiting delegation of the Council of Europe Parliamentary Assembly.

With new parliamentary elections scheduled to take place in the fall of 2005, the level of rhetoric between the government and the opposition escalated over the next several months. As part of the preparation for the elections, a new electoral alliance called Solidarity and Trust was set up in January 2005, bringing together 26 non-governmental organizations and movements plus individual figures from both the ruling Yeni Azerbaycan party and the opposition Musavat and Democratic parties. The stated purpose of Solidarity and Trust was to ensure that the November parliamentary elections would be free and fair.

A second, more specifically political bloc of three opposition political parties was also set up in March 2005. This new bloc, called the Ugur Bloc (Forum for Free Elections), brought together Musavat, the Democratic Party of Azerbaijan and the progressive wing of the divided Azerbaijan Popular Front Party. A month later, the New Policy bloc was formed by a group of prominent political and civic figures, under the leadership of Lala-Shovket Gadjieva, leader of the National Unity Liberation Movement. The group included former deputy prime minister Ali Masimov, who was also the main opposition candidate in the 1998 elections. Two weeks later, the seven Azerbaijani oppositionists who had had their prison sentences annulled by President Aliyev a month earlier announced that they were

establishing a political movement called 16 October. The group did not intend to field candidates for the November parliamentary elections but said, rather, that the purpose of the group was to further democracy based on free and fair elections. However, Rauf Arifoglu, one of the members of the new group, who is also editor of the opposition newspaper Yeni Musavat, was quoted as saying that, "if the people want a revolution, we shall bring one about."

Responding to these developments, the Council of Europe released a statement on April 25 which called the situation in Azerbaijan alarming. Decrying the almost total lack of dialogue between the authorities and the opposition, the restrictions on the freedom of assembly and expression, and the lack of pluralism on television channels, the report urged the government to ensure that the November parliamentary ballot would be free, fair, and democratic.

Two weeks later, talks took place involving the ruling Yeni Azerbaycan Party, two other pro-government parties, and four opposition parties, which produced consensus on some issues and questions on others. Following the meeting, President Aliyev issued a decree setting forth measures intended to preclude violations and falsification during the parliamentary election. The decree promised that all candidates would be provided with equal access to the media and freedom to conduct their electoral campaigns.

Yet the campaign did not go smoothly. Candidates sometimes had difficulty getting permission to hold rallies. On at least one occasion, the regional office of one of the opposition parties was attacked by persons wielding iron bars. In addition, only those parties and blocs that had registered candidates in no fewer than 60 constituencies qualified for three hours of free airtime per week on Azerbaijani State Television and the recently launched Public Television channel. The situation was further complicated by the fact that there were over 1,500 candidates vying for the 125 parliamentary seats.

After the voting, it was reported that Yeni Azerbaycan had won 63 of the 125 mandates, with independent candidates filling a further 44 seats. The Musavat Party was awarded 4 seats, Civil Solidarity three; two each went to Ana Veten and the progressive wing of the Azerbaijan Popular Front Party; and one each went to the Umid Party, Civic Unity, Civic Welfare, the Democratic Reforms Party, the Unified National Front Party, and the Great Creation Party.

After monitors from both the United States and the European Union complained about "major irregularities and fraud," however, the Azerbaijan Government was forced to backtrack. In the end, ten of the results were annulled, with new elections scheduled for May 2006. In December, the Constitutional Court endorsed the election results in 115 of the 125 constituencies. The ruling Yeni Azerbaycan held 58 of the 115 filled seats, while an additional 42 seats went to independent candidates—most of whom support the government. The opposition originally held ten seats, but the Musavat Party—which controlled four seats—quit the opposition bloc in February 2006 after it voted to participate in the parliament and field candidates for the 10 parliamentary seats to be filled in the May 13 elections. Later that same month, a sixth member of the opposition—Djamil Gasanli, deputy chairman of the progressive wing of the Azerbaijan Popular Front Party—announced that he would take up his mandate and participate in parliament.

In the end, Musavat, Adolat, and Civic Solidarity all fielded candidates in the May 13 elections. Eight of the seats went either to members of Yeni Azerbaycan or nominally independent candidates. Opposition Adolit Party Chairman Ilyas Ismailov won a seat in the rural constituency of Tovuz; the 10th seat was won by a candidate from the opposition Civic Solidarity Party. None of Musavat's 7 candidates won. The 13-person team from the OSCE reported afterward that there has been "improvement in some aspects of the process," but that there has also been "instances of interference by local authorities in the election process."

But as a result of the eclipse of the secular political opposition, many Azerbaijanis have begun to look to Islam to fill the ideological vacuum. Thousands of younger Azerbaijanis now flock to Friday Prayers at Baku's Abu-Bakr mosque. One reason for this is that active proselytizing is being carried out within the country by three competing schools of Islamic thought, the Salafi/Wahhabi school from Saudi Arabia; radical Shi'ite Islam from Iran; and the moderate Hanafi school of Islam that derives from the Turkish NGO Nur (Light). Azerbaijan is traditionally about 65% Shi'ite, but the Sunni share is gradually increasing, presumably because of the actions of the Salafi/Wahhabi school from Saudi Arabia.

This movement is not yet explicitly political, but many fear that it may become so. In the event, this trend has caused the Azerbaijani authorities to keep a close watch over religious groups and there have been arrests of several "Wahhabi" groups suspected of planning terrorist acts.

At the same time, the secular opposition parties have recently attempted to increase their relevance by creating an umbrella organization of up to 20 opposition parties. The Parliamentary Assembly of the Council of Europe (PACE) has also begun putting pressure on the Azerbaijan Government to widen the scope of permitted activities by opposition parties, including such things as representation on the election commissions. PACE has also pressed the government to free imprisoned former officials and journalists.

In March 2008, Azerbaijan held a referendum to amend 29 articles of the constitution, including an amendment that would abolish term limits for the presidency. The referendum received the support of 54% of the voters.

New presidential elections took place on October 15, 2008. Although there were six candidates for the presidency in addition to President Aliyev, all of them were non-entities whom no one gave a chance to win. Essentially, all of the major oppositional political figures, knowing that they had no chance to win after three years of double-digit economic growth, boycotted the election. In the end, Aliyev won reelection with just over 89% of the vote. It was an unusual campaign however, for there were no banners, no posters, and no rallies. President Aliyev did no campaigning himself, though he traveled about the country dealing, as he said, with matters of state.

In June 2009, the Azerbaijani parliament passed a new law dealing with non-governmental organizations (NGOs). In its original form, the proposed law imposed harsh restrictions on NGOs but, because of well-organized civil protests among rights groups in and outside of Azerbaijan, most of the offending sections were deleted before passage. It also did not hurt that Anne Derse, the American ambassador in Baku, issued a public statement warning that the legislation would "contravene international standards, result in further restrictions on freedom of speech and association, and put development of civil society in Azerbaijan at risk." Freedom House still lists Azerbaijan among its "consolidated authoritarian regimes" of the post-communist sphere. While that is probably an accurate characterization, it is still significant that civil protests can still take place and even influence actions in parliament.

New parliamentary elections took place on November 7, 2010, under the terms of a new electoral law that shortened the active canvassing campaign from 28 to 23 days. In addition, large-scale political rallies were prohibited, to be replaced by town-hall meetings. All candidates were given access to free airtime on national TV and radio, but each candidate was allotted only four minutes each evening. In addition, the Central Election Commission disqualified a large number of opposition candidates, thus denying them a place on the ballot.

In the end, the ruling Yeni Azerbaycan Party (YAP) took 71 of the 124 seats in the new parliament. An additional 42 seats were taken by political independents. The remaining 12 seats were taken by nine opposition or quasi-opposition parties—three by Civic Solidarity (CSP), two by Ana Vaten (Motherland), and one seat each by Democratic Reforms, Great Creation, Hope, Social Welfare, Civic Unity Whole Azerbaijan Popular Front and Justice. The assessment of the OSCE Election Observation Mission of the election was that "restrictions of fundamental freedoms, media bias, the dominance of public life by one party, and serious violations on election day" meant that "the conditions necessary for a meaningful democratic election were not established."

Since that time, opposition political parties that had failed to win parliamentary representation have been attempting to remedy that situation by forming new political blocs. In early 2011, several veteran opposition figures set up the Civic Movement for Democracy–Public Chamber (GDDOP), which has since acted as a sort of shadow parliament. Its purpose was to unite all those dissatisfied with the current regime. One of their demands has been for preterm parliamentary elections prior to the presidential elections scheduled to take place in October 2013. The GDDOP has also led mass protests calling for President Aliyev's resignation. In January 2012, another five extra-parliamentary parties created yet another umbrella organization, the Resistance Movement for a Democratic Society. Although these attempts to unite the political opposition could give them a better chance to win representation in parliament next time around, it is not clear that they are actually united except in their opposition to the current government.

President Aliyev's response to the political unrest has been a mixture of the use of the carrot and the stick. Twice in 2012, he issued amnesties that resulted in the freeing of persons held in prison, including individuals regarded by rights activists as political prisoners. In June, 9 such prisoners were freed, along with another 57 others; in December, the president pardoned an additional 86 prisoners, including a number of journalists. And yet, in November 2012, Azerbaijan's parliament adopted a number of amendments to the law on public gatherings which significantly increased fines for illegal demonstrators.

In early 2013, a new wave of protests was met by a new government crackdown and renewed arrests. There were also police raids on foreign-funded NGOs that included a program officer of the US-funded National Democratic Institute and

Azerbaijan

a raid on an OSCE training seminar sponsored by Germany's Friedrich Naumann Foundation. And in March the Azerbaijani government formally requested the OSCE to downgrade its Baku office from a mission to a project-coordination office.

The role of the OSCE in Azerbaijan is somewhat unusual. For a number of years, it has acted as the sponsoring agency of the ongoing talks to resolve the Azerbaijani-Armenian war over Nagorno-Karabakh; in addition, it monitors national elections to determine whether they meet international standards. The Azerbaijani government has been unhappy about the lack of progress over Nagorno-Karabakh and that may have been a factor it its decision to ask the OSCE to downgrade its mission in Baku. Or it may have been related to the fact that new presidential elections were scheduled to take place in October 2013 and President Aliyev, who intended to run for a third term, didn't want the OSCE criticizing the results. In 2015, the OSCE was forced to shutter its operations in the country entirely.

In the end, President Aliyev easily won a third term, taking 84.6% of the total vote. Jamil Hasanli, his nearest competitor, came in second with 5.5% of the vote. The election itself got mixed views. Observers from the European Parliament, focusing on the voting itself, concluded that:

Overall all around Election Day we have observed a free, fair and transparent electoral process. From what we have seen, electoral procedures on the eve and on Election Day have been carried out in a professional and peaceful way.

However, the OSCE observers, focusing on the general political conditions in Azerbaijan, concluded that the election was deeply unfair from the start. Citing the government's control over the news media and official efforts to suppress the opposition, the OSCE observers argued that the election was:

undermined by limitations on the freedom of expression, assembly and association that did not guarantee a level playing field for candidates. Continued allegations of candidate and voter intimidation and a restrictive media environment marred the campaign. Significant problems were observed throughout all stages of Election Day processes and underscored the serious nature of the shortcomings.

Azerbaijan has never held a national election that has fully met international election standards as seen by the OSCE.

Ever since Aliyev won his third term, his government has increased its efforts to silence government opponents and

reverse gains made by civil society, including foreign non-governmental organizations (NGOs). Aside from wanting to increase his personal power as president, Aliyev may be worried about potential unrest sparked by a weakening economy due to the dramatic fall in the price of oil. He may also have calculated that Western nations might not raise serious objections to his repressive policies as their attention had been diverted by the crisis in Ukraine. The International Research and Exchanges Board (IREX), a US NGO that had promoted educational exchanges with Azerbaijan and had helped establish a free and open society for 18 years, was forced to cease its operations in the country in September 2014. In December, Azeri officials closed the offices of Radio Free Europe/Radio Liberty, which is a news service funded by the US government. In a report from March 2015, the European Union sharply criticized Azerbaijan's government. The report stated that there had occurred a "regression in the democratic transition process and with regard to human rights and fundamental freedoms, for example, the freedom of religion or belief, freedom of expression, and freedom of assembly." The report added that "a number of prominent human right defenders were detained, travel bans were issued, and bank accounts of civil society organizations were frozen."

The regime has curtailed the establishment of independent media and critical journalism. In Reporters Without Borders 2018 Press Freedom Index, the state was ranked near the bottom (163rd out of 180 countries). The organization described the current climate as one of "unrelenting war" against independent journalists and bloggers. One of the most prominent victims of this "war" is Mehman Huseynov, once the most visible political blogger in

the country. In 2017, Huseynov was convicted of slandering police officers when he accused them of abducting and beating him. As he approached the end of his two-year sentence, new charges were brought up against him accusing him of attacking a prison guard. In response, Huseynov initiated a hunger strike in the prison and civil society activists outside organized a massive rally in support of the blogger on January 19, 2019. While the number of participants in the rally is disputed (organizers claim that 25,000 partook, while authorities claimed that less than 3,000 were there), it was the most visible protest in years and it gained international attention. In response to this impressive show of societal strength, the government dropped the new charges, and Huseynov was released in March 2019.

In March 2020, Azerbaijan's parliament passed an amendment to the state's law on information ostensibly aimed at limiting the spread of disinformation on the coronavirus pandemic. Under the terms of the new amendment, the owner of any internet information resource is obliged to prevent the publication of false information. According to the OSCE, the bill stipulates that it covers all information that "poses a threat to the life, health and property of the population or public safety, or to the work of life support facilities, financial, transport, communication, industrial, energy, and social infrastructure." The expansiveness of the amendment prompted Harlem Desir, the OSCE Representative on Freedom of the Media, to raise concern that journalists covering important issues unrelated to the coronavirus could be targeted by the regime under the guise of protecting the public.

Aliyev's consolidation of power has come at the expense of former regime insiders as well. On October 17, Aliyev decreed

Vice President Mehriban Aliyeva Courtesy of VUGAR AMRULLAYEV

A view of Baku with the Adjarbek Mosque   Courtesy of NOVOSTI

that the long-standing National Security Minister, Eldar Mahmudov, be sacked. The dismissal of Mahmudov, who had served as minister since 2004, was soon followed by a sweeping overhaul of the security apparatus of the state. In the weeks that followed, up to a dozen senior officials within the ministry were arrested under suspicion of corruption, and around 250 other employees were also dismissed. In December 2015, Aliyev issued a decree that formally disbanded the ministry and diverted its powers to newly created organizations, the Foreign Intelligence Service and the State Security Service. Although formally officials indicated that this restructuring was done in the interest of improving government efficiency and rooting out corruption, this episode is best understood as reflecting intra-elite regime political dynamics.

In September 2016, Azerbaijan demonstrated once again the utility of using referendum votes to legitimate continued autocratic rule. On that date, voters went to the polls to separately vote on 29 constitutional amendments initially decreed by President Aliyev. Unsurprisingly, each amendment definitively passed with no less than 89% support. These amendments serve to further extend the formal powers of the executive branch, for instance by extending the presidential term from five to seven years. They also eliminated the age requirement for a citizen to become president. This change set off widespread speculation that the president's then-19-year-old son, Heidar, may be next in-line for power.

The amendment also established the new position of vice president. Although technically, multiple vice presidents are permitted through the referendum to date only one has been appointed—to the president's wife, Mehriban Aliyeva.

This appointment establishes the First Lady as the de jure successor of Ilham Aliyev should he resign or become incapacitated. Although her appointment was challenged by opposition politicians on the grounds that her appointment violated anti-nepotism rules, Aliyeva position further ensconces the personal claim of the Aliyev family on political power in Azerbaijan.

On April 11, 2018, this personal claim was deepened when Ilham Aliyev was reelected President for the fourth time. In a sham election, Aliyev won with 86.02% of the vote. Under the terms of the new constitutional amendments, Aliyev will not have to run again until 2025.

Foreign Policy

Nagorno-Karabakh. Azerbaijan's foreign policy since independence has been held hostage by the state of war that exists with Armenia over the status of Nagorno-Karabakh, the enclave located in Western Azerbaijan which is inhabited by ethnic Armenians. That situation was further complicated when Robert Kocharian, a former president of Nagorno-Karabakh, was elected president of Armenia in March 1998. However, President Aliyev arranged to meet with President Kocharian in 2000, and they held several meetings thereafter. While these discussions did not lead to a breakthrough on Nagorno-Karabakh, both presidents believed them to be valuable enough that they should be continued.

President Aliyev's son and successor, Ilham, did very little during his first several months as president as he first of all focused on consolidating his power. His first initiative on Nagorno-Karabakh came in the fall of 2004 when his government submitted a request to the UN General

Assembly to debate the issue. At issue were four UN Security Council resolutions adopted in 1993 calling for the withdrawal of "Armenian forces" from occupied Azerbaijani territory. Azerbaijan's permanent representative to the UN, Yashar Aliyev, also accused Armenia of colonizing occupied territory by building permanent settlements there.

Separately, President Aliyev told journalists in Baku that he wanted the OSCE Minsk Group to continue to mediate a solution to the Karabakh conflict. He merely wanted the conflict to be debated more widely by international organizations, including the United Nations and the Council of Europe. Armenian Foreign Minister Vartan Oskanian responded to President Aliyev's comments to the press by reaffirming Armenia's willingness to resume Karabakh talks. He also pointed out that the "Armenian forces" referred to in the UN resolutions were troops of Nagorno-Karabakh and that no troops from Armenia were in occupied Azerbaijan. Arkadi Ghukasyan, president of the unrecognized Nagorno-Karabakh Republic, interviewed on Armenian television, also reiterated his government's position that it was "ready to negotiate with Azerbaijan in any format, with or without Armenia."

The foreign ministers of Azerbaijan and Armenia met in Sofia and Brussels in December 2004 in what was actually their fifth meeting in 2004; the Armenian foreign minister commented afterward that his meeting with the Azerbaijan foreign minister had yielded "a framework of issues that can serve as a basis" for a future peace deal. President Aliyev, taking up the issue in a New Year's address, called 2004 "a turning point" in talks over the unresolved Nagorno-Karabakh conflict, though he did add that Azerbaijan would "never make any concessions in question of its territorial integrity."

The Parliamentary Assembly of the Council of Europe debated a resolution on Nagorno-Karabakh in January 2005, though the outcome was not particularly pleasing to either side in the conflict. Although the resolution called for the withdrawal of unnamed occupying forces from districts of Azerbaijan bordering on Nagorno-Karabakh, it also called on the Azerbaijani leadership to "embark immediately and unconditionally on talks with the leadership of the unrecognized Nagorno-Karabakh Republic on the region's future status. Azerbaijan got some further bad news in March when the OSCE Minsk Group published its conclusions following an extensive tour of the occupied territories in February. Essentially, the fact-finding mission concluded that resettlement is "quite limited" and that

Azerbaijan

most of the Armenian settlers involved were displaced persons from other regions of Azerbaijan.

Although the presidents of Azerbaijan and Armenia, as well as each country's foreign ministers, continued to meet periodically over the next several years, the situation with regard to Nagorno-Karabakh remained unchanged. Then, in the spring of 2009, a rapprochement between the governments of Armenia and Turkey introduced a new element, particularly after the two governments signed two protocols in October 2009 calling for the establishment of diplomatic relations and opening of the border between the two countries. The rapprochement caused a great deal of disquiet among governmental circles in Baku but, in the end, the issue of Nagorno-Karabakh scuppered the agreement. As the Turkish government expressed it in March 2010, ratification of the two protocols could occur only after Armenia settled its disagreement with Azerbaijan over Nagorno-Karabakh. The Armenian government also suspended ratification of the two protocols "until such time as the Turkish government is ready to proceed further."

Meanwhile, representatives of the governments of Azerbaijan and Armenia have continued to meet periodically to discuss possible solutions to the Nagorno-Karabakh problem, but the stalemate remains.

Azerbaijan's oil wealth in the early 2000s prompted it to drastically increase its military expenditure, initiating an arms race with Armenia. In 2014 and 2015, reports of occasional violations of the cease-fire became more frequent. In April 2016, the most serious violation of the 1994 cease-fire to date occurred. Under conditions

that remain uncertain, fighting broke out between the Armenian and Azerbaijan forces. The fighting resulted in significant numbers of civilian and military deaths on both sides, as well claims from Azerbaijan that its forces seized disputed villages and territories.

Russia. Azerbaijan had very poor relations with Russia under the government of President Elchibey, partly because of Elchibey's nationalism and partly because he believed that Russia was pro-Armenian. Elchibey also pulled Azerbaijan out of the Commonwealth of Independent States (CIS). Heydar Aliyev reversed this policy when he came to power in 1993. Under Aliyev, Azerbaijan rejoined the CIS, and began building better relations with Russia. The cease-fire signed by Azerbaijan and Armenia in 1994 was one of the first fruits of his new policy. Since that time, Russo–Azeri relations have been correct but not warm.

Azerbaijan did resume natural gas sales to Russia in January 2010, however, and approximately one billion cubic meters of natural gas were delivered to Gazprom in 2010. Under the terms of a second agreement, signed with SOCAR, Azerbaijan's state energy firm in September 2010, Gazprom agreed to buy two billion cubic meters of natural gas in 2011 and even more in 2012.

Gazprom re-exports the gas it buys from Azerbaijan to Europe. As Pavel Sorokin, oil and gas analyst at Alfa Bank, explained, "it is much more expensive for Russia to buy gas from Azerbaijan than to produce it domestically, but the more it buys from Azerbaijan, the less others can buy." The European Union has been discussing

plans to build Nabucco, a $10 billion gas pipeline, to transport gas from the Caspian region. Thus, the primary Russian motivation for the purchases appears to be to prevent Europe from diversifying its supplies away from Russia. So far, it appears to be working.

United States. Throughout the 1990s, Azerbaijan's relations with the United States were always cool, largely because of the influence on US foreign policy of the significant Armenian Diaspora in the United States. Under this influence, the US Congress instituted a ban on US assistance to Azerbaijan in 1992, even as Armenia was becoming the second-largest recipient of American assistance, on a per capita basis, among ex-Soviet republics.

Azerbaijanis interpreted this to mean that the United States had allied itself with Armenia, and this limited the influence of the US government on Azerbaijan. Accordingly, the United States played no significant role in outside attempts to bring a peaceful resolution to the conflict over Nagorno-Karabakh until 1997 when, at the urging of both Armenia and Azerbaijan, the United States agreed to accept one of the three co-chairs of the Minsk peace talks.

This situation began to change in July 1998 when the US State Department asked Congress to lift sanctions on Azerbaijan, arguing that this would benefit American companies involved in developing energy resources in the Caspian Sea region. Although the US Senate rejected the recommendation, relations began to improve from this time onward.

After the September 11 terrorist attacks against the United States, Azerbaijan was among the first of the CIS members to offer the use of its airspace for the United States–led War on Terrorism. Wishing to include Azerbaijan in its War on Terrorism, the United States Government recommended to Congress that it waive the appropriate section of US law that banned all assistance to Azerbaijan. Congress quickly responded and President Bush signed the waiver in January 2002. Since that time, military talks have resulted in a number of agreements between the two countries, with the United States making specific commitments to provide training for the armed forces, the navy, and the air force. Perhaps most important, Mira Ricardel, deputy assistant to Secretary of Defense Donald Rumsfeld, told a press conference in Baku in March 2002 that the United States attached great importance to Azerbaijan's national security, sovereignty, and territorial integrity.

President Aliyev paid a formal visit to the United States in February 2003. Azerbaijan supported the United States on Iraq and Azerbaijan agreed to send a

The Museum of Azerbaijan Literature at Baku

contingent of 150 Azerbaijani troops to Iraq following the American defeat of the Iraqi government to guard Muslim holy sites in the cities of Karbala, Kirkuk, and Mosul. In April 2003, President Aliyev declared that Azerbaijan had an interest in eventually joining NATO.

US-Azerbaijani relations suffered somewhat at the beginning of the Obama administration, largely because of the encouragement that the Obama administration gave for the restoration of diplomatic relations between Turkey and Armenia. In an attempt to reverse this situation, Secretary of Defense Robert M. Gates paid a visit to Baku in June 2010, during which he delivered a letter from President Obama pledging a closer relationship. Following this up one month later, Secretary of State Hillary Clinton made a stop in Baku on July 4 during a five-nation tour of former Soviet bloc countries. During the visit, Clinton praised Azerbaijan's thriving economy, culture, and contributions to US military efforts in Iraq and Afghanistan. Two months later, President Obama arranged a side meeting with President Aliyev when both presidents attended the UN General Assembly meeting in New York. According to a White House press communiqué, President Obama "expressed his appreciation for Azerbaijan's contributions to supporting the ISAF mission in Afghanistan" and "reaffirmed strong US support for the OSCE Minsk Group process to resolve the Nagorno-Karabakh conflict."

Turkey. Azerbaijan's best relations are with Turkey, which closed its borders with Armenia in 1993 in support of the Azerbaijani position on Nagorno-Karabakh and in other ways has continued to cultivate good relations with Azerbaijan. Some signs of that close connection include a bilateral military agreement between the two countries, signed in May 2002, under which military aid is being provided to the Azerbaijan armed forces; somewhat related to that, the Azerbaijan Government decided in November 2002 to provide a small military contingent to serve as part of the Turkish forces in Afghanistan. The decision also enhanced the American connection, since the United States Government provided $1 million toward the expenses involved.

Israel. The development of Azerbaijan's relations with Israel, unlikely as that would seem, began in 1992 when Israel recognized the newly independent Azerbaijan; two years later, Israel opened an embassy in Baku. In 1997, President Heydar Aliyev welcomed Prime Minister Benjamin Netanyahu to Baku for an official but low-key visit. Although no official

treaty was ever signed between the two states, relations blossomed in other ways over the years as Israel became a major source of arms for the Azerbaijani military. Again, Baku never opened an embassy in Israel but relations nevertheless grew as Azerbaijan came to consider Israel to be trustworthy in security matters and routinely began exchanges of intelligence with the Jewish state. In 2009, Israeli President Shimon Peres was welcomed to Baku for an official visit, where he was received with the highest honors. Israeli Foreign Minister Avigdor Lieberman paid a two-day visit Baku in April 2012 to carry on discussions on bilateral relations. It was recently reported that Israel had signed an agreement to supply $1.6 billion in weapons to Azerbaijan.

Iran. Azerbaijan's relations with its other neighbors are for the most part correct but not cordial. Its relations with Iran, its southern neighbor, were poor until recently because Iran has refused to support Azerbaijan's attempts to isolate Armenia and, in fact, has been Armenia's largest trading partner since 1991. Religious rivalries also play a role in this relationship. Although, as in Iran, the majority of the population of Azerbaijan is Shi'a Muslim, the Azerbaijani government fears and distrusts the religious fundamentalism currently dominant in Iran. In turn, Iran worries about the fact that it has millions of its own Azeris living along the border with Azerbaijan. However, the two countries signed a cooperation agreement in 2002 on the joint struggle against terrorism, drug smuggling, and organized crime and followed this up in April 2003 with a second bilateral agreement that added border security and arms proliferation to the list. There have also been a number of economic agreements for Iranian financing of several transportation projects and a $40 million Iranian credit package for a natural-gas project in Azerbaijan.

Nature of the Regime

After briefly flirting with political pluralism, Azerbaijan has now fully consolidated itself as a closed autocracy. The regime is built around Aliyev and those with close connection to them. The space for legal opposition has been nearly obliterated. Even when opposition parties and politicians are not arrested or otherwise harassed by security personal, they find it exceedingly difficult to gain access to state-run media or to be granted permission to organize rallies. There has been some evidence that the regime has abused the Interpol Red Notice system to harass Azerbaijani citizens engaged in what it deems to be "anti-regime" activities while abroad. Making matters worse, the regime

has adopted restrictive NGO registration laws, severely limiting the space for NGOs to operate.

After several opposition politicians called for hunger strikes and demonstrations against the government after the 1998 presidential elections, the parliament passed legislation limiting the right to hold public demonstrations and imposing a sentence of up to three years for organizing or participating in an unsanctioned demonstration. The government has also used libel suits on several occasions to bankrupt newspapers owned by the opposition. The ruling party, Yeni Azerbaycan—founded by President Aliyev in 1992 as his personal power base—controls a majority of seats in the parliament. His son, Ilham, who succeeded his father in 2003, continues to use the Yeni Azerbaycan as his chief instrument for controlling the country. During the lead-up to the 2005 parliamentary elections, however, he took a number of actions aimed at facilitating a somewhat greater pluralism. Most of these actions were in response to international pressure on his government to allow fair and free elections, but the new president does appear to be somewhat more democratically oriented than his father.

On the other hand, the constitution was amended in 2008 to remove all term limits on the presidency, giving President Aliyev the unlimited right to stand for reelection. President Aliyev did stand for reelection in 2018, winning 86.02% of the vote. According to the OSCE, the election lacked "genuine competition" as challenging candidates "refrained from directly challenging or criticizing the incumbent." The observers also noted widespread irregularities, including ballot stuffing, on the day of the election. Under the terms of the constitutional amendments passed in 2016, Aliyev will have six years before he needs to stage another sham election.

Like Russia, the regime is structured as a semi-presidential system. There is a popularly elected president who is considered to be the spokesman for the nation. He is responsible for general policy, but has a prime minister who handles day-to-day affairs of government. The president is commander-in-chief of the armed forces. He also presides over the State Council and the Defense Council. The current president is Ilham Aliyev, who was first elected In October 2003 after his father withdrew as a candidate because of illness. He began his fourth term in April 2018.

The prime minister and members of the cabinet are appointed by the president, but must be confirmed by the legislature, formally known as the Milli Mejlis or National Assembly. Aliyev's prime minister is Artur Rasizade, who had held that office from 1996 to August 2003; he was

Azerbaijan

reappointed after Ilham Aliyev won his own election as president.

Before 2016, Azerbaijan had no office of the vice president. Until 2002, the constitution had specified that the speaker of the parliament became acting president in the case of the death or incapacity of the president. After a constitutional referendum, from 2002 until 2016 the prime minister was listed as the successor should the president be unable to serve. This constitutional change proved to be quite convenient as it enabled Heydar Aliyev to name his son, Ilham Aliyev, prime minister shortly before he died. Under the new constitutional amendments, up to three vice presidents can be appointed by the president. The first vice president, however, is the successor should the president be incapacitated. To date only the position of the first vice president has been filled: it is now occupied by Ilham Aliyev's wife, Mehriban Aliyeva. Azerbaijan's system of proportional representation was abolished in 2002. All 125 parliamentary seats have therefore become single-seat constituencies.

The most recent elections for the largely toothless parliament occurred in February 2020. These were snap elections held after the dissolution of previous government in December 2019. The results were entirely unsurprising with the ruling Yeni Azerbaijan (New Azerbaijan) party winning a clear majority with 70 of the 125 seats. While the elections were clearly not a democratic moment, they were significant for enabling Aliyev to replace aging politicians who had been in positions of power under his father with younger, more technocratic members of the party.

Culture

Most Azerbaijani are Shi'a Muslims, unlike their Muslim neighbors in Central Asia, who are mostly Sunni. This results from the fact that the area of Azerbaijan was part of the Persian Empire for several centuries. When it became a part of the Russian Empire at the beginning of the 19th century, however, the Azeris became merely one of the Muslim peoples of Russia.

There was no sense of national Azerbaijani identity until fairly recently, but there have been a number of famous Azeri thinkers, poets, and scientists. Abul Hasan Bakhmanyar, who lived in the 11th century, wrote a number of books on mathematics and philosophy. Abul Hasan Shirvani, a later contemporary, left behind a book on astronomy. Nezami was a later poet and philosopher.

The Azeris have an ancient musical tradition which has survived. Musicians improvise the words to songs as they play a stringed instrument called a kobuz. There are also vocal and instrumental compositions that have been kept alive in a folk tradition.

They also have modern composers with international reputations. Two of these are Uzeir Hajjibekov, author of a number of operas, and Kara Karayev, who writes ballets. The Baku Film Studio also has an international reputation. *Little Vera*, a fairly recent film, tells a depressing story of a young girl growing up as a member of a working-class family in Baku.

Although a large part of the population was still illiterate in 1917, according to the Ministry of Education there are now 20 state institutions of higher education in Azerbaijan. The largest of these is the Azerbaijan Institute of Petroleum and Chemistry.

In January 1992, the Azerbaijan National Council passed a law adopting the Latin script for the Azeri language. It acted on the basis of a recommendation from a special commission, appointed two years earlier, to look into the question. The commission, made up of a number of linguists, historians, and literary specialists, concluded that the Azeri language's phonetic "peculiarities are best 'superimposed' on the Latin script." Azerbaijan had used the Latin script in the 1920s but, under pressure from Moscow, went over to the Cyrillic script at the end of the 1930s.

Economy

Baku, now the capital and largest city, was the center of the oil industry of Imperial Russia. In 1901, the Baku fields produced over 11 million tons of oil, which was 50% of the world's oil production at the time. The fields lost much of their earlier significance after World War II, but the region still produced 3% of the Soviet Union's oil in 1991. Even then, Baku was still surrounded by oil derricks, though natural gas came to rival petroleum in significance in the last years of the Soviet Union.

Once a beautiful city that spread out along natural terraces running down to a gulf of the Caspian Sea, Baku was, by 1991, a grimy industrial city with terrible pollution problems. The emergence of Azerbaijan as an independent country has given the city new life, however. Today, it is the center of a boom associated with new oil fields that are being opened up on the seabed of the Caspian Sea. Sabrina Tavernise, a reporter for the *New York Times*, reporting on her visit to Baku in October 2008, wrote that:

most of the downtown is encased in scaffolding, high rises have mushroomed and new roads are starting to make their way through the city.

Recent drilling by international companies has resulted in identification of proven oil reserves of between 15 and 20 billion barrels beneath the Caspian Sea, with the possibility that the basin might hold between 40 and 178 billion barrels. Azerbaijan's share of this treasure trove is estimated to be worth $100 billion over the next 30 years. International companies have already signed contracts with Azerbaijan worth an estimated $60 billion.

The first oil began flowing from the Chirag Caspian field in November 1997. The Chirag field was developed between 1994 and 1997 by a consortium of Western oil companies plus Russia's LUKoil. Yet another milestone was reached in December 1998 when the first oil was pumped into the new 930-kilometer pipeline connecting Baku with the Georgian Black Sea port of Supsa. This pipeline has an annual capacity of 2.5 million metric tons. Crude oil production—9 million metric tons in 1997—rose to 11.4 million metric tons in 1998; oil production has gone up every year since that time.

Azerbaijan's ability to move crude oil to world markets remained a major bottleneck until the summer of 2006 when the first oil began flowing through the 1,091-mile Baku-Tbilisi-Ceyhan export pipeline, which was constructed by an international consortium including British Petroleum, STATOIL, and UNOCAL, with Azerbaijan's state oil company, SOCAR, holding a 25% equity stake. Since the pipeline has a throughput capacity of 50 million metric tons per year, Kazakhstan has begun to use some of this capacity for its own oil exports, though that use is limited by the lack of a pipeline connecting the Kazakh oil fields with Baku.

A second, parallel 690-kilometer gas pipeline has also recently been completed. Azerbaijan produced about 5 billion cubic meters of natural gas in 2006, but it had to import an additional 4.5 billion cubic meters from Russia to meet domestic demand. However, the government cut its natural gas imports in early 2007 after Gazprom raised the price to $230 per 1,000 cubic meters. It could do so because the Shah Deniz gas field began producing its first gas in November 2006. Shah Deniz has estimated reserves of 1.2 trillion cubic meters of gas; production was 5–6 billion cubic meters in 2007, growing to 17.86 billion cubic meters in 2013. Azerbaijan exported 5.55 billion cubic meters of natural gas in 2013. In line with long-term contracts, Azerbaijan is furnishing 1 million cubic meters a day to Georgia and 7 million cubic meters a day to Turkey. Azerbaijan had also promised to supply 8 billion cubic meters of natural gas to the Nabucco pipeline when completed, but this promise was overtaken in 2013 when the consortium developing

Shah Deniz-2 approved an investment agreement paving the way for the use of the Trans-Adriatic (TAP) gas pipeline—replacing the Nabucco pipeline project—to bring Azerbaijani natural gas to Europe. The agreement also stated that oil from the Shah Deniz-2 offshore oil field would be shipped using the Trans-Anatolian (TANAP) pipeline. Construction of TANAP began in March 2015 and is scheduled for completion in 2018. The TAP pipeline will have the capacity of providing up to 14 billion cubic meters of natural gas to Europe.

There are still diplomatic problems that need to be solved before Azerbaijan can feel free to develop all of its potential wealth. The problem is that the countries bordering on the Caspian have not been able to agree on how to divide the seabed of the Caspian. The main question under international law is whether the Caspian is a sea or a saltwater lake. If the Caspian is determined to be a saltwater lake, then, according to international law, its various resources can only be exploited on the basis of an agreement signed by all bordering states. On the other hand, if the Caspian is a sea, its resources would be divided into national sectors that each country would have the right to exploit as it pleases. All of the littoral states have already exploited oil and gas deposits off their coastlines, but lack of agreement on the status of the Caspian limits development in contested areas.

Russia and Iran had until recently contended that the Caspian is a saltwater lake. Azerbaijan and Kazakhstan, on the other hand, took the position that it is a sea. Turkmenistan, the last of the states bordering on the Caspian Sea, first sided with Kazakhstan and Azerbaijan, then switched its position in 1996 and until recently was supporting the Russian–Iranian position. The death of President Niyazov has changed that stance once again. His successor, President Berdymukhammedov, has shown some interest in finding a way around Turkmenistan's oil dependency on Russia and recently endorsed an underwater gas line across the Caspian Sea to Baku.

Russia and Iran indicated in 1998 that they might be willing to agree that the Caspian is a sea if an appropriate division of the seabed could be worked out. However, Iran continues to claim 20% of the seabed, a position rejected by Azerbaijan; Iran would be entitled to 13% if the Caspian is determined to be a sea.

Azerbaijan has signed agreements with a number of international oil companies for the development of what it considers its national sector. In addition, Azerbaijan signed an agreement with Russia in September 2002 delimiting the two countries' respective sectors of the Caspian Sea

bed. Azerbaijan has also continued talks with the Iranian Government concerning the Caspian Sea bed.

Sumgait, located 22 miles north of Baku, is Azerbaijan's most important industrial center. Major chemical and oil-drilling industries are located here. In fact, Sumgait is the primary manufacturer of oil-drilling equipment, a position it already held when Azerbaijan was part of the now-defunct Soviet Union. The resurgence of Azerbaijan's oil and natural gas industries after independence has brought renewed prosperity and much new wealth to this city.

Three other cities with significant industry are Mingechaur, Gyanja (formerly Kirovabad), and Stepanakert. Mingechaur manufactures appliances and instruments and electrical equipment of all kinds, plus textiles, shoes, and other consumer goods. Gyanja and Stepanakert manufacture consumer goods, including textiles, and things like knitwear and souvenirs. All have benefited from the growth in the standard of living over the past several years, though Stepanakert, capital of Nagorno-Karabakh, suffered badly during Nagorno-Karabakh's war to free itself from Baku's control. Today, Nagorno-Karabakh, though still technically part of Azerbaijan, is part of an economic unit with Armenia.

Most of Azerbaijan's industry was developed to process its petroleum and natural gas production. Thus, it has refineries producing gas and diesel fuel, herbicides, industrial oils, and kerosene, but it also manufactures chemical fertilizers, synthetic rubber, and plastics. All of these industries have benefited from the great growth in oil and natural gas production since independence.

Another issue is privatization. Azerbaijan was slow to begin the process of privatization, but it did initiate the privatization of companies with fewer than 50 employees after 1991. Approximately 15,000 such companies were sold between then and 1997, most of them to the managers who had run them under communism.

Finally, in March 1997, Azerbaijan launched a mass privatization program that was supposed to result in the privatization of 70% of all enterprises by the end of 1998. This was a voucher program whereby each citizen was issued a coupon book of four vouchers. (War veterans received eight vouchers.)

All enterprises that were to be privatized were turned into joint-stock companies and 55% of their shares were then auctioned off for vouchers. The vouchers were distributed between March and August 1997 and voucher auctions were held regularly after that time. By December 1997,

approximately 400 large enterprises had been privatized.

Although government plans call for the eventual privatization of all medium-scale enterprises, many large-scale enterprises will remain in state hands. This will include the state oil company, railroads, water facilities, pension funds, and the state bank. In addition, companies involved in fuel and energy production, petrochemicals, telecommunications, plus bakeries and wineries, can only be privatized by presidential decree.

In March 2001, President Aliyev gave approval for the privatization of over 100 state-owned enterprises in the chemical, machine-building, and fuel and energy sectors. While he ordered the government to determine how enterprises in the fuel and energy sectors are to be privatized, he approved the privatization of the remainder of the companies using public auctions. In a few cases, 15% of the shares were offered in closed subscriptions to staff of the enterprises concerned.

Azerbaijan is also a major producer of electric power and traditionally has exported electricity to neighboring republics. There is a handicraft industry in the south along the border with Iran. Here the Talysh, an Iranian people, live in their mountainous villages and support themselves by weaving rugs and carpets by hand in the traditional way.

Fishing has also made a major contribution to the gross domestic product in the past, though it has been declining for a number of years, largely because of the growth of pollution of the Caspian Sea, famous for its caviar-producing sturgeon. This is a problem not limited to Azerbaijan and it will take a multination effort to deal with the problem.

Agriculture is considerably less significant than industry as far as GDP is concerned, though it still provides employment for over a third of the total population. Cotton, the most valuable individual crop, is mostly exported; its importance has declined in recent years but as recently as 1998 it was the second most important export after crude oil. Other important crops include tobacco, grapes, vegetables, fruits, and nuts. There is also a small silk industry.

The Lenkoren region in southern Azerbaijan produces subtropical crops such as citrus and tea. It also produces rice and tobacco and is a major source for winter and spring vegetables.

The Naxcivan (Nakhichevan) Autonomous Republic has a semi-desert climate, but irrigation allows it to raise grapes, cotton, and grain. It is also famous for its mineral water from local springs, which is bottled and sold as far away as Moscow.

Azerbaijan

There is some concern that this great growth in government expenditures could lead to runaway inflation. In fact, the Azerbaijani government is aware of the problem, and it has been funneling part of its energy revenues into the State Oil Fund (SOFAR) since 2001. SOFAR held around $2 billion in deposits by September 2007.

Another concern is that the rapid expansion of the economy has led the banking sector to be undercapitalized and fragmented. Three banking laws passed in the past 15 years address this issue by encouraging a gradual consolidation of the banking industry. At one point, there were approximately 250 banks in Azerbaijan; by the end of 2007, this number had been reduced to 44. Even so, the 30 smallest banks control under 20% of banking assets; meanwhile, two partially state-owned banks, the International Bank of Azerbaijan and the Kapital Bank together control over half the assets of the banking sector.

Azerbaijan had the fastest growing economy in the world during the period 2005–2008, averaging 28% a year. During that time, the budget grew twelve-fold and the economy grew by more than four times. The rate of growth dropped to just over 9% in 2009, then dropped to 3.7% in 2010, largely in reaction to the worldwide economic downturn. GDP growth was about 8% in 2011, but slipped to 3.5% in 2013.

As with other petroleum dependent economies in the region, the sharp decline in global oil prices since December 2014 has been a tremendous shock to the Azerbaijani economy. After years of oil fueled economic growth, in the first quarter of 2016, the economy contracted 3.5%. The oil drop has forced the state to take bold actions in order to balance its budget without burning through its foreign exchange reserves. Most notably, in December 2015 the central bank unpegged the Azerbaijani manat from the US dollar. As Azerbaijan imports a large number of consumer goods, including material need for foodstuffs, the devaluation spiked the price of many consumer products. With limited success, the government has attempted to manage social grievances over these price increases through waiving a value-added tax (VAT) on bread and flour and raising pensions.

In September 2010, an official spokesman for the Azerbaijani government announced that the poverty rate in Azerbaijan had been brought down from 49% to 11%. During that time, more than 900,000 jobs had been created, 600,000 of them permanent. Since the economy is so dependent on oil and gas extraction, the drop in crude prices in 2014–2015 stalled the state's economy. As a result of this shock, the Central Bank has twice devalued the nation's currency, the manat, the state's largest bank, the International Bank of Azerbaijan, declared bankruptcy and the economy contracted in 2016 and 2017. Given Azerbaijan's nondiversified economy, its economic prospects remain tied to the global price of oil and gas. The EU's partial embargo on Russian crude oil and petroleum products following Russia's unprovoked invasion of Ukraine, is expected to lead increasing demand for non-Russian crude and a corresponding rise in oil prices. All of this should be good news for Azerbaijan were it not for the war that has caused significant disruptions in commercial shipping in the Black Sea. Azerbaijan uses the Supsa terminal in the Republic of Georgia to deliver its oil to the European Market. Recently, the British Petroleum, which produces the bulk of Azerbaijani oil, announced that the disruption may have to do with the war in Ukraine. According to an April 4, 2002, article in Deutche Welle, the presence of floating naval mines, which Russia and Ukraine accuse each other of deploying, makes shipping an extremely risky business because these drifting mines are said to be old and capable of detonating by light contact, even from an object as light as an air mattress. Azerbaijan has an option of using the Baku–Tbilisi–Ceyhan pipeline to export its oil. Although, it would be more costly than shipping the crude through the Supsa terminal, higher future oil prices are likely to make the switch to CPT pipeline a viable option for Azerbaijan.

The Future

In a modern case of dynastic succession, Ilham Aliyev has been president since the death of his father in 2003. He is currently serving his fourth term, having won reelection in 2018. Recent efforts to reform the constitution to eliminate the age requirement to serve as president and to establish the first vice president as the successor to the president should be seen as attempts to increase the likelihood that political power remains in the Aliyev family for the foreseeable future. This is abundantly clear when one considers that the current first vice president is Ilham Aliyev's wife.

After booming in the 2000s, Azerbaijan's oil-export based economy has slowed tremendously since 2015 and is now in jeopardy of shrinking due to the decline in world energy prices. Deteriorating economic conditions, and price hikes associated with the devaluation of Azerbaijan's currency, the manat, have spurred a number of protests across the country. Given the growing economic frustrations of the populace, from Aliyev's perspective, the release of documents in the so-called Panama Papers revealing his families extensive use of offshore companies to hide wealth acquired through secret shares in Azerbaijani companies could not have come at a worse time.

President Aliyev casts his ballot during the 2009 Azerbaijan elections

A weakening economy may explain Azerbaijan's recent suppression of human rights. In recent years, the state has silenced political opponents of the president and shut down foreign-based NGOs. It has also kept a watchful eye on religious movements of all sorts. These policies have had a chilling effect on civil society.

Azerbaijan's successful reclamation of territory in the 2020 Nagorno-Karabakh war has seemingly bolstered the Aliyev regime. In the months that followed, the state has arranged for nationalistic displays and celebrations honoring the military victory over regional rival Armenia.

Most notably an open-air park, named The Spoils of War Park, which featured equipment and vehicles seized from Armenian forces during the war, opened in Baku. The fact that the park also features cartoonish mannequins of Armenian soldiers with stereotypical features makes clear the intent of the regime is to stoke a perpetual societal war footing and to engender anti-Armeninian nationalism. Although the regime relies on aggressively nationalistic (and chauvinistic) legitimation strategy, it appears that it is finally interested in reaching a comprehensive peace deal with Armenia that would grant it territorial control over Nagorno-Karabakh. Armenians, especially followers of the opposition parties, are weary that diplomacy would establish a victor's peace at the expense of Armenia. Their fears might not be entirely unfounded. In negotiations held in May 2023 in Brussels, the Armenian side publicly stated that it intends to recognize Nagorno-Karabakh as part of Azerbaijan. For its part, the Azerbaijani side did not publicly commit to guarantee that the rights and security of Karabakh Armenians would be protected. Whether Armenians accept Azerbaijan's peace plans remains to be seen.

Georgia

Area: 26,903 sq. mi. (69,700 sq. km), slightly smaller than South Carolina.

Population: 4,900,961 (2023 estimate).

Capital City: Tbilisi (Pop. 1.080 million 2022 estimate).

Climate: Humid, subtropical in the Kolkhida Lowland (along the eastern shore of the Black Sea) and on the interior, high plateau known as the Kartalinian Plain; temperate in the high mountains to either side of the Kartalinian Plain.

Neighboring States: Russia (north), Turkey, Armenia (south), and Azerbaijan (southeast).

Official Language: Georgian; Abkhaz is the official language of Abkhazia.

Ethnic Composition: Georgian (86.8%), Azeri (6.3%), Armenian (4.5%), Other (2.3%).

Principal Religions: Orthodox Christian (83.4%); Muslim (10.7%); Armenian-Apostolic (2.9%); other (1.2%).

Chief Commercial Products: Hydroelectric power, mining, electrical equipment, metals and alloys, automobiles, electrical manufactures, instruments, wines, fruits, tea, vegetables, livestock.

Currency: lari (introduced on October 2, 1995).

Per Capita Annual Income (Purchasing Power Parity): $22247 (2023 estimate).

Recent Political Status: Soviet Republic (1921), part of Transcaucasian SSR (1922–1936), Republic of the USSR (1936–1991).

President: Salome Zourabichvili (December 16, 2018).

Prime Minister: Irakli Garibashvili (February 22, 2021).

National Flag: Large red cross superimposed on a white background with four small red crosses centered on the four fields created by the large cross.

National Holiday: May 26 (1918), date of independence from Soviet Russia.

The Land

The Republic of Georgia (Sak'art'velo) is the independent successor state to the Georgian Soviet Socialist Republic, which was one of the 15 republics of the Union of Soviet Socialist Republics. The Georgia Supreme Soviet announced the republic's intention to separate from the Soviet Union in November 1990, but it was the August 1991 failed coup against Mikhail Gorbachev that created a situation of de facto independence for Georgia. Georgia covers an area of 26,903 square miles (69,700 sq. km.). It includes the Abkhazian and Adjarian Autonomous Republics, plus the South Ossetian Autonomous Region. Of the three, only the Adjarian Autonomous Republic recognizes the authority of the central government, however; the other two have declared themselves to be independent republics.

Georgia lies at the eastern end of the Black Sea, just to the south of the Great Caucasus Mountains. Eighty-5% of the country is mountainous, the exception being a small area in the west bordering on the Black Sea known as the Kolkhida Lowland. This is the site of ancient Colchis, where Jason and the Argonauts sought the Golden Fleece. The Kolkhida Lowland is a delta region formed by the deposits of three rivers that flow through the area,

the Inguri, Rioni, and Kodori. It was once mostly swampland, but drain-age projects have turned it into a major producer of subtropical crops and winter vegetables. Here winter temperatures average 41°F and there is a plentiful year-round rainfall.

Behind Kolkhida, the land rises until it reaches two saddle ridges which connect the Great Caucasus and the Little Caucasus Mountains. Beyond that is a high plateau which runs eastward to the border of Azerbaijan. This high plateau, known as the Kartalinian Plain, is the heartland of Georgia.

Most of it is covered by a loess type soil. Drier than the western coast, it nevertheless gets sufficient rainfall to sustain agriculture. In addition, the Mtkvari (formerly Kur or Kura) River flows down out of the Little Caucasus in the southwest and then eastward across the plateau, providing plenty of water for irrigation.

Open to the warm, moist air from the Black Sea and protected on the north by the wall of the Great Caucasus Mountains, the Kartalinian Plain has winters warm enough for citrus groves to thrive. The high mountains to the north and south of this plateau are covered with forests of oak, chestnut, beech, ash, linden, alder, and Caucasian fir. Fruit trees also abound, including apples, pears, and various kinds of nuts. Dairying is practiced on the lower slopes of the mountains and on parts of the plateau. Vineyards are also widely cultivated. Grapes are sold fresh or turned into wine, brandy, or champagne.

The eastern part of the country consists of the Alasari River Valley plus a saddle

Georgia

land to the south between that valley and the Kara River Valley. This area receives only between 16 and 28 inches of rainfall per year and therefore makes use of the water from the Alasari River for irrigation.

The People

According to a recent estimate reported in the CIA World Factbook, Georgia's population is 4.9 million. Georgians make up approximately 86.8% of the population. The two largest minorities are Azeris (6.3%) and Armenians (4.5%).

Georgia is an ancient center of civilization. Archaeological excavations place the beginning of the Bronze Age here as early as 3000 B.C. The ancestors of the Georgian people emerged for the first time in the first millennium B.C. in the annals of the Assyrian Empire. The Georgian language itself is classified as one of the Caucasian languages, meaning that, as far as it known, the Georgians originated here.

Among the Georgian tribes were the Kulkha (Colchians), who once dominated most of the eastern shores of the Black Sea. Their city, Colchis, was known for its fabulous wealth and gave rise to the legend of Medea and the Golden Fleece. Colchis was later colonized by Greeks and still later incorporated into the Roman Empire.

History

Georgia converted to Christianity in the year 337. Over the next three centuries, it became a battlefield between the Byzantine Empire and Persia. In 654, however, it was conquered by the Arqab caliphs, who established an emirate in Tbilisi. In reaction to the Arab presence, the various Georgian tribes united around a princely family long prominent in the affairs of Armenia, and this family eventually brought most of Georgia under its sway. King Bagrat III (975–1014) ruled all of Georgia except for the Tbilisi emirate, and that was conquered in the year 1122 by one of his descendants, King David II ("the Builder"). The Georgian Kingdom reached its zenith under Queen Tamara (1184–1213), when it included most of the Caucasus.

The end came in 1220 with the appearance of the Mongols from the east. Eastern Georgia became part of the Mongol Empire, with only the area west of the mountains along the Black Sea maintaining its independence. The decline of the Mongol Empire brought part of the high central plateau back under Georgian control, but the new kingdom was destroyed by a fresh onslaught by Tamerlane, who created a great empire stretching across Central Asia.

The fall of Constantinople to the Ottoman Turks in 1453 isolated Georgia. In the 16th century, it, too, was incorporated into the Turkish Empire. The Turks were

in turn driven out by Shah Abba I (1587–1629), ruler of the Persian Empire. In the process, thousands of Georgian Christians were transported to distant parts of the Persian Empire. There was a brief respite after 1658, when the Persians installed the House of Mukhran as viceroys at Tbilisi, but this was brought to an end by a fresh Turkish invasion in 1722. The Persians expelled the Turks 22 years later. Another kingdom based on Georgia was installed by the Persians and lasted until near the end of the 18th century.

In 1783, Erekle, the Georgian king, signed the Treaty of Georgievsk with Catherine the Great, whereby Russia guaranteed Georgia's independence and territorial integrity in return for Erekle's acceptance of Russian authority. When Georgia was invaded by Persia in 1795, however, Russia offered no assistance. Tbilisi was

sacked in 1795 and Erekle died three years later. His son, George XII, offered the kingdom to Paul, the Russian Tsar. Paul died before the treaty could be signed, so it was Alexander I who incorporated Georgia into the Russian Empire. In spite of the treaty of 1783, Alexander I then deposed George XII and replaced him with Russian military governors. Erekle's kingdom had included only the areas of Kartalinia and Kakhetia, so other parts of Georgia were incorporated in the Russian Empire between 1810 and 1864. The Black Sea ports of Poti and Batumi were added at the time of the Russo-Turkish War of 1877–78.

Georgia's incorporation into the Russian Empire provoked a number of popular uprisings at various times, but it did have the merit of ensuring the corporate survival of the Georgian nation. Georgia also benefited economically and culturally from

An artist's concept of the medieval fortress of Queen Tamara in the towering Caucasus Mountains

253

Georgia

its connection with Russia. A railroad connecting Tbilisi with Poti on the Black Sea opened in 1872 and mines, factories and commercial farms were established with Russian and foreign capital. Alexander II's reforms also included the end of serfdom and the spread of education. Alexander III's policy of Russification fostered nationalism among the middle-class intelligentsia, however, and marked the beginning of a national revival.

A number of illegal nationalist groups were founded in the 1890s, the most important of which was the "Third Group," a Marxist group affiliated with the Russian Social Democratic Labor Party. In 1898, the Third Group recruited Joseph Dzhugashvili, better known by his later revolutionary name, Joseph Stalin. Five years later, Stalin became a Bolshevik when the Russian Social Democratic Labor Party, separated into Bolshevik and Menshevik factions at its second congress. The Georgian Marxist party, on the other hand, was controlled by Mensheviks.

Georgia saw widespread disturbances and guerrilla fighting during the 1905 Russian uprising, but these were put down by Cossacks in 1906. After the 1917 Revolution, an autonomous Transcaucasian committee was established under the authority of the Provisional Government. After the Bolshevik Revolution in the fall, however, this Transcaucasian committee, which was dominated by Mensheviks, broke with the national government and established the Transcaucasian Federal Republic on April 22, 1918. When this collapsed a month later, the Georgian National Council set up the Georgian Social Democratic Republic. The republic was under German protection for a while, but then was occupied by the British. The Georgians refused to cooperate with the British, however, and the latter departed Batumi in July 1920.

Georgia signed a treaty with the Russian Soviet Government in May 1920; Moscow then dispatched Sergei M. Kirov, a Georgian Bolshevik, to Tbilisi. Kirov's task was to undermine the Menshevik regime and prepare for a Bolshevik seizure of power. In February 1921, a Red Army under the control of two Georgian Bolshevik leaders, Joseph Stalin and Grigol K. Ordzhonikidze, entered Georgia. A Soviet regime was installed on February 25.

Georgia was incorporated into the Transcaucasian Soviet Federated Socialist Republic in March 1922 which, in turn, became a part of the Union of Soviet Socialist Republics on December 30, 1922. Stalin, who was people's commissar for nationalities in the Moscow government, carried out a purge of active nationalists, including even members of the Georgian

Communist Party. In December 1936, the Transcaucasian SFSR was formally dissolved and the Georgian Soviet Socialist Republic became one of the constituent republics in its own right.

Georgia certainly derived some benefits from its participation in the Union of Soviet Socialist Republics. Illiteracy was wiped out, schools of higher education were set up, a Georgian Academy of Sciences was established, and a great deal of industry was built. Yet the price was conformity to Marxist-Leninist ideology and a suppression of traditional Georgian culture.

When Gorbachev launched his policy of glasnost after he took over in 1985, therefore, one of his early supporters was Eduard Shevardnadze, first secretary of the Georgian Communist Party from 1972 to 1985. Shevardnadze, made a full member of the Politburo and minister of foreign affairs, became a strong voice at the center urging on Gorbachev the necessity for further reforms.

Gorbachev's reforms were endorsed and exploited as much in Georgia as any part of the Soviet Union and the Georgia Communist Party soon found itself outbid by Georgian nationalists, who did not have to worry about loyalty to Moscow. When Gorbachev decided to permit real elections in 1989, the nationalists were given their chance. A seven-party coalition called Round Table-Free Georgia won 62% of the seats in the October 1990 republic elections. They then proceeded to elect Zviad Gamsakhurdia, a longtime nationalist dissident and anti-Communist, as Georgia's head of state. The name of the country was also changed to the Republic of Georgia.

In April 1991, the Supreme Soviet declared Georgia's independence and amended the constitution to create a popularly elected, executive president. Gamsakhurdia swept the subsequent May 26, 1991, presidential elections with 86.5% of the vote.

Shortly after assuming the presidency, Gamsakhurdia began to show rather authoritarian tendencies. For example, he signed a law which made "maligning" the president a crime punishable by six years in prison. He also accused reporters of lying and had them thrown out of a news conference. And he began to attack the political autonomy enjoyed by Muslim South Ossetians in the north of the country.

When the attempted coup against Gorbachev began in August 1991, Gamsakhurdia opted for a policy of neutrality. This led to a split in the government coalition because Tengiz Sigua, the prime minister, and Gyorghi Khoshtaria, the foreign minister, publicly opposed

the coup. Gamsakhurdia dismissed both of them in the days following collapse of the coup and, when the dismissals led to popular demonstrations in the main square of Tbilisi, Gamsakhurdia ordered the National Guard to fire on the demonstrators.

When Gamsakhurdia ordered Tengiz Ketovani, the commander of the National Guard, to use force against a subsequent demonstration, the latter refused. Gamsakhurdia then fired him also, thereby driving him into the opposition.

Gamsakhurdia also abolished South Ossetia's autonomous status; in the resulting unrest, over 100 persons were killed and 50,000 Ossetians sought refuge over the mountains in North Ossetia, in the Russian Federation.

As daily demonstrations continued in Tbilisi against Gamsakhurdia, members of the government coalition began to go over to the opposition. When Gamsakhurdia ordered the arrest of Georgi Chanturia, the leader of the opposition National Democratic Party, Tengiz Sigua and Tengiz Ketovani led a series of demonstrations demanding that Gamsakhurdia resign. After anti-Gamsakhurdia demonstrators seized control of the government radio and television station on September 22, they were joined by members of the Georgia National Guard and more than 10,000 demonstrators marched on government house to demand President Gamsakhurdia's resignation.

Gamsakhurdia spent the next three months penned up in the parliament building as, outside, riots, shootings and demonstrations took place in the streets. Gamsakhurdia fled Tbilisi on January 6, making his way first to Azerbaijan and then to Chechnya. Eventually he made his way to western Georgia. Here he rallied his supporters and attempted to force his way back to power; but his remaining support was just too small.

Meanwhile the victorious opposition set up a Military Council to govern the country, with Tengiz Sigua taking the office of provisional prime minister while Tengiz Ketovani continued as commander of the National Guard. Rumors soon began to spread that Eduard Shevardnadze would return to Georgia and reenter Georgia politics. In February, Shevardnadze announced that he had agreed to serve as honorary chairman of an umbrella group called the Democratic Union. The Military Council immediately welcomed Shevardnadze's return.

In March, the Military Council relinquished power to the legislature, which set up a governing State Council to run the country until elections could take place. Shevardnadze was elected chairman of the State Council on March 10.

Georgia

In October 1992, a new legislature was elected and Shevardnadze was elected to the office of speaker of the State Council. In spite of his new title, Shevardnadze had to share power with his prime minister, Tengiz Sigua, and his defense minister, Tengiz Ketovani, the two men who arranged for his installation as chairman of the State Council in the first place.

Meanwhile, the political situation remained unstable. In June, Gamsakhurdia's supporters launched a coup to overthrow the new government. They managed to seize the television tower but were easily routed by Georgia National Guard troops. A second coup attempt, launched in November 1992, was more serious and was put down only after Russian troops were deployed on the railway running through the area. Gamsakhurdia died in Samegrelo in the western part of Georgia, an apparent suicide.

Georgia's Secessionist Movements

Shevardnadze inherited two secessionist movements from his predecessor. The first of these, South Ossetia, was set off when Gamsakhurdia attacked its autonomy, though it later became tied in with the wish to unite with neighboring North Ossetia. Tengiz Ketovani, defense minister and head of the Georgian National Guard, carried out an attack on Tskhinvali, the capital of South Ossetia in May 1992. Shevardnadze preferred a negotiated settlement, however, and responded favorably when President Boris Yeltsin offered to mediate the dispute. The two sides eventually agreed to a negotiated cease-fire which was to be policed by a joint Russian–Georgian-Ossetian force. The government of South Ossetia had declared its independence during the confrontation, however, and afterward referred to itself as the Republic of South Ossetia. A 2000 conference, organized by the Russian government brought together officials from Georgia, South Ossetia, North Ossetia, and the OSCE. The sticking point was South Ossetia's unwillingness to give up its claim to independence. In spite of subsequent talks, that remained the situation until March 2008, when Russia withdrew from the Joint Control Commission overseeing negotiations with South Ossetia. The following month, President Putin issued a decree instructing the Russian government to open political, social, and economic relations with South Ossetia.

In July 2008, Russia brought several thousand troops to the vicinity of the Georgian border for what it said was a large-scale military exercise. On August 7, the Russian peacekeeping commander in South Ossetia announced in response to reports of shelling along the South Ossetian-Georgian border that Russia

Centenarian dancers of Narta'a go to give a concert Courtesy of NOVOSTI

was unable to control the South Ossetian forces. That same day, the Russian officer who chaired the South Ossetian Security Council announced that armed groupings from North Ossetia were headed to South Ossetia to join the battle against Georgian troops.

Georgian troops entered South Ossetia at midnight on August 8. The first Russian army forces arrived in South Ossetia at about 10 a.m. By that afternoon, Georgian forces were being forced out of South Ossetia and the war rapidly escalated to other parts of Georgia. Within five days, Russian troops occupied all of northern Georgia. Russia formally recognized the "independence" of South Ossetia later in the month, announcing at the same time that its troops would remain in South Ossetia for the foreseeable future. With a population of only about 60,000, South Ossetia is not capable of being a viable state; in fact, the South Ossetian leadership, which is mainly Russian, has made it clear that its end goal is to become part of Russia.

The Abkhazian secessionist movement can be traced back to 1990 when Abkhazian nationalists began to demand greater local autonomy. In August 1992, the Abkhazian legislature voted to reinstate the region's 1925 constitution, in effect asserting its independence.

In response, Shevardnadze sent in a force of 3,000 men armed with tanks and helicopter gunships in an attempt to take control of the capital city of Sukhumi. The Abkhazian Government, headed by Vladislav Ardzinba, fled the capital, and Georgia was facing the possibility of a long period of guerrilla warfare. When President Yeltsin offered to mediate this dispute, therefore, Shevardnadze accepted and he and Ardzinba signed a cease-fire agreement in September.

The cease-fire did not hold. More fighting broke out again in October and the Abkhazians, this time supported by other mountain tribes of the Caucasus plus some Russian Cossacks, managed to gain control over a large part of northwest Abkhazia.

Russia mediated a new cease-fire in the summer of 1993 which required heavy weapons and most of the soldiers to be withdrawn from both sides. The Georgian government complied, but the Abkhazians did not. After the Georgian troops had been withdrawn from the area, the Abkhazians launched an attack on Sukhumi, the regional capital. Sukhumi fell on September 27.

In February 1994, President Yeltsin flew to Tbilisi, accompanied by General Pavel Grachev, to sign a treaty, under whose terms Georgia not only joined the CIS but also granted Russia the right to establish military bases within the country; in turn, Russia agreed to train and arm the Georgian army and to provide Georgia with 40 billion rubles ($25 million) in trade credits. A CIS peacekeeping force was to be stationed along a 13-kilometer stretch of the Inguri River, which marks the internal border between Abkhazia and the rest of Georgia. This force, which consisted entirely of Russian soldiers, was installed in July 1994.

Later in the year, the United Nations brokered a peace agreement whereby refugees from the fighting in 1993 and early 1994 were to be permitted to return to their homes and talks were to begin on a political settlement. The resulting talks broke down when the Abkhazian parliament adopted a constitution declaring the Abkhazia to be a "sovereign democratic state." Vladislav Ardzinba was also inaugurated as president on December 6.

Georgia

In March 1997, Russia backed a resolution at the CIS heads of state summit that extended the geographical area in which the CIS peacekeeping force operated and gave them more extensive powers to protect refugees attempting to return to their homes in Abkhazia. The Abkhazian leadership refused to recognize the legitimacy of the 1997 CIS resolution, however, so almost no refugees returned to their homes.

Angered, President Shevardnadze threatened to veto the extension of the mandate of the CIS peacekeeping force when it came up for renewal in July. The Georgian parliament also passed a resolution in May 1997 suggesting that Georgia leave the CIS if the 1997 CIS resolution were not implemented. Alarmed, President Yeltsin invited Shevardnadze and Abkhazian President Vladislav Ardzinba to meet with him in Moscow on August 2 for "one last serious talk." Russia announced, at the same time, that only the CIS could cancel the mandate of the CIS peacekeeping force, so that meant that the force would remain in place at least until the next CIS meeting in October. Shevardnadze accepted Yeltsin's invitation to come to Moscow, as did the Abkhazian leadership. Although Russia attempted to get the two sides to sign a peace protocol at the talks, both sides refused, so the meeting was essentially a failure.

The United Nations became actively involved in the Georgia-Abkhaz dispute during the summer of 1997. In July, the UN Secretary-General asked the United States, Germany, France, and the UK to form a Friends of Georgia group (Russia was invited as an observer) to provide a new venue for talks. This group sponsored a series of meetings between Georgia and Abkhazia which at least got the two sides to promise not to use violence or the threat of violence against each other. Georgia refused to lift its economic sanctions against Abkhazia, however, and Abkhazia refused to allow the repatriation of refugees.

The Friends of Georgia group then arranged for another round of talks in Geneva on November 17–19. Here, the Georgian and Abkhaz delegations agreed to create a coordinating commission with three working groups that would focus on security issues, repatriation, and economic and social issues. Nothing else was accomplished, however.

Abkhazia carried out new presidential elections in October 1999, which resulted in the reelection of Vladislav Ardzinba for a second term. In that same election, the people approved a referendum on the 1994 constitution which defined Abkhazia as an independent sovereign state. A few days later, the Abkhazian parliament formally adopted a statute reaffirming the region's status as an independent state.

In the summer of 2001, there was a flare-up in relations between the Georgian government and the Abkhazian authorities, but it was defused after President Shevardnadze met several times with Anri Djergenia, the prime minister of Abkhazia. At the time, Djergenia expressed his admiration for Shevardnadze, though other Abkhaz leaders were skeptical about Shevardnadze's intentions and wary of his peace proposal.

Two months later, a new crisis erupted when several hundred Georgian and Chechen fighters entered the Kodori Gorge, an area of divided control between Georgia and the Abkhazia, and began launching attacks against Abkhaz troops. The Georgian government responded by sending in 350 of its own troops to restore order. Abkhazia immediately demanded that Georgia withdraw its troops, and a similar request came from Russia. In the end, Georgia agreed to withdraw its troops in return for a UN promise that the UN Observer Mission, which had pulled out of the area in 2000 after one of its patrols was abducted, would resume patrols of the upper reaches of the Kodori Gorge. It also helped that the UN released its latest peace settlement document at this time which, while allowing Abkhazia to retain its constitution and state bodies, required it to acknowledge that it is a constituent part of Georgia.

The UN Observer Mission resumed its patrols in conjunction with the Russian peacekeeping force deployed under the CIS aegis on March 25, 2002. In return, the Georgian government promised to remove its troops from the Kodori Gorge. Even as the last Georgian troops were withdrawn, however, a series of attacks were launched against the CIS peacekeepers. Blaming

Georgia, the Russian government sent some 200 troops into the Kodori Gorge on April 12, but pulled them out two days later after President Shevardnadze personally intervened with President Putin.

Meanwhile, the UN Security Council, in renewing the mandate of the UN Observer Mission in Georgia at the end of July, called on both sides to work for a durable political solution to the conflict which would define Abkhazia's status within Georgia, based on concessions and mutual understanding. Addressing this latter point, the Georgian parliament amended the constitution in October to designate Abkhazia as an autonomous republic within Georgia. Abkhaz Prime Minister Djergenia rejected the Georgia parliament's action, however, saying that the Abkhaz would not discuss the option of autonomy within Georgia. The Abkhaz political leadership has also refused to begin talks on the UN-drafted document "Basic Principles for the Distribution of Competencies between Tbilisi and Sukhumi."

In March 2003, in a new initiative launched under UN auspices, the ambassadors in Tbilisi of the five member countries of the Friends of the UN Secretary-General group tasked with mediating a solution to the Abkhaz conflict—the United States, Russia, France, Germany, and Great Britain—met with the Abkhaz leadership to present a new proposal for solving the crisis. The Abkhaz leadership rejected the new proposals, characterizing them as an attempt to force Abkhazia to renounce its independence and revert to being an integral part of Georgia. However, a breakthrough of sorts did occur at about this same time when the Georgian and Russian presidents arranged a meeting with Abkhaz Prime Minister Gennadi

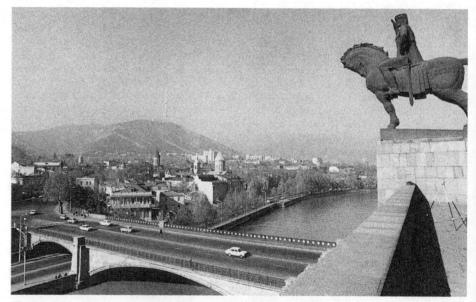

The Metekhi Bridge across the Mtkvari (Kura) River, Tbilisi   Courtesy of NOVOSTI

Gagulia (who had replaced Djergenia as prime minister in late 2002) in Sochi, Russia, on March 7. Here, agreement was reached to allow those Georgian displaced persons who fled their homes during the 1992–1993 war to be repatriated, in the first instance to Abkhazia's southernmost Gali Region and then to other districts. After the repatriation was complete, railway communication would be restored between Sochi via Abkhazia to Tbilisi and modernization would begin at the Iguri Hydroelectric Power Station. In addition, a joint Russian–Georgian–Abkhaz police force and administration was to be created for Gali, which the Abkhaz side had previously rejected. These small steps appeared to be the result of Russian pressure on the Abkhaz leadership.

There was a change in the political leadership of Abkhazia in January 2004 when Sergei Bagapsh was elected president. The new prime minister was Aleksandr Ankvab. Although Russia originally supported Bagapsh's opponent for the presidency, Bagapsh's election did not bring any significant change in Abkhazia's relations with the Georgian central government. Sergei Bagapsh died in Moscow on May 29, 2011, one week after undergoing lung surgery. His successor is Aleksandr Ankvab, who had been vice president under Bagapsh.

There was also a change in the Georgian leadership in 2004 when Mikheil Saakashvili replaced Shevardnadze as president. Saakashvili, also, was committed to bringing Abkhazia (and South Ossetia) back under central government control, but he, too, was unsuccessful. Of course, the Russian invasion of Georgia in 2008 and its subsequent recognition of the "independence" of Abkhazia and South Ossetia put an end to all such hopes for the foreseeable future.

Shevardnadze Consolidates His Power

By 1995, Shevardnadze had begun to assert a greater leadership role in the country. It also helped that Georgia was beginning to turn around again economically. That summer, Shevardnadze and his supporters pushed through a new constitution which established a presidential system. Elections for the presidency and a new legislature were set for November.

In August 1995, several persons attempted to assassinate Shevardnadze by throwing bombs at his vehicle. Although the instigators were never definitely identified, the Georgian government accused Igor Giorgadze, a former minister of security, of being behind the attempt on Shevardnadze's life. After the assassination attempt, Shevardnadze won the presidency with approximately 70% of the vote; in addition, the Union of Citizens party, the

political party Shevardnadze had founded, won a dominant position in the new parliament as well. Shevardnadze was now the dominant voice in Georgian politics.

Perhaps that explains the new attempt on President Shevardnadze's life that occurred on February 9, 1998, the second attempt within 2.5 years. President Shevardnadze was returning to his residence in his limousine, a bullet-proof Mercedes provided by the German Government, when his vehicle was fired on by a several-man hit team armed with high-caliber weaponry. In the battle that ensued, two presidential guards and one attacker were killed.

Five suspects arrested six days later were identified as supporters of ex-President Gamsakhurdia. The government eventually identified approximately 15 possible plotters, most of them Gamsakhurdia supporters. But it is still not clear what the motives of the assailants might have been or who they might have been working for. Gamsakhurdia is, of course, dead, so killing Shevardnadze would not have brought their faction back to power.

Nevertheless, a group of approximately 20 individuals who identified themselves as Gamsakhurdia supporters abducted four members of the UN observer mission in Zugdidi on February 19 and demanded the release of seven men arrested in connection with the assassination attempt. The UN hostages were released six days later.

Two months later, it became clear that the two years of stability that Georgia had enjoyed in 1996–1997 had come to an end. This time, it was renewed fighting between Georgian guerrillas and Abkhaz Interior Ministry forces in Abkhazia's southernmost province of Gali, which produced an additional 35,000 Georgian refugees.

The last event occurred in October 1998 when Georgian army units stationed in the west sector of the country mutinied, seizing several high-ranking Georgian officials as hostages. Although the insurrection failed almost immediately, it was yet another sign that political opposition to Shevardnadze continued to exist. In this case, the young officer responsible for the mutiny was later identified as a former supporter of the late President Gamsakhurdia.

New parliamentary elections took place on October 31, 1999, with several dozen parties and blocs competing for seats. Four parties/blocs surmounted the 7% barrier to participate in the division of the 150 seats distributed on a proportional basis. The pro-Shevardnadze Union of Citizens took 44% of these seats, followed by the All-Georgia Union of Revival, the vehicle of Adjar Supreme Council chairman Aslan Abashidze, which came second with 23%. The other parties/blocs that surmounted

the 7% barrier were the Labor Party and the bloc Industry Will Save Georgia, led by beer magnate Gogi Topadze.

New presidential elections took place on April 9, 2000. Seven candidates entered the race but Adjar Supreme Council Chairman Aslan Abashidze, who was expected to give Shevardnadze the greatest amount of competition, withdrew from the race two days before the balloting. As a result, President Shevardnadze won an easy reelection victory, receiving over 80% of the vote. Dzhumber Patiashvili, Shevardnadze's successor as first secretary of the Georgian Communist Party, came in second with 16%.

What should have been a triumph for Shevardnadze actually sullied his record, however. Although most observers agree that Shevardnadze would have won in any fair election, his local officials apparently worried about a poor showing and so turned to ballot-stuffing and tampering with the results. "Local governors showed too much zeal" was the way Mikheil Saakashvili, parliamentary leader of the Shevardnadze-founded Union of Citizens party, phrased it. From that time onward, Shevardnadze came under increasing attack from the political opposition, in particular the leaders of the Georgian Communist Party, the Socialist Party, the Labor Party, plus supporters of deceased former President Gamsakhurdia. These attacks by the political opposition were probably not very important.

In the summer of 2001, however, the pro-government majority split over the question of fighting corruption and began to disintegrate. By all accounts, corruption has become a very real problem with Georgia's huge shadow economy accounting, by some estimates, for 30% or more of GDP. Moreover, leading government officials had been accused of corruptly protecting important individuals in this shadow economy in return for pay-offs. Mikheil Saakashvili, an energetic young reformer who became justice minister in October 2000, made corruption an important issue when he proposed requiring government officials to reveal the source of their wealth. When senior officials criticized Saakashvili's proposal, President Shevardnadze rejected Saakashvili's proposal. Shevardnadze later pushed through a requirement that all government officials file a formal statement of their assets with the government, but this did not satisfy Saakashvili, who resigned as justice minister and subsequently went over to the opposition.

In the bitter struggle that erupted over the issue of government corruption, the Union of Citizens party first split into quarreling factions and then began to disintegrate. The Union of Citizens party had always been a curious amalgam of

Georgia

Tea leaves are harvested from tea-bush fields   Courtesy of NOVOSTI

former Soviet-era bureaucrats—now turned businessmen—who worked with Shevardnadze in the 1970s and 1980s; environmentalists who had formerly been organized into a separate, Green Party; plus a group of energetic young reformers recruited into government by Shevardnadze beginning in 1995. One of those young reformers was Mikheil Saakashvili, a lawyer who became chairman of the parliamentary faction in August 1998 at the age of 28; at the same time, he served as chairman of the parliamentary anti-corruption committee. When Saakashvili resigned as justice minister and subsequently left the party, most of the young reformers in the party left with him.

Shevardnadze resigned as chairman of the Union of Citizens in September, apparently hoping that the party might be able to hold together if he severed his connection with it. However, the opposite happened. Over the following two weeks, up to 50 deputies quit the party. It lost its majority on October 8 when the Majoritarian-Georgia's Regions faction formally withdrew its 21 deputies from the parliamentary majority bloc.

On November 1, Shevardnadze was forced to dismiss his government after a longtime ally, Zurab Zhvania, resigned his position as speaker of the parliament. The immediate issue that brought down the government was a controversial raid by state security agents against an independent television station, but the underlying issue was government abuse and corruption. The raid on the television station, Rustavi 2, was ostensibly for a tax investigation, but it was widely viewed as an attack on the independent press and it brought thousands of demonstrators into the streets. The crowds demanded the resignations of the minister for state security and the interior minister, but Shevardnadze chose to dismiss his entire cabinet instead.

In December 2001, Mikheil Saakashvili and nine other former members of the Union of Citizens formed a new faction called For Democratic Reforms. Saakashvili subsequently joined with other opposition parties to create the umbrella opposition National Movement. As a final blow, several members of the parliament faction of the Union of Citizens joined the parliamentary opposition in March 2002. Shortly afterward, a second faction led by Zurab Zhvania, former speaker of the parliament, moved into open opposition; this breakaway faction later became the United Democrats. A core section of the party continued to support Shevardnadze, however, and it was reinforced when the Tanadgoma (Support) parliamentary faction, which split from the Union of Citizens in the fall of 2001, joined the pro-government coalition.

In January 2003, a new pro-presidential majority was formed when 8 parliament factions and 15 independent deputies informally aligned to support the government. The new majority consisted of the Union of Citizens of Georgia, the Alliance for a New Georgia, Tanadgoma, the Socialists, Abkhazeti, New Abkhazia-Christian Democrats, the Majoritarians, and the Industrialists. The goals of the new majority were relatively limited—to ensure passage of the 2003 budget, to adopt the planned reform of the territorial-administrative system, and pass a new electoral law. The latter was necessary because new parliamentary elections were scheduled to take place on November 2, 2003.

As the time for the parliamentary elections approached, it became clear that the main opponents of the pro-government For a New Georgia bloc would be former allies of Shevardnadze. The most important of these was Mikheil Saakashvili, whose National Movement was contesting the elections, but nearly as important was the allied Burdjanadze-Democrats

bloc, a merger of Zurab Zhvania's United Democrats with Nino Burdjanadze's separate political organization. In all, nine blocks contested the November 2 elections. Five of the remaining six blocs ran in opposition to the government. The sixth, the Revival Party, threw its support to Shevardnadze at the last moment.

The trouble began shortly after the November 2 voting when early reports indicated that the pro-government political parties were gaining enough votes to rob Saakashvili and his allies of their hoped for electoral victory. From the beginning, Saakashvili made it clear that he and his supporters would accept nothing less than victory and he accused the government of rigging the vote. When the Central Election Commission announced the official outcome of the elections on November 19—Mr. Shevardnadze's party *For a New Georgia* came in first with 21.32% of the vote, the Revival Party came second with 18.84%—the opposition refused to accept the results.

Charging that the result had been manipulated, Mikheil Saakashvili immediately demanded that President Shevardnadze step down and that the election results be annulled. What came next was four days of demonstrations that came to be referred to as the "Rose Revolution." Shevardnadze resigned as president on November 23, and Nino Burdjanadze, speaker of the parliament, then became acting president until new presidential elections could be held. These elections were set for January 4, 2004. Separately, Georgia's highest court annulled the results of the November 2 parliamentary elections for the 150 proportional representation seats, and these elections were to take place on March 28.

Mikheil Saakashvili swept the January 4 presidential elections with 96% of the vote. Shortly after his inauguration on January 25, he had the legislature reestablish the office of prime minister. He then appointed Zurab Zhvania to this post. Zhvania served as prime minister until February 2005, when he was killed by carbon monoxide leaking from a faulty gas heater while staying at the apartment of a political colleague in Tbilisi.

Since Nino Burdjanadze already held the position of speaker of the parliament, Saakashvili and his allies controlled all of the top executive and legislative posts in the state. To guarantee that they would retain these posts, Saakashvili, Zhvania, and Burdjanadze drew up a common list for the March 28 parliamentary elections, which ran under the name of the National Movement-United Democrats. Four other blocs and 14 individual parties registered for the March 28 contest, but none of them represented the discredited Shevardnadze forces.

When the votes were tabulated, the National Movement-United Democrats

Georgia

Ex-President Mikheil Saakashvili

President Salome Zourabichvili,
the first female president of Georgia

took 67.2% of the vote. The only other party to surmount the 7% minimum required for parliamentary representation was the Industrialists-New Rightists alignment, an allied party. The only opposition in the new parliament was from among deputies who won in single member constituencies on November 2, not more than 13 deputies.

However, the results of the voting deepened a quarrel between Saakashvili and Aslan Abashidze, chairman of the Supreme Council of the Adjar Autonomous Republic and a former ally of President Shevardnadze. It had begun the previous November but escalated shortly after Saakashvili's inauguration as president. It got even worse when Saakashvili announced in March that he intended to bring the Adjar Autonomous Republic, together with the breakaway republics of Abkhazia and South Ossetia back under control of the central government.

Taking this as a challenge, Abashidze had his border police deny President Saakashvili entry at the border; Saakashvili could enter Adjaria, Abashidze said, but only if he came alone, unaccompanied by armed men. After a telephone conversation failed to resolve the differences, Saakashvili presented Abashidze with an ultimatum, in effect giving him 24 hours to accede to Saakashvili's demands. Abashidze's reply was to blow up the bridges connecting Adjaria with the rest of Georgia; thereupon Saakashvili declared a blockade of Adjaria. Moscow Mayor Yuri Luzhkov managed to defuse the quarrel temporarily after he flew to Adjaria for talks with Abashidze. This led to Saakashvili coming to Batumi, capital of Adjaria, on March 18.

When the parliamentary elections took place 10 days later, Abashidze's party, the Union for Democratic Revival (DAK), won only 6.2% of the vote. Abashidze charged that Saakashvili and his allies had manipulated the vote in order to keep the DAK out of the national parliament.

The quarrel went on for another month, with President Saakashvili insisting that Adjaria had to come back under central government control. Saakashvili secured a promise from Russia that its troops stationed in Adjaria would not support Abashidze. As the noose tightened, Abashidze finally realized that he could not win, and he fled into exile in Russia on May 6. Saakashvili immediately flew to Batumi, where he took charge of the autonomous republic. The next day, he dissolved the local parliament and established direct rule from Tbilisi. New parliamentary elections were then scheduled for June 15.

Saakashvili made it clear at this time that reestablishing central control over Adjaria was only the first step and that he was fully committed to bringing Abkhazia and South Ossetia back under central government control By stressing this position, Saakashvili established himself as a Georgian nationalist, a point he emphasized when he arranged for the body of former President Gamsakhurdia to be brought to Tbilisi from Chechnya for honorable burial.

Four years later, Abkhazia and South Ossetia continued to reject all efforts to bring them back under central government control. In fact, President Putin undermined any possibility of that occurring in the future when he announced Russia's withdrawal from the 1996 CIS sanctions treaty, which banned trade, economic, financial, transport, and other links with Abkhazia. Putin then followed up this action a month later when he issued a presidential decree instructing the Russian government to establish political, social, and economic relations with Abkhazia and South Ossetia.

Russia had always supported the two breakaway governments and 85% of the residents of Abkhazia and South Ossetia already carried Russian passports prior to these new steps by Russia. Still, the Russian actions had to be viewed by the Georgian government as being tantamount to a de facto annexation of the two territories.

This was the background to the events of August 2008 when Russia launched a war against Georgia after Georgian military forces entered South Ossetia. In retrospect, it appears that President Saakashvili fell into a trap which the Russians had carefully prepared beforehand. The provocations began in June with a series of skirmishes along the Georgian-South Ossetian border. They continued in July and included incursions of Russian military aircraft in the airspace over South Ossetia. Russia confirmed that it had sent the aircraft to "cool hotheads."

On August 7, Marat Kulakhmetov, the Russian peacekeeping commander announced that Russia had lost control over South Ossetian forces. Skirmishes between Georgian and South Ossetian forces occurred that afternoon. President Saakashvili then made the fateful decision to send military forces into South Ossetia to occupy the capital, Tskhinvali; the attack was launched just after midnight on the morning of August 8. Russia launched its own counterattack at about 10 a.m., with about 1,900 Russian troops entering Tskhinvali and Russian military aircraft attacking several villages located outside the conflict zone. Within two hours, Georgian forces were being forced back out of Tskhinvali.

On August 9, Russian jets attacked the Georgian port of Poti plus other strategic targets around Georgia. Russia also deployed its Black Sea fleet toward the port of Poti and toward Abkhazia. In Abkhazia itself, the Abkhazia militia opened a second front in the war, launching an attack against Georgian forces stationed in the Kodori gorge.

The fighting lasted five days and at the end of it Russian forces occupied the Georgian cities of Gori and Poti plus other smaller cities in northwestern Georgia. Russian forces also controlled the highway connecting eastern and western Georgia. On August 12, President Dmitry Medvedev agreed to a cease-fire plan presented by French President Nicolas Sarkozy which provided for the withdrawal of troops on both sides to their positions as of August 7. In fact, however, Russian troops do not begin to withdraw until August 20. Five days later, President Medvedev announced that Russia would recognize the independence of both Abkhazia and South Ossetia.

Georgia received the verbal support of many countries during and after the fighting, including countries such as the Baltic republics and Ukraine. The United States sent the US destroyer USS *McFaul*, which

Georgia

arrived at the port of Batumi on August 24; in addition, it promised $1 billion in humanitarian aid and to aid in reconstruction. In October, a donors' conference in Brussels resulted in pledges of more than $4.5 billion to rebuild Georgia. But these pledges were all a form of compensation; everyone recognized that Russia was now in control of the two former provinces of Georgia and had no intention of giving them up.

There have also been a number of developments dealing with domestic politics that have occurred during these years. In February 2005, Prime Minister Zhvania died by carbon monoxide poisoning. He was succeeded by Zurab Noghaideli, who had previously held the post of finance minister. Noghaideli, a political ally of Zhvania's faction in the ruling political party, held that position until November 2007. He stepped down as a result of deteriorating health. His successor was Lado Gurgenidze, formerly head of the Bank of Georgia. Gurgenidze served as prime minister from January to October 2008; he was then replaced by Grigol Mgaloblishvili, who had served for four years as Georgia's ambassador to Turkey. The change occurred as Saakashvili remade the cabinet following Georgia's defeat in its war with Russia. Gurgenidze resigned as prime minister in February 2009; the current prime minister is Mamuka Bakhtadze, who was appointed to that office on June 20, 2018.

In other domestic political developments, 10 of the opposition political parties formed a National Council in November 2007 and called for demonstrations against President Saakashvili and the Georgian government. They managed to mobilize between 40,000–50,000 sympathizers from across Georgia. Demonstrations began on November 2 and continued for the next several days. The ostensible spark that set off the demonstrations was the arrest of former Defense Minister Irakli Okruashvili shortly after he had leveled a series of damaging accusations against President Saakashvili. The National Council endorsed most of those charges, but it also demanded that government reverse a decision to postpone parliamentary elections, due in the spring of 2008, until later when they could occur at the same time as new presidential elections.

With the demonstrations continuing, President Saakashvili declared a state of emergency on November 7 after riot police used tear gas, rubber bullets, and water cannon to clear thousands of demonstrators from the streets of Tbilisi. In the process, the principal opposition television station news outlet, Imedi television, went off the air after it was taken over by a Special Forces unit. The order was issued after Badri Patarkatsishvili, owner of Imedi television, made a statement on his television station that he would "use all of his resources to overthrow the illegal state of Georgia."

After receiving harsh criticism both domestically and from abroad, President Saakashvili issued a decree setting new presidential elections on January 5, 2008. Saakashvili then resigned as president on November 25, the same day the parliament endorsed his decree on new presidential elections. Nino Burdjanadze, the parliamentary speaker, then became acting president.

Seven presidential candidates registered for the presidential elections. These included outgoing President Saakashvili; Levan Gachechiladze; the candidate of the nine-party opposition National Council; oligarch (and owner of Imedi television) Badri Patarkatsishvili; David Gamkrelidze (New Rightists); Shalva Natelashvili (Labor Party); Gia Maisashvili (Party of the Future); and Irina Sarishvili-Chanturia (Imedi). Several other candidates were rejected because they failed to turn in the required 50,000 signatures in their support. Imedi television was also permitted to begin broadcasting again on December 12.

Most Georgian voters apparently saw the election as, in effect, a vote of confidence in President Saakashvili. President Saakashvili won reelection with 53.47% of the vote; Gachechiladze, his closest challenger, received 25.69% of the vote. Badtri Patarkatsishvili came in third with 6.99% of the vote.

Although there were demonstrations demanding a second round of voting, the international community, including both the US government and the European Commission, endorsed the outcome of the vote.

New parliamentary elections took place on May 21, 2008. Under the terms of new constitutional changes made in March, the total membership of parliament was reduced from 235 to 150 members. Half of the 150 delegates were elected under the proportional system, with seats being distributed to those parties which received a minimum of 7% of the total vote; the remaining 75 delegates were elected under the Majoritarian system.

Twelve political parties and blocs contested the election. President Saakashvili's United National Movement came in first with 59.37% of the popular vote. The United Opposition bloc placed second with 17.59% of the vote. Two other parties crossed the 5% hurtle for representation, the Christian Democratic Movement, which got 8.48% of the vote, and the Labor Party, which pulled 7.53%. Although the opposition complained of irregularities in both the campaign and the voting, the United National Movement's wide margin of victory guaranteed that President Saakashvili would

Ex-Prime Minister Bidzina Ivanishvili. Although no longer prime minister, Ivanishvili remains head of the Georgian Dream coalition

continue to dominate the country's politics for the next several years.

In general, the international view of the election results was positive. Slovenia, the then-current holder of the European Union Presidency, described the elections as "encouraging." US Department of State spokesman Tom Casey said at a news briefing that "We think these elections are an improvement over the January presidential vote. And we look forward to working with the new government once formed."

Georgia's defeat in its war with Russia in August 2008 changed that equation once again, however. The first reaction of most Georgians was to rally around their political leadership, but that feeling soon evaporated. The worldwide economic crisis then began affecting Georgia by the fall of 2008. By December 2008, political opponents were blaming him for the loss of South Ossetia and Abkhazia. Moreover, one of his former allies, Nino Burdjanadze, a former speaker of the Georgian parliament, broke with Saakashvili after the August war with Russia, which she characterized as "a huge mistake." Forming her own opposition political party, the Democratic Movement-United Georgia, she became one of the more strident voices in the opposition. In April 2009, the opposition political parties began organizing daily demonstrations in Tbilisi which called on Saakashvili to resign and permit new presidential elections. Saakashvili ordered law enforcement personnel to avoid confrontations but took no further actions. In June, the opposition took control of Tbilisi's main railroad station and again Saakashvili took no action. Then, on July 20, Saakashvili proposed new democratic reforms to include new limits on the president's power and steps to strengthen the courts. Although rejected by the opposition, the demonstrations diminished after that time.

It also helped that Vice President Joe Biden arrived in Tbilisi three days later for an official visit. Biden, who had visited

Georgia one year earlier shortly after the Russian invasion, repeated the message he had delivered at that time—"I will never, never abandon you." Biden also brought the message that the United States intended to resume a combat training mission in Georgia to bring Georgian troops up to the level of NATO forces. The United States also indicated that it would consider replacing military equipment destroyed in the Russian–Georgian war. In return, Saakashvili promised to send a battalion—about 750 troops—to Afghanistan. Although the message Biden brought was for the country, not the president, the visit brought dividends to Saakashvili as well.

In March 2010, Nino Burdjanadze, leader of Georgia's opposition Democratic Movement-United Georgia Party, traveled to Moscow at the invitation of the Russian government. Her explanation for the visit was that

I took a very correct step by deciding to go to Moscow, because I consider it important, in principle, to search for an outlet to get out of the dead-end situation in which Russian-Georgian relations are now.

Other opposition political leaders also visited Moscow after the August 2008 Russian–Georgian war. Zurab Noghaideli, a former prime minister, has traveled to Russia on a number of occasions, his latest visit in May 2010. Two other opposition leaders, Koba Davitashvili and Kakha Kukava, visited Moscow in April 2010. All of them have also called for Saakashvili's resignation as president. In return, Saakashvili's supporters have branded them as "collaborators." The official Georgian government characterization was that the visits were "unpatriotic."

In 2010, Nino Burdjanadze sponsored a new umbrella opposition organization called the People's Representative Assembly. In May 2011, the People's Representative Assembly sponsored coordinated protest demonstrations demanding the resignation of the Saakashvili government; permission was given for the demonstrations to take place from May 21 to midnight on May 25, the day before the May 26 anniversary of the 1918 declaration of Georgia's independence. The protesters refused to disperse at midnight on May 25, however; as Nino Burdjanadze had made clear in an earlier speech, they stayed to prevent a government-sponsored military parade scheduled on May 26. Armed with staves, they remained in Liberty Square daring the government to act.

And so it did. Shortly after midnight, 2,000 heavily armed special forces and riot police attacked the protesters with water cannon, tear gas, and rubber bullets. Two individuals were killed—one

protester and one policeman—reportedly by a car driven away at high speed by protesters. The bodies of two more men with their hands tied behind their backs were found on May 27. Possibly beaten before death, they appeared to have died by electrocution.

While there was obviously blame on both sides, Burdjanadze's avocations of violence as a way to overthrow the Saakashvili government more or less discredited her. Nevertheless, the government came under criticism as well. Georgia's human rights ombudsman, George Tugushi, probably summed it up best. Although there were "legal grounds" for taking action against the protesters,

the use of disproportionate force was especially obvious, when in some cases the law enforcement officers were physically assaulting and in others detaining those protesters who were not offering any resistance to the police.

With President Saakashvili's term of office due to end in October 2013, the growing political opposition began preparing for new elections to the People's Representative Assembly, scheduled to take place in October 2012. In the fall of 2010, eight parties belonging to the moderate opposition formed a loose tactical alliance for political reform. What changed the equation, however, was the emergence of Bidzina Ivanishvili as a player in Georgian politics. Ivanishvili, who is worth an estimated $6.4 billion which he made in Russia during the 1990s, had transferred some of his assets to Georgia after Putin came to power and began moving against the oligarchs. At first, Ivanishvili was totally interested in business, setting up a bank, then the TV-9 television channel. To increase his total number of listeners, Ivanishvili began distributing thousands of free satellite antennas to Georgian citizens. At one time, he was viewed as a possible ally of President Saakashvili, but this changed when his television channel became a vocal critic of the president. As the election approached, Ivanishvili used his money and his influence to bring together six opposition political parties in a new coalition called Georgian Dream; he then used his great wealth to make the new coalition politically competitive.

One week before the October 1 parliamentary elections, a scandal erupted; a government insider produced a video showing systemic abuse and torture in the nation's prisons which was then broadcast on national television. President Saakashvili moved quickly to stem the damage from the prison crisis, appointing George Tugushi, the country's human rights ombudsman, in charge of

the investigation. It was not enough. On October 1, the Georgian Dream bloc won 85 seats in the 150-member People's Representative Assembly. The remaining seats went to Saakashvili's United National Movement. Bidzina Ivanishvili was formally confirmed as prime minister on October 25.

Since President Saakashvili's term of office did not come to an end until October 2013, this began Georgia's experimentation with political co-habitation. It has not been smooth. Immediately after his electoral victory, Ivanishvili called for the resignation of President Saakashvili, though he backed off after receiving harsh criticism from abroad.

But within weeks of taking office, the new government began arresting officials of the former government, charging them with various criminal offenses. The charges ranged from torture and illegal detention to abuse of office. Among those arrested were the former Defense and Interior Minister, Bacho Akhalaia and more than a dozen Ministry of Interior officials, including the head of the Department of Constitutional Security. Justifying the arrests, Ivanishvili said that he would make it a priority to investigate officials leaving the government of President Saakashvili.

Although the arrests brought some criticism from abroad, including from the US government, the arrests continued. On November 29, Archil Kbilashvili, Georgia's new prosecutor announced that his office had received more than 3,000 criminal complaints against former officials over the preceding month and he planned to triple the number of investigators in the division handling misuse of authority.

This was followed, on December 19, by the arrest of former Energy Minister Alexandre Khetagui, former Justice Minister Nika Gvaramia, and four other people—all charged in connection with an alleged $1 million bribe to avert a tax inspection that could have uncovered tax evasion by a company partly owned by the Russian energy giant RAO EES. Three days later, former Prime Minister Nika Gilauri, former Finance Minister Dmitry Gvindadze, and former Economy and Sustainable Development Minister Vera Kobalia were questioned by officials of the Ministry of Interior about alleged attempts by unspecified government agencies to bankrupt Ivanishvili's Cartu Bank. This was followed by a move in parliament to change the composition of the High Council of Justice, the body that appoints, dismisses, and disciplines judges.

Next, the Ivanishvili government stripped President Saakashvili of his private plane and reduced his household budget. The government also moved to place Saakashvili's security detail under

Georgia

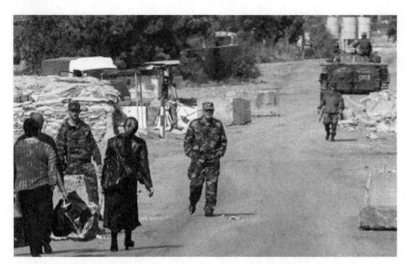

A Russian checkpoint at the South Ossetia–Georgia border

the control of the government rather than the president's office. Then, in February 2013, Prime Minister Ivanishvili's coalition canceled the president's annual address to the nation, traditionally given in the parliament chamber. Saakashvili eventually gave his report to the nation from his own office.

With new presidential elections set to occur on October 27, Prime Minister Ivanishvili announced that he himself would not stand for that office. Instead, he designated Giorgi Margvelashvili, a former education minister, as the candidate of the ruling Georgian Dream coalition. Margvelashvili's most striking quality was a lack of political experience or ambition—probably the reason Ivanishvili chose him over more experienced and politically ambitious members of the Georgian Dream coalition. Ivanishvili then announced that he would step down as prime minister after the presidential election, though the reason he gave was that he intended to devote himself to strengthen civil society. In fact, of course, he continues to dominate the government from outside through his control of the Georgian Dream coalition. Having placed his own man in the presidency, he made a point of naming his own successor as prime minister, an appointment that normally would have fallen to the new president.

Irakli Garibashvili, who was named prime minister after President Margvelashvili's inauguration on November 17, had served in the Ivanishvili administration as interior minister. A longtime protégé of Ivanishvili, he was at 31 years of age, the youngest member of the cabinet. As interior minister, it had been his task to carry out Ivanishvili's wish to destroy the legacy of the Saakashvili years and his party machine, and he had done this through a series of prosecutions of former members of the Saakashvili

government. In July 2014, the anti-corruption campaign reached its apex when cases were brought against two very high profile targets. Former Tbilisi mayor, Giorgi Ugulava, was charged with a variety of corruption offenses (and later found guilty of misspending public funds), and ex-President Saakashvili was charged with exceeding official powers during the 2007 demonstrations. Saakashvili has been out of country and thus has not formally faced trial. A major twist in this saga occurred after Saakashvili was appointed mayor of the Ukrainian region of Odessa in May 2015, prompting Margvelashvili to revoke the former president's Georgian citizenship on the grounds that the state's constitution bars dual citizenship. While officials within the Georgian Dream (GD) coalition have framed their anti-corruption campaign against former government officials as serving the public interest, many accused the coalition of engaging in a politically motivated witch-hunt and undermining state institutions.

Since Ugulava and Saakashvili were charged, public enthusiasm for the continued prosecution of UNM officials has waned and new cases have been rare. With the struggle against the UNM largely won, the loose coalition that comprised GD began to splinter. The earliest sign of this splintering occurred in November 2014, when the pro-western Free Democrats (FD) left the coalition. On March 31, 2016, the Republican Party announced that they would not remain in the coalition after scheduled elections in the fall. Perhaps the most notable signs of the divisions within the GD have been the open public showdowns between President Margvelashvili and the parliament over a number of issues, including banking laws and the length of the official election campaign season. Even though he was elected with the support of Ivanishvili, President Margvelashvili has

proven to be politically independent, and through his open feuds with the prime minister has empowered the office of the presidency. Due to the struggles in maintaining the coalition, in December 2015, Gharibashvili surprisingly announced that he was stepping down as prime minister. It fell to his successor as prime minister, Giorgi Kvirikashvili, and Ivanishvili working behind the scenes, to prepare the party for elections on October 8, 2016.

Kvirikashvili's capacity to lead the party was affirmed by the results of the election. The Georgian Dream party won a majority of seats in the parliament (115 out of 150), granting it the capability to advance its agenda relatively unhindered by opposition objections. Despite protestations of fraud by the UNM, the OSCE report of the election stated that overall the elections "were competitive, well-administered, and fundamental freedoms were generally respected." The OSCE election report did also note, however, that "[t]he calm and open campaign atmosphere was, however, impacted by allegations of unlawful campaigning and some incidents of violence. . . . Voting proceeded in an orderly manner, but counting was assessed more negatively due to procedural problems and increased tensions."

Continuing "constitutional reform" has been the major task of the newly elected parliament. Soon after convening, the parliament established a constitutional commission to explore additional reforms. On April 22, 2017, the commission proposed several significant changes that to further empower the parliament at the expense of the presidency. Specifically, the amendments will change the electoral system of Georgia from a majoritarian to a strictly proportional system, with a 5% threshold. They also eliminate the direct popular election of the president. Under the new rules, an Electoral College comprised of parliamentary and local representatives will indirectly select the president. Over the staunch objections of opposition parties, these amendments were approved by the Georgian Dream dominated parliament in September 2017. This instigated a moment of political theater as President Margvelashili vetoed the amendments on October 9 as a "one-party" document. This veto was not at all unexpected. The president had used his annual address to the nation on April 7, 2017, to criticize the efforts of Georgian Dream to pass sweeping change without bringing opposition party members on board: "Unfortunately, the ruling party refused to open up and engage in a dialogue."

The veto only served to delay the inevitable. With their dominant position in parliament, the Georgian Dream party was able to easily override the veto, and the amendments were reluctantly signed into law at the end of October by the president. His critique of the amendment process was echoed by the Venice Commission which observed that more efforts should have been made to generate consensus among stakeholders.

In general, external observers have viewed the amendments positively and necessary to transition the system to a parliamentary government. Some, including President Margvelashvili, have questioned, however, why they are not scheduled to take effect until 2024. The delay in implementation has given ammunition to those suspect that the reforms may be yet another administrative resource that the Georgian Dream is utilizing to further consolidate their hold on power.

The Georgian Dream secured a third term in government after winning 48% of the popular vote in the parliamentary elections of October 31, 2020. As a result, the party gained 50% of the seats in the 150-seat assembly, which gives it sufficient veto power to pass most laws, but not enough to amend the constitution. A coalition led by UNM came in second, winning less than 27% of the vote. All the opposition parties that entered the parliament, refused to accept the results alleging that Georgian Dream used bribery, intimidation, and falsification to steal the elections. For their part, international election observers considered the elections to be free and competitive, but also noted of certain irregularities, including the use of administrative resources by the incumbent. However, they did not go so far as the opposition parites to claim that these misconducts affected the final results in favor of the Georgian Dream. In a televised

**Former Prime Minister
Giorgi Kvirikashvili**

address from Ukraine, Saakashvili called on opposition parties, who by then took to the streets to protest the electoral results, to continue defending their votes. This was not the last time Saakashvili made headlines in Georgia, however. In an attempt to bring down his archnemesis Bidzina Ivanishvili and his Georgian Dream party, Saakashvili smuggled himself to Georgia and through his Facebook posts from Batumi tried to galvanize voters against the incumbent party in local elections which took place on October 2, 2021. After initially denying his presence on the Georgian territory, authorities eventually arrested him for illegal border crossing and sent him to prison on charges of abuse of power, the charges that Saakashvili denies and calls politically motivated.

Foreign Policy

Russia. Under Gamsakhurdia, Georgia refused to join the Commonwealth of Independent States and attempted to sever all ties with the other former Soviet republics. Shevardnadze began working for a better working relationship with Russia from the moment he returned to power in Georgia. A new treaty signed in February 1994 gave Georgia membership in the Commonwealth of Independent States and tied her to Russia militarily.

Georgia's continued struggles with its breakaway province of Abkhazia have also played an important role in its relations with Russia. Prior to 1994, Russia was inclined to support Abkhazia's attempts to break away. When Georgia agreed to join the CIS and to allow Russia to establish military bases within the country, however, Russia's position changed and, in early 1996, Russia even agreed, at the urging of the Georgian government, to impose economic sanctions on Abkhazia.

The existence of four Russian military bases in the country also had a negative effect on Georgia's relations with Russia. After negotiations, Russia agreed to close two of the bases. In the end, one of the bases was closed while the other, the Gudauta base in Abkhazia, was turned into a recreation facility for the Russian peacekeeping force deployed under CIS aegis in the Abkhaz conflict zone.

In May 2005, the foreign ministers of the Georgian and Russian governments reached agreement on a timetable for the closure of Russia's two remaining bases at Akhalkalaki and Batumi. Russia removed the last of its troops from these bases in 2008.

Another factor negatively affecting Georgian–Russian relations was the conflict in neighboring Chechnya. Russia was particularly disturbed that Georgia had permitted as many as 8,000 Chechen

refugees and perhaps 1,500 Chechen rebels to find refuge in the area of the Pankisi Gorge, an area of Georgia just south of the Chechen border where the local population speaks a language related to Chechen and is mainly Muslim. Georgia refused to extradite any Chechens or to allow Russia to send troops across the border into the area. In retaliation, Russia instituted a visa requirement for Georgian citizens in December 2000; Georgia is the only CIS country whose citizens need a Russian visa to enter the country. Moreover, Russia exempted residents of Abkhazia and South Ossetia—the two areas that rejected the authority of the Georgian government—from this visa requirement.

The Pankisi Gorge was only a minor irritant in Russian-Georgian relations prior to the terror attacks launched against the United States on September 11, 2001. As the United States began to organize its war against terrorism, however, Russia—concerned about the longtime presence of foreign radical Muslim fighters involved in the fighting in Chechnya—was among the first nations to sign on. As Russia and the United States began sharing intelligence on terrorism and, in particular, Osama bin of information that particularly stood out was the large number of Chechens who had gone to Afghanistan for training and then became part of the al-Qaeda organization. By January 2002, both the Russians and Americans had information indicating that some of these radical fighters were present in the Pankisi Gorge.

Russia first suggested a combined Russian-Georgian force to clear the area of the Pankisi Gorge of all such individuals; Georgia demurred, arguing that any military operation in the Pankisi Gorge would endanger civilians and risk bringing Russia's war in Chechnya to Georgia.

Georgia's relations with Russia went into a downward spiral in the latter part of 2005. In December 2005, Russia's natural gas monopoly Gazprom increased the price it charged Georgia to $110 per 1,000 cubic meters. The increase represented Gazprom's movement toward market pricing for natural gas and the price increase applied to Armenia, Moldova, and Ukraine as well; however, the news was not well received in Georgia—perhaps because the price increase did not apply in Abkhazia and South Ossetia, the two breakaway regions of Georgia.

Next, on January 23, 2006, two explosions in Northern Ossetia in southern Russia damaged both strands of the gas pipeline that supplied gas to Georgia, thereby cutting off gas supplies to Georgia (and Armenia) for several days. A third explosion damaged the main power line supplying electricity from Russia to Georgia. Although the breakages were

Georgia

almost certainly the result of sabotage, many Georgians were ready to believe that the Russian government arranged the explosions in order to put economic pressure on Georgia.

The third event came at the end of January when President Putin, citing a need for "universal principles," seemed to endorse independence for the Georgian breakaway provinces of Abkhazia and South Ossetia. Putin's concern was actually with a United Nations discussion with regard to the future of Kosovo, but the argument he used was that "if people believe that Kosovo can be granted full independence, why then should we deny it to Abkhazia and South Ossetia?" He went on to add that Russia would not immediately recognize Abkhazia and South Ossetia as independent states, "but such a precedent does exist." Needless to say, the Georgian government was not pleased.

The next development came on March 27, when the Russian government banned the importation of Georgian wines—claiming that the Georgian government was not maintaining adequate sanitary standards. A similar ban was applied to Moldovan wines at the same time. In April, Russia's State Health Directorate offered to lift its ban if Georgia would agree to a system of joint control over wine production in Georgia. Tbilisi considered the ban to be a form of political intimidation, however, and rejected any system of joint control. Russia then banned the importation of Georgian mineral water in May.

Two months later, with feelings running high, the Georgian parliament passed a resolution demanding the removal of all Russian peacekeeping troops from Abkhazia and South Ossetia. The Russian foreign ministry responded by calling the resolution "a provocative step directed at fueling tension, undermining the existing format for negotiations, and demolishing the legal foundations for resolving the Georgian-Abkhaz and Georgian–Ossetian conflicts peacefully."

Continuing the downward spiral, the Georgian government arrested four Russian military officers on spying charges and police surrounded a Russian military headquarters in Tbilisi demanding that a fifth Russian officer be handed over to local authorities. Russia then recalled its ambassador from Georgia. President Putin, in his first comments on the crisis, accused Georgia of "state terrorism with hostage taking." At this point, The Russian government then severed all transportation links with Georgia, including commercial flights and train service, and cut all mail delivery. At this point, President Saakashvili turned over the four Russian military officers to Karel De Gucht, the foreign minister of Belgium, who was also chairman of the OSCE. De Gucht delivered the four officers to a Russian Emergencies Ministry plane, waiting at Tbilisi airport.

But Russia continued its economic blockade even after the four Russian officers were returned and, domestically, began moving against Georgians living in Russia. Approximately 500 Georgians were deported during the first week of October and many Georgian shops, restaurants, and businesses were closed because of alleged tax violations. Gazprom also announced that future natural gas sales to Georgia would cost $230 per 1,000 cubic meters—though it indicated that it might offer a lower price if Georgia would sell Gazprom a stake in its energy sector.

In retaliation, the Georgian government stated that it would oppose further meetings dealing with Russian accession to the WTO. Two months later, Georgia reversed its position. Foreign Minister Bezhuashvili announced on December 26, 2006, that "Georgia is interested in Russia's admission to the WTO, as we need to have a reliable and civilized trade partner." He did point out, however, that it is "illogical that Georgia, a full-fledged member of WTO, is blockaded by a country that is a candidate for admission in this organization." Russia sent its ambassador back to Georgia in January 2007 and the Russian government subsequently resumed issuing visas to some categories of Georgian citizens.

Russia's support for the separatist Abkhazian and South Ossetian Governments had always been a low level irritation between the two governments, but this changed in March 2008 when President Putin announced that Russia would no longer adhere to the 1996 CIS sanctions agreement that prohibited other governments from establishing political or economic relations with Abkhazia and South Ossetia; he then issued a decree ordering the Russian government to establish political and economic relations with Abkhazia and South Ossetia. Russia had begun its slow annexation of the two territories.

Four months later, President Saakashvili responded to provocations along the South Ossetian–Georgian border by sending Georgian troops into Tskhinvali, the South Ossetian capital. Hours later, the Russians began their invasion of Georgia. Within five days, Russian troops occupied the northern half of Georgia, including the two major cities of Gori and Poti. Russia then agreed to a French proposal for a cease-fire. Russian troops were eventually pulled out of Georgian territory but remained in Abkhazia and South Ossetia, which Russia now recognized as "independent" states. In addition, President Medvedev publicly stated that the Russian government would have nothing to do with Georgia as long as Saakashvili remained president.

A change—but not a breakthrough—came on February 28, 2012, when President Saakashvili, speaking before the Georgian parliament, proposed visa-free travel for Russians. Three days later, the Russian Foreign Ministry posted a statement on its website hinting at a willingness to restore diplomatic relations with Georgia. According to the statement, Russia is interested in "strengthening ties between the peoples of Russia and Georgia" and is prepared to introduce a reciprocal visa-free regime for Georgians. The next day, President rejected the terms of the Russian offer; the prerequisite for a restoration of diplomatic relations would be Russia's recognition of Abkhazia and South Ossetia as part of Georgia.

So, no deal was struck. On the other hand, Russia and Georgia did reach a deal in December 2011 on Abkhazia and South Ossetia. Under the agreement, Russia agreed to allow an independent company to audit trade in Abkhazia and South Ossetia. This removed a Georgian veto on Russian membership in the World Trade Organization.

On October 1, 2012, Georgia obtained a new government when Bidzina Ivanishvili's Georgian Dream bloc won control of parliament. Ivanishvili, a billionaire businessman who made his money in the 1990s during Russia's period of privatization, ran on a platform of improving relations with Russia. Russia has since indicated that it was ready to discuss restoring air connections between the two countries. Yet the new Georgian government also has said that it hopes the Russian government can be persuaded to recognize Georgia's sovereignty over Abkhazia and South Ossetia. But the only concession Ivanishvili got from the Russian government was a lifting of the ban on Georgian wines and bottled water.

During the latter half of 2014 and the first half of 2015, relations between Georgia and Russia became more strained as Russia consolidated its control over South Ossetia and Abkhazia. Russia had recognized the independence of both regions after the brief 2008 war with Georgia and has kept thousands of its troops in both regions. The one positive development in this period was that in October the Russian state-controlled airline Aeroflot resumed flights between Moscow and Tbilisi for the first time since the five-day war. In February 2015, Russia enacted a "strategic partnership" with the "Republic of Abkhazia" which called for closer ties in several spheres, in particular the integration of defense and security forces. A joint Russian-Abkhaz force would patrol Abkhazia's borders, and an attack on either Russia or Abkhazia would be considered an attack on the other. Two months later, Russian President Putin and the de facto leader of South Ossetia, Leonid Tibilov, signed an "alliance and integration treaty," which assigned Russia responsibility for South Ossetia's defense and security. The pact stated that Russia would guard the borders of South Ossetia. The Georgian Foreign Ministry declared that the agreement amounted to the "actual annexation" of the region. Many Georgians fear that Russia might annex either or both regions as it did Crimea in March 2014. Georgia continues to insist that Abkhazia and South Ossetia are parts of Georgia. On May 13, 2022, the ex-president of South Ossetia, Anatoly Bibilov decreed to hold a referendum on joining Russia. However, his successor Alan Gagloev, who was elected as president of the self-proclaimed republic on May 8, scrapped the plan for the referendum that was scheduled take place on July 17, 2002. Most likely the order to cancel the referendum came down from Moscow, which has few complaints about Tbilisi, especially after the latter adopted a largely passive stance in the war between Ukraine and Russia. The Georgian government made it clear that it would not join Western countries in imposing financial and economic sanctions on Russia. The reasons for Tbilisi to adopt what it calls a "pragmatic policy" may have to do with political and economic considerations. Standing with Ukraine could have provoked Russia to annex the breakaway regions of Abkhazia and South Ossetia, and to stop trade relations with Georgia in such vital sectors as food, energy, wine, and metallurgy.

Another potential source of conflict between Georgia and Russia has to do with the Southern Gas Corridor. The proposed pipeline would deliver gas from Azerbaijan through Georgia and Turkey to south-central Europe. Russia's Gazprom would stand to lose a substantial part of its European market, and Georgia would realize a profit from transit fees once the new pipeline is completed. Construction on the pipeline commenced in March 2015. The first phase of the project was officially inaugurated on May 29, 2018.

United States. Since Gamsakhurdia began to act in an authoritarian manner domestically soon after he took power, the United States withheld diplomatic recognition, and it was only after Shevardnadze was installed as chairman of the State Council that the United States formally recognized Georgia. An embassy was opened in April 1992 and Secretary of State Baker paid an official visit to Tbilisi in May. Relations have been good ever since.

Shevardnadze made an official visit to the United States in October 2001, where he held discussions on the continuing conflict in Chechnya and Georgia's need for assistance in guarding its borders. The United States made only a general offer of military assistance at the time but, after intelligence indicated the possible presence of al-Qaeda fighters in the Pankisi Gorge, the United States offered to train four battalions of Georgian troops—approximately 1,200 men—plus provide light weapons, vehicles, and communications equipment—in all a military assistance program with a cost of $64 million. The package also included deploying 200 special operations forces to Georgia to provide the training for the four Georgian battalions. These US forces, the first of whom arrived in Georgia in May 2002, conducted four stages of antiterrorist training, each of which took approximately six months. In March 2005, the program was essentially renewed when the United States agreed to fund a further two-year training program for the Georgian military forces at a cost of approximately $65 million.

Although this was the first time that US military forces had been stationed in Georgia, it was actually only an intensification of a military relationship going back several years. Georgia had received a significant amount of military equipment, training, and financial aid from the United States over the preceding several years, and many members of Georgia's senior officer corps had received training in the United States. The United States had also provided indirect military assistance by encouraging Turkey to aid the Georgian military and to carry out military construction projects such as the rebuilding of Georgian airfields and military facilities.

This was not only related to the United States' war against terrorism. In March 2001, David Tevzadze, the Georgian defense minister, and Irakli Menagharishvili, the foreign minister, paid official visits to Washington, DC. The defense minister's talks with Defense Secretary Donald Rumsfeld focused on an expansion of bilateral military cooperation; the foreign minister, who met with Secretary of State Colin Powell, received American assurances of support in the face of Russian pressure plus a statement of the US government's commitment to the Baku-Ceyhan export pipeline.

In December 2002, Georgia and the United States signed a defense cooperation agreement which among other things allowed American military personnel to enter the country without a visa and to carry personal weapons. Implementation of the agreement was delayed by opposition in parliament, however; it then became an issue between Georgia and Russia when Russian officials attacked the agreement, charging that it "seriously upsets the balance of forces in the region and poses a threat to international security."

US–Georgian relations continued to expand in spite of Russian objections, however. Georgia approved the opening of an FBI office in the country in February 2003. In April, Georgia offered to participate in the reconstruction of Iraq. Georgia was an early supporter of the United States over Iraq, offering to provide construction materials and qualified specialists. In 2005, Georgia increased the number of troops it had in Iraq to 850, up from 156 previously.

President Bush made an official visit to Georgia in May 2005 where he hailed the Rose Revolution as a model for democracy movements everywhere. Bush's visit was a big boost for President Saakashvili, but it irritated the Russian government enough that Russian Foreign Minister Sergey Lavrov wrote a letter of complaint to Secretary of State Condoleezza Rice about it.

President Saakashvili paid an official visit to the United States in July 2006, where he received a warm welcome from President George W. Bush. In September 2006, a dozen US military officers and officials visited Tbilisi to discuss an expansion of US–Georgian military cooperation in 2007. The group also reviewed the Georgian NATO Individual Partnership Action Plan.

President Saakashvili visited the United States again in March 2008 where he met at the White House with President Bush. President Bush praised Saakashvili's aspirations to join NATO, and the NATO summit in April committed itself to "direct obligations" that Georgia would later become a full NATO member. President Saakashvili declared himself satisfied with this outcome.

Much has changed since the victory of the Georgian Dream coalition in October 2012, but the new government has repeatedly reaffirmed its unswerving commitment to the pro-Western, pro-NATO policy espoused by the previous government.

International Organizations. Georgia has been a member of the Council of Europe since January 1999, the first of the Caucasus republics to be so honored. Georgia became a full member of the World Trade Organization in June 2000. Georgia would also like to become a member of NATO. In May 2003, a NATO delegation of four military delegates arrived in Tbilisi to conduct an inspection of Georgian military facilities and to review the state of Georgia's military reforms. The North Atlantic Council formally endorsed the Georgia Membership Action Plan in October 2004. However, Sergey Lavrov, the Russian foreign minister, gave an interview in February 2007 in which he said that "we have warned Georgia, and those . . . who

Georgia

Picking citrus fruit   Courtesy of NOVOSTI

actively encourage Georgia to join NATO, that we shall not permit this."

The Georgian Dream coalition appears to be somewhat divided on how to proceed insofar as a bid for future NATO membership is concerned. In January 2014, Prime Minister Garibashvili said that Georgia's foreign policy priorities remained unchanged, but he saw no urgency in pressing for a Membership Action Plan (MAP) from NATO. Here he differed from statements made by Georgian parliament speaker David Usupashvili, who publicly made the argument that same month that Georgia should be granted a MAP at the September 2014 NATO summit in Wales.

On October 1, 2014, Georgian Prime Minister Irakli Garibashvili reiterated his nation's desire to join NATO and the European Union (EU). In June 2014, Georgia signed an Association Agreement with the EU, although the EU has not indicated a willingness to admit Georgia in the foreseeable future. Georgia's relationship with NATO is an even more delicate matter, because Georgia's eagerness to join the alliance was one cause of the 2008 war with Russia. Georgia's reliability as a future member has been demonstrated by the fact that there are close to 900 Georgian troops serving with NATO in Afghanistan. As Radio Free Europe/ Radio Liberty recently noted, on a per capita basis, Georgia's contingent is by far

the largest. To date, the country has lost 30 troops killed in the conflict. NATO continues to court Georgia as a future member, but the courtship has been slow and cautious. In January 2015, NATO Deputy Secretary-General Alexander Vershbow visited Georgia to look for a place to establish a joint Georgia–NATO training center, which could be in operation by the end of the year. Yet, NATO does not speak with one voice on the question of Georgia joining the alliance. Many in Georgia were surprised when in March 2015 French President Francois Hollande said that "France's position for the moment is to refuse any new membership."

Nature of the Regime

Georgia adopted a new constitution in 1995, which established a presidential system of government. It also created a 250-seat unicameral legislature, called the Umaghiesi Sabcho (Supreme Council). This was a purely presidential system but, in February 2004, the office of prime minister was created, with some of the powers of the president transferred to the new office of prime minister. In another change, the legislature was reduced to 150 members in 2008 and proportional representation was instituted for one-half of the seats, which were to be filled on the basis of a proportional vote with parties that received a minimum of 7% of the total electoral vote receiving seats. The remaining 75 seats continued to be filled on a first-past-the-post basis in individual constituencies.

In the summer of 2010, after several months of demonstrations and political unrest, a state commission drafted several amendments to Georgia's constitution whose purpose was to transform Georgia from a presidential to a parliamentary system. Essentially, these amendments reduced the powers of the president and transferred most of those powers to the office of prime minister. Although passed by the legislature in 2012, it was stipulated that they would go into effect in October 2013, at the time of the next presidential elections.

New parliamentary elections which took place in October 2012 were won by the Georgian Dream coalition and Bidzina Ivanishvili was named the new prime minister. This began a period of co-habitation because Mikheil Saakashvili's term of office ran until the inauguration of a new president in November 2013. The co-habitation did not go well, since the new prime minister did everything in his power to discredit the president and undo his policies. Even so, President Saakashvili managed to serve out his full term.

New presidential elections, which took place on October 17, 2013, were won by the Georgian Dream candidate, Giorgi Margvelashvili, with 62% of the vote.

Following the election, Bidzina resigned as prime minister, naming his protégé, 31-year-old Irakli Garibashvili, as his successor. Garibashvili was confirmed as prime minister in November 2013, just days after the inauguration of President Margvelashvili. Despite the support of the Georgian Dream coalition, Margvelashvili proved to be a bit of a maverick and broke publicly with the coalition on issues such as banking oversight and the start of the 2016 election season. These public squabbles and Margvelashvili's proven willingness to veto legislation have empowered the office of the presidency. It also likely contributed to Garibashvili's surprise announcement to resign as prime minister in late 2015. Garibashvili's resignation led to the elevation of the vice prime minister, Giorgi Kvirikashvili, to the post of prime minister on December 30, 2015.

In October 2016, a new parliament was elected. The Georgian Dream party won 115 out of 150 seats, leaving the UNM with only 27 seats. Two other parties, the Alliance of Patriots of Georgia (6), and Industry Will Save Georgia (1) also received seats alongside a single Independent. In October 2017, constitutional amendments were signed which will firmly establish Georgia as a proportionally elected parliamentary system as of 2024. Under the changes to the constitution, the powers of the president are greatly reduced, and the head of state will be indirectly elected.

Culture

Georgia is a land of ancient culture, a surprising amount of which has survived, considering that it was for centuries a battleground between the Persian and Byzantine Empires and, later, the Ottoman Empire. Georgian architecture is particularly interesting because of the role it played in the development of the Byzantine style of architecture.

Georgia has also had a written language since the 5th century A.D., and there are a number of great works which have survived. The earliest of these is an epic masterpiece by the poet Shota Rustaveli, called *The Knight in the Tiger's Skin*. A cultural renaissance at the end of the 19th century produced a number of poets, including Ilia Chavchavadze, Akaki Tsereteli, Vazha Pshavela, novelists such as Alexander Qazbegi, and writers like Mikhail Javakhishvili, Paolo Iashvili, Titsian Tabidze, Giorgi Leonidze, and Irakli Abashidze.

Most of these artists were later executed by Stalin when he decided in the 1930s to stamp out Georgian nationalism in his native state. Georgia has also produced important painters (Niko Pirosmanashvili, Irikli Toidze) and composers (Zakaria

Paliashvili, Meliton Balanchivadze). Vakhtang Chabukiani was the founder of the Georgian national ballet. There is also a vibrant Georgian theater and film industry. *Resurrection*, a recent surrealistic film about a Stalin-like dictator, was one specifically Georgian contribution to glasnost.

Nor should one forget Zviad Gamsakhurdia, the first anti-communist leader of the country, elected in 1990 and forced out as president at the beginning of 1992. Gamsakhurdia, the son of Georgia's best-known modern novelist, was a leading Georgian author in his own right, as well as a translator. Among the authors he translated are Shakespeare and Baudelaire. Tengiz Sigua, the former prime minister, was a professor before he entered politics, while Tengiz Ketovani is a sculptor.

Georgia has one major university, Tbilisi State University, which was founded in 1918. In addition, the Georgia Academy of Sciences, established in 1941, consists of a number of scientific institutions which conduct research throughout the republic. There is also an extensive library system. In addition, the privately run Free University in Tbilisi was set up in 2007 by Kakha Bendukidze, a Georgian who made his fortune in Russia. The new university offers courses of study in law, business, and languages. One of the unique things about the university is that each graduate is expected to pay back the university by financing the education of a new student.

Most citizens are nominal members of the Georgian Orthodox Church but the Georgian Orthodox Church does not play an important role in people's lives. Eleven years after the fall of communism, President Shevardnadze took the first step to begin reversing that condition when he and Georgian Patriarch Ilia II signed a constitutional agreement between the state and the church in October 2002. In the document, the government confirms the church's ownership of all churches and monasteries on Georgian territory except for those now privately owned. It also acknowledges the material damage inflicted on the church since the loss of autocephaly in 1811 and pledges to recompense at least part of it. Parliament is reportedly currently working on legislation which will implement the promises contained in the constitutional agreement.

Economy

Georgian industry has four main branches—mineral extraction, machine-building, chemicals, and textiles. Extensive coal deposits have been developed along the southern slopes of the Great Caucasus Mountains, particularly at Tkvarcheli and Tkibuli. Georgia also has petroleum and some natural gas. Other minerals include manganese and talc.

The machine-building industry produces railway locomotives, heavy vehicles, several types of planes, and earth moving equipment, but it also produces things like lathes and precision instruments. The chemical industry produces pharmaceuticals, synthetic fibers, and mineral fertilizers. The textile industry produces cotton, woolen and silk fabrics, and some clothing.

Agriculture contributes importantly to the economy, in spite of the fact that agricultural land is in short supply and much of it is located along mountain slopes. Major crops tend, therefore, to be labor intensive—and with a higher cash value—such as citrus fruits, tea, and nuts. Georgia produced 97% of the citrus fruits and 92% of the tea of the now defunct Soviet Union. Georgia was also a significant exporter of dairy products and canned foods. Other major agricultural products include sugar beets, tobacco, perfume oils, poultry, bees, and silkworms.

Georgia was also a major exporter of wines, brandy, and champagne to other parts of the Soviet Union, though here Armenia is a major competitor and Azerbaijan produces wines as well. Georgia had lost its entry into the Russian market even before the 2008 war which ended all relations between the two countries. Today, Georgia's exports of spirits go mainly to the European Union or other western neighbors, though they are actively working on finding new markets around the world. Between 65 and 70% of all Georgian vineyards are located in the eastern region of Georgia, called Kakheti. A second grape vine growing region is in the north-central part of Georgia, Racha-Lechkhumi. Most Georgian wineries are still relatively small but the Georgian government is actively encouraging foreign investment in the industry, resulting in some consolidation in recent years.

This state has great potential for tourism. It already has several resorts and sanatoria located on the Black Sea coast, some of which are famous for their mineral springs. In the interior, there are many monasteries and churches which qualify as architectural monuments.

The Georgian economy suffered terribly in the first years after independence, however. The gross domestic product (GDP) dropped by nearly 73% between 1991 and 1994 and inflation soared to 1,500%. Georgia was forced out of the ruble zone in late 1992 and for the next three years they made do with "coupons" issued by the state.

During those years, anecdotal evidence portrayed an economy in deep collapse. In Tbilisi, the subway didn't run most of the time because of a lack of electricity. Buildings also remained unheated for the

same reason. A female computer operator, earning the equivalent of $12 a month, commented that "that's a very good salary." Yet she also reported that butter was selling for the equivalent of $5 a pound. An academic at the Institute of Philosophy at the Georgian Academy of Sciences reported that his monthly salary was the equivalent of $3.

When Shevardnadze first took over, his government was tied down by a civil war, so it was not immediately able to launch a program of reform. The economy stabilized in 1995, then grew by 11% in 1996, by 11.3% in 1997, and by 7.9% in the first eight months of 1998. Inflation showed the same trend, dropping from 13.8% in 1996 to 7.9% in 1997, then by 3.6% in the first eight months of 1998. The average monthly wage, although still low, had begun to climb and stood at about $50 a month by the end of 1997. The currency, the lari, introduced in October 1995, also remained stable.

On the financial front, the banking system had been strengthened. Privatization, begun in 1995 then temporarily halted by a presidential decree in 1966, was restarted in July 1997 when 266 enterprises were sold. Foreign direct investment, still small, had reached $105.3 million as of October 1997. Among the firms that foreign investors bought were a brewery, a bottler, and a producer of sparkling wine.

Still there were more weaknesses than strengths. Georgia was still running budget deficits every year, though the trend was downward. More serious was the trade deficit, caused by the fact that imports were running 3.7 times the level of exports. Still, the Georgian government had the support of the IMF and the World Bank, along with the EU and the United States, and their loans financed Georgia's current account deficit. Georgia's foreign debt stood at about $1.485 billion as of October 1997.

Then came the economic collapse of Russia in September 1998 and it was not long before the Georgian economy also came under attack. The government was forced to abandon support of the currency in December 1998, resulting in a 30% loss in value within a week. It later stabilized at a little less than 2 to the $1, but the effect was to bring a sharp rise in consumer goods. The lari managed to stabilize at this level, however, and as late as the beginning of 2001 it was trading at just over 2 to the dollar. Then the political instability resulting from the collapse of the government coalition in the fall of 2001 brought the currency under renewed downward pressure and by March 2002 it had fallen to 2.35 to the dollar.

The currency might actually have fallen even further but for two actions favorable

Georgia

to Georgia that occurred in early 2001. The first was the US government's decision to grant Georgia most favored nation status, an action that gave Georgia greater access to US markets. The second was a decision by the Paris Club to grant Georgia a moratorium on debt repayment. This latter action, announced in March, re-scheduled $921.9 million of Georgian debts. Repayment was postponed until the beginning of 2004 and would then extend over a period of 15 years.

The Georgian economy started growing again in 2000, though at an anemic 1.9%. Georgia's GDP increased by 5.4% in the first six months of 2001, though it faltered in the latter part of the year after the government coalition began to fall apart in the late summer. It also did not help that fighting broke out again in the Kodori Gorge in eastern Abkhazia after the area was infiltrated by a military force made up of Georgian guerrillas and Chechen rebels. But there were other factors affecting the economy as witness the fact that industrial output actually dropped by 2.6% in the first half of 2001, that is, before any of these events occurred.

Meanwhile, the Georgian government was so strapped for funds that it failed to pay its dues for membership in international organizations. This led to Georgia's being stripped of its voting rights at UNESCO in November 2001. It was about to lose its voting rights in the United Nations in February 2003 when President Shevardnadze ordered the Georgian Foreign and Finance ministries to expedite payment of at least an initial installment of the $7 million it owed in back dues.

The economic situation showed some improvement over the next year, though things remained bleak for ordinary Georgians. In January 2005, the minimum monthly pension was raised from $7 to $15 and there are indications that the amounts of pension arrears diminished as well. Government revenues increased considerably, with the result that the 2005 budget called for revenues of $1.08 billion, approximately three times what the government was collecting just two years earlier.

The government also took a number of steps which supported economic growth in the longer run. In January 2005, the government privatized the Georgian merchant fleet by selling it to a British–Australian consortium for $161 million. The new owners pledged to increase the size of the fleet from 15 to 30 vessels, while all Georgian seamen were promised their jobs for 12 years. The government also passed a new amnesty law as a way to get rid of the "gray" market. Under its terms, businessmen who declared their previously undeclared assets and paid a 1% tax on them could not be pursued by the tax

authorities for tax debts incurred prior to 1 January 2004.

The news in 2005 was even better. First of all, the United States Government approved a grant of $295.3 million in financial aid over the following five years under the Millennium Challenge Account. Some two-thirds of the money was to go to four projects focused on the development and modernization of the infrastructure of the poorest regions of Georgia. The World Bank also approved a $13.5 million grant to support Georgia's poverty reduction program. Thirdly, the Georgian section of the Baku–Tbilisi–Ceyhan oil pipeline was completed in October 2005, and the entire pipeline was completed by the end of the year. Azerbaijan has begun filling the pipeline and the first deliveries to Ceyhan came in 2006. A second gas pipeline was completed in 2007.

The Georgian government reported that foreign investment increased by nearly 47% in 2004. Almost 87% was concentrated in Georgia's service sector, with industry a distant second. Georgia also regained its voting rights at the United Nations after it paid nearly $6 million to cover the country's UN membership dues arrears.

Georgia's economy showed a steady growth of 10% in 2007–2008, though an inflation rate of 7–8% was an increasing problem. However, the economic situation was overtaken by the Russian invasion of Georgia in August 2008. This led to a major disruption of the economy as the northern half of the country, including its major port, was occupied by Russian troops. The worldwide international economic crisis probably played a role as well, but it is difficult to sort out that particular influence from everything else that was happening. In any case, the Georgian economy contracted by approximately 7% in 2009 as foreign direct investment and worker remittances declined.

It would probably have declined more, but Georgia has been largely protected from international economic developments because of the offers of international aid that Georgia received to help in rebuilding the country after the Russian invasion. The United States Government pledged $1 billion for humanitarian aid and reconstruction. In October 2008, Georgia received pledges of an additional $4.5 billion in aid during a donors' conference held in Brussels.

GDP grew by close to 7% in the period 2010–2012. An economic slowdown started in the fourth quarter of 2012 and continued dropping throughout 2013, eventually averaging 3% for the year. Growth continued at a 2.9% rate at the beginning of 2014, but dropped to 0.2% by the end of the first quarter. According to an EBRD report, the lack of investment

plus post-election political uncertainty led to a slowdown of the economy since the end of 2012. Although Georgia is not an oil producing state, it is an important energy transit hub for oil and gas traveling from the region to Europe. The plunge in energy prices and the subsequent slowdown to the Azerbaijani economy have therefore harmed the Georgian economy. In 2014, its currency, the lari, lost 30% of its value relative to the dollar.

According to data from the World Bank, Georgia's economy grew by 10.4% in 2021. This expansion followed the Covid-19 induced 6.8% contraction in 2020. By late 2021, the country's economic output surpassed the pre-COVID-19 output levels. The country experienced a 11.3% rise in inflation by February 2022, with food and fuel prices contributing around 6% to the overall inflation.

The war in Ukraine will have an adverse effect on Geogia's economy. The country has strong trade relations with both Russia and Ukraine. As with other poor and small post-Soviet countries, Georgia is heavily reliant on Russian petroleum products, gas, and wheat. Russia accounts for 94% of all wheat flour imports. Since the start of the war, both Ukraine and Russia imposed a ban on the export of wheat to ensure domestic food security. Although Russia partially eased the ban, it caused wheat prices to soar to the point of causing panic buying in Georgia. Additionally, for many Georgians, financial remittances from Russia, which accounted for about 13% of the country's GDP in 2020, is one of the key sources of gaining livelihood. With Western sanctions causing a contraction in economic activity in Russia, the flow of remitted money is likely to dry out. The country is especially at risk of rising social discontent because of increases in wheat prices.

The Future

Georgia's economy has been performing well for more than a decade. Thanks in part to its prudent economic management, the country managed an average of 4% annual growth between 2011 and 2021. As a result, poverty declined from 59% in 2011 to 42% in 2021. However, the country remains vulnerable to external and global shocks because of its heavy reliance on tourism, remittances and trade with Russia and Ukraine. With Western sanctions causing a contraction in economic activity in Russia, the flow of remitted money is likely to dry out. The country is especially at risk of rising social discontent because of increases in the prices of wheat and gas; the two commodities it imports from Russia. The Georgian government publicly stated that it would join other Western countries in imposing sanctions against Russia. The Russian envoy in the country is reported to have praised Tbilisi's for its "balanced" reaction to the war and said that "it would not go unnoticed" in Russia. The official Moscow may have reciprocated by pressuring the de facto government of the self-proclaimed region of South Ossetia to scrap the July 17 referendum on joining Russia. Thus, in the near term, Tbilisi has one less problem to worry about as Russia won't be pursuing a "Crimean solution" for the breakaway regions of Abkhazia and South Ossetia.

Georgian politics in the medium-term will likely revolve around the newly signed constitutional amendments. These reforms have the potential to have a drastic effect upon the trajectory of Georgia as well as its neighbors. If, as proponents of the reforms claim, the reforms consolidate a parliamentary system, they may have a democratizing effect across the south Caucasus and may spur further integration with Europe. If, however, these reforms are a cynical ploy to entrench the control of the Georgian Dream Party, they may further erode popular trust and the legitimacy of Georgian political institutions. From a foreign policy perspective, President Margvelashvili and the Georgian Dream coalition are more prudent with regard to Russia than Saakashvili was, and Margvelashvili is unlikely to respond in a violent way to a provocation in either Abkhazia or South Ossetia as Saakashvili did in 2008. NATO and the European Union continue to have strong relations with Georgia, although formal accession to either organization is exceedingly unlikely in the current geopolitical climate.

In 2017, Georgia and the EU liberalized their visa regime, enabling Georgian citizens to travel visa-free in the Schengen Area. As further evidence that Georgia's future lay with Europe, this development was celebrated in Georgia. However, by spring 2018, complaints by some EU members over the number of Georgian asylum seekers seemed to put the new liberalization program in jeopardy.

Georgia has lingering anxiety over Russia's annexation of Crimea and support for the pro-Russian separatists in the war in eastern Ukraine in 2014–2015. Russia's increasing control over Abkhazia and South Ossetia raises the concern in Georgia that Russia may seek a "Crimean solution" for those regions.

CENTRAL ASIAN REPUBLICS

The Republic of Kazakhstan

Area: 1,049,155 sq. mi. (2,717,300 sq. km., almost twice the size of Alaska, second-largest state in the former USSR).

Population: 20,260,006 (2024 estimate).

Capital City: Astana [most recently known as Nur-Sultan] (1.254 million).

Climate: Continental, with very hot summers and extremely cold winters.

Neighboring States: Russia (west and north); China (east); Kyrgyzstan; Uzbekistan; and Turkmenistan (south).

Principal Languages: Kazak (Qazaq), the state language; and Russian, official: used in everyday business, designated the "language of interethnic communication."

Ethnic Composition: Kazakh (Qazaq) (71%); Russian (14.9%); Uzbek (3.3%); Ukrainian (1.9%); Other (8.9%) (2023 est.).

Principal Religion: Islam (69.3%); Christian, predominately Russian Orthodox, (17.2%); Other/None (13.5%) (2021 est.).

Chief Commercial Products: Agriculture—grain, livestock, cotton, wool. Industry—oil, coal, iron ore, mineral extraction (manganese, chromite, lead, zinc, copper, titanium, bauxite, gold, silver), tractors and other agricultural machinery, electric motors, construction materials.

Currency: tenge (issued November 1993).

Annual Per Capita Income: $35,453 (PPP, 2023 est.).

Recent Political Status: The Kazak SSR was formally a part of the Russian Soviet Federative Republic (RSFR) but in December 1936 it was proclaimed a separate constituent republic of the former USSR, remaining in that status until 1991.

Head of State: Kassym-Zhomart Tokayev (since March 20, 2019).

Head of Government: Olzhas Bektenov (since February 6, 2024).

National Day: December 16 (1991), independence from the Soviet Union).

National Flag: A golden sun rising above mountains superimposed upon a sky-blue background, with the left edge showing a stylized pattern in worked gold.

The Land

The Republic of Kazakhstan (Qazaqstan Respublikasy), successor government to the Kazakh Soviet Socialist Republic, declared its independence on December 16, 1991. The Kazakh Soviet Socialist Republic had existed only since December 1936. Its predecessor was the Kirghiz (later renamed Kazakh) Autonomous Soviet Socialist Republic, which had been founded in August 1920 as an autonomous republic of the Russian SFSR.

In spite of its size, Kazakhstan is geographically rather homogeneous. Essentially it is a great tableland, with lowlands, plains, and plateaus making up approximately 80% of the landscape. Mountainous regions in the east and southeast make up the remaining parts of the land.

Kazakhstan is a Eurasian land, with its western border beginning at the northern end of the Caspian Sea, just east of the mouth of the Volga River. It then turns slightly west and runs northward just east of the Volga River before bending northeast and skirting the southern edges of the Ural Mountains. East of the Urals, it zigzags north until it passes the Russian city of Magnitogorsk before turning eastward. After passing just south of the city of Omsk, it turns southeastward and pushes to the top ridge of the Altai Mountains. It then turns at a sharp angle and runs in a southwestern direction along the ridges of the Tarbagatay Range and the Ulu-Tau Mountains until it passes just south of the republic's former capital of Almaty. Here it turns westward and runs along the foothills, crossing the Syr Dar'ya River, until just north of Samarkand. It then crosses the Kyzylkum Desert and passes through the center of the Aral Sea, bending from there southward to reach the center of the Caspian Sea.

The western portion of the republic is dominated by the Caspian Depression. The Mogodzhar Hills, a southern extension of the Ural Mountains, separates the Caspian Depression from the Turan Plain, which stretches west-east just north of the Aral Sea. To the east of the Aral Sea is the Kyzylkum Desert. To the northeast of that, separated by the valley of the Syr Dar'ya River, is an area called the Hunger Steppe. These areas in the south are all desert and only the presence of the Syr Dar'ya River makes any agriculture possible. The northern part of Kazakhstan is known as the Kazakh Steppe, however, and here there is sufficient rainfall to support grasses. The northern part of Kazakhstan is an area of farms that concentrate on growing wheat and other cereal crops.

Some irrigation is also possible in this northern area, using water from the Ural River in the west and the Irtysh River in the east. Two smaller rivers, the Ishim and Tobol, also provide water for irrigation. Overall, the republic has over 7,000 streams and rivers, plus about 48,000 small lakes. Kazakhstan also has 1,450 miles of coastline along the Caspian Sea.

The weather is continental, with cold winters and hot summers. Temperatures in the southern part of Kazakhstan are much milder, however, with January temperatures averaging 23°–29°F. Average July temperatures are 68° in the north and 84° in the south. The area of the North has rich, black soils; south of that the soils are chestnut-brown, but still fertile. In the extreme South, soils tend to be infertile and alkaline, or sandy desert. Woodlands, found mostly in the mountains, make up only 3% of the total land surface.

The People

The population of Kazakhstan, which was an estimated 20 million, began shrinking and becoming more rural after the republic became independent at the end of 1991. The urban population dropped by 8.4% between 1989 (when the last Soviet census was taken) and 1999, while rural population dropped by a smaller 6.8%. Overall, there was a population drop of about 1.5 million in the first decade of independence. Much of the population decline can be directly attributed to the outmigration of large numbers of the new state's minority populations. That trend was reversed in recent years, however, and the population has once again begun growing.

According to an announcement by the director of the Migration and Immigration Agency in January 1999, 2.17 million persons left Kazakhstan during its first seven years of independence, while 590,000 entered the country. Approximately one million Russians, 600,000 ethnic Germans, 300,000 Ukrainians, and 70,000 Tatars emigrated during this period. Most Germans migrated to Germany, encouraged by free flights paid for by the German government. According to German government estimates, only about 170,000 ethnic Germans continue to live in Kazakhstan.

Due to the out-migration of large numbers of the state's minority population as well as natural population increase, the titular nationality has become a solid majority of the population (63.1% as of July 2016). This represents a drastic shift from the demographics of the republic during the Soviet era when Kazakhs were often a minority in their own republic. A small, but politically significant, portion of the ethnic Kazakh population growth can be attributed to the in-migration of Kazakhs from neighboring states, especially Mongolia and China. At independence, the Kazakh government launched an ambitious program of attracting members of the Kazakh diaspora, dubbed Oralmandar (returnees), by promising financial and other forms of relocation support to ethnic Kazakhs who desired to repatriate.

History

The first reference to Kazakhs living in Central Asia is found in a Russian source dated 1534. Subsequently, the Russians referred to these people as Kaisak-Kirgiz or simply Kirgiz. Undoubtedly, the reason for this is that the Russian word *Kazaky* means Cossacks and it describes Russian peasants living on the frontier. It appears, in fact, that modern Kazakhs are descendants of the old Kipchak tribes, which were part of the East-Central Asian "Golden Horde."

In the 15th century, there was a Kazakh Empire that controlled the steppe land to the east of the Caspian Sea and north of the Aral Sea, stretching eastward as far as the western approaches of the Altai Mountains. This empire lasted until the beginning of the 18th century, but then was weakened by attacks from a revived Oyrat Empire to the east. The Kazakhs were at this time organized into three principalities, the "Little Horde," "Middle Horde," and Great Horde.

When the Russians began their advance into this area in the 18th century, the Kazakhs decided to accept Russian protection against their enemies to the east. The "Little Horde" accepted Russian protection in 1731, followed by the Middle Horde in 1740 and the Great Horde in 1742.

The Kazakhs began to fear Russian control, however, and this led to a series of uprisings toward the end of the 18th century. As a result, Russia began to suppress the autonomy of the Kazakh Khans. The Khanate of the "Middle Horde" was suppressed in 1822, the "Little Horde" in 1824; and the "Great Horde" in 1848. In 1854, the Russians founded the fortress of Verna, which eventually became the modern city of Almaty. The area was administratively divided into four areas. In the latter part of the 19th century, there were large-scale settlements of Russian peasants established in the northern part of the territory.

A small Kazakh nationalist movement came into existence at the beginning of the 20th century, and a number of Kazakh deputies were elected to the first and second Russian Dumas. The first Kazakh newspaper began publication in 1910. In 1916, a revolt broke out when the Russian government ordered the mobilization of all persons between the age of 19 and 43. It was put down harshly.

After the Bolshevik seizure of power in November 1917 in Moscow, Kazakh nationalists demanded full autonomy for Kazakhstan. A Kazakh nationalist government was formed, but was suppressed in 1919–1920 when the Red Army occupied the area. The Bolsheviks did sponsor creation of the Kirgiz Autonomous Soviet Socialist Republic in August 1920, however. In 1925, the name was changed to Kazakh; in 1929, the capital was established at Almaty (formerly Alma-Ata). Kazakhstan became a Soviet Socialist Republic in December 1936.

The Kazakh Communist Party was established in 1937; Zhumabay Shayakhmetov became its first ethnic Kazakh head during World War II. He was replaced in 1954 by P. K. Ponomarenko, a Slav, because he showed insufficient support for the Moscow-sponsored newly-launched Virgin Lands campaign. Ponomarenko was replaced by Leonid Brezhnev, who remained first secretary of the Kazakh Communist Party until 1956. After he became General Secretary, Brezhnev appointed an ethnic Kazakh, Dinmukhamed Kunaev, as first secretary of the Kazakh Communist Party. He held that position until December 1986, when he was removed by Gorbachev and replaced by another Slav, Gennady Kolbin.

When word reached Almaty that Kunaev had been dismissed and was being replaced by an ethnic Russian, violent rioting broke out and several persons were killed. Gorbachev, recognizing that he had to be more sensitive to nationalist sentiments, later reassigned Kolbin and replaced him with another ethnic Kazakh.

When hardliners launched their coup against President Gorbachev on August 19, 1991, Nursultan Nazarbayev, the Kazakh political leader, condemned the action and called for Gorbachev's return. After the coup failed, Nazarbayev severed

Kazakhstan's former capital of Almaty as seen from Mt. Kok Tyube   Courtesy of NOVOSTI

271

Kazakhstan

The dam in the Maly Almaatinsky Gorge at Medeo   Courtesy of NOVOSTI

all ties with the Kazakh Communist Party and banned all political activity in government, the courts and police. The Kazakh Communist Party disbanded, but subsequently reconstituted itself as a Socialist Party. The Socialists held their first congress at Almaty in December 1991. They did not have much influence, however.

Even as the USSR began to disintegrate in late 1991, Nazarbayev strongly supported some form of continued union of the republics and, almost alone among the republic leaders, he did not press for a declaration of independence until it became clear that the old union was dead. This made sense from the point of view of Kazakhstan, for it is a large republic with a relatively small population and its economy was heavily tied to Russia. Most people still lived in the countryside and worked the land. The main industry was mineral extraction, most of which was traditionally shipped to other republics for further processing. In addition, a significant percentage of the population had ethnic ties to Russia or one of the other republics.

The Kazakh government carried out fairly extensive changes after Kazakhstan declared its independence in 1991, but the pace of change began to slow thereafter. The government still encouraged foreign investment, but there was some retrenchment on market-oriented economic changes introduced in 1991 and early 1992. In addition, terms like "pluralism" and "moving toward democracy" lost their earlier currency. The best characterization for Nazarbayev is that he is an "authoritarian modernizer" who is putting economic development before political liberalism.

On the other hand, Nazarbayev is in many ways rather pragmatic. Aware of growing nationalist currents within the country and sensitive to those feelings, he is also aware that Russian speakers still constitute 32% of the overall population. Moves to increase the use of the Kazakh language have accordingly been moderate. For example, the amount of instruction in the Kazakh language has been increased in the schools, but Russian is still the medium of instruction.

Kazakhstan's constitution designates Kazakh as the national language, but Russian is described as the language of inter-ethnic communication. The constitution also requires the president to have a good command of the Kazakh language, but does not stipulate that he be an ethnic Kazakh.

Unlike some of the European post-Soviet states, Kazakhstan lacked a sizable independence movement in the late 1980s. One could say that it was granted independence against the wishes of its elites. The lack of a mass independence movement enabled Nazarbayev to quickly consolidate his control of the political levers. Nobody challenged him at the executive level and the legislature remained compliant to his wishes. Yet Nazarbayev and appeared to favor the development of at least some political pluralism. Despite initial fears that the state's large Russian population could destabilize the country or even provoke Russian intervention, the first few years of independent Kazakhstan are notable for their lack (highlight) of acute ethnic tension.

That began to change in late 1994. On the one side, ethnic Russians began to agitate for greater recognition within the state, including the designation of Russian as the second official language, and they also began demanding the

right to dual Russian–Kazakh nationality. Nazarbayev's efforts to placate them brought a reaction from ethnic Kazakhs. For the first time, voices of criticism were heard in the Kazakh parliament. In early 1995, a majority rejected the president's proposals to give the Russian language equal status with Kazakh. The parliament also rejected a proposed law establishing procedures for the privatization of land.

These dynamics have proved to be enduring over the past two-plus decades. At the core of the tension is the definition of the Kazakhstani nation. On the one hand, Nazarbayev and the government often speak about an inclusive civic Kazakhstani identity which explicitly recognizes the state's ethnic diversity. Efforts to recognize and protect the Russian language fits squarely with this definition of the nation. On the other hand, policies are often advanced which define the state as designated to protect ethnic Kazakhs. The subsidization of ethnic Kazakh migrants interested in moving to Kazakhstan from neighboring countries is an example of this narrow and particularistic definition of the nation.

The Constitutional Court then offered Nazarbayev an unusual opportunity when it declared the March 1994 elections to be illegal on the basis that they offended the "one man, one vote" principle. Nazarbayev immediately disbanded the parliament and accepted the resignation of the government. He then announced that he would rule by decree until a new parliament was elected. Parliamentarians protested, and some threatened to form an alternative assembly. Nazarbayev, however, used the interregnum to push ahead with measures he had been unable to get through the parliament, such as privatization, enhancement of the status of the Russian language, and streamlining the tax system.

New parliamentary elections took place in December 1995. There were multiple candidates for most of the 67 seats, with the result that only 43 candidates won a majority of the votes in the first round of voting. A second round of voting then took place to fill the remaining seats. Although many of the winners ran without a party affiliation, most were, effectively, supporters of government policies.

In 1999, President Nazarbayev established a new political party, Otan, as his support base. Within a short while, 44 of the 67 members of the lower house joined Otan.

Nazarbayev had been much concerned by the out-migration of ethnic Russians since 1991. In an attempt to address their concerns and encourage them to remain, he made a number of gestures toward the Russian community. In 1994, he extended

Kazakhstan

the time when residents would have to decide whether to opt for Kazakh citizenship; when it became clear that many Russians were hesitant to relinquish their Russian citizenship, he endorsed the concept of dual Russian and Kazakh citizenship. The migration of ethnic Russians to Russia and elsewhere continues, however.

A New Capital

Another of Nazarbayev's concerns was the possibility of a separatist movement in the northern part of the country where most Russian speakers live. Attempting to address that problem, he decided in 1995 to move the capital from Almaty in the extreme southeastern part of the republic to Akmola (or Aqmola), a town of 270,000 located near the north-central portion of the country. Akmola had the advantage that it was nearer the main population and industrial centers. Moreover, the northern half of the country contains most of the country's natural resources, including oil, gas, gold, chrome, and copper, as well as much of its best farmland. Another factor that was probably taken into consideration was that ethnic Russians make up a large part of the population in northern Kazakhstan; moving the capital here may have been a way of giving them a larger stake in an independent Kazakhstan.

On the other hand, Akmola was only a provincial town in 1995 and it lacked the facilities to house a government. Over the past 15 years, therefore, whole new districts have been constructed to house the government, the parliament, the foreign embassies, and the governmental workers. This also involved constructing new luxury hotels, new residential areas, an additional business center, and an enlarged airport.

The formal move to Akmola took place in December 1997 when President Nazarbayev sent state symbols, including the flag, coat of arms, and the presidential banner, to the new capital. In fact, much of the construction ordered in 1995 remained incomplete, so most of the government ministries remained in Almaty, as did most foreign embassies. Those government officials actually transferred to Akmola had to be housed in temporary quarters for the most extent. Parliamentary deputies were assigned to hotel rooms, while government officials were put up in hostels or even kindergartens.

Although estimates of the amount of government funds invested in the new capital by this time stood at $1.5 billion, in one sense the task of constructing a new capital had only just begun. This was also reflected in the fact that the government decided to give the capital a new name. "Akmola," it turns out, means "white tomb," and it was too much of a reminder that Akmola was the site of a

The new capital at Nur-Sultan

Stalin-era forced labor camp for the wives of political prisoners during the period 1937–1945. The new name of the capital was changed to Astana (literally "Capital" in Kazakh). This uncreative name was widely believed to be little more than a placeholder until the city could be renamed after Kazakhstan's first president. Indeed, President Tokayev wasted no time initiating the change. His first official act as president upon his swearing in was to order parliament to consider renaming the capital. Dutifully, both houses unanimously agreed to amend the Constitution to change the name of the capital from Astana to Nur-Sultan in 2019. In 2022, President Tokayev signed a constitutional amendment to revert the name to Astana.

In October 1998, the Kazakh government officially selected the Japanese architect Kisho Kurokawa to produce an overall design for the new capital. The basic plan is still Kurokawa's, but there have been a number of additions to the plan as other architects have been hired for particular projects. After Kurokawa's death,

the role of chief architect was taken over by Vladimir Laptev, who has said that his plan is to create a city on the model of Berlin, but in a Eurasian style.

The Ak Orda (White Horde) Presidential Palace, completed in 2004, is an 80-meter-high square cement building faced with Italian marble and topped by a large dome; the dome sits over a yurt-like hall, also of marble and granite.

Manfredi Nicoletti of Italy designed the Kazakh Central Concert Hall, whose shape is reminiscent of the petals of a flower; the "petals" have a practical purpose, however; they act as an enclosure for the building, protecting it from the extreme weather conditions that sometimes apply in Astana. Inside, one finds a 3,500-seat concert hall, two smaller music or conference rooms able to hold 400 and 200 persons, restaurants, bars and a lobby. It was completed in 2009.

The British architectural firm of Foster and Happold designed a pyramid-shaped building known as the Palace of Peace and Reconciliation (or sometimes the Pyramid of Peace). Inaugurated in September 2006, it houses a 1,500-seat opera house, a national museum of culture, a research center for Kazakhstan's ethnic and geographical groups, plus accommodations for different religions. Foster and Happold also designed the Khan Shatyry Entertainment Center (also known as the Khan's Pavilion), which was completed in 2010; 150 meters high, its shape is that of a "giant transparent tent; as one person described it, it is "a giant conical structure, bent as though blown by the harsh winds that are notorious here"; it contains stores, a theater, a water park and seven acres of terraced gardens.

Astana is also home to Nazarbayev University. Officially founded in 2010, the

Main academic building of Nazarbayev University

Kazakhstan

Sazgen, the folk music quintet, shown at the Old Instruments Museum in Almaty

Courtesy of NOVOSTI

university represents an ambitious effort to establish a world-class institution of higher education in northern Kazakhstan. The university aims to attract the best students across the country, with the promise of free education and English language instruction from a diverse and international faculty. Located at the edge of the city against the steppe, the campus has tubes connecting academic buildings to dormitories and faculty housing so that students and faculty are able to commute back and forth to class unhindered by the harsh winter weather for which Astana is known.

Astana has a population of 1.3 million people. It still feels like a work-in-progress, however, and cranes and construction sites are ubiquitous. In summer 2017, the city hosted a world's fair, Expo 2017, on a previously undeveloped 25-hectare site. As the Expo represented a golden opportunity for the government to show off its new capital to world, it spurred the development of new infrastructure in the area of city where the pavilions are to be housed. Today, Astana has become a magnet for young professionals seeking to build a career. In addition, many migrant workers—legal and illegal—have been attracted to the city because of the intense building activity.

Autocratic Political Developments

Through 2019, there have been two laws of Kazakhstani presidential elections: (1)

they will be held early; and (2) Nazarbayev will win. Although the second of these laws will no longer hold following the perennial President's surprising retirement announcement on March 19, 2019, the second law will remain as Kazakhstan's most recent presidential election (on June 9, 2019) occurred months before their originally scheduled date. The pattern of holding snap elections was set during the second presidential election in Kazakhstan's history. These elections were originally scheduled to take place in December 2000, but were moved up to January 1999.

President Nazarbayev probably requested the legislature to take this action because he felt that, with the economy already suffering from a sharp drop in the prices of oil and steel, Kazakhstan's two chief exports, the economic situation was only likely to decline further before it got better. Nazarbayev would thus have a better chance of winning reelection if the date were moved up.

Nazarbayev was reelected with an impressive 79.78% of the vote; the election nevertheless tarnished Nazarbayev's reputation after the government refused to allow Akezhan Kazhegeldin—prime minister between 1994 and 1997—to run as one of the candidates for the presidency. As a result, the OSCE refused to send official international observers to the election and refused to recognize its results. The United

States Government also expressed its displeasure, saying in part that "the conduct of these elections has set back the process of democratization in Kazakhstan and has made more difficult the development of the important relations between our two countries."

New parliamentary elections took place in October 1999. Under a new procedure, 10 of the 67 seats in the lower chamber of the legislature (the Majilis) were allocated on a proportional basis to those political parties polling a minimum of 7% of the vote. Four parties qualified for proportional seats, the pro-presidential Otan Party with 30.5%; the Communist Party with 17.8%; the Agrarian Party with 12.6%; and the Civic Party with 10.9%. The Otan Party was the largest party in the legislature with 23 seats, down from 44 seats in the previous legislature. However, the government still had a clear majority since the Civic Party, which also supported the government, took 12 seats. The Communist Party had three seats; the Agrarian Party two; and the Republican People's Party had one. The remaining seats were held by independents, most of whom supported the government.

President Nazarbayev's tenure was marked by a frequent cycling of prime ministers. This tactic often enabled him to pin blame on government failures to the outgoing prime minister while deflecting criticism away from himself. Kazhegeldin's resignation in October 1997 demonstrates this pattern. On the same day that Kazhegeldin submitted his resignation, President Nazarbayev told the parliament that "reforms had been insufficient and in some aspects have not produced the desired results." Kazhegeldin later became a harsh critic of the president's policies and subsequently founded his own opposition party, the Republican People's Party of Kazakhstan.

Nurlan Balgimbayev, named prime minister in October 1997, had been head of the Kazakhstan National Petroleum Company prior to being named prime minister. An engineer by training, he spent the years from 1986 to 1992 in the former USSR oil and gas industry ministry in Moscow. He then spent two years in the United States, first at MIT, then at Chevron's headquarters. He was appointed Kazakh gas and oil minister in October 1994, then head of the state oil company that replaced the ministry in March 1997. Balgimbayev's term as prime minister was not smooth, and he submitted his resignation in October 1999 after harsh criticism of his policies by Marat Ospanov, the speaker of the legislature. He was subsequently named head of KazakhOil, as the Kazakhstan National Petroleum Company is now called.

**Former President
Nursultan Nazarbayev**

Interim-president Kassym-Jomart Tokayev, Balgimbayev's successor as prime minister, had previously served as deputy prime minister and foreign minister. An important factor in his selection is that he was a trained diplomat with excellent international contacts, since President Nazarbayev was, at this time, particularly interested in increasing foreign investment in the country. Tokayev served as prime minister until January 2002, when he resigned and was reappointed foreign minister. His successor was Imangali Tasmagambetov who, as a former governor of the oil-rich Atrau region in western Kazakhstan, brought firsthand knowledge of the petroleum industry to the job.

But President Nazarbayev probably selected him as prime minister because of his previous portfolio as deputy prime minister of social issues and interethnic relations. Over the previous year or so, there had been increasing political criticism of the government because of its increasing cronyism and insularity. One form this dissatisfaction took was the creation of new political parties and the merging of others to create a stronger opposition presence. President Nazarbayev's immediate reaction to these developments was to lash out against these new political entities and to treat them all as enemies.

In the case of the Forum of Democratic Forces an umbrella organization of 16 opposition political parties, including the Republican Party of Kazakhstan, headed by former Prime Minister Kazhegeldin, this was probably an accurate characterization. Kazhegeldin, who subsequently merged his party with two other parties to form the United Democratic Party, was one of the drafters of a 15-point "National Plan of Political Transformations" in January 2002, which had as its first demand that "the president must resign."

On the other hand, the center-right reformers who founded Democratic Choice for Kazakhstan in November 2001 held various positions in the government at the time—positions they subsequently lost—and they saw themselves as advocates of a gradual political liberalization which they believed was necessary to provide the economic basis for the emergence of a middle class. They never criticized Nazarbayev personally but instead expressed the hope that their goals could be achieved through the current leadership. As one of the founders of Democratic Choice for Kazakhstan, former Pavlodar Region Governor Ghalymzhan Zhaqiyanov, put it in December 2001,

we intend to mobilize public opinion and force the parliament and above all the president to accept [our program].

At first, it appeared that President Nazarbayev might attempt to co-opt his more moderate critics, but that possibility evaporated when the government ordered the arrest of two of the leaders of Democratic Choice for Kazakhstan, former Governor Zhaqiyanov and former Energy, Industry, and Trade Minister Mukhtar Ablyazov, in March. Zhaqiyanov actually took refuge in the French Embassy in Almaty to avoid arrest, which introduced an international component into the situation.

A statement issued by the political opposition after the arrest warrants were issued makes a very important point about Kazakhstan, however. As the statement pointed out, the only senior Kazakh officials to have been charged with corruption in the decade after Kazakhstan became independent were individuals whom the government considered to be members of the political opposition—Zhaqiyanov, Abliyazov, and Kazhegeldin. Kazhegeldin, charged with corruption, was sentenced to prison in absentia. He resides abroad in self-exile and may not return to Kazakhstan.

When the trials of the two leaders of Democratic Choice for Kazakhstan took place in July 2002, therefore, the verdicts were expected to be harsh and they were. Mukhtar Ablyazov, former minister for energy, industry, and trade, was sentenced to six years in prison with confiscation of all property, plus he was ordered to pay a fine of $3.6 million. Former Governor Zhaqiyanov was sentenced to seven years in jail.

Even as the trials were taking place, President Nazarbayev signed a new law on political parties which had been passed by the parliament at his request. Under the terms of the law, the number of signatures required for registration went from 3,000

to 50,000. In addition, any party that failed to enter parliament in two tries would lose its registration and be dissolved.

When the party registration program ended in April 2003, only 6 of the 19 parties that had existed up to that time had survived. Two of the parties had merged with Otan, the main government party. Six opposition parties never filed to re-register at all, while the remaining four parties were refused re-registration. Three of the four did not, indeed, qualify under the law, since they had fewer than 50,000 members.

However, the Compatriots (formerly the Russian Party) were refused registration even though they claimed 58,000 members. The government first challenged that figure; it then ordered the party to amend its political program when it filed again. The party filed yet a third time, but never achieved registration.

Thus, when the re-registration process came to an end, four of the seven surviving political parties were loyal supporters of President Nazarbayev. They were Otan, the Civic Party, the Agrarian Party, and the Aul (Village) Social Democratic Party. The surviving opposition parties were the moderate opposition Ak Zhol (Bright Path) Democratic Party, and the Communist Party.

Imanghali Tasmagambetov resigned as prime minister on June 11, 2003, after he had failed to persuade parliament to pass land privatization legislation in the form desired by President Nazarbayev. His successor, Daniyal Akhmetov, governor of Pavlodar Oblast, was appointed two days later.

Akhmetov had previously been deputy prime minister for industry, transport, and communications. Akhmetov has degrees in construction engineering and economics. Stressing the need for continuity even when governments change, Akhmetov said that he intended few ministerial changes. As his previous job would indicate, Akhmetov had a particular interest in economic development. The government's first priority would continue to be on exploitation of hydrocarbon reserves, Akhmetov stated, but the agricultural sector would need greater assistance and the government would also have to provide more support for small- and medium-sized businesses and domestic manufacturers.

Elections to the lower house of parliament took place on September 19, 2004, with a runoff election in 17 single-constituency seats on October 3. Twelve political parties were registered to participate in the elections and they put forth over 600 candidates for the 67 open single-constituency seats.

In the first round of voting, the pro-presidential Otan Party took 7 of the 10

Kazakhstan

President Kassym-Jomart Tokayev meets with Russian President Vladimir Putin

The unmet international standards the OSCE referred to included pro-government bias in the state media, voter intimidation, and restrictions on freedom of press and assembly during the campaign. It also made reference to charges of ballot stuffing, multiple voting, putting pressure on students to vote for Nazarbayev, and irregularities in the vote counting.

Despite the myriad problems with this election, it would prove to be the last competitive election (with a real, if hamstrung, choice for voters) in which Nazarbayev would partake. Kazakhstan has never held an election that met international standards. This does not mean that Nazarbayev was not popular, however; a pre-election poll by the US-based survey group Intermedia showed 70% support for the incumbent prior to the 2005 election. Thus, Nazarbayev would have been reelected in a fully free and fair election, though perhaps not with as many votes as he got.

Even so, the political system was severely shaken when Altynbek Sarsenbayev, an opposition leader, was found bound and shot outside the city of Almaty on February 13, 2006. Sarsenbayev, a former Kazakh ambassador to Russia, had been co-chairman of the opposition party Naghyz Ak Zhol (True Bright Path), an unregistered splinter group that had split off from the Ak Zhol.

According to the official investigation that followed, he, his driver, and his bodyguard were victims of a contract killing carried out by five members of a special elite unit of the National Security Committee and the man who arranged for the killing was Erzhan Utembaev, a former deputy prime minister; at the time, he was serving as the administrative head of the Senate.

Even though Utembaev claimed that Sarsenbayev had been killed for private reasons—he had impugned Utembaev's honor—his killing shook the Kazakh political system and brought about the resignation of the head of the National Security Committee.

Perhaps more importantly, the killing brought a number of moves on the part of the government that point in the direction of greater political pluralism in the country. In March 2006, President Nazarbayev issued a decree creating a state commission to develop a program of democratic reforms in Kazakhstan. Nazarbayev commented with regard to the work of the state commission that "I do not rule out that it may be necessary to conduct constitutional reform as well."

The government also agreed to cooperate with the OSCE to develop "amendments and changes" to the electoral law in line with the OSCE's December 2005

proportional seats and 37 of the single-constituency seats. Its ally, the AIST bloc of the Civic and Agrarian Parties won two of the proportional seats plus nine of the single-constituency seats. Asar (Mutual Help), the party created in 2003 by Nazarbayev's eldest daughter, Dariga Nazarbayeva, won one proportional seat and three single-constituency seats.

The only opposition party to win a seat in the parliament was Ak Zhol, which was awarded one proportional seat. Seventeen single-constituency seats were won by individuals running as independents, but 10 independents joined Otan after the election, which meant that the president's party actually controlled 53 of the 77 seats in the lower house.

Moreover, Ak Zhol announced that it was challenging the results of the elections by boycotting parliament, a position it maintained until September 2006, when the Ak Zhol deputy finally took his seat. Ak Zhol eventually broke up into two feuding factions, however, so the opposition was even further divided than it was before the elections.

New Senate elections took place on August 19, 2005. Sixteen seats were up for election; 10 seats were won by Otan while 3 additional seats went to independents.

The remaining three seats were won by Auyl, Asar, and the Civic Party, all allies of the pro-presidential Otan Party.

New presidential elections took place on December 4, 2005. Four candidates challenged President Nazarbayev for the post. Nazarbayev's main opponents were Zharmakhan Tuyakbai, head of the opposition bloc For a Just Kazakhstan, and Alikhan Baimenov, nominated by the opposition Ak Zhol. The other two candidates represented the old Communist Party and an environmental movement. In the end, President Nazarbayev won reelection with 91.1% of the vote. Tuyakbai came second with 6.6%, followed by Baimenov with 1.6%.

No one gave Nazarbayev's opponents a real chance to win, but there were problems during the campaign which reduced their chances further, in particular pressure on opposition newspapers. In the end, however, the OSCE issued a rather mild report which concluded that:

despite some improvements in the administration of this election in the pre-election period, the presidential election did not meet a number of OSCE commitments and other international standards for democratic elections.

criticisms of the presidential elections. In line with this trend, the government also registered Sarsenbayev's political party, the Naghyz Ak Zhol, in March.

In September 2006, the pro-presidential parties Otan and Asar, formally merged. Asar had been the party established by President Nazarbayev's daughter, Dariga Nazarbayeva.

That same month, a new opposition party, the National Social Democratic Party, (NSDP), was established under the leadership of Zharmakhan Tuyakbai, who ran against President Nazarbayev in the December 2005 presidential election, coming in second with 6.6% of the vote. The NSDP's platform called for an end to the government's privatization program, a lowering of the retirement age, and free universal higher education.

In January 2007, Daniyal Akhmetov resigned as prime minister and was appointed the new defense minister; his successor as prime minister was Karim Massimov, at the time of his appointment a 41-year-old economist who previously had been deputy prime minister. Massimov, describing himself as President Nazarbayev's "faithful assistant," committed himself to continuity in the principles of government, "one of the most important conditions of sustained economic and social development." Massimov—who speaks Arabic, Chinese, English, Kazakh, and Russian—appeared to be well qualified for the position.

In May 2007, President Nazarbayev submitted a series of constitutional amendments to parliament, the most important of which dealt with the system of parliamentary elections and the role of political parties. Another change reduced the president's term from seven to five years beginning with the 2012 presidential election. Parliament added a clause removing term limits for the "first president," then passed the constitutional amendments.

One amendment raised the membership of the lower house (or Majilis) from 77 to 107 seats; 98 of these seats were to be filled on a proportional basis by vote of the general populace. Those party slates receiving a minimum of 7% of the total vote were to receive seats according to the total number of votes cast for the slate. The remaining 9 seats, meant to represent minorities in the population, were filled by a separate vote in the Assembly of the Peoples of Kazakhstan. Another amendment added 8 seats to the membership of the upper house (or Senate), giving that body a total to 47 members.

New parliamentary elections took place on August 18, 2007. Although seven parties ran national slates, Nur Otan, the party of President Nazarbayev, took 88% of the total vote and all of the contested seats. None of the other parties cleared the 7% electoral barrier.

Nazarbayev's efforts to construct a soft cult of personality around himself while deflecting government failures to his underlings proved to be effective.

A poll taken in March 2008 showed that the Kazakh public had a significant degree of trust in President Nazarbayev, with over half the surveyed citizens saying that they trusted the president. The poll also indicated that this trust did not extend to the government as a whole, with the Interior Ministry, regional governors' offices, and local authorities receiving the lowest ratings. The largest complaints were about the sharp increases in prices for consumer goods such as food and fuel.

Despite its problematic human rights record and entrenched authoritarian regime, in January 2010, Kazakhstan assumed the position of chair of the Organization for Security and Cooperation in Europe (OSCE), the first post-Soviet country to do so. Its greatest challenge came in April 2010, when Kyrgyz President Kurmanbek Bakiev was deposed and replaced by a pro-reform democratic interim government. Kazakhstan reacted by closing its borders with Kyrgyzstan. On the other hand, Kazakhstan played a key role in removing Bakiev from the country; it was Kazakhstan that gave guarantees for Bakiev's safe flight to Belarus. But Kazakhstan was harshly criticized by many individuals who thought that Kazakhstan should have acted more as the chair of the OSCE and less as an ally of Russia. As Paul Quinn-Judge, the Bishkek-based director of the Central Asia Project of the International Crisis Group put it,

The Kazakh approach to Kyrgyzstan since April has been not very supportive, and that's putting it incredibly mildly. Closing the border with Kyrgyzstan after the change of power in early April was not a helpful gesture and did a lot of damage to the Kyrgyz economy.

In May 2010, the Kazakh parliament adopted constitutional amendments that conferred the title of Yelbasy (Leader of the Nation) and an array of other benefits on President Nazarbayev. Amzebek Zholshibekov, a legislator of the pro-presidential Nur Otan party, explained that "thanks to President Nazarbayev Kazakhstan is chairing the OSCE this year and will chair the Organization of the Islamic Conference" in 2011.

Perhaps it was this reasoning that caused the Kazakh parliament to vote unanimously in favor of a national referendum in January 2011 that would have kept President Nazarbayev in office until 2020, circumventing two presidential

elections. Nazarbayev rejected the proposed referendum, however, and once again called for early presidential elections to take place on April 3, 2011. Since this was nearly two years earlier than specified by the constitution, the constitution had to be amended to allow for such a vote; however, parliament quickly passed the required constitutional amendment, so Nazarbayev could have his wish. In general, the political opposition criticized the early vote on the not surprising basis that no opposition candidate would be able to get prepared for the elections in just two months, but even Nazarbayev's most committed critics could not deny the popularity of the president—in fact, a poll taken in March showed that over 90% of the people wanted Nazarbayev to stay on as president. Although some political opponents advocated a boycott of the presidential voting, three candidates were eventually got their names on the ballot to run against Nazarbayev. But it was all pro forma. When the actual balloting was over, turnout was 89.9% and Nazarbayev had been reelected with nearly 95% of the votes.

In November 2011, probably by President Nazarbayev's instigation, 52 of 107 members of the lower house of parliament (Majilis) signed a petition calling for new elections with the purpose of producing a multiparty Majilis. When President Nazarbayev issued the decree dissolving the Majilis and setting the election to take place on January 15, 2012, therefore, he also specified that the political party coming in second in the election would receive seats in the parliament even if it failed to overcome the minimum 7% barrier.

As it turned out, that stipulation was unnecessary as three parties surpassed the 7% barrier. The ruling Nur Otan party came in first with 83 seats, and so continues to dominate the Majilis, but the Ak Zhol and the Communist People's Party divided the remaining 15 elective seats between them. Kazakhstan thus has a multiparty parliament. This is no threat to President Nazarbayev's power, however, since both the Ak Zhol and the Communist People's Party are considered loyal to the president, even if they technically are in the opposition.

In September 2012, President Nazarbayev got his eighth prime minister when Karim Massimov submitted his resignation; Massimov, Kazakhstan's longest serving prime minister had held that office since January 2007. After his resignation, Massimov was appointed head of the presidential administration. His replacement, Serik Akhmetov, only served as prime minister for a little over 18 months. In April 2014, Massimov became prime minister once again. In September 2015, President Nazerbayev's daughter, Dariga

Kazakhstan

Drying astrakhan pelts of the new-born Persian lambs, used like fur for garments
Courtesy of NOVOSTI

Nazerbayeva, was named deputy prime minister.

Although Kazakhstan has long sought to frame itself to Western audiences as relatively tolerant, the regime has intermittently demonstrated that it possesses significant capacity to repress. Perhaps this was most readily apparent in December 2011, when the police fired on striking workers in the western oil town of Zhanaozen, killing at least 15. After that, various opposition figures were arrested and given jail sentences on the charge that they were attempting to overthrow the government through their support of the strikers. As the crackdowns continued, the media became a target. In December 2012, the opposition television channel K-Plus and its two websites were banned. Several other opposition newspapers were also banned at this time. The trend is continuing. *Pravdivaya Gazeta*, an independent Almaty newspaper that began publishing in 2013, was given a three-month suspension shortly after it began publishing. Slapped twice with fines, it was shut down entirely in February 2014; as the Almaty court explained, the closure was because of the newspaper's "failure to implement the court's decisions." In April 2014, the courts closed a second opposition newspaper, the *Assandi-Times*, claiming that it was owned by the banned *Respublika* newspaper company. Taking note of these developments, the Norwegian Helsinki Committee has characterized the media crackdown as "a dramatic step in the wrong direction"; it further warned that a court ban on independent media would represent "a serious blow to Kazakhstan's reputation internationally."

Kazakhstan's efforts to frame itself positively to Western observers was greatly complicated by the sordid affair dubbed "Rakhat-gate" which saw the president's family squabbles get splashed over international newspapers. Rakhat Aliyev, Nazarbayev's ex-son in law and former husband to his eldest-daughter Dariga Nazarbayeva, had once been one of the richest and most powerful men in Kazakhstan. A series of scandals and alleged criminal activity, including rumors that he was plotting a coup against his father-in-law, led him to escape the country and seek protection in Europe. After Kazakhstan found him guilty of numerous crimes in absentia, he cast himself as a persecuted reformer and published a tell-all memoir entitled "The Godfather-in-Law" that claimed to reveal the truth about Nazarbayev's criminal regime. Although Austria had refused to extradite him to Kazakhstan, in 2014 he was arrested by Austrian police on charges that he arranged the kidnapping and murder of two bankers. Before his trial began, however, he was found dead in prison under mysterious circumstances.

A new Criminal Code was introduced on January 1, 2015. The most controversial aspect of it is the criminalization of rumors, or what is called the "deliberate propagation of false information." Fines for disseminating false rumors could be as high as $54,000. In cases where rumors are considered to be a threat to national security, those convicted could be sentenced to up to a decade in prison. This harsh crackdown on freedom of expression reflects the lack of a transparent mass media (why would rumors be believed if news circulated freely?) as well as the government's fear of possible social and political instability in the face of an economy weakened by the sharp drop in the price of oil and concerns over militant Islamic movements and Russia's growing military power.

On April 26, 2015, Kazakhstan held its fifth presidential election since gaining independence, and President Nazarbayev was elected to his fifth term. In a move likely intended to ease the process of the inevitable succession, the government adapted a series of 26 Constitutional amendments in March 2017. Collectively, these amendments weaken presidential power by granting parliament and especially ministers additional autonomy and oversight responsibilities. For instance, the parliament was granted consulting power over the formation of the cabinet. While officials have claimed that these reforms are intended to democratize the system, it seems more likely that they were enacted to minimize the likelihood of a scramble for power and resources among powerful elites once Nazarbayev stepped aside. After his surprise resignation on March 19, 2019, the effectiveness of these reforms will be put to the test.

To be sure, although Nazarbayev is no longer president, he personally retains significant formal and informal power. Following the example of the longtime prime minister of Singapore, Lee Kwan Yew, Nazarbayev has taken steps to ensure that he will continue to play a significant role in shaping Kazakhstan's trajectory even after his resignation. As the head of the ruling Nur Otan power and of the Security Council, a newly empowered body that manages and organizes state power, he is well positioned to manage and coordinate political developments. Furthermore, his title of Yelbasy, enshrined in the Constitution, guarantees that he and his family are immune for any criminal or civil prosecution.

His shock resignation was immediately preceded by his decision to dismiss his government in February 2019. He justified this dismissal as driven by his frustration with the government's failure to reverse declining living standards. The move occurred in the face widespread protests instigated by the death of five sisters in a house fire in the capital. Despite the hyper-modern promise of the capital, this family lived in a house that was not yet connected into to the city's gas network, forcing the family to rely upon the stove to generate enough heat. This shocking event galvanized the country's oft-dormant civil society as it captured widespread frustrations over the state's limited regulations and under-supported social safety net. Although the sacking of the government enabled Nazarbayev to once again deflect criticism away from himself, it is doubtful that the new president, Tokayev, will have as much latitude in finding parliamentary scapegoats.

Following the June 2019 snap presidential election, Tokayev was able to claim an electoral mandate. In this unfree and unfair election, the incumbent received 70.96% percent of the votes cast. Although this result was unsurprising, it did trigger large protests in Almaty and Nur-Sultan, leading to hundreds of arrests. Additional anti-regime protests occurred throughout 2019 and into 2020, which may indicate that Kazakhstani civil society activists feel empowered by the leadership change at the heart of the government.

On January 6, 2002, an unprecedent social unrest erupted in Kazakhstan. The decision by the Kazakh government to lift the cap on liquified gas prices was a factor that sparked street protests. As in previous years, the protests began in the western oil-producing city of Zhanaozen, and later spread to 14 major cities, including Almaty, the financial hub of the country. These protests took place against the background of poor living standards caused by endemic government corruption and aggravated by the Covid-19 pandemic. Initially peaceful, the protests escalated into violent clashes with the police, especially in Almaty, where protesters worked to topple Nazarbaev's statue and burned cars. In response, Tokaev dismissed the government, reinstated the cap on gas prices, and declared a state of emergency. These measures failed to passify protesters. The more aggressive flank of the protest burned down government buildings, looted retail outlets, ransacked gas stations, attacked television stations and police departments, and seized the airport. In the western city of Atyray, protestors reportedly shouted "Shal ket," "Old man, out," in reference to Nazarbayev, whom they blamed for the country's economic woes. Branding rioters as "international terrorists," Tokaev solicited the help of the Russian-led Collective Security Treaty Organization to violently demobilize them by issuing "a shoot to kill" order. Although proper investigations are yet to take place, by some estimates, the unrest led to the death of 300 people, including 19 security officials.

The unrest presented Tokaev a rare opportunity to distance himself from Nazarbaev, and he did not miss his chance. Describing the January events as an attempted coup, Tokaev arrested several of Nazarbayev's close associates, including Massimov, the ex-chief of the National Security Committee, and his deputies for allegedly plotting the coup. Additionally, he dismissed Nazarbaev from his position as the Chairman of the Security Council and relieved his close relatives of their duties. To end Nazarbaev's legacy, Tokaev spearheaded a constitutional reform that include amendments that would omit mention of Nazarbayev as Kazakhstan's *Elbasy* and deprive the former president and his close relatives of lifetime immunity from prosecution. Additionally, the proposed changes to the constitution provide for a balance of power among the different branches of the government. On June 5, 2002, the amendments to the constitution were put for voters' approval in a nationwide referendum. According to Kazakhstan's Central Elections Commissions the turnout was 68.06%, of which 77.18% voted in favor of the amendments. Addressing voters on the eve of the vote, Tokaev described the proposed changes as laying the foundation for a New Kazakhstan or a Second Republic. Tokaev has a rare opportunity to implement meaningful political reforms. It remains to be seen whether this opportunity will be seized or squandered.

Foreign Policy

General. After the presidents of Russia, Ukraine, and Belarus agreed to formation of the Commonwealth of Independent States in December 1991, Nazarbayev was active in getting other republics to join and actually hosted the Almaty meeting where the general agreement was signed. Kazakhstan has since been an active participant in the CIS. At the same time, President Nazarbayev has been at the forefront in encouraging cooperation among the Central Asian republics. He was, for example, one of the early proponents of the Central Asian Customs Union. Uzbekistan and Kyrgyzstan were the other two original members. Tajikistan has been a member since March 1998, while Russia has observer status. The presidents and prime ministers of the Central Asian Customs Union meet periodically to work out economic differences and to discuss economic matters. The organization has facilitated economic agreements between the individual members, but the growth in economic relations was slow to develop. In the case of Uzbekistan and Kazakhstan, the annual trade turnover was about $2 billion in 2013. At the same time, hundreds of Kazakh–Uzbek companies have come into existence, creating the possibilities for greater economic cooperation. However, the fact that the foreign policies of the two republics were based on different principles made cooperation between the two republics more difficult.

Recent diplomatic developments suggest that relations between the two republics may now be changing, partly as a result of worries about regional security following the withdrawal of the United States and NATO from Afghanistan at the end of 2014. The greater cooperation between the two republics can be dated from Uzbekistan President Islam Karimov's official visit to Astana in September 2012. President Nazarbayev paid his own official visit to Tashkent on June 13–14, 2013. In their continuing discussions, the two presidents found common areas of agreement, the most important of these, as President Nazarbayev put it, is that Uzbekistan and Kazakhstan are "the key states that provide peace, security, trade and growth of well-being" in Central Asia. Nazarbayev also stressed that regional problems had to be resolved by Central Asians themselves "without the intervention of foreign powers." The two presidents signaled their new commitment to cooperation by signing a Treaty on Strategic Partnership.

United States. At independence, President Nazarbayev said that he wanted Kazakhstan to become nuclear-free. In May 1993, however, he reversed himself and asked for security guarantees from the United States, Russia, and China in return for agreeing to give up Kazakhstan's nuclear weapons. He was, he said, asking for the pledge because some Chinese textbooks showed parts of Kazakhstan as being part of China. There was also other evidence to show that at least some Kazakh officials were having second thoughts about the merits of going nuclear-free. As one of Nazarbayev's advisers pointed out, Kazakhstan would not be receiving the attentions of Secretary of State James Baker and high-ranking officials of other countries, if it didn't have nuclear weapons.

Nazarbayev paid an official visit to Washington later that same month, however, and here he agreed to the withdrawal of nuclear weapons from Kazakhstan within seven years. Kazakhstan subsequently signed both the START I agreement and the Non-Proliferation Treaty.

Nazarbayev visited the United States again in February 1994. A major purpose of this visit was, according to his advisers, to get American help in reducing Kazakhstan's dependence on Russia. It appeared that Nazarbayev was uneasy about the rise to prominence in Russia of Vladimir Zhirinovsky, an ethnic Russian from Kazakhstan. Kazakhstan was also at that time under pressure from the Russian government to regularize Russian control of the Baikonur space launch facility and several military bases.

During the visit, President Clinton promised to increase US aid to Kazakhstan from the previous year's $91 million to $311 million in 1994–1995. A number of agreements were signed, including one by President Nazarbayev formalizing Kazakhstan's adhesion to the nuclear nonproliferation treaty. Kazakhstan has since become a member of the NATO-sponsored "Partners for Peace" and has participated in military maneuvers in Central Asia.

US–Kazakh relations deteriorated somewhat in 2000–2001 in response to US criticisms of Kazakhstan's human rights record, particularly the US world human rights report for 2001, which was critical of the Kazakh government's treatment of the political opposition. That changed somewhat after the terror attacks against the United States on September 11 when President Nazarbayev became one of the first among world leaders to join the American War on Terrorism, declaring soon after September 11 that Kazakhstan was prepared to allow the use of Kazakh military bases by foreign troops involved in the War on Terrorism. Nazarbayev also paid a four-day visit to the United States in December which included a 30-minute meeting at the White House. After the meeting, Nazarbayev and President George W. Bush signed a joint statement calling for a

long-term strategic partnership and cooperation between our nations.

Military cooperation continued to expand in 2002, symbolized by the visit of

Kazakhstan

General Tommy Franks, US Forces commander in chief for the Middle East and Central Asia, to Astana in August. The United States received emergency landing permission for the airport at Almaty, Chimkent, and Lugovoi, while it promised to provide Kazakhstan with helicopters and Humvees. Military assistance to Kazakhstan for 2003 was set at $270 million.

Yet there was another side to the relationship as well. The United States has been extremely critical of the Kazakh government's harassment and arrest of political opponents and its actions to restrict press freedom. The Kazakh government was also very unhappy when US Justice Department prosecutors raised the issue of possible bribes paid to President Nazarbayev during the 1990s in connection with dispensing of oil concessions in Kazakhstan.

Still, the US government has made it clear that it favors continued cooperation in the military sphere. In November 2004, it offered $36 million to Kazakhstan to set up biological laboratories to track dangerous pathogens and diseases. The US government has also spoken favorably about the "excellent business opportunities" that exist in Kazakhstan, though it warned that corruption remained a hazard in the local business environment.

President Nazarbayev paid an official visit to the United States in September 2006. In Washington, he called for closer relations with the United States, adding that "the time is coming when our relations can be raised to an absolutely different level." In a press release, the White House said that the visit had affirmed the 2001 strategic partnership agreement between Kazakhstan and the United States. The United States also expressed its support for Kazakhstan's entry into the World Trade Organization. On November 30, 2015, Kazakhstan joined the WTO.

In recent years, Kazakhstani officials has made a concerted effort to establish warm relations with US business leaders. For instance, in April 2017 Prime Minister Bakytzhan Sagintayev visited the US to meet with representatives from Chevron. While in the US, he also visited the Silicon Valley Innovation Center and announced plans to establish a Representative Office in the valley. Of course, state visits remain highly coveted, and a means to promote Kazakhstani interests. On January 16, 2018, President Nazarbayev was welcomed to the White House for an official visit with President Donald Trump. Unlike Nazarbayev's last visit to the White House in 2006, neither president mentioned that they discussed liberty, democracy, or human rights in their private talks. Instead, their discussion focused on the

Afghanistan war, nuclear non-proliferation (especially on the Korean peninsula), and commercial relations.

Russia. Nazarbayev has always supported close relations with Russia but these relations were expanded in January 1995 when Kazakhstan and Russia signed an agreement calling for closer economic and military links. This was followed, a few days later, by a second agreement establishing a customs union between Kazakhstan, Russia, and Belarus. President Nazarbayev also signed a key accord with Russia during a visit to Moscow in July 1998 which provided for the division of the northern sector of the Caspian Sea bed between the two countries.

The five states bordering on the Caspian Sea have been unable to agree on an overall legal demarcation of the Caspian Sea bed, considered to be a precondition for the exploitation of Caspian hydrocarbon reserves. But the 1998 agreement, which applied only to areas not claimed by the other three littoral states, allowed Russia and Kazakhstan to proceed with exploitation of the northern part of the Caspian Sea. This agreement was augmented in May 2002 when the Kazakh and Russian presidents signed a protocol on the division of the Kurmangazy, Tsentralnoe, and Khvalynskoe oil and natural-gas fields in the northern Caspian. Under the protocol, Kazakhstan will get the Kurmangazy field while the other two fields will go to Russia. The protocol also defined the median line dividing the Kazakh and Russian sectors of the Caspian Sea.

Presidents Nazarbayev and Putin have met regularly over the past several years for wide-ranging discussions on topics such as the CIS Collective Security Treaty, energy cooperation, economic integration, and the weapons trade. In July 2006, the two presidents announced an agreement to create a joint venture to expand capacity of the Soviet-built Orenburg refinery in order

Naval Cemetery at the Aral Sea

to process natural gas from Kazakhstan's Karachaganak gas field.

In November 2006, Kazakh Defense Minister Akhmetov told a news conference in Astana that the top priority in Kazakhstan's new defense doctrine was participation in the Collective Security Treaty Organization (CSTO). CSTO brings together Armenia, Belarus, Kazakhstan, Kyrgyzstan, Russia, and Uzbekistan. Akhmetov then added that China and Russia "remain Kazakhstan's strategic partners under the new doctrine." He did add, however, that the doctrine accorded "serious attention to the strengthening and perfecting of cooperation with the United States and NATO."

On January 1, 2015, Kazakhstan joined Russia and Belarus in founding the Eurasian Economic Union which allows people, goods, capital, and services to travel more freely within the member states. The Union has subsequently admitted Armenia and Kyrgyzstan.

China. Economic relations between Kazakhstan and China have been growing for a number of years, based largely on China's role as a growing consumer of Kazakh energy. For instance, an oil pipeline from eastern Kazakhstan to China was completed in 2005. Kazakhstan's energy cooperation with China has continued to grow since that time. This cooperation reached a new level in September 2013, when China's President Xi Jinping visited Astana as part of a four-country tour of Central Asia prior to attending the G20 summit in St. Petersburg. During the Chinese president's visit to Astana, the two heads of state initialed more than 20 economic agreements worth more than $30 billion. These included an agreement on building a new oil refinery in Kazakhstan and a second agreement whereby China obtained shares valued at $5.5 billion in Kazakhstan's Kashagan offshore oil project. There are also plans to construct a railroad connecting the two countries. As he met with President Xi Jinping, Nazarbayev proclaimed that Kazakhstan and China had now entered an era of "strategic" relationship.

By early 2015, China's investment in Kazakhstan, which consisted largely of oil and gas pipelines, totaled $26 billion. In March, China and Kazakhstan agreed on a massive industrial development program for Kazakhstan worth another $23 billion. Two months later, President Nazarbayev and Chinese President Xi Jinping agreed to build a system of transportation routes connecting China to Europe through Kazakhstan. Kazakhstan has enormous economic potential serving simply as transit territory between East and West.

Kazakhstan

At independence, Kazakhstan inherited a long-standing border dispute with China. Throughout much of the 20th century, the border between China and the then-Soviet Union was not demarcated. A series of treaties in the mid-1990s finally delineated the border. This process enabled further political engagement between the two neighbors. Most notably, in the 2000s, China and Kazakhstan helped to found the Shanghai Cooperation Organization, which is designed to enhance Both China and Kazakhstan are founding members of the Shanghai Cooperation Organization, which is predominately designed to promote security engagement between member states.

Overall, Kazakhstan is in tricky situation vis-à-vis China. As the regional hegemon, China has tremendous leverage over Kazakhstan. At the same time, Kazakhstani officials are mindful of their population's widespread cultural anxiety and negative perceptions of China. As Bruce Pannier writing for Radio Free Europe/Radio Liberty describes in an article from June 1, 2018, this balancing act was especially noticeable following reports that Kazakhstani citizens had been detained and sent to re-education camps while in China. As Pannier recounts, the widespread reporting of these detentions forced the Kazakhstan Foreign Ministry to issue a statement following a meeting in Beijing which read: "The question of the situation of ethnic Kazakhs, who have resettled from China to Kazakhstan and have become citizens of the Republic of Kazakhstan, was raised by the Kazakh side. An urgent request was expressed about an objective and fair review of affairs and the release of those ethnic Kazakhs detained in China who have dual citizenship."

Vatican. President Nazarbayev also signed an important agreement with the Vatican during a visit there in September 1998. Essentially, the agreement grants the Roman Catholic Church full religious freedom and access to the media in Kazakhstan. This, the first such agreement that the Vatican has signed with a former Soviet republic, then provided the background for a visit that Pope John Paul II paid to Kazakhstan in September 2001. The pope celebrated a mass in Astana for 50,000 pilgrims, then met later that same day with President Nazarbayev. There are an estimated 350,000 Roman Catholics living in Kazakhstan.

Nature of the Regime
Kazakhstan adopted a new constitution in 1993 which only slightly modified the presidential-parliamentary system (modeled rather closely on that of Russia)

which had been set up after independence. The popularly elected, executive presidency was retained, but the new constitution created a 177-member parliament, with 42 seats to be filled by direct presidential appointees and another 11 by the official trade unions. In early 1995, the Constitutional Court ruled this system to be illegal because it violated the principle of "one man, one vote."

President Nazarbayev disbanded the legislature and ruled by decree while he had the electoral law redrafted to bring it into line with the decision of the Constitutional Court. The new electoral law created a bicameral parliament, made up of a completely elective lower house (or Majilis) and a partly appointed upper house (or Senate). Under the terms of the decree, seven of the Senate seats were to be filled by presidential appointment, while the remaining 32 seats were to be indirectly elected at a joint session of the representative bodies of all local government units, on the basis of two deputies from each oblast and major city.

Although a decision was made to postpone creation of the Senate until a later time, the first parliamentary elections for the lower house under the new system took place in December 1995. Many of the winning candidates ran as independents, since Kazakhstan was only beginning to create political parties at this time. When President Nazarbayev launched a new political party called Otan in 1999 as his own political platform, however, 44 deputies signed on as members.

Shortly before the 1999 parliamentary elections, new legislation was passed specifying that 10 of the 67 seats in the lower house would be allocated on a proportional basis to those political parties drawing a minimum of 7% of the national vote. In 2002, the total number of seats in the lower house was raised to 77 as of the 2004 elections, with, again, 10 of the seats to be awarded to party slates on a proportional basis.

In October 2002, elections were held for 16 seats in the Senate. A total of 33 candidates—31 men and 2 women—competed for the seats. The majority of the candidates were members of pro-presidential parties and in six of the districts the candidate ran unopposed. Since the regional councils both nominate and elect the senators, there were few surprises. For example, The Almaty city council elected the man who had been the council's secretary for the preceding eight years. Neither woman was elected. The remaining 16 senators were elected on August 19, 2005. Ten seats were won by Otan while three additional seats went to independents. The remaining three seats were won by

Auyl, Asar, and the Civic Party, all allies of the pro-presidential Otan Party.

A series of constitutional amendments passed in May 2007 specified that the size of the lower-house Majilis be 107 seats at the time of the next legislative elections; 98 Majilis seats were to be elected on the basis of proportional representation using party slates; the remaining 9 seats would be elected by the Assembly of Kazakhstan Nations.

The Majilis would be organized on the basis of party factions, with the prime minister representing the majority party in the Majilis. The Senate was increased to 47, with 15 deputies appointed by the president. Party factions would not exist in the Senate.

These same constitutional amendments reduced the term of office of the president to five years beginning at the end of President Nazarbayev's term in 2012. The amendments also gave the president the right to run for the office indefinitely; his successor, Kassym-Jomart Tokayev, will, however, be limited to two five-year terms.

The latest Majilis elections took place on March 20, 2016. Due to the economic crisis, the government dissolved in January 20, 2016 and snap-elections were called, presumably to select a government more capable of addressing fundamental economic issues. If this was indeed the impetus for the vote, the election is unlikely to have any impact as the results were nearly identical to the 2012 election results. Nur Otan won 82.2% of the vote, and received 84 seats. Ak Zhol won 7.18% of the vote and received 7 seats and the Communist People's Party of Kazakhstan won 7.14% of the vote and received 7 seats as well.

Kazakhstan has had 10 prime ministers since independence. The latest is Askar Mamin, appointed February 25, 2019.

In July 2000, parliament passed a law bestowing on the incumbent president special powers for life. Under the terms of this law, Nazarbayev will retain a permanent seat on the Security Council; he will also retain the right to address the people, parliament, and future presidents. President Nazarbayev was most recently reelected in April 2015. The election provided voters no real choice and Nazarbayev won a remarkable 98% of the vote. Significant constitutional reforms were passed in March 2017 which aimed at slightly weakening the power of the president and formally empowering the legislature. Most notably, a president's power to issue decrees that have the power of law are curtailed, and parliament is granted consulting power over the composition of the President's Cabinet. By most accounts these reforms were intended to lay the groundwork for presidential succession. It should come as no surprise, therefore, that these

Kazakhstan

amendments were adapted only months after Uzbekistan experienced a peaceful presidential succession following Islam Karimov's death. With Nazarbayev's resignation, the effectiveness of these reforms will be tested.

Culture

Kazakhs are historically a rural people. Nearly all are Muslims, but there has never been a major religious center such as can be found in Uzbekistan. There is a specific Kazakh style of clothing and interior decoration. Traditional women still tend to wear a long, wide dress with a stand-up collar and bloomers gathered at the ankle, particularly in the countryside. Elderly men wear wide, white shirts, wide trousers, and woolen or cotton robes. Young people of both sexes tend to wear European-style clothing. This is especially the case in the cosmopolitan cities of Almaty and Nur-Sultan. The large malls and shopping areas of these cities are stocked with major global brands. Kazakh homes exhibit specific Kazakh designs in stucco work and wall facings, while floors are covered with carpets. The cuisine is meat-based and shares a number of similarities with Kyrgyz food. The most popular meal is Beshbarmaq, which is boiled meat (often mutton or horse) served over noodles. The name—which translates to "five fingers"—refers to the traditional way of eating the dish without cutlery.

Because of several terrorist attacks in 2011 that were blamed on religious extremists, the Kazakh government enacted new legislation attempting to give the state greater power to regulate religious activities. Entitled "The Law on Religious Activity and Religious Associations," the new law severely tightens registration procedures for religious institutions. Although it technically applies to all religions, the real concern appears to be with the growth of interest in Islam in recent years. Many new mosques have been built in recent years and there is an increasing popularity among young girls for the hijab or Islamic head scarf. But the 2011 terrorist attacks and the first suicide attack, along with other evidence of growing Islamic extremism, appear to be the motivating factors behind the new law.

There is a growing literary and contemporary art scene. Abay Ibragim Kunanbayev, a 19th-century humanist and poet, is usually considered to be the father of Kazakh written literature. Early twentieth-century writers include Aqmet Baytursinuli, an author and newspaper editor, and Jambil Jabayev, a folk poet. The best known of the Kazakh literary figures of the Soviet period is Mukhtar Auezov, a playwright and novelist; his long novel, *Abay*, deals with Kazakh steppe life in the 19th century. It has been translated into English. Kazakhstan has recently begun developing a film industry. The 2008 film *Tulpan* won acclaim and some international awards for its reflective depiction of life in a steppe village. Kazakhstan has also produced some historical epics including 2007's *Mongol: The Rise of Genghis Khan* (co-produced with Russian and German companies) and 2011's *Myn Bala*, a state-sponsored film that dramatized the fight between Kazakhs and the Dzungars (a Mongol tribe) which occurred in the early 1700s. The latter film is explicitly nationalistic and echoes *Braveheart* in telling the story of an early independence struggle. It was released to commemorate the 20th anniversary of Kazakhstan independence.

Almaty is the largest city and the center for most higher education. The Kazakh S. M. Kirov State University is located here, as is the Abay Teachers College. Almaty also has polytechnic, agricultural, and veterinary institutes. Karaganda has a medical institute and a teachers training college. (Nazarbayev University in Nur-Sultan is a clear exception.) Other institutes of higher learning are also found in regional centers.

There is a Kazakh Academy of Sciences, founded in 1945. This has particularly encouraged scholarship in ethnographic studies of the Kazakh language and the history of Kazakh literature. It also finances industrial and agricultural research.

In October 2006, President Nazarbayev told a session of the Assembly of the Peoples of Kazakhstan that the country should consider switching the alphabet for the Kazakh language from Cyrillic to Latin. He then appointed a panel of experts to produce specific proposals on the issue. For about a decade, this proposed policy change was largely dormant with only vague references made to some future date in which the Latin alphabet would be fully adapted. In April 2017, however, the president published an article in *Egemen Kazakhstan*, an official newspaper, which stated that all government documents would use the Latin alphabet by 2025. To successfully make this date will require a significant outlay of resources to ensure that large segments of the population are not made functionally illiterate overnight.

In recent years, language has emerged as a significant social issue amongst Kazakhs. In urban areas, Russian is the first language of many ethnic Kazakhs. After decades of Kazakh-language promotion, some Kazakh speaking nationalists have grown frustrated with Russian-speaking co-ethnics. In online discussion boards, ethnic Kazakhs who cannot speak Kazakh are sometimes dismissed as inauthentic Kazakhs who have forgotten their heritage.

Economy

About 20% of the residents of the republic support themselves from agriculture or stock-raising. The northern part of Kazakhstan is a major grain growing area, with supplemental crops like fruits, vegetables, grapes, sugar beets, and potatoes being grown. Stock-raising is concentrated in the dryer area to the south of the grain belt, in the area of the grassy steppe. Cotton, tobacco, grapes, and mustard are grown in the Syr-Dar'ya and Ili River Valleys.

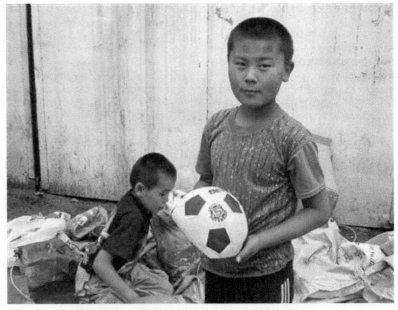

Kyrgyz boy working in Almaty's Green Market

Kazakhstan

Kazakhstan had already instituted a number of reforms in agriculture during the Gorbachev era which began to break down the old system of command control. For example, a 1987 law abolished all restrictions on the number of animals that a farmer could have. This led to an increase of about 2.5 million in the sheep and goat population and about a million additional cattle. Meat sales in the cooperative sector also quadrupled in that time. In addition, 890,000 families received plots of land in 1991 and 46,000 private houses were constructed with state assistance.

In February 1992, Nazarbayev signed a decree on privatizing the property of enterprises in the agro-industrial complex, apparently intending to end the collective and state farm system. At the time, Nazarbayev commented that Kazakhstan did not need loss-making farms. "Private farming works because it is private," he was quoted as saying. There was bitter resistance to this approach at the local level, however, and as a result parliament refused to endorse any major changes. However, the government continued to pursue policies aimed at breaking up the old agricultural units with the result that, by 1999, 75% of agricultural land was held in leasehold by individual farmers. President Nazarbayev still favored the complete privatization of farmland, but he could not get a majority of the parliament to support him on this issue. In February 2000, therefore, Nazarbayev asked parliament to give private farmers the right to use the land they lease as a pledge on the land market.

In August 2002, President Nazarbayev took up the issue again while touring grain fields outside Almaty. Promising to submit a land law to the parliament, he said that he wanted to give farmers the right to purchase agricultural land directly, or on a 10-year installment plan. Nazarbayev next submitted the issue to Kazakhstan's National Council—which comprises representatives from the government, parliament, trade unions, presidential administration, and business community. The National Council approved a draft Land Code and ordered the government to submit the final version to parliament. Discussion of the Land Code began in parliament in March 2003. Many deputies objected and over 500 amendments were added to the bill. Two months later, the bill was still under discussion. Parliament eventually passed a privatization bill, though only after passing a number of amendments. Because he was unable to persuade parliament to pass the privatization bill in the form desired by the president, Prime Minister Imangali Tasmagambetov submitted his resignation in June 2003.

The issue of land ownership has remained a tricky subject for the regime to navigate. In 2016, a national wave of protests swept over the country following a March announcement by then–Minister of the Economy, Erbolat Dosaev, that 1.7 million hectares of agricultural land would soon be put up for auction. Alongside the auction, there were plans to extend the length of time in which foreigners could lease land. Despite assurances that the foreigners would not be permitted to own any of the land, there were widespread concerns among many Kazakhstanis that the auctions would facilitate a Chinese land grab. The size and scope of the protests caught the government off-guard and spurred Nazarbayev to issue a temporary moratorium on changes to the Land Code. To better gauge (and manage) public attitudes, two new institutions were created in the wake of the protests: 1) a commission on land reform which was intended to interface between the regime and the rural population; and 2) a Ministry of Information and Communication, which would be responsible for both ensuring consistent and clear government messaging and for gauging public sentiment expressed in social media and other outlets. Although these institutions have since evolved (for instance the new ministry was dissolved and absorbed into the new Ministry of Information and Social Development) the legacy of these protests has continued to influence Kazakhstani domestic policy. At the time of writing, in spring 2021 the government was on the cusp of permanently banning foreign ownership or leasing of agricultural land.

Kazakhstan's grain belt is in the north, comprising the three oblasts of Kostanai, North Kazakhstan, and Akmola, where the capital is located. Its largest grain crop is wheat, followed by barley. This is spring wheat, with a small amount of winter wheat produced in southern Kazakhstan. The soils of northern Kazakhstan are fertile *chernozem* and *kashtan* soils, capable of producing outstanding harvests; however, it is also a region subject to frequent drought. Accordingly, grain production is marked by sharp year-to-year fluctuations. For example, the grain harvest went from 6.9 million tons in 1998—a year of drought—to 15 million tons in 1999 and 14 million tons in 2000, then climbed to 18 million tons in 2001. Kazakhstan produces a grain surplus for export in most years; it exported close to 6 million tons in 2001. Kazakhstan produced a near record grain harvest of 17.1 million tons in 2003. Because of smaller grain harvests in the neighboring republics of Russia, Ukraine, and Belarus, about half of the harvest was sold abroad. When this produced shortages at home and increases in the price of

bread, the government was forced to institute an informal ban on the export of grain in January 2004.

Kazakhstan had a large grain harvest of 20 million tons in 2007 but, as a result of the significant increase in the world price for grain in 2007, the government subsequently prohibited the export of most grains, though exceptions were made for neighboring countries such as Kyrgyzstan. To deal with the problem on a permanent basis, the government created a stabilization grain reserve which eventually grew to one million tons. When the 2008 grain harvest came in at 15.6 million tons, therefore, the government announced that 6 million tons would be available for export. The 2009 grain harvest was 21 million tons. Extremely hot weather in 2010 led to a bad drought and a sharp drop in grain production; the Kazakh government then issued a ban on the export of grain that fall. The year 2011 saw another bumper crop—22,732,000 tons, while in 2012 production dropped to 9,841,000 tons. Official estimates project a 2013 harvest of 15 million tons. Grain and flour exports for 2019 are projected to be 9 million tons.

Kazakh industry is mainly of the extractive variety. Most industry is located in the northeastern part of the republic, in and around the cities of Karaganda, Zelinograd, and Semipalatinsk. Kazakhstan has large deposits of coal and iron ore. It also produces lead, zinc, copper, chromite, nickel, molybdenum, tin, antimony, cadmium, bauxite, gold, silver, phosphates, and oil. In addition to the processing of ferrous and nonferrous metals, Kazakhstan has chemical, machine-building, cement, and textile industries. Light industries associated with agriculture include food processing and leather. Overall, about 30% of the people are employed in industry, while approximately 50% are employed in services.

In September 1991, the government approved a program for the "first stage of destatization and privatization" of state property. The program, which included a coupon mechanism, promoted privatization in trade, public catering, construction, motor transport, agriculture, consumer services, and small enterprises. Medium and large enterprises were to be converted to joint-stock companies, collective enterprises, or partnerships. In a speech to the legislature in January 1993, however, Nazarbayev spoke of mistakes associated with free-market reform in Russia and Kazakhstan and declared that a significant decree of state control and regulation would be necessary in the future. He indicated that major enterprises would be run along commercial principles, but most would remain in state hands. Most small- and medium-scale industries have been

Kazakhstan

privatized since that time, but plans to extend privatization into the areas of gas and oil, which had been stalled for a number of years, have since been reversed. Prime Minister Massimov announced in December 2007 that the Kazakh government intended to nationalize "strategic" energy assets. This has mostly taken the form of the government buying up the shares of publicly traded energy companies, but parliament also enacted a revised energy law in November 2007 which gives the Kazakh government greater authority over the work of international energy companies.

One colonial leftover that the Kazakhs are somewhat ambivalent about is the massive space complex at Baikonur Cosmodrome. There is no question but that the space program has given tremendous stimulus to the advancement of high-tech education, but it has been almost exclusively Russians, not ethnic Kazakhs, that have benefited from the program. This has bothered the government of Kazakhstan, which would like ethnic Kazakhs to be able to benefit more from its presence. A new agreement, signed in January 2004 during a visit of President Putin to Kazakhstan, extends Russia's lease to 2050. Subsidiary clauses make reference to bilateral and international use of the spaceport and provide for the presence of Kazakh police, tax authorities, and customs officers in Baikonur City.

Kazakhstan is one of the few ex-Soviet republics to have attracted significant interest among foreign investors since independence. The reason for this is that Kazakhstan has some of the largest undeveloped oil, gas, and mineral deposits on earth. By the end of 1999, foreign direct investment in the oil, gas, and mining sectors had grown to $3 billion, with an addition $1.2 billion on extraction expenditures, $1 billion invested in the construction or renovation of subsurface use facilities, and $213.7 million expended on geological surveys. In addition, Kazakhstan has commitments from foreign companies to invest more than $60 billion in the coming years. The 1998 decline in petroleum prices slowed this process, but Kazakhstan nevertheless received $1.3 billion in foreign direct investment in 1999, over one-half in the energy sector.

For example, the Chevron Corporation and the Government of Kazakhstan signed an agreement in April 1993 establishing a 40-year, $20 billion joint venture (Tengizchevroil) to develop the Tengiz and Korolev oil fields on the northeastern coast of the Caspian Sea. By June 1997, Chevron had invested $800 million in Kazakhstan and had committed itself to invest another $500 million over the next three years, with plans to invest $20 billion in the Tengiz oil field over the next 40 years. The Tengizchevroil joint venture was producing 160,000 barrels of oil a day as of June 1997 and planned to increase this to 700,000 barrels a day by 2003.

Kazakhstan's integration into the global economy was accelerated with the formal opening of the Caspian Pipeline Consortium pipeline in November 2001.

This pipeline, which runs from the Tengiz oil field in western Kazakhstan to Novorossiysk, a Russian seaport on the Black Sea, had an initial capacity of 28.2 million tons a year, which was scheduled to increase to 67 million tons. Chevron Texaco Oil, which owns a 15% stake in the Caspian Pipeline Consortium, announced afterward that it would increase its production of Kazakh oil from 13 million tons per year to 20 million tons per year by 2005, and that this would involve an investment of $1.5 billion over the following three years in the Tengizchevronoil joint venture.

In another change that occurred in February 2002, the Kazakhstan Government merged its largest oil-producing company, KazakhOil, with its largest oil-transporting company, Transport Nefti i Gaza [Oil and Gas Transportation], to produce a new closed joint-stock company, KazMuayGaz [Kazakh Oil and Gas]. The new entity controls 15% of the country's oil production capacity and more than 6,400 kilometers of oil pipelines which deliver 80% of the country's oil. The government indicated that it would also retain a 51% stake in all new gas and oil contracts. The government has said that concentration of control over oil extraction and transportation will improve the coordination of operations in the sector.

Tengizchevroil canceled plans to invest a further $3 billion into the project in November 2002 after a disagreement with the Kazakh government over funding of the planned second stage of development. The company wanted to fund the expansion out of revenues, while the government worried over the loss of taxes. Under a compromise reached in January 2003, the consortium agreed to pay $810 million to the government, of which $600 million was taxes to be paid in installments from 2003–2005. In addition, the consortium agreed to take out a loan to finance the government's share of the cost of pushing ahead with development.

Direct foreign investment in the country between 1991 and 2002 was about $13 billion. However, an October 2002 government announcement that KazMunayGaz, the national oil-and-gas company, had discovered new reserves in the Caspian Sea 80 kilometers south of the giant Kashagan field may soon make that sum seem small. In February 2004, it was announced that a consortium of international oil companies had formally agreed to invest $29 billion in developing the new oil field. Total oil reserves are now estimated to be 13 billion barrels. The oil companies involved are ENI, Royal Dutch Shell, ExxonMobil, Total of France, Conoco Phillips, and Impex of Japan. The Kazakh Foreign Ministry put US investment in Kazakhstan at $11.43 billion as of the first quarter of 2005. In March 2006, US Energy Secretary Samuel Bodman announced during a visit to Astana that US investment in Kazakhstan "could double in the next five years."

The United States Government strongly supports continued American investment in Kazakhstan; in September 2006, during President Nazarbayev's visit to Washington, it issued a press release pointing out that the United States has accounted for 30% of foreign direct investment in Kazakhstan.

Kazakhstan's export potential is still limited by the lack of pipelines to transport energy to ports, however. The Caspian Pipeline Consortium pipeline was pumping 12 million tons per year as of October 2002, so the government has pinned great hopes on the Baku-Tbilisi-Ceyhan pipeline, which began its first oil shipments in early 2006. Kazakhstan supports the idea of building an undersea oil pipeline across the Caspian Sea that would connect Aktau in Kazakhstan with Baku in Azerbaijan. The project was originally timed to coincide with the beginning of production of production at Kazakhstan's Kashagan oil field in 2009. Production at Kashagan, initially only 75,000 barrels a day, will eventually climb to 1.2 million barrels a day. Kazakhstan is currently shipping 10 million tons of oil to Baku by boat, where it is then fed into the Baku–Tbilisi–Ceyhan pipeline.

A July 2010 report in the *New York Times* indicated that Chevron had raised the *capacity* of the Tengiz oil field to 600,000 barrels a day but that actual production was only 420,000 barrels a day. The challenge is getting the oil to the market. The 1,580-kilometer Caspian Pipeline Consortium pipeline has a capacity of 600,000 barrels a day, but Chevron is limited to 420,000 barrels a day. Meanwhile, the Russian government has refused to enlarge the capacity of the pipeline because, it says, it does not have the evidence that there will be enough oil running through it to justify its cost. Some Tengiz oil is shipped by tanker across the Caspian Sea and then by overland railway tankers, but this is a much more costly means of transportation. Chevron has said that it is willing to make further production investments which would raise the

Kazakhstan

productive capacity of the Tengiz field to a million barrels a day, but it first needs to know how it will get the additional production to market.

The Kazakh government also completed the 988-kilometer Atasu-Alashankou oil pipeline linking western Kazakh oil fields with China in December 2005. Deliveries to China began in mid-2006. The initial annual capacity of the pipeline is 10 million tons. Russia's state-owned Rosneft has also begun using the pipeline to ship oil to China. The pipeline will eventually transport 20 million tons of oil a year. In 2007, President Nazarbayev announced plans to construct a 700-kilometer oil pipeline from Atasu in central Kazakhstan to the Caspian Sea coast. The pipeline will connect to the existing Atasu-Alashankou oil pipeline to China.

In May 2007, Kazakhstan, Russia, and Turkmenistan signed an agreement calling for the construction of a new pipeline along the Caspian Sea coast to transport Turkmen and Kazakh natural gas to European markets through Russia.

Kazakhstan has also proposed the construction of a new 700-kilometer canal that would connect the Caspian Sea to the Black Sea. The canal would cost an estimated $6 billion and take 10 years to build. It would, however, accommodate ships weighing up to 10,000 tons and essentially open the Caspian Sea to international commerce.

Kazakhstan's economy grew at an annual rate of 9.3% in 2004, with both its retail and financial sectors showing significant growth. Agricultural production jumped 6% in the first quarter of 2004, but that was dwarfed by a 21.5% growth in capital investments. People are obviously much poorer in the countryside; to address this disparity, the government launched a three-year program in late 2003 aimed at providing $1 billion in new investment in agriculture over the following three years.

GDP growth in 2005 was 9.4%, 10% in 2006, and 8.7% in 2007. Industrial growth slowed to 4.6% in 2005, but the construction and service sectors grew so fast in 2006 that general unemployment declined. Inflation has been a problem in the economy and this led Prime Minister Massimov to present an action plan to parliament in February 2007 aimed at achieving an inflation rate of 7.5–8% in 2007–2009. The government also took some money out of the economy in 2006 by paying off $849 million of the country's sovereign debt ahead of schedule, reducing it to $3.9 billion or 7.8% of GDP. In addition, the National Fund, created to set aside surplus energy-sector revenues, had grown to $8 billion by 2005. In January 2008, Kazakhstan's gold and currency reserves reached a new high of $38.4 billion.

The worldwide economic recession that began in 2008 has also reached Kazakhstan, though not as severely as several of its neighbors. GNP growth dropped to 3.1% in 2008, and the unemployment rate rose to about 7%. Real GNP growth was around 2% in 2009, with unemployment growing to about 8%. The Kazakh government also launched a Joint Action Plan on stabilization of the economy and financial system for 2009–2010, whose goals included support for small- and medium-sized enterprises, stabilization of the financial system, and support to socially vulnerable groups of the population. A crisis in the banking sector began in February 2009. At that time, the external debt of the banking sector was 26% of GDP, totaling about $12 billion. The BTA Bank was deemed to be in the greatest trouble, so the Kazakh government carried out a restructuring of the bank. What was unusual about the restructuring is that it was carried out without government guarantees. Instead, BTA creditors were offered various combinations of senior and subordinated debt, and a small stake in the bank's equity; the refinancing lowered the banking industry's external debt to about $4 billion.

The economy began growing again in 2010, though at a lower rate because of the 2010 crisis in the agricultural sector, caused by hot weather and the drought that resulted from it. GDP growth in 2011 was 3.5%. That figure dropped to 0.5% in 2012; although oil production showed a drop of about 1.9% for 2012, the major problem seems to be in other segments of the economy. Kazakhmyc Pic, a large producer of copper, reported a loss of $2.27 billion for the year. A drought also reduced total grain production.

The Kashagan offshore oilfield began production in September 2013 after 13 years of development, but production had to be suspended almost immediately when it was discovered that toxic gas had corroded the pipelines leading to the mainland. In February 2014, the National Bank of Kazakhstan devalued Kazakhstan's currency, the tenge, by about 20% against the dollar. The primary reason for this devaluation was a decline in the value of the Russian ruble, but deterioration in Kazakhstan's trade balance had also eaten into foreign balance reserves. In 2015, the economy slowed significantly due to the collapse of oil prices and the Russian recession. That year, the economy grew only 1.5%. In the final four months of 2015, the tenge lost around 50% of its value relative to the dollar, drastically raising the price of many goods including sugar, butter, and tea. In the wake of these shocks, there have been frequent small-scale economic protests.

President Nazarbayev has frequently spoken of the need for further economic diversification, pointing out on one occasion that "about ten mega holdings control almost 80% of Kazakhstan's total GDP. We should work to transfer the secondary functions of mega holdings to medium and small business," he argued. A spokesman later explained that "what the president has in mind is that the ten financial and oligarchic groups in Kazakhstan that control 80% of the economy should in no way influence decision making in the government and in parliament." He also suggested that parliament would consider new laws to reduce the current economic concentration, but that such laws would take two to five years to enact.

In December 2012, President Nazarbayev reiterated his position on the need for change. Setting forth the goal of making Kazakhstan one of the world's 30 most developed and prosperous nations by 2050, he announced a reorganization of the government through the creation of a new ministry in charge of regional development and the optimization of policy functions within existing structures. Nazarbayev also proposed that 11 existing pension organizations, both state-owned and private, be organized into a single pension fund. The purpose of this move was to improve the flow of money to the non-extracting sectors of the economy. At the same time, he stated that budgetary funds should be used in the future only for large-scale investment projects. He also promised further privatizations of state-owned firms. Lastly, he lifted the ban on the exploitation of newly discovered mineral deposits, thus opening this sector to private investment.

Kazakhstan also has the second-largest reserves of uranium ore in the world. In 2009, Kazakhstan accounted for 19.4% of the world's supply of uranium. Nuclear production began during the Soviet period but, after independence, a state nuclear firm, Kazatomprom, was created to handle all production. Since that time, Kazatomprom has developed a number of foreign partners, including the Canadian mining giant Cameco, which runs a joint plant with Kazatomprom for the processing of yellowcake. At this plant, sulfuric acid is injected into the ground, where it reacts with the ore. The solution is then pumped into a plant that distills it into yellowcake.

A French and Japanese conglomerate runs another joint plant to turn enriched uranium into fuel rods. Kazatomprom has also signed agreements to become China's main supplier of nuclear fuel. In addition, Kazatomprom owns a stake in Westinghouse, which gives it a piece of the reactor constructor business.

285

Kazakhstan

Kazakhstan has also signed a number of agreements with Russia in recent years. In 2006, the Zarechnoye mine, a joint uranium venture set up by Russia's Teksnabexport and Kazakhstan's Kazatomprom, began operation. The following year, the governments of Russia and Kazakhstan agreed to spend up to $3 billion to set up an enrichment facility in Siberia to produce nuclear fuel. The facility is expected to begin producing nuclear fuel in 2011. The Kazakh government is also considering building a number of nuclear plants to provide electricity to more remote parts of the country. The first project, a 600-megawatt plant costing $100 million, has been designated for the western Kazakh city of Aqtau.

One of Kazakhstan's problems that it inherited at the time of independence was the situation with regard to the Aral Sea. For the first 10 years or so of independence, Kazakhstan attempted to arrive at a common agreement with Uzbekistan, the other republic heavily affected by the drying up sea, but nothing was ever decided.

By 2000, the Aral Sea had split into two sections, with the larger sea largely in Uzbekistan and a small sea in Kazakhstan. Kazakhstan then turned to the World Bank, which agreed to help finance the Kok-Aral Dam and a series of dikes designed to create spillways to allow the flushing of excess salt from the sea while improving the overall water levels. The project began in 2001.

The project is still ongoing, with plans to repair a second dam, dig a channel to connect the two parts of the Aral Sea, and provide additional water management structures. However, the dam has already raised the level of the small Aral from 98 to 125 feet and it has expanded the Aral's surface area by 30%. The small Aral has recovered enough that commercial fishing is now again possible. Government experts warn, however, that the process has only begun and it will take decades for the small Aral to recover. No one holds out any hope for the large Aral. Some water from the small Aral already makes its way to the large Aral, but it is only the excess water from a sluice on top of the dam. The Kazakh government estimates that the small Aral will have to reach a depth of 138 feet before it will become minimally viable. When that occurs, a greater flow into the large Aral will be possible.

The Future

Kazakhstan's statehood and Kassym-Jomart Tokaev's presidency survived unprecedented political unrest that rocked the country at the start of the year. With the help of Russian troops, Tokaev's government was able to violently demobilize the unrest. Having accomplished their mission, Russian troops immediately left instead of annexing Kazakhstan, as speculated by Western and local analysts. The unrest, which started over a steep increase in fuel prices, quickly escalated into political demands with protesters calling for Tokaev's government to finally decouple itself from Nazarbaev, who was serving as a lifelong chairman of the National Security Council and leader of the ruling Nur Otan political party. Tokaev responded by dismissing Nazarbaev from the security council and purging his relatives and associates from the security services, whom he accused of masterminding the coup. He spearheaded a constitutional reform to change the system from a strong presidential rule to one where all branches of the government have equal power. The reform extends the presidential term to seven years from five, and prohibits incumbents from seeking a second term. In September 2022, Tokayev signed a constitutional amendment to revert the name of the country's capital from Nur-Sultan to Astana. On June 5, 2002, the amendments to the constitution were put for voters' approval in a nationwide referendum, in which the vast majority voted in favor of those amendments. On March 19, a snap parliamentary election for the lower chamber of parliament (Majilis) took place under a reformed electoral system, which allowed 29 of the 98 elected representatives to be self-nominated and elected by single-member constituencies. As part of a constitutional reform package, the electoral rule change appears to have been intended for increasing the representation diverse array of candidates, not merely those associated with political parties. According to Western election observers, overall contestants were able to campaign actively and freely. These are important, but by no means sufficient, steps to end Nazarbaev's legacy of misrule. That would require implementing genuine political and welfare-enhancing economic reforms. It remains to be seen whether Tokaev has the will and power to deliver on those.

The Kazakh economy has been strong in the 21st century until recently. After a period of sluggish growth caused by the pandemic, the country's economy regained a 4% growth in 2021. Although the authorities had hoped to maintain that rate for the years to come, with Western sanctions against Russia, that is unlikely to happen. The World Bank estimates that shocks associated with Western sanctions on Russia coupled with the impact of the ongoing Covid-19 pandemic are likely to reduce growth to 1.5 percent in 2002, against a previously forecast rise of 4 percent. In theory, Kazakhstan should benefit from high oil prices and a Western embargo on Russian oil. However, the Kazakh government recently downgraded its economic growth forecast for the country for the year 2002 from 3.9% to 2.1%. The main reason is that the country is unable to deliver its oil to the European market. Kazakhstan uses the Russian Black Sea port of Novorossiysk to ship most of its oil. Of the 67.6 million tons of oil that the country exported in 2021, more than 53 million tons were delivered through that port. Damages to the infrastructure in that port, which Russian officials claim was caused by the storm, led to a decline in oil production in Kazakhstan. Despite being partners within the Eurasian Economic Community, the Kazakh government publicly stated that it would not help Russia circumvent Western sanctions and to that end rebranded the oil it exports via Russian sea ports to avoid confusion and secondary sanctions fallout. Whether Russia would retaliate in response to what it might perceive as a disloyalty on the part of the Kazakh government remains to be seen. In the medium term, however, Tokayev will be tasked with implementing difficult political and economic reforms.

The Kyrgyz Republic

Area: 76,640 sq. mi. (198,500 sq. km., slightly smaller than Nebraska).
Population: 6,172,101 (2024 estimate).
Capital City: Bishkek (formerly Frunze); Pop. 1,105,000 (2023 estimate).
Climate: Temperate in the northern foothill region; subtropical in the Fergana Valley; alpine in the high southwestern plateau; and high desert in the Tian Shan Mountains along the southeastern border with China.
Neighboring States: Kazakhstan (north), Uzbekistan (west), Tajikistan (west, south-west), China (southeast).
Languages: Kyrgyz, Russian.
Ethnic Composition: Kyrgyz (73.8%), Uzbek (14.8%), Russian (5.1%), Dungan (1.1%), Others (5.2%).
Principal Religion: Islam. About 7% of the people are nominally Orthodox Christian.
Chief Commercial Products: Cotton and cottonseed oil, tobacco, livestock, wool, hides, vegetables, sugar beets, refined sugar, flour, mining enterprises, metals, textiles.
Currency: som (May 1993).
Annual Per Capita Income (Purchasing Power Parity): $6,402 (2023 est.).
Recent Political Status: Autonomous Republic within the USSR (1926), Constituent Republic of the USSR (1936–1991)
President: Sadyr Japarov (January 28, 2021).
National Day: August 31 (1991), independence from the Soviet Union.

National Flag: Red field with a yellow sun in the center having 40 rays representing the 40 Kyrgyz tribes; on the center of the sun is a red ring crossed by two sets of three lines, a stylized representation of the roof of the traditional Kyrgyz yurt.

The Land

The Kyrgyz Republic (more commonly known as Kyrgyzstan) is the independent successor state to the Kirghiz Soviet Socialist Republic. Situated on a western spur of the Tian Shan Mountains, it is a mountainous country surrounded by more mountains; most of its borders run along mountain crests. Thus, it is separated from Tajikistan by the Turkistan and Zaalay Ranges. The Kokshaal-Tau Range, a part of the Tian Shan, forms the border with the People's Republic of China.

The exception is in the southwest, where the border dips down to cross the upper reaches of the Fergana River Valley. Apart from the Fergana Valley, the only lowland areas are the downstream parts of the Chu and Talas River Valleys along the northern border. The capital, Bishtek, is located in the Chu River Valley. These lowland areas make up about 15% of the total surface of the republic.

Kyrgyzstan's most unusual geographical feature is Lake Ysykköl (Ysyk-ko), a high mountain lake found in the eastern part of the country. Set in a massive hollow much like the Fergana Valley in western Kyrgyzstan, it is surrounded by mountains with a high, alpine plateau to the west. A deep clear lake, it is rich in fish and supports fishing communities around its edges.

The People

The population of Kyrgyzstan is diverse, with Kyrgyz speakers constituting only about 70% of the population. Uzbeks, the largest minority, are around 14% of the population, with Russians a close third at around 7%. Other minorities found in the republic include Dungans, Ukrainians, Uygurs, Ukrainians, and Germans. The Kyrgyz language belongs to the Turkic group of languages. The two official languages of the country are Kyrgyz and Russian.

History

The Kyrgyz have lived in the Tian Shan Mountains at least since the 16th century and some Soviet ethnographers postulate that they arrived as early as the 12th century. Since they had no written language until recently and continued to live as a nomadic people until modern times, archaeological evidence provides most of what we know of them.

They came under the nominal control of the Kokand Khanate until about 1850, when this area became a major region of Russian colonization. Since the Kyrgyz, as nomads, had no permanent claims on the land, the Russian colonists moved in and took most of the best land, leading to an uprising in 1916, which was put down with great force.

After the Russian Revolution, this area became a part of Soviet Turkistan. In 1921, it then became part of the Turkistan Autonomous SSR of the Russian SFSR. In 1924, it was separated from the Turkistan ASSR and given the status of an autonomous oblast (area) of the Russian SFSR. Two years later, it became the Kirgiz Autonomous SSR of the Russian SFSR. It was not until December 1936 that it became a constituent republic of the USSR as the Kirgiz Soviet Socialist Republic.

Much changed during the Soviet years. The nomadic life of the people ended when they were settled on collective and state farms. Some mechanization was also introduced in the countryside, and irrigation projects increased cultivated land in the lowlands. The exploitation of minerals found in the mountains increased the number of jobs in industry and drew more of the Kyrgyz people into cities and modern life. Most preferred to remain in stock raising or farming, however, so the overwhelming majority of people in industry and in the urban areas are non-Kyrgyz.

Mikhail Gorbachev's perestroika left the republic untouched until 1990, when ethnic riots broke out in the Fergana Valley along the border with Uzbekistan. The riots left

Kyrgyzstan

200 people dead and damaged the reputation of Absamat Masaliev, the Kyrgyz Communist Party leader. Masaliev tried to repair the damage by calling on the republic's Supreme Soviet to create the office of president, to be elected by that body.

Masaliev's political opposition in the Supreme Soviet organized themselves into a new party, called Democratic Kyrgyzstan, and elected Askar Akayev instead. Akayev, a physicist by training, worked for 20 years in St. Petersburg (then Leningrad) before returning to Kyrgyzstan.

In August 1991, there was an organized attempt to depose President Akayev as part of the attempted coup against Gorbachev. The local military commander threatened to send tanks into the street and the local KGB chief attempted to arrest Akayev. The president's loyal troops surrounded the Communist Party headquarters and then had the KGB chief arrested. Akayev subsequently banned the Communist Party from government offices. When the coup failed, the Kyrgyz Communist Party dissolved itself. After his own return to power, Gorbachev asked Akayev to come to Moscow to become his vice president. He turned it down, saying that he wanted to stay in Kyrgyzstan.

As part of the further democratization of the country, the Kyrgyz Supreme Soviet modified the constitution to create an elective presidency and set new elections on October 12. Akayev's position was so strong by this time that no candidate bothered to oppose him.

The Consolidation of the Akayev Regime

Over the next two years, Akayev pushed democratic reforms and the creation of a market economy, but he was frustrated by opposition in the legislature. This led him, in February 1994, to call for a referendum in which the people were asked whether they supported his policies and wanted him to finish his term ending in 1996. Ninety-6% of those voting answered yes. Acting on this vote of confidence, Akayev dismissed the old 350-member Supreme Soviet, elected during the Soviet era in 1990, and submitted a second referendum to the people proposing a new, two-chamber "Assembly of the People of Kyrgyzstan," composed of 105 members. When the electorate approved his proposal, Akayev set new elections for February 5, 1995. Over 1,000 candidates vied for the 105 seats, about 80% of them running as independents. This produced a cooperative legislature for Akayev to work with.

Following that, Akayev pushed through a whole sheaf of constitutional amendments, many of which significantly increased his powers. New constitutional

Kyrgyz villagers celebrating Navruz, the traditional Persian New Year

amendments in 1999 changed the make-up of the legislature and created 15 seats to be elected by proportional voting on the basis of party lists.

Akayev also pushed through legislation authorizing some forms of privatization, including land. Some 61% of state-owned industrial enterprises had been privatized by May 1997 when President Akayev ended all forms of privatization after he became convinced that state-owned facilities were being sold at unjustifiably low prices. The ban lasted just under a year. In April 1998, the legislature approved a further privatization which included individual companies in telecommunications, mining and energy. Opposition to privatization continued to grow, however, and accusations were made that members of parliament had been making personal profit from the privatization process. Unfortunately, corruption is widespread enough to suggest that some of them probably were.

Kyrgyzstan was badly hurt by the collapse of the Russian ruble in 1998 and this had a negative effect on President Akayev's standing among the Kyrgyz people. As the government prepared for new parliamentary elections in February–March 2000, therefore, a major effort was made to minimize the vote for the political opposition. In the end, the actions of the authorities were so blatant that the Organization for Security and Co-operation in Europe declared the parliamentary elections so flawed that they had failed to meet international standards. Attempting to deal with the criticism, President Akayev called for a roundtable discussion with the political opposition which took place in June. Here, President

Akayev solicited suggestions on measures to stabilize the political and economic situation. He also admitted that irregularities were registered in a number of court cases with regard to the parliamentary elections.

Presidential elections were scheduled to take place in October 2000. As a result of worsening economic conditions, President Akayev's popularity had declined greatly in the previous two years and many thought he could be defeated. Feliks Kulov, who had earlier held the post of vice president, was seen by those same observers as the individual most likely to be able to defeat Akayev.

Kulov, who had also served as minister of national security and mayor of Bishkek, had earlier broken with Akayev and then founded the Ar-Namys Party. When Kulov was suddenly arrested on what most people considered to be trumped up charges, there was therefore some disquiet. This disquiet only grew when a military court reinstated the charges after Kulov had been acquitted. Kulov eventually pulled out of the presidential race—supposedly because he refused to take a required exam in the Kyrgyz language—but it probably was also because of the charges pending against him.

President Akayev eventually faced five challengers in the presidential race, none of any great stature; even so, any chance that one of them might win against Akayev was negated by the press coverage of the campaign on the part of a media almost entirely controlled by the government. In the end, Akayev won reelection with 74.47% of the vote; however, the OSCE once again declared that the presidential election had failed to comply with its standards for democratic elections.

After the results were in, Feliks Kulov, calling for cooperation with the government, told journalists that his party would avoid a confrontation with the government authorities at all costs, and added that he intended to participate in an upcoming dialogue between the authorities and political parties. In spite of his offer of cooperation, a court found him guilty in his retrial and he was sentenced to prison in January 2001. Apparently, the authorities continued to fear him even after the elections were over.

If the authorities thought that sending Kulov to prison would negatively affect his political reputation, they were plainly wrong, however. In November 2001, the leaders of the opposition Ar-Namys, Ata-Meken, Erkindik, and People's parties organized a "People's Congress" in Bishkek and symbolically elected Feliks Kulov as chairman. The "Congress" then adopted a resolution condemning the country's "authoritarian" leadership and "thoroughly corrupt" government. In addition to demanding Kulov's release from prison, they called for constitutional changes that would transfer some of the president's powers to parliament.

In January 2002, the focus of the opposition changed after the arrest of Azimbek Beknazarov, a parliament deputy from Aksy Rayon of Jalal-Abad Region in southern Kyrgyzstan. Beknazarov's constituents became convinced that the criminal charges brought against him were a sham and that the real cause of the government's actions was Beknazarov's opposition to the ratification of a border treaty with China, which ceded 95,000 hectares of disputed territory to China. His constituents therefore began organizing demonstrations demanding Beknazarov's release. These demonstrations continued until March, when they led to a clash with the government authorities in the Aksy Rayon which resulted in the death of six individuals when policemen fired on the demonstrators.

A state commission set up in April to investigate the Aksy incidents blamed government authorities on all levels and law-enforcement bodies for "political short-sightedness," and it criticized the Aksy authorities for refusing to permit pro-Beknazarov rallies. By the middle of May, when the state commission released its report, demonstrations were taking place all over Kyrgyzstan and demands were beginning to be heard for the resignation of President Akayev. Meanwhile, the border treaty with China was ratified by the lower house of parliament on May 10 and by the Senate a week later.

Hoping to calm the situation, the government issued arrest warrants for several local Aksy Rayon officials and ordered the release of Beknazarov. President Akayev

Deposed president Askar Akayev at dinner with his wife and children

followed these actions up with a national address to the Kyrgyz people. When none of these things defused the situation, Prime Minister Bakiev resigned on May 22. His replacement as prime minister, named the same day by President Akayev, was Nikolay Tanayev.

Demonstrations continued throughout the summer, with an increasing number of voices calling for President Akayev's resignation. In July, the president made another attempt to defuse the situation; calling on all political factions to engage in a dialogue with the government, he cautioned opposition politicians against exploiting current tensions for their personal political aims. He also hinted that he might be willing to cede some powers to parliament if the relevant constitutional amendments were endorsed in a nationwide referendum. In another concession, he also signed six laws recently passed by parliament, the most significant of which guaranteed the right of peaceable assembly. Prior official permission to hold rallies was no longer required, except in the vicinity of schools and hospitals.

A Constitutional Council charged with drawing up possible constitutional amendments was established by presidential decree on August 26. The Council, which met for the first time on September 4, elected Absamat Masaliev, leader of the opposition Communist Party of Kyrgyzstan, as co-chairman. The membership of the Council included the prime minister, foreign minister, speakers of the upper and lower chambers of parliament, leaders and deputies of several opposition political parties, the chairs of the Constitutional and Supreme Courts, and some NGO representatives.

The Council drew up a series of constitutional amendments which, somewhat modified, were submitted as a national

referendum on February 6. Because there had been so many calls for President Akayev's resignation, the referendum also asked the public to indicate whether they wanted the president to serve to the end of his present term in 2005. Although 12 opposition parties called for a boycott of the referendum, the final vote showed participation by 86.36% of the electorate. The referendum received a 75.5% favorable vote.

The newly approved constitutional amendments created a new 75-member unicameral parliament—all elected in single-seat constituencies—to replace the bicameral parliament as of the 2005 elections. While President Akayev was confirmed in office until the end of his term in December 2005, another amendment stripped former presidents and their families of immunity from prosecution.

Elections to the new unicameral parliament took place on February 27, 2005, with approximately 400 candidates vying for the 75 seats. Five major opposition political parties formed an electoral bloc under the leadership of Kurmanbek Bakiev, former prime minister and leader of the People's Movement of Kyrgyzstan. In the end, however, the opposition won only seven seats, with supporters of the government taking the rest. Perhaps the greatest blow was the fact that Kurmanbek Bakiev failed to win his seat in the runoff.

The opposition refused to accept the results of the parliamentary elections, and they were helped in this position by the statement by the Organization for Security and Cooperation in Europe (OSCE) that there were "significant shortcomings" in the electoral process. OSCE areas of concern included "lack of effective voter access to diverse sources of information, bias in the media, continued de-registration of candidates on minor grounds, and inaccurate and poorly maintained voter lists."

Kyrgyzstan

Kyrgyz woman in traditional headdress of a married woman making a felt rug ("shirdak")
Courtesy of Hermine Dreyfuss

Although President Akayev had announced on several occasions that he intended to step down at the end of his term as president, the opposition was also convinced that, with a two-thirds pro-government majority in parliament, Akayev would amend the constitution and run for a third term. They were reinforced in this belief by the fact that four members of the Akayev family—the president's son and daughter and his wife's two sisters—were originally awarded seats in the new parliament.

Revolution and a New President

Protest rallies began on March 14 with opponents of the government occupying government offices in several towns across the country. The largest of the protest demonstrations took place in the city of Jalal-Abad, located in the south of the country in the crowded and impoverished Fergana Valley. By March 22, protesters had completed their takeover of the south,

occupying all three regional capitals. The next day, the protests spread to Bishkek, the capital. One day later, President Akayev and his family fled Bishkek, having decided to seek sanctuary in Kazakhstan.

The next day, the Supreme Court revoked the mandate of the newly elected parliament. Hours later, Kurmanbek Bakiev was named prime minister by the old parliament and given the power to issue decrees as acting president, even though President Akayev had not resigned the presidency. That evening, as looters took to the streets, ransacking shopping centers and targeting bank machines and currency-exchange places, Bakiev began to put together a provisional government. He asked Feliks Kulov, who had been released from prison on March 24, to accept the position of coordinator of security services. Kulov's job was essentially to restore order in the country, putting an end to the looting which had broken out in the wake of the uprising. Kulov held this position

for only a few days. In his letter of resignation, he stated that he had accomplished what he had been asked to do; it is likely, however, that he was positioning himself to run against Bakiev in the upcoming presidential elections.

In another twist, Acting President Bakiev decided to recognize the legitimacy of the new parliament. This was partly because the mandate of the old parliament was due to run out on April 15, and he was concerned about the legitimacy of the revolutionary government. After Bakiev's action, the new parliament voted 54–0 to recognize Bakiev as prime minister and acting president. Since the Central Election Commission had, in the meantime, decided to annul the results in 13 constituencies, those elections would be rerun. President Akayev, now in exile in Russia, formally resigned his office on April 4.

New presidential elections were set for July 10. At first, it appeared that Bakiev and Kulov would be the two chief candidates. Instead, the two candidates met privately and then announced that Kulov had decided to withdraw from the campaign and to support Bakiev's run for the presidency; in return, Bakiev promised that he would appoint Kulov as prime minister if elected. Bakiev actually appointed Kulov to the post of acting deputy prime minister a few days later. A major factor in Kulov's withdrawal was apparently his fear that he would be unable to pass a fluency test in the Kyrgyz language, one of the requirements for all presidential candidates. Kulov's education had been primarily in Russian language schools, and he is said to have a limited fluency in Kyrgyz.

Bakiev won the July 10 presidential elections with 88.9% of the votes; he was formally sworn in as president on August 14. Since parliament was not scheduled to meet in its opening session until September 1, Bakiev appointed Kulov as acting prime minister while formally nominating him for the office of prime minister. Kulov was confirmed in office on September 1 during parliament's opening session; he received the support of 55 of the 66 deputies present.

This overwhelming vote of confidence in the new prime minister was somewhat misleading, however. When Bakiev formally presented his new government to parliament on September 26, parliament rejected 6 of the 16 cabinet nominees. Not wanting a confrontation with parliament, Bakiev submitted six new nominations for the vacant positions.

Parliament eventually confirmed his new appointees, but the political situation continued to be extremely fluid. Part of the problem was that, although everyone claimed to support an expansion of democracy and political freedoms, there was a great deal of disagreement about what that meant. Another part of the problem is that many people expected the situation to improve greatly with the departure of President Akayev; yet corruption and poverty may have actually gotten worse, aggravated by the very political instability that continued to plague the country. It also did not help that three members of parliament were murdered in the six months following collapse of the Akayev regime.

President Bakiev was probably another part of the problem; although his reputation was as a wily politician and a survivor, he has had great difficulty in maintaining a consistent political position. For example, Bakiev opposed the expansion of presidential authority which Akayev pushed through in 2003, only to reverse his position after assuming that office himself. More recently, his position has been that the presidential powers are necessary to put an end to the disorders and destabilization in the country. In November 2005, in fact, he proposed that the office of prime minister be abolished and the president made head of government. Many in parliament, on the other hand, have favored a parliamentary system with a figurehead president.

Meanwhile, this infighting has resulted in a great deal of frustration within the country and some loss of confidence in the new political leadership. Omurbek Tekebaev, the speaker of parliament, was forced to resign in February 2006 after he said of President Bakiev "he's become a disgrace, a dog; if he's a man, he should hang himself." Nor did the quarrel benefit Bakiev; a poll take at about that same time showed that 74% of those polled expressed a lack of trust in the president.

Discussions concerning the future form of government were supposed to take place under the auspices of the Constitutional Council, a 114-member body set up by parliament in April 2005. In March 2006, however, President Bakiev took control of the discussions by appointing his own working group on constitutional reform. Bakiev's instructions

Ex-Prime Minister Feliks Kulov

Ex-President Kurmanbek Bakiev

were to take the materials produced by the Constitutional Council and use them to create draft constitutions; the task force delivered three drafts to President Bakiev and Prime Minister Kulov in July 2006, prescribing presidential, parliamentary, and mixed presidential-parliamentary forms of government. All three drafts envisaged a 75-member parliament with 50 deputies elected on party slates and 25 in single-member constituencies; formerly all deputies were elected in single-member constituencies.

Bakiev also set up a new governmental body, the State Council, in April 2006. The membership of the State Council included the president, prime minister, speaker of parliament, chairpersons of the Constitutional and Supreme Courts, state secretary, head of the presidential administration, prosecutor-general, defense minister, chairman of the National Security Service, and mayor of Bishkek.

The purpose of the State Council was to bring all of the leading political personalities together and provide them with a common forum where political differences could be discussed and resolved. It didn't work out that way. Instead, parliament passed a resolution in September 2006 which declared the "tandem" arrangement between President Bakiev and Prime Minister Kulov to be unconstitutional. Lawmakers also provided President Bakiev with a number of demands: to form a coalition government; conduct rapid constitutional reforms; place the National Security Service (SNB) under governmental, rather than presidential, control; replace the director of Manas airport; remove the head of the state broadcasting corporation; open a criminal case against Janysh Bakiev, the president's brother (and former head of the SNB) in connection with the arrest of Omurbek Tekebaev (former parliamentary speaker); and give the parliamentary commission on the Tekebaev affair more powers.

This was, as it turned out, the beginning of a season of additional demands. In October, a civic forum that took place under the auspices of the opposition For Reforms presented President Bakiev with a list of nine demands. Calling for the creation of a national unity government, this list included demands that Bakiev remove all relatives from government posts; withdraw his veto of a parliamentary act transforming state television into public television; and reject participation in the Heavily Indebted Poor Countries debt-reduction initiative of the World Bank/IMF.

One month later, parliament adopted a new constitution significantly curtailing the powers of the presidency and increasing the powers of the legislature—though the curb on presidential powers was not go take effect until after the next presidential elections in 2010. Perhaps the most important change was to place the National Security Service under governmental, not presidential, control.

Two months later, on December 30, parliament reversed itself and passed a new constitution that broadened the power of the presidency—giving the president the right to appoint cabinet members without parliamentary approval and giving the president control over law-enforcement and security organs. The new constitution also gave the president the authority to nominate a new prime minister, though the nominee would have to be confirmed by parliament.

Meanwhile, a schism occurred in Prime Minister Kulov's political party, Ar-Namys, and this led him to resign his office on December 19. President Bakiev prevailed on Kulov to once again accept the office, but when he sent Kulov's name to parliament, parliament rejected the nomination twice in succession. An important reason for parliament's rejection of Kulov was that the prime minister had strongly supported the Heavily Indebted Poor Countries debt-relief program. Although

Ex-President Almazbek Atambayev

Kyrgyzstan

Kyrgyz family waiting at typical mosaic bus stop which dot the countryside. Man wears a "kalpak" hat Courtesy of Hermine Dreyfuss

about half of Kyrgyzstan's $2 billion in international debt would have been forgiven if it joined the program, a majority of parliament opposed the program, fearing it would give international financial institutions too much authority over domestic policy. Reflecting this position, the government decided in February 2007 against participation in the program.

President Bakiev's choice as Kulov's successor was Azim Isabekov, at that time minister for agriculture. Isabekov was easily confirmed, but he held the office for only two months. He resigned on March 29 after President Bakiev blocked his attempt to sack five members of his cabinet.

When President Bakiev named Isabekov as Kulov's successor, he offered Kulov "any position" in government that was not subordinate to parliament. Kulov refused and, instead, set up a new opposition movement called the United Front for a Worthy Future for Kyrgyzstan (UFFWFK). In March, Kulov announced that the UFFWFK would begin holding demonstrations calling for new presidential elections. Meanwhile, the rest of the political opposition, which was organized as the For Reforms Movement, had drawn up its own plans for demonstrations beginning

in April. When Isabekov resigned as prime minister on March 29, therefore, President Bakiev turned to Almazbek Atambayev, co-chairman of the For Reforms movement, and offered to nominate him for the office of prime minister. Atambayev accepted, and he was confirmed as prime minister on March 30.

In his maiden speech as prime minister, Atambayev harshly condemned the policies of the government over the preceding two years—"over the past two years, necessary, cardinal, steps were not taken in the economy, corruption was not vanquished, and concrete measures were not taken to raise the living standards of ordinary citizens." However, he spoke against the demands of the rest of the opposition for early presidential elections which, he said, could "provoke a split in the country."

President Bakiev tried to placate the opposition by giving in to some of their demands. In addition to rejecting participation in the Heavily Indebted Poor Countries debt-relief program, he agreed to legislation turning state television into public television.

The demonstrations called by Kulov began to have a political effect, however; after some of the demonstrators began

throwing stones at the police, the government authorized the arrest of some of the demonstration leaders. The police also raided the offices of two Kyrgyz newspapers and seized entire press runs, plus the offices of Kulov's Ar-Namys Party—acts which brought swift condemnation by organizations such as Freedom House in America.

President Bakiev's chance to counter the political opposition came in September 2007 when the Supreme Court ruled that constitutional amendments adopted in November and December 2007 were illegal, a decision that restored the 2003 constitution as the governing document. Essentially, the Supreme Court ruled that "changes or amendments to the constitution can be made only through a referendum."

When parliament responded by adopting a vote of non-confidence in the Supreme Court, President Bakiev proposed instead that a new draft constitution be submitted to a popular referendum. When that vote took place on October 21, the new constitution received overwhelming popular approval.

With a new constitution in place, President Bakiev dissolved parliament and set new elections for December 16. Under the terms of the new constitution, the membership of parliament (Supreme Council) was set at 90 seats. Individual constituencies were abolished; instead, all seats were to be filled on the basis of proportional representation. Party slates had to receive a minimum of 5% of the national vote in order to qualify; in addition, a party slate had to also win 0.5% of the vote in each of the country's seven provinces and two largest cities in order to win representation in parliament.

Prior to the elections, President Bakiev established the Ak Jol (White Path) political party as a new pro-government party. Although Bakiev was originally elected party chairman, he suspended his activities as leader, saying that the president could not participate in party politics. From the beginning, however, most people looked on the party as the party of government. If the party were successful in the following elections, Kyrgyzstan would thus join the rest of his neighbors, not excluding Russia, in having a ruling party.

In the event, Ak Jol won 46% of the vote, which gave it 71 of the 90 seats in parliament. The opposition Social Democratic Party, received 11 seats; the pro-government Communist Party of Kyrgyzstan got 8. Ata-Meken, a second opposition party, polled some 8.3% of the vote but did not qualify for any seats because it failed to win the required minimum of 0.5% of the vote in the southern city of Osh. Monitors from the OSCE criticized the election for "failing to meet democratic standards." Kimmo Kiljunen, the head of the monitoring mission, said that he was "personally disappointed that there is now a backsliding in the elector process," and he stressed that the election undermined "political pluralism" in Kyrgyzstan. The election was, of course, an important political win for President Bakiev.

The new prime minister was Igor Chudinov, a former industry and trade minister. In an interesting break with the recent past, Chudinov was an ethnic Russian who did not speak Kazakh. He was, of course, ineligible for the run for the presidency for that reason. Chudinov was apparently picked because of his business background. He was expected to place a heavy emphasis on improving core areas in agriculture, minerals, and mining.

Balancing Social Cleavages

Kyrgyz politics have always reflected underlying regional power networks. Under Akayev, who came from the Kemin district in northern Kyrgyzstan, most of the members of the government came from the north. In the 2005 Tulip Revolution, initial mobilization began in the south among followers of southern elites shut out from the lucrative presidential network. President Bakiev, on the other hand, came from a village in Jalal-Abad in the south. When he first came to power, it was with the cooperation and support of Feliks Kulov, an influential figure from the north. After Kulov's departure as prime minister, however, nearly all new members of the Bakiev government came from the south. President Bakiev apparently tried to redress that balance in May 2008 when he appointed Kulov to head a new state energy investment body shortly after Kulov had withdrawn from the opposition's alternative parliament.

Akayev also carefully and publicly managed the state's ethnic diversity. Without a traditional power base in the early years of his presidency, he was especially keen to defuse the ethnic tensions that led to the 1990 Osh riots and subsequent dismissal of Absamat Masaliev. Most explicitly, he promoted an inclusive nationalist slogan: "Kyrgyzstan Is Our Common Home." He also formed an extra-parliamentary Assembly of the People of Kyrgyzstan which represented 27 ethnic groups. The body had only limited powers, but it did provide an avenue for minority elites to have access to President Akayev. Under Akayev, a number of minority elites, especially Uzbek elites were able to build and cultivate dense patronage networks of their own. Perhaps most prominently, Uzbek businessman Kadyrjan Batyrov, served as a member of parliament representing Jalal-Abad,

The tunduk is the dome of the yurt, the traditional Kyrgyz nomadic dwelling
Courtesy of Hermine Dreyfuss

opened an Uzbek-language University and established an Uzbek cultural center to promote and protect Uzbek minority interests. Under Bakiev, the space for prominent leaders like Batyrov was squeezed. In 2007, Batyrov's political party, Rodina, was prevented from participating in parliamentary elections as a result of a dubious Central Election Commission ruling that the citizenship of several party members could not be properly verified. While ethnic minority leaders found themselves with diminished prominence, the opposite could be said about ethno-nationalist Kyrgyz leaders. Ethno-nationalists were an important base for Bakiev and many gained important titles. For instance, Adahan Madumarov, a politician who had responded to Akayev's slogan regarding "our common home" by stating that "Kyrgyz are owners of the house, the rest are tenants," served as deputy prime minister for a time under Bakiev.

Publicly, Bakiev's greatest difficulty was in combating the widespread perception that he and his family were using the office to personally enrich themselves. Indeed, his family held a myriad of important positions across several sectors. One of the president's brothers, Janysh, headed the State Protective Service; two more, Marat and Adil, worked in Kyrgyz embassies abroad. One of Bakiev's sons, Marat, was also a government official. Most notorious of all, however, was youngest son, Maxim. Maxim enjoyed a steady stream of revenue as an intermediary in fuel sales at

the US Air Base at Manas Airport. He was wealthy enough to become a part owner of Blackpool FC, an English Soccer Club. Maxim was also accused of arranging an attempted assassination on a British businessman in a dispute over gold mining. Despite, or perhaps because of, these murky dealings, Maxim was named the head of a newly formed organization entitled The Central Agency for Development, Investment, and Innovation in 2009. Nepotism is common in Central Asia, but it should be remembered that this was the main charge used to bring down President Akayev.

President Bakiev was reelected in new presidential elections which took place on July 23, 2009. There were five other contenders for the office of president, but his chief opponent was Almazbek Atambayev, the candidate of the unified opposition. President Bakiev was favored for reelection, but his reelection with 86% of the vote brought widespread charges that the election had been stolen. In fact, Almazbek Atambayev pulled out of the race on the day of the election even before the final result had been announced because, he said, "widespread fraud had ensured the incumbent's victory." Reacting to the vote, the European Union announced that "election day was marred by many problems and irregularities, including evidence of ballot-box stuffing, inaccuracies in the voter lists and some evidence of multiple voting." OSCE Election monitors also expressed disappointment over the presidential vote, concluding that the election "fell short of key standards." A major OSCE criticism was that Kyrgyzstan's journalists had "recently endured an upsurge of brutal attacks, including two this month alone, while many cases from earlier this year have still not been resolved by the authorities."

President Bakiev attempted to further consolidate his power by issuing a sweeping administrative reform in October. This brought about the resignation of Prime Minister Chudinov after the political opposition characterized the decree as another step toward boosting the president's "semi-authoritarian" powers. President Bakiev then appointed Daniyar Usenov as his new prime minister.

A Second Revolution

After a winter and early spring of rising fuel and food costs, a stagnant economy, and Russian-based media reports on the corrupt practices of the Bakiev regime, popular opinion began to turn against the president. Things came to a head on April 7, 2010, when protests began in the town of Talas after an opposition political leader, Bolot Sherniazov, was arrested. The protests then quickly spread to Bishkek,

Kyrgyzstan

the capital. The government immediately arrested most of the opposition politicians so that, when the protests turned violent in Bishkek, there were no opposition leaders available to exercise a moderating influence. Then the police began using live ammunition against the demonstrators, resulting in the death of possibly as many as 82 people, with up to an additional thousand wounded. Fearing for his life, President Bakiev fled to his political base in southern Kyrgyzstan. But he found relatively little support even there, so he fled the country on April 15, then made his way to Belarus where he was offered asylum by President Alexander Lukashenko.

Meanwhile, the major opposition political leaders, freed from arrest, had organized an interim government in Bishkek under the leadership of Roza Otunbayeva. This was made easier by the fact that the political opposition set up a National Executive as a sort of shadow government in March. Now most of them took senior positions in the new interim government.

Roza Otunbayeva, named Acting President, was a former foreign minister and former Kyrgyz ambassador to the United States. Almazbek Atambayev, an ex-prime minister and unsuccessful candidate for the presidency in 2009, was named her deputy. General Ismail Isakov was named Defense Minister; Isakov had previously served as defense minister and National Security Council secretary under Bakiev. He was also among those freed from jail after President Bakiev fled Bishkek. Bolot Sherniazov, a leader of the Ata-Meken [Fatherland] party, was named interior minister.

Soon after forming, the interim government dissolved parliament in a effort to sweep clean nodes of lingering Bakiev loyalists in Bishkek's halls of power. Of course, this meant that many of his supporters returned to their home districts and local patronage networks. Soon reports of score settling between elite networks, which sometimes had an ethnic dimension, were reported in Southern Kyrgyzstan. This period of tremendous political uncertainty turned tragically violent on June 10, when a fight in a casino between young Uzbek and Kyrgyz men in the city of Osh spilled out onto the streets. As more young Uzbek and Kyrgyz men arrived, untrue rumors that Uzbeks had perpetrated mass rapes of female Kyrgyz college students began to spread widely. Over the next two days, swarms of rioters (sometimes supported by armored vehicles) attacked Uzbek neighborhoods in Osh and a few other southern communities such as Jalal-Abad, destroying property and assailing residents. The violence subsided in a little less than a week, but the actual damage it inflicted remains highly contested and politicized. Estimated

deaths range from several hundred to several thousand, with most sources acknowledging the disproportionate suffering of the ethnic Uzbek population. According to the UN, around 400,000 individuals were displaced due to the violence, most of them Uzbeks. By most accounts, the temporary government proved incapable of responding to the violence and there were significant reports that sympathetic members of security services either directly participate in the riots or tacitly permitted the use of government equipment, including the aforementioned armored vehicles, to orchestrate acts of violence.

Another Shot at Democratization?

The new provisional government promised a new constitution giving Kyrgyzstan a parliamentary system with a ceremonial president. For this purpose, they created a 75-member Constitutional Committee that was largely made up of representatives from nongovernmental organizations. The committee also received advice from several international organizations. and this they did over the next month or so. The new constitution, produced in approximately one month, was made public on May 21; a national referendum on the new constitution took place on June 27, when it received overwhelming support.

Although the initiators of the project said that they were giving the country a parliamentary system, it might better be referred to as a modified presidential-parliamentary system. It clearly creates a presidential office that is more limited than previously, but the president still has the power to either veto or refuse to sign any laws other than laws related to budget and fiscal policy. He can also send a law back to parliament. On the other hand, he is limited to a single, six-year term.

The prime minister (and cabinet) have far more power than previously, for it is they who control the government's purse strings and with them much of the country's economic life. The prime minister is also in charge of personnel policy, finance, and licenses.

The new constitution increases the size of parliament from 90 to 120 seats. To guard against a single party amassing too much power, no party can hold more than 65 seats; this probably also means that most governments will have to be coalitions.

Parliamentary elections were set to occur every five years, and the first elections took place on October 10, 2010. The results were instructive. Total number of votes cast was approximately 1.38 million; of that number, approximately a third of all votes went to the 24 political parties that failed to achieve the required minimum of 5% of the national vote and so these people

are not represented in the parliament. Ata-Jurt (Homeland), the party which came in first with 8.69% of the vote, actually got less than 250,000 votes.

Four other political parties surmounted the 5% barrier—the Social Democratic Party, with 8.13% of the vote; the Ar-Namys (Dignity) party, with 7.64% of the vote; Respublika with 7.04% of the vote; and the Ata-Meken (Fatherland) party with 5.71% of the vote.

Forming a coalition government was difficult because the leaders of two of the winning political parties, Ata-Jurt and Ar-Namys, were on record as favoring a strong presidential form of government. But politics makes strange bed fellows. In December 2010, a new coalition government was formed with Almazbek Atambayev, head of the Social Democratic Party, as prime minister. The other three parties forming the coalition were Ar-Namys, Respublika, and Ata-Meken. The important factor that led to the inclusion of Ar-Namys into the coalition was that its main power base was in the south, the area where the other three coalition parties were weak.

It was also decided that Roza Otunbayeva would remain president until December 2011, when new presidential elections would take place. Since President Otunbayeva was not eligible for reelection, Prime Minister Atambayev, head of the Social Democratic Party, quickly became the odds-on favorite to succeed her.

Sixteen candidates competed in the October 30 presidential race, raising the question whether any candidate could win in the first round by winning over 50% of the vote. In the end, Atambayev won handsomely with 62.8% of the vote. His inauguration took place on December 1. He immediately named Omurbek Babanov, leader of Respublika, as his new prime minister.

Kyrgyzstan is still a country marked by deep political, ethnic, and regional divisions and that became clear when President Atambayev and Prime Minister Babanov opposed the reelection of Mayor Melis Myrzakmatov in Osh, the major city in the south, claiming he had contributed to the ethnic tensions that erupted in the 2010 riots. Myrzakmatov's local supporters, on the other hand, credited him with saving the city. In the end, the mayoral election took place peacefully on March 4, 2012, with Myrzakmatov easily winning reelection. It is likely that the mayor's resistance to Bishkek helped win him reelection, since it played into the growing resistance to Atambayev in southern Kyrgyzstan.

Prime Minister Babanov's government fell on August 22, 2012 when Ar-Namys and Ata-Meken withdrew from the coalition over differences with the prime minister. Thirteen days later, a new coalition came into existence when President Atambayev's

Kyrgyzstan

Social Democratic Party, signed an agreement with Ar-Namys and Ata-Meken that excluded Babanov's Respublika party from the new government. President Atambayev then named Jantoro Satybaldiev as the new prime minister.

Saltybaldiev had no party affiliation, but he was a career politician who managed to win the confidence of three presidents. A southerner, he had served as mayor of Osh in 2000–2001 and as governor of Osh Oblast in 2006–2007. However, his non-party status made him totally dependent on President Atambayev for support. Saltybaldiev submitted his resignation as prime minister on March 25, 2014, after Ata-Meken withdrew from the coalition. The presumed issue that brought about the fall of the Saltybaldiev government was disagreement over the Kumtor gold mine. Omurbek Tekebaev, leader of Ata-Meken, argued that the government took too soft a stance in negotiations, and that the government should have demanded 67% of the shares of the new company being created. The government has actually negotiated an agreement that gives the government 50% of the stock in the new entity that will control the mine.

On March 26, President Atambayev named Joomart Otorbaev as the new prime minister. This was a clever move on the part of the president, for Otorbaev was elected to parliament in October 2010 as a candidate of the Ata-Meken party. President Atambayev thus offered to Ata-Meken the prestige of having the prime minister from its party in return for accepting a compromise on the Kumtor gold mine.

Prime Minister Otorbaev was well qualified for the new position, having been a leading figure in Kyrgyz politics since the time of President Akayev, serving as deputy prime minister during the last three years of Akayev's presidency. He then served as a senior consultant to the European Bank of Reconstruction and Development until 2010, when he returned to Kyrgyzstan. He served as deputy prime minister in charge of the economy and investment from December 2011 to September 2012, when he was named first deputy prime minister, a post he was occupying when he was named prime minister. Nevertheless, on May 2, 2015, after he had served only 13 months in office, Prime Minister Otorbayev was replaced by President Atambayev with Temir Sariyev, the economy minister. Sariyev thus became the 27th prime minister since Kyrgyzstan became an independent country at the end of 1991. Temir Sariyev retained his position as PM following the October 2015 Parliamentary elections which saw the Social Democratic Party retain a plurality of seats. However, in Spring 2016, Sariyev and his cabinet

Ex-President Roza Otunbayeva

resigned as reports of corruption emerged which indicated that he had broken the law in arranging a road building contract with a Chinese firm. His successor, Sooronbay Jeenbekov assumed the role of prime minister on April 2016. His government lasted only a half-year before collapsing on October 26, 2016, when the Social Democratic Party pulled out of the ruling coalition. This move was sparked by the reluctance of two coalition partners, Ata-Meken and Onuguu Progress, to support Atambayev's proposal for Constitutional reforms. On November 9, 2016, Jeenbekov formed a new government built around a slimmer coalition, all of whom supported the amendments. A little more than a month later, a set of constitutional amendments that increased the powers of the prime minister (and weakened the powers of the president) and banned same-sex marriage were overwhelmingly approved by participating voters.

Government Change
without Revolution

In November 2017, a peaceful transfer of power occurred when former prime

minister Sooronbay Jeenbekov replaced Atambayev as president. In a rarity in Central Asia, a competitive election determined the winner. Jeenbekov won with 54.7% of the vote; the next highest vote getter, Omurbek Babanov (who also is a former prime minister), received 33.7% of the vote. The remaining vote was split between 9 other candidates. Despite its competitive nature, the presidential campaign and its aftermath have revealed some of the gaps in Kyrgyzstan's weak democratic institutions. As the designated candidate of Atambayev's Social Democratic Party of Kyrgyzstan, Jeenbekov benefited from the "administrative resources" of the state throughout the campaign.

Despite the positives associated with the peaceful transfer of power, the weakness of Kyrgyzstan's democratic institutions have been exposed in the aftermath of the election. The last weeks of the campaign were marred by serious allegations leveled against Babanov. Following a meeting between President Nursultan Nazarbayev of Kazakhstan and Babanov, Kyrgyzstani government officials accused Kazakhstan of interfering in the election. While the accusation was predominately directed against the Kazakhstani government, it also clearly was intended to mobilize nationalist Kyrgyzstani voters against Babanov. A few weeks later, Babanov gave a speech in Osh in which he apparently pandered to Uzbek voters. During the speech at the end of September, he was alleged to have stated that "if any policeman touches an Uzbek, he will be fired." Soon thereafter the GKNB—State Committee for National Security—began investigating Babanov for inciting ethnic hatred. Following the election, these allegations continued to dog the defeated

Mass protests brought down the Kyrgyz government in April 2010

295

Kyrgyzstan

opposition candidate and forced him into exile abroad. In December, his NTS TV station was raided and impounded by state officials. This act shut down the largest private TV station in Kyrgyzstan. In the spring of 2018, additional charges were brought up against Babanov, who remains abroad. To the charges of inciting ethnic hatred, he also now stands accused of plotting to incite riots as a means to seize political power. Needless to say, the persecution of a defeated political opponent is a fundamental violation of democratic norms.

More surprisingly, Jeenbekov has also used his power to also go after his former patron, Atambayev. In March 2018, the ex-president was selected as the head of the Social Democratic Party of Kyrgyzstan. During an ill-advised Q+A with reporters, he referred to himself as "an older brother" of Jeenbekov before offering criticism of "clan politics" within the current administration as well as the current president's handling of a crisis when a power plant responsible for producing electricity and heated water to Bishkek broke down during a cold snap. In the wake of these criticisms, Jeenbekov systematically fired Atambayev's allies from positions within the government. Several of these allies have subsequently been arrested on corruption charges stemming from alleged behavior while they served under Atambayev. Amongst the prominent names arrested include former presidential adviser and deputy chief of the presidential office, Ikramjan Ilmiyanov, and two former prime ministers, Sapar Isakov and Jantoro Satybaldiev.

The targeting of Atambayev intensified in May 2018, and parliament began discussing revoking the legal immunity enjoyed by former heads of state. Although efforts to revoke presidential immunity were not immediately successful, in October 2018 Kyrgyzstan's Supreme Court ruled that blanket presidential immunity violated the constitutional principle of equality before the law. The court tasked parliament with revising presidential the laws surrounding presidential powers and responsibilities. On May 16, 2019, Jeenbekov signed revised legislation into law which significantly weakens the assurance of immunity for former presidents. The legislation establishes that ex-presidents are formally immune from prosecution; however, it also grants parliament the power to strip individuals of their "ex-president" status, thereby leaving them vulnerable for prosecution. Thus, this law enables immunity for ex-presidents so long as parliament determines it does not wish to prosecute a former president.

Atambayev should have seen this legislation as a credible threat from the Kyrgyzstani government that he should quietly retire from public life. If he did perceive the credibility of the threat, he did not heed it. As documented in a June 12, 2019, article on Eurasianet, Atambayev proceeded to organize a small rally on June 8 in which he stated that "Before, parliament was different, not the chimkyruk (snot) it is today." Needless to say, this quote did not win him any more support in the legislature. On June 27, 103 out of 109 members of parliament voted to strip Atambayev of his immunity. Of course, parliamentarians cited a laundry-list of crimes he had allegedly committed while in office as the justification for their vote, not his tendency to insult them.

Following this vote, Atambayev retreated to his house outside of Bishkek and refused to submit to police requests that he come in for questioning. On August 7, elite security forces launched a botched and bloody raid on his house, which resulted in the death of one member of the special forces team. A second raid the following day finally led to Atambayev's detention. He and 13 allies face a litany of charges, including murder, hostage taking, and forced power seizure. At the time of writing however, the trial of the ex-president remains in limbo. After a series of procedural delays pushed it into spring 2020, it has been indefinitely suspended due to the declaration of a state of emergency because of the novel coronavirus.

This episode is yet another example of how in Kyrgyzstan politics revolves around personal networks rather than institutions or formal organizations. While Jeenbekov may have been insulted by Atambayev's critiques, the moves against his network are probably best seen as strategic rather than emotional. By purging Atambayev's power network, Jeenbekov is better able consolidate control around his own hand-picked circle of cronies and insiders.

A Third Revolution and a Return to Presidentialism

Following a difficult summer in which Kyrgyzstan was severely hit by the coronavirus pandemic, opposition parties called for a postponement of parliamentary elections scheduled for the fall. Jeenbekov ignored these calls and on October 4, 2020, Kyrgyzstanis went to the polls. Due to the aforementioned power struggle between Jeenbekov and Atambayev, the ruling Social Democratic Party of Kyrgyzstan split before the election. Pro-Jeenbekov members of the Social Democratic Party formed a new party officially named the Party of Democratic Socialism-Eurasian Choice "Unity," but commonly known as simply "Unity." When the polls closed, Unity received a

Ex-Prime Minister Jantoro Satybaldiev

plurality of votes, followed closely by At-Zhurt-My Homeland. However, only one opposition party (United Kyrgyzstan) received enough votes to clear the 7% electoral threshold.

These electoral results were challenged immediately by the leading opposition parties shut out of parliament, Ata Meken and the Social Democrats. Protesters gathered in Bishkek demanding the election results be annulled. On October 5, former president Atambayev was freed from prison. The next day, another imprisoned politician, Sadyr Japarov was broken out of jail. Japarov was a notorious nationalist opposition figure who had been arrested due to his involvement in a plot to kidnap a regional governor (akim) during protests demanding the nationalization of the Kumtor mine in Karakol. On October 7, one day after being freed from prison, Japarov was appointed Prime Minister. This spurred a temporary dual or even tri-power struggle, as the resignation of the old Prime Minister had yet to be formally approved by Jeenbekov and a faction of the parliament put forth a third candidate for the position.

The governance crisis led to Jeenbekov's resignation on October 15. Japarov, whose nomination to serve as Prime Minister had been rejected by the President two days earlier, declared himsekf to be the acting President, circumventing Constitutional protocol.

On January 10, 2021, Japarov's unlikely rise from the jail cell to the Presidency was formalized when he has elected president in a snap election that was held concurrently with a constitutional referendum. Japarov won the low-turnout election in a landslide, winning 79.8% of the vote. Eighteen other candidates split the remaining 20.2%.

However, less than 40% of voters turned out to this hugely important election. Not only did the election cement Japarov rise, but it also ushered in significant changes to the Kyrgyzstani Constitution. Voters, who were asked to choose whether they preferred to adopt a presidential or parliamentary system, overwhelmingly opted for presidentialism, the outcome openly favored by Japarov.

In April, a second referendum occurred with a super majority of voters supporting a draft constitution which consolidated power in the president while weakening parliament. Supporters of the referendum argued that the decade-long experiment in a mixed system with a relatively powerful parliament was destabilizing. Under the new constitution, which was formally signed on May 5, the president has the power of appointment over judges and law enforcement agencies. It also established a new consultative body, the People's Kuraltai, which some fear will diminish the role of parliament. The single-term limit of the prior constitution was also eliminated, which opposition voices have critiqued will enable Japarov to personalize power similar to those in neighboring states.

Foreign Policy

In his early years after taking power, Akayev's reputation as a genuine democrat caused some problems with his neighbors, all of whose rulers were much more conservative and still attuned to the traditional communist ways of doing things. The partial exception was Kazakhstan, whose former President, Nursultan Nazarbayev, although an ex-communist, had gained a reputation for pragmatism.

International Organizations. Kyrgyzstan was also the first ex-Soviet republic to meet World Bank and IMF requirements for obtaining finance assistance. It has received loans from the World Bank and has negotiated a full standby agreement with the IMF. In 1997, the IMF increased its credits to Kyrgyzstan. Kyrgyzstan was also the first CIS state to be invited to join the World Trade Organization, the WTO having issued the invitation to Kyrgyzstan in October 1998. Kyrgyzstan still has to ratify the accession protocols, which require it to open the country's markets to foreign goods and services.

Russia. The government of Kyrgyzstan has established fairly extensive relations with the other states of Central Asia in recent years, but it has also worked to improve relations with Russia. Kyrgyzstan's decision in May 2000 to reestablish Russian as an official language in the republic was taken partly to stem the outflow of

its Russian population, but it was an act that was also welcomed in Moscow. There were also signs that many in Kyrgyzstan viewed President Vladimir Putin as a potentially more reliable partner and ally.

In December 2002, Kyrgyzstan signed a new security pact with Russia which authorized the stationing of an air squadron consisting of 10 SU-25 and SU-27 attack jets, five training aircraft, two transport planes, and two multipurpose MI-8 helicopters plus approximately 1,000 Russian troops at the Kant military airfield near Bishkek. The air squadron was intended to support a 5,000-member rapid-reaction force then being created under the auspices of the Collective Security Treaty Organization by Russia, Kyrgyzstan, Kazakhstan, Armenia, Belarus, and Tajikistan.

In 2019, following months of rumors, Russian Foreign Minister Sergei Lavrov stated that Russia was interested in opening a second military base in Kyrgyzstan. Although Jeenbekov's government has denied that a second base was being considered, following a state visit by Vladimir Putin in March 2019, the two countries agreed to slightly expand the territory alloted to the Kant airbase in exchange for an increase in rent.

In 2014–2105, Kyrgyzstan took major steps to achieve economic integration with Russia. In April 2014, the Russian state-controlled energy giant Gazprom bought state-owned KyrgyzGas for the symbolic sum of $1. In return for losing control of KyrgyzGas, Kyrgyzstan received a pledge from Gazprom to invest $600 million in modernizing the country's energy industry. In late December 2014, Kyrgyzstan agreed to join the Russian-dominated Eurasian Economic Union (EEU) and did so in May 2015. For its membership to become official, Kyrgyzstan must upgrade border checkpoints, and the four other EEU members must approve the inclusion of Kyrgyzstan; however, these stipulations are just formalities. People, goods, capital, and services are to move freely within the EEU, which came into existence on January 1, 2015. The deal with Gazprom and Kyrgyzstan's decision to join the EEU, appear to have resolved a conflict between Uzbekistan and Kyrgyzstan. In July 2013, Uzbekistan cut off the flow of natural gas to southern Kyrgyzstan, which forced 60,000 people in Kyrgyzstan to cook and heat their homes with other fuels, including bricks of pressed animal dung. The gas dispute was particularly dangerous, because in 2010, riots between ethnic Kyrgyz and Uzbeks had engulfed southern Kyrgyzstan, especially the city of Osh, resulting in the deaths of at least 426 people. (There had been similar riots in the same area back in 1990.) Right after Kyrgyzstan agreed to join the EEU, the

gas started flowing again from Uzbekistan to Kyrgyzstan. Speculation has it that Russian President Putin cut a deal with Uzbek President Islam Karimov to resume sending gas to Kyrgyzstan.

United States. The US government showed its own support for Akayev when it opened the first US Embassy in Central Asia in Bishkek on February 1, 1992. In 1993, Kyrgyzstan received the highest amount of U.S aid on per capita basis of any of the ex-Soviet republics.

President Akayev made an unofficial seven-day visit to the United States in July 1997. Among those he met with were George Soros, a prominent American investor who subsequently invested several million US dollars in Kyrgyzstan, UN Secretary-General Kofi Annan, and IMF Deputy Managing Director Alassane Ouattara.

The September 11 terror attacks against the United States, followed by America's subsequent War on Terrorism, have had a major effect on international Kyrgyzstan's relations. Kyrgyzstan has had its own problems with radical Islam in the form of periodic incursions into the country by units of the Islamic Movement of Uzbekistan, a group with ties to the Taliban in Afghanistan and to al-Qaeda. But the government had to take into consideration its close association with Russia, so President Akayev consulted with the Russian government before the country offered the use of its airspace and airfields to the United States.

On December 6, Kyrgyzstan's Legislative Assembly voted to allow US military aircraft to use Bishkek's Manas international airport; the first American military aircraft arrived on December 19. By the middle of January, there were 250 US military personnel in residence—the first contingent of as many as 5,000 troops who would be coming from the United States, France, Italy, and Canada. A reporter who visited the air base at the end of April reported close to 2,000 soldiers there, all living in air-conditioned tents.

President Sooronbay Jeenbekov

Kyrgyzstan

About half were American; most of the rest were French, though there were also some South Korean servicemen. The main function of the air base at the time was to service the FA-18 fighter jets and French Mirages that were flying daily sorties over Afghanistan, plus the two KC-135 tankers that provided in-flight refueling for the combat jets. The personnel also serviced the Spanish, Dutch, and Danish cargo planes ferrying supplies in from Western Europe. The 420-person French contingent at Manas was replaced by an equivalent number of Danish, Dutch, and Norwegian airmen and troops in October 2002. With the departure of the French, the Mirages were replaced by 19 F-16 fighter jets.

A two-year US-Kyrgyz military cooperation agreement signed in January 2002 authorized exchange visits and joint training. The Kyrgyzstan Government was also granted $50 million in American aid for various economic and social programs; that figure was expected to double for 2003.

Secretary of Defense Donald Rumsfeld visited Kyrgyzstan in May 2002. Secretary of Treasury Paul O'Neill arrived in the middle of July. President Akayev then made an official visit to Washington in September. Although cooperation on antiterrorism was the focus of Rumsfeld's visit, both the O'Neill visit and President Akayev's own visit to Washington focused primarily on poverty-reduction strategies and Kyrgyzstan's own economic–recovery plan.

The revolutionary events of March 2005 produced a new leadership, but they only gradually began to affect Kyrgyz foreign policy. From the beginning, however, the new government began pushing for the United States to increase the amount of money it paid for the lease of the Kyrgyzstan military base being used to support allied military forces in Afghanistan.

In August 2006, the Kyrgyz government expelled two American diplomats, charging that the diplomats interfered "in the country's internal affairs." According to the American Embassy, the two diplomats had been accused of improper contacts with local NGOs. The US government denied the charges.

When the Kyrgyz government insisted on their departure, the US government declared two members of the Kyrgyz Embassy to the United States personae non grata.

The expulsions do not seem to have had an important effect on relations between the two countries. In fact, the Kyrgyz Foreign Ministry announced in March 2007 that Kyrgyzstan would be joining NATO's Planning and Review Program. Kyrgyzstan was already an active member of NATO's Partnership for Peace program.

In February 2009, however, President Bakiev announced that he was requesting the closure of the Manas air base. The announcement came immediately after a meeting with President Dmitry Medvedev in which Russia agreed to extend $2 billion in loans to Kyrgyzstan. Both Russia and Kyrgyzstan denied that Russia had demanded closure of the base as a quid pro quo, but Russia had been publicly pushing for some time for closure of the American base. However, the Kyrgyz government reversed its position on the Manas base in June 2009 after the US government agreed to more than triple its annual compensation payments for the base.

In November 2011, right after he was elected president, Almazbek Atambayev promised to close the US air base (by then officially called a "transit center") at the Manas Airport near Bishkek by 2014. Called the "gateway to Afghanistan," the facility had been used to transfer over five million troops and tens of thousands of cargo shipments into and out of Afghanistan since 2001. With NATO's presence in Afghanistan winding down, the US chose not to try to negotiate with the Kyrgyz government to hold on to its only airfield in Central Asia but instead turned it over to the Kyrgyz government in June 2014. US "peace and security" aid to Central Asia has been cut substantially since 2013. Kyrgyzstan received $32.4 million from the US government in fiscal year 2012 but only $8.4 million in 2013.

Tajikistan

Since independence, there have been regular low-level tensions between Kyrgyzstan and Tajikistan over the demarcation and security of their shared border in the Ferghana Valley. These disputes are a direct legacy of the Soviet Union's delimitation of its constituent republics. In the Soviet era, boundaries were drawn largely to reflect ethnic group concentrations, and were never intended to operate as international borders. As a result, infrastructure, such as irrigation networks and roads, was built with little regard to republic boundaries. Additionally, Uzbekistan, Tajikistan, and Kyrgyzstan each have enclaves in the Ferghana Valley.

In Spring 2021, the existence of one of Tajikistan's enclaves surrounded by Kyrgyzstan prompted a severe security crisis. In March, Kyrgyzstan's newly appointed head of the State Committee for National Security and notorious nationalist politician, Kamchybek Tashiev gave a speech in which he proposed swapping the fertile territory of Vorukh with some much less fertile land. Needless to say, this poorly formulated flippant proposal was rejected out of hand by Tajikistani officials and by the predominately ethnic Tajik population of Vorukh. In April, prescheduled Kyrgyzstani military exercises in the neighboring region of Batken further exacerbated security fears of some Tajiks in the border region. These fears manifested themselves in violence following a dispute over a Tajikistani attempted installation of security cameras at a contested water supply facility. Following a rock fight between residents on either side of the border, a loose assortment of military personnel, border guards, and civilians were mobilized on the Tajikistani side to attack Kyrgyzstani land and property. The precession of the Tajikistani response strongly suggests that there was significant degree of premeditation and preparation before the violence. At least 46 people were killed in the days-long fighting and more than 100 properties were destroyed. With the balance of the causalities on the Kyrgyzstani side, this

Kyrgyzstan protest

Kyrgyzstan

unnecessary and embarrassing incident could end up severely damaging the legitimacy of Japarov's nationalist appeal. The latest shooting along the border between Kyrgyz and Tajik border guards broke out on April 10, 2002, which left 12 Kyrgyz and 10 Tajiks nationals wounded. Although the situation was deescalated through intergovernmental talks, permanent resolution of the conflict is unlikely until authorities address the preconditions that enable bouts of border violence. These preconditions include, but are not limited to, developing and enforcing clear rules regarding the use of land, water, and grazing rights, and demarcation of state boundaries.

Nature of the Regime

Under the October 2007 constitution, Kyrgyzstan had a presidential-parliamentary form of government with the president responsible for general policy and a prime minister, responsible to the legislature, formally known as the Jorgorku Kengesh (Supreme Council), handling implementation of policy. Under that system, the president was advised by a State Council, while the prime minister presided over his cabinet. The prime minister was responsible to the Supreme Council and had to be confirmed by that body in order to hold office.

The Supreme Council was a unicameral legislature of 90 seats, all of which were filled on the basis of proportional representation; seats were apportioned to those party slates that won a minimum of 5% of the national vote, and a minimum of 0.5% of the vote in each of the country's seven regions and its two largest cities.

As a result of the April 2010 revolution that overthrew President Bakiev, the 2007 constitution was suspended and the new interim leadership, which consisted entirely of individuals who had been in the political opposition prior to April 2010, promised a new constitution giving Kyrgyzstan a parliamentary system with a ceremonial president.

For this purpose, they created a 75-member Constitutional Committee that was largely made up of representatives from nongovernmental organizations. The committee also received advice from several international organizations and this they did over the next month or so. The new constitution, produced in approximately one month, was made public on May 21; a national referendum on the new constitution took place on June 27, when it received overwhelming support.

Although the initiators of the project said that they were giving the country a parliamentary system, it might better be referred to as a modified presidential-parliamentary system. Although it creates a presidential office somewhat more limited than in the 2007 constitution, the president still has the power to either veto or refuse to sign any laws other than laws related to budget and fiscal policy; he can also send a law back to parliament for reconsideration. On the other hand, he is limited to a single, six-year term.

The prime minister (and cabinet) exercise far more power than previously, for they control the government's purse strings and so much of the country's economic life. The prime minister is also in charge of personnel policy, finance, and licenses.

The new constitution increases the size of parliament from 90 to 120 seats. To guard against a single party amassing too much power, no party can hold more than 65 seats. This probably means that most governments will be coalitions—the current situation.

Parliamentary elections were set to occur every five years, and the first elections took place on October 10, 2010. The results were instructive. Total number of votes cast was approximately 1.38 million; of that number, approximately a third of all votes went to the 24 political parties that failed to achieve the required minimum of 5% of the national vote.

Five parties won more than 5% of the national vote and so entered the parliament. Ata-Jurt (Homeland) came first with 8.69% of the vote, closely followed by the Social Democratic Party, with 8.13% of the vote. The Ar-Namys (Dignity) party came in third with 7.64% of the vote; Respublika was next with 7.04% of the vote; and the Ata-Meken (Fatherland) party came last with 5.71% of the vote.

Forming a coalition government was difficult because the leaders of two of the winning political parties, Ata-Jurt and Ar-Namys, were on record as favoring a strong presidential form of government. But politics makes strange bedfellows. In December 2010, a new coalition government was formed with Almazbek Atambayev, head of the Social Democratic Party, as prime minister. The other three parties forming the coalition were Ar-Namys, Ata-Meken, and Respublika. The important factor that led to the inclusion

Young Kyrgyz woman and child

of Ar-Namys into the coalition was that its main power base was in the south, the area where the other three coalition parties were relatively weak.

Roza Otunbayeva, a former foreign minister and former Kyrgyz ambassador to the United States, was named acting president in May 2010; after the new constitution was approved, she was named President but with a term of office that would run only until December 2011 when presidential elections would occur; it was understood that she would not run to succeed herself. New presidential elections, which took place on October 30, 2011, were won by Almazbek Atambayev, a two-time prime minister and unsuccessful candidate for the presidency in 2009. In November 2017, independent Kyrgyzstan experienced its first non-violent, procedural transfer of power when Sooronbay Jeenbekov was elected president. Even though Jeenbekov was Atambayev's choice to replace him when his term was over, according to observers the election was relatively fair and free.

Among observers, there is currently a great deal of concern that Kyrgyzstan's democratization has stalled following the state's third revolution in October 2020 and the subsequent return to a presidential system. Under the new constitution, newly elected President Japarov has expanded powers in line with the neighboring autocratic Central Asian states.

Culture

Most Kyrgyz are Muslims. An oral tradition among the people has kept alive epic cycles and lyric poetry. This has saved much that would otherwise have been lost, for the written language has been in three different forms in the 20th century. The first written language used the Arabic script, but that was abandoned after World War I and the Latin script was introduced. In 1940, Stalin forced all of the Central Asian republics to adopt the Cyrillic alphabet.

While the other Central Asian Republics have recently begun the switch back to the Latin script, President Bakiev said in April 2008 that he had rejected such a switch. According to Bakiev, financial costs played an important role in his decision, but he was also concerned that a switch might pose "a risk that the quality of education will worsen sharply in our country." According to preliminary estimates of the Education and Science Ministry, the switch to the Latin script would cost about $140 million.

Kyrgyzstan has produced two writers of note in modern times, the playwright and novelist Chinghiz Aitmatov and the playwright Kaltay Muhamedjanov. Aitmatov, who died on June 10, 2008, at the age of 79, is the author of several notable works

Kyrgyzstan

which give voice to Central Asian protagonists living in the Soviet Union, including *The Day Lasts More Than a Hundred Years* and *Jamila*. The two collaborated on the play *The Ascent of Mt. Fuji*, which has also been translated into English and was performed onstage in Washington, DC, in 1973. Its theme is the moral compromises that people had to make under Stalin.

Russian and Kyrgyz are both official languages. Newspapers and magazines are published in both Russian and Kyrgyz and radio and television broadcasts are made in both languages. National broadcasts are also received from Moscow by way of relay lines. The Russian cultural influence is, therefore, very strong. The State University of Kyrgyzstan is located in Bishtek; in December 1991, it opened a business school, support for which came partly from IBM, which donated a roomful of personal computers.

Since its emergence as an independent republic in 1991, the government of Kyrgyzstan has celebrated an epic poem of over a million verses called "Manas," parts of which may date back a thousand years. A story of a wise folk hero who unites the Kyrgyz nomads against foreign enemies, the poem has become the center of a nationalistic up swelling throughout the country, plus something more. "This is our Bible," Jenishbek Sydykov, director of linguistics and literature at the Kyrgyz National Academy of Sciences, said of it. "As a people, we are one with this poem. In our eyes, the hero Manas is just below God—and higher than Lenin ever was to us."

Economy

The Kyrgyz were once mainly nomads who pastured their herds in summer on the alpine-like slopes of the mountains where 30–40 inches of rainfall annually provide lush meadows for grazing. During the Soviet period, they were settled into villages and made part of collective or state farms. Livestock includes sheep, goats, cattle, and horses. Mare's milk is the source for *koumiss*, the local fermented drink. Pigs, bees, and rabbits are also raised in the mountains. Agriculture, practiced mainly in the lowland areas, is dependent on irrigation, since these areas receive an average of 7 inches of rainfall a year. The main crops include sugar beets, cotton, tobacco, opium poppies, and cereal grains. Agriculture contributes approximately 37% of the Gross Domestic Production (GDP). Of the main agricultural crops, only cotton and tobacco are exported in significant quantities.

The role of industry in the economy has grown greatly in recent years, and now makes up 21.9% of GDP. Extractive industries are important; Kyrgyzstan has

significant deposits of gold and rare earth minerals and is a major source of antimony and mercury ores. It also has significant deposits of lead, nepheline, mercury, bismuth, and zinc. It also has large coal reserves, which have begun to be exploited. Hydroelectric power provides about half the energy needs of the republic. It also produces petroleum and natural gas. Kyrgyzstan has approximately 6 billion cubic meters of proven natural gas reserves, but its annual production is only about 30 million cubic meters. Food processing and light industry have been developed, and the republic also manufactures machinery and instruments.

Kyrgyzstan still has a predominantly agrarian economy, however, and many of the industries developed while it was still part of the Soviet Union, such as processing cotton brought from other republics or uranium mining, were heavily dependent on trade with the other republics for survival. Thus, the break up of the Soviet Union had a particularly devastating impact on the standard of living. One effect has been that Russians, who still tend to dominate Kyrgyzstan's professional elite, have left in large numbers for Russia. In addition, most ethnic Germans living in the republic in 1991 have since left; there were 100,000 in 1991, but fewer than 11,000 today. The effect has been to leave the economy even more profoundly agrarian than it was before.

Kyrgyzstan has religiously followed the prescriptions of the World Bank and IMF since independence, liberalizing the economy and privatizing shops and some enterprises. The results, satisfactory in the beginning, earned Kyrgyzstan an invitation to join the World Trade Organization in October 1998, the first CIS state to receive such an invitation.

However, Kyrgyzstan was badly affected by the economic collapse in Russia beginning in September 1998. Russia is Kyrgyzstan's chief trading partner, accounting for 25% of Kyrgyzstan's foreign trade. As Marat Sultanov, chairman of Kyrgyzstan's National Bank, put it in October 1998, "we were prepared for the Russian crisis in Kyrgyzstan, but not on such a scale."

In spite of these negative factors, there was no economic collapse, and the government was able to continue to pay interest on treasury bills and meet its foreign debt obligations. By revising the budget to reflect the new economic situation, making greater efforts to collect taxes from enterprises, and strengthening its controls over the country's banks, it somehow made it through.

The economic situation improved slightly in the period 2000–2008, but the

weakest link remained the industrial sector. For example, a 0.5% drop in GDP for 2002 was entirely attributed to a fall in industrial production, since agricultural output actually increased by 3.5% while turnover trade increased by 8.2%. Imports increased by 31.7% and exports by 6.1%, which gave Kyrgyzstan a negative trade balance of $33.7 million. The economy improved again the next year.

The government launched a new round of large-scale privatization in December 2002, though it was not very successful. For example, an electric-lamp company being offered for $3.2 million attracted no bids at all. Other enterprises being offered for sale included the Haydarken mercury factory, a cotton plant in Osh, and a semiconductor plant in Tash-Kumyr. A Russian metals company did purchase a controlling interest in tin and tungsten mines along the southern shore of Lake Issuk-Kul, however. Speaking in November 2004, President Akayev said that Kyrgyzstan had "managed to reduce poverty by 15%" over the preceding five years.

The revolution of 2005 brought in a new, democratic government, but it also led to a lot of political instability. As a result, GDP grew by only about 1.4% in 2005 and 2.7% in 2006. On the other hand, foreign direct investment for the first nine months of 2005 showed a 33% increase over 2004.

Kyrgyzstan has never had great success attracting foreign investment, but that seems to be changing. Most importantly, it appears that the Russian government now supports Russian investments in the Kyrgyz economy. In April 2006, Russian Security Council Secretary Igor Ivanov visited Bishkek; while there, he told a press conference that Russian investment in Kyrgyzstan could reach several billion dollars in a few years. The most promising sectors, he added, were energy, gas, and metallurgy. Meeting later with President Bakiev, he said that Russia was prepared to invest up to $3 billion in Kyrgyzstan. In March 2007, the Kyrgyz government signed an agreement with the Russian and Kazakhstan Governments for construction of two Kambar-Ata hydroelectric power stations at a cost of about $2.5 billion. The Kyrgyz parliament passed the necessary implementation laws in June 2007.

In October 2008, the Kyrgyz government sold a 75% in its state-owned natural gas company, Kyrgyzgas, to Gazprom. In February 2009, President Medvedev announced during a visit to Bishtek that Russia has agreed to provide $2 billion in loans to Kyrgyzstan, though it is not clear that this offer survived the April 2010 revolution.

Private Russian companies have also begun to take a renewed interest in

Kyrgyzstan in recent years, with the result that Russian investments in Kyrgyzstan have grown significantly over the last several years. In August 2004, Russia's Unified Energy Systems signed an agreement with the Kyrgyz government to finish two massive hydropower plants in Kyrgyz at a cost of $2 billion. In February 2007, Russia's Renova Group purchased a 72.28% interest in the Kara Balta uranium-production facility.

One of Kyrgyzstan's most profitable industries is the Kumtor gold mine, located in the Tian Shan Mountains. Run by the Canadian Centerra Gold Company since 1997, Kumtor is currently accounting for about 12% of Kyrgyzstan's GDP and adding $1.9 billion to the Krygyz budget. It is also one of Kyrgyzstan's main export earners. That has not proved to be enough for some politicians, who have been pushing for renegotiation of the contract with the Canadian company. The company, which pays 14% of its gross revenues as taxes, says that it has poured $1.2 billion into the mine since 2009. The Kyrgyz government's push to renegotiate its contract with Centerra has brought an extremely negative reaction from international investors and dampened any possibility of greater foreign investment in the country. The gold mine has also become a domestic political issue as some political leaders have pushed to have the mine nationalized.

This issue led to the collapse of the Kyrgyz government in March 2014, when Ata-Meken, one of the three parties in the coalition government, withdrew its support over the issue of ownership of the Kumtor gold mine. The government was just completing negotiations with the Canadian Centerra Gold Company on an arrangement which would have given the Kyrgyz government 50% of the shares of a newly formed joint-stock company when Ata-Meken made its move. Omurbek Tekebaev, leader of Ata-Meken, insisted that the government hold out for 67% of the shares of the new company.

In 2019, mining was once again a divisive political issue. Following a series of anti-uranium mining protests, parliament voted to ban uranium exploration and mining. While this decision seems to be politically popular given widespread concern with environmental degradation and negative public health effects of uranium mining, it is unclear whether foreign companies who have invested in exploration will seek compensation or legal restitution from the government.

Kyrgyzstan has been getting international assistance for a number of years.

In May 2002, the IMF released the second tranche of a $93 million loan approved in 2001; it also agreed to write off or reschedule a portion of Kyrgyzstan's foreign debt. In March 2002, the Paris Club rescheduled $94.5 million in loans that would have come due during the period 2002–2004. Meeting in Bishkek in October 2002, the third annual Kyrgyzstan donor's conference pledged loans and grants worth $700 million for the period 2003–2005. The World Bank granted a $5 million loan to rehabilitate uranium-tailings dumps in September 2003 and made two grants of $370,000 each for feasibility studies on renovating other nuclear dumps. In August 2006, it provided a further $15 million to be used for rural reform. Kyrgyzstan also became eligible for the heavily indebted poor countries (HIPC) initiative, which allowed the government to nearly close the gap between expenditures and revenue in 2006. GDP grew about 8% annually in 2007–2008.

Kyrgyzstan made significant economic progress in 2007, but there was some regression in 2008 as two of Kyrgyzstan's imports, natural gas and grain, jumped drastically in price. The official employment figures for 2008 showed a 16.8% unemployment rate; perhaps more significant, a report by the Committee on Migration and Employment determined that 547,000 persons had gone abroad seeking work.

The 2008 worldwide recession brought a serious drop in commodity prices, and it also led to many Kyrgyz citizens working in Russia and Kazakhstan losing their jobs and their ability to send remittances back to their families in Kyrgyzstan. GDP slowed to about 2.9% in 2009 and then dropped to 0.5% in 2010. Political instability and a serious drought were also contributing factors to the decline. GDP grew at a 5.7% rate in 2011, but dropped to an estimated 1% in 2012. One factor in the decrease in GDP was a significant drop in production at the Kumtor gold mine.

Deputy Prime Minister Joomart Otorbaev was in Washington in April 2012 to attend the World Bank and IMF spring meetings. Speaking at the National Democratic Institute, a pro-democracy NGO in Washington, Otorbaev was critical of both the World Bank and IMF, accusing the two agencies of having provided delayed guidance and expertise to Kyrgyzstan on economic modernization and resource development. Speaking on the same topic during another interview, Otorbaev added that Kyrgyzstan was now looking to China for speedier help.

Western sanctions on Russia, following the invasion of Ukraine, will have an adverse effect on the economy of Kyrgyzstan. Similar to Tajikistan, the country strongly depends on Russia for the inflow of financial remittances from migrant laborers. In Kyrgyzstan and Tajikistan, remittances in 2020 totaled the equivalent of 31 percent and 27 percent of GDP, respectively. As a share of GDP, these figures equaled or even exceeded the countries' exports of goods and services. As sanctions weaken economic activity in Russia and devalue the Russian ruble, the World Bank estimates that remittances to Kyrgyzstan would fall by 33%, against a previously forecast rise of 3%.

The Future

Even if statements that the country was the "Switzerland of Central Asia" have proven to be hyperbolic, Kyrgyzstan has enjoyed far more political pluralism than any of its neighbors. By all accounts, the fact that a peaceful transfer of power following a competitive election occurred in the fall of 2017 should be seen as a momentous occasion. However, the persecution of Babanov, the defeated opponent, following the election should give observers pause. While Kyrgyzstan is not an autocracy, neither is it a stable democracy. The purge of Atambayev and his allies by Jeenbekov reveals the continued importance of personalist networks in Kyrgyzstani politics. While the clash of networks may produce pluralism, they do not necessarily lend themselves to the formation of self-reinforcing democratic institutions. Kyrgyzstan has yet to develop programmatic political parties with relatively consistent political ideologies; instead, parties are platforms for individual personalities which are regularly shed following an election.

The rapid rise of Sadyr Japaorv, who went from being a disgraced and imprisoned former member of parliament to the self-declared interim president of the country in a span of less two weeks in October 2020, is a symptom of the under-institutionalization of Kyrgyzstani politics. At the same time, his selection and later election into the presidency has many concerned that the democratization window in Kyrgyzstan is rapidly closing. At the very least, the passage of the most recent batch of constitutional amendments, which have strengthened the presidency, have signaled that Kyrgyzstan's experiment with a mixed system has come to an end.

The Republic of Tajikistan

Area: 57,250 sq. mi. (143,000 sq. km., slightly smaller than Illinois).

Population: 10,394,063 (2024 estimate).

Capital City: Dushanbe (Pop. 987,000 2023 estimate).

Climate: Continental, with sharp changes depending upon altitude.

Neighboring Countries: China (east); Afghanistan (south); Uzbekistan (west and north); and Kyrgyzstan (north).

Principal Language: Tajik has been the sole official language since 1994, but Russian is still widely used in government and business.

Ethnic Composition: Tajik (84.3%), Uzbek (13.8%), Other (2%) (2014 est.).

Principal Religion: Islam (Sunni 95%; Shi'a 3%); Other 2% (2014 est.).

Chief Commercial Products: Mining, food processing, textiles, clothing and silk; fruit and livestock. The Ghissar sheep is famous for its meat and Karakul sheep produce wool and glossy, curly lamb pelts. The Republic has tremendous existing and potential hydroelectric resources.

Currency: somoni (introduced on October 30, 2000).

Per Capita Annual Income (Purchasing Power Parity): $4,581 (2023 est.).

Recent Political Status: Autonomous Republic within the former USSR (1924) as part of Uzbek SSR; Constituent Republic of the former USSR (1929–1991).

President: Emomali Rahmon [prior to March 2007 Imamali Rakhmonov] (since November 6, 1994, and reelected October 11, 2020).

Prime Minister: Qohir Rasulzoda (appointed November 23, 2013).

National Day: September 9 (independence from Soviet Union).

National Flag: Three horizontal stripes; on top a narrow red and on the bottom a narrow green, with a broader white stripe across the center. Superimposed on the white is a golden crown with a semicircle of stars.

The Land

The Republic of Tajikistan is the independent successor state to the Tajik Soviet Socialist Republic. It declared its independence in September 1991.

Tajikistan is a small land, which includes the autonomous region of Gorno-Badakhshan. It is located in the extreme southern part of Central Asia.

It is also a mountainous land, with more than half of its territory lying above 10,000 feet. The northern border forms a loop around the western part of the Fergana Valley, running along the top ridges of the Kuramin Range in the north before turning south, crossing the valley, and then tracing its way westward along the foothills of the Zeravshan Range. Here the western and eastern borders almost meet before turning south. The western border continues south, turning somewhat westward, while the eastern border bends sharply eastward and runs along the northern slopes of the Zeravshan Range, continuing until it reaches the China border.

The center of the republic is dominated by the Turkistan Range and the slightly lower Zevavshan and Gissar Ranges. In the east are the Pamirs, which contain the highest peaks found anywhere in Central Asia. In the south, a series of transverse ridges and river valleys slope down to the Pyandzh River in Afghanistan.

Valleys make up about 10% of the land of the republic. In addition to the western part of the Fergana Valley, there are the smaller Gissar, Vakhsh, Yavansu, Obikiik, Lower Kafirnigan, and Pyandzh valleys in the south. There are also a number of small lakes in the eastern part of the country, in the Pamir Mountains. There is a dense river network. These include the stretch of the Syr Dar'ya that flows through the western part of the Fergana Valley and the upper reaches of the Amu Dar'ya. Most rivers flow northward into Central Asia.

Tajikistan has two climatic zones. The valleys are subtropical, with average July temperatures in the 80s and January temperatures hovering around freezing. Annual rainfall in the valleys is only 6–10 inches, so agriculture depends entirely on irrigation. In the highlands, average January temperatures are 0°F or below. The mountains get very little precipitation in the summer, but the high ranges get 30–60 inches in the form of snow in the winter. In the highest ranges, there are also huge glaciers that partially melt in the summer, only to be replenished in the winter. The spring and summer runoff from the mountains provides water for irrigation on the lower slopes and in the valleys.

The People

Tajikistan's estimated population as of July 2024 was over 10 million, an increase of more than three million since independence. Tajiks comprise approximately 84.3% of that figure. Uzbeks, found mainly in the northwestern and southwestern part of the republic, come next with 13.8%. The relative percentages of Tajiks and Uzbeks is not without controversy, as some Uzbeks maintain that many co-ethnics are incorrectly classified as Tajiks in official statistics. The remaining 2% of the population is composed of Russians, Kyrgyz, Turkmens, Tatars, and Arabs.

Tajik is the sole official language of the state. Tajik belongs to the southwest group of Iranian languages, which set the Tajiks off from the rest of their Central Asian neighbors. Orally, Tajik is quite similar to Dari, spoken widely in Afghanistan. Dari and Tajik differ in their written forms, however. Dari is written using a modified Arabic alphabet, while contemporary Tajik is written using a modified Cyrillic script. Because of the nature of the terrain, Tajiks actually speak a variety of dialects, depending on which part of Tajikistan they live in. The mountainous region of Gorno-Badakshan is home to a dizzying degree of linguistic diversity. At least nine distinct languages, classified as East Iranian, are spoken in the valleys of this region. Although these langauges are commonly used in day-to-day interactions within communities, the speakers generally need to use Tajik in more formal settings.

302

As a result, many of these languages are endangered.

History

The Tajiks are the descendants of Iranian-speaking people who entered Central Asia as early as 2000 B.C. They were incorporated into the Persian Empire and the subsequent Empire of Alexander the Great. The ancient kingdom of Sogdiana, conquered by the Arabs in the 8th century, was Tajik speaking. In the 10th century, an invasion of Turkic-speaking peoples overran Central Asia. Many Tajiks were assimilated at this time, with Tajik culture surviving mainly in the mountains.

The Tajiks were later brought under the control of the Emirate of Bukhara. In the 18th century, Afghanistan extended its control over the area. The Russian Empire gained control in the 1860s. Bukhara became a Russian protectorate in 1868.

After the Russian Revolution, part of the area occupied by the Tajik people was incorporated into the Turkistan Autonomous Soviet Socialist Republic, established in April 1918. When the Red Army took over Bukhara in 1920, it also claimed most of the territory of modern Tajikistan. The Red Army captured Dushanbe early in 1921. The Basmachi revolt, which began in 1922 and lasted to the summer of 1923, was an attempt to throw off communist control, but it was ultimately unsuccessful. In 1924, the communist authorities decided to divide up Central Asia along ethnic lines. This led to the creation of the Tadzhik Autonomous Soviet Socialist Republic, at the time part of the Uzbek SSR. In December 1929, the Tadzhik Autonomous SSR was separated from the Uzbek SSR and made a constituent republic in its own right.

Mountainous and isolated and divided into different tribes that had a long history of rivalry, the Tadzhik SSR was run throughout most of the Soviet period by officials sent out by Moscow. Even as late as 1990, Tajiks were a minority in the Tajik Communist Party. Gorbachev's programs of glasnost and perestroika changed that. By 1988, Tajik officials had recognized the opportunity offered by the Gorbachev reform program and had begun to implement Tajik solutions to local problems. This led the Tajik Supreme Soviet to assert Tajikistan sovereignty in August 1990.

Independence and Civil War

After the attempted coup against Gorbachev collapsed in August 1991, Kakhar Makhkamov, who had supported the coup, resigned as party leader and Chairman of the Supreme Soviet. He was replaced by Kadriddin Aslonov. Upon taking office, Aslonov resigned his membership on the Politburo of the Tajik Communist Party and issued a decree banning the Communist Party of the Soviet Union on Tajik territory.

This irritated a majority of the members of the Tajik Supreme Soviet, 95% of whom were communists. Accusing him of "unconstitutional actions," they ousted him as chairman of the Supreme Soviet. In his stead, they elected Rakhmon Nabiyev, who had been first secretary of the Tajik Communist Party before Makhkamov. At about this time also, the Dushanbe party leader gave permission for a statue of Lenin to be torn down. He, too, was ousted and a state of emergency was declared in Dushanbe. In a related development, a hastily called congress of the Tajik Communist Party "dissolved" the party and established a new Socialist Party in its stead.

This combined set of developments appeared to political opponents to prove that the communists were determined to retain power. They organized a series of protest rallies in Dushanbe where they demanded that the state of emergency be lifted, the Supreme Soviet be dissolved and new elections called, and that Nabiyev resign as Chairman of the Supreme Soviet.

On September 30, after the rallies had continued for several days, the Supreme Soviet voted to lift the state of emergency in Dushanbe. Two days later, the Supreme Soviet suspended the activities of the officially dissolved Tajik Communist Party and its successor, the Socialist Party, "until the party's participation in the coup attempt is estimated." Finally, Nabiyev submitted his resignation as Supreme Soviet chairman on October 6. Akbarsho Iskandarov took over as acting chairman. The opposition had won every one of their points.

In September, the Supreme Soviet had created a new popularly elected presidency. That election had been set for October 27, but it was then postponed until November 24. As the presidential contest began, there were ten candidates, including Rakhmon Nabiyev. Three later withdrew. There were also a number of political parties active, some registered and some not. Registered parties included the Democratic Party of Tajikistan and the Popular Movement "Rastokhez" (Revival). The Islamic Revival Party was still in limbo at this point.

The government banned all religious-oriented parties at first but then lifted the ban on October 22. At this point, a number of organizations had nominated Akbar Turajonzoda, head of the Spiritual Administration of Muslims of Tajikistan, for president. Turajonzoda's subsequent statement was therefore significant:

I support a secular parliamentary state with a free economy. Religion should be separated from the state so the sins of society cannot be attributed to Islam, which is what happened to the Communist Party.

Turajonzoda did not stand as a candidate for the presidency. When the election was finally held on November 24, 1991, Rakhmon Nabiyev won with 56.9% of the vote. His chief opponent, Davlat Khudonazarov, who had been supported by the united opposition, won 30.7% of the vote.

Nabiyev's victory in the elections did not put an end to the struggle, however. In the early spring, the Islamic-led opposition, organized as the Union of Popular Forces, launched a campaign demanding multiparty elections and more freedom of religion, though their real purpose was to drive Nabiyev from office. Responding to the threat, the Tajik parliament attempted to strengthen Nabiyev's hand by giving him the power to rule by decree. As demonstrations continued, Nabiyev declared a state of emergency. Instead of calming the situation, this brought calls for Nabiyev's resignation. In early May, opposition forces seized control of Dushanbe, the capital, and declared the creation of a revolutionary council. In a compromise, Nabiyev then lifted the state of emergency and agreed to form a "government of national reconciliation." In the new government, eight seats were assigned to an opposition coalition consisting of democrats and moderate Islamists, plus the Islamic Revival Party, whose program at that time called for the creation of an Islamic state.

Nabiyev's compromise calmed the situation briefly, but there was no reconciliation. Not only did the two disparate groupings find it difficult to work with each other; Nabiyev also found himself under attack from ex-communist allies in the northern part of the country who accused him of ceding too much power to the opposition. In addition, the central government began to lose control of the countryside as ex-communists took control of local governments in the north and Islamists took control of local governments in the south and east. Fighting then broke out between regions, eventually resulting in about 1,000 deaths.

In an attempt to restore order, Nabiyev asked the Commonwealth of Independent States to dispatch peacekeeping troops to the country. The opposition now declared open rebellion and seized control of Dushanbe. Nabiyev, taken prisoner by demonstrators as he fled to the Dushanbe airport, was forced at gunpoint to resign as president. The Islamic-democratic coalition then declared itself to be the new government and named Akbarsho Iskandarov as acting president.

Tajikistan

303

Tajikistan

The Islamic-democratic coalition was unable to consolidate its control over the country, however. The northern, and most developed, part of the country was controlled by ex-communists associated with Nabiyev and they would have nothing to do with the new government. Meanwhile the situation in Dushanbe remained so unstable that the new government was unable to convene a new session of the parliament. This government lasted two months and then resigned on November 12, 1992, turning power over to an interim council. Meanwhile the parliament, meeting in the northern town of Khojand, elected Emomali Rahmonov, a former collective farm manager, as chairman of the legislature after accepting President Nabiyev's voluntary resignation. On December 10, forces loyal to the former president took control of Dushanbe and at this time Rahmonov was designated acting president. Islamists fled to their strongholds in the mountains of eastern Tajikistan, pursued by elements of the Tajik army. Other Islamists sought refuge across the border in Afghanistan.

Rahmonov was an unlikely figure to emerge as the head of the fractured country. As a farm manager from the rural region of Kulob, he hadn't cultivated elite connections with communist party leaders across the former Soviet space. His ascension to power was through the Popular Front of Tajikistan, a coalition of warlords from the conservative power bases in Leninabad (now Khujand) and Kulob. By all accounts, it was expected that Rahmonov would simply be a puppet through which powerful warlords such as Sangak Safarov, a former felon, could reign. However, following Safarov's death in a shoot-out in 1993, Rahmonov proved adept at outmaneuvering rivals to his power.

As the civil war continued, the Tajik government received more assistance from Russia. By the fall of 1993, there were more than 20,000 Russian troops in the republic and Russia was providing subsidies amounting to 50% of the budget. Russia's interest was apparently its fear that the Islamic forces, allied with Afghan Islamic militants, would seize control of the government and establish a militant Islamic regime in Tajikistan. The Tajik government received significant assistance from the Government of Uzbekistan as well, partly for the same reason.

The government's control remained fragile, however. A reporter who visited Dushanbe in May 1994 reported that it was calm there during the day but that the streets were deserted at night and, in the distance, one heard a "chorus of automatic rifle shots. With daybreak come reports of assassinations of public figures or of men disappearing from sight."

Russian soldiers began guarding Tajikistan's border with Afghanistan in 1994. Eleven Russian soldiers were killed in skirmishes over that summer before government and opposition forces reached agreement on a cease-fire. The two sides later held talks in Islamabad which produced a cease-fire between government forces and guerillas based in the eastern mountains. From this time onward, the Russian foreign ministry supported a settlement that would reintegrate the rebels into the society.

In November 1994, the Tajik government held a combined presidential election and referendum on a new constitution. With the real opposition excluded from participating, the presidential contest was between the acting president, Rahmonov, and Abdumalik Abdulajanov, a former prime minister. Though not democratic by western standards, election observers said that the voting itself was free and fair. Rahmonov won with about 60% of the vote and the new constitution was approved as well. At this time, Rahmonov appointed Jamshed Karimov as his prime minister and announced that the government would launch a new privatization initiative. This resulted in some small-scale privatization of firms having fewer than 20 employees, mainly firms providing catering and consumer services, but the economy continued to be basically state-run.

In the early part of 1996, a split among the forces supporting the government produced a new crisis. Two regional leaders who had been supporters of President Rahmonov charged his government with incompetence and corruption and demanded its dismissal. They also demanded that he do something to improve the state of the economy. One of them, Colonel Makhmoud Khudoyberdyev, moved his troops within 10 miles from the capital, though no actual battle took place. Faced with the possibility of another civil war and informed by the Russian government that it would not intervene again to save his government, Rahmonov opened negotiations with the rebels. During the discussions, he agreed to dismiss several officials, including his first deputy prime minister, his chief of staff and a southern governor. In return, the rebels agreed to return to their barracks.

A few days later, Rahmonov dismissed his prime minister, replacing him with Yakhyo Azimov, a little-known northerner who up to this time had been a carpet factory manager. It appears that this change was made because of the poor

Spectators watch horses and riders at a popular equestrian event   Courtesy of NOVOSTI

performance of the economy. In a news conference which he called after assuming office, Azimov announced that he favored market reforms and would cooperate with international donor organizations to re-build the economy.

President Rahmonov's greater, long-term problem was how to deal with the Islamic-democratic opposition, however. No real political stability could be achieved until he either came to terms with them or found some way to defeat them or deprive them of their popular political support. Many of Rahmonov's supporters pushed for the second alternative, but this looked increasingly unrealistic to outside observers, particularly the Russians. According to Russian estimates, Rahmonov's forces controlled, at best, a third of the republic, and the war would already have been lost but for the presence of 25,000 Russian troops.

Under strong pressure from the Russian government to come to an understanding with the opposition, Rahmonov traveled to Moscow in December 1996 to meet with Sayed Abdullo Nuri, leader of the Islamic Renaissance Party, largest of the parties in the United Tajik Opposition (UTO). The talks went well and a peace agreement was signed which provided for a general amnesty and called for creation of a Reconciliation Council. When President Rahmonov got back to Dushanbe, however, he found that he was unable to sell the peace agreement to his political supporters.

Under continuing pressure from the Russian government, Rahmonov traveled to Moscow again in March 1997 for new talks with the UTO. Here, Rahmonov signed an agreement which called for integration of opposition troops into the regular Tajik armed forces. No agreement for a political reconciliation had been reached, however, so another round of talks was scheduled to begin in Tehran on April 9, 1997. No breakthrough occurred at this point, but the two sides did agree to meet again in Moscow in June. It was in Moscow that President Rahmonov, under pressure from a Russian government that had grown tired of the war and the continuing death of Russian soldiers, signed a final accord with Sayed Abdullo Nuri on June 27, aimed at ending the years of fighting in the country.

The accord created a power-sharing arrangement and legalized the parties of the UTO, including the Islamic Renaissance Party, the Democratic Party, the Rastokhez People's Movement, and the Laali Badakhshan. The accord also created a National Reconciliation Commission which was charged with laying the groundwork for elections by the end of 1998, including recommending amendments to election laws. The interim power-sharing arrangement provided that

President Emomali Rahmon

the UTO was to obtain 30% of the ministerial posts in the government. It also specified that members of the UTO were to be allowed to return to Tajikistan accompanied by their own armed guards. After the accord was signed, the two parties supporting the government—the People's Party and the Political and Economic Renewal Party—merged themselves into the National Unity Movement.

Post-Civil War Politics

Thus, the stage was set for Tajik politics to be dominated by two large political groupings, one representing President Rahmonov and his allies and the other representing the political opposition. To the extent that these two political groupings represented most of the people of Tajikistan, they created the circumstances whereby disagreements could be transferred from the battlefield to the political stage.

Implementation did not go entirely smoothly, but it appears that one major reason for this was the Tajik government's desire to assert greater control over subordinate commanders inclined to operate rather too independently of the government. This appears to have been the case with regard to Colonel Makhmoud Khudaberiyev, commander of the Tajik army's First Brigade, who was accused of launching a military coup to overthrow the government in August 1997. According to Colonel Khudaberiyev, whose First Brigade was the rapid reaction force of the presidential guard, his unit was attacked by another unit of the presidential guard, led by its commander General Gafar Mirzoyev, and he and his unit only defended themselves. Two other outbreaks of military violence seem to have had similar roots. In each case, military forces loyal to the Tajik government were able to assert their control.

A great deal of distrust continued to exist between the two sides, though they gradually managed to build a working relationship. Sayed Abdullo Nuri, head of the UTO, returned to Dushanbe in

September 1997. Akbar Turajonzoda, deputy leader of the UTO (and former head of the Spiritual Administration of Muslims of Tajikistan), finally returned to Tajikistan in March 1998 and took up his post as deputy prime minister. Turajonzoda's position put him in charge of economic and trade relations with other CIS countries.

Instances of violence continued to occur on a fairly frequent basis, though it was often caused by renegade groups flaunting the authority of the UTO. In fact, after the killing of a number of policemen at road checkpoints in March 1998, the government issued a statement accusing the leadership of the UTO of being "either unable to control its armed formations or insincere when it makes statements on its intention to establish a final peace."

It appears that, indeed, they often were not able to control these forces. In July 1998, for example, fighting even broke out between the followers of two different UTO field commanders. Deputy Prime Minister Turajonzoda managed to mediate an end to that fighting after two days. Periodic gunshots were even heard in the capital itself, with the result that almost no one went out-of-doors after dark.

Assassinations also continued to occur. In September 1998, Otakhon Latifi, a leading Tajik opposition figure who was also head of the National Reconciliation Commission sub-committee on legal issues, was shot dead by unidentified attackers as he left his home in Dushanbe. In January 1999, Tolib Boboyev, the former prosecutor-general of Leninabad Oblast, was killed by masked gunmen while visiting the home of his son.

Implementation of the terms of the peace accord was painfully slow. For example, the president acknowledged in January 1999—18 months after the signing of the final accord—that the Commission on National Reconciliation had only just begun discussions on drafting necessary amendments to the country's constitution. Progress in disarming opposition and maverick armed formations was also both tedious and slow.

The 1997 agreement ending the civil war had specified that new parliamentary elections were to take place by December 1998, but a ban on religious-oriented parties—instituted in 1993—remained a major impediment. In 1999, the government finally submitted three constitutional amendments to the people for their approval. The first authorized the formation of Islamic political parties; the second added an upper chamber to the parliament; and the third created a single seven-year term of office for the president. All three amendments were approved in a September 26 referendum. Elections to the lower chamber of the parliament were then scheduled for February 27, 2000.

Tajikistan

Grandfather shows his newly fashioned whistles to his grandson and friend

Courtesy of NOVOSTI

Meanwhile, new presidential elections had to occur by November 6, 1999, the day President Rahmonov's term was set to expire. That proved to be no simple matter. When three would-be candidates were denied registration after failing to obtain the number of signatures required by the Central Electoral Commission, they appealed their case to the Supreme Court on the grounds that local officials were actively preventing them from collecting signatures. They then demanded that the presidential elections be postponed until their appeals had been heard. When Akbar Turajonzoda, deputy head of the UTO, criticized the demands of the three candidates for a postponement, the UTO presidium expelled him from the party and demanded that he be removed from his post as first deputy opposition leader and his government position as deputy prime minister. As it turned out, Turajonzoda kept his government position.

When the three would-be candidates lost their appeal to the Supreme Court, the Islamic Renaissance Party, senior partner in the umbrella UTO, called for a boycott of the presidential election. When the election went off as planned on November 6, however, the Central Electoral Commission announced that 98% of the electoral had participated in the polling. President Rahmonov, with only nominal opposition from a candidate who had asked that his name be withdrawn from the ballot, was reelected with 96% of the vote.

The lead-up to the parliamentary elections was equally rough. First of all, the Supreme Court banned the Agrarian Party and the Party of National Unity and annulled the registration of the Justice and Development Party, the Renaissance of Tajikistan Party, and the Democratic Party of Tajikistan (Tehran Platform). In addition, the Justice Ministry refused to register the Party of the National Movement of Tajikistan and the Social Democratic Party, "Adolat Va Tarakkiyot."

In the end, six parties participated in the February 27 parliamentary elections, the ruling People's Democratic Party (64.5%), the Communist Party (20.6%), the Islamic Renaissance Party (7.48%), the Democratic Party (Almaty Platform) (3.52%), the Adolatkhoh (Justice) Party (1.35%), and the Socialist Party (1.24%). As the percentages indicate, only the first three parties surmounted the 5% minimum needed to gain proportional representation seats. A runoff election was then held on March 12 in 12 constituencies where no candidate won an overall majority in the first round of voting. A second round of voting was also scheduled in two of the 36 single-mandate constituencies where the first-round poll was declared invalid. The results of these votes showed the same pattern as the first round of voting. The ruling People's Democratic Party won a total of 30 seats, giving them just short of a majority in the lower house of parliament. This actually gave the People's Democratic Party secure control, since 15 seats were won by independents allied with the party. The remaining seats were won by the Communist Party (13 seats) and the Islamic Renaissance Party (2 seats). Three seats were unfilled.

Elections to the 33-seat Majlisi Milliy (senate), the newly created upper body of the legislature, took place on March 23, 2000. Twenty-five of the senate members were chosen by five regional assemblies, with each regional assembly selecting five members. The remaining eight senators were nominated by the president. The senate is supposed to act as a stabilizing factor on the country's politics by guaranteeing representation to each of the individual regions.

Politics and Islam

Since 2001, Tajikistan has taken advantage of the US-backed Global War on Terrorism to justify its regulation of Islamic expression and practice in the country. The Rahmon regime has sought to continue the Soviet practice of using a state institution, now known as the Council of Ulema, to separate good, moderate, and secular Islam from dangerous and foreign forms of Islam. Formally, the Council of Ulema is independent; however, it serves under the president. The institution is responsible for appointing clerics, issuing fatwas and writing the only legally permitted sermons in the state. In the early 2000s, Tajikistan instituted an annual examination of Muslim cleric and lecturers at Islamic schools and universities on their knowledge of the canons and rituals of Islam. In 2002, the government decided that it would require imams, Friday preachers, and muezzins to sit the tests as well. In addition, the government began more strenuously enforcing the constitutional provision that prohibits clergy from participating in political organizations. In Tajikistan's northern Isfara Rayon, 10 clerics were banned from preaching on the grounds that they were members of the Islamic Renaissance Party.

About a hundred alleged members of Hizb ut-Tahrir were arrested In Tajikistan in 2001. Hizb ut-Tahrir, "Party of Liberation," is an Islamic group that seeks a non-violent revolution establishing a global caliphate. Despite its denunciation of violent tactics, it has been deemed a threat by the regimes in Central Asia, and proscribed as a terrorist organization. Two of those arrested in Tajikistan's Sughd region were found with a cache of several thousand books and pamphlets calling for the overthrow of the Tajik government. With evidence that the movement was growing in northern Tajikistan, President Rahmonov launched a new campaign against the group in 2002. In July, a schoolteacher named Vakhob Khalilov was sentenced to five years' imprisonment for heading a local cell of Hizb ut-Tahrir. That same month, police detained another Hizb activist in Dushanbe. In January 2003, two Hizb ut-Tahrir members were arrested while distributing leaflets and brochures calling for the establishment of an Islamic caliphate. The following month, police uncovered an extensive illicit publishing operation in Sughd Oblast. The police announced at the time that this arrest brought to 130 the number of Hizb ut-Tahrir members arrested in Sughd Oblast. As the anti-Islamic extremist campaign continued, police announced in April that they had discovered another clandestine print shop set up by Hizb ut-Tahrir, and that this was the third such printing shop they had discovered in 2003.

An August 2005 trial resulted in nine Hizb ut-Tahrir members being given prison terms ranging from 3 to 15 years. In the first half of 2006, police arrested 42 individuals, including 20 women, as suspected members of Hizb ut-Tahrir.

Several more members of Hizb ut-Tahrir, including the leader of the movement in Tajikistan, were arrested in the summer of 2010. The leader, Yusuf Khafizov, was sentenced to 18 years in prison in January 2011. Seven other active members received prison terms between 6 and 17 years. All were found guilty of inciting ethnic and religious hatred and attempting to overthrow the government. One of the defendants' relatives admitted afterward that the group's plan was to build an Islamic state but, he insisted, only through political means, not violence.

Another Islamic extremist party that has been worrisome to the government is the Islamic Movement of Uzbekistan (IMU). The headquarters of the IMU are believed to be in Afghanistan, but it launched excursions into Kyrgyzstan from Tajikistan in 1999 and again in 2000. In July 2006, 10 suspected members of the Islamic Movement of Uzbekistan were arrested in the northern city of Khujand; 3 of the 10 were Uzbek citizens. That same year, the IMU were blamed for an attack on the Kairakkum detention center to free two suspected IMU members being held there; the head of the detention center was killed during the action. It is also believed that the IMU was responsible for killing several police officers in 2007 and 2008 in the northern town of Isfara. In September 2010, Tajikistan experienced its first terrorist bombing when two suicide bombers drove an explosives-packed car into a police station in the northern city of Khujand, killing two policemen and partially destroying the police compound; Tajik authorities blamed the attack on elements with ties to the IMU.

Since 2009, the limited space which existed for religious expression has been further restricted. That year a new law was signed that gave the government sweeping powers to regulate religion. For example, amongst the powers granted to the state were the powers to determine when and where mosques could be built, how children are educated about Islam and whether foreign religious groups can be contacted. Tajikistanis who practice Islam in a manner not explicitly approved by the regime face severe criminal punishments. A subsequent law signed in 2011 bars persons under the age of 18 from participating in any public religious activity aside from funerals. In March 2015, President Rahmon criticized women who wore "foreign" clothing, especially black veils. Since that speech, the police chief of Khatlon reported that his police "convinced" more than 1,500 women to de-veil and forcibly shaved around 13,000 men. While "foreign" fashions were being regulated by the police, the state took decisive action against the IRPT. In August, the justice ministry banned the up-until-then legally permitted Islamic party in the region. The next month, a high court ruled that the IRPT should be listed as a terrorist organization. Due to the restrictions on Muslims, as well as members of other faith groups, since 2016, the United States Commission on International Religious Freedom has classified Tajikistan as a a "country of particular concern."

Since 2015, former IRPT members have been either arrested or forced into exile. The party leader, Muhuddin Kabiri is living abroad, and the deputy head of the party, Mahmadli Hayit received a life sentence for allegedly organizing a coup against the government. The latter charges have been heavily questioned by international observers and human rights organizations who have called for his release. The round-up of IRPT members has continued into 2019. In April 2019, former IRPT member Naimjon Samiev was forcibly detained in Russia and returned to Tajikistan where he was convicted of weapons possession and of membership in a criminal and extremist group.

Tajikistan has recently stressed the threat posed by nationals traveling to Syria and Iraq to join ISIS. Although in January 2016 the regime estimated that up to 1,000 Tajiks were fighting with ISIS, the precise number of is unconfirmed. Estimates from the regime are best taken with a grain of salt, as it has an incentive to overestimate the threat posed by ISIS since efforts have been

Famous woodcarver Sirodzhitdin Nuritdinov in his studio   Courtesy of NOVOSTI

Tajikistan

made to connect ISIS with the now-banned IRPT. A video that surfaced in May 2015 was used by the government to legitimate its concern over ISIS recruitment. The head of the country's special forces, General Gulmurod Khalimov, claimed that he had defected to join ISIS in Syria as a protest against Tajikistan's religious policies, which he said were anti-Islamic. In the video, he threatened President Rahmon: "We are coming to you with slaughter, if Allah wills." According to the Russian military, in September 2017 he was killed in a Russian air strike against ISIS targets in Syria. Despite this high-level defection, there is no evidence that any other officials have followed his lead nor that there is widespread radicalization amongst Tajikistani citizens.

While ISIS activity in the country remains rare, a July 2018 attack on foreign cyclists 100 miles south of Dushanbe that left four dead grabbed international headlines. Soon after the attack, video evidence emerged that showed the attackers declaring allegiance to ISIS before carrying out the action. Despite this evidence, the Tajikistani government has insisted that the attack was organized by the IRPT. There is no evidence that the IRPT was behind this action.

The government reported that in November 2018 and May 2019, two different bloody prison riots were instigated by ISIS fighters who had returned from Syria and Iraq. In each riot, scores of people were killed. Unfortunately, due to the government's history of misleading claims about the Islamist threat it faces it is difficult to verify what exactly happened in either case. ISIS has claimed responsibility for the November riot in Khujand, but this could be a strategic claim. In the May riot, which occurred east of Dushanbe, three of those killed were imprisoned IRPT members and one was Behruz Gulmurod, the son of Gulmurod Khalimov. These two riots within a six-month period suggests an inability for the Tajikistani criminal-justice system to establish control without excessive violence.

The Drug Trade

The drug trade is another problem to which the Tajik government has given increasing attention since 2002. The Tajik government was responding to a 2002 report of the UN drug control office, whose most important conclusion was that 90% of all heroin consumed in Europe originated in Afghanistan and most of it passed through Tajikistan on its way to market. It is estimated that there are as many as 20,000 drug addicts in Tajikistan itself, at least partly because drug couriers are often paid off in illegal drugs. This has also contributed to an increase in corruption as government officials accept bribes to look the other way and allow drugs through.

Prime Minister Qohir Rasulzoda

To help fight the trafficking, the United Nations helped Tajikistan create an independent drug control agency; to keep its 350 officers honest, the UN also arranged to pay salaries for drug control officers that are equivalent to 17 times the average wage in the country.

The program has had some success; according to a 2006 report of the United Nations, "19% of the total volume of Afghanistan's drug production is smuggled north through Tajikistan, Turkmenistan, and Uzbekistan." Total seizures had dropped to 2.5 tons, including 1.2 tons of heroin, with half of the drugs seized on the Afghan border and half seized elsewhere in Tajikistan. In August 2006, police announced that they had broken up four drug-smuggling rings.

Authoritarian Politics

New elections to the 63-member lower chamber of parliament took place on February 27, 2005. Six political parties ran candidates, but only three parties—the ruling People's Democratic Party of Tajikistan (PDPT) (17 seats), the Communist Party (3 seats), and the Islamic Renaissance Party (IRP) (2 seats)—cleared the 5% barrier to win party slate seats. The PDPT won 32 of the 41 single mandate seats, with an additional seat going to the Communist Party. Five additional seats were won by independent candidates, while the remaining three seats went to a second round. The PDPT thus controlled a majority of the seats even without the support of the allied Communist Party.

New presidential elections took place on November 6, 2006. President Rahmonov stood for reelection, but the election was largely pro forma, since most of the oppositional political parties were in disarray at the time. In particular, the Islamic Renaissance Party (HNIT) was hit hard when its leader, Sayed Abdullo Nuri, died on August 9. The new leader of the party, 42-year-old Muhiddin Kabiri, decided that the party would field no candidate for the election. The leader of the second opposition party, the Democratic Party of Tajikistan (HDT), Mahmadruzi

Iskandarov, was in prison, so the party had only an acting leader. Iskandarov, who had exiled himself in Russia, was sent back to Tajikistan under murky circumstances. Arrested on charges of terrorism, the embezzlement of state funds, and the illegal storage of weapons, he was sentenced to 23 years prison in October 2005. In addition, the party split in early 2006 when part of its membership left to form a new party, Vatan, which announced it would work with the government.

Rahmatullo Zoirov, leader of the Social Democratic Party of Tajikistan, would have been a good opposition candidate, but he suffered a stroke in August 2006. In the end, there were five candidates for the presidency, but all of the parties putting up candidates were actually part of the government coalition. These included the Socialist Party, the Economic Reform Party, the Agrarian Party, and the Communist Party. President Rahmonov would probably have won reelection anyway, but against such weak candidates he managed to take 79.3% of the popular vote. After the vote, European Union monitors announced that they had seen some progress, though the election still fell short of "OSCE commitments and other international standards for democratic elections." The EU monitors were particularly concerned about the lack of meaningful competition.

Following the election, President Rahmonov reappointed Oqil Oqilov as his prime minister. The decree reappointing Oqilov also announced a restructuring of government, including abolition of 26 ministries and committees. In April 2007, three parliamentary by-elections were held; all three seats were won by the ruling People's Democratic Party. A fourth parliamentary by-election in December 2007 resulted in a win by the People's Democratic Party after the opposition Islamic Revival Party refused to field a candidate.

The other development occurred in March 2007 when the president announced that he had removed the "ov" ending from his name; henceforth, he would use the Tajik spelling of "Emomali Rahmon." Addressing a meeting of Tajik intellectuals on the traditional spring celebration of Norouz, he called on others to change their names in similar fashion. There does not appear to be any legal compulsion for adult Tajiks to change their names, but a decree issued by President Rahmon in March 2007 requires that the names of babies born to Tajik parents incorporate this change.

The change has also caused speculation as to whether the next step would be to drop the Cyrillic alphabet and revert to the use of the Arabic script at some time in the future. Thus far, all of this is mere speculation.

New parliamentary elections were held on February 28, 2010. The ruling

People's Democratic Party came in first with 71.04% of the popular vote. The Islamic Renaissance Party came in second with 8.2% of the vote, followed by the Communist Party, with 7.01% of the vote. The Agrarian Party came in third with 5.11%, followed by the Party of Economic Reform, with 5.06%. The People's Democratic Party currently holds 55 of the 63 seats; each of other parties holds 2 legislative seats.

Heavy fighting broke out in the city of Khorug, capital of the Gorno-Badakhshan Autonomous Region, in July 2012 when central government forces confronted local commanders after General Nazarov, a high-ranking security officer, died as the result of a stabbing in the city. The Tajik government blamed an illegal armed group led by border-police commander Talib Ayombekov for the killing and launched an operation against the group. In the ensuing confrontation, 48 people were killed, including 17 members of the security forces. Citizens of Khorug then threw up barricades in the city and the situation only threatened to worsen.

But clearer heads prevailed. The government promised amnesty to rebels who voluntarily laid down their weapons; Talib Ayombekov, head of one of the rebel groups, voluntarily surrendered on August 12 and called on others to lay down their arms as well. A truce with the Tajik government brought fragile stability to the region.

The Gorno-Badakhshan Autonomous Region had been the center of resistance against the government during the civil war in the 1990s and that made the threat of violence there all the more important. That is also probably why, on August 30, the Prosecutor General accused members of the opposition Islamic Renaissance Party of involvement in crimes connected to extremism and terrorism. Sayidumar Husaini, the party's deputy chairman, denounced the prosecutor's claims as part of a campaign aimed at shutting down the party. There is no evidence that the Islamic Renaissance Party was in any way connected with the events in Khorug. The changes may have had something to do with the fact that new presidential elections were set to take place on November 6, 2013.

President Rahmon was heavily favored to win reelection in any case, but it appeared that there might be something approaching a genuine race when the opposition Alliance of Reformist Forces of Tajikistan (ARFT) announced in September 2013 that they had united behind a single candidate, Oynihol Bobonazarova. The ARFT includes the country's two leading opposition parties, the Islamic Revival Party and the Social Democratic Party as well as a number of non-governmental organizations and prominent individuals.

Even more interesting is that Oynihol Bobonazarova was a 65-year-old woman lawyer and human rights activist not associated with any political party. Unfortunately, Bobonazarova was unable to obtain the required 210,000 signatures needed to qualify to get on the ballot. In the end, therefore, President Rahmon faced only five relatively unknown candidates and he won reelection with 83.9% of the vote.

Over the past few years, Rustam Emomali, President Rahmon's son, has became a shooting star in the Tajikistani political galaxy. The former star soccer player was appointed head of the State Customs Administration in November 2013 and then less than two years later, became the director of the State Agency For Financial Control and Measures Against Corruption in March 2015. After heading the anti-corruption agency for less than two years, Rustam Emomali attained his most prominent role to date when Rahmon appointed his son as the new mayor of Dushanbe. To make this move, Rahmon removed long-term mayor Mahmadsaid Ubaidulloev from the post he held for 19 years. It is widely speculated the Emomali's rapid upward trajectory indicates that he is being groomed to replace his father. Adding fuel to this line of speculation, in May 2016, the Constitution was amended to reduce the minimum age to serve as president from 35 to 30; Rustam Emomali was 29 when he became mayor of Dushanbe. Emomali is not the only member of the Rahmon family to have been appointed to a high government office. One of his daughters, Ozoda, serves as chief of staff for the President and as a senator in the parliament. Another daughter, Ruhshona Rahmonova, reportedly heads a department in the Foreign Ministry.

As the regime has grown more authoritarian, the space for opposition has drastically diminished. In June 2015, Muhiddin Kabiri, the leader of the Islamic Renaissance Party, which is the country's main opposition party, announced that he was leaving Tajikistan because he feared arrest on trumped-up charges. Kabiri's decision to leave was well timed. His party, which was completely shut out of parliament in the March 2015 elections for the first time since the signing of the peace treaty that ended the civil war, was stripped of its status as a political party in late August. The Justice Ministry claimed that the organization's limited membership justified the loss of its party status. Any possibility that the party may be reinstituted at a later date were seemingly eliminated when a new Constitutional amendment was adopted in May 2016 which banned all parties with religious platforms. Other opposition parties have also been banned in recent years, most

notably the small organization named Group 24. Collectively, these proscriptions have effectively established Tajikistan as a single party state. The government has aggressively tried to control the Internet, to which about half of the country has access. Over the past several years, it has intermittently blocked access to Facebook, YouTube, and other social media services. State media essentially acts as propaganda for the regime, and independent journalists are regularly pressured and intimated. For these reasons, in 2020, the media watchdog organization Reporters Without Borders ranked Tajikistan 161 out of 180 countries in its World Press Freedom Index. On April 23, 2017, the state control of media veered toward self-parody when journalists were instructed to use the President's full title ("the founder of peace and national unity of Tajikistan, the leader of the nation, President Emomali Rahmon") whenever he was discussed.

Western observers have long warned that the elimination of legitimate opposition, especially the religious kind, would create a fertile ground for the emergence of Sunni extremist movements bent on toppling the secular governments in central Asia. Since the banning of the Islamic Renaissance Party seven years ago, no such movement rose to pose a threat to the incumbent government in Tajikistan. To the extent the government faced a challenge to its rule, it has been in the form of periodic social uprisings in the Gorno-Badakhshan Autonomous Region, where people identify as Shi'ites, Ismaili Muslims, while most Tajikistan's population are Sunni Muslims. To be sure, the anti-government protests in the region are not a function of religious differences. Rather, the root cause appears to be government misrule. Since the truce of July 2012, the regime has increased the number of security forces in Khorug, failed to deliver on its promise to dismantle security checkpoints within the city, which have been disruptive of free movement, and arrested local residents on, perhaps dubious, charges of drug possession and trafficking. Such repressive measures were bound to raise tensions. The latest violence in the region started in January 2021, when security forces shot 29-year-old Gulbiddin Ziyobekov, a local resident who previously slapped a member of the security forces for molesting a local girl. This event triggered street protests in Khorug, which was violently demobilized by the government, resulting in more civilian deaths. Protesters accused the government of revenge killing and demanded a fair investigation into the killing of Ziyobekov. As in the past, authorities made empty promises, and continued to use coercive measures to deal with local dissent.

Tajikistan

In May 2002, Khorug became the center of anti-government rallies yet again. Local residents protested the government's verdict, which handed a young Pamiri an eight-and-a-half-year prison sentence for purportedly inciting an anti-government insurrection on social media. In a now familiar pattern, Tajik authorities forcibly removed him from Russia and handed him the sentence. Additionally, protesters demanded the resignation of the local government whom they view as a token representative. Perhaps, fearing that the protests might gain momentum, central authorities declared to launch "a special anti-terrorist operation," by dispatching more troops to the region. Owing to government's blocking of the internet in the region, it is hard to obtain reliable information about who resorted to violence first in the clashes that took place between protesters and security forces, or how many casualties there are on either side. Initial reports from the region suggest that security forces killed local residents in the Khorug and Rushan districts, the latter for attempting to block government troops from advancing toward Khorug. Among the confirmed casualties in Khorug was Mahmadboqir Mahmadboqirov, a prominent local leader whom the authorities blamed for instigating the unrest. On June 11, authorities captured Tolib Ayombekov and his associates. Foreign and local analysts are of the opinion that the real reason the government deployed security forces was to eliminate informal local authorities, such as Mahmadbokirov, who allegedly

assert Pamiris' right for self-determination. These events are unfolding against the backdrop of unfavorable economic conditions associated with a plunge in migrant remittances, and international security threats in the form of territorial disputes with Kyrgyzstan, and the presence of Islamic State militants in Afghanistan (who reportedly launched rockets into Tajikistan the same month the Tajik government launched a security operation in Khorug). Whether the incumbent regime has enough fiscal power to fend off domestic and international challenges remains to be seen.

Foreign Policy

Russia. Because of the civil war that ravaged the country between 1992 and 1997, the leaders of the Tajik government turned to the Russian government for support in order to remain in power. For several years, therefore, Tajikistan's dependence on Russia meant that it was not really able to maintain an independent foreign policy. The civil war came to an end in June 1997 when an agreement was reached with the United Tajik Opposition, but Tajikistan continued to be dependent on Russia for military assistance. A February 2001 treaty signed by the two nations regulates the status of Russian military bases in Tajikistan. As President Rakhmonov (as he was known at the time) commented at the time, "Russia is our chief strategic ally." Russian troops guarded Tajikistan's thousand-mile

border with Afghanistan until they were withdrawn in mid-2005.

President Putin paid a visit to Tajikistan in April 2003 which included a visit to a Russian military base along the Afghan border. Here Putin announced that Russia would soon bolster its military presence in Tajikistan. Currently, Russia keeps 10,000 troops stationed in the country.

President Rahmon held talks with President Putin in February 2008 following his arrival in Moscow to attend a CIS summit meeting. The two presidents discussed bilateral energy and military cooperation. President Rahmon made a point of mentioning that 183 Russian companies were currently operating in Tajikistan; he also hailed a 75% increase in bilateral trade since 2006.

In October 2012, the Tajik and Russian governments signed an agreement allowing Russian troops to stay at a military base in Tajikistan until 2042. The agreement was signed during a visit of President Putin to Dushanbe. Under the terms of the agreement, Russia will take responsibility for the "modernization and technical renovation" of Tajikistan's armed forces. As of January 2015, Tajiks were allowed to enlist in the Russian army.

United States. Tajikistan never recognized the Taliban government in neighboring Afghanistan, partly because it feared the threat which its extremist Islamic leadership represented. Tajikistan gave asylum to the Afghan opposition government and even permitted an ethnic Tajik commander from Afghanistan to bring his armed forces into the country. However, it refused to accept several thousand refugees who attempted to cross the border in the fall of 2000, and it was particularly concerned that about 12,000 of those who had been refused entry remained camped along the border for months.

When Islamic terrorists launched their attacks against the United States on September 11, 2001, therefore, the government of Tajikistan was among the first to express its willingness to cooperate with the United States in the fight against international terrorism, though it was hesitant about committing itself further because it feared for its own vulnerability. It also felt that it had to consult with the Russian government before making any specific commitments, since Tajikistan's border with Afghanistan had been guarded for years by several thousand Russian troops.

As it happened, it was Russian Defense Minister Sergei Ivanov who announced on September 25 that the Dushanbe airport would be made available to the American military "if such a necessity arises." In October, the Tajik government opened its airspace to the use of American military

Young Tajiks fill an open air Mosque

planes, but it was not until US Defense Secretary Donald Rumsfeld visited Dushanbe in November that President Rakhmonov formally agreed to allow US troops to be based in Tajikistan. Eventually, Kulyab air base, located about 200 miles south of Dushanbe, was made available for the international war against terrorism. The first Western military aircraft began arriving in December and the first use of the base was for delivering humanitarian cargos under UN colors to towns in northern Afghanistan.

The base was used primarily by a French military contingent, stationed in Tajikistan as part of the international coalition operating in Afghanistan. France also has about 400 service personnel in Dushanbe. They service three Mirage fighters and three transport planes which provide support for International Security Assistance Force operations in Afghanistan. In 2013, French forces were pulled out of Tajikistan as they withdrew from engagements in Afghanistan.

There had been discussions in 2001 about an American base in Tajikistan, but these talks were broken off when the United States opted for the Manas Air Base in northern Kyrgyzstan instead. The United States Government then launched new talks with the Tajik government in March 2003 about leasing three air bases in Tajikistan. Nothing came of the discussions.

The expansion in US-Tajik relations after September 2001 was rather impressive, however. Relations had been minimal for several years prior to September 2001; the American Embassy had actually been closed in 1998 following the embassy bombings in Africa. There has always been an ambassador accredited to Tajikistan, but he was based in Almaty, Kazakhstan and paid only periodic visits to Dushanbe. After the events of September 11, high-level American delegations visited Dushanbe on a number of occasions. In addition to granting the United States permission to use the Kulyab air base about 200 miles south of Dushanbe, the Tajik government also formally joined NATO's Partnership for Peace program, the last of the CIS members to do so. President Rakhmonov paid an official visit to the United States in December 2002 where he had separate meetings with President George W. Bush, Secretary of State Colin Powell, and CIA Director George Tenet. The talks focused on the war on international terrorism, combating drug trafficking, and economic reforms and poverty reduction in Tajikistan.

US Secretary of State Condoleezza Rice paid a one-day visit to Tajikistan in October 2005. While there, she stated explicitly that the United States did not seek a "permanent military presence in Tajikistan." That same day, Tajik Foreign Minister Talbak Nazarov committed his country to continued cooperation with the United States in international efforts to combat terrorism, extremism, and drug trafficking.

As part of this cooperation, the United States government carried out an airlift of winter supplies to Tajik border guards in January 2006. In addition to about $3 million in supplies and equipment delivered directly to Tajik border guards, the United States has a second assistance program, given under the auspices of the US Export Control and Related Border Security Program, which has furnished over $7.5 million in equipment and training to Tajikistan since 2002. In March 2006, the United States Government pledged $7.75 million to build facilities around a bridge linking Afghanistan and Tajikistan, plus another $800,000 to train Tajik security personnel with an eye to improving border security.

In 2007, the US government pledged $20 million in aid to enhance border security in Tajikistan; this was part of a program launched in mid-2005 when Russia withdrew its border troops from along the Afghan–Tajik border. In February 2009, President Rahmon announced that Tajikistan would open his country's airspace for the transit of NATO nonmilitary supplies bund for Afghanistan. In 2002, American and other NATO forces began using a Tajik air base to gain access to Afghanistan. They used the base until 2014, when they left as NATO's mission in Afghanistan wound down.

Central Asian Neighbors. In May 2006, the Government of Tajikistan formally joined the Asian Cooperation Dialogue at a meeting of member states in Doha, Qatar. The ACD brings together 30 countries for discussion of topics such as energy cooperation.

Tajikistan's relations with its Central Asian neighbors are greatly affected by differing positions on the subjects of energy and water, and poorly demarcated interstate borders. Tajikistan, lacking domestic natural gas or petroleum resources, has placed a great emphasis in developing hydroelectric power. The Government of Uzbekistan, fearing the loss of summer water for irrigation, has objected to the construction of the Rogun power plant in Tajikistan and in early 2010 it stopped freight cars bound for Tajikistan, in part, it said, because they were carrying construction materials for Rogun. Uzbekistan also objects to new hydroelectric power plants in Kyrgyzstan for the same reason. Following the death of Uzbekistani President Islam Karimov there have some signs of thawing relations between the two states; most notably, after several months of false starts in April 2017, regular flights between Tashkent and Dushanbe resumed for the first time since the early 1990s. The Governments of Turkmenistan and Kazakhstan share some of Uzbekistan's worries about water but, thus far, they have refused to support Uzbekistan over the development of new hydroelectric sources in Tajikistan and Kyrgyzstan.

While relations with Uzbekistan have improved, those with Kyrgyzstan have worsened to the point of militarized conflict. Like many other frontier areas in central Asia, about half of the 600-mile-long Kyrgyz–Tajik border has not been demarcated leading to regular flashes of cross-border violence between these nations. According to a recent PONARS memo, the frontier communities clash over water because they lack shared norms regarding water usage, clear understanding about the advantages of regulation, and a shared water authority to monitor the use and abuse of water consumption. On April 28, 2021, fighting broke out between villagers on either side of the border over irrigation water, resulting in the deaths of 36 Kyrgyz and 19 Tajik citizens. Tajik authorities installed a surveillance camera at a water distribution point near Vorukh exclave and, reportedly, this is what triggered an intercommunal dispute and the ensuing violent conflict. This was the deadliest interstate conflict in central Asia since the fall of the Soviet Union. Tajikistani troops were mobilized almost instantly and seized land in Kyrgyzstani territory near the Tajik enclave of Vorukh. To prevent further escalation, the two countries quickly declared a ceasefire, pulled back troops and promised to use diplomacy to resolve the immediate tensions. Cross-border armed clashes took place again in January and April 2002. These clashes were less severe in intensity than before and resulted in both countries signing an agreement on troop reduction near the border. Although clashes between villagers are unfortunately not infrequent on the border between Tajikistan and Kyrgyzstan, the Tajikistani military's involvement in these clashes is without precedent. Both states are co-members of two multilateral security pacts, the Collective Security Treaty Organization (CSTO) and the Shanghai Cooperation Organization (SCO), yet neither of these organizations played a role in resolving the dispute in the latest round of armed clashes.

Nature of the Regime

Tajikistan established a presidential-parliamentary form of government with a popularly elected president and a multiparty system in September 1991, shortly after it emerged as an independent republic. The subsequent struggles between

Tajikistan

the various factions that emerged led to parts of this system being changed or suppressed, but the new constitution that was approved in a popular referendum in November 1994 largely rebuilt the system put into effect in 1991.

Under this constitution, the key political figure in the system is the popularly elected president, who acts as the spokesman for the nation and establishes general policy. Next in line comes the prime minister, who is appointed by the president but must be confirmed in office by the lower chamber of the parliament. The prime minister and his cabinet are responsible for the day-to-day operation of government. Qohir Rasulzoda, the current prime minister, was appointed to that office on November 23, 2013, following President Rahmon's reelection earlier that month.

The new two-chamber parliament, created as a result of a constitutional amendment approved in 1999, represents the sovereignty of the nation. The Majilisi Namoyandagon or lower chamber has 63 members, 22 elected by party slate, and 41 in single-member constituencies. As the more popular, and therefore more powerful, chamber, it is responsible for all legislation and has final authority over the budget. Most top government officials must also be confirmed in office by the lower chamber of the parliament.

In the case of the Majlisi Milli or upper chamber, 5 regional assemblies representing Tajikistan's 5 electoral districts each elect 5 deputies. An additional 8 deputies are appointed by the president, bringing the total number of deputies to 33. Election or appointment to the upper chamber is considered an honor, so several of its deputies were selected because of their prominence in Tajik society rather than their politics. These elections, which occur every five years, last took place in February 2010.

President Rahmon, along with most of the people allied with him, were formerly leaders in the now disbanded Tajik Communist Party. In June 1997, a power-sharing agreement was reached which brought the United Tajik Opposition into the government with 30% of the seats in the cabinet plus a similar representation in other government and local administrative posts. This legalized two political groupings in the country, the National Unity Movement (made up of the People's Democratic Party and the Political and Economic Renewal Party), representing the old communist elites, and the United Tajik Opposition (which brought together the Islamic Renaissance Party, the Democratic Party, the Rastokhez People's Movement, and the Laali Badakhshan).

This interim arrangement was supposed to last until new, free elections (originally stipulated as occurring before the end of 1998). Implementation of the agreement took much longer than anyone anticipated, however, so the power-sharing arrangement was renewed for three years in 1999. New parliamentary elections finally took place in February/March 2000—and resulted in a victory by the ruling Democratic People's Party. Because of the power-sharing arrangement, however, opposition political figures continued to hold offices in government for several years; the last opposition figure stepped down in 2006.

Before the series of coups and counter-coups of 1992, Tajikistan seemed to be evolving toward an institutionalized pluralism. Some experts speculated that this was because the Tajik Communist Party had always had its organized political factions, based on differences between regional clans, and this was now coming out in the open. That trend suffered a severe setback in 1992 as first one side, then the other, resorted to force to get its way. Then the coalition of democrats and Islamists that held power briefly in 1992 was overthrown and many of its members fled into hiding, either in the mountains to the east or in Afghanistan.

After that, the new government in Dushanbe went about systematically eliminating the opposition. "It was a real blood bath," said one Western diplomat.

During the period of the civil war—between 1992 and 1996—the government was essentially an alliance of the Leninabad and Kulyab areas. Excluded were other important areas such as Garm and Badakhshan. The power-sharing arrangement set up in 1997 and renewed in 1999, which guaranteed the opposition 30% of all government and local administrative posts, also provided representation to most of those other parts of the country which had been excluded from decision-making during the period of the civil war.

By March 2002, when the power-sharing arrangement was due to expire, the country's power structure had come to realize that the power-sharing arrangement, by institutionalizing political pluralism, had made a major contribution to political stability. Shortly before it was due to expire, therefore, the original signatories got together and renewed it for an indefinite period in March 2002.

In the most recent parliamentary elections in March 2020, Rahmon's People Democratic Party unsurprisingly maintained dominant control over the legislature. The ruling party currently holds 47 of the 63 seats in the Assembly of Representatives. The remaining seats are split between alternative pro-regime parties including the Agrarian Party and the Party of Economic Reform. With the Islamic Renaissance Party barred from participating in the election, the Social Democrat Party was the sole opposition party contesting for seats. Its inability to win a single seat is illustrative of the limited opportunities for non-regime voices to have access to any power.

Despite some speculation that he would step away from the office, President Rahmon won his fifth presidential election in October 2020 in a landslide election. As with the parliamentary elections early in the year, these elections were neither free nor fair. Furthermore, the election lacked any real choice as there are no well-known viable opposition candidates, Thus, although Rahmon received 92% of the vote, this is not (necessarily) an accurate measure of his true popularity. Unfortunately, given the closed nature of the regime a true sense of his popularity is not possible to assess. In May 2016, Rahmon's grip on power was further cemented through a series of Constitutional Amendments approved in a referendum with an unbelievably high 96.6% of voters. Most notable among the 41 amendments approved was the elimination of term limits for the president, and the reduction of the minimum age to be president (from 35 to 30). The latter is widely seen as paving the way for Rahmon's son, Rustam Emomali, to succeed him earlier rather than later.

In April 2020, the succession plans were further advanced when Emomali was named the chair of the Majlisi Mili (the upper house) and, as such, is the designated successor should anything befall his father. Emomali has been groomed for this possibility for years, attaining the rank of major general in the armed forces (despite lacking military experience) and serving as the mayor of Dushanbe since 2017.

Culture

Traditional Tajik festivals have always featured songs and dances and there is also a long tradition of theatrical and circus performances. Tajik circuses specialize in tightrope walkers, conjurers, singers, and musicians. There is also a vigorous folk literature that is still being collected.

The Tajik National Theater was founded in 1929. It has nine separate theaters, performing operas, ballet, musical comedy, and puppetry. There is also a Tajik film studio that makes both feature films and documentaries. Dushanbe has had its own television center since 1960.

Two pre-Soviet Tajik cultural figures are Abdalrauf Fitrat, author of *Last Judgment*, and Sadriddin Ayni, famous for two novels, *Slaves* and *Dokhunda*. His autobiography is titled *Bukhara*. Tajik writers of the Soviet period include the poets Abu ol-Qasem Lahuti and Mirzo Tursunzade. Tursunzade won the Lenin Prize in 1960 for his poem "The Voice of Asia."

The Tajik State University, located in Dushanbe, is the largest of 10 state institutes of higher education. There are also 41 state technical colleges. There is also one private university, the Institute of Technical Innovations and Communications (ITIC), which was set up by Sadriddin Akramov, a Tajik-born US citizen. The ITIC, also known locally as the "American" university, received financial support from US and other Western foundations. The ITIC has had some difficulties with the Tajik government, which has attempted to exercise greater control over it. Part of ITIC's difficulties with the government is that its faculty includes many prominent opposition politicians and outspoken government critics. ITIC is also disliked by other educational institutions because it has made a name as a university where entrance exam results are based on students' knowledge. Bribery is rampant in most state-run institutions. In August 2010, Education Minister Abdujabor Rahmonov announced that the ITIC's license had been revoked. This action brought notes of protest from the US, British, French, and German ambassadors. The Education Ministry's decision is currently under appeal.

A Tajik Academy of Sciences was established in 1951. It now has 16 institutions and oversees 61 research institutions located in various parts of the republic. The Pamir research station, located in the Pamir Mountains in the eastern part of the country, is a major regional meteorological observatory.

Most Tajiks are Sunni Muslims of the Hanafi School, although there are some Shiite communities among the Mountain Tajiks. Throughout the Soviet era, Islam was a barely tolerated religion and there were few mosques. But Islam is as much a way of life and a culture as it is a belief, so it survived in the villages in spite of official hostility. There has been a clear revival of Islam since about 1989, with many mosques being built, but it does not appear to have a great political significance.

In 2009, the Tajik legislature passed a new law on religion. In its prologue, the law proclaims Tajikistan to be a secular state with every faith being equal. It then goes on to assert that every individual has a right to pray and follow any religion; however, it then adds that the role of the Hanafi branch of Islam in the life of Tajiks must be taken into account. The law bans the propagation of other religions and, further, imposes a new requirement that religious schools be attached to and supervised by either Friday mosques or by Orthodox churches with a congregation numbering over 15,000.

An invigorated Islam worries the government. In 2007, the government banned the wearing of Islamic head scarves (hijabs) in public schools. A separate order required males to wear suits and ties and to shave their beards. Next, the government instituted compulsory tests for clerics, followed by a ban on the fundamentalist Mavlavi group. Most recently, Tajik authorities issued an order requiring mosques to be re-registered. In enforcing this particular decree, the government closed more than 300 unregistered places of worship.

In Dushanbe, the capital, the head of the municipal department of religious affairs announced in August 2007 that new requirements for the licensing of Islamic leaders of local mosques would be imposed, including a new review process overseen by the Tajik Council of Ulemas. According to the government, the appraisal commissions were a response to a number of complaints over the "illiteracy" of Islamic leaders in the city. Opposition deputies in the Tajik parliament have protested these recent moves on the part of the government.

In May 2010, President Rahmon reinstated the State Committee on Religious Affairs to oversee the republic's religious organizations. That function had previously been assigned to the Ministry of Culture. The State Committee will be responsible for sending people on the annual hajj, maintaining the registration of mosques and churches, and regulating the import of religious literature.

In July 2010, there was a report that the Tajik government had become concerned that many parents in the eastern Tajik valley of Rasht were sending their children to local mullahs to get a basic education in religion and ethnics. According to one report, parents were concerned that public schools did not teach children the moral codes, family values, and religious principles they considered important for their children's upbringing. The government had already outlawed unsanctioned madrasahs and this appeared to be an attempt to get around that prohibition. This is also an area where there have been small-scale skirmishes between government forces and local elements that were still taking place from time to time.

Since the trend appears to be spreading, the government began carrying out raids on what they called "illegal madrasahs" in July and August 2010. Then, in February 2011, President Rahmon instructed his security services to tighten control over religious education and mosques, which he said were often used to foment religious radicalism. Then he added that some mosques had turned into "places for recruiting youths to the ranks of extremists."

In July 2013, the Tajik government's Religions Committee ordered five of the country's six legally run madrasahs temporarily closed. The ostensive reason was that the madrasahs had to obtain permission for their activities. All five suspended madrasahs are located in the northern province of Sughd on the Tajik side of the Fergana Valley, an area known for its deep Islamic roots. But it is perhaps no coincidence that, one week later, President Rahmon publicly expressed concern about "growing religious extremism" in the country.

On another topic, it was reported in 2009 that authorities were busy removing Soviet-era statues and replacing them with historical Tajik figures. Many Lenin statues have been removed—to be replaced by statues of Tajik poets, scientists or, in some cases, by fountains. In Dushanbe's central square, a monument to Ismoil Somoni, a 10th century Tajik king, now stands where a Lenin statue had previously stood. Lenin statues are still to be found in squares across Tajikistan, although authorities have suggested that they will eventually be removed.

Economy

Tajikistan is primarily an agricultural economy and its most significant crop is long-staple cotton. Cattle-raising (including sheep and goats) is also important, as is the growing of fruits, grain, and vegetables. Fruits grown include apricots, pears, apples, plums, quinces, cherries, pomegranates, and figs. Grapes and almonds are other major crops.

One of the most pressing issues for Tajikistan at independence was how to remake its agricultural system. Under the Soviet Union, Tajikistan's heavily subsidized and economically inefficient state and collective farms were responsible for producing raw materials, predominantly cotton, which were then used elsewhere. Until the mid-2000s, however, Tajikistan's agrarian reforms were largely superficial. Due in part to international pressure, since the mid-2000s there has been greater emphasis on breaking up collective and state farms and redistributing land shares to farm workers. Despite the attention to process of land reform, many farmers continue to work on farms which are collective farms in all but name. The state also technically owns all land, although some land use rights are heritable.

Tajikistan's light industry mainly involves processing agricultural products, such as cotton and silk processing, fruit canning, and wine making. Related industries include knitted goods, shoes, leather working, and carpet making. Light industry manufacturing plants tend to be small.

Its larger industry is either ore extraction or non-ferrous metallurgy. The Tajik Aluminium Company (TALCO) is the crown jewel of Tajikistan's industry. Built in 1975, its factory in Tursunzoda is the largest aluminum smelter in the region

Tajikistan

and consumes approximately 40% of the state's electricity. Tajikistan is rich in mineral deposits. It mines coal, iron, lead, zinc, antimony, mercury, gold, tin, and tungsten. Its mountains are the source of a number of non-metals, including salt, carbonates, fluorite, arsenic, quartz sand, asbestos, and precious and semiprecious stones. Petroleum and natural gas have also been discovered and are beginning to be exploited, though it still imports natural gas from Afghanistan by means of a pipeline constructed in 1974. There are a number of large hydroelectric stations plus a number of thermal electric stations. Tajikistan currently has to import some of its electricity, but it has a number of hydroelectric power plants currently under construction—most of them financed by Russia's Unified Electrical Systems.

Tajikistan has long been dependent on Uzbekistan for its natural gas, but a four-fold increase in the price of Uzbek gas between 2004 and 2010 has forced Tajikistan to cut its purchases of Uzbek gas. Therefore, the discovery of a natural gas field at Sarikamysh has been good news for the government. The field, which is estimated to contain 60 billion cubic meters of gas, is being developed by Zarubezhneftegaz, a subsidiary of the Russian giant Gazprom. The first well was drilled in December 2010. Gazprom has promised that the field would be producing 2 bcm yearly sometime between 2011 and 2013, enough to cover Tajikistan's annual consumption and make it independent of imported Uzbek gas.

Gold is mined at two sites in the northern part of the republic. Current production is fairly small, only 3.79 tons in 1991. A major new gold combine is currently under construction, however, and gold production is expected to double after it becomes operational.

Tajikistan manufactures a number of engineering or metalworking products, including looms, power transformers, cables, and agricultural and household equipment. There is also a nitrogen fertilizer plant, built in 1967. Most workers in industry are non-Tajiks.

The 1992–1997 civil war left Tajikistan with a badly damaged infrastructure and continued distrust among the political elites, but the March 2002 decision of the government to extend the power-sharing agreement with the opposition for an indefinite period probably contributed toward greater political pluralism and so was also good for the economy. The last of the opposition political figures left office in December 2006, however.

Tajikistan's economy began growing again in 1998, and that growth continued for the next decade, until 2008 when Tajikistan, like most of the world began to suffer the effect of the worldwide economic recession. GDP grew by 3.7% in 1999; it then spurted to over 9% in 2000. A severe drought in 2001 partially reversed the gains of the preceding two years, but the economy began growing again at an average of 10% over the next several years. By November 2004, President Rakhmonov was able to inform a gathering of international donors in Dushanbe that GDP had risen 50% over the preceding five years.

One project for which the Tajik government sought foreign investment was the Rogun hydroelectric power station. Originally begun in the 1980s, construction of the Rogun hydroelectric power station was halted in 1992 with the collapse of the Soviet Union. Because of the importance of the project—which would be capable of producing up to 3,600 megawatts of power, thus guaranteeing Tajikistan power independence, the Tajik government revived the project in 1999. In 2004, Russian oligarch Oleg Deripaska, owner of Russian Aluminum, promised to invest over $2 billion to complete Rogun as part of his commitment to modernize the Tajik aluminum company TadAZ (now TALCO). Deripaska failed to follow through, however, and Tajikistan canceled the deal with Deripaska in 2009, citing his failure to follow through. The Tajik government then made a commitment to complete the project on its own. To raise money for the project, the Tajik government issued $1.4 billion in stock in January 2010, eventually raising about $200 million. The World Bank provided funds to complete a feasibility study on Rogan. After officially beginning construction of the dam in 2016, Rogun remains a work in progress. Although the first turbine of the power plant opened in 2018, there are five more that are planned to open in the future. Additionally, the height of the dam is currently several hundred meters below its targeted height.

The Tajik government has also carried on negotiations with the US-based AES Corporation concerning investment in the Rogun hydroelectric power station, plus construction of electric transmission lines linking Tajikistan and Afghanistan. In addition, a related project to permit power exports to Afghanistan, which involved the construction of a 220-kilovolt power line connecting Tajikistan's Vakhsh power state with cities in Afghanistan, included financial backing from OPEC, the Islamic Development Bank, and Tajikistan's Vakhsh power station.

Russia's Unified Energy Systems (UES) has invested approximately $500 million in the construction of the Sangtuda-1 hydroelectric plant; daily electricity production of 2.4-million kilowatt hours came online in January 2008. Three more units were expected to come online in late 2008. UES has a 75% ownership in these hydroelectric plants.

However, President Dmitry Medvedev announced in February 2009 that Russia would no longer support energy projects in Tajikistan that did not have the approval of all the governments of Central Asia. This was viewed partly as a gesture to the Government of Uzbekistan, which has worried that the building of additional dams in the mountains of Tajikistan would decrease the amount of water that Uzbekistan would get for irrigation. Desultory discussions between the Uzbek and Tajik Governments on this particular topic have gone on since that time.

President Medvedev later reversed his position on support of energy projects in Tajikistan; in July 2009, he traveled to Tajikistan to participate in the unveiling of the fourth and last facility of the Sangtuda-1 Hydroelectric Plant. A press statement issued at the time characterized the power plant as "the most important project completed by the countries in the past 20 years."

China has offered Tajikistan a $200 million loan to cover construction of a hydroelectric power station in northern Tajikistan; it is also providing a $267 million loan to build the North-South electrical transmission line, and a $55 million loan to build the Lolazor-Khatlon electric transmission line. In addition, China is financing the Dushanbe-Chanak Road construction project.

In July 2006, the World Bank approved $20 million for three projects for Tajikistan in the areas of poverty reduction, state sector reform, and health. The European Union has also pledged $80 million to Tajikistan during the period 2007–2010 for poverty reduction and economic development. The European Bank for Reconstruction and Development (EBRD) for Central Asia also pledged to provide $30 million for investment projects each year. The EBRD portfolio in Tajikistan currently totals some 23 investment projects with an estimated value of $85.6 million, much of it relating to the banking sector. Agroinvestbank is 25% owned by the EBRD.

Tajikistan has one of the highest rates of population growth in Central Asia, which means that the per capita growth rate is extremely low. But poverty levels are dropping, from a figure as high as 64% just after the end of the civil war to a current level of about 35%.

One side effect of the high level of poverty in the country is that roughly half of the working age male population have left the country to seek work abroad, mainly in Russia or Kazakhstan. Though as labor migrants they are limited to the lowest-paying jobs, they have managed to send somewhere between $480 and $840 million a year back to their families, a figure that is equal to between 42 and 75% of total GDP. According to the World Bank, in recent years, Tajikistan has been the world's most remittance dependent state. As a department head at the Economic Research Institute of the Tajik Economics and Trade Ministry put it, "these migrant workers are the reason why there is no mass hunger in the country." As Western sanctions weaken economic activity in Russia and lower the value of the Russian ruble against the US dollar, Tajikistani migrants would struggle to find work or earn enough income to send home. As a result, per the World Bank estimation, remittances to Tajikistan would fall by 22% percent, compared to the original forecast rise of 2%. Although during recent economic shocks, many Tajikistani migrants continued to seek work abroad despite reduced wages, the current crisis may force them to return to Tajikistan. Given the high level of poverty and lack of good-paying jobs in Tajikistan, the decline in remittance value and the possible return of migrant laborers is a deeply worrying trend.

Tajikistan is a donor dependent state. Both the World Bank and the IMF are active in the country, and they sponsor a number of valuable programs; however, Tajikistan's foreign debt is $1.07 billion, or 30.5% of GDP, and the country has some difficulty servicing its loans. One of the World Bank projects promotes economic structural reform. In June 2005, the World Bank announced that it was allocating $50 million for projects in Tajikistan. Most of the money was to help develop the country's agricultural sector, develop water resources in the Fergana Valley, and to manage losses in the electrical power and gas sectors. In February 2006, the World Bank announced $32.5 million in grants to Tajikistan. Most of this money was to be used to improve health care and improve municipal services. The IMF also announced a new three-year program for Tajikistan which will provide up to $99 million in aid.

The Asian Development Bank, the Islamic Development Bank and the European Bank for Reconstruction and Development (EBRD) also approved loans to the Tajik government in 2006–2007. The Asian Development Bank approved $145 million in projects to be carried out during the period 2006–2008. The EBRD agreed to loan $5 million to the Tajik air carrier Tojikiston to permit it to lease two new planes.

Individual foreign countries have also been very generous. For example, Germany provided $33 million in technical and financial assistance to the Tajik government, $7 million of which was in the form of a grant. In January 2006, seven donor countries agreed to write off Tajikistan's $99 million debt to the IMF.

In January 2005, the Russian, Iranian, and Tajik Governments signed protocols to complete the construction of Tajikistan's Sangtuda-1 and Sangtuda-2 hydropower stations. Russia's Unified Energy Systems provided most of the financing for Sangtuda-1 while Iran provided almost all of the financing for Sangtuda-2. Sangtuda-1 began producing electricity in January 2008. Sangtuda-2 began producing electricity in 2011.

In April 2007, Murodali Alimardonov, the chairman of Tajikistan's National Bank announced that it was opening up the banking sector to foreign banks. Alimardonov commented that

Our banks have grown quite strong to stand up to the competition with the new banks that will enter our market; therefore we will gladly welcome them to our republic.

Alimardonov said that five foreign banks would soon receive licenses to operate in Tajikistan; one of those will be Kazakhstan's Kazkommertsbank. No other banks were named, but according to reports several foreign banks have signaled interest in working in Tajikistan.

By 2011, Tajikistan had a total of 14 banks in operation within the country. The first of these, Amonatbonk, is state-owned, while nine additional banks are local-foreign joint ventures. Four banks—Accessbank, FirstMicroBank, Kazkommertsbank, and Bank Tijarat—are 100% foreign-owned. In addition, Tajikistan has one investment bank—Somon Capital, which was opened in 2007.

Tajikistan was officially admitted to the World Trade Organization in December 2012. Tajikistan's negotiations to join the WTO went on for 11 years.

In recent years, Tajikistan's economic ties with China have become very extensive. Development projects include building roads and tunnels, exploring for oil and natural gas, and mining gold. According to Chris Rickleton writing for Eurasianet.org, the head of Tajikistan's Chamber of Commerce stated in 2014 that since 2003, Chinese-Tajik trade had grown over 6000%, from $32 million to $2 billion annually. Construction of a network of gas pipelines from Turkmenistan to China is scheduled to start soon. Tajikistan will not receive any gas from the pipeline but will receive transit fees.

The Future
Tajikistan's first five years after independence were characterized by a civil war and a collapse of most of the urban economy. The end of the civil war in 1997 has been followed by an authoritarian political stability which allowed the economy to begin growing again in 1998. In 2015, the peace deal effectively ended when the IRPT was proscribed. Whether this move indicates that the Rahmon regime feels increasingly secure or whether this action is a sign of desperation is unclear. Early fears that that the elimination of the moderate Islamic opposition would spur some Tajikistani citizens to radicalize, since they have no other option to express discontent, did not materialize Similarly, the regime's harsh crackdown on all but state-sanctioned forms of religious expression have not fostered conditions for extremist ideologies to take root underground. Instead, challenges to the regime came in the form of intermittent anti-government protests in GBAO, and community cross-border conflicts between Tajiks and Kyrgyz over water and land. These challenges might not directly threaten the survival of the incumbent regime, especially border clashes in the north. Nonetheless, they can strain the regime's fiscal resource, undermining the odds of its survival in times of severe economic downturn.

The economic prospects for Tajikistan are quite limited. Western sanctions on Russia might bode ill for the fate of the incumbent regime in Tajikistan because the country highly depends on Russia for financial remittances. The steep plunge in remittances and the inability of domestic economy to absorb labor of migrant returnees could potentially have a destabilizing effect on the country.

In the medium term, Tajikistan is facing the central dilemma of authoritarian regimes: how to manage succession. To date, President Rahmon has not explicitly stated his succession plan; however, most observers suspect that the first choice is his 32-year-old son, Rustam Emomali. Indeed, over the past few years, Rustam Emomali has gained experience in a variety of government posts—useful in building a network of supporters—and is currently chair of the upper house of parliament. As such, he would step in should his father become incapacitated or dies in office. After much speculation that Rustam Emomali was being groomed to take power as soon as the 2000 presidential election, Rahmon decided to remain in power. Ensuring that the regime insiders are confident about their prospects under the apparently favored prince if and when he replaces his father is of paramount importance for the continuation of the regime. Even so, an adverse economic condition associated with a dramatic fall in migrant remittances might throw a wrinkle into the smooth transfer of power from father to son.

Turkmenistan

Area: 186,400 sq. mi. (488,100. sq. km., as large as California and half of Oregon).

Population: 5,636,011 5,744,151 (2024 estimate).

Capital City: Ashgabat (formerly Ashkabad) Pop. 810,000 (2018 estimate).

Climate: Hot and dry summers, very cold in winter.

Neighboring Countries: Kazakhstan (north), Uzbekistan (north and east), Iran, Afghanistan (south).

Language: Turkmen.

Ethnic Composition: Turkmen (85%), Uzbek (5%), Russian (4%), Kazakh (2%), Other (4%).

Principal Religion: Islam.

Chief Commercial Products: Oil, natural gas minerals, cotton, jute, fruits (grapes), vegetables, sheep, goats.

Currency: manat (issued November 1993).

Per Capita Annual Income (Purchasing Power Parity): $8,906 (2023 estimate).

Recent Political Status: A republic was formed in 1924, but in 1925 it was incorporated into the former USSR and remained so until 1991.

Head of State: Serdar Berdimuhamedov, President.

Head of Government: Serdar Berdimuhamedov, President.

National Day: October 27 (1991), independence from USSR.

National Flag: A solid green background; superimposed against the green on the left, a red-brown fabric pattern consisting of five medallions runs slightly indented from top to bottom; to the right of that in the upper left, a crescent moon with five stars.

The Land

The Republic of Turkmenistan, independent successor state to the Turkmen Soviet Socialist Republic, declared its independence following the collapse of the attempted coup against the USSR's Gorbachev in August 1991. October 27 has been established as the official Independence Day.

Although it borders on the Caspian Sea in the west, Turkmenistan is almost entirely a land of deserts and passes. The entire central part of the republic is occupied by the largest of these, the Kara Kum, or Black Sand Desert. Topographically, it is also the southern part of the Turan Plain. Only in the south are there foothills and mountains. The Kopet-Dag forms the border with eastern Iran, while northern-reaching spurs of the Pamir Alay Mountain Ranges form the border with Afghanistan and the south part of the border with Uzbekistan. On the northeast, the Amu Dar'ya River flows along the border with Uzbekistan. It borders on the Caspian Sea in the west.

Three other rivers, the Tedzhen, Murgab and Atrek, flow north out of the southern mountains and provide water for irrigation. In the 1950s, the Kara Kum Canal was constructed from Kerki on the Amu Dar'ya northwestward across the southern part of the Kara Kum to the city of Merv and Ashgabat, the capital. It is the world's largest irrigation and shipping canal. Oases exist along the rivers plus in the foothills of the Kopet-Dag Mountains. The rest of the country is desert.

Turkmenistan has a strongly continental climate, extremely hot in summer (average of 95°F), and bitterly cold in winter (temperatures as low as –27°F). Precipitation averages 3 inches a year in the northwestern desert and 12 inches in the southern mountains. Except in oases areas, only desert vegetation grows.

The People

Turkmen make up 85% of the republic's population. The two largest minorities are Uzbeks (5%) and Russians (4%). Kazaks make up a further 2%, while there are smaller numbers of Tatars, Ukrainians, Armenians, Kara Kalpaks and Azeris. Russians, found mainly in urban areas, have been leaving the country in large numbers since independence; at the time of the 1989 census, they constituted 13% of the population. About half the people live in urban areas, the rest in rural settlements and villages. Turkmen is, as the name implies, a Turkic language.

History

The Turkmen were mostly nomads up to the time of the Russian Revolution, though some had settled in oases and taken up agriculture. Divided up into a number of tribes, their main loyalty was to their tribe or clan, with almost no sense of a Turkmen identity. The creation of the Turkmen Soviet Socialist Republic in October 1924 provided a strong impetus toward creation of a Turkmen nation. Because the nomadic tribes lacked written records, there are debates over the history and ethnogensis of the Turkmen. Turkmens boast of a rich oral tradition, with bards (known as bakshy) passing on legends and stories from generation to generation. Their main tribes were the Tekes, Ersaris, and Yomut. There were bitter rivalries between the tribes. Thus, when the Tekes were fighting a struggle to drive back the Russians in the

316

1860s and 1870s, the other tribes offered no assistance whatsoever.

In 1869, a Russian military force landed on the eastern shore of the Caspian Sea and founded a settlement at the location of present-day Krasnovodsk. Five years later, the Transcaspian military district was established. This became the Transcaspian oblast in 1881. There was fierce resistance to the Russian advance, but it was broken at the battle of Geok-Tepe in 1881. In 1899, the area was incorporated into the Governor Generalship of Turkistan.

Turkmenistan was the scene of intermittent fighting during the Russian civil war that followed the Bolshevik Revolution. Red Army troops conquered Ashgabat in July 1919 and Krasnovodsk in February 1920. The Bolsheviks organized the western part of present-day Turkmenistan as a separate oblast of the Turkistan Autonomous SSR. The remaining parts were included in the Bukharan and Khorezmian Soviet Socialist Republics. In 1924, a Turkmen Soviet Socialist Republic was formed, which took in all three Turkmen-inhabited areas. The Turkmen SSR was formally incorporated into the USSR in May 1925.

The life of the Turkmen people changed almost completely during the 70 years of the Soviet period but, through it all, the Turkmen SSR remained one of the most obedient of the constituent republics of the USSR. This began to change somewhat after Mikhail Gorbachev became General Secretary in 1985 and launched his program of glasnost and perestroika. In August 1990, the Turkmen Supreme Soviet passed a declaration of sovereignty, though there was still no real challenge to Soviet authority. However, Saparmurat Niyazov, first secretary of the Turkmen Communist Party, had the Supreme Soviet create the office of president and he was elected to that office in October 1990.

The attempted coup against Gorbachev in August 1991 changed this situation again. Following the collapse of the USSR President Niyazov issued a declaration of Turkmen independence and called for a referendum on the question, which took place on October 26. When the referendum received a 94% favorable vote, President Niyazov declared October 27 Turkmen independence day.

He confiscated all assets held by the Communist Party of the Soviet Union within the republic, but he remained first secretary of the Turkmen Communist Party, and on November 18–19, the Central Committee of the party held a plenum to consider the future. It called a party congress for December 16 and recommended that the party be renamed the Turkmen Democratic Party. This recommendation was implemented by the party congress

Ex-President Saparmurat Niyazov

when it met in December. President Niyazov was elected chairman. According to the program of the Democratic Party, it is "oriented toward market reforms, sale of the state's property and support of all forms of property."

Independence

On November 15, Niyazov, who had appointed his prime minister as the chief of a newly formed Turkmen Railroad, decided to take on direct leadership of the government himself. His assumption of the duties of the prime minister was temporary, according to a government spokesman. There was no question of abolishing the office of prime minister. By January 1992, it appeared that the deputy prime minister, Nazar Suyunov, had become the de facto head of government.

In April 1993, President Niyazov signed a decree approving a new alphabet of the Turkmen language based on Latin. This change marks the third alphabetic reform for the Turkmen language since the beginning of the century. The switch to the new Latin alphabet took place on January 1, 2000.

Over the next several years, President Niyazov was increasingly referred to in the press and in public announcements as "Turkmenbashi," or "Leader of the Turkmen." His portrait was ubiquitous, appearing in every parade float, office building, and hotel. Every park in the country had a statue of him. The purpose

was apparently to increase his popularity among the people by portraying him as a traditional tribal leader and it appeared to be working. In a referendum held in January 1994, the people were asked whether they approved extending his term of office until 2002. The final result of the vote was 1,959,408 votes for, 212 against, and 17 spoiled ballots.

Talking to a Western reporter in December 1995, Niyazov admitted that the new cult of personality had gone too far. "I admit it, there are too many portraits, pictures and monuments. I don't find any pleasure in it, but the people demand it because of their mentality."

Elections to the newly created Majlis (legislature) took place in December 1994. Since no oppositional party managed to gain official registration, the candidates were almost all members of the Democratic Party of Turkmenistan. All ran unopposed.

President Niyazov had cardiac surgery in Germany on September 1, 1997. The operation was a success and there were no complications. Five weeks later, he chaired his first cabinet meeting since the operation and later attended a ceremony commemorating the victims of the 1948 earthquake that destroyed Ashgabat. President Niyazov's mother and brothers were among the victims.

President Niyazov paid an official visit to the United States in April 1998. One agreement signed during the visit provided for Export-Import Bank credit for purchasing US-made goods, while a second provided $750,000 for a feasibility study of Trans-Caspian oil and gas lines on the Caspian Sea bed. In addition, Niyazov signed agreements with ExxonMobil on the exploration and extraction of oil in western Turkmenistan.

New parliamentary elections took place on December 12, 1999. A total of 102 candidates competed for the 50 mandates in the new parliament but, except for a few independents, all were members of the Democratic Party of Turkmenistan. After the elections, the new parliament approved an amendment to the constitution allowing Niyazov to serve as president for life. The next day, Niyazov announced that no alternatives to the Democratic Party of Turkmenistan would be allowed to exist during the next decade. Niyazov modified that position slightly in February 2001 when he announced that he would leave office no later than 2010, when he would turn 70. He promised that open elections for the presidency would be held at that time. Parliament duly passed a law setting presidential elections for 2010.

The matter came up again in August 2002 when the 3,000 delegates to the Khalk Maslakhaty enthusiastically endorsed a proposal making Niyazov president for

Turkmenistan

life. President Niyazov rejected the proposal the next day, but he then instructed the Khalk Maslakhaty to rename the months and days of the week. The Khalk Maslakhaty proceeded to rename January as Turkmenbashi (one of Niyazov's titles), April after Niyazov's mother, and September after the Rukh*name*, Niyazov's volume of spiritual writings.

Niyazov was not permitted the quiet enjoyment of his remaining years in power, however. The political situation in the country began deteriorating in the summer of 2001 when President Niyazov launched what looked like a political purge by summarily sacking four government officials, five deputy governors of provinces, and the mayor of Ashgabat.

Three months later, on October 30, 2001, he met with the members of the Turkmen diplomatic corps. As the meeting was carried live on Turkmen television, the general population saw Niyazov chastise nearly every one of Turkmenistan's ambassadors and fire two of them, the ambassadors to the United Arab Emirates and China. Two days later, Boris Shikhmuradov, the fired ambassador to China arrived in Moscow, where he issued a press statement denouncing President Niyazov's regime as "a primitive police state" which had isolated the country; he also accused Niyazov of having committed crimes, allowed crimes to be committed, and persecuted people on religious

and ethnic bases. Shikhmuradov also announced that he was creating an anti-Niyazov political organization, the People's Democratic Movement of Turkmenistan. One day later, the Turkmen Prosecutor-General's office in Ashgabat issued an indictment against Shikmuradov accusing him, among other things, of stealing $25 million worth of equipment from the state, 9,000 Kalashnikov assault rifles, and $2.5 million worth of ammunition. The Turkmenistan government later requested Shikhmuradov's extradition, but the Russian government demurred.

As it turned out, Shikhmuradov was the *second* high government official to break with Niyazov and then go on to form an anti-Niyazov political organization. The first, Avdy Kuliev, had served as foreign minister from 1990 until July 1992 and left after policy disagreements with his boss. He moved to Moscow in 1997, but when he attempted to return to Ashgabat for a visit in 1998, he was stopped upon his arrival at the airport, and then detained for five days before being sent back to Moscow. It was after his return to Moscow that he formed the Committee for National Salvation and began campaigning for Niyazov's resignation and for free and democratic elections.

In February 2002, a third former government official showed up in Moscow as a recruit to the anti-Niyazov opposition. This was Hudaiberdi Orazov, a former chairman of the Turkmen Central Bank,

who was serving as a deputy prime minister when he was fired by Niyazov in 2000. Orazov also billed himself as a reformer—"all my attempts to change the situation in the country for the better came to nothing"—but his reputation suffered when, after being indicted by the Prosecutor General's office for embezzlement, he partially admitted the charge and returned $100,000 to the state.

It was never likely that a group of opposition figures living in Moscow could threaten Niyazov's hold on power, but it appears that Niyazov was nevertheless shaken by the nature of the charges made against him. But what probably bothered him the most is that all three of these individuals seemed to be loyal subordinates while in office. Now he could only wonder how many of his other "loyal subordinates" were secretly sympathetic to one or more of the Moscow opposition. This may explain why Niyazov launched a purge of the National Security Committee (Turkmenistan's successor to the KGB) in March 2002. More than two dozen top officials were fired outright while Muhammad Nazarov, the head of the National Security Committee, was demoted from four-star general to lieutenant general. Perhaps even more significant, Nazarov, who had been very close to Niyazov, lost his other post as the president's chief legal adviser. Within days, Niyazov also fired Defense Minister Kurbandurdy Begendjev.

Inside a typical Turkmen home in Ashgabat

318

Turkmenistan

Turkomen carpets for sale in a bazaar outside of Ashgabat Courtesy of Hermine Dreyfuss

A few days later, Niyazov pushed the purge further down the ranks, dismissing two National Security Committee colonels, three lieutenant colonels, and two captains. In April, the purges spread out to other sections of the society when Niyazov dismissed another governor as the chairman of the Food Industry Association.

At the beginning of May, criminal charges were filed against Muhammad Nazarov and 21 of his subordinates in the National Security Committee. Nazarov was accused of 11 crimes, including murder, procuring prostitutes, bribe taking, and fraud. That same day, ex-Defense Minister Begendjev was charged with four counts of corruption. The trials followed quickly afterward—ex-Defense Minister Begendjev was sentenced to 10 years in prison on May 23. Nazarov, whose sentencing came on June 15, got 15 years in prison.

As the purges continued, the chairman of the National Bank and the head of the country's main television channel lost their jobs on May 6. Deputy Foreign Minister Batyr Khadykuliev was fired on June 19. The chairman of the Council for Television and Radio Broadcasting and the rector of the Institute of Culture were fired on July 29. The firings and arrests then tailed off.

On November 25, there was an apparent attempt to assassinate President Niyazov. According to the initial story, the president's motorcade came under fire about 7 a.m. at an intersection in downtown Ashgabat as he was traveling to his office. The gunman or gunmen jumped out of a

KamAZ truck—in later versions from the truck, a BMW, and a Gazel automobile—and began raking the motorcade with machine-gun fire. By the next day, the story involved the truck, two minibuses and a BMW, while more assailants ran out of nearby residential buildings and opened fire. In spite of the confusion about details, the one constant was that President Niyazov's car was untouched and he was, as he himself later reported, not even aware of the attack at the time.

From the beginning, some political opponents claimed that the attack was either staged or fabricated. Another theory propounded by Saparmurat Iklymov, former Turkmen deputy agriculture minister was that the assassination attempt had been carried out by the National Security Committee, which had been the target of a Niyazov purge in the spring. Iklymov's evidence was that the KamAZ truck used in the attempt had been confiscated in 1999 from his brother Parakhat, who left Turkmenistan the following year.

Whatever the truth about the alleged assassination attempt, President Niyazov used it to justify a renewed attack on his political opponents, a further purge of the top echelons of Turkmen society, and a general tightening up of the controls over Turkmen society. Hundreds of persons were arrested after November 25, including visitors in the country from several foreign countries, including one from the United States. Security officials even went so far as to raid the Uzbek Embassy in

Ashgabat on December 16, also searching the ambassador's residence. Their excuse was that, according to their information, Turkmen citizens involved in the attempted assassination had taken refuge in the Uzbek Embassy. When they found no one hiding there, the officers filmed a Turkmen man who had accompanied them into the building as he testified on camera to having been living in the embassy for some time. When the Uzbek Ambassador protested the violation of diplomatic immunity, the Turkmen government declared him persona non grata and expelled him from the country.

Former Foreign Minister Boris Shikhmuradov, who had secretly reentered Turkmenistan from Uzbekistan shortly before the assassination attempt, was arrested after he gave himself up to the Turkmen authorities. Shikhmuradov was subsequently sentenced to life imprisonment. Shikhmuradov's public confession, with its description of the president as "a gift given to the people from on high" and the characterization of his policies as "absolutely correct," reminded one forcefully of the Stalinist trials of the 1930s.

Over 50 more men were sentenced to long prison terms during the third week in January. These included former parliament speaker Tagandurdy Khallyev; Konstantin Shikhmuradov, brother of Boris Shikhmuradov; and former Foreign Minister Batyr Berdyev. And just as in the 1930s, President Niyazov ordered publication of the proceedings of the trials of

319

Turkmenistan

those charged in the alleged assassination attempt.

International reaction was rather uniformly negative. In its annual human rights report issued on March 31, the United States State Department described Turkmenistan as "a one-party state dominated by its president, who continues to exercise power in a Soviet-era authoritarian style." On April 16, the UN Commission on Human Rights adopted a resolution expressing its concern about limitations and violations of human rights in Turkmenistan and calling for an immediate end to mass repressions, the extra-judicial harassment of opposition figures and their families, the fabrication of evidence against people suspected of involvement in the assassination attempt, and the use of torture by law enforcement officials. The resolution also censured Turkmenistan for its lack of cooperation with international organizations. But Turkmenistan did have some support on the commission—Russia, Ukraine, Armenia, and 13 other countries all voted against the resolution.

A New President

President Niyazov died unexpectedly on December 21, 2006, apparently of a massive heart attack. That same day, it was announced that the new acting leader of Turkmenistan was Deputy Prime Minister Gurbanguly Berdymukhammedov (pronounced gur-BAHN-goo-lee bair-dee-mukh-ha-MAY-doff), who also made a nationally televised address explaining that his selection was confirmed by his fellow ministers and members of the Turkmen State Security Council. The explanation was necessary because, according to the constitution, President Niyazov's successor was supposed to be the speaker of the parliament, Ovezgeldy Atayev.

As Marina Kozlova, writer for *Business Week* wrote in January 2007, "the inner workings of Niyazov's secretive regime are difficult to decipher." So, we don't know why the speaker of parliament was placed under arrest and later sentenced to five years in prison, while a relatively little known junior minister in Niyazov's cabinet became acting president. But he did. Moreover, parliament quickly passed legislation making Berdymukhammedov eligible to run for the presidency.

Parliament set the presidential election for February 11; it then picked six candidates, including Berdymukhammedov, for the presidential poll. No actual opposition candidates were considered. All six presidential candidates said that they would continue the political course set out by President Niyazov. Berdymukhammedov announced that the election would be conducted "in accordance with the concept of democracy as understood by Niyazov. On

**President
Gurbanguly Berdymukhammedov**

Election Day, Berdymukhammedov was elected with over 89% of the vote. He was sworn in as president three days later, on February 14.

With such a beginning for an administration, there could be little basis to expect that the new leadership would introduce significant changes. Yet there have been a number of surprising reversals of policy since that time.

Berdymukhammedov did, it is true, promise during the electoral campaign that he would, one, work to improve education and that, two, he intended to engage Turkmenistan more with its neighbors even while retaining the country's neutrality.

Nevertheless, it came as a surprise when he almost immediately ordered the restoration of the 10th year of secondary education and replaced vocational training in secondary schools with physical education and social studies. In addition, he reduced teachers' work schedules and limited classroom size to 25 for secondary schools with lower ratios for primary grades.

He also announced that young people would be permitted to study in foreign universities; that teachers would be sent abroad for professional training; that foreign diplomas would again be recognized; and that the two-year work requirement for university students would be dropped.

Another presidential decree called for the opening of the first Internet cafés in Ashgabat, with more Internet cafés to be opened later in other parts of the country. The news was not all good; the fees charged in the new Internet cafés limited the number of individuals who could afford to use them.

In another change, President Berdymukhammedov instructed government officials to attend conferences and meetings abroad. This was a 180-degree change from the situation under President Niyazov, who forbade all but senior government officials from representing their country abroad.

Since that time, President Berdymukhammedov has re-opened

circus and opera performances, released prisoners, and re-opened hospitals. He has reinstituted pensions for the elderly and mandated new government payments for mothers and their infants, as well as for veterans and disabled persons.

President Berdymukhammedov also dismantled the cult of Niyazov. Most of Niyazov's portraits have been taken down; his birthday has ceased to be a national holiday; and the months of the year that had been renamed in honor of his mother and himself have had their traditional Turkmen names restored. And the great statue of Niyazov in the main square of Ashgabat is scheduled to be either removed to the edge of the city or dismantled.

Unsurprisingly, in place of the cult of Niyazov, a new cult of personality has been constructed around Berdymukhammedov. It is now his face on posters and billboards across the country. Like his predecessor, he has also claimed a nickname (albeit one slightly less grandiose than Niyazov): Arkadag ("The Protector"). In May 2015, a 23-foot statue of himself covered in 24-carat gold was unveiled. It was named "The Protector."

President Berdymukhammedov has also reversed Niyazov's policy of isolation; he has restored diplomatic relations with Azerbaijan and otherwise worked to improve relations with all of his neighbors. He has also encouraged foreign investment in the country.

President Berdymukhammedov also gave the country a new constitution in 2008. Among its more important changes, the 2,500 member Halk Maslahaty was replaced by an enlarged standing parliament, the Majlis, which now has 125 members. The constitution also gave citizens the right to form political parties, though that article required new legislation before it could come into effect. New elections, scheduled for December 2008, were therefore held under the old rules and all members of the Majlis were members of the Democratic Party of Turkmenistan with the exception of a few independents.

In February 2010, President Berdymukhammedov ordered the legislature to draft legislation authorizing a multiparty system in Turkmenistan. Eleven months later, the president again urged parliamentary deputies to accelerate their work on legislation authorizing additional political parties. The Turkmen parliament finally got around to passing the necessary legislation in January 2012.

In August 2012, the Party of Industrialists and Entrepreneurs was established by a trade organization of the same name. In 2014, the Agrarian Party was formed to represent agricultural interests.

But as in neighboring Uzbekistan, the existence of more than one party is no true sign of an emerging political pluralism. Even with multiple political parties, Turkmenistan's political system is still authoritarian. All political parties are creatures of the Turkmen state and would not be permitted to act as real opposition parties; real political opponents are still not tolerated in Turkmenistan.

New presidential elections took place on February 12, 2012, and again five years later on February 12, 2017. In both elections, President Berdymukhammedov stood for reelection against a series of token opponents (seven alternative candidates in 2012, and eight in 2012). Despite the incredible number of candidates, in both reelection bids, Berdymukhammedov received more than ninety-7% of the ballots cast. These numbers reveal the elections as shams.

Under Berdymukhammedov, Turkmenistan remains an opaque and harshly authoritarian state. Indeed, it is one of the most repressive countries in the world. There is very little freedom of speech, assembly, or religion. A concerted effort is made to keep news from the outside world from seeping in. For example, authorities remove satellite dishes from private homes. Imprisonment is used to punish political opponents. Some convicts who were arrested under Niyazov have languished in jail for many years and have no means of communicating with family members. The only ways to get an idea of life inside notorious prisons are through occasional firsthand reports and satellite imagery. Prisons are overcrowded and filthy, and prisoners can be subjected to frequent beatings. Prisons are frigid in the winter and extremely hot in the summer.

Of great concern to the government is its ongoing domestic economic crisis. Because of contract issues with Russia in 2016, and then Iran in 2017, Turkmenistan is running out of potential purchasers of its gas. These disputes have made the country dependent on China as a buyer; however, although Chinese energy needs are great, the global price of natural gas has plummeted, drastically reducing the earnings that the Turmenistani political economy had relied on since independence. To make matters worse, as Bruce Pannier reported in Radio Free Europe/Radio Liberty on March 6, 2017, the proposed line "D" pipeline between Turkmenistan and China, which had the largest capacity of any pipeline connected to Turkmenistani gas, was canceled. As Pannier also points out, this cancellation is especially damaging to Turkmenistan, since a portion of the sale of gas to China through the other smaller pipelines is currently used to pay off the debt that Turkmenistan owes to China for loans used to develop the extraction and transportation infrastructure.

The economic crisis caused by the declining value of its natural gas has begun to produce ripples domestically, and since the fall of 2016 there have been reports of shortages of basic goods such as sugar, flour, and cooking oils. Observers in the country have noted that hundreds will regularly wait in lines for hours in order to purchase bread. The challenging economic conditions led Turkmenistan to end its formally generous subsidies to its citizens on January 1, 2019: no longer would the state provide free electricity, gas, drinking water, or salt to Turkmen citizens. The cessation of this program can be seen as the end of an era in Turkmenistan. Indeed, the cuts to public goods continued into 2020: recent reports have indicated that Turkmenistan plans to end free higher education and transition to fee-based model. Since the 1990s, the Turkmenistani social contract between the state and its citizens was largely based upon the idea that citizens would accept the regime's harsh authoritarian rule in exchange for the promise that (at least some) of Turkmenistan's gas resources would be used to provide basic goods for the people. Now that this contract has been discarded it remains to be seen how the regime will attempt to legitimate itself.

In the face of these growing challenges, in April 2017 Berdymukhammedov fired a longtime energy official who has been serving as deputy prime minister for energy, Yashigeldy Kakaev. Officially, Kakaev was fired for lapses in monitoring and supervision of the sector, but most observers see the shake-up as an attempt of blame-shifting and papering over the serious structural problems at the core of Turkmenistan's economy. That being said, it is highly unlikely that Kakaev's replacement, Maksat Babayev, will fare much better.

Foreign Policy

Russia. Since emerging as an independent nation in 1991, Turkmenistan has pursued an official policy of neutrality and nonintervention in the affairs of other nations. Except for its membership in the Commonwealth of Independent States, therefore, it has refused to join any of the supranational organizations that came into existence in the region after the collapse of the Soviet Union, while its relations with its neighbors were mainly economic where they have existed at all.

Turkmenistan made a partial exception in its relations with Russia, however; in December 1995, the Government of

A catch of wild carp is hauled from the Kara Kum Canal Courtesy of NOVOSTI

Turkmenistan

Turkmenistan signed an agreement with Russia under which Russian troops took responsibility for guarding Turkmenistan's borders with Iran and Afghanistan. An accord on dual citizenship was signed by the two nations at the same time.

But even with Russia, Turkmenistan's relations were mainly economic, based on the fact that Turkmenistan is a major producer of natural gas but, until recently, was totally dependent on Russian-controlled pipelines to get its gas to world markets. This became absolutely clear in 1994 when Gazprom, with monopoly control of all of Russia's natural gas lines, raised its transit fees to such a level that Turkmenistan would have lost money on natural gas shipments to Western Europe.

Over the next several years, Turkmenistan worked to reduce its dependency on Russia by supporting projects to construct pipelines to carry its gas south through Afghanistan and Iran. Taliban control of Afghanistan ruled out use of that route in the 1990s, but a pipeline to Iran was completed in 1998. The Sarakhs-Meshhed Railroad, which was completed in 1995, provided a rail connection between Turkmenistan and Iran and led to increased trade between the two countries but, overall, it was an economic disappointment

In 2005, Turkmenistan signed an agreement with Gazprom under which the latter agreed to import between 60 and 70 billion cubic meters of natural gas a year by 2007. Gazprom originally paid $44 per 1,000 cubic meters for this gas but raised the price to $100 per 1,000 cubic meters at the beginning of 2007 at the insistence of the Turkmenistan government. In November 2007, Gazprom signed a new agreement with President Berdymukhammedov in which it agreed to pay $130 per 1,000 cubic meters of gas for the first half of 2008 and $150 for the second half of the year; Gazprom would then begin paying the European market price for future deliveries of Turkmenistan natural gas. As part of the deal, Turkmenistan committed itself to support construction of a new Russian-owned pipeline along the eastern shores of the Caspian Sea, to facilitate the export of gas from Central Asia via Russia. The new natural gas pipeline would have an annual capacity of about 20 billion cubic meters.

Gazprom then reportedly negotiated a new natural gas contract with Turkmenistan in which it agreed to purchase 50 billion cubic meters of natural gas at $340 per thousand cubic meters as of the beginning of 2009. The worldwide recession that began in late 2008 brought a sharp drop in natural gas prices, however. Gazprom, committed to paying more for Turkmenistan's natural gas than it could sell it for in Europe, decided to close down the natural gas line running from Turkmenistan in April 2009, in the process causing a major explosion that damaged the Turkmen pipeline. Gazprom then announced that it was canceling all natural gas purchases from Turkmenistan until it was able to negotiate a lower price. In December 2009, Gazprom reached an agreement with Turkmenistan to purchase 30 billion cubic meters of natural gas in 2010 for about $250 per 1,000 cubic meters. In early 2016, Russia formally suspended purchasing Turkmenistani gas. The Russian decision was economically rational, it was able to sell less natural gas to Europe than it had previously, and had alternative sources of gas, namely Uzbekistan. From the Turkmenistan perspective, this decision was quite damaging, as for many years the economy had grown dependent on selling gas to Russia.

Iran. Turkmenistan probably has the best relations with Iran of any of his neighbors, and part of that is related to the growing economic connections between the two states. President Mohammad Khatami of Iran attended a Turkmenistan-sponsored conference of the countries bordering on the Caspian Sea in Ashgabat in April 2002. Although the conference produced no agreement, the two leaders did discuss raising the throughput capacity of the Korpedzhe-Kurt-Kui gas pipeline to 13 billion cubic meters per year. In April 2006, it was announced that Iran would purchase 8 billion cubic meters of natural gas in 2006 and 14 billion cubic meters in 2007. The price was set at $65 per 1,000 cubic meters of gas.

In January 2010, the Dovietabat-Sarakhs-Khangiran natural gas pipeline opened to great fanfare with Iranian President Mahmoud Ahmadinejad traveling to Ashgabat for the occasion. This pipeline, when fully operational, will boost Turkmen gas exports to Iran to 20 billion cubic meters annually.

In September 2007, President Berdymukhammedov signed an agreement with the Governments of Kazakhstan and Iran for the joint construction of a "North-South" railroad. This second railroad, which is currently under construction, will run from Kazakhstan through Turkmenistan to Iran's Persian Gulf ports. When completed, the North-South Railroad, should provide a major new route for exports from Central Asia.

China. Turkmenistan upgraded its relations with the People's Republic of China, particularly in the economic sphere. In April 2006, during an official visit to China, President Niyazov signed an agreement with the Chinese Government on building a pipeline to export natural gas from Turkmenistan to China. This pipeline, which runs for 1,140 miles across three Central Asian republics to the Chinese border, was officially completed in December 2009. It has an annual throughput of 40 billion cubic meters. On January 1, 2017 Reuters reports that Turkmenistan cut off gas deliveries to Iran over unpaid debt for past deliveries. Although there has been talk about taking the dispute to arbitration, to date the dispute remains frozen.

United States. Relations between Turkmenistan and the United States were cool for a number of years, as the United States human rights reports were critical of President Niyazov's government on issues such as the regime's authoritarianism and its human rights record.

That changed to some extent after the terrorist attacks of September 11, but particularly after the United States launched its War on Terrorism. The United States continued to be critical of certain policies of the government, but it also expressed its gratitude for President Niyazov's early condemnation of the terror attacks and for Turkmenistan's willingness to make its airspace and territory available for humanitarian aid flights to Afghanistan.

In fact, almost all humanitarian aid going to Afghanistan prior to January 2002 passed through Turkmenistan. During a single week in November, nine planes carrying humanitarian cargo for Afghanistan landed at Ashgabat airport. In addition, the Government of Turkmenistan used its own jets to carry consignments of humanitarian aid from Ashgabat to an airport along the Afghan border.

President Niyazov also moved to establish cordial relations with the new Government of Afghanistan. Hamid Karzai, the head of Afghanistan's interim government, was welcomed to Ashgabat in March 2002. The two leaders signed a series of agreements on construction of new roads between their countries and linking their power grids so Turkmenistan could begin providing electricity to Afghanistan. The Government of Turkmenistan also promised to open an embassy in Kabul.

In April 2002, James Wolfensohn, president of the World Bank, came to Ashgabat to offer World Bank assistance in helping Turkmenistan speed up market reforms; Wolfensohn also expressed the World Bank's willingness to invest in oil and gas infrastructure as well as projects contributing to the rational use of the country's water resources.

Most of this new international openness was put on hold after the alleged attempted assassination of President Niyazov, particularly after the widespread purges that he instituted at this time. The various Color Revolutions that took place

Turkmenistan

in Georgia, Ukraine, and Kyrgyzstan in 2003–2005 created a sort of siege mentality in Turkmenistan among the political elites and a further withdrawal from international involvement. That began gradually changing again after President Berdymukhammedov was elected president in February 2007. In 2009, the Government of Turkmenistan signed a cooperation agreement with the US government under which the Government of Turkmenistan agreed to relay nonlethal goods to US and NATO troops in Afghanistan. This has led to the stationing of a small contingent of US troops in Ashgabat to assist in refueling planes that land at the Ashgabat airport.

Following a campaign by human rights organizations, in May 2018 the US Customs and Border Protection (CBP) service banned the importation of cotton picked in Turkmenistan. Although the CBP did not state the reason for the ban, it has been widely reported that it was due to the state's use of forced labor and child labor in the cotton harvest. Although there is little direct trade between the US and Turkmenistan, the ban will force apparel makers based in countries that import Turkmenistani cotton to alter their source of raw cotton for products which ultimately are destined for the US.

Azerbaijan. Turkmenistan's relations with Azerbaijan, its neighbor across the Baltic, were placed in a deep freeze in the late 1990s because of a disagreement over demarcation of the boundary between the two republics on the seabed of the Baltic that involved a potential oil field.

A change in the relationship began in March 2007, when President Berdymukhammedov proposed to President Aliyev that the two republics end the official eight-year boycott and begin talking again. For his part, Berdymukhammedov ordered the Turkmen Embassy to be reopened in Baku. The two countries were unable to reach agreement on delineation of the seabed boundary between their two republics, however. This led the Government of Turkmenistan to announce in July 2009 that it intended to take Azerbaijan to court over the disputed border demarcation. Though it subsequently relented and returned to bilateral negotiations, progress has since been slow to nonexistent. That is unfortunate, since an agreement between Turkmenistan and Azerbaijan could lead to unfreezing the stalemate that has kept the Caspian littoral states from reaching an agreement on the demarcation of the Caspian seabed. This could, in turn, launch a new wave of foreign investment in Turkmenistan as well as in Azerbaijan, and it could also lead to construction of

a pipeline connecting Turkmenistan and Azerbaijan, with the gas then flowing into the recently opened gas pipeline to Turkey. One possible harbinger of future cooperation between the two republics is that Turkmenistan purchased three oil tankers in 2010 and it began shipping Turkmen oil through the Baku-Tbilisi-Ceyhan pipeline in August of that year.

Nature of the Regime

In December 1994, Turkmenistan replaced the governmental system inherited from the Soviet era with a new system, under which the president acts as both head of state and head of government. There is no separate prime minister. The presidential term was originally set for five years, but in 1999 the legislature amended the constitution to allow Niyazov to serve for life. Niyazov announced in 2000 that he intended to serve only until he reached the age of 70, that is, until 2010, and parliament subsequently passed a law to that effect.

President Niyazov's death in December 2006 created a new situation entirely. His successor is Gurbanguly Berdymukhammedov, who began his five-year term as president on February 14, 2007. Berdymukhammedov also assumed the second position as head of government.

Under Niyazov, the Majlis (legislature) consisted of 50 members, elected for a term of five years. There was also a constitutional court and a supreme court.

There also existed an additional entity, referred to as the Khalk Maslakhaty (People's Supreme Council) which was defined as the country's supreme consultative body. It was supposed to meet annually, but met for the first time in three years in August 2002. Turkmen television explained at the time that, although it was commonly referred to as the Khalk Maslakhaty, it was more accurately referred to as the 12th joint forum of three bodies: the Congress of Elders, intended to be an advisery group to the president; the National Revival Movement of Turkmenistan, a coalition of political parties and public associations in the country; and the People's Council proper, consisting of parliamentary deputies and Niyazov's appointees. Interfax added that, according to the Turkmen constitution, the council included cabinet members, heads of local executive bodies, judges, and representatives of nongovernmental organizations.

In August 2012, a second political party, the Party of Industrialists and Entrepreneurs (PIE), came into existence. This is described as a pro-business party. Two years later, the Agrarian Party, which claims to represent agricultural interests, was formed. Both PIE and the Agrarian Party are explicitly pro-regime. Although candidates representing trade unions and women's unions serve in parliament, these

are not opposition politicians, and the associations they represent are dependent upon the regime.

In 2016, amendments to the constitution extended presidential terms from five to seven years and eliminated a formal age limit of 70 for presidential candidates. As a result of these changes and the fact that Turkmenistan has no term limits for the presidency, Berdymukhammedov now has the legal capacity to rule for life. In the same year, clear efforts began to groom President Berdymukhammedov's son, Serdar, as a potential successor. In 2016, Serdar Berdymukhammedov was elected to parliament. In subsequent years, his profile has grown and in 2018 he was named the deputy foreign minister.

In 2019 and 2020, his brief rapidly changed: first he was appointed governor of his (and his father's) home province of Ahal, and then a little more than a year later, he was named the head of the newly established ministry for construction and industry. As minister, Serdar Berdymukhammedov will be in a prime position to extracts rents from the lucrative state building projects that his office will be overseeing, and thus should be able to build a network of allies around him.

In February 2022, Gurbanguly Berdimuhamedov publicly stated that he would step down from office and called for snap elections to replace him. In the ensuing elections his son Serdar Beridmuhamedov won with 73% of the votes. Thus, Turkmenistan accomplished a peaceful transfer of power from father to son, making it the first country in modern central Asia to install a dynastic rule. Upon becoming the new president on March 19, Sardar Berdimuhamedov, announced that he would follow his father's political and economic course. For an average citizen of Turkmenistan, it means they would continue to live under miserable economic conditions and political tyranny. Serdar publicly stated that advancing gender equality would be one of his top policy priorities. Despite government's proclamations about the importance of gender equality, informal orders continue to disenfranchise women. According to these orders, women are prohibited from sitting in the front seat of taxis, male drivers are barred from offering rides to women who are not family members. Additionally, women are banned from getting beauty services, including but not limited to dyeing hair; getting manicures, fake nails, and eyelashes; lip tattoos; Botox injections; and wearing tight, revealing outfits.

Culture

Prior to the Russian Revolution, most educated Turkmen were graduates of one of the several seminaries located in Bukhara. Perhaps the most famous of

Turkmenistan

Korpeje Oil and Gas Field

these was Abdulhekim Qulmuhammed-oghli, a writer, editor, researcher and cultural organizer, who eventually joined the Communist Party. He was killed in 1937 at the time of the great Soviet purge. The level of literacy increased greatly during the Soviet era, but the straitjacket of socialist realism, instituted by Stalin in 1930, meant that most work was written "for the masses." In addition, many Turkmen writers' works were in Russian. This is true also of films, television, radio, and theater, which appeared in Russian.

As in the other post-Soviet states of Central Asia, there have been debates over what it means to be Turkmen. There has been a revitalization of "traditions" in some segments of society, which in some cases has meant old taboos are once again observed including the practice of polygamy amongst wealthy Turkmen males despite its proscription by Turkmenistan law. Most Turkmen are Sunni Muslims, but religion, though important, often is less important than tribal loyalties. Turkmenistan is still essentially a tribal culture, dominated by its five major tribes. Tribal ties, officially suppressed under communism, have once again come to the fore.

The government has also sought to reduce the influence of Russian culture since independence. The local publication of Russian-language newspapers stopped in 1992. Five years later, the government began to place restrictions on the importation of periodicals from Russia. Then it became illegal to import any publication from Russia in July 2002. The motivation for this particular governmental action was probably more political than cultural, however;

Russian publications had increasingly become very critical of President Niyazov.

Still, the move to ban all Russian publications fit into a larger pattern of governmental actions taken to isolate Turkmen citizens from foreign influence. For example, President Niyazov issued a decree in February 2003 whose effect was to severely restrict opportunities for Turkmen citizens to study abroad. Essentially, the decree stipulated that only students chosen by the Education Ministry could legally exchange manats, the national currency, for convertible currencies. Two months later, the government began dismissing all teachers who had earned their degrees from foreign institutions of higher or specialized secondary education after 1993. President Berdymukhammedov began reversing all of these policies as soon as he took over in February 2007 and that trend is expected to continue.

Turkmenistan has no great literary tradition and in recent years the most important Turkmen author was President Niyazov. His last work, *Mahribanlarim* (My Dear All), a mixture of prose and poetry, was published in October 2005. His works are unlikely to long survive his death, however.

A perhaps more typical Turkmen writer is Rahim Esenov, author of more than 20 novels. Esenov was awarded the 2006 PEN/Barbara Goldsmith Freedom to Write Award in April 2006. Esenov, then 79 years old, was permitted to travel to New York City to receive the award; he had been held in confinement in Ashgabat for two years prior to that time, however, and his novels were banned in Turkmenistan.

Esenov's most important novel is *The Crowned Wanderer*, which tells the life of Bayram Khan, a military general and man of letters from earlier Turkmen history.

Turkmenistan has three UNESCO world heritage sites within its borders. The oldest of these, Nisa, the capital of the Parthian Empire, is located about 15 kilometers from Ashgabat. The Parthian Empire was one of the most powerful civilizations of the ancient world and Nisa itself dates from 3000 B.C. Nisa lost its significance in the 3rd century A.D. Today, only the lower walls and bases of the columns remain.

The second world heritage site is the city of ancient Merv, famous as the location of the mausoleum of Sultan Sanjar. Merv is believed to have been the most populous city in the mid-12th century.

The third world heritage site is Kunyaurgench, located in northern Turkmenistan on the left bank of the Amu-Darya River. The ancient city, with its many ruins and monuments, is a large archaeological park. It borders on the modern city of Kunyaurgench.

In the first years of independence, the government tended to take a hands-off attitude toward religion. That changed when the number of Protestant Christians began to grow in the country. In 1997, the government started taking coercive actions against individual Protestant churches. Government police and security officers raided three Protestant churches in September–October 2000; congregation members had their passports confiscated, and members were warned not to attend services in the future. In February 2001, the government arrested and imprisoned a Baptist minister by the name of Shageldy Atakov. He had been serving his four-year sentence at the Seydy labor camp in northeastern Turkmenistan but was later moved to a closed prison in the town of Turkmenbashi, on the Caspian coast. Atakov's wife and children were reportedly ordered to convert from Christianity or Islam with the proviso that, if they did not, their home would be confiscated. In March 2001, the last open Baptist church in Ashgabat was seized and closed. City officials said afterward that the congregation had not complied with a 1997 requirement to re-register with the Turkmen ministry of justice.

Arranged marriages are still the norm in the society, particularly in rural areas. Traditionally, the bride and groom must belong to the same tribe. This causes problems for young people of different tribes who fall in love. Occasionally, a young man will "steal away" the girl he favors, hoping thereby to force the parents to agree. This doesn't always work, however. As one Turkmen commented, "it's no joke. Some parents sue the husband in court. Others kill the bride."

Economy

The Soviet era brought about major changes in the lives of the Turkmen people. Prior to the Russian Revolution, most Turkmen were nomads who constantly moved from place to place in search of forage for their herds. Beginning in the 1930s, great engineering projects were launched to increase the irrigated areas. These irrigated lands were organized into state farms and the Turkmen people were settled on them, their nomadic life at an end.

Cotton became the chief crop grown throughout the area. New engineering projects in the 1950s and 1960s, in particular the Kara Kum Canal, brought additional lands under cultivation and increased Turkmenistan production of cotton even further. Local reports of increasing salinity in the soil or the constant drop in the level of the Aral Sea as a result of the new engineering projects were ignored by the central planners in Moscow.

After 1985, however, Mikhail Gorbachev's reforms allowed for greater local autonomy. Beginning about 1987, Turkmenistan began an attempt to restructure its agricultural economy. Moscow was asked to lower its cotton quota somewhat, and some land was removed from cotton production and switched to other crops. Turkmenistan began to grow more grain and feed, and the number of livestock grown also increased.

The government has continued and expanded on this emphasis since independence. In December 1996, President Niyazov issued a decree dissolving the old state and collective farms, officially transforming them into "peasant associations." The decree also specified that farmers would have the right to lease land for up to 15 years free of charge.

President Niyazov's decree required lease holders to grow certain specified crops for the first two years of the lease contract. At the end of the two years, if the leaser has achieved the minimum yields contracted for, the lease holder was to be free to plant whatever crops he wanted, and could even lease the land to someone else if he chose, though he was not free to sell it.

President Niyazov fired his agriculture minister in January 1999 and named his deputy to succeed him. Some days later, the government announced a six-year program for the partial privatization of farms, plus industrial and construction companies belonging to the agro-industrial complex. The announcement did not provide many details, but it did say that the government would retain a 51% stake in the newly privatized companies.

The agricultural sector supposedly did very well in 2002 with a record grain harvest of 2.3 million tons, though official government figures for Niyazov's last years in power are now believed to have been fabricated. Even with the government's official figures, however, the cotton crop was a failure, with production under 500,000 metric tons. The 2003 cotton harvest totaled 713,200 tons, an improvement but far below the 2.2-million-ton target set by the state. That 2.2-million-ton target was undoubtedly unrealistic, but it remained the target for 2004. When the harvest came in at 700,000 tons, President Niyazov dismissed Enebai Ataeva from the posts of deputy prime minister and governor of Ahal province. Ataeva's replacement was Murat Atagarriyev, formerly chairman of the Food Industry Association of Turkmenistan.

President Berdymukhammedov has taken a more hands-off attitude with regard to agriculture and government figures are now considered to be more reliable. In March 2011, Turkmenistan state television announced that the 2010 grain harvest had been 1.5 million tons; in 1991, the program pointed out, Turkmenistan's grain production had been only 70,000 tons. The program also indicated that Turkmenistan had joined the ranks of grain exporters, and would export 217,000 tons of grain in 2010–2011. In fact, wheat production in 2012 dropped by nearly 25% and President Berdymukhammedov then fired the minister of agriculture.

Currently, agriculture accounts for 26.9% of GDP. Even more importantly, 48.2% of all workers are employed in this sector.

Today, farming is officially organized on the basis of self-governing farming associations, but the new system appears to work very much like the old system of state and collective farms. Because almost all individuals receive land on the basis of annual leases, they never get free from the state-managed system. As one peasant in Mary Province told a reporter in March 2010, "authorities tell us what to grow, when to irrigate, where to sell the crops, and for what price."

Turkmenistan is the least industrialized of all the Central Asian republics, and industry is mainly extractive, essentially gas and oil production. The petroleum industry first began to be developed in the 1930s; Turkmenistan now ranks fourth in production among CIS republics after Russia, Kazakhstan, and Azerbaijan.

According to recent estimates, Turkmenistan has the third-largest gas reserves in the world, while its estimated oil reserves in the Caspian Basin are second only to those of Kazakhstan. Unlike Kazakhstan and Azerbaijan, however, foreign investment is only now beginning to flow into the country.

Turkmenistan's natural gas reserves may actually be greater than earlier estimated. In March 2007, the government announced the discovery of a massive new natural gas field in southeastern Turkmenistan. Official sources claimed that the gas field was 10 times the size of its previously known reserves.

In January 2008, President Berdymukhammedov authorized the British consulting firm Gaffney, Cline & Associates, to assess Turkmenistan's natural gas reserves. That report, which came out in October 2008, confirmed that the Yoloten-Osman oil and gas fields in the Amu Dar'ya basin appear to have enough gas to become the world's fourth- or fifth-largest gas reserve. Turkmenistan thus has plentiful reserves, but there are problems. First, it will have to raise sufficient capital to develop the fields; secondly, it will then have to build pipelines to get the gas to international markets.

Turkmenistan exported about seven billion cubic meters of natural gas annually before independence. Some of this gas went to other republics, but much of it was exported to Western Europe. In 1994, however, Gazprom, the newly privatized Russian gas company which controlled the pipelines to Western Europe, greatly increased transit fees for Turkmen gas and cut off the government of Turkmenistan when it refused to pay the higher fees.

The Government of Turkmenistan continued to export gas to other members of the CIS for another two years, but it cut off most of these countries at the beginning of 1997 when they were unable to pay the large arrears that they had built up. This is the main explanation why gas export revenues fell to $275 million in 1997 (down from $674 million in 1996).

The situation began to change again in 1998 when construction was completed on a pipeline connecting Turkmenistan's Korpedzhe gas field and the Iranian town of Kord Kuy. This allowed Turkmenistan to export four billion cubic meters of natural gas to Iran in 1998. Natural gas exports to Iran remained stagnant for several years, but a new agreement, signed in April 2006, called for exports to Iran of 8 billion cubic meters in 2006 and 14 billion cubic meters in 2007. This latter figure was never reached, since the Korpedzhe natural gas pipeline has a maximum annual throughput of 8 billion cubic meters. The Dovletabat–Sarakhs–Khangiran natural gas pipeline, which was officially opened in January 2010, will allow the export of 20 billion cubic meters of natural gas annually to Iran when fully operational. Iran has recently had trouble making international payments and this led, in November 2012, to a temporary shutoff of gas exports to Iran. The matter was resolved in December when the two countries reached a deal whereby Turkmenistan agreed to

Turkmenistan

allow Iran to pay off $1 billion in overdue invoices through a barter arrangement.

In April 2003, President Niyazov personally negotiated a gas deal with the Russian natural-gas company Gazprom under which Gazprom agreed to purchase 10 billion cubic meters of Turkmen gas. Two years later, Gazprom negotiated a second contract which anticipated a large increase in gas imports from Turkmenistan. Gazprom originally paid $44 per 1,000 cubic meters for this gas, but raised the price to $100 per 1,000 cubic meters in 2007 at the insistence of the Turkmen government. A third agreement, negotiated in November 2007 with President Berdymukhammedov, established the principle of a gradual increase to world prices.

In late 2008, then, Gazprom reportedly negotiated a new natural gas contract with Turkmenistan in which it agreed to purchase 50 billion cubic meters of natural gas at $340 per 1,000 cubic meters as of the beginning of 2009. The worldwide recession that began in late 2008 brought a sharp drop in natural gas prices, however. Gazprom, committed to paying more for Turkmenistan's natural gas than it could sell it for in Europe, decided to close down the natural gas line running from Turkmenistan in April 2009, in the process causing a major explosion that damaged the Turkmen pipeline. Gazprom then announced that it was canceling all natural gas purchases from Turkmenistan until it was able to negotiate a lower price. In December 2009, Gazprom signed an agreement with Turkmenistan to purchase 30

billion cubic meters of natural gas in 2010 for about $250 per 1,000 cubic meters.

A new Turkmen-China natural gas pipeline, completed in December 2009, allowed Turkmenistan to begin exporting 10 billion cubic meters of natural gas annually to China. The pipeline has the capacity to carry 30–40 billion cubic meters of natural gas annually; The Turkmen government expected to reach this larger export figure by the end of 2012.

These new export markets will require the further expansion of Turkmenistan's natural gas fields. The Government of Turkmenistan has not previously permitted foreign companies to invest in land-based energy projects, but that changed in early 2010 when Turkmenistan signed agreements with a number of Asian companies to develop the South Yolotan natural gas field, which is estimated to have reserves of 4–14 trillion cubic meters. All of the South Yolotan projects are to be financed by the China Development Bank. In 2010, $3 billion was provided by the bank; the loan contains a provision for another $4 billion in loans to complete the first stage of the project. It is expected that China will be the main export destination for the gas when the South Yolotan field begins producing.

There are also indications that President Berdymukhammedov wants to involve western energy companies in Turkmenistan as well. For example, the president issued instructions in 2010 for a new production-sharing agreement to be worked out that would allow a foreign company in on the development of the Nebit-Dag oil field

in western Turkmenistan. The Italian company Eni was expected to be the first western company to have an onshore contract in Turkmenistan. The president also indicated that the government was considering bids from Chevron, TS Oil, and ConocoPhilips for development of Turkmenistan's Caspian shelf. No western energy company has been offered access to onshore development as yet, however.

In 2010, the Government of Turkmenistan purchased three oil tankers and began shipping oil through the Baku-Tbilisi-Ceyhan pipeline. The first delivery, in August 2010, was only 36,500 barrels, but plans call for oil shipments to eventually reach nearly one million barrels monthly.

Although the role of the government in the economy has not diminished very much, there has been some restructuring of industry since independence. First of all, the production of gas was made the responsibility of Turkmenbashi, a separately organized but still state-owned company. The rest of the energy sector was partially privatized (but still controlled by the state). Under this system, five separate joint-stock companies were set up with shared responsibility for energy. The first of these, Turkmenrosgaz, was responsible for gas exports. It is 51% owned by Turkmengaz, 45% by Gazprom, and 4% by a Russian trading company. The other four companies were Turkmenneft (oil production), Turkmenneftgaz (oil and gas marketing), Turkmenneftgazstroy (construction), and Turkmengeologia (exploration). In December 2005, President Niyazov abolished Turkmenneftegaz. Responsibility for gas sales was transferred to Turkmengaz, while responsibility for sales of oil and liquefied natural gas were assigned to the Turkmenbashi refinery complex. Perhaps coincidentally, these changes were initiated after it was announced that there had been a shortfall in oil production in 2005.

Little has changed in the rest of the industrial sector thus far. Some privatization of small enterprises occurred in 1992, mostly purchased by employees, but everything else remained in state hands. According to an announcement made in November 1997, by President Niyazov, 50 state-owned enterprises were auctioned off in March 1998. Half of these companies were in the textile sector, with the remainder in the energy, industry, construction, and food and fruit sectors. In 2012, the government introduced a privatization plan. Some small- and medium-size enterprises were privatized the following year; however, implementation of this reform has been slow with limited results. Turkmenistan permits joint ventures with foreign companies and some companies have been set up, particularly in textiles.

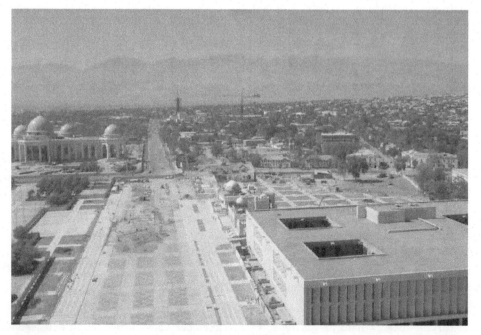

A scene in Ashgabat

Turkmenistan

Yet, bureaucratic obstacles impede international business activity.

Turkmenistan's GDP grew by an annual rate of 11% between 2007 and 2012; however, because most economic data are state secrets, government figures on economic growth are unreliable. Based on government data, GDP grew by 10.3% in 2014. The country's economy continues to depend heavily on exports of natural gas and, to a lesser extent, oil and cotton. Turkmenistan has the fourth-largest gas reserves in the world and produces around 70 billion cubic meters (bcm) of natural gas each year. Russia and Iran together purchase 15 to 20 bcm per year, but those markets are likely to decline. Both countries are focusing more attention on exploiting their own gas reserves at a time when world gas prices are declining due to abundant supply. Russian energy giant Gazprom announced that it planned to quit purchasing gas from Turkmenistan. This leaves Turkmenistan heavily dependent upon gas deliveries to China. A pipeline from Turkmenistan to China was constructed by the Chinese and began transporting gas in 2010. By the end of 2015, it is projected to deliver 55 bcm of gas per year. Turkmenistan would like to open pipelines to other countries in order not to become overly dependent on the Chinese market. Countries of the European Union are anxious to cut their reliance on Russian natural gas, so they have favored the construction of a Southern Gas Corridor pipeline from the gas-rich Caspian Sea Basin that would pass through Azerbaijan, Georgia, and Turkey (but not Russia) on its way to Europe. Work began in March 2015 on the section of the pipeline that would span Turkey (the Trans-Anatolian Pipeline or TANAP), which is now completed as of July 2019. However, no progress has been made on laying a pipeline across the Caspian Sea to tap into gas deposits in Turkmenistan, due to opposition from Russia and Iran, which also border the Caspian. Another proposed pipeline would transport gas from Turkmenistan to Afghanistan to Pakistan to India (the so-called TAPI pipeline). The main weakness of this potentially lucrative project is that the pipeline would have to traverse politically volatile regions. After numerous false starts, in December 2015 an official groundbreaking ceremony for the pipeline took place in the Karakum Desert. Officials at the ceremony expressed their optimism that the project would be completed by the end of 2019. The construction of TAPI has been slow to take off the ground,

however. After initially announcing its readiness to invest $1.1 billion into the implementation of the project, the Asian Development Bank paused its involvement until the time when the Taliban government in Afghanistan gets international recognition, which is not the horizon any time soon. In the absence of foreign investment, Turkmenistan is unlikely to foot the estimated $10 billion bill to complete the project. As of 2021, Turkmenistan exported the majority of its gas to China and a far smaller quantity to Russia.

Turkmenistan has been thrust into an economic crisis. In 2014, the state announced that residents would soon no longer be receiving gas, electricity, and water for free, although the plan is for these utilities to remain heavily subsidized. In January 2015, Turkmenistan's currency, the manat, was devalued by 19%. In the wake of the devaluation, there have been unverified reports of increasing unemployment numbers and signs of social unrest. While social dynamics within the state are generally opaque, President Berdymukhammedov's April 2016 decision to remove the Economy and Development Minister, the Trade and Foreign Economic Relations Minister, and the head of the tax service reveals a great deal of concern within the regime regarding its economic performance. The collapse of gas deals with Russia in 2016 and Iran in 2017 further sent the economy into a tailspin. Currently, gas deliveries with China represents the only reliable source of foreign currency. Despite efforts by the regime to frame the economic situation in the best possible light, the crisis has begun to hit ordinary citizens in a multitude of ways. Not only have subsidies for gas and water been eliminated but shortages of eggs, sugar, and cooking oil have been reported since the fall of 2016.

The Future

Turkmenistan is an impoverished desert country that has very large reserves of natural gas and some oil. Cotton, wheat, and other crops are intensively cultivated by about half of the population in irrigated oases. Saparmurat Niyazov served as the leader of Turkmenistan from 1985 until his death at the end of 2006. Calling himself "Turkmenbashi," the "Father of the Turkmen," he made himself the subject of a glorified personality cult. His successor, Gurbanguly Berdymukhammedov, eradicated much of that cult, and created new political parties; however, even those hoping for minor moves toward political

pluralism would be disappointed. In relatively quick fashion, Berdymukhammedov cultivated his own cult of personality. He labels himself Arkadag ("The Protector)," commands massive spectacles, and state-run television regularly celebrates his physical and intellectual capacity. Although many of the statues of Niyazov were taken down, in 2015, a 20-meter gold statue of Berdymukhammedov amount a golden horse was unveiled in the capital as school children cheered "Glory to Arkadag." Turkmenistan remains a hermit khanate, closed off from much of the rest of the world with an authoritarian, repressive government.

Turkmenistan has the smallest population of the five Central Asian states that came out of the Soviet Union and is the most ethnically homogeneous. The current economic crisis represents the most severe challenge that the regime has faced. To date, the regime has attempted to resolve the dilemma through ministerial shake-ups, which have (unsurprisingly) made no difference.

The export of natural gas continues to be Turkmenistan's largest source of income. Its reserves are estimated to be the fourth largest in the world; however, at present, only China is a reliable buyer of Turkmen gas. Iran and Russia are reducing their purchases, and both are blocking Turkmenistan's attempt to connect with the Southern Gas Corridor via a pipeline across the Caspian Sea.

The economic crisis brought on by the novel coronavirus has further taxed the regime's dwindling finances. However, this reality is not commented on by regime officials. Cabinet meetings throughout the year have insisted that the economy is growing despite the tremendous disruptions to global trade. The use of fantastical rhetoric also extends to public health statements: despite reports that patients with symptoms similar to COVID-19 have been seeking treatment across the country, officially Turkmenistan maintains that the state has no confirmed cases of the virus.

An authoritarian and repressive government, widespread corruption, and a poor education system do not present good prospects for positive development in the near future. Although Berdymukhammedov the elder is no longer the president, he holds an influential position as the head of Khalk Maslakhaty, which means the cult of personality initiatives designed around his person are likely to persist.

The Republic of Uzbekistan

Area: 186,400 sq. mi. (447,400 sq. km.; slightly larger than California).

Population: 36,520,593 (2024 estimate).

Capital City: Tashkent (Pop. 2.6 million).

Climate: Very hot and dry with average annual rainfall of only 8 inches.

Neighboring Countries: Kazakhstan (west and north); Kyrgyzstan and Tajikistan (east); Afghanistan (south); Turkmenistan (south and southwest).

Principal Languages: Uzbek and Russian.

Ethnic Composition: Uzbek (83.8%), Tajik (4.8%), Kazakh (2.5%), Russian (2.3%), Karakalpak (2.2%), Tatar (1.5%), others (2.9%) (2017 estimate).

Principal Religion: Islam (mostly Sunni).

Chief Commercial Products: Agriculture—cotton, livestock, melons, fruit, vegetables, wheat, and rice, all due to vast irrigation. Industry—natural gas, petroleum, gold, chemicals, machinery, textiles, food processing, and construction materials. Natural gas exports.

Currency: sum (Issued November 1993).

Annual Per Capita Income (Purchasing Power Parity): $8,766.

Recent Political Status: The republic was proclaimed in 1924 and became part of the USSR in 1925, which it remained until 1991.

Head of State: Shavkat Mirziyoyev (Since December 14, 2016).

Head of Government: Abdulla Aripov, Prime Minister (since December 2016).

National Day: September 1 (1991), Independence Day.

National Flag: Three equal, horizontal stripes, sky blue, white, green, separated by narrow red stripes. In the upper left against the blue, a crescent moon and to the right of it three rows of stars (3, 4, and 5), aligned on the right.

The Land

The Republic of Uzbekistan (Ozbekiston Respublikasi) is the independent successor of the Uzbek Soviet Socialist Republic, which until August 1991 was part of the USSR. Its large area stretches from west of the Aral Sea to the Fergana Valley in the east.

Uzbekistan takes in parts of the Amu Dar'ya River Valley plus the southern half of the Kysyl-Kum Desert. In the east, the republic includes the Fergana River Valley up to the foothills of the Tian Shan Mountain Range, which surrounds the valley on three sides. A landscape of little populated deserts and dry steppes, most of the population live either in the Fergana Valley or in the fertile oases along rivers flowing of the mountains to the south and southeast.

That part of Uzbekistan which lies west of the Aral Sea is known as the Ust-Urt Flatland. This area is a dry steppe land, flat and sunbaked and useful only for certain types of grazing. The Aral Sea, which Uzbekistan shares with Kazakhstan, was once the world's fourth-largest body of inland water and supported a large fishing industry. In the last 45 years or so, however, the sea and the land bordering on it have become an ecological disaster area. Since 1960, the Aral Sea has lost 60% of its water by volume and the level of the water has dropped nearly 50 feet. Each year, it drops another 9–10 inches.

The problem is that it receives its water from two main rivers, the Amu Dar'ya and the Syr Dar'ya, and those two rivers flow through 600 miles of desert and semi-desert before emptying into the Aral Sea. They form natural oases along their banks, but these cultivated areas were greatly extended in the Soviet era through new irrigation projects. Uzbekistan today has 10.75 million acres of land under irrigation, mainly along the lower reaches of the Amu Dar'ya. There are another 8.25 million acres of irrigated land in Turkmenistan, the Fergana River Valley of Kyrgyzstan and Kazakhstan. To stabilize the Aral Sea at its present level, the republics would have to agree to cut water usage sufficiently to allow the annual flow into it to grow from 11 million cubic kilometers to 35 million cubic kilometers per year. To raise it to its 1960 level, the republics would have to agree to cut out all water usage for three decades. Neither alternative is practical, so the Aral Sea will continue to shrink. Its salinity is steadily increasing.

The People

Uzbekistan is the largest of the Central Asian republics in terms of population. Uzbeks make up about 80% of the population of the country. Russians, who constitute another 5.5%, are the largest minority, followed by Tajiks (5%), Kazakhs (3%), Karakalpak (2.5%), and Tatars (1.5%). The territory also includes an autonomous region, Karakalpakstan, which was established as the "homeland" for Karakalpaks, a Turkic ethnic group. The population of

328

Uzbekistan

Tashkent, the ancient capital of Uzbekistan, shows its modern face   Courtesy of NOVOSTI

History

The territory claimed by modern Uzbekistan has been a center of civilization since ancient times, beginning with the early states of Bactria and Sogdiana. It was incorporated into the Persian Empire of Darius the Great and the Empire of Alexander the Great. Islam was introduced in the 8th century when the area was invaded by Arab forces. Incorporated into the Mongol Empire in the 13th century, it next gave birth to the Empire of Tamerlane.

The Uzbek people were late comers to the area, however, arriving probably sometime in the 15th century. They are believed to have been subordinate tribes of the Kipchak Khanate who called themselves Uzbeks in honor of the greatest of the Kipchak Khans, Uzbek or *Uzbeg*. Originally settled in the area of the Irtysh River, they began to move southeastward in the 15th century under their ruler Abu al-Khayr Khan. His grandson, Muhammad Shaybani, conquered Samarkand and most of the Syr-Dar'ya River Valley and the land south of it up to the Amu Dar'ya.

The Shaybani dynasty ruled at Samarkand until 1598, with a collateral branch ruling in Khiva (called Khwarezm until the 18th century). Another dynasty,

this territory, which is located in the far west of the country, has suffered greatly from the desiccation of the Aral Sea which has destroyed irrigation networks and fishing opportunities. Although formally an autonomous region, in practice decisions made in Tashkent determine policy in the region.

the Janids, ruled a portion of the country until the 18th century, when a reinvigorated Persia invaded and conquered Bukhara and Khiva.

The area between the Amu Dar'ya and Syr-Dar'ya was dominated by three khanates by the beginning of the 19th century— Bukhara, Khiva, and Kokand. More city-states than empires, they exercised very little control over the nomadic tribes of the desert and semi-desert. These tribes subsisted by raids on settlements to the north.

As Russian settlers pushed into the area, raids became more frequent and a problem for the Russian military which was charged with protecting the area. Building first a line of forts along the frontier, they then began retaliatory raids. Finally, they began annexing the border areas. Kokand was attacked in 1864–1865 and the emir was forced to cede Chimkent and Tashkent. In 1868, Bukhara was forced to accept the status of Russian vassal. Khiva fell in 1873. Kokand was formally annexed in 1876. The Imperial Russian government referred to the areas it had annexed as Russian Turkistan. Bukhara and Khiva continued to be semi-independent khanates.

At the time of the Russian Revolution, a Turkistan Committee of the Provisional Government was set up in Tashkent, but it was replaced in April 1918 by the Autonomous Soviet Socialist Republic of Turkistan. Lenin extended his direct control over this organization in the fall of 1919. In 1920, the semi-independent Khanates of Khiva and Bukhara were conquered by the Red Army and made into People's Republics. Khiva was transformed into a

Soviet Socialist Republic in 1923, Bukhara in 1924.

A fundamental redrawing of Central Asian boundaries along ethnic lines took place in 1924. The republics of Khiva, Turkistan, and Bukhara were abolished and five new republics were created. The Uzbekistan Soviet Socialist Republic, created in October 1924, included a large part of the Samarkand region, a large part of the Fergana Valley, part of the upper reaches of the Syr-Dar'ya River, including Tashkent and the surrounding area, plus the western plains of Bukhara. It also included the Tajik Autonomous SSR until 1929 when Tajikistan became a Soviet Socialist Republic in its own right.

Soviet rule imposed many changes on Uzbekistan; one of the most significant lasting changes was the transformation of much of the countryside into large-scale collectivized cotton farms which were responsible for producing much of the raw cotton fiber for the rest of the Soviet Union. Throughout the entire Soviet era, the Communist Party monopolized political power, so there was little chance for a political opposition to grow. Despite having little appetite for independence, the Uzbek Communist Party followed the example of other Soviet Republics when the republic adopted a resolution of sovereignty in June 1990.

Independence

Islam Karimov, the leader of the Uzbek Communist Party, sat out the August 1991 coup against Gorbachev until it became clear that it was failing. He then joined in condemning it and banned communist party cells in the armed forces, police, and civil service. Uzbekistan declared its independence on August 31. In mid-September, Karimov called a congress of the Uzbek Communist Party and had it change its name to the People's Democratic Party.

Karimov adopted Uzbek nationalist slogans, but he publicly argued that Uzbekistan was not ready for democracy or a market economy. Later, he took on some democratic trappings when he had the Uzbek Supreme Soviet create a popularly elected presidency and set elections for December 29, 1991. Other political parties became legal but they were not permitted to operate freely. The Uzbek popular front Birlik, potentially the largest opposition grouping, was not permitted to field a candidate. The Islamic Renaissance Movement, which advocated an Islamic state, was banned. Only the Erk Democratic Party, which split from Birlik in 1990, was permitted to field a candidate. Karimov won 86% of the popular vote. His opponent, Muhammad Salih, got 12.4%. In a separate referendum, 98.2% cast their votes in favor of

Uzbekistan

Gur-Emir Mausoleum, 15th century Samarkand

Uzbek independence. The following year, the Erk Democratic Party was also banned and Salih left Uzbekistan for Turkey to go into self-imposed exile.

Following independence, the government of Uzbekistan tolerated little political dissent. For instance, the government banned political demonstrations and religious-oriented political parties, and it arrested and imprisoned numerous members of the political opposition. The activities of Birlik were suspended in January 1993 and a number of its leaders were later arrested. Even the registered opposition party, Erk (Freedom), suffered tremendous harassment from the government, its newspaper shut and its bank accounts seized. Throughout the 1990s, the Karimov regime implied that without such harsh actions something something similar to the Tajikistan Civil War could break out in Uzbekistan.

Parliamentary elections took place in December 1994 under the terms of a new constitution that reduced the number of deputies from 500 to 250. The governing People's Democratic Party won 205 seats. Real oppositional political parties were not permitted to participate in the elections, but there was a second party, the National Progress Party, which was created by the government to represent business interests. It took six seats.

New presidential elections were scheduled to take place in 1996; instead, a referendum was held in March 1995 asking the people to approve an extension of the term of the president until the year 2000. This was supposed to put the elections for the presidency on the same schedule as that for the legislature.

President Karimov was elected to another five-year term in January 2000, winning with 91.9% of the vote. His only rival in the elections, Abdulhafiz Dzhalalov was personally selected by President Karimov as the alternate candidate in the election. Dzhalalov is head of the People's Democratic Party, which Karimov headed until 1996.

Having to run for reelection every five years apparently became burdensome to Karimov, however. In January 2002, he held a national referendum that extended the term of the presidency until December 2007.

President Karimov's second term of office came to an end in December 2007. Although, according to the constitution, he was ineligible to run for a third term, the Uzbek Election Commission approved his candidacy for a third term as president. The voting took place on December 23, 2007; there were three other candidates on the ballot. Since Uzbekistan had no actual opposition political parties, the candidates

were nominated by the various pro-government political parties. As an interesting aside, Dilorom Toshmuhamedova, nominated by the Party of Justice, became the first woman candidate to stand for the presidency. In the end, none of this mattered, however. Karimov easily won reelection to a third term, securing over 88% of the vote. Each of his little-known "opponents" secured only 3–4% of the vote each.

Uzbekistan and Militant Islamism

The secular political leadership of Uzbekistan has had an uneasy relationship with Islam since before independence. In the fall of 1991, before the Soviet Union collapsed, two religiously inspired activists, Tohir Yuldosh and Juma Khojiyev (later to be renamed Namangani), organized a series of rallies in the city of Namangan demanding that the local government respect Muslim traditions. Islam Karimov met with the leaders and placated their demands by promising to convert the city's Communist Party building into an Islamic center. This concession turned out to be temporary. However, in March 1992, Karimov ordered that the Islamic Center be shut down, and subsequently began repressing the activists. As a result of the repression, Yuldosh and Khojiyev fled to Tajikistan where they founded the Islamic Movement of Uzbekistan (IMU) which explicitly sought to overthrow the Karimov regime.

State-Islam relations worsened in December 1997 when several policemen were killed in the city of Namangan. Although no one claimed responsibility for the killings, the government blamed Islamic militants and launched a massive crackdown. It also enforced a 9:00 p.m. curfew in Namangan and the neighboring city of Andizhan. Following the crackdown, veiled women organized demonstrations before the presidential palace in Tashkent to protest the arrest and detention of their sons and husbands without charges. As one of the demonstrating women said of her husband, "there are no charges. He has a beard, so they accuse him of being a Wahhabi." At the time, the watchword was that the government routinely used the word Wahhabi as a catchall pejorative which it applied to all Islamic devotees.

Abid Khan Nazarov, a religious leader expelled in 1995 as the imam of an important mosque in Tashkent, said of the situation, "Government policy is becoming tougher and people are losing their tolerance. There is the danger that the situation will provoke the emergence of some terrorist group."

That may have happened on February 16, 1999, when a number of car bomb explosions rocked Tashkent with the apparent target being President Karimov. Karimov was uninjured, but 16 people were killed and another 80 were injured. The government immediately identified the IMU as the culprits and sealed the borders, however the details of the bombings remain sketchy to this date. Some critics have suggested that the bombings were more likely to have been orchestrated by some rival factions within the government itself.

Regardless of the truth of the bombings, the government efficiently used these events to instigate a further crackdown on who security forces dubbed religious extremists. A major trial took place in November 2000. Tohir Yuldosh and Juma Namangani were tried in absentia and sentenced to death. Ten others received various terms of imprisonment for their role in the bombings. Muhammad Solih, leader of the Erk party, was also tried in absentia and given a prison sentence.

The terrorist attacks of September 11 and the subsequent US-led War on Terrorism were used by the Karimov regime to justify its harsh repression of Islamic organizations. Uzbekistan, with memories of February 1999 fresh before it, became one of the first nations to throw its support behind the American-led War on Terrorism. On September 16, President Karimov offered the use of

Uzbek airspace and territory for an attack against Afghanistan and Foreign Minister Kamilov said that Uzbekistan was willing to discuss the stationing of United States troops in the country.

Uzbekistan's willingness to participate in a US military coalition surprised some people for Uzbekistan had rejected participating in any military alliances after becoming independent in 1991. However, it joined the US-led War on Terrorism because it was already carrying out a similar policy on its own. Collaborating with the US, thus served to legitimize statements made by the Uzbekistani regime regarding the existential threat of terrorism, and thereby its harsh societal crackdown. The Uzbek government knew, for example, that Juma Namangani, whom it held responsible for the February 1999 explosions, had been in Afghanistan for a number of years and had become a top officer in the Taliban militia. In the fall of 2001, he was the commander in charge of the pivotal northern city of Mazar-i-Sharif and had under him a force of 14,000 soldiers, including Arab, Tajik, Uzbek, and other foreign mercenaries and volunteers.

Namangani had served in Afghanistan 14 years earlier as an 18-year-old conscript in the Soviet military. After his service, he returned to his native city of Namangan and founded the Islamic Movement of Uzbekistan (IMU). The goal of the IMU was the formation of an Islamic state uniting the Muslims of Central Asia; from the beginning, the organization ignored the boundaries of existing states and recruited

At Uzbekistan Restaurant in Tashkent, chef Bikhadyr Iskhakov prepares a traditional Uzbek dish—*lagman,* **pasta with mutton** Courtesy of NOVOSTI

members throughout the region. In 1999, armed bands of IMU guerrillas launched attacks from Afghanistan into Tajikistan, Kyrgyzstan, and Uzbekistan. Their target was the fertile Fergana River Valley, the most densely populated area of Central Asia. When the 1999 attacks failed, they were launched again in 2000, this time with the purpose of setting up guerrilla camps in the mountains northeast of Tashkent. They made their way into the mountains, but were eventually driven out.

The American invasion of Afghanistan in the fall of 2001 ended the IMU's safe haven in Afghanistan and led to the death of Namangani himself. Yet Namangani had engendered such fear in Central Asia that Uzbekistan had closed its border with Afghanistan and did not reopen the Friendship Bridge connecting the two countries until December 2001, after it was absolutely certain that Namangani had been killed during the fighting that led up to the fall of Mazar-i-Sharif.

The IMU survived Namangani's death, but his death left the organization without a charismatic military leader. The Uzbek government thus began to focus on the Hizb ut-Tahrir, a banned Islamic extremist party committed to uniting all Central Asian Muslims in a single Islamic state by political means, as the new threat to governmental stability.

A series of bombings and attacks that extended from March 28 to April 1, 2004, and included the first known suicide bombings in Uzbekistan were believed to have been organized by Islamic militants. The first of the attacks killed 10 persons in the province of Bukhara; the next morning, female suicide bombers blew themselves up in a children's store in central Tashkent and at a nearby bus stop. As the attacks continued over the next days, the government reported that at least 47 persons had been killed, including 10 policemen and 33 militants, 7 of them women.

Four months later, on July 30, three suicide bombers blew themselves up outside the Israeli and American Embassies and at the headquarters of the Uzbek chief prosecutor. In this second case, it was eventually established that all three of the bombers were from Kazakhstan.

As the government began rounding up suspected militants, it first laid the blame on Hizb ut-Tahrir (which denied any involvement), but it then appeared that the attacks had been organized by a resurgent Islamic Movement of Uzbekistan. In fact, it is still not clear who organized and carried out the attacks. Although the government subsequently rounded up numerous suspected militants, it was already holding up to 7,000 Muslims in jail for their religious or political beliefs prior to these attacks.

Uzbekistan

Responding to the advice of the US State Department that democracy is the best cure for terrorism and the best response to the attacks would be to open up society, Uzbek Foreign Minister Sodik Saforev agreed that

more civil society, more democracy, is one of the best ways to secure profound stability and, let's say, public accord in society.

But, he then added,

We believe that what happened in Uzbekistan is part of a global activation of terrorism. We believe that its aim is to sow chaos and systematic instability.

In May 2005, violence again broke out in Uzbekistan. For several months, demonstrators had gathered outside of the courthouse in Andijon demanding the release of 23 businessmen who had organized a private charity inspired by Islamic teachings. The businessmen had been arrested and charged with membership in an extremist group named "Akramiya." By all accounts, this organization did not exist; the businessmen seem to have been arrested because their private charity threatened local power structures. In May, a group of armed men stormed the prison and released the prisoners. The prison break drew even more demonstrators to the square, most of whom were unarmed.

In response, the Uzbek government sent in soldiers with tanks who fired on the demonstrators, resulting in the deaths of several hundred individuals. The security services attempted to close off the city in an effort to round up as many demonstrators as possible. Despite their efforts, many demonstrators fled to neighboring Kyrgyzstan.

Andijon, a city of about 300,000 inhabitants located in the Fergana Valley, is in a region that has experienced worsening economic problems for a number of years, and it was the scene of at least one other demonstration in September 2004. That demonstration, which lasted several days, was set off after the authorities issued new regulations requiring bazaar sellers who sold imported goods to undergo individual registration. The bazaar sellers, many of whom were women, complained that the new regulations would increase costs to them and require them to raise their prices. Andijon's individual merchants failed to get the regulations withdrawn, however, and nearly 3,000 were left without any work at all. Thus, although the government blamed the May 2005 events on religious extremism, it appears that economic motivations played a more important role.

Students at Alisher Navoi University in Samarkand listen to a lecturer
Courtesy of NOVOSTI

In the actual trials, which took place in November 2005, the defendants all pleaded guilty to the charges and were given prison sentences ranging from 14 to 20 years. One month later, the government organized a second trial of local Uzbek officials—policemen, prison guards, soldiers, and medics—who were put on trial for dereliction of duty and negligence in connection with the May 2005 violence. There was also a third trial of 768 individuals charged with direct involvement in the violence. Unlike the first public trial, these trials have taken place behind closed doors. In addition, numerous Uzbek political and rights activists were arrested and detained by the government after the events of May 2005.

Post-Andijon Developments under Karimov

The Uzbek government also moved against foreign non-governmental organizations (NGOs) operating in the country. In June 2006, Uzbek courts ordered the closure of the American Council for Collaboration in Education and Language Study (ACCELS) for numerous violations of Uzbek law. The chief accusation was that ACCELS had sent more than 100 Uzbek students to study in the United States without informing the Uzbek government. In July, the courts closed the offices of Winrock International, a US-based agricultural NGO. Winrock's crime was

that it had financed a publication entitled "Islam and Women," which was found to denigrate national values. In August, the courts closed the Massachusetts-based NGO Partnership in Academics and Development (PAD) for proselytizing among Uzbeks. PAD had been charged with engaging in unlawful missionary activity, offering Internet access without a license, and other "violations."

There was one important exception to this general picture, however. In October 2006, the Tashkent city courts ruled in favor of two US-funded NGOs—the Cooperative Housing Foundation International and Mercy Corps—that had been charged with violating Uzbek law. These verdicts were unusual, however. Virtually all Western-funded NGOs had been forced to close by the end of 2006.

In November 2006, the Uzbek government created a special fund to control and manage foreign financial assistance to the country's media outlets. Foreign states and organizations have since been forbidden to provide grants directly to Uzbek media.

In January 2008, President Karimov issued a decree abolishing capital punishment in Uzbekistan. Particularly brutal murders and acts of terrorism will be punished by lifetime imprisonment. In the next several months, the government also released a number of human rights advocates from prison and granted the International Committee of the Red Cross permission to visit Uzbek prisons.

Sabrina Tavernise, in a May 2008 article written for the *New York Times*, characterized the situation in Uzbekistan as follows:

Uzbeks have become poorer, less educated and more isolated in the 17 years since the Soviet Union collapsed. At the same time, the most religious parts of society have been brutalized by the government.

After 2008, the economic situation in Uzbekistan increasingly began to reflect the worldwide economic downturn as hundreds of thousands of migrants working in Russia and Kazakhstan were forced home from abroad. Remittances from abroad, which had been approximately $2 billion for the first half of 2008, plunged as much as 90% toward the end of the year. Domestically, Uzbekistan's sole automaker, Uz-Daewoo, announced that its auto sales to Russia and other members of the CIS from its Asaka car plant in Andijon had plunged by 85% in the first two months of 2009. Uzbekistan's currency, the som, also came under international pressure, but the government, which maintains an official rate of soms to the dollar, instituted new controls on foreign currencies in an attempt to maintain the som's official value. The black market rate grew, however, and was running at about 1,700–1,750 soms to the dollar in 2009. As a result the government raised the official rate to 1,466.7 soms to the dollar in 2009; it then raised it to 1,588 soms to the dollar in 2010.

In 2010, the problem of alleged jihadist groups once again became a focus of government action. Throughout the country, there were several trials involving purported members of a new Islamic group called "Jihadists." In one case, 13 people were sentenced to between 6 and 10 years in prison for their alleged membership in "Jihadists." According to local and international rights groups, more than 10,000 practicing Muslims were serving long prison sentences, most on charges of attempting to overthrow the constitutional order and install a theocracy.

In that same vein, Human Rights Watch (HRW) was forced to close its office in Tashkent in March 2011; HRW had been operating in the country for 15 years. HRW's Tashkent director, Steve Swerdlow, had actually had his accreditation lifted in December 2010. "With the expulsion of Human Rights Watch," the organization said in announcing its expulsion, "the Uzbek government sends a clear message that it isn't willing to tolerate critical scrutiny of its human rights record."

President Karimov turned 73 in January 2011. Anticipating the need for a successor-in-waiting, Karimov proposed a series of constitutional amendments that would reduce the power of the presidency in favor of the office of prime minister and set up a new line of succession. Previously, the constitution called for parliament to select a successor in the event the president could not serve. Under the new provisions, the Chairman of the Senate would succeed to the presidency if the incumbent died or was unable to serve. The lower house of parliament approved the constitutional changes in March 2011. Senate action followed shortly afterward.

In June 2011, there were reports coming out of the Shanghai Cooperation Organization of a meeting between President Dmitry Medvedev and President Karimov. According to the reports, Medvedev advised Karimov to prepare for a "peaceful transfer of power," presumably by leaving office voluntarily.

Instead, the Uzbekistani parliament passed legislation in December 2011 reducing the presidential term of office from seven to five years. This change permitted Karimov to claim the right to serve two additional terms in office.

Uzbekistan held multi-candidate elections in 2014 and 2015, but the prospects for internal political reform are virtually nil, because any opposition political parties and independent candidates had no chance to participate. Two rounds of

parliamentary elections were held in late December 2014 and early January 2015. Only four parties that strongly supported President Islam Karimov and a small "green" party fielded candidates.

In March 2015, Karimov was reelected to a five-year term. According to the official results, he received 90% of the vote from 91% of eligible voters. The voters really had no choice in the election. Karimov's three "opponents" in fact were members of pro-government parties, who praised Karimov's policies during the campaign.

Meet the New Boss, Same as the Old Boss?

In late August 2016, rumors began to spread out of Tashkent that Karimov had been hospitalized. Likely because Karimov would not be able to attend the upcoming independence day celebrations on September 1, which always centered on a speech by the president, his daughter, Lola Karimova-Tillyaeva, confirmed that he had been hospitalized with a brain hemorrhage but insisted that he was recuperating. On August 29, ferghana.ru, a Moscow-based independent Internet news organization reported that Karimov had died. These reports were not addressed by the government which only admitted that Karimov was critically ill on September 2. Later that same day, anonymous diplomatic sources reported to Reuters that Karimov had died, and the Turkish Prime Minister Binali Yildirim announced his death in a televised meeting with his cabinet. At this point, the Uzbekistani government confirmed the death of the president, although with a modified timeline of his demise.

What explains the reluctance to confirm Karimov's death? In all likelihood, it boils down to the problem of transition.

Succession is an uncertain process in all authoritarian regimes, and is especially fraught for those regimes which have never before established a precedent for how the power of the executive is passed on. The delaying tactics in Uzbekistan permitted well-placed elites to privately arrange the transition to a new leader without involving the public. During this silent period, Rustam Azimov, the finance minister and possible succession candidate, was rumored to have been held in house arrest by forces close to then-Prime Minister Shavkat Mirziyoyev. Another wrinkle that likely contributed to the delayed announcement are the mass festivities that mark the country's independence day celebrations. It was likely feared that mass gatherings could become politicized had the announcement of Karimov's death preceded the independence day celebrations.

Following the announcement of Karimov's death, 59-year-old Mirziyoyev was announced as the interim president disregarding the Constitutional stipulation that Chairman of the Senate, Nigmatilla Yuldashev, was to serve in a caretaker role until new elections are called should a president be unable to complete his/her term. After serving as Hakim (governor) of two regions, Jizzakh and Samarkand, Mirziyoyev was elevated to position of Prime Minister in 2003. Although he had never been named as Karimov's official successor, his incredibly long tenure as Prime Minister and connections to Karimov's support base in Jizzakh and Samarkand, positioned him at the top of the succession pyramid. Despite his position, he was not that well-known to many citizens; according to US diplomatic cables released by WikiLeaks, as Prime Minister Mirziyoyev "instructed the state-controlled media to never show him on TV"

Women doing gold embroidery—a traditional art form—at factory in Bukhara
Courtesy of Hermine Dreyfuss

Uzbekistan

likely because he did not want Karimov to fear that he was likely to launch a palace coup. His low profile didn't harm him in the first post-Karimov presidential election, held on December 4, 2016. In that election, Mirziyoyev officially received 88.6% of the vote. Without a doubt, this percentage was carefully chosen, as it represents both overwhelming support for the incumbent, while still respectful of Karimov's position as the first president as it is slightly less than Karimov received in his last election.

The consolidation of power around Mirziyoyev signals the end of the family drama that surrounded the rise and fall of Islam Karimov's eldest daughter Gulnara. Over the past decade and a half, her fortunes resembled a soap opera. For much of that period, as her influence grew, Gulnara presented herself as a cosmopolitan celebrity and businessperson, releasing pop-music albums, partaking in international fashion shows, and cutting business deals in Tashkent. For a number of years, observers expected her to succeed her father, however, her ruthless reputation eroded elite and mass support. One US diplomatic cable released by WikiLeaks described her as "the most hated person" in the country. Within a few years, her involvement in a series of global money laundering and bribery investigations led to her being placed under house arrest in 2014. As a result of her confinement, the once ubiquitous socialite was even unable to attend her father's funeral in September 2016. In March of 2019, she was imprisoned for violating the terms of her house arrest.

Since assuming the presidency, Mirziyoyev has initiated a surprising degree of reform aimed at opening up Uzbekistan economy and normalizing relations with its neighbors. This is clearest in the foreign policy arena where he has taken steps to improve ties between

Former President Islam Karimov

Uzbekistan and its neighbors. Uzbekistan watchers were initially clued into the fact that times had changed when flights were resumed between Tashkent and Dushanbe, Tajikistan in early 2017 after a 25-year gap. In March 2018, largely at the behest of Mirziyoyev, a summit between four Central Asian leaders occurred in Astana (only Turkmen President Gurbanguly Berdymukhammedov was missing). At the meeting, the presidents stated their commitment to regional trade and cooperation on water resources. The most notable aspect of the summit is the fact that it occurred at all; it had been a decade since the last similar meeting. Promisingly, according to Kazakh President Nursultan Nazarbayev, the leaders agreed to meet annually in the spring before Navruz (Persian New Year). This has led to the initiation of flights between Tashkent and Dushanbe, Tajikistan for the first time in a quarter century.

Domestically, he has released a handful of long-serving prominent political prisoners, including Rustam Usmanov, the founder of the country's first private bank and a supporter of government opposition, after serving 19 years on trumped-up charges. Still much of the harsh security apparatus remains in place, and it is unlikely that more space for opposition candidates is forthcoming. Promised reforms to the feared National Security Service (SNB), independent Uzbekistan's successor to the KGB, have been somewhat delayed. However, in 2018, he removed the longtime head of the organization, Rustam Inoyatov, who had presided over the SNB for nearly 23 years. While Inoyatov's removal may be simply a result of Mirziyoyev's continued consolidation of power, it may also signal an intention to check the autonomy of the SNB.

Miziyoyev has also acknowledged the widespread problem of rural poverty in the country and has encouraged subsistence farming as part of the solution. One aspect of this approach which has been widely criticized is his pro-chicken policy, whereby all rural households have been encouraged to raise around 100 chickens for personal consumption as well as for profit off of selling eggs. Some reports have indicated that to initiate this policy, some part of the salary of state employees has been paid in live poultry. If true, these reports underscore the degree to which Uzbekistan's economy retains command-type elements.

Despite this qualification, some significant economic reforms have occurred. In September 2017, the government began the process of making the currency, the som, fully convertible. As a result, foreign investors are able to change local currency into foreign banknotes, incentivizing

investment and trade. Furthermore, significant steps have been taken to reform the massive cotton cultivation system and eradicate forced and child labor. In all, although one should be skeptical of talk of an "Uzbek Spring," significant reforms have occurred since the fall 2016 which have reintroduced Uzbekistan to the global system.

In February 2019, electoral reforms expanded the franchise to ex-felons and established gender quotas in the legislature. The impact of these reforms are of course limited by the lack of true democratic choice in the country. On October 24, 2021, Uzbekistan held a presidential election, which Shavkat Mirziyoyev won by a landslide, garnering 80% of the votes. Unlike in previous election, this time the incumbent candidate won by 5% less. To international election observers, it was hardly an indication of freeer and fairer elections. In fact, they faulted the process for lacking genuine opposition and pointed to numerous violations on election day.

Foreign Policy

Russia and the CIS. Uzbekistan has been a member of the Commonwealth of Independent States since it came into being and it was a founding member, along with Kazakhstan and Kyrgyzstan, of the Central Asian Customs Union. Although it continues to attend CIS meetings, Uzbekistan has been reluctant to enter into CIS agreements, and particularly economic agreements such as Russia's proposed free trade zone within the CIS.

Until recently, in fact, Uzbekistan has not placed great emphasis on the foreign affairs area, choosing instead to concentrate on domestic affairs. As an exception, it has worked to develop stronger ties with Turkey and it has maintained reasonably good relations with its Central Asian neighbors.

President Karimov's particular fear has been that Russia could continue to dominate the various Central Asian republics. For that reason, Uzbekistan placed a greater emphasis on building up its military forces than any other Central Asian republic. In addition, Uzbekistan—alone among the Central Asian Republics—never permitted Russian border guards to be stationed on its soil. On the other hand, Uzbekistan was always careful to maintain friendly relations with Russia, and even cooperated with the Russian government on occasion. In June 2000, in fact, Uzbekistan signed new military cooperation agreements that specifically spelled out additional areas of Russian–Uzbek military cooperation. One of those agreements allowed Uzbekistan to use Russian weapons testing facilities. It was

Uzbekistan

also announced at this time that further military agreements were being drafted on the training of Uzbek military personnel in Russia, the repair of all Uzbek military equipment in Russia, and the establishment of a joint venture to manufacture explosives.

A further Uzbek–Russian strategic partnership treaty, signed in June 2004, placed its emphasis on increased military cooperation, but also made reference to increased cooperation in the political, economic, and commercial spheres. In addition, Uzbekistan agreed to purchase military hardware from Russia, while Russia offered to train Uzbek officers in their use and maintenance.

Uzbek-Russian commercial ties were enhanced when LUKoil, a privately-owned Russian oil company, signed a 35-year production sharing agreement with Uzbekneftegas PSA to develop the Kandym natural gas field. Under the terms of the agreement, LUKoil agreed to provide 90% of the $1 billion investment cost of the projects. In addition, Gazprom, Russia's state-run natural gas monopoly, which negotiated an agreement to purchase the gas produced by the new consortium, committed itself to invest a further $1 billion in Uzbekistan to develop gas-condensate fields in the Ustyurt region.

As part of this realignment, Uzbekistan also reversed its earlier policy of holding Russia at arm's length. In September 2005, Russian Defense Minister Sergei Ivanov visited Uzbekistan to observe the first ever joint Russian–Uzbek military exercises. In November, Uzbekistan and Russia signed a bilateral treaty providing for long-term cooperation in trade and security. The treaty called for defense cooperation and intelligence sharing, mutual use of military facilities, and cooperation in battling terrorism and drug trafficking. In speaking about the treaty, President Karimov said that the "consolidation of Russia's presence in Central Asia would be a reliable guarantee of peace and stability in the region."

In December 2006, this cooperation was carried a step further when Uzbekistan and Russia signed a new agreement providing Russian forces with basing rights at the Navoi military airfield in Uzbekistan. The agreement gave Russia the right to deploy fighter jets and bombers at the airfield; in return, Russia agreed to upgrade the airfield's navigation systems and to provide "air-defense weaponry."

Karimov also visited China in the aftermath of Andijon, and here he heard unequivocal support for the Uzbek version of events. While there, he signed a $600 million oil joint venture with China.

In August 2006, Uzbekistan rejoined the Collective Security Treaty

View of the city of Khiva, Uzbekistan

Organization (CSTO), which it quit in 1999. CSTO—whose membership includes Russia, Armenia, Belarus, Kazakhstan, Kyrgyzstan, and Tajikistan—promotes military and political cooperation aimed at ensuring the collective security of its member states. A largely symbolic organization, its chief activity is to hold periodic antiterrorism exercises. In June 2012, The Uzbek government announced that it had again suspended its membership in the CSTO; its reason is that the CSTO ignored Uzbekistan and did not consider its views.

In February 2009, the Uzbek government announced that it had reached an agreement with Turkmenistan under which the two countries would permit non-military freight to cross their territories to Afghanistan. This appeared to be part of a new effort by Uzbekistan to improve its relations with its immediate neighbors. The Uzbek government announced at about the same time that it would cooperate in construction of the Rogun hydroelectric power station in Tajikistan and the Kambarat station in Kyrgyzstan, requiring only that an impartial international audit be made to ensure that Uzbekistan would not lose water supplies.

Relations have not proceeded smoothly, however. In December 2009, Uzbekistan left a regional power grid, further deepening energy shortages in Tajikistan and Kyrgyzstan. Two months later, in February 2010, the Uzbek prime minister wrote to the Tajik prime minister warning about the "potential damage" which might result from completion of the Rogun hydroelectric power station. "In a region facing water shortages and prone to earthquakes," he wrote, Rogun could bring "catastrophic consequences." Uzbekistan's real fear, of course, is that Tajikistan's (and Kyrgyzstan's) efforts to

develop their hydroelectric power potential to meet winter energy supply needs will result in summer water shortages and possible other ecological threats in Uzbekistan. That will possibly be the case; yet, Uzbekistan's withdrawal from the regional power grid only increases the pressure the Tajik and Kyrgyz governments feel from their own citizens to develop their hydroelectric power potential.

United States, NATO, and the EU. Relations with the United States, correct but not cordial, improved somewhat in 1999 when the two countries negotiated an agreement providing for American aid in dismantling and decontaminating a large chemical weapons testing facility located at Nukus, Uzbekistan. The United States also negotiated a separate agreement with Uzbekistan and Kazakhstan concerning a site on Vozrozhdeniya Island, in the middle of the Aral Sea, where the Soviet Union dumped hundreds of tons of anthrax bacteria in the spring of 1988. Tests performed by American military laboratories have established that the dump still contains live anthrax bacteria and is potentially extremely dangerous. This led to an "implementing arrangement with Uzbekistan," signed on October 22, 2001, under which the United States "agreed to provide technical assistance" and help pay for the removal of thousands of tons of anthrax spores dumped on Vozrozhdeniya Island.

However, the real change in US–Uzbek relations came after the terrorist attacks against the United States of September 11, 2001, when Uzbekistan became one of the first nations to sign on to the subsequent United States–led War on Terrorism. It was also among the first to open its airspace for use by US military planes.

Uzbekistan

The next several months were a heady time for US–Uzbek relations. During a meeting between President Karimov and Defense Secretary Donald Rumsfeld on October 5, Karimov gave formal approval for the use of an Uzbek military airfield and Rumsfeld provided assurances that America would protect Uzbekistan's security. Less than a week later, nearly 1,000 US troops from the Army's 10th Mountain Division were on the ground at the Hanabad air base in southern Uzbekistan.

On October 30, General Tommy Franks, commander of the military campaign against Afghanistan, visited Tashkent and met with President Karimov, plus the Uzbek defense and foreign ministers. Five days later, Defense Secretary Rumsfeld was back in Tashkent for another meeting with President Karimov. Secretary of State Colin Powell came a month later, on December 9. It was after meeting with Powell that Karimov announced the opening of the Friendship Bridge between Uzbekistan and Afghanistan.

After that, Tashkent seemingly played host to a high-level American delegation every few days. In January, a delegation of nine US Senators was followed five days later by a five-person delegation from the House of Representatives, led by Congressman Jim Kolbe. It was Kolbe who announced that the United States had awarded Uzbekistan $100 million in economic and humanitarian assistance. On January 18, another Senatorial delegation headed by Majority Leader Tom Daschle arrived in Tashkent and, like the two previous delegations, met with President Karimov.

On January 22, General Franks arrived back in Tashkent. Franks' visit was marked by a further formalization of the military cooperation between the two nations, including a plan of military visits and exchanges through the remainder of 2002. A day later, Elizabeth Jones, assistant secretary of state for European and Eurasian affairs, arrived in Tashkent for a discussion of future US–Uzbek relations. Next, General Richard Myers, chairman of the US Joint Chiefs of Staff, came to Tashkent to meet with President Karimov, followed by a US Congressional delegation led by Congressman Dave Hobson.

President Karimov then made a four-day trip to the United States in March 2002 where he met with President George W. Bush and other US government officials. The tenor in the relationship at this time can best be summed up by two actions of Secretary Powell on March 12, the same day that President Karimov was meeting with President Bush. Testifying at a congressional hearing, Secretary Powell said that "Karimov has been a solid coalition partner;" but then added, "at the same time, there are problems with respect to human rights in Uzbekistan, and we will not shrink from discussing them." That afternoon, Secretary Powell and his counterpart, Uzbek Foreign Minister Abdulaziz Komilov, signed a five-point "Strategic Partner" agreement that spelled out cooperation in the military, political, legal, humanitarian, and economic areas, plus cooperation against nuclear proliferation.

The decision of the Uzbek government to support US policy in Iraq cemented the relationship even further, especially after

A metro station in Tashkent

Courtesy of NOVOSTI

336

Uzbekistan

President Karimov declared his firm support of the US position in Iraq in March 2003 at the same time that Russia was threatening to veto a United Nations Security Council resolution supporting a military invasion of Iraq. President Karimov even went so far as to characterize an invasion of Iraq as a continuation of the antiterrorist campaign that began in Afghanistan. A month later, when a session of the US–Uzbekistan Security Cooperation Council was held in Washington, the American representatives announced the willingness of the United States to expand defense and military cooperation with Uzbekistan.

The issues of human rights and democratic reform were not dead, however. In July 2004, the US State Department announced that Uzbekistan would be denied $18 million in aid because of a "lack of progress on democratic reform." However, US diplomats afterward tried to cushion the blow by stressing that, while the United States intended to continue to offer Uzbekistan "advice and assistance" in implementing democratic reforms, the United States Government considered that it was a separate issue from that of cooperation in combating international terrorism. A US delegation headed by Lincoln Bloomfield, Assistant Secretary of State for Political and Military Affairs, and Andy Hoehn, Deputy Assistant Secretary of Defense, did visit Tashkent in October 2004 and, after discussing bilateral military cooperation in a series of high level meetings, met with President Karimov.

Uzbekistan had expanded its international relations in other areas as well during this period. In March 2002, the chief of staff of the Turkish armed forces visited Tashkent to discuss bilateral military cooperation. He brought also an offer of $1.2 million in military assistance to Uzbekistan. A few days later, NATO Deputy Secretary-General Daniel Speckhard arrived in Tashkent to meet with Defense Minister Kadyr Gulyamov. The message he brought was that NATO was ready to help Uzbekistan reorganize its military forces. In addition, he brought a NATO offer of 70 research grants to be awarded to Uzbek scientists. In April 2003, NATO held civil-emergency exercises in the Uzbek part of the Fergana Valley. Fourteen countries took part in the exercises. Uzbekistan reciprocated with a promise of full support in logistics, medical assistance, and humanitarian operations to NATO in its operations in Afghanistan.

President Karimov also welcomed German Chancellor Gerhard Schroeder to Tashkent in May 2002; he then paid a three-day visit to Japan in July, meeting with Prime Minister Junichiro Koizumi and being received by Emperor Akihito. A total of 14 documents were signed during

President Shavkat Mirziyoyev

the visit, including a joint declaration of friendship, cooperation, and strategic partnership. Three months later, Karimov welcomed Aleksander Kwasniewski, President of Poland, to Uzbekistan. The two presidents discussed, among other things, bilateral military cooperation to combat terrorism. President Karimov then paid a three-day visit to Spain in January 2003. Although the main purpose of the visit was to boost trade and attract Spanish investment in Uzbekistan, the discussions also covered political and economic cooperation as well as the war against international terrorism and drug trafficking.

Up to this time, the world emphasis on fighting terrorism meant that Uzbekistan was benefiting politically from the new relationships that developed after September 2001. Then the first of the Color Revolutions took place in Georgia in November 2003, followed by the Color Revolutions in Ukraine, and Kyrgyzstan in 2004 and 2005. The switch in emphasis from terrorism to democracy which these Color Revolutions represented led the top Uzbek leadership to question whether it was possible to cooperate with western nations over terrorism without encouraging the growth of similar democratic movements locally.

When the United States and the various member countries of the European Union called on an international investigation of the events of May 2005 and its aftermath, the Uzbek government rejected this approach as interference in its domestic affairs. Even before this time, however, the Uzbek government leadership had decided that democracy was a greater threat to the regime than terrorism, and that the contamination was coming from the west. The government accordingly began to reverse its policies of the previous three or so years and to return to its earlier policy of isolation.

The European Union's imposition of sanctions against Uzbekistan in November 2005—which included an embargo on arms and equipment which could be used for internal repression and a ban on travel by officials directly involved in the Andijon crackdown—only reinforced this policy.

Because the United States Government was also critical of Uzbekistan's handling of the events of May 2005, the continuing presence of US military forces in Uzbekistan became another irritant. In June 2005, the Uzbek government responded by placing new restrictions on United States government use of the Karshi-Khanabad air base, which the United States had been using to support its forces in Afghanistan; one month later, it gave the United States government a deadline of six months to get out entirely. It also quietly terminated most other forms of cooperation with the United States government, including counterterrorism and international cultural exchanges. In general, it applied the same new policy to the members of the European Union as well. As part of this new policy, the government also expelled most international organizations that had been active in Uzbekistan up to this time. These included Freedom House, the Eurasia Foundation, Internews, the BBC, RFE/RL, and the Soros Foundation's Open Society Institute. In March 2006, the UN High Commissioner for Refugees was told that it had to leave Uzbekistan within a month.

In early 2008, the Government of Uzbekistan apparently shifted gears once again. The reason for the shift appears to be Uzbekistan's concern that Afghanistan might once again become a security issue for Uzbekistan. The first sign of this change came in January 2008 when President Karimov welcomed Admiral William Fallon, head of the US Central Command, to Tashkent. The conversations between the two men included "issues of terrorism, illegal drug trafficking, organized crime, the fight against proliferation of weapons of mass destruction, as well as issues of securing stability in the region," according to an official statement from President Karimov's office. Two months later, the Uzbek government decided to renew limited NATO access to a military base near the city of Termez, which had been largely used by German troops to supply NATO troops in Afghanistan. No US troops would be stationed there, but they could use it en route to and from Afghanistan

One month later, President Karimov attended the NATO summit meeting in Bucharest, Romania. Addressing the NATO meeting, President Karimov praised "NATO's progressive transformation into a political structure" which he

Uzbekistan

said provided an "impetus to the further development and strengthening of Euro-Atlantic partnership." He also called for bolstering efforts to stabilize Afghanistan, "still a locus of threat to the world community." Reflecting that new viewpoint, Uzbekistan signed a treaty with NATO in 2009 essentially giving that organization permission to ship non-lethal equipment through Uzbekistan to NATO-led forces in Afghanistan.

In January 2011, President Karimov paid a visit to Brussels where he met with top-level NATO and European Union officials. During the visit, he signed a number of agreements, including one allowing the European Union to establish an office in Uzbekistan. The statement made by EU Commission President Jose Manuel Barroso after his meeting with President Karimov probably best sums up European Union (and United States) current relations with Uzbekistan:

The European Union follows a policy of critical, conditional, and comprehensive engagement with Uzbekistan. I have raised all key concerns of Europe, notably regarding human rights and fundamental freedoms. I believe it is through such a robust eye-to-eye dialogue—and not an empty-chair policy—that we can further the EU's unanimously agreed policy of engagement most effectively.

In May 2018, Uzbekistan's reentry into global politics achieved a significant milestone when President Mirziyoyev was welcomed to the White House to hold bilateral talks with President Donald Trump. This was the first invitation for Uzbekistan's head of state since the 2002, three years before the Andijon massacre. The meeting was intended to shore-up relations between the two countries, but for Uzbekistan, it also provided the opportunity to sign contracts and work out business deals to further consolidate the economic reforms taking place domestically.

The warming relations continued in 2020, when U.S. Secretary of State Mike Pompeo visited Tashkent, and praised the country's "progress on human rights issues." While in Uzbekistan, he also revealed that US planned to send Uzbekistan $2 million in assistance to bolster its financial reforms, and trade networks. This sum is dwarfed by the hefty investments made in recent years by China and Russia, indicating that although relations between the U.S. and Uzbekistan have normalized, the country is not a priority in Washington.

China. Uzbekistan's relations with China were minimal until China began seeking other sources for the increasing amounts of energy it was consuming. Uzbekistan had natural gas to sell, but no way to get it to China. In May 2007, the two countries agreed to construct a 530-kilometer natural gas pipeline connecting Uzbekistan's gas fields with China. China signed a similar agreement with Turkmenistan at the same time.

Since that time, while Uzbekistan was becoming a major supplier of natural gas to China, general trade between the two countries was growing as well. In 2012, China took 21.2% of Uzbekistan's exports, making China Uzbekistan's largest export market. By way of comparison, Russia, Uzbekistan's second most important export market, took only 14.7% of Uzbekistan's exports. China also furnished 16.6% of Uzbekistan's imports in 2012, though that put it second to Russia, the source of 20.7% of Uzbekistan's imports.

Nature of the Regime

Uzbekistan has a presidential-parliamentary system similar to those found in the other ex-Soviet republics. However, until his death in September 2016 the system was totally dominated by President Karimov since independence. At first, Karimov ruled through the Uzbek Communist Party, merely changing its name to the People's Democratic Party. In 1996, then, Karimov resigned as leader of the People's Democratic Party and began creating a facade of political pluralism. As a result, five political parties entered the Oliy Majlis (parliament). None of these were true opposition parties, however, for all five political parties were created at the initiative of President Karimov. Despite some signals of some minor reforms, there is little to indicate that anything fundamental about the regime has changed since the election of Shavkat Mirziyoyev to president on December 4, 2016. Although some political prisoners have been released and the media has been granted some more freedoms, the political system remains centralized and autocratic.

The office of prime minister is responsible for the day-to-day operations of the government. The current prime minister is Abdulla Aripov, appointed on December 14, 2016.

In December 2004, a new upper house or Senate was set up, consisting of 100 members. Sixteen of the senators are appointed by the President while the remaining 84 are indirectly elected at joint meetings of region, district, and city assemblies from among the members of those bodies. Six senators were elected from each of the country's 12 regions plus Karakalpakistan and the city of Tashkent.

The lower house, called the Legislative Chamber, has 150 members. Following electoral reforms in 2019, all seats are directly elected. In the most recent elections, five parties competed for votes and each won seats. While this pluralism may resemble appear to be democratic, all five competing parties declared their loyalty to president. The president's party, the Uzbekistan Liberal Democratic Party, received a plurality of seats (53 out 150); however, given the inability of an opposition party to compete in the election, the post-electoral coalition formation in Uzbekistan lacks the drama that can be found in other settings.

Culture

Uzbeks have a rich cultural legacy. In rural areas, traditionally men wear a robe, sometimes monochromatic and sometimes striped, and an embroidered skullcap. Women traditionally wear bright silk dresses with a shawl over the head. Rugs cover the floors of Uzbek houses and often folk art decorates the walls. There are also traditional Uzbek festivals in various times of the year when the people dress up in their finery and there is singing and dancing. Another specialty of the festivals is horse dancing. This is also the time for games and tests of strength, dexterity, and skill. And, of course, food plays a role. Some of the distinctive foods include *d'ighman* (meat with pastry in a strong broth), spicy chopped meat wrapped in a thin dough, and *plov* (rice with meat, vegetables, spices, and dried apricots).

Uzbeks are Sunni Muslims of the Hanafi School. Sufism is also practiced by some, and there is a famous Sufi School, the Naqshbandi or *tariqat-al-Khwajagan*, in Bukhara.

The government is deeply cautious of independent Islam. It regularly monitors mosques and harasses young men with beards. According to the United States Commission on International Religious Freedom (USCIRF), Uzbekistan has imprisoned as many as 12,000 Muslims who did not conform to state-sanctioned religious practices. Most of those arrested were labeled "extremists" or "terrorists." Due to its harsh repression of independent Islam, USCIRF has designated Uzbekistan a tier 1 country, indicating that its practices are "of particular concern."

The country is home to some of the world's greatest architectural treasures. Two of the most famous silk road cities are found within its borders—Samarkand and Bukhara. The former city was the capital of the Timuride Empire and hosts Amir Temur's mausoleum (Gur-e Amir), the Registan—an ancient madrasah complex—and the Bibi-Khanym Mosque. The latter city was an intellectual center of the Samanid dynasty and remains a pilgrimage destination.

Uzbekistan has produced a number of writers in the 20th century. Perhaps the best known is Abdullah Qadiri, famous for two historical novels, *Days Gone By* and *Scorpion from the Pulpit*, published in the 1920s. Qadiri was later killed in the Soviet purges of the late 1930s. The novel *Sisters*, by Asqad Mukhtar, has been translated into English. Uzbeks have also made some original contributions in modern graphic arts. Some of the ancient skills such as ornamental wall painting, wood carving and fabric printing have also been kept alive. There is an Uzbek film studio where films in the Uzbeki language are made, and the republic also has its own radio and television facilities. The Navoi Theater of Opera and Ballet in Tashkent is also famous for its productions. The country is also home to one of the most surprising art collections in the world, housed at the Savitsky Museum in Nukus. For decades, Igor Savitsky, a Russian painter and archeologist, collected and stored Soviet avant-garde artwork proscribed under the Soviet Union. Nukus' remote location enabled him to escape the attention of the Soviet authorities. The amazing story of this museum and a discussion of its contemporary struggles is told in the documentary film *The Desert of Forbidden Art*.

Economy

Uzbekistan has what is traditionally referred to as a commercial single-crop agricultural economy. What this means is that the republic is heavily dependent on the production of a single agricultural product, cotton. Uzbekistan is the world's sixth-largest producer of cotton, with its annual crop yielding just under four million bales of cotton. Under the Soviet Union, the Uzbek Republic sent the vast majority of its raw cotton fiber to firms in the northern republics to be processed and transformed into fabric. Although since 1991, some textile manufacturing has been established in independent Uzbekistan, the broad pattern of exporting the bulk of the raw cotton crop for processing elsewhere has remained durable. For instance, of the 3.8 million bales produced between May 2015 and May 2016, 2.5 million were exported. Cotton, referred to as "white gold," represents a vital source of foreign currency to the Uzbekistani regime.

Almost all agriculture is dependent on irrigation, and practically all irrigated land was organized into huge collective and state farms during the Soviet period whose sole commercial product was cotton. Most of these collectivized farms were transformed into agricultural production cooperatives in the first five years after independence; with ownership vested in the state, however, the management and efficiency of the state farms remained more or less what it had been in Soviet times.

During this period, the traditional household plots that had existed under the old communist form of agriculture have been renamed—becoming *dehkan* farms; in addition, the government created a second category of landholding—called "farmers"—which are essentially mid-sized peasant farms. The private farming that existed during these early years were largely dependent on the collective farm system both for leases and for marketing their products.

In 1998, collective farms (kolkhoz) were officially transformed into new entities known as shirkatlar. Other than the change in name, this transformation had a limited impact on rural development. Another law, the Law on Private Farms, however, did have a significant effect as it established a new legal category of farm fully separate from shirkatlar. Over a period of several years, unprofitable shirkatlar were broken up into smaller private farms.

Although by the end of the first decade of the millenium, private farms formed the backbone of agricultural production in the country, according to most observers, there is still a great deal of land reform that still needs to be completed. Farmers are not allowed to actually own land, by law, all land is owned by the state. While farmers are granted long-term leases, no land market has developed. Furthermore, there are a multiitude of reports that local officials directly influence the crop selection of farmers as a means of maintaining the production of cotton.

The republic has the second highest birth rate of Central Asia, which has resulted in a surplus rural population. As a result, rural unemployment is high. The unemployment rate in the republic was over 10% even before the collapse of the Soviet system. Although the government is pursuing programs aimed at addressing these problems, the greatest help thus far has been out-migration.

The independent Uzbek newspaper *Hurriyat* reported in April 2003 that between 500,000 and 700,000 Uzbeks had gone abroad in search of work. The newspaper also reported that the number of people leaving the country to find jobs was increasing.

According to World Bank data from 2010, around 7% of the population were emigrants (roughly 2 million Uzbekistani citizens). That number may be under reporting the true scope of migration however, since according to Russia's Federal Migration Service, in 2015 2.2 million Uzbekistani citizens were in Russia. The bulk of emigration has been to Kazakhstan and Russia, but significant emigrant populations have also temporarily settled in Ukraine, South Korea, and the European Union. Remittances sent from migrants are vital to the country's economy, according to the World Bank, in 2015 remittances accounted for 4.7% of total GDP. In 2016, the Russian Central Bank reported that from Russia alone, $2.74 billion were transferred between individuals in Russia and Uzbekistan.

Despite the significance of migrant labor to the Uzbekistani economy, in the last years of his presidency, Islam Karimov famously disparaged those citizens who sought to work abroad. As reported by Radio Free Europe/Radio Liberty, on June 20, in a televised discussion, Karimov stated, "There are very few lazy people in Uzbekistan now. I describe as lazy those who to Moscow and sweep its streets and squares. One feels disgusted with Uzbeks going there for a slice of bread." While this particular statement may have been off-the-cuff, Karimov's government had taken actions to discourage emigration, presumably to assert control over his population as well as to lessen the state's dependence on Russia.

Although Mirziyoyev's migration policy is still in formation, over a series of meetings on April 4–5, 2017 an agreement was reached with Russia to establish offices to assist Uzbek migrants working in Russia and thereby formalizing the process by which Uzbeks of various skill levels could temporarily seek work in Russia. This agreement can be seen as the clearest sign to date that Mirziyoyev is breaking with Karimov's stance on Uzbek labor migration.

Uzbekistan has large reserves of natural gas, petroleum, and coal. Proven reserves of natural gas are 1.841 trillion cubic meters, according to a January 2018 estimate. Most local industry uses natural gas. Gas is exported to Russia via a pipeline that runs from Bukhara to the area of the Urals and then on to European Russia. Gazprom, the Russian natural gas monopoly, has invested millions of dollars into the country's energy sector in the last several years. In 2007, agreement was reached to build a new natural gas pipeline along the eastern shore of the Caspian Sea, though construction has been delayed because of the worldwide economic downturn. Natural gas exports were 9.4 million cubic meters a day in 2017, the last year for which figures are available.

Petroleum is being produced in the Fergana Valley, in the area around Bukhara, and in the area south of the Aral Sea. Uzbekistan has proven petroleum reserves of about 594 million barrels. It produces about 70,000 barrels of oil a day, which is approximately half of domestic daily consumption. The Angren coal field produces coal for local use, but coal deposits have not been developed to any great extent.

Plentiful energy supplies have become the basis for some industry as well. Uzbekistan produces machines and heavy

Uzbekistan

equipment, its specialty being machinery for cotton cultivation and harvesting. Machinery for irrigation projects and road construction are also manufactured, plus some for the textile industry.

Uzbekistan also mines gold, copper, zinc and lead ores, plus uranium, tungsten, and molybdenum. Uzbekistan is among the world's top ten gold exporters, although officials do not announce gold output statistics.

It also produces fertilizers, cement, cotton textiles, coke, and chemicals. Gold made up 9.6% of all exports in 2001. The Navoi Combine, which is the country's largest producer of gold, also owns several uranium mines. Several were closed in 1995, but growing world demand and new mining techniques have recently reinvigorated the industry. Uranium production is currently about 3,000 tons a year.

Uzbekistan was the most reluctant of all the Central Asian republics to reform. In February 1994, President Karimov decreed a package of economic reforms; designed to set up a market economy, the plan called for the phasing out of subsidies on basic foodstuffs and public transport. Peasant farmers were also granted private plots of land.

This brought some improvement in the economy. Inflation decreased somewhat; foreign reserves grew; and there was a bumper cotton crop. A Mercedes-Benz joint venture began turning out its first trucks as well.

In late 1999, President Karimov began talking about additional moves to develop a market economy as a way of giving a boost to the flagging economy. He wanted to expand privatization and encourage small businesses. He also talked about

freeing the som, the Uzbek currency, and allowing it to float.

The government did sell 49% of the shares in Uzbekneftegaz, the state petroleum and natural gas company, to foreign investors—and shares in three other petroleum companies, Uzneftegazdobycha, Uznefte pererobatka, and Uzburneftegaz, were also made available to foreign investors—but little else changed.

After Uzbekistan joined the United States–led War on Terrorism in the fall of 2001, however, President Karimov found all sorts of opportunities opening up before him. It began in November when the United States Government offered an aid package worth $100 million to help Uzbekistan's currency become fully convertible.

In February 2002, the Government of Uzbekistan announced a new macroeconomic and structural reform plan, which it had worked out in consultation with the IMF. The plan called for removal of all restrictions on access to foreign exchange, unification of the exchange rates, agricultural sector reforms, and measures to improve the nation's banking system.

In April 2002, the government adopted a new commercial exchange rate which brought it just slightly under the real black-market rate; the next step came in October 2003, when the som became fully convertible.

When James Wolfensohn, president of the World Bank, met with President Karimov in Tashkent in April 2002, he proposed lending Uzbekistan $350 million over the following two years to fund projects in health, agriculture, banking, and water-resources and offered another $40 million credit agreement for a project

to improve water supplies in Samarkand and Bukhara.

To put these figures into perspective, Uzbekistan, which joined the World Bank in 1992, received a total of $494 million from the World Bank from 1992 to 2002. In September 2004, the World Bank agreed to provide another $40 million loan to finance a project to improve health care services.

A reversal of sorts occurred in March 2006, when Martin Raiser, the World Bank's country manager for Uzbekistan announced that the World Bank would not offer new loans to the government of Uzbekistan, though it would continue to service existing programs and provide technical assistance. Although Raiser stressed that there were no political reasons behind the World Bank's decision, Uzbekistan's turn away from reform after the violent events of May 2005 has clearly had a negative effect on the economy.

In a partial reversal, the World Bank announced in July 2006 that it would pursue an interim strategy of "continued engagement" with Uzbekistan over the next 12–15 months. The Bank said that this strategy "reflects the need to strengthen the poverty orientation of public policy, deepen structural reforms, and ensure broader civil society participation." The Bank indicated that its new policy might include limited new lending for global public goods and basic social services. In line with this new policy, it approved a $40 million credit to Uzbekistan to improve basic education.

Foreign investment in Uzbekistan, already the lowest on a per capita basis of any Central Asian republic, may actually have shrunk due to Uzbek government policy. To illustrate, in August 2006, the Uzbek government launched a criminal probe of Zarafshan-Newmont, an open-pit gold mining joint venture set up in 1992 by the Colorado-based Newmont Mining Corporation in partnership with the Uzbek State Committee for Geology and Mineral Resources. Two months earlier, the Uzbek government ordered Zarafshan-Newmont to pay $45 million in back taxes; they next froze the joint venture's assets and seized some of its gold. After declaring Zarafshan-Newmont bankrupt in October 2006, the government announced in February 2007 that it would be putting the company up for auction with a starting price of $139 million. The Uzbek government subsequently took control of Newmont's assets in the country.

Four months earlier, the Uzbek government authorities presented the joint venture Amantaytau Goldfields, half-owned by the British mining company Oxus Gold, with a $224.7 million claim for back taxes. The case went to arbitration, and Uzbekistan prevailed on its claims. From actions like this, it appears that the Uzbek

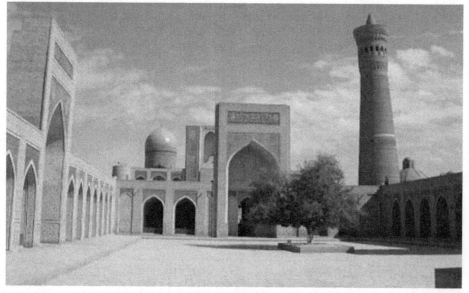

Kalyan Mosque

government intends to take full control of all gold-mining enterprises in the republic.

There is one foreign investment that appears to be paying off for Uzbekistan, however. In 2007, General Motors took over UzDaewooAuto, established in 1996 as a joint venture of Daewoo and the Uzbekistani government. GM Uzbekistan, as it became known, began manufacturing Chevrolet and GM Daewoo vehicles in Uzbekistan, most of which were exported to Russia. Export sales were badly affected at first by the 2008 economic downturn, but the situation has since reversed. GM Uzbekistan sold 45,127 cars in Russia in the first six months of 2011. This placed GM Uzbekistan in 10th place in terms of car sales on the Russian market.

According to an official government report, Uzbek GDP rose 9.7% in 2007. Industrial production grew by 11.6%, production of consumer goods by 19%. President Karimov commented that "the high economic growth figures, the drop in inflation, and improvement in the lives of citizens are a result of deeper reforms and the liberalization of the economy."

The government did create a $1 billion State Development Fund in May 2006 which, according to the decree which created it, is supposed to focus on "securing dynamic, sustainable, and balanced social and economic development, as well as conducting effective structural and investment policies."

In July 2007, President Karimov issued a decree calling for the privatization of nearly 1,000 state-owned enterprises in the chemical, electro-technical, construction materials, and agricultural machine-building sectors. In his decree, he noted that the private sector already accounted for over 75% of GDP. He must have been counting the entire agricultural sector as privatized in order to achieve this figure, however.

In 2007, Uzbekistan and Turkmenistan signed agreements with China to build a gas pipeline from Turkmenistan through Uzbekistan to Kazakhstan to China. The first gas flowed from Uzbekistan to China in 2012. Although Uzbekistan consumes 85% of the gas that it produces, China imported six billion cubic meters (bcm) of gas from Uzbekistan by the end of 2013. The supply is scheduled to reach 10 bcm by the end of 2015. The International Energy Agency, which represents 29 developed nations, estimates that if China's expansion into Central Asia continues at the current rate, China will be importing half of the region's gas by 2020.

According to official government statistics, GDP grew by 9% in 2008. The worldwide economic downturn did not affect Uzbekistan greatly, but GDP growth did drop by about a percentage point to 8.1% in 2009. GDP growth continued at about

that rate for the next three years, but dropped to 7% in 2013. A major factor appears to have been a drop in export prices.

The price of Uzbekistan's three main exports—gas, cotton, and gold—all dropped in 2014; nevertheless, the economy reportedly grew by 8.1% that year. No doubt, part of the increase was due to the increase in the volume of gas sold to China. The valuable trade with China is one important factor that prevents Uzbekistan from joining the Russian-dominated Eurasian Economic Union. If Uzbekistan joined that Union, it would have to erect trade barriers with China, which does not belong to the Union.

Uzbekistan also maintains important economic ties to Russia. It transports gas through Kazakhstan to Russia via a pipeline network controlled by the Russian energy giant Gazprom. Also, approximately four million Uzbeks work in Russia and send much of their income home. Remittances from migrant workers, in fact, account for about 12% of Uzbekistan's economy. These payments (calculated in dollars), however, declined sharply in 2014 largely as a consequence of the devaluation of the Russian ruble and are expected to diminish further in 2015. Russia's economy has weakened due to the drop in the price of its energy exports and the effect of Western sanctions. With growth rates projected to be lower in Russia, there will probably be fewer jobs there for Central Asian migrant workers.

The Ukrainian Revolution and Russia's annexation of Crimea and support for pro-Russian separatists in eastern Ukraine presented President Karimov with a dilemma. On the one hand, a grassroots revolutionary movement, such as the Euromaidan, is a cause for alarm for any authoritarian government. One the other hand, Karimov was logically wary of any circumstances that could lead to Russian expansion into former Soviet states, even though Uzbekistan does not share a border with Russia. Although it is still early in his presidency, thus far Mirziyoyev has shown more willingness to engage politically and economically with Russia than Karimov had over the last decade of his rule.

The Future

In August and September 2016, the Uzbekistani regime faced an unprecedented challenge when the only president who had ever served, Islam Karimov, died unexpectedly. Due to the low level of transparency amongst elite networks in the country, many observers feared that the transition to a new president may provoke some degree of civil unrest. However, despite some pessimistic predictions, the succession to President Shavkat Miziyoyev (which was fully completed

when he was elected in December 2017) proceeded remarkably smoothly. Mirziyoev was reelected in 2021. Under the current constitution, this would be his last term as president. However, on 30 April 2023, authorities held a referendum on proposed amendments to the constitution. The reforms introduced a range of civil liberties, but allow Mirziyoyev to extend his rule for nearly two decades. The new provision resets his term to zero, extends the presidential tenure from five to seven years, and permits him to seek reelection. The constitutional reforms sparked an unprecedented protest in Karakalpakstan, an autonomous republic in the northwest of the country. This unrest was triggered by the initial draft of the constitutional rewrite, which downgraded the republic's sovereign status by removing its right to secede from Uzbekistan. In response to the protests that erupted on July 1, 2022, resulting in the deaths of 21 people, Mirziyoyev reinstated the region's right to self-determination. Regrettably, no law enforcement personnel have been held accountable for the fatalities. However, the government convicted 61 local civil society leaders whom they believed had instigated the protest with the intention of seceding from Uzbekistan.

To date, Mirziyoyev, who was reelected in 2021, has initiated significant economic reforms, liberalizing aspects of the statist economy that had stagnated under Karimov. The thoroughness with which Mirziyoyev attacks structural problems in the economic system will be an early indication of his true political strength. In Uzbekistan's political economy, every change will likely produce losers who may threaten to pull their support of the new president. In this regard, the biggest test may be how Mirziyoyev handles cotton production. In recent years, Uzbekistan has made gestures toward becoming less dependent on cotton monoculture, and ended the systematic forced labor in the country's cotton harvest; however, a number of powerful individuals in the regime benefit enormously from the cotton extraction system and will likely resist drastic changes without some sort of pay-off. To date, it appears that Mirziyoyev is modeling his reforms on the Authoritarian Capitalism found in states like China. Navigating the liberalization of the former command economy will require deft political skill, and observers should pay close attention to this process.

As in China, economic liberalization has not gone hand-in-hand with political liberalization. Despite some recent electoral reforms, the legislature does not include opposition voices. Similarly, despite some increased press freedoms, the media is dominated by the state. In

Uzbekistan

short, Uzbekistan remains a closed authoritarian regime. Still, unlike neighboring authoritarian regimes, Tajikistan and Turkmenistan, Uzbekistan has relatively transparently addressed the public health crisis caused by Covid-19. Counterfactuals are tricky, but it is difficult to imagine that the Karimov regime would have been as open about the crisis. It will be important to watch whether the economic reforms that have been initiated in recent years will be scaled back as the state addresses the economic fallout from the pandemic.

Web Sites and Bibliography of Key English-Language Books

WEBSITES

WEBSITES OF INTERNATIONAL ORGANIZATIONS

www.un.org (Website for United Nations. Many links.)
www.unsystem.or (Official UN website)
http://europa.eu.int (EU server site)
http://europa.eu.int/comm (European Commission site)
http://www.euobserver.com (EU news)
http://www.euractiv.com (European news)
www.euractiv.com (Diverse news on EU and Europe)
www.oecd.org/daf/cmis/fdi/statist.htm (OECD site)
www.osce.org (Site of OSCE)
www.nato.int/structur/nids/nids.htm (NATO documentation, NATO Review)
www.nato.org and www.NATO.int (Web sites for NATO. Many links.)
www.wto.org (World Trade Organization site)
www.worldbank.org/html/Welcome.html (World Bank news, publications with
    links to other financial institutions)
www.ceip.org (Carnegie Endowment for International Peace, using a fully integrated
    Web-database system)
www.cia.gov/index.html (Central Intelligence Agency)
www.odci.gov/cia (Includes useful CIA publications, such as the *World Factbook* and
    maps)
www.xe.com/ucc/. (Current exchange rates)
www.state.gov (US Department of State, including country reports)
lcweb2.loc.gov/frd/cs/cshome.html (Library of Congress with coverage of over 100
    countries)
www.embassy.org/embassies (A site with links to all embassy web sites in
    Washington, DC)
www.psr.keele.ac.uk/official.htm (Collective site for governments and international
    organizations)
http://usinfo.state.gov (US Department of State)
http://www.duma.ru (Site for Russian Federation parliament)
http://www.government.gov.ru (Russian government site)
http://www.president.kremlin.ru/ (Russian president site)
http://www.eurasianet.org (News for Eurasia)
http://www.rferl.org/caucasus-report/(Site for Caucasus)
http://www.foreignpolicy.org.ua (Site for Ukrainian foreign policy)

WEBSITES OF NEWS ORGANIZATIONS AND NON-GOVERNMENTAL ORGANIZATIONS:

www.chicagotribune.com (Named best overall US newspaper online service for
    newspapers with circulation over 100,000)
www.economist.com (British weekly news magazine)
www.nytimes.com (Respected US newspaper, the *New York Times*)
www.washingtonpost.com
www.IHT.com (*International Herald Tribune*, published and distributed in Europe)
www.Europeanvoice.com (Weekly newspaper with EU and European news)
www.timeeurope.com (European edition of *Time*)
www.foreignaffairs.org (One of best-known international affairs journal)
www.cnn.com (Latest news with external links)
www.news.BBC.co.uk (British Broadcasting Corporation site)
www.c-span.org (Includes C-SPAN International)
www.reuters.com (Reuters international news service)
http://russialist.org (Johnson's Russia List, a digest of news about Russia)
www.jamestown.org (The Jamestown Foundation, a leading provider of information
    about Eurasia)
www.hrw.org (News and reports from Human Rights Watch, a highly respected or-
    ganization dedicated to improving human rights around the world)
http://imrussia.org/en (News about Russia from the Institute of Modern Russia, a
    think tank based in New York)
www.themoscowtimes.com (The only English-language daily newspaper published
    in Russia)

Bibliography

BOOKS

RUSSIA: GENERAL

Allensworth, Wayne. *The Russian Question: Nationalism, Modernization, and Post-Communist Russia*. Lanham, MD: Rowman & Littlefield Publishers, 1999; 368 p. (pb).

Bermeo, Nancy (ed.). *Liberalization and Democratization: Change in the Soviet Union and Eastern Europe*. Baltimore, MD: Johns Hopkins University Press, 1992; 200 p. (pb).

Blum, Douglas W. (ed.). *Russia's Future: Consolidation or Disintegration?* Boulder, CO: Westview Press, 1994; 173 p. (pb).

Evtuhov, Catherine et al. *A History of Russia: People, Legends, Events, Forces*. St. Charles, IL: Houghton Mifflin, 2003.

Hosking, Geoffrey A. *Russia and the Russians: A History*. Harvard University Press, 2001.

Kaiser, Robert G. *Russia: The People and the Power*. New York, NY: Pocket Books, 1974; 557 p. (pb).

Lapidus, Gail W. (ed.). *The New Russia*. Boulder, CO: Westview Press, 1994; 280 p. (pb).

Milner-Gulland, Robin R. *The Russians*. NY: Blackwell, 1999.

Remnik, David. *Lenin's Tomb: The Last Days of the Soviet Empire*. New York, NY: Vintage, 1992; 608 p. (pb).

Rozman, Gilbert (ed.). *Dismantling Communism: Common Causes and Regional Variations*. Baltimore, MD: Johns Hopkins University Press, 1992; 304 p. (pb).

Service, Robert. *A History of World Communism*. Cambridge, MA: Harvard University Press, 2007; 624 p.

Smith, Hedrick. *The New Russians*. New York, NY: Avon Books, 1991; 734 p. (pb).

HISTORY

Chamberlin, William Henry. *The Russian Revolution*. 2 vols., New York, NY: Macmillan, 1952.

Daniels, Robert V. *The Conscience of the Revolution: Communist Opposition in Soviet Russia*. Cambridge, MA: Harvard University Press, 1960; 524 p.

Davis, Nathaniel, *A Long Walk to Church: A Contemporary History of Russian Orthodoxy*. Boulder: Westview Press, 1995; 381 p. (pb)

Dmytryshyn, Basil. *A History of Russia*. Englewood Cliffs, NJ: Prentice Hall, 1977; 648. p.

Dmytryshyn, Basil. *U.S.S.R.: A Concise History*. New York, NY: Charles Scribner's Sons, 1978; 620 p.

Florinsky, Michael T. *Russia: A History and an Interpretation*. 2 vols, New York, NY: Macmillan, 1954.

Kappeler, Andreas. *The Russian Empire: A Multi-ethnic History*. Routledge, 2014.

Lieven, Dominic. *Russia against Napoleon: The True Story of the Campaigns of War and Peace*. New York, NY: Viking, 2010; 618 p.

Lincoln, W. Bruce. *Sunlight at Midnight. St. Petersburg and the Rise of Modern Russia*. NY: Basic Books, 2002.

Martin, Terry Dean. *The Affirmative Action Empire: Nations and Nationalism in the Soviet Union, 1923–1939*. Cornell University Press, 2001.

Massie, Robert K. *Catherine the Great*. New York: Random House, 2011; 625 p.

Poe, Marshall T. *The Russian Moment in World History*. Princeton University Press, 2011.

Pipes, Richard. *Russia under the Old Regime*. New York, NY: Charles Scribner's Sons, 1974; 361 p.

Radzinsky, *Alexander II: The Last Great Tsar*. New York: The Free Press, 2005; 462 p.

Riasanovsky, Nicholas. *A History of Russia*. New York, NY: Oxford University Press, 1993; 768 p.

Riasanovsky, Nicholas V. and Mark D. Steinberg, *A History of Russia*, eighth edition. New York and Oxford: Oxford University Press, 2011; 710 p. (pb)

Thompson, John M. *Russia and the Soviet Union*. (3rd ed); Boulder, CO: Westview Press, 1994; 320 p. (pb).

Treadgold, Donald W. *Twentieth Century Russia*. (8th ed); Boulder, CO: Westview Press, 1994; 498 p.

Wren, Melvin C. *The Course of Russian History*. Prospect Heights, IL: Waveland Press, 1994; 617 p. (pb).

Bibliography

THE COMMUNIST ERA

Andrew, Christopher and Vasili Mitrokhin. *The Sword and the Shield: The Mitrokhin Archive and the Secret History of the KGB.* New York: Basic Books, 1999; 700 p.

Applebaum, Anne. *Gulag: A History.* New York, NY: Doubleday, 2003; 736 p.

Arbatov, Georgi. *The System: An Insider's Life in Soviet Politics.* New York, NY: Times Books, 1993; 380 p. (pb).

Bailer, Seweryn. *Stalin's Successors: Leadership, Stability, and Change in the Soviet Union.* Cambridge, England: Cambridge University Press, 1980; 312 p. (pb).

Bailes, Kendall E. *Technology and Society under Lenin and Stalin: Origins of the Soviet Technical Intelligentsia.* Princeton, NJ: Princeton University Press, 1978; 472 p.

Berlin, Isaiah and Henry Hardy (eds.). *The Soviet Mind: Russian Culture under Communism.* Washington, DC: Brookings, 2004; 230 p.

Bidlack, Richard and Nikita Lomagin, *The Leningrad Blockade, 1941–1944: A New Documentary History from the Soviet Archives.* New Haven: Yale University Press, 2012; 486 p. (pb)

Braithwaite, Rodric. *Moscow 1941: A City and Its People at War.* New York: Alfred A. Knopf, 2006; 416 p.

Bremzen, Anya von. *Mastering the Art of Soviet Cooking: A Memoir of Food and Longing.* New York: Crown Publishers, 2013.

Breslauer, George W. *Khrushchev and Brezhnev as Leaders: Building Authority in Soviet Politics.* London, England: Allen Unwin, 1982; 318 p. (pb).

Brown, Archie. *The Rise and Fall of Communism.* New York: Ecco-HarperCollins Publishers, 2009; 736 p.

Caute, David. *The Dancer Defects: The Struggle for Cultural Supremacy during the Cold War.* New York: Oxford University Press, 2003; 788 p.

Conquest, Robert. *Stalin: A Biography.* Cambridge, MA: Harvard University Press, 2005 (pb).

Daniels, Robert V. *Trotsky, Stalin and Socialism.* Boulder, CO: Westview Press, 1991; 208 p.

Daniels, Robert Vincent. *Stalin Revolution: Foundations of Soviet Totalitarianism.* (2nd ed.) Boston, MA: Heath, 1973; 106 p.

Djilas, Milovan. *Conversations with Stalin.* New York, NY: Harcourt Brace World, 1962; 211 p.

Figes, Orlando. *The Whisperers: Private Life in Stalin's Russia.* London: Allen Lane, 2007; 740 p.

Fitzpatrick, Sheila. *Everyday Stalinism: Ordinary Life in Extraordinary Times: Soviet Russia in the 1930s.* Oxford University Press, 1999.

Gaddis, John Lewis. *George F. Kennan: An American Life.* New York: Penguin, 2011.

Gellately, Robert. *Lenin, Stalin, and Hitler: The Age of Social Catastrophe.* New York: Knopf, 2007; 720 p.

Gellately, Robert. *Stalin's Curse: Battling for Communism in War and Cold War.* New York: Knopf, 2013; 464 p.

Getty, J. Arch and Oleg V. Naumov. *The Road to Terror: Stalin and the Self-Destruction of the Bolsheviks, 1932–1939.* New Haven, CT: Yale University Press, 1999; 688 p.

Goldgeier, James M. *Leadership Style and Soviet Foreign Policy: Stalin, Khrushchev, Brezhnev, Gorbachev.* Baltimore, MD: Johns Hopkins University Press, 1994; 192 p.

Gorodetsky, Gabriel. *Grand Illusion: Stalin and the German Invasion of Russia.* New Haven, CT: Yale University Press, 1999; 424 p.

Gorbachev, Mikhail. *Memoirs.* New York, NY: Doubleday, 1996; 800 p.

Gorbachev, Mikhail. *Gorbachev on His Country and the World;* Trans. George Shriver. New York: Columbia University Press, 1999; 499 p.

Hagenloh, Paul. *Stalin's Police: Public Order and Mass Repression, 1926–1941.* Baltimore, MD: Johns Hopkins University Press, 2009.

Hill, Fiona and Clifford G. Gaddy. *The Siberian Curse: How Communist Planners Left Russia Out in the Cold.* Washington, DC: Brookings, 2003.

Hosking, Geoffrey. *Rulers and Victims: The Russians in the Soviet Union.* Cambridge, MA: Harvard University Press, 2006; 496 p.

Karcz, Jerzy F. *The Economics of Communist Agriculture: Selected Papers.* Bloomington, IN: International Development Institute, 1979; 494 p.

Keep, John. *Last of the Empires: A History of the Soviet Union, 1946–1991.* New York, NY: Oxford University Press, 1997 (pb).

Kotkin, Stephen. *Magnetic Mountain: Stalinism as a Civilization.* University of California Press, 1997.

Leitenberg, Milton. *The Soviet Biological Weapons Program.* Cambridge: Harvard University Press, 2013; 921 p.

Bibliography

Ligachev, Yegor. *Inside Gorbachev's Kremlin*. trans. Catherine A Fitzpatrick, Michele A Berdy, and Dobrochna Dyrcz-Freeman. New York, NY: Pantheon Books, 1993; 369 p.

Linden, Carl. *Khrushchev and the Soviet Leadership: With an Epilogue on Gorbachev*. Baltimore, MD: Johns Hopkins University Press, 1990; 304 p. (pb)

Montefiore, Simon Sebag. *Young Stalin*. New York: Knopf, 2007; 432p.

Rabinowitch, Alexander, *The Bolsheviks Come to Power: The Revolution of 1917 in Petrograd*. New York: W.W. Norton & Company, 1976; 393 p. (pb)

Rabinowitch, Alexander, *The Bolsheviks in Power: The First Year of Soviet Rule in Petrograd*. Bloomington: Indiana University Press, 2007; 494 p. (pb)

Satter, David. *It Was a Long Time Ago and It Never Happened: Russia and the Communist Past*. New Haven: Yale University Press, 2011; 400 p.

Service, Robert, *Lenin: A Biography*. Cambridge: Harvard University Press, 2000; 561 p. (pb)

Service, Robert. *Stalin: A Biography*. New York, Macmillan, 2005.

Snyder, Timothy. *Bloodlands: Europe between Hitler and Stalin*. New York: Basic Books, 2010; 560 p. (pb)

Taubman, William. *Khrushchev: The Man and His Era*. New York: Norton, 2003; 876 p.

Ulam, Adam B. *The Bolsheviks: The Intellectual and Political History of the Triumph of Communism in Russia*. New York, NY: Macmillan, 1965; 598 p.

Viola, Lynne. *Peasant Rebels under Stalin: Collectivization and the Culture of Peasant Resistance*. New York, NY: Oxford University Press, 1999; 328 p. (pb)

Volkogonov, Dmitri. *Autopsy for an Empire*. New York, NY: The Free Press (Simon & Schuster), 1998. 528 p.

Volkogonov, Dmitri. *Lenin: A New Biography*. New York: The Free Press, 1994; 529 p.

Volkogonov, Dmitri. *Trotsky: The Eternal Revolutionary*. New York: The Free Press, 1996 (pb).

Yakovlev, Aleksandr. *The Fate of Marxism in Russia*. trans. by Catherine A. Fitzpatrick. New Haven, CT: Yale University Press, 1993; 256 p.

SOVIET/RUSSIAN FOREIGN POLICY

Applebaum, Anne. *Iron Curtain: The Crushing of Eastern Europe 1944–1956*. New York: Doubleday, 2012; 614 p.

Arbatov, Alexei and Vladimir Dvorkin. *Beyond Nuclear Deterrence: Transforming the U.S.-Russian Equation*. Washington, DC: Carnegie Endowment for International Peace, 2006; 188 p.

Aron, Leon and Kenneth M. Jensen (eds.). *The Emergence of Russian Foreign Policy*. Herndon, VA.: United States Institute of Peace Press, 1994; 221 p. (pb)

Bain, Mervyn J. *Russian-Cuban Relations since 1992: Continuing Camaraderie in a Post-Soviet World*. Lanham, MD: Rowman & Littlefield, 2008; 182 p.

Beschloss, Michael R. and Strobe Talbott. *At the Highest Levels: The Inside Story of the End of the Cold War*. Boston, MA: Little, Brown, 1993; 498 p.

Bialer, Seweryn. *The Soviet Paradox-External Expansion, Internal Decline*. New York, NY: Alfred A. Knopf, 1986; 391 p.

Cohen, Stephen F. *Soviet Fates and Lost Alternatives: From Stalinism to the New Cold War*. New York, NY: Columbia University Press, 2009; 308p.

Deyermond, Ruth. *Security and Sovereignty in the Former Soviet Union*. Boulder: Lynn Rienner, 2008; 233 p.

Dobbs, Michael. *Six Months in 1945: FDR, Stalin, Churchill, and Truman*. New York: Knopf, 2012; 418 p.

Figes, Orlando. *The Whisperers: Private Life in Stalin's Russia*. London: Allen Lane, 2007; 740 p.

Fischer, Louis. *Russia's Road from Peace to War*. New York, NY: Harper Row, 1969; 499 p.

Fursenko, Aleksandr and Timothy Naftali. *Khrushchev's Cold War: The Inside Story of an American Adversary*. New York: Norton, 2006; 670 p.

Gaddis, John Lewis. *The Cold War: A New History*. New York: The Penguin Press, 2005; 400 p.

Goldgeier, James M. and Michael McFaul. *Power and Purpose: U.S. Policy toward Russia after the Cold War*. Washington, DC: Brookings, 2003; 450 p. (pb)

Harriman, W. Averill. *Special Envoy to Churchill and Stalin, 1941–1946*. New York, NY: Random House, 1975; 595 p.

Ivanov, Igor S. *The New Russian Diplomacy*. Washington, DC: Brookings, 2002.

Jeffrey, Mankoff. *Russian Foreign Policy: The Return of Great Power Politics*. Lanham, MD: Rowman & Littlefield, 2011.

Jonson, Lena (ed.). *Peacekeeping and the Role of Russia in Eurasia*. Boulder, CO: Westview Press, 1996; 240 p.

Kennan, George F. *Russia and the West under Lenin and Stalin*. Boston, MA: Little, Brown, 1961; 411 p.

Leffler, Melvyn P. *For the Soul of Mankind: The United States, the Soviet Union, and the Cold War*. New York: Hill and Wang, 2007; 586 p.

Lo, Bobo. *Axis of Convenience: Moscow, Beijing, and the New Geopolitics*. Washington, DC: Brookings, 2008; 277 p.

Lucas, Edward. *Deception: Spies, Lies, and How Russia Dupes the West*. London: Bloomsbury Publishing PLC, 2012.

Lucas, Edward. *The New Cold War: How the Kremlin Menaces Both Russia and the West*. London: Bloomsbury, 2008; 352 p.

Mankoff, Jeffrey. *Russian Foreign Policy: The Return of Great Power Politics*. Lanham, MD: Rowman & Littlefield, 2009; 368 p. (pb).

McFaul, Michael and James Goldgeiger. *Power and Purpose: U.S. Policy toward Russia after the Cold War*. Washington: Carnegie Endowment, 2003.

Miscamble, Wilson D. *From Roosevelt to Truman: Potsdam, Hiroshima, and the Cold War*. Cambridge: Cambridge University Press, 2006; 393 p.

Motyl, Alexander J, Blair Ruble and Lilia Shevtsova. *Russia's Engagement with the West: Transformation and Integration in the Twenty-First Century*. New York: Armonk, 2005.

Primakov, Yevgeny. *Russia and the Arabs: Behind the Scenes in the Middle East from the Cold War to the Present*. New York: Basic Books, 2009; 432 p.

Roberts, Geoffrey. *Stalin's Wars: From World War to Cold War*. New Haven: Yale University Press, 2006; 468 p.

Sarotte, Mary Elise, *1989: The Struggle to Create Post–Cold War Europe*. Princeton, NJ: Princeton University Press, 2009; 344 p.

Sebestyen, Victor. *Revolution 1989: The Fall of the Soviet Empire*. New York: Pantheon, 2009; 480 p.

Shearman, Peter (ed.). *Russian Foreign Policy since 1990*. Boulder, CO: Westview Press, 1995; 320 p. (pb).

Sherr, James. *Promise and Realism in Relations with Russia*. Washington, DC: Brookings, 2010; 40 p. (pb).

Shevtsova, Lilia. *Change or Decay: Russia's Dilemma and the West's Response*. Washington, DC: Brookings Institute Press, 2011; 260 p.

Stent, Angela. *The Limits of Partnership: US—Russian Relations in the Twenty-First Century*. Princeton, NJ: Princeton University Press, 2014; 384 p.

Tsyankov, Andrei P. *Russia's Foreign Policy*. Lanham, MD: Rowman & Littlefield, 2009,

Talbott, Strobe. *The Russia Hand: A Memoir of Presidential Diplomacy*. NY: Random House, 2002.

Trenin, Dmitri V. *The End of Eurasia: Russia on the Border between Geopolitics and Globalization*. Washington: Carnegie Endowment, 2002.

Ulam, Adam B. *Expansion and Coexistence*. New York, NY: Praeger, 1968; 797 p.

Ulam, Adam B. *The Rivals: America and Russia since World War II*. New York, NY: Viking Press, 1971; 405 p.

Von Bencke, Matthew J. *The Politics of Space: A History of U.S.-Soviet/Russian Cooperation in Space*. Boulder, CO: Westview Press, 1996; 272 p.

Wettig, Gerhard. *Changes in Soviet Policy toward the West*. Boulder, CO: Westview Press, 1991; 193 p.

Zubok, Vladislav M. *A Failed Empire: The Soviet Union in the Cold War*. Greensboro: University of North Carolina Press, 2007; 467 p.

COLLAPSE OF COMMUNISM

Aron, Leon. *Yeltsin: A Revolutionary Life*. London: HarperCollins, 2000; 934 p.

Balzer, Harley D. (ed.). *Five Years That Shook the World: Gorbachev's Unfinished Revolution*. Boulder, CO: Westview Press, 1991; 267 p. (pb).

Brown, Archie. *Seven Years That Changed the World: Perestroika in Perspective*. Cambridge, England: Oxford University Press, 2007; 350 p.

Bunce, Valerie. *Subversive Institutions: The Design and the Destruction of Socialism and the State*. Cambridge University Press, 1999.

Colton, Timothy J. *Yeltsin: A Life*. New York: Basic Books, 2008; 616 p.

Dallin, Alexander and Gail W. Lapidus (eds.). *The Soviet System: From Crisis to Collapse*. Boulder, CO: Westview Press, 1994; 725 p. (pb).

Daniels, Robert V. *Russia's Transformation: Snapshots of a Crumbling System*. Lanham, MD: Rowman & Littlefield Publishers, 1997; 256 p. (pb).

Bibliography

Gaidar, Yegor. *Collapse of an Empire: Lessons for Modern Russia*. Washington, DC: Brookings Institution Press, 2008; 332 p.

Goldman, Marshal I. *USSR in Crisis: The Failure of an Economic System*. New York, NY: Norton, 1983; 210 p. (pb).

Goldman, Marshall I. *What Went Wrong with Perestroika?* New York, NY: Norton, 1991.

Gorbachev, Mikhail. *The August Coup: The Truth and the Lessons*. New York, NY: HarperCollins, 1991; 127 p.

Jones, Anthony, Walter D. Conner, and David E. Powell (eds.). *Soviet Social Problems*. Boulder, CO: Westview Press, 1991; 337 p. (pb).

Kaiser, Robert. *Why Gorbachev Happened: His Triumphs and His Failures*. New York, NY: Simon & Schuster, 1991; 476 p.

Kotkin, Stephen. *Armageddon Averted: The Soviet Collapse 1970–2000*. New York: Oxford University Press, 2001; 258 p.

Kotkin, Stephen. *Steeltown, USSR: Soviet Society in the Gorbachev Era*. Berkeley, CA: University of California Press, 1991; 269 p.

Kotkin, Stephen. *Uncivil Society: 1989 and the Implosion of the Communist Establishment*. New York: Modern Library, 2009; 197 p.

Kull, Steven. *Burying Lenin: The Revolution in Soviet Ideology and Foreign Policy*. Boulder, CO: Westview Press, 1992; 219 p. (pb).

Nahaylo, B. and V. Svoboda. *Soviet Disunion*. New York, NY: Free Press, 1990.

O'Connor, Kevin C. *Intellectuals and Apparatchiks: Russian Nationalism and the Gorbachev Revolution*. Lanham, MD: Rowman & Littlefield, 2008; 332 p.

Odom, William E. *The Collapse of the Soviet Military*. New Haven, CT: Yale University Press, 1998; 480 p.

Pleshakov, Constantine. *There Is No Freedom without Bread: 1989 and The Civil War That Brought Down Communism*. New York: Farrar, Straus & Giroux, 2009; 289 p.

Plokhy, Serhii. *The Last Empire: The Final Days of the Soviet Union*. New York: Basic Books, 2015.

Ratnesar, Romesh. *Tear Down This Wall: A City, a President, and the Speech That Ended the Cold War*. New York, NY: Simon & Schuster, 2009; 229 p.

Shane, Scott. *Dismantling Utopia: How Information Ended the Soviet Union*. Chicago, IL: Ivan R. Dee, Inc., Publisher, 1995; 336 p.

Sharlet, Robert. *Soviet Constitutional Crisis: From De-Stalinization to Disintegration*. Armonk, NY: M. E. Sharpe, 1992; 204 p. (pb).

Sheets, Lawrence Scott. *8 Pieces of Empire: A 20-Year Journey*. New York: Crown, 2011.

Solomon, Andrew. *The Irony Tower: Soviet Artists in a Time of Glasnost*. New York, NY: Knopf, 1991; 170 p.

Trenin, Dmitri. *Post-Imperium: A Eurasian Story*. Washington, DC: Carnegie Endowment for International Peace, 2011; 270 p.

Volkogonov, Dmitri. *Autopsy for an Empire*. New York: The Free Press, 1998; 572 p.

White, Stephen. *Gorbachev and After*. New York, NY: Cambridge University Press, 1992; 327 p. (pb).

Zaslavskaya, Tatyana. *The Second Socialist Revolution: An Alternative Soviet Strategy*. Bloomington, IN: Indiana University Press, 1990; 241 p. (pb).

POLITICS

Babenko, Arkady. *One Soldier's War*. New York: Grove, 2007; 395 p.

Baker, Peter and Susan Glasser. *Kremlin Rising: Vladimir Putin's Russia and the End of Revolution*. New York: A Lisa Drew Book/Scribner, 2005; 453 p.

Barry, Donald D. (ed.). *Towards the Rule of Law in Russia: Political and Legal Reform in the Transition Period*. Armonk, NY: Sharpe, 1992.

Bjorkman, Tom. *Russia's Road to Deeper Democracy*. Washington, DC: Brookings, 2003.

Blum, Douglas W. (ed.). *Russia's Future: Consolidation or Disintegration?* Boulder, CO: Westview Press, 1994; 192 p. (pb).

Braithwaite, Rodric. *Across the Moscow River: The World Turned Upside Down*. New Haven: Yale University, 2002.

Bressler, Michael L. (ed.). *Understanding Contemporary Russia*. Boulder, CO: Lynne Rienner, 2009.

Brown, Archie and Lilia Shevtsova, eds. *Gorbachev, Yeltsin & Putin. Political Leadership in Russia's Transition*. Washington, DC: Brookings, 2001.

Colton, Timothy J. *Yeltsin: A Life*. New York: Basic Books, 2008; 616 p.

Cronberg, Tarja. *Transforming Russia: From a Military to a Peace Economy*. NY: Palgrave, 2003.

Bibliography

Cuchins, Andrew C. (ed.). *Russia after The Fall*. Washington: Carnegie Endowment, 2002.

Davis, Sue. *The Russian Far East: The Last Frontier*. NY: Routledge, 2002.

Deyermond, Ruth. *Security and Sovereignty in the Former Soviet Union*. Boulder, CO: Lynne Rienner, 2009

Dunlop, John B. *Russia Confronts Chechnya: Roots of a Separatist Conflict*. New York, NY: Cambridge University Press, 1998; 248 p. (pb).

Eckstein, Harry et al. *Can Democracy Take Root in Post-Soviet Russia?* Lanham, MD: Rowman & Littlefield Publishers, 1998; 406 p. (pb).

Evangelista, Matthew. *The Chechen Wars. Will Russia Go the Way of the Soviet Union?* Washington, DC: Brookings, 2002.

Felshtinsky, Yuri. *The Age of Assassins: The Rise and Rise of Vladimir Putin*. London: Gibson Square Books, 2008; 320 p.

Felshtinsky, Yuri and Vladimir Pribylovsky. *The Corporation: Russia and the KGB in the Age of President Putin*. New York, NY: EncantER Books, 2009.

Feltbrugge, F. J. M. *Russian Law: The End of the Soviet System and the Role of Law*. Dordrecht, The Netherlands: Martinus Nijhoff, 1993.

Fish, Steven. *Democracy from Scratch*. Princeton, NJ: Princeton University Press, 1996; 312 p. (pb).

Friedgut, Theodore H. and Jeffrey W. Hahn (eds.). *Local Power and Post-Soviet Politics*. Armonk, NY: M. E. Sharpe, 1994; 320 p. (pb).

Gall, Carlotta and Thomas DeWall. *Chechnya: Calamity in the Caucasus*. New York: NYU Press, 2000; 416 p. (pb).

Gessen, Masha. *The Man without a Face: The Unlikely Rise of Vladimir Putin*. New York: Riverhead, 2012; 314 p.

Goldman, Marshall I. *Petrostate: Putin, Power, and the New Russia*. Oxford: Oxford University Press, 2008; 256 p.

Golosov, Grigorii V. *Political Parties in the Regions of Russia: Democracy Unclaimed*. Boulder, CO: Lynne Rienner, 2004; 307 p.

Gomart, Thomas. *Russian Civil-Military Relations*. Washington, DC: Carnegie Endowment for International Peace, 2008; 120 p. (pb).

Graney, Katherine E. *Of Khans and Kremlins: Tatarstan and the Future of Ethno-Federalism in Russia*. Lanham, MD: Rowman & Littlefield, 2008; 226 p.

Hale, Henry E. *Why Not Parties in Russia?: Democracy, Federalism, and the State*. Cambridge University Press, 2005.

Hale, Henry E. *Patronal Politics: Eurasian Regime Dynamics in Comparative Perspective*. Cambridge University Press, 2014.

Hill, Fiona and Clifford Gaddy. *Mr Putin: Operative in the Kremlin*. Washington, DC: Brookings Institution Press, 2013; 400 p.

Hoffmann, David. *The Oligarchs. Wealth and Power in the New Russia*. NY: Public Affairs, 2003.

Hosking, Geoffrey. *The Russians in the Soviet Union*. Cambridge, MA: Harvard University Press, 2006; 496 p.

Jack, Andrew. *Inside Putin's Russia*. Granta Books, 2004.

Jagielski, Wojciech. *Towers of Stone: The Battle of Wills in Chechnya*. New York, NY: Seven Stories Press, 2009; 329 p.

Judah, Ben. *Fragile Empire: How Russia Fell In and Out of Love with Vladimir Putin*. New Haven: Yale University Press, 2013; 379 p.

Kasyanov, Mikhail. *Bez Putina: Politicheskie Dialogi i Yevgeniem Kiselevym [Without Putin: Political Dialogues with Yevgeny Kiselev]*. Moscow: Novaya Gazeta, 2009; 318 p.

Lapidus, Gail W. (ed.). *The New Russia: Troubled Transformation*. Boulder, CO: Westview Press, 1994; 320 p. (pb).

Lebeneva, Alena. *Can Russia Modernise? Sistema, Power Networks and Informal Governance*. Cambridge: Cambridge University Press, 2013; 310 p.

Lempert, David H. *Daily Life in a Crumbling Empire*; 2 vols. New York: Columbia University Press, 1996; 600 p. (each).

LeVine, Steve. *Putin's Labyrinth: Spies, Murder, and the Dark Heart of the New Russia*. New York: Random House, 2008; 194 p.

Lynch, Allen C. *Vladimir Putin and Russian Statecraft*. Dulles, VA: Potomac Books, 2011; 184 p.

Marsh, Christopher. *Russia at the Polls: Voters, Elections, and Democratization*. Washington: CQ Press, 2002.

McFaul, Michael et al. *Between Dictatorship and Democracy: Russian Post-Communist Political Reforms*. Washington, DC: Brookings, 2004.

Meier, Andrew. *Black Earth: A Journey through Russia after the Fall*. NY: Norton, 2004.

Meier, Andrew. *Chechnya: To the Heart of a Conflict*. New York: Norton, 2005.

Bibliography

Mendras, Marie. *Russian Politics: The Paradox of a Weak State*. New York: Columbia University Press, 2012; 349 p.

Moore, Robert. *A Time to Die. The Kursk Disaster*. London: Bantam, 2003.

Olcott, Martha Brill et al. *Getting It Wrong: Regional Cooperation and the Commonwealth of Independent States*. Washington, DC: Brookings, 2000.

Piveronus, Peter J. *Reinventing Russia: The Formation of a Post-Soviet Identity*. Lanham, MD: University Press of America, 2009; 120 p (pb).

Politkovskaya, Anna. *A Russian Diary*. New York: Random House, 2007; 272 p.

Politkovskaya, Anna. *Putin's Russia: Life in a Failing Democracy*. New York, NY: Harvill (Random House), 2005.

Putin, Vladimir. *First Person*. NY: Public Affairs, 2000.

Remington, Thomas F. *The Russian Parliament: Institutional Evolution in a Transitional Regime, 1989–1999*. Yale University Press, 2008.

Roxburgh, Angus. *The Strongman: Vladimir Putin and the Struggle for Russia*. London: I. B. Tauris, 2012; 288 p.

Robinson, Neil. *Russia. A State of Uncertainty*. NY: Routledge, 2001.

Ross, Cameron. *Federalism and Democratization in Post-Communist Russia*. Manchester: Manchester University Press, 2003.

Ross, Cameron (ed). *Russian Politics under Putin*. Manchester: Manchester University Press, 2004.

Saivetz, Carol R. and Anthony Jones. *In Search of Pluralism: Soviet and Post-Soviet Politics*. Boulder, CO: Westview Press, 1994; 174 p. (pb).

Sakwa, Richard. *Russian Politics and Society*, 3rd. ed. NY: Routledge, 2002.

Service, Robert. *Russia: Experiment with a People*. Cambridge, MA: Harvard University, 2003.

Shevtsova, Lilia. *Putin's Russia*. Revised Edition. Carnegie Endowment for International Peace, 2005; 298 p. (pb).

Shevtsova, Lilia. *Russia—Lost in Translation: The Yeltsin and Putin Legacies*. Washington, DC: Carnegie Endowment for International Peace, 2008; 388 p. (pb).

Smith, Gordon B. (ed.). *State-Building in Russia: The Yeltsin Legacy and the Challenge of the Future*. Armonk, NY: M. E. Sharpe, 1998; 224 p.

Smyth, Regina. *Candidate Strategies and Electoral Competition in the Russian Federation: Democracy without foundation*. Cambridge University Press, 2006.

Stuermer, Michael. *Putin and the Rise of Russia*. London: Weidenfeld & Nicolson, 2008.

Taylor, Brian D. *Politics and the Russian Army: Civil-Military Relations, 1689–2000*. Cambridge: Cambridge University, 2003.

Treisman, Daniel S. *After the Deluge: Regional Crises and Political Consolidation in Russia*. Ann Arbor, MI: The University of Michigan Press, 1999; 340 p.

Treisman, Daniel. *The Return: Russia's Journey from Gorbachev to Medvedev*. Simon & Schuster, 2012.

Trenin, Dmitri et al. *Russia's Restless Frontier. The Chechnya Factor in Post-Soviet Russia*. Washington, DC: Brookings, 2004.

Truscott, Peter. *Putin's Progress*. NY: Simon & Schuster, 2004.

Urban, Joan Barth. *Russia's Communists at the Crossroads*. Boulder, CO: Westview Press, 1997; 224 p. (pb).

Waller, J. Michael. *Secret Empire: The KGB in Russia Today*. Boulder, CO: Westview Press, 1994; 375 p. (pb).

Wegren, Stephen, ed., *Return to Putin's Russia: Past Imperfect, Future Uncertain*, fifth edition. Lanham: Rowman & Littlefield, 2013; 332 p. (pb)

Weiler, Jonathon. *Human Rights in Russia: A Darker Side of Reform*. Boulder, CO: Lynne Rienner, 2004.

Yeltsin, Boris. *The Struggle for Russia*. New York, NY: Times Books, 1995; 336 p.

Zyuganov, Gennady A. *My Russia: The Political Autobiography of Gennedy Zyuganov*. Armonk, NY: M.E. Sharpe, Inc, 1997; 224 p.

ECONOMY

Allina-Pisano, Jessica. *The Post-Soviet Potemkin Village: Politics and Property Rights in the Black Earth*. Cambridge University Press, 2007.

Aslund, Anders. *How Capitalism Was Built: The Transformation of Central and Eastern Europe, Russia and Central Asia*. New York: Cambridge University Press, 2007; 384 p.

Aslund, Anders and Richard Layard (eds.). *Changing the Economic System in Russia*. London, England: Pinter, 1993.

Boeva, Irina and Viacheslav Shironin. *Russians between State and Market*. Glasgow, Scotland: University of Strathclyde Centre for the Study of Public Policy, SPP 205, 1992.

Barnes, Andrew Scott. *Owning Russia: The Struggle over Factories, Farms, and Power*. Cornell University Press, 2006.

Brady, Rose. *Kapitalizm: Russia's Struggle to Free Its Economy*. New Haven, CT: Yale University Press, 1998. 320 p.

Desai, Raj M. and Itzhak Goldberg (eds.). *Can Russia Compete?: Enhancing Productivity and Innovation in a Globalizing World*. Washington, DC: Brookings, 2008; 183 p. (pb).

Ellman, Michael and Vladimir Kontorovich (eds.). *The Disintegration of the Soviet Economic System*. New York, NY: Routledge, 1994; 281 p. (pb).

Frye, Timothy. *Property Rights and Property Wrongs: How Power, Institutions, and Norms Shape Economic Conflict in Russia*. Cambridge University Press, 2017.

Gaddy, Clifford G. and Barry W. Ickes. *Russia's Virtual Economy*. Washington, DC: Brookings, 2002.

Granville, Brigitte and Peter Oppenheimer. *Russia's Post-Communist Economy*. New York: Oxford University Press, 2001; 570 p.

Gaddy, Clifford G. and Barry W. Ickes. *Russia's Addiction: The Political Economy of Resource Dependence*. Washington, DC: Brookings, 2009; 240 p. (pb).

Gaddy, Clifford G. and Barry W. Ickes. *Russia's Virtual Economy*. Washington, DC: Brookings Institution Press, 1999; 96 p. (pb).

Gilman, Martin. *No Precedent, No Plan: Inside Russia's 1998 Default*. Cambridge, MA: The MIT Press, 2010; 331 p.

Hill, Fiona and Clifford G. Gaddy. *The Siberian Curse: How Communist Planners Left Russia Out in the Cold*. Washington: Brookings, 2004.

Ioffe, Grigory and Tatyana Nefedova. *Continuity and Change in Rural Russia*. Boulder, CO: Westview Press, 1997; 328 p.

Keren, Michael and Gur Ofer (eds.). *Trials of Transition: Economic Reform in the Former Communist Bloc*. Boulder, CO: Westview Press, 1992; 308 p. (pb).

Kokh, Alfred. *The Selling of the Soviet Empire: Politics & Economics of Russia's Privatization—Revelations of the Principal Insider*. New York, NY: S.P.I. Books, 1999. (pb).

Lane, David (ed.). *The Political Economy of Russian Oil*. Lanham, MD: Rowman & Littlefield Publishers, Inc., 1999; 240 p. (pb)

Lavagne, Marie. *The Economics of Transition: From Socialist Economy to Market Economy*. New York: St. Martin's Press, 1999; 304 p.

McKinnon, Ronald. *The Order of Economic Liberalization: Financial Control in the Transition to a Market Economy*. Baltimore, MD: Johns Hopkins University Press, 1993; 224 p. (pb).

Nelson, Lynn D. and Irina Y. Kuzes. *Property to the People: The Struggle for Radical Economic Reform in Russia*. Armonk, NY: M. E. Sharpe, 1994; 280 p. (pb).

Roberts, John. *Pipeline Politics: The Caspian and Global Energy Security*. London: Chatham House, 2008; 176 p. (pb).

Stern, Jonathan P. *The Future of Russian Gas and Gazprom*. New York: Oxford University Press, 2005; 298 p.

Vinhas de Souza, Lúcio. *A Different Country: Russia's Economic Resurgence*. Budapest: Centre for European Policy Studies, 2008; 112 p. (pb).

Wegren, Stephen K. *Agriculture and the State in Soviet and Post-Soviet Russia*. Pittsburgh, PA: University of Pittsburgh Press, 1998; 246 p.

Wegren, Stephen. *The Moral Economy Reconsidered: Russia's Search for Agrarian Capitalism*. Springer, 2005.

Wengle, Susanne A. *Post-Soviet Power*. Cambridge University Press, 2015.

CULTURAL

Berlin, Isaiah and Henry Hardy (eds.). *The Soviet Mind. Russian Culture under Communism*. Washington: Brookings, 2004.

Buckley, Mary. *Redefining Russian Society and Polity*. Boulder, CO: Westview Press, 1993; 346 p. (pb).

Davis, Nathaniel. *A Long Walk to Church: A Contemporary History*. Boulder, CO: Westview Press, 1994; 381 p. (pb).

Dunlap, John B. *Russia Confronts Chechnya*. New York: Cambridge University Press, 1998; 248 p.

Gessen, Masha. *Words Will Break Cement: The Passion of Pussy Riot*. New York: Riverhead Books, 2013; 320 p.

Goscilo, Helena. *Dehexing Sex: Russian Womanhood during and after Glasnost*. Ann Arbor, MI: University of Michigan Press, 1996; 192 p. (pb).

Hilton, Alison. *Russian Folk Art*. Bloomington, IN: Indiana University Press, 1995; 320 p.

Bibliography

Hosking, Geoffrey A. *Beyond Socialist Realism: Soviet Fiction since Ivan Denisovich*. New York, NY: Holmes Meier Publishers, 1980; 260 p.

Jones, Anthony (ed.). *Education and Society in the New Russia*. Armonk, NY: M. E. Sharpe, 1994; 360 p. (pb).

Leach, Robert and Victor Borovsky (eds.). *A History of Russian Theatre*. New York, NY: Cambridge University Press, 1998; 425 p.

Marks, Steven G. *How Russia Shaped the Modern World: From Art to Anti-Semitism, Ballet to Bolshevism*. Princeton: Princeton University, 2004.

Orlov, Yuri. *Dangerous Thoughts*. New York, NY: Morrow, 1991; 339 p.

Ramet, Sabrina P. *Nihil Obstat: Religion, Politics, and Social Change in East-Central Europe and Russia*. Durham, NC: Duke University Press, 1998; 424 p. (pb).

Ramet, Sabrina P. *Rocking the State: Rock Music and Politics in Eastern Europe and Russia*. Boulder, CO: Westview Press, 1994; 317 p. (pb).

Rand, Robert. *Comrade Lawyer: Inside Soviet Justice in an Era of Reform*. Boulder, CO: Westview Press, 1991; 166 p. (pb).

Scanlan, James P. (ed.). *Russian Thought after Communism*. Armonk, NY: M. E. Sharpe, 1994; 256 p. (pb).

Segal, Harold B. *Twentieth-Century Russian Drama: From Gorky to the Present*. New York, NY: Columbia University Press, 1979; 502 p.

Shlapentikh, Vladimir. *Soviet Intellectuals and Political Power*. Princeton, NJ: Princeton University Press, 1991; 321 p.

Shneidman, N. N. *Soviet Literature in the 1970's: Artistic Diversity and Ideological Conformity*. Toronto, Canada: University of Toronto Press, 1979; 128 p.

Smeliansky, Anatoly. *The Russian Theatre after Stalin*. New York: Cambridge University Press, 1999; 270 p. (pb).

Smith, Gerald S. (ed. and trans.). *Contemporary Russian Poetry*. Bloomington, IN: Indiana University Press, 1993; 390 p.

Solzhenitsyn, Aleksandr et al. *From Under the Rubble*. trans. by A. M. Brock. Boston, MA: Little, Brown, 1975; 308 p.

Solzhenitsyn, Aleksandr. *The Gulag Archipelago: 1918–1956*. trans. by Thomas R. Whitney. New York, NY: Harper Row, 1974; 640 p. (pb).

Terras, Victor. *A History of Russian Literature*. New Haven, CT: Yale University Press, 1992; 672 p. (pb).

Yurchak, Alexei. *Everything Was Forever, until It Was No More: The Last Soviet Generation*. Princeton University Press, 2013.

Zubok, Vladislav. *Zhivago's Children: The Last Russian Intelligentsia*. Cambridge, MA: Harvard University Press/Belknap, 2009; 464 p.

EURASIAN STATES

Akiner, Shirin. *Islamic Peoples of the Soviet Union*. New York, NY: Routledge Kegan Paul, 1986; 462 p.

Allison, Roy and Lena Jonson, eds. *Central Asian Security. The New International Context*. Washington, DC: Brookings, 2001.

Aslund, Anders and Michael McFaul (eds). *Revolution in Orange: The Origins of Ukraine's Democratic Breakthrough*. Washington, DC: Carnegie Endowment for International Peace, 2006; 216 p.

Asmus, Ronald. *A Little War That Shook the World: Georgia, Russia, and the Future of the West*. New York, NY: Palgrave Macmillan, 2009; 250 p.

Banuazizi, Ali and Myron Weiner (eds.). *New Geopolitics of Central Asia*. Bloomington, IN: Indiana University Press, 1994; 288 p. (pb).

Bissell, Tom. *Chasing the Sea: Lost among the Ghosts of Empire in Central Asia*. Pantheon, 2003; 416 p.

Bremmer, Ian and Ray Taras (eds.). *Nations and Politics in the Soviet Successor States*. New York, NY: Cambridge University Press, 1993; 577 p. (pb).

Brzezinski, Zbigniew and Paige Sullivan. *Russia and the Commonwealth of Independent States: A Historical and Geopolitical Evolution*. Armonk, NY: M. E. Sharpe, 1996.

Buckley, Mary, *Post-Soviet Women: From the Baltic to Central Asia*. New York, NY: Cambridge University Press, 1997; 333 p. (pb).

Bullough, Oliver. *Let Our Fame Be Great: Journeys among the Defiant People of the Caucasus*. New York, NY: Basic Books, 2010; 496 p.

Chahin, M. *The Kingdom of Armenia*. New York, NY: Dorset Press, 1987; 332 p.

Cohen, Ariel. *Kazakhstan: The Road to Independence*. Washington, DC: Central Asia-Caucasus Institute, 2009.

Collins, Kathleen. *Clan Politics and Regime Transition in Central Asia*. Cambridge University Press, 2006.

Bibliography

Commercio, Michele E. *Russian Minority Politics in Post-Soviet Latvia and Kyrgyzstan: The Transformative Power of Informal Networks*. University of Pennsylvania Press, 2011.

Cooley, Alexander A., and John Heathershaw. *Dictators without borders: Power and Money in Central Asia*. Yale University Press, 2017.

Cornell, Svante E., Johanna Popjanevski and Niklas Nilsson. *Russia's War in Georgia: Causes and Implications for Georgia and the World*. Washington, DC: Johns Hopkins University-SAIS, 2008, 43 p.

Coulton, Timothy J. and Robert C. Tucker (eds). *Patterns of Post-Soviet Leadership*. Boulder, CO: Westview Press, 1995; 256 p. (pb).

Daly, John C. K. *Kazakhstan's Emerging Middle Class*. Washington, DC: Central Asia-Caucasus Institute, 2008; 99 p.

D'Anieri, Paul J. *Understanding Ukrainian Politics: Power, Politics and Institutional Design*. Armonk, N.Y.: M. E. Sharpe Inc, 2007.

Dawisha, Karen and Bruce Parrott (eds.). *Conflict, Cleavage and Change in Central Asia and the Caucasus*. New York, NY: Cambridge University Press, 1997; 441 p. (pb).

Denber, Rachel (ed.). *The Soviet Nationality Reader: The Disintegration in Context*. Boulder, CO: Westview Press, 1992; 635 p. (pb).

d'Encausse, Helen Careere. *Decline of an Empire: The Soviet Socialist Republics in Revolt*. trans. Martin Sokolinsky and Henry A. La Farge. New York, NY: Newsweek Books, 1978; 304 p.

Derluguian, Georgi M. *Bourdieu's Secret Admirer in the Caucasus: A World-System Biography*. University of Chicago Press, 2005.

Driscoll, Jesse. *Warlords and Coalition Politics in Post-Soviet States*. Cambridge University Press, 2015.

Enders, Wimbush S. *Soviet Nationalities in Strategic Perspective*. New York, NY: St. Martin's Press, 1985; 253 p.

Edgar, Adrienne Lynn. *Tribal Nation: The Making of Soviet Turkmenistan*. Princeton: Princeton University, 2004.

Frydman, Roman *et al*. *The Privatization Process in Russia, Ukraine and the Baltic States*. Budapest, Hungary: Central European University Press, 1993.

Gitelman, Zvi (ed.). *The Politics of Nationality and the Erosion of the USSR*. London, England: Macmillan, 1992.

Gleason, Gregory. *The Central Asian States*. Boulder, CO: Westview Press, 1997; 240 p. (pb).

Hajda, L and M. Beissinger (eds.). *The Nationalities Factor in Soviet Politics and Society*. Boulder, CO: Westview Press, 1990.

Hamilton, Daniel S. and Gerhard Mangott (eds). *The New Eastern Europe: Ukraine, Belarus, and Moldova*. Washington, DC: Johns Hopkins Press-SAIS, 2008; 292 p. (pb).

Hiro, Dilip. *Inside Central Asia: A Political and Cultural History of Uzbekistan, Turkmenistan, Kazakhstan, Kyrgystan, Tajikistan, Turkey, and Iran*. New York, NY: Overlook, 2009; 480 p.

Horák, Slavomír and Jan Sir. *Dismantling Totalitarianism? Turkmenistan under Berdimuhamedow*. Washington, DC: Johns Hopkins-SAIS, 2009; 97 p. (pb).

Hosking, Geoffrey et al. *The Road to Post-Communism: Independent Political Movements in the Soviet Union 1985–1991*. London, England: Pinter, 1992.

Hunter, Shireen. *Central Asia since Independence*. New York, NY: Praeger, 1996; 220 p. (pb).

Hunter, Shireen. *The Transcaucasus in Transition: Nation-Building and Conflict*. New York, NY: Praeger, 1994; 240 p. (pb).

Ioffe, Grigory. *Understanding Belarus and How Western Foreign Policy Misses the Mark*. Lanham, MD: Rowman & Littlefield, 2008; 272 p.

Institutions in Soviet Successor States. Cambridge University Press, 2010.

Jones, Stephen. *Georgia: A Political History since Independence*. London: I. B. Tauris, 2012; 376 p.

Khalid, Adeeb. *Islam after Communism: Religion and Politics in Central Asia*. University of California Press, 2014.

Kiev, Anna Reid. *Borderland: A Journey through the History of the Ukraine*. Boulder, CO: Westview, 2000.

King, Charles. *The Black Sea: A History*. New York: OUP Oxford, 2005.

King, Charles. *The Ghost of Freedom: A History of the Caucasus*. Oxford University Press, 2008.

King, Charles. *The Moldovans: Romania, Russia, and the Politics of Culture*. Stanford, CA: Hoover Press, 2013.

Kravchuk, Robert S. *Ukrainian Political Economy. The First Ten Years*. NY: Palgrave, 2003.

Bibliography

Krushelnycky, Askold. *An Orange Revolution: A Personal Journey through Ukrainian History*. Great Britain: Harvill Secker, 2006; 368 p. (pb)

Kurth, Helmut and Iris Kempe (eds.). *Presidential Elections and Orange Revolution's Implications for Ukraine's Transition*. Berlin: Friedrich Ebert Stiftung, 2005.

Kuzio, Taras (ed.). *Contemporary Ukraine: Dynamics of Post-Soviet Transformation*. Armonk, NY: M. E. Sharpe, 1998; 272 p. (pb).

Lentini, Peter. *Political Parties and Movements in the Commonwealth of Independent States*. Manchester, England: Lorton House, 1992.

Lieven, Anatol. *Ukraine and Russia. A Fraternal Rivalry*. Herndon, VA: U.S. Institute of Peace, 1999.

Luong, Pauline Jones. *Institutional Change and Political Continuity in Post-Soviet Central Asia: Power, Perceptions, and Pacts*. Cambridge University Press, 2002.

Luong, Pauline Jones, and Erika Weinthal. *Oil Is Not a Curse: Ownership Structure and*

Lynch, Dov. *Engaging Eurasia's Separatist States: Unresolved Conflicts and De Facto States*. Herndon, VA: United States Institute of Peace, 2004.

Mandelbaum, Michael (ed.). *The Rise of Nations in the Soviet Union: American Foreign Policy and the Disintegration of the USSR*. New York, NY: Council on Foreign Relations, 1991; 104 p. (pb).

Marat, Erica. *Labor Migration in Central Asia: Implications of the Global Economic Crisis*. Washington, DC: Johns Hopkins-SAIS, 2009; 47 p. (pb).

Markowitz, Lawrence P. *State Erosion: Unlootable Resources and Unruly Elites in Central Asia*. Cornell University Press, 2013.

Marples, David R. *Belarus: A Denationalized Nation*. Amsterdam: Harwood Academic Publishers, 1999.

Masik, Joseph R. and Robert O. Krikorian. *Armenia at the Crossroads*. Amsterdam: Harwood Academic Publishers, 1999.

McGlinchey, Eric. *Chaos, Violence, Dynasty: Politics and Islam in Central Asia*. University of Pittsburgh Pre, 2011.

McMann, Kelly M. *Corruption as a Last Resort: Adapting to the Market in Central Asia*. Cornell University Press, 2014.

Metcalf, Daniel. *The Lost Peoples of Central Asia*. London: Hutchinson, 2009; 352 p.

Miyamoto, Akira. *Natural Gas in Central Asia: Industries, Markets and Export Options of Kazakstan, Turkmenistan and Uzbekistan*. Washington, DC: The Brookings Institute Press, 1998; 100 p. (pb).

Motyl, Alexander J. *Dilemmas of Independence: Ukraine after Totalitarianism*. New York, NY: Council on Foreign Relations, 1993.

Nahaylo, B. and V. Svoboda. *Soviet Disunion*. New York, NY: Free Press, 1990.

Olcott, Martha Brill. *Central Asia's New States: Independence, Foreign Policy, and Regional Security*. Herndon, VA: United States Institute of Peace Press, 1966; 256 p. (pb).

Olcott, Martha Brill. *Central Asia's Second Chance*. Washington, DC: Carnegie Endowment for International Peace, 2005; 380 p. (pb).

Olcott, Martha Brill. *Kazakhstan. Unfulfilled Promise*. Washington, DC: Carnegie Endowment for International Peace, 2009; 322 p. (pb).

Paksoy, H. B. (ed.). *Central Asian Reader: The Rediscovery of History*. Armonk, NY: M. E. Sharpe, 1994; 216 p. (pb).

Peterson, D. J. *Troubled Lands: The Legacy of Soviet Environmental Destruction*. Boulder, CO: Westview Press, 1993; 276 p. (pb).

Radnitz, Scott. *Weapons of the Wealthy: Predatory Regimes and Elite-Led Protests in Central Asia*. Cornell University Press, 2010.

Rayfield, Donald. *Edge of Empires: A History of Georgia*. London: Reaktion Books, Ltd, 2012; 500 p.

Reeves, Madeleine. *Border Work: Spatial Lives of the State in Rural Central Asia*. Cornell University Press, 2014.

Remington, Thomas F. (ed.). *Parliaments in Transition: The New Legislative Politics in the Former USSR and Eastern Europe*. Boulder, CO: Westview Press, 1994; 246 p. (pb).

Rumer, Boris Z. *Soviet Central Asia: A Tragic Experiment*. Boston, MA: Unwin Hyman, 1989; 204 p. (pb).

Rywkin, Michael. *Moscow's Muslim Challenge: Soviet Central Asia*. Armonk, NY: M. E. Sharpe, 1990; 181 p.

Rywkin, Michael. *Moscow's Lost Empire*. Armonk, NY: M. E. Sharpe, 1994; 230 p. (pb).

Schatz, Edward. *Modern Clan Politics: The Power of "Blood" in Kazakhstan and Beyond*. University of Washington Press, 2004.

Shlapentokh, Vladimir and Munir Sendich (eds.). *The New Russian Diaspora: Russian Minorities in the Former Soviet Republics*. Armonk, NY: M. E. Sharpe, 1994; 248 p. (pb).

Bibliography

Smith, Graham et al. *Nation-Building in the Post-Soviet Borderlands: The Politics of National Identities*. New York, NY: Cambridge University Press, 1998; 312 p. (pb).

Suny, Ronald Grigor. *Looking toward Ararat: Armenia in Modern History*. Bloomington, IN: Indiana University Press, 1993; 304 p. (pb).

Suny, Ronald Grigor. *The Making of the Georgian Nation*. Bloomington, IN: Indiana University Press, 1994; 448 p. (pb).

Tongeren, Paul van et al., eds. *Searching for Peace in Europe and Eurasia: An Overview of Conflict Prevention and Peacebuilding Activities*. Boulder, CO: Lynne Reinner, 2002.

Walker, Christopher J. *Armenia: The Survival of a Nation*. New York, NY: St. Martin's Press, 1990; 476 p.

Weinthal, Erika. *State Making and Environmental Cooperation: Linking Domestic and International Politics in Central Asia*. MIT Press, 2002.

Wilson, Andrew. *Ukraine's Orange Revolution*. New Haven: Yale University Press, 2005.

Wilson, Andrew. *The Ukrainians: Unexpected Nation*. Second Edition. New Haven: Yale University, 2002.

Wolchik, Sharon and Volodymyr Zviglyanich (eds.). *Ukraine: The Search for a National Identity*. Lanham, MD: Rowman & Littlefield Publishers, 1999; 336 p. (pb)

Wolczuk, Kasia and Roman Wulczuk. *Poland and Ukraine*. Washington, DC: Brookings, 2003.

Yalcin, Resul. *Rebirth of Uzbekistan. Politics, Economy and Society in the Post-Soviet Era*. UK: Ithaca Press, 2002.

Zaprudnik, Jan. *Belarus: At a Crossroads in History*. Boulder, CO: Westview Press, 1993; 278 p. (pb).

Zevelev, Igor. *Russia and Its New Diasporas*. Herndon, VA: U.S. Institute of Peace, 2001.